The Manual to Online Public Records

The Researcher's Tool to Online Resources of Public Records and Public Information

3rd[nd] Edition

By Sankey & Hetherington

Facts ON DEMAND PRESS

Facts on Demand Press
PO Box 27869
Tempe, AZ 85285
800-929-3811
www.brbpublications.com

Facts
ON DEMAND
PRESS

The Manual to Online Public Records

The Researcher's Tool to Online Resources of Public Records and Public Information
Third Edition

PO Box 27869 • Tempe, AZ 85285 • 800.929.3811
ISBN13: 978-1-889150-60-4

Text written by: Michael L. Sankey and Cynthia Hetherington
Government Sites Sections Complied by: Michael Sankey and BRB Publications, Inc.
Cover Design by: Robin Fox & Associates

Cataloging-in-Publication Data
(Provided by Quality Books, Inc.)

Sankey, Michael L., 1949-
The manual to online public records : the researcher's tool to online resources of public records and public information / by Sankey & Hetherington. -- 3rd ed.
p. cm.
Includes index.
1st ed. gives Hetherington first on t.p.
ISBN 978-1-889150-60-4

1. Electronic public records--United States--Directories. 2. Public records--United States--Directories. 3. Internet research. I. Hetherington, Cynthia. II. Hetherington, Cynthia. Manual to online public records. III. Title. IV. Title: Online public records.

JK468.P76H43 2013 025.06'973
QBI13-600076

We are Proud to Present to You

The Manual to Online Public Records

3rd Edition

Cynthia Hetherington & Michael Sankey

June, 2013

Table of Contents

The Read Me Page

The depth and scope of information that exists online about people, businesses, and places is staggering. These cyber trails record major events in people's lives – from birth to the first car and house, to death, wills, and probate. Add to this the paths of the social networks and search engines that reflect an abundance of willingly shared personal information. It is no wonder that today's society treats public record information as a commodity.

With literally thousands of public record and public information sources accessible on the web by anyone, how do you know which sites are useful and which ones are fluff? What facts should be taken into consideration when you evaluate the information they offer? If you think that just because something is on the Internet it must be true and complete, you are living in a vacuum.

The goal of this manual is to provide you with facts and procedures you can use to improve your business operation or your public record searching. These pages will assist you in finding and compiling information on individuals and business entities. More importantly, this Manual will assist not only in **where** to find records, but also **how to search** for information and **how to evaluate** the reliability and worthiness of web sources.

How to Use This Book to Your Best Advantage

The chapters in *The Manual to Online Public Records* will lead you to many, many diverse and accurate sources of records. A brief review of how this content flows will make it easier for you to find specific material you need. Below are short summaries of each chapter with explanations on their applications.

Chapter 1 - Short primer on public records and guidance on how to evaluate an online source.

If you are a novice to public records, the entire chapter is a must read. Even if you consider yourself a public records guru, the section on evaluation is very definitely worth reviewing.

Chapter 2 - How to use search engines to your advantage.

Anyone can do a "Google Search." But knowing how to the conduct technologically superior searches will not only save time, but also reap richer results.

Chapter 3 - How to use social media sites to your advantage.

How to best employ social media sites when investigating or researching people and events is a science. With a focus on Facebook, Twitter and LinkedIn, this chapter examines search techniques, shortcuts, and investigating tools. To keep abreast of the latest Web 2.0 (and beyond) developments one must kept informed.

Chapter 4 - Record types profiled in alpha order with specific "how to search" tips.

All record types are described herein. The chapter is filled with a mix of government agency and vendor online sources. A key point is keep in mind is when the public record topic involves the state and county level agencies profiled in Chapter 6, then that is where you will find these source URLs. For example Chapter 4 tells you how to search for court records, but Chapter 6 profiles the online sources of these county and state court records.

Chapter 5 - An analysis of vendors; how to find, evaluate, and a selected list.

Dissecting vendor types and how to choose the right vendor are often overlooked analysis tools, but are contained herein. Tips on where to find vendors are included along with select list of vendors connected to categories of government records sites profile in Chapter 6.

Chapter 6 - The online sites found at the state and county levels.

This is the largest chapter. Presented state-by-state in an easy to use format, the chapter examines what is available online from the state and local government agencies. Free online access and fee-based systems are denoted, all within the type or category of records available.

Chapter 7 - How to obtain records from the Federal Court System

This chapter explains how the Federal Court System works, what data is available electronically, and how to access case files stored at the Federal Archives.

Some Straight Talk

How many of these six statements about public record searching do you believe are true?

- It's all free online. Why should I have to pay for it?
- I can find all the information I need using Google.
- To do a criminal record search, all I need is a national database; I don't need to go to the courthouse.
- I do background checks for employers, but I am not governed by the Fair Credit Reporting Act because I do not provide credit reports.
- To do comprehensive public record searching online all I need is my $29 membership web account that lets me search 35,000+ databases of public records.
- Certain record types may be open to the public in one state, but in another state they are not.

The first five statements above represent common myths thought to be true by individuals looking for easy solutions to finding public records. If you are someone who practices due diligence when using public records for decision-making, you likely know **only the last statement is true.**

Regardless if you use public records for decision-making on the job or if you are a casual record searcher – this book will help you and likely change the way you search for public records.

Chapter 1

Public Record Fundamentals and Online Evaluation Techniques

This Chapter has two sections.

- The first part examines key concepts that are critical to know when searching public records.
- The latter half of this chapter examines how to analyze the value and worthiness of an online site.

An understanding of the material in this chapter will help and guide you through the rest of the book.

Inside This Chapter:

- Part One: A Primer
  - The "Types" of Data You Will Find Online
  - The Sources of Public Records
  - Searching Private Sources
  - Searching Government Sources
  - Record Indexing and the Importance of Identifiers
  - About Record Fees and Charges
- Part Two: How to Evaluate the Worthiness of Online Content
  - The Competitive Edge
  - Analyze the Search Mechanics
  - Analyze the Viewable Data
  - Analyze the Disclaimer
  - Putting it Altogether

Part One – A Primer

The "Types" of Data You Will Find Online

An understanding of the differences among the following *types* of information is important to an overall discussion and review of online record sources. The boundaries between these records continually undergo intense scrutiny by record-keepers and the public.

Public Record

Public records are records of incidents or actions filed or recorded with a government agency for the purpose of notifying others – the public – about the matter. For example, deeds are recorded in order to keep track of who owns property. Mortgages are recorded to indicate there is a lien on the property. Prospective buyers and lenders search these records to verify ownership and if the property is subject to liens or easements. These records are public; anyone requiring details about your property may review or copy these documents.

Public Information

Your telephone book listing is an example of **public information**; that is, you freely furnished the information to ease the flow of commercial and private communications. Another example is when people place information about themselves on social network sites such as Facebook or LinkedIn. And when you sign up for the discount card at the local grocery store you have made information about yourself publically available to entities purchasing marketing lists.

Knowing the difference between these two terms will help you understand some of the differences between online sites and how they gather their datasets.

Personal Information

The topic of whether personal information should be made available online and by whom and to whom goes well beyond the focus of this book. Suffice it to say that **personal information** may be found in either public records or in public information. To a limited extent such information will remain private unless it is disclosed to some outside entity that could make it public.

Having some element of viewable personal identifiers on public records is a must to properly identify the correct person or to match public records to the right individual.

The Sources of Public Records

Online access to public records comes in several varieties and packages, but searching really boils down to two primary resources:

1. **Government Agencies**
2. **Private Sector - Record Vendors.**

An important point to make is that access is not necessarily always instant. Online access portals can be an instant path to viewable or downloadable record data, or a conduit to first view an index and then order the needed information.

Adding to the mystique of public record is the simple fact that all government records are not computerized. Some county level agencies still use paper and other media forms. The process of converting current and older government record to an electronic format is an ongoing function in many government jurisdictions.

Searching Private Sources

Public Record Vendor Sites

Chapter 5 describes the five definable and distinct main categories of public record professionals: distributors, gateways, search firms, verification or screening firms, and local record document retrievers. (Note that private investigation firms may fall in multiple categories depending on range of services.) Knowledge of how each these vendor categories operates and how they work with clients is invaluable.

The online vendors who create and maintain their proprietary databases of public records do so in several ways. They may purchase records in bulk from specific government agencies, or obtain through online data extraction, or even in limited circumstances send personnel to a government office to make photo copies or enter data into a laptop computer.

Selecting the right record vendor for your particular search needs is a 'science.' Before you sign up with every interesting online vendor that catches your eye, try to narrow your search to the type of vendor suitable for your record needs. Many specialized vendors are mentioned throughout this book.

The "People Search" Data Broker Site

Referred to as "consumer sites" in this book, there are many commercial sites geared towards finding personal and public information such as telephone numbers, emails, or addresses of old friends and family members. Using their free public information data or links as a draw, these sites will try to sell searches to consumers. Often these searches are a search of multiple free sites at the same time, thus offering a convenience service. Some consumer sites charge a "membership fee" for the convenience of searching multiple free sites at once. Other consumer sites will include their own proprietary data with other public record data into a specialized search. The amount of free data they provide is often tied to how aggressive their SEO (Search Engine Optimization) is maintained.

Specialized Web Resources

Using the web for any extensive research will involve knowledge of search engines, directories, media site, social networking sites, and using effective search strategies. The creative use of web resources is an art. Knowing where to find special topic web pages is important, but knowing **how to use these pages** to your advantage is even more important. Chapters 2 and 3 scrutinize these tools.

Searching Government Sources

There are five important truths about searching public records online from government agencies—

1. More than 30% of state and county government maintained public records are not available online.
2. Government sites can be free or fee-based. Generally, the fee-based sites are more robust.
3. Most government public record websites that are free to search contain no personal identifiers beyond the name.
4. Often the searchable and viewable information found online is limited to name indexes and summary data rather than document images. Most access sites – especially the free access sites – permit the former, not the latter.
5. Just because records are accessible in your state or county, do not assume the same accessibility exists in the next county or state.

Keep these truths in mind and your public record searching will lead to better results.

The Accessibility Paradox

Truth #5 above, referred to as the *accessibility paradox*, adds to the mystique of access government public records via any access method.

In some states a specific category of records is severely restricted and therefore those records are not "public," while the very same category of records may be 100% open in other states. This is particularly true for criminal histories, motor vehicle records, and non-certified vital records. As your public record searching takes you from state-to-state and county-to-count, keep this concept in mind.

Record Indexing and the Importance of Identifiers

The term *record index* is used often throughout this book. A record index points to a location or file number where documents, such as recordings, case files, deeds, and articles of incorporation are kept. The index often shows key summary facts also. If you are searching an unfamiliar location, then the presentation of the index is one of first items you need to check. A public record index can be electronic, but also can exist on-site on card files, in books, on microfiche, etc. A record index can be organized in a variety of ways – by name, by year, by case or file number, or by name and year. Depending on the type of public record, an alpha index could be by plaintiff and/or defendant, by grantor and/or grantee, by address, by year, etc.

An important fact to take note of is: the primary search that government agencies provide is a search of the index. When someone tells you "I can view xxx county court records online," this person is most likely talking about searching an index summary of records and not about the all files and pages contained within a case history.

Identifiers on Records

The lack of identifiers displayed when searching online is a real problem for employers or financial institutions who require a certain high level of accuracy in their due diligence. The existence of any possible adverse information must be checked by a hands-on search to insure the proper identity of the subject. Even then identifiers may be removed.

Government agencies who offer online access on a fee or subscription basis – usually to pre-approved requesters – are more apt to disclose personal identifiers such as the date of birth than the free access sites. Very few give Social Security Numbers and those that do usually cloak or mask the first five digits. Some now even cloak the month and day of the birth and only release the year. For example, most U.S. District Court and Bankruptcy Court PACER search systems give little (sometimes only the last four digits of SSN and no DOB) or no personal identifiers at all on search results, thus making a reliable "name search" nearly impossible.

What If the Index Doesn't Have Matching Identifiers?

You will often find that an online index of government agencies records does not contain a personal identifier. In that situation, one must search within in the record file itself or in associated paperwork.

For example, let us say you are searching for a record on Joe B. Cool with a DOB of 01/01/1985. And let us say the index gives you an index showing a possible record match of J Cool with no DOB, and another possible match with a Joseph Cool with a partial DOB match. The next step is to examine the two files. The file content may contain the matching personal identifiers you seek. If you are a professional and the highest form of accuracy is vital, then you may have times where a common name requires you to view dozens of files.

The Redaction Trend

Redaction is simply removing or hiding certain elements within a record itself or the record index. Often news stories appear related to ongoing privacy debates and efforts to remove personal identifiers from public records.

In some cases, the anticipated cost of redacting records is forcing government agencies to instead block public access to their records. At the same time government officials understand the importance and benefits attached to the openness of public records. The balance of privacy interests versus public jeopardy goes beyond the purposes of this book; however, the key points here are to be aware of change and know that redactions can and will alter public record searching procedures.

About Record Fees and Charges

Public records are created by incidents or transactions. It costs money (time, salaries, supplies, etc.) to record, store, and track these events. Although public records may be free of charge to view, they are not necessarily free of charge when obtaining file copies. Fees may be expected if government personnel must perform searches onsite.

The common charges found at government agencies – whether searching is performed online or on site – include: copy fees (to make copies of documents); search fees (for clerical personnel to search for the record); certification fees (to certify a document as being accurate and coming from the particular agency); and expedite fees (to place you at the "front of the line").

Subscription Accounts or Pay as You Order

Payment for records, at either at government sites or vendor sites, is usually done through a subscription account or pay as you go using a credit card.

The use of subscription accounts is more common than people may be aware. Also, many agencies, such as state motor vehicle agencies, only provide online record access to pre-approved, high-volume, ongoing accounts. Typically, this contractual access involves fees and a specified, minimum amount of usage.

A number of the online agencies profiled in Chapter 6 provide access to information on a pay-as-you-go basis, often requiring a credit card payment. Some agencies will give you a glimpse of the index or docket, but will charge a fee for the record copy. Some allow the record to be printed on the spot; others may only mail it.

Fees can and do vary widely from jurisdiction to jurisdiction for even the same record type. Copy fees vary from $.10 to $10 per page, search fees range from under a dollar to as much as $65.

BRB's online Public Record Research System (PRRS found at www.brbpublications.com) relates the specific fees involved with all record access methods for more than 20,000 government agencies.

Part 2 – How to Evaluate the Worthiness of Online Content

This section presents concrete ideas and facts to improve your analysis of your public record searching. If you are a professional and the use of public records is important to your operation, analyzing the value of the searchable content presented by either a government agency or a vendor is a must.

The Competitive Edge

Today everyone is trying to either save a buck or find an edge over their competition. Finding the best online resources is a constant quest. Typical questions often asked are "How much does it cost?" and "Is the data current?"

But the questions that need to be asked and answered are:

- Is 'x' a primary source or a secondary source?
- Is an online search of 'x' equivalent to an onsite search?

Firms who have taken the time to ask these questions and analyze the data to find answers to determine the rate of return for using certain online systems are not going to give their analysis away freely. Sure, you can ask a colleague for a recommendation, but you are not going get full scale information on a post on a social media site or list serve. The data is much too valuable.

The Three Keys to Evaluation

There are three primary consideration areas when evaluating searchable record content for your needs—

1. **Search Mechanics**
2. **The Viewable Data**
3. **The Severity of the Disclosure**

The data found in this section will certainly help you provide better service to your clients and possibly save you money. And perhaps more importantly, the recommendations and cautions will help lessen your exposure to possibilities of being involved in litigation.

1. Analyze the Search Mechanics

Check the "Name Field" Logistics

How does the search work when searching by name? Are there wild cards? How do you handle a search when the record could be under the name of Tom or Thomas? Will the use of a middle initial help? One of the easiest and quickest ways to find answers is to look for *a help me* or *searching tips* section. They are not always evident, but even if available, they are often ignored. A researcher who is in a hurry and does not want to be bogged done by reading instructions displays an attitude that will eventually lead to trouble.

Another common problem in the name field is the inconsistency of how business names are shown in a name field. If you are searching for records on *The ABC Company*, do you search under both "The…" and "ABC…"?

A recommendation is to test the site using some prior, successful searches from the site. In this way you can experiment with different 'ways in' and keep track of your results.

Searchable by All Involved Parties?

Let's say you are looking for liens or civil litigation facts on a subject. Using a free online search of a government database, you perform your search and find no hits. So you report to your client there is no record on file. But what if you were not aware for this particular database source that when multiple parties are involved the record is only searchable by the first name entered on the list of defendants? Perhaps this sounds a bit far-fetched, but unfortunately this situation is more common than you might think. For example there is a free New York statewide search of the civil index which reportedly operates in this manner.

The recommendation is to use previously completed searches that contain multiple parties and re-search by all party names. Determine for yourself if a site's searchable index includes all the names or parties involved or not.

Use of the DOB Field

Are you looking for leads on the whereabouts of someone - or are you preparing a report that will be submitted to an attorney which could be used in court? Can you get by on just the name and year of birth?

If the DOB is critical to your search and it is available as a search component on the search site you are using or evaluating, great. But try the same search without entering data in the DOB field and see what results are now produced. Consider the possibility that more possibilities of records under the same subject name could be found. And in the process you may even find a missing middle initial or an address that previously had not surfaced.

The reality is that in certain types of databases the DOB may appear sporadically on records or in the index. This is especially true for civil court case records. If you have a common name, to find the DOB you may need to pull and examine the full case file or call the attorney, as that may be the only way to determine if the record you found belongs to the subject of your search.

Redaction can also change the outcome of using a DOB on a search. For example, in Wyoming a State Rule effective January 1, 2011 directed redaction of the birth day and birth month on public record pleadings and exhibits filed at the courts. From that date forward, the courts have two copies of each document – one public copy that is redacted, and one non-public that contains the full DOB and SSN. But what is also important is the fact some Wyoming court judges have directed their courts to redact these partial identifiers on **all** prior cases filed, not just since 01/01/11. And how would you know this if you were using an un-informed consumer vendor site?

Can You Search Using Multiple Case Types or Case Date Fields?

Much like searching all involved parties, these are other key components of a search site that need to be tested if you want to use it for serious research. The site may have a drop down box, but you cannot always rely on the "all" choice. It is a good idea to test with known cases and see if there are any anomalies or patterns that surface.

Will the Search Subject be Notified?

Some states have laws that require the subject to be informed when certain types of inquiries are made which includes identifying the requester. This is extremely important if your inquiry is sub rosa or if the subject's discovery of the search could lead to any embarrassment. Examples include driving records in North Dakota and criminal records from the AOCFastCheck system in Kentucky.

2. Analyze the Viewable Data

How Far Back?

Obviously it is beneficial to know the record retention period – how far back records are maintained. Let's say you are hired to do a seven-year search on a subject in a number of locations. You assume all of your sources go back that far, but one of them only goes back five years and you did not know or check. If the record search connected research involving litigation or background, an incomplete data is used, are you prepared for the possible legal exposure you or your client will face?

With a little effort you can often find the throughput listed on a site and it is well worth the effort to do so. Chapter 6 provides examples where the throughput varies widely from county to county on a state's judiciary online site. Check out Indiana, Kansas, and North Dakota.

This is an important factor which helps determine if an online resource should be used only as a secondary or supplemental search, opposed to being a primary search source.

How Current

Of course you can also look for indications of when the page was revised and for signs of indicators (press releases, statistics) showing that the site is regularly maintained. But you need to take it a step farther.

Knowing how "fresh" the information is – when it was last updated and through what date – is an important search factor. Any answer except a clear, concise date is inadequate. A vendor may claim it updated an index of records last week, but what if this data still reflects a sixty-day delay or data entry backlog. If there is an investigation of an incident in progress by an occupational licensing board, will your online resource show the latest results?

This update gap is extremely common with state criminal record agencies such as the State Police or Department of Public Safety who receive and hold criminal case information received from the courts. See the Criminal Record Repository section in Chapter 4 for some eye-opening statistics from a recent U.S. Department of Justice Study.

Another example is the time lag in the Los Angeles online system. There is a lag time in Los Angeles of 1 to 2 weeks between the event and the posting of content onto their online accessible criminal record system. Let's say you are a background screening firm and this database is all you use to search Los Angeles. Using this resource you inform your client, an employer, the record on a particular name is clear. However there was a recent conviction for a bad felony not yet reported online, but clearly shown at the courthouse. In the event this person is hired and does wrong to a member of the public, who is liable if this newly hired person harms someone? Per the FCRA, the background screening firm has exposure because the rule is the background screening firm must use the most *up-to-date system*. (Not the most reliable or best system, but the most up-to-date-system.)

Why take the chance? Make sure the level of due diligence you require matches the results of the search you perform.

Confirm the Sources and Geographic Boundaries of the Search

Look for a disclosure statement confirming the sources that encompass the database you are searching. If the site belongs to a vendor, look for verification material regarding the completeness of the data. Judging the reliability of a database site includes knowing facts about the system's data boundaries.

Statewide or Partial State or Single County

If you are using a state government public record site, confirm if the search is truly statewide or just encompasses one or certain counties. And if supposedly statewide is it truly 100% statewide with all counties reporting back to a specific date threshold?

Always look for a disclosure statement confirming the geographic sources that encompass the database you are searching.

For example as you will learn in Chapter 6, there are 32 states that provide some type of centralized online access platform to court record information in that state. But if you assume each of these sites is all inclusive and an online search is equivalent to searching each county court in-person, you are badly mistaken. Check Arizona. Check Arkansas.

So if a vendor is supplying you with an "instant criminal record search" in Arizona, you better look again on what the true coverage is. You know the old adage about the word *assume,* it certainly applies here.

Countywide or Single County Agency

The same concept described above can be applicable within a county (or parish, etc.). Records within a geographic region are not necessarily co-mingled. This is especially true for upper and lower courts. For example, in Virginia there is one online system for the Circuit Courts Court (upper) case records, one for the District Courts (lower). In Ohio the upper court (Court of Common Pleas) may have a countywide system online, but the lower courts (Municipal Courts) are not included.

Consider the searching recorded documents and property-related records in New Hampshire. The recording officers are Register of Deeds (for real estate only) and Town/City Clerk (for farm-related UCCs). The following names are identical for both a town/city and a county - Grafton, Hillsborough, Merrimack, Strafford, and Sullivan. The following unincorporated towns do not have a Town Clerk, so all liens are located at the corresponding county: Cambridge (Coos), Dicksville (Coos), Green's Grant (Coos), Hale's Location (Carroll), Millsfield (Coos), and Wentworth's Location (Coos).

The message here is if you are looking for records in an unfamiliar state or county, you could be in trouble unless you first do your homework.

Be Aware of "Garbage In and Garbage Out"

As good as some sites are and may pass your tests with flying colors, the fact remains that many public records are created by humans doing data entry. There are always going to be errors and typos such as missed characters or transposed digits or letters.

But if you have a good inkling of the pluses and minuses of a site and make use of 'wild cards' you will run a better chance to pick up results that would not otherwise appear.

3. Analyze the Disclaimer

Does the site you are using have a different bias or purpose than your intent? Many government websites offering online record access include a warning or disclosure stating that the data can have errors and/or should be used for informational purposes only. The common reaction is often "yeah, so what?"

But have you ever considered the severity of a site's disclaimer in relationship to your record searching due diligence needs? Is the disclaimer merely a CYA courtesy warning, or should this site truly not be used as a primary search site? Is there something wrong? What if you provide research to an attorney and you use a statewide civil records site in South Dakota and you are not aware prohibits the use of the site if the data is resold? Any possible exposure there?

Below are several examples of disclaimers from statewide court judicial sites.

Disclaimer from Washington (www.courts.wa.gov/jislink/?fa=jislink.agreement)

This is part of the license agreement that all online users must sign:

> "Disclosure Statement - You agree to provide a disclosure statement to each customer, client, or other third party at the time any information from JIS-Link is provided to them. You agree that a statement is displayed or provided every time information is provided which states, at a minimum:
>
> The data or information provided is based on information obtained from the Washington State courts as of __________ (insert date the information was obtained from JIS-Link). The Administrative Office of the Courts and the Washington Courts:
>
> 1) Do not warrant that the information is accurate or complete except for court purposes;
>
> 2) Make no representations regarding the identity of any persons whose names appear in the information; and
>
> 3) Deny liability for any damages resulting from release or use of the data or information.
>
> The user should verify the information by personally consulting the "official" record reposing at the court of record."

A search from this Washington site using their JIS-Link product is commonly known to be *on-site equivalent* – meaning a search made using this system provides the same results as a search performed at the local courthouse using a public access terminal. But the warning still exists. So if you are receiving instant WA records from a vendor using this site, are you also receiving this notification?

Disclaimer from Rhode Island (http://courtconnect.courts.state.ri.us)

This is from the Adult Criminal Information Database maintained by the Rhode Island Judiciary. This is a free search.

> "This website is provided as an informational service only <u>and does not constitute and should not be relied upon as an official record and/or schedule of the court.</u> Since the full date of birth and other personally identifying information is not included in this service, the information contained herein shall not be relied upon to confirm a person's identity or a person's criminal record for any purpose including, but not limited to, background checks or employment."

In other words the Judiciary is telling you this site should not be used for a background check. What is your exposure if this is the only site you are using in RI? Any red flags come to mind?

The message here is that sites with disclaimers such as the one above in Rhode Island should be considered as supplemental or secondary sources only, especially if you are performing record searching that requires strict due diligence. For example, using a web source for a criminal record search, with such a disclaimer, usually indicates the search by itself will not comply with the Federal Fair Credit Reporting Act which regulates pre-employment screening.

Putting it Altogether

Everyone is not going to have the same criteria or due diligence needs. Therefore use the following checklist as a guide to help evaluate what is going to work best for your operation.

✓ Analyze Your Product/Service Requirements

The best way to start is to make a couple of lists.

1. List what you are required to provide, such as what have promised to do for your clients.
2. List all the evaluation categories mentioned previously that carry any degree of importance to you. Differentiate those that are mandatory to your needs and which ones that are supplemental.

You can even take this a step further: Create a matrix spreadsheet document and assign point values based on level of importance. Compare this analysis to the level of service or coverage you have promised to your clientele. What level of due diligence is your client expecting? Have you allocated enough costs (time and fees) in a search to properly to the job?

✓ Monitor Your Core Sites

Keeping track of online sites is like herding cats. As the saying goes - the only constant in life is change. Changes can be good or bad. Sites often add more content or more search criteria. But they can take content away too. And new sites can always pop-up. Here is an example. At the BRB Publications web page we provide the public the links to free government search sites. In 2012 we added or modified over 1,700 sites.

The key here is after you create your own analysis matrix and list of core sites, do not park and sit on your analysis for 2 years.

✓ Make a Statement - What is Your Best Practice

Do you have an internal best practice statement that details the necessary components you or our firm perceives to be required in order to consider a web source as a **primary search**? What components, or lack of, lead to classifying a site as being **secondary**? Do you have a similar best practice statement provided to clients about your online research - or do you use a statement that is basically something to the effect that *we do the best we can*?

Below are four questions to ask yourself about your own best practices. Your answers will dictate some insight to your current online research procedures.

- How Do You Measure the Worthiness?
- Do You Cut Corners? If so, Where?
- Do You Monitor or Evaluate Sites
- How Will your Results Hold Up in Court?

Hopefully, this chapter has given you insight on how to analyze your record searching procedures. Chapters to follow will place you on the road to becoming an expert.

The next two chapters explore how to use search engines, social networks, and media sites.

Chapter 2

Using Traditional Search Engines for Locating Public Information

This chapter examines the creative searching features and offerings provided by search engines. Using these advanced techniques greatly enhances the searching of public information.

Note the next chapter examines how to use search engines to find social network users and content.

Inside This Chapter:

- The Reliance on Search Engines
- Getting the Most Out of Google
- Other Useful Google Tools
- Other Worthy Search Engines
- Using eBay.com
- Craigslist Searching
- SearchTempest.com & Claz.org
- Bing.com
- Zoominfo.com
- Wayback Machine on Archive.org
- Summary

The Reliance on Search Engines

The Internet has come a long way since the days of command line searching through services like Gopher, Veronica, Jughead, and Archie. Now with billions of index-able webpages, modern search engines exist as viable search tools for locating public records and public information.

Online researchers rely on search engines to search webpages for specified keywords and then return a list of those webpages where the keywords were found. Answers can be found instantly with almost zero effort. However, the simplicity in using these easy tools often takes away from the technologically superior searches that can be conducted and reap richer results. Many users will plug in a word or phrase and hit the "Search" button without much thought as to running a smarter search. Some will take advantage of adding quotes around phrases or common expressions, but most just type and go. Also missed are the other search tools created by these services such as mapping, news, videos, etc.

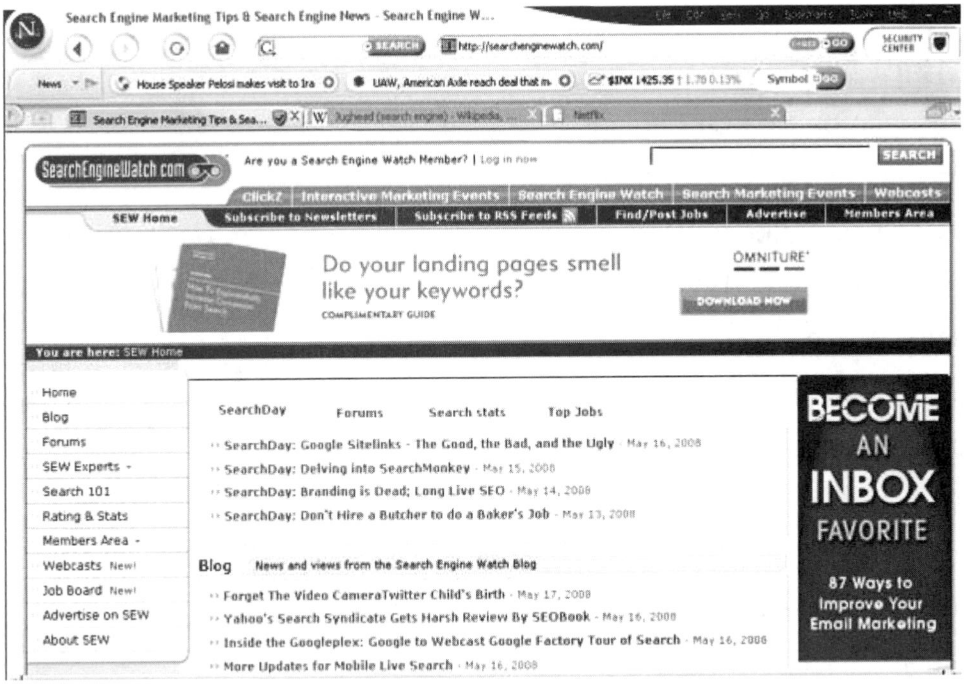

Among the earliest engines developed are Yahoo.com, Altavista.com, and Google.com. There are several online resources that excel in helping you understand the history of these engines as well as learn more about their functionality, how they rank pages, how to use these resources to their best ability, and what else is on the horizon in the searcher's world. Check out online reviews on searchenginewatch.com (above). Find anything by Gary Price (the Invisible Web guru) and Chris Sherman (founder of Searchenginewatch.com), and look for Ran Hock's *The Extreme Searcher's Internet Handbook,* which is a handy resource for any new searcher, for more information.

The balance of this chapter examines the advanced search features of those search engines with the most robust and useful offerings for expertly searching public information.

Getting the Most Out of Google

As the market-share leader of free search tools on the Internet, Google certainly gets a good deal of use. However, it is probably one of the most under-utilized search engines available. There are numerous enhancements that go well beyond merely pushing words through and clicking "Google Search" or "I'm Feeling Lucky." An accomplished investigator should know how to use Google's advanced-search features, operators, and how to take advantage of its advanced search feature settings and preferences settings.

Using Google's Preferred Results

For example, one way to save a lot of time and not miss vital hits is to set the *Number of Results* from 10 (the default) to 100. (This is also recommended for other search engines.)

To do this, go to the first screen of Google.com, click on *Preferences*, which is to the right of the search engine box or upper right-hand corner (sometimes looks like a sprocket), and then slide down to *Number of Results*. Here you see a choice to use the pull down menu which should have 10 showing in the box. Change that to 100 and click the *Save Preferences* button at the bottom of the page. Then every time you use Google, it will give you 100 results per page.

Number of Results
Google's default (10 results) provides the fastest results.
Display 100 results per page.

The *Preferences* option (see *Settings*) also allows you to specify the default tolerance for "safe searching filtering." Google's *SafeSearch* blocks webpages containing explicit sexual content from appearing in search results. The filter options are:

- Use strict filtering (filter both explicit text and explicit images)
- Use moderate filtering (filter explicit images only—default behavior)
- Do not filter my search results

Google Operators

Using Google operators will smarten a search and enable you to find the right link faster. Look in the first column in the table below for the bolded characters known as operators. They help define or "narrow" a search.

This Search	Operator	Google Finds Pages Containing ...
cooking Italian	None	Both the words cooking and Italian but not together or in order
vegetarian **OR** vegan	**OR**	Information on vegetarian or vegan
"Can I get a witness"	""	The exact phrase "Can I get a witness"
Henry +8 Great Britain	+	Information about Henry the Eighth (8), weeding out other kings of Great Britain
automobiles ~glossary	~	Glossaries about automobiles as well as dictionaries, lists of terms, terminology, etc.
salsa -dance	-	The word "salsa" but NOT the word "dance" (note the space before the hyphen)

salsa-dancer	-	All forms of the term, whether spelled as a single word, a phrase, or hyphenated (note the lack of a space)
define:congo	**define:**	Definitions of the word "congo" from the Web
site:virtuallibrarian.com	**site:**	Searches only one website for expression, in this case virtuallibrarian.com
filetype:doc	**filetype:**	Find documents of the specified type, in this case MS Word documents
link:virtuallibrarian.com	**link:**	Find linked pages, i.e. show pages that point to the URL

Also available on Google are the common mathematical operators you would use on your computer. The following symbols between any two numbers will automatically perform a math function.

Symbol	Function
+	Addition
-	Subtraction
*	Multiplication
/	Division

Other *Advanced Google Operators* can be located through the *Advanced Search Page* or performed right in the search box.

Google operators can also be **combined**. Follow the example below:

site:hp.com filetype:pdf "5010 LaserJet" printer FAQ

This search is directed to the Hewlett Packard website; looking for Adobe Acrobat PDF file of Frequently Asked Questions file regarding the 5010 LaserJet printer.

A great resource for search help for beginners to experts is www.googleguide.com. There are dozens more operators and search techniques to use.

Proximity Searching

When an **asterisk** "*" is used between words or expressions, Google offers a very effective proximity searching feature. Used between two expressions, proximity will return results that are within 15 words of each other.

For example, a search for **"cynthia hetherington" investigator** returned 755 matches in Google.

Whereas, the search **"cynthia hetherington" * investigator** resulted in 24 matches.

Hence, the expression "cynthia hetherington" did appear on the same web page as "investigator" 755 times, but it only occurred in close proximity to "investigator" 24 times out of the 755 matches.

Common Phrase Searching

For English language searches, consider the common colloquialisms people use in everyday language. With email, text messaging, and other basic device communications, writing has turned into an extension of speaking. People no longer think about what they are writing; as far as grammar is concerned, they tend to write like they speak. Thus shorthand and common expressions are found. Below are common expressions used to create phrase searching.

- I hate XXX (my job, my mom, my school, my employer)
- Better than XXX (<restaurant>, <product>, <any proper noun>)

- I love XXX (my job, my mom, my school, my employer)
- XXX was the nicest (<geography/location>, <company or person>)
- XXX was the worst
- XXX was off the charts
- XXX was off the hook
- XXX was off the map
- XXX was such a jerk/babe/<expletive>
- XXX was so hot/stupid/boring

An example search in Google for "Better than Disney" returned hits such as:

- Is Disney Land better than Disney World?
- Nick [Nickelodeon's children's network] is slightly better than Disney

Be inventive and consider how you would describe a similar topic, then run your search in the same style using quotes to contain the phrases.

Other Useful Google Tools

Beyond Web searching, Google also offers image searching, news searching, books, maps, products, translations, documents, calendars, etc. as shown in the screen below. We will review how to use three of the more useful Google tools for record searching.

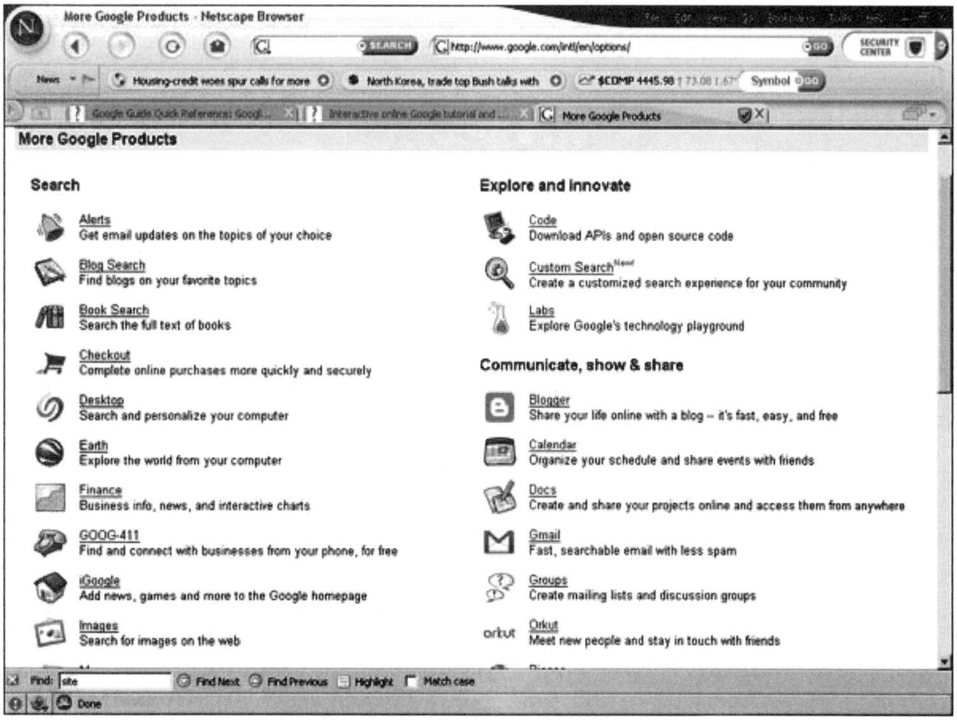

Google Alerts

Google Alerts are one of the handiest tools that Google offers. Google Alerts sends emails automatically when there are new Google results for your submitted list of search terms. The results are culled from Google News, Web, Blogs, Video, and Groups.

The easiest way to get to the Alerts feature in Google.com is simply at google.com/alerts. Type in your search query – such as a proper name, expression or phrase search. Be sure to use Google Operators described earlier in order to filter and smarten your search results.

You can set up your alert to email you: 1) as the event is found or 2) once a day or 3) once a week. You can also use the "Result Type" pull down menu to select what types of sources you want Google to use when creating the alerts. The image on the right below indicates the choices.

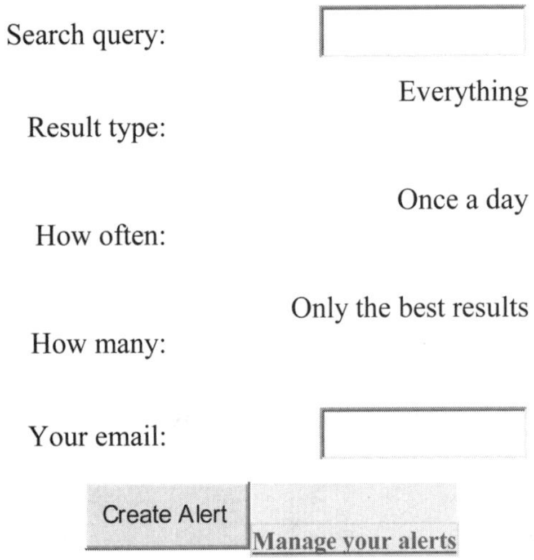

Google Images

Image searching in Google can return a host of interesting results. Using the same type of text search queries, the *Advanced Image Searching* offers limiters by image type; such as black and white, color, drawing, and has a search feature for finding just faces and just news content.

The *Faces* only feature is helpful at narrowing down large result matches, and the *News Content* feature is terrific considering the image search takes place only within media and press oriented websites.

Normally, news and media searches are conducted on databases such as LexisNexis or Factiva, where images have been stripped out of the stories.

The screen image on the next page indicates the many search possibilities and parameters that Google Images offers.

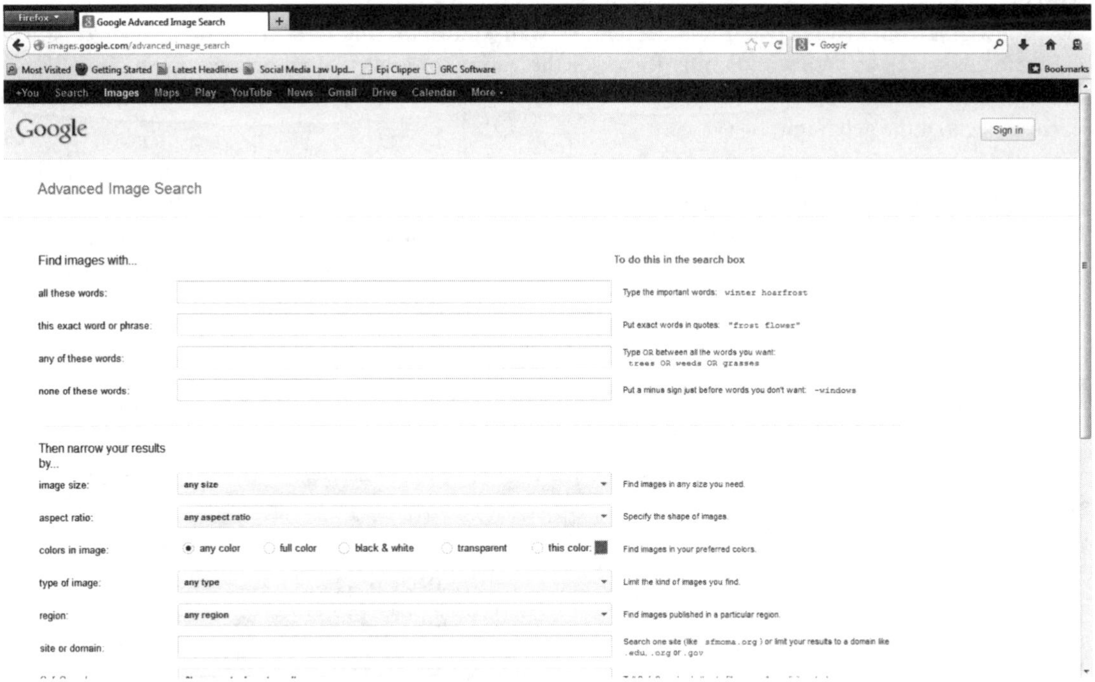

You can also "Search by image" by selecting the small camera in the in the images.google.com search box. From here you either paste your image URL or upload the photo from your desktop. Google will look for images that are exactly the same, similar or holding the same content (i.e. filename, tagged name).

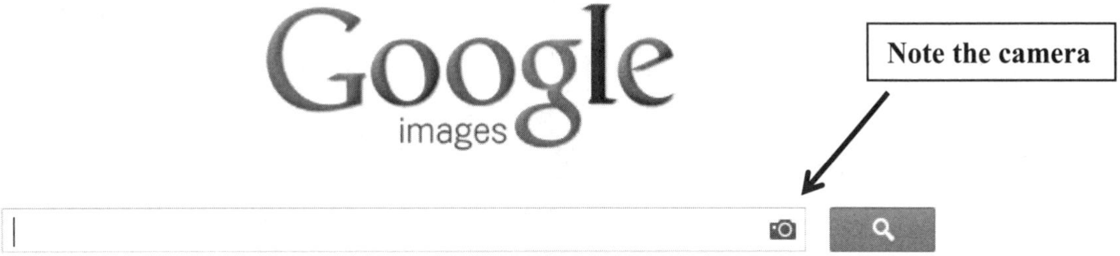

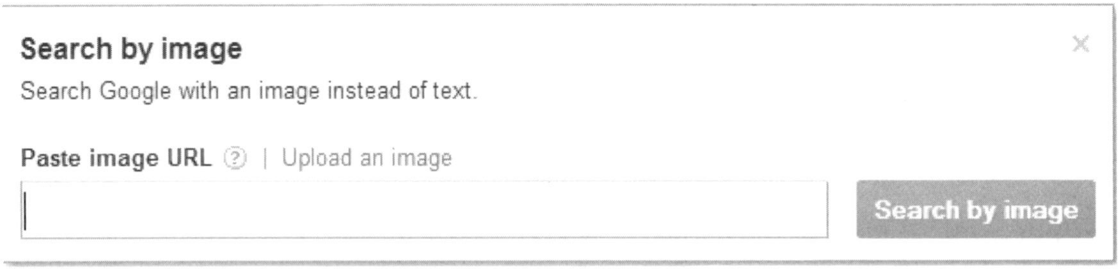

Google Maps Tool

Google Maps is a great tool that is quite useful beyond the well-known *driving directions* and the *Where Is* features. To become acquainted, search an area with familiarity to see the variety of tools that go beyond directions of East to West. The *My Maps* tab offers tools that allow you to customize your own searches and really "zero in" on certain geographical aspects of the geography.

The image below shows how a search can be narrowed to show real estate listings, user contributed photos (with Picasa Web Album or Panoramio), and places of interest. The distance measurement tool is handy when trying to establish the length between two points on the map and has various measurement methods offered. For example, the distance between Minneapolis and St. Paul Minnesota is 8.73084 mi or 128.052 football fields, 13.1711 верста, 281.019 pools, etc.

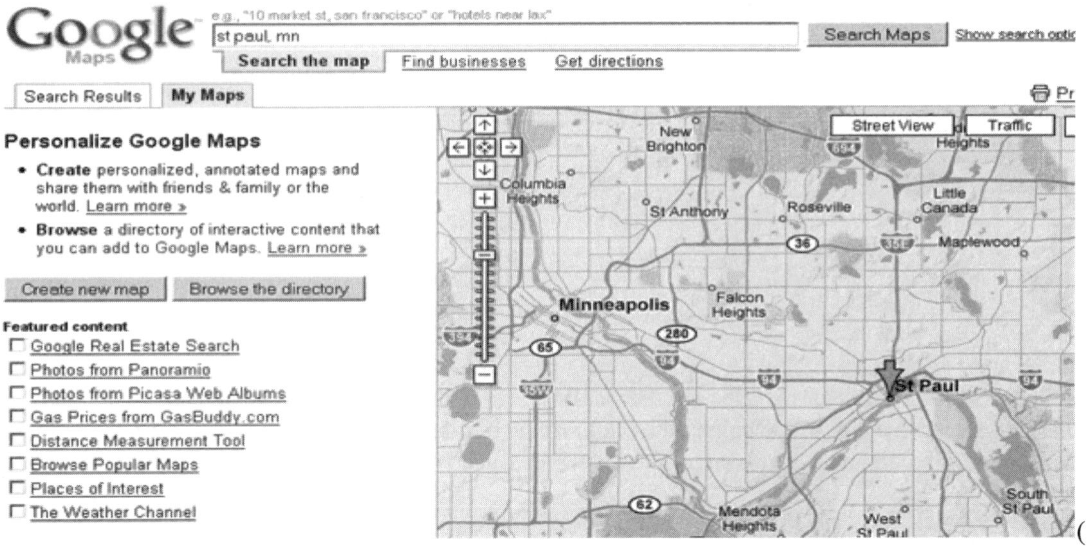

Other Worthy Search Engines

Other traditional search engines with valuable searching features for public information research include—

- Ask.com
- Bing.com
- Copernic.com (a fee-based resource)
- Yahoo.com

Using eBay

Ebay and its partner Paypal offer over a decade's worth of information on their users.

Using the eBay site as a research tool often leads to a treasure trove of information about a subject.

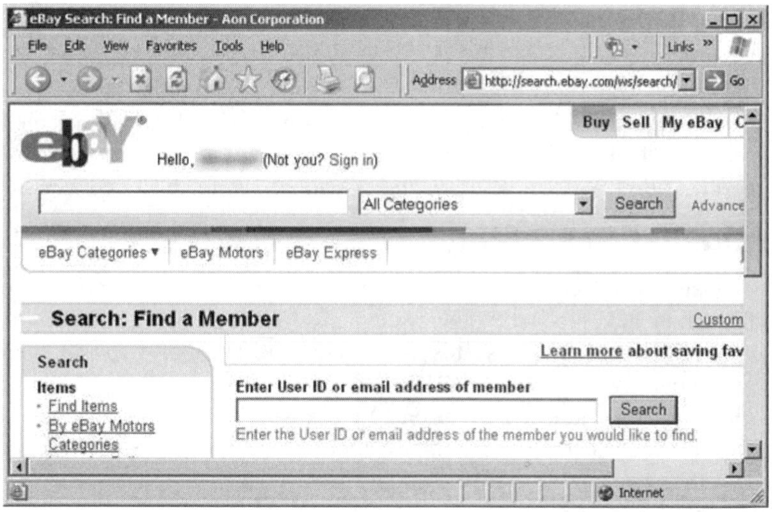

Here is how to search by a person's name, email address, or best of all, the first half of an email address, which is very likely also the person's username, on eBay.

- Go to *Advanced Search* from the homepage, upper right-hand corner
- Choose *Find a Member* from the left-hand column
- Type in the first half of the person's personal email address. For example, for crazybird@gmail.com, type "crazybird"

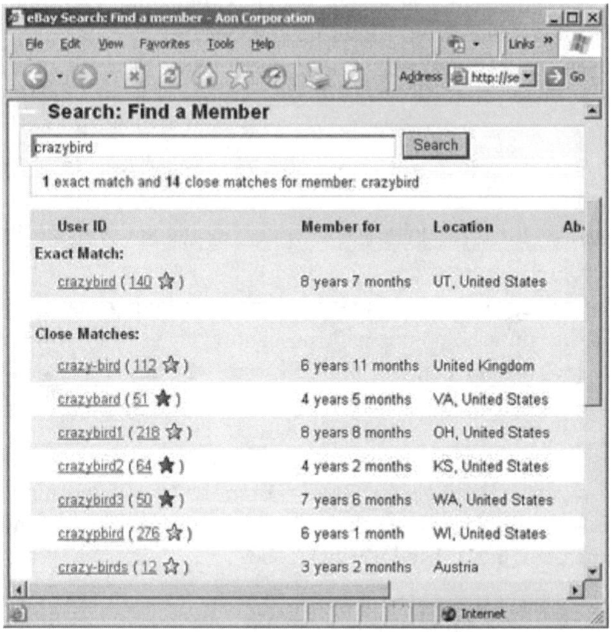

The results screen shows one perfect match for "crazybird" in Utah. This person has held this account with eBay.com for over eight years.

Note: Remember to take into account that this could be a mismatch, especially if the name is a common one like "baseballfan" or "nascarfanatic."

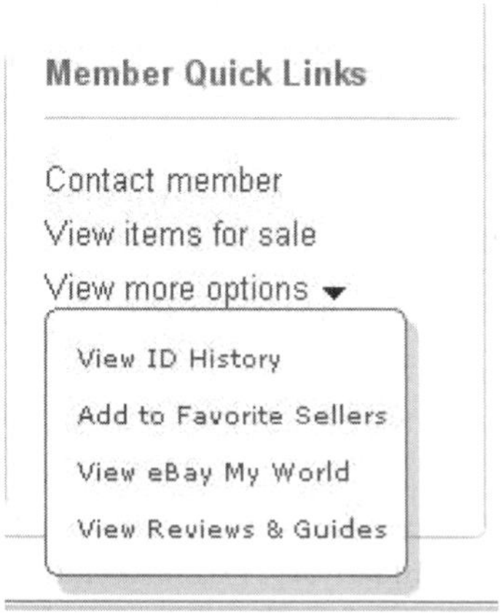

If you think you have a match to your person, visit the person's online profile on eBay and read EVERYTHING they have on their page. Insight can be developed by looking at the items they've bought and sold and by reviewing all comments made to and by the individual.

Once you gather comments, click over to the *Feedback Profile* for the individual. Down the right-hand side are a few selectable items under *Member Quick Links*. Look at *View ID History* to see if the member changed an ID in eBay in the past ten years. You can also *Add to Favorite Sellers* to be alerted when that person places new items for sale on eBay.

Craigslist Searching

The site www.craigslist.org is an online emporium *or* a flea market, depending on your perspective. The large want-ad listings include products, garage-sale items, rental properties, houses for sale, services, and personal ads. The catch to correctly searching Craigslist is its geographic restriction. If you are interested in items in San Francisco, that is the only geographic location you should search under; example is http://sfbay.craigslist.org. Craigslist will *not* allow you to search multiple jurisdictions at once. To expand your search, you have to specify Northern California or name another area. Or you can use SearchTempest.com.

SearchTempest.com & Claz.org

Tired of hunting around Craigslist for your suspect's posts, stolen goods, or to see if your hard-to-find sports memorabilia is anywhere to be found? Craigslist itself does not offer a way to search across broad geographic areas. Lo and behold a search engine to the rescue: Craigshelper.com. This service is now known as SearchTempest.com, also Claz.org (formerly Craigslook.com).

You can search by distance (in miles) to a zip code, pick multiple cities, type of sale, and if you want eBay and Amazon results. A search on *'Dukes of Hazard' from New Jersey* brought up results as far as Monterey Bay, California. Of course, one of the key reasons to search within eBay or Craigslist is not only to find your Dukes of Hazard memorabilia – but to discern if your subject is using auction Web sites and services with a unique user account.

Once you have conducted your search, an added bonus to SearchTempest is that if your search is something you want to be alerted about future sales of, click on the RSS option in the upper right hand corner named "Feeds For This Search." An .OPML file will be created which you can drag into your email browser, and it will create a folder marked with the title of your search. Anytime a sale matching your original criteria appears through Searchtempest.com, your RSS inbox will show a new message.

Bing.com

Introduced by Microsoft, Bing is the latest search engine to take on the formidable pace-setters Google and Yahoo. Bing focuses on four key areas: shopping, local, travel, and health.

A number of features and benefits of this new search engine are reviewed below. It is worth mentioning that Bing's interface is rather pleasant with a photo backdrop, which is fine on a computer with no bandwidth issues. However, large image files are always a burden when you are strictly looking for content, not bells and whistles. Bing's PDA version – accessible by Blackberry, iPhone, and similar devices – opens with a plain-text screen.

Bing Search Features and Settings

Go straight to *Preferences* in the right-hand corner and change the settings for *Results* from 10 to 50 (the highest number). The search box can contain up to 150 characters, including spaces. The standard stop words ("a," "the," "and," etc.) can be included in your search if they're used in quoted phrases, e.g., "The Di Vinci Code."

One odd feature was the increase of results when searching with quotes against a name. A search without quotes on **Cynthia Hetherington** returned 60,500 results, whereas a search with the quotes returned 179,000 results.

Although the algorithm is not clear, it is possible Bing uses a proximity command as a default when searching one or more expressions. This would make sense to limit bad results such as a document that lists "Cynthia Nixon" at the top of the webpage and "Hetherington Smith LLP" six pages later. A nice feature brought back to use in database searching is the Boolean terms "or" and "not." By default, search engines tend to assume the "and" (e.g., chocolate "and" cake), and the "not," which can also be represented as a "–" (minus) in the query. Although the "or" (represented as "|") gets a little lost in the advanced features, it is good to see Bing highlighting this little-used but resourceful feature.

Bing has brought back parentheses to allow you to combine expressions to be included or not. This is great for intelligence investigators who suffer due to popular names flooding their results. For example, **Bill Gates** returns 24 million hits. Add **(Gates Foundation)** to the search and you are limited to 700,000 results. If you subtract (or **NOT Gates Foundation**), the results jump back up, but the results will be significantly less than the original 24 million.

On the right-hand side of the results page, if you mouse over the returned links, you will see your search expression as it appears within the context of the website that was found. Other links offered on that page are also revealed.

Zoominfo

Another great source for free searching is Zoominfo.com. Information is collated from websites that the Zoominfo's software *bots* – also known as intelligent agents – have captured and matched to a particular person or company. You can search by company, person, or industry. This is truly one of the most useful specialist search engines on the Internet. You can locate an abundance of *who's who* straight from www.zoominfo.com. Keep in mind though that this information is being generated from other websites and needs to be verified.

Searching on Cynthia's name, Zoominfo produces what looks like a resume with business experience, association connections, education credentials, and photos in some cases.

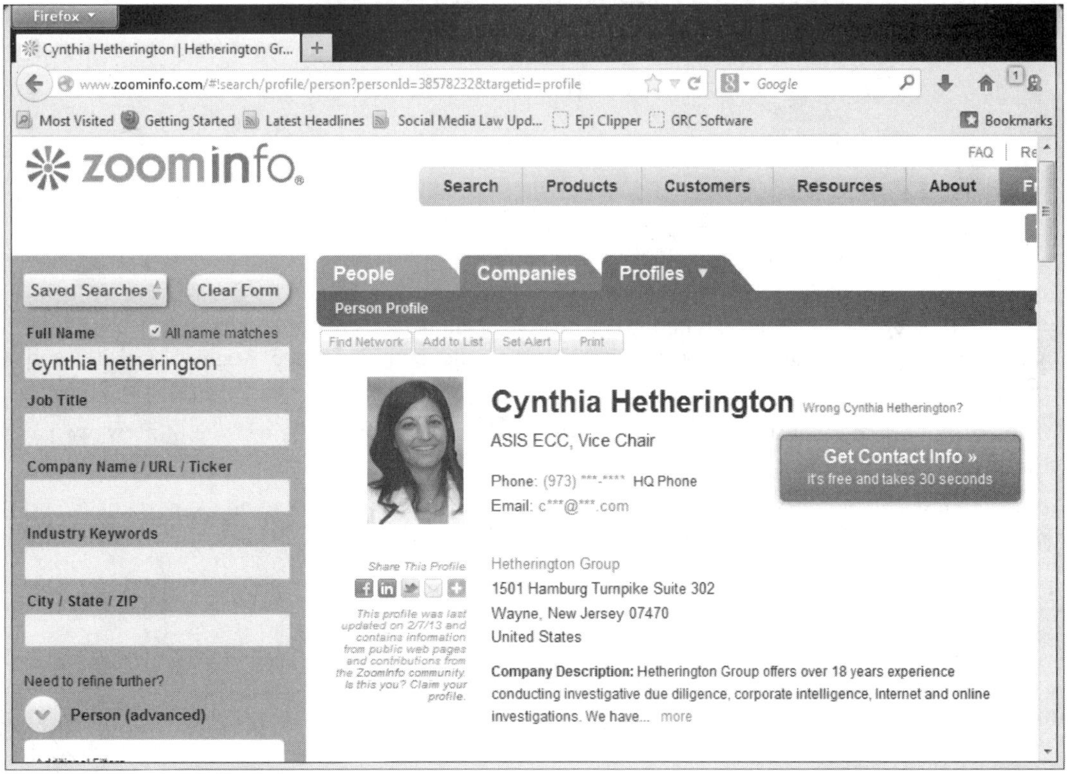

The information found in the left-hand column is produced from the web matches Zoominfo agents found on the right-hand side. These articles, website matches, and directory listings all are assembled into the resume-like profile you see above.

Keep in mind that when searching by a personal name, there may be several matches in the results list. Be sure to look at each one because Zoominfo.com may not connect the dots between two profiles and merely list the names separately. For example, Cynthia Hetherington has twelve separate line entries including some listed as Cindy Hetherington. Look at each line item to insure that you do not miss any important or random information on your subject.

One problem when using Zoominfo is attempting to look up a very common name. There will be thousands of results. The best approach is to search a common name in the *advance search section* and narrow results down by combining name and company name.

Wayback Machine on Archive.org

The mission of Archive.org is "...to help preserve those artifacts and create an Internet library for researchers, historians, and scholars. The Archive collaborates with institutions including the Library of Congress and the Smithsonian."

Archive.org offers researchers and historians a view of a website as captured by the Wayback Machine on a specific date. A web address is entered into the search parameter creating a results page. In the case of http://www.data2know.com, this website has been continually archived since August 18, 2000 and as recently as January 14, 2013.

From January 1, 1996 to August 18, 2007, the Wayback Machine recorded the website http://www.data2know.com on the following dates:

The asterisks shown on the screen capture to follow denote that a change occurred on the www.data2know.com website. Hence from November 22, 2002 to February 7, 2003, there were no alterations of site.

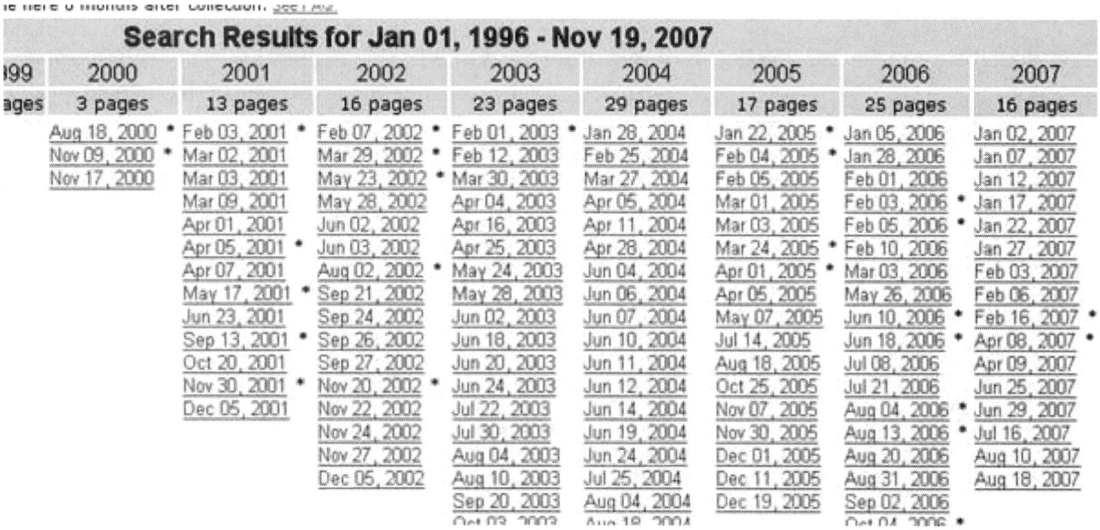

Search Results for Jan 01, 1996 - Nov 19, 2007

2000	2001	2002	2003	2004	2005	2006	2007
3 pages	13 pages	16 pages	23 pages	29 pages	17 pages	25 pages	16 pages
Aug 18, 2000	Feb 03, 2001	Feb 07, 2002	Feb 01, 2003	Jan 28, 2004	Jan 22, 2005	Jan 05, 2006	Jan 02, 2007
Nov 09, 2000	Mar 02, 2001	Mar 29, 2002	Feb 12, 2003	Feb 25, 2004	Feb 04, 2005	Jan 28, 2006	Jan 07, 2007
Nov 17, 2000	Mar 03, 2001	May 23, 2002	Mar 30, 2003	Mar 27, 2004	Feb 05, 2005	Feb 01, 2006	Jan 12, 2007
	Mar 09, 2001	May 28, 2002	Apr 04, 2003	Apr 05, 2004	Mar 01, 2005	Feb 03, 2006	Jan 17, 2007
	Apr 01, 2001	Jun 02, 2002	Apr 16, 2003	Apr 11, 2004	Mar 03, 2005	Feb 05, 2006	Jan 22, 2007
	Apr 05, 2001	Jun 03, 2002	Apr 25, 2003	Apr 28, 2004	Mar 24, 2005	Feb 10, 2006	Jan 27, 2007
	Apr 07, 2001	Aug 02, 2002	May 24, 2003	Jun 04, 2004	Apr 01, 2005	Mar 03, 2006	Feb 03, 2007
	May 17, 2001	Sep 21, 2002	May 28, 2003	Jun 06, 2004	Apr 05, 2005	May 26, 2006	Feb 06, 2007
	Jun 23, 2001	Sep 24, 2002	Jun 02, 2003	Jun 07, 2004	May 07, 2005	Jun 10, 2006	Feb 16, 2007
	Sep 13, 2001	Sep 26, 2002	Jun 18, 2003	Jun 10, 2004	Jul 14, 2005	Jun 18, 2006	Apr 08, 2007
	Oct 20, 2001	Sep 27, 2002	Jun 20, 2003	Jun 11, 2004	Aug 18, 2005	Jul 08, 2006	Apr 09, 2007
	Nov 30, 2001	Nov 20, 2002	Jun 24, 2003	Jun 12, 2004	Oct 25, 2005	Jul 21, 2006	Jun 25, 2007
	Dec 05, 2001	Nov 22, 2002	Jul 22, 2003	Jun 14, 2004	Nov 07, 2005	Aug 04, 2006	Jun 29, 2007
		Nov 24, 2002	Jul 30, 2003	Jun 19, 2004	Nov 30, 2005	Aug 13, 2006	Jul 16, 2007
		Nov 27, 2002	Aug 04, 2003	Jun 24, 2004	Dec 01, 2005	Aug 20, 2006	Aug 10, 2007
		Dec 05, 2002	Aug 10, 2003	Jul 25, 2004	Dec 11, 2005	Aug 31, 2006	Aug 18, 2007
			Sep 20, 2003	Aug 04, 2004	Dec 19, 2005	Sep 02, 2006	

The correct date that the website was captured is in the web address. Wayback Machine records their captures as follows:

http://web.archive.org/web/YYYYMMDDhhmmss/www.website.com/index.html

The phrase "YYYYMMDDhhmmss" is equal to the "year month date hour minute second." Hence, in http://web.archive.org/web/20050403055101/www.data2know.com/index.html the code 20050403055101 equals the exact date and time of April 3, 2005 5:51:01 AM

Summary

What seems like a new phenomenon to many, websites have opened doors for researchers to discover an online bevy of information on individuals' activities and antics. Although, I say "new," which the traditional Web still looks, acts and feels like, it is over twenty years old. With that length of age attributed to it, user histories have been stored for just as long. Hence eBay transactions from 1996 are still accessible. Google.com searches from its earliest days are stored in logs somewhere. Services like Zoominfo.com and Archive.org are preserving websites long gone from their servers.

To uncover valuable information it takes imagination and creative searching along with the ability to know where these services are, what they cover, and how long they have been around to uncover valuable information.

With this abundance of historical information on the Worldwide Web, an individual's online activity can easily, though lightly, be researched. Couple the online profile that is developed through these searches with any press releases and media found through online news channels and a public records search, as outlined in the rest of this book, and it will result in enough information for a very robust profile.

The next generation – the Web 2.0 social network sites – is a whole new resource of potential information and is explored in the next chapter. This is the side of the "Public Information" search mentioned in Chapter 1. Web 2.0's social networks are 'the best of the best' for a researcher. This is where individuals post not only their preferences, likes and dislikes, hobbies, sports, and interests, but also they are diarists sharing their life stories in a very public way.

The next chapter examines how "once what was private and inane" is now "public and the new reality."

Chapter 3

Researching Social Networks

Reference.yourdictionary.com provides an interesting definition of social networks:

> "To define social networking, we need only look at our lives, for though the term is relatively new, the concept is as old as humanity itself. As long as there are people, there will be social networks – individuals connecting with other individuals to form groups, groups connecting with other groups to form larger groups, and then individuals from one group connecting with individuals from another group to form an entirely different group… We are all in some kind of social network, whether it's a family, a neighborhood, a religious organization or a sports team; we know people who know other people. It's simply a natural human phenomenon. However, as the world has become better connected across geographical and cultural boundaries, we've had to devise more creative ways to stay connected and form new relationships."

Inside This Chapter:

- The Quest for Public Exposure
- Facebook
- Pinterest
- Instagram
- Myspace
- Blog.com
- Linkedin
- Twitter
- Flickr
- Using Search Engines to Find Social Network Users and Information
    - Pipl
    - Yoname
    - Lococitato
    - Other Recommended Search Engines
- Using Search Engines to Find Content
    - Icerocket
    - Technorati
    - SocialMention
    - Kurrently
    - Bing.com/Social
- Summary

The Quest for Public Exposure

Social networks are a representation of Web 2.0 programming. Developers have created a way for end users, regardless of their ability, to tailor an environment to share stories through text, sound, and pictures.

Popular social networking sites known as weblogs ("blogs" for short), such as Twitter.com and Facebook.com, have opened up the Web to individuals who want to participate on the Internet but do not have the technical knowhow, time, money to create a website.

Blogs allow for simple input, storage, and are easily searchable. A blog about Italian cooking could be created for free in minutes. Once available, the author selects certain keywords, known as tags, to help draw traffic to their blog. These keywords are updated as the blog grows; so, for instance, specific restaurants can be named, recipes, points of interest, or *whatever* subject the author wants to focus on.

Other social network tools like Youtube.com or Flickr.com are video and photo sites. They allow users to express themselves by uploading imagery and sharing whatever they feel like with the world. These services also encourage tagging (labeling or indexing) the photo or video in order to make it searchable. For example, photos of the San Diego Zoo would be tagged with 'San Diego' and 'zoo' thereby creating fast links for anyone using a search tool to look for either topic.

In comparison, a webpage is fully index-able, but there is nothing really guiding the reader to what the author wants to call attention to. Tags are focused and direct *versus* the hit or miss word match you get from full-page indexing. This is not to say that blogs are not indexed by the full page. Google and other traditional search engines still scan and index the full pages of blogs, but specialized engines like Icerocket.com and Technorati.com put the heavier emphasis on the tags indicated by the author, resulting in better search results.

As an investigative source, this is a super benefit for those who are looking for individuals based on a username, hobby, or location.

A Trick of the Trade

A convenient trick recommended by Cynthia is to go to gmail.com, hotmail.com, or yahoo.com and create an email account that you can use for registration on various social network sites. This email is referred to as your "throw away email account" because you are able to move through the various sites and services without exposing your actual everyday email account to spam or unwanted emails. In other words, when you are tired of it, throw it away.

To summarize, social networks use the latest web development programming to make the Internet more accessible for those who were otherwise technically challenged. Anyone can get involved by creating an account for themselves and communicating with the world in the form of a blog, or they can create an account with a video service or photo service in order to share images and videos.

Let's examine what is possible in what social networks offer and how they can be used for locating information about a person or topic.

Facebook

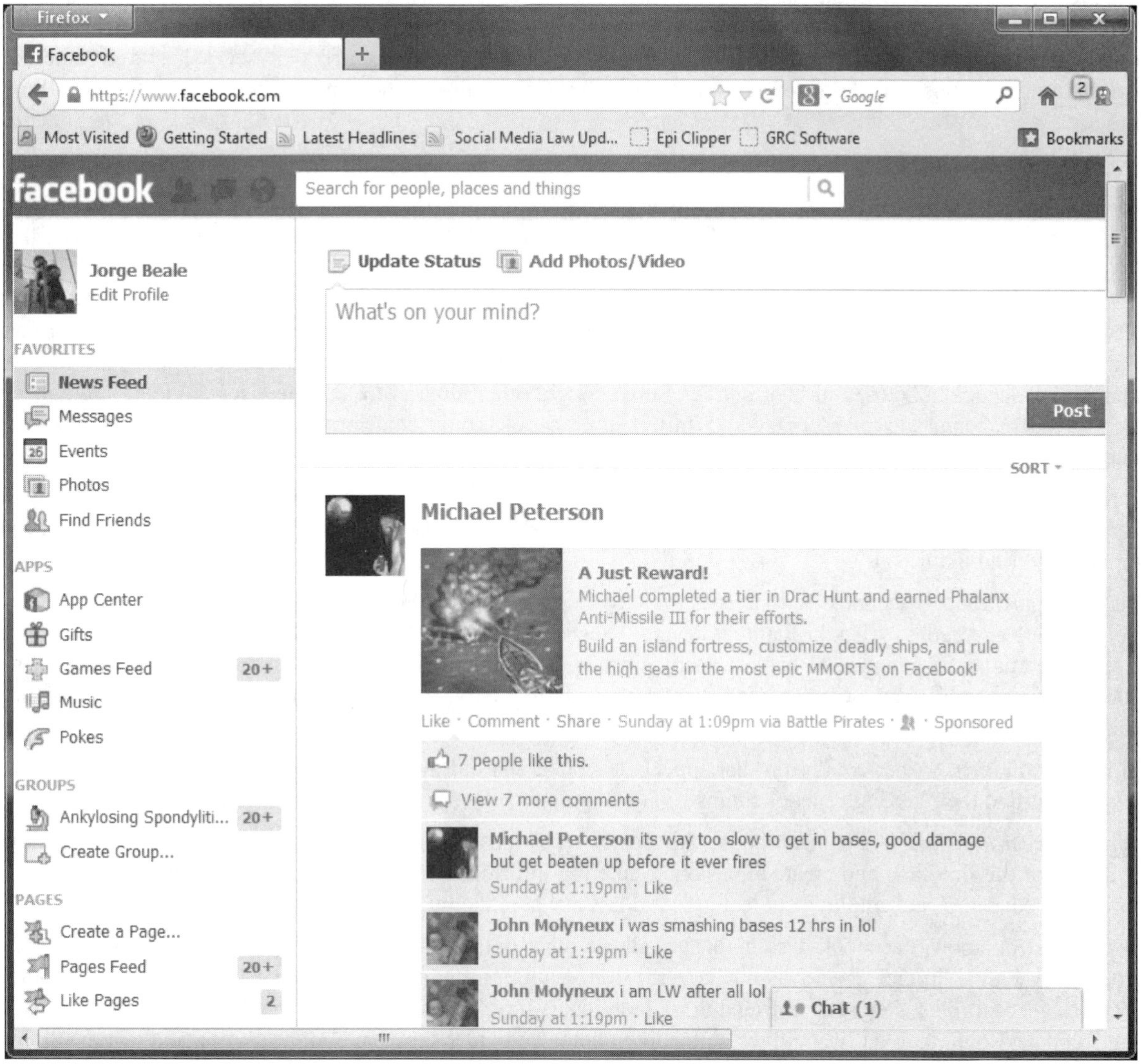

Even though there are thousands of social networks spanning corporate worlds, embedded in geographic regions, or focused in cultural norms to attract specific masses, Facebook.com is the go-to leader in social networking.

Facebook's latest statistics are astounding. Some of the top numbers are:

- More than 900 million active users
- 50% of active users log on to Facebook.com in any given day

That means hundreds of millions of people from all over the planet are logging in and checking Facebook daily, and that is just the daily active users!

There are still several hundred million users who are only occasional participants in the service. It is no wonder every investigator wants to learn about using Facebook in their investigations. This issue will start by doing its best to help you understand the users and their perspective when using Facebook. Then we'll later discuss Facebook as an investigative tool, and finally we'll talk about the legal issues involved, terms of service, and common sense to investigating with this tool because even though there are 200 million active inhabitants, it is still the Wild West of the Internet.

Understanding the Facebook User

Keep in mind the Web has been around for over a dozen years, and for most of that time, the only participants were those individuals who could create web pages, edit them, FTP them, and had a place to house them (i.e. www.mycompany.com). Maybe there were 10 out of 200 people who could and would do this regularly. The Web was their domain, and it was an exclusive club for programmers and geeks. Then the earlier blogs began to appear as social networks such as Xanga.com and Tribe.net, and soon enough the masses started getting wind and wanted to try it out. The real WOW came when Myspace.com hit the scene and "all those young people" started sharing information about their bands, schools, photos, and their antics. Sure enough, other blogs were out there for the more journalistic types, such as typepad.com and livejournal.com. In this zone people could contribute their thoughts and opinions, but not much else.

Here is where social networking stayed for a long time until Facebook arrived. It is a perfect marriage of blogging ideas, thoughts, and opinions, coupled with the ability upload photos, videos, reference other websites, and most importantly, find old friends.

The best part about Facebook is that it is so easy to use that getting into the action is no longer exclusive to programmers and geeks. Also, brilliant by design, Facebook is a very clean and non-intimidating Web presence so the older generations are not turned off by flashy images or blaring tunes jumping out at them suddenly. In a very Google'esqe manner, they have modeled their design in simplicity, where Myspace thrives on action and noise (i.e. Yahoo.com).

So here we have it. A perfect design that appeals to young and old, offers free access to friends and family, and will help people find their lost high school chums.

Ahh... *Facecrack!* This is the phenomenon that occurs when a user first signs on with their authentic credentials. They sit down for the first time and create an account; entering information like what books and movies they enjoy, marital status, and education and employment history. And this is where the little addiction to Facecrack starts.

Next thing you know, Facebook has aggregated all the other graduates from their high school and offered them up as people they should "friend" (which is now a verb, along with unfriending, in Webster's Dictionary). Given the natural curiosity of most folks, they start to friend these individuals if only to see how they aged. Next, the new user is posting status updates about their daily activities, uploading photos and videos, playing online games, and commenting on their friends' walls.

Investigating Techniques

The chief component of the Facecrack addict, and even the occasional Facebook user, is that they usually do not consider what they are writing on their walls and in their profiles to be an open source. When a participant updates their profile, in their mind's eye they see a specific entity reading that information. Usually this entity looks, smells, sounds, and acts just like themselves and their friends. They might not be aware that complete strangers, bosses, competitors, ex-lovers, and potentially future suitors might be peeking in on their updates. Even now, I just took a break, looked at my own Facebook profile, and saw one member advising everyone to turn on an afternoon soap opera, another telling everyone she's "taking Ruby to the vet," and others were either quoting historical phrases or lyrics or were complaining that it is only Thursday instead of the weekend. Nothing too offensive, however, I wonder if any of these self-confessors ever consider "what if my mother or boss could read this?" And that's the investigative key! They aren't asking those questions. They are blindly updating and informing the world of their activity, family updates, and photos, and it is up to the investigator to look and see if they can uncover any information from these profiles. Is it taking advantage of them? Not really. No one forced the user to open an account and broadcast their lives. Also, when the accounts are set up, they have the option to completely lock unknown parties out! Facebook is very clear on their privacy set ups.

Indeed, when Facebook offers someone an account, they are given the option to set passwords and permit only certain other users, friends, and networks into their profile. Originally, the default was to permit "friends and networks" to see a profile. When networks were originally set up with a profile, the user would add Central New Jersey, San Francisco Bay, or another regionally specific network to identify what area of the country they were most interested in and most likely from. If I were investigating them, I would make sure I was in the same regional network as they are. Then because of the "friends and networks" default, I could in most cases view their entire profile, including photos and wall posts.

Apparently this was not a great secret because the nice folks at Facebook caught on and quickly stopped allowing regional network selection, eliminating this way of viewing someone's profile without actually friending them.

The other method might not be a method so much as a tactic. When used wisely, it can return some rich gains, and by all means, has worked for me more times than not. However, when it does not work, it can either leave you hanging or have a backlash which can compromise your whole case. Try friending your target. This direct route is dangerous so consider this section like a mine-field and treat it with the same respect you would if you had to tread across said mine-field wearing a blindfold. In other words, here is the disclaimer, *do not try this if you are unsure of the outcome!*

Using an account created specifically for Facebook investigations (more on terms of service later), I have a profile that is not exactly as forthcoming as my own personal account. You can create variations on your own real account for learning purposes and see what I mean. Mine is for my dog, Java. Java has discussions, friends, and photos, but if you look for her in Facebook searches, you won't find much out there because she's pretty good at setting up her security preferences.

When we come to a person's profile we need to look into, the first thing I'll check is the photo. This little feature, which is always set to public unless they uncheck it, is a huge resource all by itself. Surveillance investigators can't help but love getting people's photos from Facebook. Second, do they have any fan pages listed? Are they a fan of In and Out Burger and Arbor Day Fund? Final thing to check is the friend's list. If the list is available (again this is normally defaulted to show friends), then I can scan the entire list and look for other associates I might be trying to develop or family members based on same last name.

After examining the list of friends for any known associates, matching family names to garner leads, I will then take a gander at how many friends this target has. Using the following statistics that Facebook.com provides, we see most persons have 130 friends.

- Average user has 130 friends on the site
- Average user sends 8 friend requests per month
- Average user spends more than 55 minutes per day on Facebook
- Average user clicks the Like button on 9 pieces of content each month
- Average user writes 25 comments on Facebook content each month
- Average user becomes a fan of 4 Pages each month
- Average user is invited to 3 events per month
- Average user is a member of 13 groups

If my target has more than 130 friends, or anything above 100 friends, they are probably not too discerning about whom they are friending. Anything above 200 friends and I'm considering that the user really isn't paying attention to the quality of friend they are letting in, but is just interested in clicking "accept" or trying to build some larger number of friends. Whatever the reason, we use the numbers as a cue.

If they are hovering at the lower end, I will start sending invitations to friend my target's friend list. Java's profile picture is of a cute dog with plush toy. She's hard to resist and often gets invited in without question. Even so, not everyone is gullible, so she'll eventually get questioned to which she will usually ignore that user and find another. Once Java has enough friends (10 or so) of my target, she'll then try to directly friend the target. The target user will see the invite, see that they have 10 friends in common, and (since it's man's nature to not be confrontational) will hopefully invite her in.

If my target has hundreds of friends, I don't bother with the extra friending. The user is not really checking who they are letting in so I go right for it.

On the other hand, if the user has less than 100 friends, or if they have ignored my friend requests, another measure is necessary. From the investigation I have to date, I try to find the hobbies, sports, and interests of the target, and try to pre-empt and predict what fan pages they might be part of. Indeed, I might have discerned their fan pages right away when I saw their initial profile, so I'll use this. I join their fan pages. No, by being in the same fan network I cannot view their profile, but it will give credibility when I try to friend them. What I am doing is morphing my profile to match the target's profile so I become appealing and someone they want to connect to.

What if they have very minimal information, a handful of friends, and seem intimidating to even approach? Then I don't bother. They are probably not using Facebook as much as I think and aren't worth the effort to try to read their wall. If you do attempt to friend a target with little activity, they might catch on that you are not a friendly friend but more of an investigative one, or a nuisance, depending on the situation.

Using Sense and Caution

This brings us to the common sense step. Just because people are using Facebook, does not mean they are spilling their secrets, exchanging intellectual property, or talking about their finances openly. Most of the discussions we've seen over the years remind me of barroom chatter. People who are mildly comfortable with each other exchange the day's events, some pleasantries, some flirtations, and the occasional political flare-up. They discuss sports, cheer their teams, swap vacation pictures, and cajole their neighbors. If a tragedy has occurred, you'll see them reaching out for support.

Finally, and most importantly, in the last few months Facebook has changed its privacy settings. The default is now open source versus the closed source it used to be. So before you go through any of these methods, first and foremost check the person's profile to see if it is even locked down. You might be surprised that what you thought would be an insurmountable task to see what they are writing about, turns out to be a few mouse clicks away!

In closing I want to talk about the terms of service. Facebook is an amazing application that hosts 2/3rds the size of the US population every day in active users. You can imagine the security troubles, breeches, and nuisances they see on an hourly basis. They do their best with setting policies for privacy, making the users responsible for their own network security settings, and putting in place a clear set of terms.

As with most software applications, very few users actually read the terms of service before jumping in and hardly realize that the terms change often, even after they have signed on and agreed to them. Yet the terms of service are very clear about creating false profiles under Section 4, ("You will not provide any false personal information on Facebook, or create an account for anyone other than you without permission."), and in the law enforcement guidelines sent out, they are equally clear that if they identify a false profile for the purpose of an investigation, they will remove it.

Of course, you will see hundreds of pages of fictional characters and dead celebs who all have active Facebook accounts. Look up Julia Child and you'll see she's Facebook-ing from the grave.

Pinterest

Pinterest.com is a digital bulletin board for cool and interesting things. Users find images they like and pin them to their own boards. Similar to a teenager's bedroom walls full of posters and rock show ticket stubs, a Pinterest.com user finds images, inspirational sayings, keepsakes, and other memorabilia and pins it to their Pinterest account. According to the Nielsen 2012 study (http://blog.nielsen.com/nielsenwire/social/2012), Pinterest.com users increased by over 1,000% by the end of 2012. At this writing they had about 11 million users, all of who spend about 90+ minutes per month on the site.

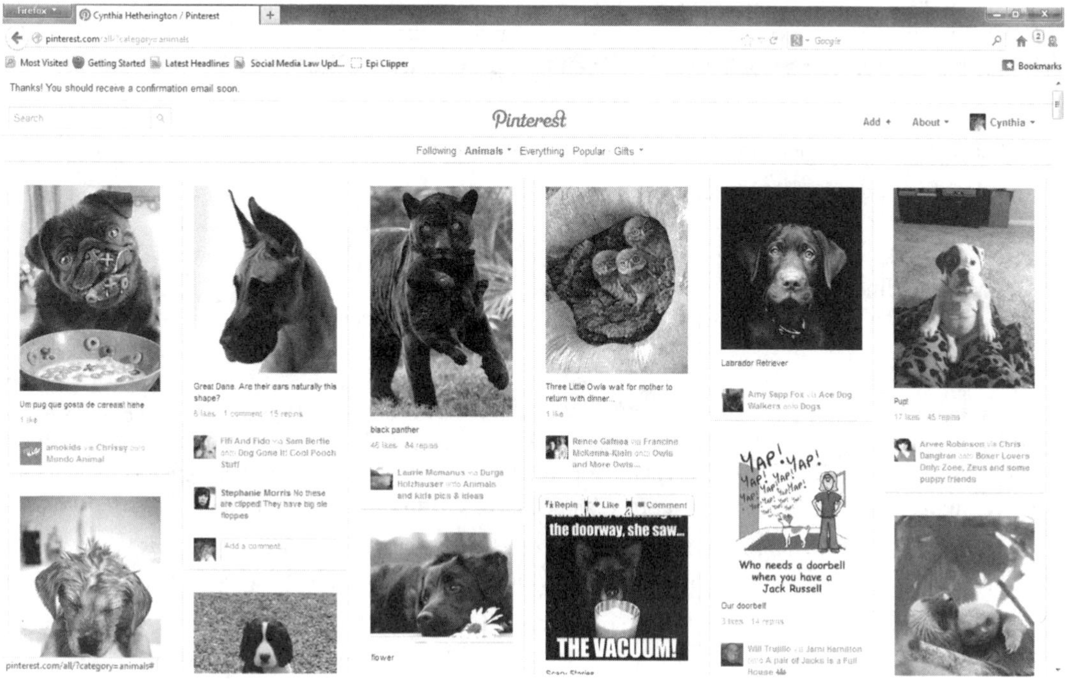

Investigator Takeaways

- If you know the username of the individual, try it after the pinterest.com/USERNAME
- If you don't know their username, go to Facebook.com or Twitter.com to find their username
- Once you are in their account, you can make an assessment of their likes and dislikes
- Often times a link to their Twitter and Facebook account is available
- Who they are following and who follows them is also available
- "Repins from" is not necessarily a friend

Notes to Users

To protect your own account follow these privacy settings which can be found under the Options section.

- Choose whether your profile page is available to search engines
- Go to *Settings* and turn on the "Prevent Search Engines from including your profile in their search results"
- Do not connect your account with Facebook or Twitter
- Do not use the same user id as Facebook or Twitter

Instagram

Instagram.com is a free online photo-sharing and social networking service that enables its users to take a picture, apply a digital filter to it, and share it on a variety of social networking services, including its own and other leading sites such as Facebook or Twitter. Users can add hashtags (the "#" sign in front of a word designating it to be a topic) to photos and make comments. Once the photo is uploaded others can make comments and like the photo.

Investigator Takeaways

- If you know the username of the individual, try it after the instagram.com/USERNAME
  - Go to Facebook to find their username
- If they are sharing their photos, you will get a firsthand account of personal information
- If they haven't set their account to private, you will see who they follow and who follows them

Notes to Users

In order to set any features, you need to work off your device. After logging into your account:

- Click on the sprocket in the upper right hand corner
- Scroll to "Photos are Private" and select ON
- Also review Share Settings in the same menu
- Here you will find Facebook, Twitter, and Tumblr, to name a few
- The site does not work well with older versions of Internet Explorer

Myspace

Myspace.com was one of the earliest and most popular social networking sites on the Web. Begun as a tool for local musicians to share songs, gig dates, and information about themselves with their fans, Myspace quickly took off as the go-to site for anyone who considers themselves hip. The largest portion of its subscriber base is teenagers and young adults. However, plenty of seniors, adults, and professional service firms – hiring agencies – also use Myspace.

Use your *throw away email address* to create an account on Myspace.com. Your account allows you to move smoothly through the various users' pages, viewing their photos and videos as well as interacting with them as necessary.

Once logged in, utilize the search engine at the top of the page. Be sure to change the pull down menu on the right of the search box from **People** to **Myspace.com**, forcing the search to look within Myspace.com only.

Recommended searches are a person's name (yes, many do post their full name), the person's username, the town the person lives in, the school attended, or the employer's name. All of these items are generally self-reported within the user's profile. These profiles can be extremely revealing. It is amazing how much information is disclosed including occupation, employer, sexual preference, marriage status, birthdays, and personal tastes in music, movies, and hobbies.

Beyond what the profile owner writes about themselves on their page, information can be discerned from the dialog between themselves and their friends – those people in the extended networks. Happy birthday messages are very common. One can learn much about the author's social life, where they hang out, with whom, and what crazy events occurred because these individuals talk pretty openly about themselves. Beyond looking at the user's profile, look as well at their friends' profiles for messages posted to their friends.

The next pieces of useful information are the videos and pictures. Many details can be extracted just from looking at pictures. The surroundings, titles of the photos, and other interesting tell-tale facts can be found.

What can be discerned from the snapshot of this fellow's Myspace page is his full name, employer's name, where he lives, and what he looks like. Looking deeper into his photos are references to bars in NY City that he appears to be visiting.

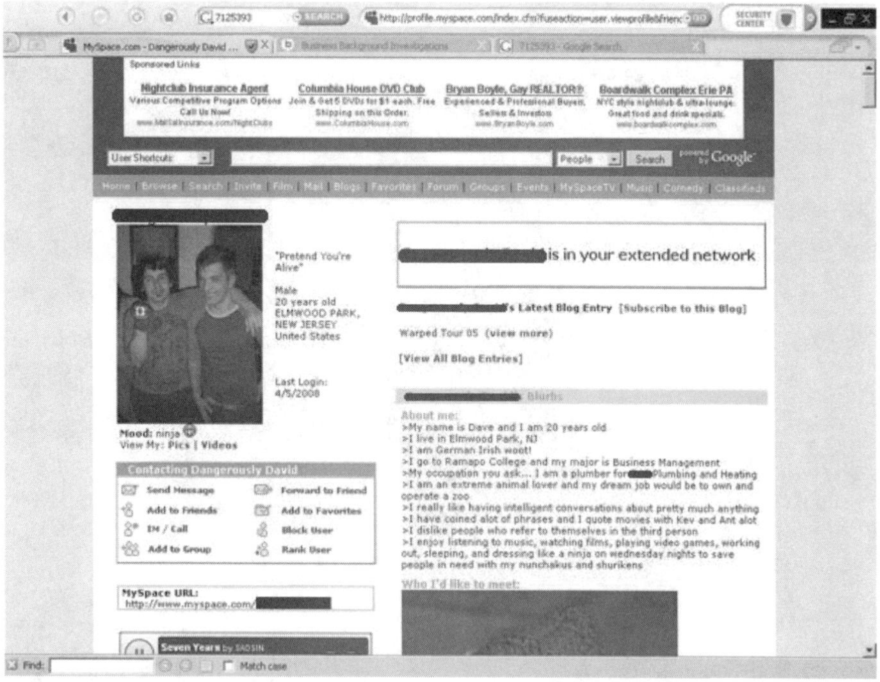

Other spaces that share this type of information and may be searched in a similar fashion are—

- Facebook.com
- Friendster.com
- Yahoo360.com
- Twitter.com
- Youtube.com

Blog.com

Blog.com is just one of many websites to create your own web log, also known as a blog. As the following image portrays, a person can create a blog in three easy steps.

1. The first is to signup, which in the case of blog.com is a simple name, address, and email registration.
2. Second, the blog is created by giving a name and specifying what the topic is. For example, Business Background Investigations is a blog about conducting due diligence on companies. The title of this blog is hetheringtongroup.blog.com. Its initial setup only took minutes.
3. The last step is to tailor the blog's appearance by maneuvering through a selection of pre-established fonts, colors, backgrounds, and layouts.

The entire process is point and click.

These blogs are not search engines in themselves, but instead offer searchable interfaces on their own sites. If they do not have a search engine within their own domain, then make sure to use Technorati.com and Icerocket.com to reach these services. Or try this trick with Google.com. Run a search as follows—site:blog.com <username, expression, person's name, whatever you are looking for>

The "site:domain.xxx" narrows down your search to just that particular domain, Yahoo.com for example.

Similar sites to blog.com include typepad.com, journalspace.com, xanga.com, and livejournal.com. Also, a directory of free blog registry sites and tools can be found at diarist.net.

Linkedin

Linkedin.com is the professional social network, targeting adults who want to share and network their business experience. In reality, both adults and young people can register in any service, however the focus of Linkedin.com is more concerned about professional networking than social networking.

An amazing amount of information is posted on Linkedin pages. The obvious data that jumps out includes the name, location, and work position. Also discoverable items may include one's education, past employment, affiliations to associations, particular networking groups, and any posted recommendations.

Individuals can be quite revealing about themselves on Linkedin, and they offer up probably too much personal information.

A popular social network tool very similar to Linkedin is Spoke.com.

Below is the Linkedin page for co-author Cynthia Hetherington.

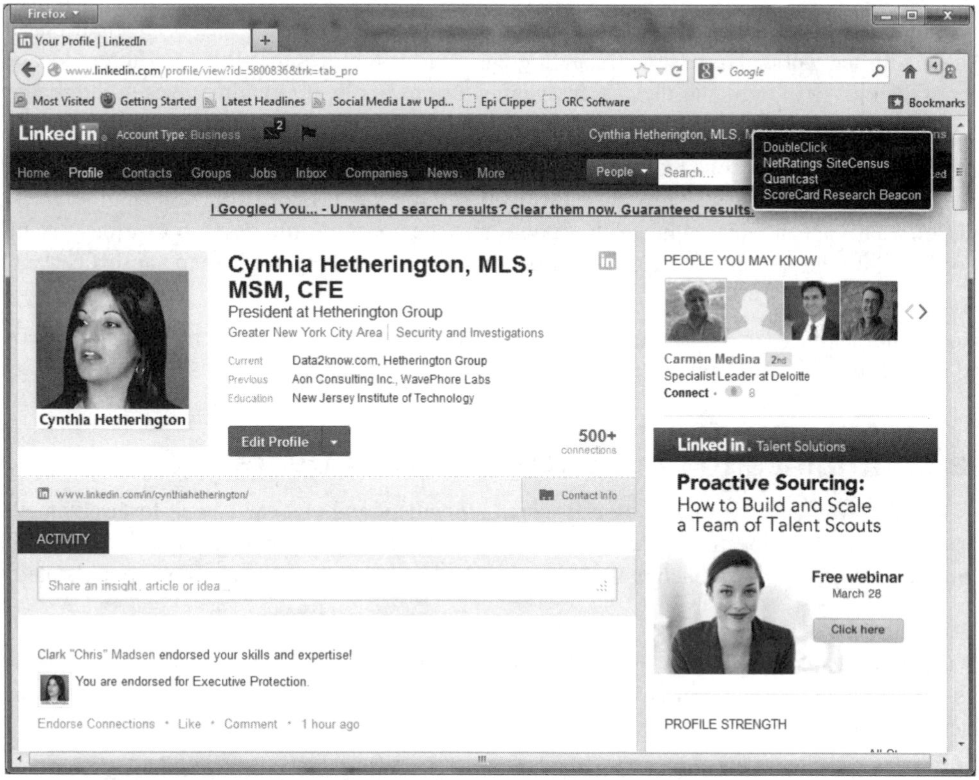

LinkedIn and Diploma Mills

An interesting background check search is a diploma mill search on Linkedin. Go to LinkedIn's *Advanced Search* and in the education section enter the known name of a college **Diploma Mill** such as **Almeda**. A Diploma Mill is a non-accredited school offering degrees for sale with little or no academic requirements (just money). For a few hundred dollars, Almeda grants 'degrees' based on one's life experiences. You will be amazed by the number of people (thousands) who tout their education credentials from Almeda on their Linkedin profile.

Twitter

In 144 characters or less you can blast your thoughts, opinions, and ideas – or absolute nonsense – to the world via Twitter.com. Although many are quick to discredit the value of Twitter for investigative uses, the truth is that this service is probably one of the best resources to arrive online since Google. When someone decides it is a good time to complain about their job, boss, or spouse, they might do this openly on Twitter. Perhaps a Tweet stems from an incident such as an accident or pandemonium erupting (perhaps due to workplace and school violence). Those tweets are all archived and searchable!

You can search directly in Twitter via search.twitter.com. What is key about Twitter? The content is real time – and so are search results. Potentially, you can find information posted within seconds. Also helpful is the ability to geo-locate Twitter posters based on tweets. You can look for mentions of wine tasting near Sonoma County with a search that looks like this >>> #winetasting near:"sonoma county, ca" within:15mi

You can also use the advanced search (http://twitter.com/search-advanced) in Twitter to make it easier as well.

Flickr

Flickr.com, Photobucket.com, Picassa.com, Kodak.com, and similar online services offer great places to park digital images to share with the world. These services are a great idea for families that live in different locations who want to share images of the kids or of events as they are happening. For example, if Grandma lives in Florida, and the grandkids are in New York, the parents can send Grandma a link to Flickr.com after they celebrate a holiday.

However Grandma is not the only one looking at these photos and many of them are not of kids at holidays. Anyone can find office workers at office parties taking snapshots of their cubes or office spaces and sharing way too much on the business side of what happens internally. Such a photo may demonstrate the desktop of a busy right handed (mouse position) working gal who is using Microsoft Outlook email and working on perhaps an office layout or marketing campaign.

The trick to searching in Flickr and other such sites is to search by company name, personal name, username (if known), and also add phrases like "at work" or "at school" or "on the job." Be imaginative.

Using Search Engines to Find Social Network Users

Searching in social networks is twofold. You can search by content and you can search for username. Though Google is an excellent search tool for locating the actual social network profile, it is not very good for searching the posts and content within a social network site. Each of the following are located at ".com" unless otherwise stated.

Pipl

Considered the best search engine for user's social network accounts, Pipl.com has been the go-to source for investigators for several years. It can be searched by full name, email address, and even phone number. Though Pipl.com does not find every last social network site and location, its coverage is very thorough.

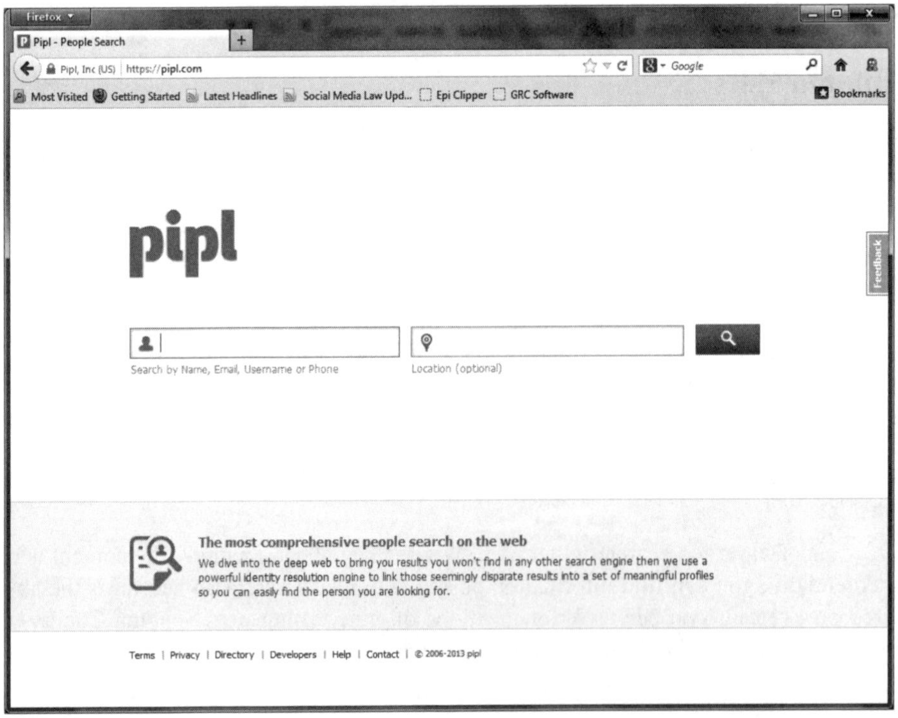

Yoname

If you are not familiar with which social networks your search subject may be involved with, then search out Yoname.com. Here you can search by full name, email address, and even phone number.

Whichever term you select, your search will use the following social network sites as shown on the example to follow and will return whatever matches the name, email address, or number you entered.

Warning – If you search by email address, that person will receive an email from Yoname.com stating someone was looking for them. It will not say who searched them, just that the search was conducted.

Lococitato

Lococitato.com is an easy to use application and an excellent resource to discover who a person's friends are and to whom the person chats with – providing the user has not made their network of friends and profile "private."

Lococitato.com, sold specifically to law enforcement and security professionals, works for Facebook, Twitter, YouTube, and Myspace.

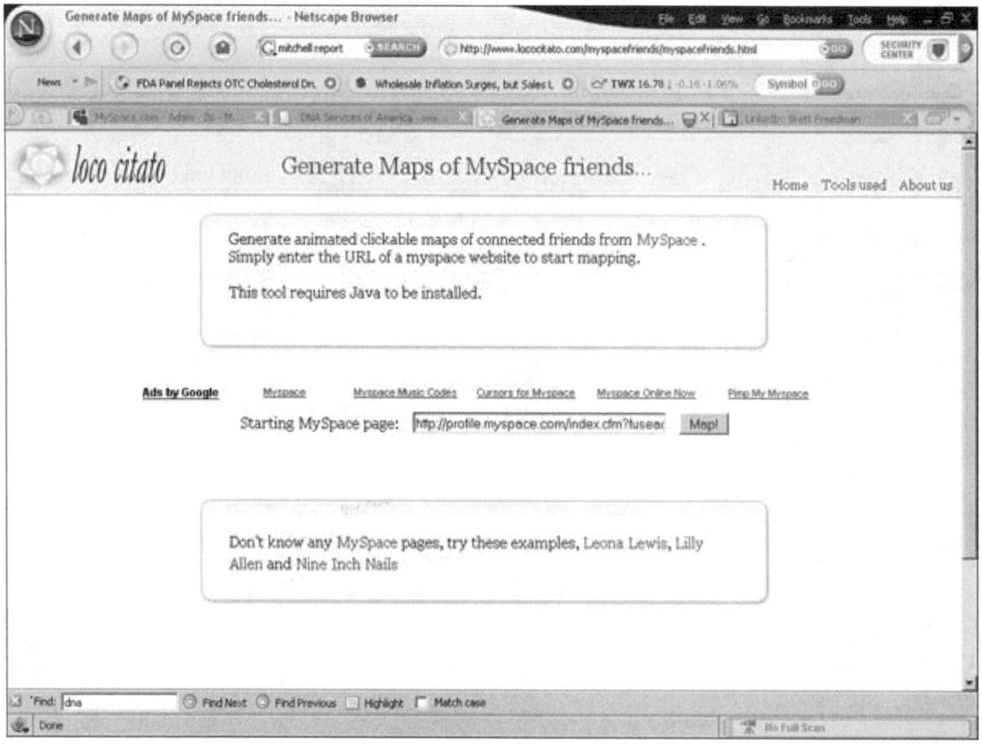

Using the URL you have copied from the Myspace or Facebook entry, open up Visualizer and plug in that address to expand the network.

From here you can mouse over the buttons that pop up at the same time, and you will see a quick snapshot of the person that is being connected, as in the example below with Kristen Nicole.

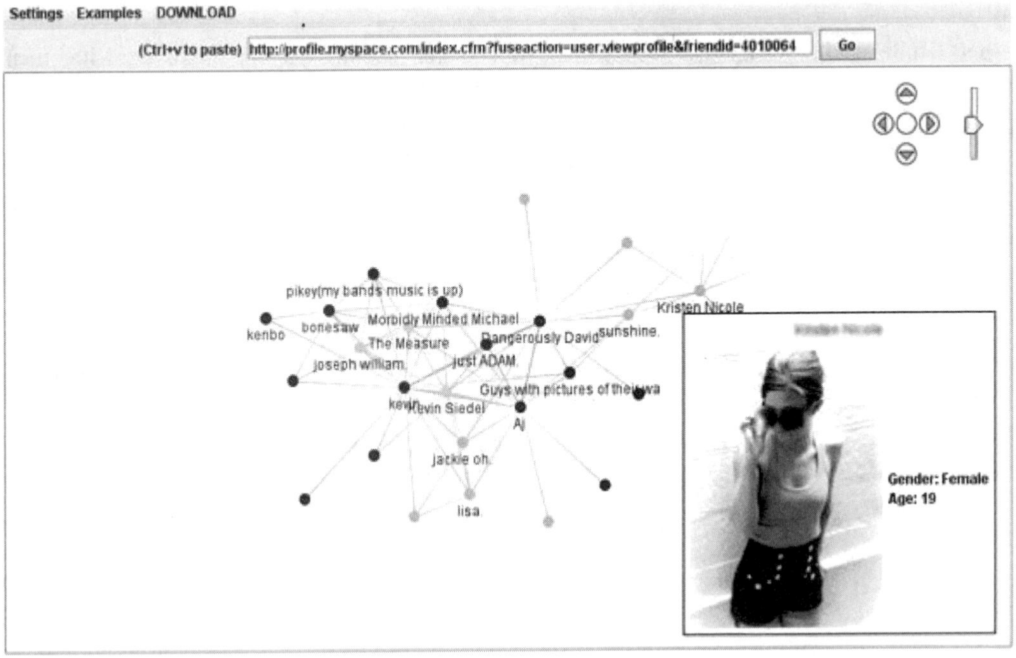

The incredibly useful feature of this is that not only do you see who is connected to our subject, but who amongst them are also connected to each other. This helps establish groups of friends or colleagues. Often times you can discern who is in school together, who works together, or what cliques are rejoined through their social network site.

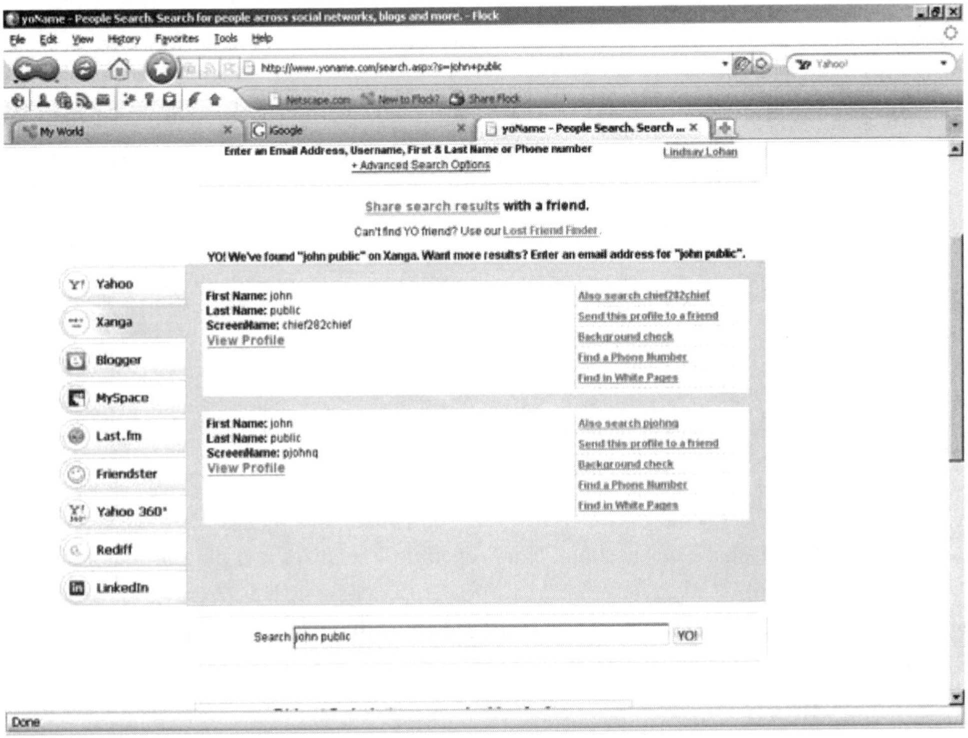

The sample search to the left is on the made-up name 'John Public.' This search shows that yoname.com located results matching that name in Yahoo, Xanga, Blogger, Myspace, and other similar social networks.

Other Recommended Search Engines

Other search engines for locating user accounts are:

- Google
- Spokeo
- Yasni
- Yatedo
- 123People
- Foupas

Using Search Engines to Find Content

Icerocket

Icerocket.com offers a unique array of useful tools for the blogger and the researcher. Backed by Mark Cuban, owner of the Dallas Mavericks and avid blogger himself (see www.blogmaverick.com), this resource was created to track what people were searching for. Icerocket.com focuses primarily on blog sites, using sites' meta-tagging to categorize and index the content within the blogs. In this way a search can be conducted by keyword, which allows us to capture any relevant matches found on a site and will prioritize those matches that are marked as tagged searches.

For example, let us say a blog is written about places to eat in Seattle. It names several Italian, Spanish, and French specific restaurants by design, such as—

Seattle Italian Restaurants
- La Trattatoria

Seattle Spanish Restaurants
- Papi's Cocina

All the words will be captured by the search bot and indexed. However, if the writer tags or self- indexes this post as Italian Restaurants, Spanish Restaurants, etc., it will move up in rank in our Icerocket search results.

From the observer's perspective, one can watch the search terms being typed in by users to see what interests the average person and what they look for.

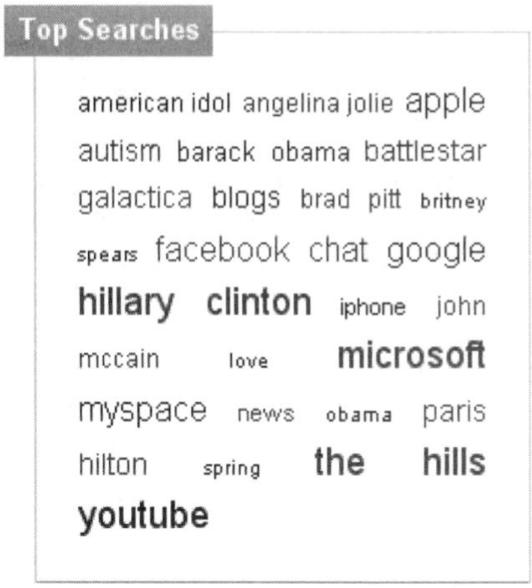

The real benefit to Icerocket is the search engine. Icerocket searches through blogs, image directories, and most importantly, Myspace. Even though you can search directly in Myspace, using the Icerocket search engine tool for Myspace searches often presents a more comfortable search environment since it is a more traditional search.

Icerocket does allow you to narrow down your blog searches through the advanced search link *or* by using the search operators such as Title, Author, and Tag to find blogs you desire.

Hence, a search would look like, **title: "public records"** and the results would require that *public records* show up in the title. The other examples are: **author: "Cynthia Hetherington"** will return all mentions written by "Cynthia Hetherington" and **tag:Yankees** will return all posts tagged "Yankees."

These advanced search features can be combined. For example, search using *title: "Public Records" author: "Cynthia Hetherington"* to locate all blog posts by Cynthia Hetherington with Public Records in the title.

Icerocket searches against Facebook, Twitter, blogs, and images and organizes its information by time and date of posting. This is an excellent resource for investigators who are limited in what they can search in their office thanks to the firewall blocking popular tools like YouTube and Facebook. You won't be able to open the links, but at least you can search those sites unhindered and get a results list.

Icerocket.com is a perfect way to search Twitter if your company firewall will not let you access Twitter.com directly.

Technorati

Technorati.com is the "Google" of blog search engines; meaning this is the market-share leader, at least for now. Technorati is the search engine for websites like YouTube, Myspace, Blog.com, Xanga.com, etc. Technorati covers almost 100 million blogs daily and offers a rich search engine that enables one to narrow down a results list efficiently.

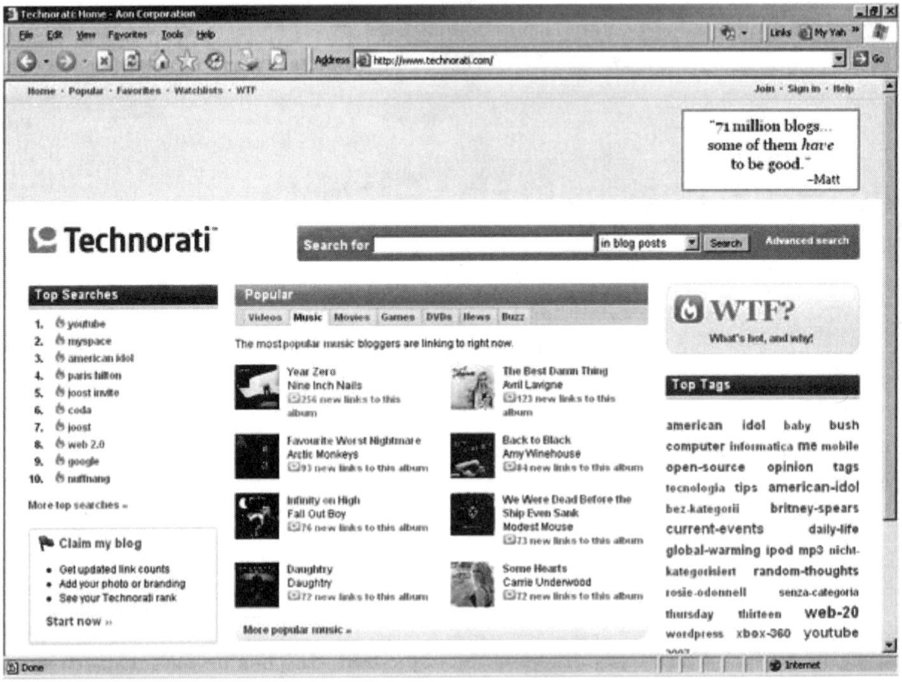

Using a particular topic is a must when searching Technorati and Icerocket thoroughly

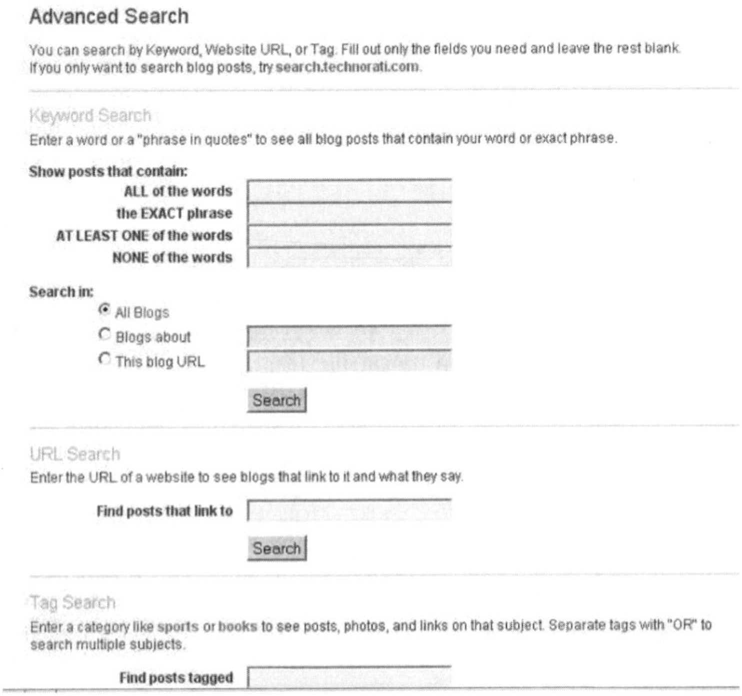

Using the *Advanced Search* option, the search can be narrowed down to a particular blog, perhaps to search for the one or two times a topic was mentioned by a single blogger. Also, search by tag (explained further in Icerocket.com) to sites linked to a particular blog and by the usual phrase or single-word search.

Other Twitter Resources

Monitter.com

Monitter.com offers you three simultaneous searches on Twitter posts.

Addictomatic.com

Addictomatic.com tracks RSS feeds, blog posts, Twitter, Flickr, other social networking sites, and news. However, you will not locate the historical information as shown from a traditional search engine results list.

SocialMention

Socialmention.com goes beyond Twitter, Facebook, and Google+ by including a larger number of blogs and microblogs. They organize information in several methods. There is the standard date/time or relevance results list, but SocialMention also offers several analytical features such as sentiment (putting posts into positive, negative, or neutral categories based on the linguistics of the post). Top keywords are also highlighted. The best feature of SocialMention is the ability to set up an RSS feed to your email service by choosing the RSS button on the right hand side of the screen. Searches you are interested in conducting often, for example a brand or company name, you can have sent to your RSS folder in your email server.

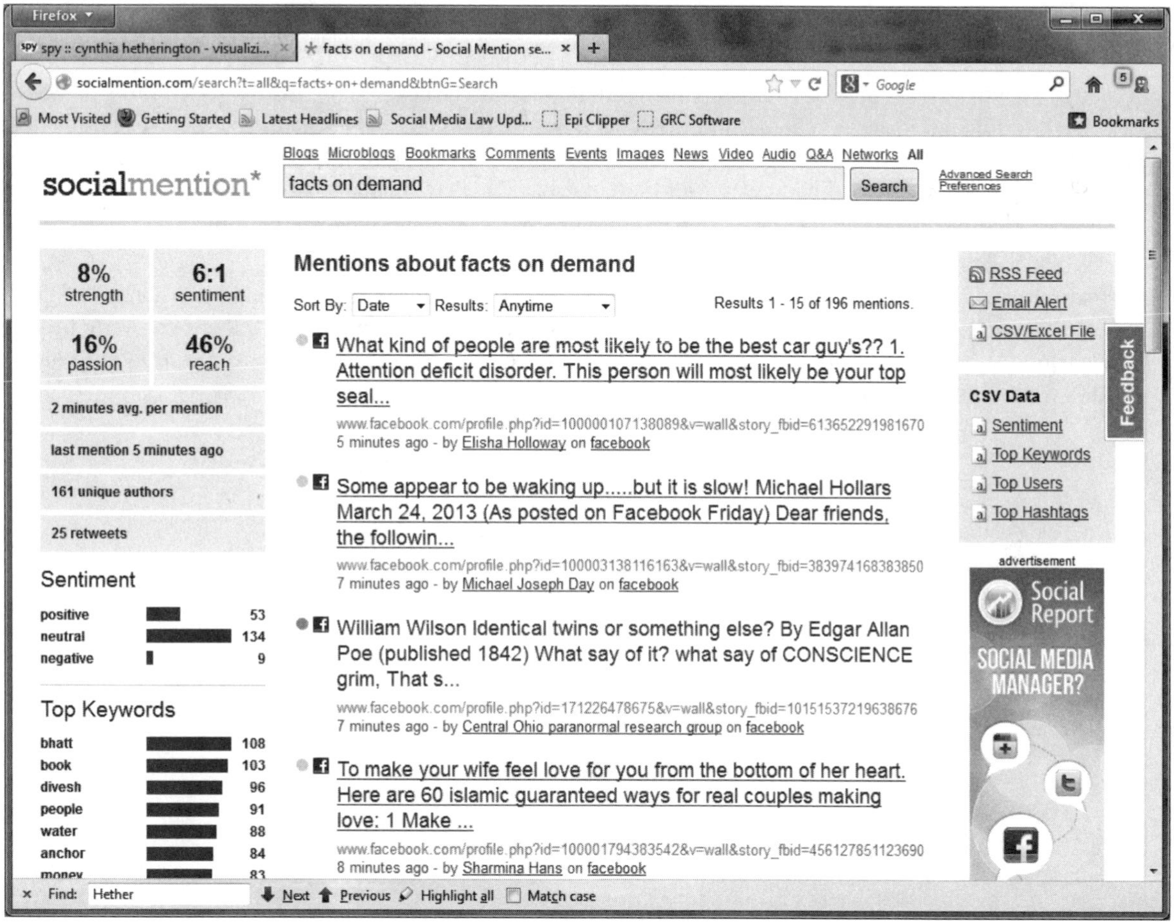

To learn about new social networks or for locating social networks that focus on individual cultures, social groups, and country specific blogs – visit Wikipedia.org at http://en.wikipedia.org/wiki/List_of_social_networking_websites.

Kurrently

Kurrently.com searches Twitter, Facebook, and Google+ with keyword searches. You can organize your results lists by date/time or relevance. It used to offer an RSS feed and may again in the future.

Bing.com/Social

Bing's Social Search has a unique relationship with Facebook, so not only can you focus on content searching, but it is rather handy for locating profiles in Facebook that have been privatized. The primary focus is indexing content from Facebook, Twitter, and Google+ by date/time or relevance.

Summary

In today's identity theft-aware environment, there are privacy advocates arguing for tighter controls on SSNs, personal identifiers, health and financial records, and any other piece of information that can be misused. The irony is while these advocates fight for discretion and privacy of an individual's personal information, that person is "out there" sharing even more than identifiers and addresses with the entire universe! Individuals, as we have seen through Web 2.0 and social networks, are living online. They rely on the Web to relay their stories, carry their message, and carve out a bit of themselves virtually to anyone everywhere who would log in.

As researchers, it is to our benefit to take advantage of these self-exposing persons and keep abreast of the latest Web 2.0 (and beyond) developments in order to keep informed. From this point forward, there can only be more service offerings on the Web to take advantage of. Some good advice is to learn the resources outlined in this chapter and stay tuned to what is on the horizon.

Chapter 4

Resources and Search Tips by Topic

This Chapter presents key public record and public information topics in an alphabetical order index. From ***Archives*** to ***Worker's Compensation,*** *t*he resources listed herein are a mix of searchable government sites and private company sites. Chapter 6 provides specific data found at the state, county /parish or local government levels, such as courts or recorder's offices.

Inside This Chapter:

- Archives
- Aviation Records
- Banks & Financial Institutions
- Business Entity Records
- Copyrights
- Court Records (includes civil, criminal, etc. records)
- Court Records of Native Americans
- Court Records on Statewide Judicial Systems
- Criminal Records at State Repositories
- Elections: Candidates, PACs, Lobbyists, and Voters
- Environmental Information
- Federal Agencies
- Federal Sanctions & Watch Lists
- Genealogy Resources
- GIS and Mapping
- Incarceration Records
- Internal Revenue Service (IRS) Records
- Media Resources
- Military Records
- Missing Persons
- Most Wanted Lists
- Motor Vehicle Records (includes drivers, vehicles, vessels, accident reports, etc.)
- Occupations & Licensing Boards
- Patents
- Privacy and Privacy Rights Resources
- Recalls, Products and Safety
- Recorded Documents, Judgments, and Liens (includes UCC filings)
- Securities and Securities Dealers
- Sexual Offender Registries
- Tax Assessor and Collector Records
- Telephone Numbers
- Trademarks & Service Marks
- Unclaimed Funds
- Vital Records (includes SSA Death Index and Obituaries)
- Voter Registration
- Workers' Compensation
- World Wide Web

Archives

Federal Archives

The National Archives and Records Administration (NARA) is America's record keeper and it serves as the archival arm of the federal government. NARA not only preserves documents and materials related to the U.S., but also ensures people can access the information.

In addition, through its Electronic Records Archives (ERA), NARA manages, preserve, and provides access to the growing number of electronic Government records. ERA will keep essential electronic Federal records retrievable, readable, and authentic.

The NARA web page at www.archives.gov has detailed information regarding documents and images, and how to research or order documents. To find all of the NARA locations and affiliated sites visit www.archives.gov/locations. Also see the **Military Records** section later in the chapter.

The Federal Record Centers (FRCs), part of NARA, hold closed case files from Federal U.S. District Courts civil and criminal and Bankruptcy Courts. See Chapter 7 (Searching Federal Court Records) for the locations and information on how to obtain these cases files.

State Archives

Every state has an Archives agency that collects and preserves historical government records, and makes them available for public use. The websites for the states' archives are found in the next chapter.

Aviation Records

Government Record Sources

Besides regulations and policies, the **Federal Aviation Administration (FAA)** site at www.faa.gov provides a myriad of data about aircraft including registration and ownership, airports, air traffic, training and testing. The FAA site is the also the main government information center regarding certification for pilots and airmen. One may find current flight delay information nationwide and accident incident data here at the site.

The Federal National Transportation Safety Board (NTSB) maintains an aviation accident database from 1962 forward about civil aviation accidents and selected incidents within the U.S., its territories and possessions, and in international waters. Six different queries are available. Preliminary reports are posted within days; final reports may take months before posted. Some information prior to 1993 is sketchy. See www.ntsb.gov/aviationquery/index.aspx.

The Canadian government site to search Canadian Civil Aircraft Register and aircraft information is wwwapps2.tc.gc.ca/saf-sec-sur/2/CCARCS/aspscripts/en/menu.asp.

For information of foreign countries, the **International Civil Aviation Organization** (www.icao.int) maintains aircraft registration standards for participating countries.

Private Record Sources

Leading private information resource centers for searching hundreds of indexed categories including news, reference data, flights, pilot certifications, and regulatory overviews include these sites:

- Landings.com is an excellent news and overall reference resource.

- Jane's Transportation News and Reference site at www.janes.com/products/janes/transport/index.aspx is well known for its aviation related content. IHS, a global information supplier, acquired Jane's Information Group in June 2007.
- ARGUS International services include charter operator ratings and due diligence program, market intelligence data and research services, and aviation consulting. See www.aviationresearch.com.

Banks & Financial Institutions

Office of the Comptroller of the Currency

The Office of the Comptroller of the Currency (OCC), a bureau of the U.S. Department of the Treasury, charters, regulates, and supervises all national banks and federal savings associations. The OCC also supervises federally chartered branches and agencies of foreign banks that may not be members of the Federal Reserve System. The Office of Thrift Supervision is now part of the OCC. Under the **Licensing** tab at www.occ.gov one can find lists of banks by name, and by city and state.

The OCC has the statutory authority to take action against Institution-Affiliated Parties (IAPs) including:

- Officers, directors, and employees,
- A bank's controlling stockholders, agents, and certain other individuals.

Information may be requested on formal enforcement actions against the above entities for violations of laws, rules or regulations, unsafe or unsound practices, violations of final orders, violations of conditions imposed in writing, and for IAP breaches of fiduciary duty. Search **enforcement actions** at http://apps.occ.gov/EnforcementActions.

Federal Deposit Insurance Corporation (FDIC)

The Federal Deposit Insurance Corporation (FDIC) insures deposits in banks and thrift institutions for at least $250,000 and identifies, monitors and addresses risks to the deposit insurance funds when a bank or thrift institution fails. The FDIC Institution Directory is found at www2.fdic.gov/idasp/index.asp. The FDIC has the statutory authority to take enforcement actions against the following entities —

- FDIC-insured state chartered banks that are not members of the Federal Reserve System
- FDIC-insured branches of foreign banks
- Officers, directors, employees, controlling shareholders, agents, and certain other categories of individuals (institution-affiliated parties) associated with such institutions

The FDIC **Enforcement Decisions and Orders** (ED&O) contains the full text of the formal enforcement actions against financial institutions that are regulated by the FDIC or against their affiliated parties. The ED&O is updated on a monthly basis. To view enforcement actions, go to https://www5.fdic.gov/EDO/index.html.

Federal Reserve Board

The Federal Reserve (www.federalreserve.gov) is the central bank of the U.S. As such it supervises and has the statutory authority to take formal enforcement actions against the following entities —

- State member banks
- Bank holding companies
- Non-bank subsidiaries of bank holding companies

- Edge and agreement corporations
- Branches and agencies of foreign banking organizations operating in the United States and their parent banks
- Officers, directors, employees, and certain other categories of individuals associated with the above banks, companies, and organizations (referred to as "institution-affiliated parties")

The Federal Reserve can take formal **enforcement actions** against the entities listed above for violations of laws, rules, or regulations, unsafe or unsound practices, breaches of fiduciary duty, and violations of final orders. Since August 1989, the Federal Reserve has made all final enforcement orders public. Search at www.federalreserve.gov/apps/enforcementactions/search.aspx.

The **National Information Center (NIC)**, part of the Federal Reserve System, is a central repository of data about banks and other institutions that the Federal Reserve has a supervisory, regulatory, or research interest. This includes both domestic and foreign banking organizations which operate in the U.S. The USBA Search allows one to search for an institution's current and non-current information by name and location. Those two sites above are accessible from main site at www.ffiec.gov/nicpubweb/nicweb/NicHome.aspx.

National Credit Union Administration

The National Credit Union Administration (NCUA) is an independent federal agency that charters and supervises federal credit unions. The web page at www.ncua.gov offers plenty of research and data access.

Business Entity Records

Businesses are formed in many shapes and sizes. They may be organized as corporation, limited liability companies, partnerships, limited liability partnerships, etc. They can be designated for-profit or not-for-profit. And they can be a public company (selling shares of ownership to the public) or non-public.

Searching Publicly Owned (Traded) Companies

There are two important facts to know about finding information about publicly traded companies:

1. Publicly traded companies operating in the U.S. are required by federal law to register with the Securities and Exchange Commission (SEC).
2. However if a publicly traded company does not meet certain "thresholds," then it submits filings with a state regulatory securities agency instead of the SEC.

A registration statement is filed with the appropriate securities exchanges and state securities regulators. This public document discloses information on the management and financial condition of the entity, and describes how the proceeds of the offering will be used.

Either the SEC or these state agencies monitor the registered companies for any irregularities or potential fraudulent behavior.

This section examines first how to find information on publicly traded companies at the federal level, then how to find information at the state level on both public and privately held companies at the state level. This is followed by an analysis of key vendors who offer excellent reference data online in this subject area.

The Federal Level: EDGAR and the SEC

Publicly traded companies must inform the public the complete truth about their businesses' financial data. All non-exempt companies (see below), foreign and domestic, are required to file registration statements, periodic reports, and other forms with the SEC. As of May 6, 1996, these reports are filed electronically using EDGAR – the **E**lectronic **D**ata

Gathering **A**nalysis and **R**etrieval system. Thus, EDGAR is an extensive repository of U.S. corporation information available and anyone can access and download this information for free. The reports that entities must file include the following:

- 10-K – an annual financial report that includes audited year-end financial statements.
- 10-Q – a quarterly, unaudited report.
- 8K – a report detailing significant or unscheduled corporate changes or events.
- Securities offering, trading registrations, and final prospectus.
- DEF-14 – a definitive proxy statement offering director names, their compensation and position.

The list above is not all-inclusive. Other miscellaneous reports include items dealing with security holdings by institutions and insiders. Access to these documents often leads to a wealth of informative data about these companies.

The record searching site at EDGAR is www.sec.gov/edgar/searchedgar/webusers.htm. EDGAR offers a guide on how to search publicly traded companies at www.sec.gov/investor/pubs/edgarguide.htm.

Several private vendors offer access to EDGAR records combined with some added features and searching flexibilities. Recommended sites include www.edgr.com, www.secinfo.com, and www.lexisnexis.com.

For more information about other SEC databases including access to enforcement actions, see the *Securities and Securities Dealers* section later in this chapter.

Searching Business Records at with State Agency Level

In general, businesses that are not public companies are registered at the state level, usually with at the Secretary of State office. The types of business entities that have records available at the state level include:

- Corporations (including Foreign and Non-Profit)
- Partnerships (Limited, Limited Liability, and General)
- Limited Liability Companies
- Franchises
- *Trade Names, Fictitious Names, Assumed Names

*Fictitious names and trade names can be registered at either the local (county or city) or state level, depending on the state's specifications.

Every state provides a business search tool on the web to find information on state-registered business entities. Usually these look-ups are free and include all business entities types, including non-profits. You will find these URLs in Chapter 6. Also visit www.brbpublications.com for free searching links by state.

While most states have one central agency that oversees business entity records and filings, there are several exceptions of note.

- **Arizona** – The Corporation Commission oversees corporation and LLC records. The Secretary of State oversees all partnerships including LPs and LLPs; as well as trademarks, servicemarks, and trade names.
- **South Carolina** – The Corporation Division oversees corporation, LP, LLP, LLC, trademark and servicemark records. The Department of Revenue oversees annual reports and records of directors for corporation; those records are only available from this agency.
- **Kansas** – Kansas does not have statutes requiring or permitting the registration or filing of DBAs or fictitious names.

Searching Non-Profits

Private foundations, charities, non-profits, churches, hospitals, schools, or publicly-supported organizations all are subject to special considerations regarding federal taxes. These entities file different forms with the IRS and all must contribute detailed financial and member information, which can be a great asset for the online intelligence investigator.

The information regarding officers and the financials in a non-profit organization is completely transparent in the Form 990 - an annual report that certain federally tax exempt organizations must file with the IRS. Form 990 provides information on the filing organization's mission, programs, finances, and beyond. For example, on Part 8 of the Form all the trustees are listed, which can be a great investigative lead.

Searching these entities at the state level is much like searching the for-profits entities, but these online sources can actually provide added depth to investigators and researchers. Whether you are looking to reveal experts in the field, local interests to a region, or the financial participation of a particular foundation, these organizations can open a bevy of investigative leads. Finding out what organizations or affiliations a person belongs to can give insight into that person's character. Categories can include religious, athletic, health, child focused, or specific-interest related. For example, there are two non-profit associations dedicated just to avocados!

What is also good to know is there are several vendors who specialize in providing material and content about on non-profits. These firms are profiled later in this section.

Searching Franchise Records

Franchises are regulated by both the Federal Trade Commission (FTC) and by state regulatory agencies. (See *Blue Sky Laws* below.) If the franchise involves a public offering, then records may also be in the SEC database.

A key public record document associated with a franchise is the Uniform Franchise Offering Circular (UFOC). Usually this document may be obtained from a state agency or from a vendor, but not the FTC.

The International Franchise Association (IFA) is a great resource of in-depth information about franchising and finding Franchise Members by topic or service. See www.franchise.org.

State Regulatory Agencies and Blue Sky Laws

Every state has securities laws – often referred to as **"Blue Sky Laws"** – designed to protect investors against fraud. These laws, which do vary from state to state, typically require companies making small offerings to register these offerings before they can be sold in a particular state.

Records of the filings by companies registering under Blue Sky Laws, as well as any records of legal actions, are held by designated state regulatory securities agencies. These agencies oversee the licensing and regulation of securities broker-dealers, agents, investment advisers and investment adviser representatives, and financial planners. The agencies also protect investors against securities fraud by taking enforcement actions

These records are open to the public and can be a great source of data when searching for assets, ownership records, or doing background investigations.

A links list to all the state regulatory agencies home pages is found at the North American Securities Administrators Association web page at www.nasaa.org/about-us/contact-us/contact-your-regulator/. Another vendor source with a breakdown of states' Blue Sky laws is www.seclinks.com/id16.html.

More Online Searching Tips

An initial search for a business entity's records usually starts there with a record index. An index "hit" will lead to a document file number or images of documents. Most states merge the indices of all their registered business entities (corporations, partnerships, LLCs, LLPs, etc.) and registered business names into one index. Usually this index is searchable online.

A good researcher must become familiar with the alphabetizing system in use, regardless if the search is on-site or online. For example, knowing the answers to the questions below can prove to be crucial.

- How to search when a company name starts with the word *The*. Should you search for *The* ABC Company or search by ABC Company, *The* ?
- Know the procedure when a company name starts with a number. Is the number alphabetized as a word? Are listings with numbers found at the front or the end of the index?
- Watch for key words indicating name changes, former entities, or related companies. For example, if a company is known as YESS Embroidery and Screenprinting, it would be worthwhile to search for YESS Embroidery, YESS Screenprinting, YESS Screenprinting and Embroidery, The YESS Company, etc. Also, ascertain if the use of an "&" in place of the word "and" will modify the search results.
- Know the capacity for error and forgiving of typos. If you can pull an alphabetical index list, make sure that screenprinting is not listed as scrrenprinting or even screen printing, etc.
- Many large companies with offices or clients in multiple states will incorporate in Delaware or Nevada.

Information found in a registration file typically includes the date of registration, status, name and address of the registered agent and, sometimes, the names and addresses of officers, directors or principals. The registered agent is the person authorized to receive legal papers such as service of process. The registered agent can be a company attorney, a principal, or a designated third party who specializes in representing business entities.

The registration file can hold a myriad of other company documents. For example, a corporation registration file will typically include the articles of incorporation, annual reports, merger documents, name changes, and termination papers. Partnership and LLC filings may include similar documents with details such as how decisions are made, how profits are distributed, and names and addresses of all limited and general partners or owners. **Finding this material is a good way to find the affiliates of a search subject.**

All state agencies provide a **business name check** so that a new entity can make sure the name is not already used by an existing business entity. Many offer this service online. Performing a business name check is often a good way to find where a business is located and may lead to additional information about a business.

Checking to see if a company is currently registered and filings are current is called a **status check.** If an entity's registration is current and there are no problems, a document known as a Good Standing may be purchased. If available, articles of incorporation including amendments as well as copies of annual reports also may provide useful information about an entity or business owner. Know that corporate records may not be a good source for a business address because most states allow corporations to use a registered agent (third party) as their address for service of process.

Using a Company's Web Page as a Resource

Do not underestimate the usefulness of news stories, press releases, and other data displayed a company's website. The "About Us" section may accurately offer company history and ownership information. However, it is best to verify any company-produced literature. Given that investigators always verify their leads, take a look to see what is on the website that may offer clues.

Recommended Non-Government Resources

Of course every major stockbrokerage firm offers some free information on the web about publicly traded. Search engines Yahoo! and Google also provide in-depth data on publicly traded companies. Also, check out *The Motley Fool* at www.fool.com and the *Investors Business Daily* at www.investors.com. The site at www.annualreports.com provides access to annual reports.

Finding the ownership and records of private companies can be a difficult task. The entity may be registered at the state, but minimal public disclosure and required forms may be available.

Key analysis points to learn more about a company is to determine who the administration is, what type of financials can be obtained, how many locations there are, and in what type of industry it is involved. There are numerous online services to research both large and small corporations. The given for large companies is that *the bigger they are, the easier it is to gather information on them.* The tasking issues are discerning the volumes of data and deciding on what is valuable and current and what is not. Researching the target company by using online database vendors is a must. To the plus, there are a number of vendors who profile both public and private companies. Hoovers.com and Manta.com are different, but both provide excellent sites. Local Chambers of Commerce and Better Business Bureaus may be useful; to find their local offices go to www.worldchambers.com and www.bbb.org.

When the question comes down to "who owns whom?" two valuable resources for finding the ultimate parent of a company are recommended—

- The Directory of Corporate Affiliations at www.corporateaffiliations.com owned by LexisNexis.
- Who Owns Whom at https://solutions.dnb.com/wow presented by Dun & Bradstreet.

The next portion of this section takes an in-depth look at some of the most comprehensive vendors and vendor products.

ThomasNet

One of the most powerful resources for searching **industrial information, products and services** is ThomasNet (www.thomasnet.com). From the home page you can also link to the Thomas Global Register then search worldwide industrial Information from more than 610,000 suppliers worldwide.

Dun & Bradstreet

With more than 100 million companies in its database, Dun & Bradstreet is the largest international provider of business reports. Very small, one-man companies and very large, mega corporations are found in its international collection. Researchers and investigators who conduct a lot of due diligence or research company data often will find D&B is worth the starting subscription price of several thousand dollars. However, you can find search for the address of a company for free. At www.dnb.com, see the "Find a Company" search box. This "Find a Company" search box extends to international searches. See if your company is listed.

Here are some practical reasons that illustrate the need to use D&B—

- Fraudulent companies often share fax numbers, even though they generate new phone numbers for business. **Always search for the fax**!
- Searching by the principal's name will often show former company interests or current company interests.
- Dun & Bradstreet automatically does Soundex searching. The name Bill will generate William hits.
- Address searches will show other companies listed at the same address, including mail drops and suspicious addresses.

If you cannot afford D&B directly, you can access their reports through one of B&B's resellers, such as Dialog, SkyMinder, LexisNexis and Bureau van Dijk. If you are a licensed investigator with Thomson Reuters CLEAR, TLO or Accurint, they resell D&B reports. However, keep in mind that direct service subscribers get much better pricing.

Kompass.com

Kompass originated in Switzerland and is now present in 70 countries with a very reasonably priced collection of information on more than two million companies globally. Subscribers can locate the executives of companies, obtain addresses, corporate structures, names of key figures, company turnover information, company descriptions, product names and services, trade and brand names, and location of branches. Kompass offers free searches for the following topics—

- Region – Geographically locate all companies
- Products/Services – Type of product (i.e. clocks, telephones, hamburgers)
- Companies – Name of company
- Trade names – Name of product
- Executives – Search by person at the top
- Codes – NAICS, SIC and other government-related codes

SkyMinder.com

SkyMinder, an incredible aggregator of other corporate business and credit reports, supplies online credit and business information on more than 50 million companies in 230 countries. SkyMinder is also one of the best places to buy inexpensive D&B header reports.

A complete source list for Skyminder can be found at www.skyminder.com/basic/info_sources.asp. The source list includes a note on how often the data is updated for each of the 40+ sources.

Bureau van Dijk (BvDEP)

Because there is so much that Bureau van Dijk (www.bvdinfo.com) has to offer, cataloging its many databases is difficult. With unique names such as Orbis and Osiris, each database product is matched with services that are country-specific such as for Ruslana (Russia), Sabi (Spain) and Jade (Japan).

For example, Orbis contains comprehensive information on companies worldwide, with an emphasis on private company information. The information is sourced from more than 40 different information providers, all experts in their regions or disciplines. With its descriptive information and company financials, Orbis displays extensive detail on items such as news, market research, ratings and country reports, scanned reports, ownership and mergers and acquisitions data.

Orbis provides several different reports for a company. You can view a summary report, a report that automatically compares a company to its peers or view more detailed reports that are taken from BvDEP's specialist products. More detailed information is available for listed companies, banks and insurance companies, and major private companies, more detailed information is available.

Their other Bureau databases can be examined by visiting their brochure library online at www.bvdinfo.com/About-BvD/Brochure-Library

CLEAR – Thomson Reuters

CLEAR is a very strong investigative platform designed for professionals who need detailed record information about individuals and companies. Provided by Thomson Reuters, CLEAR has a vast collection of public records in their proprietary database.

CLEAR also provides other useful search tools including access to cell phone and utility data, as well as blogs, news and more from social network sites.

The CLEAR platform is especially helpful for corporate security, collections, insurance investigations, and for law enforcement and government personnel.

Visit https://clear.thomsonreuters.com/clear_home/index.jsp.

Resources for Searching Non-Profits and Foundations

GuideStar (www.guidestar.org) is a great starting point to find detailed financial information about non-profits. It also offers free access to basic information on 1.8 million non-profits. Registration is required. GuideStar's fee-searching content includes searchable data from IRS Forms 990 and the IRS Business Master File, including comprehensive facts on employee compensation and grant activity.

Below are several other recommended organizations that are quite helpful for finding information on non-profits.

Capital Research Center (CRC) www.capitalresearch.org, established in 1984 to study non-profit organizations, provides a free database search of non-profits including associated activists and directors.

The Foundation Center is a national organization that serves as an authoritative source of information on foundation and corporate giving. See http://foundationcenter.org.

Enterprise Resources Database website provides fundraising tools with plenty of good information on how to find qualified prospects to donate money and help with fundraising. The site's search of qualifying potential donors is a quite useful as reference resource for finding personal and business assets and financial relationships. See www.practitionerresources.org.

NOZA is advertised as the world's largest searchable database of charitable donors. They help subscribers find donations. See www.nozasearch.com.

Charity Navigator is an independent charity evaluator, with ongoing evaluations on over 6,000 of the largest charities in the U.S. See www.charitynavigator.org.

Civil Court Records

See **Court Records** and **Court Records on Statewide Systems**

Copyrights

The United States Copyright Office administers the copyright system, see www.copyright.gov. The U.S., the Copyright Law (www.loc.gov/copyright/title17/) governs the use of these copyrighted: literary works; musical works including words; dramatic works including music; pantomimes and choreographic works; pictorial, graphic, and sculptural works; motion pictures and other audiovisual works; sound recordings; architectural work, but ***not*** titles, names, short phrases, and slogans; familiar symbols or designs; variations of typographic ornamentation, lettering, or coloring; mere listings of ingredients or contents; ideas; procedures; methods; systems; processes; concepts; principles; discoveries; devices; works of common property, nor containing no original authorship like calendars, rulers, and public lists or tables.

About Copyrights and Authorship

Since 1978, copyright protection exists from the time the work is created in fixed form and ordinarily given a term enduring for the author's life plus 70 years after. For works made for hire, and for anonymous and pseudonymous the duration of a copyright is 95 years from publication or 120 years from creation, whichever is shorter. The copyright for the work of authorship immediately becomes the property of the author who created the work. Only the author or those deriving their rights through the author can rightfully claim copyright. In the case of works made for hire, the employer and not the employee is considered the author.

Where to Search

A free search the Library of Congress database is found at www.copyright.gov/rb.html.

A copyright availability search is one of many national, international IP, trademark, and copyright services provided for a fee from Thomson Compumark at http://compumark.thomson.com/do/cache/off/pid/13.

Search Canadian copyrights free at: http://strategis.ic.gc.ca/app/cipo/copyrights/displaySearch.do?language=eng.

Court Records

Court records are one of the most widely sought types of public record in the U.S. This section provides an in-depth review of how court records maintain and how to search. Also see:

- **Court Records: State Judicial Systems** later in this chapter.
- **Criminal Records Section** later in this chapter.
- **Federal Court Records** in Chapter 7.
- The **individual state, county and local courts providing online access** are profiled in Chapter 6.

Researching court records is complicated because of the extensive diversity of the courts and their record keeping systems. Courts exist at four levels: federal, state, county (or parish), and local municipalities and all four levels can be found within the same county.

Each state has its own court system, created by statutes or constitution to enforce state civil and criminal laws. Sometimes the terms *state court* and *county court* can be a source of confusion because state trial courts are located at county courthouses. Within this book the phrase *state courts* refers to the courts belonging to the state court systems; and *county courts* refers to those courts administrated by county authority. Local municipal courts can be managed by the local city, town or village government whose laws they enforce. Some lower level courts are called justice courts.

The Term "County Courts" and Courts at Parishes, Boroughs, and Certain Cities

In Louisiana the word Parish is equivalent to what is a county in another state. Alaska is organized by Boroughs. In Colorado, Missouri, and Virginia a city may have the same jurisdictional authority of a county. Rather than continually restate these facts, assume when the text is speaking of county courts that these other courts are included.

How State Courts Operate

Before searching an online index of court records you should first familiarize yourself with basic court structures and procedures. And an important first step in determining where a court case is located is to know how the structure of the court system in that particular state. The general structure of all state court systems has four tiers:

1. Appellate courts
2. Intermediate appellate courts
3. General jurisdiction trial courts
4. Limited jurisdiction trial courts

The two highest levels, **appellate** and **intermediate appellate** courts, only hear cases on appeal from the trial courts. "Opinions" of these appellate courts are of particular interest to attorneys seeking legal precedents for newer cases. However, opinions can be useful to record searchers because they summarize facts about the case that will not show on an index or docket.

General jurisdiction trial courts oversee a full range of civil and criminal litigation, usually handling felonies and higher dollar civil cases. The general jurisdiction courts often serve as the appellate courts for cases appealed from limited jurisdiction courts and even from the local courts. Many court researchers refer to general jurisdiction courts as upper courts.

Limited jurisdiction trial courts come in several varieties. Many limited jurisdiction courts handle smaller civil claims (such as $15,000 or less), misdemeanors, and pretrial hearings for felonies. Localized municipal courts are also referred to as courts of limited jurisdiction. Many court researchers refer to limited jurisdiction courts as lower courts.

A number of states, Iowa for instance, have consolidated their general and limited court structure into one combined court system.

Some courts – sometimes called special jurisdiction courts – have general jurisdiction but are limited to one type of litigation. An example is the Court of Claims in New York which only processes liability cases against the state.

Searching Tip: The Online State Judicial Systems

Every state has an administrative agency that oversees the upper three levels and, depending the type of court, the fourth level as well.

This agency is important because actually more counties and courts are found online on systems managed by this agency, then found at the local county level. For more information about searching these sites see the **Court Records on Statewide Judicial Systems** section later in this chapter.

Watch for Divisions and Name Variations

The structure of the court system and the names used for courts often vary widely from state-to-state. Civil and criminal records may be handled by different divisions within a court or sometimes by completely different courts with different names. For example, in Tennessee the Chancery Court oversees civil cases but criminal cases are tried in Circuit Courts, except in districts with separate Criminal Courts as established by the state legislature. In Iowa the District Court is the highest trial court whereas in Michigan the District Court is a limited jurisdiction court.

Municipal, Town, and Village Courts

Localized courts preside over city or town misdemeanors, infractions, and ordinance violations at the city, town or township level. Sometimes these courts may be known as justice courts. Notable is the state of New York where nearly 1,400 Town and Village Justice Courts handle misdemeanors, local ordinance violations, and traffic violations including DWIs.

In most states there is a distinction between state-supported courts and the local courts in terms of management, funding, and sharing of web pages.

How Courts Maintain Records

Case Numbering and Record Index

When a case is filed, a case number is assigned. Use of a case number is the primary indexing method in every court. Therefore, to search specific case file documents, you will need to know – or find – the applicable case number.

Be aware that case numbering procedures are not necessarily consistent throughout a state court system. One district may assign numbers by district while another may assign numbers by location (division) within the district, or by judge. Remember: case numbers appearing in legal text citations may not be adequate for searching unless they appear in the proper form for the particular court in which you are searching.

Unless you know the exact case number, to search for a record or to determine if a record exists the index is one of first items you need to check. A public record index can be electronic, but also can exist on-site on card files, in books, on microfiche, etc. A record index can be organized in a variety of ways – by name, by year, by case or file number, or by name and year. A record index points to a location or file number of the case. The same type of index system exists for other types of public records such as recordings, deeds, and articles of incorporation.

A record index can be electronic, but also can exist on-site on card files, in books, on microfiche, etc. A record index can be organized in a variety of ways – by name, by year, by case or file number, or by name and year. Depending on the type of public record, an alpha index could be by plaintiff and/or defendant, by grantor and/or grantee, by address, etc.

The Docket Sheet – A Key Information Resource

Information from cover sheets and from documents filed as a case goes forward is recorded on the *docket sheet*. Thus the docket sheet, sometimes called a register of actions, is a running summary of a case history. Each action, such as motions, briefs, exhibits, etc., and are recorded in chronological order. While docket sheets differ somewhat in format from court to court, the basic information contained on a docket sheet is consistent. Docket sheets will contain:

- Name of court, including location (division) and the judge assigned;
- Case number and case name;
- Names of all plaintiffs and defendants/debtors;
- Names and addresses of attorneys for the plaintiff or debtor;
- Nature and cause (e.g., statute) of action.
- Date and summary of all materials and motions filed in a case
- Case outcome (disposition)

Most courts enter the docket data into a computer system. Within a state or judicial district, the courts may be linked together via a single computer system.

An important fact to take note of is: **the primary search that government agencies provide is a search of the index.** When someone tells you "I can view xxx county court records online," this person is most likely talking about searching an index summary of records and not about the actual document pages contained in the case history file.

But docket sheets from cases closed before the advent of computerization may not be in the computer system. And in some locations all docket information is non-computerized. Media formats include microfilm, microfiche, index cards, and paper that may even be hand-written.

The Case Disposition

The term *disposition* is frequently used when discussing or searching court records. The case disposition refers to the final outcome of a case - such as a judgment in a civil matter or if a party is determined to be guilty in a criminal matter.

There are some cases where decisions were rendered, but the results are not recorded or the case file number is removed from the index. In certain situations, a judge can order the case file sealed or removed – expunged – from the public repository. Examples include if a defendant enters a diversion program (drug or family counseling), or a defendant makes restitution as part of a plea bargain; these cases may not be searchable. The only way to gain direct access to these types of case filings is through a subpoena. However, savvy researchers and investigators will sometimes search news media sources if need be.

Use of Identifiers and Redaction

Identifiers are important to record searching. They serve two different although related purposes.

1. The identifiers of the subject must be used to analyze a public record for the purpose of determining if the record is about that subject. Perhaps the records are indexed by the last name and also by either the DOB or part of a SSN. If so, a searcher with a DOB or SSN will have a more accurate search result.

2. The identifiers act as an important safeguard for both the requesting party and the subject of the search. There is always the chance that the "Harold Johnson" on whom a given repository has a record is not the same "Harold Johnson" on whom a check has been requested. The possibility of a misidentification can be decreased substantially if other identifiers can match the individual to the record. Providing an identifier as simple as just the middle initial is likely to help identify the correct Harold Johnson.

The federal, state, and local agencies that maintain court record systems make substantial efforts to protect the public from identity theft and limit the disclosure of certain personal information such as Social Security Numbers, phone numbers, and addresses. Many agencies now redacting their records. Redaction is simply removing or hiding certain elements within a record itself or the record index.

Often the redaction will not apply to the DOB on the records. At least part of the DOB is necessary to determine the proper identity of someone who has a common name. There are plenty of news stories about how someone was denied a job because a background check was done and the wrong information was reported, wrong information pertaining to someone else with the same name. The balance of privacy interests versus public jeopardy goes beyond the purposes of this book. However, the key point here is to be aware of change and know that redactions can and will alter public record searching procedures.

The Types of Court Cases Found Online

Below is a summary of the types of court cases and records found at the state or local level. Note that bankruptcies are not found on this list because bankruptcy cases are filed at the federal level.

- **Civil Actions** - For money damages usually greater than $5,000. Also, some states have designated dollar amount thresholds for upper or lower (limited) civil courts. Most civil litigation involves torts or contract.
- **Small Claims** - Actions for minor money damages, generally under $5,000, no juries involved.
- **Criminal Felonies** - Generally defined as crimes punishable by one year or more of jail time. There can be multiple levels or classes.
- **Criminal Misdemeanors** - Generally defined as minor infractions with a fine and less than one year of jail time. Misdemeanors also have multiple levels or classes.
- **Probate** - Estate matters, settling the estate of a deceased person, resolving claims and distributing the decedent's property.
- **Eviction Actions** - Landlord/tenant actions, can also known as an unlawful detainer, forcible detainer, summary possession, or repossession.
- **Domestic Relations** – Sometimes known as *Family Law*, with authority over family disputes, divorces, dissolutions, child support or custody cases.
- **Juvenile** – Authority over cases involving individuals under a specified age, usually 18 years but sometimes 21.
- **Traffic** – May also have authority over municipal ordinances.
- **Specialty Courts** – Water, equity in fiduciary questions, tort, contracts, tax, etc.

More about Civil Court Cases

A civil case usually commences when a plaintiff files a complaint with a court against defendants. The defendants respond to the complaint with an answer. After this initial round, there may be literally hundreds of activities before the court issues a judgment. These activities can include revised complaints and their answers, motions of various kinds, discovery proceedings (including depositions) to establish the documentation and facts involved in the case. All of these activities are listed on a docket sheet, which may be a piece of paper or a computerized index.

Once a civil court issues a judgment, either party may appeal the ruling to an appellate division or court. In the case of a money judgment, the winning side can usually file it as a judgment lien with the county recorder. Appellate divisions usually deal only with legal issues and not the facts of the case.

One common problem when searching civil records is that they often show very few, if any, personal identifiers on the index or case files. Sometimes extensive research is required to properly determine the identity of a person subject of a search.

About Judgments

When a judgment is rendered in court, the winning party usually files and records a lien notice (called an Abstract of Judgment in many states) against real estate owned by the defendant or party against whom the judgment is given. Sometimes judgments can be used to garnish wages or can be placed on bank accounts.

Judgments can be searched at the local or county level usually in the same index as real estate records. See the *Recorded Documents, Judgments, and Liens* section.

Searching Tip: Watch for Overlapping Jurisdictions

In some states, the general jurisdiction court and the limited jurisdiction court have overlapping dollar amounts for civil cases. That means a case could be filed in either court. Check both courts; never assume.

More about Criminal Court Cases

In a criminal case, the plaintiff is a government jurisdiction. The government brings the action against the defendant for violation of one or more of its statutes. The term disposition refers to the final outcome of a criminal court case. A disposition is an important piece of information on a criminal record or record index, along with the defendant's name, some type of personal identifier, the charge, and the case number. This is also a key term when legal use of records is governed by state laws and the federal FCRA (Fair Credit Reporting Act). The information that could be disclosed on a criminal record includes the arrest record, criminal charges, fines, sentencing and incarceration information.

Criminal court records are eventually submitted to a central repository controlled by a state agency such as the State Police or Department of Public Safety. See *Criminal Record Repositories* later in this chapter.

There is a huge difference on the record access procedures between the state repositories and the courts. Records maintained by the court are generally open to the public, but not all state criminal record repositories open their criminal records to the public.

Eight Tips for Searching Court Records Online

1. Be Aware Not All Courts Are Online

A surprising number of courts do not have computerized record keeping. Per the latest statistics taken from the Public Record Research System 68% of civil courts and 65% of criminal courts are online. (Makes you wonder about the so-called instant national database check some online vendors are selling!)

2. Online Searching is Generally Limited to Docket Sheets

Most courts that offer online access limit the search to the docket sheet data. But checking a courthouse's computer online docket index is the quickest way to find if case records exist online. Just be sure to check all name variations and spelling variations.

Case document images are not generally available online because courts are still experimenting and developing electronic filing and imaging. Generally, copies of case documents are only on-site.

3. Learn the Index and What Data is Viewable

There are question you need to ask and to be answered: How far back does the index go? Are all cases online? How current is the index - real time? With 24 hours? With 7 days? What identifiers are needed to search and are shown on results? Is the search countywide, or do other courts in the county need to be searched?

For example, most civil courts index records by both plaintiffs and defendants, but some only index by the defendant name. A plaintiff search is useful, for example, to determine if someone is especially litigious.

4. Understand the Search Mechanics

Most civil courts index records by both plaintiffs and defendants, but some only index by the defendant name. A plaintiff search is useful, for example, to determine if someone is especially litigious. Look for any help screens that may offer advice, such as the use of wildcards. If the search lets you provide a partial name that helps you find records that may have name spelling variances. For civil cases, the usual reasonable requirement is a defendant (or plaintiff) name – full name if it is a common name – and the time frame to search – e.g., 1993-2002. For criminal cases, the court may require more identification, such as date of birth (DOB), to ascertain the correct individual.

5. Be Aware of Restricted Records

Courts have types of case records, such as juvenile and adoptions, which are not released without a court order. Records may also be sealed form view or expunged. The presiding judge often makes a determination of whether a particular record type is available to the public. Some criminal court records include the arresting officer's report. In some locations this information is regarded as public record, while in other locations the police report may be sealed.

6. Watch for Multiple Courts as Same Location

When the general jurisdiction and limited jurisdiction courts are in the same building and use the same support staff, chances are the record databases are combined as well. But that does not necessarily mean you will receive a search of both databases and pay for one search unless you ask for it. Do not assume a search is countywide.

7. Watch for Overlapping Jurisdictions on Civil Limits

In some states, the general jurisdiction court and the limited jurisdiction court have overlapping dollar amounts for civil cases. That means a case could be filed in either court. Check both courts; never assume.

8. Look for the Lag Time

Depending on the level of due diligence needed, a good searcher needs to know what the time delay is for posting records. Is it a week or more (such as in Los Angeles) or 24 hours, or in real time? This is important if the search is conducted in connection with litigation or hiring matters.

Court Records of Native Americans

Native American Tribes are indigenous, sovereign entities and are not governed by state or federal courts. Therefore court records pertaining to tribal matters or regarding incidents occurring on tribal land will not be found in the state or federal courts. But there is an excellent online resource about tribal court and law matters.

The Tribal Court Clearinghouse

Sponsored by the Tribal Institute, the Tribal Court Clearinghouse is a comprehensive website resource for American Indian and Alaska Native Nations, tribal justice systems, victim services providers, tribal service providers, and others involved in the improvement of justice in Indian country. The *Tribal Law* tab provides direct links to many resources including Tribal Courts, Tribal Court Decisions, and Law Enforcement resources. The Tribal Institute also does a great job of listing and describing the many federal government agencies and native organizations involved with Native Americans. This very useful site is found at www.tribal-institute.org/index.htm

Court Records on Statewide Judicial Systems

The online court records obtainable from this venue are widespread, often free, and overall very worthwhile.

As mentioned previously, every state has a judicial branch that oversees that state's trial and appellate court system. The name of the agency will vary, but it is often known as the Administration Office of the Courts (AOC) or State Court Administrator' Office.

Knowing about this agency and their online services is important because thru the AOC more counties and courts are online than from the individual county-based systems. Consider these overall statistics about state judicial systems and the state courts at the county level:

- 28 States Offer Online Access to Both Civil and Criminal Records
- 3 State Offer Access to Only Online Civil Records
- 2 State Offer Access to Only Online Criminal Records
- 17 State Have Online Access to Neither

The specific states and sites with web access are profiled Chapter 6.

These Systems are Not Created Equal - Know the State-by-State Variations

Online researchers must be aware that there are many nuances to these searches. The value of a "statewide" court search varies by state. Consider these evaluation points:

- Pay for free or both? While some of the free searches are good, the adage *you pay for what you get* can certainly apply here.
- Is the search a statewide search?
- Are counties may not be on the system.
- Is the throughput post and is there uniformity? For example, one county may have cases dating back for seven years, while another county may have only two years of history.
- Are Identifiers shown? The lack of identifiers to properly identify a subject varies widely from state-to-state. A lack of is especially apparent on the free access search systems.
- And perhaps the most important evaluation point: Is an online search equivalent to searching onsite? The level of your due diligence and need for accuracy will determine if using an online site that is in reality a supplemental search is sufficient for your needs. This of course is true for ANY online site for ANY type of public record.

The Only Game in Town for Online Criminal Searches?

A search from one of these court systems can be a particularly useful criminal record search tool in those states – such as New York, North Carolina, or Utah – that do not permit a search at the state criminal records repository agency (see the next section).

Of course these court systems can be useful in those states that do offer access to the state criminal records repository agency because often the court data is usually much more current than form the repository – especially when not submitting fingerprints.

Beside the content in Chapter 6, a resource for in-depth details about each state's court system including access to the AOC databases is the BRB Publication's Public Record Research System at www.brbpublications.com.

Criminal Records at State Repositories

This section is limited to a discussion to specific state criminal record database repositories. Additional information about criminal records or criminal related records is found at:

- **Court Records**
- **Court Records on Statewide Judicial Systems**
- **Incarceration Records**
- **Sexual Offender Registries**
- **Federal Agency Sanctions & Watch Lists**
- **Federal Courts (Chapter7)**

All states have a central repository of criminal records of those individuals who have been subject to that state's criminal justice system. The database is managed by a state law enforcement agency often called the State Police or the Department of Public Safety. The exact name varies from state-to-state. Often these state record repositories are designated as the state's Official Source for performing a background check. This can be a problem for non-fingerprint checks, as you will learn below.

The information at the state repository is submitted by state, county, parish, and municipal courts as well as from local law enforcement. Information forwarded to the state includes notations of arrests and charges, sometimes the disposition, and from law enforcement agencies a set of fingerprints.

Criminal-related records exist in other state repositories including incarceration (prison) systems, sexual predator registries, and on federal government sanction and watch lists. These venues are examined elsewhere in this chapter. And there are vendors who collect and maintain proprietary databases of criminal record information gathered from as many of the above mentioned sources as possible.

Availability of Records to the Public Varies by State

In general, the criminal records are public when at the courts. But when the records are forwarded to the state repositories there are often restrictions placed on access by the general public. For example, per the Public Record Research System from BRB Publications, only 27 states release criminal records (name search) to the general public without consent of the subject, 17 states require a signed release from the subject, and 6 states require submission of fingerprints.

Detailed information about each state's online system is presented in Chapter 6.

Facts about Accuracy and Completeness, Especially When Fingerprints Not Submitted

Many employers and state licensing boards depend on state criminal record repositories as a primary resource when performing a criminal record background check. Here is the rub: a search of the state criminal record database may not be as accurate as assumed. There are three key reasons why the completeness, consistency, and accuracy of state criminal record repositories could be suspect—

- Inability to Match Dispositions with Arrest Records
- Timeliness of Receiving Arrest and Disposition Data
- Timeliness of Entering Arrest and Disposition Data into the Repository

The basis for this concern is supported by facts contained in a Study released in November 2011 by the Bureau of Justice Statistics of the U.S. Department of Justice[1]. Consider the following findings from this Study—

- 9 states reported that 25% or more of all dispositions received could NOT be linked to the arrest/charge information in the state criminal record database.
- A total of 1,753,623 unprocessed or partially processed court disposition forms were reported by 18 states.
- 27 states reported a significant backlog for entering court disposition data into the criminal history database.

The content in the table below was obtained directly from this Study. Note this information should not be confused with criminal data held by the state's courts systems.

State	Number of unprocessed or partially processed court disposition forms on hand	% Arrests in last 5 years in DB that have final dispositions Recorded	Average # of Days between occurrence of final felony court disposition and receipt of data by repository	Average # of Days between receipt of final felony court disposition and entry in state database
AL	unknown	62%	1	146
AK	67,445	n/a	n/a	n/a
AR		76%	30	2
AZ		72%	21	2
CA	30,000	11%		55
CO		22%	n/a	n/a
CT	unknown	95%	2	2
DE		90%	0	0
DC		n/a	n/a	n/a
FL		61%	37	1
GA	4,400	80%	30	7
HI	155,466	84%	8	0
IA	2,500	84%	7	7
ID		45%	1	1
IL		55%	n/a	n/a

[1] The statistics herein are taken directly from the U.S. Department of Justice, Bureau of Justice Statistic's Survey of State Criminal History Information Systems, 2010 (released November 2011) found at www.ncjrs.gov/app/publications/abstract.aspx?ID=259283.

State	Number of unprocessed or partially processed court disposition forms on hand	% Arrests in last 5 years in DB that have final dispositions Recorded	Average # of Days between occurrence of final felony court disposition and receipt of data by repository	Average # of Days between receipt of final felony court disposition and entry in state database
IN	3,000	47%	unknown	1
KS	75,274	45%	555	665
KY	100	18%	1-90	1-90
LA	5,000	n/a	n/a	n/a
MA		n/a	1	1
MD		80%	1	1
ME		45%	14	14
MI		n/a	1	1
MN		54%	2	1
MO	263,228	72%	n/a	54.5
MS		13%	n/a	5
MT		59%	36	30
NC		89%	3	1
ND		86%	n/a	n/a
NE		71%	1	1
NH	35,000	n/a	n/a	n/a
NJ	64,937	70%	3	7
NM		n/a	n/a	n/a
NV	522	29%	unknown	unknown
NY		94%	0	0
OH	500	63%	30-60	35-65
OK		37%	30	30
OR		67%	7	7
PA	160,428	65%	unknown	n/a
RI	unknown	95%	unknown	unknown
SC		n/a	7	1
SD		n/a	15	1
TN		n/a	n/a	n/a
TX		74%	30	1
UT	761,462	71%	1	1
VA		86%	14	14
VT		85%	17	24
WA		92%	403	1-66

State	Number of unprocessed or partially processed court disposition forms on hand	% Arrests in last 5 years in DB that have final dispositions Recorded	Average # of Days between occurrence of final felony court disposition and receipt of data by repository	Average # of Days between receipt of final felony court disposition and entry in state database
WI	4,456	89%	10	1
WV	119,901	90%	180	180
WY		985%	30-45	2

Please don't misunderstand the message here – there are certainly good reasons for performing a search of a state repository record database. A statewide search covers a wider geographic range than a county search. And a state search is certainly less expensive than a separate search of each county. Many states do have strong database systems. But for proper due diligence for performing a criminal record search, using a state search AND a county search of criminal records AND a search from a vendor's proprietary database should be considered. This is extremely critical for employers making hiring decisions in states with legislative limitations on using criminal records without dispositions or using misdemeanor records.

Death Records

See the **Vital Records** section for information regarding death records, the Social Security Administration' Death Index, and about obituary records. Also see **Genealogy Records** section.

Elections: Candidates, PACs, Lobbyists, and Voters

There are numerous federal, state, and local public records associated with the election process and many of these records are viewable online. For example the lists of register voters are not often online, but can be downloaded and purchased for certain uses. All states consider campaign finance and disclosure documents as public record and these documents are often viewable online.

Voter Registration

Voting registration records are public record sources of the voting history, the addresses, and sometimes telephone numbers of individual voters. Every state has a central election agency or commission, and all have a central repository of voter information collected from the local level agencies per federal mandate HAVA (Help America Vote Act of 2002, Public Law 107-252).[2]

In general, voter registration records are publicly accessible at the local level, and not so accessibly at the state level. Roughly 2/3's of states will only release voter registration information to those with a political or research purpose. Political purposes include purchase by political parties or candidates to solicit votes.

[2] South Dakota is exempt from HAVA.

As shown in Chapter 6, a handful of states offer an online search which is usually of a voter's status. A few public record vendors offer online access to their proprietary database of voter records. Perhaps the best known vendor that specializes in voter registration records is Aristotle.com. Record data released generally includes name, address and telephone numbers, unless specifically blocked by the registrant. We believe all states and local agencies block the release of Social Security Numbers.

Campaign Finance and Disclosure

Candidates for state and local office are subject to the campaign finance laws. Once a candidate raises, receives or expends more than designated threshold in a year, the candidate is required to register and report form whom the funds are raised. That same is true for committees working on behalf of political parties or candidate or for specific political measures.

All of this information is public record and it is generally found online.

PACs: Political Action Committee

The purpose of a Political Action Committee (PAC) is to raise money in the support of (or against) political candidates, legislation and ballot items. PACs usually represent businesses large or small, or special interest groups such as unions or the NRA, etc. PACs must register at the state or federal level, depending on the purpose of the PAC, and follow pre-set guidelines. Since PACs are a matter of public record, the registration information and donations are searchable by the public.

State PAC online resources are usually with the same agency that oversees elections, but sometimes PACs are managed by a totally different state agency. The sources are shown in Chapter 6. Federal level sites are covered later within this section.

Lobbyists

Lobbyists are individuals paid to communicate with public office holders in order to influence government decisions. As with PACs, lobbyists must be registered at the government level where they are trying to influence votes. The registration of lobbyists is a matter of public record.

In some states lobbyists are registered with the same agency that oversees elections, in other the lobbyist records are with a different agency, such as an agency that over sees ethics of legislative-related people and entities. The resources for online access to lobbyist data are shown in Chapter 6 within the appropriate section.

Federal Agency Resources

Federal Election Commission (FEC)

The Federal Election Commission (FEC) administers and enforces the Federal Election Campaign Act (FECA), which is the statute that governs the financing of federal elections. To locate information about the political donations go to the Federal Election Commission's website at www.fec.gov. There are some excellent search tools offered under the *Campaign Finance Disclosure Portal*. Also, try the *Search* tab for your favorite celebrity name

Internal Revenue Service

The IRS monitors what can be deducted as donations to a PAC or by a PAC. At the web page one can search by name of employer for all electronic and paper submissions of Form 8871 Political Organization Notice of Section 527 Status, and Form 8872 Political Organization Report of Contributions and Expenditures. Also searchable from this site are the paper submissions of Form 990 Return of Organizations Exempt from Income Tax - the form filed by many public charities and other exempt organizations. See http://forms.irs.gov/app/pod/basicSearch/search?execution=e2s1.

Lobbyists & Laws

Lobbyists must register with the Senate to disclose who hired them, how much they are paid, what issues or bills they are lobbying on, and the federal agencies they are contacting. There is no search web page of registered lobbyists. To research laws, click on the *Public Disclosure* tab at www.senate.gov.

The Office of the Clerk for the U.S. House of Representatives maintains a web page at http://lobbyingdisclosure.house.gov that offers information about lobbying at the House, but the organization does not offer a searchable online database.

Agent for a Foreign Principal for Political Reasons

The Foreign Agents Registration Act (FARA) requires individuals acting as agents of foreign principals in a political or quasi-political capacity to make periodic public disclosure of their relationship with the foreign principal, as well as activities, receipts and disbursements in support of those activities. Many searching features are provided at www.fara.gov.

Private Sector Resources

OpenSecrets.org is an extremely useful site. Per their web page "...is the nation's premier research group tracking money in U.S. politics and its effect on elections and public policy. Nonpartisan, independent and nonprofit, the organization aims to create a more educated voter, an involved citizenry and a more transparent and responsive government."

Another recommended site is FollowTheMoney.org which is maintained by the National Institute on Money in State Politics. The Institute provides a searchable database with substantive profiles on candidates and issues, insightful reports and reliable data for all 50 states. This excellent web page also has many, many other database searches available on a subscription basis only.

Also, a great searchable directory of lobbying firms is found at LobbyData.com. Search by name, the agency involved or by issue.

The **Vote Smart** site at www.vote-smart.org/index.htm tracks campaign contributions for more than 13,000 candidates and elected officials nationwide and includes voting records and evaluations by special interest groups.

Environmental Information

Many environmental public records held by the government rest at two locations: the **Environmental Protection Agency** and the **National Library of Medicine**. The content to follow looks at each agency and public records associated with health hazards. At the end of this section, be sure to check out **Scorecard**, a pollution information site.

Environmental Protection Agency (EPA)

The EPA's Environmental Facts Warehouse at www.epa.gov/enviro is an excellent starting place to search for environmental information related to locations. There are nine *Topic Searches*, each with the ability to find data by Zip Code, or by city and state.

Below are descriptions of more useful search sites and features provided by the EPA.

- EnviroMapper combines interactive maps and aerial photography to display various types of environmental information, including air releases, drinking water, toxic releases, hazardous wastes, water discharge permits, and Superfund sites. The site creates maps at the national, state, and county levels that can be linked to environmental text reports. Go to www.epa.gov/emefdata/em4ef.home.

- The EPA's Office of Enforcement and Compliance Assurance (OECA) works with EPA regional offices, state governments, tribal governments and other federal agencies on compliance with the nation's environmental laws. Two useful starting pages are offered. The Compliance Home is www.epa.gov/compliance/index-c.html. The Enforcement Home is www.epa.gov/enforcement/index.html.
- OECA also offers online access to its database called Enforcement & Compliance History Online (ECHO). Search the database for inspection, violation, enforcement action, and penalty information about compliance and enforcement information on approximately 800,000 regulated facilities. ECHO can be found at www.epa-echo.gov/echo. For a web search of cases and settlements go to http://cfpub.epa.gov/compliance/cases.
- Federal law requires facilities in certain industries which manufacture, process, or use significant amounts of toxic chemicals, to report annually on their releases of these chemicals to the EPA Toxics Release Inventory Program. *Superfund sites* are those throughout the United States and its territories which contain substances that are either designated as hazardous under the Comprehensive Environmental Response, Compensation and Liability Act (CERCLA), or identified as such under other laws. For information about the Superfund sites on the National Priorities List, email superfund.docket@epa.gov. Superfund sites are at http://cfpub.epa.gov/supercpad/cursites/srchsites.cfm. Search EPA Records of Decisions (ROD) at www.epa.gov/superfund/sites/rods.

National Library of Medicine (NLM)

Household Products Database

This resource indicates the chemical ingredients found in household products and who manufactures specific brands. The database contains information on over 7,000 products. Email tehip@teh.nlm.nih.gov or visit http://householdproducts.nlm.nih.gov.

TOXMAP

TOXMAP (http://toxmap.nlm.nih.gov/toxmap/main/index.jsp) is a Geographic Information System (GIS) using maps of the U.S. to help users visually explore data from the EPA's Toxics Release Inventory (TRI) (www.epa.gov/tri/) and Superfund Programs. Maps at www.epa.gov/superfund/sites/npl show locations of national priorities of the known releases or threatened releases of hazardous substances, pollutants, or contaminants in the U.S. Users can search the system by chemical name, chemical name fragment, and/or location (such as city, state, or ZIP code). TOXMAP also overlays map data such as U.S. Census population information, income figures from the Bureau of Economic Analysis, and health data from the National Cancer Institute (www.cancer.gov) and the National Center for Health Statistics (www.cdc.gov/nchs).

TOXNET

TOXNET, the Toxicology Data Network, provides multiple databases on toxicology, hazardous chemicals, environmental health, and toxic releases. The free access at http://toxnet.nlm.nih.gov provides easy searching to a great many databases.

Tox Town

This interactive web page is a great source of non-technical descriptions of chemicals, assorted links to selected, authoritative chemical information, and lists everyday locations where one might find toxic chemicals. Visit http://toxtown.nlm.nih.gov.

Private Sector Sites

One can find a variety of informative 'whistle blower sites' on the web, usually supported by a law firms. Below are two non-attorney firm organizations worthy of mention.

Scorecard

Scorecard is a very popular, non-government web resource for information about pollution problems and toxic chemicals. Per their web page, one may learn about the pollution problems in community and learn who is responsible. See which geographic areas and companies have the worst pollution records. Visit http://scorecard.goodguide.com/.

Oceana

Oceana is the largest international organization dealing with on ocean conservation. Their scientists work closely with teams of economists, lawyers and advocates to achieve conservation results for the oceans. See http://oceana.org/en.

Federal Agencies

We could add 800 pages to this book with data about many, many federal agencies. Instead, we offer the two best starting points.

USA.Gov

This is a terrific online tool for government records because it is the U.S.A. Government's search engine. Over 100 different online functions that can be performed via this government interface, from opting out of direct marketing databases to locating zip codes. If you want to file a complaint against a government agency or take a virtual White House tour, it is probably available online through links on usa.gov.

The Government Printing Office

For those truly interested in getting to the source of federal information, start with the Government Printing Office located at gpo.gov. You can search for a publication by name, author, keyword or subject. A search for "Public Records" as a Subject returned a number of matches. These are not necessarily online and waiting for you to click and grab, however many are. Actually, this site will tell you which government depository library has a hard copy physically on the shelf or if it can be acquired through your local library.

The government spends billions of dollars every year on industry analysis, medical trials, land management studies, etcetera. Always consider a government document when conducting any form of research. If it can be studied, the government has a report on it! These reports are significantly cheaper (often free!) compared to expensive market-research reports.

Federal Sanctions & Watch Lists

This section examines public record databases of individuals and companies that have sanctions, violations, enforcement actions, or warnings initiated against them by one of these federal government departments—

- Consolidated Export Screening List with Export Specific Lists From:
  - Department of Commerce Department
  - Department of State
  - Department of the Treasury
- FDA - Food & Drug Administration
- GSA – Government Services
- Human Health Care Services Department

- Justice Department
- Labor Department
- OSHA - Occupational Safety & Health Administration
- State Department
- Treasury Department

Note: To find enforcement actions taken by the Federal Reserve, see the *Banks & Financial Institutions* Section. To find enforcement action involving stocks and securities see the *Securities and Securities Dealers* Section.

Consolidated Export Screening List – Six Lists

A downloadable file at http://export.gov/ecr/eg_main_023148.asp has six consolidated export screening lists from the Departments of Commerce, State and the Treasury into one spreadsheet relevant to import/export transactions. The purpose is as an aide to industry in conducting electronic screens of potential parties to regulated transactions. The six lists are described below.

Commerce Department, Bureau of Industry and Security (BIS)

1. Denied Persons List

The Denied Persons List is meant to prevent the illegal export of dual-use items before they occur and to investigate and assist in the prosecution of violators of the Export Administration Regulations.

2. Unverified List

This list of parties whom BIS has been unable to verify in some manner in prior transaction, includes names and countries of foreign persons who in the past were parties to a transaction with respect to which BIS could not conduct a pre-license check ("PLC") or a post-shipment verification ("PSV") for reasons outside of the U.S. Government's control.

3. Entity List

The Entity List, is a list of parties whose presence in a transaction can trigger a license requirement under the Export Administration Regulations. The original purpose was to inform the public of entities whose activities imposed a risk of diverting exported and re-exported items into programs related to weapons of mass destruction. Now the list includes those with any license requirements imposed on the transaction by other provisions of the Export Administration Regulations. The list specifies the license requirements that apply to each listed party.

Department of State:

4. Nonproliferation Sanctions List

This shows parties who have been sanctioned under various statutes per the Bureau of International Security. Note webpage is updated as appropriate, but the Federal Register is the only official and complete listing of nonproliferation sanctions determinations.

5. AECA Debarred List

Per the Directorate of Defense Trade Controls, this displays entities and individuals prohibited from participating directly or indirectly in the export of defense articles, including technical data and defense services. Pursuant to the Arms Export Control Act (AECA) and the International Traffic in Arms Regulations (ITAR), the AECA Debarred List includes persons convicted in court of violating or conspiring to violate the AECA and subject to "statutory debarment" or persons established to have violated the AECA in an administrative proceeding and subject to "administrative debarment."

Department of the Treasury:

6. Specially Designated Nationals List

Per the Office of Foreign Assets Control, the **Specially Designated Nationals List** shows parties who may be prohibited from export transactions based on OFAC regulations.

FDA – Food & Drug Administration

The FDA regulates scientific studies designed to develop evidence to support the safety and effectiveness of investigational drugs (human and animal), biological products, and medical devices. Physicians and other qualified experts ("clinical investigators") who conduct these studies are required to comply with applicable statutes and regulations intended to ensure the integrity of clinical data on which product approvals are based and, for investigations involving human subjects, to help protect the rights, safety, and welfare of these subjects.

FDA Enforcement Report Index – Recalls, Market Withdrawals, and Safety Alerts

The FDA Enforcement Report, published weekly, contains information on actions taken in connection with agency regulatory activities. Data includes Recalls and Field Corrections, Injunctions, Seizures, Indictments, Prosecutions, and Dispositions. A record of Enforcement Reports going back 8 years is found at the agency's web page at www.fda.gov/Safety/Recalls/EnforcementReports/default.htm.

Visit www.fda.gov/Safety/Recalls/default.htm for the most significant recalls, market withdrawals and safety alerts of products; all listed are based on the extent of distribution and the degree of health risk

Debarment List

The FDA maintains a list at www.fda.gov/ICECI/EnforcementActions/FDADebarmentList/default.htm of individuals and entities that are prohibited from introducing any type of food, drug, cosmetics or associated devices into interstate commerce.

Disqualified or Restricted Clinical Investigator List

A disqualified or totally restricted clinical investigator is not eligible to receive investigational drugs, biologics, or devices. Some clinical investigators have agreed to certain restrictions with respect to their conduct of clinical investigations. See www.fda.gov/ICECI/EnforcementActions/ucm321308.htm

GSA – Government Services

Excluded Party List

The Excluded Parties List System (EPLS) contains information on individuals and firms excluded by various Federal government agencies from receiving federal contracts or federally approved subcontracts and from certain types of federal financial and non-financial assistance and benefits. Note that individual agencies are responsible for their data.

EPLS is now provided by the System for Award Management (SAM), which is combining federal procurement systems and the Catalog of Federal Domestic Assistance into one new system. See www.sam.gov/portal/public/SAM/

Human Health Services, Department of

Excluded Individuals/Entities (LEIE)

The LEIE maintained by the Office of Inspector General (OIG) for the Department of Human Health Services is a list of currently excluded parties. The exclusions are based on convictions for program-related fraud and patient abuse, licensing board actions, and default on Health Education Assistance Loans. The searchable database is found at http://exclusions.oig.hhs.gov/. A downloadable version is at https://oig.hhs.gov/exclusions/exclusions_list.asp.

Justice Department

There are a number of Divisions within the Justice Department that maintain news articles, stories, records lists, and most wanted lists that can be very useful for research and investigation purposes.

Bureau of Alcohol, Tobacco, Firearms and Explosives

Below are two online resources:

- Federal Firearms License Validator - https://www.atfonline.gov/fflezcheck
- ATF Most Wanted List - www.atf.gov/most-wanted

Bureau of Investigation (FBI)

The FBI's Most Wanted Site at www.fbi.gov/wanted/wanted_by_the_fbi contains numerous lists to search, including kidnappings, missing persons, unknown bank robbers, and others.

Drug Enforcement Administration (DEA)

Search DEA fugitives at www.justice.gov/dea/fugitives.shtml by major metro areas. Also, major international fugitives and captured fugitives are found here.

Labor Department: Labor and Labor Unions

The Office of Labor-Management Standards (OLMS) in the U.S. Department of Labor is the Federal agency responsible for administering and enforcing most provisions of the Labor-Management Reporting and Disclosure Act of 1959, as amended (LMRDA). Note that OLMS does not have jurisdiction over unions representing solely state, county, or municipal employees. OLMS responsibilities include:

- Public Disclosure of Reports
- Compliance Audits
- Investigations
- Education and Compliance Assistance

The OLMS Internet Public Disclosure Room web page www.dol.gov/olms/regs/compliance/rrlo/lmrda.htm enables users to view and print reports filed by unions, union officers and employees, employers, and labor relations consultants.

Occupational Safety & Health Administration (OSHA)

The purpose of the Occupational Safety & Health Administration (OSHA) is to insure employee safety and health in the U.S. by setting and enforcing standards in the workplace. OSHA partners with the states for inspections and enforcements, along with education programs, technical assistance and consultation programs.

There are a number of searchable databases at OSHA (www.osha.gov). For example, search by establishment name for information on over 3 million inspections conducted since 1972 at see www.osha.gov/pls/imis/establishment.html. You can also search by the North American Industry Classification Code (NAIC) or the Standard Industrial Classification Code (SIC).

Another useful search is of the Accident Investigation database at www.osha.gov/pls/imis/accidentsearch.html. This database contains abstracts dating back to 1984 and injury data dating back to 1972.

State Department

ITAR Debarred List

A list compiled by the State Department of parties who are barred by the International Traffic in Arms Regulations (ITAR) (22 CFR §127.7) from participating directly or indirectly in the export of defense articles, including technical data or in the furnishing of defense services for which a license or approval is required, is found at www.pmddtc.state.gov/compliance/debar.html.

Nonproliferation Sanctions Lists

The State Department maintains lists of parties that have been sanctioned under various statutes and legal authority. See www.state.gov/t/isn/c15231.htm.

Treasury Department

Specifically Designated Nationals (SDN) List

The U.S. Department of the Treasury, Office of Foreign Assets Control (OFAC) publishes a list of individuals and companies owned or controlled by, or acting for or on behalf of, targeted foreign countries, terrorists, international narcotics traffickers, and those engaged in activities related to the proliferation of weapons of mass destruction.

www.treasury.gov/resource-center/sanctions/SDN-List/Pages/default.aspx.

Federal Contractor & Vendor Eligibility Sites

An avenue of public record data sometimes overlooked is the licensing of individual and businesses to do business for the U.S. government. Below are two resources from this agency.

1. Central Contractor Registration (CCR)

The Central Contractor Registration (CCR) registers all companies and individuals that sell services and products to, or apply for assistance from, the federal government. The 450,000+ registrants at CRR are searchable online using a DUNS number, company name, or other criteria.

CCR is now provided by the System for Award Management (SAM), which is combining federal procurement systems and the Catalog of Federal Domestic Assistance into one new system. See https://www.sam.gov/portal/public/SAM.

2. Online Representations and Certifications Application (ORCA)

The ORCA system allows contractors to enter company data regarding certification needed on federal contracts. This is a publicly accessible database, but it does require the subject's DUNS number.

ORCA is now provided by the System for Award Management (SAM) as described above.

Small Business Administration (SBA)

The SBA maintains a database of Dynamic Small Business (DSBS) that, while primarily self-certified, does indicate certifications relating to 8(a) Business Development, HUBZone or Small Disadvantaged Business status. Visit http://dsbs.sba.gov/dsbs/search/dsp_dsbs.cfm

To find woman-owned, veteran-owned, and service disabled veteran-owned specific profiles in this same SBA database go to the Quick Market Search screen at http://dsbs.sba.gov/dsbs/search/dsp_quicksearch.cfm.

Genealogy Resources

(Also see the **Vital Records Section**.)

Perhaps the most well-known resource of genealogical information is the Church of Jesus Christ of Latter-day Saints (Mormon Church). The Church has been actively gathering and preserving genealogical records worldwide for over 100 years. One may access genealogy records on-site at churches across the nation and on foreign soil. The genealogy site is www.familysearch.org.

There are several other, huge genealogical sites that have collected public record information along with historical documents from various sources. Below are a few recommended sites and starting points for genealogy record searching, presented in alphabetical order.

- Archives.com provides access to over 1 billion historical records.
- Cyndi's List at www.cyndislist.com has cross-referenced and categorized numerous links.
- The Generations Network has multiple sites, see
  - www.ancestry.com
  - http://search.ancestry.com/search/default.aspx
  - http://searches.rootsweb.ancestry.com www.genealogy.com
  - www.myfamily.com
- The National Genealogical Society in Arlington, VA www.ngsgenealogy.org.

GIS and Mapping

GIS is the acronym used for Geographic Information System. Commonly associated with maps, GIS data can be displayed in a variety of product types with many associated uses. GIS can link and layer data attributes to specific criteria, such as addresses to people or parcels to building. GIS property details are used by the assessing offices at the county or municipality level for taxation and real estate associated matters.

Although they may appear intimidating, GIS mapping websites maintained by these government offices usually have a search mechanism for finding parcels, addresses, and sometimes, but not always, property owner names. A GIS website's search feature is not always displayed prominently, but many local assessor sites provide this service.

For more information about GIS visit www.gis.com. A private site that does an excellent job of maintaining links is www.netronline.com.

Find GIS searching sites at the local level by state in Chapter 6.

Incarceration Records

Incarceration records are criminal-related records of inmates housed or formerly housed at jails and prisons.

Prisons records refer to inmates held in state prisons and federal prisons. The details found in prison records vary widely by location and content. Of course those convicted of federal crimes are place in a federal prison, those for a state crime in a state prison.

Since jails are usually found at the local level and hold a variety of inmates, *jail records* are often a mix of persons with misdemeanor sentences and persons being held until transport to a state of federal facility. Jails records are probably the least useful to professional record searchers.

An excellent website devoted to information about prisons and corrections facilities "...with the most comprehensive database of vendor intelligence in corrections..." is the Corrections Connection (www.corrections.com).

Federal Prison System

The Federal Bureau of Prisons web page offers a searchable Inmate Locator and a Facility Locator at www.bop.gov. The Inmate Locator contains records on inmates incarcerated or released from 1982 to present.

State Prison Systems

Each state has a government agency that manages the corrections departments and prisons. These state agencies consider the inmate records to be public and will process information requests. Many states offer web pages with inmate locators or look-ups. The level of information available varies widely from state to state. All the searchable state sites are listed in Chapter 6.

Vendor Resources

The web pages of several private companies are great resources to information and find links and searchable inmate locators to state prison systems.

An excellent website devoted to information about prisons and corrections facilities "...with the most comprehensive database of vendor intelligence in corrections..." is the Corrections Connection (www.corrections.com).

VINELink.com, by Appriss Inc., is the online resource of VINE (Victim Information and Notification Everyday), the National Victim Notification Network. The primary objective of this site is to help crime victims obtain timely and reliable information about criminal cases and the custody status of offenders. From the map page a user can search for offenders in practically every state in the U.S. by name or identification number. As you will see in Chapter 6, many state incarcerations agencies offer links on their web pages to VINELink.

Other web pages of several private companies are great resources to find links and searchable inmate locators to state prison systems. Check www.theinmatelocator.com and www.inmatesplus.com. Also most of the free public record links lists sites (such www.brbpublications.com and http://publicrecords.searchsystems.net) offer a wealth of searching links.

Internal Revenue Service (IRS) Records

Most IRS records are not public – there is only a handful of record types that may be accessed.

Charitable Organizations

Exempt Organizations Select Check is an online search tool that allows users to select an exempt organization and check certain information about its federal tax status and filings. See www.irs.gov/Charities-&-Non-Profits/Exempt-Organizations-Select-Check.

Seized Property

Check what the IRS is auctioning at www.ustreas.gov/auctions/irs.

Verification of Income

The Income Verification Express Service (IVES) program is used by mortgage lenders and others within the financial community to confirm the income of a borrower during the processing of a loan application. The written consent of the taxpayer is required. These approved entities may obtain a full return or just the income informational info (the W-2). Visit http://www.irs.gov/Individuals/IVES-Enrollment-Procedures.

TheWorkNumber.com is a private company service for obtaining proof of employment or income. The site is owned by Equifax.

Liens

See the **Recorded Documents, Judgments, and Liens** section.

Media Resources

The media is an often overlooked resource for finding clues to public records and public record trails. Researching 24-hour news outlets, press releases, company announcements, trade journals and magazines is a great way to find many leads. Below are some research sources and tips that should prove helpful. Also keep in mind that although many resources are online, a good starting point is often the local library.

News Journalism

Links to thousands of newspapers, radio and TV stations, magazines, and foreign outlets are found at two excellent web pages: www.editorandpublisher.com and www.newslink.org.

A web page specializing in magazine stories is www.highbeam.com.

Without a doubt the leading trade association for journalists is the **Investigative Reporters & Editors, Inc**. This organization promotes high standards while providing educational services to reporters, editors and others interested in investigative journalism. Visit the IRE web page at www.ire.org.

CNN provides a web page to obtain transcripts of broadcasts. Visit http://transcripts.cnn.com/TRANSCRIPTS/.

Back Issues in Print

The United States Book Exchange is a non-profit organization which supplies back issues of scholarly periodicals, trade journals, popular magazines and other serials to libraries worldwide. Visit them at www.usbe.com.

Another good resource for finding locations and stores selling back issues of a magazine is presented at www.trussel.com/books/magdeal.htm.

Other Web Resources

Fee-Based Resources

One of the advantages of the fee-based resources is the length of time stories are kept available. Depending on the service, some vendors maintain comprehensive data dating back 40 years or more. The following entities are highly recommended by Cynthia Hetherington:

- EBSCO (www.ebsco.com)
- Factiva from Dow Jones (www.factiva.com)

- InfoTrac (www.infotrac.com)
- ProQuest (www.proquest.com)

Free Resources

Websites that offer free access to news stories usually allow searching by either topic or by location. Here are four sites excellent for investigations.

These sites are organized **by topic**.

- Newspaper Archive (www.newspaperarchive.com). Use their seven-day free trial to see if this works for you.
- Google News (news.google.com). Offers current news (within 30 days) and is an excellent source for local news with approximately 4,500 news sources worldwide.

These sites are organized **by location**.

- NewsLibrary.com enables a search by location and by available news on a specific topic.
- ThePaperBoy.com includes national and international locations.

Military Records

National Personnel Records Center (NPRC)

Military service records are kept by the National Personnel Records Center (NPRC) which is under the jurisdiction of the National Archives and Records Administration.

Recent military service and medical records are **not online**. The type of information released to the general public is dependent upon the veteran's authorization. However, most veterans and their next-of-kin can obtain free copies of their DD Form 214 (Report of Separation) and other records in several ways. Another key form used when searching military records is form SF-180 (or a signed release). See www.archives.gov/veterans/military-service-records.

Military Branches - Internet Sources

The Official Sites include—

www.army.mil	U.S. Army
www.af.mil	U.S. Air Force
www.navy.mil	U.S. Navy
www.marines.mil	U.S. Marine Corps
www.arng.army.mil	Army National Guard
www.ang.af.mil	Air National Guard
www.uscg.mil/default.asp	U.S. Coast Guard

National Gravesite Locator

The Nationwide Gravesite Locator maintained by the U.S. Department of Veterans Affairs includes burial records from many sources. Go to http://gravelocator.cem.va.gov.

Missing Persons

A links list of missing persons compiled by state agencies is free at www.ancestorhunt.com/missing-persons.htm. View the FBI Kidnapping and Missing Persons Investigations web page free at www.fbi.gov/wanted/kidnap. The privately operated Doe Network lists international missing persons and unidentified victims at www.doenetwork.org. Another private site – America's Most Wanted at www.amw.com – features links to missing persons and missing children profiles at www.amw.com.

Most Wanted Lists

Many federal agencies (and some international agencies) have a web page with a Most Wanted List often with name searching capabilities. A web page with links to lists maintained by the FBI, U.S. Marshall, the Bureau of Alcohol, Tobacco, and Firearms (ATF), The Drug Enforcement Administration (DEA), and even the U.S. Postal Service is found at www.usa.gov/Citizen/Topics/MostWanted.shtml.

A quick way to find each state's Most Wanted Lists is at www.ancestorhunt.com/most-wanted-criminals-and-fugitives.htm. Another excellent profile site is America's Most Wanted at www.amw.com

Where found, County Sheriff websites often provide data on County Most Wanted individuals. These same sheriff websites may include missing persons, sexual predators, warrants, arrests, DUIs and other types of local pages as a public service.

Motor Vehicle Records

Motor vehicle records are essential decision-making tools used by many industries and groups, particularly insurance companies, trucking firms, employers, lenders, and private investigators. In general, motor vehicle records can be made public only if personal information is not disclosed, depending on the type of record and the laws of a particular state.

The types of records characterized as motor vehicle records include—

- Driving history (sometimes known as an MVR)
- Driver license status
- Accident report
- Traffic ticket
- Vehicle registration, status
- Vehicle title (ownership), title history, liens
- Vessel registration
- Vessel title, title history, liens
- VIN – Vehicle Identification Number

In general, the databases for each of these record types are maintained by state agencies, but in some jurisdictions a local agency is empowered to process record requests.

Four Critical Guidance Tips

Before proceeding with a review of motor vehicle record searching procedures and online access, there are four important rules to consider regarding these records—

1. There is NO national, all inclusive database of motor vehicle records.
2. Each state maintains its own separate database(s) of licensed drivers, vehicle registrations, vehicle ownership, accident reports, and other associated records.
3. Sometimes there are different state agencies within a state that manage separate record system. For example, in Texas driver licensing and driver records are governed by the Department of Public Safety, but vehicle ownership and registration is governed by the Department of Motor Vehicles.
4. The federal Driver's Privacy Protection Act (DPPA) sets specific standards when personal information can be included on a record, dependent upon the purpose of the record request. All states comply with DPPA. Some more stringent. A copy of DPPA can be found at http://uscode.house.gov/download/pls/18C123.txt or www.mvrdecoder.com.

Driving Records

A driving record is a historical index of a driver's moving violation convictions, accidents, and license sanctions. Depending on the state's record reporting procedure, an MVR can show activity anywhere from 3 years to a lifetime.

A driving record is often referred to as an **MVR.** The acronym MVR comes from the phrase "Motor Vehicle Record" or "Moving Violation Records." However, state motor vehicle agencies do not always refer to a driving record as an MVR, they may consider this term to mean a vehicle record. So if talking to someone at a state motor vehicle department about records, be sure you are clear on what you want or mean.

Personal information found on a driving record may include the licensee's address, height, weight, date of birth. As a rule, Social Security Numbers and medical information are always redacted and never released to record requesters. As mentioned, the release of personal information (PI) on motor vehicle records is governed by the DPPA, based on the premise if there is a permissible use or if the consent of the subject is given, then PI is released.

However, the level of compliance with the Act is inconsistent from state-to-state; some states have stricter policies than the Act never release certain pieces personal information to the public regardless of the permissible use.

About Online Access

All states offer online access to driving records, but there are many caveats. To receive DPPA-compliant records, the requester must qualified, be pre-approved, and often there is a minimum daily or monthly order level. If the requester is not DPPA-Compliant, certain states offer record access, but records are *sanitized* – meaning without personal information included.

Electronic access methods vary widely depending upon how orders are grouped or submitted, and by the media type. States provide interactive processing (results of a record request is shown immediately), electronic batch processing (usually using FTP - File Transfer Protocol - technology), or both.

The License Status Report

A status report – the top or header portion of a driving record – can sometimes be obtained as a separate record. The license status report generally indicates three important pieces of information:

1. The type or class of license issued which in turn tells what types of vehicles (commercial, non-commercial, motorcycle) can be operated. Different commercial license classes regulate the size or weight of the vehicle licensed to be driven.

2. Any special conditions placed on the license holder. These permissions and limitations are known as endorsements and restrictions. A typical restriction is a requirement to have "corrective lenses" when driving. Another example is a CDL license may have an endorsement that regulates if hazardous material can be hauled.

3. If the license is valid or under suspension or revocation.

A handful of states offer online status checks. Some are free and some are for a fee, as indicated in the state profiles in Chapter 6.

Accident or Crash Reports

Note many states use the term "crash reports" and will bristle if you use the term "accident reports."

There are usually two types of accident records for each incident – the reports filed by the citizens involved and the reports prepared by the investigating officers. Copies of a citizen's accident report are not usually available to the public and are not reviewed herein. The profiles in Chapter 6 refer to reports prepared by the investigating officer.

A good rule of thumb is that accident records must be obtained from the agency that investigated the incident. If that agency is part of the same agency that holds driving records, then DPPA guidelines are followed with regards to honoring record requests.

Typical information found on a state accident report includes drivers' addresses and license numbers as well as a description of the incident. Only a handful of states offer online access to accident reports.

Vehicle Records

There are many similarities between accessing driving records and accessing vehicle records, especially if records are administered by the same agency that handles driver records. Regardless of which agency oversees vehicle recordkeeping, record access is affected by DPPA as described for driving records. However, not every state offers online access. A few states offer status checks, as indicated in Chapter 6.

Normally these categories of vehicle records are available:

- Ownership and title
- Registration and license plate data
- Vehicle identification numbers (VINs)
- Liens

Ownership and title records of vehicles can generally be obtained as either a current record, or as a historical record showing all previous owners. Title data can indicate if a vehicle was at one time a junk vehicle or if the vehicle was once a subject of title washing (previously branded as a salvage or flood-damaged vehicle), or perhaps a government vehicle previously. **Liens** generally are part of the title record, but know that in some states the liens on vehicles are recorded at the county or at the Secretary of State's Office where UCCs are filed.

Registration data is usually limited to the current year. Searches of license plates, to find the registered own of a vehicle is not a public record search, there must be a disclosed permissible use.

The same description above holds true for **vessel records** if the vessels are administered by the same motor vehicle agency. When watercraft and watercraft records are governed by a different government agency, the access policies are usually not governed by DPPA. In these states certain records may be more open to access, but generally access is governed by administrative rules or even by statute.

Vehicle record data that includes personal identifiers is never sold for marketing purposes, per DPPA.

About the VIN

VIN stands for "vehicle identification number." This number is internationally recognized as the way to identify an individual vehicle. When buying a used vehicle, many people and dealers check the history of a vehicle from a vendor to help make an informed decision about the quality and value of the vehicle. The VIN is the key identifier used. Vehicles have a metal plate stamped with unique VIN located somewhere on the dashboard or door, but the VIN may also be found attached to other locations on the vehicle.

A VIN consists of 17 characters (vehicles manufactured before 1981 may have fewer characters) in a highly coded but strict format structure. A code table that shows all the possible meanings for each position is a very extensive document, and it changes frequently. Web resources to decode a VIN include:

- www.autocheck.com
- www.cardetective.com
- www.decodethis.com

Vessels Records

Vessels and watercraft that weigh more than five tons are registered with the U.S. Coast Guard, www.st.nmfs.noaa.gov/st1/CoastGuard. Another handy location to search for larger vessels, or to search by lien or title, is the Coast Guard's National Vessel Documentation Center found at www.uscg.mil/hq/g-m/vdoc/poc.htm.

Smaller vessels, usually those for pleasure or sport, are registered through a state motor vehicle department or a state environmental agency such as a Fish & Game Department. Usually but not always the same state agency that administers vehicle records also administers vessel records. In some states vessel records are controlled by an entirely different state government department or division.

The types of vessel records available from state agencies are very similar, with different terms used sometimes for the registration or plate type data. Not all states title watercraft, and those that do generally only require titles if the vessel is over a certain length or motorized or both. Similar requirements may be imposed when registration is mandatory. Also, in some states the liens on vehicles are recorded at the county or at the Secretary of State's Office where UCCs are filed.

For in-depth, detailed information about each state's procedures regarding all types of motor vehicle records, see The MVR Access and Decoder Digest. [3]

Occupations & Licensing Boards

The process of regulating people who have professional occupations and businesses which required licenses is intended to protect the public from fraud and the unqualified. Information about these people and entities is often (but not always) a matter of public record and is often found online.

Types of Agencies Involved

Professional Occupations can be registered, certified, or licensed. In general there are there types of regulatory agencies involved in this process.

1. Private Entities

A certification body is a private association that has set the licensing or certification standards for many professions. The issuance of professional licenses can be based on completion of the requirements of professional associations An

[3] Published annually by BRB Publications, www.brbpublications.com

example is the American Institute of Certified Public Accountants, which sets the standards for becoming a Certified Public Accountant (CPA). It does not license as CPA in a state (see below) .

In addition, there are many professional designations issued by associations that are not recognized as official licenses by government, but are of interest to the professionals within an industry. For example, the initials "CFE" indicate an individual is a Certified Fraud Examiner and has met the minimum requirements for that title from the Association of Certified Fraud Examiners.

To find other resources that may oversee credentialing, see the *Trade Associations* section later in this chapter.

2. State Agencies

A state agency can administer the registration, certification, and occupational licensing of an individual intending to offer specified products or services in the designated area. If registration alone is required, there may not be a certification status showing that the person has met minimum requirements. Using the CPA example above, the New York State Education Department, Office of the Professions, oversees the preparation, licensure, and practice of its CPAs.

Businesses may also fall under the administration of state entity, per statute. For example, a state may require business registration for an entity to do business or offer specified products or services in a designated area, such as registering a liquor license. Some business license agencies require testing or a background check. Others merely charge a fee after a cursory review of the application.

Often the state agencies are referred to as **licensing boards**. Sometimes many, many boards are under the direction of one specific branch of regulatory government. An example is health care related vocations.

3. Local Entities

Local county and municipal government agencies may require business registrations and permits in order for companies to operate (construction, signage, sell hot dogs on a street corner, etc.) within their borders. If you must check on local registrations and permits, call the offices at both the county (try the county recording office) and municipal level (try city hall) to find out what type of registrations may be required for the person or business you are investigating. Several of the free links lists sites will connect you to online searching sites when available.

Widespread Online Access

Per the BRB Publications database of occupational licensing boards, there are over 8,750 individual job titles or businesses that are administered for licensing, registration or certification by nearly 2,000 different state entities. **Some level of online searching exists for names and even enforcement actions on over 5,500 occupations or businesses.**

The online sites are listed in Chapter 6.

What Information May Be Available

An agency may be willing to release part or all of the following—

- Field of Certification
- Status of License/Certificate
- Date License/Certificate Issued
- Date License/Certificate Expires
- Current or Most Recent Employer
- Social Security Number
- Address of Subject
- Complaints, Violations or Disciplinary Actions

The Council on Licensure, Enforcement, and Regulation (CLEAR)

An excellent organizational resource for entities or individuals involved in the licensing, non-voluntary certification or registration of hundreds of regulated occupations is the Council on Licensure, Enforcement, and Regulation (CLEAR) See www.clearhq.org.

Patents

United States Patent and Trademark Office

Most patent applications filed on or after November 29, 2000, will be published 18 months after the filing date of the application. Otherwise, all patent applications withheld until the patent is issued or the application is published. After the application has been published, the public may request a copy of the application file. After the patent is issued, the Office file containing the application and all correspondence leading up to issuance of the patent is made available in the Files Information Unit for inspection by anyone, and copies of these files may be purchased.

Search the United States Patent and Trademark office (USPTO) databases at www.uspto.gov/patents/process/search. Also for full-text patent information on U.S. patents granted since 1976 and full-page images since 1790 see http://patft.uspto.gov. Note that the text-searchable patent database begins with patents granted since 1976. Patents issued from 1790 through 1975 are searchable only by patent number, issue date, and current US classifications. Also, be aware neither assignment changes nor address changes recorded at the USPTO are reflected in the patent full-text or the patent full-page images.

The Patent Application Information Retrieval (PAIR) system provides a filing status check of a patent application. Actually a number of different searches from PAIR are accessible from the home page above. The site also permits third parties to obtain information on published applications on issued patents, status of maintenance fee payments, and if a re-issue application or re-examination request has been filed.

Private Resources

The World Intellectual Property Organization (WIPO) is a specialized agency of the United Nations dedicated to promoting the effective use and protection of intellectual property worldwide. WIPO offers an international patent search at http://patentscope.wipo.int/search/en/search.jsf.

Also, check out www.intellogist.com/wiki/Compare:Patent_Search_System (a unique site that lists and compares patent search systems), www.freepatentsonline.com, and www.patentgenius.com.

Privacy and Privacy Rights Resources

Do Not Call & Opt Out Sites of Note

Listed below are several of the most effective organizations that assist the public to remove their names and addresses from marketing list organizations—

- National Do Not Call Registry - https://www.donotcall.gov
- Optout Prescreen.com - https://www.optoutprescreen.com/?rf=t
  (To opt-out or opt-in for offers of credit or insurance)
- Direct Marketing Association Email Opt Out - https://www.dmachoice.org/MPS/
- Report Unsolicited Faxes - http://transition.fcc.gov/eb/tcd/ufax.html

Privacy Rights Advocates

There are a number of organizations who specialize in representing the privacy interests of the consumer. You will find that some of these groups are extremely one-sided in their approach to many issues and view all vendors as data aggregators who cause harm by violating the privacy rights of unsuspecting individuals. However, there are organizations with a balanced view. They do understand of the legitimacy of information requests from businesses based on with permissible use or permission or per statute, but at the same time are vibrant watchdogs monitoring that the information is used correctly. These listed are thought of very highly for their excellent programs to help individuals who have privacy concerns or have been wronged.

Privacy Rights Clearinghouse

This non-profit organization provides a myriad of information for consumers about privacy topics and is a strong voice for consumer advocacy issue. The web page at www.privacyrights.org displays excellent information on many topics. The organization also acknowledges the importance of balancing privacy implications with legitimate protection needs for the public good.

Privacy Rights publishes a list of "data brokers" at https://www.privacyrights.org/online-information-brokers-list. The majority of the 240+ entities listed provide "consumer site" services.

World Privacy Forum

This is another top organization with plenty of informative data on their web page. They specialize, among other topics, in protecting medical information. www.worldprivacyforum.org

PrivacyExchange

PrivacyExchange.org, produced by The Center for Social & Legal Research, is an excellent and informative global information resource. www.privacyexchange.org

Recalls, Products and Safety

Six federal agencies with very different jurisdictions together created www.recalls.gov. Searching is arranged by these topics: boats, consumer products, cosmetics, environment, food, medicine, and motor vehicle. Various search capabilities are offered. You can do a name search or use the tabs to find lists of recalls by product type.

See www-odi.nhtsa.dot.gov/cars/problems/recalls/recallsearch.cfm, a useful government site dedicated to vehicle recall issues site.

The FDA is very involved with product recalls and withdrawals and safety alerts. The site at www.fda.gov is home to many search services and search options.

Another great resource is the U.S. Consumer Product Safety Commission site at www.cpsc.gov.

Real Estate Records

(See **Recorded Documents, Judgments and Liens** below.)

Recorded Documents, Judgments, and Liens

Recorded documents, judgments and liens are among the most popular types of public records sought online. This data can show proof of ownership (deed to your house) or show when an asset is used as collateral for a loan (mortgage on your house). Finding recorded documents and lien notices is a necessity to making informed business-related decisions and these documents lead to a virtual treasure trove of data. Private investigators and attorneys research liens and recorded documents when doing an *Asset Lien* search because a lien search will often lead to finding other liens which in turn could lead to finding other assets.

The function of searching liens and recorded documents in the U.S. public record is truly an art because there are over 3,600 locations in the U.S. where one may file a lien notice or record a document. The locations can be at any of three levels: local municipality, county or parish, or state agency. These jurisdictions maintain indices to these recorded documents. Some government agencies maintain an overall index of all recorded documents and liens notices, while others maintain a series of separate indices within the same office. In other words, a researcher must know the particular index to search for a particular record. A good searcher knows to search ALL the indices.

The publicly recorded documents most often accessed are generally related to:

- Real Estate Transactions
- Uniform Commercial Code (UCC) Filings
- Judgments
- Other Liens (including federal and state tax liens, mechanics liens, etc.)

That does not imply that other records such as vital records, voter registration rolls, and fictitious names are inconsequential – far from it. Before examining each of the key documents types, let's look at some essential facts related to searching these documents.

The Difference Between Personal Property and Real Property

An important first distinction when searching recorded public records is to know the difference between personal property and real property. This is because documents related to real property generally are recorded in different locations than personal property records.

Personal property includes items such as bank accounts, vehicles, jewelry, computers, etc. This property can be collateral or 'consumer goods.' Often when personal property is given as collateral, the lender will secure the loan by filing a **Uniform Commercial Code (UCC)** financing statement on the asset.

Real property involves real estate related assets such as homes, apartment building, land, etc. A **mortgage** is an example of a recorded document that secures the associated loan to finance real property.

Types of Liens and Security Interests

Liens - With or Without Consent

A lien is a lawful claim or right against property or funds for payment of a debt or for services rendered. There are two types of liens that are recorded: those **with consent (voluntary)** or **without consent (involuntary)**.

Examples of liens placed with the consent of an asset holder include mortgages, loans on car and vessels, and Uniform Commercial Code filings on business assets such as equipment or accounts receivable.

Examples of liens placed without the consent of an asset holder include federal and state tax liens, mechanic's liens, and liens filed on assets as the result of judgments issued by courts.

The Grantor-Grantee Index

Perhaps the most commonly used term to describe an index of recorded documents at a county/parish/city/town recorder's office is the **Grantor-Granter Index**.

The Grantor is the party that is a transferring title or some type of interest that involves a recording. The Grantee is the party that is the recipient of the title, interest or document. For example, if you purchase or re-finance real estate and borrow money from a bank, an instrument called a mortgage or deed of trust is generally involved. You, the borrower, are the Grantor since you giving a lien on the property to the bank. The bank is recorded as the Grantee since it is the recipient of the interest in the property as collateral for the loan. Sometimes the Grantor-Grantee Index is known as the Forward-Reverse or Direct-Indirect Index.

About Judgments

When a judgment is rendered in court, the winning party usually files and records a lien notice (called an *Abstract of Judgment* in many states) against real estate owned by the defendant or party against whom the judgment is given. Sometimes judgments can be used to garnish wages or can be placed on bank accounts.

Judgments can be searched at the local or county level usually in the same index as real estate records. Many times judgments are bought and sold as commodities. An *Assignment of Judgment* is the transfer of the title and interest in a judgment from one person to another person.

The Search Location Problem

Keeping state laws variations and filing locations straight is a major challenge to the professional public record searching specialist. Where to search for recorded documents and property liens can be a perplexing puzzle. Just because a mailing address is Schenectady NY doesn't mean the property is located in Schenectady County. The property could be physically located in neighboring Albany County. **The fact is over 8,000 of the 45,000 or so ZIP Codes cross county lines.** Having access to an enhanced ZIP Code/place name/county locator product is a must. Finding involuntary liens—such as federal and state tax liens—and UCC filings can be even harder.

So, unless you know exactly where the real or personal property is located, and you are certain that everyone else who has filed or recorded liens also knows where to go, you may have a problem. You may have to search more than one county, town, city (or even state) to find the property or liens you need to know about. But knowing about the County Rule helps.

In most states, transactions are recorded at one designated recording office in the county where the property is located. But the key word in the last sentence is *most,* because there are exceptions. And if a researcher is not aware of the exceptions key mistakes can be made in filing or searching which could affect borrower and lenders in a very negative manner.

An excellent overview of important searching tips to have in hand when searching for liens and recorded documents is an article titled *The County Rule* written by the late Mr. Carl R. Ernst, founder of Ernst Publishing.[4] While this article is somewhat old, it is still very pertinent.

The County Rule, by Carl R. Ernst

Where to search for recorded documents usually isn't a difficult problem to overcome in everyday practice. In most states, these transactions are recorded at one designated recording office in the county where the

[4] Ernst Publishing publishes two extensive industry manuals - *The UCC Filing Guide* and *The Real Estate Recording Guide.* Visit www.ernstpublishing.com for more information.

property is located.

We call this the "County Rule." It applies to types of public records such as real estate recordings, tax liens, Uniform Commercial Code (UCC) filings, vital records, and voter registration records. However, as with most government rules, there are a variety of exceptions which are summarized here.

The Exceptions

The five categories of exceptions to the County Rule (or Parish Rule, if searching in Louisiana) are listed below [Editor's Note: details for each state are listed in the State Profiles Section which follows.]—

Special Recording Districts (AK, HI)

Multiple Recording Offices (AL, AR, IA, KY, ME, MA, MS, TN)

Independent Cities (MD, MO, NV, VA)

Recording at the Municipal Level (CT, RI, VT)

Identical Names—Different Place (CT, IL, MA, NE, NH, PA, RI, VT, VA)

The Personal Property Problem and the Fifth Exception

The real estate recording system in the U.S. is self-auditing to the extent that you generally cannot record a document in the wrong recording office. However, many documents are rejected for recording because they are submitted to the wrong recording office. There are a number of reasons why this occurs, one of which is the overlap of filing locations for real estate and UCC.

Finding the right location of a related UCC filing is a different and much more difficult problem from finding a real estate recording. In the majority of states, the usual place to file a UCC financing statement is at the Secretary of State office—these are called central filing states. In the dual and local filing states, the place to file, in addition to the central filing office, is usually at the same office where your real estate documents are recorded. However, where there are identical place names referring to two different places, it becomes quite confusing, so hence, the fifth exemption.

Searching Real Estate Records

Every local entity (i.e. county, parish or town recorder of Deeds) records documents that transfer or encumber title. Many county, city, and parish government jurisdictions provide online access to indices of real estate records and recorded documents. Most sites are free if viewing an index, but an increasing number of government agencies will charge a fee to view or print an image or copy of a page within the file.

As with other types of public records, many investigators and researchers use these online resources as a pre-search or preliminary search, especially if dealing with an uncommon name.

Keep in mind there are a number of private companies who compile and maintain these records. Some offer free searching on the web as a way to drive users to their web pages. Some vendors offer bulk data for resale. Vendors are a very comprehensive resource to obtain electronic records.

There are a number of web pages that information on the property of specific homes (addresses). Check www.zillow.com and www.trulia.com. For interactive map information, check out http://nationalmap.gov.

Types of Real Estate Recorded Documents Found Online

There many types of lien notices and recorded documents related to real estate files. Below are common names for documents that a public record researcher may find when searching real estate records. This list is certainly not all inclusive; there are many, many more. Also keep in mind that name variations will occur from state to state.

- **Deed of Trust or Mortgage of Deed of Trust** Generally a mortgage that secures a debt, and names three parties - the borrower (trustor), the beneficiary (lender), and the trustee who holds title to real property under the terms of a deed of trust.
- **Bill of Sale** A Bill of Sale will be recorded to show the transfer of most any kind of personal property.
- **Assignment of Deed of Trust** A transfer or sale of a Deed of Trust from the current lender (beneficiary) to a new beneficiary.
- **Abstract of Judgment** A court issued money judgment to secure payment to the creditor, usually creates a general lien on real property of the judgment debtor.
- **Declaration of Homestead** A document recorded by either a homeowner or head of household on their primary residence to protect his home from forced sale in satisfaction of certain types of creditors' claims.
- **Mechanic's Lien** A document recorded to create a lien in favor of persons contributing labor, material, supplies, etc., to a work of improvement upon real property.
- **Notice of Default** A notice to show that the borrower under a mortgage or deed of trust is behind in payments.
- **Notice of Lis Pendens** A notice that litigation is pending in court which may affect the title of the real estate involved.
- **Notice of Trustee's Sale** This document is recorded to notify the public of pending the foreclosure sale by the trust for non-payment or non-performance of the conditions of the deed of trust.
- **Power of Attorney** This document delegates the authority of an entity to an agent (attorney-in-fact) to allow this agent to act behalf of the entity in a designated capacity.
- **Quitclaim Deed** A form of deed that conveys or releases any interest that the grantor may have acquired in real property. Many times this type of deed is issued without title insurance.
- **Reconveyance** The instrument releases the loan that was a lien against real property. Can also be called a satisfaction of the loan or a release of lien or a release of mortgage.
- **Satisfaction of Mortgage** Release of the loan that was a lien against real property. This document may also be called a release of mortgage.
- **Subordination Agreement** This document is recorded when a current lender agrees to makes their encumbrance deed of trust beneath or junior to another loan. These loans are sometimes called seconds.
- **Trustee Deed in Lieu of Foreclosure** Document indicates the transfer of real property from the defaulting borrower to the beneficiary (lender) in lieu of foreclosure.
- **Trustee's Deed** A deed given by the trustee when the real property is sold under the power of sale in a deed of trust in a foreclosure proceeding.
- **Writ or Notice of Levy** A document to notify a party served with writ of execution that specific property is being taken to satisfy a debt.

Real Estate Records and the County Rule

Remember the earlier section on the County Rule? The second, third and fourth County Rules are very important to observe when searching real estate records in the states listed below.

- **Multiple Recording Offices**. In these states, some counties have more than one recording office; AL, AR, IA, KY, LA, ME, MA, MS, and TN.
- **Independent Cities.** Four states (MD, MO, NV, and VA) have independent cities that should be treated just as if they are counties. For example, St Louis City and St. Louis County are separate jurisdictions with separate sets of data.
- **Recording at the Municipal Level.** In CT, RI, and VT the recording jurisdiction is the town, not the county. The county clerk's office does not record documents.

Uniform Commercial Code

Uniform Commercial Code (UCC) filings are to personal property what mortgages are to real estate property. UCCs indicate where personal property, usually business related, is secured as collateral. A UCC recording allows potential lenders to be notified that certain assets of a debtor are already pledged to secure a loan or lease. Therefore, examining UCC filings is an excellent way to find many types of assets, security interests, and financiers.

Most state UCC websites provide a free search of the index. A few will permit free access to images, but most states charge a fee to access the full records, which usually involves a subscription service and registration, login, and password. Delaware is the only state that does not offer online access to an index of UCC records, except through certain contracted firms.

Chapter 6 gives the searchable web address for each state's central repository. Also, for specific links and updated information, visit the free public record searching sites found at www.brbpublications.com.

A number of private companies compile their own proprietary database of UCC and tax lien records or offer real time online services. Vendors are a very comprehensive resource to obtain electronic records over multiple jurisdictions, see Chapter 5.

UCC Searching Tips

Most UCC filings against businesses are found at the state where a business is organized, not where the collateral or chief executive offices are located. Most UCCs files against individuals are files in the state where the person resides. Therefore, you will need to know where a company is organized in order to know where to find recent UCC filings against it. (However federal tax liens are still generally filed where the chief executive office is located.)

The location to search UCC records changed dramatically in many states in July 2001 with the enactment of **Revised Article 9**. Prior to that date UCC documents were recorded either at a centralized state agency or at a local recording office. Since July 2001 all UCC documents are filed recorded at a state level agency with the exception of certain real estate filings such as farm-related real estate (see Searching Real Estate Related UCC Collateral to follow).

Until June 30, 2001, liens on certain types of companies required dual filing (must file at BOTH locations) in some states, and records could be searched at BOTH locations. As of July 1, 2001, UCC filings other than those that go into real estate records were no longer filed at the local filing offices. According to the UCC Filing Guide (see www.ernstpublishing.com) less than 3% of UCC filings are done so at the local level.

Although there are significant variations among state statutes, the state level is now the best starting place to uncover liens filed against an individual or business, but it is not the only place to search. Strict due diligence may require a local search also, depending on the state, how many years back you wish to search, and the type of collateral. The best technique is to check both locales of records.

As a result of Revised Article 9 (Secured Transactions) of the Uniform Commercial Code, **the general rules for searching of UCC records** are as follows:

- Except in former local filing states, a search at the state level is adequate to locate all legally valid UCC records on a subject.
- Credit due diligence searching requires use of flexible search logic provided either by the state agency or private database vendors.
- Mortgage record searches will include any real estate related UCC filings.

Note that over the past several years, states' filing offices have been busy gaining legislative approval for implementing the additional amendments to Article 9. The changes go into effect July 1, 2013. These changes should not affect searching, but will provide uniformity on how names are recorded on the filings.

Searching Real Estate-Related UCC Collateral Online

UCC financing statements applicable to real estate related collateral must be filed where real estate and mortgage records are kept, which is generally at the county level — except in Connecticut, Rhode Island, and Vermont where the Town/City Clerk maintains these records.

In general, the definition of real estate related UCC collateral is any property that in one form is attached to land, but that in another form is not attached. For the sake of simplicity, we can define the characteristics of two broad types of property that meet this definition:

1. Property that is initially attached to real property, but then is separated. Three specific types of collateral have this characteristic: minerals (including oil and gas), timber, and crops. These things are grown on or extracted from land. While they are on or in the ground they are thought of as real property, but once they are harvested or extracted they become personal property. Some states have a separate central filing system for crops.
2. Property that is initially personal property, but then is attached to land, is generally called fixtures. Equipment such as telephone systems or heavy industrial equipment permanently affixed to a building are examples of fixtures. It is important to realize that what is a fixture, like beauty, is in the eye of the beholder, since it is a somewhat vague definition.

UCC financing statements applicable to real estate related collateral must be filed where real estate and mortgage records are kept, which is generally at the county level — except in Connecticut, Rhode Island, and Vermont where the Town/City Clerk maintains these records.

Tax Liens

Tax liens are non-consensual liens placed by a government agency for non-payment of taxes. Of course the federal government and every state all impose taxes, such as sales, income, withholding, unemployment, and/or personal property. When these taxes go unpaid, the appropriate state agency can file a lien on the real or personal property of the subject.

Tax liens filed against individuals are frequently maintained at separate locations from those liens filed against businesses. For example, many number of states require liens filed against businesses to be filed at a central state location (i.e., Secretary of State's office) and liens against individuals to be filed at the county level (i.e., Recorder, Registrar of Deeds, Clerk of Court, etc.).

Searching Tips for Federal and State Tax Liens

Tax liens filed against individuals are frequently maintained at separate locations from those liens filed against businesses. For example, many number of states require liens filed against businesses to be filed at a central state location (i.e., Secretary of State's office) and liens against individuals to be filed at the county level (i.e., Recorder,

Registrar of Deeds, Clerk of Court, etc.). So when searching tax liens, first and foremost one must realize there are actually are four location possibilities in play:

1. Federal Tax Liens on Individuals
2. Federal Tax Liens on Businesses
3. State Tax Liens on Individuals
4. State Tax Liens on Businesses

Also, Federal tax liens are filed at the location of the taxpayer's principal address, which is not the same rule applied for UCC filings. So Federal tax liens will not necessarily be filed (recorded) at the same location/jurisdiction as a state tax lien. These variances are shown in the *Recording Offices Summaries* section later in Chapter 6. In general, state tax liens on personal property will be found where UCCs are filed and tax liens on real property will be found where real property deeds are recorded, with few exceptions.

Another point to consider is that the IRS files their federal tax liens under the name of the taxpayer. But that name may be different than the name used on the filing papers when a business entity was registered.

Unsatisfied state and federal tax liens may be renewed if prescribed by individual state statutes. However, once satisfied, the time the record will remain in the repository before removal varies by jurisdiction. Many states will show a release of lien filing rather than deleting the original recording of the lien.

Other Types of Recorded Documents

There are numerous types of documents that can be recorded and are not related to real estate or personal property. Many of these documents are found at the same recording office that records real estate liens, and often times they appear in the same index. Mentioned below are several significant types.

Fictitious Names or Assumed Names

If a person operates a business not organized as a corporation, partnership, LLC, etc., under a name other his own, then it has a fictitious name. For example if Joe Cool is doing business as Costabunch General Store, that business name must be registered. Depending on the state, this registration can take place at municipal, county or state. A fictitious name is also known as a **DBA** – meaning *Doing Business As*.

Forcible Detainer

A Forcible Detainer is a landlord's lien against a tenant's property for unpaid rent or damages. Sometimes the document is filed to essentially 'give notice.' If the tenant does not comply within a designated time period, the landlord can forcibly move the tenant's belongings off the property, usually with the assistance of local law enforcement.

Searching for evidence of a Forcible Detainer is part of the tenant screening process, which is governed by the federal Fair Credit Reporting Act (FCRA).

Vital Records

Birth certificates, death certificates, marriages licenses, and divorce decrees are often recorded at the local level and then forwarded to centralized state agency. These records may be available from both locations - local and state. Sometimes the local level is the only place to obtain a certified copy of a marriage or divorce action. Non-certified copies are often available online at the local level. See the *Vital Records Section* later in this chapter.

Wills

Many people record their Last Will and Testament at the local recorder's office. Some people confuse a probate court with this function. A probate court is not a recording office, but has records concerning decedents which include their wills (if any) and lists of assets.

Securities and Securities Dealers

Federal Level

While federal agencies oversee the regulatory and compliance issues which deal with publicly traded securities or with security dealers, there are several private entities with great authority as well. All of these agencies have the authority to investigate issues related to compliance or improprieties. Hence, these agencies are excellent resources to search for enforcement actions. Perhaps the most well-known government agency is the Securities and Exchange Commission (SEC).

SEC – Securities & Exchange Commission

The SEC oversees the participants in the securities world, including securities exchanges, securities brokers and dealers, investment advisors, and mutual funds. The SEC offers a number of useful online search sites through **EDGAR** at www.sec.gov/edgar/searchedgar/webusers.htm. See data presented earlier in this chapter under *Business Entity Records: Edgar and the SEC.*

Enforcement Actions: SEC-related enforcement actions are viewable online at www.sec.gov/divisions/enforce/enforceactions.shtml. These actions include civil lawsuits brought by the Commission in Federal court, administrative proceedings as instituted and/or settled, opinions issued by Administrative Law Judges in contested administrative proceedings, and opinions on appeals issued by the Commission on appeal of Initial Decisions or disciplinary decisions issued by self-regulatory organizations (e.g., NYSE or NASD).

Litigation Actions: The SEC page at http://www.sec.gov/litigation.shtml contains specific links to information on SEC enforcement actions including reportsa of investigations, trading suspensions, opinions issued by the Commission, briefs filed by SEC staff, trading suspensions, and notices concerning the creation of investors' claims funds in specific cases.

Financial Industry Regulatory Authority (FINRA)

Formerly the National Association of Securities Dealers (NASD), the Financial Industry Regulatory Authority (FINRA) is a resource to investigate brokers and brokerage firms. FINRA oversees over 4,700 brokerage firms, 167,000 branch offices, and more than 635,000 registered securities representatives. FINRA is probably the largest non-governmental regulator for all securities firms doing business in the U.S.

The website at www.finra.org offers *BrokerCheck®* which provides name searching of an individual or of a brokerage firm registered in FINRA. The user can download an eight-page Adobe Acrobat PDF file that outlines the subject's history, including employment. Brokerage firms are searchable for any disciplinary actions taken against a company, or brokers who are involved with arbitration awards, disciplinary, and regulatory events. You can reach FINRA at 301-590-6500.

North American Securities Administrators Association (NASAA)

The North American Securities Administrators Association (NASAA) is devoted to investor protection. Members of NASAA are state securities regulators. They license firms and their agents, investigate violations of state and provincial law, file enforcement actions when appropriate, and educate the public about investment fraud. NASAA members also participate in multi-state enforcement actions and information sharing.

The NASAA web page (http://www.nasaa.org/) is a great resource of links to individual state, provincial, and territorial jurisdictions for securities laws, rules and regulations. Headquartered in Washington DC, NASAA can be reached at 202-737-0900.

CRD and IARD

The Central Registration Depository (CRD) is a centralized filing system of licensed broker-dealers. The CRD was developed by state securities regulators, NASAA, FINRA, and the SEC. CRD reports are available through state regulatory authorities. CRD's computerized database contains the licensing and disciplinary histories on more than 650,000 securities professionals and 5,200 securities firms. IARD is the acronym for the Investment Advisor Registration Depository system is to investment advisers what the CRD is to broker-dealers.

More information and useful search links are located under the Industry Resources tab at the NASAA web page.

National Futures Association (NFA)

The National Futures Association (NFA) is a self-regulatory organization meant to safeguard the U.S. futures industry. The NFA web page offers name searching of individuals or firms. Results indicate any arbitration or regulatory action filed against any NFA listed individual or firm. Visit www.nfa.futures.org or call the Chicago headquarters at 312-781-1300.

Securities Class Action Clearinghouse

The Securities Class Action Clearinghouse provides detailed information relating to the prosecution, defense, and settlement of federal class action securities fraud litigation. The Clearinghouse maintains an index of than 40,600 complaints, briefs, filings, and other litigation-related materials. This content is maintained by the Stanford Law School and Cornerstone Research. Visit http://securities.stanford.edu.

State Level

Every state has its own securities laws – often referred to as **"Blue Sky Laws**" – designed to protect investors against fraud. The records of the filings by companies registering under the Blue Sky Laws, as well as any records of legal actions, are held by designated *state regulatory securities agencies*.

These state agencies also usually license and hold records of brokerage firms, their brokers, and investment adviser representatives doing business there.

Although these records are open to the public they are not generally found online. Those states with searchable online sites are shown in Chapter 6.

To find each state's address and web page, we suggest to visit the North American Securities Administrators Association (see above) or to view the links found at www.seclinks.com/id16.html.

Sexual Offender Registries

Sexual offenses include aggravated sexual assault, sexual assault, aggravated criminal sexual contact, endangering the welfare of a child by engaging in sexual conduct, kidnapping, and false imprisonment. Under Megan's Law, sex offenders are classified in one of three levels or tiers based on the severity of their crime as follows: Tier 3 (high); Tier 2 (moderate); and Tier 1 (low).

Sex offenders must notify authorities of their whereabouts or when moving into a community.

Usually, the state agency that oversees the criminal record repository also administrates the Sexual Offender Registry (SOR) and offers a free search of registered sexual offenders who are living within the particular state. These state web pages are shown in Chapter 6.

The creation of the National Sexual Offender Registry (www.nsopr.gov) is the result of coordinated efforts by the Department of Justice and the state agencies hosting public sexual offender registries. The website has a national query to obtain information about sex offenders through a number of search options including name, Zip Code, county, and city or town. The site also has an excellent, detailed overview of each state's SOR policies and procedures.

Tax Assessor and Collector Records

In every county, parish, or local municipality there is an official – often called the Assessor – who is required by law to determine the value of all taxable property in a jurisdiction for property taxing purposes. This official publishes assessment reports and provides it to property owners with valuation notices. The official may also be known as the Auditor or Property Valuator.

Records of unpaid property taxes can be found in the office of the Treasurer or Tax Collector.

All of records are very public, very valuable, and often accessible online. Usually tax assessment records are searchable by name or by legal description (plat number), and not necessarily by the address.

Chapter 6 shows the searchable web pages to several thousand assessor type sites.

There are several private sites that offer links lists to Tax Assessor offices. The site at www.pulawski.net is very easy to use and indicates when pages are last updated. Another excellent site specializing in listing tax assessors and recorder offices with web pages offering record searching capabilities is http://publicrecords.netronline.com. And the site at www.brbpublications.com provides address, phone number home page, and free searching links.

Telephone Numbers

This section has two very distinctly different section parts, yet relevant to this topic.

Assignment of Area Codes - North American Numbering Plan (NANPA)

NANPA is the integrated telephone numbering plan serving the United States, its territories, and 18 other North American countries; Canada, Bermuda, Anguilla, Antigua & Barbuda, the Bahamas, Barbados, the British Virgin Islands, Cayman Islands, Dominica, Dominican Republic, Grenada, Jamaica, Montserrat, St. Kitts and Nevis, St. Lucia, St. Vincent and the Grenadines, Trinidad and Tobago, and Turks & Caicos.

While regulatory authorities in each participating country have plenary authority over numbering resources, the participating countries share numbering resources cooperatively. Thus NANPA holds overall responsibility for the administration of NANPA numbering resources, subject to directives from regulatory authorities in the countries that share participate in the NANP. See www.nanpa.com/index.html.

Key online searches include:

- **Area Code Maps** - Select a state and see area code boundaries.
- **Central Office Code Assignments** - Find out what codes are assigned or available for assignment in each geographic area code
- **Area Code Search** - Get information about individual area codes, including dialing plans and pointers to planning letters with split/overlay information.

Links to Yellow and White Pages and Directories

There are a number of web resources that provide name look-ups to find phone numbers. But the "problem" is some of sites take you through a search procedure then at the point of obtaining the phone number they attempt to charge a fee

PLUS try to sell you other public record details about the person. We are purposely not recommending these commercial, consumer sites in this book. Below are several recommended search sites that do provide telephone numbers freely with a name search. The sites also offer a reverse phone look-up.

- www.superpages.com
- www.addresses.com
- www.anywho.com
- http://ypng.infospace.com (great for *Yellow Page* look-ups)

Other very worthwhile vendor search tools include:

- Dun & Bradstreet's www.zapdata.com offers phone mailing-list services. Through various public records, news accounts, and telephone interviews, D&B has amassed a large amount of very specific contact information that can be purchased by the batch or in small doses. The lists are targeted for marketing purposes but investigators can use purchased lists to locate a target or subject by occupation, geography, or hobby.
- FoneFinder is a service tool providing the location and basic service provider for a telephone number. Search by the telephone number or by city or ZIP Code at www.fonefinder.net.

Trademarks & Service Marks

United States Patent and Trademark Office

The U.S. Patent and Trademark Office (USPTO) reviews trademark applications to determine if an applicant meets the requirements for federal registration. The USPTO does not decide who has the right to *use* a mark. Even without a registration, someone may still *use* any mark adopted to identify the source of your goods and/or services.

Once a registration is issued, it is up to the owner of a mark to enforce their rights in the mark based on ownership of a federal registration.

The Electronic Business Center offers trademark and status searching at www.uspto.gov/ebc/index_tm.html. There is no fee to search, but charges are incurred for certified copies.

Other Key Resources

An astounding list of international trademark resources is found at www.ggmark.com/#International_Trademark_Law.

A rather comprehensive service for finding intellectual property and international trademark registries is www.ipmenu.org.

Unclaimed Funds

Unclaimed funds refers to money, stocks, bonds, dividends, utility deposits, vendor payments, gift certificates and insurance proceeds held by state or federal agencies who are looking for rightful owners.

Every state has an agency, sometimes called the Unclaimed Property Division, responsible for holding and returning these assets to the rightful owners. Nearly every one of these state agencies provides a link to find unclaimed monies. A link to each state's search site is provided Chapter 6 under the *Useful State Links* section.

National links list are easily found on the web. A great resource is the National Association of Unclaimed Property Administrators (NAUPA), a non-profit organization affiliated with the National Association of State Treasurers. Click on the map to find state sites. Another important feature that NAUPA offers is its list of various U.S. government agencies that hold unclaimed assets.

At the ANUPA at www.unclaimed.org one may do national searches or find a profile of the state agency responsible for holding unclaimed funds, including a link to the state's free web search page.

Another recommended vendor is Missing Money at www.missingmoney.com.

Uniform Commercial Code

(See the **Recorded Documents and Liens Section**.)

Vessels and Boats

(See the **Motor Vehicle Records Section.**)

Vital Records

(Also see the **Genealogy Resources Section** earlier in this chapter.)

Usually birth, death, marriage and divorce records can be searched at the local (county) level and/or at the state vital records office, which is usually part of a state health agency. If a certified copy is needed then birth, death and marriage certificates can usually be obtained from the state agency; divorce certificates from the county or local entity.

Vital records are not necessarily public records. Many states place limitations, ranging from 50 to 100 years, before records are fully open. Therefore these "newer" records are not usually found online. In general, birth records are the most restrictive, death records the least restrictive, and marriage and divorce records somewhere in between. But the degree of restrictiveness may also depend on if a certified record is needed or if merely a computer printout will suffice.

But online ordering is often offered. State agencies that provide online ordering or host searchable databases of older records are listed in Chapter 6.

Recommended Vendors

There are several national vendors who specialize in providing vital records to clients, with a special emphasis on doing so on an expedited basis. Perhaps the most well-known, one-stop shop is VitalChek.com, a LexisNexis company. VitalChek has relationships with nearly all the state vital record agencies and a number of local agencies. They offer a means to order and receive records in an expedited manner.

Another vendor with similar services is Vitalrec.com found at http://vitalrec.com. This web page provides some excellent links and good basic searching information about each state. The site has direct ties to Ancestry, a vendor specialized in genealogy records.

Another excellent site with a mixture of old and new records is www.archives.com. There is an annual subscription fee per year, but you have unlimited access to over 1 billion historical records.

The web abounds with marriage record sources, most of which are genealogy based. Besides the sites mentioned above, try www.genealinks.com.

Death Records & the Death Index of U.S. Social Security Administration

The Social Security Death Index (SSDI) contains the records of deceased persons who were assigned a SSN. Data is generated from the master death file of the U.S. Social Security Administration (SSA). The data is not searchable from a SSA site but a number of vendors purchase the data and make it available to the public.

Use Caution

Please note that the SSA does not have a death record for all persons. The SSA's Master Death File (DMF) used as a verification tool is good, but the absence of a particular person does not guarantee the person is alive. For example, effective November 1, 2011, the SSA no longer includes state death records in the DMF. Further, since the SSA no longer adds these entries, the SSA decided to remove 4.2 million existing state records from the DMF in November 2011. This removal represented a little over 4.7% of the entire database. One of the significant pieces of information removed, which came from the state records data added to the DMF, was the last known residence (state, county) of a subject.

The law governing this action is found at www.ssa.gov/OP_Home/ssact/title02/0205.htm. Section 205(r) prohibits the SSA from disclosing state death records it receives, except in limited circumstances.

A good free search source is from an Ancestry.com site at http://search.ancestry.com/search/db.aspx?dbid=3693. Links to free search sites is found at http://genealogy.about.com/od/free_genealogy/a/ssdi.htm.

Obituaries

The database searches offered by Obituary Central at www.obitcentral.com includes include not only obituaries, but also cemetery searches. The data gets stronger as you go further back in time. The site shows many resources and other links of interest. News and media databases like LexisNexis, Factiva and Dialog are great resources for looking up obituaries going back 20 years.

Also, search obituaries at http://search.ancestry.com/oldsearch/obit/.

The Nationwide Gravesite Locator

The Nationwide Gravesite Locator is maintained by the U.S. Department of Veterans Affairs. The site includes burial records from many sources, see http://gravelocator.cem.va.gov/.

Voter Registration

See **Elections: Politics, Lobbyists, and Voters**

Workers' Compensation

Workers' compensation benefits are paid to people who have suffered an injury during the performance of their jobs. Every state has an agency that administrates workers' compensation cases and records; there is no national database.

A workers' compensation record of an incident may contain the date of the incident, employer, insurance company, type of injury, body part injured, time lost, and if there is a job-related disability. Obviously, these records are useful in background investigations and fraud cases. However, most records are considered to be confidential or at least certain portions of each case file are. They're usually only released to parties involved in a case or by subpoena. Generally what is considered public record by some states is limited to determining if a subject has filed a claim, and decisions, awards or orders in disputed cases. The handful of states will release some type of workers' compensation information online, the sites are indicated in Chapter 6.

Another piece of information about worker's compensation found perhaps more frequently online is the ability to do a status check of an employer - to determine if the employer has current coverage. The states that offer online access to some limited information are shown in Chapter 6.

World Wide Web

Web Page Registry Public Records

There are plenty of useful resources with public information about web pages. A number of source report who owns a URL and how to contact them, the webmaster, the software, and even if an address has been blacklisted.

Search for a URL at http://whois.domaintools.com to find physical details about a website including meta description, registry creation and expiration dates, server details, webmaster contact info, and its all-important basic WhoIs record of the registrant.

InterNIC.net provides public information on domain names and other useful information on web topics such as viruses, IP address, website content, registries. Also InterNIC provides a simple WhoIs lookup.

Another good IP search site is ARIN at https://www.arin.net/resources/services/.

VeriSign.com provides a list of North American website registrars.

For an analytical profile of a website, visit http://nerdydata.com.

Other Recommended Web Page Resources and Tools

- The Internet Corporation for Assigned Names and Numbers (ICANN) is a network of inter-related sites who manage the naming system for the millions of internet sites. See www.icann.net.
- The Network Solutions WhoIs page at www.networksolutions.com/whois conveniently tells you if a name is available or not and under what suffix, also lets you search for expired domain names.
- An excellent tool for analyzing a website is the NetSolutions' WhoIs search at www.networksolutions.com/whois/index.jsp. Results include who owns or registered a site, the IP address, a screen capture of the home page, traffic ranking, more.
- To find out if anyone is imitating your site or stealing your content check out www.copyscape.com.
- Use the Xenu web check tool for reports on URLs and broken links. Go to http://home.snafu.de/tilman/xenulink.html and download the free Xenu's Link Sleuth. You can check the status of a list of URLs by posted a list on the site and Xenu will generate a report.
- To find the IP address (e.g. 200.100.100.80) you are using on your computer go to www.palserv.com/ipdisp.html or www.whatismyipaddress.com.
- To find information about an email address, check www.newultimates.com/email.
- Historical web pages can be found at the WayBack Machine at http://archive.org/index.php.
- Another web searching resource is Search Engine Showdown at www.searchengineshowdown.com.

Chapter 5

Using Online Public Record Vendors

The purpose of this chapter is to familiarize you with the types of public record vendors in the business marketplace and to help you determine the right vendor for your record needs.

Before you sign-up for every interesting online consumer site that catches your eye, we suggest some key points and techniques in order to narrow your search to the type of site or vendor that best suits your needs.

Inside This Chapter:

- Step 1: Recognize the Types of Vendors
- Step 2: Recognize Difference Between Consumer and Professional Sites
- Web Data Extraction & Screen Scraping Technology
    - Web Data Extraction (a.k.a. screen scraping) and Online Public Records Article by John Kloos
- Vendors and Privacy Concerns
- Four Questions to Ask
- The Advantages Online Public Record Vendors Provide
- The Instant Web-Based Background Checks
- Where to Find a Vendor
- Resource List of Selected Vendors

Step 1: Recognize the Types of Vendors

Finding the right vendor or web page for your needs starts with having knowledge of the types of vendors and how they work with clients.

Essentially public record vendors can be categorized as follows:

- **Distributors (with proprietary databases)**
- **Gateways**
- **Search Firms**
- **Verification Firms**
- **Record Retrievers**

Distributors: Vendors with Proprietary Databases

Distributors, generally, are automated public record dealers who combine public sources of bulk data and/or online access to develop their own in-house database products. Also sometimes called *data brokers*, they collect or buy public record information from government repositories. They may also purchase and hold records from other distributors, or from public information vendors, like phone companies, then combine the content in ways useful to their clients. There are hundreds of these vendors in the U.S. that collect, warehouse, and sell public record information.

Some distributors will work with professionals as clients; others will target everyday people or consumers as clients.

Distributors can often be categorized as follows:

1. **Vertical:** collecting multiple data types on a local or regional basis; or
2. **Horizontal:** collecting a single-purpose type of info, collected on regional or national basis; or
3. **Both Vertical and Horizontal**.

An example of a Vertical distributor is iDocket.com. This Texas-based company offers online access to many types of court records from 300+ courts in Texas

An example of a Horizontal Distributor is Aristotle, www.aristotle.com. Aristotle purchases voter registration records nationwide and sells customized, authorized lists to political candidates and political parties.

An example of a distributor who is both Vertical and Horizontal is LexisNexis, www.lexisnexis.com, a company with multiple divisions who offers access to many and varied nationwide databases for a wide variety of clients.

This is a key point: **When a database vendor sells data, the vendor is bound by the same disclosure laws attached to the original government repository.** Access restrictions can range from *zero* for recorded documents, level three sexual predators, to severe for voter registrations, vehicle ownership (for vehicle recall notifications), etc.

Gateways

Gateways are similar to distributors except gateways do not warehouse records – they merely provide a sophisticated method to electronically access existing databases from other locations or hosts.

Therefore gateways provide their clients with an automated electronic access to 1) multiple proprietary database vendors or 2) government agency online systems. Gateways thus provide 'one-stop shopping' for multiple geographic areas and/or categories of information. Gateways are very evident on the Internet, advertising access to records for many different purposes.

Gateways may provide their services using direct connection to one source, or may use multiple sources. This is often done on a simultaneous basis using what is known as data extraction, or now often referred to as *screen scraping*. Later in this chapter you will find an excellent article, written by Mr. John Kloos, containing a detailed description about data extraction.

Many gateways are the resulting service from of a contractual relationship with a government agency and a chosen vendor. A number of states outsource certain record access services and other business services, such as license registrations or motor vehicle record access, to gateways. For example, the National Information Consortium (www.nicusa.com) has over thirty individual state affiliates that provide online access to a variety of state-held records. Many of these state affiliates are mentioned in Chapter 6. To view the site of an NIC affiliate, visit www.nebraska.gov and click on "Become a Subscriber." Keep in mind, the state's data still resides with the state. The NIC affiliate is merely offering a sophisticated electronic conduit or *gateway* to the records.

Companies can be both distributors and gateways. For example, a number of online database companies are both primary distributors of corporate information and also gateways to real estate information from other primary distributors.

Search Firms

Search firms are very prominent on the web. They furnish clients with public record search and document retrieval services. They obtain the records by either using distributors or gateways, or by going direct to government agencies. The key point is their services are not always online oriented since not all records are online, or copies of documents must be obtained. Search firm often have built their own network of on-site specialists, (see Record Retrievers below). Search firms combine online proficiency with document retrieval expertise. Search firms may focus either on one geographic region – like New England – or on one specific type of public record information – like criminal records. There are literally hundreds of search firms in the U.S.

Many search firms provide services not only on an ongoing basis to businesses and clients, but also to the general consumer market.

Verification Firms

Verification firms provide services to employers and businesses when the search subject has given consent for the verification. This category includes pre-employment screening firms, tenant screening firms, and motor vehicle vendors.

These firms normally provide services to clients who have a permissible use to the record data, usually per statute. For example, the access to and use of the various public records provided by pre-employment and tenant screening firms are subject to provisions in the Fair Credit Reporting Act (FCRA). Also, what personal information states provide on motor vehicle records is governed by the Drivers Privacy Protection Act (DPPA).

Since verification firms usually only perform their services for clients who have first received consent from the subject, they do not warehouse or collect data to be resold. The service provided by a pre-employment screening company is often called a background screen or a background report. Their service should not be confused with 'an investigation' as provided by private investigators (see below) or with search firms who provide general public record searches.

There are probably about 1,000 true pre-employment screening firms in the U.S., not counting the many private investigators who also offer these records as part of their services. This number also does not include the many online consumer sites or consumer links sites where you can do a broad but limited instant background check on people.

About Private Investigation Agencies

Many private investigators and agencies provide record retrieval services (see below) or search firm services (see above). In fact the principal and/or employees of a search firms or verification firms often have a state-issued private investigators license.

Since private investigators research and analyze information about legal, financial, and personal matters they often use public records and reports results findings from public record searches within the final reports provided to clients. They may investigate or verify a subject's background, find missing persons, or investigate cyber-crimes.

Record Retrievers

A different vendor somewhat similar to a search firm is known as a l*ocal document retriever* or simply, a r*ecord retriever*. Retrievers are hands-on researchers for hire who visit government agencies in-person. Their clients request name searches or document retrieval services usually for legal compliance, hiring, lending, real estate abstracting, or for litigation purposes. Retrievers do not usually review or interpret the results or issue reports in the sense that investigators or verifications firms do. The retriever's primary function is to return the results of searches and document copies. Retrievers tend to be localized, but there are companies who offer a national network of retrievers and/or correspondents. Since retrievers go directly to the agency, they may be relied upon for their strong knowledge on record searching in a local area.

The 500+ members of the Public Record Retriever Network (PRRN) are listed by state and counties served at www.PRRN.us. This organization has a set industry standards for the retrieval of public record documents. Members operate under a Code of Professional Conduct. Using one of these record retrievers is an excellent way to quickly access records in jurisdictions where online access is not available.

Step 2: Recognize the Difference Between a Consumer and Professional Site

The Internet is filled with web pages offering low-cost record searching deals claiming to have the most overall records available. How do you gauge the degree of differentiation between these "public record web stores?" How do you know which site is going to give you the best overall search or service?

First, one must realize there are some websites that specialize in providing services to "consumers" and some vendor sites that specialize in providing services to "professionals." And second, one must recognize the pluses and minuses of using each of these types of sites.

About Consumer-Oriented Sites

Consumer sites are great for finding personal information such as telephone numbers or addresses of old friends and family members. Sometimes these sites are referred to as *People Search* websites and are usually categorized as either distributors or gateways. A one-stop-shop to search many web pages at the same time certainly has its advantages as a quick, instant way to find low-cost public records information about someone, such as a neighbor, or a person dating a relative.

Consumer sites generally can be quite useful if their limitations are kept in mind. An example of an excellent people search site is PeopleSmart.com, a site that understands all records are not online and offers other means to obtain records if and when needed.

But in general, consumer sites are rarely used by professionals who require a deeper due diligence need when searching public records. So what are concerns if using a consumer site? The limitations often boil down to issues about completeness, timeliness, legal compliance, and searching techniques. Even if a site purports to be updated frequently, the question is "how old is the data in the update?" Also, watch out for misleading statements in the marketing material. For example, there are few truly national databases because many government agencies do not sell records to vendors. In fact some agencies cannot because they are not yet computerized. As mentioned previously, if 33% of courts' felony records are not online, then how accurate is a so-called instant national criminal check?

About Professional-Oriented Search Sites

Like consumer sites, professional sites can be Distributors or Gateways. However, what separates the *consumer site users* from *professional site users* is often the purpose of the record search and level of due diligence required. Using data sources with a high degree of currency and authenticity is a must when performing a full-scale background check, a pre-employment background screen, or an asset and lien search.

Finding professional search sites is not always easy. A Google search on *driving records* or *driving record check* will find many service companies, but you are probably not going to find the industry icons. The fact is, there is a very limited number of driving record vendors who offer high-volume pricing with true national coverage because these vendors limit their services to specific clientele, such as the insurance or trucking industries or pre-employment screening companies. They do not show up prominently in search engine results. You won't often see Google ads posted by these vendors. But a Google search will find plenty of vendors looking to sell to those with an occasional need.

About the Vendors Shown in This Book

If you have not figured this out by now, let's be blunt. This book is filled with references to professional sites and largely ignores consumer sites. For example, the recommended sites and vendors listed in Chapter 4 are included because their services and expertise are specific to the topics covered within chapter. The vendor list at the end of this chapter is certainly not finite, but they were selected because the type of records they provide are closely connected with many of the public records profiled in the next chapter. It is not the purpose of this book to prove a lengthy list of consumer-oriented sites, per the definitions above.

For more information about how to analyze a site, be it consumer or professional, see page 7.

Web Data Extraction & Screen Scraping Technology

An old concept with a new application is being used by a number of vendors today. This technology is known as web data extraction, but the name in vogue is *Screen Scraping.*

Below is an informative article written by Mr. John Kloos, President of BackChecked LLC, Phoenix, AZ www.backchecked.com. Mr. Kloos is very well-known within the background screening industry. He has served on the Board of Directors of the National Association of Professional Background Screeners and is a frequent speaker on industry topics. We sincerely thank Mr. Kloos for allowing us to reprint his article.

Web Data Extraction (a.k.a. screen scraping) and Online Public Records by John Kloos

As soon as the first public records became available online in the late 1990's you can be sure that somewhere some computer programmer started thinking about a way to automate the process of searching them. After all, what's better than not having to go to the court house? How about not having to manually enter the search parameters into the various court websites? Instead, let a computer program do the grunt work!

Fast forward to today. We find a growing number of for-profit public records research companies doing exactly this, utilizing a process known as *Web Data Extraction.* Although predictable and probably unstoppable, this trend is not without its controversy and it is important to understand what is behind it all.

Let's start with the technology that makes it possible.

Web Data Extraction – What is it?

In the public records research marketplace, this technology is often referred to as *Screen Scraping*. In fact, *Screen Scraping* is a term dating to the 1960's when programmers wrote processes to read or "scrape" text from computer terminals so that it could be used by other programs. *Web Data Extraction* is a much more sophisticated technology that incorporates the automated scheduling, extraction, filtering, transformation and transmission of targeted data available via the Internet. To say that a well-deployed *Web Data Extraction* system is performing *Screen Scraping* is like calling a modern refrigerator an ice box.

An example of a relatively simple *Web Data Extraction* application is the free service Google provides for repeatedly searching news articles on a specific topic. Because I am in the Background Screening Industry, I use Google to conduct a daily search for articles that include the phrase "background check." Every morning, I am greeted with an email that lists new articles, complete with links to each one. Nice.

An example of a more complex *Web Data Extraction* application would be collecting competitive data in your marketplace. Are there any new announcements by your competitors? What new products are they selling? What's available in their on-line catalogues? Are their prices changing? Have they formed any new partnerships? Are there any newcomers to the industry? Obviously, the technology behind this type of application is much more sophisticated than the *Google News* search mentioned above.

With the shear amount of information available via the Internet, it's no surprise that a large number of off-the-shelf *Web Data Extraction* tools are now available at a very reasonable cost. Both start-up and industry veterans in the public records research market now utilize these platforms. Others have developed custom systems. The benefits are obvious: reduced costs and shorter turn-around times. But, what are the risks?

Web Data Extraction in Online Public Records Research

The first factor to consider in Public Records Research is that the stakes can be high. Consider the consequences of missing data while conducting competitive analysis compared to the ramifications of missing a felony record while doing a background check. Perhaps this is the single greatest reason that the public records industry has been slow to adopt this new technology. There is a well-established comfort level with direct human involvement in conducting searches, even when that search is conducted online.

Another reality to consider is that state and county jurisdictions are not necessarily pleased that *Web Data Extraction* technology is being used to search records on their websites that were designed and implemented to serve humans. In addition to the fear that their sites may be overloaded by technology that is much faster than the typical human's ability to point and click, there is a legitimate concern that public records will be systematically extracted and used to populate commercial databases.

In an effort to thwart *Web Data Extraction* systems, many government agencies have equipped their sites with a challenge-response test, known as a CAPTCHA. Coined in 2000 by a group from Carnegie Mellon University, this acronym stands for "Completely Automated Public Turing test to tell Computers and Humans Apart." It works by presenting the user with a purposely distorted image that contains letters and/or numbers. In order to gain access to the desired data, the characters must be re-entered by the user. Of course, as with almost any roadblock they encounter, smart programmers have found ways to beat the CAPTCHA test, resulting in a back and forth battle that is sure to continue far into the future.

Despite the current controversy it is likely that the use of *Web Data Extraction* systems will continue to expand. The economics are simply too compelling to believe otherwise. Consider what would happen if you were to hold a contest between a well-implemented Web Data Extraction system and a well-rested human record retriever. The task: perform 1,000 searches on a county website that provides full online access. The end results should be identical. However, the *Web Data Extraction* system is going to finish the job in less than an hour. It won't get tired. It won't make an error while copying results. It won't get distracted by a phone call. And it won't call you to complain that it can't be expected to search every possible variation of Mickey Johannes MacDougal.

This does not mean to suggest the days of the human Record Retriever are finished. Not all records are available online nor is there any guarantee that you will be able to find a Web Data Extraction system that meets your standards.

Evaluating Public Record Providers Who Utilize Web Data Extraction Systems

If you routinely rely on third party providers to conduct public records research, you will eventually encounter a provider that employs *Web Data Extraction* for at least some jurisdictions. In this case, there a few key questions to ask.

1. Does the provider have the proper domain expertise in public records research?

Even the brightest computer programmers are unlikely to develop a good system if there is no one to educate them and provide detailed requirements and quality assurance tests. It's important that experienced public records researchers have provided this expertise and that they have remained involved in on-going development.

2. Does the provider keep current with changes at the jurisdictions being searched?

Unlike with system interfaces developed between cooperative partners, county and state jurisdictions are under no obligation to inform operators of a *Web Data Extraction* system that a change has been made to their site. It's important that the provider constantly monitor government sites for changes that can affect the outcome of a search.

3. Is the provider committed to monitoring and complying with the legal restrictions contained on each site?

Although they may be providing public records, each jurisdiction maintains its own policies regarding use of their public data. These policies are presented in text format for examination by a human. The provider must be aware of these policies and commit to remaining compliant.

4. Does the provider have a comprehensive test plan to ensure that results from automated activity are equal to that of a human researcher?

To maintain confidence that it is working properly, any automated system needs to be tested continuously. Since the cost of running test searches is low in an automated system, beware of a provider who is unwilling to accommodate tests against known results on a regular basis.

Conclusion

Although very controversial just a few years ago, Web Data Extraction has become mainstream. Most of the larger public research providers are utilizing the technology in some way, melding it with legacy systems that support traditional methods. Furthermore, new providers have emerged in the past few years, specializing in the technology and providing service in only those jurisdiction where Web Data Extraction can be counted on to get the complete job done.

Still, Web Data Extraction in the public records market is not so mature that you should take it for granted. Make sure it's right for your particular needs. It can also be valuable to demonstrate your knowledge of the technology whenever contacting new vendors or reviewing current providers.

Vendors and Privacy Concerns

Personal information is part of public records. Therefore personal information may also be found within the databases of distributors or often shown in the results presented by gateways and search firms. Of course the extent of the data displayed varies from state to state or county to county.

Using one of the news media sites mentioned in the previous chapter, one can search and find many news stories related to concerns about personal information and incorrect data affecting people lives. But the point here is not to present a pros and cons discussion about personal information shown or of privacy and redaction, but rather to mention different ways vendors deal with privacy issues and problems.

One problem that often surfaces is when the originating government source sells its data to a vendor, then after the fact the government agency corrects or removes personal information. When the vendor is not notified of changes or does not update the content, then incorrect data on a person or subject would be reported.

Some vendors do offer consumers the chance to opt out or opt out the personal information in the vendor database. But if the data is removed, then there must also be a way to re-remove it the next time the database is updated from the originating agency.

Some database vendors will permanently offer to redact personal information, but will charge a fee to do so.

For a more detailed discussion and excellent suggestions on other ways people can remove personal data or opt out, visit the web page for PrivacyRights.org.

Four Questions to Ask

Putting it all together, to help narrow your search to the type of vendor for your needs, ask yourself the following four questions—

1. What is the Frequency of Usage?

Setting up an account with a primary distributor such as LexisNexis or Westlaw will give you an inexpensive per search fee, but the monthly minimum requirements may be cost prohibitive to the casual requester who would be better off using a vendor who accesses that distributor.

2. What is the Complexity of the Search?

The importance of hiring a vendor who understands and can interpret the information increases with the complexity of the search. Pulling a corporation record in Arizona is not difficult, but doing an online criminal record search in Arizona, when only a portion of the criminal records are online even when using 4 different sources, is not as easy.

Thus, part of the answer to determining which vendor or type of vendor to use is to first understand what is and is not available from government agencies. Without knowing what is available and what restrictions apply, you cannot guide the search process effectively nor control the cost. Once you are comfortable knowing the kinds of information available in the public record, you are in a position to find the best method to access the information you need.

3. What are the Geographic Boundaries of the Search?

Many national primary distributors and gateways combine various local and state databases into one large comprehensive system. If your record searching is narrowed by a region or locality, then an online source that specializes in a specific geographic region may be an alternative. Keep in mind that many national firms allow you to order a search online even though results cannot be delivered immediately. Some hands-on local searching may be required.

4. What is the Throughput and Currency of the Data?

Common sense dictates if you need to perform a search going back 10 years then the site you use had better go back that far. Never assume. Look for the answers to these two facts - how far back and how often updated. If you cannot find the answer then call the vendor.

One of the leading vendor sites in Texas for accessing court records is iDocket.com. This vendor makes a point of detailing how far records go back (http://idocket.com/cgi-bin/db2www/cntysince.mbr/run) and when the most recent cases were added (http://idocket.com/cgi-bin/db2www/cntyfiled.mbr/run).

The Advantages Online Public Record Vendors Provide

As explained, vendors must buy the data from the government agencies or from other vendors. So, what are the advantages of using a vendor instead of "going direct" to a government agency? There are many—

- One-stop shopping for many or all states or record types
- Speed of access - often instantaneously
- Experts on state compliance issues
- Help with reading or deciphering records
- Technical communication experts
- Provide uniform record format
- Provide customized software to access and receive
- Understand the "how fast - how much" needs of clients

The Instant Web-Based Background Checks

Pre-employment screening firms, also known as Consumer Reporting Agencies (CRAs), must abide by the provisions in the Fair Credit Reporting Act (FCRA). In addition there are a myriad of state laws and compliance rules that go beyond the regulations imposed by FCRA. CRAs do have a web presence and do advertise their services. And yes, CRAs will use the services of database criminal record vendors who provide very impressive supplemental yet useful searches.

But there are also many *consumer sites* offering to do background checks that sound a little too inviting. These sites often advertise they can do an instant, national background check to learn about anyone's past. There is no mention of the FCRA. And since there is no true national database of criminal records and 33% of the felony courts are not online, the reality is the promotional wording these sites use is often very misleading.

So how do you determine if a web vendor is truly an FCRA-Complaint background screening service or a database distributer with a great marketing presence? If you find a site using any of the marketing schemes listed below, then a giant red flag should pop up in your mind and you need to take a closer look—

1. Charging membership fees for unlimited access to national background data

The most common type of site is charging a $29 to $35 fee for a one- to five-year membership term. Sites even offer an affiliate program where you set up your own site to sell memberships to others. But there is some benefit. These sites provide the ability to simultaneously search hundreds of free government sites at once; but there are no magic or special databases used. The membership fee is paying for a sophisticated hits or links to a series of free search pages belonging to others. Problems are currency of the data and how national is "national?"

2. Show endorsement by a phony or suspect trade association

Several of the suspect public records membership sites tout an endorsement from a national association of private investigators. Do a Google search on that association's name. Read the results. Some are phony.

3. Promote what amounts to non-FCRA compliant employment screening

Any public record professional will tell you that you cannot purchase a "background check" on a new hire for $15 and be truly protected from a negligent hiring lawsuit. Nor will the vendor likely be in compliance with the Federal Fair Credit Reporting Act (FCRA). You may be able to do quick record search from a couple web pages or court repository, or from a supplementary database vendor, but that does not equate to fulfilling the due diligence necessary in a professional pre-employment background check.

The bottom line is to use caution and common since if using one of these sites.

Where to Find a Vendor

Using a Search Engine

This is a good way to find a consumer site vendor. These vendors thrive based on the strength of their SEO (Search Engine Optimization). Also, this is a good way to find many of the vertical-type vendors mentioned in Chapter 4. Picking a topic like Aviation or Unclaimed Funds will likely lead you to many of the entities mentioned in that chapter.

But this is not necessarily true for professional-oriented sites. If your business has a high volume need for a core state or county record such as court records, UCC fillings, or driving records, it is unlikely you will find the nation's leading vendors with a simple Google search. However there are other avenues (beside the last portion of this chapter).

Word of Mouth and Social Media

Reaching out to colleagues or networking on social media sites such as LinkedIn is a good way to find vendor alternatives.

Using a Trade Association Site

Trade Association websites often provide a wealth of information. They are useful for not only industry knowledge, but also for finding members and entities with strong ties as vendors. Here is a representative list of 90 national associations with strong ties to public records or public record searching you can comb through.

Acronym	Organization	Website
USFN	America's Mortgage Banking Attorneys	http://imis.usfn.org
AALL	American Assn of Law Librarians	www.aallnet.org/default.aspx
AAMVA	American Assn of Motor Vehicle Administrators	www.aamva.org
AAPL	American Assn of Professional Landmen	www.landman.org
AAJ	American Association For Justice	www.justice.org/
ABA (2)	American Banking Assn	www.aba.com/default.htm
ABI	American Bankruptcy Institute	www.abiworld.org
ABA	American Bar Assn	www.americanbar.org/aba.html
ABFE	American Board of Forensic Examiners	www.acfei.com
ABWA	American Business Women' Association	www.abwa.org
AICPA	American Institute of Certified Public Accountants	www.aicpa.org/Pages/Default.aspx
AIPLA	American Intellectual Property Law Assn	www.aipla.org/Pages/default.aspx
ALTA	American Land Title Assn	www.alta.org
ALA	American Library Assn	www.ala.org
AMA	American Management Assn	www.amanet.org/default.aspx
APA (2)	American Psychological Assn	www.apa.org
ASIS	American Society for Industrial Security	www.asisonline.org
ASLET	American Society of Law Enforcement Trainers	www.aslet.org
ASSE	American Society of Safety Engineers	www.asse.org
ATA	American Trucking Associations	www.truckline.com/Pages/Home.aspx
ACFE	Assn of Certified Fraud Examiners	www.acfe.com
ACA	Assn of Collectors and Collection Professionals	www.acainternational.org
AFIO	Assn of Former Intelligence Officers	www.afio.com
AIIP	Assn of Independent Information Professionals	www.aiip.org
APG	Assn of Professional Genealogists	www.apgen.org
ARELLO	Assn of Real Estate License Law Officials	https://www.arello.org/
CII	Council of Intl Investigators	www.cii2.org
DMA	Direct Marketing Assn	www.the-dma.org/index.php
ESA	Electronic Security Association	www.alarm.org/
EAA	Environmental Assessment Assn	www.eaa-assoc.org/
EPIC	Evidence Photographers Intl Council	www.epic-photo.org
FBINAA	FBI National Academy Assn	www.fbinaa.org
IIAA	Independent Insurance Agents of America	www.independentagent.com/default.aspx
IREM	Institute of Real Estate Management	www.irem.org
IAAI	Intl Assn of Arson Investigators	www.fire-investigators.org
IAHSS	Intl Assn of Healthcare Security & Safety	www.iahss.org
IALEIA	Intl Assn of Law Enforcement Intelligence Analysts	www.ialeia.org
NASIR	Intl Assn of Security & Investigative Regulators	www.iasir.org
INA	Intl Nanny Assn	www.nanny.org
INOA	Intl Narcotics Officers Assn	www.ineoa.org
INTA	Intl Trademark Assn	www.inta.org/Pages/Home.aspx
ION	Investigative Open Network	www.ioninc.com

Acronym	Organization	Website
LES	Licensing Executive Society	www.lesusacanada.org/
MBA	Mortgage Bankers Assn	hwww.mbaa.org/default.htm
NALS	NALS…the Assn of Legal Professionals	www.nals.org
NAC	National Assn of Counselors	http://nac.lincoln-grad.org
NACRC	National Assn of County Recorders, Elec. Officials And Clerks	www.nacrc.org/
NACM	National Assn of Credit Managers	www.nacm.org
NAFE	National Assn of Female Executives	www.nafe.com
NAFI	National Assn of Fire Investigators	www.nafi.org
NAHB	National Assn of Home Builders	www.nahb.org
NAHRO	National Assn of Housing & Redevelopment Officials	www.nahro.org
NAIS	National Assn of Investigative Specialists	www.pimall.com/nais/
NALFM	National Assn of Law Firm Marketers	www.legalmarketing.org
NALA	National Assn of Legal Assistants	www.nala.org
NALI	National Assn of Legal Investigators	www.nalionline.org
NALSC	National Assn of Legal Search Consultants	www.nalsc.org
NAMSS	National Assn of Medical Staff Svcs	www.namss.org
NAPBS	National Assn of Professional Background Screeners	www.napbs.com
NAPPS	National Assn of Professional Process Servers	www.napps.org
NAPIA	National Assn of Public Insurance Adjustors	www.napia.com
NAREIT	National Assn of Real Estate Investment Trusts	www.reit.com
NAR	National Assn of Realtors	www.realtor.com
NARPM	National Assn of Residential Property Managers	www.narpm.org
NAUPA	National Assn of Unclaimed Property Administrators	www.unclaimed.org
NAWBO	National Assn of Women Business Owners	www.nawbo.org
NCRA	National Consumer Reporting Assn	www.ncrainc.org
NCISS	National Council of Investigation & Security Services	www.nciss.org
NCRA	National Court Reporters Assn	www.ncra.org/
NDIA	National Defender Investigator Assn	www.ndia.net
NFIB	National Federation of Independent Businesses	www.nfib.com
NFPA	National Federation of Paralegal Associations	www.paralegals.org/
NGS	National Genealogical Society	www.ngsgenealogy.org
NHRA	National Human Resources Assn	www.humanresources.org/website/c/
NICB	National Insurance Crime Bureau	https://www.nicb.org/
NLG	National Lawyers Guild	www.nlg.org
NASA	National Multifamily Resident Information Council	www.nmric.org/
NPPRA	National Public Record Research Assn	www.nprra.org
NSA	National Sheriffs' Assn	www.sheriffs.org
PBUS	Professional Bail Agents of the United States	www.pbus.com
PIHRA	Professionals in Human Resources Assn	www.pihra.org
PRRN	Public Record Retriever Network	www.prrn.us
PRIA	Public Records Information Professionals Assn	www.pria.us
SCIP	Society of Competitive Intelligence Professionals	www.scip.org

Acronym	Organization	Website
SFSA	Society of Former Special Agents of the FBI	www.socxfbi.org
SHRM	Society of Human Resources Management	www.shrm.org
SILA	Society of Insurance License Administrators	www.sila.org
SIIA	Software & Information Industry Assn	www.siia.net
SLA	Special Libraries Assn	www.sla.org
W.A.D	World Assn of Detectives	www.wad.net

Resource List of Selected Vendors

Of course there are many more public record vendors than the 135+ firms appearing in this section. The reason these particular companies were chosen is because they provide either a Proprietary Database or offer a non-intervention Gateway to the government public record categories shown in Chapter 6.

Also, to find additional information and profiles on many more professional vendors and record searchers, go to www.brbpublications.com/pubrecsites_ven.asp.

Record Information Categories

This index consists of 11 Information Categories. The vendors are listed alphabetically within each category. Each listing includes geographic coverage area and the vendor's web address. Note that PR signifies Puerto Rico, ITL signifies International.

- Bankruptcy
- Corporate/Business Entity
- Criminal Information
- Driver and/or Vehicle
- Licenses/Registrations/Permits
- Litigation/Judgments/Tax Liens
- Real Estate/Assessor
- Uniform Commercial Code
- Vessels
- Vital Records
- Voter Registration

This is a best efforts presentation. Please keep in mind that the Region column primarily refers of online access from a gateway of proprietary database. Many of these firms offer additional services, including the ability to process requests to obtain records onsite or in-person in more states.

Bankruptcy

Vendors - Bankruptcy	Web Page	Region
Accurint (LexisNexis)	www.accurint.com	US
BANKO (LexisNexis)	https://www.banko.com/app/bnk/main	US
CaseClerk.com	www.caseclerk.com/search/default.htm	TN, US
CCH Washington Service Bureau	www.wsb.com	US
CourtLink (LexisNexis)	www.lexisnexis.com/courtlink/online/	US
CSC - Corporation Service Company	https://www.cscglobal.com/global/web/csc/home	MN

Vendors - Bankruptcy	Web Page	Region
Dun & Bradstreet	www.dnb.com/us/	US
Equifax Credit Services	www.equifax.com/business/en_us	US
Haines & Company Inc	www.haines.com	US
IQ Data Systems	www.iqdata.com	US
KnowX	www.knowx.com	US
LexisNexis	www.lexisnexis.com	US
Motznik Information Services	www.motznik.com	AK
OPENonline	www.openonline.com	US
Record Information Services Inc	www.public-record.com	IL
Red Vision	www.redvision.com	CA, FL, MD, TX
Research Archives.com	www.researcharchives.com	US
TLO	www.tlo.com/	US
Tracers Information Specialists Inc	www.tracersinfo.com	US
UCC Direct Services	www.uccdirectservices.com	US
US SEARCH.com	www.ussearch.com/consumer/index.jsp	US
Virtual Docket LLC	www.virtualdocket.com	DE
WestLaw CourtExpress.com (D.C.)	http://courtexpress.westlaw.com	US
WestlawNext	http://web2.westlaw.com	US

Corporate/Business Entity

Vendors - Corporate/Business Entity	Web Page	Region
Accurint LexisNexis	www.accurint.com	US
Accutrend Data Corporation	www.accutrend.com	US
Alacra	www.alacra.com	US, FR, GB, ITL
Attorneys Title Insurance Fund	www.thefund.com/portal/	FL
Background Information Services Inc.	www.bisi.com	CO
Better Business Bureau	www.bbb.org	US
Capitol Lien Records & Research Inc	www.capitollien.com	MN, WI, US
CCH Washington Service Bureau	www.wsb.com	US
CountryWatch Inc	www.countrywatch.com	ITL
CSC - Corporation Service Company	https://www.cscglobal.com/global/web/csc/home	MN
Derwent Information - Thomson Search Svcs	http://thomsonreuters.com/products_services/legal/legal_products/intellectual_property/	US
Dialog (Thomson)	www.dialog.com	US, ITL
Dun & Bradstreet	www.dnb.com/us/	US
GuideStar	www.guidestar.org/	US
Hoovers Inc	www.hoovers.com	US
infogroup/infoUSA.com -	www.infousa.com/	US
IQ Data Systems	www.iqdata.com	US (28 +/- states)
IRB - International Research Bureau	www.irb-online.com	US
KnowX	www.knowx.com	US
Kompass USA Inc	www.kompass-intl.com	US
Legal Solutions - Thomson Reuters	http://legalsolutions.thomsonreuters.com/law-products/	US

Vendors - Corporate/Business Entity	Web Page	Region
LexisNexis	www.lexisnexis.com	US
LocatePlus.com Inc	https://www.locateplus.com/welcome.asp	US
MegaCriminal Database	www.megacriminal.com/	CA
Motznik Information Services	www.motznik.com	AK
OPENonline	www.openonline.com	US
Pallorium Inc	www.pallorium.com	US, PR
Research Archives.com	www.researcharchives.com	US
SEAFAX Inc	www.seafax.com	US
Thomson Compumark	http://trademarks.thomsonreuters.com/	US
TLO	www.tlo.com	US
Tracers Information Specialists Inc	www.tracersinfo.com	US
UCC Direct Services	www.uccdirectservices.com	US
US SEARCH.com	www.ussearch.com/consumer/index.jsp	US
USADATA	www.usadata.com	US
WestlawNext	http://web2.westlaw.com	US

Criminal Information

Vendors - Criminal Records	Web Page	Region
Accurint (LexisNexis)	www.accurint.com	US
Alacourt.com	https://v2.alacourt.com/	AL
Appriss Inc/VineLink	www.appriss.com/VINE.html	US
Background Information Services Inc.	www.bisi.com	CO
backgroundchecks.com	https://www.backgroundchecks.com/	US
CaseClerk.com	www.caseclerk.com/search/default.htm	TN, US
Circuit Court Express	https://www.wvcircuitexpress.com/Default.aspx	WV
Confi-Chek	www.confi-chek.com	CA
CourtLink (LexisNexis)	www.lexisnexis.com/courtlink/online/	TX, OR, WA, NC, MD, US
CourtSearch.com	https://www.courtsearch.com/	NC
Criminal Information Services Inc	www.criminalinfo.com	US
Data Divers	www.edatadivers.com	
Data-Trac.com	www.data-trac.com	US
DCS Information Systems	www.dcsinfosys.com/	US
DEXTER	www.bergconsultinggroup.com/products/criminal-records-searches/	US
Doxpop	https://www.doxpop.com/prod/	IN
Fetch Technologies	www.fetch.com/	US
iDocket.com	www.idocket.com	TX
Innovative Enterprises	www.knowthefacts.com/	US
IQ Data Systems	www.iqdata.com	US (42 +/- states)
IRB - International Research Bureau	www.irb-online.com	US
Judici	www.judici.com	IL
KellPro Inc	www.kellpro.com	OK
KnowX	www.knowx.com	US
MegaCriminal Database	www.megacriminal.com	US (18 +/- states)

Vendors - Criminal Records	Web Page	Region
Motznik Information Services	www.motznik.com	AK
National Background Data	/www.nationalbackgrounddata.com/marketing/home.html	US
OPENonline	www.openonline.com	OH,IN,MI
Rapidcourt.com - NC Recordsonline.com	www.rapidcourt.com	NC, US
SJV & Associates	www.sjvassoc.com	US
Tracers Information Specialists Inc	www.tracersinfo.com	US
US SEARCH.com	www.ussearch.com/consumer/index.jsp	US (45+/- states)
USIS	www.usis.com/commercialservices/default.htm	US
Virtual Docket LLC	www.virtualdocket.com	DE
WestLaw CourtExpress.com (D.C.)	http://courtexpress.westlaw.com	US (31 +/- states)
XPOFACT	www.xpofact.com	MN

Driver and/or Vehicle Vital Records

Venders - Driver and/or Vehicle	Web Page	Region
American Driving Records - ADR	www.mvrs.com	US
AutoDataDirect, Inc	www.add123.com	FL
CARFAX	www.carfaxonline.com	US
CourtSearch.com	https://www.courtsearch.com/	NC
Datalink Services Inc	https://www.imvrs.com/	CA
Data-Trac.com	www.data-trac.com	US
DCS Information Systems	www.dcsinfosys.com/	TX
Explore Information Services	www.exploredata.com/	US
First InfoSource	https://secure.firstinfosource.com	MO
HireRight Record Services (formerly DAC)	www.hireright.com	US
iiX (Insurance Information Exchange)	www.iix.com	US
IRB - International Research Bureau	www.irb-online.com	US
LexisNexis	www.lexisnexis.com/risk/solutions/motor-vechicle-records.aspx	US
LocatePlus.com Inc	https://www.locateplus.com/welcome.asp	US
Logan Registration Service Inc	www.loganreg.com/Welcome.aspx	CA, US
MDR/Minnesota Driving Records	www.mdrecords.us	MN, US
Motznik Information Services	www.motznik.com	AK
National Background Data	www.nationalbackgrounddata.com/marketing/home.html	US
Pallorium Inc	www.pallorium.com	US
Records Research Inc	www.recordsresearch.com	CA, US
SAMBA	www.samba.biz/	US
Softech International Inc	www.softechinternational.com	US
Tracers Information Specialists Inc	www.tracersinfo.com	US
WestlawNext	http://web2.westlaw.com	US

Licenses/Registrations/Permits

Vendors - Licenses/Registrations/Permits	Web Page	Region
Accutrend Data Corporation	www.accutrend.com	US
Capitol Lien Records & Research Inc	www.capitollien.com	MN, WI, US
E-Merges.com	www.emerges.com	17 or more states
IQ Data Systems	www.iqdata.com	CA
KnowX	www.knowx.com	US
LexisNexis	www.lexisnexis.com	US
MegaCriminal Database	www.megacriminal.com/	CA
Motznik Information Services	www.motznik.com	AK
Record Information Services Inc	www.public-record.com	IL
Thomson Compumark	http://trademarks.thomsonreuters.com/	US
TLO	www.tlo.com/	US
WestlawNext	http://web2.westlaw.com	US

Litigation/Judgments/Liens

Vendors - Litigation/Judgments/Liens	Web Page	Region
Accurint (LexisNexis)	www.accurint.com	US
Alacourt.com	https://v2.alacourt.com/	AL
Attorneys Title Insurance Fund	www.thefund.com/portal/	FL
Background Information Services Inc.	www.bisi.com	CO
BANKO (LexisNexis)	https://www.banko.com/app/bnk/main	US
Capitol Lien Records & Research Inc	www.capitollien.com	MN, WI, US
CaseClerk.com	www.caseclerk.com/search/default.htm	TN, US
Circuit Court Express	https://www.wvcircuitexpress.com/Default.aspx	WV
CourthouseDirect.com	http://courthousedirect.com/courth/	US
CourtLink (LexisNexis)	www.lexisnexis.com/courtlink/online/	US
CourtSearch.com	https://www.courtsearch.com/	NC
CSC - Corporation Service Company	https://www.cscglobal.com/global/web/csc/home	MN
Data-Trac.com	www.data-trac.com	US
DCS Information Systems	www.dcsinfosys.com/	US
Doxpop	https://www.doxpop.com/prod/	IN
Dun & Bradstreet	www.dnb.com/us/	US
eCCLIX.com	https://ecclix.com/	KY
Equifax Credit Services	www.equifax.com/business/en_us	US
Foreclosure Freesearch.com	www.foreclosurefreesearch.com	US
iDocket.com	www.idocket.com	TX
Infocon Corporation	www.infoconcorporation.com	PA
IQ Data Systems	www.iqdata.com	US
IRB - International Research Bureau	www.irb-online.com	US
Judici	www.judici.com	IL
KellPro Inc	www.kellpro.com	OK
KnowX	https://www.knowx.com	US
Law Bulletin Information Network	www.lawbulletin.com	IL
LexisNexis	www.lexisnexis.com	US

Vendors - Litigation/Judgments/Liens	Web Page	Region
LocatePlus.com Inc	https://www.locateplus.com/welcome.asp	US
MasterFiles	www.masterfiles.com/	US
Metrolist, Inc	www.metrolist.com	CO
Motznik Information Services	www.motznik.com	AK
MyFloridaCounty.com	www.myfloridacounty.com	FL
National Service Information	www.nsii.net	IN, OH, WI, US
OPENonline	www.openonline.com	US
Public Data Corporation	www.pdcny.com	NY
Rapidcourt.com - NC Recordsonline.com	www.rapidcourt.com/	NC, US
Realty Data Corp	www.realtydata.com	US
Record Information Services Inc	www.public-record.com	IL
Red Vision	www.redvision.com	FL, TX
TitleSearcher.com	www.titlesearcher.com	TN
TLO	www.tlo.com/	US
Tracers Information Specialists Inc	www.tracersinfo.com	US
UCC Direct Services	www.uccdirectservices.com	US
Virtual Docket LLC	www.virtualdocket.com	DE
WestLaw CourtExpress.com	http://courtexpress.westlaw.com	US
WestlawNext	http://web2.westlaw.com	US

Real Estate/Assessor

Vendors - Real Estate/Assessor	Web Page	Region
Accurint (LexisNexis)	www.accurint.com	US
AccuriZ.com	www.accuriz.com/index.aspx	US (22 states)
ACS Inc, Landaccess.com	www.landaccess.com	OH
ARCountyData.com	www.arcountydata.com	AR
Attorneys Title Insurance Fund	www.thefund.com/portal/	FL
Capitol Lien Records & Research Inc	www.capitollien.com	MN, WI, US
Courthouse Retrieval System Inc	www.crsdata.net/default.aspx	AL, NC, TN
CourthouseDirect.com	http://courthousedirect.com/courth/	US
DataQuick	http://ww3.dataquick.com	US
DCS Information Systems	www.dcsinfosys.com/	TX
DigitalCourthouse	http://digitalcourthouse.com/search.asp	WV
eCCLIX.com	https://ecclix.com	KY
Environmental Data Resources, Inc (EDR)	www.edrnet.com	US
eTitleSearch	www.etitlesearch.com	AR, ID, IA,MT, MO
First American Data Tree	www.datatree.com/	US
FIS Data Svcs - IDM Corporation	www.sitexdata.com/Home/RealEstate.aspx	US
Foreclosure Freesearch.com	www.foreclosurefreesearch.com	US
Haines & Company Inc	www.haines.com	US
Infocon Corporation	www.infoconcorporation.com	PA
infogroup/infoUSA.com	www.infousa.com	US
IQ Data Systems	www.iqdata.com	US (38 States)
KnowX	www.knowx.com	US
Law Bulletin Information Network	www.lawbulletin.com	IL-Central Counties

Vendors - Real Estate/Assessor	Web Page	Region
LexisNexis	www.lexisnexis.com	US
MasterFiles	www.masterfiles.com/	US
Merlin Information Services	https://www.merlindata.com/index.asp	US
Metro Market Trends Inc	www.mmtinfo.com	FL, AL
Metrolist, Inc	www.metrolist.com	CO
Motznik Information Services	www.motznik.com	AK
MyFloridaCounty.com	www.myfloridacounty.com	FL
NETR Real Estate Research and Information	www.netronline.com	US
OPENonline	www.openonline.com	US
Pallorium Inc	www.pallorium.com	US
Plat System Services Inc	www.platsystems.com	MN-Central
Property Info	http://portal.propertyinfo.com/	US
Public Data Corporation	www.pdcny.com	NY
real-info.com	www.real-info.com/index.asp	US
Realty Data Corp	www.realtydata.com	US
Record Information Services Inc	www.public-record.com	IL
Red Vision	www.redvision.com	AZ, CA, CO
SKLD Information Services LLC	www.skld.com	CO-14 counties
Tapestry	https://tapestry.fidlar.com	IL, IN, KS, MI, MN, WI
TitleSearcher.com	www.titlesearcher.com	TN
TitleX.com	www.titlex.net	TX
TLO	www.tlo.com/	US
tnrealestate.com	www.tnrealestate.com	TN
Tracers Information Specialists Inc	www.tracersinfo.com	US
UCC Direct Services	www.uccdirectservices.com	US
US SEARCH.com	www.ussearch.com/consumer/index.jsp	US
US Title Search Network	www.ustitlesearch.net/	TN
USADATA	www.usadata.com	US
Vision Appraisal Technology	www.visionappraisal.com	CT, ME, MA, NH, NY, PA, RI, VA, VT
WestlawNext	http://web2.westlaw.com	US

Uniform Commercial Code

Vendors - Uniform Commercial Code	Web Page	Region
Accurint (LexisNexis)	www.accurint.com	US
ACS Inc, Landaccess.com	www.landaccess.com	OH
Background Information Services Inc.	www.bisi.com	CO
Capitol Lien Records & Research Inc	www.capitollien.com	MN, WI, US
CSC - Corporation Service Company	https://www.cscglobal.com/global/web/csc/home	US
Dun & Bradstreet	www.dnb.com/us/	US
eCCLIX.com	https://ecclix.com/	KY
IQ Data Systems	www.iqdata.com	CA
KnowX	www.knowx.com	US
Law Bulletin Information Network	www.lawbulletin.com	IL-Central

Vendors - Uniform Commercial Code	Web Page	Region
Legal Solutions - Thomson Reuters	http://legalsolutions.thomsonreuters.com/law-products/	US
LexisNexis	www.lexisnexis.com	US
LocatePlus.com Inc	https://www.locateplus.com/welcome.asp	US
Motznik Information Services	www.motznik.com	AK
National Service Information	www.nsii.net	IN, OH, WI, US
OPENonline	www.openonline.com	US
Public Data Corporation	www.pdcny.com	NY
TLO	www.tlo.com/	US
Tracers Information Specialists Inc	www.tracersinfo.com	US
UCC Direct Services	www.uccdirectservices.com	US
WestlawNext	http://web2.westlaw.com	US

Vessels

Vendors - Vessels	Web Page	Region
AutoDataDirect, Inc	www.add123.com	FL
E-Merges.com	www.emerges.com/	US
First InfoSource	https://secure.firstinfosource.com	MO
KnowX	www.knowx.com	US
LexisNexis	www.lexisnexis.com	US
LocatePlus.com Inc	https://www.locateplus.com/welcome.asp	US
Motznik Information Services	www.motznik.com	AK
Pallorium Inc	www.pallorium.com	US
Research Archives.com	www.researcharchives.com	US
UCC Direct Services	www.uccdirectservices.com	US
US SEARCH.com	www.ussearch.com/consumer/index.jsp	US
WestlawNext	http://web2.westlaw.com	US

Voter Registration

Vendors - Voter Registration	Web Page	Region
ARISTOTLE International	www.aristotle.com/	US
E-Merges.com	www.emerges.com/	US

Reminder:

Of course there are many more public record vendors than the 135+ firms appearing in this section. The reason these particular companies were chosen is because they provide either a Proprietary Database or offer a non-intervention Gateway to the government public record categories shown in Chapter 6.

This is a best efforts presentation. Please keep in mind that the Region column primarily refers of online access from a gateway of proprietary database. Many of these firms offer additional services, including the ability to process requests to obtain records onsite or in-person in more states. .

Also, to find additional information and profiles on many more professional vendors and record searchers, go to www.brbpublications.com/pubrecsites_ven.asp.

Chapter 6

State and Local Government Online Sources

Individual state chapters have been compiled into an easy to use format that details when records or record indices may be searched online.

Within each state's section, these four sub-chapter sections are presented in this order:

1. State Public Record Agencies
2. State Licensing and Regulatory Boards
3. County Courts
4. County Recorder, Assessor, & Other Sites of Note

Only agencies with online access are listed.

If the agency provides a fee-based system you will see $$$ appearing at the end of the profile. Be aware that some agencies provide both a pay and a free system.

Be sure to review the Structure and Online Access notes found at the beginning of each state's Courts and Recorder's Office sections. This is a good place to find out about statewide or multi-jurisdictional online systems. At the county (parish) level, if there is a statewide site that encompasses all county jurisdictions - look for a master section of text.

To save paper and the redundancy of displaying the same language for each county listing - a summary may be displayed at the beginning of that section.

One last tip...remember that just because records are maintained in a certain way in your state or county do not assume that any other county or state does things the same way.

Note: All of the information found in this Chapter and in Chapter 7 is supplied by BRB Publications.

- For an updated list of free links list of all the government agencies, visit www.brbpublications.com and click on the Free Public Record Searches link.
- For those of you who need much more detailed information about the government agencies, BRB provides *The Public Record Research System (PRRS)*. For details, go to the same web page and click on the Subscription Products link.

Alabama

Capital: Montgomery
Montgomery County
Time Zone: CST
Population: 4,822,023
# of Counties: 67

Useful State Links

Website: www.alabama.gov
Governor: www.governor.alabama.gov
Attorney General: www.ago.state.al.us
State Archives: www.archives.state.al.us
State Statutes and Codes: www.legislature.state.al.us/prefiled/prefiled.html
Legislative Bill Search: www.legislature.state.al.us
Unclaimed Funds: www.treasury.state.al.us/up/

State Public Record Agencies

Criminal Records

Alabama Bureau of Investigation, Identification Unit - Record Checks, http://dps.alabama.gov/Home/ This agency recommends that searchers contact http://background.alabama.gov/. This is a subscription service with a $25.00 search fee and a $75 annual fee. Employers using a CRA must be registered first and CRA must also be approved. This service also includes arrest only records and is in real-time. This site is considered to be the official search site for the state. A fugitive search is offered at http://dps.alabama.gov/Community/wfSearch.aspx?Type=25. **$$$**

Sexual Offender Registry

Department of Public Safety, Sexual Offender Registry, http://dps.alabama.gov/Community/Default.aspx Sex offender data and a felony fugitives list are available online at the home page above. Search by name, ZIP, city or county. Missing persons and felony fugitives are also shown.

Incarceration Records

Alabama Department of Corrections, Central Records Office, www.doc.alabama.gov Information on current inmates only is available online. Location, AIS number, physical identifiers, and projected release date are released. The database is updated weekly. Inmates sentenced as Youthful Offenders are not included in this search. The site, available from the home page, is extremely slow to load.

Corporation, LP, LLC, LLP, Trade Names, Trademarks/Servicemarks

Secretary of State, Business Services Division, www.sos.alabama.gov/BusinessServices/BusinessEntities.aspx Search business entities free at www.sos.alabama.gov/vb/inquiry/inquiry.aspx?area=Business%20Entity. Search trademarks by applicant name or trademark number or description at www.sos.state.al.us/vb/inquiry/inquiry.aspx?area=Trademarks. Also, search securities department administrative actions lists free at http://asc.state.al.us/Issued-Orders.htm.

Uniform Commercial Code, Federal & State Tax Liens

UCC Division - SOS, UCC Records, www.sos.alabama.gov/BusinessServices/UCC.aspx There are online searches offered from the home page. Both a free, simple search and an advanced fee-based search are offered. The advanced search provides images, the free search does not. The free search offers access to the index by debtor name, or filing number. The advanced search is available to the public (credit card required) or to subscribers at a slightly lower feet. Search by name is $15.00 and $1.00 per page. Search by filing number for just $1.00 per page. Also there is a $9.75 electronic fee per transaction. Plus, non-subscribers must pay $4.50 fee and $.10 per page portal fee. Subscribers pay a $3.50 portal fee an no fee per page. **$$$** *Other Options:* Bulk sale by CD for $1,500 plus $300 a week for updates. No images.

Vital Records

Center for Health Statistics, Record Services Division, www.adph.org/vitalrecords/ Online ordering is available from the webpage through a service provider www.vitalchek.com. Check their sites for fees and turnaround times. **$$$**

Driver Records

Department of Public Safety, Driver Records-License Division, http://dps.alabama.gov/Home/wfContent.aspx?ID=30&PLH1=plhHome-DriverLicense Alabama.gov is designated the state's agent for online access of state driving records. A Subscriber Registration Agreement must be submitted. Both Alabama.gov and the Alabama DPS must approve all subscribers. There is a $75.00 annual administrative fee for new accounts and the search fee is $7.75 per record. The driver license number is needed to search. The system, open 24 hours daily, is Internet-based. Alabama.gov (Alabama Interactive) can be reached at 2 N. Jackson St, #301, Montgomery AL, 36104, (866) 353-3468. **$$$**

Vehicle Ownership & Registration

Motor Vehicle Division - Records Unit, Alabama Dept. of Revenue, www.revenue.alabama.gov/motorvehicle/index.cfm There are four search services available at www.revenue.alabama.gov/motorvehicle/mvinfo.html. A Vehicle Information Check is offered, it provides limited vehicle information, but includes lienholder data. Both a Registration Record search and a Title Record search are offered as well. Also an Abandoned Motor Vehicle Information Service is provided. Occasional requesters may use a credit card for the $6.00 fee per search. Ongoing users may access as approved, subscribers of Alabama Interactive - the NIC affiliate for the state. Subscribers also may be eligible to use other premium services such as obtaining a driving record, a vehicle VIN check, and a criminal record check, and for filing UCCs. **$$$**

Accident Reports

Alabama Department of Public Safety, Crash Records, http://dps.alabama.gov/Home/ Once the report has been identified and ordered, it is accessible online in a document format for seven days from the date of purchase. The fee for online purchase is $17.00 which includes a $2 processing fee above the $15.00 state fee. Visit https://www.alabamainteractive.org/dps_crash_report/welcome.action. **$$$**

Voter Registration, Lobbyists, PACs

Secretary of State-Elections Division, PO Box 5616, www.alabamavotes.gov/ PAC resources can be searched at www.sos.alabama.gov/vb/election/pacsrch1.aspx. Download the PAC list at www.alabamavotes.gov/downloads/election/fcpa/paclist.pdf. Download the PAC list at www.alabamavotes.gov/downloads/election/fcpa/paclist.pdf. The list of current lobbyists is at http://doa.alaska.gov/apoc/TrainingReports/lobbyist.html. Archived registered lobbyist list at http://ethics.alabama.gov/news2.aspx *Other Options:* Bulk requests can be ordered from this office for voter data from all 67 counties. Call 334-242-7222 for fees and breakdowns of customized requests.

Occupational Licensing Boards

Abortion/Reproductive Health Ctr .... http://ph.state.al.us/facilitiesdirectory/(S(n5lch3ny55g2s445agq20245))/Default.aspx
Accountant-CPA.. www.asbpa.alabama.gov/register/register.asp
Accountant-Non-Licensee........................... www.asbpa.alabama.gov/register/register.asp
Ambulatory Surgery Ctr .... http://ph.state.al.us/facilitiesdirectory/(S(n5lch3ny55g2s445agq20245))/Default.aspx
Anesthesiologist Assistant .... www.albme.org/licenseesearch.html#howtouse
Architect .... www.boa.state.al.us/RosterSearch/Search.aspx
Assisted Living Facility Speciality Care........ http://ph.state.al.us/facilitiesdirectory/(S(n5lch3ny55g2s445agq20245))/Default.aspx
Attorney.. www.alabar.org/oldirectory/
Audiologist.. www.abespa.org/files/roster.pdf
Bank .... www.bank.state.al.us/bank_search.aspx
Birthing Center .... http://ph.state.al.us/facilitiesdirectory/(S(n5lch3ny55g2s445agq20245))/Default.aspx
Cerebral Palsy Center.................................. http://ph.state.al.us/facilitiesdirectory/(S(n5lch3ny55g2s445agq20245))/Default.aspx
Certified Lead Firm...................................... www.adph.org/lead/assets/RRPweblist.pdf
Certified Renovator Training Provider.......... www.adph.org/lead/assets/RRPTrainingProviders.pdf
Chiropractor .... https://www.alabamainteractive.org/asbce_licverification/welcome.action
Clinical Nurse Specialist .... https://www.abn.alabama.gov/abnonline/License_LookUp.aspx
Contractor, General/Subcontractor .... http://genconbd.alabama.gov/DATABASE-SQL/roster.aspx
Cosmetologist www.aboc.state.al.us/Search1.htm
Counselor, Professional .... www.abec.state.al.us/
Dental Hygienist... www.dentalboard.org/pdf/2013%20Directory%20of%20Active%20Hygienists.pdf
Dentist.. www.dentalboard.org/pdf/2013%20Directory%20of%20Active%20Dentists.pdf
Dietitian/Nutritionist .... www.boed.alabama.gov/license_search/search_form.aspx
Electrical Contractor.................................... www.aecb.state.al.us/Search.aspx
Electrician, Journeyman.............................. www.aecb.state.al.us/Search.aspx

Embalmer	www.fsb.alabama.gov/pdfs/2013/AlabamaActiveLicenseFuneralDirectorsandEmbalmers020113.pdf
Engineer/Engineer in Training	www.bels.alabama.gov/LicenseeSearch/searchmenu.asp
Esthetic'n Student/Instruct/Sch'l/Salon	www.aboc.state.al.us/Search1.htm
Facilities	www.apob.alabama.gov/pages/directory.htm
Firefighter	www.alabamafirecollege.net/
Forester	http://asbrf.alabama.gov/vs2k5/rosterofforesters.aspx
Funeral Director	www.fsb.alabama.gov/pdfs/2013/AlabamaActiveLicenseFuneralDirectorsandEmbalmers020113.pdf
Funeral Service Establishments	www.fsb.alabama.gov/pdfs/2013/AlabamaActiveLicenseFuneralEstablishments020113.pdf
Gas Fitter	www.pgfb.state.al.us/Inquiry.aspx
Geologist	www.algeobd.alabama.gov/roster_search.asp
Heating/Air Conditioning Contractor	www.hvacboard.state.al.us/Construction.aspx
Home Builder	www.hblb.alabama.gov/content/Search/search.aspx
Home Health Agency	http://ph.state.al.us/facilitiesdirectory/(S(n5lch3ny55g2s445agq20245))/Default.aspx
Home Inspector	www.inspectorseek.com/
Home Medical Equip. Svcs. Provider	www.homemed.state.al.us/
Hospice	http://ph.state.al.us/facilitiesdirectory/(S(n5lch3ny55g2s445agq20245))/Default.aspx
Hospital	http://ph.state.al.us/facilitiesdirectory/(S(n5lch3ny55g2s445agq20245))/Default.aspx
Independent Clinical Labs	http://ph.state.al.us/facilitiesdirectory/(S(n5lch3ny55g2s445agq20245))/Default.aspx
Insurance Adjuster	https://sbs-al.naic.org/Lion-Web/jsp/sbsreports/AgentLookup.jsp
Insurance Agent/Broker/Producer	https://sbs-al.naic.org/Lion-Web/jsp/sbsreports/AgentLookup.jsp
Insurance Corp./Co./Partnership	https://sbs-al.naic.org/Lion-Web/jsp/sbsreports/CompanySearchLookup.jsp
Interior Designer	www.idboard.alabama.gov/search/start.aspx
Interpreter	www.albit.state.al.us/search/Roster.aspx
Landscape Architect	www.abela.state.al.us/architects.html
Lead Abatement Contractor/Professional	www.adph.org/lead/
Legal/Dental Svc Representative	https://sbs-al.naic.org/Lion-Web/jsp/sbsreports/AgentLookup.jsp
Lobbyist, Archived Registered Lobbyist	http://ethics.alabama.gov/news2.aspx
LPG-Liquef'd Petrol'm Gas Broker	www.lpgb.state.al.us/Search.htm
Manicurist Salon/Sch'l/Student/Instruct'r/	www.aboc.state.al.us/Search1.htm
Marriage/Family Therapist/Supervisor	www.mft.state.al.us/search.aspx
Massage Therapist	www.almtbd.state.al.us/roster_search.asp
Medical Gas Piper	www.pgfb.state.al.us/Inquiry.aspx
Mental Health Center	http://ph.state.al.us/facilitiesdirectory/(S(n5lch3ny55g2s445agq20245))/Default.aspx
Midwife	https://www.abn.alabama.gov/abnonline/License_LookUp.aspx
Mobile Home Manufacturer	www.amhc.alabama.gov/
Mobile Home Set-up/Instal./Seller	www.amhc.alabama.gov/
Motor Club Representative	https://sbs-al.naic.org/Lion-Web/jsp/sbsreports/AgentLookup.jsp
Notary Public	www.sos.state.al.us/vb/inquiry/inquiry.aspx?area=Notaries%20Public
Nurse-LPN/RN	https://www.abn.alabama.gov/abnonline/License_LookUp.aspx
Nursing Disciplinary Action	https://www.abn.alabama.gov/abnonline/License_LookUp.aspx
Nursing Home	http://ph.state.al.us/facilitiesdirectory/(S(n5lch3ny55g2s445agq20245))/Default.aspx
Nursing Home Administrator	www.alboenha.state.al.us/logon.html
Nutritionist	www.boed.alabama.gov/license_search/search_form.aspx
Occupational Therapist/Assistant	www.asbot.state.al.us/search.htm
Optometrist	http://optometry.alabama.gov/Search.aspx
Organ Procurement Ctr	http://ph.state.al.us/facilitiesdirectory/(S(n5lch3ny55g2s445agq20245))/Default.aspx
Orthotist	www.apob.alabama.gov/pages/directory.htm
Osteopathic Physician	www.albme.org/licenseesearch.html#howtouse
Pesticide Applicator/Dealer	http://agi.alabama.gov/pestappannounce
Pharmacist/Technician/Intern/Extern	https://www.cebroker.com/public/pb_index.aspx
Pharmacy Store	https://www.cebroker.com/public/pb_index.aspx
Physical Therapist/Therapist Asst	www.pt.state.al.us/License/searchform.asp
Physician/Medical Doctor/Assistant	www.albme.org/licenseesearch.html#howtouse
Physiological Lab, Clinical	http://ph.state.al.us/facilitiesdirectory/(S(n5lch3ny55g2s445agq20245))/Default.aspx
Plumber	www.pgfb.state.al.us/Inquiry.aspx

Podiatrist	www.podiatryboard.alabama.gov/current_licensees.html
Pre-Need Sales Agent	https://sbs-al.naic.org/Lion-Web/jsp/sbsreports/AgentLookup.jsp
Prosthetist	www.apob.alabama.gov/pages/directory.htm
Real Estate Agent/Seller	http://arec.alabama.gov/professionals/licensing/license-search
Real Estate Appraiser	http://reab.state.al.us/appraisers/searchform.asp
Real Estate Broker	http://arec.alabama.gov/professionals/licensing/license-search
Registered Nurse Practitioner	https://www.abn.alabama.gov/abnonline/License_LookUp.aspx
Rehabilitation Center	http://ph.state.al.us/facilitiesdirectory/(S(n5lch3ny55g2s445agq20245))/Default.aspx
Renal Disease Terminal Treatment Ctr	http://ph.state.al.us/facilitiesdirectory/(S(n5lch3ny55g2s445agq20245))/Default.aspx
Residential Treatment Facilities	http://ph.state.al.us/facilitiesdirectory/(S(n5lch3ny55g2s445agq20245))/Default.aspx
Rural Primary Care Hospital	http://ph.state.al.us/facilitiesdirectory/(S(n5lch3ny55g2s445agq20245))/Default.aspx
School Superintendent	www.alsde.edu/html/super_listing.asp?menu=none&footer=general
Senior Volunteer, Medical	www.albme.org/licenseesearch.html#howtouse
Shampoo Assistant	www.aboc.state.al.us/Search1.htm
Sleep Disorder Center	http://ph.state.al.us/facilitiesdirectory/(S(n5lch3ny55g2s445agq20245))/Default.aspx
Social Worker	www.abswe.state.al.us/Lic_Search/search.asp
Social Worker, Private Practice	www.abswe.state.al.us/Lic_Search/search.asp
Soil Classifier	http://swcc.alabama.gov/pages/soil_classifiers.aspx?sm=b_c
Special Purpose License, Medical	www.albme.org/licenseesearch.html#howtouse
Speech Pathologist/Audiologist	www.abespa.org/files/roster.pdf
Sports Agent	www.sos.state.al.us/Downloads/dl1.aspx
Steamship Agencies	www.asdd.com/
Stevedoring Companies	www.asdd.com/
Surgeon/Assistant	www.albme.org/licenseesearch.html#howtouse
Surplus Line Broker	https://sbs-al.naic.org/Lion-Web/jsp/sbsreports/AgentLookup.jsp
Surveyor, Land	www.bels.alabama.gov/LicenseeSearch/searchmenu.asp
Transliterator	www.albit.state.al.us/search/Roster.aspx
X-ray (Portable) Supplier	http://ph.state.al.us/facilitiesdirectory/(S(n5lch3ny55g2s445agq20245))/Default.aspx

State and Local Courts

State Court Structure: **Circuit Courts** are the courts of general jurisdiction and exclusive jurisdiction on civil matters over $10,000. **District Courts** are the limited jurisdiction in civil matters. Civil cases between $3,000 and $10,000 may be concurrent and heard at either court, depending on local practice. Barbour, Coffee, Jefferson, St. Clair, Talladega, and Tallapoosa Counties have two court locations within the county. Jefferson County (Birmingham), Madison (Huntsville), Marshall, and Tuscaloosa Counties have separate criminal divisions for Circuit and/or District Courts. All counties have separate probate courts.

Appellate Courts: One may view Civil Appeals, Criminal Appeals, and Reporter Decisions at http://2.alalinc.net/, a subscription is required. Attorneys may subscribe to the Appellate Court's Online Information Service at https://acis.alabama.gov.

Statewide Court Online Access: All courts participate in the system described below.

The state courts generally promote use of a vendor. *ON-DEMAND Access to Alabama State Trial Court Records* is a subscription service that provides access to criminal, civil, small claims, state traffic, domestic relations and child support case information. A name search is $9.99 which includes details on one case; each additional case is $9.99. A case number search is $9.99. Images are $5.00 for the first 20 pages and $.50 per page each add'l. There is a case monitoring service offered as well; $29.99 for a Circuit Court case and $19.99 for a District Court case. To sign up visit https://pa.alacourt.com/default.aspx

County Sites (other than the statewide site mentioned above):

Baldwin County

Probate Court

Probate records are accessible at www.deltacomputersystems.com/al/al05/probatea.html.

Mobile County

Probate Court

Online access to the probate record index is free at http://probate.mobilecountyal.gov/.

Search **City of Mobile Municipal Court** records at www.cityofmobile.org/mcourts/index.php.

Monroe County
Probate Court
Online access to the probate record index is free at http://probate.mobilecountyal.gov/.

Montgomery County
Probate Court
Probate and **marriage** index available free at www.mc-ala.org/ElectedOfficials/ProbateJudge/ProbateResources/Pages/ProbateRecordsSearch.aspx.

Morgan County
Probate Court
Search probate records at http://morgancountyprobate.com/DesktopDefault.aspx?tabindex=5&tabid=99.

Recorders, Assessors, and Other Sites of Note

Recording Office Organization: 67 counties, 71 recording offices. **The recording officer is the Judge of Probate**. Four counties have two recording offices- Barbour, Coffee, Jefferson, and St. Clair. Federal and state tax liens on personal property of businesses are filed with the Secretary of State. Other federal and state tax liens are filed with the County Judge of Probate.

Statewide or Multi-Jurisdiction Access: There is no statewide system for access to recorded documents, but a increasing number of counties offer free online access to recorded documents as well as tax assessor data, and property info on GIS-mapping sites.

- Access property assessment data for 11 counties at GIS-mapping and land database company eMapsPlus at http://emaps.emapsplus.com/. Free search counties are: Autauga, Bibb, Dallas, Franklin, Lamar, Lawrence, Macon, Madison, Perry, Tuscaloosa, and Washington.
- Access property assessment data free from 13 counties (Baldwin, Blount, Clay, Colbert, Cullman, DeKalb, Escambia, Etowah, Jackson, Lauderdale, Lee, Madison, Morgan, and St. Clair) from Delta Computer Systems at www.deltacomputersystems.com/search.html.

Note: The two statewide sites mentioned below are useful. To avoid redundancy they are not mentioned in the county profiles to follow.

- Access to individual county lists of the Transcripts of Tax Delinquent Property is at http://revenue.alabama.gov/advalorem/transcript/transcript.cfm. This site has data for all counties and is not listed in the profiles below.
- The Secretary of State's Lands and Trademarks Division offers free access to county-by-county tract books which reflect the original ownership of Alabama lands, see www.sos.state.al.us/GovtRecords/Land.aspx. This site has data for all counties and is not listed in the profiles below.

County Sites:

Autauga County ***Property Taxation and/or GIS Records*** Access the GIS-property info database and Tax Office free at http://emaps.emapsplus.com/.

Baldwin County ***Recorded Documents*** www.co.baldwin.al.us/PageView.asp?PageType=R&edit_id=3 Access to recordings, deeds, and UCCs at www.deltacomputersystems.com/AL/AL05/INDEX.HTML.
Property Taxation and/or GIS Records Property tax data and property appraiser records at www.deltacomputersystems.com/AL/AL05/INDEX.HTML.

Bibb County ***Property Taxation and/or GIS Records*** Access the GIS-property info database and Tax Office free at http://emaps.emapsplus.com/.

Blount County ***Property Taxation and/or GIS Records*** Public records available from the Revenue Commissioner's Office at www.blountrevenue.com/?page_id=28 includes property and assessment records. Also, property tax data and GIS/mapping at www.deltacomputersystems.com/AL/AL05/INDEX.HTML.

Bullock County ***Property Taxation and/or GIS Records*** Access to records free at www.qpublic.net/al/bullock/.

Butler County ***Property Taxation and/or GIS Records*** Access to GIS/mapping for free at www.alabamagis.com/Butler/.

Chambers County ***Recorded Documents*** www.chamberscountyal.gov/departments/circuit-clerk/probate/ Access real estate and UCC data online by subscription for $65.00 monthly fee. Records are live and go back 5 years. For info, call 334-864-4384. **$$$**

Property Taxation and/or GIS Records Access parcel data on the GIS-mapping site free at www.chamberscountymaps.com/. Password required for full data.

Chilton County ***Property Taxation and/or GIS Records*** Access to GIS/mapping free at www.alabamagis.com/Chilton/.

Clay County ***Property Taxation and/or GIS Records*** Property tax data records at www.deltacomputersystems.com/AL/AL05/INDEX.HTML.

Cleburne County ***Property Taxation and/or GIS Records*** Access to GIS/mapping for a fee at www.alabamagis.com/Cleburne/. Must also install plug-in \"Flagship\" before use.**$$$**

Coffee County (Both Divisions) ***Recorded Documents*** www.coffeecounty.us/ Subscription access to all recorded indices available, $25.00 signup fee, view images at $.75 each or less, print images $.25 each. Data is same as appears on PAT. See http://sysconononline.com/?page_id=71. **$$$**

Property Taxation and/or GIS Records Search tax status by name at www.coffeecountyrevenue.com/search.aspx.

Colbert County ***Recorded Documents*** www.colbertprobatejudge.org/ Subscription access to all recorded records indexes available, $25.00 signup fee, view images at $.75 each or less, print images $.25 each. Data is same as appears on PAT. See http://sysconononline.com/?page_id=71. **$$$**

Property Taxation and/or GIS Records Access property tax records free at www.deltacomputersystems.com/AL/AL20/INDEX.HTML. Also, access to GIS/mapping free at www.waalex.com/webgis/colb_gismap.html.

Conecuh County ***Property Taxation and/or GIS Records*** Access to GIS/mapping for free at www.alabamagis.com/conecuh/.

Covington County ***Property Taxation and/or GIS Records*** Access property tax records at www.alabamagis.com/covington/frameset.cfm. Access to GIS/mapping for free at www.alabamagis.com/covington/.

Cullman County ***Recorded Documents*** Subscription access to recorded record indices, $25.00 signup fee, view images at $.75 each or less, print images $.25 each. Data is same as appears on PAT. See http://sysconononline.com/?page_id=71. **$$$**

Property Taxation and/or GIS Records Access the GIS-property info database and Tax Office free at www.cullmanrevenuecom.com/. Click on Search and Pay Taxes. Also, access to property taxes and GIS/mapping free at www.deltacomputersystems.com/AL/AL25/INDEX.HTML.

Dale County ***Recorded Documents*** http://dalecountyal.org/Home.aspx Subscription access to recorded record indices, $25.00 signup fee, view images at $.75 each or less, print images $.25 each. Data is same as appears on PAT. See http://sysconononline.com/?page_id=71. **$$$**

Property Taxation and/or GIS Records Access to property tax searches free at http://dalecountyrevenuecommissioner.com/v3.aspx. Can also choose motor vehicle taxes.

Dallas County ***Property Taxation and/or GIS Records*** Access the GIS-property info database and Tax Office free at http://emaps.emapsplus.com/. Also, access to tax record information free at www.dallascountyproperty-tags.com/search.aspx?type=p.

De Kalb County ***Property Taxation and/or GIS Records*** A login name and account and credit card is required to view assessment, appraisal, property tax data at www.deltacomputersystems.com/AL/AL28/index_revenue.html.**$$$**

Elmore County ***Property Taxation and/or GIS Records*** Access to taxpayer search data free at www.elmorerevenuecommissioner.com/search.aspx.

Escambia County ***Property Taxation and/or GIS Records*** Access to the county property appraisal data is free at www.escpa.org/default.aspx. Click on record search. Also can click on Maps for GIS/mapping for free. Also, access to propert taxes and appraisal free at www.deltacomputersystems.com/AL/AL30/INDEX.HTML.

Etowah County ***Recorded Documents*** http://etowahcounty.org/department/id/12/ Access to parcel records free at http://isv.kcsgis.com/al.etowah/#/SearchOptions.

Property Taxation and/or GIS Records Access to property data and tax records for free at www.deltacomputersystems.com/AL/AL31/INDEX.HTML.

Fayette County ***Property Taxation and/or GIS Records*** Access parcel data on the GIS/mapping site free at www.alabamagis.com/Fayette/.

Franklin County ***Property Taxation and/or GIS Records*** Access the GIS-property info database and Tax Office free at http://emaps.emapsplus.com/.

Geneva County ***Recorded Documents*** www.genevacounty.us/aboutGenevaCounty/countyGovernment/probatejudge.aspx Subscription access to recorded record indices, $25.00 signup fee, view images at $.75 each or less, print images $.25 each. Data is same as appears on PAT. See http://sysconline.com/?page_id=71. **$$$**

Property Taxation and/or GIS Records Access to GIS/mapping for free at www.alabamagis.com/Geneva/Frameset.cfm.

Henry County ***Property Taxation and/or GIS Records*** Access parcel data on the GIS-mapping site free at www.alabamagis.com/Henry/. Must download Mapguide Viewer Software first.

Houston County ***Recorded Documents*** http://houstoncountyprobate.org/ Subscription access to recorded record indices, $25.00 signup fee, view images at $.75 each or less, print images $.25 each. Data is same as appears on PAT. See http://sysconline.com/?page_id=71. **$$$**

Property Taxation and/or GIS Records Access to property record search and GIS/mapping parcel viewer for free at www.houstoncounty.org/index.php#.

Jackson County ***Recorded Documents*** www.jacksoncountyal.com/probate.html Access to deeds and records free at www.deltacomputersystems.com/AL/AL39/drlinkquerya.html.

Property Taxation and/or GIS Records Access Rev Commission property tax lookup free at www.deltacomputersystems.com/AL/AL39/INDEX.HTML. Also, search the property tax assessment and taxes at www.jacksoncountyrevenue.com/propertytaxes/.

Jefferson County (Both Divisions) ***Recorded Documents*** Access to records for a fee at http://jeffconlinelandrecord.jccal.org/ailis/index.html. Monthly subscription fee is $100.00 unlimited or $2.00 per page, minimum $3.00 per document. **$$$**

Property Taxation and/or GIS Records The site at http://www.jeffcointouch.com/ecourthouse provides free searches to tax appraisal data and maps. Search assessment data by name or parcel # or address.

Lamar County ***Property Taxation and/or GIS Records*** Access the GIS-property info database and Tax Office free at http://emaps.emapsplus.com/.

Lauderdale County ***Property Taxation and/or GIS Records*** Access to property appraisal data and property taxes are free at www.deltacomputersystems.com/AL/AL41/INDEX.HTML.

Lawrence County ***Property Taxation and/or GIS Records*** Access the GIS-property info database and Tax Office free at http://emaps.emapsplus.com/.

Lee County ***Property Taxation and/or GIS Records*** Access to property appraisal records and property tax data is free at www.deltacomputersystems.com/AL/AL43/INDEX.HTML. Also, access parcel data on the GIS-mapping site free at www.alabamagis.com/lee/. Password required for full data.

Limestone County ***Recorded Documents*** www.probate.limestonecounty.net/ Subscription access to recorded record indices, $25.00 signup fee, view images at $.75 each or less, print images $.25 each. Data is same as appears on PAT. See http://sysconline.com/?page_id=71. **$$$**

Macon County ***Property Taxation and/or GIS Records*** Free property record searches at www.qpublic.net/al/macon/search.html. Also, access the GIS-property info database and Tax Office free at http://emaps.emapsplus.com/.

Madison County ***Recorded Documents*** http://madisoncountyal.gov/probate/ Access to the judge of probate's recording index is free at http://probate.co.madison.al.us/. Land records including images go back to 1971; marriage and military discharges back to 1976.

Property Taxation and/or GIS Records Access assessor, appraiser data and land and lot books free at www.deltacomputersystems.com/AL/AL47/INDEX.HTML. Also, access the GIS-property info database and Tax Office free at http://emaps.emapsplus.com/.

Marion County ***Property Taxation and/or GIS Records*** Access parcel data on the GIS-mapping site free at www.marioncountymaps.com/.

Marshall County ***Recorded Documents*** www.marshallco.org/index.php Access to deeds by grantor/grantee free at www.deedlookup.org/.

Property Taxation and/or GIS Records Access property data free at www.landlookup.org/.

Mobile County ***Recorded Documents*** www.probate.mobilecountyal.gov/ Access real estate, grantor/grantee, deed records and more back to 2000 free at www.mobilecounty.org/probatecourt/recordssearch.htm. Also, search real and personal property, estate claims, and election results. Search marriages at http://records.mobile-county.net/Login.aspx?SessionExpired=I.

Property Taxation and/or GIS Records Access real property and personal property tax records free at www.mobile-propertytaxal.com/bill_search.shtml. Also, City of Mobile property ownership data is free at http://maps.cityofmobile.org/gis/webmapping.aspx.

Greg Norris ***Property Taxation and/or GIS Records*** Access to property tax search and pay for free at www.monroecountyonline.com/PropertyTaxSearch.

Montgomery County ***Recorded Documents*** www.mc-ala.org/ElectedOfficials/ProbateJudge/Pages/Default.aspx Free access to records index found at www.mc-ala.org/ElectedOfficials/ProbateJudge/ProbateResources/Pages/ProbateRecordsSearch.aspx.

Property Taxation and/or GIS Records Access the property tax and assessment info using the left side choices at http://revco.mc-ala.org/.

Morgan County ***Recorded Documents, Marriage Records*** www.morgancountyprobate.com/DesktopDefault.aspx Access the probate office index of recordings free at www.morgancountyprobate.com/DesktopDefault.aspx?tabindex=5&tabid=99.Land records go back to 1999.
Property Taxation and/or GIS Records Access property appraiser data free at www.deltacomputersystems.com/AL/AL52/INDEX.HTML.

Perry County ***Property Taxation and/or GIS Records*** Access the GIS-property info database and Tax Office free at http://emaps.emapsplus.com/.

Pickens County ***Property Taxation and/or GIS Records*** Access parcel data on the GIS/mapping site free at www.alabamagis.com/Pickens/. Must download Mapguide Viewer Software first.

Pike County ***Property Taxation and/or GIS Records*** Access GIS/mapping property data free at www.alabamagis.com/Pike/. Also, access to property records free at www.pikerevenue.com/search.aspx?type=p.

Russell County ***Property Taxation and/or GIS Records*** Access the GIS-property info database and Tax Office free at http://russellcountyrevenuecommissioner.com/search.aspx.

St. Clair County (Both Districts) ***Property Taxation and/or GIS Records*** Access to property appraiser data and assessor date free at http://www.deltacomputersystems.com/AL/AL59/INDEX.HTML.

Shelby County ***Recorded Documents, Notary Records*** www.shelbyal.com/index.aspx?nid=285 Access to the probate court recording data is free at www.shelbyal.com/index.aspx?nid=289. Marriage license is index only. No images.
Property Taxation and/or GIS Records Search property tax records free at https://ptc.shelbyal.com/caportal_mainpage.aspx.

Sumter County ***Property Taxation and/or GIS Records*** Access to GIS/mapping free at www.alabamagis.com/Sumter/disclaimer.cfm.

Tallapoosa County ***Property Taxation and/or GIS Records*** Access parcel data on the GIS-mapping site free at www.alabamagis.com/tallapoosa/. Password required for full data.

Tuscaloosa County ***Recorded Documents*** www.tuscco.com Access to the recorder's database is free at www.tuscco.com/recordroom/. Also included are incorporations, bonds, discharges, exemptions. Probate court, miscellaneous. Must purchase images.
Property Taxation and/or GIS Records Access the GIS-property info database and Tax Office free at http://emaps.emapsplus.com/. Also, access tax sale and other records free at www.tuscco.com/recordroom/.

Walker County ***Recorded Documents*** www.walkercounty.com Subscription access to recorded record indices, $25.00 signup fee, view images at $.75 each or less, print images $.25 each. Data is same as appears on PAT. See http://sysconline.com/?page_id=71. **$$$**
Property Taxation and/or GIS Records Access parcel data on the GIS-mapping site free at www.alabamagis.com/walker/. Must download Mapguide Viewer Software first. Password required for full data.

Washington County ***Property Taxation and/or GIS Records*** Access the GIS-property info database and Tax Office free at http://emaps.emapsplus.com/.

Wilcox County ***Property Taxation and/or GIS Records*** Access to GIS/mapping for free at www.alabamagis.com/Wilcoxgov/disclaimer.cfm.

Winston County ***Property Taxation and/or GIS Records*** Access parcel data on the GIS-mapping site free at www.alabamagis.com/winston/. Must download Mapguide Viewer Software first. Password required for full data.

Reminder:

Access to individual county lists of the Transcripts of Tax Delinquent Property is at http://revenue.alabama.gov/advalorem/transcript/transcript.cfm. This site has data for all counties and is not listed in the profiles above.

The Secretary of State's Lands and Trademarks Division offers free access to county-by-county tract books which reflect the original ownership of Alabama lands, see www.sos.state.al.us/GovtRecords/Land.aspx. This site has data for all counties and is not listed in the profiles above.

Alaska

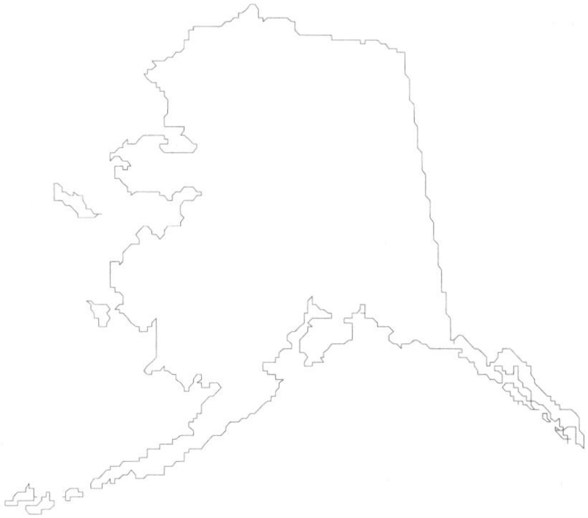

Capital: Juneau
Juneau Borough
Time Zone: AK (Alaska Standard Time)
Population: 731,449
# of Boroughs/Divisions: 23

Useful State Links

Website: www.alaska.gov
Governor: www.gov.state.ak.us
Attorney General: www.law.state.ak.us
State Archives: www.archives.state.ak.us
State Statutes and Codes: www.legis.state.ak.us/basis/folio.asp
Legislative Bill Search: www.legis.state.ak.us/basis/folio.asp
Bill Monitoring: www.legis.state.ak.us/basis/btmf_login.asp?session=24
Unclaimed Funds: www.dor.alaska.gov/treasury/programs/programs/index.aspx?23050

State Public Record Agencies

Sexual Offender Registry

Department of Public Safety, Statewide Services Div-SOCKR Unit, www.dps.state.ak.us/sorweb/Sorweb.aspx Name searching and geographic searching is available at the website. This is the primary search offered by the agency.

Incarceration Records

Alaska Department of Corrections, DOC Classification Office, www.correct.state.ak.us No online searching available from this agency, but it promotes a private company with a free search of DOC inmates and offenders at https://www.vinelink.com/vinelink/siteInfoAction.do?siteId=2001.

Corporation, LP, LLC, LLP, Trademarks/Servicemarks, Fictitious/Assumed Name

Corporation Section, Department of Commerce, Community & Econ Dev, http://commerce.alaska.gov/occ/home_corporations.html At http://commerce.alaska.gov/CBP/Main/SearchInfo.aspx, search and download status information on corps, LLCs, LLP, LP (all both foreign and domestic), registered and reserved names. Search by entity name, registered agent name, or by officer name. Search by entity name, registered agent name, or by officer name. Also, search Dept of Commerce Securities Dept. Disciplinary actions at www.dced.state.ak.us/bsc/orders.htm. Search business licenses at http://commerce.alaska.gov/CBP/Main/CBPLSearch.aspx?mode=BL. *Other Options:* The business license database can be downloaded from the web.

Uniform Commercial Code

UCC Central File Systems Office, State Recorder's Office, www.ucc.alaska.gov/ One can search by debtor or secured party name, date, document number or document type at http://dnr.alaska.gov/ssd/recoff/searchUCC.cfm. There is no fee. Images of UCC document files/recorded from July 1, 2008 forward are available on the Internet. Inactive UCCs (UCCs that are more than one year past their date of lapse) are purged from the database on an annual schedule. Images of mining documents (Index Code MI, Document Type - Mining) and deed documents (Index Code D, Document Type - Deeds) recorded from January 1, 1973 forward are now available at http://dnr.alaska.gov/ssd/recoff/searchRO.cfm. Official certified copies must be requested and paid for through the recording district office where the plat was recorded. *Other Options:* CDs or FTPs of document images can be purchased from the State Recorder's Office (907-269-8878). Also this office provides a number of excellent searches at http://dnr.alaska.gov/ssd/recoff/searchRO.cfm.

Vital Records

Department of Health & Social Services, Bureau of Vital Statistics, http://dhss.alaska.gov/Pages/default.aspx Records may be ordered online via a state-designated vendor at www.vitalchek.com. There are additional fees. Use of credit card required. **$$$**

Workers' Compensation Records

Workers' Compensation, www.labor.state.ak.us/wc/wc.htm Requests may be submitted online - all 07-6121 Form requirements still apply. Also, submit via email at workerscomp@alaska.gov. Emails are checked every workday. *Other Options:* Microfiche is available at $50.00 per fiche, prepaid.

Driver Records

Division of Motor Vehicles, Attn: Research, http://doa.alaska.gov/dmv/ Online access costs $10.00 per record. This is for pre-approved, ongoing requesters only. Inquiries may be made at any time, 24 hours a day. Batch inquiries may call back within thirty minutes for responses. Search by the first four letters of driver's name, license number and date of birth. Note this is not a web-based system. **$$$**

Voter Registration, Campaign & Financial Disclosures

Division of Elections, www.elections.alaska.gov Search campaign disclosures records at https://webapp.state.ak.us/apoc/searchcampaigndisclosure.jsp. Search public official and legislative financial disclosure at https://webapp.state.ak.us/apoc/. *Other Options:* The agency offers the complete voter registration database on CD-ROM for $21. Individual districts (there are 40) can be purchased on disk for $21.00 per district. Statewide lists are created every Friday.

Occupational Licensing Boards

Accountant-CPA.. www.commerce.state.ak.us/occ/search3.htm
Acupuncturist www.commerce.state.ak.us/occ/search3.htm
Aircraft-related Occupation .... www.faa.gov/licenses_certificates/airmen_certification/sport_pilot/
Anesthesia Permit, Dental www.commerce.state.ak.us/occ/search3.htm
Approved Fingerprinters .... www.dps.alaska.gov/Statewide/background/fingerprinters.aspx
Architect/Land Surveyors............................. www.commerce.state.ak.us/occ/search3.htm
Athletic Event Promoter www.commerce.state.ak.us/occ/search3.htm
Athletic Trainer.. www.commerce.state.ak.us/occ/search3.htm
Attorney... https://www.alaskabar.org/servlet/content/member_directory.html
Audiologist/Hearing Aid Dealer www.commerce.state.ak.us/occ/search3.htm
Bail Bondsman .... www.commerce.state.ak.us/ins/apps/producersearch/InsLicStart.cfm
Banks/Financial Institutions-Disciplinary Orders........www.commerce.state.ak.us/bsc/orders.htm
Barber www.commerce.state.ak.us/occ/search3.htm
Barber Shop Owner/Sch'l/Instruc................ www.commerce.state.ak.us/occ/search3.htm
Big Game, Hunting Guide/Assist/Transporte.............www.commerce.state.ak.us/occ/search3.htm
Boxer... www.commerce.state.ak.us/occ/search3.htm
Boxing Physician... www.commerce.state.ak.us/occ/search3.htm
Boxing/Wrestling Personnel........................ www.commerce.state.ak.us/occ/search3.htm
Certified Septic Installer .... http://dec.alaska.gov/water/wwdp/onsite/pdf/rptCurrentCI.pdf
Child Care Provider/Home/Center https://dpasysops.dhss.alaska.gov/FindProviderVS8/zSearch.aspx
Chiropractor www.commerce.state.ak.us/occ/search3.htm
Collection Agency/Operator www.commerce.state.ak.us/occ/search3.htm
Concert Promoter.. www.commerce.state.ak.us/occ/search3.htm
Construction Contractor www.commerce.state.ak.us/occ/search3.htm
Contractor, Civil/Elect./Mech./Mining/Petrol. www.commerce.state.ak.us/occ/search3.htm
Contractor, Residential www.commerce.state.ak.us/occ/search3.htm
Cosmetologist/Hairdresser.......................... www.commerce.state.ak.us/occ/search3.htm
Cosmetology Shop Owner/School/Instructorwww.commerce.state.ak.us/occ/search3.htm
Counselor, Professional www.commerce.state.ak.us/occ/search3.htm
Defibrillator Technician .... http://dhss.alaska.gov/dph/Emergency/Pages/ems/default.aspx
Dentist/Dental Examiner/Dental Hygienist... www.commerce.state.ak.us/occ/search3.htm
Dietitian/Nutritionist.................................... www.commerce.state.ak.us/occ/search3.htm
Disciplinary Orders..................................... www.commerce.state.ak.us/bsc/orders.htm
Drug Distributor/Drug Room www.commerce.state.ak.us/occ/search3.htm
Electrical Administrator www.commerce.state.ak.us/occ/search3.htm
Emergency Medical Technician .... http://dhss.alaska.gov/dph/Emergency/Pages/ems/default.aspx
Engineer.. www.commerce.state.ak.us/occ/search3.htm
Esthetician.. www.commerce.state.ak.us/occ/search3.htm

Funeral Director/Establishment.................... www.commerce.state.ak.us/occ/search3.htm
Geologist.. www.commerce.state.ak.us/occ/search3.htm
Guide/Outfitter, Hunting www.commerce.state.ak.us/occ/search3.htm
Hairdresser/Esthetician www.commerce.state.ak.us/occ/search3.htm
Hearing Aid Dealer....................................... www.commerce.state.ak.us/occ/search3.htm
Home Inspector.. www.commerce.state.ak.us/occ/search3.htm
Independent Adjuster.................................... www.commerce.state.ak.us/ins/apps/producersearch/InsLicStart.cfm
Insurance Agent/Producer/Occupation........ www.commerce.state.ak.us/ins/apps/producersearch/InsLicStart.cfm
Landscape Architect www.commerce.state.ak.us/occ/search3.htm
Lobbyist/Lobbyist Employer.......................... http://doa.alaska.gov/apoc/TrainingReports/lobbyist.html
Marriage & Family Therapist......................... www.commerce.state.ak.us/occ/search3.htm
Mechanical Administrator............................. www.commerce.state.ak.us/occ/search3.htm
Midwife... www.commerce.state.ak.us/occ/search3.htm
Mortician/Embalmer..................................... www.commerce.state.ak.us/occ/search3.htm
Naturopathic Physician www.commerce.state.ak.us/occ/search3.htm
Notary Public.. http://ltgov.alaska.gov/treadwell/notaries.html
Nurse Anesthetist... www.commerce.state.ak.us/occ/search3.htm
Nurse-RN/LPN/Nurses Aid www.commerce.state.ak.us/occ/search3.htm
Nursing Home Administrator......................... www.commerce.state.ak.us/occ/search3.htm
Occupational Therapist/Assistant www.commerce.state.ak.us/occ/search3.htm
Optician, Dispensing www.commerce.state.ak.us/occ/search3.htm
Optometrist... www.commerce.state.ak.us/occ/search3.htm
Osteopathic Physician www.commerce.state.ak.us/occ/search3.htm
Paramedic.. www.commerce.state.ak.us/occ/search3.htm
Parenteral Sedation Permit (Dental)............ www.commerce.state.ak.us/occ/search3.htm
Pesticide Applicator/Dealer.......................... www.kellysolutions.com/ak/
Pesticide Permit, Registration...................... www.kellysolutions.com/ak/
Pharmacist/Pharmacist Intern...................... www.commerce.state.ak.us/occ/search3.htm
Pharmacy/Technician www.commerce.state.ak.us/occ/search3.htm
Physical Therapist/Assistant........................ www.commerce.state.ak.us/occ/search3.htm
Physician/Doctor, Surgeon/Assistant........... www.commerce.state.ak.us/occ/search3.htm
Pilot, Aircraft.. http://registry.faa.gov/aircraftinquiry/NNum_Inquiry.aspx
Pilot, Marine www.commerce.state.ak.us/occ/search3.htm
Podiatrist... www.commerce.state.ak.us/occ/search3.htm
Process Server.. www.dps.alaska.gov/Statewide/PermitsLicensing/docs/CPSlist.pdf
Psychologist/Psycholog'l Assistant.............. www.commerce.state.ak.us/occ/search3.htm
Real Estate Agent/Broker/Assoc.................. www.commerce.state.ak.us/occ/search3.htm
Real Estate Appraiser.................................. www.commerce.state.ak.us/occ/search3.htm
Reinsurance Intermediary Broker/Mgr......... www.commerce.state.ak.us/ins/apps/producersearch/InsLicStart.cfm
School Administrator.................................... www.eed.state.ak.us/TeacherCertification/CertificationsSearch.cfm
School Special Service .... www.eed.state.ak.us/TeacherCertification/CertificationsSearch.cfm
Social Worker/Clinical.................................. www.commerce.state.ak.us/occ/search3.htm
Speech/Language Pathologist...................... www.commerce.state.ak.us/occ/search3.htm
Surplus Line Broker...................................... www.commerce.state.ak.us/ins/apps/producersearch/InsLicStart.cfm
Surveyor, Land... www.commerce.state.ak.us/occ/search3.htm
Tattoo Artist/Body Piercer www.commerce.state.ak.us/occ/search3.htm
Teacher.. www.eed.state.ak.us/TeacherCertification/CertificationsSearch.cfm
Transporter, Game....................................... www.commerce.state.ak.us/occ/search3.htm
Underground Storage Tank Worker/Contr.... www.commerce.state.ak.us/occ/search3.htm
Vessel Agent.. www.commerce.state.ak.us/occ/search3.htm
Veterinarian/Veterinary Technician.............. www.commerce.state.ak.us/occ/search3.htm
Viatical Settlement Broker............................ www.commerce.state.ak.us/ins/apps/producersearch/InsLicStart.cfm
Waste Water System Operator .... https://myalaska.state.ak.us/dec/water/opcert/Home.aspx?p=OperatorSearch
Wrestler.. www.commerce.state.ak.us/occ/search3.htm

State and Local Courts

State Court Structure: Alaska has a unified, centrally administered, and totally state-funded judicial system with 4 Judicial Districts. Municipal governments do not maintain separate court systems. Alaska has 19 boroughs or home rule cities or combination borough and home rule cities. Also 12 home rule cities do not directly coincide with the 4 Judicial Districts. In other words, judicial boundaries cross borough boundaries.

The four levels of courts in the Alaska Court System are the Supreme Court, the Court of Appeals, the Superior Court, and the District Court. Magistrate Courts preside over certain District Court matters. The magistrate is a judicial officer of the District Court.

The Supreme Court and Court of Appeals are appellate courts, while Superior Courts and District Courts are trial courts. The Superior Court Probate is handled by Superior Courts.

The Superior Court is a trial court for both criminal and civil cases. The District Court hears cases that involve hear state misdemeanors and violations of city and borough ordinances, first appearances and preliminary hearings in felony cases, record vital statistics (in some areas of the state), civil cases valued up to $100,000, small claims cases ($10,000 maximum), cases involving children on an emergency basis, and domestic violence cases.

Appellate Courts: The page at www.courts.alaska.gov gives access to Appellate opinions. Also, the site at http://government.westlaw.com/akcases/ provides access to opinions of the Alaska Supreme Court and Alaska Court of Appeals.

Statewide Court Online Access: All courts participate in the system described below.

The case summary and docket information for Alaska trial courts is found on Courtview at www.courtrecords.alaska.gov/eservices. Records available include civil criminal, traffic and wills. One may search by name, case number or ticket number, and give a date range on the DOB. Although all courts participate, the dates of the earliest available cases vary by court.

Caution: The site has had a history of problems recently regarding the display of certain pieces of data and also access to e-filings. See www.courts.alaska.gov/cvinfo.htm#problems to view the latest on these problems.

Other Sites: None – no individual courts offer online access to court records.

Recorders, Assessors, and Other Sites of Note

Recording Office Organization: The 23 Alaskan counties are called boroughs. However, real estate recording is is done by 34 Recording Districts under a system that was established at the time of the Gold Rush (1893-1916). Some of the Districts are identical in geography to boroughs such as the Aleutian Islands, but other boroughs and districts overlap. Therefore, you need to know which recording district any given town or city is located in. A helpful website is http://dnr.alaska.gov/ssd/recoff/findYourDistrict.htm

Statewide or Multi-Jurisdiction Access: The state Recorder's Office at the Dept. of Natural Resources provides a search site for all Recorder's Offices in the state. See below.

- Search recorded documents by many ways including name, date, doc #, doc type,, plat, survey, free on the statewide system at http://recorder.alaska.gov/searchRO.cfm. Search entire state or by recording district. Images go back to June, 2001; index to 2000. The agency is working on a film converison with plans to display images back to 1973.

Local Sites Other Than Statewide Site Mentioned Above:

Anchorage District ***Property, Taxation Records*** Access appraisal data free at www.muni.org/pw/public.html.

Fairbanks District ***Property, Taxation Records*** Access to the Fairbanks North Star Borough property database is free online at www.co.fairbanks.ak.us/Assessing/propsearch.aspx.

Juneau District ***Property, Taxation Records*** Access to City of Juneau Property Records database is free online at www.juneau.org/assessordata/sqlassessor.php.

Homer District ***Property, Taxation Records*** Access borough tax assessor rolls free at http://ak-kenai-property.governmax.com/propertymax/rover30.asp.

Kenai District ***Property, Taxation Records*** Access to Kenai Peninsula Borough Assessing Dept. Public Information Search Page is free at www.borough.kenai.ak.us/assessingdept/Default.htm.

Seldovia District, c/o Homer District ***Property, Taxation Records*** Access borough tax assessor rolls is free at http://ak-kenai-property.governmax.com/propertymax/rover30.asp. Also, view Parcel Maps by pdf or tiff free at www2.borough.kenai.ak.us/Assessingdept/maps.htm. Parcel file downloads are also available. Plat maps and surveys are free on the statewide system at http://recorder.alaska.gov/search.cfm.

Seward District ***Property, Taxation Records*** Access borough tax assessor rolls is free at http://ak-kenai-property.governmax.com/propertymax/rover30.asp.

Kodiak District ***Property, Taxation Records*** Search property assessor real property records free at www.kodiakak.us/. Click on \"Real Property Records.\"

Palmer District ***Property, Taxation Records*** Access borough property and property tax data free at www.matsugov.us/myproperty//

Talkeetna District, c/o Palmer District ***Property, Taxation Records*** Access borough property and property tax data free at www.matsugov.us/myproperty/.

Skagway District, c/o Juneau District ***Property, Taxation Records*** A citywide assessor is free at www.juneau.org/index.php

Reminder:

Search recorded documents statewide or by recording district in many ways including name, date, doc #, doc type,, plat, survey, free on the statewide system at http://recorder.alaska.gov/searchRO.cfm. Images go back to June, 2001; index to 2000. The agency is working on a film converison with plans to display images back to 1973.

Arizona

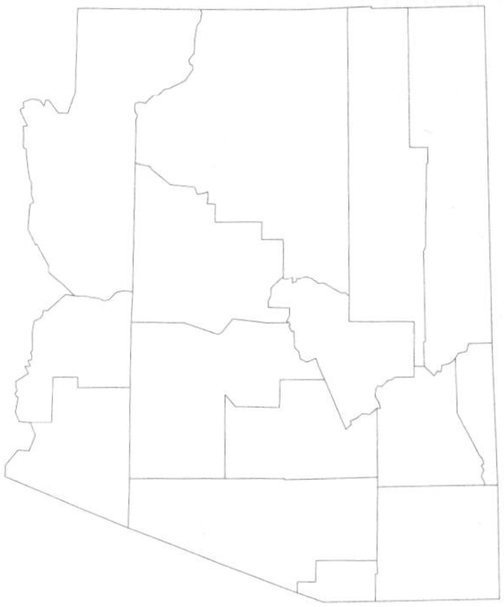

Capital: Phoenix
Maricopa County
Time Zone: MST
Population: 6,553,255
# of Counties: 15

Useful State Links

Website: http://az.gov
Governor: www.governor.state.az.us
Attorney General: www.azag.gov
State Archives: www.lib.az.us/archives/
State Statutes and Codes: www.azleg.state.az.us/ArizonaRevisedStatutes.asp
Legislative Bill Search: www.azleg.state.az.us/Bills.asp
Bill Monitoring: http://alistrack.azleg.state.az.us/
Unclaimed Funds: www.azunclaimed.gov/

Editor's Tip: Arizona, which is on Mountain Standard Time, does not observe Daylight Savings Time rules. Thus, from the first Sunday in April to the last Sunday in October, nearly all Arizona locations will have the same clock time as Pacific Daylight Time, the same time as in California.

But there are exceptions. Some Arizona Indian Reservation offices may observe Daylight Savings Time. Notable is the Navajo Nation Indian Reservation in northeastern Arizona. This does not include the Hopi Indian Reservation, which is surrounded by the Navajos.

State Public Record Agencies

Sexual Offender Registry

Department of Public Safety, Sex Offender Compliance, www.azdps.gov/Services/Sex_Offender/ Searching of Level 2 and Level 3 offenders is available online at https://az.gov/app/sows/home.xhtml. Search for an individual by name, or search by ZIP Code or address for known offenders. The site also lists, with pictures, absconders who are individuals whose whereabouts are unknown. *Other Options:* A download is available from the webpage for $25.00.

Incarceration Records

Arizona Department of Corrections, Records Department, www.azcorrections.gov/ For online search, you must provide last name, first initial or ADC number. Any add'l identifiers are welcomed. Location, ADC number, physical identifiers and sentencing information are released. Inmates admitted and released from 1972 to 1985 may not be searchable on the web. Also available is ADC Fugitives - an alphabetical Inmate Datasearch listing of Absconders and Escapees from ADC.

Corporation, LLC Records

Corporation Commission, Corporation Records, www.azcc.gov/divisions/corporations/ STARPAS, functioning 24/7 is a resource for searching the index and viewing documents (without SSNs). Go to http://starpas.azcc.gov/scripts/cgiip.exe/WService=wsbroker1/main.p. Another site, https://edocket.azcc.gov/, gives access to the Corporation Commission's official dockets and rule-making proceedings, referred herein as cases or dockets.

Also, search Corp Commission's Securities Division Actions, Orders and Admin. Decisions pages at www.azcc.gov/divisions/securities/enforcement/. *Other Options:* To purchase the database or in bulk, see www.azcc.gov/Divisions/Corporations/starpas1/rec2003.pdf. Call 602-364-4433.

Partnerships, LP, LLP, Trademarks/Servicemarks, Trade Names

Secretary of State, Trademarks/Tradenames/Limited Partnership Division, www.azsos.gov/business_services/TNT/Default.htm The website links to three searchable databases. One searches for Registered Names, Trade Names, and Trademarks. Also available is the full Trade Name and Trademark index in data format. Other lists the registered names in alpha order and states the type of records available. Another way to obtain this data is from http://starpas.azcc.gov/scripts/cgiip.exe/WService=wsbroker1/main.p - from the Corp Commission. *Other Options:* Bulk purchase is available on CD or microfiche.

Uniform Commercial Code, Federal & State Tax Liens

UCC Division, Secretary of State, www.azsos.gov/business_services/UCC/ The UCC record index can be searched for free at www.azsos.gov/scripts/ucc_search.dll. Searching can be done by debtor, secured party name, or file number. Images are available on records since 5/1994. SSNs have been redacted. Filings that exist before May 1994 have fiche locations at the bottom of the details page. *Other Options:* The agency offers six options of bulk database purchases. Requests must be in writing using their request form which can be downloaded from the web.

Sales Tax Registrations

Revenue Department, Transaction (Sales) Tax Licenses and Registration, www.azdor.gov/ Search sales tax registrations by tax number online free at https://www.aztaxes.gov/default.aspx?target=LicenseVerification. Must be eight digits.

Birth Certificates, Death Records

Department of Health Services, Vital Records Section, www.azdhs.gov/vitalrcd/index.htm Records may be ordered online via www.vitalchek.com, a state-endorsed vendor. Images of birth certificates from 1887 to 1934 are available free online at http://genealogy.az.gov. Death certificates 1878-1959 are also available. **$$$**

Driver Records

Motor Vehicle Division, Correspondence Unit, www.azdot.gov/mvd/index.asp Arizona's commercial online system (MVRRS) is interactive and batch and open 24 hours daily. Fee is $3.25 per record. This system is primarily for those requesters who qualify per DPPA. For more information call 602-712-7235. Interactive records have a fee of $6.00 (39-month) and $8.00 (5-year). This includes all portal fees. For more information about MVRRS, contact the Electronic Data Services Unit by email at eds@azdot.gov or call 602-712-7235. The site also permits licensed driver to view their own record. Fee is $3.00 and use of a credit card is required. Visit www.servicearizona.com. CDL holders and/or persons applying for a CDL who submitted their medical certification may review the status of their certification at www.azdot.gov/mvd/medicalreview/cdlstatus.asp. **$$$**

Vehicle Ownership & Registration

Motor Vehicle Division - Director's Office, Record Services Section, www.azdot.gov/mvd/index.asp The Motor Vehicle Record Request System (MVRRS) is the single access point for electronic title and registration records. This is only for authorized users. There is a $1.25 "portal fee" added to the normal record $3.00 charge. For more information contact the Electronic Data Services Units at 602-712-7235 or eds@azdot.gov. The MVD also offers access for vehicle owners to view and print their own title and registration records. The fee is $3.00 per record and use of a credit card is required. Visit www.servicearizona.com. **$$$** *Other Options:* Check the attorney general's stolen vehicle list free at https://theftaz.azag.gov/.

Voter Registration, Campaign Finance, PAC, Lobbyists

Secretary of State, Election Division, www.azsos.gov/election/ A search of candidates' campaign finance is found at www.azsos.gov/cfs/CandidateSummarySearch.aspx. SuperPAC Committees are found at www.azsos.gov/cfs/SuperPACList.aspx. A search of lobbyists is at www.azsos.gov/scripts/Lobbyist_Search.dll.

Occupational Licensing Boards

Accountant-CPA/PA/Firm .... www.azaccountancy.gov/CPADirectory/CPASearch.aspx
Acupuncturist .... www.azacupunctureboard.us/ASPSearch.html
Acupuncturist School .... www.azacupunctureboard.us/schools.html
Adoption Investigator/Searcher.................... www.azcourts.gov/cld/ConfidentialIntermediaryProgram.aspx
Adult Care Home Manager .... www.aznciaboard.us/managers.html
Advance Fee Loan Broker .... http://azdfi.gov/Consumers/Licensees/LicenseeList.html
Aerial Applicator, Pesticide .... www.kellysolutions.com/az/Pilots/index.asp
Agricultural Grower/Seller/Permit................. www.kellysolutions.com/az/RUPBuyers/index.asp
Agricultural Pest Control Advisor .... www.kellysolutions.com/az/PCA/index.asp
Aircraft Use Fuel Dealer/Mfg........................ https://www.aztaxes.gov/default.aspx
Ambulance Service, Air............................... http://azdhs.gov/bems/documents/ambulance/air/LicensedAirProviders.pdf

Ambulance Service, Ground	http://azdhs.gov/bems/documents/ambulance/ground/con-provider-list.pdf
Ambulatory Surgical Ctr	www.azdhs.gov/als/search/index.htm
Amusement Park/Printing/Advertising	https://www.aztaxes.gov/default.aspx
Animimal Crematory	www.vetbd.state.az.us/divisions/default.aspx
Applicator, Pesticide, Private/Commercial	www.kellysolutions.com/AZ/Applicators/index.asp
Appraisal Management Company	www.appraisal.state.az.us/AMCs.aspx
Appraiser, Real Estate/Personal Property	https://www.aztaxes.gov/default.aspx
Architect	www.btr.state.az.us/listings/professional_registrant2.asp
Assayer	www.btr.state.az.us/listings/professional_registrant2.asp
Assisted Living Facility/Manager	www.azdhs.gov/als/search/index.htm
Attorney	www.azbar.org/FindaLawyer
Audiologist	www.azdhs.gov/als/search/index.htm
Bank, State Chartered	http://azdfi.gov/Consumers/Licensees/LicenseeList.html
Barber School/Instruction	www.azbarberboard.us/schools.html
Barber/Barber Shop	www.azbarberboard.us/dir.html
Behavior Analyst	www.psychboard.az.gov/PsySearch.asp?licenseTypeId=2
Behavioral Health Emerg'y/Resi. Svcs	www.azdhs.gov/als/databases/
Behavioral Outpatient Clinic/Rehab	www.azdhs.gov/als/databases/
Bingo Operation	https://www.aztaxes.gov/default.aspx
Bondsman (Insurance)	https://az.gov/app/doilookup/
Bone Densitometer Operator	https://az.gov/app/mrtbe/certificatesearch.xhtml
Cannabis/Control'd Substance Dealer	https://www.aztaxes.gov/default.aspx
Charity	www.azsos.gov/scripts/Charity_Search.dll
Charter School	www.ade.az.gov/charterschools/search/
Child Care	www.azdhs.gov/als/search/index.htm
Child Residential Home	www.azdhs.gov/als/databases/providers_cc.pdf
Chiropractor/Acupuncturist	www.azchiroboard.us/ASPSearch.html
Citrus Broker	www.azda.gov/cfv/CompanysWithCurrentLicenses.pdf
Clinic, Recovery Care	www.azdhs.gov/als/search/index.htm
Clinic, Rural Health	www.azdhs.gov/als/search/index.htm
Clinical Laboratory	https://app.azdhs.gov/BFS/LABS/ELBIS/ArizonaCertifiedLabs/
Collection Agency	http://azdfi.gov/Consumers/Licensees/LicenseeList.html
Commercial Leasing	https://www.aztaxes.gov/default.aspx
Confidential Intermediary	www.azcourts.gov/Portals/26/CIP/pdf/2011/012811CIDirectory.pdf
Consumer Lender	http://azdfi.gov/Consumers/Licensees/LicenseeList.html
Contractor	https://elicense02.az.gov/app/roc/#
Cosmetologist/Nail Technician	https://azboc.irondata.com/datamart/mainMenu.do;jsessionid=AD0F4358E9FB3F8E198567F9D8F0F20D
Cosmetology/Salon/School/Instruct'r	www.beautyschoolsdirectory.com/find/index.php?search=Y&t=ALL&st=AZ
Counselor, Professional	http://azbbhe.us/verifications.htm
Court Reporter	www.azcourts.gov/Portals/26/CourtReporter/pdf/2011/71911CRDirectory.pdf
Credit Union, State Chartered	http://azdfi.gov/Consumers/Licensees/LicenseeList.html
Crematory/Funeral Establishment	www.azfuneralboard.us/dir.html
Day Care Establishment	http://hsapps.azdhs.gov/ls/sod/SearchProv.aspx?type=CC
Debt Management Company	http://azdfi.gov/Consumers/Licensees/LicenseeList.html
Defensive Driving Instructor	www.azcourts.gov/drive/SchoolandInstructorCertificationInformation.aspx
Defensive Driving School	www.azcourts.gov/drive/ListofCertifiedSchools.aspx
Deferred Presentment Company	http://azdfi.gov/Consumers/Licensees/LicenseeList.html
Dental Office	https://azbod.glsuite.us/glsuiteweb/clients/azbod/public/WebVerificationSearch.aspx
Dentist/Assistant/Hygienist	https://azbod.glsuite.us/glsuiteweb/clients/azbod/public/WebVerificationSearch.aspx
Denturist/Denture Technologist	https://azbod.glsuite.us/glsuiteweb/clients/azbod/public/WebVerificationSearch.aspx
Detoxification Service	www.azdhs.gov/als/databases/
Developmentally Disab'd Group Home	www.azdhs.gov/als/search/index.htm
Dispensing Naturopath	www.aznd.gov/agency/pages/directorysearch.asp
Drug Mfg/Wholesaler	https://az.gov/app/pharmacy/search.xhtml
Drug, Retail non-prescription	https://az.gov/app/pharmacy/search.xhtml

Dry Well Registration .... www.azdeq.gov/databases/drywellsearch.html
Embalmer/Cremationist/Assistant/Intern...... www.azfuneralboard.us/dir.html
Emergency Medical Tech/Instructor .... http://azdhs.gov/bems/certification/index.htm
Engineer.. www.btr.state.az.us/listings/professional_registrant2.asp
Environmental Laboratory........................... https://app.azdhs.gov/BFS/LABS/ELBIS/ArizonaCertifiedLabs/
Equine Dental Practitioners .... www.vetbd.state.az.us/equine.aspx
Escrow Agent.. http://azdfi.gov/Consumers/Licensees/LicenseeList.html
Family Day Care Home............................... www.azdhs.gov/als/databases/providers_cc.pdf
Feed Dealer/Wholesaler/Distribution .... www.kellysolutions.com/az/feeddealers/index.asp
Fertilizer Dealer/Distribution, Commercial ... www.kellysolutions.com/az/FertDealers/index.asp
Fertilizer Product... www.kellysolutions.com/AZ/Fertilizer/fertilizerindex.asp
Fiduciary.. www.azcourts.gov/Portals/26/fiduciary/2011/71911FiduciaryDirectory.pdf
Food Establishment.www.maricopa.gov/EnvSvc/envwebapp/business_search.aspx?as_page_title=Food%20Establishments%20Search&as_type=Food
Fruit Broker .... www.azda.gov/cfv/CompanysWithCurrentLicenses.pdf
Funeral Director .... www.azfuneralboard.us/dir.html
Funeral Pre-Need Trust Company.............. http://azdfi.gov/Consumers/Licensees/LicenseeList.html
Geologist... www.btr.state.az.us/listings/professional_registrant2.asp
Group Home, Development Disabled .... www.azdhs.gov/als/search/index.htm
Group Home, Small..................................... www.azdhs.gov/als/search/index.htm
Health Clinic.. www.azdhs.gov/als/search/index.htm
Health Screening Service .... https://app.azdhs.gov/BFS/LABS/ELBIS/ArizonaCertifiedLabs/
Hearing Aid Dispenser................................ www.azdhs.gov/als/search/index.htm
Highway Engineer....................................... www.btr.state.az.us/listings/professional_registrant2.asp
Home Health Agency .... www.azdhs.gov/als/search/index.htm
Home Inspector... www.btr.state.az.us/listings/professional_registrant2.asp
Homeopathic Physician .... www.azhomeopathbd.az.gov/phy_dir.html
Hospice .... www.azdhs.gov/als/search/index.htm
Hospital .... www.azdhs.gov/als/search/index.htm
Hospital, Adv'd Life Support (EMS) .... http://azdhs.gov/bems/documents/hospitals/CertifiedALSBaseHospitals.pdf
Infirmary .... www.azdhs.gov/als/search/index.htm
Insurance Producer..................................... https://az.gov/app/doilookup/
Investment Advisor/Rep. .... www.adviserinfo.sec.gov/(S(f3iim33mmpytaq5552khgte3))/IAPD/Content/Search/iapd_Search.aspx
Juvenile Group Home .... www.azdhs.gov/als/search/index.htm
Landscape Architect .... www.btr.state.az.us/listings/professional_registrant2.asp
Laser Light Show .... https://www.aztaxes.gov/default.aspx
Legal Document Preparer............................ http://azcourts.gov/Portals/26/LDP/2010/2011/12611LDPDirectory.pdf
Liquor Producer/Whlse .... www.azliquor.gov/query/query.cfm
Liquor Retail Co-Operative/Agent/Mgr......... www.azliquor.gov/query/query.cfm
Lobbyist... www.azsos.gov/scripts/Lobbyist_Search.dll
Long Term Care Facility.............................. www.azdhs.gov/als/search/index.htm
Lottery Retailer.. www.arizonalottery.com/FindARetailer.html
Mammography Technologist........................ https://az.gov/app/mrtbe/certificatesearch.xhtml
Manufactured Home Dealer/Mfg................. www.dfbls.az.gov/omh.aspx
Marriage & Family Therapist........................ http://azbbhe.us/verifications.htm
Massage Therapy School .... www.npbomex.az.gov/school_directory.asp
Medical Facility.. www.azdhs.gov/als/search/index.htm
Medical Gas Dist/Supplier........................... https://az.gov/app/pharmacy/search.xhtml
Mentally Retarded Care Facility.................. www.azdhs.gov/als/search/index.htm
Midwife .... www.azdhs.gov/als/databases/providers_mw.pdf
Mobile Home Dealer/Broker/Seller .... www.dfbls.az.gov/omh/licensing/salesperson.aspx
Mobile Home Installer/Mfg. .... www.dfbls.az.gov/omh.aspx
Money Transmitter .... http://azdfi.gov/Consumers/Licensees/LicenseeList.html
Mortgage Banker/BrokerCommercial........... http://azdfi.gov/Consumers/Licensees/LicenseeList.html
Motor Vehicle Dealer/Sales Finance............ http://azdfi.gov/Consumers/Licensees/LicenseeList.html
Naturopathic Medical Asst. .... www.aznd.gov/agency/pages/directorysearch.asp

Naturopathic Physician .... www.aznd.gov/agency/pages/directorysearch.asp
Naturopathic School.................................... www.aznd.gov/PDF/School%20nov%2020120001.pdf
Neuro Rehab Center.................................. www.azdhs.gov/als/search/index.htm
Notary Public.. www.azsos.gov/scripts/Notary_Search.dll
Nuclear Medicine Technologist.................... https://az.gov/app/mrtbe/certificatesearch.xhtml
Nurse-LPN/RN/Aide................................... https://www.azbn.gov/OnlineVerification.aspx
Nursing Care Inst Administrator.................. www.aznciaboard.us/administrators.html
Occupational Therapist/Assistant .... www.occupationaltherapyboard.az.gov/licensee_directory/default.asp
Off-Track Betting/Wagering Facility .... www.azracing.gov/OTB/otbsitesbyarea.pdf
On Site Worker/Superv'r .... www.btr.state.az.us/listings/professional_registrant2.asp
Optical Establishment .... www.do.az.gov/directory/default.asp
Optician .... www.do.az.gov/directory/default.asp
Optometrist... www.optometry.az.gov/directory.asp
Osteopathic Physician .... www.azmd.gov/GLSPages/DoctorSearch.aspx
Osteopathic Physician/Surgeon.................. www.azdo.gov/GLSPages/DoctorSearch.aspx
Out-Patient Physical Therapy .... www.azdhs.gov/als/search/index.htm
Out-Patient Surgical Center........................ www.azdhs.gov/als/search/index.htm
Outpatient Treatment Clinic .... www.azdhs.gov/als/search/index.htm
P&C Managing Agent, Life/Disability .... https://az.gov/app/doilookup/
Packer, Fruit/Vegetable .... www.azda.gov/cfv/CompanysWithCurrentLicenses.pdf
Pesticide Applicator/Supv./Advisor .... www.sb.state.az.us/PCProfSearch.php
Pesticide Company .... www.sb.state.az.us/PCBusSearch.php
Pesticide Custom Applicator....................... www.kellysolutions.com/az/CustomAppl/index.asp
Pesticide Distribution/Seller .... www.kellysolutions.com/az/Dealers/index.asp
Pesticide Registration .... www.kellysolutions.com/az/pesticideindex.htm
Pharmacist/Pharmacy Intern....................... https://az.gov/app/pharmacy/search.xhtml
Physical Therapist/Therapist Asst............... www.ptboard.az.gov/public1/pages/ptSearchEngine.asp
Physician/Assistant/Intern/Resident............ www.azmd.gov/GLSPages/DoctorSearch.aspx
Physiotherapist... www.azchiroboard.us/ASPSearch.html
Pipeline .... https://www.aztaxes.gov/default.aspx
Plant Operator.. www.azdeq.gov/databases/opcertsearch.html
Podiatrist .... www.podiatry.state.az.us/dir.htm
Political Action Committee .... www.azsos.gov/cfs/SuperPACList.aspx
Post-Secondary Educ Institution................. http://azppse.state.az.us/Licensee/LicenseeSearch.aspx
Post-Secondary Voc. Program, Private .... http://azppse.state.az.us/Licensee/LicenseeSearch.aspx
Pre-Need Endorsement, Establishm't.......... www.azfuneralboard.us/dir.html
Pre-Need Salesperson................................ www.azfuneralboard.us/dir.html
Premium Finance Company .... http://azdfi.gov/Consumers/Licensees/LicenseeList.html
Preschool/Headstart Facility .... http://hsapps.azdhs.gov/ls/sod/SearchProv.aspx?type=CC
Private Investigator .... http://webapps.azdps.gov/public_inq/sgrd/ShowLicenseStatus.action
Process Server, Private www.azcourts.gov/Portals/26/PPS/procsvrsactivelist05022013.pdf
Property Tax Agent..................................... www.appraisal.state.az.us/directory/Default.aspx
Psychologist.. www.psychboard.az.gov/PsySearch.asp?licenseTypeId=2
Radiation Handler/Machine......................... https://az.gov/app/mrtbe/
Radiologic Technologist.............................. https://az.gov/app/mrtbe/certificatesearch.xhtml
Radiology Practical Technologist................. https://az.gov/app/mrtbe/certificatesearch.xhtml
Real Estate Agent/Broker/Sales .... http://159.87.254.2/publicdatabase/SearchIndividuals.aspx?mode=2
Real Estate Appraiser................................. www.appraisal.state.az.us/directory/Default.aspx
Real Estate School/Course......................... http://159.87.254.2/publicdatabase/SearchSchools.aspx?mode=3
Recovery Center... www.azdhs.gov/als/search/index.htm
Registered Medical Assistant...................... www.azhomeopathbd.az.gov/asst_dir.asp
Rehabilitation Agency .... www.azdhs.gov/als/search/index.htm
Remediation Specialist .... www.btr.state.az.us/listings/professional_registrant2.asp
Renal Disease Facility .... www.azdhs.gov/als/search/index.htm
Rental of Personal Property........................ https://www.aztaxes.gov/default.aspx

Respiratory Therapist................................. https://az.gov/app/rce/appstatus-inquiry.xhtml
Restaurant/Bar... https://www.aztaxes.gov/default.aspx
Retail Sales Outlet .... https://www.aztaxes.gov/default.aspx
Risk Management Producers...................... https://az.gov/app/doilookup/
Sales Finance Company............................. http://azdfi.gov/Consumers/Licensees/LicenseeList.html
Sanitarian.. www.azdhs.gov/phs/oeh/rs/pdf/ActiveAZSanitarians.pdf
Savings and Loan, Chartered .... http://azdfi.gov/Consumers/Licensees/LicenseeList.html
Scanner, Electronic System........................ http://azdwm.gov/dwm/pv/Inspection_Search.asp
Security Guard .... http://webapps.azdps.gov/public_inq/sgrd/ShowLicenseStatus.action
Seed Dealer .... www.kellysolutions.com/az/SeedDealers/index.asp
Seed Labeler.. www.kellysolutions.com/az/SeedLabelers/index.asp
Social Worker... http://azbbhe.us/verifications.htm
Solar Energy Device .... https://www.aztaxes.gov/default.aspx
Speech Pathology....................................... www.azdhs.gov/als/search/index.htm
Speech-Language Pathologist.................... www.azdhs.gov/als/search/index.htm
Subdivision Public Report.......................... http://159.87.254.2/publicdatabase/SearchDevelopments.aspx?mode=2
Substance Abuse Counselor .... http://azbbhe.us/verifications.htm
Surety... https://az.gov/app/doilookup/
Surplus Line Broker.................................... https://az.gov/app/doilookup/
Surveyor, Land... www.btr.state.az.us/listings/professional_registrant2.asp
Telemarketing Firm .... www.azsos.gov/business_services/TS/
Timbering .... https://www.aztaxes.gov/default.aspx
Tobacco Product Distributor .... https://www.aztaxes.gov/default.aspx
Transporting/Towing Company................... https://www.aztaxes.gov/default.aspx
Travel Agent, Limited .... https://az.gov/app/doilookup/
Treatment Clinic.. www.azdhs.gov/als/search/index.htm
Trust Company... http://azdfi.gov/Consumers/Licensees/LicenseeList.html
Trust Div. of Chartered Financial Inst. .... http://azdfi.gov/Consumers/Licensees/LicenseeList.html
Vendor.. https://www.aztaxes.gov/default.aspx
Veterinary Medicine/Surgery....................... www.vetbd.state.az.us/divisions/default.aspx
Veterinary Premise (Hospital)..................... www.vetbd.state.az.us/divisions/default.aspx
Veterinary Technician .... www.vetbd.state.az.us/divisions/default.aspx
Waste Water Facility Operator.................... www.azdeq.gov/databases/opcertsearch.html
Water Distribution System Operator .... www.azdeq.gov/databases/opcertsearch.html
Well Drilling Firm.. www.azwater.gov/azdwr/default.aspx
Well Registration/Construction.................... https://gisweb.azwater.gov/waterresourcedata/
X-Ray Supplier (Portable)........................... www.azdhs.gov/als/search/index.htm

State and Local Courts

State Court Structure: The **Superior Court** is the court of general jurisdiction and acts as an appellate court for Justice and Municipal courts. The Superior Court hears felony, misdemeanor (if not heard elsewhere), civil, property cases of $1,000 or more, eviction, probate, estate, divorce and naturalization issues. Justice Courts and Municipal Courts generally have separate jurisdiction over lessor case types. Estate cases are handled by Superior Court.

Appellate Courts: The page at www.azcourts.gov gives access to Appellate opinions and summaries.

About Court Online Access: There is no single source of statewide access but a near statewide system exists.

- **The Public Access to Court Case Information** online system provided by Administrative Office of the Courts (AOC) contains information about court cases for a majority of the courts in Arizona. **But courts not covered include certain courts in the counties with the highest populations: Pima, Yavapai and Maricopa counties.** Information provided includes detailed case information (i.e., case type, charges, filing and disposition dates), the parties in the case (not including victims and witnesses), and the court mailing address and location. Plus municipal courts are not included. For more information go to http://apps.supremecourt.az.gov/publicaccess/. Please note the site has a strong disclaimer which states in part "...not all cases from a participating court may be included....information should not be used as a substitute for a thorough background search of official public records..."

County Sites Not Part of the Public Access Site Mentioned Above:

Maricopa County

Superior Court www.clerkofcourt.maricopa.gov/

Civil: Public access at http://apps.supremecourt.az.gov/publicaccess/caselookup.aspx. *Criminal:* Access to criminal dockets is free at www.superiorcourt.maricopa.gov/docket/index.asp. Case file docket can be printed. Search by first and last name or by business name or by case number. Images not shown. Access is now also available at the Public Access system at http://apps.supremecourt.az.gov/publicaccess/. Due to name variations and aliases, online search result dockets can be misinterpreted - use caution.

All Justice Courts http://justicecourts.maricopa.gov/Locations/index.aspx

Civil: Access court index free on countywide site at www.superiorcourt.maricopa.gov/docket/JusticeCourtCases/caseSearch.asp. Can be incomplete dockets, also expired data online. *Criminal:* Online access same as civil, however chance of DOB appearing is greater.

Pima County

Superior Court www.cosc.co.pima.az.us

Civil: Online access to superior court records is free at www.agave.cosc.pima.gov/PublicDocs/. Search by name, business name, or by case number.

Pima County Consolidated Justice Court www.jp.pima.gov/

Civil: Online access is free http://jp.co.pima.az.us/casesearch/CaseSearch.aspx. You can search docket information for civil, criminal or traffic cases by name, docket or citation number. This site does not include the other Justice Courts in this county. *Criminal:* same This site does not include the other Justice Courts in this county. The system shows the month and year, but not day of birth. It costs $3.00 to obtain the complete DOB.

Yavapai County

Prescott Justice Court www.prescottjpcourt.com

Civil: Access to City and Justice court records is free at www.prescottjpcourt.com/csp/pcc/csp1.csp. *Criminal:* Access to City Court and Justice Court records is free at www.prescottjpcourt.com/csp/pcc/csp1.csp.

Recorders, Assessors, and Other Sites of Note

Recording Office Organization: 15 counties, 16 recording offices (the Navajo Nation Recorder is the 16th office and covers northern parts of Apache and Navajo Counties). Recording officers are the County Recorders. Recordings are usually placed in a Grantor/Grantee index. Federal and state tax liens on personal property of businesses are filed with the Secretary of State. Federal and state tax liens on individuals are filed with the County Recorder.

Statewide or Multi-Jurisdiction Access: There is no statewide access site. Most county assessor offices do offer online access. There is one vendor offering access to county recorder public documents free for Apache, Cochise, Graham, Greenlee, LaPaz, Navajo and Santa Cruz Counties. See www.thecountyrecorder.com.

County Sites:

Apache County ***Recorded Documents*** www.co.apache.az.us/Recorder/ Access to the recorder is free at www.thecountyrecorder.com/Disclaimer.aspx. Index goes back to 1985.

Property, Taxation Records Access assessor search page free at www.co.apache.az.us/parcelsearch/parcelsearch.aspx.

Cochise County ***Recorded Documents*** www.co.cochise.az.us/recorders/Default.htm Access the recorder office document search site free at www.thecountyrecorder.com/Disclaimer.aspx. Index goes back to 1985.

Property, Taxation Records Access the treasurer's back tax list free at www.cochise.az.gov/cochise_treasurer.aspx?id=68&ekmensel=c580fa7b_148_0_68_4.

Coconino County ***Recorded Documents*** www.coconino.az.gov/index.aspx?nid=319 Access the recorder system free at http://eaglerecorder.coconino.az.gov/recorder/web/. Documents are $1.00 to print; images back to 3/1999. Computer indexing from 1/1983 to present. For official or certified copies or inquiries on documents prior to 1983 please contact office at 928-679-7850 or 800-793-6181. **$$$**

Property, Taxation Records Search assessor data at http://assessor.coconino.az.gov/assessor/web/. Also, access to parcel viewer free at http://gismaps.coconino.az.gov/parcelviewer/. Must register to create and print reports for properties free of charge.

Gila County ***Recorded Documents*** www.gilacountyaz.gov/government/recorder/index.php Access to grantor/grantee index from EagleWeb for a small fee go to http://recorder.gilacountyaz.gov/recorder/web/. **$$$**

Property, Taxation Records Search assessor property data and sales free at https://parcelsearch.gilacountyaz.gov/. Also, access to GIS/mapping free at www.gilacountyaz.gov/government/assessor/maps_and_record_surveys.php.

Graham County ***Recorded Documents*** www.graham.az.gov/Graham_CMS/Recorder.aspx?id=2414 Access to recorder records is at www.thecountyrecorder.com/Disclaimer.aspx. Index goes back to 1982, unofficial images go back to 1982.

Property, Taxation Records Access the assessor database of property and assessments free at http://72.165.8.87/parcelsearch/parcelsearch.aspx.

Greenlee County ***Recorded Documents*** www.co.greenlee.az.us/recorder/ Access to recorder records is free at www.thecountyrecorder.com/Disclaimer.aspx. Indexes back to 1977, unofficial images back to 1977.

Property, Taxation Records Search treasurer's tax lien sale list free at www.co.greenlee.az.us/treasurer/taxlien.pdf.

La Paz County ***Recorded Documents*** www.co.la-paz.az.us/ Access to the recorder documents at www.thecountyrecorder.com/Disclaimer.aspx. Index back to 1984.

Maricopa County ***Property, Taxation Records*** Assessor database is at http://mcassessor.maricopa.gov/assessor//NewParcel/Default.aspx. Also, perform tax appeal lookups at SBOE site at www.sboe.state.az.us/cgi-bin/name_lookup.pl. Search treasurers tax data and parcels by number free at http://treasurer.maricopa.gov/.

Mohave County ***Recorded Documents, Death Records*** www.mohavecounty.us/ContentPage.aspx?id=129 Access the Recorder's System free at http://eagleweb.co.mohave.az.us/recorder/web/login.jsp. Registration-password required; sign-up with IT Dept, x4357.

Property, Taxation Records Online access to the Assessor's property database is free at http://legacy.co.mohave.az.us/depts/assessor/prop_info.asp. A sales history also available. Tax maps at http://legacy.co.mohave.az.us/taxmaps/default.asp/. Property sales history back to 2000 free at http://legacy.co.mohave.az.us/1moweb/depts_files/assessor_files/saleshist.asp. Also, the treasurer's tax sale parcel search is at http://legacy.co.mohave.az.us/depts/treas/tax_sale.asp.

Navajo County ***Recorded Documents*** www.navajocountyaz.gov/recorder/ Access to the recorder's database at www.thecountyrecorder.com/Disclaimer.aspx. Index goes back to 1989; unofficial images to 1995.

Property, Taxation Records Access property assessor database free at www.navajocountyaz.gov/assessor/. Search the Navajo County assessor back tax auction list free at http://www.navajocountyaz.gov/bos/backtaxauction.aspx. Also, a Tax Lien Auction list is at found at www.navajocountyaz.gov/treasurer/delinquentlist.aspx

Pima County ***Recorded Documents*** www.recorder.pima.gov/ Access to records for free at http://service.recorder.pima.gov/publicdocuments/.

Property, Taxation Records Records on the Pima County Tax Assessor database are free at www.asr.co.pima.az.us/links/frm_AdvancedSearch_v2.aspx?search=Parcel. A name/parcel/property tax lookup may be performed free on the SBOE site at www.sboe.state.az.us/cgi-bin/name_lookup.pl.

Pinal County ***Recorded Documents*** http://pinalcountyaz.gov/Departments/Recorder/Pages/Recorder.aspx Access to the recorder's index is free at http://pinalcountyaz.gov/DEPARTMENTS/RECORDER/Pages/DocumentSearch.aspx.

Property, Taxation Records Search the assessor's property tax database free at www.pinalcountyaz.gov/Departments/Assessor/Pages/ParcelInfoSearch.aspx. Also, access to the county treasurer's database of tax liens, tax bills, and tax sales is free at http://pinalcountyaz.gov/Departments/Treasurer/Pages/TaxBillSearch.aspx.

Santa Cruz County ***Recorded Documents*** www.co.santa-cruz.az.us/recorder/index.html Access to the recorder's database of indices is free at www.thecountyrecorder.com/Disclaimer.aspx. Index back to 1986.

Property, Taxation Records Access County Assessor data free at http://parcelsearch.co.santa-cruz.az.us/parcelsearch.aspx.

Yavapai County ***Recorded Documents*** www.yavapai.us/recorder/ Access to the recording office Eagle Web database is free at http://eweb.co.yavapai.az.us/recorder/web/. Records from 1976 to present; images from 1976 to present.

Property, Taxation Records Assessor and land records on County GIS database are free at www.yavapai.us/mis/gis-mapping-applications/.

Yuma County ***Property, Taxation Records*** Access county assessment sales data free at http://treasurer.yumacountyaz.gov/treasurer/treasurerweb/search.jsp.

Arkansas

Capital: Little Rock
Pulaski County
Time Zone: CST
Population: 2,949,131
# of Counties: 75

Useful State Links

Website: http://portal.arkansas.gov/
Governor: www.governor.arkansas.gov
Attorney General: www.ag.state.ar.us
State Archives: www.ark-ives.com
State Statutes and Codes: www.lexisnexis.com/hottopics/arcode/Default.asp
Legislative Bill Search: www.arkleg.state.ar.us/SearchCenter/Pages/historicalbil.aspx
Unclaimed Funds: 'http://auditor.ar.gov/Pages/default.aspx

State Public Record Agencies

Criminal Records

Arkansas State Police, Identification Bureau, www.asp.arkansas.gov Online access available to only employers or their agents (with written consent on file), and professional licensing boards. A subscriber account with the Information Network of Arkansas (INA) is required, a $95 annual fee is imposed. The search fee is $22.00. Searches are conducted by name. Search results includes registered sex offenders. For more info on this online service, see https://www.ark.org/criminal/index.php. Accounts must maintain the signed release documents in-house for three years. Visit https://www.ark.org/subscribe/index.php for an excellent overview of all record types available. Results show felony and misdemeanor conviction record, any pending Arkansas felony arrests within the last three years, and whether the person is a registered sex offender or is required to be registered. **$$$**

Sexual Offender Registry

Arkansas Crime Information Center, Sexual Offender Registry, http://acic.org/citizens/Pages/sexOffenderInfo.aspx Searching is available at http://acic.org/offender-search/index.php. Search by name or location (county). Includes Level 3 and Level 4 offenders. Subscribers to the Information Network of Arkansas (INA) can download the database for $.10 per record. Visit www.arkansas.gov/sub_services.php. The annual subscription fee is $75.00; other record services are available. *Other Options:* Download the SOR data at https://www.ark.org/Registration/so_bulk.php. Fee is $.10 per record. **$$$**

Incarceration Records

Arkansas Department of Corrections, Records Supervisor, http://adc.arkansas.gov/Pages/default.aspx The online access at http://adc.arkansas.gov/inmate_info/index.php has many search criteria capabilities. Subscribers to the Information Network of Arkansas (INA) can download the database for $.10 per record. Visit www.arkansas.gov/sub_services.php. The annual subscription fee is $75.00; other record services are available. *Other Options:* The inmate access web page offers a download of the inmate database. Fee includes an annual INA subscription of $75.00 plus $0.10 per record enhanced access fee. The file is updated weekly. **$$$**

Corporation, Fictitious Name, LLC, Partnerships (LP, LLP LLLP, Foreign)

Secretary of State, Business & Commercial Service Division, www.sos.arkansas.gov/BCS/Pages/default.aspx The Internet site permits free searching of many types of business entity records at www.sos.arkansas.gov/BCS/Pages/default.aspx#bcsonlineservices. More extensive record searching is available in a fee-based format from Arkansas.gov). There is annual subscription is $95.00; other record services are available. The site also provides Franchise Tax filings, with both batch and single request services. Also, search securities companies registered with the state at www.securities.arkansas.gov/star/portal/arasd/portal.aspx. *Other Options:* Subscribers can download lists for $.10 per record with a $10.00 minimum, or obtain bulk downloads for $2000 per month. Visit www.arkansas.gov/sub_services.php; other record services are available. **$$$**

Trademarks/Servicemarks

Secretary of State, Trademarks Section, www.sos.arkansas.gov/BCS/Pages/trademarkServiceMark.aspx Searching is available at no fee at www.sos.arkansas.gov/corps/trademk/index.php. Search by name, owner, city, or filing number. Search via email at corprequest@sos.arkansas.gov *Other Options:* Records can be provided in bulk for $.50 per page. Call 501-682-3409 or visit website for details. **$$$**

Uniform Commercial Code, Federal Tax Liens

UCC Division - Commercial Svcs, Secretary of State, www.sos.arkansas.gov/BCS/Pages/uniformCommercialCodeServices.aspx Subscribers of Arkansas.gov can search by file number or debtor name; subscription fees and search fees involved. See www.sos.arkansas.gov/aboutOffice/Pages/SoSOnlineServices.aspx for subscription details. **$$$** *Other Options:* A download of UCC data is available via Arkansas.gov to subscribers. Fee is $2,000.00 per month for weekly, bi-weekly or monthly downloads.

Vital Records

Arkansas Department of Health, Division of Vital Records, www.healthy.arkansas.gov/Pages/default.aspx Orders can be placed via a state designated vendor. Go to www.vitalchek.com. Extra fees are involved. **$$$** *Other Options:* Research projects require the approval of the director.

Workers' Compensation Records

Workers Compensation Commission, Operations/Compliance, www.awcc.state.ar.us To perform an online claim search, one must be a subscriber to Arkansas.gov. Records are from May 1, 1997 forward. There is an annual $95 subscriber fee. Each record request is $3.50; if more than 20 are ordered in one month, the fee is $2.50 each request over 20. For more information, visit www.awcc.state.ar.us/electron.html or https://www.ark.org/subscribe/index.php. **$$$** *Other Options:* Subscribers to t Arkansas.gov can obtain a bulk download s for a one-time $5000 fee then $100 per month. Visit www.arkansas.gov/sub_services.php. Annual subscription is $95.00; other record services are available.

Driver Records

Department of Driver Services, Driving Records Division, www.dfa.arkansas.gov/offices/driverServices/Pages/default.aspx Access is available through Arkansas.gov. The system offers both batch and interactive service. The system is only available to INA subscribers who have statutory rights to the data. The record fee is $8.50 for insurance record or $11.50 for commercial record. Visit www.arkansas.gov/sub_services.php. The annual subscription fee is $95.00, other record services are available. AR drivers may purchase their own record, to view and print, online at https://www.ark.org/personal_tvr/index.php. The same fees apply. The date the DL was issued is required with name, DOB, DL#, and partial SSN. **$$$** *Other Options:* A commercial Driver Watch is a available to subscribers who have statutory rights to the data. Companies who wish to monitor the driving record status of their employees may set up profiles and have the system notify them of a change in driving status. **$$$**

Vehicle Ownership & Registration

Office of Motor Vehicles, MV Title Records, www.dfa.arkansas.gov/offices/motorVehicle/Pages/default.aspx Approved, DPPA compliant accounts may access records online by VIN, plate, or title number. The fee is $1.50. Name searches and certificated documents may be ordered. For further info, go to www.arkansas.gov/sub_services.php. There is a $95 annual subscription fee, other records are also available. **$$$** *Other Options:* The bulk purchase of records, except for recall or statistical purposes, is prohibited.

Accident Reports

Arkansas State Police, Crash Records Section, www.asp.state.ar.us/divisions/rs/rs_crash.html Information is available from https://www.ark.org/grs/app/asp. There is no fee to view, but a PDF copy may be purchased for $12.00. Search by name, license number and/or date range. Once purchased, reports will be available for 30 days and may be repeatedly accessed with an Order ID. For further information regarding the contents of the report, please contact the Arkansas State Police at 501-618-8130. Credit card is required, unless requester is subscriber to Arkansas.gov. Available records date back to 01/02/2000, but not all crash reports are available for online purchase. **$$$**

Voter Registration, Campaign Finance, PAC, Lobbyists

Secretary of State, Voter Services, www.sos.arkansas.gov/elections/Pages/default.aspx Search one's voter registration information at https://www.voterview.ar-nova.org/VoterView/RegistrantSearch.do. Name and DOB required. A financial disclosure search for all election related entities, including lobbyists, PACs and candidates, is found at www.sos.arkansas.gov/filing_search/index.php/filing/search/new *Other Options:* The voter registration CD is available for $2.50. If bulk data is requested on other formats, including paper, the cost is considerably higher. **$$$**

Occupational Licensing Boards

Accountant-CPA.. http://arboa.glsuite.us/GLSuiteWeb/Clients/ARBOA/Public/LicenseeSearch.aspx
Acupuncturist .... www.asbart.org/licensees.htm
Alcohol/Drug Abuse Program......www.healthy.arkansas.gov/programsServices/hsLicensingRegulation/HealthFacilityServices/Pages/ProviderLists.aspx
Architect .... https://www.ark.org/asbalaid/index.php/arch/search_indv
Asbestos Inspector/Planner .... www.adeq.state.ar.us/compsvs/webmaster/databases.htm

Asbestos Training Provider/Removal Provider............www.adeq.state.ar.us/compsvs/webmaster/databases.htm
Athletic Trainer (Sports) .... www.aratb.org/search.php
Athletic Trainer/Agent (Health).................... www.aratb.org/search.php
Attorney... https://attorneyinfo.aoc.arkansas.gov/info/attorney_search/info/attorney/attorneysearch.aspx
Auctioneer.. https://www.ark.org/auct_ds/app/index.html
Audiologist.. www.arkansas.gov/abespa_licv/app/enter.html
Bank... www.sos.arkansas.gov/corps/search_all.php
Barber College/Instructor .... www.arbarber.com/barber_college_list.html
Barber/Barber Technician .... www.arbarber.com/licensing/index.html
Birthing Center...........................www.healthy.arkansas.gov/programsServices/hsLicensingRegulation/HealthFacilityServices/Pages/ProviderLists.aspx
Boiler Operator/Inspector/Installer/Repairer.........https://www.ark.org/rosterdl/index.php?agency=dol_boilel
Cemetery, Perpetual Care .... www.securities.arkansas.gov/star/portal/arasd/portal.aspx
Certified Mediator.. https://courts.arkansas.gov/administration/adr/certified-mediators
Charitable Annuity....................................... http://insurance.arkansas.gov/is/companysearch/cosearch.asp
Check Casher .... www.asbca.org/collect_search/
Check Seller/Money Services www.securities.arkansas.gov/page/339/money-services
Chemical, List 1, Wholesale Distr. .... www.ark.org/asbp/roster/index.php
Child Care Provider..................................... https://dhs.arkansas.gov/dccece/cclas/FacilitySearch.aspx
Chiropractor .... www.arkansas.gov/asbce/applicants_licensees/licensees.html
Collection Agency/ Collector/Mgr................ www.asbca.org/collect_search/
Contractor .... www.arkansas.gov/clb/search.php
Counselor, Professional.............................. www.accessarkansas.org/abec/search.php
Court Interpreters .... https://courts.arkansas.gov/directories/court-interpreters-registry
Court Reporter .... www.arkansas.gov/court_reporters/search/index.php
Dental Assistant .... https://www.ark.org/asbde_darenewal/app/roster.html
Dental Hygienist.. www.dentalboard.arkansas.gov/ddsroster/search.php
Dentist... www.dentalboard.arkansas.gov/rdhroster/search.php
Drugs, Legend, Wholesale Distr. .... www.ark.org/asbp/roster/index.php
Electrician Journeyman/ Master/Contractor. https://www.ark.org/labor/electrician/search.php
Embalmer/Embalmer Apprentice .... www.arkansas.gov/fdemb/
Emergency Medical Tech/Paramedic .... https://www.ark.org/dhhsems/index.php
Employee Leasing Firm .... http://insurance.arkansas.gov/is/companysearch/cosearch.asp
Engineer/Engineer in Training .... www.arkansas.gov/pels/search/search.php
Farm Mutual Aid Assoc............................... http://insurance.arkansas.gov/is/companysearch/cosearch.asp
Fire Equipment Inspector/Repairer............. www.arfireprotection.org/roster/index.html
Fire Extinguisher Sprinkler Inspector........... www.arfireprotection.org/roster/index.html
Forester... https://www.ark.org/foresters_rsearch/app/enter.html
Funeral Director/Apprentice .... www.arkansas.gov/fdemb/
Funeral Home/Crematory .... www.arkansas.gov/fdemb/
Ginseng Dealers .... http://plantboard.arkansas.gov/PlantIndustry/Pages/LicenseHolders.aspx
HMO Medicare.. http://insurance.arkansas.gov/is/companysearch/cosearch.asp
Home Inspector... www.ahib.org/
Homebuilders.. www.arkansas.gov/clb/search.php
Hospice Facility...........www.healthy.arkansas.gov/programsServices/hsLicensingRegulation/HealthFacilityServices/Documents/providers/HOSPICE.pdf
Hospital Medical Service............................. http://insurance.arkansas.gov/is/companysearch/cosearch.asp
Insurance Agency .... www.sos.arkansas.gov/corps/search_all.php
Insurance Company.................................... http://insurance.arkansas.gov/is/companysearch/cosearch.asp
Insurance Sales Agent................................ https://a5w.insurance.arkansas.gov/AIDSearches/agent.a5w
Investment Advisor...................................... www.securities.arkansas.gov/star/portal/arasd/portal.aspx
Landscape Architect .... www.arkansas.gov/asbla/find_landscape_architect.html
Landscape Contractors............................... http://plantboard.arkansas.gov/PlantIndustry/Pages/LicenseHolders.aspx
Life Care.. http://insurance.arkansas.gov/is/companysearch/cosearch.asp
Lobbyist... www.sos.arkansas.gov/filing_search/index.php/filing/search/new
Marriage & Family Therapist....................... www.accessarkansas.org/abec/search.php
Massage Therapy Tech/masseur/m'use...... www.arkansasmassagetherapy.com/Roster.htm

Medicaid Provider	https://www.medicaid.state.ar.us/InternetSolution/provider/enroll/enroll.aspx
Medical Corporation	www.armedicalboard.org/public/verify/default.aspx
Midwife	https://www.ark.org/arsbn/statuswatch/index.php/nurse/search/new
Mortgage Loan Broker/Company	www.securities.arkansas.gov/star/portal/arasd/portal.aspx
Motor Club	http://insurance.arkansas.gov/is/companysearch/cosearch.asp
Motor Vehicle Dealer/Distributor	www.armvc.com/dealers/search.php
Motor Vehicle Mfg/Rep, New	www.armvc.com/mfg_dist/search.php
Moxibustion Provider	www.asbart.org/licensees.htm
Multiple Employee Welfare Assoc	http://insurance.arkansas.gov/is/companysearch/cosearch.asp
Notary Public	www.sos.arkansas.gov/corps/notary/index.php
Nurse Anesthetist	https://www.ark.org/arsbn/statuswatch/index.php/nurse/search/new
Nurse-LPN	https://www.ark.org/arsbn/statuswatch/index.php/nurse/search/new
Nursery Dealers	http://plantboard.arkansas.gov/PlantIndustry/Documents/Licensed_Nursery_Dealers.htm
Nurseryman	http://plantboard.arkansas.gov/PlantIndustry/Pages/LicenseHolders.aspx
Nursing Home Facility	www.arhspa.org/agency_decisions.html
Occupational Therapist/Assistant	www.armedicalboard.org/public/verify/default.aspx
Optometrist	www.arbo.org/index.php?action=findanoptometrist
Oriental Medicine	www.asbart.org/licensees.htm
Orthotist/Orthotist Assistant	www.healthy.arkansas.gov/opp/verification/index.php
Osteopathic Physician	www.armedicalboard.org/public/verify/default.aspx
P & C Company	http://insurance.arkansas.gov/pclh/pcweb.asp
Pedorthist	www.healthy.arkansas.gov/opp/verification/index.php
Pharmacist/Intern/Technician	www.ark.org/asbp/roster/index.php
Pharmacy, Hospital/Institution	www.ark.org/asbp/roster/index.php
Pharmacy, Specialty	www.ark.org/asbp/roster/index.php
Pharmacy-In-State or Out-of-State, Retail	www.ark.org/asbp/roster/index.php
Physical Therapist	www.arptb.org/ptroster/search.php
Physician/Medical Doctor/Surgeon/Assistant	www.armedicalboard.org/public/verify/default.aspx
Political Action Committee	www.sos.arkansas.gov/filing_search/index.php/filing/search/new
Pre-Need Seller	http://insurance.arkansas.gov/is/companysearch/cosearch.asp
Prosthetist/Assistant	www.healthy.arkansas.gov/opp/verification/index.php
Psychologist/Examiner	http://psychologyboard.arkansas.gov/licenseeInfo/Pages/default.aspx
Pump Installer	www.arkansas.gov/awwcc/
Real Estate Agent/Broker/Sales	https://www.ark.org/arec_renewals/index.php/search/agent
Real Estate Appraiser	www.arkansas.gov/alcb/search.php
Reins Intermediary	http://insurance.arkansas.gov/is/companysearch/cosearch.asp
Reinsurer	http://insurance.arkansas.gov/is/companysearch/cosearch.asp
Respiratory Care Practitioner	www.armedicalboard.org/public/verify/default.aspx
School Principal/Admin/Super	https://www.ark.org/ina_renewalservices/teachers/licensure.aspx
Securities Agent/Broker/Dealer	www.securities.arkansas.gov/star/portal/arasd/portal.aspx
Securities Exemption	www.securities.arkansas.gov/star/portal/arasd/portal.aspx
Security Mutual Fund	www.securities.arkansas.gov/star/portal/arasd/portal.aspx
Service Contract Provider	http://insurance.arkansas.gov/is/companysearch/cosearch.asp
Social Worker	www.accessarkansas.org/swlb/search/index.html
Solid Waste Facility Operator	www.adeq.state.ar.us/compsvs/webmaster/databases.htm
Speech Pathologist	www.arkansas.gov/abespa_licv/app/enter.html
Supplier of Legend Device/Med Gas	www.ark.org/asbp/roster/index.php
Supplier of Med Equipment	www.ark.org/asbp/roster/index.php
Surplus Lines Insurer	http://insurance.arkansas.gov/is/companysearch/cosearch.asp
Surveyor, Land/Surveyor-in-Training	www.arkansas.gov/pels/search/search.php
Teacher	https://www.ark.org/ina_renewalservices/teachers/licensure.aspx
Water Supply Operator	www.healthy.arkansas.gov/eng/autoupdates/oper/operlistall.xls
Water Well Driller	www.arkansas.gov/awwcc/

State and Local Courts

State Court Structure: **Circuit Courts** are the courts of general jurisdiction and are arranged in 28 circuits. Circuit Courts consist of five subject matter divisions: criminal, civil, probate, domestic relations, and juvenile. A Circuit Clerk handles the records and recordings, however some counties have a County Clerk that handles probate. **District Courts**, formerly known as Municipal Courts before passage of Amendment 80 to the Arkansas Constitution, exercise countywide jurisdiction over misdemeanor cases, preliminary felony cases, and civil cases in matters of less than $5,000, including small claims. The City Courts operate in smaller communities where District Courts do not exist and exercise citywide jurisdiction.

Appellate Courts: Opinions and Citations are available online at https://courts.arkansas.gov.

About Court Online Access: There is no statewide access. A handful of counties individually offer online access to dockets or images. The AOC has a growing number of Courts participating in a limited online docket look-up by name or case number called CourtConnect at https://caseinfo.aoc.arkansas.gov. Two systems are offered:

1. 20+ Circuit Courts and one District Court provide fairly detailed information that goes back in time a good number of years. The system provides links to case images for some records. Cases available include civil, criminal, domestic relations, and probate. If you do not provide a DOB, there is no DOB provided.
2. There are 26 other Circuit Courts that provide very limited data online - all cases are not included. Limited information is available online for court records. What is shown for these courts is only the data as provided on paper coversheets to the Administrative Office of the Courts and the participating Circuit Court may not report all case types on paper. The searches are not onsite equivalent. If you do not provide a DOB, there is no DOB provided.

County Sites:

Arkansas County

Circuit Court - Northern District www.arcocircuitclerk.com/

Civil: Click on document search from the home page. Although this service leads to Title Searcher, the court has placed court records on this system. There is a monthly fee of $70.00 for unlimited searching and a $3.00 fee to view an image plus an $.25 per name Images are available from 2005, the docket index goes back to 1996. Includes both Districts in this county. Also, Limited docket info is free at https://caseinfo.aoc.arkansas.gov/cconnect/PROD/public/ck_public_qry_main.cp_main_idx.**$$$** *Criminal:* same **$$$**

Circuit Court - Southern District www.arcocircuitclerk.com/

Civil: Click on document search from the home page. Although this service leads to Title Searcher, the court has placed court records on this system. There is a monthly fee of $70.00 for unlimited searching and a $3.00 fee to view an image. Images are available from 2005, the docket index goes back to 1996. Includes both Districts in this county. Also, Limited docket info is free at https://caseinfo.aoc.arkansas.gov/cconnect/PROD/public/ck_public_qry_main.cp_main_idx.**$$$** *Criminal:* same**$$$**

Ashley County

Circuit Court

Civil: Limited docket info is free at https://caseinfo.aoc.arkansas.gov/cconnect/PROD/public/ck_public_qry_main.cp_main_idx. Only data shown is data provided on paper coversheets to the Administrative Office of the Courts and it is uncertain if the court reports all case types on paper. *Criminal:* same

Baxter County

Circuit Court

Civil: Limited docket info is free at https://caseinfo.aoc.arkansas.gov/cconnect/PROD/public/ck_public_qry_main.cp_main_idx. Only data shown is data provided on paper coversheets to the Administrative Office of the Courts and it is uncertain if the court reports all case types on paper. *Criminal:* same

Benton County

Circuit Court http://bentoncountyar.gov/BCAdminM1.aspx?/BCAdminSecond.aspx?m=Circuit

Civil: Search civil court docket information free at http://records.co.benton.ar.us:5061/ *Criminal:* Search criminal court docket information free at http://records.co.benton.ar.us:5061/

Bradley County

Circuit Court

Civil: Limited docket info is free at https://caseinfo.aoc.arkansas.gov/cconnect/PROD/public/ck_public_qry_main.cp_main_idx. Only data shown is data provided on paper coversheets to the Administrative Office of the Courts and it is uncertain if the court reports all case types on paper. *Criminal:* same

Calhoun County

Circuit Court

Civil: Limited docket info is free at https://caseinfo.aoc.arkansas.gov/cconnect/PROD/public/ck_public_qry_main.cp_main_idx. Only data shown is data provided on paper coversheets to the Administrative Office of the Courts and it is uncertain if the court reports all case types on paper. *Criminal:* same

Chicot County

Circuit Court

Civil: Limited docket info is free at https://caseinfo.aoc.arkansas.gov/cconnect/PROD/public/ck_public_qry_main.cp_main_idx. Only data shown is data provided on paper coversheets to the Administrative Office of the Courts and it is uncertain if the court reports all case types on paper. *Criminal:* same

Clark County

Circuit Court

Civil: Search by name or case number at https://caseinfo.aoc.arkansas.gov/cconnect/PROD/public/ck_public_qry_main.cp_main_idx. Submit DOB for a name search, but DOB not provided in results. Limited images available. Probate and domestic relations data also at this site. *Criminal:* Search by name or case number at https://caseinfo.aoc.arkansas.gov/cconnect/PROD/public/ck_public_qry_main.cp_main_idx. Submit DOB for a name search, but DOB not provided in results. Limited images available.

Cleveland County

Circuit Court

Civil: Limited docket info is free at https://caseinfo.aoc.arkansas.gov/cconnect/PROD/public/ck_public_qry_main.cp_main_idx. Only data shown is data provided on paper coversheets to the Administrative Office of the Courts and it is uncertain if the court reports all case types on paper. *Criminal:* same

Columbia County

Circuit Court www.countyofcolumbia.net/circuit-clerk/

Civil: Limited docket info is free at https://caseinfo.aoc.arkansas.gov/cconnect/PROD/public/ck_public_qry_main.cp_main_idx. Only data shown is data provided on paper coversheets to the Administrative Office of the Courts and it is uncertain if the court reports all case types on paper. *Criminal:* same

Conway County

Circuit Court

Civil: Search by name or case number at https://caseinfo.aoc.arkansas.gov/cconnect/PROD/public/ck_public_qry_main.cp_main_idx. Submit DOB for a name search, but DOB not provided in results. Limited images available. Probate and domestic relations data also at this site. *Criminal:* Search by name or case number at https://caseinfo.aoc.arkansas.gov/cconnect/PROD/public/ck_public_qry_main.cp_main_idx. Submit DOB for a name search, but DOB not provided in results. Limited images available.

Craighead County

Jonesboro Circuit Court http://craigheadcounty.org/content/circuit-court-clerk

Civil: Search by name or case number at https://caseinfo.aoc.arkansas.gov/cconnect/PROD/public/ck_public_qry_main.cp_main_idx. Submit DOB for a name search, but DOB not provided in results. Limited images available. Probate and domestic relations data also at this site. *Criminal:*

Lake City Circuit Court - Eastern District

Civil: Search by name or case number at https://caseinfo.aoc.arkansas.gov/cconnect/PROD/public/ck_public_qry_main.cp_main_idx. Submit DOB for a name search, but DOB not provided in results. Limited images available. Probate and domestic relations data also at this site. *Criminal:* Search by name or case number at https://caseinfo.aoc.arkansas.gov/cconnect/PROD/public/ck_public_qry_main.cp_main_idx. Submit DOB for a name search, but DOB not provided in results. Limited images available.

Crawford County

Circuit Court www.crawford-county.org/circuit_clerk.aspx

Civil: Search by name or case number at https://caseinfo.aoc.arkansas.gov/cconnect/PROD/public/ck_public_qry_main.cp_main_idx. Submit DOB for a name search, but DOB not provided in results. Limited images available. *Criminal:* same

Cross County

Circuit Court www.crosscountyar.org/page.php?id=2

Civil: Search by name or case number at https://caseinfo.aoc.arkansas.gov/cconnect/PROD/public/ck_public_qry_main.cp_main_idx. Includes probate and domestic violence. Submit DOB for a name search, but DOB not provided in results. Limited images available. *Criminal:* Same.

Dallas County

Circuit Court

Civil: Limited docket info is free at https://caseinfo.aoc.arkansas.gov/cconnect/PROD/public/ck_public_qry_main.cp_main_idx. Only data shown is data provided on paper coversheets to the Administrative Office of the Courts and it is uncertain if the court reports all case types on paper. *Criminal:* same

Desha County

Circuit Court

Civil: Limited docket info is free at https://caseinfo.aoc.arkansas.gov/cconnect/PROD/public/ck_public_qry_main.cp_main_idx. Only data shown is data provided on paper coversheets to the Administrative Office of the Courts and it is uncertain if the court reports all case types on paper. *Criminal:* same

Drew County

Circuit Court

Civil: Limited docket info is free at https://caseinfo.aoc.arkansas.gov/cconnect/PROD/public/ck_public_qry_main.cp_main_idx. Only data shown is data provided on paper coversheets to the Administrative Office of the Courts and it is uncertain if the court reports all case types on paper. *Criminal:* same

Faulkner County

Circuit Court www.faulknercounty.org/

Civil: Search by name or case number at https://caseinfo.aoc.arkansas.gov/cconnect/PROD/public/ck_public_qry_main.cp_main_idx. Submit DOB for a name search, but DOB not provided in results. Limited images available. Probate and domestic relations data also at this site.s data also at this site. *Criminal:* same

Garland County

Circuit Court www.garlandcounty.org/

Civil: Search by name or case number at https://caseinfo.aoc.arkansas.gov/cconnect/PROD/public/ck_public_qry_main.cp_main_idx. Submit DOB for a name search, but DOB not provided in results. Limited images available. Probate and domestic relations data also at this site.s data also at this site. *Criminal:* same

Grant County

Circuit Court

Civil: Search by name or case number at https://caseinfo.aoc.arkansas.gov/cconnect/PROD/public/ck_public_qry_main.cp_main_idx. Submit DOB for a name search, but DOB not provided in results. Limited images available. Probate and domestic relations data also at this site. *Criminal:* Search by name or case number at https://caseinfo.aoc.arkansas.gov/cconnect/PROD/public/ck_public_qry_main.cp_main_idx. Submit DOB for a name search, but DOB not provided in results. Limited images available.

Greene County

Circuit Court

Civil: Limited docket info is free at https://caseinfo.aoc.arkansas.gov/cconnect/PROD/public/ck_public_qry_main.cp_main_idx. Only data shown is data provided on paper coversheets to the Administrative Office of the Courts and it is uncertain if the court reports all case types on paper. *Criminal:* same

Hempstead County

Circuit Court http://hempsteadcountyar.com/circuitclerk.html

Civil: Search Probate (not civil) by name or case number at https://caseinfo.aoc.arkansas.gov/cconnect/PROD/public/ck_public_qry_main.cp_main_idx. Submit DOB for a name search, but DOB not provided in results. Limited images available. *Criminal:*

Hot Spring County

Circuit Court

Civil: Search by name or case number at https://caseinfo.aoc.arkansas.gov/cconnect/PROD/public/ck_public_qry_main.cp_main_idx. Submit DOB for a name search, but DOB not provided in results. Limited images available. Probate and domestic relations data also at this site.s data also at this site. *Criminal:* same

Malvern Local District Court

Civil: Search by name or case number at https://caseinfo.aoc.arkansas.gov/cconnect/PROD/public/ck_public_qry_main.cp_main_idx. Submit DOB for a name search, but DOB not provided in results. Limited images available. *Criminal:* same

Howard County

Circuit Court

Civil: Limited docket info is free at https://caseinfo.aoc.arkansas.gov/cconnect/PROD/public/ck_public_qry_main.cp_main_idx. Only data shown is data provided on paper coversheets to the Administrative Office of the Courts and it is uncertain if the court reports all case types on paper. *Criminal:* same

Independence County

Circuit Court www.independencecircuitclerk.com/

Civil: Online access to recorded judgments (not court records) available by subscription; see www.independencecircuitclerk.com/node/6 for details.**$$$**

Jackson County

Circuit Court

Civil: Limited docket info is free at https://caseinfo.aoc.arkansas.gov/cconnect/PROD/public/ck_public_qry_main.cp_main_idx. Only data shown is data provided on paper coversheets to the Administrative Office of the Courts and it is uncertain if the court reports all case types on paper. *Criminal:* same

Johnson County

Circuit Court

Civil: Limited docket info is free at https://caseinfo.aoc.arkansas.gov/cconnect/PROD/public/ck_public_qry_main.cp_main_idx. Only data shown is data provided on paper coversheets to the Administrative Office of the Courts and it is uncertain if the court reports all case types on paper. *Criminal:* same

Lafayette County

Circuit Court

Civil: Limited docket info is free at https://caseinfo.aoc.arkansas.gov/cconnect/PROD/public/ck_public_qry_main.cp_main_idx. Only data shown is data provided on paper coversheets to the Administrative Office of the Courts and it is uncertain if the court reports all case types on paper. *Criminal:* same

Lee County

Circuit Court

Civil: Search by name or case number at https://caseinfo.aoc.arkansas.gov/cconnect/PROD/public/ck_public_qry_main.cp_main_idx. Submit DOB for a name search, but DOB not provided in results. Limited images available. Probate and domestic relations data also at this site. *Criminal:* same

Lincoln County

Circuit Court

Civil: Limited docket info is free at https://caseinfo.aoc.arkansas.gov/cconnect/PROD/public/ck_public_qry_main.cp_main_idx. Only data shown is data provided on paper coversheets to the Administrative Office of the Courts and it is uncertain if the court reports all case types on paper. *Criminal:* same

Little River County

Circuit Court

Civil: Limited docket info is free at https://caseinfo.aoc.arkansas.gov/cconnect/PROD/public/ck_public_qry_main.cp_main_idx. Only data shown is data provided on paper coversheets to the Administrative Office of the Courts and it is uncertain if the court reports all case types on paper. *Criminal:* same

Logan County

Circuit Court

Civil: Search by name or case number at https://caseinfo.aoc.arkansas.gov/cconnect/PROD/public/ck_public_qry_main.cp_main_idx. Submit DOB for a name search, but DOB not provided in results. Limited images available. Probate and domestic relations data also at this site. *Criminal:* Search by name or case number at https://caseinfo.aoc.arkansas.gov/cconnect/PROD/public/ck_public_qry_main.cp_main_idx. Submit DOB for a name search, but DOB not provided in results. Limited images available.

Lonoke County

Circuit Court www.lonokecountycircuitclerk.com/

Civil: Limited docket info is free at https://caseinfo.aoc.arkansas.gov/cconnect/PROD/public/ck_public_qry_main.cp_main_idx. Only data shown is data provided on paper coversheets to the Administrative Office of the Courts and it is uncertain if the court reports all case types on paper. *Criminal:* same

Madison County

Circuit Court

Civil: Limited docket info is free at https://caseinfo.aoc.arkansas.gov/cconnect/PROD/public/ck_public_qry_main.cp_main_idx. Only data shown is data provided on paper coversheets to the Administrative Office of the Courts and it is uncertain if the court reports all case types on paper. *Criminal:* same

Marion County

Circuit Court

Civil: Limited docket info is free at https://caseinfo.aoc.arkansas.gov/cconnect/PROD/public/ck_public_qry_main.cp_main_idx. Only data shown is data provided on paper coversheets to the Administrative Office of the Courts and it is uncertain if the court reports all case types on paper. *Criminal:* same

Miller County

Circuit Court

Civil: Search by name or case number at https://caseinfo.aoc.arkansas.gov/cconnect/PROD/public/ck_public_qry_main.cp_main_idx. Submit DOB for a name search, but DOB not provided in results. Limited images available. Probate and domestic relations data also at this site. Online access to circuit court dockets by subscription through RecordsUSA.com. Credit card, username and password is required; choose either monthly or per-use plan. Visit the website for sign-up or call Rob at 888-633-4748 x17 for information.**$$$** *Criminal:* Search by name or case number at https://caseinfo.aoc.arkansas.gov/cconnect/PROD/public/ck_public_qry_main.cp_main_idx. Submit DOB for a name search, but DOB not provided in results. Limited images available.**$$$**

Nevada County

Circuit Court

Civil: Search by name or case number at https://caseinfo.aoc.arkansas.gov/cconnect/PROD/public/ck_public_qry_main.cp_main_idx. Submit DOB for a name search, but DOB not provided in results. Limited images available. Probate and domestic relations data also at this site. *Criminal:* same

Ouachita County

Circuit Court

Civil: Limited docket info is free at https://caseinfo.aoc.arkansas.gov/cconnect/PROD/public/ck_public_qry_main.cp_main_idx. Only data shown is data provided on paper coversheets to the Administrative Office of the Courts and it is uncertain if the court reports all case types on paper. *Criminal:* same

Polk County

Circuit Court

Civil: Limited docket info is free at https://caseinfo.aoc.arkansas.gov/cconnect/PROD/public/ck_public_qry_main.cp_main_idx. Only data shown is data provided on paper coversheets to the Administrative Office of the Courts and it is uncertain if the court reports all case types on paper. *Criminal:* same

Pulaski County

Circuit Court www.pulaskiclerk.com/

Civil: Search by name or case number at https://caseinfo.aoc.arkansas.gov/cconnect/PROD/public/ck_public_qry_main.cp_main_idx. Submit DOB for a name search, but DOB not provided in results. Limited images available. Probate and domestic relations data also at this site.s data also at this site. *Criminal:* same

Randolph County

Circuit Court

Civil: Limited docket info is free at https://caseinfo.aoc.arkansas.gov/cconnect/PROD/public/ck_public_qry_main.cp_main_idx. Only data shown is data provided on paper coversheets to the Administrative Office of the Courts and it is uncertain if the court reports all case types on paper. *Criminal:* same

Saline County

Circuit Court

Civil: A court records index search is free at https://www.ark.org/grs/app/saline but fees are changed for record copies. Annual subscription account is $75.00 and the cost per record is $1.00. Search by name or case number at https://caseinfo.aoc.arkansas.gov. Submit DOB for a name search, but DOB not provided in results. Limited images available.**$$$** *Criminal:* same Search by name or case number at https://caseinfo.aoc.arkansas.gov/cconnect/PROD/public/ck_public_qry_main.cp_main_idx. Submit DOB for a name search, but DOB not provided in results. Limited images available. Probate and domestic relations data also at this site. **$$$**

Scott County

Circuit Court

Civil: Access to civil case information at https://caseinfo.aoc.arkansas.gov/cconnect/PROD/public/ck_public_qry_main.cp_main_idx. *Criminal:* Access to criminal case information at https://caseinfo.aoc.arkansas.gov/cconnect/PROD/public/ck_public_qry_main.cp_main_idx.

Searcy County

Circuit Court

Civil: Search by name or case number at https://caseinfo.aoc.arkansas.gov/cconnect/PROD/public/ck_public_qry_main.cp_main_idx. Submit DOB for a name search, but DOB not provided in results. Limited images available. Probate and domestic relations data also at this site.s data also at this site. *Criminal:* same

Sebastian County

All Circuit Courts - Greenwood Division www.sebastiancountyonline.com

Civil: An index search to civil records, domestic relations, and probate from 1998 forward is at www.sebastiancountyonline.com/. This is tricky to find. Click on the 'site map' and choose 'Circuit Clerk.' The public access password and user is shown. Only attorneys may view the DOBs, they must secure a special password before access. *Criminal:* The criminal record index from 1998 forward is at www.sebastiancountyonline.com/. This is tricky to find. Click on the 'site map' and choose 'Circuit Clerk.'

All District Court www.sebastiancountyonline.com

Civil: The index to civil records, domestic relations, and probate from 1998 forward is at www.sebastiancountyonline.com/. Click on Greenwood District Court. *Criminal:* The index to criminal records from 1985 forward is at www.sebastiancountyonline.com/. Click on Greenwood District Court.

Sevier County

Circuit Court

Civil: Limited docket info is free at https://caseinfo.aoc.arkansas.gov/cconnect/PROD/public/ck_public_qry_main.cp_main_idx. Only data shown is data provided on paper coversheets to the Administrative Office of the Courts and it is uncertain if the court reports all case types on paper. *Criminal:* same

Sharp County

Circuit Court

Civil: Court has outsourced online access to for probate and court orders to www.etitlesearch.com/. The data is mostly recorded documents, fees are involved.**$$$**

St. Francis County

Circuit Court

Civil: Search by name or case number at https://caseinfo.aoc.arkansas.gov/cconnect/PROD/public/ck_public_qry_main.cp_main_idx. Submit DOB for a name search, but DOB not provided in results. Limited images available. Probate and domestic relations data also at this site. *Criminal:* same

Union County

Circuit Court

Civil: Online access to circuit court dockets by subscription through RecordsUSA.com. Credit card, username and password is required; choose either monthly or per-use plan. Visit the website for sign-up or call Rob at 888-633-4748 x17 for information. Only data shown is data provided on paper coversheets to the Administrative Office of the Courts and it is uncertain if the court reports all case types on paper.**$$$** *Criminal:* same**$$$**

Van Buren County

Circuit Court www.vanburencountycircuitclerk.com/

Civil: Search by name or case number at https://arep2.aoc.arkansas.gov/cconnect/PROD/public/ck_public_qry_main.cp_main_idx. Submit DOB for a name search, but DOB not provided in results. Probate and domestic relations data also at this site.s data also at this site. *Criminal:* same

Washington County

Circuit Court www.co.washington.ar.us

Civil: Search case index online from the home page. Includes probate records. There is a guest sign-in, but detailed information is via a commercial system, fee is $50.00 per month prepaid. Civil cases indexed from 1992 forward. Search pre-1973 court indices free at www.co.washington.ar.us/ArchiveSearch/CourtRecordSearch.asp.**$$$** *Criminal:* Search case index online from the home page. Includes probate records. There is a guest sign-in, but detailed information is via a commercial system, fee is $50.00 per month prepaid. Cases indexed from 1992 forward. Pre-1933 criminal court indices free at www.co.washington.ar.us/ArchiveSearch/CourtRecordSearch.asp. Note that these cases are very old. **$$$**

Yell County

Dardanelle Circuit Court

Civil: Search by name or case number at https://caseinfo.aoc.arkansas.gov/cconnect/PROD/public/ck_public_qry_main.cp_main_idx. Submit DOB for a name search, but DOB not provided in results. Limited images available. Probate and domestic relations data also at this site. *Criminal:* same

Recorders, Assessors, and Other Sites of Note

Recording Office Organization: 75 counties, 85 recording offices. The recording officer is the Clerk of Circuit Court who is Ex Officio Recorder. 10 counties have 2 recording offices - Arkansas, Carroll, Clay, Craighead, Franklin, Logan, Mississippi, Prairie, Sebastian, and Yell. Federal tax liens on personal property of businesses are filed with the Secretary of State. Other federal and all state tax liens are filed with the Circuit Clerk.

Statewide or Multi-Jurisdiction Access: There is no statewide access to assessor or tax collector data; however, all counties cooperate with at least one commercial vendor. These vendors are summarized below.

- One can research county property information including property sales histories, commercial and residential building descriptions, and legal descriptions at www.arcountydata.com. 48 counties involved. There is a one-time signup fee of $200 for all counties plus $.10 per minute usage. Also at this site there is a free public search of Assessor (25 counties) and Tax Collector (23 counties) records.
- Search by name or address or parcel number data free for 31 county assessor offices at www.actdatascout.com/.
- Search assessor real estate and tax info for free at www.countyservice.net for 49 counties.
- Subscription access to real property records for all Arkansas counties is available from DataScoutPro at www.datascoutpro.com. There are various subscription plans up to $150 monthly for all.
- A fee service to property title information for 16 participating counties is at http://etitlesearch.com/. Fees vary depending on the county.

County Sites:

Arkansas County (Both Districts) ***Recorded Documents*** www.arcocircuitclerk.com Access to online document searches at www.arcocircuitclerk.com/node/3. Fees are $70.00 monthly for unlimited access or $3.00 per viewed image + $.25 per name searched. Can also call 866-604-3673 for more information. **$$$**

Property, Taxation Records Access tax collector data and limited assessor data at www.arcountydata.com/. Both free and a subscription service offered. See the description at beginning of this section for details. Search assessor real estate and property tax records free at www.countyservice.net.**$$$**

Ashley County ***Property, Taxation Records*** Access property data free at www.actdatascout.com/default.aspx?ci=1. Subscription for deeper info is $20 per month. Search assessor real estate and property tax records free at www.countyservice.net.**$$$**

Baxter County ***Recorded Documents*** www.baxtercounty.org/clerk.php For a fee access land records at http://etitlesearch.com/. You can do a name search; Fees vary depending on the usage. **$$$**

Property, Taxation Records Access tax collector data and limited assessor data at www.arcountydata.com/. Both free and a subscription service offered. See the description at beginning of this section for details. Search assessor real estate and property tax records free at www.countyservice.net.**$$$**

Benton County ***Recorded Documents*** http://bentoncountyar.gov/BCAdminSecond.aspx?m=Circuit Circuit court data for a fee at https://gov.propertyinfo.com/AR-Benton/#. Fee is $60.00 per month per account or can do a non subscribers payment of $.50 per page. Also, for a fee access land records at http://etitlesearch.com/. You can do a name search; Fees vary depending on the usage. **$$$**

Property, Taxation Records Access tax collector data and limited assessor data at www.arcountydata.com/. Both free and a subscription service offered. See the description at beginning of this section for details. Search assessor real estate and property tax records free at www.countyservice.net. Also, access to GIS/mapping for free at www.co.benton.ar.us/GIS/Create.aspx.**$$$**

Boone County ***Recorded Documents*** http://boonecountyar.com/page.php?id=2 Land records are at http://etitlesearch.com. You can do a name search; choose from $45.00 monthly subscription or per click account. **$$$**

Property, Taxation Records Access tax collector data and limited assessor data at www.arcountydata.com/. Both free and a subscription service offered. See the description at beginning of this section for details. Search assessor real estate and property tax records free at www.countyservice.net.**$$$**

Bradley County ***Property, Taxation Records*** Access tax collector data and limited assessor data at www.arcountydata.com/. Both free and a subscription service offered. See the description at beginning of this section for details. Search assessor real estate and property tax records free at www.countyservice.net.**$$$**

Calhoun County ***Property, Taxation Records*** Access tax collector data and limited assessor data at www.arcountydata.com/. Both free and a subscription service offered. See the description at beginning of this section for details. Search assessor real estate and property tax records free at www.countyservice.net.**$$$**

Carroll County (Both Districts) ***Property, Taxation Records*** Access tax collector data and limited assessor data at www.arcountydata.com/. Both free and a subscription service offered. See the description at beginning of this section for details. Search assessor real estate and property tax records free at www.countyservice.net.**$$$**

Chicot County ***Property, Taxation Records*** Access tax collector data and limited assessor data at www.arcountydata.com/. Both free and a subscription service offered. See the description at beginning of this section for details.. Search assessor real estate and property tax records free at www.countyservice.net.**$$$**

Clark County ***Property, Taxation Records*** Access property data free at www.actdatascout.com/default.aspx?CI=3. Subscription required for deeper info is $20 per month. Search assessor real estate and property tax records free at www.countyservice.net.**$$$**

Clay County (Both Districts) ***Property, Taxation Records*** Access tax collector and assessor data for a fee at www.arcountydata.com/. Registration and logon is required to search records. One-time setup fee-$200 plus $.10 per minute usage. For signup or info call 479-631-8054 or visit the website.**$$$**

Cleburne County ***Recorded Documents*** For a fee access land records at http://etitlesearch.com/. You can do a name search; Fees vary depending on the usage. **$$$**

Property, Taxation Records Access property data free at www.actdatascout.com/. Subscription for deeper info is $20 per month. Search assessor real estate and property tax records free at www.countyservice.net.**$$$**

Columbia County ***Property, Taxation Records*** Access tax collector data and limited assessor data at www.arcountydata.com/. Both free and a subscription service offered. See the description at beginning of this section for details. Search assessor real estate and property tax records free at www.countyservice.net.**$$$**

Conway County ***Property, Taxation Records*** Access property data free at www.actdatascout.com/default.aspx?CI=6. Subscription for deeper info is $20 per month. Search assessor real estate and property tax records free at www.countyservice.net.**$$$**

Craighead County ***Recorded Documents*** http://craigheadcounty.org/content/circuit-court-clerk Access recording office land data at www.etitlesearch.com; registration required, fee based on usage. **$$$**

Property, Taxation Records Access tax collector data and limited assessor data at www.arcountydata.com/. Both free and a subscription service offered. See the description at beginning of this section for details. Search assessor real estate and property tax records free at www.countyservice.net.**$$$**

Craighead County ***Recorded Documents*** http://craigheadcounty.org/content/circuit-court-clerk Access recording office land data at www.etitlesearch.com/; registration required, fee based on usage. **$$$**

Property, Taxation Records Access tax collector data and limited assessor data at www.arcountydata.com/. Both free and a subscription service offered. See the description at beginning of this section for details. Search assessor real estate and property tax records free at www.countyservice.net.**$$$**

Crawford County ***Recorded Documents*** www.crawford-county.org/ For a fee access land records at http://etitlesearch.com/. You can do a name search; Fees vary depending on the usage. **$$$**

Property, Taxation Records Access tax collector data and limited assessor data at www.arcountydata.com/. Both free and a subscription service offered. See the description at beginning of this section for details. Search assessor real estate and property tax records free at www.countyservice.net.**$$$**

Crittenden County ***Property, Taxation Records*** Access tax collector data and limited assessor data at www.arcountydata.com/. Both free and a subscription service offered. See the description at beginning of this section for details. Search assessor real estate and property tax records free at www.countyservice.net.**$$$**

Cross County ***Recorded Documents*** www.crosscountyar.org/page.php?id=2 The agency sends requesters to the Laredo system. Fees are based on a flat rate by usage ranging from $50 to $250 per month. The same vendor offers the Tapestry program with a $5.95 search fee and copies for

$.50 per page. You can pay as you go with a credit card or be billed monthly with a $25.00 monthly minimum. Visit at www.fidlar.com or call 800-747-4600 at ext 271 or 324. **$$$**

Property, Taxation Records Access property data free at www.actdatascout.com/. Subscription for deeper information. Search assessor real estate and property tax records free at www.countyservice.net.**$$$**

Dallas County ***Recorded Documents*** Access to recorded documents for a fee at www.titlesearcher.com/countyHomepages.php?state=AR. Subscription fees apply. **$$$**

Property, Taxation Records Access tax collector data and limited assessor data at www.arcountydata.com/. Both free and a subscription service offered. See the description at beginning of this section for details. Search assessor real estate and property tax records free at www.countyservice.net.**$$$**

Desha County ***Recorded Documents*** To search records at just this county, the agency sends requesters to the Laredo system Fees are based on a flat rate by usage ranging from $50 to $250 per month plus a slight per minute if usage is surpassed. Coverage for multiple counties is offered by the Tapestry program from the same vendor. There is a $5.95 fee per search and copies can be generated for $.50 per page. You can pay as you go with a credit card or be billed monthly with a $25.00 monthly minimum. Visit at www.fidlar.com or call 800-747-4600 at ext 271 or 324. **$$$**

Property, Taxation Records Access tax collector data and limited assessor data at www.arcountydata.com/. Both free and a subscription service offered. See the description at beginning of this section for details. Search assessor real estate and property tax records free at www.countyservice.net.**$$$**

Drew County ***Property, Taxation Records*** Search property data at www.actdatascout.com/default.aspx?ci=9. 4 levels of pricing starting at $10 for 24 hours, to $150 per month.**$$$**

Faulkner Circuit Clerk ***Recorded Documents*** www.faulknercounty.org/index.php?option=com_content&view=article&id=8&Itemid=11 Access to records free at https://caseinfo.aoc.arkansas.gov/cconnect/PROD/public/ck_public_qry_main.cp_main_idx. No Real Estate records online as of 3/5/13.

Property, Taxation Records Access tax collector data and limited assessor data at www.arcountydata.com/. Both free and a subscription service offered. See the description at beginning of this section for details.**$$$**

Franklin County (Both Districts) ***Property, Taxation Records*** Access property data free at www.actdatascout.com/. Subscription for deeper info is $20 per month. Search assessor real estate and property tax records free at www.countyservice.net. Search an older system at www.arcountydata.com/. Franklin's records have not been updated since 01.01.2009. Login and password required. There is a one-time $200 setup and access charges.

Fulton County ***Property, Taxation Records*** Access tax collector data and limited assessor data at www.arcountydata.com/. Both free and a subscription service offered. See the description at beginning of this section for details. **$$$**

Garland County ***Recorded Documents*** https://gov.propertyinfo.com/AR-Garland/ Access to document images and index information for a fee at https://gov.propertyinfo.com/AR-Garland/. **$$$**

Property, Taxation Records Access property data free at www.actdatascout.com/. Subscription for deeper info is $20 per month.**$$$**

Grant County ***Property, Taxation Records*** Access tax collector data and limited assessor data at www.arcountydata.com/. Both free and a subscription service offered. See the description at beginning of this section for details. Search assessor real estate and property tax records free at www.countyservice.net.**$$$**

Greene County ***Property, Taxation Records*** Access tax collector data and limited assessor data at www.arcountydata.com/. Both free and a subscription service offered. See the description at beginning of this section for details. **$$$**

Hempstead County ***Recorded Records Records*** www.hempsteadcountyar.com/circuitclerk.html For a fee access land records at http://etitlesearch.com/. You can do a name search; Fees vary depending on the usage. **$$$**

Property, Taxation Records Access property data free at www.actdatascout.com/. Subscription for deeper info is $20 per month.**$$$**

Hot Spring County ***Property, Taxation Records*** Access property data free at www.actdatascout.com/. Subscription for deeper info is $20 per month.**$$$**

Howard County ***Property, Taxation Records*** Access tax collector data and limited assessor data at www.arcountydata.com/. Both free and a subscription service offered. See the description at beginning of this section for details. Search assessor real estate and property tax records free at www.countyservice.net.**$$$**

Independence County Circuit Clerk ***Recorded Documents*** www.independencecircuitclerk.com/ For a fee access land records at http://etitlesearch.com/. You can do a name search; Fees vary depending on the usage. Also, online access to be available by subscription from Title Searcher at www.independencecircuitclerk.com/node/6; $70.00 monthly, $3 per viewed image. **$$$**

Property, Taxation Records Access property data free at www.actdatascout.com/. Subscription for deeper info is $20 per month. Search assessor real estate and property tax records free at www.countyservice.net.**$$$**

Izard County ***Property, Taxation Records*** Access tax collector data and limited assessor data at www.arcountydata.com/. Both free and a subscription service offered. See the description at beginning of this section for details. Also, visit www.countyservice.net/assess.asp?id=izatax for free look-ups but address is required.**$$$**

Jackson County ***Property, Taxation Records*** Access property data free at ttp://www.actdatascout.com/. Subscription for deeper info is $20 per month.**$$$**

Jefferson County ***Property, Taxation Records*** Access tax collector data and limited assessor data at www.arcountydata.com/. Both free and a subscription service offered. See the description at beginning of this section for details. Search assessor real estate and property tax records free at www.countyservice.net.**$$$**

Johnson County ***Property, Taxation Records*** Access tax collector data and limited assessor data at www.arcountydata.com/. Both free and a subscription service offered. See the description at beginning of this section for details. Search assessor real estate and property tax records free at www.countyservice.net.**$$$**

Lafayette County ***Property, Taxation Records*** Access property data free at www.actdatascout.com/default.aspx?ci=16. Subscription for deeper info is $20 per month. Search assessor real estate and property tax records free at www.countyservice.net.**$$$**

Lawrence County ***Property, Taxation Records*** Access property data free at www.actdatascout.com. Subscription for deeper info is $20 per month. Search assessor real estate and property tax records free at www.countyservice.net.**$$$**

Lee County ***Property, Taxation Records*** Access tax collector data and limited assessor data at www.arcountydata.com/. Both free and a subscription service offered. See the description at beginning of this section for details. **$$$**

Little River County ***Recorded Documents*** To search records at just this county, the agency sends requesters to the Laredo system Fees are based on a flat rate by usage ranging from $50 to $250 per month plus a slight per minute if usage is surpassed. Coverage for multiple counties is offered by the Tapestry program from the same vendor. There is a $5.95 fee per search and copies can be generated for $.50 per page. You can pay as you go with a credit card or be billed monthly with a $25.00 monthly minimum. Visit at www.fidlar.com or call 800-747-4600 at ext 271 or 324. **$$$**

Property, Taxation Records Access property data free at www.actdatascout.com/. Subscription for deeper info is $20 per month. Access tax collector data free at www.arcountydata.com/. Subscription required for depper info. Search assessor real estate and property tax records free at www.countyservice.net.**$$$**

Logan County (Both Districts) ***Property, Taxation Records*** Access tax collector data and limited assessor data at www.arcountydata.com/. Both free and a subscription service offered. See the description at beginning of this section for details. Also, visit www.countyservice.net/assess.asp?id=logtax for free look-ups but address is required.**$$$**

Lonoke County ***Recorded Documents*** www.lonokecountycircuitclerk.com For a fee access land records at http://etitlesearch.com/. You can do a name search; Fees vary depending on the usage. **$$$**

Property, Taxation Records Access tax collector data and limited assessor data at www.arcountydata.com/. Both free and a subscription service offered. See the description at beginning of this section for details. Search assessor real estate and property tax records free at www.countyservice.net.**$$$**

Madison County ***Recorded Documents*** www.madisoncircuitclerk.com Access to land records for a fee at www.titlesearcher.com/. Must register and pay fees before searching records. **$$$**

Property, Taxation Records Access property data free at www.actdatascout.com/default.aspx?ci=20. Subscription for deeper info is $20 per month.**$$$**

Marion County ***Property, Taxation Records*** Access tax collector data and limited assessor data at www.arcountydata.com/. Both free and a subscription service offered. See the description at beginning of this section for details. **$$$**

Miller County ***Recorded Documents*** To search records at just this county, the agency sends requesters to the Laredo system Fees are based on a flat rate by usage ranging from $50 to $250 per month plus a slight per minute if usage is surpassed. Coverage for multiple counties is offered by the Tapestry program from the same vendor. There is a $5.95 fee per search and copies can be generated for $.50 per page. You can pay as you go with a credit card or be billed monthly with a $25.00 monthly minimum. Visit at www.fidlar.com or call 800-747-4600 at ext 271 or 324. **$$$**

Property, Taxation Records Access property data free at www.actdatascout.com/default.aspx?ci=21. Access tax collector data free at www.arcountydata.com/. Registration and logon is required to search full collector records. Signup fee-$200 plus $.10 per minute usage. For signup or info call 479-631-8054 or visit the website.**$$$**

Mississippi County (Both Districts) ***Recorded Documents*** www.mcagov.com/offices/circuit-chancery-court-clerk For a fee access land records at http://etitlesearch.com/. You can do a name search; Fees vary depending on the usage. **$$$**

Property, Taxation Records Access to property assessment records is free at www.dsmone.com/missco/.

Monroe County ***Property, Taxation Records*** A Access tax collector data and limited assessor data at www.arcountydata.com/. Both free and a subscription service offered. See the description at beginning of this section for details. Search assessor real estate and property tax records free at www.countyservice.net. **$$$**

Montgomery County ***Property, Taxation Records*** Access property data free at www.actdatascout.com/. Subscription for deeper info is $20 per month.**$$$**

Newton County ***Property, Taxation Records*** Acce Access tax collector data and limited assessor data at www.arcountydata.com/. Both free and a subscription service offered. See the description at beginning of this section for details. **$$$**

Ouachita County ***Property, Taxation Records*** Access tax collector data and limited assessor data at www.arcountydata.com/. Both free and a subscription service offered. See the description at beginning of this section for details. Search assessor real estate and property tax records free at www.countyservice.net.

Perry County ***Property, Taxation Records*** Access property data free at www.actdatascout.com/. Subscription for deeper info is $20 per month.**$$$**

Phillips County ***Recorded Documents*** For a fee access land records at http://etitlesearch.com/. You can do a name search; Fees vary depending on the usage. **$$$**

Property, Taxation Records Access property data free at www.actdatascout.com/. Subscription for deeper info is $20 per month.**$$$**

Pike County ***Property, Taxation Records*** Access tax collector data and limited assessor data at www.arcountydata.com/. Both free and a subscription service offered. See the description at beginning of this section for details. **$$$**

Poinsett County ***Property, Taxation Records*** Access tax collector data and limited assessor data at www.arcountydata.com/. Both free and a subscription service offered. See the description at beginning of this section for details. Search assessor real estate and property tax records free at www.countyservice.net.**$$$**

Polk County ***Recorded Documents*** Online access to land records is by subscription through RecordsUSA.com. Images are available. Visit the website for sign-up or call Rob at 888-633-4748 x17 for info. **$$$**

Property, Taxation Records Access property data free at www.actdatascout.com/. Subscription for deeper info is $20 per month. Also, access tax collector data free at www.arcountydata.com/. Subscription required for deeper data. Search assessor real estate and property tax records free at www.countyservice.net.**$$$**

Pope County Circuit Clerk ***Recorded Documents*** www.popecountyar.com/circuit_clerk.html For a fee access land records at http://etitlesearch.com/. You can do a name search; Fees vary depending on the usage. **$$$**

Property, Taxation Records Access tax collector data and limited assessor data at www.arcountydata.com/. Both free and a subscription service offered. See the description at beginning of this section for details. Also, free access to assessor data is at www.countyservice.net/assess.asp?id=poptax but address is required.**$$$**

Prairie County (Both Districts) ***Property, Taxation Records*** Search assessor real estate and property tax records free at www.countyservice.net.

Pulaski County ***Recorded Documents, Voter Registration, Marriage Records*** www.pulaskiclerk.com/ At the main web page, Click on Searches for the free search of voter registration, and vital records data. Real estate information is found at http://69.152.184.8/oncoreweb/. Also, for a fee access land records at http://etitlesearch.com/. You can do a name search; Fees vary depending on the usage. **$$$**

Property, Taxation Records Access tax collector data and limited assessor data at www.arcountydata.com/. Both free and a subscription service offered. See the description at beginning of this section for details. Also, search current Personal Property free at www.countyservice.net/assess.asp?id=PULTAX.**$$$**

Randolph County ***Property, Taxation Records*** Search property and personal property data free at www.countyservice.net/. Also, access property data free at www.actdatascout.com/default.aspx?ci=29. Subscription for deeper info is $20 per month.**$$$**

St. Francis County ***Recorded Documents*** For a fee access land records at http://etitlesearch.com/. You can do a name search; Fees vary depending on the usage. **$$$**

Property, Taxation Records Access tax collector data and limited assessor data at www.arcountydata.com/. Both free and a subscription service offered. See the description at beginning of this section for details. Also, search assessor real estate and property tax records free at www.countyservice.net/stftax.asp but free search requires address.**$$$**

Saline County ***Recorded Documents*** www.salinecounty.org/index.php?option=com_content&view=article&id=18&Itemid=16 For a fee access land records at http://etitlesearch.com/. You can do a name search; Fees vary depending on the usage. **$$$**

Property, Taxation Records Access tax collector data and limited assessor data at www.arcountydata.com/. Both free and a subscription service offered. See the description at beginning of this section for details. Search assessor records free at www.countyservice.net/assess.asp?id=saltax, free search requires address. Search tax collector records free at https://www.ark.org/salinecounty/index.php.**$$$**

Scott County ***Property, Taxation Records*** Access tax collector data and limited assessor data at www.arcountydata.com/. Both free and a subscription service offered. See the description at beginning of this section for details. **$$$**

Searcy County ***Recorded Documents*** Access to land records for a fee at www.titlesearcher.com/. **$$$**

Property, Taxation Records Subscription access to property data available at www.datascoutpro.com/county.aspx?CI=30. Search assessor real estate and property tax records free at www.countyservice.net.**$$$**

Sebastian County (Both Districts) ***Recorded Documents*** www.sebastiancountyonline.com To search records at just this county, the agency sends requesters to the Laredo system Fees are based on a flat rate by usage ranging from $50 to $250 per month plus a slight per minute if usage is surpassed. Coverage for multiple counties is offered by the Tapestry program from the same vendor. There is a $5.95 fee per search and copies can be generated for $.50 per page. You can pay as you go with a credit card or be billed monthly with a $25.00 monthly minimum. Visit at www.fidlar.com or call 800-747-4600 at ext 271 or 324. **$$$**

Property, Taxation Records Access tax collector data and limited assessor data at www.arcountydata.com/. Both free and a subscription service offered. See the description at beginning of this section for details. Also, search property and personal property data free at www.countyservice.net/.**$$$**

Sevier County ***Recorded Documents*** www.seviercountyar.com/county-circuit-clerk.html To search records at just this county, the agency sends requesters to the Laredo system Fees are based on a flat rate by usage ranging from $50 to $250 per month plus a slight per minute if usage is surpassed. Coverage for multiple counties is offered by the Tapestry program from the same vendor. There is a $5.95 fee per search and copies can be generated for $.50 per page. You can pay as you go with a credit card or be billed monthly with a $25.00 monthly minimum. Visit at www.fidlar.com or call 800-747-4600 at ext 271 or 324. **$$$**

Property, Taxation Records Access property data free at www.actdatascout.com. Subscription for deeper info is $20 per month.**$$$**

Sharp County ***Recorded Documents*** For a fee access land records at http://etitlesearch.com/. You can do a name search; Fees vary depending on the usage. **$$$**

Property, Taxation Records Access tax collector data and limited assessor data at www.arcountydata.com/. Both free and a subscription service offered. See the description at beginning of this section for details. Search assessor real estate and property tax records free at www.countyservice.net.**$$$**

Stone County ***Property, Taxation Records*** Access assessor data free at www.arcountydata.com/. Registration and logon is required to search full assessor records. Signup fee-$200 plus $.10 per minute usage. For signup or info call 479-631-8054 or visit the website. Also, access to property records free at http://countyrecordsdirect.com/default.aspx?ci=76. Search assessor real estate and property tax records free at www.countyservice.net. **$$$**

Union County ***Recorded Documents*** http://unioncountyar.com/circuit-clerk/ The agency sends requesters to the Laredo system. Fees are based on a flat rate by usage ranging from $50 to $250 per month. The same vendor offers the Tapestry program with a $5.95 search fee and copies for $.50 per page. You can pay as you go with a credit card or be billed monthly with a $25.00 monthly minimum. Visit at www.fidlar.com or call 800-747-4600 at ext 271 or 324. **$$$**

Property, Taxation Records Access to real estate records for free at http://unioncountyar.com/assessor/. On the left hand side of page is the search mode, can search by parcel number, last name or address.

Van Buren County ***Recorded Documents*** www.vanburencountycircuitclerk.com/ Access land records at www.vanburencountycircuitclerk.com/node/6. Unlimited access $135 monthly or pay $4.00 per viewed image plus $.50 to view each name searched. **$$$**

Property, Taxation Records Access tax collector data and limited assessor data at www.arcountydata.com/. Both free and a subscription service offered. See the description at beginning of this section for details. Search tax payments free at https://www.ark.org/vanburencounty/index.php and use name search to locate property owner. Search assessor real estate and property tax records free at www.countyservice.net.**$$$**

Washington County ***Recorded Documents, Vital Records Records*** www.co.washington.ar.us Search Clerk's records and index at www.co.washington.ar.us/eSearch/User/Login.aspx?ReturnUrl=%2feSearch%2findex.aspx. Can sign-in as guest for minor information, for more detailed information must subscribe. Also, search court record archives at www.co.washington.ar.us/ArchiveSearch/CourtRecordSearch.asp. Also, for a fee access land records at http://etitlesearch.com/. You can do a name search; Fees vary depending on the usage. **$$$**

Property, Taxation Records Search property records for free at www.co.washington.ar.us/PropertySearch/MapSearch.asp. Also, access tax collector data free at www.arcountydata.com/. Registration and fees required for deeper info. Search assessor real estate and property tax records free at www.countyservice.net.**$$$**

White County ***Property, Taxation Records*** Access tax collector data and limited assessor data at www.arcountydata.com/. Both free and a subscription service offered. See the description at beginning of this section for details. Also, free access to assessor records at www.countyservice.net/assess.asp?id=whitax\\. Address required.**$$$**

Woodruff County ***Recorded Documents*** For a fee access land records at http://etitlesearch.com/. You can do a name search; Fees vary depending on the county. **$$$**

Yell County (Both Districts) ***Property, Taxation Records*** Access tax collector data and limited assessor data at www.arcountydata.com/. Both free and a subscription service offered. See the description at beginning of this section for details. **$$$**

California

Capital: Sacramento
Sacramento County
Time Zone: PST
Population: 38,041,430
# of Counties: 58

Useful State Links

Website: www.ca.gov/
Governor: http://gov.ca.gov
Attorney General: http://oag.ca.gov
State Archives: www.sos.ca.gov/archives/archives.htm
State Statutes and Codes: www.leginfo.ca.gov/calaw.html
Legislative Bill Search: www.leginfo.ca.gov/bilinfo.html
Bill Monitoring: www.leginfo.ca.gov/cgi-bin/postquery?maison=$prfx&nro=$num&act=10
Unclaimed Funds: https://scoweb.sco.ca.gov/UCP/

State Public Record Agencies

Sexual Offender Registry

Department of Justice, Sexual Offender Program, www.meganslaw.ca.gov/ This online search CANNOT be used for pre-employment purposes unless the applicant is applying for a job that deals specifically with vulnerable people. The web page offers online searching by a sex offender's specific name or by geographic location including ZIP Code, county or within a predetermined radius of a selected address, park, or school. The site provides access to information on more than 63,500 persons required to register in California as sex offenders. Specific home addresses are displayed on more than 33,500 offenders.

Incarceration Records

Dept of Corrections, Corrections & Rehabilitation ID Unit, www.cdcr.ca.gov Identification Unit / Inmate Locator is free at http://inmatelocator.cdcr.ca.gov/. The name and either the DOB or Corrections Number must be provided.

Corporation, LLC, LP, LLP

Secretary of State, Information Retrieval/Certification Unit, www.sos.ca.gov/business/ The website at http://kepler.sos.ca.gov/ offers access to business entity information including corporation, LLC, and LP. Information available includes status, file number, date of registration, jurisdiction and agent for service of process. The file is updated weekly. Also, a Publicly Traded Disclosure search is at www.ptsearch.sos.ca.gov/app/basic_search.html. And one may search securities companies registered with the state at http://134.186.208.228/caleasi/pub/exsearch.htm. *Other Options:* Information regarding bulk lists and other forms of records access is available by contacting the Sec. of State's Information Technology Division at 916-653-8905.

Trademarks/Servicemarks

Secretary of State, Trademark Unit, www.sos.ca.gov/business/ts/ One may request a search via email to tm@sos.ca.gov. *Other Options:* Microfilm is sold on monthly basis with year contract.

Uniform Commercial Code, Federal & State Tax Liens

Business Programs Division, UCC Section, www.sos.ca.gov/business/ucc/ UCC Connect provides an online service at https://uccconnect.sos.ca.gov/acct/acct-login.asp to conduct a variety of inquiries and place orders for copies and debtor search certificates on records and submit UCC filings. Ongoing requesters can become subscribers. Fees are based on name inquires ($5.00 per name) and images viewed ($1.00). The web page has a complete list of fees and excellent FAQ section. Click on the Help tab. **$$$** *Other Options:* The database is available for purchase, daily updates are available for an additional fee on a yearly subscription basis. The web page has prices.

Sales Tax Registrations

Board of Equalization, Sales and Use Tax Department, www.boe.ca.gov The Internet site provides a permit verification service at https://efile.boe.ca.gov/boewebservices/verification.jsp?action=SALES. Permit number is needed. System is open 5AM to midnight. *Other Options:* Lists, available for a fee, are sorted in a number of ways including CA Industry Code. For further information and fees, call the Technical Services Division at 916-445-5848

Death Records

State Department of Health Svcs, Office of Vital Records - MS 5103, www.cdph.ca.gov/Pages/default.aspx Access death records 1940 thru 1997 at http://vitals.rootsweb.ancestry.com/ca/death/search.cgi.

Workers' Compensation Records

Division of Workers' Compensation, Headquarters, www.dir.ca.gov/dwc/dwc_home_page.htm Members of the public may search the Division of Workers' Compensation's database for information on active disputed workers' compensation cases (20% of cases) using the Electronic Adjudication Management System's (EAMS). This is an informational only. There is no name searching, and it is not in real time. Go to www.dir.ca.gov/dwc/eams/EAMS_PublicInformationSearch.htm.

Driver Records

Department of Motor Vehicles, Information Services Branch, www.dmv.ca.gov The department offers online access, a $10,000 one-time setup fee is required. Entities who order from an online vendor must also be pre-approved and other fees are involved. The fee is $2.00 per record. The system is available 24 hours, 7 days a week. For more information call 916-657-5582. **$$$** *Other Options:* Employers may monitor their drivers in the Pull Notice Program. The DMV informs the organization when there is activity on enrolled drivers. Visit the web page for details.

Vehicle, Vessel Ownership & Registration

Department of Motor Vehicle, Information Release Unit, www.dmv.ca.gov 24 hour online access is limited to certain Authorized Vendors. Requesters may not use data for direct marketing, solicitation, nor resell for those purposes. A bond of $50,000 is required, and a $10,000 one-time permit fee is mandatory. Records are $2.00 ea. For additional information, contact the Electronic Access Administration Section at 916-657-5582. **$$$** *Other Options:* California offers electronic delivery of registration information within special parameters. Release of information is denied for commercial marketing purposes.

Voter Registration, Campaign Finance, PACs, Lobbyists

Secretary of State, Elections Division, www.sos.ca.gov/elections/ Cal-Access provides financial information supplied by state candidates, donors, lobbyists, and others. Records of campaign finance can be viewed at http://cal-access.sos.ca.gov/campaign/. Find data on PACs and major donors at http://cal-access.ss.ca.gov/Campaign/Committees/. To find persons spending $5,000 or more to influence legislation or administration see http://cal-access.ss.ca.gov/Lobbying/Payments/. Data on lobbyists is found at http://cal-access.ss.ca.gov/Lobbying/. *Other Options:* The state will sell CDs with all or portions of the statewide voter registration database for political or pre-approved purposes. Call for details.

Occupational Licensing Boards

Accountant-CPA/Firm .... www.dca.ca.gov/cba/lookup.shtml
Acupuncturist .... www2.dca.ca.gov/pls/wllpub/wllqryna$lcev2.startup?p_qte_code=AC&p_qte_pgm_code=6500
Adoption Agency .... https://secure.dss.cahwnet.gov/ccld/securenet/ccld_search/ccld_search.aspx
Agricultural Engineer .... www.bpelsg.ca.gov/consumers/lic_lookup.shtml
Air Conditioning Contractor https://www2.cslb.ca.gov/OnlineServices/CheckLicenseII/CheckLicense.aspx
Alarm Firm/Employee/Mngr .... www.bsis.ca.gov/online_services/verify_license.shtml
Appraiser, Real Estate .... www.orea.ca.gov/html/SearchAppraisers.asp
Apprentice Program, Skilled Labor .... www.dir.ca.gov/databases/das/aigstart.asp
Architect .... www2.dca.ca.gov/pls/wllpub/wllqryna$lcev2.startup?p_qte_code=GEN&p_qte_pgm_code=0600
Asbestos Consultant/Surveillance .... www.dir.ca.gov/databases/doshcaccsst/caccsst_query_1.html
Asbestos Contractor .... www.dir.ca.gov/databases/doshacru/acrusearch.html
Asbestos Trainer .... www.dir.ca.gov/databasedown.asp
Asbestos Worker/Trainee .... www.dir.ca.gov/DOSH/ACRU/TP_AsbestosTrainingCertificates.html
Attorney .... http://members.calbar.ca.gov/fal/MemberSearch/FindLegalHelp
Audiologist .... www2.dca.ca.gov/pls/wllpub/wllqryna$lcev2.startup?p_qte_code=LIC&p_qte_pgm_code=7700
Automobile Dealer/Repair .... www.bar.ca.gov/70_SiteWideInfo/02_Tools/03_VerifyLicense.html
Bank Agencies/Facility/Branches, Foreign .. www.dfi.ca.gov/licensees/otherstate/default.asp
Bank, State Chartered .... www.dfi.ca.gov/licensees/
Bank, State Chartered, Industr'l .... www.dfi.ca.gov/directory/

Barber Instructor/School	www2.dca.ca.gov/pls/wllpub/wllqryna$lcev2.startup?p_qte_code=FRM&p_qte_pgm_code=3300
Barber/Barber Shop/Apprentice	www2.dca.ca.gov/pls/wllpub/wllqryna$lcev2.startup?p_qte_code=IND&p_qte_pgm_code=3300
Baton Training Facility/Instruct	www.bsis.ca.gov/online_services/verify_license.shtml
Brake & Lamp Adjuster/Station	www.bar.ca.gov/70_SiteWideInfo/02_Tools/03_VerifyLicense.html
Building Contr., General-Class B	https://www2.cslb.ca.gov/OnlineServices/CheckLicenseII/CheckLicense.aspx
Business/Industrial Developm't Firm	www.dfi.ca.gov/directory/
Cabinet/Millwork Contractor	https://www2.cslb.ca.gov/OnlineServices/CheckLicenseII/CheckLicense.aspx
Car Washing/Polishing	www.dir.ca.gov/databases/dlselr/carwash.html
Care Facility for Chronically Ill	https://secure.dss.cahwnet.gov/ccld/securenet/ccld_search/ccld_search.aspx
Care Facility, Children, Transitional	https://secure.dss.cahwnet.gov/ccld/securenet/ccld_search/ccld_search.aspx
Cemetery, Cemetery Broker/Seller	www.cfb.ca.gov/consumer/lookup.shtml
Child Care Center	https://secure.dss.cahwnet.gov/ccld/securenet/ccld_search/ccld_search.aspx
Chiropractic Corp./Satellite/Referal Svc	www.chiro.ca.gov/onlineservices_licsearch.htm
Chiropractor	www.chiro.ca.gov/onlineservices_licsearch.htm
Clinic Pharmaceutical Permit	www.pharmacy.ca.gov/online/verify_lic.shtml
Community Treatment Facility	https://secure.dss.cahwnet.gov/ccld/securenet/ccld_search/ccld_search.aspx
Concrete Contractor/Company	https://www2.cslb.ca.gov/OnlineServices/CheckLicenseII/CheckLicense.aspx
Conscious Sedation Permit	www2.dca.ca.gov/pls/wllpub/wllquery$.startup
Construction Permit, Excava'n/Shoring	www.dir.ca.gov/dosh/PermitHolder/PermitHolder.asp
Continuing Education Provider	www.bbs.ca.gov/quick_links/weblookup.shtml
Contractor, Business/Individual	https://www2.cslb.ca.gov/OnlineServices/CheckLicenseII/CheckLicense.aspx
Cosmetician/Cosmetologist	www2.dca.ca.gov/pls/wllpub/wllqryna$lcev2.startup?p_qte_code=IND&p_qte_pgm_code=3300
Cosmetology School	www2.dca.ca.gov/pls/wllpub/wllqryna$lcev2.startup?p_qte_code=FRM&p_qte_pgm_code=3300
Cosmetology/Electrology Firm/Instr.	www2.dca.ca.gov/pls/wllpub/wllqryna$lcev2.startup?p_qte_code=IND&p_qte_pgm_code=3300
Court Reporter/Shorthand Reporter	www2.dca.ca.gov/pls/wllpub/wllqryna$lcev2.startup?p_qte_code=CSR&p_qte_pgm_code=8100
Crane Operator	www.dir.ca.gov/databases/crane/cranesearch.html
Credit Union	www.dfi.ca.gov/licensees/cu/default.asp
Cremated Remains Disposer	www.cfb.ca.gov/consumer/lookup.shtml
Crematory	www.cfb.ca.gov/consumer/lookup.shtml
Day Care, Adult/Child	https://secure.dss.cahwnet.gov/ccld/securenet/ccld_search/ccld_search.aspx
Dental Anesthesia Permit	www2.dca.ca.gov/pls/wllpub/wllquery$.startup
Dental Assistant, Extended Function	www.dbc.ca.gov/verification/license_verification.shtml
Dental Assistant/Hygienst	www.dbc.ca.gov/verification/license_verification.shtml
Dental Registered Provider	www.dbc.ca.gov/verification/license_verification.shtml
Dentist	www.dbc.ca.gov/verification/license_verification.shtml
Dentist Fictitious Name	www2.dca.ca.gov/pls/wllpub/wllquery$.startup
Development Corporation	www.dfi.ca.gov/directory/
Driving School/Instructor	http://dmv.ca.gov/olinq2/welcome.do
Drug Wholesaler/Drug Room	www.pharmacy.ca.gov/online/verify_lic.shtml
Drywall Contractor	https://www2.cslb.ca.gov/OnlineServices/CheckLicenseII/CheckLicense.aspx
Earthwork/Paving Contractor	https://www2.cslb.ca.gov/OnlineServices/CheckLicenseII/CheckLicense.aspx
Electrical Contr. & Electric Sign Contr.	https://www2.cslb.ca.gov/OnlineServices/CheckLicenseII/CheckLicense.aspx
Electrologist	www2.dca.ca.gov/pls/wllpub/wllqryna$lcev2.startup?p_qte_code=IND&p_qte_pgm_code=3300
Electrology School	www2.dca.ca.gov/pls/wllpub/wllqryna$lcev2.startup?p_qte_code=FRM&p_qte_pgm_code=3300
Electronic & Appliance Repair	www2.dca.ca.gov/pls/wllpub/wllqryna$lcev2.startup?p_qte_code=SSA&p_qte_pgm_code=3900
Elementary School Teacher	https://educator.ctc.ca.gov/esales_enu/start.swe?SWECmd=GotoView&SWEView=CTC+Search+View+Web
Elevator Installation Contractor	https://www2.cslb.ca.gov/OnlineServices/CheckLicenseII/CheckLicense.aspx
Embalmer/Embalmer Apprentice	www.cfb.ca.gov/consumer/lookup.shtml
Engineer (various disciplines)	www.bpelsg.ca.gov/consumers/lic_lookup.shtml
Esthetician	www2.dca.ca.gov/pls/wllpub/wllqryna$lcev2.startup?p_qte_code=IND&p_qte_pgm_code=3300
Family Child Care Home	https://secure.dss.cahwnet.gov/ccld/securenet/ccld_search/ccld_search.aspx
Farm Labor Contractor	www.dir.ca.gov/databases/dlselr/farmlic.html
Fencing Contractor	https://www2.cslb.ca.gov/OnlineServices/CheckLicenseII/CheckLicense.aspx
Firearm Permit	www.bsis.ca.gov/online_services/verify_license.shtml
Firearm Training Facility/Instr.	www.bsis.ca.gov/online_services/verify_license.shtml

Flooring/Floor Covering Contractor	https://www2.cslb.ca.gov/OnlineServices/CheckLicenseII/CheckLicense.aspx
Foster Family Agency	https://secure.dss.cahwnet.gov/ccld/securenet/ccld_search/ccld_search.aspx
Funeral Director/Establishment	www.cfb.ca.gov/consumer/lookup.shtml
Funerary Training Establ./Apprentice	www.cfb.ca.gov/consumer/lookup.shtml
Garment Manufacturer	www.dir.ca.gov/databases/dlselr/Garmreg.html
Geologist	www2.dca.ca.gov/pls/wllpub/wllqryna$lcev2.startup?p_qte_code=GEO&p_qte_pgm_code=5100
Geologist, Engineering	www2.dca.ca.gov/pls/wllpub/wllqryna$lcev2.startup?p_qte_code=GEO&p_qte_pgm_code=5100
Geologist/Geologist, Engineering	www2.dca.ca.gov/pls/wllpub/wllqryna$lcev2.startup?p_qte_code=GEO&p_qte_pgm_code=5100
Geophysicist	www2.dca.ca.gov/pls/wllpub/wllqryna$lcev2.startup?p_qte_code=GEO&p_qte_pgm_code=5100
Geophysicist	www2.dca.ca.gov/pls/wllpub/wllqryna$lcev2.startup?p_qte_code=GEO&p_qte_pgm_code=5100
Glazier	https://www2.cslb.ca.gov/OnlineServices/CheckLicenseII/CheckLicense.aspx
Group Home	https://secure.dss.cahwnet.gov/ccld/securenet/ccld_search/ccld_search.aspx
Healing Art Supervisor	www.apps.cdph.ca.gov/rhbxray/
Hearing Aid Dispenser	www2.dca.ca.gov/pls/wllpub/wllqryna$lcev2.startup?p_qte_code=HA&p_qte_pgm_code=6700
Hearling Aid Dispenser	www2.dca.ca.gov/pls/wllpub/wllqryna$lcev2.startup?p_qte_code=HA&p_qte_pgm_code=6700
Heating & Warm-Air Vent. Contr.	https://www2.cslb.ca.gov/OnlineServices/CheckLicenseII/CheckLicense.aspx
Home Furnishings	www2.dca.ca.gov/pls/wllpub/wllqryna$lcev2.startup?p_qte_code=LIC&p_qte_pgm_code=5710
Horse Racing (license type)	www.chrb.ca.gov/licensing.html
Hospital Pharmaceutical Exemptee	www.pharmacy.ca.gov/online/verify_lic.shtml
Hydrogeologist	www2.dca.ca.gov/pls/wllpub/wllqryna$lcev2.startup?p_qte_code=GEO&p_qte_pgm_code=5100
Hydrogeologist	www2.dca.ca.gov/pls/wllpub/wllqryna$lcev2.startup?p_qte_code=GEO&p_qte_pgm_code=5100
Hypodermic Needle & Syringe Dist	www.pharmacy.ca.gov/online/verify_lic.shtml
Infant Center	https://secure.dss.cahwnet.gov/ccld/securenet/ccld_search/ccld_search.aspx
Instructors	www.guidedogboard.ca.gov/consumers/license_lookup.shtml
Insulation/Acoustical Contractor	https://www2.cslb.ca.gov/OnlineServices/CheckLicenseII/CheckLicense.aspx
Insurance Adjuster	www.insurance.ca.gov/0200-industry/0200-prod-licensing/0200-current-lic-info/
Insurance Agent/Broker/Producer	www.insurance.ca.gov/license-status/index.cfm
Insurance Company	www.insurance.ca.gov/0200-industry/0070-check-license-status/index.cfm
Insurance2 Agent/Broker	www.insurance.ca.gov/0200-industry/0070-check-license-status/index.cfm
Investment Advisor	www.corp.ca.gov/FSD/licensees/default.asp
Land Surveyor-in-Training	www.bpelsg.ca.gov/consumers/lic_lookup.shtml
Landscape Architect	www.latc.ca.gov/consumers/search.shtml
Landscaping Contractor	https://www2.cslb.ca.gov/OnlineServices/CheckLicenseII/CheckLicense.aspx
Lawyer Referral Service	www.calbar.ca.gov/Public/LawyerReferralServicesLRS.aspx
Legal Specialization Provider	http://lawhelpca.org/
Lobbyist/Lobbying Firm/Employer	http://cal-access.ss.ca.gov/Lobbying/
Locksmith/Locksmith Company	www.bsis.ca.gov/online_services/verify_license.shtml
Mammographic Facility	www.apps.cdph.ca.gov/rhbxray/
Manicurist	www2.dca.ca.gov/pls/wllpub/wllqryna$lcev2.startup?p_qte_code=IND&p_qte_pgm_code=3300
Marriage & Family Therapist	www.bbs.ca.gov/quick_links/weblookup.shtml
Masonry Contractor	https://www2.cslb.ca.gov/OnlineServices/CheckLicenseII/CheckLicense.aspx
Medical Evaluator	www.dir.ca.gov/databases/dwc/qmestartnew.asp
Midwife	www2.dca.ca.gov/pls/wllpub/wllqryna$lcev2.startup?p_qte_code=LM&p_qte_pgm_code=6200
Money Order Issuer	www.dfi.ca.gov/licensees/moneytransmitters/default.asp
Notary Education Vendor	http://notaryeducation.sos.ca.gov/
Notary Public	www.sos.ca.gov/business/notary/notary-online-listing.htm
Nuclear Medicine Technologist	www.apps.cdph.ca.gov/rhbxray/
Nurse Temporary or Intern	https://www.dca.ca.gov/webapps/rn/tlverif.php
Nurse-RN	www2.dca.ca.gov/pls/wllpub/wllqryna$lcev2.startup?p_qte_code=RN&p_qte_pgm_code=7800
Nursing Continued Edu Provider	www2.dca.ca.gov/pls/wllpub/wllqryna$lcev2.startup?p_qte_code=RN&p_qte_pgm_code=7800
Nursing Home Administrator	www.apps.cdph.ca.gov/cvl/SearchPage.aspx
Occupational Therapist/Assistant	www2.dca.ca.gov/pls/wllpub/wllqryna$lcev2.startup?p_qte_code=OT&p_qte_pgm_code=1475
Optician, Dispensing	www2.dca.ca.gov/pls/wllpub/wllqryna$lcev2.startup?p_qte_code=D&p_qte_pgm_code=6400
Optometric Corporation	www2.dca.ca.gov/pls/wllpub/wllqryna$lcev2.startup?p_qte_code=GEN&p_qte_pgm_code=6900
Optometrist	www2.dca.ca.gov/pls/wllpub/wllqryna$lcev2.startup?p_qte_code=GEN&p_qte_pgm_code=6900

Optometry Practice/Branch Office	www2.dca.ca.gov/pls/wllpub/wllqryna$lcev2.startup?p_qte_code=GEN&p_qte_pgm_code=6900
Ornamental Metal Contractor	https://www2.cslb.ca.gov/OnlineServices/CheckLicenseII/CheckLicense.aspx
Osteopath	www.opsc.org/displaycommon.cfm?an=1&subarticlenbr=9
Painting/Decorating Contractor	https://www2.cslb.ca.gov/OnlineServices/CheckLicenseII/CheckLicense.aspx
Parking/Highway Improvement Contr.	https://www2.cslb.ca.gov/OnlineServices/CheckLicenseII/CheckLicense.aspx
Patrol Operator, Private	www.bsis.ca.gov/online_services/verify_license.shtml
Payment Instrument Issuer	www.dfi.ca.gov/directory/
Pesticide Applicator/Operator/Field Rep	www2.dca.ca.gov/pls/wllpub/wllqryna$lcev2.startup?p_qte_code=EMP&p_qte_pgm_code=8400
Pharmaceutical Dist., Out-of-State	www.pharmacy.ca.gov/online/verify_lic.shtml
Pharmaceutical Whlse./Exemptee	www.pharmacy.ca.gov/online/verify_lic.shtml
Pharmacist/Pharmacist Intern	www.pharmacy.ca.gov/online/verify_lic.shtml
Pharmacy/Pharmacy Technician	www.pharmacy.ca.gov/online/verify_lic.shtml
Photogrammetrist	www.bpelsg.ca.gov/consumers/lic_lookup.shtml
Physical Therapist/Assistant	www2.dca.ca.gov/pls/wllpub/wllqryna$lcev2.startup?p_qte_code=PT&p_qte_pgm_code=6800
Physician Assistant	www.pac.ca.gov/forms_pubs/online_services/license_lookup.shtml
Physician/Medical Doctor/Surgeon	www.mbc.ca.gov/lookup.html
Plastering Contractor	https://www2.cslb.ca.gov/OnlineServices/CheckLicenseII/CheckLicense.aspx
Plumber	https://www2.cslb.ca.gov/OnlineServices/CheckLicenseII/CheckLicense.aspx
Podiatrist	www.bpm.ca.gov/licensing/index.shtml
Premium Finance Company	http://search.dre.ca.gov/integrationaspcode/
Private Investigator	www2.dca.ca.gov/pls/wllpub/wllqryna$lcev2.startup?p_qte_code=PSE&p_qte_pgm_code=2420
Psychiatric Technician	www.bvnpt.ca.gov/license_verification.shtml
Psychologist, Educational	www.bbs.ca.gov/quick_links/weblookup.shtml
Psychologist/Assistant	www2.dca.ca.gov/pls/wllpub/wllqryna$lcev2.startup?p_qte_code=PSX&p_qte_pgm_code=7300
Public Works Trainer	www.dir.ca.gov/databases/das/pwaddrstart.asp
Radioactive Material Licensee	www.apps.cdph.ca.gov/rhbxray/
Radiologic Technologist	www.apps.cdph.ca.gov/rhbxray/
Real Estate Agent/Seller/Broker/Corp	http://search.dre.ca.gov/integrationaspcode/
Refrigeration Contractor	https://www2.cslb.ca.gov/OnlineServices/CheckLicenseII/CheckLicense.aspx
Repossessor Agency/Mgr./Employee	www.bsis.ca.gov/online_services/verify_license.shtml
Representative (Banking) Foreign	www.dfi.ca.gov/licensees/otherstate/default.asp
Residential Care/Facility for Adult/Elderly	https://secure.dss.cahwnet.gov/ccld/securenet/ccld_search/ccld_search.aspx
Respiratory Care Practitioner	www2.dca.ca.gov/pls/wllpub/wllqryna$lcev2.startup?p_qte_code=RCP&p_qte_pgm_code=7600
Roofing Contractor	https://www2.cslb.ca.gov/OnlineServices/CheckLicenseII/CheckLicense.aspx
Sanitation System Contractor	https://www2.cslb.ca.gov/OnlineServices/CheckLicenseII/CheckLicense.aspx
Savings & Loan Association	http://search.dre.ca.gov/integrationaspcode/
School Administrative Service	www.ctc.ca.gov/credentials/default.html
Schools	www.guidedogboard.ca.gov/consumers/license_lookup.shtml
Secondary School Teacher	https://educator.ctc.ca.gov/esales_enu/start.swe?SWECmd=GotoView&SWEView=CTC+Search+View+Web
Securities Broker/Dealer	www.corp.ca.gov/FSD/licensees/default.asp
Security Guard	www2.dca.ca.gov/pls/wllpub/wllqryna$lcev2.startup?p_qte_code=G&p_qte_pgm_code=2420
Service Contract Seller, Appliance	www2.dca.ca.gov/pls/wllpub/wllqryna$lcev2.startup?p_qte_code=SSA&p_qte_pgm_code=3900
Sheet Metal Contractor	https://www2.cslb.ca.gov/OnlineServices/CheckLicenseII/CheckLicense.aspx
Shelter, Temporary	https://secure.dss.cahwnet.gov/ccld/securenet/ccld_search/ccld_search.aspx
Smog Check Station/Technician	www.bar.ca.gov/70_SiteWideInfo/02_Tools/03_VerifyLicense.html
Social Rehabilitation Facility	https://secure.dss.cahwnet.gov/ccld/securenet/ccld_search/ccld_search.aspx
Social Worker, Clinical	www.bbs.ca.gov/quick_links/weblookup.shtml
Solar Energy Contractor	https://www2.cslb.ca.gov/OnlineServices/CheckLicenseII/CheckLicense.aspx
Specialty Contractor-Class C	https://www2.cslb.ca.gov/OnlineServices/CheckLicenseII/CheckLicense.aspx
Speech Pathologist Asst./Audiologist Aide	www2.dca.ca.gov/pls/wllpub/wllqryna$lcev2.startup?p_qte_code=LIC&p_qte_pgm_code=7700
Speech-Language Pathologist	www2.dca.ca.gov/pls/wllpub/wllqryna$lcev2.startup?p_qte_code=LIC&p_qte_pgm_code=7700
Steel Contractor	https://www2.cslb.ca.gov/OnlineServices/CheckLicenseII/CheckLicense.aspx
Studio Teacher	www.dir.ca.gov/databases/dlselr/StudTch.html
Support Center, Adult	https://secure.dss.cahwnet.gov/ccld/securenet/ccld_search/ccld_search.aspx
Surgical Clinic Pharm., Nonprofit	www.pharmacy.ca.gov/online/verify_lic.shtml

Surveyor, Land	www.bpelsg.ca.gov/consumers/lic_lookup.shtml
Swimming Pool Contractor	https://www2.cslb.ca.gov/OnlineServices/CheckLicenseII/CheckLicense.aspx
Talent Agency	www.dir.ca.gov/databases/dlselr/Talag.html
Tax Preparer	www.ctec.org/PreparerVerify.aspx
Thrift & Loan Company	http://search.dre.ca.gov/integrationaspcode/
Tile Contractor, Ceramic/Mosaic	https://www2.cslb.ca.gov/OnlineServices/CheckLicenseII/CheckLicense.aspx
Traffic Violator School Lecense/Provider	www.dmv.ca.gov/vehindustry/ol/drschool.htm
Trainer, Public Works	www.dir.ca.gov/databases/das/pwaddrstart.asp
Travelers Checks Issuer	www.dfi.ca.gov/licensees/moneytransmitters/default.asp
Trust Company	www.dfi.ca.gov/directory/
Veterinarian/Technician/Vet. Hospitals	www2.dca.ca.gov/pls/wllpub/wllqryna$lcev2.startup?p_qte_code=VTX&p_qte_pgm_code=9010
Veterinary Food/Animal Drug Retailer	www.pharmacy.ca.gov/online/verify_lic.shtml
Viatical Settlement Insurer	www.insurance.ca.gov/0100-consumers/0030-licensee-info/0040-viatical-settlements/
Vocational Nurse	www.bvnpt.ca.gov/license_verification.shtml
Water Well Driller	https://www2.cslb.ca.gov/OnlineServices/CheckLicenseII/CheckLicense.aspx
X-Ray Technician/Equipment (Registration)	www.apps.cdph.ca.gov/rhbxray/

State and Local Courts

State Court Structure: **Superior Courts** have jurisdiction over all felonies, misdemeanors, traffic matters, and all civil cases including family law, probate, juvenile, and general civil matters. Some courts known as **Limited Jurisdiction Superior Courts** generally hear civil cases under $25,000. But it is important to note that Limited Courts may try minor felonies.

Appellate Courts: The page at www.courts.ca.gov provides access to all opinions from the Supreme Court and Appeals Courts from 1850 to present. Click on *Case Information.*

About Court Online Access: There is no statewide online access available for the trial court record index. However, a number of counties have their own online access system and some provide web access at no fee. Of note, the Los Angeles County has an extensive free and fee-based online system at www.lasuperiorcourt.org. The fee based service has separate charges for a name search or for downloading a case file. The free portion is only available if you know the case number.

County Sites:

Alameda County

All Superior Court Locations www.alameda.courts.ca.gov/

Civil: Online access to calendars, limited civil case summaries and complex litigations are free from Domain Web at the website. Search limited cases by number; litigations by case number. Images are also available for Probate cases for documents filed after January 31, 2006, except for conservatorships, guardianships and confidential documents. *Criminal:* At the website, search "Find Your Court Date" to determine if a name has an upcoming court date.

Butte County

All Superior Court Locations www.buttecourt.ca.gov

Civil: Limited case index searching by name is free at www.buttecourt.ca.gov/online_index/cmssearch.cfm. There is also a calendar lookup at www.buttecourt.ca.gov/calendarlookup/cmscalendarlookup.cfm. *Criminal:* Limited case index searching by name is free online at www.buttecourt.ca.gov/online_index/cmssearch.cfm. There is also a calendar lookup, see above.

Colusa County

All Superior Court Locations www.colusa.courts.ca.gov

Civil: The actual web search site is http://cms.colusa.courts.ca.gov/ for a civil or family case index search. Can search by name or case number. *Criminal:* The actual web search site is http://cms.colusa.courts.ca.gov/ for a criminal or traffic case index search. Can search by name or case number.

Contra Costa County

All Superior Court Locations www.cc-courts.org

Civil: With registration, use Open Access to view Civil, Probate, Family and Small Claims information is free at http://icms.cc-courts.org/iotw/. Also, lookup your court case info free at http://icms.cc-courts.org/tellme/. Online civil search results include month/year of birth.

El Dorado County

All Superior Court Locations www.eldoradocourt.org/

Civil & Criminal: Access alpha Case Index lists back to year 2000 free at www.eldoradocourt.org/caseindex/case_index.aspx. Search monthly calendars free at http://eldocourtweb.eldoradocourt.org/calendar.aspx.

Fresno County

All Superior Court Locations - Civil www.fresnosuperiorcourt.org

Civil: Access to civil general and limited, probate, family law, and small claims cases is free at www.fresnosuperiorcourt.org/case_info/. Unlawful Detainer cases are not available for sixty days after the complaint is filed with the court. In cases filed in the Civil Department, the three initials of the judge assigned to the case are being listed at the end of the case number on documents.

Glenn County

Superior Court www.glenncourt.ca.gov

Civil: Search case index at www.glenncourt.ca.gov/online_index/. *Criminal:* same

Kern County

All Superior Court Locations www.kern.courts.ca.gov

Civil: Search civil records free at www.kern.courts.ca.gov/home.aspx. Civil case info and calendars on special kiosk computers located at every court location and at website. *Criminal:* Access defendant database free at www.co.kern.ca.us/courts/crimcal/crim_index_def.asp; Results show year of birth only; old records being added. Current court calendars free at www.co.kern.ca.us/courts/crim_index_case_info_cal.asp. Access defendant hearings schedule at www.co.kern.ca.us/courts/crimcal/crim_hearing_srch.asp. Also, search sheriff inmate list at www.kern.courts.ca.gov/case-menu-main.asp. Click on "inmate search."

Lassen County

All Superior Court Locations www.lassencourt.ca.gov

Civil: The courts provides a free index search at www.lassencourt.ca.gov/index.php?option=com_wrapper&view=wrapper&Itemid=137. The search includes civil and family law. Search by name or case number. *Criminal:* The courts provides a free index search at www.lassencourt.ca.gov/index.php?option=com_wrapper&view=wrapper&Itemid=137. The search includes criminal and traffic. Search by name or case number.

Los Angeles County

All Los Angeles Superior Court Locations - Civil www.lasuperiorcourt.org

Civil: There are two search services at https://www.lasuperiorcourt.org/onlineservices/LAECourtOnlineIndex.htm. Both are fee based. A civil party name search returns a list of litigant names, corresponding case types, filing dates, filing locations, and number of available imaged documents; fee is $4.75 per record. One may also download civil case document images. The fee is per case file is $7.50 for first 10 pages, then $.07 each add'l page with a maximum of $40.00. Unlimited (over 25K) civil, probate and family law records go back to 1983, unlimited civil to 1991, small claims 1992 to present. A free case summary search is at https://www.lasuperiorcourt.org/onlineservices/civilIndex; the case number is needed. **$$$**

All Los Angeles Superior Court Location - Criminal www.lasuperiorcourt.org

Search felony & misdemeanor defendant index for a fee at https://www.lasuperiorcourt.org/OnlineServices/criminalindex/index.asp. Online search fee is $4.oo to $4.75 a search based on volume. If available, the counts, current charges, disposition and disposition dates are shown. **$$$**

Marin County

Superior Court www.marincourt.org/

Civil: Access to the court index back to the 1970s is free at www.marincourt.org/PublicIndex/Default.aspx or http://public.marincourt.org/publicindex/default.aspx. *Criminal:* Access to the court index back to the 1970s is free at www.marincourt.org/PublicIndex/Default.aspx or http://public.marincourt.org/publicindex/default.aspx

Mendocino County

All Superior Court Locations www.mendocino.courts.ca.gov

Civil: Search index at www.mendocino.courts.ca.gov/caseindex.html. Not all indices are online. *Criminal:* Search index at www.mendocino.courts.ca.gov/caseindex.html. A separate search must be performed for records prior to 2000.

Monterey County

All Superior Court Locations www.monterey.courts.ca.gov

Civil: Access court data free at https://www.justicepartners.monterey.courts.ca.gov/Public/JPPublicIndex.aspx. Search calendars at https://www.justicepartners.monterey.courts.ca.gov/Public/JPPublicCalendarSearch.aspx, When searching court record index online there could be missing identifiers, and computer systems are not always up-to-date, and do not have as wide a date range as when searching onsite.

Napa County

Superior Court - Criminal www.napa.courts.ca.gov

Civil: Access to tentative rulings is online free at www.napa.courts.ca.gov/Civil/civil_tentative.asp. These only go back about 1 week. Civil calendars are also online. *Criminal:* Online access (BUT no name search) to criminal and traffic index is at https://secure.napa.courts.ca.gov/UnifiedLookup/UnifiedCaseLookup.html. Results return name and case number.

Nevada County

All Superior Court Locations www.nevadacountycourts.com/

Civil: Access to case calendar is free at http://nevadacountycourts.com/cgi/dba/casecal/db.cgi. *Criminal:* same

Orange County

All Superior Court - Civil Locations www.occourts.org

Civil: Access civil case index and calendars free at www.occourts.org/online-services/case-access/. Family court calendars also shown. Civil, small claims, probate cases index for the county can be purchased on CD; index goes back to 12/31/01 or can be purchased on monthly basis.

All Superior Court - Criminal Locations www.occourts.org

Criminal: Online access to criminal, traffic and calendars free at www.occourts.org/online-services/case-access/. Search results include dispositions, dismissals, sentences, and participants, but no DOB. Index rarely goes back beyond 2002. Also shows names, aliases, and Court True name. The case index can be purchased on CD; index goes back to 12/31/01 or can be purchased on monthly basis.

Placer County

All Superior Court - Civil Locations www.placer.courts.ca.gov/

Civil: An online index search is available at www.placer.courts.ca.gov/case-search.html for cases back to 1999. Data is updated once a week.

All Superior Court - Criminal Locations www.placer.courts.ca.gov/

Civil: An online index search is available at www.placer.courts.ca.gov/case-search.html for cases back to 1999. *Criminal:* An online index search is available at www.placer.courts.ca.gov/case-search.html for cases back to 1999. Data is updated once a week.

Riverside County

All Superior Court - Civil Locations www.riverside.courts.ca.gov/

Civil: The fee for a name search from http://public-access.riverside.courts.ca.gov/OpenAccess/ is $1 for 1 search, $3.50 for 2-5 searches, or $5 for 6-10 searches. A flat fee of $250 per month provides an unlimited number of online searches. To view or print civil court documents, the fee is $1.00 per page 1st 5 pages, then $.40 ea add'l with cap of $40. If a civil case number is provided, the register of actions for that case may be viewed free of charge.**$$$**

All Superior Court - Criminal Locations www.riverside.courts.ca.gov/

Criminal: The fee for a name search from http://public-access.riverside.courts.ca.gov/OpenAccess/ is $1 for 1 search, $3.50 for 2-5 searches, or $5 for 6-10 searches. A flat fee of $250 per month provides an unlimited number of online searches. Criminal case images are not provided. Email courtweb1@riverside.courts.ca.gov or contact the Executive Office at 951-955-5536 to establish an account. **$$$**

Sacramento County

Superior Court www.saccourt.ca.gov/

Civil: Access court records back to 1993 free at https://services.saccourt.com/indexsearchnew/. Includes civil, probate, small claims, unlawful detainer, family as well as criminal. *Criminal:* Access criminal records back to 1989 free at https://services.saccourt.com/indexsearchnew/. May also search using DOB.

San Bernardino County

All Superior Court Locations www.sb-court.org/

Civil: Online access to civil cases is free at www.sb-court.org/Divisions/Civil/CaseInformationOnline.aspx. Access to limited Probate Notes is free at www.sb-court.org/Divisions/Probate/ProbateNotes.aspx. Online results show DOB month and year only. *Criminal:* Access to criminal cases and traffic is free at hhttp://206.169.61.205/openaccess/criminal/default.aspdefault.asp. Includes calendars. Note that this Internet service is provided "as is", with no warranties, express or implied, including the implied warranty of fitness for a particular purpose, the court does not guarantee or warrant the completeness. Caution.

San Diego County

All Superior Court Locations - Civil www.sdcourt.ca.gov

Online search for case information for civil and probate cases initiated after 01/01/2008 is free at www.sdcourt.ca.gov/portal/page?_pageid=55,1056871&_dad=portal&_schema=PORTAL. Also lists calendars and new filings. *Criminal:* Online search for case information, calendars, and new filings is free at http://courtindex.sdcourt.ca.gov/CISPublic/enter.

San Francisco County

Superior Court - Civil www.sfsuperiorcourt.org/

Civil: The San Francisco Superior Court offers online queries by case number, name search, and tentative rulings to the Register of Actions. Documents included for cases in the following departments: Civil, Family Law, Probate, and Small Claims. Visit www.sfsuperiorcourt.org/index.aspx?page=467

San Joaquin County

All Superior Court Locations www.stocktoncourt.org/courts/

Civil: Civil: Free access to civil and family case summaries countywide, with name searching, at www.stocktoncourt.org/courts/caseinquiry.htm. Records to family law, juvenile court, guardianship and conservatorship, mental health, criminal, civil harassment, workplace violence prevention are not available online. *Criminal:* Access only calendars free at www.stocktoncourt.org/courts/caseinquiry.htm. Effective 04/01/2011 access to historical records was removed.

San Mateo County

All Superior Court Locations www.sanmateocourt.org

Civil: Online access is free at www.sanmateocourt.org/midx/. *Criminal:* Search all county case records including criminal for free at www.sanmateocourt.org/midx/. Also, search traffic citations at https://www.sanmateocourt.org/traffic/.

Santa Barbara County

All Superior Court Locations - Civil www.sbcourts.org/index.asp

Civil: Search general civil index 1975 to present or limited civil from 1997 free at www.sbcourts.org/pubindex/. Also, a CD-Rom of monthly court indices from all divisions is for $40.00.

Santa Clara County

All Superior Court Locations - www.sccsuperiorcourt.org

Civil: Civil, Family, Probate, and Small Claims case records and court calendars are free online at www.sccaseinfo.org/. CD-Rom is also available, fee-$150.00. *Criminal:* Access to the criminal case index is at www.scscourt.org/court_divisions/criminal/index_search.asp. Traffic and Local Ordinance case information is at www.sccaseinfo.org.

Santa Cruz County

All Superior Court locations - Civil www.santacruzcourt.org

Civil: Access civil records free at www.santacruzcourt.org/Case%20Info/index.htm. Includes civil, small claims, family law, probate. Access using case number or party name. When searching online court record there could be missing identifiers, and computer systems are not always up-to-date, and do not have as wide a date range as when searching onsite.

Shasta County

All Superior Court Locations www.shastacourts.com

Civil: Access to civil division index free back to 1993 at http://caselookup.shastacourts.com:8080/cgi-bin/webcase01r. Search by case, name, or date. Also, the county offers access to the Integrated Justice System (IJS), this is meant for attorneys and requires a password. And registration.**$$$** *Criminal:* Access to the criminal docket index is free back to 1993 at http://caselookup.shastacourts.com:8080/cgi-bin/webcase01r. Search by case, name, or date.

Siskiyou County

All Superior Court Locations www.siskiyou.courts.ca.gov

Civil: Access to county superior court records is free at www.siskiyou.courts.ca.gov/CaseHistory.asp. Includes traffic but not juvenile. *Criminal:* Online access to criminal and traffic records is same as civil

Solano County

All Superior Court Locations www.solano.courts.ca.gov/

Civil: Online access to countywide civil record index is free online. Click on Court Connect from the home page. Also, civil tentative rulings and probate notes are available. Online search provides a case number and limited docket entry information, no personal identifiers except name. Online search request does not allow for add'l identifiers. Missing records can be avoided with an in person search for some case types. *Criminal:* Online access to countywide court record index (back to year 2000 generally) is free at http://courtconnect.solanocourts.com/courtconnect/ck_public_qry_main.cp_main_idx. Online search provides a case number and limited docket entry information, no personal identifiers except name. Online search request does not allow for add'l identifiers. Missing records, often older felonies, can be avoided with an in person search.

Sonoma County

Superior Court www.sonomasuperiorcourt.com/index.php

Civil: Limited search free at www.sonomasuperiorcourt.com/index.php for court calendars, cases recently filed, tentative rulings. *Criminal:* Search free calendars directly at www.sonomasuperiorcourt.com/index.php. Online index does not provide register of actions, just case number and parties. Goes back 3 months

Stanislaus County

Superior Court www.stanct.org/

Civil: Search yearly case index by name and year at http://caseindex.stanct.org/. Also, Superior Court Case Index is available alphabetically in a 2-CD set. Case Index is updated quarterly and includes cases filed 1900-1999, and 2000-present day. Cost is $15.00 per each 2-CD set, which includes S&H. *Criminal:* Access the yearly case indices free at http://caseindex.stanct.org/.1 Superior Court Case Index is available alphabetically in a 2-CD set. Case Index is updated quarterly and includes cases filed 1900-1999, and 2000-present day. Cost is $15.00 per each 2-CD set, which includes S&H. **$$$**

Sutter County

Superior Court - Civil www.suttercourts.com

Civi & Criminal: Access calendars free at www.suttercourts.com/unprotected/Calendar/themed.asp.

Tehama County

All Superior Court Locations www.tehamacourt.ca.gov

Civil: Search by name or case number at http://cms.tehamacourt.ca.gov/. Daily calendars also online. Cases online starting with NSC or NCI are at Red Bluff; SSC or SCI are at Corning. *Criminal:* same as civil.

Tulare County

Superior Court www.tularesuperiorcourt.ca.gov

Civil: Daily calendar and civil tentative rulings and probate recommendations at www.tularesuperiorcourt.ca.gov. *Criminal:* Daily calendar at www.tularesuperiorcourt.ca.gov.

Tuolumne County

Superior Court - Criminal www.tuolumne.courts.ca.gov

Criminal: Access criminal records by case number of DR# at www.tuolumne.courts.ca.gov; click on "Criminal Division."

Ventura County

All Superior Court Locations www.ventura.courts.ca.gov

Civil: Access to case information, calendars and dockets is free at www.ventura.courts.ca.gov/via/CaseSearch.aspx. Search by defendant or plaintiff name, case number, or date. Search probate at www.ventura.courts.ca.gov/probate.html. *Criminal:* Access to case information back to 1995, calendars and dockets is free at https://secured.countyofventura.org/courtservices/CourtServiceHome.aspx.

Yolo County

Superior Court www.yolo.courts.ca.gov/

Civil: Calendars are online free at www.yolocourts.com/calendar_daily.html. Search Probate Notes at www.yolocourts.com/probate_notes.html. *Criminal:* Access criminal and traffic records free at http://secure.yolo.courts.ca.gov:80/GetWeb/YoloCrimTrafStart.html but no name searching; search by case number or DL only, DOB requested. Also, calendars are free at www.yolocourts.com/calendar_daily.html.

Recorders, Assessors, and Other Sites of Note

Recording Office Organization: 58 counties, 58 recording offices. The recording officer is the County Recorder. Recordings are usually located in a Grantor/Grantee or General Index. Federal and state tax liens on personal property of businesses are filed with the Secretary of State. Other federal and state tax liens are filed with the County Recorder, and state tax liens on individuals can be found at both the Sec of State and county.

Statewide or Multi-Jurisdiction Access: There is no statewide system. A number of counties offer online access to assessor and real estate information.

County Sites:

Alameda County ***Real Estate, Deed, Lien, Fictitious Name, Voter Status Records*** www.acgov.org/auditor/clerk/ Access the clerk-recorder's official public records and fictitious name databases for free at http://rechart1.acgov.org/. Also, check voter registration status at www.acgov.org/rov/voter_reg_lookup.htm.

Property, Taxation Records Access to the Property Assessment database is free at www.acgov.org/MS/prop/index.aspx but no name searching. Also, GIS/mapping for free at www.acgov.org/assessor/maps.htm. Also, property tax data is found at www.acgov.org/propertytax/online.htm.

Amador County ***Recorded Documents Records*** www.co.amador.ca.us/index.aspx?page=94 Access to the county's recorded documents is free at www.criis.com/cgi-bin/doc_search.cgi?COUNTY=amador&YEARSEGMENT=current&TAB=1.

Property, Taxation Records Access GIS/mapping for free at www.co.amador.ca.us/index.aspx?page=287&parent=931. Also, tax sale data is at www.co.amador.ca.us/index.aspx?page=132; search by year.

Butte County Clerk/Recorder ***Real Estate, Fictitious Business Name Records*** http://clerk-recorder.buttecounty.net Access to the recorder's database of official documents is free at http://clerk-recorder.buttecounty.net/Riimsweb/Asp/ORInquiry.asp. Records go back to 1988. Marriages, births and deaths are no longer available.

Property, Taxation Records View property tax data free at www.buttecounty.net/Online%20Services.aspx. Also, access to tax sales lists is free through a private company at www.bid4assets.com/.

Calaveras County ***Property, Taxation Records*** Access property tax data free at http://calaverasgov.us/QuickLinks/PropertyInfo.aspx. No name searching. Also, access GIS Project of property data free at http://calaverasgov.us/Departments/HZ/TechnologyServices/GIS.aspx. Click on \"New GIS Viewer\". No name searching.

Colusa County ***Property, Taxation Records*** Access to parcel searches for free at http://assr.parcelquest.com/PQGov/StdSearch.aspx?username=abccol&password=def&coassr=WAYNE%20ZOLLER.

Contra Costa County ***Recorded Documents Records*** www.ccclerkrec.us/connect/site/ Recorder office records are at www.criis.com/contracosta.html# for a fee. Fictitious Business names are at www.criis.com/cgi-bin/fbn_search.cgi?COUNTY=contracosta&YEARSEGMENT=current&TAB=1 for a fee. **$$$**

Property, Taxation Records Access to GIS/mapping records for free at www.ccmap.us/interactive_maps.aspx.

El Dorado County ***Recorded Documents, Fictitious Name Index Records*** www.edcgov.us/CountyClerk/ Access to the Recorder's index is free at www.edcgov.us/Government/CountyClerk/Recorded_Document_Lookup.aspx.

Property, Taxation Records Parcel, tax, and personal property information available free at http://main.edcgov.us/CGI/WWB012/WWM400/A.

Fresno County ***Real Estate, Deed, Lien, Mortgage, Birth, Death Records*** www.co.fresno.ca.us/Departments.aspx?id=186 Access to the recorder database is free at www.criis.com/fresno.html.

Property, Taxation Records Download the Assessment Roll at www.co.fresno.ca.us/DepartmentPage.aspx?id=12324.

Humboldt County ***Property, Taxation Records*** Download GIS data from http://co.humboldt.ca.us/planning/maps/datainventory/gisdatalist.asp. There is a myriad of data available.

Imperial County ***Recorded Documents, Marriage Records*** www.imperialcounty.net/Recorder/Default.htm Access the Recorder's Official records index free at http://implookup.imperialcounty.net/. Index goes back to 4/1/1986, but no images available. Fictitious business names are at www.imperialcounty.net/Recorder/FBN/Fbn_Page.htm. Index available from 01/01/2006 to present.

Property, Taxation Records A GIS-mapping site can assist you in finding parcel data free at www.geovieweronline.net/website/icpublic/viewer.htm but no name searching.

Inyo County ***Real Estate, Lien Records*** www.inyocounty.us/Recorder/Clerk-Recorder.html Access to recorded documents free at www.criis.com/cgi-bin/doc_search.cgi?COUNTY=inyo&YEARSEGMENT=current&TAB=1. Documents from 1982 to present. Also, access to fictitious business search free at www.criis.com/cgi-bin/fbn_search.cgi?COUNTY=inyo&YEARSEGMENT=current&TAB=1. Documents from 1990 to present.

Kern County ***Recorded Documents, Fictitious Business Name Records*** http://recorder.co.kern.ca.us/index.php Search recorders database of deeds free at http://recorderonline.co.kern.ca.us/. Also, search county clerk's fictitious business name database free at www.co.kern.ca.us/ctyclerk/dba/default.asp. Search county recent sales data at http://kerndata.com.

Property, Taxation Records Assessor database records available free at http://assessor.co.kern.ca.us/propertysearch/index.php. Search tax collector data at www.kcttc.co.kern.ca.us/payment/mainsearch.aspx.

Kings County ***Property, Taxation Records*** A subscription-based access system is available at www.countyofkings.com/acr/Assessor/online_access.html. There is a $50 one-time set-up fee. There are no monthly fees. Access is $.15 per screen. Data available includes ownership including history, taxes, assessor maps, and boat and airplane information.**$$$**

Lake County ***Real Estate, Grantor/Grantee, Deed, Lien, Mortgage Records*** www.co.lake.ca.us/Government/Directory/Assessor-Recorder.htm Limited index display of official records can be accessed at http://acm.co.lake.ca.us/recorder/cms_recordssearch.asp.

Property, Taxation Records Parcel records on the GIS Mapping site available by clicking on Lake County Base Maps free at http://gis.co.lake.ca.us/. No name searching.

Lassen County ***Real Estate, Deed Records*** www.lassencounty.org/govt/dept/county_clerk/County_Recorder.asp Access to the recorder index only is free at http://clerk.co.lassen.ca.us/recorder/web/ with registration or logon free as Public User. Recorded documents go back to 7/1985.

Property, Taxation Records Access to real estate for a fee at http://assr.parcelquest.com/PQGov/StdSearch.aspx?username=abclas&password=def Also, access to tax sales lists is free through a private company at www.bid4assets.com/.**$$$**

Los Angeles County ***Fictitious Business Names Records*** www.lavote.net/Default.cfm?Splash=NO Search fictitious business names for free at www.lavote.net/CLERK/FBN_Search.cfm.

Property, Taxation Records Property database subscription access at http://assessor.lacounty.gov/extranet/outsidesales/online.aspx. $100 monthly for maintaining the account, plus $1.00 per inquiry/screen, and $75.00 signup fee. Also search property/assessor data free at http://assessor.lacounty.gov/extranet/datamaps/pais.aspx.**$$$**

Madera County ***Property, Taxation Records*** Access parcel and ownership data free on the GIS-mapping site free at http://63.192.182.23/parcelview/pv_blank.aspx?g=.

Marin County ***Real Estate, Grantor/Grantee, Deed Records*** www.co.marin.ca.us/depts/AR/Main/Recorder.cfm Search the county Grantor/Grantee index free at www.co.marin.ca.us/depts/AR/RiiMs/index.asp. Also, search the real estate sales by month and year at www.co.marin.ca.us/depts/AR/main/Sales.cfm. Search business names by type at www.marin.org/bizmo/.

Property, Taxation Records Search the property tax database at www.co.marin.ca.us/depts/AR/COMPASS/index.asp, there is no name searching.

Mendocino County ***Property, Taxation Records*** A free property tax search is at www.co.mendocino.ca.us/tax/cgi-bin/pTax.pl. Must search by street address or parcel number - name search not available.

Merced County ***Real Estate, Grantor/Grantee, Deed Records*** www.co.merced.ca.us/index.aspx?NID=239 Access to the recorder official records index PARIS system is free at www.recorder.merced.ca.us/.

Property, Taxation Records Search parcel maps at www.co.merced.ca.us/index.aspx?NID=196. Search by fee parcel number or assessment number at www.co.merced.ca.us/index.aspx?NID=193 but no name searching.

Mono County ***Property, Taxation Records*** Access property data free at www.monocounty.ca.gov/departments/assessor/public_inquiry.html, but no name searching. GIS searching provided at https://gis.mono.ca.gov/site/data.

Monterey County Recorder ***Real Estate, Grantor/Grantee, Deed, Lien Records*** www.co.monterey.ca.us./recorder/ Access the county PARIS system including official records and fictitious business names free at http://65.249.61.8/. Official records go back to 1978. When searching recorded documents online there could be missing identifiers, and computers are not always up-to-date, and do not have as wide a date range as when searching onsite.

Property, Taxation Records Search assessment data free at http://000sweb.co.monterey.ca.us/assessor/asmt-query.htm but no name searching. The county tax defaulted property list is at www.co.monterey.ca.us/taxcollector/Auction_Internet.html.

Napa County ***Real Estate, Grantor/Grantee, Deed, Judgment, Lien, Voter Registration Records*** www.countyofnapa.org/Recorder-Clerk/ Access \"Official Records\" by subscription; fee- $3600 per year. Index goes back to 1/1976; images back to 1/1976. Also, search Official Records Inquiry site for real estate and Grantor/Grantee index back to 1/1976 free at http://services.countyofnapa.org/OfficialRecordsPublic/. **$$$**

Property, Taxation Records Search assessor's property tax payments free at www.countyofnapa.org/PropertyTaxPayments/, but no name searching. Also, search for property data for free at www.countyofnapa.org/assessorparceldata/. Also search for property data on the GIS-mapping site free at www.countyofnapa.org/Assessor/.

Nevada County ***Real Estate, Deed, Judgment, UCC, Fictitious Name, Index Recorded Maps Records*** www.mynevadacounty.com/nc/recorder Access to the county clerk database of recordings and assumed names is free at http://recorder.nevcounty.net/oncoreweb/. Also, subscription access to the recorders full database is $200 per month fee. This is only the index, cannot view images online. **$$$**

Property, Taxation Records Access to parcel data and maps free at www.mynevadacounty.com/nc/assessor/Pages/Home.aspx.. Also, view and pay property tax records at www.mynevadacounty.com/ttc/index.cfm?ccs=1614&cs=4357.

Orange County ***Recorded Documents Records*** http://ocgov.com/gov/clerk/ Orange County Grantor/Grantee index is free online at https://cr.ocgov.com/recorderworks/. Records are from 1982 to present. Also, search fictitious business names at https://efbn.ocgov.com/eFBNweb/default.aspx.

Property, Taxation Records Search property tax records at http://tax.ocgov.com/tcweb/search_page.asp; no name searching. Also, search tax parcel data, aircraft, and vessels free at http://tax.ocgov.com/tcweb/search_page.asp but no name searching.

Placer County ***Recorded Documents Records*** www.placer.ca.gov/Departments/Recorder.aspx Recorder office index records are free at https://portal1.recordfusion.com/countyweb/login.do?countyname=Placer.

Property, Taxation Records Assessor's property assessment data free at www.placer.ca.gov/Departments/Assessor/Assessment%20Inquiry/Assessment%20Inquiry%20Iframe.aspx. Also, search GIS data at http://lis.placer.ca.gov/gis.asp?s=1000&h2=545.

Riverside County ***Real Estate, Grantor/Grantee, Deed, Lien, Judgment, Mortgage, Fictitious Name Records*** http://riverside.asrclkrec.com Search Grantor/Grantee index and recorded data at http://riverside.asrclkrec.com/OSVitalChekmsg.asp. Also, access to county fictitious name database is free at http://riverside.asrclkrec.com/OSfbn.asp. **$$$**

Property, Taxation Records Access property tax data free at http://pic.asrclkrec.com/Default.aspx but no name searching.

Sacramento County ***Real Estate, Grantor/Grantee, Deed, Fictitious Names, Business License, Voter Registration Records*** www.ccr.saccounty.net/Pages/default.aspx Access Clerk-recorder Grantee/Grantor index back to 1965 for free at www.erosi.saccounty.net/Inputs.asp. The county's site is www.ccr.saccounty.net/Pages/e-ROSI.aspx. Search fictitious names at https://apsonline.saccounty.net/CitizenAccess/SACCO_FBNSearch.aspx.

Property, Taxation Records Search property tax & parcels at www.eproptax.saccounty.net/; no name searching. Also, find property data at http://assessorparcelviewer.saccounty.net/GISViewer/Default.aspx; no name searching. Search treasurer tax sale, tax bill, and fictitious names free at www.saccounty.net/PropertyTaxes/default.htm.

San Benito County ***Property, Taxation Records*** Access to GIS/mapping for free at www.lynxgis.com/sanbenitoco/.

San Bernardino County ***Recorded Documents Records*** www.sbcounty.gov/arc/index2.html Auditor/Controller Grantor/Grantee recording index back to 1980 is free at http://acrparis.co.san-bernardino.ca.us/cgi-bin/odsmnu1.html/input. Recorder online search does not show actual doc. Search fictitious business names at http://170.164.50.51/fbn/index.html.

Property, Taxation Records Records on the County Assessor database are free at www.mytaxcollector.com/trSearch.aspx. No name searching. Property can also be searched on PIMS system at www.co.san-bernardino.ca.us/assessor/DataSales.asp. This is a subscription service.

San Diego County ***Recorded Documents, Fictitious Name Records*** http://arcc.co.san-diego.ca.us/arcc/default.aspx From the home page above or at http://arcc.co.san-diego.ca.us/services/grantorgrantee/search.aspx search for recorded documents and property sales. Search fictitious business names at https://arcc.co.san-diego.ca.us/services/fbn/search.aspx.

Property, Taxation Records From the county home page above or at https://arcc.co.san-diego.ca.us/services/parcelmap/search.aspx search for assessor data on the parcel mapping site. Search for property sales data at http://arcc.co.san-diego.ca.us/services/propsales/propsales_search.aspx; no name searching. Assessor date also available in bulk, see https://arcc.co.san-diego.ca.us/subscription/login.aspx or call 619-685-2455.**$$$**

San Francisco County ***Real Estate, Deed, Real Estate, Lien, Judgment Records*** www.sfassessor.org/ Search recorders database free at http://criis.com/sanfrancisco.html. Records from 1990 to present. Limited vital statistic data is searchable at www.sfgenealogy.com/sf/, a privately operated site.

Property, Taxation Records For recorded documents for free at http://criis.com/sanfrancisco.html.

San Joaquin County ***Real Estate, Grantor, Grantee Records*** www.co.san-joaquin.ca.us/assessor_recorder/ Access to grantor/grantee database free at www.co.san-joaquin.ca.us/Recorder/grantorgrantee.aspx

Property, Taxation Records Access property data on the GIS-mapping site free at www.sjmap.org/mapapps.asp, but no name searching.

San Luis Obispo County ***Real Estate, Grantor/Grantee, Deed, Judgment, Lien, Mortgage, Fictitious Business Name, Records*** www.slocounty.ca.gov/clerk Search the recorder database for free at http://clerk.slocounty.ca.gov/officialrecords/Search.aspx.

Property, Taxation Records Access property information search free at www.slocounty.ca.gov/Page81.aspx. Also, parcel map records free at http://assessor.slocounty.ca.gov/pisa/.

San Mateo County ***Real Estate, Grantor/Grantee, Deed, Property Tax, Fictitious Name Records*** www.smcare.org Access the recorder's grantor/grantee index free at www.smcare.org/apps/LandDocs/grantee_index.asp. Also, search fictitious business names at www.smcare.org/clerk/fictitious/default.asp.

Property, Taxation Records Records on county property tax data site is free at http://smctweb1.co.sanmateo.ca.us/index.html, view secured or unsecured.

Santa Barbara County ***Real Estate, Grantor/Grantee, Deed, Lien Records*** www.sbcrecorder.com/Home.aspx Search the recorder's grantor/grantee index at www.sbcrecorder.com/ClerkRecorder/GrantorGranteeIndex.aspx.

Property, Taxation Records Access to assessor online property info system (OPIS) in free at www.sbcassessor.com/Assessor/AssessorRealEstateServices.aspx but no name searching. Records go back to 1989. Also, search property tax bills at http://taxes.co.santa-barbara.ca.us/propertytax.asp; click on View Breakdown of Secured Property Tax Bills. No name searching.

Santa Clara County ***Real Estate, Grantor/Grantee, Deed, Fictitious Business Name, Birth Records*** www.sccgov.org/sites/rec/Pages/Office-of-the-Clerk-Recorder.aspx Access to the County Clerk-Recorder database is free at www.clerkrecordersearch.org/. Search births 1905-1995 free at www.mariposaresearch.net/php/. Also, search fictitious business names for free at www.clerkrecordersearch.org/cgi-bin/FBNSearch.html/input. Also, search the tax collector database at http://payments.scctax.org/payment/jsp/startup.jsp. No name searching.

Property, Taxation Records Search the assessment roll free a https://www.sccassessor.org/index.php/online-services/property-search/real-property.

Santa Cruz County ***Real Estate, Deed, Grantor/Grantee Records*** www.co.santa-cruz.ca.us/rcd/ Access to the recorder's official records is free at http://clerkrecorder.co.santa-cruz.ca.us/. Online indexes go back to 1978. Images from 4/1/97.

Property, Taxation Records Access the assessor's parcel data free at http://sccounty01.co.santa-cruz.ca.us/ASR/. No name searching. Also, search for property data using the GIS map at http://gis.co.santa-cruz.ca.us.

Shasta County ***Deeds, Liens, Judgments, Vital Records Records*** www.co.shasta.ca.us/index/recorder_index.aspx See www.co.shasta.ca.us/riimspublic/Asp/ORPublicInquiry.asp for free access to index. Search by name, document type or document ID. Records available for viewing from 1/2/1924 to present. This agency links online requesters to www.vitalchek.com/.

Property, Taxation Records Search assessor documents for free at www.co.shasta.ca.us/index/assessor_index/assessment_inquiry.aspx#. Records on the City of Redding Parcel Search By Parcel Number Server are free at http://cor400.ci.redding.ca.us/nd/gow3lkap.ndm/input. CA state law has removed owner names.

Sierra County ***Property, Taxation Records*** Access to tax sales lists is free through a private company at www.bid4assets.com/.

Siskiyou County ***Recorded Documents Records*** www.co.siskiyou.ca.us/Assessor/recorder.aspx Access to index from 1974 to current found at www.criis.com/siskiyou.html. No images available. Also at this site are fictitious business searches.

Solano County ***Real Estate, Grantor/Grantee, Deed, Judgment, Lien Records*** www.solanocounty.com Access the recorder's indexes free at http://recorderonline.solanocounty.com. Access recorded data free at http://recorderonline.solanocounty.com/cgi-bin/odsmnu1.html/input.

Property, Taxation Records Access to Treasurer/tax collector property taxes and tax sales for free at www.solanocounty.com/depts/ttcc/default.asp.

Sonoma County ***Real Estate, Deed, Lien, UCC, Voter Registration Records*** www.sonoma-county.org/recorder/aboutus.asp Access recorder index records free at http://deeds.sonoma-county.org/. No images on this system. Also, with address, ZIP, and DOB search voter registration records free at http://vote.sonoma-county.org/voter_registration_status.aspx?sid=1009.

Property, Taxation Records Access assessor information free at http://sonoma-county.org/assessor/.

Stanislaus County ***Property, Taxation Records*** Access property assessment data free at www.co.stanislaus.ca.us/assessor/assessor-disclaimer2.shtm but no name searching. Fuller data for professional service companies is available by subscription.

Sutter County ***Real Estate, Grantor/Grantee, Deed, Fictitious Name Records*** www.suttercounty.org Access the recorder database free at www.suttercounty.org/apps/recordsquery/clerk/. Records go back to 12/29/1994.

Property, Taxation Records Access assessment and property tax records free at www.suttercounty.org/doc/apps/recordsquery/recordsquery but no name searching.

Tehama County ***Real Estate, Grantor/Grantee, Deed, Lien Records*** www.co.tehama.ca.us/index.php?option=com_content&task=view&id=19&Itemid=24&phpMyAdmin=EnoGFkv%2Cc7dMRvqgsDQTPHxadm3&phpMyAdmin=dbe9156cbc4ca14cb7aebd15243fd0e1 Search recorder's official public record indexes free at http://tehamapublic.countyrecords.com/.

Property, Taxation Records Search property tax data on the county unsecured tax information lookup at www.co.tehama.ca.us/index.php?option=com_chronocontact&chronoformname=view_pay_taxes&Itemid=122.

Trinity County ***Fictitious Business Name Records*** www.trinitycounty.org/Departments/assessor-clerk-elect/clerkrecorder.htm Access to the Recorder's fictitious business names database is free at http://halfile.trinitycounty.org. For user name, enter \"fbn\"; leave password field empty.

Tulare County ***Recorded Documents Records*** www.tularecounty.ca.gov/clerkrecorder/ Search the recorders database including births, marriages, deaths free at http://riimsweb.co.tulare.ca.us/riimsweb/Asp/ORInquiry.asp. Subscription fee for all images and recorder's services is $780/00 per month. **$$$**

Property, Taxation Records Search treasurer/tax collector property data free at www.co.tulare.ca.us/government/treasurertax/mytaxes/default.asp; no name searching.

Tuolumne County ***Recorded Documents Records*** http://portal.co.tuolumne.ca.us/psp/ps/TUP_ASSESSOR/ENTP/h/?tab=DEFAULT Access the recorder grantor/grantee index at https://www.records.co.tuolumne.ca.us/. Logon using 'web' for free access; turn off your pop-up blocker.

Ventura County ***Recorded Documents, Fictitious Name Records*** http://recorder.countyofventura.org/county-recorder/ Access the county clerk & recorder database free at http://recorder.countyofventura.org/county-recorder/official-records/.

Property, Taxation Records Search property tax data for free at http://prop-tax.countyofventura.org/ but no name searching. Also, access to parcel maps free at http://assessor.countyofventura.org/research/mappage.asp.

Yolo County ***Real Estate, Deed, Lien, Birth, Death, Fictitious Business Name, Marriage Records*** www.yolorecorder.org Access to recordings on the county clerk database are free at www.yolorecorder.org/recsearch. County Fictitious Business Name at www.yolorecorder.org/recording/fictitious/lookup. Search City of Davis business licenses free at http://cityofdavis.org/ed/business/.

Property, Taxation Records With an address, look up parcel numbers free at www.yolocounty.org/Index.aspx?page=344. Search for parcels free at www.yolocounty.org/index.aspx?page=587.

Yuba County ***Real Estate, Deed, Judgment, Lien Records*** www.co.yuba.ca.us/departments/clerk/ Access recorded document index free at www.co.yuba.ca.us/services/Land%20Records/. Online records go back to 1989.

Property, Taxation Records Access to property records is free at www.co.yuba.ca.us/services/Parcel%20Search/, but no name searching.

Colorado

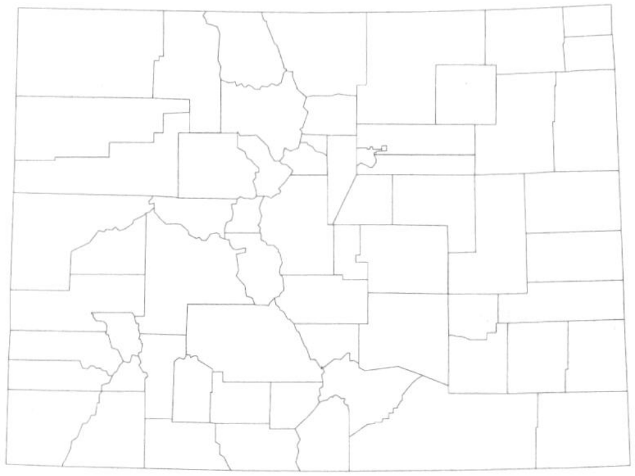

Capital: Denver
Denver County
Time Zone: MST
Population: 5,187,582
# of Counties: 64

Useful State Links

Website: www.colorado.gov
Governor: www.colorado.gov/governor
Attorney General: www.coloradoattorneygeneral.gov
State Archives: www.colorado.gov/dpa/doit/archives
State Statutes and Codes: www.state.co.us/gov_dir/leg_dir/olls/colorado_revised_statutes.htm
Legislative Bill Search: www.leg.state.co.us/Clics/CLICS2010A/csl.nsf/MainBills?openFrameset
Unclaimed Funds: www.colorado.gov/treasury/gcp/

State Public Record Agencies

Criminal Records

CO Bureau of Investigation, State Repository, Identification Unit, www.colorado.gov/cs/Satellite/CDPS-CBIMain/CBON/1251621089773 There is an Internet access athttps://www.cbirecordscheck.com/(X(1)S(uj0bbb3vwrhxgd55mcvlwf3q))/Index.aspx?CLS=N. Requesters must use a credit card, an account does not need to be established. However, account holders may set up a batch system. The fee is $6.85 per record. Account holders must place a minimum of $200 in the account. Arrests which are not supported by fingerprints will not be included in this database. Note warrant information, sealed records, and juvenile records are not available to the public. $$$

Sexual Offender Registry

Colorado Bureau of Investigation, SOR Unit, http://sor.state.co.us/?SOR=home.caveat The website gives access to only certain high-risk registered sex offenders in the following categories: Sexually Violent Predator (SVP), Multiple Offenses, Failed to Register, and adult felony conviction.

Incarceration Records

Colorado Department of Corrections, Offender Records, www.doc.state.co.us Search the Inmate Locater at www.doc.state.co.us/oss/. This is not a historical search; only active offenders and parolees are listed. Also, one may email locator requests from this URL - www.doc.state.co.us/contact?nid=49.

Corporation, LLC, LP, LLP, LLLP, Trademarks/Servicemarks, Fictitious/Assumed Name, Trade Name

Secretary of State, Business & Licensing, www.sos.state.co.us There are a variety of searches available from the home page including a business search, lobbyist search, and a charity & fundraiser search. Several other sites, not from this agency, are worthy of mention herein. Search securities dept. enforcement action at www.colorado.gov/cs/Satellite/DORA-SD/CBON/DORA/1251627123688. Search for charitable nonprofit members of CANPO at www.coloradononprofits.org/help-desk-resources/geographic-information-system/. *Other Options:* Various information is available as a one time order or via subscription. Transmittal can be through CDs, tapes or FTP.

Uniform Commercial Code, Federal Tax Liens

Secretary of State, UCC Division, https://www.sos.state.co.us/ucc/pages/home.jspx There are a number of search options at https://www.sos.state.co.us/ucc/pages/home.jspx. There a standard search, advanced search, a master list of Farm Product related filings, and one can also validate or certify a search. More extensive data is also available via subscription for ongoing business requesters. *Other Options:* Various information is available as a one time order or via subscription. Transmittal can be through CDs, tapes or FTP. The program may be delayed due to the redaction of SSNs.

Sales Tax Registrations

CO Dept of Revenue, Taxpayer Service Division, www.taxcolorado.com You can verify a sales tax license or exemption number at https://www.colorado.gov/revenueonline/_/#2.

Vital Records

Department of Public Health & Environment, Vital Records Section HSVR-A1, www.colorado.gov/cs/Satellite/CDPHE-CHEIS/CBON/1251593016787 Records can be ordered online from state designated vendor. Go to https://www.vitalchek.com/default.aspx. **$$$**

Driver Records

Division of Motor Vehicles, Driver Control/Traffic Record Room 150, www.colorado.gov/revenue/dmv Colorado Interactive, 600 17th Street, Ste. 2150 South, Denver, CO 80202, 800-970-3468, www.colorado.gov is the entity designated by the state to provide online access to driving records to registered users. Both interactive and batch processing is offered. Requesters must be approved per state compliance requirements with DPPA. There is an annual $75.00 registration fee, records are $2.00 each. Submit DL and either last name or DOB. For more information visit www.colorado.gov/registration/. The Colorado Interactive person to contact for more information is Amy Sawyer at 303-534-3468 extension 102. **$$$**
Other Options: A driver monitoring program is offered by Colorado Interactive.

Voter Registration, Campaign and Finance Disclosures

Department of State, Elections Department, www.sos.state.co.us/pubs/elections/main.htm Verify voter registration status at https://www.sos.state.co.us/voter-classic/secuRegVoterIntro.do. An overall search site with many options is at http://tracer.sos.colorado.gov/PublicSite/Search.aspx. View campaign finance documents at www.sos.state.co.us/ImageView/MainSearch.do?division=5. Search registered lobbyists at www.sos.state.co.us/lobby/Home.do. *Other Options:* The entire database of voter registration is available on CD-ROM. The cost is $500. No customization is available.

GED Certificates

GED Testing Program, www.cde.state.co.us/cdeadult/GEDindex.htm Requesters must first open an account. With an Authentication Code, access is provided from the web page at https://diplomasender.com/Default.aspx **$$$**

Occupational Licensing Boards

Accountant-CPA .... https://www.colorado.gov/dora/licensing/Lookup/LicenseLookup.aspx
Acupuncturist .... https://www.colorado.gov/dora/licensing/Lookup/LicenseLookup.aspx
Addiction Counselor .... https://www.colorado.gov/dora/licensing/Lookup/LicenseLookup.aspx
Alcohol Wholesalers .... www.ttb.gov/foia/xls/frl-alcohol-wholesalers-ak-to-fl.htm
Architect .... https://www.colorado.gov/dora/licensing/Lookup/LicenseLookup.aspx
Asbestos Abatement Contr'r www.colorado.gov/cs/Satellite/CDPHE-AP/CBON/1251594599673
Asbestos Disposal Site www.colorado.gov/cs/Satellite/CDPHE-AP/CBON/1251594599673
Attorney .... www.coloradosupremecourt.com/Search/AttSearch.asp
Audiologist .... https://www.colorado.gov/dora/licensing/Lookup/LicenseLookup.aspx
Bail Bond Agent .... https://www.sircon.com/ComplianceExpress/Inquiry/consumerInquiry.do?nonSscrb=Y
Barber .... https://www.colorado.gov/dora/licensing/Lookup/LicenseLookup.aspx
Bus, Charter/Scenic/Children's .... www.dora.state.co.us/pls/real/puc_permit.search_form
CDL Third-Party Tester/School www.colorado.gov/cs/Satellite/Revenue-MV/RMV/1186129986882
Charitable Organization .... www.sos.state.co.us/ccsa/CcsaInquiryMain.do
Child Care Facility .... www.colorado.gov/apps/cdhs/childcare/lookup/index.jsf
Chiropractor .... https://www.colorado.gov/dora/licensing/Lookup/LicenseLookup.aspx
Collection Agency/Debt Collector .... www.coloradoattorneygeneral.gov/ca
Common Carrier/Contract Carrier .... www.dora.state.co.us/pls/real/puc_permit.search_form
Cosmetologist/Manicurist .... https://www.colorado.gov/dora/licensing/Lookup/LicenseLookup.aspx
Counselor, Professional .... https://www.colorado.gov/dora/licensing/Lookup/LicenseLookup.aspx
Dentist/Dental Hygienist .... https://www.colorado.gov/dora/licensing/Lookup/LicenseLookup.aspx
Drug Company (DRU) Mfg/Dist/Whlse .... https://www.colorado.gov/dora/licensing/Lookup/LicenseLookup.aspx
Electrical Contractor/Contractor Registration .... https://www.colorado.gov/dora/licensing/Lookup/LicenseLookup.aspx
Electrician Journeyman/Master .... https://www.colorado.gov/dora/licensing/Lookup/LicenseLookup.aspx
Engineer/Engineer Intern .... https://www.colorado.gov/dora/licensing/Lookup/LicenseLookup.aspx
Fundraising Consultant .... www.sos.state.co.us/ccsa/PfcInquiryCriteria.do
HazMat Carrier .... www.dora.state.co.us/pls/real/puc_permit.search_form

Hearing Aid Dealer .... https://www.colorado.gov/dora/licensing/Lookup/LicenseLookup.aspx
Household Goods/Property Carrier .... www.dora.state.co.us/pls/real/puc_permit.search_form
Insurance Agency/Agent .... https://www.sircon.com/ComplianceExpress/Inquiry/consumerInquiry.do?nonSscrb=Y
Insurance/Casualty Company .... https://www.sircon.com/ComplianceExpress/Inquiry/consumerInquiry.do?nonSscrb=Y
Investment Advisor .... www.adviserinfo.sec.gov/IAPD/Content/Search/iapd_Search.aspx
Land Surveyor/Land Surveyor Intern .... https://www.colorado.gov/dora/licensing/Lookup/LicenseLookup.aspx
Life Insurance Company .... https://www.sircon.com/ComplianceExpress/Inquiry/consumerInquiry.do?nonSscrb=Y
Limousine .... www.dora.state.co.us/pls/real/puc_permit.search_form
Lobbyist/Volunteer .... www.sos.state.co.us/lobby/SearchLobbyist.do
Manufactured Housing Dealer/Mfg www.colorado.gov/cs/Satellite/DOLA-Main/CBON/1251590375290
Manufacturer Housing Inspector/Installer www.colorado.gov/cs/Satellite/DOLA-Main/CBON/1251590375290
Marriage & Family Therapist .... https://www.colorado.gov/dora/licensing/Lookup/LicenseLookup.aspx
Mental Health Psychotherap't, Unlicensed .... https://www.colorado.gov/dora/licensing/Lookup/LicenseLookup.aspx
Midwife .... https://www.colorado.gov/dora/licensing/Lookup/LicenseLookup.aspx
Notary Public .... https://www.sos.state.co.us/NotaryPublic/verifyNotarySearch.do
Nurse-RN/LPN .... https://www.colorado.gov/dora/licensing/Lookup/LicenseLookup.aspx
Nurses Aide .... https://www.colorado.gov/dora/licensing/Lookup/LicenseLookup.aspx
Nursing Home Administrator .... https://www.colorado.gov/dora/licensing/Lookup/LicenseLookup.aspx
Off-Road Charter .... www.dora.state.co.us/pls/real/puc_permit.search_form
Optometrist .... https://www.colorado.gov/dora/licensing/Lookup/LicenseLookup.aspx
Outfitter-River .... https://www.colorado.gov/dora/licensing/Lookup/LicenseLookup.aspx
Pharmacist/Pharmacist Intern .... https://www.colorado.gov/dora/licensing/Lookup/LicenseLookup.aspx
Pharmacy Limited License .... https://www.colorado.gov/dora/licensing/Lookup/LicenseLookup.aspx
Pharmacy/Out-of-State/In-State/PDO .... https://www.colorado.gov/dora/licensing/Lookup/LicenseLookup.aspx
Physical Therapist .... https://www.colorado.gov/dora/licensing/Lookup/LicenseLookup.aspx
Physician/Assistant .... https://www.colorado.gov/dora/licensing/Lookup/LicenseLookup.aspx
Plumber Journeyman/Master/Resid'l .... https://www.colorado.gov/dora/licensing/Lookup/LicenseLookup.aspx
Podiatrist .... https://www.colorado.gov/dora/licensing/Lookup/LicenseLookup.aspx
Psychiatric Technician .... https://www.colorado.gov/dora/licensing/Lookup/LicenseLookup.aspx
Psychologist .... https://www.colorado.gov/dora/licensing/Lookup/LicenseLookup.aspx
Public Adjuster .... https://www.sircon.com/ComplianceExpress/Inquiry/consumerInquiry.do?nonSscrb=Y
Real Estate Agent/Broker/Seller .... http://eservices.psiexams.com/crec/search.jsp
Real Estate Appraiser .... http://eservices.psiexams.com/crec/search.jsp
Reinsurance Intermediary Manager .... https://www.sircon.com/ComplianceExpress/Inquiry/consumerInquiry.do?nonSscrb=Y
Respiratory Therapist .... https://www.colorado.gov/dora/licensing/Lookup/LicenseLookup.aspx
School Administrator/Principal .... https://www.colorado.gov/cde/licensing/Lookup/LicenseLookup.aspx
School Special Service Associate .... https://www.colorado.gov/cde/licensing/Lookup/LicenseLookup.aspx
Securities Broker/Dealer-Stock Broker .... www.finra.org/Investors/ToolsCalculators/BrokerCheck/index.htm
Ski Lift .... https://www.colorado.gov/dora/licensing/Lookup/LicenseLookup.aspx
Social Work .... https://www.colorado.gov/dora/licensing/Lookup/LicenseLookup.aspx
Solicitor, Paid .... https://www.sos.state.co.us/ucc/pages/home.jspx
Substitute Teacher .... https://www.colorado.gov/cde/licensing/Lookup/LicenseLookup.aspx
Surgical Assistant/Technologist .... https://www.colorado.gov/dora/licensing/Lookup/LicenseLookup.aspx
Surplus Lines Seller .... https://www.sircon.com/ComplianceExpress/Inquiry/consumerInquiry.do?nonSscrb=Y
Teacher/Substitute/Vocational Ed .... https://www.colorado.gov/cde/licensing/Lookup/LicenseLookup.aspx
Towing Carrier .... www.dora.state.co.us/pls/real/puc_permit.search_form
Tramway .... https://www.colorado.gov/dora/licensing/Lookup/LicenseLookup.aspx
Travel Ticker Seller .... https://www.sircon.com/ComplianceExpress/Inquiry/consumerInquiry.do?nonSscrb=Y
Vehicle Dealer .... www.dmv.ca.gov/vehindustry/ol/drschool.htm
Veterinarian .... https://www.colorado.gov/dora/licensing/Lookup/LicenseLookup.aspx
Wireman, Residential .... https://www.colorado.gov/dora/licensing/Lookup/LicenseLookup.aspx

State and Local Courts

State Court Structure: **District Courts** hear civil cases in any amount (District and County Courts have overlapping jurisdiction over civil cases involving less than $15,000), as well as domestic relations, criminal, juvenile, probate, and mental health cases. District court decisions may be appealed to the Colorado Court of Appeals and in some cases directly to the Colorado Supreme Court).

County Courts handle civil cases under $15,000, misdemeanors, traffic infractions, felony complaints (which may be sent to District Court), protection orders, and small claims. County court decisions may be appealed to the District Court.

Water Courts have exclusive jurisdiction over cases relating to the determination of water rights, use and administration of water, and all other water matters. There are seven Water Courts - one per major river basins - located in Weld, Pueblo, Alamosa, Montrose, Garfield, Routt, and La Plata counties.

The **Denver Court System** differs from those in the rest of the state, in part because Denver is both a city and a county. The Denver County Court functions as a municipal and a county court and is paid for entirely by Denver taxes, rather than by state taxes. The Denver County Court is not part of the state court system; the District Court is.

Municipal Courts only have jurisdiction over traffic, parking, and ordinance violations. Denver is the only county where the **Probate Court** and **Juvenile Court** is separate from the District Court.

Appellate Courts: The page at www.courts.state.co.us gives access to Appellate opinions and summaries.

About Court Online Access: Statewide online access to the dockets is available directly from several state-designated vendors who were designated by the Colorado Judicial Branch. A register of actions available on commercial sites include civil, civil water, small claims, domestic, felony, misdemeanor, and traffic cases. Fees vary. See www.courts.state.co.us/Administration/Program.cfm/Program/11

The limited jurisdiction Denver County Court is not in the statewide system, but has its own separate online access system, see below.

County Sites (not including the statewide site mentioned above):

Delta County

Combined Courts http://7thjudicialdistrictco.org/trial-courts/delta/

Civil: Civil case look-up at http://7thjudicialdistrictco.org/docket-search/. Weekly dockets only available. *Criminal:* Criminal case index at http://7thjudicialdistrictco.org/docket-search/. Weekly dockets only available.

Denver County

County Court - Civil Division https://www.denvercountycourt.org/

Civil: Online search of Denver County Civil Division court cases is at www.denvergov.org/apps/newcourt/court_select.aspx. Search by name, business name, or case number. DOBs do not always appear on Denver online results. A subscription account is also available via www.courts.state.co.us where daily trial court dockets can be searched free. One week of dockets available free at www.courts.state.co.us/Courts/County/Dockets.cfm/County_ID/3.**$$$**

County Court - Criminal Division https://www.denvercountycourt.org/

Criminal: Criminal case index and dockets at www.denvergov.org/apps/newcourt/court_select.aspx where Denver case histories go back at least 10 years; results include case, party and action information. Also,a search of warrants is provided. A subscription account is also available via www.courts.state.co.us where daily trial court dockets can be searched free but DOBs do not always appear on Denver online results. **$$$**

El Paso County

El Paso Combined Court www.elpasocountycourts.com/

Civi & Criminal: Order record copies from the page at www.elpasocountycourts.com/public_data_request_form.htm. **$$$**

Moffat County

Moffat County Combined Court www.courts.state.co.us/Courts/County/Choose.cfm

Access the sheriff's sex offender list at www.moffatcountysheriff.com/offender_login.htm. **$$$**

Pitkin County

9th District & County Courts www.courts.state.co.us/Courts/County/Choose.cfm

Probate: Search probate 1881-1953 at www.colorado.gov/dpa/doit/archives/probate/pitkin_probate.htm.

Recorders, Assessors, and Other Sites of Note

Recording Office Organization: 63 counties, 63 recording offices. The recording officer is the County Clerk and Recorder. November 15, 2001, Broomfield City and County came into existence, derived from portions of Adams, Boulder, Jefferson and Weld counties. To determine if an address is in Broomfield County, you may parcel search by address at the Broomfield County Assessor search site at www.broomfield.org/maps/IMS.shtml

Statewide or Multi-Jurisdiction Access: There is no statewide access to recorded documents or tax assessment data. A number of individual counties do offer access.

- 17 Colorado counties offer free access to property assessor basic tax roll records and sometimes sales at www.qpublic.net/. Participating counties are shown below.
- The state archives site at www.colorado.gov/dpa/doit/archives/inh_tax/index.html provides limited "inheritance tax" records for 14 Colorado counties. However, records extend forward only to 1940s.

County Sites:

Adams County ***Recorded Documents, Marriage, Death Records*** www.co.adams.co.us/index.aspx?nid=140 Search recorded documents free at http://apps.adcogov.org/oncoreweb/default.aspx.

Property, Taxation Records from the Adams County Assessor database are free at www.gis.co.adams.co.us/quicksearch/.

Alamosa County ***Recorded Documents, Marriage Records*** www.alamosacounty.org/index.php?option=com_content&view=article&id=24&Itemid=48 Access to recording data back to 1985 is by subscription to I County; fee is $250.00 per month; for info and sign up, contact the Recording office. **$$$**

Property, Taxation Access property data free at www.qpublic.net/co/alamosa/search.html. Subscription required for full data.

Arapahoe County ***Recorded Documents*** www.co.arapahoe.co.us/Departments/CR/index.asp Access to the recorders database is free at www.co.arapahoe.co.us/oncoreweb/Search.aspx. Unofficial images are now available online for the year 1998 and forward. No fee for unofficial images, non-certified-$.25 per page, certified copies-$.25 per page plus $1.00 per document. A convenience fee of $2.00 is added to all orders. **$$$**

Property, Taxation Centrally assessed tax data is available free at www.co.arapahoe.co.us/Apps/Tax/Default.aspx but no name searching. Search business personal property free at www.co.arapahoe.co.us/apps/PersProp/PersPropForm.asp. Search other tax/parcel data by category free at www.co.arapahoe.co.us/ and click on Online Tools. Search county foreclosures free at www.co.arapahoe.co.us/Apps/ForeClosure/index.aspx.

Archuleta County ***Recorded Documents*** www.archuletacounty.org/index.aspx?nid=84 Access to record data is by internet subscription, fee is $250 monthly. Call Recording office for further info and sign-up. 24 hr search $15.00 plus credit card service fee, copies are $.25 per image printed. Credit cards accepted are Visa, M/C, (credit card fee is 3.5%), Discover and AMEX (credit card fee is 3.7%). **$$$**

Property, Taxation Search index data free at http://64.234.218.210/cgi-bin/colorado_links.cgi?county=archuleta. Also search assessor data by name or address via the free mapping site at http://assessorrecords.archuletacounty.org/.

Baca County Clerk ***Recorded Documents*** www.springfieldcolorado.com/bacacountygov.html Search recorded documents at www.thecountyrecorder.com/Disclaimer.aspx. Index goes back to 1997.

Bent County ***Recorded Documents, Vital Records*** Access to recorded data is available by subscription. Fee is $150 per month. To print documents, an add'l fee of $.25 per page applies. To sign-up, contact Patti Nickell; a sign up form will be faxed to you. **$$$**

Property, Taxation Access assessor records free at www.qpublic.net/co/lasanimas/search.html. Search by parcel number, location, or owner name.

Boulder County ***Recorded Documents*** www.bouldercounty.org/dept/clerkrecorder/pages/default.aspx Recorder data for free at http://recorder.bouldercounty.org/countyweb/login.do?countyname=Boulder. Can use Guest login. **$$$**

Property, Taxation Search property tax records at www.bouldercounty.org/property/assess/pages/proprecsearch.aspx.

Broomfield County ***Recorded Documents*** www.broomfield.org/index.aspx?NID=191 Search recorded documents free at https://egov.broomfield.org/recorder/web/.

Property, Taxation Access to the property database portal is free at www.ci.broomfield.co.us/maps/IMS.shtml. Search by address or parcel ID only. Also, Treasurer's tax assessment data free at https://info.ci.broomfield.co.us/Tax/. but no name searching. Also, to GIS/mapping for free at http://gis.broomfield.org/apps/parcelsearch.

Chaffee County ***Recorded Documents*** www.chaffeecountyclerk.org/ Access to records for a fee at http://icounty.org/. **$$$**

Property, Taxation Search assessor database free at http://assessorsearch.chaffeecounty.org/RWDataMartPropertyInquiry/Inquiry.aspx.

Cheyenne County ***Recorded Documents*** www.co.cheyenne.co.us/countydepartments/clerkandrecorder.htm The agency sends online requesters of recorded documents to www.thecountyrecorder.com/Disclaimer.aspx. Index goes back to 1995, unofficial images go back to 1995.

Property, Taxation Search the county property sales lists free at www.co.cheyenne.co.us/countydepartments/assessor.htm. Lookups at bottom of webpage. Also, access the assessor final tax roll free at http://qpublic.net/co/cheyenne/. A subscription is required to view sales, legal info, and more.**$$$**

Clear Creek County ***Recorded Documents*** www.co.clear-creek.co.us/index.aspx?nid=104 Access to records free at https://erecording.co.clear-creek.co.us/clearcreekrecorder/web/. Recorded documents from 8/30/83 to present. Images are not available at this time.

Property, Taxation Access to property record search database for free at http://assessor.co.clear-creek.co.us/Assessor/web/.

Conejos County ***Recorded Documents*** www.conejoscounty.org/Webpages/crhome.html Access to recorder office index back to 1978 is by subscription, $100 per month. Call recorder for signup and info. Fee is $150.00 per month plus $.10 per document. **$$$**

Property, Taxation A property search is offered at www.co.pueblo.co.us/cgi-bin/webatrallbroker.wsc/atrpropertysearchall.html. A vendor provides data from the final tax roll free at http://qpublic.net/co/conejos/. There are 3 levels of subscription service based on your needs.**$$$**

Costilla County ***Recorded Documents*** www.colorado.gov/cs/Satellite/CNTY-Costilla/CBON/1251593793203 Access to daily/monthly subscription at http://icounty.org/. All documents available from 1997-2013. Documents prior to 1997 coming soon. **$$$**

Property, Taxation Access assessor property data free at http://64.234.218.210/cgi-bin/colorado_links.cgi?county=costilla. Also, access to Assessor property search for free at www.co.pueblo.co.us/cgi-bin/webatrallbroker.wsc/ackatrcos.p.

Crowley County ***Property, Taxation*** Access data from the final tax roll free at http://qpublic.net/co/crowley/. Subscription required for full property data and sales. Also, access property assessment data by subscription at http://64.234.218.210/cgi-bin/colorado.pl.**$$$**

Custer County ***Recorded Documents*** http://custercountygov.com/index.php?pg=clerk Access to land record searching for a fee at http://icounty.org/. **$$$**

Property, Taxation Access assessor final tax roll data free at www.qpublic.net/co/custer/search.html. Subscription required for full property data and sales. **$$$**

Delta County ***Recorded Documents, Death, Marriage, DOT Release Records*** www.deltacounty.com/index.aspx?nid=4 Access recorder records free at http://clerk.deltacounty.com/Search.aspx. Alpha indexing goes back to 1988. With reception number you can pull images back to 1883.

Property, Taxation Access Assessor data on the GIS site for free at http://itax.deltacounty.com/assessor/web/ .

Denver County ***Foreclosures Records*** www.denvergov.org/Default.aspx?alias=www.denvergov.org/clerkandrecorder Search foreclosures at www.denvergov.org/apps4/eForeclosures.

Property, Taxation Assessor database at www.denvergov.org/property. Search business personal property atwww.denvergov.org/apps/perspropertyapplication/persproperty.asp www.denvergov.org/apps/perspropertyapplication/persproperty.asp. Also, search real estate property tax data for free at www.denvergov.org/treasurypt/PropertyTax.asp. Search foreclosures at www.denvergov.org/.

Dolores County ***Recorded Records*** www.dolorescounty.org/government/dolores_county_clerk_and_recorder.html Access to Recorder's office records free at www.thecountyrecorder.com/Disclaimer.aspx. Index goes back to 1996.

Property, Taxation Assessor information and free search at www.qpublic.net/co/dolores/index.html. Subscription and log-on required for legal information, go to http://64.234.218.210/cgi-bin/colorado.pl for new subscriber sign-up.**$$$**

Douglas County ***Recorded Documents, Marriage Records*** www.douglas.co.us/clerk/ Access to recorders index is free at http://apps.douglas.co.us/OnCoreWeb/.

Property, Taxation Records on the county assessor database are free at www.douglas.co.us/assessor/. You may also download related list data from the site. Locate parcels free at http://publicstaging.douglas.co.us/website/default.htm.

Eagle County ***Recorded Documents, Vital Records*** www.eaglecounty.us/Clerk/ Search clerk and recorder data free at http://acclaim.eaglecounty.us/. The agency sends requesters to the Laredo system. The same vendor offers the Tapestry program with a $5.95 search fee and copies for $.50 per page. You can pay as you go with a credit card or be billed monthly with a $25.00 monthly minimum. Visit at www.fidlar.com or call 800-747-4600 at ext 271 or 324. **$$$**

Property, Taxation Search comps sales at www.eaglecounty.us/Assessor/Comparable_Sales_Data/.

Elbert County ***Recorded Documents*** www.elbertcounty-co.gov Access to records search at http://elbertco.tyler-esubmittal.com/recorder/web/. Free is access to recorded documents without images, User ID and Password required for view/print images, based on subscription type. **$$$**

Property, Taxation Search Assessor data free at http://elbertco.tyler-esubmittal.com/assessor/web/ but no name searching; free registration required.

El Paso County ***Recorded Documents*** http://car.elpasoco.com/Pages/default.aspx Search the grantor/grantee index at http://car2.elpasoco.com/rcdquery.asp. Search marriage index back to 5/1/1991 on a separate lookup page. Also, search marriage index 1/1985 to 5/1991 free on the OPR - Official Public Records - search page.

Property, Taxation Records on the county Assessor database are free at http://land.elpasoco.com.

Fremont County ***Recorded Documents, Marriage Records*** www.fremontco.com/clerkandrecorder/index.shtml Search recorded document index free at https://erecords.fremontco.com/recorder/web/. Indexed back to 1987. Registered users may purchase single documents by credit card for $.25 per page plus a $.50 processing fee. Wills can be recorded here. When the agency completes its digitizing program, the index and most images will be available to 1861, now they go back to 1994. UCCs not included. The agency also offers a subscription program of images, which can be pre-paid. There is a monthly and usage fee. Call or email susan.justus@fremontco.com. **$$$**

Property, Taxation Access the assessors property and sales database free at http://qpublic.net/fremont/. There are 3 levels of subscription service based on needs. A subscription based service is also at http://assessor.fremontco.com:82/assessor/web/.

Garfield County ***Recorded Documents*** www.garfield-county.com/Index.aspx?page=562 Access recording data free at https://act.garfield-county.com/recorder/web/.

Property, Taxation Search the assessor and treasurer property and tax data free at https://act.garfield-county.com/assessor/web/. Also, you may search assessor sales data by subscription at https://act.garfield-county.com/assessor/web/login.jsp?submit=Enter+EagleWeb. Also, access PDF parcel maps and property information free at http://gismaps.garfield-county.com/parcelmap/.**$$$**

Gilpin County ***Marriage Records*** www.co.gilpin.co.us Access to county marriage records from 1864 to 1944 is free at www.colorado.gov/dpa/doit/archives/marriage/gilpin_index.htm.

Property, Taxation Assessor data, GIS/mapping and research of property information at www.co.gilpin.co.us/Assessor/default.htm.

Grand County ***Recorded Documents, Marriage Records*** http://co.grand.co.us/Clerk/clerkand.htm Access to Clerk-Recorder index is free at http://co.grand.co.us/aptitude/oncoreweb/

Property, Taxation Access assessor data free at www2.co.grand.co.us/assessor_lookup/. Access the assessor database free at http://co.grand.co.us/Assessor/Download_Page.html.

Gunnison County ***Recorded Documents*** www.gunnisoncounty.org/clerk_recorder.html Access records for a fee at https://www.idocmarket.com/Sites. **$$$**

Property, Taxation Access to property records and sales list for free at www.qpublic.net/co/gunnison/search1.html.

Hinsdale County ***Recorded Documents*** www.hinsdalecountycolorado.us/clerk.html Access to records for a fee at icounty.org contact the Clerk's office for application. **$$$**

Property, Taxation Access to 2012 Tax rolls, vacant land sales, commercial sales and residential sales for free at www.hinsdalecountycolorado.us/assessor.html. Go to bottom of page under Information.

Huerfano County ***Recorded Documents*** www.huerfano.us/Clerk_s_Office.php Access to Recorder database records free at www.thecountyrecorder.com/Disclaimer.aspx. Index goes back to 1997.

Property, Taxation Access to online maps free at http://maps.huerfano.us:8008/onlinemaps/.

Jefferson County ***Recorded Documents*** http://jeffco.us/cr/index.htm Search the recorder's records for free at https://landrecords.co.jefferson.co.us/. Index goes back to 1963; images to 1994.

Property, Taxation Records on the county Assessor database are free at http://jeffco.us/ats/splash.do. No name searching.

Kiowa County ***Recorded Documents*** www.kiowacounty-colorado.com/kiowa_county_clerk_&_recorder.htm Access to recording index is free from a 3rd party company at www.thecountyrecorder.com/Disclaimer.aspx. Index goes back only to July, 2001.

Kit Carson County ***Property, Taxation*** Access data from the final tax roll free at http://qpublic.net/co/kitcarson/. There are 3 levels of subscription service based on your needs.

Lake County ***Recorded Documents*** www.lakecountyco.com/clerkandrecorder/ Online subscription available-contact Rachele at 719-486-4131. **$$$**

Property, Taxation Access county assessor property data free at http://64.234.218.210/cgi-bin/colorado_links.cgi?county=lake or at http://qpublic.net/co/lake/index.html.

La Plata County ***Recorded Documents*** www.co.laplata.co.us/departments_and_elected_officials/clerk_recorder Access to online index and images are free at https://papervision.laplata.co.us/PVE.aspx. If printing access is requested the fee is $100.00 for unlimited copies. Must have user name and password. **$$$**

Property, Taxation Property information is available at http://eagleweb.laplata.co.us/assessor/web/. Also, records on the county Real Estate Parcel Search Page are free at www.laplatainfo.com/search2.html. This is basic property data but for sales and tax data, there is a subscription service for $20.00 per month, credit cards accepted.**$$$**

Larimer County ***Recorded Documents, Voter Registration Records*** www.larimer.org/clerk/ Search the county Public Record Databases (indexing only-no images) for free at www.larimer.org/databases/index.htm. Search registered voter list free at https://larimer.org/depts/clerkr/elections/voter_inquiry.cfm?.

Property, Taxation Search assessor and property data free at www.larimer.org/assessor/propertyExplorer/propertyexplorer.html. Download free FlashPlayer8. Also, search assessor and property data free at www.co.larimer.co.us/assessor/query/search.cfm. Search treasurer data free at www.larimer.org/treasurer/query/search.cfm but no name searching.

Las Animas County ***Property, Taxation*** Access data from the final tax roll free at http://qpublic.net/co/lasanimas/. There are 3 levels of subscription service based on your needs. **$$$**

Lincoln County ***Recorded Documents*** http://lincolncountyco.us/clerk_recorder/clerk_recorder.html Assess to documents free at www.thecountyrecorder.com/Disclaimer.aspx. Index goes back to 1997.

Property, Taxation Access data from the final tax roll free at http://qpublic.net/co/lincoln/. There are 3 levels of subscription service based on your needs.**$$$**

Logan County ***Recorded Documents, Birth, Death, Marriage Records*** www.logancountyco.gov/?page_id=100 Enter the recorder's database site at www.logancountyco.gov/?page_id=100, registration and username/password required to view and print images. Sub fee is $300 per month. **$$$**

Property, Taxation Access to assessor property data is free at www.logancountycoaat.com/Search/Disclaimer2.aspx.

Mesa County ***Recorded Documents*** www.mesacounty.us Search the recorder's Grantor/Grantee index free at http://apps.mesacounty.us/oncore/Search.aspx.

Property, Taxation GIS/mapping and property data at http://gis.mesacounty.us/interactive.aspx.

Mineral County ***Property, Taxation*** Access data from the final tax roll free at http://qpublic.net/co/mineral/. There are 3 levels of subscription service based on your needs.**$$$**

Moffat County ***Recorded Documents*** www.colorado.gov/cs/Satellite/CNTY-Moffat/CBON/1251574651173 Online records available online for $250.00 per month or $12.50 per day (24 hours). Contact Debbie Winder for more information. **$$$**

Property, Taxation Access to assessor property data free at www.colorado.gov/cs/Satellite/CNTY-Moffat/CBON/1251574785611. Also, search the treasurer's tax database free at http://moffat.visualgov.com/SearchSelect.aspx.

Montezuma County ***Recorded Documents, Marriage, Death Records*** www.co.montezuma.co.us/newsite/clerkhome.html Access recorded records data back to 6/3/1996 free at http://eagleweb.co.montezuma.co.us/recorder/web/. Index only. For more detail image view and print web subscription for $350.00 per month.

Property, Taxation Access county property tax data and property sales free at www.co.montezuma.co.us/newsite/itax.html. Subscription service also available. Also, search property data on new GIS-mapping site at www.co.montezuma.co.us/newsite/gismaps.html.**$$$**

Montrose County ***Recorded Documents*** www.montrosecounty.net/index.aspx?nid=72 Access to records free at http://oncore.montrosecounty.net/. No images.

Property, Taxation Access to Property Information EagleWeb System is free at http://eagleweb.co.montrose.co.us/eagleassessor/web/splash.jsp.

Morgan County ***Recorded Documents, Marriage Records*** www.co.morgan.co.us/CountyClerk.html Access the recorder's online index free as a public user or by subscription for images for $300 per year at www.co.morgan.co.us/recorder/web/splash.jsp. **$$$**

Property, Taxation Search the assessor database free at www.co.morgan.co.us/assessor/web/. Must register with username and password before using database.

Otero County ***Recorded Documents*** www.oterogov.com/ Access to recorded data is by subscription only. Fee is $200 per month or $20.00 per day plus $.25 per page for copies printed. Contact the Clerk/Recorder office for more info and sign-up. **$$$**

Property, Taxation Access property data free at www.qpublic.net/co/otero/search.html.

Ouray County ***Recorded Documents, Marriage Records*** http://ouraycountyco.gov/clerk.html Access the record data free at http://ouraycountyrecording.org/OnCoreWeb/Search.aspx.

Property, Taxation Access recorder data free at http://ouraycountyassessor.org/assessor/web/. With registration, you may also create and print reports for properties free of charge.

Park County ***Property, Taxation*** Records on the county Assessor database are free at www.parkco.org/Search2.asp, including tax data, owner, address, building characteristics, legal and deed information.

Pitkin County ***Recorded Documents*** www.pitkinclerk.org/ Search recorded documents free at www.pitkinclerk.org/oncoreweb/. Also, probate records from 1881 to 1953 are at www.colorado.gov/dpa/doit/archives/probate/pitkin_probate.htm. Divorce records 1931 to 1964 are at www.colorado.gov/dpa/doit/archives/divorce/1pitkin.htm.

Property, Taxation Records on the county Assessor database are free at www.pitkinassessor.org/Assessor/.

Pueblo County ***Recorded Documents, Marriage Records*** http://county.pueblo.org/government/county/elected-office/clerk-and-recorder Access clerk & recorder index of recorded docs at http://erecording.co.pueblo.co.us/recorder/web/. Search documents recorded since 05/01/1991.

Property, Taxation Access county assessor data free at www.co.pueblo.co.us/cgi-bin/webatrbroker.wsc/ackatr.p.

Rio Blanco County ***Recorded Documents*** www.co.rio-blanco.co.us/clerkandrecorder/recording.php Access to records free at http://acclaimweb.co.rio-blanco.co.us/.

Property, Taxation Access assessor property data free at www.co.rio-blanco.co.us/assessor/.

Rio Grande County ***Recorded Documents*** www.riograndecounty.org/index.php?option=com_content&view=article&id=9&Itemid=7 Access to records for a fee at http://icounty.org/. **$$$**

Property, Taxation Access to GIS/mapping for free to go www.co.pueblo.co.us/cgi-bin/webatrallbroker.wsc/ackatrrig.p.

Routt County ***Recorded Documents, Property Sale Records*** www.co.routt.co.us/index.aspx?nid=133 Search records free on the County Recorder Office archives database at http://pioneer.co.routt.co.us/aptitude/oncoreweb/. For unlimited usage and downloads, you must register, for a fee. See www.co.routt.co.us/index.aspx?nid=140 for details. **$$$**

Property, Taxation Records on the county Assessor are free at http://agner.co.routt.co.us/assessohttp://agner.co.routt.co.us/assessor/taxweb/. Treasurer records free at http://agner.co.routt.co.us:8080/treasurer/web/.

Saguache County ***Recorded Documents*** www.saguachecounty.net/index.php/clerk-a-recorder-home Access Recorder database free at www.thecountyrecorder.com/Disclaimer.aspx. Index goes back to 1994; unofficial images back to 1996.

Property, Taxation Search Assessor tax roll database free at www.qpublic.net/co/saguache/.**$$$**

San Juan County ***Recorded Documents*** www.sanjuancountycolorado.us/clerk--recorder.html Access to recording index is free from a 3rd party company at www.thecountyrecorder.com/Disclaimer.aspx. Index goes back to 1997.

Property, Taxation Access to county online property search for free at www.co.pueblo.co.us/cgi-bin/webatrallbroker.wsc/atrpropertysearchall.html.

San Miguel County ***Recorded Documents*** www.sanmiguelcounty.org/departments/clerk/index.html Access to recording index is free from a 3rd party company at www.thecountyrecorder.com/Disclaimer.aspx. Index goes back to 1990, unofficial images back to 1990.

Property, Taxation Assessor data is viewable online at http://sanmiguel.valuewest.net/. The tax database is at http://sanmiguel.visualgov.com/. A database of property foreclosures is at http://foreclosures.sanmiguelcounty.org/. All searches are free.

Sedgwick County ***Recorded Documents*** www.sedgwickcountygov.net/index.php?option=com_content&view=category&layout=blog&id=23&Itemid=35 Access to recorded records free at www.thecountyrecorder.com/Disclaimer.aspx. Index goes back to 1973.

Property, Taxation Access data from the final tax roll free at http://qpublic.net/co/sedgwick/. There are 3 levels of subscription service based on your needs.**$$$**

Summit County ***Property, Taxation*** Access to the GIS-mapping site property data is free at www.co.summit.co.us/index.aspx?NID=354. Also, access to foreclosure property search free at http://apps.co.summit.co.us/foreclosure_search/index.aspx.

Teller County ***Recorded Documents*** www.co.teller.co.us Access the county clerk real estate database free at www.thecountyrecorder.com/Disclaimer.aspx. Index goes back to 1918.

Property, Taxation Search the assessor database free at www.co.teller.co.us/assessor/databasehome.aspx.

Washington County ***Recorded Documents*** www.co.washington.co.us/clerk.htm Access to recorded records for free to go www.thecountyrecorder.com/Disclaimer.aspx. Index goes back to 1996.

Property, Taxation Access data from the final tax roll free at http://qpublic.net/co/washington/index-search.html. There are 3 levels of subscription service based on your needs.

Weld County ***Real Estate, Deed, Grantor/Grantee Records*** www.co.weld.co.us/Departments/ClerkRecorder/index.html Access to records go to https://searchicris.co.weld.co.us/recorder/web/. Query is free but for advanced search must subscribe. **$$$**

Property, Taxation Access assessor data, property sales, ownership listings, transfers, property cards free at www.co.weld.co.us/Departments/Assessor/PropertyInformationSearches.html Search property data on the map server database free at http://propertyinfo.co.weld.co.us/.

Yuma County ***Deeds, Plats, etc. Records*** www.yumacounty.net/clerk_recorder.html Access to online records for a fee at https://idoc.csa-inc.net/yumaco/default.aspx. **$$$**

Property, Taxation Access data from the final tax roll free at http://qpublic.net/co/yuma/. There are 3 levels of subscription service based on your needs. **$$$**

Connecticut

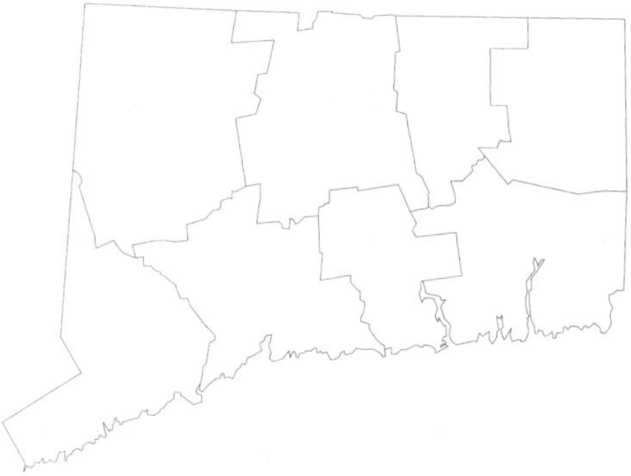

Capital: Hartford
Hartford County
Time Zone: EST
Population: 3,590,347
# of Counties: 8

Useful State Links

Website: www.ct.gov
Governor: www.governor.ct.gov/malloy/site/default.asp
Attorney General: www.ct.gov/ag/site/default.asp
State Archives: www.cslib.org/archives/
State Statutes and Codes: www.cga.ct.gov/asp/menu/Statutes.asp
Legislative Bill Search: www.cga.ct.gov/asp/menu/Search.asp
Bill Tracking: www.cga.ct.gov/aspx/cgapublicbilltrack/cgapublicbilltrack.aspx
Unclaimed Funds: www.ctbiglist.com/

State Public Record Agencies

Sexual Offender Registry

Department of Public Safety, Sex Offender Registry Unit, www.communitynotification.com/cap_office_disclaimer.php?office=54567 The search site is www.icrimewatch.net/index.php?AgencyID=54567. There are many search options including by Internet name. *Other Options:* Record data can be purchased in bulk.

Incarceration Records

Connecticut Department of Corrections, Public Information Office, www.ct.gov/doc/site/default.asp Current inmates may be searched at www.ctinmateinfo.state.ct.us/searchop.asp. DOB is shown. It is extremely important to note that a person's current incarceration does not necessarily indicate they have been convicted of a crime, as Connecticut's correctional system also holds those who are awaiting trial.

Corporation, LP, LLC, LLP, Statutory Trust, Trademarks/Servicemarks

Secretary of the State, Commercial Recording Division, www.sots.ct.gov/sots/site/default.asp Click on the CONCORD option at the website for free access to corporation and UCC records. The system is open from 7AM to 11PM. You can search by business name, business ID or by filing number. The web also offers online filing. Go to www.concord-sots.ct.gov/CONCORD/index.jsp. Search securities division enforcement actions at www.ct.gov/dob/cwp/view.asp?a=2246&q=401762. *Other Options:* Bulk data is available on disk, there are many options. Please call for details.

Uniform Commercial Code, Federal & State Tax Liens

UCC Division, Secretary of State, www.concord-sots.ct.gov/CONCORD/index.jsp An free index search is offered at www.concord-sots.ct.gov/CONCORD/index.jsp. *Other Options:* Bulk lists and CDs are available for purchase. Call the Financial Area at 860-509-6165.

Vital Records

Department of Public Health, Vital Records Section MS# 11VRS, www.ct.gov/dph/site/default.asp Online ordering is provided by a designated vendor - www.vitalchek.com. **$$$**

Driver Records

Department of Motor Vehicles, Copy Records Unit, www.ct.gov/dmv/site/default.asp Electronic access is provided to approved businesses that enter into written contract. The contract requires a $37,500 prepayment deposit for the first 2,500 records.. Fee is $15.00 per record. The address is part of the record. For more information, call 960-263-5424. Also, search disposed conviction and bond forfeitures at www.jud2.ct.gov/crdockets/SearchByDefDisp.aspx by Geographical Area court. Links include pending case lookup pages and docket/calendar lookup pages. **$$$** *Other Options:* Batch requests are available for approved users, write to Data Access at the above address.

Vehicle Ownership & Registration

Department of Motor Vehicles, Copy Record Unit, www.ct.gov/dmv/site/default.asp There is no online access to full records, but one may check registration expiration dates by entering the plate number at www.dmvselfservice.ct.gov/RegistrationVerificationService.aspx. *Other Options:* Vehicle record information is available on a volume basis to approved businesses that enter into a written agreement and approved use. The contract requires an annual fee and a surety bond. For more information, write to Data Access at the address above.

Accident Reports

Department of Public Safety, Reports and Records Unit, www.ct.gov/despp/cwp/view.asp?a=4212&q=494530 Access online is available via a designated vendor; see www.docview.us.com. A $6.00 convenience fee is added. **$$$**

Voter Registration, Campaign Finance & Committees

Secretary of State, Election Services Division, www.sots.ct.gov/sots/site/default.asp Search campaign finance and committee fundraising at the Campaign Reporting Information System at http://seec.ct.gov/eCris/DocumentSearch/DocumentSearchHome.aspx?seecNav=| Political committees are shown at www.ct.gov/seec/lib/seec/committeelists/ongoing_political_committees.pdf. *Other Options:* An electronic file of all registered voters is available for $300. The agency does not offer geographic customization.

Occupational Licensing Boards

Accountant-CAP/Firm .... https://www.elicense.ct.gov/Lookup/LicenseLookup.aspx
Acupuncturist .... https://www.elicense.ct.gov/Lookup/LicenseLookup.aspx
Airport/Heliport .... www.ct.gov/dot/cwp/view.asp?a=1390&Q=292426&dotPNavCtr=|40038|#40038
Alcohol/Drug Counselor .... https://www.elicense.ct.gov/Lookup/LicenseLookup.aspx
Appraiser, MVPD/MVR .... www.ct-clic.com
Architect/Architectural Firm .... https://www.elicense.ct.gov/Lookup/LicenseLookup.aspx
Asbestos Consultant/Contractor .... www.ct.gov/dph/cwp/view.asp?a=3140&q=417040&dphNav_GID=1889&dphPNavCtr=|#47059
Asbestos Worker/Supvr .... www.ct.gov/dph/cwp/view.asp?a=3140&q=417040&dphNav_GID=1889&dphPNavCtr=|#47059
Association Manager .... https://www.elicense.ct.gov/Lookup/LicenseLookup.aspx
Athletic Promoter .... www.ct.gov/dcp/cwp/view.asp?a=4308&q=507962
Attorney/Attorney Firm www.jud2.ct.gov/attorneyfirminq/AttorneyFirmInquiry.aspx
Audiologist .... https://www.elicense.ct.gov/Lookup/LicenseLookup.aspx
Automobile Glass Technician .... https://www.elicense.ct.gov/Lookup/GenerateRoster.aspx
Automobile Insurance Adjuster .... www.ct-clic.com
Bail Bond Agent .... www.ct-clic.com
Bail Bondsman .... www.ct.gov/dps/lib/dps/special_licensing_and_firearms/licensed_bondsman.pdf
Bail Enforcement Agent .... www.ct.gov/dps/lib/dps/special_licensing_and_firearms/licensed_bea.pdf
Bail Enforcement Instructor .... www.ct.gov/dps/lib/dps/special_licensing_and_firearms/bea_instructors.pdf
Bakery .... https://www.elicense.ct.gov/Lookup/LicenseLookup.aspx
Bank & Trust Company .... www.ct.gov/dob/cwp/view.asp?a=2239&Q=298138&dobNAV_GID=1659&dobNav=|
Bank Branch/Banking Office .... www.ct.gov/dob/cwp/view.asp?a=2239&Q=298138&dobNAV_GID=1659&dobNav=|
Bank CEO .... www.ct.gov/dob/cwp/view.asp?a=2239&Q=298138&dobNAV_GID=1659&dobNav=|
Barber .... https://www.elicense.ct.gov/Lookup/LicenseLookup.aspx
Bazaar/Raffle Permit .... www.ct-clic.com/
Bedding Mfg/Renovation .... https://www.elicense.ct.gov/Lookup/GenerateRoster.aspx
Bedding Supply/Sterilizer .... https://www.elicense.ct.gov/Lookup/GenerateRoster.aspx
Beekeeper .... www.ct.gov/caes/cwp/view.asp?a=2818&q=376964#Beekeeper
Beverage/Water Bottler .... https://www.elicense.ct.gov/Lookup/GenerateRoster.aspx
Bingo Registration .... www.ct-clic.com/
Boxer/Boxing Professional .... www.ct.gov/dcp/cwp/view.asp?a=4308&q=507962
Building Contractor .... www.ct.gov/dcp/cwp/view.asp?a=4308&q=507962
Casino/Occupation .... www.ct-clic.com/
Casualty Adjuster .... www.ct-clic.com
Caterer/Concessioner, Liquor .... https://www.elicense.ct.gov/Lookup/LicenseLookup.aspx

Charitable Solicitor .... https://www.elicense.ct.gov/Lookup/LicenseLookup.aspx
Check Cashing Service .... www.ct.gov/dob/cwp/view.asp?a=2239&Q=298138&dobNAV_GID=1659&dobNav=|
Child Caring Agency/Facility .... www.dir.ct.gov/dcf/Licensed_Facilities/listing_CCF.asp
Child Placing Agency .... www.dir.ct.gov/dcf/Licensed_Facilities/listing_CPA.asp
Child Psychiatric Clinic/Outpatient .... www.dir.ct.gov/dcf/Licensed_Facilities/listing_OPCC.asp
Chiropractor .... https://www.elicense.ct.gov/Lookup/LicenseLookup.aspx
Cigarette Seller/Distributor/Manufacturers... www.ct.gov/drs/cwp/view.asp?a=2015&q=295694&drsPNavCtr=|#43204
Closing Out Sale .... https://www.elicense.ct.gov/Lookup/GenerateRoster.aspx
Collection Agency .... www.ct.gov/dob/cwp/view.asp?a=2239&Q=298138&dobNAV_GID=1659&dobNav=|
College/University-State Supported .... www.ctohe.org/HEWeb/CollegesList.asp
Contractor, Mechanical/Major .... https://www.elicense.ct.gov/Lookup/GenerateRoster.aspx
Controlled Substance Lab .... https://www.elicense.ct.gov/Lookup/LicenseLookup.aspx
Cosmetologist .... https://www.elicense.ct.gov/Lookup/LicenseLookup.aspx
Counselor, Professional .... www.ct.gov/dph/site/default.asp
Credit Union .... www.ct.gov/dob/cwp/view.asp?a=2239&Q=298138&dobNAV_GID=1659&dobNav=|
Day Treatment Facility, Extended .... www.dir.ct.gov/dcf/Licensed_Facilities/listing_EDT.asp
Debt Adjuster .... www.ct.gov/dob/cwp/view.asp?a=2239&Q=298138&dobNAV_GID=1659&dobNav=|
Dental Anesthesia/Sedation Permittee .... https://www.elicense.ct.gov/Lookup/LicenseLookup.aspx
Dentist/Dental Hygienist .... https://www.elicense.ct.gov/Lookup/LicenseLookup.aspx
Dietician/Nutritionist .... https://www.elicense.ct.gov/Lookup/LicenseLookup.aspx
Dog Racing Owner/Trainer .... www.ct-clic.com/
Drug/Cosmetic Whlse/Mfg .... https://www.elicense.ct.gov/Lookup/LicenseLookup.aspx
Druggist Liquor Permittee .... https://www.elicense.ct.gov/Lookup/LicenseLookup.aspx
Electrical Contr./Inspector .... www.ct.gov/dcp/cwp/view.asp?a=4308&q=507962
Electrical Journeyman/Apprentice .... https://www.elicense.ct.gov/Lookup/GenerateRoster.aspx
Electrical Sign Installer .... www.ct.gov/dcp/cwp/view.asp?a=4308&q=507962
Electrician .... www.ct.gov/dcp/cwp/view.asp?a=4308&q=507962
Electrologist/Hypertricologist .... https://www.elicense.ct.gov/Lookup/LicenseLookup.aspx
Elevator Inspector/Mechanic .... https://www.elicense.ct.gov/Lookup/GenerateRoster.aspx
Embalmer .... https://www.elicense.ct.gov/Lookup/LicenseLookup.aspx
Emergency Med Svc Professional .... https://www.elicense.ct.gov/Lookup/LicenseLookup.aspx
EMS First Responder .... https://www.elicense.ct.gov/Lookup/LicenseLookup.aspx
EMS Instructor .... https://www.elicense.ct.gov/Lookup/LicenseLookup.aspx
Engineer/Engineer-in-Training .... https://www.elicense.ct.gov/Lookup/GenerateRoster.aspx
Family Residence, Permanent .... www.dir.ct.gov/dcf/Licensed_Facilities/listing_PFR.asp
Fire Protection Inspector/Contractor .... https://www.elicense.ct.gov/Lookup/GenerateRoster.aspx
Fire Sprinkler Technician .... https://www.elicense.ct.gov/Lookup/GenerateRoster.aspx
Fund Raiser, Paid .... https://www.elicense.ct.gov/Lookup/LicenseLookup.aspx
Funeral Director/Home .... https://www.elicense.ct.gov/Lookup/LicenseLookup.aspx
Gasoline Dealer, Retail .... https://www.elicense.ct.gov/Lookup/LicenseLookup.aspx
Glazier .... https://www.elicense.ct.gov/Lookup/GenerateRoster.aspx
Hairdresser .... https://www.elicense.ct.gov/Lookup/LicenseLookup.aspx
Hazardous Waste Transporter .... www.ct.gov/deep/cwp/view.asp?a=2718&q=455558&depNav_GID=1967&depNav=|
Health Care Center Insurer .... www.ct-clic.com
Health Club .... https://www.elicense.ct.gov/Lookup/GenerateRoster.aspx
Hearing Instrument Specialist .... https://www.elicense.ct.gov/Lookup/LicenseLookup.aspx
Heating/Piping/Cooling Cont./Journey'n .... https://www.elicense.ct.gov/Lookup/GenerateRoster.aspx
Home Heating Fuel Dealer .... https://www.elicense.ct.gov/Lookup/LicenseLookup.aspx
Home Improvement Contr/Seller .... https://www.elicense.ct.gov/Lookup/GenerateRoster.aspx
Home Inspector .... https://www.elicense.ct.gov/Lookup/GenerateRoster.aspx
Homemaker Companion .... https://www.elicense.ct.gov/Lookup/GenerateRoster.aspx
Homeopathic Physician .... https://www.elicense.ct.gov/Lookup/LicenseLookup.aspx
Honey Bee Registration .... www.ct.gov/caes/cwp/view.asp?a=2818&q=376964#Beekeeper
Hypnotist .... https://www.elicense.ct.gov/Lookup/GenerateRoster.aspx
Insurance Adjuster/Public Adjuster .... www.ct-clic.com

Insurance Agent, Fraternal/Consultant........ www.ct-clic.com
Insurance Appraiser.................................... www.ct-clic.com
Insurance Company/Producer..................... www.ct-clic.com
Interior Designer.. https://www.elicense.ct.gov/Lookup/GenerateRoster.aspx
Interstate Land Sale.................................... https://www.elicense.ct.gov/Lookup/LicenseLookup.aspx
Investment Advisor/Agent........................... www.ct.gov/dob/cwp/view.asp?a=2239&Q=298138&dobNAV_GID=1659&dobNav=|
Juice Producer.. https://www.elicense.ct.gov/Lookup/LicenseLookup.aspx
Land Sale, Interstate................................... https://www.elicense.ct.gov/Lookup/LicenseLookup.aspx
Landscape Architect/Land Surveyor............ https://www.elicense.ct.gov/Lookup/LicenseLookup.aspx
Lead Consultant.. www.ct.gov/dph/cwp/view.asp?a=3140&q=417040&dphNav_GID=1889&dphPNavCtr=|#47059
Legalized Gaming Occupation..................... www.ct-clic.com/
Liquor License... https://www.elicense.ct.gov/Lookup/LicenseLookup.aspx
Liquor Mfg/Dist/Whlse................................. https://www.elicense.ct.gov/Lookup/LicenseLookup.aspx
Liquor Permittee.. https://www.elicense.ct.gov/Lookup/LicenseLookup.aspx
Liquor Store/Broker/Shipper........................ https://www.elicense.ct.gov/Lookup/LicenseLookup.aspx
Loan Company, Small................................. www.ct.gov/dob/cwp/view.asp?a=2239&Q=298138&dobNAV_GID=1659&dobNav=|
Lobbyist.. https://www.oseapps.ct.gov/NewLobbyist/security/loginhome.aspx
Lottery/Sales Agent..................................... www.ct-clic.com/
Marriage & Family Therapist........................ https://www.elicense.ct.gov/Lookup/LicenseLookup.aspx
Marshall, State.. www.jud.ct.gov/faq/marshals.htm
Martial Arts Facility...................................... https://www.elicense.ct.gov/Lookup/GenerateRoster.aspx
Massage Therapist...................................... https://www.elicense.ct.gov/Lookup/LicenseLookup.aspx
Mausoleum.. https://www.elicense.ct.gov/Lookup/LicenseLookup.aspx
Medical Gas/Vacuum System...................... https://www.elicense.ct.gov/Lookup/GenerateRoster.aspx
Medical Response Technician..................... https://www.elicense.ct.gov/Lookup/LicenseLookup.aspx
Midwife.. https://www.elicense.ct.gov/Lookup/LicenseLookup.aspx
Mobile Home Park/Seller............................ https://www.elicense.ct.gov/Lookup/LicenseLookup.aspx
Money Forwarder... www.ct.gov/dob/cwp/view.asp?a=2239&Q=298138&dobNAV_GID=1659&dobNav=|
Money Order/Travelers Check Issuer.......... www.ct.gov/dob/cwp/view.asp?a=2233&q=297862&dobNAV_GID=1663
Mortgage Broker/Lender............................. www.ct.gov/dob/cwp/view.asp?a=2239&Q=298138&dobNAV_GID=1659&dobNav=|
Naturopathic Physician............................... https://www.elicense.ct.gov/Lookup/LicenseLookup.aspx
New Home Construction Contr.................... https://www.elicense.ct.gov/Lookup/GenerateRoster.aspx
Nurse-Advance Registered Practice........... https://www.elicense.ct.gov/Lookup/LicenseLookup.aspx
Nurse-LPN/Aide.. https://www.elicense.ct.gov/Lookup/LicenseLookup.aspx
Nursery Plant/Dealer.................................... www.ct.gov/caes/cwp/view.asp?a=2818&q=376964#Nurseries
Nursing Home Administrator........................ https://www.elicense.ct.gov/Lookup/LicenseLookup.aspx
Occupational Therapist/Assistant................ https://www.elicense.ct.gov/Lookup/LicenseLookup.aspx
Off-Track Betting... www.ct-clic.com/
Optical Shop.. https://www.elicense.ct.gov/Lookup/LicenseLookup.aspx
Optician... https://www.elicense.ct.gov/Lookup/LicenseLookup.aspx
Optometrist.. https://www.elicense.ct.gov/Lookup/LicenseLookup.aspx
Osteopathic Physician................................ https://www.elicense.ct.gov/Lookup/LicenseLookup.aspx
Paramedic... https://www.elicense.ct.gov/Lookup/LicenseLookup.aspx
Perfusionist... https://www.elicense.ct.gov/Lookup/LicenseLookup.aspx
Pesticide Applicator..................................... www.kellysolutions.com/CT/Applicators/index.htm
Pesticide-related Business........................... www.kellysolutions.com/CT/Business/index.htm
Pharmacist/Pharmacist Intern...................... https://www.elicense.ct.gov/Lookup/LicenseLookup.aspx
Pharmacy/Technician.................................. https://www.elicense.ct.gov/Lookup/LicenseLookup.aspx
Physical Therapist/Assistant........................ https://www.elicense.ct.gov/Lookup/LicenseLookup.aspx
Physician/Medical Doctor/Assistant............ https://www.elicense.ct.gov/Lookup/LicenseLookup.aspx
Pipefitter.. www.ct.gov/dcp/cwp/view.asp?a=4308&q=507962
Plumber... https://www.elicense.ct.gov/Lookup/GenerateRoster.aspx
Podiatrist... https://www.elicense.ct.gov/Lookup/LicenseLookup.aspx
Premium Finance Company........................ www.ct-clic.com
Private Investigator/Agency......................... www.ct.gov/dps/lib/dps/special_licensing_and_firearms/licensed_pi_security_companies.pdf

Private Occupational & Hospital-Based Schools...........www.ctohe.org/POSA/
Psychologist... https://www.elicense.ct.gov/Lookup/LicenseLookup.aspx
Public Service Technician........................... https://www.elicense.ct.gov/Lookup/GenerateRoster.aspx
Radiographer .... https://www.elicense.ct.gov/Lookup/LicenseLookup.aspx
Real Estate Agent/Broker/Sales .... https://www.elicense.ct.gov/Lookup/LicenseLookup.aspx
Real Estate Appraiser .... https://www.elicense.ct.gov/Lookup/LicenseLookup.aspx
Real Estate Educ. Provider......................... https://www.elicense.ct.gov/Lookup/LicenseLookup.aspx
Reinsurance Intermediary........................... www.ct-clic.com
Rental Car Company.................................. www.ct-clic.com
Respiratory Care Practitioner...................... https://www.elicense.ct.gov/Lookup/LicenseLookup.aspx
Risk Purchasing/Retention Group............... www.ct-clic.com
Sales Finance Company............................. www.ct.gov/dob/cwp/view.asp?a=2239&Q=298138&dobNAV_GID=1659&dobNav=|
Sanitarian .... https://www.elicense.ct.gov/Lookup/LicenseLookup.aspx
Savings & Loan Association .... www.ct.gov/dob/cwp/view.asp?a=2239&Q=298138&dobNAV_GID=1659&dobNav=|
School Principal/Superintendent................. www.csde.state.ct.us/public/csde/reports/SuperintendentContacts.asp
Securities Agent/Broker/Dealer................... www.finra.org/index.htm
Security Company Firearms Instructor .... www.ct.gov/dps/lib/dps/special_licensing_and_firearms/certified_security_officers_firearms_instructors-
.... blue_cards.pdf
Security Company, Private .... www.ct.gov/dps/lib/dps/special_licensing_and_firearms/licensed_pi_security_companies.pdf
Security Officer Instructor .... www.ct.gov/dps/lib/dps/special_licensing_and_firearms/approved_cj_security_instructor_(public).pdf
Security Service .... www.ct.gov/dps/lib/dps/special_licensing_and_firearms/licensed_pi_security_companies.pdf
Sheet Metal Contr/Journeyman .... https://www.elicense.ct.gov/Lookup/GenerateRoster.aspx
Shorthand Court Reporter........................... https://www.elicense.ct.gov/Lookup/GenerateRoster.aspx
Social Worker... https://www.elicense.ct.gov/Lookup/LicenseLookup.aspx
Solar Energy Contr/Journeyman................. https://www.elicense.ct.gov/Lookup/GenerateRoster.aspx
Solid Waste Facility Operator .... www.ct.gov/deep/cwp/view.asp?a=2718&q=455558&depNav_GID=1967&depNav=|
Speech Pathologist.................................... https://www.elicense.ct.gov/Lookup/LicenseLookup.aspx
Sprinkler Layout Technician........................ https://www.elicense.ct.gov/Lookup/GenerateRoster.aspx
Student Athlete Agent .... https://www.elicense.ct.gov/Lookup/GenerateRoster.aspx
Surplus Lines Broker.................................. www.ct-clic.com
Teacher.. http://sdeportal.ct.gov/CECSFOI/FOILookup.aspx
Telecommunication Technician .... https://www.elicense.ct.gov/Lookup/GenerateRoster.aspx
Television/Radio License .... https://www.elicense.ct.gov/Lookup/GenerateRoster.aspx
Utilization Review Company .... www.ct-clic.com
Vehicle Dealer/Repairer.............................. www.ct.gov/dmv/cwp/view.asp?a=799&q=401814&dmvPNavCtr=|#48712
Vending Machine Operator.......................... https://www.elicense.ct.gov/Lookup/LicenseLookup.aspx
Vendor, Itinerant... https://www.elicense.ct.gov/Lookup/GenerateRoster.aspx
Veterinarian.. https://www.elicense.ct.gov/Lookup/LicenseLookup.aspx
Viatical Settlement Broker/Provider .... www.ct-clic.com
Water Distribution System Operator .... https://www.elicense.ct.gov/Lookup/LicenseLookup.aspx
Water Treatment Plant Operator................. https://www.elicense.ct.gov/Lookup/LicenseLookup.aspx
Weigher.. https://www.elicense.ct.gov/Lookup/LicenseLookup.aspx
Weights/Measures Dealer/Repair/Regul'r.... https://www.elicense.ct.gov/Lookup/LicenseLookup.aspx
Well Driller.. https://www.elicense.ct.gov/Lookup/LicenseLookup.aspx
Winery Farm... https://www.elicense.ct.gov/Lookup/LicenseLookup.aspx
Wrestler/Wrestling Manager .... www.ct.gov/dcp/cwp/view.asp?a=4308&q=507962

State and Local Courts

State Court Structure: The Superior Court is the sole court of original jurisdiction for all causes of action, except for matters over which the Probate Courts have jurisdiction as provided by statute. The state is divided into 13 Judicial Districts, 20 Geographic Area Courts, and 13 Juvenile Districts. The Superior Court - comprised primarily of the Judicial District Courts and the Geographical Area Courts - has 5 divisions: Criminal, Civil, Family, Juvenile, and Administrative Appeals. When not combined, the Judicial District Courts handle felony and civil cases while the Geographic Area Courts handle misdemeanors, and most handle small claims. Divorce records are maintained by the Chief Clerk of the Judicial District Courts. Probate is handled by city Probate Courts and those courts not part of the state court system. In May, 2006 the state centralized all small claims cases to the Centralized Small Claims Office. This location holds all records since that date.

Appellate Courts: Opinions from the Supreme and Appellate courts are available at www.jud.state.ct.us/opinions.htm..

About Court Online Access: There is a statewide system for each of serveral Types of records.

- The Judicial Branch offers web look-up to case docket information at www.jud.ct.gov/jud2.htm. Case look-ups are segregated into **five types; civil/family, criminal/motor vehicle, housing** (see below), **juvenile**, and **small claim**s. Search statewide or by location for civil; only by location for criminal. The year of birth shows for criminal, but not for civil. The criminal and motor vehicle case docket data is available on cases up to ten years after a disposition or bond forfeiture occurred. The web page states civil cases are available from no less than one year and no more than ten years after the disposition date depending on location, but the number is usually closer to ten. There may be missing or unviewable data on the online system if the civil case was e-filed
- **Youthful Offender** cases are not shown on the criminal/motor vehicle look-ups. To search statewide, leave the location field blank. For housing (landlord/tenant) cases, search by name, address, or docket number.
- **Criminal** searches are generally considered to be onsite equivalent - civil searches are not.
- Note the **Housing** case record search at www.jud.ct.gov/housing.htm is available only for Hartford, New Haven, New Britain, Bridgeport, Norwalk and Waterbury districts. However, Case records for summary process matters in Tolland and Meriden Judicial Districts can be found using the Civil/Family look-up.

There are no individual Connecticut courts offering online access beyond the statewide sites mentioned above.

Recorders, Assessors, and Other Sites of Note

Recording Office Organization: 8 counties and 169 towns/cities. There is no county recording in Connecticut, all recording is at the town/city level. The recording officer is the Town/City Clerk. Be careful not to confuse searching in the following towns/cities as equivalent to a countywide search (since they have the same names): Fairfield, Hartford, Litchfield, New Haven, New London, Tolland, and Windham.

Statewide or Multi-Jurisdiction Access: A number of towns offer free access to assessor information. The State's Municipal Public Access Initiative has produced a website usefule of Town and Municipality general information at www.munic.state.ct.us.

Several private database companies provide access from various Connecticut jurisdictions. See below.

- A private vendor provides assessor property records, usually free for 100 participating jurisdiction at www.vgsi.com/vision/Applications/ParcelData/Home.aspx. Note this URL will give you the main site to VISION Government Solutions and then you must click on each individual town for the data. The ensuing URL begins with data.visionappraisal.com for each town.
- Retrieve and review real property data and assessments free for 8 Connecticut towns at www.prophecyone.us/index_prophecy.php. A fee is charged for records. There is no name searching.

Local Sites, Organized by County:

Fairfield County

Bethel Town ***Recorded Documents*** www.bethel-ct.gov/content/117/452/default.aspx Access to records for a fee at https://connecticut-townclerks-records.com/User/Login.aspx?ReturnUrl=%2fIndex.aspx. Must register before use. **$$$**
Property, Taxation Access to the Assessor's database for free at http://bethel.univers-clt.com/. GIS is at http://107.20.209.214/bethelct_public/default.html.

Bridgeport Town ***Recorded Documents*** www.bridgeportct.gov/content/89019/89914/default.aspx Access to land record indexes for free, go to https://www.uslandrecords.com/ctlr/. To view any image there is a charge of $2.00 per page for all the pages of the document. Images are available from 1985 to present. **$$$**

Property, Taxation Search town assessor database for free at http://data.visionappraisal.com/BridgeportCT/. Also, access to GIS/mapping free at http://gis.cdm.com/website/bridgeportct/.

Brookfield Town ***Property, Taxation*** Search town assessor database at http://data.visionappraisal.com/BrookfieldCT/DEFAULT.asp. Free registration for full data.

Danbury City ***Recorded Documents, Maps, Marriage, Trade Names, Deaths, Civil Union Records*** www.ci.danbury.ct.us/content/21015/21087/21135/default.aspx Access to records free at http://tc.ci.danbury.ct.us/external/LandRecords/protected/SrchQuickName.aspx.

Property, Taxation Access assessor property data free at http://data.visionappraisal.com/DanburyCT/DEFAULT.asp

Darien Town ***Property, Taxation*** Access to Assessor's database for free at http://darien.ias-clt.com/parcel.list.php.

Easton Town ***Property, Taxation*** Access property data free at www.prophecyone.us/index_prophecy.php?town=Easton. No name searching. Also, access to online property field cards at www.equalitycama.com/towns/Towns.htm. Click on Easton.**$$$**

Fairfield Town ***Recorded Documents*** www.fairfieldct.org Access to land record indexes for free, go to https://www.uslandrecords.com/ctlr/. To view any image there is a charge of $2.00 per page for all the pages of the document. Images are available from 2000 to present. **$$$**

Property, Taxation Access assessor property data free at http://data.visionappraisal.com/FairfieldCT/DEFAULT.asp Also, access to the Grand List for 2008, 2009, 2010 and 2011 found at www.fairfieldct.org/taxfaq.htm.

Greenwich Town ***Recorded Documents*** www.greenwichct.org/Government/Departments/Town_Clerk/ Access to land record indexes for free, go to https://www.uslandrecords.com/ctlr/. To view any image there is a charge of $2.00 per page for all the pages of the document. Images are available from 1985 to present. **$$$**

Property, Taxation Search current tax records free at www.greenwichct.org/Government/Departments/Assessor/#. Click on view and pay taxes. You may also search real estate, personal property, and motor vehicles.

Monroe Town ***Recorded Documents*** www.monroect.org/townclerk.aspx Access to index search free at https://www.uslandrecords.com/ctlr/controller;jsessionid=C2F46A4635FDEDA84559ECAAD230DFBF. Images available from 1988 to present. For more detailed information you must subscribe for a fee. **$$$**

Property, Taxation Access to Tax search information for free at www.monroect.org/TaxInformation.aspx. No name search.

New Canaan Town ***Real Estate, Maps, Trade names Records*** www.newcanaan.info/content/9490/293/329/default.aspx Access to land records free at www.newcanaan.info/content/9490/293/329/6878/default.aspx.

New Fairfield Town ***Property, Taxation*** Access the assessor database free at http://data.visionappraisal.com/NewfairfieldCT/DEFAULT.asp.

Newtown Municipal Ctr ***Real Estate Records*** www.newtown-ct.gov/Public_Documents/NewtownCT_Clerk/index Access to land records free at https://connecticut-townclerks-records.com/User/Login.aspx?ReturnUrl=%2fIndex.aspx/. Records dates are: Land records 01/01/1900-01/27/2010; Maps 02/23/2006-01/21/2010; Trade name 07/13/2004-07/13/2004

Property, Taxation Access property data free at www.prophecyone.us/index_prophecy.php?town=Newtown. No name searching. Search the town assessor's database free at http://data.visionappraisal.com/newtownCT/DEFAULT.asp.**$$$**

Norwalk City ***Real Estate, Deed, Lien, Marriage, UCC Records*** www.norwalkct.org/index.aspx?nid=155 Access to the town clerk's Official Records is free at www.norwalkct.org/index.aspx?NID=163.

Property, Taxation Access to Norwalk property records is free at www.norwalkct.org/index.aspx?NID=163.

Redding Town ***Recorded Documents*** www.townofreddingct.org/Public_Documents/ReddingCT_Clerk/index Access to recorded document index free at www.townofreddingct.org/Public_Documents/ReddingCT_Clerk/SEARCH%20PUBLIC%20RECORDS. To get images, must subscribe for a fee. Images viewable from 12/10/02 to present. **$$$**

Property, Taxation Access to GIS/mapping free at http://ags.cdm.com/redding/. Search the city assessor database at http://data.visionappraisal.com/ReddingCT/DEFAULT.asp. Free registration required.

Ridgefield Town ***Property, Taxation*** For property assessments for free at www.prophecyone.us/index_prophecy.php. Email general questions to the assessor at assessor@ridgefieldct.org.

Stamford City ***Trade Name, City Businesses Records*** www.stamfordct.gov/town-clerk Search the city registry of trade names for free at http://cityofstamford.org/apps/tradenames/.

Property, Taxation Access assessor tax data free at http://gis.vgsi.com/stamfordct/ or at http://apps.cityofstamford.org/tax/.

Stratford Town ***Recorded Documents*** www.townofstratford.com/content/39832/39846/39945/default.aspx Access to town records for a fee at https://connecticut-townclerks-records.com/User/Login.aspx?ReturnUrl=%2fIndex.aspx. Must subscribe to use. Index goes back to 1984 and images go back to 1991. **$$$**

Property, Taxation Search town assessor database free at http://data.visionappraisal.com/StratfordCT/DEFAULT.asp.

Trumbull Town ***Recorded Documents*** www.trumbull-ct.gov/content/10623/10655/11079/default.aspx Free access to land records available at http://71.11.0.182/External/LandRecords/protected/SrchQuickName.aspx. Land record index from 1/1/50 to present, trade names from 3/24/30 to present.
Property, Taxation Search the assessor database free at http://data.visionappraisal.com/TrumbullCT/DEFAULT.asp. Also, free access to GIS/mapping at http://ags2.cdm.com/trumbullct/.

Weston Town ***Recorded Documents, Marriage, Death, Trade Name Records*** www.westonct.gov/townhall/27652/27718/28002 Access the Town Clerk's index records free at www.westonlandrecords.com/.
Property, Taxation Search the town assessor's database free at http://data.visionappraisal.com/westonCT/DEFAULT.asp.

Westport Town ***Land Records, Deed, Lien, Maps/Surveys, Death, Marriage, Civil Union, Trade Name, Burial, Liquor Licenses Records*** www.westportct.gov/index.aspx?page=134 Search a variety of public record indexes only at www.westportct.gov/index.aspx?page=634 including land records back to 5/17/94, civil unions back to 2005, deaths and marriages to 1949, maps/surveys to 1886, trade names to 8/8/24, burials back to 2006. Subscribers can view and print images of land records and trade names for a fee. **$$$**
Property, Taxation Search assessor data free at http://data.visionappraisal.com/WestportCT/DEFAULT.asp. Also, search property data free on the GIS-mapping site at https://geopower.jws.com/westport/.

Wilton Town ***Recorded Documents*** www.wiltonct.org/departments/clerk/clerk.html Access to land record indexes for free, go to https://www.uslandrecords.com/ctlr/. To view any image there is a charge of $2.00 per page for all the pages of the document. Images are available from 1985 to present. **$$$**
Property, Taxation Search the town assessor database free at http://data.visionappraisal.com/WiltonCT/DEFAULT.asp.

Hartford County

Avon Town ***Recorded Documents*** www.town.avon.ct.us/Public_Documents/AvonCT_Clerk/clerk Access land data (index) and trade names free at www.town.avon.ct.us/Public_Documents/AvonCT_Clerk/clerk.
Property, Taxation Access to property data is free at www.avonassessor.com/index.shtml.

Berlin Town ***Land Records Records*** www.town.berlin.ct.us/content/195/245/default.aspx Access the recorders index free at http://65.75.60.205/resolution/.
Property, Taxation Search the Town of Berlin Geographic and Property Network for property maps and abutting property at http://berlingis.com/. Search town assessor database at http://data.visionappraisal.com/BerlinCT/DEFAULT.asp. Free registration for full data.

Bloomfield Town ***Property, Taxation*** Access to Assessor's online database free at www.qpublic.net/ct/bloomfield/search.html.

Bristol City ***Recorded Documents*** www.ci.bristol.ct.us/index.aspx?nid=281 Access to land records free at http://cottweb.ci.bristol.ct.us/External/User/Login.aspx?ReturnUrl=%2fExternal%2fLandRecords%2fprotected%2fSrchQuickName.aspx.
Property, Taxation Search town assessor database free at http://data.visionappraisal.com/BristolCT/DEFAULT.asp.

Burlington Town ***Recorded Documents*** http://burlingtonct.us/departments/burlington-town-clerk.php Access to records for a fee at https://connecticut-townclerks-records.com/User/Login.aspx?ReturnUrl=%2fIndex.aspx. **$$$**
Property, Taxation Search town assessor database free at http://data.visionappraisal.com/BurlingtonCT/DEFAULT.asp.

Canton Town ***Real Estate, Trade Names, Death Records Records*** www.townofcantonct.org Access to land records, maps/surveys and death records free at https://connecticut-townclerks-records.com/User/Login.aspx?ReturnUrl=%2fIndex.aspx.
Property, Taxation Search of property address, search by owner name, or search sales at www.cantonassessor.com.

East Granby Town ***Real Estate Records*** http://eastgranbyct.org/town-clerk.html Access to Town Clerks portal for a fee at https://connecticut-townclerks-records.com/User/Login.aspx?ReturnUrl=%2fIndex.aspx **$$$**
Property, Taxation Access to property tax for free at www.my-tax-bill.info/cgi-local/looktax.pl?ID=EG. Also, access to GIS/mapping free at http://eastgranbyct.org/area-maps.html.

East Hartford Town ***Recorded Documents*** http://easthartfordct.gov/Public_Documents/EastHartfordCT_Clerk/index Access to land record indexes for free, go to https://www.uslandrecords.com/ctlr/. To view any image there is a charge of $2.00 per page for all the pages of the document. Images are available from 1985 to present. **$$$**
Property, Taxation Access to GIS/mapping for free at http://ceo.fando.com/easthartford/.

East Windsor Town ***Property, Taxation*** Access property data free at www.prophecyone.us/index_prophecy.php. No name searching. Also, access to online property field cards at www.equalitycama.com/towns/Towns.htm. Click on East Windsor.**$$$**

Enfield Town ***Recorded Documents*** http://enfield-ct.gov/content/91/148/default.aspx Access real estate records free at https://app7.enfield.org/.

Property, Taxation Access assessor property data free at http://data.visionappraisal.com/EnfieldCT/DEFAULT.asp Also, search for parcel data free on the GIS-mapping site at http://ags2.cdm.com/fl/enfieldct/main.html.

Farmington Town ***Recorded Documents*** www.farmington-ct.org/town_services/town_clerk/index.html Access to land and indexed information for a fee, go to https://connecticut-townclerks-records.com/User/Login.aspx?ReturnUrl=%2fIndex.aspx. **$$$**

Property, Taxation Access property assessor data free at www.farmington-ct.org/landrecords/search.php.

Glastonbury Town ***Recorded Documents*** www.glastonbury-ct.gov Access town clerks recorded document index free at http://tcweb.glastonbury-ct.gov/wb_or1/disclaim.asp. Online land record indexes go back to 1973.

Property, Taxation Access assessor property data free at http://data.visionappraisal.com/GlastonburyCT/DEFAULT.asp

Granby Town ***Property, Taxation*** Access assessor property data free at http://data.visionappraisal.com/GranbyCT/DEFAULT.asp

Hartford City ***Recorded Documents*** www.hartford.gov/townclerk Access to land record indexes for free, go to https://www.uslandrecords.com/ctlr/. To view any image there is a charge of $2.00 per page for all the pages of the document. Images are available from 1985 to present. **$$$**

Property, Taxation Search city assessor data free at http://assessor1.hartford.gov/Default.asp?br=exp&vr=6.

Manchester Town ***Recorded Documents*** www.townofmanchester.org/Town_Clerk/ Access to the town records for free to go http://tcweb.townofmanchester.org/External/LandRecords/protected/SrchQuickName.aspx.

Property, Taxation Search the town assessor database at http://data.visionappraisal.com/ManchesterCT/DEFAULT.asp. Free registration required. Also, click on TOMnet Public parcel viewer to search property free at www.manchestergis.com/ but no name searching.

Marlborough Town ***Property, Taxation*** Search the assessor database free at http://data.visionappraisal.com/MarlboroughCT/DEFAULT.asp. Free registration required.

New Britain Town ***Real Estate Records*** www.newbritainct.gov/index.php/city-services/town-clerk.html Access to land record indexes only, free at http://landrecords.newbritainct.gov/

Property, Taxation Search the city assessor database at http://data.visionappraisal.com/NewbritainCT/DEFAULT.asp. Free registration required.

Newington Town ***Real Estate, Trade names, Deed, GIS/maps Records*** www.newingtonct.gov/content/78/118/148/2078.aspx Access to online database search for free to go www.newingtonct.gov/content/78/118/148/8210/default.aspx.

Property, Taxation Access to assessor property records is free at www.newingtonct.gov/content/78/118/120/7768.aspx.

Plainville Town ***Recorded Documents*** www.plainvillect.com/pages/page_content/town_departments_town%20clerk.aspx Access to records for a fee at https://connecticut-townclerks-records.com/User/Login.aspx?ReturnUrl=%2fIndex.aspx. **$$$**

Property, Taxation Access town assessor property data free at http://plainville.univers-clt.com/.

Rocky Hill Town ***Recorded Documents, Marriage, Death, Trade Name, Map Records*** www.rockyhillct.gov/DeptPages/tc.htm Access to the Town Clerk's Index Search is free at www.rockyhillct.gov/resolution/. Land records go back to 1973; Marriages/Deaths to 1990; trade names to 1987; maps to 1982.

Property, Taxation Access to property data/GIS/mapping for free at www.mapsonline.net/rockyhillct/web_assessor/search.php#sid=2d31363c2f9346353df303f8622f1447. Also, access to GIS/mapping free at www.mapsonline.net/rockyhillct/.

Simsbury Town ***Recorded Documents*** www.simsbury-ct.gov/town-clerk Access to records for a fee at https://connecticut-townclerks-records.com/User/Login.aspx?ReturnUrl=%2fIndex.aspx. **$$$**

Property, Taxation For property assessments for free at www.prophecyone.us/index_prophecy.php. No name searches. Also, access to online property field cards at www.equalitycama.com/tvweb/mainsearch.aspx?city=Simsbury.**$$$**

South Windsor Town ***Recorded Documents*** www.southwindsor.org Access to records for a subscription fee go to https://connecticut-townclerks-records.com/User/Login.aspx?ReturnUrl=%2fIndex.aspx. Click on Town of South Windsor. **$$$**

Property, Taxation Search the town Assessor's database at http://data.visionappraisal.com/SouthwindsorCT/DEFAULT.asp.

Southington Town ***Recorded Documents, Voter Registration Records*** www.southington.org/content/17216/17534/default.aspx Access to state town clerk data for a fee at https://connecticut-townclerks-records.com/User/Login.aspx?ReturnUrl=%2fIndex.aspx. Access the voter registration lookup free at www.southington.org/content/17216/17323/default.aspx. **$$$**

Property, Taxation Access town assessor records free at http://data.visionappraisal.com/SouthingtonCT/DEFAULT.asp. Also, access to GIS/mapping free at www.southingtongis.com/.

Suffield Town ***Property, Taxation*** Search the town assessor's database at http://data.visionappraisal.com/SuffieldCT/DEFAULT.asp.

West Hartford Town ***Real Estate, Deed, Lien, Trade names, Foreclosure, Maps Records*** www.westhartford.org/living_here/town_departments/town_clerk/index.php Access to records free at http://cotthosting.com/ctwesthartford/User/Login.aspx?ReturnUrl=%2fctwesthartford%2fDefault.aspx. Choose option to \"Sign in as a guest\".
Property, Taxation Access to the assessor property records on the GIS-mapping site is free at http://host.appgeo.com/westhartfordct/. Also, search the assessor database free at http://data.visionappraisal.com/WesthartfordCT/DEFAULT.asp. Also, lookup property tax data using address or name searching free at http://data.visionappraisal.com/Westhavenct/DEFAULT.asp.

Wethersfield Town ***Property, Taxation*** Access to property data is free after free registration at http://data.visionappraisal.com/WethersfieldCT/DEFAULT.asp. Free registration required.

Windsor Locks Town ***Recorded Documents*** www.windsorlocksct.org/page.php?pid=22 Access to records for a fee at https://connecticut-townclerks-records.com/User/Login.aspx?ReturnUrl=%2fIndex.aspx. **$$$**
Property, Taxation Search the town assessor database free at http://data.visionappraisal.com/WINDSORLOCKSCT/DEFAULT.asp.

Windsor Town ***Real Estate, Grantor/Grantee, Deed Records*** http://townofwindsorct.com/townclerk/ Search the town clerk's land records index for free at http://townofwindsorct.com/townclerk/index.php?page=68. Index goes back to 1970. Town services search page at www.townofwindsorct.com/.
Property, Taxation Search the town GIS database at http://info.townofwindsorct.com/gis/.

Litchfield County

Barkhamsted Town ***Property, Taxation*** Search town assessor database at http://data.visionappraisal.com/BethlehemCT/DEFAULT.asp.

Bethlehem Town ***Property, Taxation*** Search town assessor database at http://data.visionappraisal.com/BethlehemCT/DEFAULT.asp. Free registration for full data.

Canaan Town ***Property, Taxation*** Search town assessor database at http://data.visionappraisal.com/CanaanCT/DEFAULT.asp. Free registration for full data.

Colebrook Town ***Property, Taxation*** Assessor property data free at http://data.visionappraisal.com/ColebrookCT/DEFAULT.asp

Cornwall Town ***Recorded Documents*** www.cornwallct.org/town_offices.html Access records for a fee at www.webtownhall.com. **$$$**

Goshen Town ***Property, Taxation*** Assessor property data free at http://data.visionappraisal.com/GoshenCT/DEFAULT.asp

Harwinton Town ***Property, Taxation*** Search the town assessor's database free at http://data.visionappraisal.com/HarwintonCT/DEFAULT.asp.

Kent Town ***Property, Taxation*** Access to property assessor data is at http://data.visionappraisal.com/KentCT/DEFAULT.asp. Free registration required.

Litchfield Town ***Property, Taxation*** Search town assessor property data free at http://gis.vgsi.com/LitchfieldCT/.

Town of Morris ***Real Estate, Vital Registry Records*** www.morris.webtownhall.com/Departments/TownClerk/tabid/67/Default.aspx Access to land records for a fee at https://www.webtownhall.com/Default.aspx. Find and Click on Town of Morris. Subscription fees are $4.99 per day, $29.99 per month, $170.94 semi annually and $323.89 annually. **$$$**
Property, Taxation Access assessor data free with registration at http://data.visionappraisal.com/MorrisCT/DEFAULT.asp

New Hartford Town ***Recorded Documents*** www.town.new-hartford.ct.us Access real estate, assumed names records for free at http://cotthosting.com/ctnewhartford/LandRecords/protected/SrchQuickName.aspx.
Property, Taxation Access to GIS/mapping for free at www.newhartfordgis.com/.

New Milford Town ***Property, Taxation*** Search the town assessor database at http://data.visionappraisal.com/NewMilfordCT/DEFAULT.asp. Free registration required.

Norfolk Town Clerk ***Property, Taxation*** Access to assessor's online database for free at http://data.visionappraisal.com/NorfolkCT/DEFAULT.asp.

Roxbury Town ***Property, Taxation*** Access to property data free at http://data.visionappraisal.com/RoxburyCT/DEFAULT.asp.

Salisbury Town Clerk ***Land Records,Recorded Documents*** www.salisburyct.us/offices/townclerk Access to town portals for a fee at https://connecticut-townclerks-records.com/User/Login.aspx?ReturnUrl=%2fIndex.aspx. Then click on Town of Salisbury. Can sign in as a guest, to get detailed images must subscribe. **$$$**

Sharon Town ***Real Estate Records*** www.sharonct.org/index.php?option=com_content&view=article&id=70&Itemid=80 Access to Town Clerk records for a fee at https://connecticut-townclerks-records.com/User/Login.aspx?ReturnUrl=%2fIndex.aspx. **$$$**

Property, Taxation Access assessor data free after registration at http://data.visionappraisal.com/SharonCT/DEFAULT.asp.

Thomaston Town ***Property, Taxation*** Search property data free at www.prophecyone.us/index_prophecy.php?town=Thomaston, but no name searching.**$$$**

Torrington City ***Property, Taxation*** Also, access to online property field cards at www.equalitycama.com/towns/Towns.htm. Click on Torrington.**$$$**

Warren Town ***Recorded Documents*** http://warren.webtownhall.com/Departments/TownClerk/tabid/181/Default.aspx Access land records for a fee at http://landrecordsearch.webtownhall.com/. **$$$**
Property, Taxation Access assessor property data free at http://data.visionappraisal.com/warrenct/DEFAULT.asp

Washington Town ***Property, Taxation*** Access to the Grand Lists for Real Estate, Motor Vehicles and Personal Property for free at http://www.washingtonct.org/assessor.html.

Watertown Town ***Property, Taxation*** Access property data free at http://data.visionappraisal.com/watertownct/DEFAULT.asp.

Winchester Town ***Property, Taxation*** Access town property tax data free at http://data.visionappraisal.com/WinchesterCT/DEFAULT.asp. Also sometimes known as Winchester.

Woodbury Town ***Property, Taxation*** Access to online property field cards at www.equalitycama.com/towns/Towns.htm. Click on Woodbury.**$$$**

Middlesex County

Chester Town ***Recorded Documents*** www.chesterct.org/departments/townclerk.htm Access to recorded documents for a fee at https://connecticut-townclerks-records.com/User/Login.aspx?ReturnUrl=%2fIndex.aspx **$$$**
Property, Taxation Also, access to online property field cards at www.equalitycama.com/towns/Towns.htm. Click on Chester**$$$**

Clinton Town ***Recorded Documents*** http://clintonct.org/town_clerk.php Access to records for a fee at https://connecticut-townclerks-records.com/User/Login.aspx?ReturnUrl=%2fIndex.aspx. Can see index for free, charges for copies. **$$$**
Property, Taxation Access assessor property data free at http://data.visionappraisal.com/ClintonCT/DEFAULT.asp

Cromwell Town Clerk ***Recorded Documents*** www.cromwellct.com/Town%20Departments/TownClerk.htm Access to land record indexes for free, go to https://www.uslandrecords.com/ctlr/. To view any image there is a charge of $2.00 per page for all the pages of the document. Images are available from 1985 to present. **$$$**
Property, Taxation Access assessor property data free at http://data.visionappraisal.com/CromwellCT/DEFAULT.asp

Deep River Town ***Recorded Documents*** www.deepriverct.us/Pages/DeepRiverCT_Clerk/index Access to record indexes free at https://connecticut-townclerks-records.com/User/Login.aspx?ReturnUrl=%2fIndex.aspx. For images, must subscribe for a fee. **$$$**
Property, Taxation Access to property records for free at http://data.visionappraisal.com/DeepRiverCT/DEFAULT.asp.

Durham Town ***Property, Taxation*** Access the assessor's database at http://durham.univers-clt.com.

East Haddam Town ***Recorded Documents*** www.easthaddam.org/index.cfm?fuseaction=trees.treePage&treeID=97 Access to records for a fee at https://uslandrecords.com/uslr/UslrApp/index.jsp. Will start online on 4/1/2013. **$$$**
Property, Taxation Search town assessor database free at http://data.visionappraisal.com/EastHaddamCT/DEFAULT.asp.

Essex Town ***Real Estate, Deed, Lien, Mortgage Records*** www.essexct.gov/departments/townclerk.html Access to records for a fee at https://connecticut-townclerks-records.com/User/Login.aspx?ReturnUrl=%2fIndex.aspx. Access to records for a fee go to https://connecticut-townclerks-records.com/User/Login.aspx?ReturnUrl=%2fIndex.aspx. **$$$**
Property, Taxation Access assessor property data free at http://data.visionappraisal.com/EssexCT/DEFAULT.asp Also, access to on-line property viewer, GIS/mapping free at www.mapgeo.com/EssexCT/.

Haddam Town ***Property, Taxation*** Access the Assessor database free after email registration at http://rmsreval.com/login.asp?town=Haddam. Data may be old. Also, search town assessor database at http://data.visionappraisal.com/HaddamCT/DEFAULT.asp. Free registration for full data.

Killingworth Town ***Recorded Documents*** www.townofkillingworth.com/offices/town_clerk.html Access to records for a fee at https://connecticut-townclerks-records.com/User/Login.aspx?ReturnUrl=%2fIndex.aspx. **$$$**
Property, Taxation Access property data free at www.prophecyone.us/index_prophecy.php?town=Killingworth. No name searching. This is a demo site for a subscription vendor, this town just happens to be free. Also, access to online property field cards at www.equalitycama.com/towns/Towns.htm. Click on Killingworth.**$$$**

Middlefield Town ***Property, Taxation*** Search the town assessor database free at http://data.visionappraisal.com/MiddlefieldCT/DEFAULT.asp.

Middletown City ***Real Estate Records*** www.middletownct.gov/content/117/123/181/default.aspx Access to indices for land records for a fee at https://connecticut-townclerks-records.com/User/Login.aspx?ReturnUrl=%2fIndex.aspx. The land record indices on this site range from January 1, 1969 to today's date. Images of documents are available from August 29, 2005 to the present. **$$$**

Property, Taxation Access GIS/mapping for free at http://gis.cityofmiddletown.com/middletownct/. Also, access to property data free at http://middletown.univers-clt.com/, also no name searching.

Old Saybrook Town ***Recorded Documents*** www.oldsaybrookct.org To access records for a fee at https://connecticut-townclerks-records.com/User/Login.aspx?ReturnUrl=%2fIndex.aspx. **$$$**

Town of Portland ***Property, Taxation*** Access to Assessors data for free at www.portlandct.org/.

Westbrook Town ***Property, Taxation*** Access to property records for free at http://data.visionappraisal.com/WestbrookCT/DEFAULT.asp.

New Haven County

Ansonia City ***Property, Taxation*** Access to GIS/mapping for free at http://ansonia.mapxpress.net/.

Bethany Town ***Property, Taxation*** For property assessments for free at www.prophecyone.us/index_prophecy.php. Also, access to online property field cards at www.equalitycama.com/towns/Towns.htm. Click on Bethany.

Branford Town ***Recorded Documents*** www.branford-ct.gov/Town%20Clerk.htm Access to town clerk's recording records is free at http://deeds.branford-ct.gov/External/LandRecords/protected/SrchQuickName.aspx. Land records go back to 7/1993; trade names indexes and images back to 2005. Maps go back to 1959. To subscribe for images go to https://connecticut-townclerks-records.com/User/Login.aspx?ReturnUrl=%2fIndex.aspx. **$$$**

Property, Taxation Search the town assessor database at http://data.visionappraisal.com/BranfordCT/DEFAULT.asp.

Cheshire Town ***Property, Taxation*** Access property data free at www.prophecyone.us/index_prophecy.php?town=Cheshire. No name searching. Also, access to online property field cards at www.equalitycama.com/towns/Towns.htm. Click on Cheshire.**$$$**

East Haven Town ***Property, Taxation*** Access property data free at www.prophecyone.us/index_prophecy.php?town=East%20Haven. Also, access to online property field cards at www.equalitycama.com/towns/Towns.htm. Click on East Haven.**$$$**

Guilford Town ***Recorded Documents*** www.ci.guilford.ct.us Access to land records free at http://ctguilford.cotthosting.com/.

Property, Taxation Access property data by address, or legal free at For property assessments for free at www.prophecyone.us/index_prophecy.php. Also, access to online property field cards at www.equalitycama.com/towns/Towns.htm. Click on Guilford.**$$$**

Hamden Town ***Property, Taxation*** Search the town assessor's database free at http://data.visionappraisal.com/hamdenCT/DEFAULT.asp.

Madison City ***Property, Taxation*** Search the city assessor database free at http://data.visionappraisal.com/MadisonCT/DEFAULT.asp. Also, access property data free at www.nereval.com/OnlineDatabases.aspx.

Meriden City ***Property, Taxation*** Search by parcel ID or address for property assessor data at www.cityofmeriden.org/. Click on Property Searches. Also, search property data free on a private site at www.nereval.com/OnlineDatabases.aspx. Also, access parcel data free at http://gis.ci.meriden.ct.us/website/default.asp.

Middlebury Town ***Property, Taxation*** Access assessor and property data free at http://data.visionappraisal.com/MiddleburyCT/DEFAULT.asp. Free registration required.

Milford City ***Recorded Documents*** www.ci.milford.ct.us/Public_Documents/MilfordCT_clerk/index Access to state portal for records for a fee at https://connecticut-townclerks-records.com/User/Login.aspx?ReturnUrl=%2fIndex.aspx. **$$$**

Property, Taxation Search the city assessor's database at http://data.visionappraisal.com/MilfordCT/DEFAULT.asp.

Naugatuck Town ***Property, Taxation*** Search assessor database free at http://data.visionappraisal.com/NaugatuckCT/DEFAULT.asp.

New Haven City ***Recorded Documents*** www.cityofnewhaven.com/TownClerk/index.asp Access to land record indexes for free, go to https://www.uslandrecords.com/ctlr/. To view any image there is a charge of $2.00 per page for all the pages of the document. Images are available from 1985 to present. **$$$**

Property, Taxation Search the city assessor database free at http://data.visionappraisal.com/NewhavenCT/DEFAULT.asp.

North Branford Town ***Recorded Documents*** www.townofnorthbranfordct.com/town_services/town_clerk.htm Access to records for a fee at https://connecticut-townclerks-records.com/User/Login.aspx?ReturnUrl=%2fIndex.aspx. **$$$**

Property, Taxation Search assessor records at http://data.visionappraisal.com/NorthBranfordCT/DEFAULT.asp. Free registration required Also, access to GIS/mapping free at http://107.20.209.214/NorthBranfordCT_Public/index.html.

North Haven Town ***Real Estate, Tradename Certs Records*** www.town.north-haven.ct.us/TownHallDepts/TownClerk.asp Access to land records free at http://69.177.104.220/resolution/.

Property, Taxation Access property data free at http://north-haven.univers-clt.com. Also, access to property assessment data for free at http://data.visionappraisal.com/NorthHavenCT/DEFAULT.asp.

Orange Town ***Recorded Documents*** www.orange-ct.gov/govser/townclerk.htm Access to records for a fee at https://connecticut-townclerks-records.com/User/Login.aspx?ReturnUrl=%2fIndex.aspx. Indexes free, images and copies for a fee. Index goes back to 1972 and images go back to approx 1996. **$$$**

Property, Taxation Access to property assessment free at http://data.visionappraisal.com/OrangeCT/DEFAULT.asp.

Oxford Town ***Recorded Documents*** www.oxford-ct.gov Access to records for a fee at https://connecticut-townclerks-records.com/User/Login.aspx?ReturnUrl=%2fIndex.aspx. **$$$**

Property, Taxation Access property data free at www.prophecyone.us/index_prophecy.php?town=Oxford. No name searching. Access to property assessment free at http://data.visionappraisal.com/OxfordCT/DEFAULT.asp.**$$$**

Prospect Town ***Property, Taxation*** Access property data free at www.prophecyone.us/index_prophecy.php?town=Prospect. No name searching. Also, access to online property field cards at www.equalitycama.com/towns/Towns.htm. Click on Prospect.**$$$**

Seymour Town ***Property, Taxation*** Access to GIS/mapping for free at www.seymourgis.com/.

Southbury Town ***Property, Taxation*** For property assessments for free at www.prophecyone.us/index_prophecy.php. Click on Southbury. No name searches. Also, search the town Assessor's database at http://data.visionappraisal.com/SouthburyCT/DEFAULT.asp. Also, access to online property field cards at www.equalitycama.com/towns/Towns.htm. Click on Southbury.**$$$**

Waterbury City ***Recorded Documents*** www.waterburyct.org/content/9569/9605/9640/default.aspx Real Estate records and lien lists can be accessed for free at www.waterburyct.org/content/9569/9605/9640/10285.aspx.

Property, Taxation Also, access to online property field cards at www.equalitycama.com/towns/Towns.htm. Click on Waterbury. Also, access to GIS/mapping free at http://gis.waterburyct.org/GIS/Maps_Assessor.asp.

West Haven City ***Property, Taxation*** Search the town assessor's database free at http://data.visionappraisal.com/Westhavenct/DEFAULT.asp.

Wolcott Town ***Real Estate Records*** www.wolcottct.org/pages/page_content/secondary_town-departments_town-clerk_town-clerks-office.aspx Access to land records and other recorded information for a fee at https://connecticut-townclerks-records.com/User/Login.aspx?ReturnUrl=%2fIndex.aspx **$$$**

Property, Taxation Access property data free at www.prophecyone.us/index_prophecy.php?town=Wolcott. No name searching.**$$$**

Woodbridge Town ***Property, Taxation*** Search the town assessor's database at http://data.visionappraisal.com/WoodbridgeCT/DEFAULT.asp.

New London County

Colchester Town ***Recorded Documents*** www.colchesterct.gov/Pages/ColchesterCT_Dept/CTC/index Access to records for a fee at https://connecticut-townclerks-records.com/User/Login.aspx?ReturnUrl=%2fIndex.aspx. **$$$**

Property, Taxation Search town assessor database at http://data.visionappraisal.com/ColchesterCT/DEFAULT.asp. Free registration for full data.

East Lyme Town ***Property, Taxation*** Assessor property data free at http://data.visionappraisal.com/EastLymeCT/DEFAULT.asp

Griswold Town ***Real Estate Records*** www.griswold-ct.org Access to Town Clerks Portal for a fee to go https://connecticut-townclerks-records.com/User/Login.aspx?ReturnUrl=%2fIndex.aspx **$$$**

Property, Taxation Search town assessor database at http://data.visionappraisal.com/GriswoldCT/DEFAULT.asp. Free registration for full data.

Groton Town ***Recorded Documents*** www.groton-ct.gov/depts/twnclk/ Access to record indexes free at https://connecticut-townclerks-records.com/User/Login.aspx?ReturnUrl=%2fIndex.aspx. There is a charge to view and print documents. **$$$**

Property, Taxation Access property data free at http://gis.groton-ct.gov/Disclaimer.asp. Click on Interactive Mapping, then Property Viewer, then owner name. Records back to 1990. Search list of tax payments for 2010 free at www.town.groton.ct.us/taxes/listing.asp.

Lebanon Town ***Property, Taxation*** Access to GIS/mapping for free at www.mainstreetmaps.com/CT/Lebanon/.

Montville Town ***Land Records, Maps/Surveys, Death, Marriage, Civil Union, Trade Name Records*** www.townofmontville.org/Content/Town_Clerk/ Access to recorders databases are available for a fee at https://connecticut-townclerks-records.com/User/Login.aspx. **$$$**

Property, Taxation Access assessor data free at http://data.visionappraisal.com/MontvilleCT/DEFAULT.asp.

New London City ***Property, Taxation*** Search the city assessor's database free at http://data.visionappraisal.com/newlondonct/DEFAULT.asp. Also, access to GIS/mapping free at http://host.appgeo.com/sccog/Default.aspx. Select New London Town.

North Stonington Town ***Property, Taxation*** Access to GIS/mapping for free at www.northstoningtongis.com/.

Norwich City ***Real Estate, Deed Records*** www.norwichct.org Also, access to the clerk's town land records is online by subscription. Index goes back to 1929 and images to 1997. Fee is $350.00 per year; sign-up online at www.norwichct.org/content/43/280/81/249.aspx or call 860-823-3734. **$$$**
Property, Taxation Search the city assessor's database free at http://data.visionappraisal.com/NorwichCT/DEFAULT.asp. Also, access to property data to be available soon at www.nereval.com/OnlineDatabases.aspx.

Old Lyme Town ***Property, Taxation*** Search the town Assessor's database at http://data.visionappraisal.com/OLDLYMECT/DEFAULT.asp. Also, access to GIS/mapping free at www.mapgeo.com/OldLymeCT/.

Preston Town ***Property, Taxation*** Access assessor data free at http://data.visionappraisal.com/PrestonCT/DEFAULT.asp.

Salem Town ***Property, Taxation*** Access to database for free at http://data.visionappraisal.com/SalemCT/DEFAULT.asp. Also, access to GIS/mapping free at http://host.appgeo.com/sccog/.

Stonington Town ***Land Records, Maps/Surveys, Trade Name, Marriage, Death, Civil Union Records*** www.townofstonington.com/Pages/StoningtonCT_Clerk/index Access the clerks' index free at https://connecticut-townclerks-records.com/User/Login.aspx?ReturnUrl=%2fLandRecords%2fprotected%2fSrchQuickName.aspx.
Property, Taxation Access to GIS/mapping data free at http://gis.stonington-ct.gov/mapxpress/. Search the town assessor's database free at http://data.visionappraisal.com/stoningtonCT/DEFAULT.asp.

Voluntown Town ***Property, Taxation*** Access to records free at http://data.visionappraisal.com/VoluntownCT/DEFAULT.asp.

Waterford Town ***Property, Taxation*** Access property data free at www.prophecyone.us/index_prophecy.php. but no name searching. Also, search the assessor database free at http://data.visionappraisal.com/WaterfordCT/DEFAULT.asp. Also, access to online property field cards at www.equalitycama.com/towns/Towns.htm. Click on Waterford.**$$$**

Tolland County

Andover Town ***Property, Taxation*** Search town assessor database at http://data.visionappraisal.com/AndoverCT/DEFAULT.asp. Free registration for full data.

Bolton Town ***Property, Taxation*** Also, access to online property field cards at www.equalitycama.com/towns/Towns.htm. Click on Bolton.**$$$**

Columbia Town ***Property, Taxation*** Access to GIS/mapping free at www.wincog-gis.org/ags_map/default.asp?town=Columbia. Also, access assessor property data free at http://data.visionappraisal.com/ColumbiaCT/DEFAULT.asp.

Coventry Town ***Property, Taxation*** Access assessor and property data free at http://ceo.fando.com/coventry/. Also, access to GIS/mapping free at www.wincog-gis.org/.

Ellington Town ***Real Estate, Deed, Mortgage, Map Records*** http://ellington-ct.gov/Plugs/town_clerk.aspx Access land records at https://connecticut-townclerks-records.com/User/Login.aspx?ReturnUrl=%2fIndex.aspx, indexes online are free, images online for a fee). **$$$**
Property, Taxation Access assessor property data free at http://data.visionappraisal.com/EllingtonCT/DEFAULT.asp

Hebron Town ***Recorded Documents*** www.hebronct.com/townclerkofc.htm Access to index search is for free, go to https://www.uslandrecords.com/ctlr/. Images are charged at a rate of $2.00 per page for all the pages of the document. Document images are available from 1988 to present. **$$$**
Property, Taxation Access property data free at www.prophecyone.us/index_prophecy.php?town=Hebron. No name searching.**$$$**

Mansfield Town ***Property, Taxation*** Access property and GIS-Mapping free at www.mainstreetmaps.com/CT/Mansfield/.

Somers Town Recorded Documents www.somersct.gov/townclerk.cfm Access to records for a fee at https://connecticut-townclerks-records.com/User/Login.aspx?ReturnUrl=%2fIndex.aspx. **$$$**
Property, Taxation Search the town assessor's database free at http://data.visionappraisal.com/somersCT/DEFAULT.asp.

Stafford Town ***Real Estate, Deed, Lien Records*** www.staffordct.org/clerk.php Access town clerk land records back to 1/03/1977 free at http://records.staffordct.org/Resolution/search_menu.asp but free registration is required.

Property, Taxation Access assessor property data free at http://stafford.univers-clt.com. Search the town assessor's database free at http://data.visionappraisal.com/StaffordCT/DEFAULT.asp.

Tolland Town ***Property, Taxation*** Search town assessor database free at http://data.visionappraisal.com/TollandCT/DEFAULT.asp.

Union Town ***Property, Taxation*** Search the town assessor's database free at http://data.visionappraisal.com/unionCT/DEFAULT.asp.

Willington Town ***Property, Taxation*** Search the town assessor's database free at http://data.visionappraisal.com/willingtonCT/DEFAULT.asp. Also, access to GIS/mapping free at www.wincog-gis.org/ags_map/default.asp?town=Willington.

Windham County

Ashford Town ***Recorded Documents*** www.ashfordtownhall.org/government/admin-and-finance/town-clerk/ Access to records for a fee at https://connecticut-townclerks-records.com/User/Login.aspx?ReturnUrl=%2fIndex.aspx. **$$$**
Property, Taxation Access to property assessment free at http://data.visionappraisal.com/AshfordCT/DEFAULT.asp.

Brooklyn Town ***Recorded Documents*** www.brooklynct.org/townclerk.htm Access to land record indexes for free, go to https://www.uslandrecords.com/ctlr/. To view any image there is a charge of $2.00 per page for all the pages of the document. Images are available from 1985 to present. **$$$**
Property, Taxation Access assessor database records free at www.rmsreval.com/login.asp?town=Brooklyn. Free email registration required. No name searching. Data may be old. Search the assessor database free at http://data.visionappraisal.com/brooklynCT/DEFAULT.asp.

Canterbury Town ***Property, Taxation*** Access assessor property data free at http://data.visionappraisal.com/CanterburyCT/DEFAULT.asp

Chaplin Town ***Real Estate Records*** www.chaplinct.org/index.php?option=com_content&view=article&id=1198&Itemid=571 Access to Town Clerks portal for a fee at https://connecticut-townclerks-records.com/User/Login.aspx?ReturnUrl=%2fIndex.aspx **$$$**
Property, Taxation Access assessor property data free at http://data.visionappraisal.com/ChaplinCT/DEFAULT.asp

Eastford Town Clerk ***Property, Taxation*** Access to town mapping for free at www.townhallmaps.com/eastford%20ct/index.html.

Hampton Town ***Property, Taxation*** Access property data free after registration at http://data.visionappraisal.com/HamptonCT/DEFAULT.asp.

Killingly Town ***Property, Taxation*** Access assessor records of real estate sales for free at www.killingly.org/index.asp?Type=B_LIST&SEC={2FE9A391-3E41-49FB-B060-D1895327F9CF}.

Plainfield Town ***Property, Taxation*** Access to parcel searches for free at http://gis.vgsi.com/plainfieldct/. Also, access to GIS/mapping free at www.plainfieldct.org/onlinemap.asp.

Pomfret Town ***Property, Taxation*** Search town assessor database free at http://data.visionappraisal.com/PomfretCT/DEFAULT.asp.

Putnam Town ***Property, Taxation*** Access assessor property data free after registration at http://data.visionappraisal.com/PutnamCT/DEFAULT.asp.

Sterling Town ***Property, Taxation*** Access to Assessor's database for free at http://sterling.ias-clt.com/parcel.list.php. Also, access to GIS/mapping free at http://107.20.209.214/sterlingct_public/default.html.

Thompson Town ***Recorded Documents*** www.thompsonct.org/hidden-dept-town-clerk Access to land record indexes for free, go to https://www.uslandrecords.com/ctlr/. To view any image there is a charge of $2.00 per page for all the pages of the document. Images are available from 1985 to present. **$$$**
Property, Taxation Search the town assessor database free at http://data.visionappraisal.com/ThompsonCT/DEFAULT.asp.

Windham Town ***Recorded Documents*** www.windhamct.com/department.htm?id=i9g86evd&m=boards Access to records free at www.searchiqs.com/ctwin/. Must pay to print.
Property, Taxation Access assessor valuation data free at http://windham.univers-clt.com/.

Woodstock Town ***Property, Taxation*** Search the assessor database at http://data.visionappraisal.com/WoodstockCT/DEFAULT.asp.

Delaware

Capital: Dover
Kent County
Time Zone: EST
Population: 917,092
# of Counties: 3

Useful State Links

Website: http://delaware.gov
Governor: http://governor.delaware.gov/index.shtml
Attorney General: http://attorneygeneral.delaware.gov/
State Archives: http://archives.delaware.gov/
State Statutes and Codes: http://delcode.delaware.gov/
Legislative Bill Search: http://legis.delaware.gov/
Unclaimed Funds: www.revenue.delaware.gov/unprop/unprop_lists.shtml

State Public Record Agencies

Sexual Offender Registry

Delaware State Police, Sex Offender Central Registry, http://dsp.delaware.gov/StateBureauofIdentification.shtml#Sexoff Statewide registry can be searched at https://desexoffender.dsp.delaware.gov/SexOffenderPublic/. Be patient as sometimes it takes a while for the page to open. The site gives the ability to search by last name, Development, and city or Zip Code. Any combination of these fields may be used; however, a search cannot be performed if both a city and Zip Code are entered.

Corporation, LLC, LP, LLP, General Partnerships, Trademarks/Servicemarks

Secretary of State, Corporation Records, www.corp.delaware.gov/ Check an entity name for corporate status, file number, incorporation/formation date, registered agent name, address, phone number and residency from www.corp.delaware.gov/. A search of Trade, Business, or Fictitious names is found at http://courts.delaware.gov/superior//trade_names.stm. Note this is from the courts, not from the Sec. of State. Also, the DE Department of Finance provides a free search of business licenses at https://dorweb.revenue.delaware.gov/bussrch/.

Sales Tax Registrations

Finance Department - Div. Rev., Gross Receipt Tax Registration, http://revenue.delaware.gov/ Search for a business license at https://dorweb.revenue.delaware.gov/bussrch/

Vital Records

Department of Health, Office of Vital Statistics, www.dhss.delaware.gov/dhss/dph/ss/vitalstats.html Access available at vitalchek.com, a state designated vendor. **$$$**

Workers' Compensation Records

Labor Department, Industrial Accident Board, http://dia.delawareworks.com/workers-comp/ To check on an employer's insurance history visit http://dia.delawareworks.com/workers-comp-search.php.

Driver Records

Division of Motor Vehicles, Driver Services Department, www.dmv.de.gov/ The Direct Access Program is provided 24 hours via the web. The fee is $15.00 per record. Searches are done by submitting the driver's license number. Requesters must be pre-approved, a signed contract application is required. Online searching is by single inquiry only; no batch request mode is offered. For more information about establishing an account, call Ms. Jackson 302-744-2726. **$$$**

Vehicle Ownership & Registration

DMV - Administration, Vehicle Records, www.dmv.de.gov/ The Direct Access Program is provided 24 hours via the web. The fee is $15.00 per name. Requesters must be pre-approved; a signed contract application is required. Online searching is by single inquiry only; no batch request mode is offered. For more information about establishing an account, call M. Jackson at 302-744-2726. This program is strictly monitored and not available for non-permissible uses. **$$$**

Voter Registration, Campaign Finance

Commissioner of Elections, Voter Registration Records, http://elections.delaware.gov/ A list of PACs is found at http://elections.delaware.gov/information/campaignfinance/pdfs/PAC%20List.pdf. View reports submitted by candidates or committees at http://elections.delaware.gov/information/campaignfinance/pdfs/PAC%20List.pdf. *Other Options:* As stated, the entire state voter registration database is available on CD for $10. The file is provided in Access. Candidates who filed to run for office may request the Statewide CD at no cost.

Occupational Licensing Boards

Accountant-CPA https://dpronline.delaware.gov/mylicense%20weblookup/Search.aspx
Adult Entertainment https://dpronline.delaware.gov/mylicense%20weblookup/Search.aspx
Aesthetician https://dpronline.delaware.gov/mylicense%20weblookup/Search.aspx
Amateur Boxing-related https://dpronline.delaware.gov/mylicense%20weblookup/Search.aspx
Architect https://dpronline.delaware.gov/mylicense%20weblookup/Search.aspx
Athletic Agent https://dpronline.delaware.gov/mylicense%20weblookup/Search.aspx
Athletic Trainer https://dpronline.delaware.gov/mylicense%20weblookup/Search.aspx
Attorney, List of Passing Applicants .... www.courts.delaware.gov/forms/download.aspx?id=49378
Audiologist https://dpronline.delaware.gov/mylicense%20weblookup/Search.aspx
Barber https://dpronline.delaware.gov/mylicense%20weblookup/Search.aspx
Bodyworker https://dpronline.delaware.gov/mylicense%20weblookup/Search.aspx
Boxer/Boxing Professional https://dpronline.delaware.gov/mylicense%20weblookup/Search.aspx
Charitable Gaming Permittee https://dpronline.delaware.gov/mylicense%20weblookup/Search.aspx
Chiropractor https://dpronline.delaware.gov/mylicense%20weblookup/Search.aspx
Cosmetologist https://dpronline.delaware.gov/mylicense%20weblookup/Search.aspx
Counselor, Elem./Second'y School .... https://deeds.doe.k12.de.us/public/deeds_pc_findeducator.aspx
Counselor, Professional https://dpronline.delaware.gov/mylicense%20weblookup/Search.aspx
Deadly Weapons Dealer https://dpronline.delaware.gov/mylicense%20weblookup/Search.aspx
Dental Hygienist https://dpronline.delaware.gov/mylicense%20weblookup/Search.aspx
Dentist https://dpronline.delaware.gov/mylicense%20weblookup/Search.aspx
Dietician/Nutritionist https://dpronline.delaware.gov/mylicense%20weblookup/Search.aspx
Electrical Inspector https://dpronline.delaware.gov/mylicense%20weblookup/Search.aspx
Electrician https://dpronline.delaware.gov/mylicense%20weblookup/Search.aspx
Electrologist https://dpronline.delaware.gov/mylicense%20weblookup/Search.aspx
Emergency Medical Tech/Paramedic https://dpronline.delaware.gov/mylicense%20weblookup/Search.aspx
Engineer/Firm .... www.dape.org/App/peRoster.asp
Funeral Director https://dpronline.delaware.gov/mylicense%20weblookup/Search.aspx
Gaming Control https://dpronline.delaware.gov/mylicense%20weblookup/Search.aspx
Geologist https://dpronline.delaware.gov/mylicense%20weblookup/Search.aspx
Hearing Aid Dealer/Fitter https://dpronline.delaware.gov/mylicense%20weblookup/Search.aspx
Insurance Adjuster/Advisor .... https://sbs-de.naic.org/Lion-Web/jsp/sbsreports/AgentLookup.jsp?submit=Licensee+Lookup
Insurance Agent/Consultant .... https://sbs-de.naic.org/Lion-Web/jsp/sbsreports/AgentLookup.jsp?submit=Licensee+Lookup
Insurance Broker/Dealer/Company .... https://sbs-de.naic.org/Lion-Web/jsp/sbsreports/AgentLookup.jsp?submit=Licensee+Lookup
Insurance Entity .... https://sbs-de.naic.org/Lion-Web/jsp/sbsreports/AgentLookup.jsp?submit=Licensee+Lookup
Investment Adviser/Firm .... www.adviserinfo.sec.gov/IAPD/Content/Search/iapd_Search.aspx
Landscape Architect https://dpronline.delaware.gov/mylicense%20weblookup/Search.aspx
Library/Media Specialist .... https://deeds.doe.k12.de.us/public/deeds_pc_findeducator.aspx
Liquid Waste Hauler www.dnrec.delaware.gov/wr/Information/GWDInfo/Documents/Class%20F%20list.pdf
Lobbyist .... www.delawaregov.us/pic/index.cfm?ref=74391
Massage https://dpronline.delaware.gov/mylicense%20weblookup/Search.aspx

Medical Practice https://dpronline.delaware.gov/mylicense%20weblookup/Search.aspx
Mental Health Counselor https://dpronline.delaware.gov/mylicense%20weblookup/Search.aspx
Midwife https://dpronline.delaware.gov/mylicense%20weblookup/Search.aspx
Nail Technician https://dpronline.delaware.gov/mylicense%20weblookup/Search.aspx
Nurse https://dpronline.delaware.gov/mylicense%20weblookup/Search.aspx
Nursing Home Administrator https://dpronline.delaware.gov/mylicense%20weblookup/Search.aspx
Nutritionist https://dpronline.delaware.gov/mylicense%20weblookup/Search.aspx
Occupational Therapist/Assistant https://dpronline.delaware.gov/mylicense%20weblookup/Search.aspx
Optometrist .... www.arbo.org/index.php?action=findanoptometrist
Osteopathic Physician https://dpronline.delaware.gov/mylicense%20weblookup/Search.aspx
Pesticide Applicator .... www.kellysolutions.com/de/Applicators/index.htm
Pesticide Business .... www.kellysolutions.com/de/Business/index.htm
Pesticide Dealer .... www.kellysolutions.com/de/Dealers/index.htm
Pesticide, Registered .... www.kellysolutions.com/de/pesticideindex.htm
Pharmacist https://dpronline.delaware.gov/mylicense%20weblookup/Search.aspx
Pharmacy/Pharmacy-related Business https://dpronline.delaware.gov/mylicense%20weblookup/Search.aspx
Physical Therapist/Assistant https://dpronline.delaware.gov/mylicense%20weblookup/Search.aspx
Physician Assistant https://dpronline.delaware.gov/mylicense%20weblookup/Search.aspx
Physician/Medical Doctor/Surgeon https://dpronline.delaware.gov/mylicense%20weblookup/Search.aspx
Pilot, River https://dpronline.delaware.gov/mylicense%20weblookup/Search.aspx
Plumber https://dpronline.delaware.gov/mylicense%20weblookup/Search.aspx
Podiatrist https://dpronline.delaware.gov/mylicense%20weblookup/Search.aspx
Psychological Assistant https://dpronline.delaware.gov/mylicense%20weblookup/Search.aspx
Psychologist https://dpronline.delaware.gov/mylicense%20weblookup/Search.aspx
Public Officer .... https://egov.delaware.gov/lobs/
Radiation Technician .... http://dhss.delaware.gov/dhss/dph/hsp/files/orcradtechreg.pdf
Radiologic Technologist .... http://dhss.delaware.gov/dhss/dph/hsp/files/orcradtechreg.pdf
Real Estate Agent/Broker https://dpronline.delaware.gov/mylicense%20weblookup/Search.aspx
Real Estate Appraiser https://dpronline.delaware.gov/mylicense%20weblookup/Search.aspx
Respiratory Care Practitioner https://dpronline.delaware.gov/mylicense%20weblookup/Search.aspx
School Admin. Supervisor/Asst. .... https://deeds.doe.k12.de.us/public/deeds_pc_findeducator.aspx
School Counselor .... https://deeds.doe.k12.de.us/public/deeds_pc_findeducator.aspx
School Principal/Superintendent .... https://deeds.doe.k12.de.us/public/deeds_pc_findeducator.aspx
Social Worker https://dpronline.delaware.gov/mylicense%20weblookup/Search.aspx
Speech Pathologist/Audiologist https://dpronline.delaware.gov/mylicense%20weblookup/Search.aspx
Surplus Lines Broker .... https://sbs-de.naic.org/Lion-Web/jsp/sbsreports/AgentLookup.jsp?submit=Licensee+Lookup
Surveyor, Land https://dpronline.delaware.gov/mylicense%20weblookup/Search.aspx
Teacher .... https://deeds.doe.k12.de.us/public/deeds_pc_findeducator.aspx
Veterinarian https://dpronline.delaware.gov/mylicense%20weblookup/Search.aspx

State and Local Courts

State Court Structure: The **Superior Court** has original jurisdiction over criminal and civil cases except equity cases. The Superior Court has exclusive jurisdiction over felonies and drug offenses, except drug offenses involving minors, and offenses involving possession of marijuana.

The **Court of Common Pleas** has jurisdiction in civil cases where the amount in controversy, exclusive of interest, does not exceed $50,000. In criminal cases, the Court of Common Pleas handles all misdemeanors occurring in the state except certain drug-related offenses and traffic offenses. Appeals may be taken to the Superior Court.

Court of Chancery cases consist largely of corporate matters, trusts, estates, and other fiduciary matters, disputes involving the purchase and sale of land, questions of title to real estate, and commercial and contractual matters in general.

The **Family Court** has jurisdiction over juvenile, child neglect, custody, guardianship, adoptions, divorces and annulments, property divisions, and separation agreements.

The **Justice of the Peace Court** jurisdiction will vary by court – not all courts have the same jurisdiction. Depending of the court, it may handle civil cases in which the disputed amount is less than $15,000, landlord/tenant proceedings, certain misdemeanors including DUIs and Truancy, and most motor vehicle cases (excluding felonies). The Court may act as Committing magistrates for all crimes.

Alderman's Courts usually have jurisdiction over misdemeanors, municipal ordinances, and traffic offenses that occur within their town limits.

Appellate Courts: Chancery, Superior, Common Pleas, and Supreme Courts opinions and orders are available free online at http://courts.delaware.gov/opinions/?ag=all courts.

About Court Online Access: There are a number of statewide sites.

- For a free site to search trial court **civil** case information and judgments. Go to http://courtconnect.courts.delaware.gov/public/ck_public_qry_main.cp_main_idx. Note the site states *Any commercial use of data obtained through the use of this site is strictly prohibited.* Basically gives parties, case number, and status. There are no identifiers shown.
- A search of **Probat**e records is at http://archives.delaware.gov/collections/probate.shtml.
- Supreme, Superior. Common Pleas Courts **calendars** are available free at http://courts.delaware.gov/calendars.
- **Probate** records are found at http://archives.delaware.gov/collections/probate.shtml.
- In the Superior Court in each county there is a Prothonotary which is where the registration of **Business, Trade and Fictitious Names** must be filed. There is a free online access page to this data, go to http://courts.delaware.gov/Superior/trade_names.stm.
- Access to e-filed civil records from the **Chancery Courts** is available online by subscription through LexisNexis eFlex system used for filing. See http://courts.delaware.gov/efiling/index.stm.

There are no individual Delaware courts offering online access beyond the statewide sites mentioned above.

Recorders, Assessors, and Other Sites of Note

Recording Office Organization: Delaware has 3 counties and 3 recording offices. The recording officer is the County Recorder. Federal tax liens on personal property of businesses are filed with the Secretary of State. Other federal and all state tax liens on personal property are filed with the County Recorder. Financing statements are filed at the state level - Secretary of State, UCC Division - except for real estate related collateral which are filed only with the County Recorder.

Statewide or Multi-Jurisdiction Access: There is no statewide online system for county recorded documents. However each county has an affiliated site. Searching is free, but each site requires registration and a monthly fee to access documents.

County Sites:

Kent County ***Recorded Documents*** www.co.kent.de.us/Departments/RowOffices/Recorder/index.htm Search the Registry of Deeds at https://de.uslandrecords.com/delr/DelrApp/index.jsp. A subscription account is also available at $50.00 per month, other charges may be involved. **$$$**

Property, Taxation Records Locate parcels on the GIS-mapping site free at http://66.173.241.168/kent_co/ but no name searching and you must chose a 'hundred.'

New Castle County ***Recorded Documents, Marriage Records*** www2.nccde.org/deeds/default.aspx Free text searches to the Recorder of Deeds database found at www2.nccde.org/deeds/Search/default.aspx. Must sign up with a credit card to view images. Fee is $1.00 per page or $100.00 per month per user, unlimited use. **$$$**

Property, Taxation Records County property data is found at www3.nccde.org/parcel/search/. No name searching.

Sussex County ***Recorded Documents*** www.sussexcountyde.gov/dept/rod/ Search the Registry of Deeds at https://de.uslandrecords.com/delr/DelrApp/index.jsp. A subscription account is also available at $50.00 per month, other charges may be involved. **$$$**

Property, Taxation Records Access tax info free at www.sussexcounty.net/e-service/propertytaxes/. Search parcels on GIS-mapping site free at http://map.sussexcountyde.gov/. Search current sheriff sale list free at www.sussexcountyde.gov/dept/sheriff/. Search county tax data free at www.sussexcountyde.gov/e-service/propertytaxes/index.cfm?resource=search_page.

District of Columbia

Time Zone: EST
Population: 632,323
# of Divisions/Counties: 1

Useful State Links

Website: www.dc.gov
Mayor: http://mayor.dc.gov/page/mayors-welcome
Attorney General: http://oag.dc.gov/
District Archives: http://os.dc.gov/service/district-columbia-archives
District Statutes and Codes: http://dc.gov/DC/Government/DC+Courts+&+Laws/DC+Laws
District Municipal Regulations: http://os.dc.gov/os/cwp/view,a,1206,q,522357,osNav,%7C31374%7C.asp
Legislative Bill Search: http://dccouncil.us/legislation/current
Unclaimed Funds: http://cfo.dc.gov/service/unclaimed-property

State Public Record Agencies

Sexual Offender Registry

Metropolitan Police Department, Sex Offender Registry Unit, http://mpdc.dc.gov/service/sex-offender-registry A list of Class A & **$$$** registered sex offenders is provided at http://mpdc.dc.gov/service/search-sex-offender-registry.

Incarceration Records

District of Columbia Department of Corrections, DC Jail Records Office, http://doc.dc.gov/ The agency directs online searching to a third party at https://www.vinelink.com/vinelink/siteInfoAction.do?siteId=9900.

Corporation, LP, LLC, Trade Name, Fictitious Name

Corporations Division, Department of Consumer & Regulatory Affairs, http://dcra.dc.gov/DC/DCRA Check to see if a business is licenses at http://cpms.dcra.dc.gov/BBLV/default.aspx. *Other Options:* For information concerning lists and bulk file purchases, contact the Office of Information Services.

Uniform Commercial Code, Federal & State Tax Liens, Recorded Documents

UCC Recorder, District of Columbia Recorder of Deeds, http://otr.cfo.dc.gov/page/ucc-uniform-commercial-code-filings Search the index by name or document number at https://gov.propertyinfo.com/DC-Washington/. This is a vendor site promoted by this agency. Data is provided from 1921 forward. Both a non-subscriber system (which requires registration) and a subscriber account are offered. Subscribers receive unlimited view of index data and pay $2.00 per document, plus a $175 fee per month. A registered "non-subscriber" pays no fee to view documents and $4.00 per document mage downloaded. Registration is required. Use of a credit card is required. Note that this system provided access to all recorded documents - not just UCC filings. **$$$**

Birth Certificates, Death Records

Department of Health, Vital Records Division, http://doh.dc.gov/service/death-certificates Orders may be placed online via a state designated vendor at www.vitalchek.com. Also, a Nationwide Gravesite Locator is located at http://gravelocator.cem.va.gov/. Includes VA, national, state, military, veteran, DOI, and where grave is marked with a government grave marker. **$$$**

Driver Records

Department of Motor Vehicles, Driver Records Division, http://dmv.dc.gov Online requests are taken throughout the day and are available in batch the next morning after 8:15 am. There is no minimum order requirement. Fee is $13.00 per record; only the ten-year record is sold. This system is restricted to high volume, ongoing users. Each requester must be approved, sign a contract and pay a $3,500 annual fee. Billing is a "bank" system which draws from pre-paid account. For more information, call 202-727-5692. There is driver license number verification site at https://public.dmv.washingtondc.gov/BusinessPages/DL/DriverLicenseVerification.aspx. Also, DC drivers may obtain their driving record at http://dmv.dc.gov/node/152992. **$$$**

Vehicle Ownership & Registration

Department of Motor Vehicles, Vehicle Records, http://dmv.dc.gov DC provides a Vehicle Registration Verification at https://public.dmv.washingtondc.gov/BusinessPages/VR/VehicleRegistrationVerification.aspx and an Out-of-State Title Status at https://public.dmv.washingtondc.gov/scripts/VS/OutOfStateTitleStatus.aspx. *Other Options:* Bulk requests can be obtained for commercial purposes upon approval by the Director, Department of Motor Vehicles if it is determined that the requested use "is for the public interest." Commercial purposes are not permitted. **$$$**

Campaign Finance, Lobbyists

Office of Campaign Finance, Frank D. Reeves Municipal Building, www.ocf.dc.gov/ Financial Reports Images Searches available at www.ocf.dc.gov/IMAGING/SEARCHIMAGES.ASP. Contributions and expenditures records are searchable at www.ocf.dc.gov/dsearch/dsearch.asp. Search lobbyists activities at www.ocf.dc.gov/serv/lobbying_activity.asp.

Voter Registration

DC Board of Elections, Voter Registration Records, www.dcboee.org/home.asp One may check voter registration status at www.dcboee.org/voter_info/reg_status/. Name, DOB and ZIP are required. *Other Options:* Records can be purchased on CD. A variety of data is available from party registration to voter history. Minimum fee $2 for CD. Call 202-727-2525 for details. Form at www.dcboee.org/pdf_files/Data_Request_Form.pdf. **$$$**

Occupational Licensing Boards

Acupuncturist .... http://app.hpla.doh.dc.gov/weblookup/
Addiction Counselor .... http://app.hpla.doh.dc.gov/weblookup/
Appraiser, Real Estate .... https://www.asc.gov/National-Registry/FindAnAppraiser.aspx
Attorney .... www.dcbar.org/find_a_member/index.cfm
Bank .... http://disb.dc.gov/service/verify-financial-institution-or-representative-licensed-disb
Barber .... www.asisvcs.com/indhome_fs.asp?CPCAT=1309STATEREG
Boxing Event/Professional .... www.asisvcs.com/indhome_fs.asp?CPCAT=BX09STATEREG
Check Casher .... http://disb.dc.gov/service/verify-financial-institution-or-representative-licensed-disb
Chiropractor .... http://app.hpla.doh.dc.gov/weblookup/
Cosmetologist .... www.asisvcs.com/indhome_fs.asp?CPCAT=2009STATEREG
Counselor, Professional .... http://app.hpla.doh.dc.gov/weblookup/
Dance Therapist .... http://app.hpla.doh.dc.gov/weblookup/
Dentist/Dental Hygienist .... http://app.hpla.doh.dc.gov/weblookup/
Dietitian/Nutritionist .... http://app.hpla.doh.dc.gov/weblookup/
Electrician .... www.asisvcs.com/indhome_fs.asp?CPCAT=3609STATEREG
Engineer .... www.asisvcs.com/indhome_fs.asp?CPCAT=EN09STATEREG
Funeral Director .... www.asisvcs.com/indhome_fs.asp?CPCAT=FN09STATEREG
Insurance Broker/Agent/Company .... http://disb.dc.gov/service/verify-financial-institution-or-representative-licensed-disb
Lobbyist .... http://ocf.dc.gov/WebsiteReports/filertype.asp
Massage Therapist .... http://app.hpla.doh.dc.gov/weblookup/
Midwife .... http://app.hpla.doh.dc.gov/weblookup/
Money Lender .... http://disb.dc.gov/service/verify-financial-institution-or-representative-licensed-disb
Money Transmitter .... http://disb.dc.gov/service/verify-financial-institution-or-representative-licensed-disb
Mortgage Broker/Lender .... http://disb.dc.gov/service/verify-financial-institution-or-representative-licensed-disb
Naturopath .... http://app.hpla.doh.dc.gov/weblookup/
Notary Public .... http://dcatlas.dcgis.dc.gov/agencyapps/notary.aspx
Nurse, LPN/RN .... http://app.hpla.doh.dc.gov/weblookup/
Nursing Home Administrator .... http://app.hpla.doh.dc.gov/weblookup/
Occupational Therapist .... http://app.hpla.doh.dc.gov/weblookup/
Optometrist .... http://app.hpla.doh.dc.gov/weblookup/
Osteopath .... http://app.hpla.doh.dc.gov/weblookup/
Pharmacist/Pharmacy .... http://app.hpla.doh.dc.gov/weblookup/
Physical Therapist .... http://app.hpla.doh.dc.gov/weblookup/

Physician, Assistant .... http://app.hpla.doh.dc.gov/weblookup/
Plumber .... www.asisvcs.com/indhome_fs.asp?CPCAT=4909STATEREG
Podiatrist .... http://app.hpla.doh.dc.gov/weblookup/
Political Campaign Contributor .... http://ocf.dc.gov/WebsiteReports/filertype.asp
Psychologist .... http://app.hpla.doh.dc.gov/weblookup/
Real Estate Agent/Broker/Seller .... https://www.asisvcs.com/services/licensing/Dcopla/LicRenewals/LrIndex.asp?CBCAT=0909BR
Real Estate Appraiser .... https://www.asc.gov/Resources-For/Real-Estate-Appraisers/RealEstateAppraiser.aspx
Recreational Therapist .... http://app.hpla.doh.dc.gov/weblookup/
Respiratory Care .... http://app.hpla.doh.dc.gov/weblookup/
Sales Finance Company .... http://disb.dc.gov/service/verify-financial-institution-or-representative-licensed-disb
Security Agency/Guard http://mpdc.dc.gov/mpdc/cwp/view,a,1242,q,566954.asp
Social Worker .... http://app.hpla.doh.dc.gov/weblookup/
Taxi Insurer .... http://dctaxi.dc.gov/page/taxicab-insurance-companies

Courts

DC Court Structure: The **Superior Court** handles all local trial matters and consists of five divisions: Civil, Criminal, Family, Probate, and Domestic Violence.

The **Civil Division** is divided into four branches: the Civil Actions Branch, the Quality Review Branch, the Landlord and Tenant Branch and the Small Claims Branch. The **Criminal Division** hears all local criminal matters including felony, misdemeanor, and serious traffic cases. The **Family Court** Operations Division receives and processes the following types of cases: child abuse and neglect, juvenile delinquency, adoption, divorce, custody, guardianship, visitation, paternity, child support, termination of parental rights, as well as mental health and habilitation. The **Probate Division** has jurisdiction over estates guardianships of minors and of incapacitated adults.

Appellate Online Access: The Court of Appeals opinions are at www.dccourts.gov/internet/welcome.jsf.

The DC Courts:

Superior Court - Civil www.dccourts.gov/internet/welcome.jsf
Civil: Access civil records free at www.dccourts.gov/internet/CCO.jsf. Although the system provides case summary data it does not provide images, address, SSNs, DOB, and phone numbers. The public information on the Remote Access to Case Dockets (RACD) System reflects the docket entries in civil, criminal, domestic violence and tax cases, probate, disclaimers of interest, major litigation, wills and foreign estate proceedings.

Superior Court - Criminal www.dccourts.gov/internet/welcome.jsf
Criminal: Access criminal case information free at www.dccourts.gov/internet/CCO.jsf. Although the system provides case summary data does not provide images, address, SSNs, DOB, and phone numbers.Some sentencing and dockets are incorrect compared to onsite court re The public information on the Remote Access to Case Dockets (RACD) System reflects the docket entries in civil, criminal, domestic violence and tax cases, probate, disclaimers of interest, major litigation, wills and foreign estate proceedings.

Civil Division - Small Claims and Conciliation Branch www.dccourts.gov/internet/welcome.jsf
Civil: Access civil records free at www.dccourts.gov/internet/CCO.jsf. Although the system provides case summary data it does not provide images, address, SSNs, DOB, and phone numbers.

Superior Court - Landlord & Tenant Branch www.dccourts.gov/internet/public/aud_civil/lease.jsf
Civil: Access information using the civil record index at www.dccourts.gov/internet/CCO.jsf. There is no fee. Although the system provides case summary data it does not provide images, address, SSNs, DOB, and phone numbers.

Recorder, Assessor

Recording Office: ***Real Estate, Deed, Judgment, Lien, UCC Records*** http://otr.cfo.dc.gov/service/otr-recorder-deeds
The Recorder of Deeds, an administration of the Office of Tax and Revenue, is the official repository of all land records and general public instruments for the District of Columbia. Federal tax liens and all DC tax liens regardless if on businesses or indviduals are filed with the Recorder. Search the index by name or document number at https://gov.propertyinfo.com/DC-Washington/. This is a vendor site promoted by this agency. Data is provided from 1921 forward. Both a non-subscriber system (requires registration) and a subscriber account are offered. Subscribers receive unlimted view of index data and pay $2.00 per document, plus a $175 fee per month. A registered \"non-subscriber\" pays no fee to view documents and $4.00 per document image downloaded. Registration is required. Use of a credit card is required. Also, search the real property database and real estate sales database at http://otr.cfo.dc.gov/page/real-property-tax-database-search. **$$$**

Property, Taxation: Search the real property tax database at http://otr.cfo.dc.gov/page/real-property-tax-database-search.

Florida

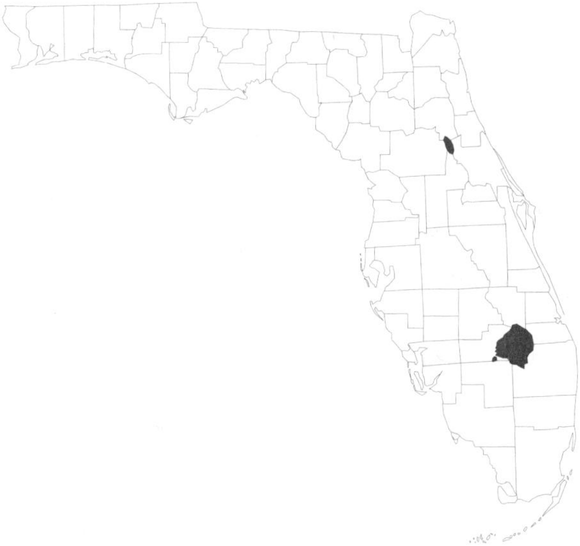

Capital: Tallahassee
Leon County
Time Zone: EST

Florida's ten western-most counties are CST:
They are: Bay, Calhoun, Escambia, Gulf, Holmes,
Jackson, Okaloosa, Santa Rosa, Walton, Washington.

Population: 19,317,568
# of Counties: 67

Useful State Links

Website: www.myflorida.com
Governor: www.flgov.com/
Attorney General: http://myfloridalegal.com
State Archives: http://dlis.dos.state.fl.us/index.cfm
State Statutes and Codes: www.flsenate.gov/Laws/Statutes
Legislative Bill Search: www.leg.state.fl.us
Unclaimed Funds: https://www.fltreasurehunt.org/

State Public Record Agencies

Criminal Records

Florida Department of Law Enforcement, User Services Bureau/Criminal History Srvs, www.fdle.state.fl.us Criminal history information may be ordered over the Department Program Internet site at https://web.fdle.state.fl.us/search/app/default. The $24.00 fee applies. These records are not certified. Credit card ordering will return records to your screen or via email. Search multiple types of state's wanted list at http://pas.fdle.state.fl.us/pas/pashome.a. Included stolen vehicles, boats, plates, etc. **$$$**

Sexual Offender Registry

Florida Department of Law Enforcement, Florida Offender Registration and Tracking Svcs, http://offender.fdle.state.fl.us/offender/homepage.do Search the registry from the web page. Searching can be done by name or by geographic area.

Incarceration Records

Florida Department of Corrections, Central Records Office, www.dc.state.fl.us Extensive search capabilities are offered at www.dc.state.fl.us/inmateinfo/inmateinfomenu.asp. Click on Inmate Population Information Search. Bulk data may be purchased on a CD.

Corporation, LP, LLC, Trademarks/Servicemarks, Fictitious Names, Federal Tax Liens

Division of Corporations, Department of State, www.sunbiz.org The state's excellent Internet site gives detailed information on all corporate, trademark, limited liability company and limited partnerships; fictitious names; and lien records. Images of filed documents are available from 1996/7 to present. *Other Options:* The agency offers downloadable record information from the web page. Data is released quarterly. See www.sunbiz.org/corp_pur.html.

Uniform Commercial Code

UCC Filings, FLORIDAUCC, Inc, www.floridaucc.com The Internet site www.floridaucc.com/UCCWEB/SearchDisclaimer.aspx? allows access for no charge. Search by name or document number, for records 1997 to present. TIFF images of Florida UCC filings can be downloaded from the Internet for all filings from 1997 to present. Tax Liens are not included with UCC filing information. *Other Options:* Microfilm reels and CD's of images are available for bulk purchase requesters. Call for more information.

Workers' Compensation Records

Workers Compensation Division, Data Quality Section, www.myfloridacfo.com/wc/ A myriad of information is available at www.myfloridacfo.com/wc/databases.html. Access to the claims history database is provided, all personal information has been redacted.

Driver Records

Division of Motorist Services, Bureau of Records, www.flhsmv.gov/ Record access online has been privatized through Network Providers. Requesters with 5,000 or more records per month are considered Network Providers. Requesters with less than 5,000 requests per month (called Individual Users) are directed to a Provider. Call 850-617-2014 to become a Provider. A list of providers is found at http://flhsmv.gov/data/internet2.html. The state fee is as stated above; Providers add a service fee, which varies by vendor. Online requests are processed on an interactive basis. Check the status of any Florida driver license free at https://services.flhsmv.gov/DLCheck/. Simply enter the driver license number. **$$$** *Other Options:* This agency will process batch data via FTP for approved users. Contact DataProcessingUnit@flhsmv.gov.

Vehicle Ownership & Registration

Division of Motorist Services, Record Information & Research Unit -MS91, www.flhsmv.gov/html/titlinf.html For a free vehicle status check enter the title # or VIN to check vehicle status at https://services.flhsmv.gov/MVCheckWeb/. A personalized license plate inquiry at https://services.flhsmv.gov/MVCheckPersonalPlate/ lets user know availability. Florida has contracted to release detailed vehicle information through approved Network Providers. Accounts must first be approved by the state. For each record accessed, the charge is $50. to $1.25 plus a transactional fee. The link to the list of vendors on the Dept web site is at http://flhsmv.gov/data/internet2.html. **$$$**

Accident Reports

DHSMV-, Crash Records-MS-28, www.flhsmv.gov/ Crash reports can be purchased online at www.buycrash.com, a state designated vendor. The fee is $16.00, use of a credit card or PayPal is required. **$$$** *Other Options:* List or bulk purchase is available by special request.

Voter Registration, Campaign Finance & Contributions, PACs

Dept of State - Division of Elections, 500 South Bronough St, http://election.dos.state.fl.us A number of searches are provided at http://election.dos.state.fl.us/campaign-finance/cam-finance-index.shtml including filed campaign documents, contribution and expenditure records, and PACs *Other Options:* The only format for bulk release of voter reg. records is via DVD for $5.00. The content includes name, address, party, gender, voting history, and the telephone if provided on registration or if not marked confidential.

Occupational Licensing Boards

Accountant-CPA https://www.myfloridalicense.com/wl11.asp
Acupuncturist http://ww2.doh.state.fl.us/irm00praes/praslist.asp
Air Ambulance .... www.doh.state.fl.us/demo/ems/emslookup.html
Air Conditioning Contractor/Svc https://www.myfloridalicense.com/wl11.asp
Alcoholic Beverage Permit https://www.myfloridalicense.com/wl11.asp
Ambulance Service .... www.doh.state.fl.us/demo/ems/emslookup.html
Animal Registra'n (Marks/Brands) .... www.freshfromflorida.com/ai/adc/adc_livestock_brands.shtml
Architect/Architectural Firm https://www.myfloridalicense.com/wl11.asp
Athletic Agent https://www.myfloridalicense.com/wl11.asp
Athletic Trainer http://ww2.doh.state.fl.us/irm00praes/praslist.asp
Attorney .... www.floridabar.org/names.nsf/MESearch?OpenForm
Auctioneer/Auction Firm https://www.myfloridalicense.com/wl11.asp
Audiologist http://ww2.doh.state.fl.us/irm00praes/praslist.asp
Automobile Repossessor .... http://licgweb.doacs.state.fl.us/access/individual.html
Bank .... https://real.flofr.com/ConsumerServices/FinancialInstitutions/InstSrch.aspx
Barber/Barber Assist./Shop https://www.myfloridalicense.com/wl11.asp
Boxer https://www.myfloridalicense.com/wl11.asp
Building Code Administrator https://www.myfloridalicense.com/wl11.asp
Building Contractor https://www.myfloridalicense.com/wl11.asp
Building Inspector https://www.myfloridalicense.com/wl11.asp
Cemetery .... https://apps.fldfs.com/fclicense/searchpage.aspx
Cemetery Lot Salesperson .... https://apps.fldfs.com/fclicense/searchpage.aspx
Child Care Center .... http://dcfsanswrite.state.fl.us/Childcare/provider/
Chiropractic-related Occupation http://ww2.doh.state.fl.us/irm00praes/praslist.asp
Chiropractor http://ww2.doh.state.fl.us/irm00praes/praslist.asp

Clinical Lab Personnel	http://ww2.doh.state.fl.us/irm00praes/praslist.asp
Community Assoc. Manager	https://www.myfloridalicense.com/wl11.asp
Company in Receivership	www.myfloridacfo.com/Receiver/companyInfo/company_list.asp
Construction Qualified Business	https://www.myfloridalicense.com/wl11.asp
Continuing Edu Provider-Medical	http://ww2.doh.state.fl.us/irm00praes/praslist.asp
Contractor, General, Residential	https://www.myfloridalicense.com/wl11.asp
Cosmetologist, Nails/Salon	https://www.myfloridalicense.com/wl11.asp
Credit Union	https://real.flofr.com/ConsumerServices/FinancialInstitutions/InstSrch.aspx
Crematory	https://apps.fldfs.com/fclicense/searchpage.aspx
Day Care/Child Care Ctr/Nursery Sch'l	http://dcfsanswrite.state.fl.us/Childcare/provider/
Dentist/Dental Assistant	http://ww2.doh.state.fl.us/irm00praes/praslist.asp
Dietician/Nutritionist	http://ww2.doh.state.fl.us/irm00praes/praslist.asp
Drywall/Gypsum Specialty Contr.	https://www.myfloridalicense.com/wl11.asp
Electrical Contractor	https://www.myfloridalicense.com/wl11.asp
Electrologist/Electrologist Facility	http://ww2.doh.state.fl.us/irm00praes/praslist.asp
Elevator Certificates of Operation	https://www.myfloridalicense.com/wl11.asp
Embalmer	https://apps.fldfs.com/fclicense/searchpage.aspx
Emergency Medical Technician	www.doh.state.fl.us/demo/ems/emslookup.html
Employee Leasing Company	https://www.myfloridalicense.com/wl11.asp
Engineer, Engineering Firm	https://www.myfloridalicense.com/wl11.asp?mode=0&SID=
Finance Company, Consumer	www.flofr.com/StaticPages/VerifyALicense.htm
Firearm Instructor/School/Agency	https://licgweb.doacs.state.fl.us/account_maintenance/index.html
Firearm License, Statewide	http://licgweb.doacs.state.fl.us/access/individual.html
Food Services Establishment	https://www.myfloridalicense.com/wl11.asp
Fumigation Performance Special ID	www.flaes.org/aes%2Dent/
Funeral Director, Home	https://apps.fldfs.com/fclicense/searchpage.aspx
Gas Line Specialty Contractor	https://www.myfloridalicense.com/wl11.asp
Geologist/Geology Firm	https://www.myfloridalicense.com/wl11.asp
Hair Braider	https://www.myfloridalicense.com/wl11.asp
Hearing Aid Specialist	http://ww2.doh.state.fl.us/irm00praes/praslist.asp
Home Improvement Financer	www.flofr.com/StaticPages/VerifyALicense.htm
Hotel/Restaurant	https://www.myfloridalicense.com/wl11.asp
In Home Family Day Care Center	http://dcfsanswrite.state.fl.us/Childcare/provider/
Insect Sting Treatment Specialist	www.doh.state.fl.us/demo/ems/emslookup.html
Installment Seller, Retail	www.flofr.com/StaticPages/VerifyALicense.htm
Insurance Adjuster/Agent/Title Agent	www.myfloridacfo.com/data/aar_alis1/
Insurance-related Company	www.floir.com/companysearch/
Interior Design Business/Individual	https://www.myfloridalicense.com/wl11.asp
Internal Pollutant Storage Tank Lining	https://www.myfloridalicense.com/wl11.asp
International Bank Office	https://real.flofr.com/ConsumerServices/FinancialInstitutions/InstSrch.aspx
Investment Advisor	www.flofr.com/StaticPages/VerifyALicense.htm
Kickboxer	https://www.myfloridalicense.com/wl11.asp
Labor Organization, Business Agent	https://www.myfloridalicense.com/wl11.asp?mode=0&SID=
Land Sale, Condominiums	https://www.myfloridalicense.com/wl11.asp
Landscape Architecture Firm/Individ'l	https://www.myfloridalicense.com/wl11.asp
Landscape Maint./Pest Mgmt Co.	www.flaes.org/aes%2Dent/
Liquor Store	https://www.myfloridalicense.com/wl11.asp
Lobbyist/Lobby Principal	www.leg.state.fl.us/lobbyist/index.cfm?RequestTimeout=500&Mode=Lists&Submenu=2&Tab=lobbyist
Lodging Establishment	https://www.myfloridalicense.com/wl11.asp
Marriage & Family Therapist	http://ww2.doh.state.fl.us/irm00praes/praslist.asp
Massage Therapist/School/Facility	http://ww2.doh.state.fl.us/irm00praes/praslist.asp
Mechanical Contractor	https://www.myfloridalicense.com/wl11.asp
Medical Doctor, Limited	http://ww2.doh.state.fl.us/irm00praes/praslist.asp
Medical Faculty Member	http://ww2.doh.state.fl.us/irm00praes/praslist.asp
Mental Health Counselor	http://ww2.doh.state.fl.us/irm00praes/praslist.asp

Midwife	http://ww2.doh.state.fl.us/irm00praes/praslist.asp
Mobile Home	https://www.myfloridalicense.com/wl11.asp
Money Transmitter	www.flofr.com/StaticPages/VerifyALicense.htm
Monument Dealer	https://apps.fldfs.com/fclicense/searchpage.aspx
Mortgage Broker/Firm	www.flofr.com/StaticPages/VerifyALicense.htm
Mortgage Business School	www.flofr.com/StaticPages/VerifyALicense.htm
Motel/Restaurant	https://www.myfloridalicense.com/wl11.asp
Nail Specialist	https://www.myfloridalicense.com/wl11.asp
Naturopath, Naturopathic Physician	http://ww2.doh.state.fl.us/irm00praes/praslist.asp
Notary Public	http://notaries.dos.state.fl.us/not001.html
Nuclear Radiology Physicist	http://ww2.doh.state.fl.us/irm00praes/praslist.asp
Nurse/Practical/Aide	http://ww2.doh.state.fl.us/irm00praes/praslist.asp
Nursing Home Administrator	http://ww2.doh.state.fl.us/irm00praes/praslist.asp
Nutrition Counselor	http://ww2.doh.state.fl.us/irm00praes/praslist.asp
Occupational Therapist	http://ww2.doh.state.fl.us/irm00praes/praslist.asp
Optician/Optician Apprentice	http://ww2.doh.state.fl.us/irm00praes/praslist.asp
Optometrist	http://ww2.doh.state.fl.us/irm00praes/praslist.asp
Orthotist/Prosthetist	http://ww2.doh.state.fl.us/irm00praes/praslist.asp
Osteopathic Physician	http://ww2.doh.state.fl.us/irm00praes/praslist.asp
Paramedic	www.doh.state.fl.us/demo/ems/emslookup.html
Pari-Mutuel Wagering	https://www.myfloridalicense.com/wl11.asp
Pedorthist	http://ww2.doh.state.fl.us/irm00praes/praslist.asp
Pest Control, Structural/Operator	http://app1.flaes.org/ceu/
Pesticide Applicator/Dealers/Companies	http://app1.flaes.org/ceu/
Pharmacist, Consulting	http://ww2.doh.state.fl.us/irm00praes/praslist.asp
Pharmacist/Pharmacist Intern	http://ww2.doh.state.fl.us/irm00praes/praslist.asp
PHPC Public Health Pest Control	www.flaes.org/aes%2Dent/
Physical Therapist/Assistant	http://ww2.doh.state.fl.us/irm00praes/praslist.asp
Physician/Medical Doctor/Assistant	http://ww2.doh.state.fl.us/irm00praes/praslist.asp
Physicist-Medical	http://ww2.doh.state.fl.us/irm00praes/praslist.asp
Pilot, State/Deputy	https://www.myfloridalicense.com/wl11.asp
Plumbing Contractor	https://www.myfloridalicense.com/wl11.asp
Pollutant Storage System Contr.	https://www.myfloridalicense.com/wl11.asp
Polygraph Assn Member	www.floridapolygraph.org/members
Polygraph PCSOT Examiner	www.floridapolygraph.org/members/pcsot_certified
Polygraphist, Certified	www.floridapolygraph.org/members/certified
Precision Tank Tester	https://www.myfloridalicense.com/wl11.asp
Preneed Seller, Funeral	https://apps.fldfs.com/fclicense/searchpage.aspx
Private Investigator/Agency/School	http://licgweb.doacs.state.fl.us/access/individual.html
Psychologist/Ltd License Psycholog't	http://ww2.doh.state.fl.us/irm00praes/praslist.asp
Racing, Dog/Horse	https://www.myfloridalicense.com/wl11.asp
Radiologic Physician	http://ww2.doh.state.fl.us/irm00praes/praslist.asp
Radiologist	http://ww2.doh.state.fl.us/irm00praes/praslist.asp
Real Estate Agent/Broker/Sales	https://www.myfloridalicense.com/wl11.asp
Real Estate Appraiser	https://www.myfloridalicense.com/wl11.asp
Recovering Agent/School/Instruct./Mgr.	http://licgweb.doacs.state.fl.us/access/individual.html
Respiratory Care Therapist/Provider	http://ww2.doh.state.fl.us/irm00praes/praslist.asp
Roofing Contractor	https://www.myfloridalicense.com/wl11.asp
Sales Finance Company	www.flofr.com/StaticPages/VerifyALicense.htm
Savings & Loan Association, Charter	https://real.flofr.com/ConsumerServices/FinancialInstitutions/InstSrch.aspx
School Psychologist	http://ww2.doh.state.fl.us/irm00praes/praslist.asp
Securities Agent Broker Dealer Office	www.flofr.com/StaticPages/VerifyALicense.htm
Security Officer/Instructor/School	http://licgweb.doacs.state.fl.us/access/agency.html
Sheet Metal Contractor	https://www.myfloridalicense.com/wl11.asp
Social Worker, Clinical/Master	http://ww2.doh.state.fl.us/irm00praes/praslist.asp

Solar Contractor	https://www.myfloridalicense.com/wl11.asp
Solid Waste Facility Operator	http://appprod.dep.state.fl.us/www_rcra/reports/handler_sel.asp
Specialty Structure Contractor	https://www.myfloridalicense.com/wl11.asp
Speech-Language Pathologist	http://ww2.doh.state.fl.us/irm00praes/praslist.asp
Surveyor, Mapping	https://www.myfloridalicense.com/wl11.asp
Swimming Pool/Spa Contr./Svc	https://www.myfloridalicense.com/wl11.asp
Talent Agency	https://www.myfloridalicense.com/wl11.asp
Teacher	www.fldoe.org/edcert/public.asp
Therapeutic Radiologic Physician	http://ww2.doh.state.fl.us/irm00praes/praslist.asp
Tobacco Wholesale	https://www.myfloridalicense.com/wl11.asp
Trust Company	https://real.flofr.com/ConsumerServices/FinancialInstitutions/InstSrch.aspx
Underground Utility Contractor	https://www.myfloridalicense.com/wl11.asp
Veterinarian/Veterinary Establishment	https://www.myfloridalicense.com/wl11.asp
Visiting Mental Health Faculty	http://ww2.doh.state.fl.us/irm00praes/praslist.asp
X-Ray Podiatric Assistant (certified)	http://ww2.doh.state.fl.us/irm00praes/praslist.asp
Yacht & Ship Broker/Salesman	https://www.myfloridalicense.com/wl11.asp

State and Local Courts

State Court Structure: The trial jurisdiction of **Circuit Courts** includes, among other matters, original jurisdiction over felonies, civil disputes involving more than $15,000, estates, minors and persons adjudicated as incapacitated, juveniles tax disputes; title and boundaries of real property; suits for declaratory judgments. Circuit Courts also have general trial jurisdiction over matters not assigned by statute to the county courts and also hear appeals from county court cases.

The trial jurisdiction of **County Courts** includes civil disputes involving $15,000 or less, misdemeanors, traffic and small claims.

Appellate Courts: Search Supreme Court dockets at http://jweb.flcourts.org/pls/docket/ds_docket_search%20. Search Docket Appeals at http://199.242.69.70/pls/ds/ds_docket_search.

About Court Online Access: There is no statewide access to trial court data. A number counties offer free access to court docket from links provided by www.myfloridacounty.com. Also a number of courts offer online access of recorded civil judgment liens via https://www.myfloridacountycom. Some of the sites are free, others have fees are involved when ordering copies. For those fee sites save $1.50 per record by becoming a subscriber. MyFloridaCounty.com is maintained and operated by the Florida Association of Court Clerks Services Group.

County Sites:

Alachua County

Circuit & County Courts - Criminal www.alachuacounty.us/Depts/Clerk/Pages/Clerk.aspx/

Criminal: Search limited criminal and traffic citations at https://www.alachuaclerk.org/court_records/.

Circuit & County Courts - Civil www.alachuacounty.us/Depts/Clerk/Pages/Clerk.aspx

Civil: Search civil records free at https://www.alachuaclerk.org/court_records/. Also, access to an index of judgments & recorded documents at www.myfloridacounty.com. Fees involved to order copies; Also, search the probate index (no images) and other ancient records free at www.alachuaclerk.org/Archive/default.cfm. Court accepts record requests by email llr@alachuacounty.org.**$$$**

Baker County

Circuit & County Courts http://208.75.175.18/clerk/

Civil: Access civil, probate, guardianship, and small claims records at https://www2.myfloridacounty.com/ccm/?county=02.**$$$**

Circuit & County Courts - Criminal http://208.75.175.18/clerk/

Criminal: Access the circuit-wide criminal quick lookup at http://circuit8.org. Account and password is required; restricted usage. Call the court for details. Access index of felony, misdemeanor, and traffic records at https://www2.myfloridacounty.com/ccm/?county=02.

Bay County

Circuit Court www.baycoclerk.com

Civil: Search the court cases, including traffic and probate, for free at www.baycoclerk.com/courts/case-search/. Also, access an index of judgments, liens, recorded documents at www.myfloridacounty.com. Fees involved to order copies; save $1.50 per record by becoming a subscriber. **$$$**

Criminal: Search court cases free at www.baycoclerk.com/courts/case-search/.

County Court www.baycoclerk.com

Civil: Search the court cases, including traffic and probate, for free at www.baycoclerk.com/courts/case-search/. Florida Attorneys may request secure access subscription and access information by emailing CIS@baycoclerk.com. Also, access an index of judgments, liens, recorded documents at www.myfloridacounty.com. Fees involved to order copies; save $1.50 per record by becoming a subscriber. **$$$** *Criminal:* Search the courts case database free at www.baycoclerk.com/courts/case-search/.

Bradford County

Circuit Court www.bradfordcountyfl.gov/clerkIndex.html

Civil: A free search is offered at https://www2.myfloridacounty.com/ccm/?county=04. This is county wide. Search by name or SSN.**$$$** *Criminal:* A free seacrh is offered at https://www2.myfloridacounty.com/ccm/?county=04. This is county wide. Search by name or SSN.

County Court www.bradfordcountyfl.gov/clerkIndex.html

Civil: A free search is offered at https://www2.myfloridacounty.com/ccm/?county=04. This is county wide. Search by name or SSN. Access an index of judgments (not dockets) is at www.myfloridacounty.com. Fees involved to order copies; save $1.50 per record by becoming a subscriber.**$$$**

Brevard County

Circuit Court http://brevardclerk.us/

Civil: Access public information of the records index free at https://vweb1.brevardclerk.us/facts/facts_search.cfm. Attorneys of record have access to images per a separate account. A subscription account is also available, see http://brevardclerk.us/official-re One may request copies and pay for research at https://vweb1.brevardclerk.us/webapps_ssl/rcrc/default.cfm. Overall, online civil records can be searched by name or case number from 1987 to present. *Criminal:* Access public information of the records index free at https://vweb1.brevardclerk.us/facts/facts_search.cfm. Attorneys of record have access to images per a separte account. A subcription account is also available, see http://brevardclerk.us/official-reco One may request copies and pay for research at https://vweb1.brevardclerk.us/webapps_ssl/rcrc/default.cfm.

County Court - Misdemeanor http://brevardclerk.us/

Criminal: Access public information of the records index free at http://webinfo4.brevardclerk.us/facts/facts_splash.cfm. Attorneys of record have access to images per a separte account. A subcription account is also available, see http://brevardclerk.us/official-re

Broward County

Circuit & County Courts www.clerk-17th-flcourts.org/ClerkWebsite/welcome2.aspx

Civil: Basic information is free at www.clerk-17th-flcourts.org/ClerkWebsite/welcome2.aspx. Search by name, case number or case type. There is also a premium case subscription service available to registered users and free to one-time users. Direct email record requests to eclerk@browardclerk.org. *Criminal:* Basic information free at www.clerk-17th-flcourts.org/ClerkWebsite/welcome2.aspx. Search by name, case number or case type. Also, there is a "Premium Access" for detailed case information; requires a fee, registration and password. Call 954-831-5654 for information or visit the website. Also, direct email record requests to eclerk@browardclerk.org.

Calhoun County

Circuit & County Court https://www.myfloridacounty.com/ori/index.do

Civil: Access civil, probate, guardianship, and small claims records at https://www2.myfloridacounty.com/ccm/?county=07.**$$$** *Criminal:* Access index of felony, misdemeanor, and traffic records at https://www2.myfloridacounty.com/ccm/?county=07.

Charlotte County

Circuit & County Courts - Civil Division http://co.charlotte.fl.us/Default.aspx

Civil: Access civil court records free at http://co.charlotte.fl.us/Default.aspx#null. Also, access an index of judgments, liens, recorded documents at www.myfloridacounty.com fees for copies.

Circuit & County Courts - Criminal Division http://co.charlotte.fl.us/Default.aspx

Criminal: Access index free at http://co.charlotte.fl.us/Default.aspx#null. Name only required to search.

Citrus County

Circuit Court www.clerk.citrus.fl.us/nws/home.jsp?section=1&item=1

Civil: View court record index (no images) free at http://search.clerk.citrus.fl.us/courts/login.asp; Subscription system giving full identifiers also available. Also there is an index of judgments, liens, recorded documents at www.myfloridacounty.com. Fees involved to order copies; save $1.50 per record by becoming a subscriber.**$$$** *Criminal:* View court record index (no images) free at www.clerk.citrus.fl.us/courts/search. Also, see www.clerk.citrus.fl.us/nws/home.jsp?section=1&item=17 for a subscription system giving full address and DOB identifiers also available. **$$$**

County Court www.clerk.citrus.fl.us/nws/home.jsp?section=1&item=1

Civil: View court record index (no images) free at http://search.clerk.citrus.fl.us/courts/login.asp; Subscription system with identifiers also available. Free index search does not give DOB or full address, subscription system does. Access an index of judgments, liens, recorded documents at www.myfloridacounty.com/services/officialrecords_intro.shtml; Fees involved to order copies; save $1.50 per record by becoming a subscriber. *Criminal:* View court record index (no images) free at www.clerk.citrus.fl.us/home.jsp; Subscription system with identifiers also available. Free index search does not give DOB or full address, subscription system does. **$$$**

Clay County

Circuit Court www.clayclerk.com/

Civil: Clerk of the circuit court provides free access to record index of civil actions and judgments at http://odysseypa.tylerhost.net/Clay/default.aspx. Also, from an approved vendor, access an index of judgments, liens, recorded documents at www.myfloridacounty.com. Fees involved to order copies; save $1.50 per record by becoming a subscriber. *Criminal:* Access to criminal record index is free at http://odysseypa.tylerhost.net/Clay/default.aspx.

County Court http://clayclerk.com/default.html

Civil: Access civil records back to 1992 free at http://clayclerk.com/OdysseyPA/default.aspx. Also, access an index of judgments, liens, recorded documents at www.myfloridacounty.com. Fees involved to order copies; save $1.50 per record by becoming a subscriber. **$$$** *Criminal:* Access criminal records free at http://clayclerk.com/OdysseyPA/default.aspx.

Collier County

Circuit & County Court www.collierclerk.com/

Civil: Online access is free at www.collierclerk.com/RecordsSearch/CourtRecords. Records include probate, traffic and domestic. Search dockets at www.collierclerk.com/RecordsSearch/Dockets. Data is viewable only, no printing. The Circuit Court is now allowing attorneys and state agencies online access to court cases with images. See instructions at www.collierclerk.com/pdf/CMSeFilingInstructions. Subscription agreement and fees involved.**$$$** *Criminal:* Search the criminal record index at http://apps.collierclerk.com/public_inquiry/Search.aspx. Data is viewable only, no printing.

Columbia County

Circuit & County Courts www.columbiaclerk.com/

Civil: Access to County Clerk of Circuit Court records is at https://www2.myfloridacounty.com/ccm/?county=12 *Criminal:* Access to County Clerk of Circuit Court felony, misdemeanor, and traffic records is at https://www2.myfloridacounty.com/ccm/?county=12

De Soto County

Circuit & County Courts www.desotoclerk.com

Civil: Free access to civil information, marriage/divorce, small claims, traffic/parking, Muni ordinances, domestic relations, name changes, foreclosures from 1980 to present at www.desotoclerk.com. Access civil, probate, guardianship, and small claims records at https://www2.myfloridacounty.com/ccm/?county=14. **$$$** *Criminal:* Traffic Criminal cases are free at www.desotoclerk.com/dpa/cvweb.asp. Access index of felony, misdemeanor, and traffic records at https://www2.myfloridacounty.com/ccm/?county=14.

Dixie County

Circuit & County Courts https://www.myfloridacounty.com/ori/index.do

Civil: Access to County Clerk of Circuit Court records is at https://www2.myfloridacounty.com/ccm/?county=15 *Criminal:* Access to index of felony, misdemeanor and traffic records is at https://www2.myfloridacounty.com/ccm/?county=12.

Duval County

Circuit & County Courts www.duvalclerk.com/ccWebsite/

Civil: Access court records back to 1986 from all courts in the county free at https://core.duvalclerk.com/welcome/. One must create a log-in first. Also, access an index of judgments, liens, recorded documents at https://www.myfloridacounty.com/. Fees involved to order copies; save $1.50 per record by becoming a subscriber.**$$$** *Criminal:* Access court records back to 1986 from all courts in the county free at https://core.duvalclerk.com/welcome/. One must create a log-in first.

Escambia County

Circuit & County Courts www.escambiaclerk.com/clerk/index.aspx

Civil: Online access to county clerk records is free at http://public.escambiaclerk.com/xml/xml_web_1a.asp. Search by name, citation, or case number. Small claims, traffic, and marriage data also available. Access an index of judgments, liens, recorded documents at www.myfloridacounty.com. Fees involved to order copies; save $1.50 per record by becoming a subscriber.

Criminal: Online access to felony, criminal traffic and municipal ordinance records is free at http://public.escambiaclerk.com/xml/xml_web_1a.asp. Search by name, citation, or case number.

Flagler County

Circuit & County Courts www.flaglerclerk.com/

Civil: Access clerk's civil records free at www.flaglerclerk.com/courtrecords.htm. Also, access an index of judgments, liens, recorded documents at www.myfloridacounty.com. Fees involved to order copies. Also, you may email record requests to rmlo@flaglerclerk.com.**$$$** *Criminal:* Access clerk's criminal records free at www.flaglerclerk.com/courtrecords.htm.

Franklin County

Circuit & County Courts www.franklinclerk.com

Civil: Access index and records free at https://www2.myfloridacounty.com/ccm/?county=19. Circuit goes back to 3/1997; County to 10/1998; Probate back to 2/1982. Also, access an index of judgments with other recorded documents at https://www3.myfloridacounty.com/official_records/index.html. Fees involved to order copies; save $1.50 per record by becoming a subscriber.**$$$** *Criminal:* Access index and records free at https://www2.myfloridacounty.com/ccm/?county=19. Felony goes back to 3/4/1984; Misdemeanors back to 1989. Also, access criminal records by subscription at https://www.myfloridacounty.com/subscription/. Fees are involved. **$$$**

Gadsden County

Circuit & County Courts www.gadsdenclerk.com/

Civil: The index of civil court judgments is free to view from the County Clerk at www.gadsdenclerk.com/unifiedcourtweb/. Also, subscription access an index of judgments, liens, recorded documents at www.myfloridacounty.com. Fees involved to order copies; save $1.50 per record by becoming a subscriber.**$$$** *Criminal:* The index of criminal and traffic case files is free to view at www.gadsdenclerk.com/unifiedcourtweb/.

Gilchrist County

Circuit & County Courts www.gilchristclerk.com/

Civil: Search judgments and liens online at http://records.gilchrist.fl.us/oncoreweb/. Access to County Clerk of Circuit Court records is at https://www2.myfloridacounty.com/ccm/?county=21

Criminal: Access to County Clerk of Circuit Court records is at https://www2.myfloridacounty.com/ccm/?county=12

Glades County

Circuit & County Courts www.gladesclerk.com/

Civil: Access civil, probate, guardianship, and small claims records at https://www2.myfloridacounty.com/ccm/?county=22.**$$$** *Criminal:* Access index of felony, misdemeanor, and traffic records at https://www2.myfloridacounty.com/ccm/?county=22.

Gulf County

Circuit & County Courts http://gulfclerk.com/

Civil: Access an index of civil judgments and small claims at https://www2.myfloridacounty.com/ccm/?county=23. Fees involved to order copies; save $1.50 per record by becoming a subscriber. Circuit civil goes back to 7/31/1984, County civil to 3/31/1986.**$$$** *Criminal:* Access an index of felony and misdemeanor cases at https://www2.myfloridacounty.com/ccm/?county=23. Fees involved to order copies; save $1.50 per record by becoming a subscriber. Records go back to 2/22/1979 for felony, 4/6/1973 for misdemeanor and 01/04 **$$$**

Hamilton County

Circuit & County Courts

Civil: Access an index of judgments (not dockets) is at www.myfloridacounty.com. Fees involved to order copies; save $1.50 per record by becoming a subscriber. **$$$**

Hardee County

Circuit & County Courts www.hardeeclerk.com/

Civil: Access to civil, domestic, small claims, guardianship, and probate is available at https://www2.myfloridacounty.com/ccm/?county=25. Records go back at least 25 years. *Criminal:* Access to felony, misdemenaor, traffic is available at https://www2.myfloridacounty.com/ccm/?county=25. Records go back at least 25 years. Felony records go back to 9/17/1973.

Hendry County

Circuit & County Courts www.hendryclerk.org/

Civil: Access civil and guardianship case dockets free back to 05/1992 at https://www2.myfloridacounty.com/ccm/?county=26. Fees involved to order copies; save $1.50 per record by becoming a subscriber.**$$$** *Criminal:* Access felony to 6/18/1985, misdemeanor to 5/19/1986, and traffic to 08/21/1988 free at https://www2.myfloridacounty.com/ccm/?county=26.

Hernando County

Circuit & County Courts http://hernandoclerk.com/

Civil: Online access to court records is free at https://www2.myfloridacounty.com/ccm/do/personSearch?county=27. Online records may go as far back as 1/1983. Searchable online record index for court records often does not provide identifiers and addresses. Fees involved to order copies; save $1.50 per record by becoming a subscriber. *Criminal:* same **$$$**

Highlands County

Circuit & County Courts www.hcclerk.org/Home.aspx

Civil: Access to county clerk civil and probate records is free at www.hcclerk.org/Home/Search-Court-Records.aspx back to 1991. Also includes small claims, probate, and tax deeds. Access civil, probate, guardianship, and small claims records at https://www2.myfloridacounty.com/ccm/?county=28. *Criminal:* Subscribe for access to court records at http://courts.hcclerk.org/iquery/. Access free index of felony, misdemeanor, and traffic records at https://www2.myfloridacounty.com/ccm/?county=28. **$$$**

Hillsborough County

Circuit & County Courts www.hillsclerk.com/publicweb/home.aspx

Civil: Online access to records at http://pubrec10.hillsclerk.com/default.aspx. Can also search family law and probate. Searchable online record index for court records often does not provide identifiers and addresses. Order case files from www.hillsclerk.com/publicweb/Search_Court_Records.aspx (for a fee). Access index of judgments, liens, recorded documents at www.myfloridacounty.com. Fees involved to order copies; save $1.50 per record by becoming a subscriber. **$$$** *Criminal:* Online access to Progress Dockets records is free at www.hillsclerk.com/publicweb/Search_Court_Records.aspx. Searchable online record index for court records often does not provide identifiers and addresses. One may also order case files online, for a fee, from the same URL. **$$$**

Holmes County

Circuit & County Courts https://www.myfloridacounty.com/ori/index.do

Civil: Access to County Clerk of Circuit Court records is at https://www2.myfloridacounty.com/ccm/?county=30 Note that there is a disclaimer that states this search should not be used as an authoritative public record. *Criminal:* same

Indian River County

Circuit & County Courts www.clerk.indian-river.org

Civil: Free access to the index for civil, family, and probate is at http://public.indian-river.org/. Full access to court records is via the clerk's subscription service. Fee is $25.00 per month. For information about the fee access, call Gary at 772-567-8000 x1216. **$$$** *Criminal:* Free access to the index for criminal and traffic is at http://public.indian-river.org/. Full access to court records is via the clerk's subscription service. Fee is $25.00 per month. **$$$**

Jackson County

Circuit & County Courts www.jacksonclerk.com/

Civil: Access civil, probate, guardianship, and small claims at https://www2.myfloridacounty.com/ccm/?county=32. Access an index of judgments (not dockets) is at www.myfloridacounty.com. Fees involved to order copies; save $1.50 per record by becoming a subscriber. **$$$** *Criminal:* Access index of felony, misdemeanor, and traffic at https://www2.myfloridacounty.com/ccm/?county=32.

Jefferson County

Circuit & County Courts www.jeffersonclerk.com/

Civil: Access to County Clerk of Circuit Court records is at https://www2.myfloridacounty.com/ccm/?county=33 *Criminal:* same

Lafayette County

Circuit & County Courts https://www.myfloridacounty.com/ori/index.do

Civil: Access civil, probate, guardianship, and small claims records at https://www2.myfloridacounty.com/ccm/?county=34. Fees involved to order copies; save $1.50 per record by becoming a subscriber. **$$$** *Criminal:* Access civil, probate, guardianship, and small claims records at https://www2.myfloridacounty.com/ccm/?county=34.

Lake County

Circuit & County Courts www.lakecountyclerk.org/

Civi & Criminal: Online access to Court records free at www.lakecountyclerk.org/record_searches/court_records_agreement.aspx. Civil records back to 1985; Circuit records back to 9/84. Also, previous 2-weeks civil records and divorces on a private site at http://extra.orlandosentinel.com/publicrecords/search.asp.

Lee County

Circuit & County Courts www.leeclerk.org

Civil: Access records free at www.leeclerk.org, click on Courts then Search Court Cases. Online records go back to 1988. Includes traffic, felony, misdemeanor, civil, small claims and probate. Access an index of judgments, liens, recorded documents at www.leeclerk.org or www.myfloridacounty.com. Search free but fees involved to order certified copies; save the per-record copy fee by becoming a subscriber; sub fee is $25.00 per month. **$$$** *Criminal:* same

Leon County

Circuit & County Courts www.clerk.leon.fl.us

Civil: Search all types of civil and traffic cases free at http://cvweb.clerk.leon.fl.us/index.asp. Access an index of judgments, liens, recorded documents at www.myfloridacounty.com. Fees involved to order copies; save $1.50 per record by becoming a subscriber. **$$$** *Criminal:* Search traffic infraction cases free at http://cvweb.clerk.leon.fl.us/index.asp. Also access an inmate search at http://lcso.leonfl.org/jailinfo/inmate_search.asp.

Levy County

Circuit & County Courts www.levyclerk.com

Civil: Judgments available on the Clerk of the Circuit Court Official Records Index free at http://oncore.levyclerk.com/oncoreweb/.

Liberty County

Circuit & County Courts www.libertyclerk.com/

Civil: The docket index is available at https://www2.myfloridacounty.com/ccm/?county=39. Also, access an index of judgments with other recorded documents at https://www3.myfloridacounty.com/official_records/index.html. Fees involved to order copies; save $1.50 per record by becoming a subscriber. **$$$** *Criminal:* same

Madison County

Circuit & County Courts www.madisonclerk.com/

Civil: Access civil, probate, guardianship, and small claims records at https://www2.myfloridacounty.com/ccm/?county=40. *Criminal:* Same as civil

Manatee County

Circuit & County Courts www.manateeclerk.com

Civil: Access public court record index and images at clerk's office free at www.manateeclerk.org. Both a public access and a subscription service is offered. Civil record available from July 18, 2001. Also, you may direct email record requests to lori.tolksdorf@manateeclerk.com.**$$$** *Criminal:* same as civil. Felony records available from June 5, 2002; misdemeanor from Jan. 2003. **$$$**

Marion County

Circuit & County Courts www.marioncountyclerk.org/public/

Civil: Online access to county clerk records is free at www.marioncountyclerk.org/public/index.cfm?Pg=casesearch. Click on 'Search Records Now." Also, access an index of judgments, liens, recorded documents at www.myfloridacounty.com. Fees involved to order copies; save $1.50 per record by becoming a subscriber. **$$$** *Criminal:* Online access to county clerk records is free at www.marioncountyclerk.org/public/index.cfm?Pg=casesearch. Click on 'Search Records Now." Felony, misdemeanor and traffic case information available since 1991.

Martin County

Circuit & County Courts www.martinclerk.com/

Civil: Access civil, probate, guardianship, and small claims records at https://www2.myfloridacounty.com/ccm/?county=43. Search all court records free at www.martinclerk.com/ccis_disclaimer.htm. Also includes small claims, recordings, other document types. Search online by name. There is a disclaimer - the information provided is not official record. *Criminal:* Access index of felony, misdemeanor, and traffic records at https://www2.myfloridacounty.com/ccm/?county=43. Search all court records free at www.martinclerk.com/ccis_disclaimer.htm. Search online by name. Online results include partial address, sex, race, alias. There is a disclaimer - the information provided is not official record.

Miami-Dade County

Circuit & County Courts - Civil www.miami-dadeclerk.com/courts_civil.asp

Civil: Clerk of Court's online services- choose between Standard (free) and Premier fee-based services. Subscribers to the Premier service may access 3 advanced options: Civil/Family/Probate, Public Records, Traffic. Fees based on # of units purchased; minimum $5.00 in advance. Also, though limited, search felony, misdemeanor, civil and county ordinance violations free at www2.miami-dadeclerk.com/CJIS/CaseSearch.aspx.**$$$**

Circuit & County Courts - Criminal www.miami-dadeclerk.com/

Criminal: Free and Premier fee-based online services available. Though limited, search felony, misdemeanor, civil and county ordinance violations free at www2.miami-dadeclerk.com/CJIS/CaseSearch.aspx. Subscribers to the Clerk's Premier Services may Access advanced options in 3 of the Clerk's internet-based systems: Civil/Family/Probate, Public Records, Traffic. Fee is $.25 per search, in advance. Also, search traffic cases free at www.miami-dadeclerk.com/spirit/publicsearch/defnamesearch.asp. **$$$**

Monroe County

Circuit & County Courts https://gov.propertyinfo.com/fl-monroe/

Civil: Online access to civil cases is free at https://gov.propertyinfo.com/fl-monroe/searchCivilCases.asp. Subscription is required for viewing full document library. Also, search probate cases free at https://gov.propertyinfo.com/fl-monroe/searchProbateCases.asp.**$$$** *Criminal:* Online access to criminal records is free at https://gov.propertyinfo.com/fl-monroe/searchTrafficCriminalCases.asp. Includes traffic cases online. Subscription is required for viewing full document library. **$$$**

Nassau County

Circuit & County Courts www.nassauclerk.com

Civil: Search civil cases free back to 1989 and perhaps earlier at www.nassauclerk.com/cocoa/. Access an index of judgments, sentences, county commitments, uniform state commitments, disposition notices and nolle prosecution only at www.myfloridacounty.com. Fees involved to order copies; save $1.50 per record by becoming a subscriber.**$$$** *Criminal:* Search criminal and traffic cases free at www.nassauclerk.com/cocoa.

Okaloosa County

Circuit & County Courts www.clerkofcourts.cc

Civil: Civil record index search is free at www.clerkofcourts.cc/benchmarkweb2/Home.aspx. Records go back to 1/83. Search civil index by defendant or plaintiff, date, or file type. Also, access an index of judgments, liens, recorded documents back to 11/1986 at www.myfloridacounty.com. Fees involved to order copies; save $1.50 per record by becoming a subscriber. **$$$** *Criminal:* Limited criminal record docket is at www.clerkofcourts.cc/benchmarkweb2/Home.aspx.

Okeechobee County

Circuit & County Courts www.clerk.co.okeechobee.fl.us/

Civil: Index of judgments and recorded documents can be searched at http://204.215.37.218/wb_or1/. Also, access to County Clerk of Circuit Court records is at https://www2.myfloridacounty.com/ccm/?county=47 *Criminal:* same

Orange County

Circuit & County Courts http://myorangeclerk.com/enu/Pages/orange-county-clerk-of-court-home.aspx

Civil: The free Myclerk Case Inquiry System is at http://myclerk.myorangeclerk.com/default.aspx. Civil and Probate records available. Also, only previous 2-weeks civil records on a private site at http://extra.orlandosentinel.com/publicrecords/search.asp. *Criminal:* Access criminal records free on the Myclerk Case Inquiry System at http://myclerk.myorangeclerk.com/default.aspx.

All County Courts - Apopka Branch http://myorangeclerk.com/

Civil: The free Myclerk Case Inquiry System is at http://myorangeclerk.com/criminal/iclerk_disclaimer.shtml. Civil and Probate records available. Also, previous 2-weeks civil records on a private site at http://extra.orlandosentinel.com/publicrecords/search.asp. *Criminal:* Access criminal records free on the Myclerk Case Inquiry System at http://myorangeclerk.com/criminal/iclerk_disclaimer.shtml.

Osceola County

Circuit Court - Civil www.osceolaclerk.com/

Civil: Online access to court records on the Clerk of Circuit Court database is free at http://198.140.240.34/pa/ and at http://online.osceolaclerk.org/benchmarkweb. Also, access an index of judgments, liens, recorded documents at www.myfloridacounty.com. Also, access an index of judgments, liens, recorded documents at www.myfloridacounty.com. Fees involved to order copies; save $1.50 per record by becoming a subscriber .**$$$**

County Court - Civil www.osceolaclerk.com

Civil: Online access to court records on the Clerk of Circuit Court database is free at http://198.140.240.34/pa/ and at http://online.osceolaclerk.org/benchmarkweb.

Circuit & County Courts - Criminal Division www.osceolaclerk.com

Criminal: Online access to court records on the Clerk of Circuit Court database is free at http://198.140.240.34/pa/ and at http://online.osceolaclerk.org/benchmarkweb.

Palm Beach County

Circuit Court - Civil Division www.mypalmbeachclerk.com/

Civil: Access to the countywide online remote system is free. Civil index goes back to '88. Records also include probate, traffic and domestic. Also, civil records are free at http://courtcon.co.palm-beach.fl.us/pls/jiwp/ck_public_qry_main.cp_main_idx. Records include criminal and traffic.

County Court - Civil Division www.mypalmbeachclerk.com/

Civil: Access to the civil record index is free at http://courtcon.co.palm-beach.fl.us/pls/jiwp/ck_public_qry_main.cp_main_idx.. Civil index goes back to '88. Records also include probate, traffic and domestic. Also the court offers a more detailed record, there is no fee per record, but a one-time registration fee is charged. Also Downloadable civil and criminal reports are available for purchase. **$$$**

Circuit & County Courts - Criminal Division www.mypalmbeachclerk.com/circuitcriminal.aspx

Criminal: Access to the countywide criminal online system is available at www.mypalmbeachclerk.com/courtrecords.aspx. Record index available also includes civil, probate, traffic and domestic.

Pasco County

Circuit & County Courts www.pascoclerk.com/

Civil: Access court records free at www.pascoclerk.com/public-courts-svcs-info.asp. Also, access to County Clerk of Circuit Court records is at https://www2.myfloridacounty.com/ccm/?county=51. *Criminal:* Access the criminal docket index at www.pascoclerk.com/public-courts-svcs-info.asp. This online record index often does not provide identifiers or case info may be restricted, i.e. sexual offenses. Watch for insufficient case numbers. Also, access to County Clerk of Circuit Court records is at https://www2.myfloridacounty.com/ccm/?county=51

Pinellas County

Circuit & County Courts - www.pinellasclerk.org

Civil: Access clerk's criminal & other data free at https://ccmspa.pinellascounty.org/PublicAccess/default.aspx. Fees were eliminated on Oct 1, 2012. Another county free site is at https://ccmspa.pinellascounty.org/PublicAccess/default.aspx. Also, access index of judgments and recorded docs at www.myfloridacounty.com. Fees to order copies; subscribers save $1.50 per record. Also, access to Civil records go to https://public.co.pinellas.fl.us/login/loginx.jsp. **$$$** *Criminal:* Access criminal court records at https://public.co.pinellas.fl.us/justice/GEInput.jsp.

Polk County

Circuit & County Courts - www.polkcountyclerk.net/

Civil: Free online access to dockets at https://ori2.polk-county.net/ct_web1/search.asp. Searchable online record index does not provide addresses; in-person search at court will only provide most recent address. Also, access to County Clerk of Circuit Court records is at https://www2.myfloridacounty.com/ccm/?county=53.**$$$** *Criminal:* Access to County Clerk of Circuit Court records is free at www.polkcountyclerk.net/. Criminal index goes back to 1991; Online record index may not provide addresses; in-person search at court only provides most recent address. Access index of felony, misdemeanor, and traffic records at https://www2.myfloridacounty.com/ccm/?county=53.

Putnam County

Circuit & County Courts - Civil Division www.putnam-fl.com/coc/

Civil: Access to the countywide remote online system requires $400 setup fee and $40. monthly charge plus $.05 per minute over 20 hours. Civil records go back to 1984. System includes criminal and real property records. Contact Putnam County IT Dept at 386-329-0390 to register. Also, access a free index of dockets at https://www.putnam-fl.com/peas/public_menu.php. Access civil, probate, guardianship, and small claims records at https://www2.myfloridacounty.com/ccm/?count**$$$**

Circuit & County Courts - Criminal Division www.putnam-fl.com/coc/

Access to the countywide criminal online system requires $400 setup fee and $40. monthly charge plus $.05 per minute over 20 hours. Criminal records go back to 1972. System includes civil and real property records. Contact 386-329-0390 to register. Access a free index of dockets at https://www.putnam-fl.com/peas/public_menu.php. Also, you may direct email criminal record requests to gailwillis@putnam-fl.us. Access index of felony, misdemeanor, and traffic records at **$$$**

Santa Rosa County

Circuit & County Courts - Civil Division https://www.myfloridacounty.com/ori/index.do

Access to the record index is https://www2.myfloridacounty.com/ccm/?county=57. Circuit civil goes back to 12/28/1974. County civil to 4/14/1986. Small claims, probate/guardianship, domestic relations/family are also available.

Circuit & County Courts - Criminal Division www.santarosaclerk.com

Access to the record index is offered at www2.myfloridacounty.com/ccm/?county=57. Felony records go back to 3/19/1976. Misdemeanor records to 10/26/1979.

Sarasota County

Circuit & County Courts - Civil www.sarasotaclerk.com

Civil: Civil and DV case dockets from the Clerk of Circuit Court database are free at www.clerk.co.sarasota.fl.us/srqapp/civilinq.asp. Probate court dockets are at www.clerk.co.sarasota.fl.us/srqapp/probinq.asp. Also see the clerk's judgment/official document search for images back 10 years. Also, access an index of judgments, liens, recorded documents at www.myfloridacounty.com. Fees involved to order copies; save $1.50 per record by becoming a subscriber. **$$$**

Circuit & County Courts - Criminal www.sarasotaclerk.com

Criminal: Criminal and traffic case dockets from the Clerk of the Circuit Court database are free online at http://courtweb.co.sarasota.fl.us/crimapp/criminq.asp. Missing records can be avoided with an in person search. Images are often available on or after 09/09/2002.

Seminole County

Circuit & County Courts www.seminoleclerk.org

Civil: Access to judgment records is free at http://officialrecords.seminoleclerk.org/. Images related to Probate cases are not available on the Clerk's website. The court does not provide a DOB on name search results either online or on the public terminal. *Criminal:* Access criminal dockets free at www.seminoleclerk.org, click on Criminal Dockets Search. Partial DOB shown.

St. Johns County

Circuit & County Courts - Civil Division www.clk.co.st-johns.fl.us/

Civil: Also, data free at http://doris.clk.co.st-johns.fl.us/uc_web_live/default.aspx. Access an index of judgments, liens, recorded documents at www.myfloridacounty.com. Fees involved to order copies; save $1.50 per record by becoming a subscriber at $25.00 per month. **$$$**

Circuit & County Courts - Criminal Division www.clk.co.st-johns.fl.us/

Criminal: Search docket index free at http://doris.clk.co.st-johns.fl.us/benchmarkweb/. Search by name or case number.

St. Lucie County

Circuit & County Courts - Civil Division www.stlucieclerk.com/circuitcivil/circuitcivil.htm

Civil: The site has 2 access modes - a free public site and a subscriber "Electronic Access Account" option. Both are available to the public. On the public site one may download complete record listing for a small fee. The subscription access provides much more The cost for an Electronic Access Account is $240 annually if payment is made by direct withdrawal and $260 annually if any other form of payment is used. See http://casesearch.slcclerkofcourt.com/PublicSearch/.**$$$**

Circuit & County Courts - Criminal Division www.stlucieclerk.com/Criminal/Criminal.htm

The site has 2 access modes - a free public site and a subscriber "Electronic Access Account" option. Both are available to the public. On the public site one may download complete record listing for a small fee. The subscription access provides much more The cost for an Electronic Access Account is $240 annually if payment is made by direct withdrawal and $260 annually if any other form of payment is used. See http://casesearch.slcclerkofcourt.com/PublicSearch/. **$$$**

Sumter County

Circuit & County Courts - Civil Division www.sumterclerk.com/index.cfm/civil

Civil: Access an index of civil, probate and domestic relationship records at https://www2.myfloridacounty.com/ccm/?county=60. Circuit Civil dates back to 3/2/1989. County Civil to 3/7/1998.

Circuit & County Courts - Criminal Division www.sumterclerk.com/index.cfm/

Criminal: Access an index of felony, criminal traffic and misdemeanor records at https://www2.myfloridacounty.com/ccm/?county=60. Felony records available from 2/10/1958, misdemeanor from 02/06/1985, traffic from 05/13/1991. Race, sex, city and ZIP Shown.

Suwannee County

Circuit & County Courts www.suwclerk.org/mambo/

Civil: Access to civil judgment records is available by subscription at https://www.myfloridacounty.com/official_records/index.html.**$$$**

Taylor County

Circuit & County Courts https://www.myfloridacounty.com/ori/index.do

Civil: Access an index of judgments (not docket) is at www.myfloridacounty.com. Fees involved to order copies; save $1.50 per record by becoming a subscriber.

Union County

Circuit & County Courts http://circuit8.org

Civil: Access an index of judgments (not dockets) is at www.myfloridacounty.com. Fees involved to order copies; save $1.50 per record by becoming a subscriber. Access civil, probate, guardianship, and small claims records free at https://www2.myfloridacounty.com/ccm/?county=63.**$$$** *Criminal:* Access the circuit-wide criminal quick lookup at http://circuit8.org. Account and password is required; restricted usage. Also, limited free search of felony, misdemeanor, and traffic records is at https://www2.myfloridacounty.com/ccm/?county=63. **$$$**

Volusia County

Circuit & County Courts - Civil Division www.clerk.org

Civil: There is both a free and pay site. Access to the countywide Clerk of Circuit Court record index for 1982 to present is free at www.clerk.org/cm/publicrecords/publicrecords.jsp. Also, access an index of judgments, liens, recorded documents at www.myfloridacounty.com with fees for copies.**$$$**

Circuit & County Courts - Criminal Division www.clerk.org

Criminal: There is both a free and pay site. Access to the countywide Clerk of Circuit Court record index for 1982 to present is free at www.clerk.org/cm/publicrecords/publicrecords.jsp. Access to restricted data is $100 setup fee. Access to the database of Citation Violations and 24-hour Arrest Reports for 1990 forward is free at www.clerk.org/index.html.

Wakulla County

Circuit & County Courts www.wakullaclerk.com

Civil: Access to County Clerk of Circuit Court records is at https://www2.myfloridacounty.com/ccm/?county=65 *Criminal:* same

Walton County

Circuit & County Courts http://clerkofcourts.co.walton.fl.us

Civil: Access final judgments or orders on closed cases at http://orsearch.clerkofcourts.co.walton.fl.us/ORSearch/. Also, access to County Clerk of Circuit Court records is at https://www2.myfloridacounty.com/ccm/?county=66. *Criminal:* Access felony judgments of guilt only at http://clerkofcourts.co.walton.fl.us/ORSearch/. Also, access to County Clerk of Circuit Court records is at https://www2.myfloridacounty.com/ccm/?county=66.

Washington County

Circuit & County Courts https://www.myfloridacounty.com/ori/index.do

Civil: Access an index of judgments (not dockets) is at www.myfloridacounty.com. Fees involved to order copies; save $1.50 per record by becoming a subscriber.**$$$** *Criminal:*

Recorders, Assessors, and Other Sites of Note

Recording Office Organization: 67 counties, 67 recording offices. The recording officer is the Clerk of the Circuit Court. All transactions are recorded in the "Official Record," a grantor/grantee index. Some counties will search by type of transaction while others will return everything on the index.

Federal tax liens on personal property of businesses are filed with the Secretary of State. All other federal and state tax liens on personal property are filed with the county Clerk of Circuit Court. Usually tax liens on personal property are filed in the same index with UCC financing statements and real estate transactions.

Since October 1, 2002, any person preparing or filing a document for recording in the Official Record may not include a Social Security Number in such document unless required by law. The Clerk of the Circuit Court cannot place an image or copy of the following documents on a publicly available website for general public display: military discharges; death certificates; court files, records or papers relating to Family Law, Juvenile Law, or Probate Law cases.

Any person has the right to request the Clerk/County Recorder to redact/remove his or her Social Security Number from an image or copy of an Official Record that has been placed on such Clerk/County Recorder's publicly available website.

Statewide or Multi-Jurisdiction Access: There are numerous county agencies that provide online access to records, but the nearly statewide system MyFlorida.com predominates. MyFloridaCounty.com is maintained and operated by the Florida Association of Court Clerks Services Group. See description below.

- MyFloridaCounty.com, maintained and operated by the Florida Association of Court Clerks Services Group, offers free access to at least 61 county Circuit Clerks of Court recorded indexes, including real estate records, liens, judgments, marriages, deaths at https://www.myfloridacounty.com/. Fees involved to order copies, but $1.50 per record by becoming a subscriber. Subscription fee is $120.00 per year plus monthly transaction fees for copies.

County Sites:

Alachua County ***Recorded Documents, Marriage Records*** www.alachuacounty.us/Depts/Clerk/Pages/Clerk.aspx Access Clerk's recording database free at www.alachuacounty.us/Depts/Clerk/PublicRecords/Pages/PublicRecords.aspx. Index goes back to 1971; images to 1990. Also, search county property by various methods free at www.acpafl.org/. Search ancient records -pre-1940 plats, pre-1970 marriages, deeds, transcriptions, more- free at www.alachuaclerk.org/archive/default.cfm. Access index of recordings at https://www.myfloridacounty.com/ but registration and fees required for images. Records go back to 5/4/1959. **$$$**

Property, Taxation Search Appraiser's Property pages free at www.acpafl.org/. Tax Deed Sales search and GIS search also here. Property also at www.emapsplus.com/FLAlachua/maps/. Sales data free at www.acpafl.org/salessearch.asp. Tax deed sales- www.alachuacounty.us/Depts/Clerk/TaxDeeds/Pages/TaxDeedSales.aspx. Tax rolls- http://alachuataxcollector.governmax.com/collectmax/collect30.asp.

Baker County ***Recorded Documents*** http://208.75.175.18/clerk/ Access an index of recorded documents at https://www.myfloridacounty.com/. Fees involved to order copies; save $1.50 per record by becoming a subscriber. Records go back to 1/1/1985. Also, access to public records free at http://208.75.175.18/oncoreweb/Search.aspx. **$$$**

Property, Taxation Search assessor data free at www.emapsplus.com/FLBaker/maps/. Also, search appraiser data free at www.bakerpa.com/index_disclaimer.asp. Also, name search the Tax Collector database free at http://70.84.137.66/~baker/search.html.

Bay County ***Recorded Documents, Death, Marriage Records*** www.baycoclerk.com Access to the Clerk of the Circuit Court Recordings database is free at www.baycoclerk.com/courts/case-search/. Search court judgments and probate free at http://records2.baycoclerk.com/oncoreweb/Search.aspx. Also, access an index of recorded documents at https://www.myfloridacounty.com/. Fees involved to order copies; save $1.50 per record by becoming a subscriber. Records go back to2/18/1986. **$$$**

Property, Taxation Search property appraiser data free at www.baypa.net/search.html. Also, Search the tax collector data at http://tc.co.bay.fl.us//

Bradford County ***Recorded Documents, Marriage Records*** www.bradfordcountyfl.gov/clerkIndex.html Access an index of recorded documents at www.myfloridacounty.com. Fees involved to order copies; save $1.50 per record by becoming a subscriber. Records back to 1/5/1969. **$$$**

Property, Taxation Search the property appraiser database at www.bradfordappraiser.com/. Also, search assessor data free at www.emapsplus.com/FLBradford/maps/.

Brevard County ***Recorded Documents, Marriage Records*** http://brevardclerk.us/ Free access to the index is at http://web1.brevardclerk.us/oncoreweb/search.aspx. Also, the clerk offers an electronic fully automated case tracking system at https://vweb1.brevardclerk.us/FACTS/facts_search.cfm?CFID=25505312&CFTOKEN=39545041. Also, access clerk's tax lien (1981-95), land records (1995-) & indexed records 1981-9/30/1995; Registration/password required for full data. Access marriage indices 1938 to 10/2006 free at http://199.241.8.125/index.cfm?FuseAction=MarriageLicenses.Home Also, access an index of recorded documents at https://www.myfloridacounty.com/. Fees involved to order copies; save $1.50 per record by becoming a subscriber. Records go back to 10/2/1995. **$$$**

Property, Taxation Access property tax and personal property records free at https://www.brevardpropertyappraiser.com/mainhtml/mapsdata.asp. Access parcels and property/GIS free at www.emapsplus.com/FLBrevard/maps/. Property Sales & tax records at https://www.brevardpropertyappraiser.com/asp/disclaimer.asp. Also, tax deed sale lists free at http://199.241.8.125/index.cfm?FuseAction=TaxDeedAuctions.TaxDeedSales.

Broward County ***Recorded Documents*** www.broward.org/RecordsTaxesTreasury/Records/Pages/Default.aspx Access to the county records Public Search database 1978-present is free at http://205.166.161.12/oncoreV2/.

Property, Taxation Access assessor and property/GIS free at www.emapsplus.com/FLBroward/maps/. Also, search property tax data for free at www.bcpa.net/RecMenu.asp.

Calhoun County ***Recorded Documents, Historical Indexes Records*** www.calhounclerk.com/ Access an index of recorded documents at www.myfloridacounty.com. Fees involved to order copies; save $1.50 per record by becoming a subscriber. Records go back to 4/16/1945. Access to Historical Indexes free at www.calhounclerk.com/historical.html. **$$$**

Property, Taxation Search assessor's data free at http://calhounpa.net and click on \"Search Records.\"

Charlotte County ***Recorded Documents, Marriage Records*** www.co.charlotte.fl.us/Default.aspx Search recorded data and marriages free at http://208.47.160.77/or/Search.aspx. Access index of recorded documents at www.myfloridacounty.com. Fees involved to order copies; subscribers save $1.50 per record. Records go back to 4/20/1964. Also, access to records for free go to http://ccor.co.charlotte.fl.us/or/Search.aspx. **$$$**

Property, Taxation Property records are free at www.ccappraiser.com/record.asp. Search Assessor and property/GIS free at www.emapsplus.com/FLCharlotte/maps/. Sales records are on the tax collector database free at https://www.bidcharlottecounty.com/.

Citrus County ***Recorded Documents, Marriage, Probate, Military Discharge, Tax Deed Sale Records*** www.clerk.citrus.fl.us/nws/home.jsp?section=1&item=1 Access to the Clerk of Circuit Court recording records is free at http://search.clerk.citrus.fl.us/. Also, download land sales data free at www.pa.citrus.fl.us/pls/apex/f?p=100:1:1912304870588522. Access recorded documents index at https://www.myfloridacounty.com. Fees involved to order copies; save $1.50 per record by becoming a subscriber. Records go back to 4/21/1959. View tax deed sales at www.clerk.citrus.fl.us/nws/home.jsp?section=8&item=88. **$$$**

Property, Taxation Search property appraiser and personal property records free at www.pa.citrus.fl.us/pls/apex/f?p=100:20:13497745880047::NO:::. Also, download land sales data by year free. Search property and other related-tax records free at https://www.citrus.county-taxes.com/tcb/app/main/home.

Clay County ***Recorded Documents, Marriage Records*** www.clayclerk.com Access to recording records free at http://clayclerk.com/oncoreweb4251/. Index goes back to 5/27/1958. Also, access an index of recorded documents at www.myfloridacounty.com. Fees involved to order copies. Records go back to 12/26/1911. **$$$**

Property, Taxation Access property appraiser records free at www.ccpao.com/newsite/disclaimer.html. Also, search assessor data free at www.emapsplus.com/FLClay/maps/. Search treasurer RE and tangibles personal property at http://fl-clay-taxcollector.governmax.com/collectmax/collect30.asp. Tax search free at http://fl-clay-taxcollector.governmax.com/collectmax/collect30.asp?sid=6A7673E3DD1B47718CAEB0B266079A55.

Collier County Clerk of Courts ***Recorded Documents, Vital Records Records*** www.collierclerk.com/ Access court, lien, real property, UCCs and vital records free at www.collierclerk.com/. Lending agency data available. Also, access recorded document index at www.myfloridacounty.com. Fees involved to order copies; save $1.50 per record by becoming a subscriber. Records go back to 4/1/1981. **$$$**

Property, Taxation Access Property Appraiser data free at www.collierappraiser.com/. Also property assessor/GIS free at www.emapsplus.com/FLCollier/maps/. Search property tax roll at www.colliertax.com/search/.

Columbia County ***Recorded Documents, Marriage, Death Records*** www.columbiaclerk.com/ Access Clerk of Circuit Courts recording database index free at www.columbiaclerk.com/htm/or-disclaimer.html. Generally, documents go back to 1987. Also, access an index of recorded documents at https://www.myfloridacounty.com/. Fees involved to order copies; save $1.50 per record by becoming a subscriber. Records go back to 5/18/1955. **$$$**

Property, Taxation Search property appraiser records free at http://g2.columbia.floridapa.com/GIS/Search_F.asp?. Also, search property assessor data free at www.emapsplus.com/FLColumbia/maps/. Also, search the tax rolls and occupational licenses for free at http://fl-columbia-taxcollector.governmax.com/collectmax/collect30.asp

De Soto County ***Recorded Documents*** www.desotoclerk.com Access an index of recorded documents at https://www.myfloridacounty.com/. Fees involved to order copies; save $1.50 per record by becoming a subscriber. Records go back to 11/20/1901. Also, access to court records free at www.desotoclerk.com/Disclaimer.htm. **$$$**

Property, Taxation Access the property appraiser data free at http://qpublic.net/desoto/search.html. Also, search property assessor/GIS free at www.emapsplus.com/FLdesoto/maps/.

Dixie County ***Recorded Documents*** www.dixieclerk.com/ Access an index of recorded documents at https://www.myfloridacounty.com/. Fees involved to order copies; save $1.50 per record by becoming a subscriber. Records go back to 11/10/1917. **$$$**

Property, Taxation Access assessor's property data free at www.qpublic.net/dixie/search.html.

Duval County ***Recorded Documents*** www.duvalclerk.com/ccWebsite/recordSearch.page Access Clerk of Circuit Court and City of Jacksonville Official Records index free at www.duvalclerk.com/ccWebsite/recordSearch.page. This site also includes OnCore (official records). Access an index of recorded documents at https://www.myfloridacounty.com. Fees involved to order copies. Records go back to 9/8/1791. **$$$**

Property, Taxation Search Property Appraiser records free at http://apps.coj.net/pao_propertySearch/Basic/Search.aspx. Search parcel data free at http://maps.coj.net/jaxgis/ click on Duval Maps. Also, access Property Assessor/GIS data free at www.emapsplus.com/Flduval/maps/. Search tax collector real estate, personal property data free and Occupational licensing at http://fl-duval-taxcollector.governmax.com/collectmax/collect30.asp.

Escambia County ***Recorded Documents, Vital Records Records*** www.escambiaclerk.com/clerk/coc_official_records.aspx Access to the Clerk of Court Public Records database is free at www.escambiaclerk.com/clerk/coc_online_public_records.aspx. This includes grantor/grantee index and marriage, traffic, court records, tax sales. Access an index of recorded documents at https://www.myfloridacounty.com/. Fees involved to order copies; save $1.50 per record by becoming subscriber. Records go back to 12/31/1899. **$$$**

Property, Taxation Search the property appraiser records and sales, condos and subdivisions free at www.escpa.org/cama/Search.aspx. Also, access the tax collector's Property Tax database free at http://escambiataxcollector.governmaxa.com/collectmax/collect30.asp.

Flagler County ***Recorded Documents, Marriage, Death, Military Discharge, Property Sale Records*** www.flaglerclerk.com Search recording records free at www.flaglerclerk.com/oncoreweb/Search.aspx. Also, name search the tax collector tax records site free at http://fl-flagler-taxcollector.governmax.com/collectmax/collect30.asp. Check property sales at www.qpublic.net/flagler/flaglersearch.html. The state recorders' meta-search site is free at www.myflaglercounty.com/. Click on Official Records. Also, access an index of recorded documents at https://www.myfloridacounty.com. Fees involved to order copies; save $1.50 per record by becoming a subscriber. Records go back to 2/9/1961. **$$$**

Property, Taxation Search appraiser property data free at www.flaglerpa.com/search.html. Also, search Property Assessor/GIS free at www.emapsplus.com/FLflagler/maps/.

Franklin County ***Recorded Documents*** www.franklinclerk.com/ Access an index of recorded documents at https://www.myfloridacounty.com/. Fees involved to order copies; save $1.50 per record by becoming a subscriber. 1/1/1900. **$$$**

Property, Taxation Property record search form appraiser is free at http://qpublic.net/franklin/.

Gadsden County ***Recorded Documents*** www.gadsdenclerk.com/ Access to official records index is free at http://69.21.116.234/chronicleweb/. Records go back to 1985. Also, access an index of recorded documents at https://www.myfloridacounty.com. Fees involved to order copies; save $1.50 per record by becoming a subscriber. Records go back to 1/1/1949.

Property, Taxation Access to the property appraiser database is free at www.qpublic.net/gadsden/search.html. Search property sales at www.qpublic.net/gadsden/gadsdensearch.html. Also, search tax collector records at http://fl-gadsden-taxcollector.governmax.com/collectmax/collect30.asp.

Gilchrist County ***Recorded Documents, Marriage Records*** www.gilchristclerk.com/ Access an index of recorded documents at https://www.myfloridacounty.com/. Fees involved to order copies. Records go back to 11/30/1912. **$$$**

Property, Taxation Access to the property appraiser database is free at www.qpublic.net/gilchrist/search.html.

Glades County ***Recorded Documents*** www.gladesclerk.com/ Access an index of recorded documents at https://www.myfloridacounty.com/. Fees involved to order copies; save $1.50 per record by becoming a subscriber. Records go back to 1/3/1989. **$$$**

Property, Taxation Search Property Assessor/GIS free at www.emapsplus.com/FLglades/maps/. Also, sales searches are at www.gcpaonline.net/; click on Search.

Gulf County ***Recorded Documents, Marriage, Death Records*** http://gulfclerk.com/ Access an index of recorded documents at www.myfloridacounty.com/. Fees involved to order copies; save $1.50 per record by becoming a subscriber. Records go back to 8/10/1925. **$$$**

Property, Taxation Access to the property appraiser database is free at www.gulfpa.com/.

Hamilton County ***Recorded Documents*** www.hamiltoncountyflorida.com/cd_clerk.aspx Access an index of recorded documents at https://www.myfloridacounty.com. Fees involved to order copies; save $1.50 per record by becoming a subscriber. Records go back to 1/3/1984. **$$$**

Property, Taxation Access to the property appraiser database is free at www.hamiltoncountytaxcollector.com/SearchSelect.aspx.

Hardee County ***Recorded Documents*** www.hardeeclerk.com/ Access recorded documents index and images at www.myfloridacounty.com. Fees involved to order copies; save $1.50 per record by becoming a subscriber. Records go back to 8/5/1976. **$$$**

Property, Taxation Access to the property appraiser data is free at www.qpublic.net/hardee/search.html. Search assessor data on the GIS site free at www.emapsplus.com/Flhardee/maps/.

Hendry County ***Recorded Documents*** www.hendryclerk.org Access indexes of official records at https://www.myfloridacounty.com. Fees involved to order copies; save $1.50 per record by becoming a subscriber. Records go back to 1/29/1980. **$$$**

Property, Taxation Access the property appraiser database at www.hendryprop.com/GIS/Search_F.asp. Also, search Property Assessor/GIS free at www.emapsplus.com/FLhendry/maps/.

Hernando County ***Recorded Documents, Marriage, Tax Deeds Records*** http://hernandoclerk.com/ Access to the clerk's Official Records database at http://hernandoclerk.com/. Click on Official Records Search Your browser must be JavaScript enabled. Includes recordings, marriages, and court records, but domestic relations judgments/court papers not viewable. Also, access recorded document index at https://www2.myfloridacounty.com/ccm/do/personSearch?county=27. Fees involved to order copies; save $1.50 per record by becoming a subscriber. Records go back to 1/1/1900. **$$$**

Property, Taxation Access to property record search for free at http://g2.hernando.floridapa.com/GIS/Search_F.asp?REFERER=www.hernandocounty.us/pa/propertysearch.asp. Also, access to list of lands available for taxes for free at http://hernandoclerk.com/official-records/list-of-lands/.

Highlands County ***Recorded Documents*** www.hcclerk.org/Home.aspx Access an index of recorded documents at https://www.myfloridacounty.com/. Fees involved to order copies; save $1.50 per record by becoming a subscriber. Records go back to 6/20/1901. Also, records from the county recording database is free at http://records.hcclerk.org/OncoreWeb/. **$$$**

Property, Taxation Property appraiser records are free at www.appraiser.co.highlands.fl.us/search/index.shtml; tangible personal property records available. Also, county tax collector database free at https://www.highlands.county-taxes.com/tcb/app/re/accounts.

Hillsborough County ***Recorded Documents*** www.hillsclerk.com/publicweb/home.aspx Access recorded document index at https://www.myfloridacounty.com/; fees involved to order copies; subscribers save $1.50 per record. Domestic relations judgments/court papers not viewable. Records go back to 1/1/1900. Call 813-276-8100 x4444 for info. Also, access records for free at http://pubrec3.hillsclerk.com/oncore/Search.aspx. Images are from 1965 to present. **$$$**

Property, Taxation Search property appraiser records free at www.hcpafl.org/CamaDisplay.aspx. Also, search for similar tax data free on the tax collector site at www.hillstax.org/taxapp/property_information.asp. Search property on GIS site at http://propmap3.hcpafl.org/main.asp?cmd=ZOOMFOLIO&folio.

Holmes County ***Recorded Documents*** www.holmesclerk.com/ Access an index of recorded documents at https://www.myfloridacounty.com/. Fees involved to order copies; save $1.50 per record by becoming a subscriber. Records go back to 5/11/1979. **$$$**

Property, Taxation Access property appraiser data free including property, sales and sales lists free at http://qpublic.net/holmes/.

Indian River County ***Recorded Documents*** www.clerk.indian-river.org Access to Clerk's recording indices are free at http://ori.indian-river.org/. Records go back to 1983. Full court records from the Clerk of the Circuit Court is at their fee site; subscriptions start at $25.00 per month. For info about free and fee access, call 772-226-1204. Also, access an index of recorded documents at https://www.myfloridacounty.com/. Fees involved to order copies; save $1.50 per record by becoming a subscriber. **$$$**

Property, Taxation Appraiser records free at www.ircpa.org/. Also, search Property Assessor/GIS free at www.emapsplus.com/FLindianriver/maps/.

Jackson County ***Recorded Documents, Marriage, Probate/Guardianship Records*** www.jacksonclerk.com/ Access an index of recorded documents at https://www.myfloridacounty.com. Fees involved to order copies. Records go back to 1/4/1900.

Property, Taxation Search property tax data for free at www.jacksoncountytaxcollector.com/SearchSelect.aspx. Also, access to property records free at www.qpublic.net/jackson/search.html.

Jefferson County ***Recorded Documents, Marriage Records*** www.jeffersonclerk.com/ Access an index of recorded documents at https://www.myfloridacounty.com. Fees involved to order copies; save $1.50 per record by becoming a subscriber. Records go back to 1/1/1958. **$$$**

Property, Taxation Access Property Appraiser data free at www.jeffersonpa.net/GIS/Search_F.asp. Sales searches are also available. Search the tax collector database free at www.jeffersoncountytaxcollector.com/SearchSelect.aspx.

Lafayette County ***Recorded Documents*** www.lafayetteclerk.com/ Access an index of recorded documents at https://www.myfloridacounty.com. Fees involved to order copies; save $1.50 per record by becoming a subscriber. Records go back to 1/3/1979. **$$$**

Property, Taxation Search appraiser's property data free at http://g2.lafayettepa.com/GIS/Search_F.asp. Also, search property sales free at http://g2.lafayettepa.com/GIS/Search_F.asp?SalesReport.

Lake County ***Recorded Documents, Marriage Records*** www.lakecountyclerk.org Access the county clerk official records database free at http://officialrecords.lakecountyclerk.org/acclaimweb/search?target=_blank. Records go as far back as 1887. Also, marriage records back to 8/1887 are www.lakecountyclerk.org/, click on Court Records in the Recortds Seach column. Also, access an index of recorded documents at https://www.myfloridacounty.com. Fees involved to order copies; save $1.50 per record by becoming a subscriber. Records go back to 10/11/1884. **$$$**

Property, Taxation Search the County Property Assessor parcel and tax data also property sales free at www.lakecopropappr.com/. Also, search property on the tax collector site free at http://laketaxcollector.governmax.com/collectmax/collect30.asp.

Lee County ***Recorded Documents, Marriage, Business Tax Records, Records*** www.leeclerk.org Search deeds, mortgages, marriage records at http://apps.leeclerk.org/OR/Search.aspx. Access an index of recorded documents at https://www.myfloridacounty.com. Fees involved to order copies; save $1.50 per record by becoming a subscriber. Records go back to 1/11/1900. **$$$**

Property, Taxation Search property tax rolls for either real estate or personal property at www.leetc.com/taxes.asp?c=taxes. A tax certificate search is at www.leetc.com/search_criteria.asp?searchtype=TC. Search property assessor/GIS free at www.emapsplus.com/FLlee/maps/ or the new GIS site at http://gissvr.leepa.org/GeoView/GeoView.aspx.

Leon County ***Recorded Documents, Marriage Records*** www.clerk.leon.fl.us Real Estate, lien, and foreclosure records from the County Clerk are free at http://cvimage.clerk.leon.fl.us/official_records/index.asp. Marriages are at http://cvweb.clerk.leon.fl.us/index_marriage.html. Also, access an index of recorded documents at https://www.myfloridacounty.com. Fees involved to order copies; save $1.50 per record by becoming a subscriber. Records go back to 8/23/1906. **$$$**

Property, Taxation Search Property Appraiser database records free at www.leonpa.org/searchGeneral.cfm. Search tax collector rolls at www.leontaxcollector.net/disclaimer.asp?AcctNo=

Levy County ***Recorded Documents*** www.levyclerk.com Access the Clerk of Circuit Court recording database free at http://oncore.levyclerk.com/oncoreweb/Search.aspx. Search by name, book/page, file number or document type. Also, access an index of recorded documents at https://www.myfloridacounty.com. Fees involved to order copies; save $1.50 per record by becoming a subscriber. Records go back to 1/1983. **$$$**

Property, Taxation Access to the property appraiser data is free at www.qpublic.net/levy/, also has sales searches. Also search tax collector and property data free at http://fl-levy-taxcollector.governmax.com/collectmax/collect30.asp and click on Tax Search; also has tax sales.

Liberty County ***Recorded Documents*** www.libertyclerk.com/ Access an index of recorded documents at https://www.myfloridacounty.com/. Fees involved to order copies; save $1.50 per record by becoming a subscriber. Records go back to 1/2/1990. **$$$**

Property, Taxation Access assessor property records free at www.qpublic.net/liberty/.

Madison County ***Recorded Documents*** www.madisonclerk.com/ Access an index of recorded documents at www.myfloridacounty.com. Fees involved to order copies; save $1.50 per record by becoming a subscriber. Records go back to 1/1/1990. **$$$**

Property, Taxation Access property assessor and sale data free at www.madisonpa.com/GIS/Search_F.asp.

Manatee County ***Recorded Documents, Death, Marriage, Condominium Records*** www.manateeclerk.com Access to search and view real estate and recordings records free from the Clerk of Circuit Court and Comptroller's database at www.manateeclerk.com/Searches/OfficialRecordsDisclaimer.aspx. Also, access to service that includes recordings and probate available at www.manateeclerk.org/Home/tabid/57/Default.aspx. Also, access an index of recorded documents at www.myfloridacounty.com. Fees involved to order copies; save $1.50 per record by becoming a subscriber. Records go back to 1/3/1978. **$$$**

Property, Taxation Search Property Assessor/GIS data free at www.emapsplus.com/FLmanatee/maps/. Property Appraiser records free at www.manateepao.com/Search/GenericSearch.aspx.

Marion County Clerk ***Recorded Documents, Death, Marriage Records***
www.marioncountyclerk.org/public/index.cfm?Pg=ClerkOfCourt Search recorder records free at http://216.255.240.38/wb_or1/or_sch_1.asp. Also, access an index of recorded documents at https://www.myfloridacounty.com/. Fees involved to order copies; save $1.50 per record by becoming a subscriber. Records go back to 1/24/1989. **$$$**

Property, Taxation Access the Appraiser property search from the home page. Search county tax rolls free at https://www.mariontax.com/itm.asp. Also, access property data free at www.marioncountyfl.org/MSTU/assessment.aspx.

Martin County ***Recorded Documents*** www.martinclerk.com/ Access to the clerk of the circuit court recordings database are free at http://216.255.240.38/wb_or1/or_sch_1.asp. Access an index of recorded documents at www.myfloridacounty.com. Fees involved to order copies; save $1.50 per record by becoming a subscriber. Records go back to 1/2/1986. Also, access to official records public search at http://clerk-web.martin.fl.us/. Available is public search and enhanced public search (for a fee). **$$$**

Property, Taxation Records on the county property appraiser database are free at www.pa.martin.fl.us/. Choose \"Real Property Searches.\" Personal property searches are also available, and more. Also, county tax collector data files are free at https://taxcol.martin.fl.us/itm/. Also, search Property Appraiser/GIS free at www.emapsplus.com/FLmartin/maps/.

Dade County ***Recorded Documents, Marriage, Voter Registration Records*** www.miami-dadeclerk.com/ Access records and index free at http://miamidade.gov/wps/portal. Recorded docs atwww2.miami-dadeclerk.com/public-records/. Access voter registration check site free at www.miamidade.gov/elections/.

Property, Taxation Access assessor data free at www.miamidade.gov/pa/property_search.asp. Also, lookup property tax free at www.miamidade.gov/proptax/home.asp. Search assessor property and GIS site free at www.emapsplus.com/FLDade/maps/. Tax collector records free at www.co.miami-dade.fl.us/proptax/.

Monroe County ***Recorded Documents*** https://gov.propertyinfo.com/FL-Monroe/ Access to the clerk of circuit courts database is free at https://gov.propertyinfo.com/FL-Monroe/.

Property, Taxation Access to property appraiser data is free on the GIS-mapping site at www.mcpafl.org/GISMaps.aspx. Also, search property tax and tax deed sales free at www.monroetaxcollector.com/.

Nassau County ***Recorded Documents, Marriage Records*** www.nassauclerk.com Access recorders database free at www.nassauclerk.com/publicrecords/oncoreweb/. Also, access an index of recorded documents at www.myfloridacounty.com. Fees involved to order copies; save $1.50 per record by becoming a subscriber. Records go back to 9/28/1982. **$$$**

Property, Taxation Access property data free at www.nassauflpa.com/. Search Property Assessor/GIS free at www.emapsplus.com/FLnassau/maps/.

Okaloosa County ***Recorded Documents, Marriage Records*** www.clerkofcourts.cc Access clerk's land and official records for free at http://officialrecords.clerkofcourts.cc/; includes marriage, civil, traffic records. Also, access an index of recorded documents at www.myfloridacounty.com. Fees involved to order copies; save $1.50 per record by becoming a subscriber. Records go back to 1/1/1900.

Property, Taxation Access property appraiser records and sales lists free at www.okaloosapa.com/. Access tax collector data at https://www.okaloosa.county-taxes.com/tcb/app/pt/main. Access property data on the GIS-mapping site free at http://webgis.co.okaloosa.fl.us/okaloosagis/viewer.htm.

Okeechobee County ***Recorded Documents*** www.clerk.co.okeechobee.fl.us Also, access an index of recorded documents at www.myfloridacounty.com. Fees involved to order copies; save $1.50 per record by becoming a subscriber. Records go back to 6/4/1923. Also, search the Clerk of Courts Tax Deed data free at http://204.215.37.218/wb_or1/or_sch_1.asp. **$$$**

Property, Taxation Search assessor data on the GIS site free at www.okeechobeepa.com/GIS/Search_F.asp?GIS. Also, search property on the private GIS site at www.emapsplus.com/FLOkeechobee/maps/.

Orange County ***Recorded Documents*** www.occompt.com Real Estate, Lien, and Marriage records on the county Comptroller database are free at https://officialrecords.occompt.com/recorder/. Lending Agency data available.

Property, Taxation Access appraiser records free at www.ocpafl.org/Searches/ParcelSearch.aspx#%23. Search appraiser site free www.ocpafl.org/default.aspx includes tax sales. Search Property on the GIS site at www.emapsplus.com/FLorange/maps/.

Osceola County ***Recorded Documents*** http://osceolaclerk.com/ Search recorded documents at www.myfloridacounty.com. Fees involved to order copies; save $1.50 per record by becoming a subscriber. Records go back to 1/1/1900. Also, recording/land records at http://osceolaclerk.com/. **$$$**

Property, Taxation Subscription required for property appraiser records at www.osceolataxcollector.com/. Also, with registration & password, access Occ. licenses and tax collector data.**$$$**

Palm Beach County ***Recorded Documents, Vital Records Records*** www.mypalmbeachclerk.com/ Access clerk's recording database free at www.mypalmbeachclerk.com/. Records go back to 1968; images back to 1968; includes marriage records 1979 to present. Also, access an index of recorded documents at www.myfloridacounty.com. Fees involved to order copies; save $1.50 per record by becoming a subscriber. Records go back to 1/1/1968. **$$$**

Property, Taxation Access property appraiser records at www.co.palm-beach.fl.us/papa/aspx/GeneralSearch/GeneralSearch.aspx. Search real estate, property tax, personal property data at www.taxcollectorpbc.com/i&p_property.shtml. Also, search property/GIS free at www.emapsplus.com/FLpalmbeach/maps/. Search tax deeds at http://taxcollectorpbc.manatron.com/Tabs/PropertyTax.aspx.

Pasco County ***Recorded Documents, Vital Records Records*** www.pascoclerk.com Several sources available. Access to real estate, liens, marriage records requires $25 annual fee plus a $50 deposit. Billing rate is $.05 per minute, $.03 evenings. For info, call 352-521-4529. Domestic relations judgments/court papers not viewable online. Also, free access to indexes and copies at www.pascoclerk.com/. Click on \"public records.\" Also, access an index of recorded documents at www.myfloridacounty.com. Fees involved to order copies; save $1.50 per record by becoming a subscriber. Records go back to 1/2/1985. **$$$**

Property, Taxation Access property appraiser data and sales data and maps free at http://appraiser.pascogov.com. Search tax records, personal property, business taxes at www.pascotaxes.com/search/prclsearch.asp.

Pinellas County ***Recorded Documents*** www.pinellasclerk.org/aspInclude2/ASPInclude.asp?pageName=index.htm Access recorded document index at https://www.myfloridacounty.com/. Fees involved to order copies. Domestic relations judgments/court papers not viewable online. Records go back to 4/8/1988. Also, access to official court records free at https://public.co.pinellas.fl.us/login/clerkloginx.jsp. Guest access is limited to 100 transactions per day. For full range access you can subscribe. **$$$**

Property, Taxation Assessor property records are free at www.pcpao.org/. Also, search tax collector data free at https://www.pinellas.county-taxes.com/tcb/app/pt/main/. Tax deed sales lists are at www.pinellasclerk.org/tributeweb/searchcases.aspx.

Polk County ***Recorded Documents*** www.polkcountyclerk.net/ Search the county clerk database for free at www.polkcountyclerk.net/disclaimer.aspx?prev=244. Also, access an index of recorded documents at www.myfloridacounty.com. Fees involved to order copies; save $1.50 per record by becoming a subscriber. Records go back to 4/16/1900.

Property, Taxation Access appraiser property tax, personal property, and sales data free at www.polkpa.org/CamaDisplay.aspx.

Putnam County ***Recorded Documents*** www.putnam-fl.com/coc/ Access an index of recorded documents at www.myfloridacounty.com. Fees involved to order copies; save $1.50 per record by becoming a subscriber. Records go back to 1/2/1974. Also, access to official records free at https://www.putnam-fl.com/peas/public_disclaimer.php. **$$$**

Property, Taxation Access to GIS/mapping for free at www.putnam-fl.com/app/index.php?option=com_content&view=article&id=47&Itemid=57. Also, search the online tax rolls at www.putnam-fl.com/app/index.php?option=com_content&view=category&layout=blog&id=35&Itemid=74. No name searching.

St. Johns County ***Recorded Documents, Probate Records*** www.clk.co.st-johns.fl.us/ Access to the county Clerk of Circuit Court recording database is free at http://doris.clk.co.st-johns.fl.us/oncoreweb/. Includes civil and probate records, UCCs, and other public records. Also, access an index of recorded documents at www.myfloridacounty.com. Fees involved to order copies; save $1.50 per record by becoming a subscriber. Records go back to 1/21/1989. **$$$**

Property, Taxation Access county property appraiser database free at www.sjcpa.us/Disclaimer%20CAMA%20Search.html. Also, search Property/GIS free at www.emapsplus.com/FLstjohns/maps/.

St. Lucie County ***Recorded Documents, Marriage, Fictitious Name Records*** www.stlucieclerk.com/ Access public records including recorded documents at http://casesearch.slcclerkofcourt.com/PublicSearch/. Click the SLCC Departments link. Direct link to recorded documents is http://oncore.slcclerkofcourt.com/oncorewebnew/. Also, access an index of recorded documents at www.myfloridacounty.com. Fees involved to order copies; save $1.50 per record by becoming a subscriber. Records go back to 8/10/1900. **$$$**

Property, Taxation Access property appraiser records free at www.paslc.org/. Click on \"Real estate\" or \"Personal property\" for search options. Also, search assessor property data free at www.emapsplus.com/FLStLucie/maps/.

Santa Rosa County ***Recorded Documents, Marriage, Death Records*** www.santarosaclerk.com/ Access the Clerk's index of recorded documents at http://oncoreweb.srccol.com/oncoreweb/. Or, go to www.myflorida.com/ where you may search the index free; fees involved to order copies or view images. Records go back to 12/20/1909. **$$$**

Property, Taxation Access the appraiser property records free at www.srcpa.org/property.html. Also, search the real estate tax collector data for free at http://santarosataxcollector.governmax.com/collectmax/collect30.asp.

Sarasota County ***Recorded Documents, Vital Records*** www.sarasotaclerk.com/ Access Clerk of Circuit Court recordings database free at www.clerk.co.sarasota.fl.us/oprapp/oprinq.asp. Other public records included in this URL. Also, access an index of recorded documents at www.myfloridacounty.com. Fees involved to order copies; save $1.50 per record by becoming a subscriber. Records go back to 1/2/1990. **$$$**

Property, Taxation Access property appraiser data free at www.sc-pa.com/content/search_real_property.asp; includes subdivision/condominium sales. Also, search tax collector and occ licenses at http://sarasotataxcollector.governmax.com/collectmax/collect30.asp. Search property assessor/GIS data free at www.emapsplus.com/FLsarasota/maps/.

Seminole County ***Recorded Documents, Marriage Records*** www.seminoleclerk.org Access the county clerk of circuit court's recordings database free at http://officialrecords.seminoleclerk.org/.

Property, Taxation Property appraisal tax records free at www.scpafl.org/. Access property and real estate tax data free at http://seminoletax.org/Tax/TaxSearch.shtml. Also, GIS free at www.emapsplus.com/FLseminole/maps/. Search tax collector personal property and real estate records free at http://seminoletax.org.

Sumter County ***Recorded Documents*** www.sumterclerk.com/ Also, access an index of recorded documents at www.myfloridacounty.com. Fees involved to order copies; save $1.50 per record by becoming a subscriber. Records go back to 1/1/1900. **$$$**

Property, Taxation Access property assessor data free at www.sumterpa.com/. Also, search tax collector and occupational licenses for free at http://sumtertaxcollector.governmax.com/collectmax/collect30.asp. Also, tax deed, foreclosures and other sales lists are available in pdf format.

Suwannee County ***Recorded Documents, Marriage, Death Records*** www.suwclerk.org Access of the county clerk of circuit database index is free at www.suwclerk.org/. This directs you to the statewide database; search index free; subscription required for documents. Also, document index for variety of recordings free at http://151.213.249.227/oncoreweb/ which includes County Official Records. Access an index of recorded documents at www.myfloridacounty.com. Fees involved to order copies; save $1.50 per record by becoming a subscriber. Records go back to 6/21/1943. **$$$**

Property, Taxation Search property assessor data free at http://g2.suwanneepa.com/GIS/Search_F.asp?GIS. Also, search on the GIS-mapping site at www.emapsplus.com/FLSuwannee/maps/. Also, search the tax collector database free at http://fl-suwannee-taxcollector.manatron.com/ also register to view tax deed sale records.

Taylor County Clerk of Courts ***Recorded Documents*** www.taylorclerk.com/ Also, access an index of recorded documents at www.myfloridacounty.com. Fees involved to order copies; save $1.50 per record by becoming a subscriber. Records go back to 1/2/1990. Also, check voter registration for names free at https://www.voterfocus.com/vfvoters.php?county=taylor. **$$$**

Property, Taxation Access to tax collector tax roll data free at http://fl-taylor-taxcollector.governmax.com/collectmax/collect30.asp. Also, access to public records search free at http://67.158.152.37/PublicInquiry/Search.aspx?Type=Name.

Union County ***Recorded Documents*** www.unionclerk.com/ Access an index of recorded documents at www.myfloridacounty.com. Fees involved to order copies; save $1.50 per record by becoming a subscriber. Records go back to 1/3/1983. **$$$**

Property, Taxation Access assessor's records free at www.qpublic.net/union/search.html. Check tax records free at http://unioncountytaxcollector.com; click on \"Tax Record Search\" to search by name, parcel number, or address. Search property sales free at http://g2.union.floridapa.com/GIS/Search_F.asp?SalesReport. Also, search the GIS-mapping site for assessor property data free at http://g2.union.floridapa.com/GIS/Search_F.asp?GIS or www.emapsplus.com/FLUnion/maps/.

Volusia County ***Recorded Documents*** www.clerk.org/index.html Recording data is free at www.clerk.org/. Click on Search Public Records. Recorder indices go back to 1990. Arrest ledger, tax deed sales and citations also at this website. County also offers full real estate, lien, court and vital records on a commercial site; set up is $100 with $25 monthly. For info, contact clerk. Also, access index of recorded documents at www.myfloridacounty.com. Fees involved to order copies; save $1.50 per record by becoming a subscriber. Records go back to 4/4/1988. **$$$**

Property, Taxation Access property search free at http://webserver.vcgov.org/vc_search.html. Also search property assessor/GIS free at www.emapsplus.com/FLVolusia/maps/.

Wakulla County ***Recorded Documents, Death, Marriage Records*** www.wakullaclerk.com/ Access an index of recorded documents at www.wakullaclerk.com/oncoreweb/. Also, the Clerk's office has plat images online free at www.wakullaclerk.com/plats.asp. Also, access index of recorded documents at https://www.myfloridacounty.com/. Fees involved to order copies; save $1.50 per record by becoming a subscriber. Records go back to 9/26/1989. **$$$**

Property, Taxation Access assessor property data free at www.qpublic.net/wakulla/search1.html. Access clerk of court's foreclosure monthly lists and Tax Deed Sales free at www.wakullaclerk.com/index.asp. Click on Link in Quick Links Section. Search tax collector data free at www.wakullacountytaxcollector.com/SearchSelect.aspx.

Walton County ***Recorded Documents, Vital Records Records*** http://clerkofcourts.co.walton.fl.us/ Records back to 1/1976 on the County Clerk database are free at http://orsearch.clerkofcourts.co.walton.fl.us/ORSearch/. Access an index of recorded documents at https://www.myfloridacounty.com/. Fees involved to order copies; save $1.50 per record by becoming a subscriber. Records go back to 8/2/1971. **$$$**

Property, Taxation Property appraiser records are free at www.qpublic.net/walton/search1.html. Also, search tax collector data free at http://fl-walton-taxcollector.governmaxa.com/collectmax/collect30.asp.

Washington County ***Recorded Documents*** www.washingtonclerk.com/ Also, access an index of recorded documents at www.myfloridacounty.com. Fees involved to order copies; save $1.50 per record by becoming a subscriber. Records go back to 1/2/1981.

Property, Taxation Search the property appraiser sales and tax records for free at www.qpublic.net/washington/index-pa-search.html. Also, search the tax collector records for free at www.qpublic.net/wctc/index-tc-search.html.

Georgia

Capital: Atlanta
Fulton County
Time Zone: EST
Population: 9,919,945
# of Counties: 159

Useful State Links

Website: www.georgia.gov
Governor: http://gov.georgia.gov/
Attorney General: www.law.state.ga.us
State Archives: http://sos.georgia.gov/archives/
State Statutes and Codes: www.flsenate.gov/Laws/Statutes
Legislative Bill Search: www.leg.state.fl.us/
Bill Monitoring: https://www.ciclt.net/sn/clt/gatrack/default.aspx?ClientCode=gatrack
Unclaimed Funds: https://www.etax.dor.ga.gov/unclaimedproperty/main.aspx

State Public Record Agencies

Criminal Records

Georgia Bureau of Investigation, Attn: GCIC, http://gbi.georgia.gov/georgia-crime-information-center The Georgia Technology Authority (GTA) provides an online system called Georgia Felon Search. The search returns the top five closest matches based on the criteria entered. See http://gta.georgia.gov/georgia-felon-search. The search will verify whether individuals have committed and been convicted for felony offenses in the State of Georgia. The fee is $15.00, and ongoing requesters may set up an account. If questions, call 404-463-2300 (note this is a different phone number than listed above). **$$$**

Sexual Offender Registry

Georgia Bureau of Investigations, GCIC - Sexual Offender Registry, http://services.georgia.gov/gbi/gbisor/disclaim.html Records may be searched at http://services.georgia.gov/gbi/gbisor/SORSearch.jsp. Earliest records go back to 07/01/96. Close to 80% of registered offenders have photographs on the web site. Searches may be conducted for sex offenders, absconders, and predators.

Incarceration Records

Georgia Department of Corrections, Inmate Records Office - 6th Fl, East Tower, www.dcor.state.ga.us The website has an extensive array of search capabilities. Click on Find an offender. You can search by the GDC ID, case number, or by name with a variety of personal identifiers. One may search current inmates of those not currently incarcerated.

Corporation, LP, LLP, LLC, Not-for-Profits

Sec of State - Corporation Division, Record Searches, http://sos.georgia.gov/corporations/ Records are available from the corporation database at http://soskb.sos.state.ga.us/corp/soskb/csearch.asp. The corporate database can be searched for free by entity name or registered agent. Other services include name reservation, filing procedures, downloading of forms/applications. Also, search securities companies registered with the state at https://secure.sos.state.ga.us/myverification/. **$$$**

Trademarks/Servicemarks

Secretary of State, Trademark Division, http://sos.georgia.gov/corporations/trademarks.htm A record database is searchable from http://sos.georgia.gov/corporations/marksearch.htm. The DB is updated daily. Pending applications are not listed. Search by registration #, mark name, description, connection, owner, or classification.

Uniform Commercial Code

GA Superior Court Clerks' Cooperative Authority, https://www.gsccca.org/learn/projects-programs/ucc-system Free name searching is available at https://www.gsccca.org/search. Also search by secured party, tax payer ID, date, or file number. In order to view images, ongoing requesters can open a subscription account. There is a monthly charge of $9.95 and a $.25 fee per image for unlimited access to images. Billing is monthly. Requests for certified searches are offered for $10.00 per name. The system is open 24 hours daily. The website also includes searches of the real estate index w/images, lien index, and notary index. Visit https://www.gsccca.org/search. **$$$** *Other Options:* The entire UCC Central Index System can be purchased on a daily, weekly, biweekly basis. For more information, contact the Director's office.

Vital Records

Department of Human Resources, Vital Records Unit, http://health.state.ga.us/programs/vitalrecords/index.asp Records may be ordered online through an approved vendor - www.vitalchek.com. The credit card fee applies. **$$$** *Other Options:* The death index is available for the years 1919-1998 on microfiche for $50.00 or more.

Workers' Compensation Records

State Board of Workers Compensation, http://sbwc.georgia.gov/ Verify is an employer has coverage at https://www.ewccv.com/cvs/.

Driver Records

Department of Driver Services, Driver's Services Section, www.dds.ga.gov Electronic record access is available for insurance, employment, credit, rental car agency and for a Limited Rating Information (LRI) only available to the insurance industry. For each purpose and use, a requester will be assigned a separate user-ID and password. Both the $6.00 three-year history and $8.00 seven-year history are available online. A LRI is $1.70. Requesters must complete several applications and user agreement forms. See https://onlinemvr.dds.ga.gov/mvr/gettingcert.aspx or call 404-463-2300 and ask for Bulk Sales. Also, one may conduct an immediate, free driver's license status check at https://online.dds.ga.gov/DLStatus/default.aspx. **$$$**

Vehicle Ownership & Registration

DOR - Motor Vehicle Division, Research Unit, http://motor.etax.dor.ga.gov/ Online subscription access available to Georgia dealers only; registration is required. **$$$**

Accident Reports

Department of Transportation, GDOT Crash Reporting Unit, www.dot.ga.gov/statistics/CrashData/Pages/default.aspx The agency has outsourced the online purchase of accident reports through a private vendor. See www.buycrash.com. Users can search for their crash reports utilizing a number of search options including their name, date of crash, road of occurrence and VIN. This agency also accepts mail requests, a form is at the web page. The fee for reports will vary between $5.00 and $12.00 depending on the investigating agency that is supplying the report to the DOT. **$$$**

Vessel Ownership & Registration

Georgia Dept of Natural Resources, License and Boat Registration Unit, www.georgiawildlife.com/boating A download of the boat registration information by county or statewide is available on the web. The exact URL is at https://hfwa.centraltechnology.net/gdnr_vrs/downloads/boatData.do. You must have MS Access or Excel. Online files are available for subscribers at https://jc.activeoutdoorsolutions.com/. **$$$**

Voter Registration, Campaign Finance, PACs

Secretary of State - Elections Division, 1104 West Tower, http://sos.georgia.gov/elections/ Name and DOB needed to search unofficial registration information at http://mvp.sos.state.ga.us/. The results will provide address and district-precinct information; no SSNs released. Campaign contribution and disclosure reports are searchable at http://sos.georgia.gov/elections/campaign_disclosures/disclosure.htm. This includes PACs. *Other Options:* Voter Registration CDs, Internet files, disks, and paper lists are available for purchase for non-commercial purposes. For fees go to http://sos.georgia.gov/elections/voter_registration/voter_reg_lists.htm. **$$$**

Occupational Licensing Boards

Accountant-CPA .... https://secure.sos.state.ga.us/myverification/
Acupuncturist .... https://services.georgia.gov/dch/mebs/jsp/index.jsp
Air Conditioning Contractor .... https://secure.sos.state.ga.us/myverification/
Animal Technician, Veterinary .... https://secure.sos.state.ga.us/myverification/
Architect .... https://secure.sos.state.ga.us/myverification/
Athletic Agent .... https://secure.sos.state.ga.us/myverification/
Athletic Trainer .... https://secure.sos.state.ga.us/myverification/
Attorney .... www.gabar.org/membership/membersearch.cfm
Auctioneer/Auction Dealer .... https://secure.sos.state.ga.us/myverification/
Audiologist .... https://secure.sos.state.ga.us/myverification/
Barber/Barber Shop .... https://secure.sos.state.ga.us/myverification/

Cemeteries	https://secure.sos.state.ga.us/SBROrders/
Charity	https://secure.sos.state.ga.us/sbrorders/
Chiropractor	https://secure.sos.state.ga.us/myverification/
Coin-operated Machine	https://gtc.dor.ga.gov/_/#1
Cosmetologist/Cosmetology Shop	https://secure.sos.state.ga.us/myverification/
Counselor	https://secure.sos.state.ga.us/myverification/
Court Reporter	www.georgiacourts.org/agencies/bcr/
Dental Hygienist	https://secure.sos.state.ga.us/myverification/
Dentist	https://secure.sos.state.ga.us/myverification/
Detox Specialist	https://services.georgia.gov/dch/mebs/jsp/index.jsp
Dietitian	https://secure.sos.state.ga.us/myverification/
Drug Whlse/Retail/Mfg (Hospital)	https://secure.sos.state.ga.us/myverification/
Electrical Contractor	https://secure.sos.state.ga.us/myverification/
Embalmer	https://secure.sos.state.ga.us/myverification/
Emergency Medical Technician	https://sendss.state.ga.us/sendss/!ems_lic_query
Engineer	https://secure.sos.state.ga.us/myverification/
Esthetician	https://secure.sos.state.ga.us/myverification/
Family Therapist	https://secure.sos.state.ga.us/myverification/
Financial Statement (Ethics Dept.)	http://media.ethics.ga.gov/Search/Lobbyist/Lobbyist_ByName.aspx
Forester	https://secure.sos.state.ga.us/myverification/
Funeral Director/Apprentice	https://secure.sos.state.ga.us/myverification/
Funeral Establishment	https://secure.sos.state.ga.us/myverification/
Geologist	https://secure.sos.state.ga.us/myverification/
Hearing Aid Dealer/Dispenser	https://secure.sos.state.ga.us/myverification/
Home Inspector	www.gahi.com/FindGAHIInspector.html
Insurance Adjuster	www.gainsurance.org/Agents/AgentStatus.aspx
Insurance Agent/Counselor	www.gainsurance.org/Agents/AgentStatus.aspx
Insurance Company	http://oci.ga.gov/Agents/AgencyStatus.aspx
Insurance Education Providers	www.gainsurance.org/Agents/Home.aspx
Interior Designer	https://secure.sos.state.ga.us/myverification/
Investment Advisor Firm	https://secure.sos.state.ga.us/SBR_Weblookup_Prod/Search.aspx
Landscape Architect	https://secure.sos.state.ga.us/myverification/
Liquor Control	https://gtc.dor.ga.gov/_/#1
Liquor Retailer	https://gtc.dor.ga.gov/_/#1
Lobbyist	http://media.ethics.ga.gov/Search/Lobbyist/Lobbyist_ByName.aspx
Low Voltage Contractor	https://secure.sos.state.ga.us/myverification/
Manicurist	https://secure.sos.state.ga.us/myverification/
Marriage Counselor	https://secure.sos.state.ga.us/myverification/
Motor Fuel Distributor	https://gtc.dor.ga.gov/_/#1
Nail Care	https://secure.sos.state.ga.us/myverification/
Notary Public	http://search.gsccca.org/notary/search.asp
Nuclear Pharmacist	https://secure.sos.state.ga.us/myverification/
Nurse-RN/LPN	http://sos.ga.gov/myverification/
Nursing Home Administrator	https://secure.sos.state.ga.us/myverification/
Occupational Therapist/Assistant	https://secure.sos.state.ga.us/myverification/
Optician, Dispensing	https://secure.sos.state.ga.us/myverification/
Optometrist	https://secure.sos.state.ga.us/myverification/
Osteopathic Physician	https://services.georgia.gov/dch/mebs/jsp/index.jsp
Perfusionist	https://services.georgia.gov/dch/mebs/jsp/index.jsp
Pesticide Applicator	www.kellysolutions.com/ga/Applicators/index.htm
Pesticide Contractor/Employee	http://agr.georgia.gov/pesticide-contractors.aspx
Pharmacist	https://secure.sos.state.ga.us/myverification/
Pharmacy School, Clinic Researcher	https://secure.sos.state.ga.us/myverification/
Physical Therapist/Therapist Asst.	https://secure.sos.state.ga.us/myverification/
Physician Assistant	https://services.georgia.gov/dch/mebs/jsp/index.jsp

Physician Teacher	https://services.georgia.gov/dch/mebs/jsp/index.jsp
Physician/Medical Doctor	https://services.georgia.gov/dch/mebs/jsp/index.jsp
Plumber Journeyman/Contractor	https://secure.sos.state.ga.us/myverification/
Podiatrist	https://secure.sos.state.ga.us/myverification/
Poison Pharmacist	https://secure.sos.state.ga.us/myverification/
Private Investigator	https://secure.sos.state.ga.us/myverification/
Prosthetist	https://services.georgia.gov/dch/mebs/jsp/index.jsp
Psychologist	https://secure.sos.state.ga.us/myverification/
Public Adjuster	www.gainsurance.org/Agents/Home.aspx
Real Estate Agent/Seller/Broker	www.grec.state.ga.us/clsweb/realestate.aspx
Real Estate Appraiser	www.grec.state.ga.us/clsweb/appraiser.aspx
Real Estate Community Assn. Mgr.	www.grec.state.ga.us
Real Estate Firm	www.grec.state.ga.us/clsweb/company.aspx
Rebuilder of Motor Vehicles	https://secure.sos.state.ga.us/myverification/
Respiratory Care Practitioner	https://services.georgia.gov/dch/mebs/jsp/index.jsp
Salvage Pool Operator	https://secure.sos.state.ga.us/myverification/
Salvage Yard Dealer	https://secure.sos.state.ga.us/myverification/
School Librarian	https://secure.sos.state.ga.us/myverification/
Securities Salesperson/Dealer	https://secure.sos.state.ga.us/sbrorders/
Security Guard/Agency	https://secure.sos.state.ga.us/myverification/
Shorthand Court Reporter/Stenomask	www.georgiacourts.org/agencies/bcr/
Social Worker	https://secure.sos.state.ga.us/myverification/
Speech-Language Pathologist	https://secure.sos.state.ga.us/myverification/
Surplus Line Broker	www.gainsurance.org/Agents/AgentStatus.aspx
Surveyor, Land	https://secure.sos.state.ga.us/myverification/
Teacher	www.gapsc.com/Certification/Lookup.aspx
Tobacco Seller	https://gtc.dor.ga.gov/_/#1
Used Car Dealer	https://secure.sos.state.ga.us/myverification/
Used Car Parts Dist.	https://secure.sos.state.ga.us/myverification/
Utility Contractor	https://secure.sos.state.ga.us/myverification/
Veterinarian/Veterinary Technician	https://secure.sos.state.ga.us/myverification/
Waste Water Lab Analyst	https://secure.sos.state.ga.us/myverification/
Waste Water System Operator	https://secure.sos.state.ga.us/myverification/
Wastewater Collection System Operator	https://secure.sos.state.ga.us/myverification/
Wastewater Industrial	https://secure.sos.state.ga.us/myverification/
Water Distribution System Operator	https://secure.sos.state.ga.us/myverification/
Water Laboratory Operator	https://secure.sos.state.ga.us/myverification/
Water Operator Class 1-4	https://secure.sos.state.ga.us/myverification/

State and Local Courts

State Court Structure: The Georgia court system has five classes of trial-level courts: the Magistrate, Probate, Juvenile, State, and Superior courts. In addition, there are approximately 370 municipal courts operating locally. The **Superior Court**, arranged in 49 circuits, is the court of general jurisdiction. It has exclusive, constitutional authority over felony cases, divorce, equity and cases regarding title to land. The Superior Court will also assume the role of a **State Court** if the county does not have one. **State Courts** exercise limited jurisdiction within one county. These judges hear misdemeanors including traffic violations, issue search and arrest warrants, hold preliminary hearings in criminal cases and try civil matters not reserved exclusively for the Superior Courts.

Magistrate Courts have jurisdiction for bad checks, arrest warrants, preliminary hearings, and county ordinance violations and can also issue arrest warrants and set bond on all felonies. The Magistrate Court has jurisdiction over civil actions under $15,000, also one type of misdemeanor related to passing bad checks. Two counties (Bibb and Richmond) have Civil/Magistrate courts with varied civil limits.

Municipal Courts try municipal ordinance violations, issue criminal warrants, conduct preliminary hearings, and may have concurrent jurisdiction over shoplifting cases and cases involving possession of one ounce or less of marijuana.

The jurisdiction of **Juvenile Courts** extends to delinquent children under the age of 17 and deprived or unruly children under the age of 18. Juvenile courts have concurrent jurisdiction with Superior Courts in cases involving capital felonies, custody and child support cases, and in proceedings to terminate parental rights. The Juvenile Court also has jurisdiction over minors committing traffic violations or enlisting in the military services, consent to marriage for minors, and cases involving the Interstate Compact on Juveniles. Note the Superior Courts have original jurisdiction over those juveniles who commit certain serious felonies.

Probate Courts can, in certain jurisdictions, issue search and arrest warrants, and hear miscellaneous misdemeanors, or local ordinance violations.

Appellate Courts: Opinions and summaries are available from the web page at www.gasupreme.us.

About Court Online Access: There is no statewide online access available. Less than 15% of the trial courts offer online access to court docket data.

County Sites:

Bibb County

Superior Court www.co.bibb.ga.us/superiorcourtclerk/superiorcourtclerk.aspx

Civil: A subscription service is offered at https://bibbclerkindexsearch.com/external/User/Login.aspx?ReturnUrl=%2fexternal%2findex.aspx. Fee is $299.40 for a year, $24.95 for one month, or $7.95 per day. Includes civil and criminal. In general, images are avail Court calendars online at www.co.bibb.ga.us/CalendarDirectory/CalendarDirectory.asp.**$$$** *Criminal:* same Search the District Attorney's criminal case index at www.co.bibb.ga.us/da/criminalcases/. The Superior court calendars are at www.co.bibb.ga.us/CalendarDirectory/CalendarDirectory.asp. **$$$**

State Court www.co.bibb.ga.us/StateCourt/StateCourt.aspx

Civil: Search civil court calendars online at www.co.bibb.ga.us/StateCourtClerk/Civil/Default.htm. Website hopes to have access to full court record indexes in the future. *Criminal:* Search the State Court criminal docket at www.co.bibb.ga.us/StateCourt/StateCourt.aspx. Also, search the District Attorney's criminal case index at www.co.bibb.ga.us/da/criminalcases/.

Civil & Magistrate Court www.co.bibb.ga.us/magcourtcivil/Default.aspx

Civil: Access the index at www.co.bibb.ga.us/magcourtcivil/cmcasesearch.aspx. Search by name or case number back to 1980.

Bryan County

Superior & State Court www.bryancountyga.org/

Civil: The civil index is searchable at http://74.93.54.101/publiccmsearch/. No images provided. *Criminal:* The criminal index is searchable at http://74.93.54.101/publiccmsearch/. No images provided.

Chatham County

Superior Court www.chathamcourts.org/SuperiorCourt.aspx

Civil: Search county civil dockets and cases free at www.chathamcourts.org/Home.aspx. *Criminal:* Search county criminal dockets and cases free at www.chathamcourts.org/Home.aspx.

State Court www.chathamcourts.org/StateCourt.aspx

Civil: Search county civil dockets and cases free at www.chathamcourts.org/Home.aspx. Two systems are offered. *Criminal:* Search county criminal dockets and cases free at www.chathamcourts.org/Home.aspx. Two systems are offered.

Calhoun County

Superior Court www.calhouncourtclerk.com/

Civil: Court civil calendars by month available at the website.

Chatham County

Superior & State Court www.chathamcourts.org/SuperiorCourt.aspx

Civil: Search county civil dockets and cases free at www.chathamcourts.org/Home.aspx. *Criminal:* Search county criminal dockets and cases free at www.chathamcourts.org/Home.aspx.

Clarke County

Superior & State Court www.athensclarkecounty.com/index.aspx?nid=324

Civil: Public access available to the docket from the home page. *Criminal:* same

Clayton County

Superior Court www.claytoncountyga.gov/courts/clerk-of-superior-court.aspx

Civil: Online access is the same as criminal, see below. *Criminal:* Search records free at www.claytoncountyga.gov/courts/court-case-inquiry.aspx. Court calendars at www.claytoncountyga.gov/courts/court-calendars.aspx. Searches and records also available on the statewide system.

State Court www.claytoncountyga.gov/courts/clerk-of-state-court.aspx

Criminal: Search criminal database by name or case at http://weba.co.clayton.ga.us/casinqsvr/htdocs/index.shtml. Results shows year of birth. Index goes back to 1999.

Cobb County

Superior Court www.cobbsuperiorcourtclerk.com

Civil: Civil indexes and images from Clerk of Superior Court are free at www.cobbsuperiorcourtclerk.org/courts/Civil.htm. Search by name, type or case number. Data updated Fridays. Images go back thru 2004. *Criminal:* Criminal indexes and images from Clerk of Superior Court are free at www.cobbsuperiorcourtclerk.org/courts/Criminal.htm. Search by name, type or case number. Data updated Fridays but indexing can be nearly a month behind.

Coweta County

Superior Court www.coweta.ga.us/Index.aspx?page=199

Civil: Access court records free online at http://sccweb.coweta.ga.us/cmwebsearchppp/. *Criminal:* same

State Court www.coweta.ga.us/Index.aspx?page=197

Civil: Online access to index provided at www.coweta.ga.us/Index.aspx?page=1301. View case dockets by entering the case number, party's name, and/or CSE number. *Criminal:* Online access to index provided at www.coweta.ga.us/Index.aspx?page=1301. Includes traffic. View case dockets by entering the case number, party's name, and/or CSE number.

Dade County

Superior Court www.dadegaclerkofcourt.com/

Civil: The court provides access to docket information at www.dadesuperiorcourt.com/webFormFrame.aspx?page=main. Also, the home page provides case calendars. *Criminal:* same

De Kalb County

Superior Court www.co.dekalb.ga.us/superior/index.htm

Civil: Online access is free at www.ojs.dekalbga.org. *Criminal:* Online access is free at www.ojs.dekalbga.org. Jail and inmate records are also available.

State Court http://web.co.dekalb.ga.us/StateCourt/index.html

Civil: Online access is free at www.ojs.dekalbga.org. Also, current court calendars free at www.dekalbstatecourt.net. *Criminal:* Online access is free at www.ojs.dekalbga.org. Jail and inmate records also available. Also, current court calendars free at www.dekalbstatecourt.net.

Dodge County

Superior Court www.dodgeclerkofcourt.com/

Criminal: There is a subscription service offered for online access, however this is only made available to attorneys. The fee is 3140 per year. Please call the Clerk's office for details.**$$$**

Fayette County

Superior & State Court www.fayetteclerk.com/

Civil: Search dockets free at www.fayetteclerkofcourt.com/webFormFrame.aspx?page=main. *Criminal:* same

Fulton County

Superior Court - Civil www.fcclk.org

Civil: Access Clerk of Superior Court Judicial civil records free at www.fcclkjudicialsearch.org/CivilSearch/civfrmd.htm. Search by either party name, case number, and date range. Search includes status, attorney. Images provided. Also a Hearing Search free at www.fcclkjudicialsearch.org/judicialsearch/CVHearSearch/cvhearfrmd.htm.

Gwinnett County

Superior & State Court www.gwinnettcourts.com/

Civil: Online access to court case index is free at www.gwinnettcourts.com/home.asp#partycasesearch/. Search by name or case number. *Criminal:* same

Harris County

Superior Court www.harrisclerkofcourt.com/

Civil: Access court records by subscription; for information and signup contact Lisa Culpeper at 706-628-4944. **$$$** *Criminal:* same**$ $$**

Henry County

Superior Court www.co.henry.ga.us/SuperiorCourt/index.shtml

Civil: The court provides a free docket search at https://hcwebb.boca.co.henry.ga.us/SuperiorCMWebSearch/. Search by name or case number, or associated party. The DOB is not shown, it is hard to identify common names if used for a specific name search. *Criminal:* The court provides a free docket search at https://hcwebb.boca.co.henry.ga.us/SuperiorCMWebSearch/. Search by name or case number.

Liberty County

Superior & State Court www.libertyco.com

Civil: The docket index is available for no charges, includes magistrate records as well. Go the home page and click on Docket Search. Record available from 1986 forward. Search by case number or party name. *Criminal:* Online access same as described for criminal. Some entries have DOB, usually are traffic.

Madison County

Superior Court www.madisonclerkofcourt.com/

Civil: Search the docket index at www.madisonsuperiorcourt.com/webFormFrame.aspx?page=main, records go to 1998. *Criminal:* Search the criminal docket index at www.madisonsuperiorcourt.com/webFormFrame.aspx?page=main, records go to 1998.

Muscogee County

Superior & State Court www.muscogeecourts.com

Civil: Current dockets in pdf format are free at www.muscogeecourts.com. There is no historical data available online. *Criminal:* same

Richmond County

Superior Court www.augustaga.gov/index.aspx?nid=804

Civil: Access court index free at www.augustaga.gov/index.aspx?NID=421 for records 2001 forward. *Criminal:* Access court index free at www.augustaga.gov/index.aspx?NID=421 for records 2001 forward.

State Court www.augustaga.gov/index.aspx?nid=818

Civil: Name search civil dockets free at www.augustaga.gov/index.aspx?NID=421. *Criminal:* Name search of misdemeanor cases is free at www.augustaga.gov/index.aspx?NID=421.

Walker County

Superior & State Court

Civil: Access to civil records for free go to http://walker.gaclerkofcourt.net/webFormFrame.aspx?page=main. *Criminal:* Access to criminal records for free to go http://walker.gaclerkofcourt.net/webFormFrame.aspx?page=main.

Recorders, Assessors, and Other Sites of Note

Recording Office Organization: 159 counties, 159 recording offices. The recording officer is the Clerk of Superior Court. All transactions are recorded in a "General Execution Docket." All tax liens on personal property filed with the county Clerk of Superior Court in a "General Execution Docket" (grantor/grantee) or "Lien Index."

Statewide or Multi-Jurisdiction Access: The first two sites below provide data for all counties.

1. The Georgia Superior Court Clerk's Cooperative Authority (GSCCCA) at https://www.gsccca.org/search offers free access to certain recorded documents for all Georgia counties. The Real Estate Index contains property transactions from all counties since January 1, 1999. There are both free and Premium (pay) services offered. The Lien Index includes liens filed on real and personal property. Throughout varies, but is generally from January 10, 2002. The UCC Index contains financing statement data from all counties since January, 1995 and can be searched by name, taxpayer ID, file date and file number. Additionally, the actual image of the corresponding UCC statement can be downloaded for a fee. Visit the GSCCCA website for details.
2. Basic assessor and property records are available free via www.gaassessors.com for all Georgia counties for parcel data, tax digest data, and GIS maps.
3. At http://qpublic.net/ga county parcel data is available either as a free service (limited data) or through a subscription service (all available features). An example of what data is available by subscription is available at their web page. Also see the web page for the counties currently involved.

County Sites Other Than the Two Statewide Sites Mentioned Above (#1 and #2)

Baldwin County ***Property, Taxation Records*** Property searching available free at http://baldwinta.com/ or www.qpublic.net/ga/baldwin/.

Bartow County ***Property, Taxation Records*** Access to property assessment data for free at www.qpublic.net/ga/bartow/. Also, access to GIS/mapping free at www.bartowmaps.org/taxdata/maps.asp.

Bibb County ***Property, Taxation Records*** Free property records search at www.co.bibb.ga.us/TaxAssessors/index1.html. Also, search for property ownership for free at www.co.bibb.ga.us/engineering/property/search.htm. Also, Ad Valorem tax statements at www.co.bibb.ga.us/TaxBills/Searchpage.asp.

Chatham County ***Property, Taxation Records*** Search the assessor database for property sales for free at http://propertysales.chathamcounty.org/

Cherokee County ***Recorded Documents*** www.cherokeega.com See www.gsccca.org/search/ for Deed, Lien and UCC indexes. Also, access recording records free at http://deeds.cherokeega.com/Search.aspx.

Property, Taxation Records Free property records search from the Tax Assessor's Database at http://taxassessor.cherokeega.com/taxnet/ Also, access to property records for free at www.qpublic.net/ga/cherokee/. For more detailed information must subscribe for a fee. **$$$**

Clayton County ***Property, Taxation Records*** Search search property card index free at http://weba.co.clayton.ga.us/cluserver/htdocs/index.shtml. Access to real property and personal property records free at www.claytoncountyga.gov/departments/tax-assessor/property-search-information.aspx.

Cobb County ***Recorded Documents*** www.cobbsuperiorcourtclerk.org/index.htm Property records on the County Superior Court Clerk website are free at www.cobbsuperiorcourtclerk.org/home.asp. Search by name, address, land description, instrument type, or book & page; includes court records. Also, see www.gsccca.org/search/ for online access to Deed, Plat and UCC indexes.
Property, Taxation Records Property tax records search for free at www.cobbtax.org/Forms/HtmlFrame.aspx?mode=content/mainpage_taxes.htm. Also, search for parcel data on the GIS-mapping site free at http://portal.cobbcountyga.gov/index.php?option=com_content&view=article&id=29&Itemid=94. Also, property appraisal search and tax maps free at www.cobbassessor.org/Main/Home.aspx.

Crawford County ***Property, Taxation Records*** Access GIS-mapping system free at www.crawfordcountyga.org/site/index.php?cID=88. Also, access to property records free at www.qpublic.net/ga/crawford/.

Dade County ***Recorded Documents*** www.dadegaclerkofcourt.com Attorney access to clerk records is available at www.dadeclerkofcourt.com for a fee. Contact Kathy D Page for more information. Calendars are also available for no fee. **$$$**

De Kalb County ***Property, Taxation Records*** Search real estate data for free at http://web.co.dekalb.ga.us/PropertyAppraisal/realSearch.asp. Also, access to property appraisal searches for free at www.qpublic.net/ga/dekalb/.

Dougherty County ***Recorded Documents*** www.albany.ga.us/content/1800/2887/2985/default.aspx Access to the clerk of courts Dept. of Deeds public menu is at www.albany.ga.us/content/1800/2889/3011/3506/default.aspx. Click on "Real Estate." Also, see www.gsccca.org/search/ for online access to Deed and UCC indexes.

Douglas County ***Property, Taxation Records*** Access property data and gis-mapping free at http://douglas.binarybus.com/. Access to parcel data search for free at www.qpublic.net/ga/douglas/.

Effingham County ***Property, Taxation Records*** Access assessor and parcel records free at www.effinghamcounty.org/. Access to GIS/mapping free at www.effinghamcounty.org/Departments/GIS/CountyMaps/tabid/1573/Default.aspx.

Fayette County ***Recorded Documents*** www.fayetteclerk.com Search by name or instrument number for various records free at http://fccottweb.fayettecountyga.gov/external/LandRecords/protected/SrchQuickName.aspx.
Property, Taxation Records Records on the County Assessor database are free on the GIS-mapping site at www.fayettecountymaps.com/.

Floyd County ***Property, Taxation Records*** Access property data via the GIS-mapping site free at http://gis.romega.us/app/. Also, access database free at www.qpublic.net/ga/floyd/. Subscription available for advanced searches and advanced parcel searches for a fee.**$$$**

Forsyth County ***Recorded Documents*** www.forsythclerk.com/ See www.gsccca.org/search/ for free access to Deeds back to 1999, Liens back to 2004, and UCCs back to 1995, plats back to 2004. Also, search land records, liens, plats, and trade names free at http://resolution.forsythco.com/.

Glynn County ***Property, Taxation Records*** Access the county assessor property tax records free on the GIS mapping site at http://glynn.binarybus.com. A subscription service also available with deeper data.**$$$**

Gordon County ***Property, Taxation Records*** Access property data free at http://gordon.binarybus.com/lookup/. Also, search property tax payment database free at https://gordon.paytaxes.net//customer/enhanced_property_tax_search.php.

Gwinnett County ***Property, Taxation Records*** Access to GIS/mapping for free at www.gwinnettassessor.manatron.com/IWantTo/PropertyGISSearch.aspx.

Habersham County ***Property, Taxation Records*** Search property/GIS data free at www.emapsplus.com/GAHabersham/maps/. Click on Owner to name search. Also, access to property records for free at www.qpublic.net/ga/habersham/.

Hall County ***Property, Taxation Records*** Access property data free on the GIS site at http://gis1.hallcounty.org/Public/PublicRedirect/default.htm. Also, access to property records for free at www.qpublic.net/ga/hall/.

Henry County ***Recorded Documents*** www.co.henry.ga.us/SuperiorCourt/ See www.gsccca.org/search/ for free access to Deeds back to 1999, Liens back to 2004, and UCCs back to 1995, plats back to 2004.
Property, Taxation Records Search property tax data free at www.qpublic.net/ga/henry/.

Houston County ***Recorded Documents*** www.houstoncountyga.com/government/houston-county-superior-court.aspx See www.gsccca.org/search/ for free access to Deeds back to 1999, Liens back to 2004, and UCCs back to 1995, plats back to 2004. Also, the clerks recording indices of plats, land records, liens is free at http://70.166.66.197/resolution/. Pre-1998 real estate and pre-1994 financing statements are also available.

Jasper County ***Property, Taxation Records*** Access Property Records free at www.jaspercountyboa.org/ click on Search Records. Also, access to property records for free at www.qpublic.net/ga/jasper/.

Madison County ***Recorded Documents*** www.madisonclerkofcourt.com/ See www.gsccca.org/search/ for free access to Deeds back to 1999, Liens back to 2004, and UCCs back to 1995, plats back to 2004. Also, access to records free at www.madisonsuperiorcourt.com/webFormFrame.aspx?page=main.

Property, Taxation Records Access assessor property data free at www.qpublic.net/ga/madison/. Also, search tax bill data free at https://madison.paytaxes.net/customer/enhanced_property_tax_search.php.

Muscogee County ***Recorded Documents*** www.muscogeecourts.com/ See www.gsccca.org/search/ for Deed, Lien and UCC indexes.

Property, Taxation Records Access assessor property records free at http://ccga1.columbusga.org/PropertyInformation.nsf/.

Peach County ***Property, Taxation Records*** Subscribe to the GIS-mapping site for property data at www.peachcountymaps.com/. For registration and password, contact the Tax Office at 478-825-5924. **$$$**

Pickens County ***Property, Taxation Records*** Access assessor property records free at www.qpublic.net/ga/pickens/. Also, access records on the mapping site free at www.tscmaps.com/mg/ga/pickens/index.asp.

Richmond County (Augusta-Richmond) ***Property, Taxation Records*** Access GIS Maps at http://gisweb.augustaga.gov/gisweb/default.aspx. Access Real Estate Property Search System at http://mapweb.augustaga.gov/augusta/. Search parcels by owner name, address, subdivision, and parcel number. Also, access records for free at www.qpublic.net/ga/richmond/

Troup County ***Property, Taxation Records*** Troup County property records for free (limited data) at www.qpublic.net/ga/troup/. For more detailed information must subscribe for a fee. Also, access to property records free at http://property.troupcountyga.org/.**$ $$**

Walton County ***Property, Taxation Records*** Search property tax data at www.waltoncountytax.com/taxSearch. Access county maps free at www.georgiagis.com/walton/. Also, access to property search data free at www.qpublic.net/ga/walton/. For more detailed information must subscribe for a fee. **$$$**

Warren County ***Property, Taxation Records*** Access assessor property records free at www.qpublic.net/ga/warren/. Also, access assessor parcel data free on the Central Savannah River Area GIS site at www.csrardc.org/. Click on Search then County then choose Warren.

Whitfield County ***Recorded Documents*** www.whitfieldcountyga.com/coc/clerk.htm See www.gsccca.org/search/ for free access to Deeds back to 1999, Liens back to 2004, and UCCs back to 1995, plats back to 2004. Also, access to deeds, plats, etc free at http://whitfieldmst.whitfieldcountyga.com:8085/searchext/

Property, Taxation Records Access to property tax data is available free at www.whitfieldcountyga.com/Indexgis.htm. A subscription service is also available for professions requiring full property data. **$$$**

Hawaii

Capital: Honolulu
Honolulu County
Time Zone: HT
Population: 1,595,728
# of Counties: 4

Useful State Links

Website: http://portal.ehawaii.gov
Governor: http://governor.hawaii.gov
Attorney General: http://ag.hawaii.gov
State Archives: http://ags.hawaii.gov/archives
State Statutes and Codes: http://hawaii.gov/lrb/
Legislative Bill Search: www.capitol.hawaii.gov
Unclaimed Funds: https://www.ehawaii.gov/lilo/app

State Public Record Agencies

Criminal Records

Hawaii Criminal Justice Data Center, Criminal Record Request, http://ag.hawaii.gov/hcjdc/ Online access is available at eCrim at https://ecrim.ehawaii.gov/ahewa/. There is no fee to view the results of your search; the option is available to purchase a certified copy of the record for $15.00. However, in the future there will be a $5.00 fee per search for criminal records on eCrim. An implementation date has yet to be set due to a technical delay. Registration is required. Questions are directed to 808-587-4220. The same content is offered on public access terminals at five local police stations WITH exception that the online does not allow a SSN search, but the on-site locations do. **$$$** *Other Options:* A Bulk Criminal Data Download is available for $24,000/year. There is a minimum one year subscription. See http://portal.ehawaii.gov/subscriber-services.html.

Sexual Offender Registry

Hawaii Criminal Justice Data Center, Sexual Offender Registry, http://sexoffenders.ehawaii.gov/sexoffender/welcome.html Search at http://sexoffenders.ehawaii.gov/sexoffender/search.html. Search by name, street or ZIP Code. *Other Options:* Download all sex offender data for the state of Hawai'i. for $600. Contact the office above.

Incarceration Records

Hawaii Department of Public Safety, Inmate Classification, http://dps.hawaii.gov/about/divisions/corrections/ The inmate locator is outsourced to a vendor service - see https://www.vinelink.com/vinelink/siteInfoAction.do?siteId=50000.

Corporation, LP, LLC, LLP, Trade Name, Assumed Name, Trademarks/Servicemarks

Dept of Commerce and Consumer Affairs, Business Registration Division, http://hawaii.gov/dcca/breg Online access to business names is available at http://hawaii.gov/dcca/breg/online/. There are no fees, the system is open 24 hours. For assistance during business hours, call 808-586-2727. One can also search to see if business qualifies for a Good Standing report. Tax license searching is free at https://dotax.ehawaii.gov/tls/app. Search by name, ID number of DBA name. PDF copies may be purchased for $3.00. Thru the web page at business.ehawaii.gov, the agency provides a Mobile App to search a business name, find information or purchase filed documents. Use your device and the website will display a Mobile App version. *Other Options:* Bulk data can be purchased online through http://ehawaiigov.com/. The List Builder program allows one to build a customized list of registered businesses. Visit the website or call 808-587-4220 for more information.

Uniform Commercial Code, Federal & State Tax Liens, Real Estate Recordings

UCC Division, Bureau of Conveyances, http://dlnr.hawaii.gov/boc/ All of the available searches and images from this agency are available at http://dlnr.hawaii.gov/boc/online-services/. Search the all the indices from 1976 forward by grantor, grantee, business name. Includes real estate recordings. However, this system may be temporarily closed for UCC filings. A temporary site has been set up at www.iaca.org/secured-transactions/forms/. However, this system may be temporarily closed for UCC filings.

Birth Certificates

State Department of Health, Vital Records Section, http://hawaii.gov/health/vital-records/ Requests may also be placed for birth and marriage certificates on a limited basis through https://www.ehawaii.gov/doh/vitrec/exe/vitrec.cgi. There is an additional $1.50 fee for requests made through the Internet, use of a credit card is required. **$$$**

Marriage Certificates

State Department of Health, Vital Records Section, http://hawaii.gov/health/vital-records/ Requests may be placed for birth and marriage certificates on a limited basis through the Internet at https://www.ehawaii.gov/doh/vitrec/exe/vitrec.cgi. Results are mailed. There is an additional $1.50 fee for requests made through the Internet, use of a credit card is required. **$$$**

Driver Records

Traffic Violations Bureau, Driving Records, www.courts.state.hi.us/ Online ordering by DPPA complaint requesters is available from the state-designated entity - Hawaii Information Consortium (HIC). The record fee is $23.00 per record plus a $75.00 annual subscription fee is required. Record requests are accepted via FTP. Results, if clear, are returned via FTP. Results with hits on convictions on the record are returned on paper. Visit their website at www.ehawaii.gov/dakine/docs/subscription.html or call HIC at 808-695-4620 for more information. Name checks of traffic court records may be ordered from the court. **$$$** *Other Options:* HIC offers a driver monitoring program. The fee is $.15 per driver per month. Call 808-695-4620 or 4624 for further details.

Vessel Ownership & Registration

Land & Natural Resources, Division of Boating & Recreation, http://hawaii.gov/dlnr/dbor/dbor.html Go to http://hawaii.gov/dlnr/dbor/, click on DOBOR On-line Registration System, and at ensuing page click on Public Search tab to view registration data. Search by vessel name, hull number or vessel number. A name search is not offered.

Campaign Finance

Campaign Spending Commission, 235 S. Beretania Street, Room 300, http://hawaii.gov/campaign/ Campaign spending reports for all candidate committees and PACS are viewable at http://hawaii.gov/campaign/. This includes enforcement reports and court rulings. Also see the State Ethics Commission at http://hawaii.gov/ethics/findisc.

Financial Disclosures, Lobbyists

State Ethics Commission, 1001 Bishop Street, Suite 970, http://hawaii.gov/campaign/ Financial disclosures are found at http://hawaii.gov/ethics/findisc. Gift disclosures are found at http://hawaii.gov/ethics/giftdisc. Lobbyist filings are found at http://hawaii.gov/ethics/lobby.

Occupational Licensing Boards

Accountant-CPA/PA.................................... http://pvl.ehawaii.gov/pvlsearch/app
Acupuncturist .... http://pvl.ehawaii.gov/pvlsearch/app
Architect/Landscape Architect .... http://pvl.ehawaii.gov/pvlsearch/app
Attorney... www.hsba.org/Find_a_lawyer.aspx
Auction .... http://pvl.ehawaii.gov/pvlsearch/app
Bank/Bank Agency/Office .... http://hawaii.gov/dcca/dfi/regulate/regulate/
Barber Shop .... http://pvl.ehawaii.gov/pvlsearch/app
Barber/Barber Apprentice .... http://pvl.ehawaii.gov/pvlsearch/app
Boxer... http://pvl.ehawaii.gov/pvlsearch/app
Cemetery... http://pvl.ehawaii.gov/pvlsearch/app
Chiropractor .... http://pvl.ehawaii.gov/pvlsearch/app
Collection Agency .... http://pvl.ehawaii.gov/pvlsearch/app
Condominium Hotel Operator .... http://insurance.ehawaii.gov/ils/app
Condominium Managing Agent................... http://insurance.ehawaii.gov/ils/app
Contractor .... http://pvl.ehawaii.gov/pvlsearch/app
Cosmetologist/School/Shop/Instructor......... http://pvl.ehawaii.gov/pvlsearch/app
Credit Union .... http://hawaii.gov/dcca/dfi/regulate/regulate/
Dental Hygienist... http://pvl.ehawaii.gov/pvlsearch/app
Dentist... http://pvl.ehawaii.gov/pvlsearch/app

Elected Officials Financial Disclosure	http://hawaii.gov/ethics/findisc
Electrician	http://pvl.ehawaii.gov/pvlsearch/app
Electrologist	http://pvl.ehawaii.gov/pvlsearch/app
Emergency Medical Personnel	http://pvl.ehawaii.gov/pvlsearch/app
Employment Agency	http://pvl.ehawaii.gov/pvlsearch/app
Engineer	http://pvl.ehawaii.gov/pvlsearch/app
Escrow Company	http://hawaii.gov/dcca/dfi/regulate/regulate/
Financial Services Loan Company	http://hawaii.gov/dcca/dfi/regulate/regulate/
Guard/Agency	http://pvl.ehawaii.gov/pvlsearch/app
Hearing Aid Dealer/Fitter	http://pvl.ehawaii.gov/pvlsearch/app
Insurance Adjuster/Agent/Producer/Solicitor	http://insurance.ehawaii.gov/ils/app
Lobbyist	http://hawaii.gov/ethics/lobby
Marriage & Family Therapist	http://pvl.ehawaii.gov/pvlsearch/app
Massage Therapist/Establishment	http://pvl.ehawaii.gov/pvlsearch/app
Mechanic	http://pvl.ehawaii.gov/pvlsearch/app
Mortgage Broker/Solicitor	http://pvl.ehawaii.gov/pvlsearch/app
Motor Vehicle Dealer/Broker/Repair	http://pvl.ehawaii.gov/pvlsearch/app
Naturopathic Physician	http://pvl.ehawaii.gov/pvlsearch/app
Nurse/RN/LPN/Aide	http://pvl.ehawaii.gov/pvlsearch/app
Nursing Home Administrator	http://pvl.ehawaii.gov/pvlsearch/app
Occupational Therapist	http://pvl.ehawaii.gov/pvlsearch/app
Optician, Dispensing	http://pvl.ehawaii.gov/pvlsearch/app
Optometrist	http://pvl.ehawaii.gov/pvlsearch/app
Osteopathic Physician	http://pvl.ehawaii.gov/pvlsearch/app
Pest Control Field Rep/Operator	http://pvl.ehawaii.gov/pvlsearch/app
Pesticide Dealer/Product	http://hdoa.hawaii.gov/pi/pest/
Pharmacist/Pharmacy	http://pvl.ehawaii.gov/pvlsearch/app
Physical Therapist	http://pvl.ehawaii.gov/pvlsearch/app
Physician/Medical Doctor/Assistant	http://pvl.ehawaii.gov/pvlsearch/app
Pilot, Port	http://pvl.ehawaii.gov/pvlsearch/app
Plumber	http://pvl.ehawaii.gov/pvlsearch/app
Podiatrist	http://pvl.ehawaii.gov/pvlsearch/app
Private Investigator/Agency	http://pvl.ehawaii.gov/pvlsearch/app
Psychologist	http://pvl.ehawaii.gov/pvlsearch/app
Real Estate Agent/Broker/Sales	http://insurance.ehawaii.gov/ils/app
Real Estate Appraiser	http://pvl.ehawaii.gov/pvlsearch/app
Savings & Loan Association	http://hawaii.gov/dcca/dfi/regulate/regulate/
Savings Bank	http://hawaii.gov/dcca/dfi/regulate/regulate/
Social Worker	http://pvl.ehawaii.gov/pvlsearch/app
Speech Pathologist/Audiologist	http://pvl.ehawaii.gov/pvlsearch/app
Tattoo Artist/Tattoo Shop	http://hawaii.gov/health/environmental/sanitation/tattoo.html
Timeshare	http://pvl.ehawaii.gov/pvlsearch/app
Travel Agency	http://pvl.ehawaii.gov/pvlsearch/app
Trust Company	http://hawaii.gov/dcca/dfi/regulate/regulate/
Veterinarian	http://pvl.ehawaii.gov/pvlsearch/app

State and Local Courts

State Court Structure: Hawaii's trial level is comprised of **Circuit Courts** (includes Family Courts) and **District Courts**. These trial courts function in four judicial circuits: First (Oahu), Second (Maui-Molokai-Lanai), Third (Hawaii County), and Fifth (Kauai-Niihau). The Fourth Circuit was merged with the Third in 1943.

Circuit Courts are general jurisdiction and handle all jury trials, felony cases, and civil cases over $25,000, also probate and guardianship. There is con-current jurisdiction with District Courts in civil non-jury cases that specify amounts between $10,000-

$25,000.The District Court handles criminal cases punishable by a fine and/or less than one year imprisonment, landlord/tenant, traffic, DUI cases, civil cases up to $25,000, and small claims ($5,000 limit). The Family Court Division rules in all legal matters involving children, such as delinquency, waiver, status offenses, abuse and neglect, termination of parental rights, adoption, guardianships and detention. Also hears traditional domestic-relations cases, including divorce, nonsupport, paternity, uniform child custody jurisdiction cases and miscellaneous custody matters.

Appellate Courts: One may view opinions and decisions from the Supreme & Appeals courts at www.courts.state.hi.us.

Statewide Court Online Access: There are two free online access systems. Click on "Search Court Records" at www.courts.state.hi.us then follow the instructions below.

- Click on *Ho'Ohiki*. This page offers civil and criminal case information from the Circuit and Family Courts and certain civil information in the District Courts. Search by name or case number. Most courts offer access back to mid 1980s. A list by Circuit and type of record is found at www.state.hi.us/jud/pdf/hoohiki_data_content.pdf.
- Traffic records are available online, click on *eCourt Kokua* at the home page. This system also provides access to case information from the Hawaii Intermediate Court of Appeals, and the Hawaii Supreme Court. Note that juvenile traffic records are not available online.

There are no additional county sites for court records other than mentioned above.

Recorder and Assessor

Recording Office Organization: All UCC financing statements, tax liens, and real estate documents are filed centrally with the Bureau of Conveyances at http://hawaii.gov/dlnr/boc located in Honolulu. Details of searching below.

Statewide (All Counties) Access:

Records of recorded are available for either searching or downloading in bulk on the Bureau of Conveyances (http://hawaii.gov/dlnr/boc) statewide system at https://boc.ehawaii.gov/docsearch/nameSearch.html. Records are generally available from 1976 forward. Certified document copies may also be ordered. **$$$**

Other Sites (not mentioned above):

Hawaii County ***Property, Taxation Records*** Access to property tax data for free at www.hawaiipropertytax.com/Main/Home.aspx. Click on the Property Search tab. There are no name searches. Access to TMK and Subdivision Maps is free at www.hawaiicounty.gov/rpt-tmk-sub.

Honolulu County ***Property, Taxation Records*** Access to real property assessment and tax billing info free at www.honolulupropertytax.com/Main/Home.aspx. Click on the Property Search tab. There is no name searches.

Kauai County ***Property, Taxation Records*** Access to property search data for free at www.qpublic.net/hi/kauai/. Must register. Access to property tax data for free at www.hawaiipropertytax.com/Main/Home.aspx. Click on the Property Search tab. There are no name searches

Maui County ***Property, Taxation Records*** To see real property tax assessments free at www.mauipropertytax.com/. Search by location address, name, parcel number and map, also included sales search and list. Also, access to tax map images free at www.mauicounty.gov/index.aspx?NID=757. Access to parcel related data downloadable extracts from www.co.maui.hi.us/index.aspx?nid=1032.

Idaho

Capital: Boise
Ada County
Time Zone: MST

Idaho's ten northwestern-most counties are PST:
They are: Benewah, Bonner, Boundary, Clearwater, Idaho, Kootenai, Latah, Lewis, Nez Perce, Shoshone.

Population: 1,499,402
# of Counties: 44

Useful State Links

Website: www.idaho.gov/
Governor: http://gov.idaho.gov
Attorney General: www.ag.idaho.gov/index.html
State Archives: http://history.idaho.gov/idaho-state-archives
State Statutes and Codes: www.legislature.idaho.gov/statutesrules.htm
Legislative Bill Search: www.legislature.idaho.gov
Unclaimed Funds: http://tax.idaho.gov/ucp_search_idaho.htm

State Public Record Agencies

Sexual Offender Registry

State Repository, Central Sexual Offender Registry, http://isp.idaho.gov/sor_id/ Search records at http://isp.idaho.gov/sor_id/search.html. Inquires can be made by name, address, or by county or ZIP Code. Mapping is also available. Lists of violent and non-compliant offenders are viewable.

Incarceration Records

Idaho Department of Correction, Records Bureau, www.idoc.idaho.gov/ This database search at https://www.accessidaho.org/public/corr/offender/search.html provides in-depth information about offenders currently under Idaho Department of Correction jurisdiction meaning only those incarcerated, on probation, or on parole. Names of individuals who have served time and satisfied their sentence will appear - their convictions will not. If you need additional basic offender record information, contact inquire@idoc.idaho.gov.

Corporation, LP, LLP, LLC, Trademarks/Servicemarks, Assumed Name

Secretary of State, Corporation Division, www.sos.idaho.gov/corp/corindex.htm Business Entity Searches at www.accessidaho.org/public/sos/corp/search.html?SearchFormstep=crit. This is a free Internet service open 24 hours daily. Includes not-for-profit entities. Trademarks may be searched at www.accessidaho.org/public/sos/trademark/search.html. *Other Options:* There are a variety of formats and media available for bulk purchase requesters. Requesters can subscriber to a monthly CD update.

Uniform Commercial Code, Federal & State Tax Liens

UCC Division, Secretary of State, www.sos.idaho.gov/ucc/uccindex.htm There is a free limited search at https://www.accessidaho.org/secure/sos/liens/search.html. We recommend professional searchers to subscribe to the extensive commercial service at this site. The fee is $3.00 per name searched with a $95.00 annual subscription fee. Note there is a 1-2 day delay before new filings are available online. **$$$** *Other Options:* A full extract of the data file is available for download,

Sales Tax Registrations

Revenue Operations Division, IO/Records Management, www.tax.idaho.gov/ Email requests are accepted at leola.rees@tax.id.gov,

Vital Records

Vital Records, www.healthandwelfare.idaho.gov/Health/VitalRecordsandHealthStatistics/tabid/1504/Default.aspx The agency has made the death index of records from 1911 - 1956 available at http://abish.byui.edu/specialCollections/fhc/Death/searchForm.cfm. There is no fee. Also, requests can be made online via a vendor - vitalchek.com. Additional fees involved. **$$$**

Driver Records

Idaho Transportation Department, Driver's Services, www.itd.idaho.gov/dmv/ Note: Access Idaho refers to driving records as 'Driver License Records' or DLRs and refers to records related to vehicle title or registration as MVRs. Idaho offers online access (CICS) to the driver license files through its portal provider, Access Idaho. Fee is $9.56 per record. There is an annual $95.00 subscription fee. Idaho drivers can also order their own record from this site, fee is $9.56, subscription nor required. There is a free DL status check at https://www.accessidaho.org/secure/itd/reinstatement/signin.html. A free HAZMAT status check is at https://www.accessidaho.org/secure/itd/motorcarrier/unitsearch/hazmat/tportal/search.html. Must have Carrier Acct #. **$$$** *Other Options:* Idaho offers bulk retrieval of basic drivers license information with a signed contract. For information, call 208-334-8602.

Vehicle Ownership & Registration, Vessel Ownership

Idaho Transportation Department, Vehicle Services, http://itd.idaho.gov/dmv/vehicleservices/vs.htm Idaho offers online and batch access to registration and title files through its portal provider Access Idaho. Records are $8.50 per record. For more information, call 208-332-0102 or visit https://www.accessidaho.org/online_services. There is a $95 annual subscription fee. Interestingly, be aware that Access Idaho refers to vehicle-related as MVRs; they do not mean driving records. **$$$** *Other Options:* Idaho offers bulk retrieval of registration, ownership, and vehicle information with a signed contract. For more information, call 208-334-8601.

Accident Reports

Idaho Transportation Department, Traffic and Highway Safety-Accident Records, One may view and print reports at https://www.accessidaho.org/secure/itd/ohs/crashreports/search.html. The total fee is $9.00. It may take several weeks before new records are available on this system. **$$$** *Other Options:* Computer files may be purchased with prepaid deposit plus computer charges. However, the file will not contain addresses, citation information, or drivers' license numbers and other personal information. Annual databases may be purchased.

Voter Registration, Campaign Finance Disclosure, Lobbyists

State Elections Office, Sec of State, www.sos.idaho.gov/elect/eleindex.htm A list of lobbyists and expenditures is found at www.sos.idaho.gov/elect/lobbyist/lobinfo.htm. Election campaign and finance disclosure, including PACs, is searchable at www.sos.idaho.gov/elect/finance.htm. Some files are downloadable. To check to see if registered go to www.idahovotes.gov/YPP_NEW/AmIRegistered.aspx. Must have full last name, partial first name is allowed and must have date of birth, also must know in what county registered.

Occupational Licensing Boards

Accountant Firm .... http://isba.idaho.gov/htm/firmsearch.htm
Accountant-CPA/LPA .... http://isba.idaho.gov/htm/accountantsearch.htm
Acupuncturist .... https://secure.ibol.idaho.gov/eIBOLPublic/LPRBrowser.aspx
Applicator, Pesticide, Private/Commercial ... www.agri.state.id.us/Categories/Pesticides/licensing/licenseLookUp.php
Appraiser, Real Estate/Residential/Trainee . https://secure.ibol.idaho.gov/eIBOLPublic/LPRBrowser.aspx
Architect/Architectural Examiners .... https://secure.ibol.idaho.gov/eIBOLPublic/LPRBrowser.aspx
Assignee (Lender) .... http://finance.idaho.gov/LicenseeSearch.aspx
Athlete Agent .... https://secure.ibol.idaho.gov/eIBOLPublic/LPRBrowser.aspx
Athletic Commission/Boxing/Martial Arts ..... https://secure.ibol.idaho.gov/eIBOLPublic/LPRBrowser.aspx
Athletic Trainer .... https://isecure.bom.idaho.gov/BOMPublic/LPRBrowser.aspx
Attorney .... http://isb.idaho.gov/licensing/attorney_roster.cfm
Audiologist .... https://secure.ibol.idaho.gov/eIBOLPublic/LPRBrowser.aspx
Backflow Assembly Tester .... https://secure.ibol.idaho.gov/eIBOLPublic/LPRBrowser.aspx
Bank .... http://finance.idaho.gov/LicenseeSearch.aspx
Barber/Barber Shop/Instructor/School .... https://secure.ibol.idaho.gov/eIBOLPublic/LPRBrowser.aspx
Boxing/Wrestling Event/Professional .... https://secure.ibol.idaho.gov/eIBOLPublic/LPRBrowser.aspx?Profession=ATC&DefaultBoard=Y
Building Inspector .... https://data.dbs.idaho.gov/etrakit2/Search.aspx?grp=aec
Chemigator .... www.agri.state.id.us/Categories/Pesticides/licensing/licenseLookUp.php
Chiropractor .... https://secure.ibol.idaho.gov/eIBOLPublic/LPRBrowser.aspx
Clinical Nurse Specialist .... http://ibn.idaho.gov/IBNPublic/LPRBrowser.aspx
Collection Agency/Collector .... http://finance.idaho.gov/CollectionAgency/CollectionAgencyLicense.aspx
Construction Mgr, Public Works .... https://data.dbs.idaho.gov/etrakit2/Idaho_LicenseSearch.aspx

Consumer Loan Co. & Credit Seller	http://finance.idaho.gov/ConsumerFinance/ConsumerCreditLicense.aspx
Contracting Business	https://secure.ibol.idaho.gov/eIBOLPublic/LPRBrowser.aspx
Contractor, Public Works	https://data.dbs.idaho.gov/etrakit2/Idaho_LicenseSearch.aspx
Contractor, Registered	https://secure.ibol.idaho.gov/eIBOLPublic/LPRBrowser.aspx
Cosmetics Dealer, Retail	https://secure.ibol.idaho.gov/eIBOLPublic/LPRBrowser.aspx
Cosmetologist/Cosmetology Salon, School	https://secure.ibol.idaho.gov/eIBOLPublic/LPRBrowser.aspx
Counselor, Clinical	https://secure.ibol.idaho.gov/eIBOLPublic/LPRBrowser.aspx
Counselor, Debt/Credit	http://finance.idaho.gov/ConsumerFinance/ConsumerCreditLicense.aspx
Counselor, Professional	https://secure.ibol.idaho.gov/eIBOLPublic/LPRBrowser.aspx
Credit Seller	http://finance.idaho.gov/LicenseeSearch.aspx
Credit Union	http://finance.idaho.gov/LicenseeSearch.aspx
Crematory	https://secure.ibol.idaho.gov/eIBOLPublic/LPRBrowser.aspx
Dentist, Dental Hygienist/Asst/Specialists	http://isbd.idaho.gov/search.html
Denturist Intern/Establishment	https://secure.ibol.idaho.gov/eIBOLPublic/LPRBrowser.aspx
Dietitian	https://isecure.bom.idaho.gov/BOMPublic/LPRBrowser.aspx
Drinking Water Professionals	https://secure.ibol.idaho.gov/eIBOLPublic/LPRBrowser.aspx
Driving Business	https://secure.ibol.idaho.gov/eIBOLPublic/LPRBrowser.aspx
Elections & Campaign Disclosure	www.sos.idaho.gov/eid/index.htm
Electrolysis, Electrolysis Instructor	https://secure.ibol.idaho.gov/eIBOLPublic/LPRBrowser.aspx
Elevator Installation/Repairmen	https://data.dbs.idaho.gov/etrakit2/Idaho_ElevatorSearch.aspx
Endodontist	http://isbd.idaho.gov/search.html
Engineer	www.ipels.idaho.gov/rostersearch.cfm
Escrow Licensee	http://finance.idaho.gov/Escrow/EscrowLicense.aspx
Esthetician, Esthetician Instructor	https://secure.ibol.idaho.gov/eIBOLPublic/LPRBrowser.aspx
Euthanasia Agency	http://bovm.idaho.gov/license_search/
Euthanasia Technician	http://bovm.idaho.gov/license_search/
Finance Company	http://finance.idaho.gov/LicenseeSearch.aspx
Fire Sprinkler System Contractor	www.doi.idaho.gov/sfm/SprinklerContractorList.aspx
Fireworks License	www.doi.idaho.gov/sfm/FireworksVendorList.aspx
Food Establishment Studied	http://cdhd.idaho.gov/EH/food/fooddb_gui.cfm
Funeral Director/Dir. Trainee	https://secure.ibol.idaho.gov/eIBOLPublic/LPRBrowser.aspx
Funeral Establishment	https://secure.ibol.idaho.gov/eIBOLPublic/LPRBrowser.aspx
Geologist	https://secure.ibol.idaho.gov/eIBOLPublic/LPRBrowser.aspx?Profession=GEO&DefaultBoard=Y
Glamour Photography Studio	https://secure.ibol.idaho.gov/eIBOLPublic/LPRBrowser.aspx
Guide	http://fishandgame.idaho.gov/ifwis/ioglb/
Hearing Aid Fitter/Dealer	https://secure.ibol.idaho.gov/eIBOLPublic/LPRBrowser.aspx
Insurance Producer, Broker	www.doi.idaho.gov/Insurance/search.aspx
Insurer, Domestic/Mutual/Foreign	www.doi.idaho.gov/Insurance/search.aspx
Investment Advisor	http://finance.idaho.gov/Securities/SecuritiesLicense.aspx
Landscape Architect	https://secure.ibol.idaho.gov/eIBOLPublic/LPRBrowser.aspx
Lobbyist	www.sos.idaho.gov/elect/lobbyist/lobinfo.htm
LPG Dealer/Facility	https://secure.ibol.idaho.gov/eIBOLPublic/LPRBrowser.aspx
Mail Order Pharmacy List	http://bop.idaho.gov/verify_licensee/verify_licensee.cfm
Marriage & Family Counselor	https://secure.ibol.idaho.gov/eIBOLPublic/LPRBrowser.aspx
Medical Resident	https://isecure.bom.idaho.gov/BOMPublic/LPRBrowser.aspx
Medical, Temporary	https://isecure.bom.idaho.gov/BOMPublic/LPRBrowser.aspx
Midwife	https://secure.ibol.idaho.gov/eIBOLPublic/LPRBrowser.aspx
Money Transmitter	http://finance.idaho.gov/MoneyTransmitter/MoneyTransmitterLicense.aspx
Mortgage Broker/Banker	http://finance.idaho.gov/LicenseeSearch.aspx
Mortgage Company	http://finance.idaho.gov/Mortgage/MortgageLicense.aspx
Mortgage Loan Originator	http://finance.idaho.gov/Escrow/EscrowLicense.aspx
Mortician Temporary Permit	https://secure.ibol.idaho.gov/eIBOLPublic/LPRBrowser.aspx
Mortician/Mortician Resi. Trainee	https://secure.ibol.idaho.gov/eIBOLPublic/LPRBrowser.aspx
Nail Technician/Instructor	https://secure.ibol.idaho.gov/eIBOLPublic/LPRBrowser.aspx
Naturopath	https://secure.ibol.idaho.gov/eIBOLPublic/LPRBrowser.aspx

Notary Public	www.sos.idaho.gov/online/notary/notarySearch.jsp
Nurse Anesthetist	http://ibn.idaho.gov/IBNPublic/LPRBrowser.aspx
Nurse-LPN/RN	http://ibn.idaho.gov/IBNPublic/LPRBrowser.aspx
Nursing Care (Skilled) Facility	https://secure.ibol.idaho.gov/eIBOLPublic/LPRBrowser.aspx
Nursing Home Administrator	https://secure.ibol.idaho.gov/eIBOLPublic/LPRBrowser.aspx
Occupational Therapist/Assistant	https://isecure.bom.idaho.gov/BOMPublic/LPRBrowser.aspx
Optometrist	https://secure.ibol.idaho.gov/eIBOLPublic/LPRBrowser.aspx
Oral/Maxillofacial Surgeon	http://isbd.idaho.gov/search.html
Orthodontist	http://isbd.idaho.gov/search.html
Osteopathic Physician	https://isecure.bom.idaho.gov/BOMPublic/LPRBrowser.aspx
Outfitter	http://fishandgame.idaho.gov/ifwis/ioglb/
Payday Lender	http://finance.idaho.gov/LicenseeSearch.aspx
Pediatric Dentist	http://isbd.idaho.gov/search.html
Pest Control Consultant	www.agri.state.id.us/Categories/Pesticides/licensing/licenseLookUp.php
Pesticide Applicat'r/Oper'r/Dealer/Mfg	www.agri.state.id.us/Categories/Pesticides/licensing/licenseLookUp.php
Pharmacist/Pharmac't Intern/Preceptor	http://bop.idaho.gov/verify_licensee/verify_licensee.cfm
Physical Therapist/Assistant	https://isecure.bom.idaho.gov/BOMPublic/LPRBrowser.aspx
Physician Assistant	https://isecure.bom.idaho.gov/BOMPublic/LPRBrowser.aspx
Physician/Medical Doctor	https://isecure.bom.idaho.gov/BOMPublic/LPRBrowser.aspx
Plumbing Apprentice/Journeyman	https://data.dbs.idaho.gov/etrakit2/Search.aspx?grp=license
Plumbing Inspector/Contractor	https://data.dbs.idaho.gov/etrakit2/Search.aspx?grp=license
Podiatrist	https://secure.ibol.idaho.gov/eIBOLPublic/LPRBrowser.aspx
Polysomnography Technician/Trainee	https://isecure.bom.idaho.gov/BOMPublic/LPRBrowser.aspx
Prosthodontist	http://isbd.idaho.gov/search.html
Psychologist	https://secure.ibol.idaho.gov/eIBOLPublic/LPRBrowser.aspx
Psychology Service Extender	https://secure.ibol.idaho.gov/eIBOLPublic/LPRBrowser.aspx
Real Estate Agent/Broker/Company	http://irec.idaho.gov/licensee-search.html
Real Estate Appraiser	https://secure.ibol.idaho.gov/eIBOLPublic/LPRBrowser.aspx
Real Estate Instructor/School	http://irec.idaho.gov/licensee-search.html
Residential Care Administrator, Facility	https://secure.ibol.idaho.gov/eIBOLPublic/LPRBrowser.aspx
Respiratory Therapist	https://isecure.bom.idaho.gov/BOMPublic/LPRBrowser.aspx
Securities Broker/Seller/Issuer/Dealer	http://finance.idaho.gov/Securities/SecuritiesLicense.aspx
Shorthand Reporter	https://secure.ibol.idaho.gov/eIBOLPublic/LPRBrowser.aspx
Social Worker	https://secure.ibol.idaho.gov/eIBOLPublic/LPRBrowser.aspx
Speech/Language Pathologist	https://secure.ibol.idaho.gov/eIBOLPublic/LPRBrowser.aspx
Surveyor, Land	www.ipels.idaho.gov/rostersearch.cfm
Temporary Medical	https://isecure.bom.idaho.gov/BOMPublic/LPRBrowser.aspx
Title Loan Lender	http://finance.idaho.gov/LicenseeSearch.aspx
Trust Company	http://finance.idaho.gov/LicenseeSearch.aspx
Utility Regulator Gas/Water/Power/Phone	www.puc.idaho.gov/fileroom/uis%20internet%20reports.htm
Veterinarian/Veterinary Technician	http://bovm.idaho.gov/license_search/
Waste Water Professionals	https://secure.ibol.idaho.gov/eIBOLPublic/LPRBrowser.aspx
Waste Water Treatment Operator	https://secure.ibol.idaho.gov/eIBOLPublic/LPRBrowser.aspx
Water Collection Operator	https://secure.ibol.idaho.gov/eIBOLPublic/LPRBrowser.aspx
Water Distribution Operator	https://secure.ibol.idaho.gov/eIBOLPublic/LPRBrowser.aspx
Water Rights Examiner	www.idwr.idaho.gov/WaterManagement/WaterRights/Examiners/examiners.htm
Water Treatment Operator	https://secure.ibol.idaho.gov/eIBOLPublic/LPRBrowser.aspx
Water Well Driller	www.idwr.idaho.gov/apps/well/licensedwelldrillers/
Wrestler	https://secure.ibol.idaho.gov/eIBOLPublic/LPRBrowser.aspx?Profession=ATC&DefaultBoard=Y

State and Local Courts

State Court Structure: **District Courts** have original jurisdiction over felony criminal cases and civil actions if the amount involved is more than $10,000, and hear appeals of decisions of the Magistrate Division. District judges may also hear domestic relation cases, such as divorces and child custody matters, but in most counties, such cases are handled by Magistrate judges.

The **Magistrate Courts** hears probate matters, divorce proceedings, juvenile proceedings, initial felony proceedings through the preliminary hearing, criminal misdemeanors, infractions, civil cases when the amount in dispute does not exceed $10,000. Magistrates also hear Small Claims cases, established for disputes of $4,000 or less. See at www.isc.idaho.gov/overview.pdf.

Appellate Courts: One may view Supreme Court and Appellate Court opinions from www.isc.idaho.gov/opinions.

Statewide Court Online Access: **All courts** participate in the free access to trial court record index at https://www.idcourts.us/repository/start.do. Records are searchable by name statewide or by individual county, and by case number. Results date back to 1995 or further depending on the county. Online results include identifiers year of birth and middle initial. The following personal information is not released: DL, address, and first 6 characters of the SSN. This online service is not thought to be equivalent to an onsite search at the courthouse.

Note: No individual Idaho courts offer online access, other than as described above.

Recorders and Assessors

Recording Office Organization: 44 counties, 44 recording offices. The recording officer is the County Recorder. Many counties utilize a grantor/grantee index containing all transactions recorded with them. Until July 1, 1998, state tax liens were filed at the local county recorder. Now they are filed with the Secretary of State who has all active case files. Federal tax liens on personal property of businesses are filed with the Secretary of State. Other federal tax liens are filed with the county recorder.

Statewide or Multi-Jurisdiction Access: Few counties offer web access, as shown below. There is no statewide system.

Ada County Recorder ***Recorded Documents*** Access to recorder's index is free at www.adaweb.net/recsearch/.

Property, Taxation Search the property assessor database for property data free at www.adacountyassessor.org/propsys/. No name searching.

Bannock County ***Property, Taxation*** Access to GIS/mapping free at www.bannockcounty.us/zoning/disclaimer1.htm.

Boise County ***Property, Taxation*** Access to property data for free at http://property.boisecounty.us/. If you have an account, login, otherwise you may use the username and password of public1 (for both) to sign-in.

Bonner County ***Property, Taxation*** Maps and downloadable GIS data are available free at www.co.bonner.id.us/gis/index.html.

Canyon County ***Recorded Documents*** www.canyonco.org/Elected-Officials/Clerk/Recorder.aspx Access to Recorder's database search free at http://rec-search.canyonco.org/Recording/search.asp.

Property, Taxation Access to property searches and GIS/mapping info for free at http://gis.canyonco.org/flexviewers/Test/. No name searches.

Custer County ***Property, Taxation*** Access to GIS/mapping free at www.greenwoodmap.com/custer/.

Fremont County ***Property, Taxation*** Access to maps and tax assessor data free at http://www.co.fremont.id.us/mapserver/.

Idaho County ***Property, Taxation*** Free access to the county parcels found at http://gis.idaho.gov/tax/Countysupport/Idaho.html.

Jefferson County ***Property, Taxation*** Access to GIS/mapping for free at www.co.jefferson.id.us/gis_mapping.php.

Jerome County ***Property, Taxation*** The county wide data available for sale. This includes ownership, land, and improvement records. This information is available on CD or can be uploaded to an FTP site. Please contact the Jerome County Assessor's Office for more information.

Kootenai County ***Property, Taxation*** Access assessor data free on the mapping site at www.kcgov.us/departments/mapping/mapSearch/. Login as Guest to search without registration.

Lemhi County ***Recorded Documents*** www.lemhicountyidaho.org/clerkauditors.htm Subscription service available, call 208-756-2815. **$$$**

Property, Taxation Access to GIS/mapping for free at http://apps.gis.idaho.gov/tax/Google/Parcels/Lemhi.html.

Lewis County ***Property, Taxation*** Access property data for free at http://apps.gis.idaho.gov/tax/Google/Parcels/Lewis.html.

Payette County ***Recrded Documents*** www.payettecounty.org Access to recorded documents is free at www.payettecounty.org/clerk/imagesilo.html. Username is "public" and password is "look."

Property, Taxation Access to property tax information for free to go www.payettecounty.org/treasurer/Propertytaxlink.htm. Must use their User ID and Password provided on this page.

Illinois

Capital: Springfield
Sangamon County
Time Zone: CST
Population: 12,875,255
# of Counties: 102

Useful State Links

Website: www.illinois.gov
Governor: www.illinois.gov/gov
Attorney General: www.ag.state.il.us
State Archives: www.cyberdriveillinois.com/departments/archives/databases/home.html
State Statutes and Codes: www.ilga.gov/legislation/ilcs/ilcs.asp
Legislative Bill Search: www.ilga.gov/legislation/default.asp
Unclaimed Funds: https://www.treasurer.il.gov/programs/up/up_search.asp

State Public Record Agencies

Criminal Records

IL State Police Bureau of Identification, Bureau of Identification, www.isp.state.il.us/crimhistory/chri.cfm Online access costs $10.00 per name or $16.00 if fingerprints submitted electronically ($20 if fingerprints submitted manually); discounts for quantities. It takes about one month to set up an account. Upon signing an interagency agreement with ISP and establishing an escrow account, users can submit inquiries by email. Responses are sent back in 24 to 48 hours by either email or fax. Visit www.isp.state.il.us/services/convictioninquiries.cfm to enroll. There is a free search for entities that have participated in methamphetamine manufacturing - go to www.isp.state.il.us/meth/. **$$$**

Sexual Offender Registry

Illinois State Police, SOR Unit, www.isp.state.il.us/sor/ The website provides an online listing of sex offenders required to register in the State of Illinois. The database is updated daily and allows searching by name, city, county, or ZIP Code.

Incarceration Records

Illinois Department of Corrections, www2.illinois.gov/idoc/Pages/default.aspx Click on Inmate Search at the website or at www2.illinois.gov/idoc/Offender/Pages/default.aspx. *Other Options:* A CD of data since 1982 may be purchased for $45. Send request to FOIA Officer at address above.

Corporation, LLC, LP, LLP, LLLP, RLLP, Trade Names, Assumed Name

Department of Business Services, Corporate Department, www.ilsos.net The website gives free access to corporate and LLC status at www.ilsos.gov/corporatellc/. A commercial access program is also available. Fees vary. Potential users must submit in writing the purpose of the request. Submit your request to become involved in this program to the Director's Office. Search the database for registrations of LP, LLP, LLLP, and RLLP at www.ilsos.gov/lprpsearch/. **$$$** *Other Options:* List or bulk file purchases are available. Contact the Director's office for details.

Uniform Commercial Code, Federal Tax Liens

Secretary of State, UCC Division, www.cyberdriveillinois.com An index search is offered at www.ilsos.gov/UCC/. No images are available. *Other Options:* The entire database can be purchased and for $2500 with weekly updates at $200 per week. A CD update service for images is available for $250 per month.

Sales Tax Registrations

Revenue Department, Sales & Use Tax Services, www.tax.illinois.gov/ One may verify a registered business at https://www.revenue.state.il.us/app/bgii/. Whether an IL tax number or license number for FUIN is needed.

Birth Certificates

IL Department of Public Health, Division of Vital Records, www.idph.state.il.us/vitalrecords/index.htm Records may requested from www.vitalchek.com, a state-endorsed vendor. Also, detailed instructions are at the website. Requests are processed within 3-5 days. **$$$**

Death Records

IL Department of Public Health, Division of Vital Records, www.idph.state.il.us/vitalrecords/index.htm Records may be requested from www.vitalchek.com, a state-endorsed vendor. Detailed instructions are at the website. Also, the state archives database of Illinois Death Certificates 1916-1950 is available free at www.cyberdriveillinois.com/departments/archives/databases/idphdeathindex.html. **$$$**

Marriage Certificates, Divorce Records

Department of Public Health, Division of Vital Records, www.idph.state.il.us/vitalrecords/index.htm There is a free online search of a statewide Marriage Index for 1763-1900 found at the Illinois State Archives website at www.cyberdriveillinois.com/departments/archives/databases/marriage.html.

Workers' Compensation Records

IL Workers' Compensation Commission, www.iwcc.il.gov Case information for any case is available at www.iwcc.il.gov/caseinfo.htm.

Driver Records

Abstract Information Unit, Drivers Services Department, www.cyberdriveillinois.com/ A program for high volume, approved users is available. Records are $12.00 each. Call 217-785-3094 for further information. Also, there is a special, free page that parents or guardians may use to view the driving record of their children under 18. Go to https://www.ilsos.gov/parentalaccess/. **$$$** *Other Options:* Overnight cartridge batch processing may be available to high volume users (there is a 200 request minimum per day). Call 217-785-3094 for more information.

Vehicle Ownership & Registration

Vehicle Services Department, Vehicle Record Inquiry, www.cyberdriveillinois.com Online access to records is not available, but Illinois provides a free Title and Registration Status Inquiry at www.ilsos.gov/regstatus. *Other Options:* This agency will sell customized, bulk requests upon approval of purpose and with a signed contract. Contact the Data Processing Division in Room 400.

Accident Reports (Crash Reports)

Illinois State Police, Patrol Records Section, www.isp.state.il.us One may request and pay for a copy of a crash report online using a credit card. Go to www.isp.state.il.us/traffic/crashreports.cfm. There is an additional $1.00 fee plus the $5.00 per record fee for this service. Credit cards are accepted for payment online. Using E-PAY, one may also request, pay for and receive the traffic crash report by email. **$$$**

Voter Registration, Campaign Finance & Disclosure, PACs

IL State Board of Elections, Voter Registration Services, www.elections.state.il.us At www.elections.state.il.us/, click on the search option to find many searchable data sets dealing campaign finance and contributions. Search committees and PACs at www.elections.state.il.us/CampaignDisclosure/CommitteeSearch.aspx. A general contributions search is at www.elections.state.il.us/campaigndisclosure/ContributionsSearchByAllContributions.aspx One may verify registration at www.elections.il.gov/votinginformation/registrationlookup.aspx.

Occupational Licensing Boards

Accountant-CPA.. https://www.idfpr.com/licenselookup/licenselookup.asp
Acupuncturist.. https://www.idfpr.com/licenselookup/licenselookup.asp
Alarm Contractor.. https://www.idfpr.com/licenselookup/licenselookup.asp
Alcohol Abuse Counselor........................... www.iaodapca.org/wp-content/uploads/2012/05/MembershipDirectory.pdf
Ambulatory Surgical Treatment Center........ www.idph.state.il.us/healthcarefacilities/astc.htm
Amusement Attraction/Ride........................ www.state.il.us/agency/idol/Listings/Carnlist.htm
Animal Breeder.. http://dnr.illinois.gov/DNRDirectMonitor/VendorListing.aspx
Aquaculturist.. www.dnr.illinois.gov/LPR/Pages/CommercialLicensesFees.aspx
Architect.. https://www.idfpr.com/licenselookup/licenselookup.asp
Armed Security Agency/Agent.................... https://www.idfpr.com/licenselookup/licenselookup.asp
Athletic Trainer.. https://www.idfpr.com/licenselookup/licenselookup.asp
Attorney.. https://www.iardc.org/lawyersearch.asp

Auctioneer	https://www.idfpr.com/LicenseLookUp/LicenseLookup.asp
Audiologist	https://www.idfpr.com/licenselookup/licenselookup.asp
Bank	www.obrelookupclear.state.il.us/default.asp?Division=11&Profession=73&status=3
Barber	https://www.idfpr.com/licenselookup/licenselookup.asp
Bilingual Teacher, Transitional	https://sec1.isbe.net/ecs/aspapps/teachersearch.asp
Bingo Operation	www.iltax.com/CharityGaming/Bingo-Participants.htm
Boiler Repair Firms	www.sfm.illinois.gov/commercial/boilers/licensedrepair.aspx
Bull Ride	www.state.il.us/agency/idol/Listings/Carnlist.htm
Bungee Jump	www.state.il.us/agency/idol/Listings/Carnlist.htm
Business Broker	www.ilsos.gov/brokersearch/
Business Opportunity Offering	www.ilsos.gov/brokersearch/
Carnival	www.state.il.us/agency/idol/Listings/Carnlist.htm
Charitable Game	www.iltax.com/CharityGaming/Charitable-Participants.htm
Check Seller/Distributor	https://www.idfpr.com/LicenseLookUp/LicenseLookup.asp
Chiropractor	https://www.idfpr.com/licenselookup/licenselookup.asp
Classr'm Training Course, Basic	https://www.idfpr.com/licenselookup/licenselookup.asp
Collection Agency	https://www.idfpr.com/licenselookup/licenselookup.asp
Controlled Substance Registrant	https://www.idfpr.com/licenselookup/licenselookup.asp
Cosmetologist	https://www.idfpr.com/licenselookup/licenselookup.asp
Counselor/Clinical Prof Counselor	https://www.idfpr.com/licenselookup/licenselookup.asp
Dentist/Dental Hygienist	https://www.idfpr.com/licenselookup/licenselookup.asp
Design Firm	https://www.idfpr.com/licenselookup/licenselookup.asp
Dietitian/Nutrition Counselor	https://www.idfpr.com/licenselookup/licenselookup.asp
Driver Training School	www.cyberdriveillinois.com/departments/drivers/driver_education/commercial_driver_training/cdlcertschools.pdf
Drug Distributor/Wholesale	https://www.idfpr.com/licenselookup/licenselookup.asp
Early Childhood Teacher	https://sec1.isbe.net/ecs/aspapps/teachersearch.asp
Elevator Contractor/Inspector/Company	www.sfm.illinois.gov/commercial/elevators/licensees.aspx
Engineer/Engineer Intern	https://www.idfpr.com/licenselookup/licenselookup.asp
Engineer/Structural	https://www.idfpr.com/licenselookup/licenselookup.asp
Environmental Health Practitioner	https://www.idfpr.com/licenselookup/licenselookup.asp
Esthetician/Euthansaia Tech	https://www.idfpr.com/licenselookup/licenselookup.asp
Fire Equipment Distributor	www.sfm.illinois.gov/documents/R_FIREDST1_WEB.pdf
Firearms Trainer	https://www.idfpr.com/licenselookup/licenselookup.asp
Fish Dealer	www.dnr.illinois.gov/LPR/Pages/CommercialLicensesFees.aspx
Fisherman, Commercial	www.dnr.illinois.gov/LPR/Pages/CommercialLicensesFees.aspx
Funeral Director/Embalmer	https://www.idfpr.com/licenselookup/licenselookup.asp
Fur Buyer/Tanner/Dyer	http://dnr.illinois.gov/DNRDirectMonitor/VendorListing.aspx
Gambling Addiction Counselor	www.iaodapca.org/wp-content/uploads/2012/05/MembershipDirectory.pdf
Gaming Exclusion List	www.igb.state.il.us/xclude/
Gaming/Gambling Supplier	www.igb.state.il.us/Pending/ILSUPPUBweb.pdf
Geologist	https://www.idfpr.com/licenselookup/licenselookup.asp
Go-kart track	www.state.il.us/agency/idol/Listings/Carnlist.htm
Home Health Aide (CNAs-ASHHA)	www.idph.state.il.us/nar/home.htm
Home Health Care Agency	www.idph.state.il.us/healthcarefacilities/homehealth_list.htm#hha
Home Inspector	https://www.idfpr.com/LicenseLookUp/LicenseLookup.asp
Home Medical Equip Provider	https://www.idfpr.com/licenselookup/licenselookup.asp
Hospital	www.idph.state.il.us/healthcarefacilities/hospital_list.htm
Hunting Area Operator	www.dnr.illinois.gov/LPR/Pages/CommercialLicensesFees.aspx
Insurance Producer	https://sbs-il.naic.org/Lion-Web/jsp/sbsreports/AgentLookup.jsp
Interior Designer	https://www.idfpr.com/licenselookup/licenselookup.asp
Investment Adviser	www.finra.org/Investors/ToolsCalculators/BrokerCheck/index.htm
Land Sale Developer	https://www.idfpr.com/licenselookup/licenselookup.asp
Landscape Architect	https://www.idfpr.com/licenselookup/licenselookup.asp
Lead Contractor	http://app.idph.state.il.us/Envhealth/Lead/LeadProfessionalListing.asp
Lead Risk Assessor/Insp./Supr.	http://app.idph.state.il.us/Envhealth/lead/LeadProfessionalListing.asp

Lead Training Provider................................ http://app.idph.state.il.us/Envhealth/lead/LeadProfessionalListing.asp
Liquor License, Retail/Dist./Mfg. www2.state.il.us/lcc/tdq.asp
Loan Broker.. www.ilsos.gov/brokersearch/
Lobbyist... www.cyberdriveillinois.com/departments/index/lobbyist/home.html
Locksmith .... https://www.idfpr.com/licenselookup/licenselookup.asp
Long Term Care Insurance Firm................. https://sbs-il.naic.org/Lion-Web/jsp/sbsreports/AgentLookup.jsp
Marriage & Family Therapist....................... https://www.idfpr.com/licenselookup/licenselookup.asp
Massage Therapist...................................... https://www.idfpr.com/licenselookup/licenselookup.asp
Medical Corporation .... https://www.idfpr.com/licenselookup/licenselookup.asp
Mental Health Counselor www.iaodapca.org/wp-content/uploads/2012/05/MembershipDirectory.pdf
Mortgage Banker/Broker............................. www.obrelookupclear.state.il.us/default.asp?Division=11&Profession=73&status=3
Nail Technician... https://www.idfpr.com/licenselookup/licenselookup.asp
Naprapath .... https://www.idfpr.com/licenselookup/licenselookup.asp
Notary Public.. www.ilsos.gov/notary/
Nuclear Medicine Technologist................... https://www.state.il.us/iema/dns.asp
Nurse-LPN/RN/APN................................... https://www.idfpr.com/licenselookup/licenselookup.asp
Nurses Aide.. www.idph.state.il.us/nar/home.htm
Nursing Home, Administrator...................... https://www.idfpr.com/licenselookup/licenselookup.asp
Occupational Therapist, Aide...................... https://www.idfpr.com/licenselookup/licenselookup.asp
Optometrist... https://www.idfpr.com/licenselookup/licenselookup.asp
Orthotist.. https://www.idfpr.com/licenselookup/licenselookup.asp
Osteopathic Physician .... https://www.idfpr.com/licenselookup/licenselookup.asp
Pawnbroker .... https://www.idfpr.com/LicenseLookUp/LicenseLookup.asp
Pedorthist.. https://www.idfpr.com/licenselookup/licenselookup.asp
Perfusionist .... https://www.idfpr.com/licenselookup/licenselookup.asp
Pharmacist/Pharmacy .... https://www.idfpr.com/licenselookup/licenselookup.asp
Physical Therapist/Assistant, Aide.............. https://www.idfpr.com/licenselookup/licenselookup.asp
Physician/Medical Doctor............................ https://www.idfpr.com/licenselookup/licenselookup.asp
Podiatrist .... https://www.idfpr.com/licenselookup/licenselookup.asp
Police Trainer/Training Facility.................... www.ptb.state.il.us/training/training_lawenforcement.htm
Polygraph/Deception Detect.Examiner........ https://www.idfpr.com/licenselookup/licenselookup.asp
Private Investigator .... https://www.idfpr.com/licenselookup/licenselookup.asp
Private Security Contractor .... https://www.idfpr.com/licenselookup/licenselookup.asp
Psychologist... https://www.idfpr.com/licenselookup/licenselookup.asp
Psychology Business .... https://www.idfpr.com/licenselookup/licenselookup.asp
Pull Tab Operator.. www.iltax.com/CharityGaming/Pulltab-Participants.htm
Racetrack/Authorized Agent www2.illinois.gov/irb/Pages/Licensing.aspx
Radiation Therapist..................................... https://www.state.il.us/iema/dns.asp
Radon Measurement Laboratories/Detectors https://www.state.il.us/iema/radon/MeasurementLabs.asp
Real Estate Agent/Broker/Seller .... https://www.idfpr.com/LicenseLookUp/LicenseLookup.asp
Real Estate Appraiser .... https://www.idfpr.com/LicenseLookUp/LicenseLookup.asp
Red Tag Tank .... http://webapps.sfm.illinois.gov/ustsearch/Redtagtanks.aspx
Rehabilitation Aide .... https://www.idfpr.com/licenselookup/licenselookup.asp
Respiratory Care Practitioner...................... https://www.idfpr.com/licenselookup/licenselookup.asp
Roofer, Roofing Contractor .... https://www.idfpr.com/licenselookup/licenselookup.asp
Savings & Loan Association .... https://www.idfpr.com/LicenseLookUp/LicenseLookup.asp
Savings Bank .... https://www.idfpr.com/LicenseLookUp/LicenseLookup.asp
Securities Salesperson/Dealer.................... www.cyberdriveillinois.com/departments/securities/subjectindex.html
Security Force .... https://www.idfpr.com/licenselookup/licenselookup.asp
Security Guard Firm/Agency....................... https://www.idfpr.com/licenselookup/licenselookup.asp
Shorthand Reporter.................................... https://www.idfpr.com/licenselookup/licenselookup.asp
Ski Lift, Tram .... www.state.il.us/agency/idol/Listings/Carnlist.htm
Social Worker... https://www.idfpr.com/licenselookup/licenselookup.asp
Special Teacher https://sec1.isbe.net/ecs/aspapps/teachersearch.asp
Speech-Language Pathologist.................... https://www.idfpr.com/licenselookup/licenselookup.asp

Stock Broker	www.finra.org/Investors/ToolsCalculators/BrokerCheck/index.htm
Substance Abuse Counselor	www.iaodapca.org/wp-content/uploads/2012/05/MembershipDirectory.pdf
Surgical Technician	https://www.idfpr.com/licenselookup/licenselookup.asp
Surveyor/Land	https://www.idfpr.com/licenselookup/licenselookup.asp
Taxidermist	www.dnr.illinois.gov/LPR/Pages/CommercialLicensesFees.aspx
Teacher, Substitute Teacher	https://sec1.isbe.net/ecs/aspapps/teachersearch.asp
Timber Buyer	www.dnr.state.il.us/law3/timber.htm
Timeshare	https://www.idfpr.com/licenselookup/licenselookup.asp
Timeshare/Land Sales	https://www.idfpr.com/LicenseLookUp/LicenseLookup.asp
Trust Company	www.obrelookupclear.state.il.us/default.asp?Division=11&Profession=73&status=3
Underground Storage Tank	http://webapps.sfm.illinois.gov/ustsearch/Search.aspx
Veterinarian	https://www.idfpr.com/licenselookup/licenselookup.asp
Weighing/Measure Device Serviceman/Companies	www.agr.state.il.us/regulation/inspection/WM_RR_Comp_Scales.pdf

State and Local Courts

State Court Structure: The **Circuit Court** is the Unified Trail Court in Illinois and has jurisdiction for all matters properly brought before it and shares jurisdiction with the Supreme Court to hear cases relating to revenue, mandamus, prohibition, and habeas corpus. Illinois is divided into twenty-three circuits. Five are single county circuits (Cook, Will, DuPage, Lake, and McHenry) and the remaining eighteen circuits comprise as few as two and as many as twelve counties each. There are two types of judges in the Circuit Court: circuit judges and associate judges. Circuit judges, elected for six years, can hear any kind of case. An associate judge can hear any case, except criminal cases punishable by a prison term of one year or more (felonies).

Probate is handled by the Circuit Court in all counties.

Appellate Courts: Opinions and dockets for the Supreme and Appellate Courts are available from www.state.il.us/court.

Statewide Court Online Access: There is no statewide public online system available to trial courts. However at least 64 counties endorse and are participating with a vendor. The site at www.judici.com provides a free index search and a premium subscription service with more detailed information. Available data includes: litigant information; criminal charges, dispositions, and sentences; civil judgments, and case minutes. Visit the site to find the participating counties; they are shown by map and with a drop-down box. More counties will likely be added.

County Sites:

Adams County

Circuit Court www.co.adams.il.us

Civil: Online access is same as described under criminal records. Direct email search requests to rfrese@co.adams.il.us.**$$$** *Criminal:* Online access is free at www.judici.com/. A premium fee service is also available with multi-county search capabilities and other features. Case files are available from 1987. Direct email search requests to rfrese@co.adams.il.us. The county inmate list and warrant list is at the home page. **$$$**

Alexander County

Circuit Court www.state.il.us/court/CircuitCourt/CircuitMap/1st.asp#Alexander

Civil & Criminal: Online access is free at www.judici.com/. A premium fee service is also available with multi-county search capabilities and other features. Case files are available from 1986. **$$$**

Bond County

Circuit Court www.bondcountyil.com/circuitclerk/

Civi: &Criminal: Online access is free at www.judici.com/. A premium fee service is also available with multi-county search capabilities and other features. Case files are available from 1987. **$$$**

Boone County

Circuit Court www.boonecountyil.org

Civi: & Criminal: Search cases since 08/23/1993 free online at www.judici.com/courts/cases/case_search.jsp?court=IL004015J. Also, a premium fee service is available.**$$$**

Bureau County

Circuit Court www.bccirclk.gov/

Civil: Online access to Judicial Circuit records is free at https://www.judici.com/courts/cases/index.jsp?court=IL006015J *Criminal:* Online access to Judicial Circuit records is free athttps://www.judici.com/courts/cases/index.jsp?court=IL006015J.

Carroll County

Circuit Court www.15thjudicialcircuit.com

Civil: Access is free to civil, small claims, probate and traffic records at www.judici.com/courts/index.jsp?court=IL008015J. Records go back to 1988. A premium fee service is also available.**$$$** *Criminal:* same as civil **$$$**

Champaign County

Circuit Court www.cccircuitclerk.com

Civil: Access to the circuit clerk's case query online system called PASS is now free at https://secure.jtsmith.com/clerk/clerk.asp. Online case records go back to '92. A vendor provides online access via subscription is a $59 setup fee plus annual subscription of $240 for this county, or $300/yr for all 7 counties - Champaign, DeKalb, Kendall, LaSalle, Madison, Sangamon, and Will. Visit www.clericusmagnus.com/.**$$$** *Criminal:* same **$$$**

Christian County

Circuit Court www.christiancountyil.com/

Civil: Online access is same as described under criminal records.**$$$** *Criminal:* Online access is free at www.judici.com/. A premium fee service is also available with multi-county search capabilities and other features. Case files are available from 1987.**$$$**

Clark County

Circuit Court www.clarkcountyil.org/circuit_clerk.htm

Civil & Criminal: Access court index and records free from 1989 forward at www.judici.com/courts/cases/case_search.jsp?court=IL012015J.**$$$**

Clay County

Circuit Court www.claycountyillinois.org/index.aspx?page=14

Civil & Criminal: Search cases free at www.judici.com/courts/cases/case_search.jsp?court=IL013015J. Also, a premium fee service is available. **$$$**

Clinton County

Circuit Court www.fourthcircuitil.com/

Civil & Criminal: Search cases free online at www.judici.com/courts/cases/index.jsp?court=IL014015J. Also, a premium fee service is available. **$$$**

Coles County

Circuit Court www.judici.com/courts/index.jsp?court=IL015025J

Civil: Access civil, small claims, probate and traffic records for free at www.judici.com/courts/index.jsp?court=IL015025J, to 1989. A premium fee service is also available. **$$$** *Criminal:* same as civil **$$$**

Cook County

Circuit Court Civil - All Districts www.cookcountyclerkofcourt.org

Civil: Search full case dockets free at www.cookcountyclerkofcourt.org and click on Online Case Info. Among the choices are dockets, case snapshots, probate and traffic. Search by name, number, or date. Data includes attorneys, case type, filing date, the amount of damages sought, division/district, and most current court date. **$$$**

Crawford County

Circuit Court www.crawfordcountycentral.com/circuitclerk/index.htm

Civil: Access is free to civil, small claims, probate and traffic records at www.judici.com/courts/cases/index.jsp?court=IL017015J. Premium fee service also available. **$$$** *Criminal:* Criminal records access is free at www.judici.com/courts/cases/index.jsp?court=IL017015J.

Cumberland County

Circuit Court

Civil: Online access is free at www.judici.com/courts/cases/index.jsp?court=IL003015J. Premium/fee service is also available. **$$$** *Criminal:* same **$$$**

De Kalb County

Circuit Court www.circuitclerk.org/

Civil: Online access to civil court records is the same as criminal, see below. **$$$** *Criminal:* Online access via subscription requires a setup fee plus annual subscription of $240 for this county, or $300/yr Visit www.clericusmagnus.com or www.janojustice.com or call 800-250-9884 for details ands signup. **$$$**

De Witt County

Circuit Court www.dewittcountyill.com/clerk.htm

Civil: Online access is same as described under criminal records.**$$$** *Criminal:* Online access is free at www.judici.com/. A premium fee service is also available with multi-county search capabilities and other features. Case files are available from 1989. **$$$**

Douglas County

Circuit Court

Civil: Online access is same as described under criminal records. **$$$** *Criminal:* Online access is free at www.judici.com/. A premium fee service is also available with multi-county search capabilities and other features. Case files are available from 1989. **$$$**

Edgar County
Circuit Court
Civil: Access is free to civil, small claims, probate and traffic records from 1992 forward at www.judici.com/courts/cases/case_search.jsp?court=IL023015J. A premium fee service also available.**$$$** *Criminal:* same**$$$**

Edwards County
Circuit Court
Civil: Online access is same as described under criminal records. **$$$** *Criminal:* Online access is free at www.judici.com/. A premium fee service is also available with multi-county search capabilities and other features. Case files are available from 2000. **$$$**

Effingham County
Circuit Court www.fourthcircuitil.com/
Civil: Access is free to civil, small claims, probate and traffic records from 1987 forward at www.judici.com/courts/cases/index.jsp?court=IL025015J. A premium fee service also available.**$$$** *Criminal:* Same as civil $$$

Fayette County
Circuit Court www.fourthcircuitil.com/
Civil: Access court index and records from 1988 forward free at www.judici.com/courts/cases/case_search.jsp?court=IL026015J.**$$$** *Criminal:* same**$$$**

Ford County
Circuit Court
Civil: Online access is same as described under criminal records.**$$$** *Criminal:* Online access is free at www.judici.com/. A premium fee service is also available with multi-county search capabilities and other features. Criminal and civil case files are available from March 2000, traffic records from 1989.**$$$**

Franklin County
Circuit Court
Civil: Access is free to civil, small claims, probate and traffic records at www.judici.com/courts/cases/index.jsp?court=IL028015J. A premium fee service also available. **$$$** *Criminal:* same as civil. **$$$**

Grundy County
Circuit Court
Civil: Access is free to civil, small claims, probate and traffic records at www.judici.com/courts/cases/case_search.jsp?court=IL004015J. Premium fee service also available. **$$$** *Criminal:* same **$$$**

Hamilton County
Circuit Court
Civil: Online access is same as described under criminal records. **$$$** *Criminal:* Online access is free at www.judici.com/. A premium fee service is also available with multi-county search capabilities and other features. Case files are available from 2000. **$$$**

Henry County
Circuit Court www.henrycty.com/Departments/CircuitClerk/tabid/86/Default.aspx
Civil: Online access is free at www.judici.com/. A premium fee service is also available with multi-county search capabilities and other features. Case files are available from 1989. **$$$** *Criminal:* same **$$$**

Iroquois County
Circuit Court www.judici.com/courts/index.jsp?court=IL038025J
Civil: Search cases free online at www.judici.com/courts/cases/index.jsp?court=IL038025J. A premium fee service is also available.**$$$** *Criminal:* Access criminal records free at www.judici.com/courts/cases/index.jsp?court=IL038025J.**$$$**

Jackson County
Circuit Court www.circuitclerk.co.jackson.il.us/index-2.html
Civil: Online access is same as described under criminal records.**$$$** *Criminal:* Online access is free at www.judici.com/courts/cases/case_search.jsp?court=IL039015J. A premium fee service is also available with multi-county search capabilities and other features. Case files are available from 1985.**$$$**

Jefferson County
Circuit Court
Civil: Online access is same as described under criminal records.**$$$** *Criminal:* Online access is free at www.judici.com/. A premium fee service is also available with multi-county search capabilities and other features. Case files are available from 1987.**$$$**

Jersey County

Circuit Court www.jerseycounty-il.us

Civil: Court records may be accessed free at www.jerseycounty-il.us, click on Court Record Search. Also, online access is free at www.judici.com/. A premium fee service is also available with multi-county search capabilities and other features. Case files available from 1990.**$$$** *Criminal:* same **$$$**

Jo Daviess County

Circuit Court www.jodaviess.org/

Civil: Online access is same as described under criminal records.**$$$** *Criminal:* Online access is free at www.judici.com/. A premium fee service is also available with multi-county search capabilities and other features. Case files are available from 1992.**$$$**

Johnson County

Circuit Court

Civil: Online access is same as described under criminal records.**$$$** *Criminal:* Online access is free at www.judici.com/. A premium fee service is also available with multi-county search capabilities and other features. Case files are available from April 1987.**$$$**

Kane County

Circuit Court www.cic.co.kane.il.us

Civil: Online access at http://kocis.countyofkane.org/KOCIS/KOCIS.html#. Electronic results may include DL number**$$$** *Criminal:* same **$$$**

Kankakee County

Circuit Court www.co.kankakee.il.us/circuitclerk.html

Civil: Online access to the civil dockets is free at http://173.165.39.26/eservices/home.page. Note the data entry requirements if searching by case number. There are search options for range of DOB and File Date. *Criminal:* Online access to the criminal dockets is free at http://173.165.39.26/eservices/home.page. Note the data entry requirements if searching by case number. Includes Traffic. There are search options for range of DOB and File Date.

Kendall County

Circuit Court

Civil: Online access to civil court records is the same as criminal, see below.**$$$** *Criminal:* Online access via subscription requires a setup fee plus annual subscription of $240 for this county, or $300/yr for all participating IL counties - Champaign, DeKalb, Kendall, LaSalle, Madison, Sangamon, Will. Visit www.clericusmagnus.com or www.janojustice.com or call 800-250-9884 for details ands signup. **$$$**

La Salle County

Circuit Court - Civil Division www.lasallecounty.com

Civil: A vendor provides online access via subscription is a $59 setup fee plus annual subscription of $240 for this county, or $300/yr for all counties - Champaign, Dekalb, Kendall, Madison, Sangamon, Will and Winnebago. Visit www.clericusmagnus.com/.**$$$**

Circuit Court - Criminal Division www.lasallecounty.com

Criminal: Online access via subscription requires a setup fee plus annual subscription of $240 for this county, or $300/yr for all participating IL counties - Champaign, DeKalb, Kendall, LaSalle, Madison, Sangamon, Will. Visit www.clericusmagnus.com or www.janojustice.com or call 800-250-9884 for details and signup. **$$$**

Lawrence County

Circuit Court

Civil: Online access is same as described under criminal records.**$$$** *Criminal:* Online access is free at www.judici.com/. A premium fee service is also available with multi-county search capabilities and other features. Case files are available from 1999.**$$$**

Lee County

Circuit Court

Civil: Online access is same as described under criminal records.**$$$** *Criminal:* Online access is free at www.judici.com/. A premium fee service is also available with multi-county search capabilities and other features. Case files are available from 1987. **$$$**

Livingston County

Circuit Court http://livingstoncountyil.gov/?page_id=91

Civil: Probate along with divorce, traffic, miscellaneous remedy cases, law, all in separate indexes at this same address. Search cases free online at www.judici.com/courts/cases/case_search.jsp?court=IL053015J. Also, a premium fee service is available. Records back to 2000.**$$$** *Criminal:* Search cases free online at www.judici.com/courts/cases/case_search.jsp?court=IL053015J. Also, a premium fee service is available. Records back to 2000. **$$$**

Logan County

Circuit Court www.co.logan.il.us/circuit_clerk/

Civil: Online access is same as described under criminal records.**$$$** *Criminal:* Online access is free at www.judici.com/courts/cases/case_search.jsp?court=IL054025J. A premium fee service is also available with multi-county search capabilities and other features. Case files are available from 1987.**$$$**

Macon County

Circuit Court www.cclerk.co.macon.il.us/

Civil: Access to court records is free at http://search.co.macon.il.us/templates/searchcaseinfo.htm. Search docket information back to 04/96. Includes traffic, probate, family, small claims. *Criminal:* Access to court records is free online at http://search.co.macon.il.us/templates/searchcaseinfo.htm. Search docket information back to 04/96.

Macoupin County

Circuit Court www.macoupincountyil.gov/circuit_clerk.htm

Criminal: Online access is free at www.judici.com/. A premium fee service is also available with multi-county search capabilities and other features. Case files are available from 1994.**$$$**

Madison County

Circuit Court - Civil/Misdemeanor Division www.co.madison.il.us

Civil: A free docket search is offered at www.co.madison.il.us/CircuitClerk/eMagnusLite.shtml. Search by name, case number or DL#. A vendor provides online access via subscription is a $59 setup fee plus annual subscription of $240 for this county, or $300/yr for all 7 counties - Champaign, Dekalb, Kendall, Madison, Sangamon, Will and Winnebago. Visit www.clericusmagnus.com/.**$$$** *Criminal:* Online access to misdemeanor records is free at www.co.madison.il.us/CircuitClerk/eMagnusLite.shtml. Search by name, case number or DL#. **$$$**

Circuit Court - Felony Division http://madisoncountycircuitcourt.org/courts/criminal/

Criminal: same Online access via subscription requires a setup fee plus annual subscription of $240 for this county, or $300/yr for participating IL counties - Champaign, DeKalb, Kendall, LaSalle, Madison, Sangamon, Will. Visit www.clericusmagnus.com. **$$$**

Marion County

Circuit Court www.fourthcircuitil.com/

Civil: Online access is same as described under criminal records.**$$$** *Criminal:* Online access is free at www.judici.com/. A premium fee service is also available with multi-county search capabilities and other features. Case files are available from 1988.**$$$**

Marshall County

Circuit Court www.marshallcountyillinois.com/home/ElectedOfficials/CircuitClerk.aspx

Civil: Online access is same as described under criminal records.**$$$** *Criminal:* Online access is free at www.judici.com/. A premium fee service is also available with multi-county search capabilities and other features. Case files are available from 1987.**$$$**

Mason County

Circuit Court www.masoncountyil.org

Civil: Online access is free at www.judici.com/. A premium fee service is also available with multi-county search capabilities and other features. Case files are available from 1987.**$$$** *Criminal:* same**$$$**

McHenry County

Circuit Court www.co.mchenry.il.us/departments/circuitclerk/Pages/index.aspx

Civil: Access to civil, traffic and domestic records is the same as criminal, see below. One may order copies online from the home page, same copy and search fees apply.**$$$** *Criminal:* Free docket search is at http://68.21.116.46/wow65/runApp?id=0. For complete case file information, access to records on the subscription system requires $750 license fee and $92.50 set-up fee, plus $50 per month. Records date back to 1990 with civil, criminal, probate, traffic, and domestic records. For more info, call 815-334-4302. **$$$**

McLean County

Circuit Court www.mcleancountyil.gov

Criminal: Free public access at http://webapp.mcleancountyil.gov/webapps/PublicAccess/pubac_main.htm. System has traffic as well as criminal index. Full years of Circuit Clerk data are available from 1991-present.

Mercer County

Circuit Court www.mercercountyil.org/

Civil: Online access is same as described under criminal records.**$$$** *Criminal:* Online access is free at www.judici.com/. A premium fee service is also available with multi-county search capabilities and other features. Case files are available from 1988.**$$$**

Montgomery County

Circuit Court www.montgomeryco.com/index.php/circuit-court-clerk

Civil: Online access is same as described under criminal records.**$$$** *Criminal:* Online access is free at www.judici.com/. A premium fee service is also available with multi-county search capabilities and other features. Case files are available from 1992.**$$$**

Morgan County

Circuit Court

Civil: Online access is same as described under criminal records.**$$$** *Criminal:* Online access is free at www.judici.com/. A premium fee service is also available with multi-county search capabilities and other features. Case files are available from 1990.**$$$**

Moultrie County

Circuit Court www.circuit-clerk.moultrie.il.us

Civil: Online access is same as described under criminal records.**$$$** *Criminal:* Online access is free at www.judici.com/. A premium fee service is also available with multi-county search capabilities and other features. Case files are available from June 1990.**$$$**

Ogle County

Circuit Court www.oglecircuitclerk.org/

Civil: Online access is free at www.judici.com/. A premium fee service is also available with multi-county search capabilities and other features. Case files are available from 1994.**$$$** *Criminal:* Online access is free at www.judici.com/courts/cases/case_search.jsp?court=IL071015J. A premium fee service is also available with multi-county search capabilities and other features. Case files are available from 1989. **$$$**

Piatt County

Circuit Court www.piattcounty.org/

Civil: Online access is free at www.judici.com/. A premium fee service is also available with multi-county search capabilities and other features. Case files are available from 1999.**$$$** *Criminal:* same**$$$**

Pike County

Circuit Court www.pikeil.org/

Civil: Online access is free at www.judici.com/. A premium fee service is also available with multi-county search capabilities and other features. Case files are available from 1991.**$$$** *Criminal:* same**$$$**

Pope County

Circuit Court

Civil: Online access is free at www.judici.com/. A premium fee service is also available with multi-county search capabilities and other features. Case files are available from 1989.**$$$** *Criminal:* Online access is free at www.judici.com/. A premium fee service is also available with multi-county search capabilities and other features. Case files are available from 1987.**$$$**

Pulaski County

Circuit Court

Civil: Online access is free at www.judici.com/. A premium fee service is also available with multi-county search capabilities and other features. Case files are available from 1986.**$$$** *Criminal:* same**$$$**

Putnam County

Circuit Court

Civil: Online access is free at www.judici.com/. A premium fee service is also available with multi-county search capabilities and other features. Case files are available from 1990.**$$$** *Criminal:* same **$$$**

Richland County

Circuit Court

Civil: Online access is free at www.judici.com/. A premium fee service is also available with multi-county search capabilities and other features. Case files are available from 1999.**$$$** *Criminal:* same **$$$**

Rock Island County

Circuit Court www.rockislandcounty.org/CircuitClerk/CivilDiv/Home/

Civil: Full access to court records on the remote online system requires contract and fees. Civil, criminal, probate, traffic, and domestic records can be accessed by name or case number. Online access is free at www.judici.com/. A premium fee service is also available with multi-county search capabilities and other features. Case files are available from 1989.**$$$** *Criminal:* same **$$$**

Saline County

Circuit Court

Civil: Online access is free at www.judici.com/. A premium fee service is also available with multi-county search capabilities and other features. Case files are available from 1986.**$$$** *Criminal:* same **$$$**

Sangamon County

Circuit Court www.sangamoncountycircuitclerk.org

Civil: Online access to civil records is the same as criminal, see below. A daily court docket is found at www.infax.com/docket/sangamoncountydocket/.**$$$** *Criminal:* Online access via subscription requires a setup fee plus annual subscription of $240 for this county, or $300/yr for all participating IL counties - Champaign, DeKalb, Kendall, LaSalle, Madison, Sangamon, Will. Visit www.clericusmagnus.com or www.janojustice.com or call 800-250-9884 for details ands signup. A free search is also offered at http://67.128.239.91/sccc/Home.sc, but this is a limited search and not official unless certified. **$$$**

Schuyler County

Circuit Court

Civil: Online access is free at www.judici.com/. A premium fee service is also available with multi-county search capabilities and other features. Case files are available from 1988.**$$$** *Criminal:* same **$$$**

Shelby County

Circuit Court www.fourthcircuitil.com/

Civil: Online access is free at www.judici.com/. A premium fee service is also available with multi-county search capabilities and other features. Case files are available from 1988.**$$$** *Criminal:* same**$ $$**

Stark County

Circuit Court

Civil: Online access is free at www.judici.com/. A premium fee service is also available with multi-county search capabilities and other features. Case files are available from 2000.**$$$** *Criminal:* same **$$$**

Stephenson County

Circuit Court www.co.stephenson.il.us/circuitclerk/

Civil: Online access is free at www.judici.com/. A premium fee service is also available with multi-county search capabilities and other features. Case files are available from 1989.**$$$** *Criminal:* same **$$$**

Tazewell County

Circuit Court www.tazewell.com/

Civil: Online access is free at www.judici.com/. A premium fee service is also available with multi-county search capabilities and other features. Case files are available from Feb. 1989.**$$$** *Criminal:* same**$$$**

Union County

Circuit Court www.fjc-il.org/UN.html

Civil: Online access is free at www.judici.com/. A premium fee service is also available with multi-county search capabilities and other features. Case files are available from 1986.**$$$** *Criminal:* same **$$$**

Vermilion County

Circuit Court www.co.vermilion.il.us

Civil: Search the index at www.judici.com/courts/cases/case_search.jsp?court=IL092015J. Records are current to 1989. Premium fee service also available.**$$$** *Criminal:* Search the index at www.judici.com/courts/cases/case_search.jsp?court=IL092015J. Records are current to 1989.**$$$**

Wabash County

Circuit Court

Civil: Online access is free at www.judici.com/. A premium fee service is also available with multi-county search capabilities and other features. Case files are available from 2000.**$$$** *Criminal:* same **$$$**

Washington County

Circuit Court

Civil: Online access is free at www.judici.com/. A premium fee service is also available with multi-county search capabilities and other features. Case files are available from 1997.**$$$** *Criminal:* same**$ $$**

Wayne County

Circuit Court www.illinoissecondcircuit.info/county_wayne.html

Civil: Online access is free at www.judici.com/. A premium fee service is also available with multi-county search capabilities and other features. Case files are available from 1988.**$$$** *Criminal:* same **$$$**

White County

Circuit Court www.whitecounty-il.gov/

Civil: Online access is free at www.judici.com/. A premium fee service is also available with multi-county search capabilities and other features. Case files are available from 1992.**$$$** *Criminal:* same **$$$**

Whiteside County

Circuit Court www.whiteside.org/circuit-clerk/

Civil: Online access is free at www.judici.com/. A premium fee service is also available with multi-county search capabilities and other features. Case files are available from 1989.**$$$** *Criminal:* same **$$$**

Will County

Circuit Court www.willcountycircuitcourt.com

Civil: Online access to civil court records is the same as criminal, see below. **$$$** *Criminal:* A free online name search of the docket is at http://66.158.72.242/pa/cms/Signoff.php. Also a subscription service with an annual fee of $240 for this county, or $300/yr for all participating IL counties is offered. Counties are: Champaign, DeKalb, Kendall, LaSalle, Madison, Sangamon, Will. Visit www.clericusmagnus.com or www.janojustice.com or call 800-250-9884 for details and signup. **$$$**

Williamson County

Circuit Court www.state.il.us/court/CircuitCourt/default.asp

Civil: Online access is free at www.judici.com/. A premium fee service is also available with multi-county search capabilities and other features. Case files are available from 1986. Also, court calendars available free at http://williamsoncountycourthouse.com/p/calendars.php.**$$$** *Criminal:* same **$$$**

Winnebago County

Circuit Court www.cc.co.winnebago.il.us

Civil: Online access to civil court records is the same as describe for criminal - see that section. Cases are available from 1988. *Criminal:* Online access is at www.cc.co.winnebago.il.us/caseinfo.asp?P=I. Complete case files are available from 1980. Traffic citations, DUIs, and ordinance violations are available from 1996. The web page offers an excellent User's Guide that explains how to fully use the system. Court calendars are also available.

Woodford County

Circuit Court

Civil: Online access to civil cases same as criminal, see below. **$$$** *Criminal:* Online access is free at www.judici.com/. A premium fee service is also available with multi-county search capabilities and other features. Case files are available from 2000.**$$$**

Recorders, Assessors, and Other Sites of Note

Recording Office Organization: 102 counties, 102 recording offices. The recording officer is the County Recorder, but some counties prefer the name Recorder of Deeds. Many counties utilize a grantor/grantee index containing all transactions. Cook County had separate offices for real estate recording and UCC filing until they combined offices June 30, 2001. Since that date only UCC extension, amendments or terminations can be filed on exisiting UCCs, with exception of UCCs on real estate related collateral whch are still filed here.

Statewide or Multi-Jurisdiction Access: A number of counties offer online access. There is no statewide system, but there is agency-supported vendor as indicated below.

- Thirty-four counties are connected to the recorded land data subscription service from the Tapestry system. Coverage for multiple counties is offered. There is a $5.95 fee per search and copies can be generated for $.50 per page. You can pay as you go with a credit card or be billed monthly with a $25.00 monthly minimum. Visit at https://tapestry.fidlar.com.

County Sites:

Adams County ***Recorded Documents*** www.co.adams.il.us Access to records for a fee at https://tapestry.fidlar.com/Tapestry2/Default.aspx. Contact 309-794-3283 or kylec@fidlar.com forsubscription information. Search fee is $5.95 each, printed images $.50 each unless otherwise noted. **$$$**

Property, Taxation Records Access property data free at www.emapsplus.com/ILAdams/maps/, including name searching.

Boone County ***Recorded Documents*** www.boonecountyil.org/department/clerk Access to records for a fee at https://tapestry.fidlar.com/Tapestry2/Default.aspx. Contact 309-794-3283 or kylec@fidlar.com forsubscription information. Search fee is $5.95 each, printed images $.50 each unless otherwise noted. **$$$**

Property, Taxation Records Property assessments/tax info is free at www.boonecountyil.org/department/assessment. Also, access to property data is free at http://booneil.devnetwedge.com/wedge/. Also, access to GIS/mapping for free at www.boonecountyil.org/department/gis. Access land data on commercial site - PropertyMax - at http://booneilpropertymax.governmaxa.com/propertymax/rover30.asp. Subscription packages from $20.00 per month.**$$$**

Bureau County ***Recorded Documents*** www.bureaucountyclerk.com/ Access to records for a fee at https://tapestry.fidlar.com/Tapestry2/Default.aspx. Contact 309-794-3283 or kylec@fidlar.com forsubscription information. Search fee is $5.95 each, printed images $.50 each unless otherwise noted. **$$$**

Property, Taxation Records Access to property tax, parcel info and property sales for free at www.fikeandfike.com/propertytax/Home/Home.aspx.

Carroll County ***Recorded Documents*** www.carroll-county.net/index.asp?Type=B_BASIC&SEC={001FFB74-9846-4774-BCF2-566081E09851} Access to records for a fee at https://tapestry.fidlar.com/Tapestry2/Default.aspx. Contact 309-794-3283 or kylec@fidlar.com forsubscription information. Search fee is $5.95 each, printed images $.50 each unless otherwise noted. **$$$**

Cass County ***Property, Taxation Records*** Search assessor property data for a fee on the GIS system at http://beacon.schneidercorp.com/.

Champaign County ***Recorded Documents*** www.co.champaign.il.us/recorder/recorder.htm Access to records for a fee at https://tapestry.fidlar.com/Tapestry2/Default.aspx. Contact 309-794-3283 or kylec@fidlar.com forsubscription information. Search fee is $5.95 each, printed images $.50 each unless otherwise noted. **$$$**

Property, Taxation Records Search property tax records free at www.co.champaign.il.us/ccao/Assessors.htm. Also, search the treasurer's real estate property tax database free at www.co.champaign.il.us/taxlookup, but no name searching.

Christian County ***Recorded Documents*** http://christiancountyil.com/countyclerk/index.html Access to records for a fee at https://tapestry.fidlar.com/Tapestry2/Default.aspx. Contact 309-794-3283 or kylec@fidlar.com forsubscription information. Search fee is $5.95 each, printed images $.50 each unless otherwise noted. **$$$**

Property, Taxation Records Access to property tax data for free at www.fikeandfike.com/propertytax/Christian/MainMenu.aspx?c=11.

Clark County ***Property, Taxation Records*** Access to GIS/mapping for free at http://clark.il.bhamaps.com/.

Clinton County ***Recorded Documents*** https://www.clintonco.illinois.gov/county_clerk.htm The agency sends requesters to the Laredo system. Fees are based on a flat rate by usage ranging from $50 to $250 per month. The same vendor offers the Tapestry program with a $5.95 search fee and copies for $.50 per page. **$$$**

Coles County ***Recorded Documents*** www.co.coles.il.us/CoClerk/default.htm Record index from the recorder's database back to 1978 is free at https://www.illandrecords.com/illr/il029/index.jsp. Fees apply to see images and make copies. **$$$**

Property, Taxation Records Access property tax data free at www.fikeandfike.com/propertytax/Home/Home.aspx?c=15.

Cook County Recorder ***Recorded Documents*** www.ccrd.info/ Search Grantor/Grantee index and locate property data at www.ccrd.info/CCRD/il031/index.jsp. Fee for documents. Search DIMS database of recordings since 10/1985; registration and fees apply. While online recorded images require a fee, in person does not. Includes Treasurer's Current Year Tax System APIN and DuPage recorder. Sign-up info is at www.ccrd.info/CCRD/il031/index.jsp. Also, you may purchase the real estate transfer list; $100 per year on disk or $50 if you pick-up at agency. Also, access to records for a fee at https://tapestry.fidlar.com/Tapestry2/Default.aspx. Contact 309-794-3283 or kylec@fidlar.com forsubscription information. Search fee is $5.95 each, pringed images $.50 each unless otherwise noted. **$$$**

Property, Taxation Records Online search and retrieval of parcel data with GIS pictures of residential and nonresidential properties as well as prior and current assessment values are available. Also, search assessor data at www.cookcountyassessor.com but no name searching.

Crawford County ***Property, Taxation Records*** Access to property sales reports for free at www.crawfordcountycentral.com/webedit/index.php?p=assessor_sales&t=table.

De Kalb County ***Property, Taxation Records*** Search property assessor data free at www.dekalbcounty.org/GIS/TASDisclaimer.html Also, access to GIS/mapping free at www.dekalbcounty.org/GIS/GISWebDisclaimer.html.

De Witt County ***Property, Taxation Records*** Access property tax data free at www.fikeandfike.com/propertytax/Home/Disclaimer.aspx?c=20&n=Dewitt.

Douglas County ***Property, Taxation Records*** Access to record searches for free at http://douglas.illinoisassessors.com/. Subscription available for advanced searches and advanced parcel searches for a fee.**$$$**

Du Page County ***Recorded Documents*** www.dupageco.org/recorder/ Access to records for a fee at https://tapestry.fidlar.com/Tapestry2/Default.aspx. Contact 309-794-3283 or kylec@fidlar.com forsubscription information. Search fee is $5.95 each, printed images $.50 each unless otherwise noted. **$$$**

Property, Taxation Records Search Wheatland Township records at http://wheatlandassessor.com/SD/wlt/content/default.aspx?ID=6. Search Wayne Township records at www.waynetownshipassessor.com/. Search Bloomingdale Township property records at www.bloomingdaletownshipassessor.com/. Search Addison Township records at http://addisontownship.com/SD/addison/content/Detail.aspx?ID=2&CID=893fc6c7-629a-4b82-bf31-955cedae7efc. No name searches in any of these sites.

Effingham County ***Property, Taxation Records*** Access to tax parcel data is free or by subscription to the GIS site at www.co.effingham.il.us/GIS.html.**$$$**

Ford County ***Property, Taxation Records*** Access to property search data for free at http://il-ford-assessor.governmax.com/svc/

Fulton County ***Recorded Documents*** Access to records for a fee at https://tapestry.fidlar.com/Tapestry2/Default.aspx. Contact 309-794-3283 or kylec@fidlar.com forsubscription information. Search fee is $5.95 each, printed images $.50 each unless otherwise noted. **$$$**

Gallatin County ***Recorded Documents*** Access to records for a fee at https://cotthosting.com/ILPortal/User/Login.aspx?ReturnUrl=%2fILPortal%2fIndex.aspx. **$$$**

Henderson County ***Property, Taxation Records*** Access to Assessor's database information free at http://henderson.illinoisassessors.com/.

Henry County ***Recorded Documents*** www.henrycty.com/Departments/Recorder/tabid/184/Default.aspx Access to records for a fee at https://tapestry.fidlar.com/Tapestry2/Default.aspx. Contact 309-794-3283 or kylec@fidlar.com forsubscription information. Search fee is $5.95 each, printed images $.50 each unless otherwise noted. **$$$**

Property, Taxation Records Access to the assessor property database is free at www.henrycty.com/Departments/Assessments/AssessmentsSearch/tabid/141/Default.aspx. Access the treasurer's tax payment data free at www.henrycty.com/Departments/Treasurer/tabid/94/Default.aspx. Search county foreclosure list free at www.foreclosure.com/search.html?rsp=6252&st=IL&cno=073.

Jackson County ***Recorded Documents*** www.co.jackson.il.us/index.php/clerk-and-recorders-office Access to records for a fee at https://tapestry.fidlar.com/Tapestry2/Default.aspx. Contact 309-794-3283 or kylec@fidlar.com forsubscription information. Search fee is $5.95 each, printed images $.50 each unless otherwise noted. **$$$**

Jo Daviess County ***Recorded Documents*** www.jodaviess.org/index.asp?Type=B_BASIC&SEC={3DAA2673-44BE-41BA-B4AF-94B575DF38CF} Access to records for a fee at https://tapestry.fidlar.com/Tapestry2/Default.aspx. Contact 309-794-3283 or kylec@fidlar.com forsubscription information. Search fee is $5.95 each, printed images $.50 each unless otherwise noted. **$$$**

Kane County ***Recorded Documents*** www.countyofkane.org/Pages/default.aspx Access recorders real estate records free at www.kanecountyrecorder.net/lrs/Source/Home.aspx. Online images of recorded documents are unofficial; documents acquired in person or through the copy center 630-232-5944 are official.

Property, Taxation Records Search the Tax Assessment database at www.co.kane.il.us/TaxAssessment/. Search by parcel number or address only; no name searching.

Kankakee County ***Recorded Documents*** www.k3countyrecorder.com/ Access to records for a fee at https://tapestry.fidlar.com/Tapestry2/Default.aspx. Contact 309-794-3283 or kylec@fidlar.com forsubscription information. Search fee is $5.95 each, printed images $.50 each unless otherwise noted. The Treasurer offers a free property inquiry at http://treasurer.k3county.net/propertyinquiry.pl. **$$$**

Property, Taxation Records The Treasurer offers a free property inquiry at http://treasurer.k3county.net/.

Kendall County ***Recorded Documents*** www.kendallcountyrecorder.net/ Access to land records free at www.kendallcountyrecorder.net/lrs/Source/Home.aspx.

Property, Taxation Records Search property data free at www.co.kendall.il.us/assessors/property_tax_inquiry.html. Search tax data by name or parcel number.

Knox County ***Recorded Documents*** www.co.knox.il.us/ Access to records for a fee at https://tapestry.fidlar.com/Tapestry2/Default.aspx. Contact 309-794-3283 or kylec@fidlar.com forsubscription information. Search fee is $5.95 each, printed images $.50 each unless otherwise noted. **$$$**

Lake County ***Real Estate, Grantor/Grantee, Deed, Lien, Mortgage, Judgment, Lis Penden Records*** www.lakecountyil.gov/recorder/Pages/default.aspx Access to county recorded documents is by subscription; Index back to 1980; images back to 1800's. See website for information. **$$$**

Property, Taxation Records Search property by address or legal description for free on the GIS-mapping site at http://gis2.co.lake.il.us/maps/.

La Salle County ***Recorded Documents*** www.lasallecounty.org/recorder/index.htm Access to records for a fee at https://tapestry.fidlar.com/Tapestry2/Default.aspx. Contact 309-794-3283 or kylec@fidlar.com for subscription information. Search fee is $5.95 each, printed images $.50 each unless otherwise noted. **$$$**

Lee County ***Recorded Documents*** www.leecountyil.com Access to records for a fee at https://tapestry.fidlar.com/Tapestry2/Default.aspx. Contact 309-794-3283 or kylec@fidlar.com forsubscription information. Search fee is $5.95 each, printed images $.50 each unless otherwise noted. **$$$**

Livingston County ***Property, Taxation Records*** Free parcel search at http://livingston.illinoisassessors.com/search.php. For more detailed information, must subscribe for a fee. Contact the assessor's office for subscription information.**$$$**

Logan County ***Property, Taxation Records*** Search the tax assessor database at http://loganil.devnetwedge.com/wedge/. Access to GIS/mapping for free at www.centralilmaps.com/LoganGIS/. Also, access property data free at www.co.logan.il.us/treasurer/.

McHenry County ***Recorded Documents*** www.co.mchenry.il.us/departments/Recorder/Pages/index.aspx Access to records for a fee at https://tapestry.fidlar.com/Tapestry2/Default.aspx. Contact 309-794-3283 or kylec@fidlar.com for subscription information. Search fee is $5.95 each, printed images $.50 each unless otherwise noted. Also, access to land record search free at http://68.21.116.60/freewebsearch/default.aspx. **$$$**

Property, Taxation Records Records on the County Treasurer Inquiry site are free at www.mchenrytreasurer.org/common/countydpt/treas/default.aspx. Sheriff's foreclosure list is free at www.mchenrysheriff.org/side-nav-pages/side-nav-item-5.aspx.

McLean County ***Recorded Documents*** http://mcleancountyil.gov/index.aspx?nid=94 Access to recorder official records for free at http://webapp.mcleancountyil.gov/External/User/Login.aspx?ReturnUrl=%2fexternal%2findex.aspx. A registered user account required. Also, access county parcel and mobile home lots free at http://webapp.mcleancountyil.gov/webapps/(X(1)S(q2ps32as0vcpxa45wumlwh55))/Tax/MobileHomeSearch.aspx?AspxAutoDetectCookieSupport=1; no name searching. Also, search unclaimed property list at www.mcleancountyil.gov/index.aspx?nid=560.

Property, Taxation Records Access to parcel information for free at http://webapp.mcleancountyil.gov/webapps/(X(1)S(qsmw0wq4byg5el552yikfv55))/Tax/TaxParcelInfo.aspx?AspxAutoDetectCookieSupport=1.

Macon County ***Recorded Documents*** www.co.macon.il.us/recorder.php Searching recorded data free at http://173.15.61.162/.

Property, Taxation Records Access the county GIS mapping site by address at www.gis.co.macon.il.us/.

Macoupin County ***Recorded Documents*** www.macoupincountyil.gov/county_clerk.htm Recorded land documents, including images, will be available from 1/1/2001 to present. The account will have a username and password. Fees are 30 day Sub=$25.00, 180 day Sub=$125.00 and 1 year Sub=$200.00. Call the Recorder's office at X708 to set up account. The search site is at www.macoupincountyil.gov/county_clerk_remote.htm. **$$$**

Property, Taxation Records Access to parcel search for free at http://macoupin.il.bhamaps.com/.

Madison County ***Recorded Documents*** www.co.madison.il.us Access to records for a fee at https://tapestry.fidlar.com/Tapestry2/Default.aspx. Contact 309-794-3283 or kylec@fidlar.com for subscription information. Search fee is $5.95 each, printed images $.50 each unless otherwise noted. **$$$**

Property, Taxation Records Free parcel data at http://reweb1.co.madison.il.us/Forms/Search.aspx. Search by name, address or parcel number.

Marion County ***Recorded Documents*** Access to records for a fee at https://tapestry.fidlar.com/Tapestry2/Default.aspx. Contact 309-794-3283 or kylec@fidlar.com for subscription information. Search fee is $5.95 each, printed images $.50 each unless otherwise noted. **$$$**

Marshall County ***Property, Taxation Records*** Access to assessor property records is by subscription; $20 per month, minimum of 3 months. Contact the Assessor office for signup- 309-246-2350. Also, access to property tax data free at www.fikeandfike.com/propertytax/Marshall/MainMenu.aspx?c=59.**$$$**

Mason County ***Property, Taxation Records*** Access to real estate data for free to go www.masoncountyil.org/page39.html, includes farm card data and parcel data.

Monroe County ***Recorded Documents*** www.monroecountyil.org/index.aspx?nid=115 Access to records for a fee at https://tapestry.fidlar.com/Tapestry2/Default.aspx. Contact 309-794-3283 or kylec@fidlar.com for subscription information. Search fee is $5.95 each, printed images $.50 each unless otherwise noted. **$$$**

Property, Taxation Records Access to IL property tax data for free at www.fikeandfike.com/propertytax/home/Home.aspx Also, access to GIS/mapping free at www.mocoil.org/index.aspx?nid=74

Montgomery County ***Recorded Documents*** www.montgomeryco.com/countyclerk/ Access to records for a fee at https://tapestry.fidlar.com/Tapestry2/Default.aspx. Contact 309-794-3283 or kylec@fidlar.com for subscription information. Search fee is $5.95 each, printed images $.50 each unless otherwise noted. **$$$**

Morgan County ***Recorded Documents*** www.morgancounty-il.com/County-Clerk.html Access recording office land data at www.etitlesearch.com/; registration required, fee based on usage. Also, access to land data for a fee go to https://tapestry.fidlar.com/Tapestry2/Search.aspx. The cost of a search is $5.95, cost of printed page is $.50. **$$$**

Property, Taxation Records Access to property records for free at http://beacon.schneidercorp.com/

Moultrie County ***Recorded Documents*** Access to records for a fee at https://tapestry.fidlar.com/Tapestry2/Default.aspx. Contact 309-794-3283 or kylec@fidlar.com for subscription information. Search fee is $5.95 each, printed images $.50 each unless otherwise noted. **$$$**

Ogle County ***Recorded Documents*** http://oglecountyclerk.org/ Access to records for a fee at https://tapestry.fidlar.com/Tapestry2/Default.aspx. Contact 309-794-3283 or kylec@fidlar.com for subscription information. Search fee is $5.95 each, printed images $.50 each unless otherwise noted. **$$$**

Property, Taxation Records Search assessor property data for a fee on the GIS system at http://beacon.schneidercorp.com/ but registration and username required for a name search. Also, access to 2011 property assessments free at www.oglecounty.org/soa/alphalist2010all.pdf.**$$$**

Peoria County ***Recorded Documents*** www.peoriacounty.org/deedsrecorder/ Recorder's office has a subscription service with web access to land records and other official documents; call Recorder for details. **$$$**

Property, Taxation Records Access to property tax database for free at http://66.99.203.101/assessor/realasp1.asp.

Perry County ***Recorded Documents*** http://perrycountyclerk.com/ Access to records for a fee at https://tapestry.fidlar.com/Tapestry2/Default.aspx. Contact 309-794-3283 or kylec@fidlar.com for subscription information. Search fee is $5.95 each, printed images $.50 each unless otherwise noted. **$$$**

Pulaski County ***Property, Taxation Records*** Access to property tax data for free at www.fikeandfike.com/propertytax/Home/Home.aspx?c=77.

Randolph County ***Recorded Documents*** http://randolphcountyclerk.com/ Access to records for a fee at https://tapestry.fidlar.com/Tapestry2/Default.aspx. Contact 309-794-3283 or kylec@fidlar.com for subscription information. Search fee is $5.95 each, printed images $.50 each unless otherwise noted. **$$$**

Rock Island County ***Recorded Documents*** www.rockislandcounty.org/Recorder/Home/ Access to records for a fee at https://tapestry.fidlar.com/Tapestry2/Default.aspx. Contact 309-794-3283 or kylec@fidlar.com for subscription information. Search fee is $5.95 each, printed images $.50 each unless otherwise noted. Also, access for a fee to eRecording Partners Network go to www.erecordingpartners.net/. **$$$**

Property, Taxation Records Access to property tax searches at www.rockislandcounty.org/TaxSearch/. Moline Town assessor records are free at www.molinetownship.com/OnlineSearch/Search.asp. No name searching.

St. Clair County ***Recorded Documents*** www.co.st-clair.il.us/government/officials/Pages/recorder.aspx Access to land records is free at http://216.182.182.50/ILStClair/DirectSearch/Default.aspx Also, access to records for a fee at https://tapestry.fidlar.com/Tapestry2/Default.aspx. Contact 309-794-3283 or kylec@fidlar.com forsubscription information. Search fee is $5.95 each, pringed images $.50 each unless otherwise noted. **$$$**

Property, Taxation Records Access parcel data free at www.co.st-clair.il.us/departments/assessor/Pages/parcel.aspx.

Sangamon County ***Recorded Documents*** www.sangamoncountyrecorder.com/ Access to records for a fee at https://tapestry.fidlar.com/Tapestry2/Default.aspx. Contact 309-794-3283 or kylec@fidlar.com for subscription information. Search fee is $5.95 each, printed images $.50 each unless otherwise noted. **$$$**

Property, Taxation Records View the status of property tax payments or property assessments at http://tax.co.sangamon.il.us/SangamonCountyWeb/index.jsp

Shelby County ***Recorded Documents*** www.shelbycounty-il.com/countyclerkandrecorder.htm Access to records for a fee at https://tapestry.fidlar.com/Tapestry2/Default.aspx. Contact 309-794-3283 or kylec@fidlar.com for subscription information. Search fee is $5.95 each, printed images $.50 each unless otherwise noted. **$$$**

Stephenson County ***Property, Taxation Records*** Access to property search for free at http://taxrecords.co.stephenson.il.us/propertyinquiry.pl.

Tazewell County ***Property, Taxation Records*** Access to property information for free at http://il-tazewell-assessor.governmax.com/propertymax/rover30.asp.

Vermilion County ***Recorded Documents*** www.vercounty.org/recorder.htm Access real estate records at https://www.illandrecords.com/illr/il183/index.jsp. There is a $5.00 fee per doc found and $5.00 fee to view it, or you may subscribe for $1000 per month. Also, access to records for a fee at https://tapestry.fidlar.com/Tapestry2/Default.aspx. Contact 309-794-3283 or kylec@fidlar.com forsubscription information. Search fee is $5.95 each, pringed images $.50 each unless otherwise noted. **$$$**

Property, Taxation Records Access property data free on the gis-mapping site at www.vcgis.org/. Find information on subscribing to the county's property tax database at www.vercounty.org/TechServ/taxinquiry.pdf.

Warren County ***Recorded Documents*** www.warrencountyil.com/countyOffice.php?officeID=7 Access to records for a fee at https://tapestry.fidlar.com/Tapestry2/Default.aspx. Contact 309-794-3283 or kylec@fidlar.com for subscription information. Search fee is $5.95 each, printed images $.50 each unless otherwise noted. **$$$**

Wayne County ***Real Estate, Grantor/Grantee Records*** Access to records for a fee at www.fidlar.com, click on \"Laredo\" link to download. To become a Laredo Subscriber contact the Wayne County Clerk/Recorders office. For more information contact Kyle Cogdil at kylec@fidlar.com or Katie Nickel at katien@fidlar.com or call 800-747-4600 x271 for Kyle or x324 for Katie. **$$$**

Whiteside County ***Recorded Documents*** www.whiteside.org/recorder/ Access to records for a fee at https://tapestry.fidlar.com/Tapestry2/Default.aspx. Contact 309-794-3283 or kylec@fidlar.com for subscription information. Search fee is $5.95 each, printed images $.50 each unless otherwise noted. **$$$**

Property, Taxation Records Search assessor property data for a fee on the GIS system at http://beacon.schneidercorp.com/?site=WhitesideCountyIL.$$$

Will County ***Real Estate, Deed, Lien, Mortgage, Voter Registration, UCC, Judgment Records*** www.willcountyrecorder.com Access to the Recorder's real estate and lien records back to 1965 free at www.willcountyrecorder.com; fees apply for full data and to print copies. **$$$**

Property, Taxation Records Access to property/parcel number for free at www.willcountysoa.com/disclaimer.aspx.

Williamson County ***Recorded Documents*** www.williamsoncountycourthouse.com/p/county_clerk.php Access to records for a fee at https://cotthosting.com/ILPortal/User/Login.aspx?ReturnUrl=%2filportal%2fIndex.aspx. **$$$**

Winnebago County ***Recorded Documents*** http://wincoil.us/departments/recorder/ Access to records for a fee at https://tapestry.fidlar.com/Tapestry2/Default.aspx. Contact 309-794-3283 or kylec@fidlar.com for subscription information. Search fee is $5.95 each, printed images $.50 each unless otherwise noted. Also, search parcel data free on the treasurer search site free at http://treasurer.wincoil.us/ **$$$**

Property, Taxation Records Access county parcel and assessment data free at http://assessor.wincoil.us/assessment/search/. Also, search parcel data free on the treasurer search site free at http://treasurer.wincoil.us/ Also, access property data via the GIS-mapping site free at http://ims.wingis.org/. Also, search Rockford Township assessment data free at www.rockfordtownshipassessor.net/propertysearch.asp.

Indiana

Capital: Indianapolis
Marion County
Time Zone: EST

11 western Indiana counties are CST and observe DST. They are: Gibson, Jasper, Laporte, Lake, Newton, Porter, Posey, Spencer, Starke, Vanderburgh, Warrick. The remainder are EST and do not observe DST except for Clark, Dearborn, Floyd, Harrison, Ohio.

Population: 6,537,334
# of Counties: 92

Useful State Links

Website: www.in.gov
Governor: www.in.gov/gov
Attorney General: www.in.gov/attorneygeneral
State Archives: www.in.gov/icpr
State Statutes and Codes: www.in.gov/legislative/ic/code/
Legislative Bill Search: www.in.gov/apps/lsa/session/billwatch/billinfo
Bill Monitoring: www.in.gov/apps/lsa/session/billwatch/
Unclaimed Funds: https://www.indianaunclaimed.com/apps/ag/ucp/index.html

State Public Record Agencies

Criminal Records

Indiana State Police, Criminal History Records, www.IN.gov/isp/ The agency offers a Limited Criminal History that contains only felonies and Class A misdemeanor arrests, based upon county participation. See available at www.in.gov/ai/appfiles/isp-lch/. Using a credit card, the search fee is $16.32. Subscribers to accessIndiana can obtain records for $15.00 per search or for no charge if statutorily exempt, or $7.00 with a government exemption. Response of No Records Found is an official search result. **$$$**

Sexual Offender Registry

Sex and Violent Offender Directory Registry, C/O Indiana Sheriffs' Association, www.indianasheriffs.org/ The website has a searching capabilities by name and city or county at www.icrimewatch.net/indiana.php. Local sheriffs maintain and update sex offender registration information including the information found on this site.

Incarceration Records

Indiana Department of Correction, IGCS, Records Section, Room E-334, www.in.gov/idoc/ At the website, click on Offender Locator or visit www.in.gov/apps/indcorrection/ofs/ofs. To search online provide either first and last name or the inmate number.

Corporation, LP, LLC, LLP, Fictitious/Assumed Name

Corporation Division, Secretary of State, www.in.gov/sos/business/index.htm You can conduct Business Entity Name Searches, Name Availability Checks and acquire official Certificates of Existence or Authorization from www.in.gov/sos/business/index.htm. When downloading images, there is no fee for copy or certification. The site also gives access to UCC records. Frequent users of Business Services Online should subscribe to IN.Gov at www.ai.org/ai/business/. Also, search securities companies registered with the state at www.in.gov/apps/sos/securities/sos_securities. *Other Options:* Monthly lists of all new businesses are available online, as are bulk data and specialized searches. Look for Special Business Entity Search Orders at the website. See www.in.gov/accounts/2332.htm.

Trademarks/Servicemarks

Secretary of State, Trademark Division, www.in.gov/sos/business/index.htm Visit www.in.gov/sos/business/2374.htm. This database contains information regarding the status of all trademarks on file with the state of Indiana. Access is free. Results allow one to view application, certificate or the mark. *Other Options:* One may download the database and purchase monthly or weekly updates. See www.in.gov/ai/appfiles/sos-trademark-bulk/ for prices and details.

Uniform Commercial Code

UCC Division, Secretary of State, www.in.gov/sos/business/index.htm You may browse lien records at https://secure.in.gov/sos/bus_service/online_ucc/browse/default.asp. There is no charge. An official search may be performed for $4.08, use of credit card required. Ongoing requesters should subscribe to IN.Gov at www.ai.org/accounts/, then fee to obtain record is $3.00. Subscribers can also purchase customized data for as little as $25.00 per 1,000 records; example is all liens on a secured party in a date range. Filing services are also available to subscribers. **$$$** *Other Options:* The master data table with images is available for $3,000; if updated weekly then $25,000 annually; if updated monthly then $15,000 annually. Call 800-236-5446.

Sales Tax Registrations

IN Dept of Revenue, Sales Tax Registrations, www.in.gov/dor/ A look-up to tax delinquent business is found at www.in.gov/apps/dor/rrmc/Default.aspx.

Birth and Death Records

State Department of Health, Vital Records Office, www.in.gov/isdh/20243.htm Records may be ordered online via the website, but the requester must still fax a photo copy of an ID before the record request is processed. Also, records may requested from www.vitalchek.com, a state-endorsed vendor. **$$$**

Workers' Compensation Records

Workers Compensation Board, www.in.gov/wcb/ Two searches are offered. Search Disputed Claims at https://wcbnec03.wcb.state.in.us/search.asp. Search for the First Report of Injury at https://wcbnec03.wcb.state.in.us/jcn.asp. This search will only give the accident number.

Driver Records

BMV-Driving Records, 100 N Senate Ave, www.IN.gov/bmv/ IN.gov is the state owned interactive information and communication system which provides batch and interactive access to driving records. Subscribers must be approved and enter into an agreement on usage. There is an annual $95.00 fee. The fee is $7.50 per record. For more information, call 317-233-2010 or visit www.in.gov/accounts. Subscribers may also validate one's IN driver's license for $1.00 per transaction. Note that a person of record may obtain his/her own record at www.myBMV.com by creating an account and sufficiently establishing identity. The record can be viewed (but not printed) free of charge. **$$$**

Vehicle, Vessel Ownership & Registration

Bureau of Motor Vehicles, Records, www.in.gov/bmv/ Subscribers may search the Indiana Bureau of Motor Vehicles database for title and lien information by VIN and SSN or by title # and SSN. Requesters must be approved and sign an agreement on usage. Visit www.in.gov and click on Account Center. The fee is $5.00 per record for a title and lien search, and $15.00 for a vehicle registration search. One must be a subscriber paying the annual fee of $95.00. If not a subscriber, one may purchase either of these two records using a credit card for $16.32 per record. **$$$**

Accident Reports

Crash Records Section, c/o Open Portal Solutions, https://www.buycrash.com/Public/Home.aspx Crash reports can be purchased online at www.buycrash.com, a state designated vendor. The fee is $12.00, use of a credit card or PayPal is required. **$$$** *Other Options:* For information about bulk file purchasing, contact the Data Section at 317-233-5133.

Voter Registration, Campaign Finance, PACs

Election Division, www.in.gov/sos/elections/ Campaign finance reports are viewable at www.in.gov/sos/elections/2394.htm. This includes PACs.

GED Certificates

Dept of Workforce Development, 10 N Senate Ave #10, www.in.gov/dwd/adulted.htm No online access available. Records may be requested from https://www.diplomasender.com. A credit card is needed. Request must be ordered by the test taker. Employers and third parties must receive an email and/or Authentication Code from the test taker to then access the authorized documents. Turnaround time is 1-3 days. **$$$.**

Occupational Licensing Boards

Accountant-CPA .... https://mylicense.in.gov/EVerification/Search.aspx
Acupuncturist .... https://mylicense.in.gov/EVerification/Search.aspx
Alcoholic Beverage Dealer/Mfg/Dist/Retail/employee www.in.gov/ai/appfiles/atc-license-lookup/
Appraiser, Real Estate/Gen/Residential ...... https://mylicense.in.gov/EVerification/Search.aspx

Appraiser, Trainee/Temp .... https://mylicense.in.gov/EVerification/Search.aspx
Architect .... https://mylicense.in.gov/EVerification/Search.aspx
Asbestos Contractor .... https://mylicense.in.gov/eVerification/
Asbestos Disposal Mgr/Worker .... https://mylicense.in.gov/eVerification/
Asbestos Inspector/Supvr./Designer .... https://mylicense.in.gov/eVerification/
Asbestos Mgmt Planner .... https://mylicense.in.gov/eVerification/
Asbestos Training Provider .... https://mylicense.in.gov/eVerification/
Athletic Trainer .... https://mylicense.in.gov/EVerification/Search.aspx
Attorney www.in.gov/judiciary/ble/2361.htm
Auctioneer .... https://mylicense.in.gov/EVerification/Search.aspx
Audiologist .... https://mylicense.in.gov/EVerification/Search.aspx
Bank & Trust Company .... http://extranet.dfi.in.gov/dfidb/deplist.aspx
Barber/Barber Instructor .... https://mylicense.in.gov/EVerification/Search.aspx
Boxer .... https://mylicense.in.gov/EVerification/Search.aspx
Boxing Occupation .... https://mylicense.in.gov/EVerification/Search.aspx
Check Casher .... http://extranet.dfi.in.gov/dfidb/nondeplist.aspx
Child Care Center .... https://secure.in.gov/apps/fssa/carefinder/index.html
Child Care Home/Provider .... https://secure.in.gov/apps/fssa/carefinder/index.html
Chiropractor .... https://mylicense.in.gov/EVerification/Search.aspx
Clinical Nurse Specialist .... https://mylicense.in.gov/EVerification/Search.aspx
Collection Agency .... www.in.gov/apps/sos/securities/sos_securities
Cosmetologist .... https://mylicense.in.gov/EVerification/Search.aspx
Credit Union .... http://extranet.dfi.in.gov/dfidb/deplist.aspx
Dental Anesthetist/Hygienist .... https://mylicense.in.gov/EVerification/Search.aspx
Dentist .... https://mylicense.in.gov/EVerification/Search.aspx
Dietitian .... https://mylicense.in.gov/EVerification/Search.aspx
Electrologist .... https://mylicense.in.gov/EVerification/Search.aspx
Embalmer .... https://mylicense.in.gov/EVerification/Search.aspx
EMS Providers .... www.in.gov/dhs/files/prov_name.pdf
Engineer/Engineering Intern .... https://mylicense.in.gov/EVerification/Search.aspx
Environmental Health Specialist .... https://mylicense.in.gov/EVerification/Search.aspx
Esthetician .... https://mylicense.in.gov/EVerification/Search.aspx
Funeral/Cemetery Director .... https://mylicense.in.gov/EVerification/Search.aspx
Grain Bank/Warehouse www.in.gov/isda/2399.htm
Grain Buyer www.in.gov/isda/2399.htm
Hazardous Waste Facility/Handler .... https://mylicense.in.gov/EGov/
Health Services Administrator .... https://mylicense.in.gov/EVerification/Search.aspx
Hearing Aid Dealer .... https://mylicense.in.gov/EVerification/Search.aspx
Home Inspector .... www.in.gov/pla/hi.htm
Hypnotist .... https://mylicense.in.gov/EVerification/Search.aspx
Industrial Authority, State .... http://extranet.dfi.in.gov/dfidb/deplist.aspx
Insurance Agent/Consultant .... https://www.sircon.com/ComplianceExpress/Inquiry/consumerInquiry.do?nonSscrb=Y
Investment Advisor .... www.in.gov/apps/sos/securities/sos_securities
Landscape Architect .... https://mylicense.in.gov/EVerification/Search.aspx
Lead Inspector/Contractor .... https://mylicense.in.gov/eVerification/
Lead Project Designer/Supervisor .... https://mylicense.in.gov/eVerification/
Lead Risk Assessor/Lead Worker .... https://mylicense.in.gov/eVerification/
Lead Training Course Provider .... https://mylicense.in.gov/eVerification/
Lender, Small .... http://extranet.dfi.in.gov/dfidb/nondeplist.aspx
Loan Broker/Firms .... www.in.gov/apps/sos/securities/sos_securities
Lobbyist, Executive Branch .... https://secure.in.gov/apps/ilrc/registration/browse
Lobbyist, Legislative .... https://secure.in.gov/apps/ilrc/registration/browse
Manicurist .... https://mylicense.in.gov/EVerification/Search.aspx
Marriage & Family Therapist .... https://mylicense.in.gov/EVerification/Search.aspx
Medical Residency Permit .... https://mylicense.in.gov/EVerification/Search.aspx

Mental Health Counselor	https://mylicense.in.gov/EVerification/Search.aspx
Midwife	https://mylicense.in.gov/EVerification/Search.aspx
Money Transmitter	http://extranet.dfi.in.gov/dfidb/nondeplist.aspx
Notary Public	https://myweb.in.gov/SOS/notaryapp/Common/NotarySearch.aspx?isReapplying=0
Nurse-RN/LPN	https://mylicense.in.gov/EVerification/Search.aspx
Nursing Home Administrator	https://mylicense.in.gov/EVerification/Search.aspx
Occupational Therapist/Assistant	https://mylicense.in.gov/EVerification/Search.aspx
Optometrist	https://mylicense.in.gov/EVerification/Search.aspx
Optometrist Drug Certification	https://mylicense.in.gov/EVerification/Search.aspx
Osteopathic Physician	https://mylicense.in.gov/EVerification/Search.aspx
Pawnbroker	http://extranet.dfi.in.gov/dfidb/nondeplist.aspx
Pesticide Applicator	www.isco.purdue.edu/pesticide/index_pest1.html
Pesticide Registered Products	http://npirspublic.ceris.purdue.edu/state/state_menu.aspx?state=IN
Pesticide Technician/Consultant	www.isco.purdue.edu/pesticide/index_pest1.html
Pharmacist/Pharmacist Intern	https://mylicense.in.gov/EVerification/Search.aspx
Pharmacy Technician	https://mylicense.in.gov/EVerification/Search.aspx
Physical Therapist/Therapist Asst	https://mylicense.in.gov/EVerification/Search.aspx
Physician Assistant	https://mylicense.in.gov/EVerification/Search.aspx
Physician/Medical Doctor	https://mylicense.in.gov/EVerification/Search.aspx
PI Company Employee	https://mylicense.in.gov/EVerification/Search.aspx
Placement Officer, School	http://dc.doe.in.gov/public/EducatorLookup/TeacherInquiry.aspx
Plumber/Plumbing Contractor	https://mylicense.in.gov/EVerification/Search.aspx
Podiatrist	https://mylicense.in.gov/EVerification/Search.aspx
Polygraph Examiner	www.indianapolygraphassociation.com/members.asp
Private Investigator	https://mylicense.in.gov/EVerification/Search.aspx
Psychologist	https://mylicense.in.gov/EVerification/Search.aspx
Radiologic Technologist	https://mylicense.in.gov/EVerification/Search.aspx
Radon Testers/Mitigators	https://mylicense.in.gov/EVerification/Search.aspx
Real Estate Agent/Broker/Seller	https://mylicense.in.gov/EVerification/Search.aspx
Real Estate Appraiser	https://mylicense.in.gov/EVerification/Search.aspx
Rental Purchase Lender	http://extranet.dfi.in.gov/dfidb/nondeplist.aspx
Respiratory Care Practitioner	https://mylicense.in.gov/EVerification/Search.aspx
Savings & Loan	http://extranet.dfi.in.gov/dfidb/deplist.aspx
School Administr'r/Principal/Director	http://dc.doe.in.gov/public/EducatorLookup/TeacherInquiry.aspx
School Counselor	http://dc.doe.in.gov/public/EducatorLookup/TeacherInquiry.aspx
School Nurse	http://dc.doe.in.gov/public/EducatorLookup/TeacherInquiry.aspx
Securities Agent/Sales	www.finra.org/Investors/ToolsCalculators/BrokerCheck/index.htm
Securities Broker/Dealer	www.in.gov/apps/sos/securities/sos_securities
Shampoo Operator	https://mylicense.in.gov/EVerification/Search.aspx
Social Worker	https://mylicense.in.gov/EVerification/Search.aspx
Social Worker, Clinical	https://mylicense.in.gov/EVerification/Search.aspx
Solid Waste Facility	https://mylicense.in.gov/EGov/
Speech Pathologist	https://mylicense.in.gov/EVerification/Search.aspx
Surveyor, Land	https://mylicense.in.gov/EVerification/Search.aspx
Teacher	http://dc.doe.in.gov/public/EducatorLookup/TeacherInquiry.aspx
Trust Company	http://extranet.dfi.in.gov/dfidb/deplist.aspx
Veterinarian	https://mylicense.in.gov/EVerification/Search.aspx
Veterinary Tech	https://mylicense.in.gov/EVerification/Search.aspx
Warehouse, Agricultural, etc.	www.in.gov/isda/2399.htm
Waste Tire Processor/Transporter	https://mylicense.in.gov/EGov/
Waste Water Treatm't Plant Operator	https://mylicense.in.gov/EGov/
Yard Waste Composting Facility	https://mylicense.in.gov/EGov/

State and Local Courts

State Court Structure: Indiana has 92 counties, and 90 of these counties comprise their own circuit, with their own **Circuit Court**. The remaining two small counties (Ohio and Dearborn counties) have combined to form one circuit. Circuit courts traditionally heard all civil and criminal cases and have unlimited trial jurisdiction, except when exclusive or concurrent (shared) jurisdiction is conferred upon other courts. Circuit Courts also have appellate jurisdiction over appeals from City and Town Courts.

The majority of Indiana trial court cases are held in the **Superior Courts** and almost all Indiana counties have Superior Courts in addition to their Circuit Court. For the most part Superiors Courts also have general jurisdiction but their trial jurisdiction and organization varies from county to county. They can hear all civil and criminal cases, and small claims and minor offense cases.

In counties without Superior Courts, the Circuit Courts in addition to all other cases, also handle small claims cases, such as civil disputes involving less than $6,000 and minor offenses, such as misdemeanors, ordinance violations, and Class D felonies.

Appellate Courts: Decisions and case records from the Supreme and Appellate Courts are viewable online from www.in.gov/judiciary.com.

Statewide Court Online Access: There is no overall statewide system, but there are two systems in use with extensive county participation. They are described below.

- Implementation of an online record search system available for the public, called Odyssey, has over thirty counties courts as well as a number of city and town courts on the system with plans for more to be added. Visit http://mycase.in.gov/default.aspx. One may search for 1) Criminal and Citation case records; or 2) Civil, Family and Probate case records. **However, proceed with caution - see below.**
  - When searching the public access site by case number, it is possible that cases matching the case number entered may not appear in the search results depending on the exact format entered in the search form and the exact format entered into Odyssey.
  - Local users of this system indicate the system sometimes has flaws and is notorious for displaying wrong records on a multi-record subject.
  - Note the Court has determined that dates of birth will not be displayed in Public Access.
  - Check the disclaimer. See cautionary statements at beginning of this section.
- Also, a vendor is working closely with many counties to provide electronic access at http://www.doxpop.com/prod/. Full access to case record information requires registration and subscription, the fees range from $30.00 to $1,020.00 per month depending on number of searches. In general, the service does not provide case files or images, as the IN courts are cautious about providing this material. Therefore an onsite search may be necessary to pull case file information, especially if a case involves a civil judgment. At least 77 counties are participating, including a number of City Courts.

County Sites:

Adams County

Circuit & Superior Court

Civil: Access civil records by subscription to Doxpop at https://www.doxpop.com/prod/court/. Free index search. Records available from 06/1990, tax warrants from 2002. $$$ *Criminal:* Access criminal record docket by subscription to Doxpop at https://www.doxpop.com/prod/court/. Free index search. Records available from 06/1990**$$$**

Allen County

Circuit & Superior Court www.allencounty.us/courts/clerk-of-the-courts

Civil: Access civil records by subscription to Doxpop at https://www.doxpop.com/prod/court/. Free index search. The Probate, and Family indices, plus the record index from the New Haven City Court, are available at http://mycase.in.gov/default.aspx. $$$ *Criminal:* The criminal and citation record index available at http://mycase.in.gov/default.aspx. Free index search. Includes New Haven City Court,**$$$**

Bartholomew County

Circuit & Superior Court www.bartholomewco.com

Civil: Online subscription service at https://www.doxpop.com/prod/. Fees involved. Records date from 5/85. $$$ *Criminal:* same **$$$**

Benton County

Circuit & Superior Court

Civil: The record index is available at http://mycase.in.gov/default.aspx. Only several years of records are available. See cautionary statements at beginning of this section. *Criminal:* same

Blackford County

Circuit & Superior Court

Civil: The record index is available at http://mycase.in.gov/default.aspx. But only several years of records are available. See cautionary statements at beginning of this section. *Criminal:* The record index is available at http://mycase.in.gov/default.aspx But only several years of records are available. .

Boone County

Circuit & Superior Court I & II http://boonecounty.in.gov/Default.aspx?tabid=103

Civil: Access the civil docket index by name or case number at http://courtviewpa.boonecounty.in.gov/pa/. *Criminal:* Access the criminal docket index by name or case number at http://courtviewpa.boonecounty.in.gov/pa/.

Brown County

Circuit Court

Civil: Fee access to civil chronological back to 1993 is by subscription at https://www.doxpop.com/prod/; free access limited to only current open cases, case summary only. $$$ *Criminal:* Fee access to criminal chronological back to 1993 is by subscription at www.doxpop.com; free access limited to only current open cases. **$$$**

Carroll County

Circuit & Superior Court

Civil: The record index is available at http://mycase.in.gov/default.aspx. But only several years of records are available. See cautionary statements at beginning of this section. *Criminal:* The record index is available at http://mycase.in.gov/default.aspx. But only several years of records are available, from 4/2010.

Cass County

Circuit & Superior Court www.co.cass.in.us/dav/courts/circuit.html

Civil: The record index is available at http://mycase.in.gov/default.aspx. See cautionary statements at beginning of this section. *Criminal:* same

Clark County

Circuit & Superior Court www.co.clark.in.us/governmentdirectory.html

Civil: The record index is available at http://mycase.in.gov/default.aspx. But only several years of records are available. See cautionary statements at beginning of this section. *Criminal:* same

Clay County

Circuit & Superior Court www.claycountyin.gov/metadot/index.pl

Civil: Online subscription service at https://www.doxpop.com. Fees involved. A limited free search of open cases is available. Online index goes back to 9/1994; images to 8/2000. $$$ *Criminal:* **$$$**

Clinton County

Circuit & Superior Court

Civil: Online subscription service at https://www.doxpop.com. Fees involved. Records date from 01/91. A limited free search of open cases is available. The record index is available at http://mycase.in.gov/default.aspx. But only several years of records are available. See cautionary statements at beginning of this section. $$$ *Criminal:* same as civil. **$$$**

Daviess County

Circuit & Superior Court

Civil: Online subscription service at https://www.doxpop.com. Fees involved. Records date from 02/94. A limited free search of open cases is available. $$$ *Criminal:* **$$$**

Decatur County

Circuit & Superior Court www.decaturcounty.in.gov

Civil: Online subscription service at https://www.doxpop.com. Fees involved. A limited free search of open cases is available. Online records go back to 12/1998. $$$ *Criminal:* **$$$**

DeKalb County

Circuit & Superior Court 1 & 2

Civil: Search the civil, family and probate docket by case number, party name or attorney name at http://mycase.in.gov/default.aspx *Criminal:* Access court record index free at http://mycase.in.gov/default.aspx. .

Delaware County

Circuit Court www.co.delaware.in.us/clerk/

Civil: Online subscription service at https://www.doxpop.com. Fees involved. Records date from 1/89. A limited free search of open cases is available. Index from Muncie City court also available online. $$$ *Criminal:* Also, an online subscription service is at www.doxpop.com. Fees involved. Records date from 01/89. A limited free search of open cases is available. An index from the Muncie City court is also available online. **$$$**

Dubois County

Circuit & Superior Court www.duboiscountyin.org/

Civil: Online subscription service at https://www.doxpop.com. Fees involved. Records date back to 10/1993. A limited free search of open cases is available. $$$ *Criminal:* **$$$**

Elkhart County

All Circuit & Superior Courts www.elkhartcountyindiana.com/Departments/Clerk/index.htm

Civil: Online subscription service at https://www.doxpop.com. Fees involved; $39.00 per month. Records date from 01/92. A limited free search of open cases is available. Search the civil, family, and probate index at http://mycase.in.gov/default.aspx. The site does not disclose how far back records are kept. **$$$** *Criminal:* same Search the criminal index at http://mycase.in.gov/default.aspx. **$$$**

Fayette County

Circuit & Superior Court http://connersvillecommunity.com/Fayette_County/Justice_System/Clerk_of_Courts

Civil: A free name-only without identifiers search of the recorded document index from 01/1990 forward is at https://www.doxpop.com/prod/. A subscription is necessary to obtain detailed information, images available from 01/1990 as well. $$$

Floyd County

Circuit & Superior Court www.floydcounty.in.gov/

Civil: Search the index at http://mycase.in.gov/default.aspx. Includes Family and Probate records. The site does not disclose how far back records are kept. See cautionary statements at beginning of this section. *Criminal:* Search the index at http://mycase.in.gov/default.aspx. .

Fountain County

Circuit Court

Civil: Online subscription service at https://www.doxpop.com. Fees involved. Records date from 9/95. A limited free search of open cases is available. Note that index for Attica City Court is available at http://mycase.in.gov/default.aspx. The site does not disclose how far back records are kept. See cautionary statements at beginning of this section. **$$$**

Franklin County

Circuit Court

Civil: Online subscription service at https://www.doxpop.com. Fees involved. Records date from 04/2000.. $$$

Fulton County

Circuit Court/Superior Court www.co.fulton.in.us/Circuit%20Court/index.htm

Civil: Online subscription service at https://www.doxpop.com. Fees involved. Records date back to 1/1999. $$$

Gibson County

Circuit & Superior Court

Civil: Online subscription service at https://www.doxpop.com. Fees involved. Superior records date from 1/96.; circuit from 05/05. A limited free search of open cases is available. $$$ *Criminal:* same **$$$**

Grant County

Circuit & Superior Court www.grantcounty.net

Civil: Online subscription service at https://www.doxpop.com. Fees involved. Records date back to 8/1989. A limited free search of open cases is available. Also, search the civil, family, and probate index at http://mycase.in.gov/default.aspx. Gas City Court also included. The site does not disclose how far back records are kept. See cautionary statements at beginning of this section. **$$$** *Criminal:* **$$$**

Greene County

Circuit & Superior Court

Civil: Civil, probate and family docket index search is free at http://mycase.in.gov/default.aspx. The site does not disclose how far back records are kept. See cautionary statements at beginning of this section. *Criminal:* Criminal docket index search is free at http://mycase.in.gov/default.aspx. The site does not disclose how far back records are kept.

Hamilton County

Circuit & Superior Court www.hamiltoncounty.in.gov/department/index.php?structureid=13

Civil: Online subscription service at https://www.doxpop.com. Fees involved. Records date from 01/1987 to 9/21//2009. Note that newer cases and updates to existing cases for Hamilton County are no longer be updated on Doxpop. New civil, family and probate cases are now shown at http://mycase.in.gov/default.aspx, also there is a separate search for the Carmel City Court and Fishers Town Court. $$$ *Criminal:* same Case dockets are shown at http://mycase.in.gov/default.aspx, also there is a separate search for the Carmel City Court and Fishers Town Court. The site does not disclose how far back records are kept. See cautionary statements at beginning of this section. **$$$**

Hancock County

Circuit & Superior Court

Civi & Criminal: Online subscription at https://www.doxpop.com. Fees involved, records date from 7/98. Limited free search of open cases available. **$$$**

Harrison County

Circuit Court www.harrisoncounty.in.gov/index.php/local-government-our-offices-and-leadership/office-listings/clerk

Civil: Search the civil, family and probate docket by case number, party name or attorney name at http://mycase.in.gov/default.aspx. Not very many years are online. The site does not disclose how far back records are kept. See cautionary statements at beginning of this section. *Criminal:* Search docket date at http://mycase.in.gov/default.aspx, only a few years are offered. The site does not disclose how far back records are kept.

Hendricks County

Circuit & Superior Court www.co.hendricks.in.us/

Civil: Online docket found at www.co.hendricks.in.us/. There is an index to the Plainfield Town Court dockets at http://mycase.in.gov/default.aspx. *Criminal:* Search docket online at www.co.hendricks.in.us/. There is an index to the Plainfield Town Court dockets at http://mycase.in.gov/default.aspx.

Henry County

Circuit Courts I, II, & III www.henryco.net/

Civil: Record index is available at http://mycase.in.gov/default.aspx, for no fee. Online subscription service at https://www.doxpop.com. Fees involved. Records date back to 1/1991. A limited free search of open cases is available. Personal identifiers usually but not always include DOB and middle initial. **$$$** *Criminal:* same **$$$**

Howard County

Circuit & Superior Court http://co.howard.in.us/clerk1/

Civil: Online subscription service at https://www.doxpop.com. Fees involved. Records date from 07/94. A limited free search of open cases is available. **$$$** *Criminal:* same **$$$**

Huntington County

Circuit & Superior Court www.huntington.in.us/county/

Civil: Search the civil, family and probate docket by case number, party name or attorney name at http://mycase.in.gov/default.aspx. Not very many years are online. There is a separate look-up for the Roanoke Town Court. *Criminal:* Same as civil.

Jackson County

Circuit & Superior Courts www.jacksoncounty.in.gov/index.aspx?nid=268

Civil: Search the civil, family, and probate index at http://mycase.in.gov/default.aspx. The site does not disclose how far back records are kept. *Criminal:* The index is searchable online at http://mycase.in.gov/default.aspx. sThe site does not disclose how far back records are kept.

Jasper County

Superior & Circuit Courts www.jaspercountyin.gov/Default.aspx?tabid=58

Civil: Search the civil, family, and probate index at http://mycase.in.gov/default.aspx. The site does not disclose how far back records are kept. *Criminal:* Same as civil See cautionary statements at beginning of this section.

Jay County

Circuit & Superior Court www.co.jay.in.us

Civil: Online subscription service at https://www.doxpop.com. Fees involved. Records date from 03/94. A limited free search of open cases is available. **$$$** *Criminal:* same **$$$**

Jefferson County

Circuit & Superior Court www.jeffersoncounty.in.gov/superiorcourt/index.php

Civil: Access civil records by subscription to Doxpop at https://www.doxpop.com/prod/court/. Free index search. Data available from March 1995. $$$ *Criminal:* same. **$$$**

Jennings County

Circuit Court

Civil: Search the civil, family, and probate index at http://mycase.in.gov/default.aspx. The site does not disclose how far back records are kept. *Criminal:* Search the criminal index at http://mycase.in.gov/default.aspx. The site does not disclose how far back records are kept.

Johnson County

Circuit & Superior Court http://co.johnson.in.us/courts/

Civi & Criminal: Online subscription service at https://www.doxpop.com. Fees involved. Records date from 08/89. A limited free search of open cases is available. The record index from the Greenwood City and Franklin City Court is available at http://mycase.in.gov/. Records do not go back far. **$$$**

Knox County

Circuit & Superior Court

Civil: Search the civil, family, and probate index at http://mycase.in.gov/default.aspx. The site does not disclose how far back records are kept. Note information displayed on this site is not to be considered or used as an official court record and may contai Note that the Bicknell City Court has its dockets online here also. *Criminal:* Search the index at http://mycase.in.gov/default.aspx. The site does not disclose how far back records are kept. See cautionary statements at beginning of this section.

Kosciusko County

Circuit & Superior Court www.kcgov.com/

Civil: Online subscription service at https://www.doxpop.com. Fees involved. Data goes back to 10/1991. $$$ *Criminal:* same **$$$**

La Porte County

Circuit & Superior Court www.laportecounty.org/JudiciaryLaw/CircuitClerks/

Civil: Online subscription service at https://www.doxpop.com. Fees involved. Records date from 03/98. A limited free search of open cases is available. Search the civil, family, and probate index at http://mycase.in.gov/default.aspx. The site does not disclose how far back records are kept. **$$$** *Criminal:* same Search the criminal index at http://mycase.in.gov/default.aspx. The site does not disclose how far back records are kept. **$$$**

LaGrange County

Circuit & Superior Court www.lagrangecounty.org/

Civil: Online subscription service at https://www.doxpop.com. Fees involved. Records date back to 1/1990. A limited free search of open cases is available. **$$$** *Criminal:* same **$$$**

Lake County

Circuit & Superior Court www.lakecountyin.org/index.jsp

Civil: Online search for docket records available at https://www.lakecountyin.org/portal/media-type/html/user/anon/page/online-docket. Search free but $.25 per page copy fee with $1.00 minimum. Results do not show the DOB. $$$ *Criminal:* Online search of docket records at https://www.lakecountyin.org/portal/media-type/html/user/anon/page/online-docket. Search free but $.25 per page copy fee with $1.00 minimum. The DOB often will show on results screen. **$$$**

Lawrence County

Circuit & Superior Court

Civil: Access civil records by subscription to Doxpop at https://www.doxpop.com/prod/court/. Free index search. **$$$** *Criminal:* Access criminal docket by subscription at Doxpop at https://www.doxpop.com/prod/court/. Free index search. **$$$**

Madison County

Circuit & Superior Court www.madisoncty.com/CountyOffices.html

Civil: Free online docket look-up service at http://mycase.in.gov/default.aspx. Also, access civil records by subscription to Doxpop at https://www.doxpop.com/prod/court/. Free index search, includes look up from Alexandria City and Anderson City courts. **$$$** *Criminal:* Free online service at http://mycase.in.gov/default.aspx. Also, access criminal records by subscription to Doxpop at https://www.doxpop.com/prod/court/. Free index search, includes look up from Alexandria City and Anderson City courts. **$$$**

Marion County

Circuit & Superior Court www.indy.gov/egov/county/clerk/Pages/home.aspx

Civil: Search names online for free at /www.civicnet.net/court_records.html. See the web for fees, as there are many ways to order. One may be subscriber or use a credit card for a one-time search. Marriage records included. Also, search Townships of Center, Lawrence, Franklin, Perry, Warren, Wayne, and Washington; Beech Grove City and Cumberland town court dockets free at http://mycase.in.gov/default.aspx. **$$$** *Criminal:* Search names online at https://www.biz.indygov.org/criminal_court_records.html. See the web for fees, as there are several ways to order. One may be a subscriber or may use a credit card for a one-time search. **$$$**

Marshall County

Circuit & Superior Court 1 & 2 www.co.marshall.in.us/?page_id=275

Civil: Online subscription service at www.doxpop.com/prod/. Fees involved. Records date from 09/88. A limited free search of open cases is available.**$ $$** *Criminal:* same **$$$**

Martin County

Circuit Court

Civil: Access civil records by subscription to Doxpop at https://www.doxpop.com/prod/court/. Free index search. **$$$** *Criminal:* Access criminal docket by subscription to Doxpop at https://www.doxpop.com/prod/court/. Free index search. **$$$**

Miami County

Circuit & Superior Courts www.miamicountyin.gov

Civil: Online subscription service at https://www.doxpop.com. Fees involved. Records date from 03/98. A limited free search of open cases is available. Note that the Town of Bunker Hill index is free to search at http://mycase.in.gov/default.aspx. $$$ *Criminal:* **$$$**

Monroe County

Circuit Court www.co.monroe.in.us/tsd/Justice/CircuitCourt.aspx

Civil: Search the civil, family, and probate index at http://mycase.in.gov/default.aspx. The site does not disclose how far back records are kept. *Criminal:* Search the criminal index at http://mycase.in.gov/default.aspx. The site does not disclose how far back records are kept. .

Montgomery County

Circuit & Superior Court www.montgomeryco.net

Civil: Online subscription service at https://www.doxpop.com. Fees involved. Records date from 01/90. A limited free search of open cases is available. $$$ *Criminal:* **$$$**

Morgan County

Circuit & Superior Court www.morgancounty.in.gov/

Civil: Online subscription service at https://www.doxpop.com. Fees involved. Records date from 01/1997. A limited free search of open cases is available. Data is uploaded every 10 minutes. $$$ *Criminal:* Online subscription service at https://www.doxpop.com. Fees involved. Records date from 01/1997. A limited free search of open cases is available. $$$

Newton County

Circuit & Superior Court

Civil: Access civil records by subscription to Doxpop at https://www.doxpop.com/prod/court/. Free index search. Records available from 1991. $$$ *Criminal:* Access criminal record docket by subscription to Doxpop at https://www.doxpop.com/prod/court/. Free index search. Records available from 01/1991. Includes search of tax warrants from 2/2/2008 forward. $$$

Noble County

Circuit, Superior I & Superior II Court www.nobleco.org/

Civil: Access court records free at http://noble.nasaview.com/terms.php. *Criminal:* same

Owen County

Circuit Court

Civil: Search the civil, family, and probate index at http://mycase.in.gov/default.aspx. The site does not disclose how far back records are kept. *Criminal:* The record index is available at http://mycase.in.gov. See cautionary statements at beginning of this section.

Parke County

Circuit Court

Civil: Search the civil, family, and probate index at http://mycase.in.gov/default.aspx. The site does not disclose how far back records are kept. *Criminal:* Search the criminal index at http://mycase.in.gov/default.aspx. The site does not disclose how far back records are kept.

Perry County

Circuit Court www.perrycountyin.org/

Civil: Online subscription service at https://www.doxpop.com. Fees involved. Records date back to 7/1997. $$$ *Criminal:* same **$$$**

Pike County

Circuit Court

Civil: Online subscription service at https://www.doxpop.com. Fees involved. A limited free search of open cases is available. $$$ *Criminal:* same **$$$**

Porter County

Circuit Court www.porterco.org

Civil: Subscription access to court records is available via Enhanced Access for $50 per month, $25 each add'l user, see www.porterco.org/index.php?id=enhancedaccess or call 219-465-3547. **$$$** *Criminal:* same Also, search the county infractions and ordinances index at http://mycase.in.gov/default.aspx. The site does not disclose how far back records are kept. **$$$**

Superior Court www.porterco.org/

Civil: Subscription access to court records is available via Enhanced Access for $50 per month, $25 each add'l user, see www.porterco.org/index.php?id=enhancedaccess or call 219-465-3547 . $$$ *Criminal:* same Also, search the county infractions and ordinances index at http://mycase.in.gov/default.aspx. The site does not disclose how far back records are kept. **$$$**

Posey County

Circuit & Superior Court

Civil: Search the civil, family, and probate index at http://mycase.in.gov/default.aspx. The site does not disclose how far back records are kept. *Criminal:* Search the criminal index at http://mycase.in.gov/default.aspx. The site does not disclose how far back records are kept.

Putnam County

Circuit & Superior Court

Civil: Online subscription service at https://www.doxpop.com. Fees involved. Records date from 01/92. A limited free search of open cases is available. **$$$** *Criminal:* same **$$$**

Randolph County

Circuit & Superior Court www.randolphcounty.us/

Civil: Online subscription service at https://www.doxpop.com. Fees involved. Records date from 06/94. A limited free search of open cases is available. Also, the Union City Court index is searchable at http://mycase.in.gov/default.aspx. **$$$** *Criminal:* same **$$$**

Ripley County

Circuit Court www.ripleycounty.com/clerk/

Civil: Online subscription service at https://www.doxpop.com. Fees involved. Records date from 07/1993. A limited free search of open cases is available. **$$$** *Criminal:* same **$$$**

Rush County

Circuit & Superior Court www.rushcounty.in.gov/Public/Home/index.cfm

Civil: Search the civil, family, and probate index at http://mycase.in.gov/default.aspx. The site does not disclose how far back records are kept. *Criminal:* Search the criminal index at http://mycase.in.gov/default.aspx. The site does not disclose how far back records are kept.

Scott County

Circuit & Superior Court

Civil: Search the civil, family, and probate index at http://mycase.in.gov/default.aspx. The site does not disclose how far back records are kept. *Criminal:* Search the criminal index at http://mycase.in.gov/default.aspx. The site does not disclose how far back records are kept.

Shelby County

Circuit & Superior Court www.co.shelby.in.us/

Civil: Online subscription service at https://www.doxpop.com. Fees involved. Records date from 07/1995. A limited free search of open cases is available. Also search the civil, family, and probate index at http://mycase.in.gov/default.aspx. The site does not disclose how far back records are kept. **$$$** *Criminal:* same Also, search the criminal index at http://mycase.in.gov/default.aspx. The site does not disclose how far back records are kept. **$$$**

Spencer County

Circuit Court www.spencercounty.in.gov/

Civil: Online subscription service at https://www.doxpop.com. Fees involved. Records date from 1/02. $$$ *Criminal:* **$$$**

St. Joseph County

Circuit & Superior Court

Criminal: The record index for infraction ordinances only is available at http://mycase.in.gov/ .

Starke County

Circuit Court www.co.starke.in.us/circuit-court/

Civil: Online subscription service at www.doxpop.com/prod/. Fees involved. Records date back to 9/2005 A limited free search of open cases is available. DOB on internet results shows year of birth only. Also- the Knox City Court index is viewable at http://mycase.in.gov/default.aspx. **$$$** *Criminal:* Online subscription service at www.doxpop.com/prod/. Fees involved. Records date back to 9/2005 A limited free search of open cases is available. Also- the Knox City Court index is viewable at http://mycase.in.gov/default.aspx. **$$$**

Steuben County

Circuit & Superior Court www.steubencounty.com/departments/court/court.aspx

Civil: Search the civil, family, and probate index at http://mycase.in.gov/default.aspx. The site does not disclose how far back records are kept. *Criminal:* Search the criminal index at http://mycase.in.gov/default.aspx. The site does not disclose how far back records are kept.

Sullivan County

Circuit & Superior Court

Civil: Online subscription service at https://www.doxpop.com. Fees involved. Records date from 04/1999. A limited free search of open cases is available. **$$$** *Criminal:* same **$$$**

Tippecanoe County

Circuit & Superior Court www.tippecanoe.in.gov/department/?structureid=19

Civil: Online access to docket summary of court records through CourtView is free at www.tippecanoe.in.gov/eservices/home.page. The date of birth and social security number are not included on most records. *Criminal:* Online access to docket summary of court records through CourtView is free at www.tippecanoe.in.gov/eservices/home.page.. The date of birth and social security number are not included on most records.

Tipton County

Circuit Court www.tiptoncounty.in.gov/

Civil: Search the docket by case number, party name or attorney name at http://mycase.in.gov/default.aspx. Also the Tipton City Index is available. *Criminal:* Online access by free service at http://mycase.in.gov/default.aspx. Includes criminal and citations. Also the Tipton City Index is available. .

Union County

Circuit Court

Civil: Search the docket by case number, party name or attorney name at http://mycase.in.gov/default.aspx. Also, online subscription service at https://www.doxpop.com. Fees involved. Records date from 02/00. A limited free search of open cases is available. $$$ *Criminal:* Search the docket by case number, party name or attorney name at http://mycase.in.gov/default.aspx. Also, online subscription service at https://www.doxpop.com. Fees involved. Records date from 02/00. A limited free search of open cases is available.

Vanderburgh County

Circuit & Superior Court www.vanderburghgov.org/index.aspx?page=66

Civil: Access civil records by subscription to Doxpop at https://www.doxpop.com/prod/court/. Free index search. **$$$** *Criminal:* Access criminal index by subscription to Doxpop at https://www.doxpop.com/prod/court/. Free index search. **$$$**

Vermillion County

Circuit Court

Civil: Online subscription service at https://www.doxpop.com. Fees involved. Records date from 07/1999. A limited free search of open cases is available. **$$$** *Criminal:* same**$ $$**

Vigo County

Circuit Court www.vigocounty.in.gov/

Civil: Online subscription service at https://www.doxpop.com. Fees involved. Records date from 04/96. A limited free search of open cases is available. The Terre Haute City Court index is searchable free at http://mycase.in.gov/default.aspx. **$$$** *Criminal:* Same as civil. **$$$**

Wabash County

Circuit & Superior Court

Civil: Online subscription service at https://www.doxpop.com . Fees involved. Records date from 08/89. A limited free search of open cases is available. **$$$** *Criminal:* same **$$$**

Warren County

Circuit Court

Civil: Search the docket by case number, party name or attorney name at http://mycase.in.gov/default.aspx. Cases here are only since Oct 2008. *Criminal:* Online access by free service at http://mycase.in.gov/default.aspx. Includes criminal and citations. Reportedly, case info available are only since Oct 2008.

Warrick County

Circuit & Superior Court www.warrickcounty.gov/

Civil: Online subscription service at https://www.doxpop.com . Fees involved. Records date from 06/87. A limited free search of open cases is available. $$$ *Criminal:* Online subscription service at https://www.doxpop.com. Fees involved. Records date from 08/89. A limited free search of open cases is available. $$$

Washington County

Circuit & Superior Court www.washingtoncounty.in.gov

Civil: Search the docket by case number, party name or attorney name at http://mycase.in.gov/default.aspx. *Criminal:* Online access by free service at http://mycase.in.gov/default.aspx. Includes criminal and citations. .

Wayne County

Circuit & Superior Court www.co.wayne.in.us/courts/

Civil: Access records via subscription service at https://www.doxpop.com. Fees involved. Records date from 3/90; a limited free search of open cases is available. **$$$** *Criminal:* same **$$$**

Wells County

Circuit & Superior Court www.wellscounty.org/superiorcourt.htm

Civil: Online subscription service to courts at https://www.doxpop.com. Fees involved. A limited free search of open cases is available. Online index goes back to 1/2000. **$$$** *Criminal:* Online access to Bluffton city criminal records is the same as civil. **$$$**

White County

Circuit Court

Civil: Online subscription service at https://www.doxpop.com. Fees involved. Index goes back to 1/2006. A limited free search of open cases is available. **$$$**

Superior Court http://home.whitecountyindiana.us/index.php?option=com_content&view=category&id=52&Itemid=60

Civil: Online subscription service at https://www.doxpop.com. Fees involved. Index goes back to 1/2006. A limited free search of open cases is available. **$$$** *Criminal:* same **$$**

Whitley County

Circuit & Superior Court www.whitleygov.com/courts/

Civil: Online subscription service at https://www.doxpop.com. Fees involved. Records date from 01/1999. A limited free search of open cases is available. **$$$** *Criminal:* same **$$$**

Recorders, Assessors, and Other Sites of Note

Recording Office Organization: 92 counties, 92 recording offices. The recording officer is the County Recorder but see the office of the Circuit Clerk for state tax liens on personal property. Many counties utilize a "Miscellaneous Index" for tax and other liens. All federal tax liens on personal property are filed with the County Recorder. State tax liens on personal property are filed with Circuit Clerk in a different office than the Recorder.

Vendor Multi-Jurisdiction Sites: These sites are shown on the appropriate county profiles.

1. Over 36 counties, access recorder land data by subscription on either the Laredo system using subscription and fees (accessible from the County web page) or the Tapestry System using credit card. See https://tapestry.fidlar.com/Tapestry2/Default.aspx; There is a $5.95 search fee and a $.50 per image fee. There is a $.75 per print page fee.
2. Access a free name-only without identifiers search of recorded documents at http://www.doxpop.com/prod/. A subscription is necessary to obtain detailed information. There are 25 counties available.
3. Search assessor property data free on the GIS system at http://beacon.schneidercorp.com for approximately 19 participating counties..

Three Government Statewide Sites: There are three government sites that provide a wealth of information dealing with property assessment, taxes and ownership. Each site gives the ability to search by name or property on a county basis.

a. Property Assessed Value: www.in.gov/dlgf/4931.htm

b. Property Sales Disclosures: www.in.gov/dlgf/5584.htm

c. Property Tax Bill - Past Dues: www.in.gov/dlgf/4929.htm

County Sites (To Avoid Redundancy, the Three Government Sites are Omitted on All Profiles.)

Adams County ***Recorded Documents*** www.adams-county.com/county-offices/view/recorders-office A free name-only without identifiers search of recorded document index from 1/1990 forward at www.doxpop.com/prod/common/ViewCountyDetails?countyId=18001. A subscription is necessary to obtain detailed information, images available from 1/1990. **$$$**

Property, Taxation Access to GIS/mapping site free at www.adams-county.com/adams-county/online-data. Also, access to property tax database free at http://web1.adams-county.com/pti_release/search.aspx.

Allen County ***Recorded Documents*** www.allencountyrecorder.us/Home.aspx Access to records for a fee at https://tapestry.fidlar.com/Tapestry2/Default.aspx. Contact 309-794-3283 or kylec@fidlar.com for subscription information. Search fee is $5.95 each, printed images $.50 each unless otherwise noted. Also, a free name-only without identifiers search of the recorded document index from 1970 forward is at https://www.doxpop.com/prod/. A subscription is necessary to obtain detailed information, images available from 1970 as well. **$$$**

Property, Taxation Access property database card data free at www.allencounty.us/view-property-record-cards. No name searches. Also, access to tax maps free at www.acimap.us/pati/.

Bartholomew County ***Recorded Documents*** www.bartholomew.in.gov/index.php/recorder-about-us Access to index free at https://www.uslandrecords.com/uslr/UslrApp/index.jsp. Images are available online for a fee.

Property, Taxation Access to county Public Access Geographic Information System is free at http://gis.bartholomewco.com/ and you must have an email for free registration and login.

Benton County Recorder ***Property, Taxation*** Access to GIS/mapping for free at http://benton.in.wthgis.com/.

Blackford County ***Recorded Documents*** http://gov.blackfordcounty.org/pages.asp?Page=Recorder&PageIndex=367 A free name-only without identifiers search of recorded document index from 1/1992 forward at www.doxpop.com/prod/common/ViewCountyDetails?countyId=18009. A subscription is necessary to obtain detailed information, images available from 9/2000. **$$$**

Property, Taxation Access property data at http://beacon.schneidercorp.com/.

Boone County ***Recorded Documents*** www.boonecounty.in.gov/Default.aspx?tabid=151 Access to records free at https://www.uslandrecords.com/inlr/. Land records index from 1/94 to present.

Property, Taxation Search for property data free on the GIS-mapping site at http://boonecounty.in.gov/Default.aspx?tabid=57. At map, click on 'Search for' at bottom left and choose 'parcels' to search by name.

Brown County ***Recorded Documents*** http://browncounty-in.gov/Departments/Recorder.aspx Access to land records indexes for free, go to https://www.uslandrecords.com/inlr/controller;jsessionid=D045DECE7EB28EB0063332BFEEB247E9. Indexes available from 7/88 to present. Image access is currently not available online.

Cass County ***Recorded Documents*** www.co.cass.in.us/dav/recorder/recorder.html Access to case records free at http://mycase.in.gov/default.aspx. Click on Case County. Also, access to records for a fee at https://tapestry.fidlar.com/Tapestry2/Default.aspx. Contact 309-794-3283 or kylec@fidlar.com forsubscription information. Search fee is $5.95 each, pringed images $.50 each unless otherwise noted. **$$$**

Clark County ***Property, Taxation*** Online access to property records is available at http://in10.plexisgroup.com/ecama/index.cfm. Also, access to GIS/mapping free at http://clarkin.egis.39dn.com/#.

Clinton County ***Property, Taxation*** Search assessor property data for a fee on the GIS system at http://beacon.schneidercorp.com/. Registration and username required.**$$$**

Crawford County ***Recorded Documents*** Access to records for a fee at https://tapestry.fidlar.com/Tapestry2/Default.aspx. Contact 309-794-3283 or kylec@fidlar.com for subscription information. Search fee is $5.95 each, printed images $.50 each unless otherwise noted. **$$$**

Daviess County ***Property, Taxation*** Online access to property records is available at http://in14.plexisgroup.com/ecama/index.cfm.

Dearborn County ***Recorded Records*** www.dearborncounty.org/Government/County-Offices/Recorders-Office A free name-only without identifiers search of recorded document index from 1/2000 forward at www.doxpop.com/prod/common/ViewCountyDetails?countyId=18029. A subscription is necessary to obtain detailed information, images available from 1/2000. **$$$**

Property, Taxation Access to free property search go to http://in-dearborn-assessor.governmaxa.com/propertymax/rover30.asp?sid=145F8570692B4E9199A9F98FC4374FAF.

Decatur County ***Recorded Documents*** www.decaturcounty.in.gov/recorder/recorder.htm A free name-only without identifiers search of recorded document index from 1/1994 forward at www.doxpop.com/prod/common/ViewCountyDetails?countyId=18031. A subscription is necessary to obtain detailed information, images available from 1/1994. **$$$**

Property, Taxation Access county property data for free at http://beacon.schneidercorp.com/

DeKalb County ***Recorded Documents*** www.co.dekalb.in.us/department/?fDD=30-0 Access to records for a fee at https://tapestry.fidlar.com/Tapestry2/Default.aspx. Contact 309-794-3283 or kylec@fidlar.com for subscription information. Search fee is $5.95 each, printed images $.50 each unless otherwise noted. **$$$**

Property, Taxation Access to Assessor database information for free at www.xsoftin.com/dekalb/.

Delaware County ***Recorded Documents*** www.co.delaware.in.us/department/?fDD=32-0 Access to records for a fee at https://tapestry.fidlar.com/Tapestry2/Default.aspx. Contact 309-794-3283 or kylec@fidlar.com for subscription information. Search fee is $5.95 each, printed images $.50 each unless otherwise noted. **$$$**

Property, Taxation Access to property searches for free at http://munsan.spinweb.net/parcel/.

Dubois County ***Recorded Documents*** www.duboiscountyin.org/offices/recorder.html A free name-only without identifiers search of recorded document index from 04/1994 forward at www.doxpop.com/prod/common/ViewCountyDetails?countyId=18037. A subscription is necessary to obtain detailed information, images available from 12/1999 **$$$**

Property, Taxation Access property search information free at www.duboiscountyassessor.com/propertymax/rover30.asp?sid=79C1E2BF77634A9E9EF8FFA2648F0D2D.

Elkhart County ***Real Estate, Deed, Lien, GIS/mapping, Recorded Documents*** www.elkhartcountyindiana.com/Departments/Recorder/index.htm Access to simple guest browse at www.elkhartcountyindiana.com/departments/recorder/LandRecords.htm. **$$$**

Property, Taxation Search parcel data for free at www.macoggis.com/ and includes Michiana area which is St Joseph and Elkhart Counties.

Fayette County ***Property, Taxation*** Access assessor property record cards and tax records free at www.co.fayette.in.us/auditor.htm.

Floyd County ***Recorded Documents*** www.floydcountyrecorder.com/ Access to records for a fee at https://tapestry.fidlar.com/Tapestry2/Default.aspx. Contact 309-794-3283 or kylec@fidlar.com for subscription information. Search fee is $5.95 each, printed images $.50 each unless otherwise noted. **$$$**

Fountain County ***Recorded Documents*** A free name-only without identifiers search of recorded document index from 6/1992 forward at www.doxpop.com/prod/common/ViewCountyDetails?countyId=18045. A subscription is necessary to obtain detailed information, images available from 1/2003. **$$$**

Property, Taxation Access the assessor property tax and property sales data free at http://in-fountain-assessor.governmax.com/propertymax/rover30.asp.

Franklin County ***Recorded Documents*** www.franklincounty.in.gov/countyoffices/recorder/ A free name-only without identifiers search of recorded document index from 1/2002 forward at www.doxpop.com/prod/common/ViewCountyDetails?countyId=18047. A subscription is necessary to obtain detailed information, images available from 1/2002. **$$$**

Property, Taxation Access the GIS web map free at http://thinkopengis.franklin.in.wthengineering.com/. To name search, click on Parcel.

Gibson County ***Property, Taxation*** Access property assessor parcel data free at http://beacon.schneidercorp.com/.

Grant County ***Recorded Documents*** http://recorder.grantcounty27.us/ Voter registration is at http://voters.grant.in.uinquire.us/nxweb.exe; registration, login, and password required. Search tax records at https://indiana-countyrecorders-records.com/User/Login.aspx?ReturnUrl=%2fIndex.aspx. Also, access to recorders portal for a fee go to http://indiana-countyrecorders-records.com. Fees are available at this site. **$$$**

Property, Taxation Access to GIS data is found at http://grantin.egis.39dn.com/#.

Hamilton County ***Recorded Documents*** www.hamiltoncounty.in.gov/department/index.php?structureid=27 A free name-only without identifiers search of recorded document index from 01/1987 forward at www.doxpop.com/prod/common/ViewCountyDetails?countyId=18057. A subscription is necessary to obtain detailed information, images available from 2/1996. **$$$**

Property, Taxation Access parcel and tax info for free at www2.hamiltoncounty.in.gov/apps/reports/defaulttax2.asp.

Hancock County ***Recorded Documents*** http://hancockcoingov.org/hancock-county-government-departments/hancock-county-indiana-recorder.html A free name-only without identifiers search of recorded document index from 01/1990 forward at www.doxpop.com/prod/common/ViewCountyDetails?countyId=18059. A subscription is necessary to obtain detailed information, images available from 1/2001. **$$$**

Property, Taxation Access to the assessor property data is free on the gis-mapping site at http://beacon.schneidercorp.com/?site=HancockCountyIN. Click on Search to search by name. Also, sales disclosure data is free at http://hancockcoingov.org/hancock-county-assessor-sales-disclosure.html. Also, search City of Greenfield property data free at http://beacon.schneidercorp.com/.

Harrison County ***Property, Taxation*** Access property and assessor data free on the GIS-mapping search site at http://harrisonin.egis.39dn.com/#.

Hendricks County ***Recorded Documents*** www.co.hendricks.in.us/recorder.html Access to records for a fee at https://tapestry.fidlar.com/Tapestry2/Default.aspx. Contact 309-794-3283 or kylec@fidlar.com for subscription information. Search fee is $5.95 each, printed images $.50 each unless otherwise noted. **$$$**

Property, Taxation Access to county property data on the GIS mapping site is free at www.co.hendricks.in.us/DWLookup/DW_Parcel_Search.asp. Also, search the GIS mapping for Town of Plainfield data free at http://beacon.schneidercorp.com.

Henry County ***Recorded Documents*** www.henryco.net/index.php?option=com_content&view=article&id=20&Itemid=23 A free name-only without identifiers search of recorded document index from 01/1990 forward at www.doxpop.com/prod/common/ViewCountyDetails?countyId=18065. A subscription is necessary to obtain detailed information, images available from 1/1991. **$$$**

Property, Taxation Access property assessment and GIS-mapping lookup free at www.henrycogis.org/geomoose/henrygis.html#. Also, search the property tax payment site free at https://pay.paygov.us/EndUser/PaymentAgency.aspx?action=view&transactionTypeId=168.

Howard County ***Recorded Documents*** www.howardcountyrecorder.com/ Access to records for a fee at https://tapestry.fidlar.com/Tapestry2/Default.aspx. Contact 309-794-3283 or kylec@fidlar.com for subscription information. Search fee is $5.95 each, printed images $.50 each unless otherwise noted. **$$$**

Property, Taxation Search assessor property data free on the GIS system at http://beacon.schneidercorp.com/ with registration and username required.**$$$**

Huntington County ***Recorded Documents*** www.huntington.in.us/county/department/?fDD=41-0 Access to records for a fee at https://tapestry.fidlar.com/Tapestry2/Default.aspx. Contact 309-794-3283 or kylec@fidlar.com for subscription information. Search fee is $5.95 each, printed images $.50 each unless otherwise noted. **$$$**

Property, Taxation Access to the assessor property data is free on the gis-mapping site at http://gis.huntington.in.us/.

Jackson County ***Property, Taxation*** Access to property tax, GIS/mapping and assessment info for free at http://thinkopengis.jackson.in.wthengineering.com/. This is a private website.

Jasper County ***Property, Taxation*** Access to GIS/mapping free at http://thinkopengis.jasper.in.wthengineering.com/.

Jay County ***Recorded Documents*** www.jaycounty.net/recorder.asp A free name-only without identifiers search of recorded document index from 01/1997 forward at www.doxpop.com/prod/common/ViewCountyDetails?countyId=18075. A subscription is necessary to obtain detailed information, images available from 1/1997. **$$$**

Property, Taxation Access to GIS-mapping property data is free at http://jayin.egis.39dn.co/ and click on Query to name search.

Jennings County ***Recorded Documents*** www.jenningscounty-in.gov/ A free name-only without identifiers search of recorded document index from 11/91 forward at www.doxpop.com/prod/common/ViewCountyDetails?countyId=18079. A subscription is necessary to obtain detailed information, images available from 11/91. **$$$**

Property, Taxation Access to the assessor property data is free on the gis-mapping site at http://thinkopengis.jennings.in.wthtechnology.com/.

Johnson County ***Property, Taxation*** Access to the assessor GIS database of property and sales data is free at http://beacon.schneidercorp.com/.

Kosciusko County ***Recorded Documents*** www.kcgov.com/department/index.php?fDD=20-0 A free name-only without identifiers search of recorded document index from 01/1991 forward at www.doxpop.com/prod/common/ViewCountyDetails?countyId=18085. A subscription is necessary to obtain detailed information, images available from 2/1992. **$$$**

Property, Taxation Access to property records on the searchable GIS mapping site at http://beacon.schneidercorp.com/?site=KosciuskoCountyIn. Also, access to Sales Disclosure free at www.stats.indiana.edu/sdf/search_r2/.

LaGrange County ***Recorded Documents*** www.lagrangecounty.org Access to records for a fee at https://tapestry.fidlar.com/Tapestry2/Default.aspx. Contact 309-794-3283 or kylec@fidlar.com for subscription information. Search fee is $5.95 each, printed images $.50 each unless otherwise noted. **$$$**

Property, Taxation Access assessor's data and search free at http://in-lagrange-assessor.governmax.com/propertymax/rover30.asp.

Lake County ***Property, Taxation*** Access property tax data online at http://in-lake-assessor.governmaxa.com/propertymax/rover30.asp. Search free as Guest, but no name searching. Subscription service allows name searching; sub fee is $19.95 per month.

La Porte County ***Recorded Documents*** www.laportecounty.org/ Access to records for a fee at https://tapestry.fidlar.com/Tapestry2/Default.aspx. Contact 309-794-3283 or kylec@fidlar.com for subscription information. Search fee is $5.95 each, printed images $.50 each unless otherwise noted. **$$$**

Property, Taxation Access to parcel searches for free at www.xsoftin.com/. Also, access to GIS/mapping free at http://beacon.schneidercorp.com/?site=LaPorteCountyIN

Madison County ***Recorded Documents*** www.madisoncty.com/Recorder.html Access to records for a fee at https://tapestry.fidlar.com/Tapestry2/Default.aspx. Contact 309-794-3283 or kylec@fidlar.com for subscription information. Search fee is $5.95 each, printed images $.50 each unless otherwise noted. **$$$**

Marion County ***Recorded Documents*** www.indy.gov/EGOV/COUNTY/RECORDER/Pages/home.aspx Access to records for a fee at www.biz.indygov.org/. Records date back to 1964; images from 1964. Federal tax liens and UCC data available. Also, access recording office land data at www.etitlesearch.com/. Registration required, fee based on usage. **$$$**

Property, Taxation Property tax information is free at http://cms.indygov.org/MyAssessedValue/.**$$$**

Marshall County ***Recorded Documents*** www.co.marshall.in.us/?page_id=200 A subscription is necessary to obtain detailed information, images available from 01/1996. **$$$**

Property, Taxation Search property data free at http://beacon.schneidercorp.com/.

Miami County ***Recorded Documents*** www.miamicountyin.gov/ Access to records for a fee at https://tapestry.fidlar.com/Tapestry2/Default.aspx. Contact 309-794-3283 or kylec@fidlar.com for subscription information. Search fee is $5.95 each, printed images $.50 each unless otherwise noted. **$$$**

Property, Taxation View GIS, tax and property information at www.miamicountyin.gov/GIS39dn.htm.

Monroe County ***Property, Taxation*** Access to GIS/Maps information for free at www.co.monroe.in.us/tsd/GIS.aspx.

Montgomery County ***Recorded Documents*** www.montgomeryco.net/department/?fDD=12-0 A free name-only without identifiers search of recorded document index from 01/1995 forward at www.doxpop.com/prod/common/ViewCountyDetails?countyId=18107. A subscription is necessary to obtain detailed information, images available from 1/1995. **$$$**

Property, Taxation Access to property tax and property assessment data for free at http://beacon.schneidercorp.com/?site=MontgomeryCountyIN Also, access to GIS/mapping free at www.montgomeryco.net/department/?fDD=20-0.

Morgan County ***Recorded Documents*** www.morgancounty.in.gov A free name-only without identifiers search of recorded document index from 05/1994 forward at www.doxpop.com/prod/common/ViewCountyDetails?countyId=18109. A subscription is necessary to obtain detailed information, images available from 5/2004. **$$$**

Property, Taxation Access to GIS/mapping for free at http://morgan-in.egis.39dn.com/

Newton County ***Property, Taxation*** Access assessor's property database free at http://beacon.schneidercorp.com/Application.aspx?AppID=295&LayerID=3320&PageTypeID=1&PageID=2029#.

Noble County ***Recorded Documents*** www.noblecountyrecorder.com/ Access to records for a fee at https://tapestry.fidlar.com/Tapestry2/Default.aspx. Contact 309-794-3283 or kylec@fidlar.com for subscription information. Search fee is $5.95 each, printed images $.50 each unless otherwise noted. Access the township land ownership roster for free at www.noblecountyrecorder.com/downloads/Land_Ownership_Roster.pdf. **$$$**

Ohio County ***Property, Taxation*** Access property data free at http://in-ohio-assessor.governmaxa.com/propertymax/rover30.asp. Click on property search, then search by owner, address or parcel number.

Owen County ***Recorded Documents*** www.owencounty.in.gov/index.php?q=content/recorder Access to records for a fee at https://tapestry.fidlar.com/Tapestry2/Default.aspx. Contact 309-794-3283 or kylec@fidlar.com for subscription information. Search fee is $5.95 each, printed images $.50 each unless otherwise noted. **$$$**

Parke County ***Recorded Documents*** www.parkecounty-in.gov/?q=node/24 A free name-only without identifiers search of recorded document index from 03/1996 forward at www.doxpop.com/prod/common/ViewCountyDetails?countyId=18121. A subscription is necessary to obtain detailed information, images available from 12/06. **$$$**

Property, Taxation Access to property tax information for free at www.in.gov/dlgf/4931.htm.

Perry County ***Recorded Documents*** Access to records for a fee at https://tapestry.fidlar.com/Tapestry2/Default.aspx. Contact 309-794-3283 or kylec@fidlar.com for subscription information. Search fee is $5.95 each, printed images $.50 each unless otherwise noted. **$$$**

Porter County ***Recorded Documents*** www2.porterco.org/home/departments/recorder/ Access to records for a fee at https://tapestry.fidlar.com/Tapestry2/Default.aspx. Contact 309-794-3283 or kylec@fidlar.com for subscription information. Search fee is $5.95 each, printed images $.50 each unless otherwise noted. **$$$**

Property, Taxation Access to property assessment data and sales is free at www.xsoftin.com/porter/parcelsearch.aspx.

Posey County ***Recorded Documents*** www.poseycountygov.org/offices/recorder/?id=17 Access to records for a fee at https://tapestry.fidlar.com/Tapestry2/Default.aspx. Contact 309-794-3283 or kylec@fidlar.com for subscription information. Search fee is $5.95 each, printed images $.50 each unless otherwise noted. **$$$**

Property, Taxation Access to property search information for free at http://in-posey-assessor.governmax.com/svc/default.asp?.

Putnam County ***Recorded Documents*** www.co.putnam.in.us/Recorder.html A free name-only without identifiers search of recorded document index from 01/1992 forward at www.doxpop.com/prod/common/ViewCountyDetails?countyId=18133. A subscription is necessary to obtain detailed information, images available from 1/1993. **$$$**

Randolph County ***Recorded Documents*** www.randolphcounty.us/departments/recorder A free name-only without identifiers search of recorded document index from 01/1993 forward at www.doxpop.com/prod/common/ViewCountyDetails?countyId=18135. A subscription is necessary to obtain detailed information, images available from 5/2003. **$$$**

Property, Taxation Access to property/parcel Information for free at http://in-randolph-assessor.governmax.com/propertymax/rover30.asp

Ripley County ***Recorded Documents*** www.ripleycounty.com/recorder/ Access to records for a fee at https://tapestry.fidlar.com/Tapestry2/Default.aspx. Contact 309-794-3283 or kylec@fidlar.com for subscription information. Search fee is $5.95 each, printed images $.50 each unless otherwise noted. **$$$**

Rush County ***Recorded Documents*** www.rushcounty.in.gov/Public/CountyOffices/Recorder/index.cfm A free name-only without identifiers search of recorded document index from 08/97 forward at www.doxpop.com/prod/common/ViewCountyDetails?countyId=18139. A subscription is necessary to obtain detailed information, images available from 12/98. **$$$**

Property, Taxation Access to parcel searches for free at www.xsoftin.com/rush/parcelsearch.aspx.

St. Joseph County ***Recorded Documents*** www.stjosephcountyindiana.com/departments/SJCRecorder/default.htm Access to records for a fee at https://tapestry.fidlar.com/Tapestry2/Default.aspx. Contact 309-794-3283 or kylec@fidlar.com for subscription information. Search fee is $5.95 each, printed images $.50 each unless otherwise noted. Also, land records search free at http://216.117.11.48/DirectSearch/default.aspx. **$$$**

Property, Taxation Search parcel data for free at www.macoggis.com/ and includes Michiana area which is St Joseph and Elkhart Counties. Also, access to property searches free at http://in-stjoseph-assessor.governmax.com/propertymax/rover30.asp?sid=54EAF07AEF604116BF196165E12A7E63

Shelby County ***Recorded Documents*** www.co.shelby.in.us/Default.aspx?alias=www.co.shelby.in.us/recorder A free name-only without identifiers search of recorded document index from 5/1998 forward at www.doxpop.com/prod/common/ViewCountyDetails?countyId=18145. A subscription is necessary to obtain detailed information, images available from 5/1998. **$$$**

Spencer County ***Recorded Documents*** www.spencercounty.in.gov/pages.cfm?Departmentid=408 Access to records for a fee at https://tapestry.fidlar.com/Tapestry2/Default.aspx. Contact 309-794-3283 or kylec@fidlar.com for subscription information. Search fee is $5.95 each, printed images $.50 each unless otherwise noted. **$$$**

Starke County Recorder ***Property, Taxation*** Access to GIS/mapping for free at http://thinkopengis.starke.in.wthtechnology.com/ and at http://beacon.schneidercorp.com/?Site=StarkeCountyIN/.

Steuben County ***Property, Taxation*** Access the GIS mapping site at http://beacon.schneidercorp.com/?site=SteubenCountyIN.

Sullivan County ***Recorded Documents*** A free name-only without identifiers search of recorded document index from 7/2004 forward at www.doxpop.com/prod/common/ViewCountyDetails?countyId=18153. A subscription is necessary to obtain detailed information. **$$$**

Tippecanoe County ***Recorded Documents*** www.tippecanoe.in.gov/department/?structureid=9 Access to records for a fee at https://tapestry.fidlar.com/Tapestry2/Default.aspx. Contact 309-794-3283 or kylec@fidlar.com for subscription information. Search fee is $5.95 each, printed images $.50 each unless otherwise noted. **$$$**

Property, Taxation Access to tax and assessment databases for free at www.tippecanoe.in.gov/egov/apps/services/index.egov?path=details&action=i&id=50. Also, access to the county GIS-mapping site free for the county and the city of Lafayette at http://gis.tippecanoe.in.gov/public/. Access parcel sales at https://www.tippecanoe.in.gov/assessor/parcelsearch/indexDT.asp

Tipton County ***Property, Taxation*** Search assessor property data free on the GIS system at the Tipton county site or http://beacon.schneidercorp.com/.

Union County ***Recorded Documents*** www.unioncountyin.gov/recorder A free name-only without identifiers search of recorded document index from 8/2005 forward at www.doxpop.com/prod/common/ViewCountyDetails?countyId=18161. A subscription is necessary to obtain detailed information, images available from 8/2005. **$$$**

Property, Taxation Access to GIS/mapping for free to http://union.in.wthgis.com/.

Vanderburgh County ***Recorded Documents*** www.vanderburghgov.org/Index.aspx?page=69 Access to records for a fee at https://tapestry.fidlar.com/Tapestry2/Default.aspx. Contact 309-794-3283 or kylec@fidlar.com for subscription information. Search fee is $5.95 each, printed images $.50 each unless otherwise noted. **$$$**

Property, Taxation Access assessor property database free at www.vanderburghassessor.org/NewDisclaimer.aspx.

Vermillion County ***Recorded Documents*** www.vermilliongov.us/home.html A free name-only without identifiers search of recorded document index from 8/1994 forward at www.doxpop.com/prod/common/ViewCountyDetails?countyId=18165. A subscription is necessary to obtain detailed information, images available from 12/1997. **$$$**

Property, Taxation Access to GIS/mapping for free at http://thinkopengis.vermillion.in.wthtechnology.com/>

Vigo County ***Recorded Documents*** www.vigocounty.in.gov/office/?fDD=19-0 A free name-only without identifiers search of recorded document index from 11/96 forward at www.doxpop.com/prod/common/ViewCountyDetails?countyId=18167. A subscription is necessary to obtain detailed information, images available from 12/2001. **$$$**

Property, Taxation Access county and Terra Haute property data by parcel, name or address at http://beacon.schneidercorp.com/?site=VigoCountyIN.

Wabash County ***Property, Taxation*** Access property data free from the Property List at http://assessor.wabash.in.datapitstop.us. Click on Property Information.

Warrick County ***Recorded Documents*** www.warrickcounty.gov/Departments/Recorder.aspx Access to records for a fee at https://tapestry.fidlar.com/Tapestry2/Default.aspx. Contact 309-794-3283 or kylec@fidlar.com for subscription information. Search fee is $5.95 each, printed images $.50 each unless otherwise noted. **$$$**

Property, Taxation Access property data free at www.warrickcounty.gov/Departments/Assessor.aspx. GIS Map information available at http://thinkopengis.warrick.in.wthengineering.com/.

Washington County ***Recorded Documents*** www.washingtoncounty.in.gov/washington-county-indiana-government Access to land records free at http://216.182.182.50/INWashington/DirectSearch/Default.aspx.

Property, Taxation Access to GIS/mapping for free at http://washington.in.wthgis.com/.

Wayne County ***Recorded Documents, Marriage Records*** http://co.wayne.in.us/recorder/ A free name-only without identifiers search of recorded document index from 1/1994 forward at www.doxpop.com/prod/common/ViewCountyDetails?countyId=18177. A subscription is necessary to obtain detailed information, images available from 4/2000. Also, marriage records from the County Clerk's office being added irregularly to the website at www.co.wayne.in.us/marriage/retrieve.cgi. Records are from 1811 forward. **$$$**

Property, Taxation Access county property records free at http://prc.co.wayne.in.us. Also, search current property tax records free at the gis-mapping site at www.gis.co.wayne.in.us/. Free registration required. Also, access sheriff tax sale list free at www.co.wayne.in.us/legals/sales.html.

Wells County ***Property, Taxation*** Access assessor records free on the GIS-mapping site at http://beacon.schneidercorp.com/?site=WellsCountyIN. At the map page, click on Search to search by name.

White County ***Recorded Documents*** Access to records for a fee at https://tapestry.fidlar.com/Tapestry2/Default.aspx. Contact 309-794-3283 or kylec@fidlar.com forsubscription information. Search fee is $5.95 each, printed images $.50 each unless otherwise noted. Also, a free name-only without identifiers search of the recorded document index from 01/1990 forward is at https://www.doxpop.com/prod/. A subscription is necessary to obtain detailed information, images available from 01/1990 as well. **$$$**

Property, Taxation Property and tax data is available at http://in-white-treasurer.governmax.com/collectmax/collect30.asp?sid=4D9AE443CCE84C4FA4A1037D62330980.

Whitley County ***Recorded Documents*** www.whitleygov.com/department/?fDD=4-0 Access to records for a fee at https://tapestry.fidlar.com/Tapestry2/Default.aspx. Contact 309-794-3283 or kylec@fidlar.com for subscription information. Search fee is $5.95 each, printed images $.50 each unless otherwise noted. **$$$**

Property, Taxation Search assessor property data free on the GIS system at http://beacon.schneidercorp.com/.

There are three government sites that provide a wealth of information dealing with property assessment , taxes and ownership. These sites are not shown on the profiles, for the sake of avoiding redundancy

a. **Property Assessed Value: www.in.gov/dlgf/4931.htm**

b. **Property Sales Disclosures: www.in.gov/dlgf/5584.htm**

c. **Property Tax Bill - Past Dues: www.in.gov/dlgf/4929.htm**

Iowa

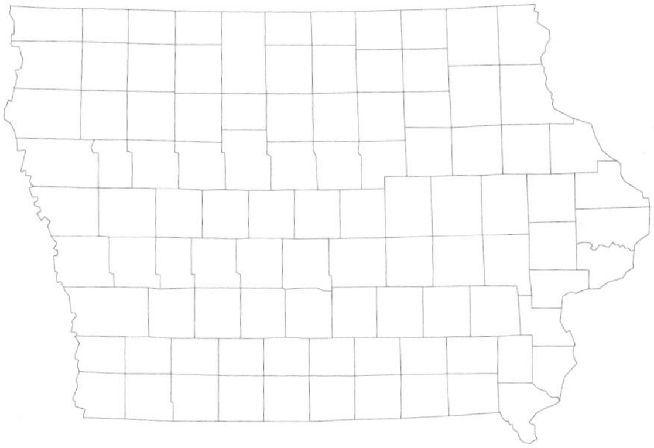

Capital: Des Moines
Polk County
Time Zone: CST
Population: 3,074,186
# of Counties: 99

Useful State Links

Website: www.iowa.gov/
Governor: www.governor.iowa.gov
Attorney General: www.state.ia.us/government/ag
State Archives: www.iowahistory.org
State Statutes and Codes: https://www.legis.iowa.gov/IowaLaw/statutoryLaw.aspx
Legislative Bill Search: www.legis.state.ia.us
Bill Monitoring: https://www.legis.iowa.gov/Legislation/BillTracking/billTrackingTools.aspx
Unclaimed Funds: www.greatiowatreasurehunt.com/search.cfm

State Public Record Agencies

Criminal Records

Division of Criminal Investigation, Support Operation Bureau, http://www.dps.state.ia.us/DCI/index.shtml The Iowa Department of Public Safety, Division of Criminal Investigation's (DCI) Criminal History Record Check website at https://iowacriminalhistory.iowa.gov/default.aspx provides a criminal record check. This website will not provide criminal history data on any arrest information that is older than 18 months without a final disposition or any completed deferred judgment information. The fee for a criminal history record check obtained through this website is $15.00. *Other Options:* Although this agency does not offer online access, there is online free access to the statewide Iowa Judicial System courts database at http://www.iowacourts.gov/.

Sexual Offender Registry

Division of Criminal Investigations, SOR Unit -, http://www.iowasexoffender.com/ The website permits name searching, enables a requester to be notified on the movement of an offender, and provides a map of registrants. RSS feed and aite API also available. There are approx. 5,400 registrants listed on this website.

Incarceration Records

Iowa Department of Corrections, 510 E 12th Street, http://www.doc.state.ia.us At the agency website, click on Offender Information for an inmate search. *Other Options:* Bulk records are not available. This was a mis-use of the deferred judgment records by vendors, and database purchases are no longer offered.

Corporation, LLC, LP, Fictitious Name, Trademarks/Servicemarks

Secretary of State - Business Services Div, 321 E 12th Street, http://sos.iowa.gov/ For free searching, click on Search Databases from home page. *Other Options:* This agency will sell the records in database format. Call the number listed above and ask for Karen Ubaldo for more information.

Uniform Commercial Code, Federal Tax Liens

UCC Division - Sec of State, 321 E 12th Street, http://sos.iowa.gov/ Visit http://sos.iowa.gov/search/ucc/search.aspx?ucc. This search uses the filing office standard search logic for UCC or federal tax liens. It allows one to print a certified lien search report. By default the search reveals all liens that have not reached their lapse date. UCC searches have the option to include liens that have lapsed within the past year. An additional, alternative search is at http://sos.iowa.gov/search/uccAlternative/search.aspx. This is helpful in finding names that are similar too but not exactly the same as the name searched. *Other Options:* This agency will sell the database of records. Call the number listed above and ask for Karen Ubaldo.

Vital Certificates

Iowa Department of Public Health, Bureau of Vital Records, http://www.idph.state.ia.us/apl/health_statistics.asp#vital The agency promotes a vendor - www.vitalchek.com - as the online means to order records. Additional fees ($13.00) involved and use of credit card required. **$$$**

Driver Records

Department of Transportation, Driver Service Records Section, http://www.iowadot.gov/mvd/ The state requires that all ongoing requesters/users access records via IowaAccess. The fee is $8.50 per record, the service is interactive or batch. Requesters must be approved and open an account. The records contain personal information, so requesters must comply with DPPA. For more information, contact IowaAccess at 515-323-3468 or 866-492-3468. Iowa drivers may view their own record online for free at https://mymvd.iowadot.gov/Account/Login. The fee to order a certified record is $7.00, use of a credit card or debit card is required. **$$$**

Vehicle Ownership & Registration

Department of Transportation, Office of Vehicle Services, http://www.iowadot.gov/mvd/ Online access is available to those who qualify per DPPA including dealers, Iowa licensed investigators and security companies. There is no fee. All accounts must register and be pre-approved per DPPA. Write to the Office of Motor Vehicle, explaining purpose/use of records. *Other Options:* Iowa makes the entire vehicle file or selected data available for purchase. Weekly updates are also available for those purchasers. Requesters subject to DPPA requirements. For more information, call 515-237-3110.

Campaign Finance, PACs

Iowa Ethics & Campaign Disclusre Board, 510 E 12th St, Ste 1A, http://www.iowa.gov/ethics/ Search campaign disclosure reports at https://webapp.iecdb.iowa.gov/publicview/ContributionSearch.aspx. Search by individual, candidate, party or PAC.

Occupational Licensing Boards

Accountant-CPA .... https://eservices.iowa.gov/licensediniowa/index.php?pgname=pubsearch
Acupuncturist .... www.medicalboard.iowa.gov/find_physician/index.html
Adoption Investigator/Searcher .... www.dhs.iowa.gov/Partners/Partners_Providers/FindAProvider/LicensingAdoptFC.html
Alcoholic Beverage Retail/Whlse/Mfg .... https://elicensing.iowaabd.com/LicenseSearch.aspx
Ambulance/Air Ambulance/Transport .... www.idph.state.ia.us/ems/report_get_service_list.asp
Anesthesiologist .... www.medicalboard.iowa.gov/find_physician/index.html
Appraiser .... https://eservices.iowa.gov/licensediniowa/index.php?pgname=pubsearch
Architect .... https://eservices.iowa.gov/licensediniowa/index.php?pgname=pubsearch
Asbestos Contractor/Worker www2.iwd.state.ia.us/LaborServices/LabrAsbs.nsf
Asbestos Project Designer/Planner www2.iwd.state.ia.us/LaborServices/LabrAsbs.nsf
Athletic Trainer .... https://eservices.iowa.gov/licensediniowa/index.php?pgname=pubsearch
Attorney .... https://www.iacourtcommissions.org/icc/
Audiologist .... https://eservices.iowa.gov/licensediniowa/index.php?pgname=pubsearch
Bank .... www.idob.state.ia.us/
Barber .... https://eservices.iowa.gov/licensediniowa/index.php?pgname=pubsearch
Chiropractor .... https://eservices.iowa.gov/licensediniowa/index.php?pgname=pubsearch
Controlled Substance Registrant .... www.state.ia.us/ibpe/verification.html
Cosmetol'y Salon/School/Instruct .... https://eservices.iowa.gov/licensediniowa/index.php?pgname=pubsearch
Cosmetologist .... https://eservices.iowa.gov/licensediniowa/index.php?pgname=pubsearch
Crematory .... https://eservices.iowa.gov/licensediniowa/index.php?pgname=pubsearch
Day Care .... https://ccmis.dhs.state.ia.us/ClientPortal/ProviderSearch.aspx
Debt Management Company .... www.idob.state.ia.us/license/lic_default.htm
Delayed Deposit Service Business .... www.idob.state.ia.us/license/lic_default.htm
Dental Assistant .... www.state.ia.us/dentalboard/practitioners/dental-assistants/registered-dental-assistants.html#Registration_verifications_
Dietitian .... https://eservices.iowa.gov/licensediniowa/index.php?pgname=pubsearch
Drug Distributor/Whlse./Mfg. .... www.state.ia.us/ibpe/verification.html
Electrologist .... https://eservices.iowa.gov/licensediniowa/index.php?pgname=pubsearch
Emergency Med Tech-Paramedic .... www.idph.state.ia.us/ems/report_get_provider_list.asp
EMS Provider/Service/Bureau Staff .... www.idph.state.ia.us/ems/report_get_provider_list.asp
Engineer .... https://eservices.iowa.gov/licensediniowa/index.php?pgname=pubsearch
Esthetician .... https://eservices.iowa.gov/licensediniowa/index.php?pgname=pubsearch
Excursion Gambling Boat .... www.iowa.gov/irgc/
Finance Company .... www.idob.state.ia.us/license/lic_default.htm

First Response Paramedic	www.idph.state.ia.us/ems/report_get_provider_list.asp
Foster Care	www.dhs.iowa.gov/docs/LicFacs.xls
Funeral Director/Home	https://eservices.iowa.gov/licensediniowa/index.php?pgname=pubsearch
Group Foster Care	www.dhs.iowa.gov/docs/LicFacs.xls
Hearing Aid Dispenser/Dealer	https://eservices.iowa.gov/licensediniowa/index.php?pgname=pubsearch
Insurance Agency/Company	https://sbs-ia.naic.org/Lion-Web/jsp/sbsreports/AgentLookup.jsp
Insurance Producer	https://sbs-ia.naic.org/Lion-Web/jsp/sbsreports/AgentLookup.jsp
Landscape Architect	https://eservices.iowa.gov/licensediniowa/index.php?pgname=pubsearch
Lobbyist	http://coolice.legis.iowa.gov/Cool-ICE/default.asp?Category=Matt&Service=Lobby
Manicurist	https://eservices.iowa.gov/licensediniowa/index.php?pgname=pubsearch
Marriage & Family Therapist	https://eservices.iowa.gov/licensediniowa/index.php?pgname=pubsearch
Massage Therapist	https://eservices.iowa.gov/licensediniowa/index.php?pgname=pubsearch
Medical Doctor	www.medicalboard.iowa.gov/find_physician/index.html
Mental Health Counselor	https://eservices.iowa.gov/licensediniowa/index.php?pgname=pubsearch
Money Transmitter	www.idob.state.ia.us/license/lic_default.htm
Mortgage Banker/Broker	www.idob.state.ia.us/license/lic_default.htm
Mortgage Loan Service	www.idob.state.ia.us/license/lic_default.htm
Mortuary Science	https://eservices.iowa.gov/licensediniowa/index.php?pgname=pubsearch
Nail Technologist	https://eservices.iowa.gov/licensediniowa/index.php?pgname=pubsearch
Notary Public	http://sos.iowa.gov/search/notary/search.aspx
Nuclear Medicine Technologist	www.idph.state.ia.us/IdphRadHealth/PermitsToPractice.aspx
Nurse-Advance Registered Practice	https://eservices.iowa.gov/PublicPortal/Iowa/IBON/public/license_verification.jsp
Nurse-LPN	https://eservices.iowa.gov/PublicPortal/Iowa/IBON/public/license_verification.jsp
Nursing Home Administrator	https://eservices.iowa.gov/licensediniowa/index.php?pgname=pubsearch
Occupational Therapist/Assistant	https://eservices.iowa.gov/licensediniowa/index.php?pgname=pubsearch
Optometrist	https://eservices.iowa.gov/licensediniowa/index.php?pgname=pubsearch
Orthopedic Doctor	www.medicalboard.iowa.gov/find_physician/index.html
Osteopathic Physician	www.medicalboard.iowa.gov/find_physician/index.html
Pari-Mutuel Race Track Enclosure	www.iowa.gov/irgc/
Pediatrician	www.medicalboard.iowa.gov/find_physician/index.html
Pesticide Commercial Applicator	www.kellysolutions.com/ia/Business/index.asp
Pesticide Commercial Certification	www.kellysolutions.com/ia/Applicators/index.asp
Pesticide Dealer	www.kellysolutions.com/ia/Dealers/index.asp
Pesticide Private Applicator	www.kellysolutions.com/ia/Applicators/index.asp
Pharmacist/Pharmacist Tech/Intern	www.state.ia.us/ibpe/verification.html
Pharmacy	www.state.ia.us/ibpe/verification.html
Physical Therapist/Assistant	https://eservices.iowa.gov/licensediniowa/index.php?pgname=pubsearch
Physician Assistant	https://eservices.iowa.gov/licensediniowa/index.php?pgname=pubsearch
Physician/Medical Doctor	www.medicalboard.iowa.gov/find_physician/index.html
Podiatrist	https://eservices.iowa.gov/licensediniowa/index.php?pgname=pubsearch
Podiatry Radiographer	www.idph.state.ia.us/IdphRadHealth/PermitsToPractice.aspx
Psychiatrist	www.medicalboard.iowa.gov/find_physician/index.html
Psychologist	https://eservices.iowa.gov/licensediniowa/index.php?pgname=pubsearch
Radiation Therapist/Technologist	www.idph.state.ia.us/IdphRadHealth/PermitsToPractice.aspx
Radon Laboratories	www.idph.state.ia.us/Radon/Certified.aspx
Radon Measurement Specialist	www.idph.state.ia.us/Radon/Certified.aspx
Radon Mitigation Specialist	www.idph.state.ia.us/Radon/Certified.aspx
Real Estate Agent/Broker/Sales	https://eservices.iowa.gov/licensediniowa/index.php?pgname=pubsearch
Real Estate Appraiser	https://eservices.iowa.gov/licensediniowa/index.php?pgname=pubsearch
Respiratory Therapist	https://eservices.iowa.gov/licensediniowa/index.php?pgname=pubsearch
School Coach	https://www.iowaonline.state.ia.us/boee/
School Counselor	https://www.iowaonline.state.ia.us/boee/
School Principal/Superintendent	https://www.iowaonline.state.ia.us/boee/
Shorthand Reporter	https://www.iacourtcommissions.org/icc/

Social Worker ..... https://eservices.iowa.gov/licensediniowa/index.php?pgname=pubsearch
Speech Pathologist/Audiologist ..... https://eservices.iowa.gov/licensediniowa/index.php?pgname=pubsearch
Surveyor, Land ..... https://eservices.iowa.gov/licensediniowa/index.php?pgname=pubsearch
Tattoo Artist ..... https://eservices.iowa.gov/licensediniowa/index.php?pgname=pubsearch
Teacher ..... https://www.iowaonline.state.ia.us/boee/
Waste Water Lagoon/Treatm't Oper'tor ..... https://programs.iowadnr.gov/wwisard/home.aspx
Water Distribution/Treatment Operator ..... https://programs.iowadnr.gov/wwisard/home.aspx
Well Driller ..... https://programs.iowadnr.gov/wwisard/home.aspx

State and Local Courts

State Court Structure: The District Court is the court of general jurisdiction. Vital records were moved from the courts to the County Recorder's office in each county.

Appellate Courts: One may view Supreme Court and Appellate Court opinions from www.iowacourts.gov.

Statewide Court Online Access: All courts participate in the system described below.

- District criminal, civil (including divorce cases with financials/custody data), probate, and traffic information is available from all 99 Iowa counties at www.iowacourts.gov/Online_Court_Services/Online_Docket_Record/index.asp. Name searches are available on either a statewide or specific county basis. Names of juveniles aged 10 to 17 will only appear for completed cases with a guilty verdict. There is no fee for basic information.
- A $25.00 per month subscription system (Advanced Case Search) is offered which provides more detailed information. While this is an excellent site with much information and are updated daily, note that the historical records are provided from different starting dates per county. Also, images are not shown. The DOB is not entered when searching, but is often shown on search results.

Note: No individual Iowa courts offer online access, other than as described above.

Recorders and Assessors

Recording Office Organization: All 99 counties, 100 recording offices. Lee County has two recording offices. The recording officer is the County Recorder. Many counties utilize a grantor/grantee index containing all transactions recorded with them. Federal tax liens on personal property of businesses are filed with the Secretary of State. Other federal and all state tax liens on personal property are filed with the County Recorder.

Vendor Multi-Jurisdiction Sites:

- A links list for assessor records for most Iowa counties plus cities of Ames, Cedar Rapids, Davenport, Dubuque, Iowa City, and Souix City is at www.iowaassessors.com.
- Search basic assessor property data free on the GIS system at http://beacon.schneidercorp.com/. Registration and username required, fees may apply.

Government Statewide Site: Recorded documents for all counties are available on the state system.

- Provided by the Iowa county Recorders Association, the Iowa Land Records system at http://iowalandrecords.org/portal offers statewide searching and pdf images of deeds, liens, even UCCs and judgments. While free now, the site states this service may begin charging at any time. There is also features for monitoring new documents and saving documents.

County Sites (To Avoid Redundancy, the Above Government Site is Omitted on All Profiles.):

Adair County ***Property, Taxation Records*** Access to the assessor database of property and sales data is free at http://adair.iowaassessors.com/.

Allamakee County

Property, Taxation Records Search assessor property data and/or GIS sites for free at http://beacon.schneidercorp.com. For detailed information, must subscribe for a fee.**$$$**

Appanoose County ***Property, Taxation Records*** Search assessor property data and/or GIS sites for free at http://beacon.schneidercorp.com. For detailed information, must subscribe for a fee.**$$$**

Audubon County ***Property, Taxation Records*** Search assessor property data and/or GIS sites for free at http://beacon.schneidercorp.com. For detailed information, must subscribe for a fee.**$$$**

Benton County ***Property, Taxation Records*** Search assessor property data and/or GIS sites for free at http://beacon.schneidercorp.com. For detailed information, must subscribe for a fee.**$$$**

Black Hawk County ***Property, Taxation Records*** Access to the assessor database of property and sales data is free at www.co.black-hawk.ia.us/depts/bhentry.htm but no name searching. Also, search the tax delinquencies list free, manually at www.co.black-hawk.ia.us/depts/treasurer.html.

Boone County ***Property, Taxation Records*** Search assessor property data and/or GIS sites for free at http://beacon.schneidercorp.com. For detailed information, must subscribe for a fee.**$$$**

Bremer County ***Property, Taxation Records*** Search assessor property data and/or GIS sites for free at http://beacon.schneidercorp.com. For detailed information, must subscribe for a fee.**$$$**

Buchanan County ***Property, Taxation Records*** Access county property data free at http://buchanan.iowaassessors.com/ but no name searching. Includes property sales.

Buena Vista County ***Property, Taxation Records*** Search the property assessor and Ag sales databases for free at www.bvcountyiowa.com/index.php/assessors. Sales searches also.

Calhoun County ***Property, Taxation Records*** Access to the assessor database of property and sales data is free at www.calhoun.iowaassessors.com/.

Carroll County ***Property, Taxation Records*** Access to the assessor database of property and sales data, plus GIS/mapping is free at www.co.carroll.ia.us/Assessor/property_records.htm.

Cass County ***Property, Taxation Records*** Search assessor property data and/or GIS sites for free at http://beacon.schneidercorp.com. For detailed information, must subscribe for a fee.**$$$**

Cedar County ***Property, Taxation Records*** Search county property and sales data free at http://cedar.iowaassessors.com/.

Cerro Gordo County ***Real Estate, Deed, Lien Records*** www.co.cerro-gordo.ia.us Access to recorded documents at www.co.cerro-gordo.ia.us/document_search/docindex_search.cfm. Also, with registration you search county land records on the statewide site at https://iowalandrecords.org/portal/clris/SwitchToCountiesTab. **$$$**

Property, Taxation Records Access to the County and Mason City property records is free at www.co.cerro-gordo.ia.us/property_search/property_search.cfm.

Cherokee County ***Recorded Documents*** http://cherokeecountyiowa.com/offices/recorder/index.htm An inquiry of recorded documents is at http://lti.gmdsolutions.com/cherokee/rindex.html. At https://iowalandrecords.org/portal/clris/SwitchToCountiesTab, an index of recorded land records is available from 1/2000, images available from 03/2002. Also, access to real estate and tax information free at http://lti.gmdsolutions.com/cherokee/index.html.

Property, Taxation Records Access to real estate and tax information for free at http://lti.gmdsolutions.com/cherokee/index.html. Search county property and sales data free at http://cherokee.iowaassessors.com/.

Chickasaw County ***Property, Taxation Records*** Search assessor property data and/or GIS sites for free at http://beacon.schneidercorp.com. For detailed information, must subscribe for a fee.**$$$**

Clarke County ***Property, Taxation Records*** Search parcels free on the GIS-mapping site at www.clarkecoiagis.com/clarke/.

Clay County ***Property, Taxation Records*** Search assessments, parcels, and sales free at http://clay.iowaassessors.com/. Also, search tax sale certificates free at http://lti.gmdsolutions.com/clay/tindex.html. Also, search land and tax database free at http://lti.gmdsolutions.com/clay/index.html.

Clayton County ***Property, Taxation Records*** Search county property records free at http://clayton.iowaassessors.com/. Search assessor property data and/or GIS sites for free at http://beacon.schneidercorp.com. For detailed information, must subscribe for a fee.**$$$**

Clinton County ***Property, Taxation Records*** Access to the assessor database of property and sales data is free at www.qpublic.net/clinton/search1.html. Search assessor property data and/or GIS sites for free at http://beacon.schneidercorp.com. For detailed information, must subscribe for a fee.**$$$**

Crawford County ***Property, Taxation Records*** Search county property records free at http://crawford.iowaassessors.com/ but no name searching or sales info until you subscribe.**$$$**

Dallas County ***Property, Taxation Records*** Access to the assessor database of property and sales data is free at http://assessorweb.co.dallas.ia.us/Searchv3.aspx. At http://iowalandrecords.org/portal/clris/SwitchToCountiesTab, view an index of recorded land records from 1/2004.

Davis County ***Property, Taxation Records*** Search assessor property data and/or GIS sites for free at http://beacon.schneidercorp.com. For detailed information, must subscribe for a fee.**$$$**

Delaware County ***Property, Taxation Records*** Search assessor property data and/or GIS sites for free at http://beacon.schneidercorp.com. For detailed information, must subscribe for a fee. Also, access to assessor data free at http://delaware.iowaassessors.com/.**$$$**

Des Moines County ***Property, Taxation Records*** Access to the assessor database of property and sales data is free at www.dmcgis.com/.

Dickinson County ***Property, Taxation Records*** Search assessor property data and/or GIS sites for free at http://beacon.schneidercorp.com. For detailed information, must subscribe for a fee.**$$$**

Dubuque County ***Recorded Documents*** www.dubuquecounty.org/Recorder/tabid/105/Default.aspx Access recorder general, tax lien, and corporations indexes free at http://cotthosting.com/iadubuque/LandRecords/protected/SrchQuickName.aspx. Also, at http://iowalandrecords.org/portal/clris/SwitchToCountiesTab, view index and images of recorded land records from 1/1987.
Property, Taxation Records Search assessor property data and/or GIS sites for free at http://beacon.schneidercorp.com. For detailed information, must subscribe for a fee.**$$$**

Emmet County ***Property, Taxation Records*** Search assessor property data and/or GIS sites for free at http://beacon.schneidercorp.com. For detailed information, must subscribe for a fee.**$$$**

Fayette County ***Property, Taxation Records*** Search assessor property data and/or GIS sites for free at http://beacon.schneidercorp.com. For detailed information, must subscribe for a fee.**$$$**

Floyd County ***Property, Taxation Records*** Search assessor property data and/or GIS sites for free at http://beacon.schneidercorp.com. For detailed information, must subscribe for a fee. Also, access property and sales data is free at www.floydcoia.org/features/gis.asp.**$$$**

Franklin County ***Property, Taxation Records*** Search assessor property data and/or GIS sites for free at http://beacon.schneidercorp.com. For detailed information, must subscribe for a fee.**$$$**

Greene County ***Property, Taxation Records*** Access to the assessor database of property and sales data is free at http://greene.iowaassessors.com. Also, access to GIS/mapping free at http://greeneia.mygisonline.com/.

Grundy County ***Property, Taxation Records*** Search assessor property data and/or GIS sites for free at http://beacon.schneidercorp.com. For detailed information, must subscribe for a fee.**$$$**

Guthrie County ***Property, Taxation Records*** Access to the assessor database of property and sales data is free at http://guthrie.iowaassessors.com/. Also, search assessor property data and/or GIS sites for free at http://beacon.schneidercorp.com. For detailed information, must subscribe for a fee.**$$$**

Hamilton County ***Real Estate, Deed, Lien, UCC, Judgment Records***
www.hamiltoncounty.org/Hamilton%20County%20Recorder%20Homepage.html At https://iowalandrecords.org/portal/clris/SwitchToCountiesTab, view an index of recorded land records from 7/02.
Property, Taxation Records Search assessor property records and residential and commercial sales free at http://hamilton.iowaassessors.com/.

Hancock County ***Property, Taxation Records*** Access to a parcel search for free at http://hancock.iowaassessors.com/.

Hardin County ***Property, Taxation Records*** Search assessor property data and/or GIS sites for free at http://beacon.schneidercorp.com. For detailed information, must subscribe for a fee.**$$$**

Harrison County ***Property, Taxation Records*** Search assessor property data and/or GIS sites for free at http://beacon.schneidercorp.com. For detailed information, must subscribe for a fee.**$$$**

Henry County ***Property, Taxation Records*** Search assessor property data and/or GIS sites for free at http://beacon.schneidercorp.com. For detailed information, must subscribe for a fee.**$$$**

Howard County ***Property, Taxation Records*** Access to assessor records for free at http://howard.iowaassessors.com/.

Humboldt County ***Property, Taxation Records*** Assessor property records and sales free at http://humboldt.iowaassessors.com/.

Iowa County ***Property, Taxation Records*** Access to the assessor database of property and sales data is free at http://iowa.iowaassessors.com/. Also search free at http://lti.gmdsolutions.com/iowa/index.html. Search Tax Sale Certificates free at http://lti.gmdsolutions.com/iowa/tindex.html.

Jackson County ***Property, Taxation Records*** Search assessor property data and/or GIS sites for free at http://beacon.schneidercorp.com. For detailed information, must subscribe for a fee.**$$$**

Jasper County ***Property, Taxation Records*** Access to the assessor database of property and sales data is free at http://jasper.iowaassessors.com/. Search assessor property data and/or GIS sites for free at http://beacon.schneidercorp.com. For detailed information, must subscribe for a fee.**$$$**

Jefferson County ***Property, Taxation Records*** Access to the assessor database of property and sales data is free at http://jefferson.iowaassessors.com/.

Johnson County ***Recorded Documents*** www.johnson-county.com/dept_recorder.aspx?id=1155 Access the recorders data free at http://recorder.johnson-county.com/External/LandRecords/protected/SrchQuickName.aspx. Images and indexes go back to 11/1983, Book 670 and are updated daily. At https://iowalandrecords.org/portal/, view index of recorded land records from 2004, images from 2/27/2004. Must register before use.

Property, Taxation Records Search assessor property data and/or GIS sites for free at http://beacon.schneidercorp.com. For detailed information, must subscribe for a fee. Also, access to Iowa City assessor and property data is free at http://iowacity.iowaassessors.com.**$$$**

Jones County ***Property, Taxation Records*** Search assessor property data and/or GIS sites for free at http://beacon.schneidercorp.com. For detailed information, must subscribe for a fee.**$$$**

Keokuk County ***Property, Taxation Records*** Search assessor property data and/or GIS sites for free at http://beacon.schneidercorp.com. For detailed information, must subscribe for a fee.**$$$**

Kossuth County ***Property, Taxation Records*** Access to the assessor database of property and sales data is free at www.co.kossuth.ia.us/assessor/assessor.htm. Also, access to assessor data free at http://kossuth.iowaassessors.com/.

Lee County ***Property, Taxation Records*** Search assessor property data and/or GIS sites for free at http://beacon.schneidercorp.com. For detailed information, must subscribe for a fee.**$$$**

Linn County ***Recorded Documents*** www.linncountyrecorder.com At https://iowalandrecords.org/portal/clris/SwitchToCountiesTab, view an index of recorded land records from 1/1990, images from 1/1990. Also, access to recorder database free at http://cotthosting.com/ialinn/LandRecords/protected/SrchQuickName.aspx.

Property, Taxation Records Access to the assessor database of property data is free at http://linn.iowaassessors.com/. Also, access to City of Cedar Rapids property data is free at www.cedar-rapids.info/assessor/pmc/. No name searching.

Louisa County ***Property, Taxation Records*** Search assessor property data and/or GIS sites for free at http://beacon.schneidercorp.com. For detailed information, must subscribe for a fee.**$$$**

Lucas County ***Property, Taxation Records*** Access to assessor's database for free at http://lucas.iowaassessors.com/.

Lyon County ***Property, Taxation Records*** Access to the assessor database of property and sales data is free at http://lyon.iowaassessors.com/.

Madison County ***Real Estate, Grantor/Grantee, Deed, Mortgage, Lien Records*** www.madisoncoia.us At https://iowalandrecords.org/portal/clris/SwitchToCountiesTab, view an index of recorded land records from 1/1987. Also, search free at http://lti.gmdsolutions.com/madison/rindex.html

Property, Taxation Records Access the assessor database of property data free at http://lti.gmdsolutions.com/madison/index.html. Also search free at http://madison.iowaassessors.com/. Search tax sales certificates free at http://lti.gmdsolutions.com/madison/tindex.html.

Mahaska County ***Property, Taxation Records*** Search assessor property data and/or GIS sites for free at http://beacon.schneidercorp.com. For detailed information, must subscribe for a fee.**$$$**

Marion County ***Property, Taxation Records*** Search assessor property data and/or GIS sites for free at http://beacon.schneidercorp.com. For detailed information, must subscribe for a fee.**$$$**

Marshall County ***Property, Taxation Records*** Access to the assessor property record card system and sales data is free at www.co.marshall.ia.us/assessor/cgi/frameset.cgi. Also, access to GIS/mapping free at www.marshallgis.org/marshallgis/.

Mills County ***Property, Taxation Records*** Access to GIS/mapping for a fee at www.millscoia.us/realestatemain.htm. Also, search assessor property data and/or GIS sites for free at http://beacon.schneidercorp.com. For detailed information, must subscribe for a fee.**$$$**

Mitchell County ***Property, Taxation Records*** Access to assessor's database for free at http://mitchell.iowaassessors.com/.

Monona County ***Property, Taxation Records*** Search assessor property data and/or GIS sites for free at http://beacon.schneidercorp.com. For detailed information, must subscribe for a fee.**$$$**

Monroe County ***Property, Taxation Records*** Access to assessor's database for free at http://monroe.iowaassessors.com/

Montgomery County ***Property, Taxation Records*** Search assessor property data and/or GIS sites for free at http://beacon.schneidercorp.com. For detailed information, must subscribe for a fee.**$$$**

Muscatine County ***Property, Taxation Records*** Search assessor property data and/or GIS sites for free at http://beacon.schneidercorp.com. For detailed information, must subscribe for a fee.**$$$**

O'Brien County ***Property, Taxation Records*** Access to assessor's database for free at http://obrien.iowaassessors.com/.

Page County ***Property, Taxation Records*** Search assessor property data and/or GIS sites for free at http://beacon.schneidercorp.com. For detailed information, must subscribe for a fee.**$$$**

Palo Alto County ***Property, Taxation Records*** Access to parcel data for free at http://beacon.schneidercorp.com/?site=PaloAltoCountyIA. Also, access to assessor's database for free to go http://paloalto.iowaassessors.com/.

Plymouth County ***Property, Taxation Records*** Access the assessor database of property and sales data free at http://plymouth.iowaassessors.com/.

Pocahontas County ***Property, Taxation Records*** Search assessor property data and/or GIS sites for free at http://beacon.schneidercorp.com. For detailed information, must subscribe for a fee.**$$$**

Polk County ***Recorded Documents*** www.polkrecorder.com/ Access to the Recorder's Index Search is free at https://iowalandrecords.org/portal/clris/SwitchToCountiesTab. Must have Username and Password. Also, access to deeds, liens, etc. free at http://landrecords.polkcountyiowa.gov/LandRecords/protected/SrchQuickName.aspx. Index records from 1992 to present; view/print documents from 7/1/2002 to present; No vital record or Military information is available online.

Property, Taxation Records Access to the Polk County assessor database is free at www.assess.co.polk.ia.us/web/basic/search.html. Search by property or by sales. Also, download residential, commercial, or agricultural data free at www.assess.co.polk.ia.us/web/basic/exports.html.

Pottawattamie County ***Recorded Documents*** www.pottcounty.com/departments/recorder/overview/ Access to real estate parcel information free at www6.pottcounty.com/government/recorder/recorder-search.php.

Property, Taxation Records Records on the County Courthouse/Council Bluffs property database and sales are free at www.pottco.org/. Search by owner name, address, or parcel number. Records since 7/1/89, images since 10/20/2002.

Poweshiek County ***Property, Taxation Records*** Search assessor property data and/or GIS sites for free at http://beacon.schneidercorp.com. For detailed information, must subscribe for a fee.**$$$**

Ringgold County ***Property, Taxation Records*** Email questions to assessor@ringgoldcounty.us.

Sac County ***Property, Taxation Records*** Assessor's property records online for a small fee; contact the Auditors Office at 712-662-7310 or visit www.saccounty.org/features/gis.asp. Also, search assessor property data and/or GIS sites for free at http://beacon.schneidercorp.com. For detailed information, must subscribe for a fee.**$$$**

Scott County ***Recorded Documents*** www.scottcountyiowa.com At https://iowalandrecords.org/portal/clris/SwitchToCountiesTab, view an index of recorded land records from 1/1989 to current. Also see http://cotthosting.com/iascott/LandRecords/protected/SrchQuickName.aspx; includes land, lien, plats, incorporations, trade names, and UCCs back to 1/1989.

Property, Taxation Records Access to assessor property records is free at www.scottcountyiowa.com/query.php. Also, sheriff sales lists free at www.scottcountyiowa.com/sheriff/sales.php.

Shelby County ***Property, Taxation Records*** Search assessor property data and/or GIS sites for free at http://beacon.schneidercorp.com. For detailed information, must subscribe for a fee.**$$$**

Sioux County ***Property, Taxation Records*** Access property data information free at www.siouxcounty.org/departments/assessor.php. Click on Online Services. Also, search the treasurer's property tax records online by subscription; for info please contact Micah Van Maanen at 712-737-6818, http://treasurer.siouxcounty.org/.**$$$**

Story County ***Property, Taxation Records*** Search assessor property data and/or GIS sites for free at http://beacon.schneidercorp.com. For detailed information, must subscribe for a fee.**$$$**

Tama County ***Property, Taxation Records*** Access to the assessor database of property and sales data is free at http://tama.iowaassessors.com/.

Union County ***Property, Taxation Records*** Search assessor property data and/or GIS sites for free at http://beacon.schneidercorp.com. For detailed information, must subscribe for a fee.**$$$**

Van Buren County ***Property, Taxation Records*** Search parcel data information free at http://vanburen.iowaassessors.com/.

Wapello County ***Property, Taxation Records*** Search assessor property and sales data free at http://wapello.iowaassessors.com/.

Warren County ***Property, Taxation Records*** Search assessor property data and/or GIS sites for free at http://beacon.schneidercorp.com. For detailed information, must subscribe for a fee.**$$$**

Washington County ***Property, Taxation Records*** Access to the assessor database of property and sales data is free at http://washington.iowaassessors.com.

Wayne County ***Property, Taxation Records*** Access to parcel searches for free at www.wayne.iowaassessors.com/.

Webster County ***Property, Taxation Records*** Access to the assessor database of property and sales data is free at http://webster.iowaassessors.com/. Also, property data is free at www.webstercountyia.org/.

Winnebago County ***Property, Taxation Records*** Search assessor property data and/or GIS sites for free at http://beacon.schneidercorp.com. For detailed information, must subscribe for a fee. Also, access to records free at https://iowalandrecords.org/portal/clris/SwitchToSearchSimpleTab#firstLevelTabs.**$$$**

Winneshiek County ***Property, Taxation Records*** Search assessor property data and/or GIS sites for free at http://beacon.schneidercorp.com. For detailed information, must subscribe for a fee.**$$$**

Woodbury County ***Property, Taxation Records*** Search assessor property data and/or GIS sites for free at http://beacon.schneidercorp.com. For detailed information, must subscribe for a fee.**$$$**

Worth County ***Property, Taxation Records*** Access to assessor's database for free at http://worth.iowaassessors.com/.

Wright County ***Property, Taxation Records*** Search assessor property and sales data free at http://wright.iowaassessors.com/. Also, search assessor property data and/or GIS sites for free at http://beacon.schneidercorp.com. For detailed information, must subscribe for a fee.**$$$**

Reminder:

Recorded documents for all counties are available on the state system.

Provided by the Iowa county Recorders Association, the Iowa Land Records system at http://iowalandrecords.org/portal offers statewide searching and pdf images of deeds, liens, even UCCs and judgments. While free now, the site states this service may begin charging at any time. There are also features for monitoring new documents and saving documents.

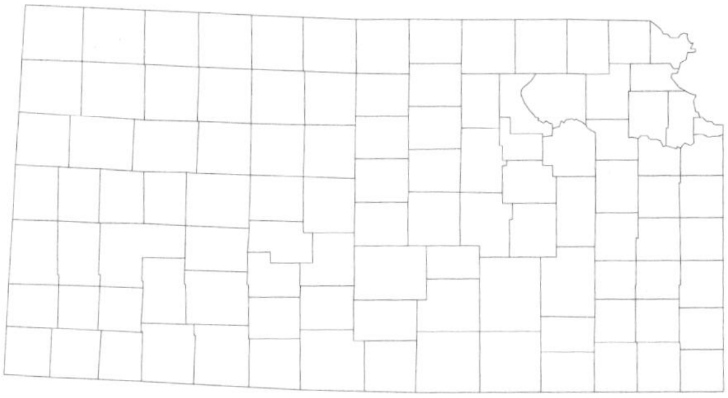

Kansas

Capital: Topeka
Shawnee County

Time Zone: CST

Kansas' five western-most counties are MST:
They are: Greeley, Hamilton, Kearny, Sherman, Wallace.

Population: 2,885,905

# of Counties: 105

Useful State Links

Website: www.kansas.gov
Governor: http://governor.ks.gov/
Attorney General: http://ag.ks.gov/home
State Archives: www.kshs.org
State Statutes and Codes: www.kslegislature.org/legsrv-statutes/index.do
Legislative Bill Search: www.kslegislature.org/li/
Unclaimed Funds: www.kansascash.com/prodweb/up/unclaimed-property.php

State Public Record Agencies

Criminal Records

Kansas Bureau of Investigation, Criminal Records Division, www.kansas.gov/kbi/ Anyone may obtain non-certified criminal records online at www.accesskansas.org/kbi/criminalhistory/. The system is also available for premium subscribers of accessKansas. The fee is $20.00 per record; credit cards accepted online. The system is unavailable between the hours of midnight and 4 AM daily. **$$$**

Sexual Offender Registry

Kansas Bureau of Investigation, Offender Registration, www.accesskansas.org/kbi/offender_registry/ Searching is available at the website. All open registrants are searchable. The information contained in a registration entry was provided by the registrant. Neither the Kansas Bureau of Investigation (KBI) nor the sheriff's office can guarantee the accuracy of this information. The online Offender Registry is for notification and public information only, and does not contain all offender required to register by law, nor does it contain all information about any offender's criminal history.

Incarceration Records

Kansas Department of Corrections, Dir. Of Communications, www.dc.state.ks.us/ Web access to the database known as KASPER gives information on offenders who are: currently incarcerated; under post-incarceration supervision; and, who have been discharged from a sentence. The database does not have information available about inmates sent to Kansas under the provisions of the interstate compact agreement. Go to www.dc.state.ks.us/kasper. Also, view the escapee list at www.dc.state.ks.us/kasper/index.htm. *Other Options:* Bulk lists are available on CD for $.01 per record.

Corporation, LP, LLC

Sec. of State - Business Srvs, Memorial Hall, 1st Floor, www.sos.ks.gov/business/business.html Free entity searching from a link at https://www.kansas.gov/bess. Search by company name or business entity ID numbers. Also search charitable organizations at this site.

Trademarks/Servicemarks

Secretary of State, Trademarks/Servicemarks Division, www.kssos.org/business/trademark/trademark_search.aspx Free searching by a variety of ways (keyword, owner, trademark, etc.) at www.kssos.org/business/trademark/trademark_search.aspxbusiness/trademark/trademark_search.aspx.. *Other Options:* For bulk file purchase call Ann at 785-296-6271.

Uniform Commercial Code, Federal & State Tax Liens

Secretary of State - UCC Searches, Memorial Hall, 1st Fl, www.sos.ks.gov/business/business.html One must be a subscriber. UCC records are $10.00 per record plus $1.00 per copy. Go to www.sos.ks.gov/other/ucc_debtor_search_requests.html or for more information call at 800-4-KANSAS. The system is open 24 hours daily. The subscription requires a modest annual fee. This is the same online system used for obtaining business entity records and driving records. **$$$** *Other Options:* Records in a bulk or database format is available from the subscription mentioned above.

Vital Records

Kansas State Department of Health & Environment, Office of Vital Statistics, www.kdheks.gov/vital/ Records may be ordered online via a state designated vendor VitalChek at www.vitalchek.com. **$$$**

Accident Reports

Kansas Highway Patrol, GHQ - Records Section, www.kansashighwaypatrol.org/about/contact.html The Kansas Highway Patrol Crash Log online application at https://www.accesskansas.org/ssrv-khp-crashlogs/index.do allows one to retrieve any crash log posted, but only for the last 30 days. Search the crash logs by date, county, and type of crash. Crash reports cannot be sent electronically. **$$$**

Driver Records

Department of Revenue, Driver Control Bureau, www.ksrevenue.org/vehicle.html There is a free DL status check at https://www.kdor.org/DLStatus/login.aspx?ReturnUrl=%2fdlstatus%2fsecure%2fdefault.aspx. Kansas has contracted with the Kansas.gov (800-452-6727) to service all electronic media requests of driver license histories at www.kansas.gov/subscribers/. The fee per record is $6.00 for batch requests or $6.60 for immediate inquiry. There is an annual subscription fee of $95. Billing is monthly. If not paid via EFT, a 3% surcharge is added. The system is open 24 hours a day, 7 days a week. Batch requests are available at 7:30 am (if ordered by 10 pm the previous day). **$$$** *Other Options:* Kansas offers a monitoring system or notification program for insurance companies to monitor any changes that occur during the month for records with a traffic conviction and/or administrative action added to the record.

Vehicle Ownership & Registration

Division of Vehicles, Title and Registration Bureau, www.ksrevenue.org/vehicle.html The fee is $6.50 to search by title number or by plate number or by VIN. No name searching is permitted. Visit www.kansas.gov for a complete description of obtaining records from accessKansas (800-452-6727), the state authorized vendor. There is an annual $95 fee to access records from Kansas, note many other records are available, including driving records. **$$$**

Voter Registration, Campaign Finance. PACs, Lobbyists

Secretary of State - Elections Division, Memorial Hall, 1st Floor, www.kssos.org Check campaign finance including spending and contribution, individual candidates, and PACs at www.sos.ks.gov/elections/cfr_viewer/cfr_examiner_entry.aspx. Lobbyists data is shown at www.kssos.org/elections/elections_lobbyists.html. Search polling place location by voter information at https://myvoteinfo.voteks.org/. *Other Options:* This agency will sell the voter registration database for political purposes by CD or email. The entire DB is $200.00 or purchase by subdivision. The form is at www.kssos.org/forms/elections/CVR.pdf. Email bryan.caskey@sos.ks.gov if questions.

Occupational Licensing Boards

A Accountant Firm.. www.da.ks.gov/boa/SearchforFirms.aspx
Accountant-CPA.. www.da.ks.gov/boa/searchforindividual.aspx
Adult Care Home Administrator.................. https://www.kdhehealthlicense.org/
Alcohol License.. www.ksrevenue.org/abccontact.html
Alcohol/Drug Counselor.............................. https://www.kansas.gov/bsrb-verification/index.do
Ambulance Attendant.................................. www.ksbems.org/ems/?page_id=477
Ambulance Service.................................... www.ksbems.org/ems/?page_id=18
Architect.. www.kansas.gov/roster-search/index.html
Athletic Trainer.. www.docboard.org/ks/df/kssearch.htm
Audiologist.. https://www.kdhehealthlicense.org/
Body Piercer.. www.accesskansas.org/kboc/LicenseeDatabase.htm
Charity Organization.................................. www.kscharitycheck.org
Chiropractor.. www.docboard.org/ks/df/kssearch.htm
Clinical Psychotherapist.............................. https://www.kansas.gov/bsrb-verification/index.do
Cosmetic Facility.. www.accesskansas.org/kboc/LicenseeDatabase.htm
Cosmetologist/Technician........................... www.accesskansas.org/kboc/LicenseeDatabase.htm
Cosmetology School Instructor.................... www.accesskansas.org/kboc/LicenseeDatabase.htm
Cosmetology-related School........................ www.accesskansas.org/kboc/SchoolListing.htm
Counselor, Professional.............................. https://www.kansas.gov/bsrb-verification/index.do

Crematory .... www.kansas.gov/ksbma/listings.html
Dental Hygienist.. www.kansas.gov/dental-verification/index.do
Dentist... www.kansas.gov/dental-verification/index.do
Dietitian .... https://www.kdhehealthlicense.org/
Electrologist.. www.accesskansas.org/kboc/LicenseeDatabase.htm
Embalmer.. www.kansas.gov/ksbma/listings.html
Engineer... www.kansas.gov/roster-search/index.html
Esthetician.. www.accesskansas.org/kboc/LicenseeDatabase.htm
Funeral Director/Assis't Financial Dir.......... www.kansas.gov/ksbma/listings.html
Funeral Establishment .... www.kansas.gov/ksbma/listings.html
Geologist.. www.kansas.gov/roster-search/index.html
Home Health Aide .... www.ksnurseaidregistry.org
Insurance Agent.. http://towerii.ksinsurance.org/agent/agent.jsp?pagnam=agentsearch
Insurance Company.................................... http://towerii.ksinsurance.org/agent/agency.jsp?pagnam=agencysearch
Landscape Architect .... www.kansas.gov/roster-search/index.html
Lobbyist.. www.kssos.org/elections/elections_lobbyists.html
Marriage & Family Therapist....................... https://www.kansas.gov/bsrb-verification/index.do
Medical School.. www.docboard.org/ks/df/kssearch.htm
Medication Aide... www.ksnurseaidregistry.org
Nail Technician.. www.accesskansas.org/kboc/LicenseeDatabase.htm
Nurse.. www.kansas.gov/ksbn-verifications/
Nurses Aide... www.ksnurseaidregistry.org
Occupational Therapist/Assistant .... www.docboard.org/ks/df/kssearch.htm
Optometrist... https://www.accesskansas.org/ssrv-optometry/index.html
Osteopathic Physician .... www.docboard.org/ks/df/kssearch.htm
Permanent Cosmetic Technician................ www.accesskansas.org/kboc/LicenseeDatabase.htm
Pesticide Applicator.................................... www.ksda.gov/pesticides_fertilizer/content/170
Pharmacist .... https://www.accesskansas.org/pharmacy_verification/index.html
Physical Therapist/Assistant....................... www.docboard.org/ks/df/kssearch.htm
Physician/Medical Doctor/Assistant............ www.docboard.org/ks/df/kssearch.htm
Podiatrist .... www.docboard.org/ks/df/kssearch.htm
Private Investigator .... https://www.accesskansas.org/ssrv-kbi-pi-verify/index.do
Psychologist.. https://www.kansas.gov/bsrb-verification/index.do
Psychologist, Masters Level .... https://www.kansas.gov/bsrb-verification/index.do
Radiologic Technologist.............................. www.docboard.org/ks/df/kssearch.htm
Real Estate Agent/Seller/Broker .... https://www.kansas.gov/krec-verification/index.do
Real Estate Appraiser................................. www.kansas.gov/appraiser-directory/index.do
Respiratory Therapist/Student .... www.docboard.org/ks/df/kssearch.htm
Social Worker.. https://www.kansas.gov/bsrb-verification/index.do
Speech/Language Pathologist.................... https://www.kdhehealthlicense.org/
Surveyor, Land.. www.kansas.gov/roster-search/index.html
Tanning Facility... www.accesskansas.org/kboc/LicenseeDatabase.htm
Tattoo Artist.. www.accesskansas.org/kboc/LicenseeDatabase.htm
Teacher... https://svapp15586.ksde.org/TLL/SearchLicense.aspx
Tobacco Registration/License..................... www.ksrevenue.org/abccontact.html
Veterinarian.. www.accesskansas.org/veterinary/listing.html

State and Local Courts

State Court Structure: The **District Court** is the court of general jurisdiction. with general original jurisdiction over all civil and criminal cases, including divorce and domestic relations, damage suits, probate and administration of estates, guardianships, conservatorships, care of the mentally ill, juvenile matters, and small claims. **Municipal Courts** deal with city ordinances; cases usually involve traffic and other minor offenses.

Appellate Courts: Published opinions and case information from the Appellate Courts and Supreme Court are available at www.kscourts.org.

Statewide Court Online Access: All courts participate in the system described below.

- Commercial online access for civil, criminal, and traffic records is available for District Court Records from the state's judicial system managed by Kansas.gov. Note that Sedgwick County cases prior to 2003 and Wyandotte County Cases prior to July 2004 are not available on the system and there are certain limitations with Johnson County (see below).
- Record searching is offered to the general public and a subscription account is also available. The fee is $1.00 per search, per county, PLUS $1.00 per case retrieved for view. Users may perform a name search of multiple counties. A credit card is required for payment, unless the requester has a subscription. Subscribers pay an annual $95 subscription fee and receive monthly billing. Interestingly, Johnson County records are available only to subscribers—if a requester uses the public site paying with a credit card, Johnson County records are NOT available.
- When doing a name search, be aware virtually no personal identifiers are shown on index results; for example the DOB is not shown. The case number is given. Case file images are not displayed. Subscribers have access to other records such as the state criminal record repository and motor vehicle records (if qualified.)
- For additional information or a registration packet, telephone 800-4-KANSAS (800-452-6727) or visit the web page at https://www.kansas.gov/countyCourts/.

Other County Sites (not mentioned above):

Anderson County

District Court www.franklincoks.org/4thdistrict/

*A*ccess to old probate court records is free at www.kscourts.org/dstcts/4anprrec.htm as well as on the subscription service. Access marriage records by alpha search up to 8/29/2001 free at www.kscourts.org/dstcts/4anmarec.htm.

Johnson County

District Court www.jococourts.org/

Civil: Search Johnson County District Court records available free at www.jococourts.org with index back to 1980. *Criminal:* same as civil.

Recorders and Assessors

Recording Office Organization: 105 counties, 105 recording offices. The recording officer is the Register of Deeds. Many counties utilize a "Miscellaneous Index" for tax and other liens, separate from real estate records. Federal tax liens on personal property of businesses are filed with the Secretary of State. Other federal tax liens and all state tax liens on personal property are filed with the county Register of Deeds.

Statewide or Multi-Jurisdiction Access: A number of counties allow online access to recorder records. There is no statewide system.

County Sites:

Allen County ***Real Estate, Deed Records*** www.ksrods.org The agency sends requesters to the Laredo system. Fees are based on a flat rate by usage ranging from $75 to $400 per month. The same vendor offers the Tapestry program with a $5.95 search fee and copies for $.50 per page. Visit at www.fidlar.com or call 800-747-4600 at ext 271 or 324. **$$$**

Property, Taxation Access to property tax information for free at http://ks388.cichosting.com/tax/.

Anderson County ***Property, Taxation*** Access to property ownership map website free at http://jade.kgs.ku.edu/orka2/IntroPage.aspx.

Atchison County ***Property, Taxation*** Search the property and tax database free at www.atchisoncountyks.org/Appraisal.aspx. Not regularly updated. Also, access to property ownership data free at http://jade.kgs.ku.edu/orka2/CoSelect.aspx?co=.

Barton County ***Property, Taxation*** Access the County Property value list by address then name at www.bartoncounty.org/appr/PROPVALS.pdf. Also, access to property ownership maps free at http://jade.kgs.ku.edu/orka2/CoSelect.aspx?co=.

Bourbon County ***Recorded Documents*** www.bourboncountyks.org/index.php/government/register-of-deeds Access recordings on the Deeds Management System paid subscription service at http://bourboncountyks.org/dms_online_search.htm. User name and password required; contact Register of Deeds to register. **$$$**

Property, Taxation Access to property data index for a fee at www.bourboncountyks.org/parcel_search.htm. Contact Appraiser's office at 620-223-3800 x36 for subscription information. Also, search property tax information free at https://dms.bourboncountyks.org/ols/tax/Search/search_tax.aspx.**$$$**

Brown County ***Recorded Documents*** http://ks-brown.manatron.com/RegisterofDeeds/tabid/5348/Default.aspx Access to recorded docs and tax records and ORION online is currently under development; see http://ks-brown.manatron.com/RegisterofDeeds/DMSOnline/tabid/5617/Default.aspx. Contact Register's Office at 785-742-7602 for more information. Registration fee is $250.00 per year. **$$$**

Property, Taxation Search assessment data free or by subscription at www.brown.kansasgov.com/parcel/. Basic searches free, more detailed searches are subscription.**$$$**

Butler County ***Recorded Documents*** www.bucoks.com/Directory.aspx?did=17 An index of recorded real estate records from 1993 forward is available at http://maps.bucoks.com/depts/regdeeds/disclaimer.htm.

Cherokee County ***Property, Taxation*** Assess to county parcel data for free at www.cherokee.kansasgov.com/parcel/. Can search as Public and contact Appraiser's Office to register.**$$$**

Clark County ***Property, Taxation*** Access to Appraisal's parcel search is free at www.clark.kansasgov.com/parcel/. Click on parcel search public for free information. A tax roll search is free at www.ecountyworks.com/clark/.

Clay County ***Property, Taxation*** Access to property lookup for free at www.claycountykansas.org/property_lookup.

Cloud County ***Property, Taxation*** Access to parcel data for free at www.cloud.kansasgov.com/parcel/. Also, access to tax search data free at www.cloud.kansasgov.com/tax/.

Coffey County ***Marriage Records*** www.coffeycountyks.org/service13.html Access to marriage records is by alpha search up to 1/18/2001 for free at www.kscourts.org/dstcts/4osmarec.htm.

Property, Taxation Access to GIS/mapping free at www.coffeycountyks.org/service14a.html.

Cowley County ***Property, Taxation*** Search property data free at www.cowleycounty.org/parcel/V2RunLev2.asp?submit1=OK.

Crawford County ***Real Estate, Deed, Lien Records*** www.crawfordcountykansas.org/cco.nsf/web/County-Register-of-Deeds The agency sends requesters to the Laredo system. Fees are based on a flat rate by usage ranging from $75 to $400 per month. The same vendor offers the Tapestry program with a $5.95 search fee and copies for $.50 per page. Pay as you go with a credit card or be billed monthly $25.00 monthly minimum. Visit www.fidlar.com or call 800-747-4600 x271 or x324. Index and images go back to 1989. **$$$**

Property, Taxation Access to parcel search for free at www.crawfordcountykansas.org/cco.nsf/web/Appraiser. Must register to enter.

Dickinson County ***Property, Taxation*** Access to GIS/mapping for free at www.dkcoks.org/index.aspx?NID=419.

Doniphan County ***Property, Taxation*** Access to GIS/mapping for free at https://doniphan.integritygis.com/.

Douglas County ***Real Estate, Deed, Lien, Voter Registration Records*** www.douglas-county.com/depts/rd/rd_home.aspx Register of Deeds data by subscription; for info and signup call IT Dept at 785-832-5183/5299. **$$$**

Property, Taxation Two sites provide free access to assessor records. Find County Property Appraiser records at www.douglas-county.com/online_services/valuestaxes/disclaimer.asp Also, view parcel property on GIS free at www.douglas-county.com/online_services/online_services_gis.aspx.

Ellis County ***Property, Taxation*** Access to assessor property data is available free at www.ellis.kansasgov.com/parcel/.

Ellsworth County ***Property, Taxation*** Email questions to ew_county_appraiser@wan.kdor.state.ks.us.

Finney County ***Real Estate, Lien, Deed, Mortgage, Plat Records*** www.finneycounty.org/index.aspx?nid=147 Access to records for fee go to http://ks-finneycounty.civicplus.com/index.aspx?NID=379; $360.00 per year; contact office at 620-272-3628.. **$$$**

Ford County ***Property, Taxation*** Property information including parcels and taxes for free are available at www.fordcounty.net/appraisal/index.html.

Franklin County ***Property, Taxation*** Access to a parcel search, tax search and maps is free at www.franklin.kansasgis.com/Welcome/Index.asp.

Geary County ***Property, Taxation*** With registration or without, you can search the parcel search database free at www.geary.kansasgis.com/Welcome/Index.asp.

Grant County ***Property Tax Records*** www.grantcoks.org/index.aspx?nid=126 Access to property tax search free at www.ecountyworks.com/grant/.

Gray County ***Recorded Documents*** www.grayco.org/Government/RegisterofDeeds/tabid/3921/Default.aspx Access to record searches free at www.grayco.org/.

Property, Taxation Access to tax and parcel searches free at www.grayco.org/.

Harvey County ***Property, Taxation*** Access property tax records from the appraiser and treasurer free at www.harvey.kansasgis.com/Tax/TaxSearch.asp.**$$$**

Jackson County ***Property, Taxation*** Access to GIS/mapping, parcel search and tax search for free at http://ks-jackson.manatron.com/Appraiser/tabid/5916/Default.aspx.

Jefferson County ***Recorded Documents*** www.jfcountyks.com/index.aspx?nid=352 To search records at just this county, the agency sends requesters to the Laredo system Fees are based on a flat rate by usage ranging from $50 to $250 per month plus a slight per minute if usage is surpassed. Coverage for multiple counties is offered by the Tapestry program from the same vendor. There is a $5.95 fee per search and copies can be generated for $.50 per page. You can pay as you go with a credit card or be billed monthly with a $25.00 monthly minimum. Visit at www.fidlar.com or call 800-747-4600 at ext 271 or 324. **$$$**

Property, Taxation Access parcel data free at http://138.210.72.133/jflgis/Welcome/index.asp.

Johnson County ***Property, Taxation*** Search records on the Land Records database free at http://land.jocogov.org/default.aspx. No name searching.

Leavenworth County ***Real Estate, Deed, Lien Records*** www.leavenworthcounty.org/home.asp The agency sends requesters to the Laredo system. Fees are based on a flat rate by usage ranging from $50 to $250 per month. The same vendor offers the Tapestry program with a $5.95 search fee and copies for $.50 per page. You can pay as you go with a credit card or be billed monthly with a $25.00 monthly minimum. Visit at www.fidlar.com or call 800-747-4600 at ext 271 or 324. **$$$**

Property, Taxation Free search of county parcel data at www.leavenworth.kansasgov.com/parcel/.

Linn County ***Property, Taxation*** Access to parcel searches for free at www.linn.kansasgov.com/parcel/.

Lyon County ***Real Estate Records*** www.lyoncounty.org/Register_of_Deeds.html To search records at just this county, the agency sends requesters to the Laredo system Fees are based on a flat rate by usage ranging from $50 to $250 per month plus a slight per minute if usage is surpassed. Coverage for multiple counties is offered by the Tapestry program from the same vendor. There is a $5.95 fee per search and copies can be generated for $.50 per page. You can pay as you go with a credit card or be billed monthly with a $25.00 monthly minimum. Visit at www.fidlar.com or call 800-747-4600 at ext 271 or 324. **$$$**

Property, Taxation Access parcel data free at http://beacon.schneidercorp.com/?site=LyonCountyKS.

McPherson County ***Property, Taxation*** Search property tax data free at http://68.88.172.233/tax/re_index.htm.

Marion County ***Property, Taxation*** Access property tax records free at www.marion.kansasgov.com/Tax/TaxSearch.asp.

Marshall County ***Property, Taxation*** Access property values free at www.marshall.kansasgov.com/Parcel/.

Meade County ***Property, Taxation*** Access to parcel search login go to www.meade.kansasgis.com/crs/DisclaimerReg.asp. Is a public search for minimal images or login for a fee. Also, access to county tax search free at www.meade.kansasgis.com/Tax/TaxSearch.asp.**$$$**

Miami County ***Recorded Documents*** www.miamicountyks.org/register.html The agency sends requesters to the Laredo system. Fees are based on a flat rate by usage ranging from $50 to $250 per month. The same vendor offers the Tapestry program with a $5.95 search fee and copies for $.50 per page. You can pay as you go with a credit card or be billed monthly with a $25.00 monthly minimum. Visit at www.fidlar.com or call 800-747-4600 at ext 271 or 324. **$$$**

Property, Taxation Access property data and cemetery data free at http://beacon.schneidercorp.com/?site=MiamiCountyKS. Registration, username and password required.

Mitchell County ***Property, Taxation*** Access to county tax search for free at www.mitchell.kansasgov.com/Tax/. Also, access to parcel searches free at www.mitchell.kansasgov.com/parcel/.

Montgomery County ***Property, Taxation*** Access to parcel search for free at www.montgomery.kansasgov.com/parcel/. Must register for access.

Morton County ***Recorded Documents*** www.mtcoks.com/register/register.html For information on subscriptions, contact the Register of Deeds office. **$$$**

Nemaha County ***Property, Taxation*** Access property data free or by registering for full subscription access at www.nemaha.kansasgov.com/parcel/. Click on 'Parcel Search Level One' for free access and name search. Subscription service for full data is $200 per year.

Neosho County ***Property, Taxation*** Access to parcel search for free at www.neosho.kansasgov.com/parcel/.

Osage County ***Property, Taxation*** Online access to the registered user application is at www.osageco.org/Services/Documents/tabid/3637/Default.aspx. Fee is $150.00 annually. Also, access to county records free at www.osage.kansasgis.com/crs/DisclaimerReg.asp.**$$$**

Ottawa County ***Property, Taxation*** Search property data for free at www.ottawa.kansasgov.com/parcel/. Also, search county tax records free at www.ottawa.kansasgov.com/tax/.

Pawnee County Register of Deeds ***Property, Taxation*** Access the parcel search site for free at www.pawnee.kansasgis.com/Welcome/Index.asp.

Pottawatomie County ***Recorded Documents*** www.pottcounty.org Contact office regarding yearly fee and contract information. **$$$**
Property, Taxation Access county parcel search free at www.pottawatomie.kansasgov.com/parcel/. For fuller data, obtain username and password from Appraiser's Office. Also search GIS maps free at www.pottcounty.org/PottCoKsMaps/Default.aspx.

Reno County ***Property, Taxation*** Parcel Information, Election Results, Tax Information, Tax Sale information free at www.renogov.org/.

Republic County ***Property, Taxation*** Access to parcel/property records for free at www.republiccounty.org/parcel// Also, access to property tax data free at www.ecountyworks.com/republic/index.php.

Riley County ***Real Estate, Deed, Lien, UCC Records*** www.rileycountyks.gov Access to recorder office land data is by subscription; Fee is $100 per year plus $.50 per page printed. Records go back to 1850. Registration through the Recorder's Office **$$$**
Property, Taxation Access to online appraisal data for free at www.rileycountyks.gov/index.aspx?NID=84.

Russell County ***Property, Taxation*** Access assessor property data and GIS/mapping for free at www.dkcoksgis.org/RSOrka/.

Saline County ***Property, Taxation*** Access property data free at www.saline.org/Appraiser/ParcelHome.aspx. Also, access to GIS/mapping is free at http://jade.kgs.ku.edu/orka2/IntroPage.aspx.**$$$**

Scott County ***Property, Taxation*** Access parcel data free at www.scottcityks.org/county_parcel.html.

Sedgwick County ***Real Estate, Deed, Property Sale, Lien Records*** www.sedgwickcounty.org/deeds/ Access to the exhaustive County online system (all departments) require a $225 set up fee, $49 monthly fee and a per transaction fee of $.09. For info on this and county record access generally, call 316-660-9860. Also, access recorder deeds free at https://rod.sedgwickcounty.org. Also, access marriage, civil, small claims, misc civil and probate records with subscription at www.kansas.gov/index.php. **$$$**
Property, Taxation Search property appraisal/tax data at https://ssc.sedgwickcounty.org/taxinfowebapp/disclaimerform.aspx.

Seward County ***Property, Taxation*** Access to records free at www.seward.kansasgov.com/parcel/. Must register.

Shawnee County ***Property, Taxation*** Access the residential property list free at www.co.shawnee.ks.us/AP/R_prop/Disclaimer.shtm; commercial at www.co.shawnee.ks.us/ap/C_prop/Disclaimer.shtm. Also search the county mapping site for parcel owner and map data at http://gis.snco.us/publicgis/.

Smith County ***Property, Taxation*** Search parcel data or tax data for free at www.smithcoks.com/Appraiser/tabid/4239/Default.aspx.

Sumner County ***Property, Taxation*** Search property and building info free on the GIS site at www.sumner.kansasgis.com/Welcome/Index.asp. Also, perform a level one tax search free at www.sumner.kansasgis.com/Tax/TaxSearch.asp.

Wabaunsee County ***Property, Taxation*** Access to the assessor parcel search data is at www.wabaunsee.kansasgov.com/parcel/; registration is asked for full data, but you may search basic data for free. To subscribe, phone 785-765-3508. Also, access the treasurer's property tax data free at www.wabaunsee.kansasgov.com/.**$$$**

Woodson County ***Property, Taxation*** Access property data free or by registering for full subscription access at www.woodson.kansasgov.com/parcel/. Click on 'Parcel Search Public' for free access and name search. Subscription service for full data is $200 per year.

Wyandotte County ***Real Estate, Deed, Lien, Judgment Records*** www.wycokck.org The agency sends requesters to the Laredo system. Fees are based on a flat rate by usage ranging from $50 to $250 per month. The same vendor offers the Tapestry program with a $5.95 search fee and copies for $.50 per page. You can pay as you go with a credit card or be billed monthly with a $25.00 monthly minimum. Visit at www.fidlar.com or call 800-747-4600 at ext 271 or 324. **$$$**
Property, Taxation The property dial-up services requires a $20 set up fee, $5 monthly minimum and $.05 each transaction. Lending agency info also available. Contact Louise Sachen 913-573-2885 for signup. There is a real estate search and a parcel search at www.wycokck.org/dept.aspx?id=886&menu_id=552&banner=15284. **$$$**

Kentucky

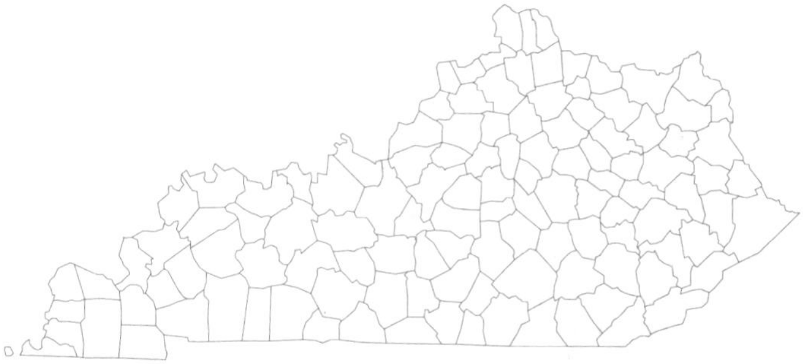

Capital: Frankfort
Franklin County

Time Zone: EST

Kentucky's forty western-most counties are CST.

CST counties are– Adair, Allen, Ballard, Barren, Breckinridge, Butler, Caldwell, Calloway, Carlisle, Christian, Clinton, Crittenden, Cumberland, Daviess, Edmonson, Fulton, Graves, Grayson, Hancock, Hart, Henderson, Hickman, Hopkins, Livingstone, Logan, Marshall, McCracken, McLean, Metcalfe, Monroe, Muhlenberg, Ohio, Russell, Simpson, Todd, Trigg, Union, Warren, Wayne, and Webster.

Population: 4,241,474

# of Counties: 120

Useful State Links

Website: http://kentucky.gov

Governor: http://governor.ky.gov

Attorney General: http://ag.ky.gov

State Archives: http://kdla.ky.gov/Pages/default.aspx

State Statutes and Codes: http://lrc.ky.gov/statrev/frontpg.htm

Legislative Bill Search: www.lrc.ky.gov/legislation.htm

Legislative Bill Watch: http://kentucky.gov/services/pages/billwatch.aspx

Unclaimed Funds: https://secure.kentucky.gov/treasury/unclaimedProperty/Default.aspx

State Public Record Agencies

Sexual Offender Registry

Kentucky State Police, Sex Offender Registry:, www.kentuckystatepolice.org/sor.htm Access is available at http://kspsor.state.ky.us/. All registrants are listed. Online searches must provide one of the following fields: Last Name, City, ZIP, or County. *Other Options:* None

Incarceration Records

Kentucky Department of Corrections, Offender Information Services, http://corrections.ky.gov/Pages/default.aspx The website http://corrections.ky.gov/communityinfo/Pages/KOOL.aspx provides information on current inmates as a service to the public. Note it can take as long as 120 days for the data to be current. *Other Options:* The IT Department has the database available on CD available; call 502-564-4360.

Corporation, LP, LLP, LLC, Assumed Name Records

Secretary of State, Corporate Records - Records, http://sos.ky.gov/business/ A number of distinct searches are available at https://app.sos.ky.gov/ftsearch/. Search business filings and records and also business organizations. Also search by registered agent, founding or current officer name. Another good search site for business filings is http://sos.ky.gov/business/filings/online/. Also, search securities companies registered with the state at http://fi.ky.gov/scr/ifs/old/sec/default.asp. *Other Options:* Monthly lists of new corporations are available at www.sos.ky.gov/business/bulkdata/.

Trademarks/Servicemarks

Secretary of State, Trademarks Service Marks Section, http://sos.ky.gov/business/trademarks/ Free, searchable database at http://apps.sos.ky.gov/business/trademarks/. *Other Options:* Bulk data available by request. Call for info and fees.

Uniform Commercial Code

UCC Branch, Secretary of State, http://sos.ky.gov/business/ucc/ UCC record searching is offered free of charge at the website or see https://app.sos.ky.gov/ftucc/(S(crvwfp55fuuzyljdzdh3viuy))/search.aspx. Search by debtor name or file number. SSNs are withheld from the online system. *Other Options:* Monthly, weekly or daily lists of new UCC filing are available at **www**.sos.ky.gov/business/bulkdata/.

Birth Certificates

Department for Public Health, Vital Statistics, http://chfs.ky.gov/dph/vital/ Records may be ordered online via a state designated vendor at www.vitalchek.com. **$$$**

Death Records

Department for Public Health, Vital Statistics, http://chfs.ky.gov/dph/vital/ In cooperation with the University of Kentucky, there is a searchable death index at http://ukcc.uky.edu/vitalrec/. This is for non-commercial use only. Records are from 1911 through 1992. Also, there is a free genealogy site at http://vitals.rootsweb.ancestry.com/ky/death/search.cgi. Death Indexes from 1911-2000 are available. Search by surname, given name, place of death, residence, or year. Records may be ordered online via a state designated vendor at www.vitalchek.com. **$$$**

Marriage Certificates

Department for Public Health, Vital Statistics, http://chfs.ky.gov/dph/vital/ In cooperation with the University of Kentucky, a searchable index is available on the Internet at http://ukcc.uky.edu/vitalrec/. The index runs from 1973 through 1993. This is for non-commercial use only. Records may be ordered online via a state designated vendor at www.vitalchek.com. **$$$** *Other Options:* Contact Libraries and Archives.

Divorce Records

Department for Public Health, Vital Statistics, http://chfs.ky.gov/dph/vital/ In cooperation with the University of Kentucky, there is a searchable index on the Internet at http://ukcc.uky.edu/vitalrec/. This is for non-commercial use only. The index is for 1973-1993. Records may be ordered online via a state designated vendor at www.vitalchek.com. **$$$** *Other Options:* Contact Libraries and Archives.

Driver Records

Division of Driver Licensing, Attention: MVRs, http://transportation.ky.gov/Driver-Licensing/Pages/default.aspx There are 2 systems, both accessible from Kentucky.gov. Requesters who are permitted to obtain personal information can order by batch. Fee is $5.00 per record, billing is monthly. Accounts must be approved by the Commissioner's office. For more details, call Kentucky.gov at 502-875-3733 or email support@kentucky.gov. Information about this service is not available on the web. Three-year records without personal information can be obtained on an interactive basis at http://dhr.ky.gov/DHRWeb/. A $5.00 fee applies and use of a credit card is required. **$$$**

Vehicle, Vessel Ownership & Registration

KY Transportation Cabinent, Division of Motor Vehicle Licensing, https://mvl.ky.gov/MVLWeb/ Electronic access is available to approved, ongoing requesters with a permissible use. The system, run by Kentucky.gov, is open 24/7 and provides immediate results after requests are sent. The fee is $0.44 per record. Requesters must be approved by the Commissioner's office and have an account with Kentucky.gov. There is a $75.00 annual subscription fee. For more information, call Kentucky.gov at 502-875-3733 or visit http://kentucky.gov/register/Pages/subscribe.aspx. **$$$** *Other Options:* Kentucky has the ability to supply customized bulk delivery of vehicle registration information. The request must be in writing with the intended use outlined. For more information, call 502-564-5301.

Accident Reports

State Police, Criminal Ident. & Records Branch, http://kentuckystatepolice.org/ Online reports are outsourced to a vendor at https://www.buycrash.com/Public/Home.aspx. The DL # or the badge number of the investigating Officer is required to search. The fee is $10.00. Use of a credit card or PayPal is required. **$$$** *Other Options:* Specific accident statistics may be obtained by phoning the statistics coordinator.

Campaign Finance & Disclosure, PACs and Contributors

Registry of Election Finance, http://kref.ky.gov/ The agency offers a searchable database of all records for 1998 to present at **www**.kref.state.ky.us/krefsearch/. When candidates submit financial records by using electronic filing software, the disbursement figures are available to download. Lobbyist data at the Ethics Commission at http://klec.ky.gov/reports/employersagents.htm.

Voter Registration

State Board of Elections, http://elect.ky.gov/Pages/default.aspx The agency offers a voter information status search at https://cdcbp.ky.gov/VICWeb/index.jsp. First name, last name and DOB are required. For questions, contact sheila.walker@ky.gov. *Other Options:* Bulk lists data is available on CD-Rom, labels or lists for eligible persons, pursuant to state statutes. See http://elect.ky.gov/requestforvoterreg/Pages/default.aspx.

GED Certificates

Kentucky Adult Education, GED Program, http://kyae.ky.gov/students/ged.htm Requests are accepted from postsecondary institutions, employers and employment agencies by submitting the form found at https://ged.ky.gov and a signed released must be submitted. Individuals may request online by completing the individual form at https://ged.ky.gov. **$$$**

Occupational Licensing Boards

Accountant-CPA/Company .... https://secure.kentucky.gov/renewalservices/cpa/lookup.aspx
Addiction Psychiatrist MD .... http://web1.ky.gov/GenSearch/LicenseSearch.aspx?AGY=5
Alcohol/Drug Counselor https://web1.ky.gov/OnPPub/Verification.aspx
Anesthesiologist .... http://web1.ky.gov/GenSearch/LicenseSearch.aspx?AGY=5
Art Therapist https://web1.ky.gov/OnPPub/Verification.aspx
Athlete Agent https://web1.ky.gov/OnPPub/Verification.aspx
Athletic Trainer, Medical .... http://web1.ky.gov/gensearch/LicenseSearch.aspx?AGY=21
Attorney www.kybar.org/26
Auctioneer, Livestock, Ltd. .... http://web1.ky.gov/gensearch/LicenseSearch.aspx?AGY=3
Auctioneer, Tobacco, Ltd. .... http://web1.ky.gov/gensearch/LicenseSearch.aspx?AGY=3
Auctioneer/Auctioneer Apprentice .... http://web1.ky.gov/gensearch/LicenseSearch.aspx?AGY=3
Audiologist https://web1.ky.gov/OnPPub/Verification.aspx
Bank .... http://dfiweb.ky.gov/dfipublic/
Check Casher/Seller .... http://dfiweb.ky.gov/dfipublic/
Child Care Facility http://chfs.ky.gov/NR/rdonlyres/14A77B8F-F406-4055-B765-43C7674599D3/0/LicensedChildCareCenterDirectory5102010.xls
Chiropractor .... http://web1.ky.gov/gensearch/LicenseSearch.aspx?AGY=22
Clean-Up Contractor of Meth Lab .... http://waste.ky.gov/SFB/MethLabCleanup/Documents/ListofContractors.pdf
Cosmetologist .... www.hnslicense.net
Cosmetology School .... www.kbhc.ky.gov/schools.htm
Counselor, Pastoral/Professional https://web1.ky.gov/OnPPub/Verification.aspx
Credit Union .... http://dfiweb.ky.gov/dfipublic/
Dental Hygienist .... http://web1.ky.gov/gensearch/LicenseSearch.aspx?AGY=11
Dental Laboratory .... http://web1.ky.gov/gensearch/LicenseSearch.aspx?AGY=13
Dentist .... http://web1.ky.gov/gensearch/LicenseSearch.aspx?AGY=9
Dialysis Technician .... https://secure.kentucky.gov/kbn/bulkvalidation/basic.aspx
Dietitian/Nutritionist https://web1.ky.gov/OnPPub/Verification.aspx
Electrical Contractor/Inspector .... http://ky.joportal.com/License/Search/license_lookup.asp
Engineer/Land Surveyor Firm .... http://apps.kyboels.ky.gov/SearchableRoster.aspx
Esthetician .... www.hnslicense.net
Exterminator .... www.kyagr.com/pesticide/agr_pco.aspx
Geologist https://web1.ky.gov/OnPPub/Verification.aspx
Hearing Instrument Specialist https://web1.ky.gov/OnPPub/Verification.aspx
Home Health Aid .... https://secure.kentucky.gov/kbn/bulkvalidation/basic.aspx
Home Inspector .... https://ky.joportal.com/License/Search
HVAC Contractor/Journeyman/Master/Mechanic.......... http://ky.joportal.com/License/Search/license_lookup.asp
Insurance Agent .... http://insurance.ky.gov/Agent/Default.aspx
Insurance CE Provider .... http://insurance.ky.gov/static_info.aspx?static_id=73&Div_id=2
Interior Designer .... https://secure.kentucky.gov/cidRosterSearch/
Legislative Employer of Lobbyists .... http://apps.klec.ky.gov/searchregister.asp
Liquor License .... https://dppweb.ky.gov/ABCStar/portal/abconline/page/License_Lookup/portal.aspx
Loan Company, Comm/Industrial .... http://dfiweb.ky.gov/dfipublic/
Lobbyist .... http://klec.ky.gov/reports/employersagents.htm
Malt Beverage Distributor .... https://dppweb.ky.gov/ABCStar/portal/abconline/page/License_Lookup/portal.aspx
Marriage & Family Therapist https://web1.ky.gov/OnPPub/Verification.aspx
Medical Specialist MD http://web1.ky.gov/gensearch/
Midwife .... https://secure.kentucky.gov/kbn/bulkvalidation/basic.aspx

Milk Inspector	www.rs.uky.edu/regulatory/inspectors/
Mortgage Broker/Loan Company	www.nmlsconsumeraccess.org/
Nail Technician	www.hnslicense.net
Notary Public	http://apps.sos.ky.gov/adminservices/notaries/(X(1)S(jawm0t55avmais55gtrhkavd))/Login.aspx
Nurse Anesthetist/Clinical Specialist	https://secure.kentucky.gov/kbn/bulkvalidation/basic.aspx
Nurse Work Permit	https://secure.kentucky.gov/kbn/bulkvalidation/basic.aspx
Nurse-RN/LPN/Aide	https://secure.kentucky.gov/kbn/bulkvalidation/basic.aspx
Nursing Home Administrator	https://web1.ky.gov/OnPPub/Verification.aspx
Occupational Therapist/Assistant	https://web1.ky.gov/OnPPub/Verification.aspx
Ophthalmic Dispenser	https://web1.ky.gov/OnPPub/Verification.aspx
Optician/Apprentice	https://web1.ky.gov/OnPPub/Verification.aspx
Optometrist	http://web1.ky.gov/gensearch/LicenseSearch.aspx?AGY=8
Osteopathic Physician	http://web1.ky.gov/gensearch/
Pesticide Applicator/Dealer	www.kyagr.com/pesticide/agr_pco.aspx
Pharmacist/Pharmacy	https://secure.kentucky.gov/pharmacy/licenselookup/
Physical Therapist/Assistant	http://pt.ky.gov/LicenseSearch/Pages/default.aspx
Physician Assistant	http://web1.ky.gov/gensearch/LicenseSearch.aspx?AGY=20
Physician/Medical Doctor/Surgeon	http://web1.ky.gov/gensearch/
Plumber	http://ky.joportal.com/License/Search/license_lookup.asp
Podiatrist	http://web1.ky.gov/gensearch/LicenseSearch.aspx?AGY=24
Private Investigator	https://web1.ky.gov/OnPPub/Verification.aspx
Property Valuation Administrator	http://revenue.ky.gov/NR/rdonlyres/A49D334B-21F9-43E5-9D64-9EBF57681D4F/0/pvadirectoryJan06.pdf
Proprietary Education School	https://web1.ky.gov/OnPPub/Verification.aspx
Psychiatrist MD	http://web1.ky.gov/gensearch/
Psychologist	https://web1.ky.gov/OnPPub/Verification.aspx
Radiation Operator/Technologist	http://chfs.ky.gov/dph/radiation.htm
Real Estate Agent/Broker/Sales	https://secure.kentucky.gov/KREC/databasesearch
Real Estate Appraiser	http://kreab.ky.gov/Pages/KLAMC.aspx
Real Estate Brokerage/Firm	http://krec.ky.gov/Pages/default.aspx
Retired LPN	http://kbn.ky.gov/apply/retired.htm
School Administrator	https://wd.kyepsb.net/EPSB.WebApps/KECI/
School Guidance Counselor	https://wd.kyepsb.net/EPSB.WebApps/KECI/
School Media Librarian	https://wd.kyepsb.net/EPSB.WebApps/KECI/
School Nurse	https://wd.kyepsb.net/EPSB.WebApps/KECI/
School Social Worker/Psychologist	https://wd.kyepsb.net/EPSB.WebApps/KECI/
Securities Agent/Broker/Dealer	www.finra.org/Investors/ToolsCalculators/BrokerCheck/index.htm
Securities, Agent of Issuer	www.finra.org/Investors/ToolsCalculators/BrokerCheck/index.htm
Sexual Assault Nurse Examiner	https://secure.kentucky.gov/kbn/bulkvalidation/basic.aspx
Social Worker	https://secure.kentucky.gov/renewalservices/kbsw/lookup.aspx
Speech-Language Pathologist	https://web1.ky.gov/OnPPub/Verification.aspx
Teacher	https://wd.kyepsb.net/EPSB.WebApps/KECI/
Trust Company	http://dfiweb.ky.gov/dfipublic/
Veterinarian	https://web1.ky.gov/OnPPub/Verification.aspx

State and Local Courts

State Court Structure: The **Circuit Court** is the court of general jurisdiction and hears civil matters involving more than $5,000, capital offenses and felonies, land dispute title cases and contested probate cases. The **Family Court** is a division of the Circuit Court and has concurrent jurisdiction with certain domestic abuse matters.

The **District Court** is the court of limited jurisdiction and handles 90% of all court matters including juvenile, city and county ordinances, misdemeanors, violations, traffic offenses, probate of wills, arraignments, felony probable cause hearings, small claims ($2,500 or less), civil cases involving $5,000 or less, voluntary and involuntary mental commitments and cases relating to domestic violence and abuse.

Appellate Courts: Search opinions and case information from the Supreme Court and Court of Appeals at http://courts.ky.gov/research/.

Statewide Court Online Access: All courts participate in the system described below.

- The KY Admin. Office of Courts provides a criminal record online ordering system called AOCFastCheck (http://courts.ky.gov/aoc/AOCFastCheck.htm), which is part of the same system described above. The fee is $20.00 per record (effective July 1, 2012). This is not an interactive system; requesters receive an e-mail notification when the results are available. A vender, designated by the state, handles the credit card transactions and charges a reported 5% surcharge.
- The following case types are not available - juvenile, mental health, and civil/domestic violence.
- **Two Cautionary Notes:**
  - The AOC is NOT the state mandated official site for criminal records. State law dictates that the Kentucky State Police Records Branch is responsible for holding records with confirmed dispositions, not the AOC.
  - The subject of the search is notified of the request, sent a copy of the record, and is given the name of the requester.
- A very limited free search is provided at http://apps.kycourts.net/CourtRecords. Search by party name, case number, or by citation number. Few historical records are provided. Most of the cases lists are pending. Results shown are only the name and case number. A free search site for daily court calendars by county is found at http://apps.kycourts.net/dockets.
- Registered members of the KY Bar may review pending cases at http://apps.kycourts.net/courtrecordsKBA/.

Note: No individual Kentucky courts offer online access, other as described above.

Recorders, Assessors, and Other Sites of Note

Recording Office Organization: 120 counties, 122 recording offices. The recording officer is the County Clerk. Kenton County has two recording offices. All federal and state tax liens on personal property are filed with the County Clerk, often in an "Encumbrance Book."

Statewide or Multi-Jurisdiction Access: A number of counties offer free access to assessor or real estate records. Several other counties offer commercial systems. There is no statewide system. There are two vendors worth emntioning.

- Access to recorded documents is provided to 12 Kentucky counties by a vendor at www.kylandrecords.com/. Fees are involved.
- Access to property data for 12 Kentucky counties for a fee is available from www.pvdnetwork.com/websiteLinks.html. A subscription is required.

County Sites:

Adair County ***Recorded Land Records*** www.adaircounty.ky.gov/cogov/departments/coclerk.htm Access to land records for a fee at www.kylandrecords.com/.

Allen County ***Property, Taxation Records*** General property valuation information available at www.allenpva.ky.gov/.

Anderson County ***Property, Taxation Records*** Access to property records and GIS/mapping for a fee are found at www.pvdnetwork.com/PVDNet.asp?SiteID=100.**$$$**

Barren County ***Property, Taxation Records*** Access to property records for free (limited data) go to http://qpublic5.qpublic.net/ky_barren_taxroll.php. For all available features must subscribe to service for a fee. Free lists of deliquent taxes for 2012 available at http://174.141.82.110/DTaxPDFs/barrendTaX.pdf.**$$$**

Bath County ***Recorded Land Records*** http://bath.clerkinfo.net/ Access to land records for a fee at www.kylandrecords.com/.

Bell County ***Property, Taxation Records*** The Property Value Assessor's office coordinates property assessments. Please call 606-337-2720.

Boone County ***Real Estate, Deed, Lien, UCC, Marriage Records*** www.boonecountyclerk.com/ Access the county clerk database through eCCLIX, a fee-based service; $200.00 sign-up and $65.00 monthly. Records go back to 1989; images to 1998. For info, see the website or call 502-266-9445. **$$$**

Property, Taxation Records Assessor property data is available at http://boonepva.ky.gov/.

Bourbon County ***Recorded Land Records*** www.bourbon.clerkinfo.net/ Access to land records for a fee at www.kylandrecords.com/. **$$$**

Boyd County ***Real Estate, Deed, Lien Records*** www.boydcountyclerk.com/contact.stm Access to the County Clerk online records requires a $sign-up plus $60.00 per month, records date back to 1/1979. Lending agency data is available. For info, contact Debbie Jones, Clerk or Kathy Fisher at 606-739-5116. **$$$**

Property, Taxation Records Access to tax rolls for free at http://qpublic5.qpublic.net/ky_boyd_taxroll.php.

Boyle County ***Property, Taxation Records*** Access to tax rolls for free at http://qpublic5.qpublic.net/ky_boyle_taxroll.php. For more product you can pay for subscription for 120 records-$100, 300 records-$200, 600 records-$400, 1200 records-$750. Also, access to delinquent tax bills list for free at www.boyleky.com/tax/BoyleDt.pdf.

Bracken County ***Property, Taxation Records*** Access to records for free (limited data) at http://qpublic5.qpublic.net/xsub_mapsync_search.php?county=ky_bracken. For more detailed information must subscribe for a fee.**$$$**

Breckinridge County ***Real Estate, Deed, Lien, Mortgage Records*** Access to land index back to 1996 and images to by subscription at www.titlesearcher.com/countyInfo.php?cnum=S99. **$$$**

Property, Taxation Records Access to property search data for free at www.qpublic.net/ky/breckinridge/search.html. For deeper information, subscription is available for a fee.**$$$**

Butler County ***Property, Taxation Records*** Access to tax roll/parcel data for free (limited data) or for all available features on subscription (pay) go to http://qpublic5.qpublic.net/ky_butler_taxroll.php.**$$$**

Caldwell County ***Real Estate, Deed, Lien, Marriage, UCC Records*** www.caldwellcounty.ky.gov/elected/coclerk.htm Register to receive free username and password to search recording indexes free at http://216.135.47.158/recordsearch/.

Calloway County ***Property, Taxation Records*** Access to property data is free at www.ccpva.org/search.aspx.

Campbell County ***Recorded Documents Records*** www.campbellcountykyclerk.org/ Access to records for a fee at www.campbellcountykyrecords.org/. Must sign-up with login and password. **$$$**

Property, Taxation Records Search county clerk and PVA records at www.campbellcountykyrecords.org/. Login and password are required. Also, access to the Property Valuation Administrator assessment search at www.campbellcountykypva.org/. Search by any or all: owner name, parcel ID, street name, street number, property type, district, sale date, sale price, deed book, deed page.**$$$**

Carroll County ***Delinquent Taxes Records*** www.carrollcountygov.us/clerk.asp Access to delinquent taxes free at www.carrollcountygov.us/pdfs/2011%20del%20taxes.pdf.

Carter County ***Recorded Land Records*** www.cartercounty.ky.gov/elected/county/coclerk.htm Access to land records for a fee at www.kylandrecords.com/.

Christian County ***Real Estate, Deed, Marriage, Tax Lien, UCC, Will Records*** www.christiancountyky.gov/qcms/index.asp?Page=county%20clerk Access recorded docs by subscription; username and password required. Contact Betty via county clerk's office, request must be in writing. $60 monthly fee. Marriage index back to 1973, Wills back to 8/2002, mortgage index 1940-1984, mortgage and land recording index and images back to 1987. **$$$**

Property, Taxation Records Access property tax data by subscription at http://christianpva.com/wps-html/TaxRoll/; fees starts as low as $50 for 60 records.**$$$**

Clark County ***Property, Taxation Records*** Online access by subscription, call office for info and signup.**$$$**

Clay County ***Recorded Land Records*** www.claycounty.ky.gov/ Access to land records for a fee at www.kylandrecords.com/.

Clinton County ***Recorded Land Records*** www.clinton.clerkinfo.net/ Access to land records for a fee at www.kylandrecords.com/.

Crittenden County ***Property, Taxation Records*** Access to data is available by subscription, fees start at 120 hits for $100. per 12 months; see www.crittendenpva.com/wps-html/TaxRoll/.**$$$**

Daviess County ***Property, Taxation Records*** Access to property records for free at www.daviesskypva.org.

Elliott County ***Property, Taxation Records*** Access to records for a fee at http://qpublic5.qpublic.net/ky_asearch.php?county=ky_elliott.**$$$**

Estill County ***Delinquent Tax List Records*** www.estillky.com/county_clerk.html Access to delinquent tax list free at www.estillky.com/county_clerk.html.

Fayette County ***Property, Taxation Records*** Search property index free at http://qpublic7.qpublic.net/ky_fayette_search2.php. No name searching. Subscription fees have been dropped, tax roll/property search info is now free.**$$$**

Floyd County ***Recorded Records*** Access to land records online for a fee at http://search.mainstreet-tech.com/Search/UserAnon/ChooseCounty.aspx?CCodeRedir=1. Contact Brad Crane at Main Street Technology at 872-910-9789. **$$$**

Franklin County ***Property, Taxation Records*** Access to property index is free at www.franklincountypva.com/PublicSearch/tabid/673/Default.aspx. A subscription is required for full data; $150 per 6 months or $250 per year. Also, access to property records and GIS/mapping for a fee are found at www.pvdnetwork.com/PVDNet.asp?SiteID=100.**$$$**

Fulton County ***Property, Taxation Records*** Access to Tax Roll data on for a fee and sign-up go to www.fultonpva.com/index.php?p=login.**$$$**

Garrard County ***Recorded Documents Records*** www.garrardcounty.ky.gov/elected/coclerk.htm Access to records for a fee at www.landrecordskentucky.com/. **$$$**

Property, Taxation Records Also, access to property records and GIS/mapping for a fee are found at www.pvdnetwork.com/PVDNet.asp?SiteID=100.

Grant County ***Property, Taxation Records*** Access property index free at http://qpublic5.qpublic.net/ky_grant_taxroll.php. Subscription required for GIS map and full data.**$$$**

Graves County ***Property, Taxation Records*** Access to property tax roll for free at www.qpublic.net/ky/graves/.

Grayson County ***Delinquent taxes Records*** http://graysoncountyclerk.ky.gov/ A pdf name list of delinquent taxes is presented from the home page.

Green County ***Recorded Documents Records*** http://greencountyclerk.com/ Access to recorded documents for a fee at http://greencountyclerk.com/. **$$$**

Hancock County ***Recorded Documents Records*** www.hancockky.us/Government/hcadbldg.htm Access to court records free at http://apps.kycourts.net/CourtRecords/. Search by party, case or citation.

Property, Taxation Records View Delinquent tax list free at www.hancockky.us/Government/DelTaxBill.htm.

Hardin County ***Real Estate, Deed, Mortgage, Marriage, Will, Assumed Name Records*** www.hccoky.org Access the Clerk's permanent and temporary records search page free at www.hccoky.org/eSearch/User/Login.aspx?ReturnUrl=%2feSearch%2fLandRecords%2fprotected%2fSrchQuickName.aspx. Deeds go back to 1976; mortgages to 1974.

Property, Taxation Records Search County Parcels at www.hardincountypva.com/parcelsearch.asp. Property maps available at www.hardincountypva.com/propertymaps.asp. Form for requests for reproduction of public records found at www.hardincountypva.com/pdfs/repreq.pdf.

Harrison County ***Property, Taxation Records*** Also, access to property records and GIS/mapping for a fee are found at www.pvdnetwork.com/PVDNet.asp?SiteID=100.**$$$**

Hart County ***Property, Taxation Records*** Access to property tax/assessment records for free at http://qpublic5.qpublic.net/ky_asearch.php?county=ky_hart. Must register and pay a fee for detailed records.**$$$**

Henderson County ***Recorded Records*** www.hendersonky.us/clerk.php Access to records for a fee at www.titlesearcher.com/countyInfo.php?cnum=K4. **$$$**

Property, Taxation Records Access county property assessment index free at http://qpublic.net/ky/henderson/search.html. For full data, a subscription is required.

Henry County ***Property, Taxation Records*** Also, access to property records and GIS/mapping for a fee are found at www.pvdnetwork.com/PVDNet.asp?SiteID=100.**$$$**

Hopkins County ***Property, Taxation Records*** Access property assessment index free at http://qpublic5.qpublic.net/ky_gsearch.php?county=ky_hopkins. Subscription available for more detailed information at http://qpublic5.qpublic.net/ky_hopkins_login.php?subscribe=1.

Jefferson County ***Real Estate, Grantor/Grantee, Deed, Lien, Will, Voter Registration Records*** www.jeffersoncountyclerk.org/ Access county land records free at www.landrecords.jcc.ky.gov/records/S0Search.html. Images go back to 6/1992. Check voter registration by name free at https://cdcbp.ky.gov/VICWeb/index.jsp.

Property, Taxation Records Access to the county property valuation administrator's assessment roll is free at http://jeffersonpva.ky.gov/property-search/. No name searching. There is also a subscription service for a fee, click on choose a plan at same site.**$$$**

Jessamine County ***Property, Taxation Records*** Access to property and sales searches free at www.jessaminepva.com/?page_id=90.

Johnson County ***Property, Taxation Records*** Access to records (limited) free at http://qpublic5.qpublic.net/ky_johnson_taxroll.php. Subscription service (all available features) available for a fee.**$$$**

Kenton County (Both Districts) ***Property, Taxation Records*** Access the county Property Valuation database at http://kcor.org/. Search for free by using "Guest Access." For full, professional property data you may subscribe; fee for username and password is varied depending on Clerk's, PVA or both records required. **$$$**

Laurel County ***Property, Taxation Records*** Access the property records free at www.qpublic.net/ky/laurel/search.html.

Lawrence County ***Property, Taxation Records*** Access to property records and GIS/mapping for a fee are found at www.pvdnetwork.com/PVDNet.asp?SiteID=100.**$$$**

Lewis County ***Recorded Documents Records*** http://lewiscountyclerk.ky.gov Access to records for a fee at http://kylandrecords.com/. **$$$**

Logan County ***Property, Taxation Records*** Access to property tax and property sale information for a fee at http://qpublic5.qpublic.net/ky_logan_taxroll.php.**$$$**

Lyon County ***Property, Taxation Records*** Access to tax roll information for free at http://qpublic5.qpublic.net/ky_lyon_taxroll.php.

McCracken County ***Property, Taxation Records*** Access to GIS/mapping for free at http://map-gis.org/disclaimer.

Madison County ***Property, Taxation Records*** Access to property tax records for free at www.madisoncountyky.us/index.php/2013-01-09-16-12-51/2013-01-09-22-17-57/property-tax-records.

Marion County ***Deeds, Mortgages, Wills, Marriages, Oil & Gas Leases, Misc Records*** www.marioncounty.ky.gov/elected/coclerk.htm Access records lookup free at www.marioncountykyclerk.com/. Click on DocSearch.

Marshall County ***Recorded Land Records*** Access to land records for a fee at www.kylandrecords.com/.

Property, Taxation Records Access to PVA property data requires registration, username and password at http://marshallpva.ky.gov/PVA/. Subscription fees apply. For info call 270-527-4728 or email marshallpva@ky.gov.**$$$**

Mason County ***Real Estate, Deed, Tax Lien, Plat, Mortgage, Misc Records*** http://masoncountyclerkky.com/ Access to records for a fee at http://masoncountyclerkky.com/. Must register for subscription, click on Land Records. Fee is: Initial account set-up fee-$200.00, base account (1 user)- $65 monthly; Add'l users-$10.00 monthly. **$$$**

Meade County ***Real Estate, Deed, Lien, Judgment, Marriage, Will Records*** www.countyclerk.meadecounty.ky.gov/ Access to recorder office records index and images is by internet subscription; fee is $50 monthly; signup through recorder office, contact Katrina. Index back to 1828, images to late 1960's. No images of wills, marriages, judgments or liens. **$$$**

Mercer County ***Property, Taxation Records*** Access to online subscription for tax roll access for a fee at www.mercercountypva.com/ContactUs/SubscriberApplication/tabid/763/Default.aspx. Fees are $250.00-1 year; each add'l sub $125.00-1 year each; short term $50.00-1 month each. Also, access to property records and GIS/mapping for a fee are found at www.pvdnetwork.com/PVDNet.asp?SiteID=100.**$$$**

Metcalfe County ***Deed, Plat, Will, Misc, Mortgage, Oil/Gas Lease Records*** www.metcalfecountyclerk.com/ Access to county records free at http://66.38.36.76/recordsearch/.

Montgomery County ***Property, Taxation Records*** Access to PVA property data requires registration, username and password at www.montgomerypva.com/. Subscription fees apply.**$$$**

Muhlenberg County ***Property, Taxation Records*** Access to property record searches for free at http://qpublic.net/ky/muhlenberg/search.html.

Nelson County ***Property, Taxation Records*** Access the property records free at www.nelsoncountypva.com/PublicSearch.aspx. Also, access to property records and GIS/mapping for a fee are found at www.qpublic.net/ky/nelson/search.html (limited information is provided to guests for free, but to access entire database you must subscribe to website).**$$$**

Nicholas County ***Property, Taxation Records*** Access to records for a fee at http://qpublic5.qpublic.net/ky_nicholas_taxroll.php.**$$$**

Ohio County ***Property, Taxation Records*** Access to property records and GIS/mapping for a fee are found at www.pvdnetwork.com/PVDNet.asp?SiteID=100.**$$$**

Oldham County ***Real Estate, Lien, UCC, Marriage Records*** http://oldhamcountyclerkky.com/ Access to the database is through eCCLIX database, a fee-based service; $200.00 sign-up & $65.00 monthly. Real estate records and marriages go back to 1980. UCC images to 2/97. For info, see http://oldhamcounty.state.ky.us/ecclix.stm or call 502-266-9445. **$$$**

Property, Taxation Records Access property index free at www.oldhampva.com/. Subscription required for full data; 25 docs for $25; 50 docs for $50; 75 docs for $75; 150 docs for $150; 300 docs for $250 and 600 docs for $350. Also, access to property tax records free at http://qpublic5.qpublic.net/ky_oldham_taxroll.php.**$$$**

Owen County ***Real Estate, Deed, Lien, Mortgage Records*** www.owencounty.ky.gov/clerk/ Access to index back to 1986 and images back to 1986 by subscription at www.titlesearcher.com/countyInfo.php?cnum=T66. **$$$**

Pendleton County ***Property, Taxation Records*** Access to property records and GIS/mapping for a fee are found at www.pvdnetwork.com/PVDNet.asp?SiteID=100.**$$$**

Powell County ***Recorded Land Records*** www.powellcounty.ky.gov/elected/coclerk.htm Access to Kentucky land records for a fee at www.kylandrecords.com/. Must purchase a subscription. **$$$**

Pulaski County ***Property, Taxation Records*** Access to property index is free at www.qpublic.net/ky/pulaski/.

Rowan County ***Property, Taxation Records*** Access to county tax rolls requires registration and password; fees apply, see http://qpublic5.qpublic.net/ky_rowan_login.php. 120 records over 12 months is $100, up to 1200 records for $750.**$$$**

Russell County ***Recorded Land Records*** www.russell.clerkinfo.net/ Access to land records for a fee at www.kylandrecords.com/.
Property, Taxation Records Access to tax roll data for free (limited) go to http://qpublic5.qpublic.net/ky_russell_taxroll.php. For detailed information (all available features) must subscribe for a fee.**$$$**

Scott County ***Recorded Records*** www.scottcountyclerk.com A subscription service available (Software Management LLC) at: 800-466-9445. **$$$**
Property, Taxation Records Access property data after registration at http://scpva.com/resources.html.**$$$**

Shelby County ***Real Estate, Deed Records*** www.shelbycountyclerk.com Access is via the eCCLIX subscription system at www.shelbycountyclerk.com/ecclix.stm. Images go back to 1960; index to 1960. Sign-up fee is $100 plus $65 per month for unlimited access. For more info, phone 502-266-9445. **$$$**
Property, Taxation Records Access to property index is free at www.qpublic.net/ky/shelby/. A subscription is required for full data.**$$$**

Taylor County ***Recorded Documents Records*** www.tcclerk.com/ Access to entire index and selected images free at www.tcclerk.com/index.cfm. Images include deeds and mortgages from 1982 to present; Marriages from 1977 and all documents imaged from 2000.

Union County ***Mortgage, Deeds, Plats, Misc Documents Records*** www.unioncounty.ky.gov/index.php/countygovernment/countyclerk Access to records for a fee at https://cotthosting.com/kyunionexternal/User/Login.aspx?ReturnUrl=%2fkyunionexternal%2fIndex.aspx.Must have user ID and password. **$$$**

Warren County ***Real Estate, Deed, Lien, UCC, Marriage, Mortgage, Plat, Will Records*** http://warrencounty.state.ky.us Access the county clerk database through eCCLIX, a fee-based service; $200.00 sign-up and $65.00 monthly. Records go back to 1997; images to 1971. For info, see the website or call 502-843-5307 (Records Dept). **$$$**
Property, Taxation Records Property data available at http://warrencounty.state.ky.us/ecclix.htm for a fee. Must sign-up with eCCLIX@.**$$$**

Wayne County ***Recorded Documents Records*** www.waynecounty.ky.gov/elected/clerk.htm Access to records free at www.waynecountyky.com/. Must register before use. Must also install Alternatiff image view in order to view images. Can get this program at this site.
Property, Taxation Records Access to property tax records for free at http://taxbills.g-uts.com/(S(e1sqz455mkuxf255cgi22v55))/default.aspx?siteid=20&taxbill=1. Access to property records and GIS/mapping for a fee are found at www.pvdnetwork.com/PVDNet.asp?SiteID=100.**$$$**

Webster County ***Recorded Land Records*** http://webstercountyclerk.ky.gov/ Access to land records for a fee at www.kylandrecords.com/. **$$$**
Property, Taxation Records Access GIS-mapping and property data free at http://kygeonet.ky.gov/pva/webster/viewer.htm but no name searching; parcel number required.

Wolfe County ***Recorded Land Records*** Access to land records for a fee at www.kylandrecords.com/.

Woodford County ***Property, Taxation Records*** Access to property records and GIS/mapping for a fee are found at www.pvdnetwork.com/PVDNet.asp?SiteID=100. **$$$**

Louisiana

Capital: Baton Rouge
East Baton Rouge Parish
Time Zone: CST
Population: 4,601,893
# of Parishes: 64

Useful State Links

Website: www.louisiana.gov
Governor: www.gov.state.la.us
Attorney General: /www.ag.state.la.us
State Archives: www.sos.louisiana.gov/tabid/53/Default.aspx
State Statutes and Codes: www.legis.la.gov/legis/LawSearch.aspx
Legislative Bill Search: www.legis.state.la.us
Unclaimed Funds: https://www.treasury.state.la.us/ucpm/UP/index.asp

Primary State Agencies

Criminal Records

State Police, Bureau of Criminal Identification, www.lsp.org/index.html Authorized agencies can utilize LAAPPS and submit their information and receive a response instantaneously provided
there is no criminal history information. The site is https://laapps.dps.louisiana.gov/. No record responses are returned in 24 hours. Fingerprints can be submitted electronically and you will receive a response
within 5 to 7 business days provided there is no criminal history information. A state check is $26.00, add $10 if fingerprints. **$$$**

Sexual Offender Registry

State Police, Sex Offender and Child Predator Registry, www.lsp.org/socpr/default.html Search by name, ZIP Code, city or parish or view the entire list at the website. Also search by city, school area or parish. Also, email requests are accepted, use SOCPR@dps.state.la.us.

Incarceration Records

Department of Public Safety and Corrections, PO Box 94304, www.corrections.state.la.us Currently, the Department does not have inmate locator capabilities. However, the web page refers searchers to www.vinelink.com. Also, search for fugitives at http://doc.la.gov/fugitives.

Corporation, LP, LLP, LLC, Trademarks/Servicemarks

Commercial Division, Corporation Department, www.sos.la.gov/ Search by individual's name or charter's name or document number at the web page listed above. Instructions are given. **$$$** *Other Options:* Bulk sale of corporation, LLC, partnership, and trademark information is available for approved entities. For more info, call 225-925-4704.

Uniform Commercial Code, Federal Tax Liens

Secretary of State, UCC Division, www.sos.la.gov/tabid/99/Default.aspx An annual $400 fee gives unlimited access to UCC filing information at Direct Access 24/7. However, the agreements states that the purchaser can only use the data for internal purposes, and data is not transferable. Although federal tax liens are filed at the parish level, they do appear on the index of this service. State tax liens do not appear on this database search. For further information, visit www.sos.la.gov/Portals/0/Newdirectaccessapp-fill.pdf or call the number above or 225-922-1193 **$$$** *Other Options:* If one needs a paper copy of a federal or state tax lien, it must be obtained at the local parish.

Birth, Death Records

Vital Records Registry, Office of Public Health, www.dhh.louisiana.gov/index.cfm/subhome/21 Orders can be placed online at www.vitalchek.com, a state-approved vendor. **$$$**

Driver Records

Dept of Public Safety and Corrections, Office of Motor Vehicles, www.expresslane.org There are two methods. The commercial requester, interactive mode is available from 7 AM to 9:30 PM daily. There is a minimum order requirement of 2,000 requests per month. A bond or large deposit is required. Fee is $6.00 per record. Users must post a bond or submit a deposit; thereafter, the state bills monthly. Users also must pass background checks and vetting. For more information, call 225-922-0017. Also, individuals may view and print their own record at https://omv.dps.state.la.us/pp_odr/odr.asp. The fee is $17.00 and requires a credit card. **$$$**

Accident Reports

Louisiana State Police, Traffic Records Unit - A27, www.lsp.org/technical.html#traffic One may purchase a crash report from the request link at www.lsp.org. The request requires first and last name, date of crash, and parish location of crash. A login/ID must be created to finalize the transaction. The fee is $8.50. The requester may print a PDF version of the report. Records go back five years. Use of a credit card is required. **$$$**

Voter Registration

Louisiana Secretary of State, Voter Registration Div, www.sos.la.gov/tabid/68/Default.aspx One may request list information online at www.sos.la.gov/tabid/156/Default.aspx. Charges and descriptions of file formats are given. Also request via email at voterlistrequest@sos.la.gov. Campaign Finance Reports and data on lobbyists are available for online viewing on the Louisiana Ethics Administration's website at www.ethics.state.la.us. **$$$** *Other Options:* The agency will sell the database statewide or by parish per request. Media formats include email, labels, CD, and paper lists. There are no restrictions regarding purchasing for marketing purposes. Email questions to cate.mcritchie@sos.louisiana.gov.

Voter Registration

Louisiana Board of Ethics, PO Box 4368, www.ethics.state.la.us/ Campaign Finance Reports, opinions, PAC lists, and outstanding fines, lobbyist data and more are available using the Tabs at http://ethics.la.gov/default.aspx.

Occupational Licensing Boards

Accountant-CPA.. https://elicense.cpaboard.la.gov/lookup/Default.asp
Acupuncturist .... www.lsbme.louisiana.gov/apps/verifications/lookup.aspx
Addiction Counselor.................................. www.la-adra.org/index.php/2012-05-25-02-39-47
Adult Residential Care .... https://webapps.dss.state.la.us/carefacility/index
Alcoholic Beverage Vendor............................ http://atcpub.license.louisiana.gov/
Architect/Architectural Firm......................... www.lastbdarchs.com/roster.htm
Athletic Trainer..................................... www.lsbme.louisiana.gov/apps/verifications/lookup.aspx
Attorney... www.lsba.org/MembershipDirectory/MembershipDirectory.asp?Menu=MD
Auctioneer Schools................................... www.lalb.org/approved_schools.php
Auto Buyer/Salesman/Dealer, New & Used. https://license.lumvc.louisiana.gov/Lookup/LicenseLookup.aspx
Automobile Parts Dealer, Used........................ https://license.lumvc.louisiana.gov/Lookup/LicenseLookup.aspx
Automotive Dismantler & Parts Recycler..... https://license.lumvc.louisiana.gov/Lookup/LicenseLookup.aspx
Bank... www.ofi.state.la.us
Bond For Deed Agency................................. www.ofi.state.la.us
Brokerage Firm www.lrec.state.la.us/view-education-record-124/
Burglar Alarm Contractor .... http://sfm.dps.louisiana.gov/lic_contractors.htm#3
Cemetery... www.lcb.state.la.us/search.html
Check Casher .... www.ofi.state.la.us
Chemical Engineer.................................... https://renewals.lapels.com/Lookup/LicenseLookup.aspx
Child Residential Care .... https://webapps.dss.state.la.us/carefacility/index
Chiropractor .... www.lachiropracticboard.com/licensees.htm
Clinical Lab Personnel .... www.lsbme.louisiana.gov/apps/verifications/lookup.aspx
Collection Agency .... www.ofi.state.la.us
Construction Project, +$50000....................... www.lslbc.louisiana.gov/findcontractor_type.htm
Consumer Credit Grantor............................. www.ofi.state.la.us
Contractor .... www.lslbc.louisiana.gov/findcontractor.asp
Contractor, General/Subcontractor.............. www.lslbc.louisiana.gov/findcontractor_type.htm

Cosmetologist/Cosmetology Instructor .... www.lsbc.louisiana.gov/Public/Default.aspx
Counselor, Professional (LPC) .... www.lpcboard.org/LPC_new.php
Credit Repair Agency.................................. www.ofi.state.la.us
Credit Union .... www.ofi.state.la.us
Day Care Facility... https://webapps.dss.state.la.us/carefacility/index
Dentist/Dental Hygienist.............................. www.lsbd.org/licenseverification.htm
Dietitian .... www.lbedn.org/searchlbedn.asp
Drug Distributor, Wholesale .... www.lsbwdd.org/
Electrical Engineer .... https://renewals.lapels.com/Lookup/LicenseLookup.aspx
Engineer/Engineer Intern/Firm..................... https://renewals.lapels.com/Lookup/LicenseLookup.aspx
Environmental Engineer.............................. https://renewals.lapels.com/Lookup/LicenseLookup.aspx
Esthetician.. www.lsbc.louisiana.gov/Public/Default.aspx
Exercise Physiologist, Clinical .... www.lsbme.louisiana.gov/apps/verifications/lookup.aspx
Fire Alarm Contractor.................................. http://sfm.dps.louisiana.gov/lic_contractors.htm#3
Fire Extinguisher Contractor .... http://sfm.dps.louisiana.gov/lic_contractors.htm#3
Fire Protection Sprinkler Contractor............ http://sfm.dps.louisiana.gov/lic_contractors.htm#3
Foster Care/Adoption Care .... https://webapps.dss.state.la.us/carefacility/index
Home Improvem't Cont'r +$75,000 .... www.lslbc.louisiana.gov/findcontractor_type.htm
Home Inspector... http://lsbhi.state.la.us/results.php
Insurance Agent/Broker/Producer/LHA/PC.. www.ldi.state.la.us/search_forms/searchforms.html
Interior Designer.. http://lsbid.org/licensees.asp
Investment Advisor...................................... www.ofi.louisiana.gov/
Land Surveyor/Surveyor Intern/Firm........... https://renewals.lapels.com/Lookup/LicenseLookup.aspx
Lender .... www.ofi.state.la.us
Lobbyist... http://ethics.la.gov/LobbyistLists.aspx
Manicurist.. www.lsbc.louisiana.gov/Public/Default.aspx
Marriage and Family Therapist .... www.lpcboard.org/LMFT_new.php
Massage Therapist...................................... https://www.labmt.org/find_a_therapist
Maternity Home... https://webapps.dss.state.la.us/carefacility/index
Medical Gas Piping Installer .... www.spbla.com/rosters.asp
Midwife .... www.lsbme.louisiana.gov/apps/verifications/lookup.aspx
Mold Remediation .... www.lslbc.louisiana.gov/findcontractor_type.htm
Motor Auction .... https://license.lumvc.louisiana.gov/Lookup/LicenseLookup.aspx
Motor Vehicle Crusher/Shredder .... https://license.lumvc.louisiana.gov/Lookup/LicenseLookup.aspx
Motor Vehicle Mfg/Distributor...................... https://license.lumvc.louisiana.gov/Lookup/LicenseLookup.aspx
Motored Products, New .... https://license.lumvc.louisiana.gov/Lookup/LicenseLookup.aspx
Notary Public... www.sos.la.gov/tabid/502/Default.aspx
Notification Filer www.ofi.state.la.us/Notification%20Licensees.htm
Nuclear Engineer .... https://renewals.lapels.com/Lookup/LicenseLookup.aspx
Nuclear Medicine Technologist................... www.lsrtbe.org/search.cfm
Nurse-LPN .... www.lsbpne.com/license_verification.phtml
Nurse-RN .... https://services.lsbn.state.la.us/services/service.asp?s=1&sid=8
Nurses Aide... www.labenfa.com/
Nursing Home Administrator....................... www.labenfa.com/
Nutritionist .... www.lbedn.org/searchlbedn.asp
Occupational Therapist/Technologist.......... www.lsbme.louisiana.gov/apps/verifications/lookup.aspx
Optometrist.. www.arbo.org/index.php?action=findanoptometrist
Osteopathic Physician .... www.lsbme.louisiana.gov/apps/verifications/lookup.aspx
Payday Lender.. www.ofi.state.la.us/
Pharmacist/Pharmacy................................. https://secure.pharmacy.la.gov/Lookup/LicenseLookup.aspx
Pharmacy Intern (College).......................... https://secure.pharmacy.la.gov/Lookup/LicenseLookup.aspx
Pharmacy Tech/Candidate .... https://secure.pharmacy.la.gov/Lookup/LicenseLookup.aspx
Pharmacy/Hospital...................................... https://secure.pharmacy.la.gov/Lookup/LicenseLookup.aspx
Physical Therapist/Therapist Asst............... www.laptboard.org/locations/
Physician/Medical Doctor/Assistant............ www.lsbme.louisiana.gov/apps/verifications/lookup.aspx

Plumber Journeyman/Master	www.spbla.com/rosters.asp
Podiatrist	www.lsbme.louisiana.gov/apps/verifications/lookup.aspx
Prevention Specialist (Social Work)	www.la-adra.org/index.php/2012-05-25-02-39-47
Private Investigator/Agency	www.lsbpie.com/
Psychologist	www.lsbep.org/verifications.php
Radiation Therapy Technologist	www.lsrtbe.org/search.cfm
Radiographer/Radiologic Technologist	www.lsrtbe.org/search.cfm
Radiologic Technologist, Private	www.lsbme.louisiana.gov/apps/verifications/lookup.aspx
Real Estate Agent/Broker/Sales	www.lrec.state.la.us/view-education-record-124/
Real Estate Appraiser	www.lreasbc.state.la.us/dbfiles/appraiserinfo.htm
Residential Construction +$50,000	www.lslbc.louisiana.gov/findcontractor_type.htm
Respiratory Therapist/Therapy Tech.	www.lsbme.louisiana.gov/apps/verifications/lookup.aspx
Securities Salesperson/Dealer	www.ofi.louisiana.gov/
Social Worker/Clinic Supervisor	www.labswe.org/searchlabswe.asp
Solicitor	www.ldi.state.la.us/search_forms/searchforms.html
Speech Pathologist/Audiologist	www.lbespa.org/searchlbespa.asp
Substance Abuse Counselor	www.la-adra.org/index.php/2012-05-25-02-39-47
Vocational Rehabilitation Counselor	http://lrcboard.org/licensee_database.asp
Water Supply Piping	www.spbla.com/rosters.asp
X-Ray Technician	www.lachiropracticboard.com/licensees.htm

Note: For all occupations related to Licensed Horticulture Professionals, Landscape Architect/Contractor, Arborist, and Florists see: www.ldaf.state.la.us/portal/Offices/AgriculturalEnvironmentalSciences/HorticultureQuarantinePrograms/LouisianaHorticultureCommission/FindaLicensedProfessional/tabid/287/Default.aspx

State and Local Courts

State Court Structure: The trial court of general jurisdiction in Louisiana is the District Court. A District Court Clerk in each Parish holds all the records for that Parish. Each Parish has its own clerk and courthouse. **City Courts** are courts of record and handle misdemeanors, limited civil, juvenile, traffic and evection. The amount of civil is concurrent with the District Court based where the amount in controversy does not exceed $15,000 to $50,000 depending on the court. (See CCP 4843 - http://www.legis.state.la.us/lss/lss.asp?doc=112087).

In criminal matters, City Courts generally have jurisdiction over ordinance violations and misdemeanor violations of state law. City judges also handle a large number of traffic cases.

Parish Courts exercise jurisdiction in civil cases worth up to $10,000 to 25,000 and criminal cases punishable by fines of $1,000 or less, or imprisonment of six months or less. Cases are appealable from the Parish Courts directly to the courts of appeal. A municipality or local may have a **Mayor's Court** or **Justice of the Peace Court** which handle certain traffic cases and minor infractions.

Appellate Courts: Search opinions at www.lasc.org/opinion_search.asp. Supreme Court Dockets going back approx. 2 years are shown at www.lasc.org/docket/default.asp.

Statewide Court Online Access: There is no statewide system open to the public for trial court dockets, but a number of parishes offer online access.

Acadia Parish

15th District Court www.acadiaparishclerk.com

Civil: Online access to record information is by subscription. There is a set-up fee and a monthly fee. Call the court for details. **$$$** *Criminal:* same **$$$**

Ascension Parish

23rd District Court www.ascensionclerk.com/default.aspx

Civil: Access to civil judgments, etc, available by subscription; $100 set-up charge single user; $250 multiple user up to 5, plus $50.00 monthly and $.50 per image printed; includes recorded document index; see www.ascensionclerk.com/onlineservices.aspx. **$$$** *Criminal:* Access to criminal case data available by subscription; $100 set-up charge single user; $250 multiple user up to 5, plus $50.00 monthly and $.50 per image printed; includes civil and recorded document index; see www.ascensionclerk.com/onlineservices.aspx. **$$$**

Assumption Parish

23rd District Court www.assumptionclerk.com/

Civil: The site is at https://esearch.assumptionclerk.com/Esearch/User/Login.aspx?ReturnUrl=%2fesearch%2fIndex.aspx. Registration is required. Registration is $50 per month or $500 a year with $1.00 per page to print images. Another way in is at http://97.89.251.18/qGov/Main/Index.aspx?bRepopForm=True. Please note that there may be records that have been assigned Official numbers but not yet completely indexed or available on this search. **$$$**

Criminal: The site is at https://esearch.assumptionclerk.com/Esearch/User/Login.aspx?ReturnUrl=%2fesearch%2fIndex.aspx. Registration is $50 per month or $500 a year with $1.00 per page to print images. Please note that there may be records that have been assigned Official numbers but not yet completely indexed or available on this search. **$$$**

Avoyelles Parish

12th District Court

Civil: An online subscription service to record images is available at http://cotthosting.com/laavoyelles. Monthly rate is $75.00, other fees are $.50 for each printed page plus a service fee to use PayPal. **$$$** *Criminal:* same **$$$**

Beauregard Parish

36th District Court www.beauregardclerk.org/

Civil: Search the index free at www.beauregardclerk.org/search-our-records. *Criminal:* same

Bienville Parish

2nd District Court http://clerk.bienvilleparish.org/

Civil: An online subscription service to view images is available. Contact the Clerk of Court for details and pricing. **$$$** *Criminal:* same **$$$**

Bossier Parish

26th District Court www.bossierclerk.com

Civil: Access to the Parish Clerk of Court online records requires $85 setup fee and a $35 monthly flat fee, see the home page. Civil, criminal, probate (1982 forward), traffic and domestic index information is by name or case number. Call 318-965-2336 for more information. The system occasionally has records missing or lack identifiers that would otherwise be found in person. **$$$** *Criminal:* same

Caddo Parish

1st District Court www.caddoclerk.com

Civil: Online access to civil records back to 1994 and name index back to 1984 is through county internet service. Registration and $100 set-up fee and $30 monthly usage fee is required. Marriage and recording information is also available. Online images $.25 each to print. For information and sign-up, call 318-226-6523. The online system for the District Court may occasionally have court records missing or lack identifiers that would otherwise be found in person. **$$$** *Criminal:* Online access to criminal record index back to 1994 and name index back to 1984 is through county internet service. Registration and $100 set-up fee and $30 monthly usage fee is required. Marriage and recording information is also available.

Shreveport City Court www.shreveportla.gov/citycourt/

Civil: Search records at www.shreveportla.gov/citycourt/ for free. Click on Civil Tools to start.

Calcasieu Parish

14th District Court www.calclerkofcourt.com

Civil: Online access to civil records is the same as criminal, see below. *Criminal:* Online access to court record indices is free at http://207.191.42.34/resolution/. Registration and password required. Full documents requires $100.00 per month subscription.

Cameron Parish

38th District Court

Civil: Online access is offered, but by contract only and fees involved. Call Susan Racca at 337-775-5316 for details. **$$$** *Criminal:* same **$$$**

De Soto Parish

42nd District Court www.desotoparishclerk.org/

Civil: Access index via a web-based subscription service. Search index, view, & print image fee is $100.00 per month, plus a one-time setup fee of $150.00. Contact Jayme, Katie or Valerie at 318-872-3110 to set-up an account of visit www.desotoparishclerk.org/online.html. **$$$** *Criminal:* same **$$$**

East Baton Rouge Parish

19th District Court www.ebrclerkofcourt.org

Civil & Criminal: Online access to the clerk's database is by subscription.. Setup fee is $100.00 plus $50.00 per month for 1st password, $25.00 for each add'l passwords. Call MIS Dept at 225-389-5295 for info or visit the website. **$$$**

Baton Rouge City Court www.brgov.com/dept/citycourt/

Civil: Access city court's database including attorneys and warrants free at from the web page. *Criminal:* Access city court's criminal dockets database and warrants free at http://brgov.com/dept.citycourt.

East Feliciana Parish

20th District Court www.eastfelicianaclerk.org/court.html

Civil: Online subscription service is available. $400.00 per quarter permits access to viewable documents; $250 per quarter permits access in indices. This database also includes recordings, conveyances, mortgages, and marriage records. **$$$** *Criminal:* Criminal online also requires a subscription for full access, must be approved. Call for details. **$$$**

Elberia Parish

16th District Court www.iberiaclerk.com

Civil: Search the civil index back to 01/01/09 and probate to 01/01/2000 at www.iberiaclerk.com/resolution/default.asp. A user ID and password are required, it may be necessary to call for help on obtaining. *Criminal:* search criminal record index from 01/01/2000 to the last day of the previous month. A user ID and password are required, it may be necessary to call for help on obtaining.

Iberville Parish

18th District Court www.ibervilleclerk.com/

Civil: Access to civil records online by subscription, contact clerk for details. See page at http://cotthosting.com/laiberia/User/Login.aspx?ReturnUrl=%2flaiberia%2findex.aspx. Fee for printed images. **$$$** *Criminal:* Access to criminal records online by subscription, contact clerk for details. See page at http://cotthosting.com/laiberia/User/Login.aspx?ReturnUrl=%2flaiberia%2findex.aspx. Fee for printed images. **$$$**

Jefferson Parish

24th District Court www.jpclerkofcourt.us

Civil: Access to court records on JeffNet is $100, plus $50.00 monthly, $.25 per printed page. Includes recordings, marriage index, and assessor rolls. For further information and sign-up, visit the website and click on "Jeffnet" or call 504-364-2976. **$$$** *Criminal:* Access to court records on JeffNet is $100, plus $50.00 monthly, $.25 per printed page. **$$$**

Lafayette Parish

15th District Court www.lafayetteparishclerk.com

Civil: Access to the remote online system requires $100 setup fee plus $65 subscription fee per month. Civil index goes back to 1986. For more information, call 337-291-6435 or visit www.lafayetteparishclerk.com/onlineIndex.cfm. The. system includes scanned images and pleadings back to May 2006. **$$$** *Criminal:* Access to crimianl and traffic index back to 1986 on the remote online system requires $100 setup fee plus $65 subscription fee per month. There is a $10.00 fee per printed minute entry, but not charge for printing other documents. For more information, call 337-291-6435 or visit www.lafayetteparishclerk.com/onlineIndex.cfm. **$$$**

Lafourche Parish

17th District Court www.lafourcheclerk.com/

Civil: Wills from 1817 and court orders from 07/01/1994 are available on a subscription system at www.lafourcheclerk.com/recordsSearch.html. Note this site does NOT include the civil docket. **$$$** *Criminal:*

Livingston Parish

District Court www.livclerk.org

Civil: Civil indexing is available to online subscribers. Civil images are available to online subscribers with a Louisiana Bar Number. Call 225-686-2216 for more information. **$$$** *Criminal:* Online access is available to local attorneys only, with registration, call 225-686-2216 x1107. $50.00 per year fee for online access. **$$$**

Natchitoches Parish

10th District Court www.npclerkofcourt.org/

Civil: With username and password to WebView you can search and access civil records, judgments. $50 setup fee, then $50.00 monthly, plus $.50 per image. Includes conveyance and marriage records. Direct subscription inquires to Linda Cockrell at 318-352-8152. **$$$** *Criminal:*

Orleans Parish

District Court www.orleanscdc.com/

Civil: CDC Remote provides access to civil case index from 1985 and First City Court cases as well as parish mortgage and conveyance indexes. Case files are not provided. The annual fee is $500 or monthly is $100. Credit cards are accepted. Call 504-592-9264 for more information. **$$$** *Criminal:* same

New Orleans City Court www.orleanscdc.com/

Civil: CDC Remote provides access to First City Court cases from 1988 as well as civil cases, parish mortgage and conveyance indexes. The fee is $250 or $300 per year. Call 504-592-9264 for more information. **$$$**

Ouachita Parish

4th District Court www.opclerkofcourt.com/

Criminal: A subscription service to the record index is at www.opclerkofcourt.com/online_records.htm. There is a one day ($12.50) or one month ($100) or one year ($1080) unlimited access fee to the index and images. There is an additional $.50 per page fee to print. Establish an account with a credit card. **$$$**

Plaquemines Parish

25th District Court www.plaqueminesparishclerkofcourt.com/

Civil: Search the docket index online from the home page. *Criminal:* same

Sabine Parish

11th District Court www.sabineparishclerk.com/

Civil: Access civil and succession-probate court records by subscription at www.sabineparishclerk.com/pages/online-access. The $100 per month fee includes access to conveyance, mortgage, marriage records. Civil suits go back to 1/1985; Probate to 1920. **$$$** *Criminal:* Access to criminal records for subcribers available at http://cotthosting.com/lasabineqgov/main/login.aspx. There is a $100.00 per month fee. **$$$**

St. Bernard Parish

34th District Court http://judgefernandez.com/index.php

Civil: Search Civil record suits back to 1/1989 free at http://records.stbclerk.com/User/Login.aspx. *Criminal:* Search criminal index back to 1/1989 free at http://records.stbclerk.com/User/Login.aspx.

St. Charles Parish

29th District Court www.stcharlesgov.net/

Civil: This is the same subscription system described under criminal records. However, civil records are much more current, generally within 1 week old. **$$$** *Criminal:* Note the onliine system has old data - criminal record data up to and not beyond 13/31//2006. The log-in page is at https://records.stcharlesparish-la.gov/User/Login.aspx?ReturnUrl=%2findex.aspx. Images to 1999, index to 1988. Fee is $50 per month plus $1.00 per page for copies. All fees paid by credit card. **$$$**

St. Landry Parish

27th District Court www.stlandry.org

Civil: Online subscription access program to civil cases is available. The fee ranges from $50.00 to $300 per month. Includes civil court records back to 1997, also includes land indexes and images. Contact the court or visit the web page for details. **$$$** *Criminal:*

St. Martin Parish

16th District Court www.stmartinparishclerkofcourt.com

Civil: The online system is by subscription only, Fee is $100 per month. Data available images back to 1989/1990. Judgments are found with Recorder's Office data indices available at www.stmartinparishclerkofcourt.com. **$$$** *Criminal:* The online system is by subscription only, Fee is $100 per month. Data available images back to 1989/1990. Note if both civil and criminal data wanted, then fee is $200 per month. **$$$**

St. Tammany Parish

22nd District Court www.sttammanyclerk.org/main/index.asp

Civil: Internet access to civil records is from the Clerk of Court. $50 initial setup fee, $50.00 per month and $.35 to print a page. For information, call Kristie Howell at 985-809-8787. Civil index goes back to 1992; images to 1995. Search index free at https://www.sttammanyclerk.org/liveapp/default.asp. **$$$** *Criminal:* Internet access to criminal records is s from the Clerk of Court. $50 initial setup fee, $50.00 per month and $.35 to print a page. For information, call Kristie Howell at 985-809-8787. **$$$**

Tangipahoa Parish

21st District Court www.tangiclerk.org

Civil: Online access to index of civil records is at www.tangiclerk.org/. You can "Sign in as a Guest" to view indexes at no cost; images are only available with a paid subscription). Index back to 1974. When civil data is shown is dependent on the type of subscription, be sure to read this information on the site. **$$$**

Terrebonne Parish

32nd District Court www.terrebonneclerk.org/

Civil: An online subscription is offered (see home page) to civil and criminal dockets. No images are provided. The rate is $50 per month. Subscribers can also obtain land records with or without images, for additional fees. One may print for $1.00 per page. **$$$** *Criminal:* An online subscription is offered (see home page) to civil and criminal dockets. No images are provided. The rate is $50 per month. Sunscribers can also obtain land records with or without images, for additional fees. One may print for $1.00 per page. Note that there is no option to subscribe to only civil or only criminal. **$$$**

Union Parish

3rd District Court www.upclerk.com/

Civil: From the home page click on "Court Records Search." This is a subscription service based on a one day ($15), one month ($100), or one year ($1080) basis. Civil and probate available ffom 06/09/2001 forward. **$$$** *Criminal*: same as civil **$$$**

Washington Parish

22nd District Court www.wpclerk.org/CustomPage.aspx?Title=Home

Civil: The records, including file images are searchable online. The fee is $100 per month to view plus $1.00 for each printed page. Sign-up is at https://search.wpclerk.org/external/User/Login.aspx?ReturnUrl=%2fexternal%2findex.aspx. **$$$** *Criminal:* same as civil. **$$$**

Webster Parish

26th District Court www.websterclerk.org/

Civil: Access court records by subscription; fee is $50.00 per month for index searches and images. Civil index goes back to 01/1986; images back to 2005. Sub includes criminal, probate, civil, traffic, also marriages and conveyances. Login, signup or find more information at www.websterclerk.org/records.html. **$$$** *Criminal:* Access to criminal index and images is included in the general subscription service described in the civil section, above. The criminal subscription index goes back to 11/28/1992; images go back to early 2007. **$$$**

Recorders, Assessors, and Other Sites of Note

Recording Office Organization: 64 parishes, 64 recording offices. One parish – St. Martin – has two non-contiguous segments. In Orleans Parish, deeds are recorded in a different office from mortgages. All federal and state tax liens are filed with the Clerk of Court. Parishes usually file tax liens on personal property in the same index. However, tax liens are not kept on the same statewide database as UCCs.

Statewide Access: **There is one free, government-based statewide system for property tax and assessment records that serivces all parishes.**

The statewide system at www.latax.state.la.us/Menu_ParishTaxRolls/TaxRolls.aspx offers free access to assessor parish tax roll data, but not all are updated to the current year.

Note a number of parishes offer online access to recorded documents. Most are commercial fee systems but newer systems are allowing for free index searching, then charge a fee for images of usually $1.00 each.

County Sites Other Than the Statewide System Mentioned Above:

Acadia Parish ***Recorded Documents, Marriage Records*** www.acadiaparishclerk.com Online subscription access to records available for a fee. Go to www.acadiaparishclerk.com/on-line_service.htm for the contract form. **$$$**

Property, Taxation Records Access to property data free at www.acadiaassessor.org/SiteDisclaimer.aspx.

Ascension Parish ***Recorded Documents, Judgment Records*** www.ascensionclerk.com/default.aspx Access available by subscription; $100 set-up charge single user; $250 multiple user up to 5, plus $50.00 monthly and $.50 per image printed; see www.ascensionclerk.com/onlineservices.aspx. **$$$**

Assumption Parish ***Recorded Documents, Probate, Marriage Records*** www.assumptionclerk.com/ Online access by subscription at https://esearch.assumptionclerk.com/Esearch/User/Login.aspx?ReturnUrl=%2fesearch%2fIndex.aspx. Civil & Probate go back to 1/1/01, marriages back to 1/2/62; mortgages to 1/8/1981. User ID and password required. **$$$**

Property, Taxation Records Email to assessor@assumptionassessor.com.

Avoyelles Parish ***Recorded Documents*** www.laclerksofcourt.org/Parishs/avoyellesparish.htm Access to land record at http://cotthosting.com/laavoyelles/User/Login.aspx?ReturnUrl=%2flaavoyelles%2fIndex.aspx. A monthly service fee of $75.00 is charged. Contact the Clerk's Office for application at 318-253-7523. **$$$**

Beauregard Parish ***Recorded Documents*** www.laclerksofcourt.org/Parishs/Beauregardparish.htm Access to recorded documents for a fee at https://cotthosting.com/labeauregard/User/Login.aspx?ReturnUrl=%2flabeauregard%2fIndex.aspx. **$$$**

Bienville Parish ***Recorded Documents*** http://clerk.bienvilleparish.org/index.php Access to records for a fee at http://clerk.bienvilleparish.org/ucc.php, or contact Eddie Holmes at 318-263-2123 X10 for more subscription information. Conveyance records from 2/13/13 to present; mortgage records from 1/1/86 to present; civil records from 7/1/89 to present. The dates for all records will broaden as they continue to integrate older records into the digital system. **$$$**

Bossier Parish ***Real Estate, Deed, Marriage, Civil, Criminal Records*** www.bossierclerk.com Access to the clerk's WebView System is by subscription; one-time signup fee is $50 plus $35 per month, plus small fee per image printed. Monthly billing. Mortgages go back to 1984, marriages to 1843, courts back to 1980s; see http://209.209.204.34/WebInquiry/login.aspx?ReturnUrl=%2fWebInquiry%2fDefault.aspx. This online system may occasionally have records missing or lack identifiers that would otherwise be found in person. **$$$**

Property, Taxation Records Free public address search available at www.bossierparishassessor.org/cgi-bin/pro_search.pl. Access to full data requires username and login ID, signup online; fee amounts to less than $1.00 per day. For more information, call 318-221-8718.

Caddo Parish ***Real Estate, Deed, Lien, Marriage, Mortgage Records*** www.caddoclerk.com Access to the Parish online records requires a $100 set up fee plus $30 monthly fee; $.25 per image. Mortgages and indirect conveyances index dates back to 1981; direct conveyances date back to 1914. Lending agency data is available. Mortgage images back to 1/1995. Also, access marriage licenses free back to 1937; use username

\"muser\" and password \"caddo.\" Signup and info at www.caddoclerk.com/remote.htm or call 318-226-6523. Online system may occasionally have records missing or lack identifiers that would otherwise be found in person. **$$$**

Property, Taxation Records Search assessor property free at https://www.caddoassessor.org/publicsearch/Search.aspx.

Calcasieu Parish ***Recorded Documents, Marriage Records*** www.calclerkofcourt.com Online access to court record indices is free at www.calclerkofcourt.com/dept.asp?cid=196. Registration and password required. Full documents requires $100.00 per month subscription. Go to www.calclerkofcourt.com/dept.asp?cid=335 for dates on hav far back the they go. **$$$**

Property, Taxation Records Access to GIS/mapping free at www.cppj.net/index.aspx?page=120.

Cameron Parish ***Recorded Documents*** For subscription service contact Susan Racca. **$$$**

De Soto Parish ***Real Estate, Deed, Judgment, Lien, Mortgage Records*** www.desotoparishclerk.org/ Access Clerk of Court records index by subscription at www.desotoparishclerk.org/online.html; set-up fee is $250.00 plus $100 per month for index, doc viewing, and images. Conveyance images and index back to 1843. Other public records included in this URL. **$$$**

East Baton Rouge Parish ***Real Estate, Deed, Lien, Marriage, Judgment, Map Data Index Records*** www.ebrclerkofcourt.org/ Access to online records requires a $100 set up fee with a $5 monthly fee and $.33 per minute of use. Four years worth of data is kept active on the system. Lending agency data is available. For info, contact Robin White at 225-389-7851. **$$$**

East Feliciana Parish ***Real Estate, Lien, Mortgage, Marriage Records*** www.eastfelicianaclerk.org/ Access to online records requires a subscription, $100 set up fee with a $50 monthly usage fee for indices or $100.00 per month for indices plus images, in quarterly advances. Conveyances go back to 1962, mortgages to 1981; viewable back to 6/18/1982. Marriages go back to 1987, viewable free to 1995, and miscellaneous index goes back to 1984. For info, contact clerk's office at 225-683-5145 or visit www.eastfelicianaclerk.org/. **$$$**

Iberia Parish ***Real Estate, Conveyance, Deed, Mortgage, Lien, Marriage Records*** www.iberiaclerk.com Access to the Parish online records requires a $100.00 monthly usage fee. Lending agency data is available. For info, contact Mike Thibodeaux at 337-365-7282. Registration is also required for the Clerk's index search at http://cotthosting.com/laiberia/User/Login.aspx?ReturnUrl=%2flaiberia%2findex.aspx which includes civil, conveyances, criminal, marriages back to 2000, mortgages back to 1959, and probate back thru 2000 **$$$**

Iberville Parish ***Real Estate, Deed Records*** www.ibervilleparish.com Access to records for a fee at http://ibervilleclerk.com/html_pages/online.html. Monthly subscription fee charged. **$$$**

Jackson Parish ***Real Estate, Grantor/Grantee, Deed, Mortgage, Lien, Judgment, Marriage Records*** www.jacksonparishclerk.org/ Access to the clerk's WebView Online Records system is available by subscription; $50 installation and account setup fee plus $50.00 per month usage fee; Sub form at http://72.149.195.202/Webinquiry_Jackson/(s2uty0ioozzflf45tewwkeb5)/subscribe.aspx. **$$$**

Jefferson Parish ***Real Estate, Deed, Marriage Records*** www.jpclerkofcourt.us Access to the clerk's JeffNet database is by subscription; set-up fee is $100.00 plus $50.00 monthly and $.50 per image printed. Mortgage and conveyance images go back to 1971 and changing; index to 1967. Marriage and property records go back to 1992. For info, visit https://ssl.jpclerkofcourt.us/JeffnetSetup/default.asp. Also, search inmates and offenders on a private site at https://www.vinelink.com/vinelink/siteInfoAction.do?siteId=19002 **$$$**

Property, Taxation Records Search the assessor property rolls free at www.jpassessor.com. Call Donna Richoux at 504-364-2900 for fee info.

Jefferson Davis Parish ***Recorded Documents*** www.jeffdavisclerk.com/ Conveyance/Mortgage records are available online with a subscription, Contact the Clerk's office or www.jeffdavisclerk.com/contract-form.html to subscribe and the DocuNet Service Terms and Conditions. **$$$**

Lafayette Parish ***Real Estate, Deed, Mortgage, Lien, UCC Records*** www.lpclerk.com/ Access to Parish online records requires a $100 set up fee plus $65 per month. Conveyances date back to 1936; mortgages to 1948; other records to 1986. Lending agency data is available. **$$$**

Property, Taxation Records Also, assessor property data is free at http://lafayetteassessor.com/PropertySearch.cfm, but no name searching.

Lafourche Parish ***Mortgage, Maps, Conveyance, Misc., Marriage, Wills, Charters Records*** http://lafourcheclerk.com/ Access to public records for a fee at http://lafourcheclerk.com/recordsSearch.html. This is a subscription fee to be paid by credit card online. Contact person is Vernell J Autin. **$$$**

Lincoln Parish ***Property, Taxation Records*** Access property assessor data at http://assessor.lincolnparish.org/WebTaxRoll/Default.aspx with free registration. Also, search by owner name for parcel and property data free on the GIS-mapping site at http://gis.lincolnparish.org. Also,

Livingston Parish ***Real Estate, Deed, Lien, Judgment, UCC, Plat Records*** https://www.livclerk.org Access the clerk's search pages for a fee at https://www.livclerk.org/external/User/Login.aspx?ReturnUrl=%2fexternal%2findex.aspx. User name and password required to search; $1.00 per page fee for printing of images. $50.00 yearly fee for an account. For assistance, call Vanessa Barnett at 225-686-2216 x1107 or 225-505-8200 (cell). **$$$**

Morehouse Parish ***Property, Taxation Records*** Also, at www.morehouseassessor.org/propertyinformation.htm, eTaxroll users are required to register online to obtain a Username and Password. Once registered, you may have limited access (3 searches per day) or you may register as a commercial user.**$$$**

Natchitoches Parish ***Recorded Documents, Marriage Records*** www.npclerkofcourt.org/ With username and password to WebView you can search and access marriage and property records back to 1976. $50 setup fee, then $50.00 monthly, plus $.50 per image. Direct subscription inquires to http://12.197.249.67/WebInquiry_Natchitoches/(15uiy35543h142fjh25zo3nv)/login.aspx?ReturnUrl=%2fwebinquiry_natchitoches%2fdefault.aspx. **$$$**

Property, Taxation Records Access assessor property data free at www.natchitochesassessor.org/SearchProperty.aspx.

Orleans Parish, Conveyance ***Recorded Documents, Birth, Death Records*** www.orleanscdc.com/regcon.html Access the Parish online records requires a $500 yearly subscription fee. Records date back to 1989. Access includes real estate, liens, civil, 1st city court records. For info/signup, phone 504-592-9264. Conveyances back to 1989, mortgages to 9/21/97. **$$$**

Ouachita Parish ***Recorded Documents, Marriage Records*** www.opclerkofcourt.com/ Access to online access for a fee at www.opclerkofcourt.com/online_records.htm. Other public records included in this URL. **$$$**

Property, Taxation Records Access to assessor property data is free at https://www.opassessor.com/. A subscription is required to view full details, legal description, etc.; fee is determined by number of logins. **$$$**

Plaquemines Parish ***Real Estate Records*** www.plaqueminesparishclerkofcourt.com/ Access to record searches free at https://cotthosting.com/laplaquemines/User/Login.aspx?ReturnUrl=%2flaplaquemines%2fIndex.aspx. For more detailed information must sign up and pay fees. **$$$**

Pointe Coupee Parish ***Property, Taxation Records*** Also, access to the assessments free at www.ptcoupeeassessor.com/Library/Library.asp. Can search by name, address, parcel number, subdivision or section, township and range.

Rapides Parish ***Real Estate Records*** www.rapidesclerk.org Access to subscription service contact Ken Parks at 318-619-5816. **$$$**

Property, Taxation Records With registration, username and password you may search the eTaxroll site free at www.rapidesassessor.org/propertyinformation.htm.

Red River Parish ***Recorded Documents*** Subscription service available, contact Clerks' Office at 318-932-6741. **$$$**

Richland Parish ***Real Estate, Deeds, Mortgage Records*** http://laclerksofcourt.org/Parishs/richlandparish.htm Access to record images free at https://www.uslandrecords.com/lalr/controller;jsessionid=D4E97782B76A36DCBE6720120BB4E616. Images available from 8/03 to present. For unlimited view of any document available online there is a fee of $200.00. per month, or $2.00 per page for view of any document available. **$$$**

Sabine Parish ***Mortgages, Conveyances, Marriage, Successions, Civil Suits Records*** www.sabineparishclerk.com/ Access deeds, civil court and succession-probate court records by subscription along with conveyance, mortgage records at https://cotthosting.com/lasabine/User/Login.aspx?ReturnUrl=%2flasabine%2fIndex.aspx. Conveyance index goes back to 6/1963, mortgage index goes back to 6/1968. Civil suits go back to 1/1985 **$$$**

St. Bernard Parish ***Recorded Documents*** http://stbclerk.com/?s=Clerk+of+court Search clerk's court and recording records indexes free at http://records.stbclerk.com/User/Login.aspx?ReturnUrl=%2fLandRecords%2fprotected%2fSrchQuickName.aspx. Mortgages back to 1974, marriages to 4/1938, conveyances and partnerships back to 1974, courts and chattel back to 1/1989, Misc. and bonds and partnerships back to 1974.

St. Charles Parish ***Mortgage, Marriage Records*** www.stcharlesgov.net/index.aspx?page=58 Access to subscription for records go to https://records.stcharlesparish-la.gov/User/Login.aspx?ReturnUrl=%2findex.aspx. Fee is $50.00 per month plus $1.00 per page to print. Conveyance indices & images from 1960-present; mortgage indices 1958-present; mortgage images 1973-present; marriage license indices 2000-present. **$$$**

St. John the Baptist Parish ***Property, Taxation Records*** Also, access property data free at www.stjohnassessor.org/PropertySearch.aspx.

St. Landry Parish ***Real Estate, Deed, Mortgage, Conveyance Records*** www.stlandry.org/ Access to recorder office land records is by subscription; fee is $35-50 per month. Data includes mortgages and conveyances, also perhaps court records. For registration and password contact Ms Lisa at Clerk of Court office, extension 103. **$$$**

St. Martin Parish ***Mortgage, Conveyance Records*** www.stmartinparishclerkofcourt.com Access to online conveyance and mortgage records on subscription, contact Tricia at 337-394-2210. **$$$**

Property, Taxation Records Access to GIS/mapping records free at www.geoportalmaps.com/atlas/stmartin/. Also, assess to 2010 tax roll for free at www.stmartinassessor.org/propsrch_disclaim.html.

St. Tammany Parish ***Real Estate, Deed, Mortgage, Lien, Marriage Map Records*** www.sttammanyclerk.org/main/index.asp Full access to clerk's Premium Service requires a fee. Records date back to 1961; viewable images on conveyances back to 1976. For info, go to https://www.sttammanyclerk.org/secure/. **$$$**

Property, Taxation Records Search assessor and property value database free at www.stassessor.org/assessor.php.

Tangipahoa Parish ***Conveyances, Civil Suits, Marriage, Mortgage, Oaths, Successions, Misc. Records*** www.tangiclerk.org Access to Parish online records found at https://www.tangiclerk.org/eSearch/User/Login.aspx?ReturnUrl=/esearch/default.aspx for sign up info. Indexes available at no cost, Images are only available with a paid subscription. **$$$**

Property, Taxation Records The county offers a subscription service which includes a mapping service with assessor property information.**$$$**

Terrebonne Parish ***Property, Taxation Records*** Search tax roll data for free at www.tpcg.org/view.php?f=assessor&p=disclaimer&goto=f:assessor,p:taxroll_main. Also, access to a subscription that will allow you to access up-to-date tax assessments and other information in real time go to www.tpcg.org/view.php?f=assessor&p=instructions for instructions. **$$$**

Union Parish ***Marriages, UCC, Conveyance, Mortgage, Probate, Civil, Criminal, Misc. Records*** www.upclerk.com/ Access to the online subscription found at http://cotthosting.com/LAUnion/User/Login.aspx?ReturnUrl=%2flaunion%2fIndex.aspx and follow directions to sign-up. Credit cards accepted. **$$$**

Property, Taxation Records Access property index free at www.unionparishassessor.com/online_property_search.htm but for full data registration and fees based on usage are required.

Vermilion Parish ***Recorded Documents*** www.vermilionparishclerkofcourt.com/ Access to mortgage records for a fee at http://sites.deltacomputersystems.com/home/la57/. Index includes records for conveyances from 1978-present, mortgages from 1960-present, Brossard Index from 1/1/1885-12/13/1959. Images from 2003-present. **$$$**

Washington Parish ***Recorded Documents*** www.wpclerk.org/CustomPage.aspx?Title=Home Access to subscription to records for a fee at https://search.wpclerk.org/external/User/Login.aspx?ReturnUrl=%2fexternal%2findex.aspx **$$$**

Property, Taxation Records

Webster Parish ***Real Estate, Deed Records*** www.websterclerk.org/ Access to records for a fee at https://records.websterclerk.org/User/Login.aspx?ReturnUrl=%2findex.aspx. **$$$**

West Baton Rouge Parish ***Recorded Records*** www.wbrclerk.org/ Access to records free at www.wbrclerk.org/CatSubCat/CatSubCatDisplay.asp?p1=139&p2=Y&p7=0&p8=1010&p9=CSC1. Sign in as a Guest. For more detailed records a subscription for a fee is available. **$$$**

Property, Taxation Records Access view your assessments, digital maps and qualified sales for free at www.wbrassessor.org/. Also,

West Feliciana Parish ***Real Estate Records*** www.westfelicianaclerkofcourt.org/ Access to public records for a fee at https://cotthosting.com/lawestfeliciana/User/Login.aspx?ReturnUrl=%2flawestfeliciana%2fIndex.aspx. Must have user ID and password. **$$$**

Property, Taxation Records Also, local property tax for free at www.wfassessor.com/component/option,com_wrapper/Itemid,48/. Also, access to GIS/mapping free at www.wfassessor.com/component/option,com_wrapper/Itemid,51/.

Reminder:

There is one free, government-based statewide system that serivces all parishes for property tax and assessment records.

The statewide system at www.latax.state.la.us/Menu_ParishTaxRolls/TaxRolls.aspx offers free access to assessor parish tax roll data, but not all are updated to the current year.

Maine

Capital: Augusta
Kennebec County
Time Zone: EST
Population: 1,329,192
# of Counties: 16

Useful State Links

Website: www.maine.gov/
Governor: www.maine.gov/governor/lepage
Attorney General: ww.maine.gov/ag/
State Archives: www.maine.gov/sos/arc/
State Statutes and Codes: www.mainelegislature.org/legis/statutes/
Legislative Bill Search: www.mainelegislature.org/LawMakerWeb/search.asp
Unclaimed Funds: www.maine.gov/treasurer/unclaimed_property/

State Public Record Agencies

Criminal Records

State Bureau of Investigation, State House Station #42, www5.informe.org/online/pcr/ One may request a record search from the web. Results are usually returned via e-mail in 2 hours. Fee is $31.00 and use of credit card required unless requester is an in-state subscriber to InforME, then fee is $21.00 per record. There is a $75.00 annual fee to be a subscriber. **$$$**

Sexual Offender Registry

State Bureau of Identification, Sex Offender Registry, http://sor.informe.org/cgi-bin/sor/index.pl Search at http://sor.informe.org/cgi-bin/sor/index.pl. Information is only provided for those individuals that are required to register pursuant to Title 34-A MRSA, Chapter 15. Records date to 01/01/82 and forward. The date of the last address verification is indicated next to the registrant's address.

Incarceration Records

Maine Department of Corrections, Inmate Records, www.maine.gov/corrections/ One may also do a search by sending an email to Corrections.Webdesk@maine.gov. Include your full name, address, and reasons for the search. Public information is provided. There is no direct online access available at this time (check website for updated information).

Corporation, LP, LLP, LLC, Trademarks/Servicemarks, Assumed Name

Secretary of State, Reports & Information Division, www.maine.gov/sos/cec/corp/ A free search of basic information about the entity including address, corporate ID, agent, and status is found at https://icrs.informe.org/nei-sos-icrs/ICRS. A commercial subscriber account also gives extensive information and ability to download files. Also, search securities Division Enforcement Actions and Consent Agreements free at www.maine.gov/pfr/securities/enforcement.shtml. **$$$** *Other Options:* Bulk data purchase is available, a list of available databases for sale if found at the web. Monthly lists of new entities filed with this office are also available. Call 207-624-7752 or view www.maine.gov/sos/cec/corp/miscellaneous.html.

Uniform Commercial Code, Federal & State Tax Liens

Secretary of State, UCC Records Section, www.maine.gov/sos/cec/ucc/index.html There is a free search of the index to search only the debtor name or name variations at www.maine.gov/sos/cec/ucconline/index.htm. For search and purchase of official UCC documents and fees visit https://www10.informe.org/ucc/search/begin.shtml. Four different searches are offered. If no record found, the fee is still incurred. Records lag one week, meaning records will appear one week after filing. **$$$** *Other Options:* UCC Bulk Database: $1,200 for all; $1,500 for–images; $600 monthly download; $300 weekly download; $500 weekly images.

Sales Tax Registrations

Maine Revenue Services, Sales, Fuel & Special Tax Division, www.maine.gov/revenue/ Maine Revenue Service provides an online Sales and Service Provider Tax Lookup Program. This program can be used to determine whether a customer's Resale Certificate or Sales Tax Exemption Certificate is currently valid. See https://portal.maine.gov/certlookup/.

Birth Certificates

Department of Health and Human Services, Office of Vital Records, www.maine.gov/dhhs/mecdc/public-health-systems/data-research/vital-records/index.shtml Records may be ordered online via www.vitalchek.com, a designated vendor. **$$$** *Other Options:* Physical birth lists are available for purchase, excluding restricted information.

Death Records

Department of Health and Human Services, Office of Vital Records, www.maine.gov/dhhs/mecdc/public-health-systems/data-research/vital-records/index.shtml Search death records for 1960 thru 12/31/2009 at https://portal.maine.gov/death/archdev.death_archive.search_form. Also, a free genealogy site at http://vitals.rootsweb.ancestry.com/me/death/search.cgi has Death Indexes from 1960-1997. Search by surname, given name, place or year. *Other Options:* Bulk file purchases are available, with the exclusion of restricted data.

Marriage Certificates

Department of Health and Human Services, Office of Vital Records, www.maine.gov/dhhs/mecdc/public-health-systems/data-research/vital-records/index.shtml Records are available from 1892 thru 2009 at https://portal.maine.gov/marriage/archdev.marriage_archive.search_form. *Other Options:* Bulk file purchasing is available, with restricted data excluded.

Workers' Compensation Records

Workers Compensation Board, www.maine.gov/wcb/ Not online - but requests are accepted by email - sandra.wade@maine.gov. Records may be returned by email upon request. **Y** *Other Options:* Computer data is available, but requests are screened for purpose.

Driver Records

BMV - Driver License Services, 101 Hospital Street, www.maine.gov/sos/bmv/ Access is through InforME via the Internet. There are two access systems. Casual requesters can obtain records that have personal information cloaked. There is a subscription service for approved requesters, records contain personal information. There is a subscription service for approved requesters, records contain personal information as records are released per DPPA. The fee for either system is $7.00 per request for a 3-year record and $12.00 for a 10-year record. There is a $95.00 annual fee for the subscription service. A myriad of other state government records are available. Visit www.informe.org/bmv/drc/ or call 207-621-2600. **$$$** *Other Options:* The state offers "Driver Cross Check" - a program for employers, to provide notification when activity occurs on a specific record.

Vehicle Ownership & Registration

Department of Motor Vehicles, Registration Section, www.maine.gov/sos/bmv/ Maine offers online access to title and registration records via InforME. Fee is $5.00 per record. Search title records by VIN or title number. Search registration records by name and DOB, or by plate number. Records are available as interactive online or FTP with a subscription account. There are many other services available with the subscription. There is a $75.00 annual fee. Contact InforME at info@informe.org or visit the web page. **$$$**

Accident Reports

Maine State Police, Traffic Division, https://www1.maine.gov/online/mcrs/ Records from 01/2003 forward may be ordered from www.informe.org/mcrs/ for $10.00 per record. If you do not have a subscription to InforME, then a credit card must be used. Resulting reports is either returned by mail, or emailed in a PDF format. Search by name, date of birth, crash location, crash date, or investigating agency (police department). These reports may include officer narratives. Records prior to 2003 must be ordered as a manual search. **$$$** *Other Options:* Subscribers may purchase monthly database updates or use the "Crash Tracker" notification program for no charge.

Campaign Finance, PACs, Lobbyists

Commission on Ethics & Election Practices, www.mainecampaignfinance.com/public/home.asp This site allows the public to view the campaign finance data for the State of Maine. There are several options for searching, viewing and printing campaign finance report information. Data available includes information on PACs and lobbyists. All searches and downloads are available from www.mainecampaignfinance.com/public/home.asp.

Occupational Licensing Boards

Accountant-CPA.. www.maine.gov/pfr/professionallicensing/professions.htm
Acupuncturist .... www.maine.gov/pfr/professionallicensing/professions.htm
Alcohol/Drug Abuse Counselor.................... www.maine.gov/pfr/professionallicensing/professions.htm
Alcoholic Beverage Distributor.................... www.maine.gov/dps/liqr/active_licenses.htm

Ambulatory Surgical Ctr	http://pfr.informe.org/ALMSOnline/
Architect	www.maine.gov/pfr/professionallicensing/professions.htm
Assisted Living Facility	https://gateway.maine.gov/dhhs-apps/rcare/
Athletic Trainer	www.maine.gov/pfr/professionallicensing/professions.htm
Attorney	www.mebaroverseers.org/dynamic/attorney_search.aspx
Auctioneer	www.maine.gov/pfr/professionallicensing/professions.htm
Barber	www.maine.gov/pfr/professionallicensing/professions.htm
Boiler	www.maine.gov/pfr/professionallicensing/professions.htm
Charitable Solicitation	www.maine.gov/pfr/professionallicensing/professions.htm
Child Care Resource/Day Care	www.childcarechoices.me/ccchoices/SearchForChildcare.aspx#noback
Chiropractor	www.maine.gov/pfr/professionallicensing/professions.htm
Cosmetologist	www.maine.gov/pfr/professionallicensing/professions.htm
Counselor	www.maine.gov/pfr/professionallicensing/professions.htm
Dental Hygienist/Radiographer	http://pfr.informe.org/ALMSOnline/
DentistDenturist	http://pfr.informe.org/ALMSOnline/
Dietitian	www.maine.gov/pfr/professionallicensing/professions.htm
Electrician	www.maine.gov/pfr/professionallicensing/professions.htm
Elevator/Tramway	www.maine.gov/pfr/professionallicensing/professions.htm
Employee Leasing Company	http://pfr.informe.org/ALMSOnline/
EMS Authorized Training Centers	www.maine.gov/ems/training_materials.html
Engineer/Intern	https://www.maine.gov/professionalengineers/database.shtml
Forester	www.maine.gov/pfr/professionallicensing/professions.htm
Funeral Service	www.maine.gov/pfr/professionallicensing/professions.htm
Geologist	www.maine.gov/pfr/professionallicensing/professions.htm
HMO	www.maine.gov/pfr/insurance/
Home Health Care Svc Agency	http://pfr.informe.org/ALMSOnline/
Hospice	http://pfr.informe.org/ALMSOnline/
Hospital	http://pfr.informe.org/ALMSOnline/
Insurance Adjuster	http://pfr.informe.org/ALMSOnline/
Interior Designer	www.maine.gov/pfr/professionallicensing/professions.htm
Intermediate Care Facility (Retarded)	http://pfr.informe.org/ALMSOnline/
Interpreter	www.maine.gov/pfr/professionallicensing/professions.htm
Investment Advisor/Representative	www.adviserinfo.sec.gov/(S(y3q5na452bz35455zy55yenk))/IAPD/Content/Search/iapd_Search.aspx
Landscape Architect	www.maine.gov/pfr/professionallicensing/professions.htm
Liquor License, On & Off Premise	www.maine.gov/dps/liqr/active_licenses.htm
Liquor Store/Wholesaler	www.maine.gov/dps/liqr/active_agency_liquor_stores.htm
Lobbyist	www.mainecampaignfinance.com/Public/entity_list.asp?TYPE=LCB
Lottery Retailer	www.mainelottery.com/players_info/where_to_buy.html
Manufactured Housing	www.maine.gov/pfr/professionallicensing/professions.htm
Massage Therapist	www.maine.gov/pfr/professionallicensing/professions.htm
Naturopathic Physician	www.maine.gov/pfr/professionallicensing/professions.htm
Notary Public	www5.informe.org/online/notary/search/
Nurse/Practical	http://pfr.informe.org/ALMSOnline/
Nursing Home	http://pfr.informe.org/ALMSOnline/
Nursing Home Administrator	www.maine.gov/pfr/professionallicensing/professions.htm
Occupational Therapist/Assistants	www.maine.gov/pfr/professionallicensing/professions.htm
Oil & Solid Fuel Professional/Company	www.maine.gov/pfr/professionallicensing/professions.htm
Optometrist	http://pfr.informe.org/ALMSOnline/
Osteopathic Physician Extender	www.docboard.org/me-osteo/df/index.htm
Osteopathic Physician/Physician Asst	www.docboard.org/me-osteo/df/index.htm
Osteopathic Resident/Intern	www.docboard.org/me-osteo/df/index.htm
Pharmacist	www.maine.gov/pfr/professionallicensing/professions.htm
Physical Therapist	www.maine.gov/pfr/professionallicensing/professions.htm
Physician/Medical Doctor/Assistant	www.docboard.org/me/licensure/dw_verification.html
Plumber	www.maine.gov/pfr/professionallicensing/professions.htm

Podiatrist	www.maine.gov/pfr/professionallicensing/professions.htm
Polygraph Examiner	www.maine.gov/dps/Polygraph%20Licenses/Licensed%20Polygraph%20OPERATORS%20Non-MCJA.doc
Preferred Provider Organization	www.maine.gov/pfr/insurance/
Propane/LP Gas Technician	www.maine.gov/pfr/professionallicensing/professions.htm
Psychologist	www.maine.gov/pfr/professionallicensing/professions.htm
Radiologic Technician	www.maine.gov/pfr/professionallicensing/professions.htm
Re-insurer, Approved	http://pfr.informe.org/ALMSOnline/
Real Estate Appraiser	www.maine.gov/pfr/professionallicensing/professions.htm
Real Estate Broker	www.maine.gov/pfr/professionallicensing/professions.htm
Renal Disease (End Stage) Facility	http://pfr.informe.org/ALMSOnline/
Respiratory Care Therapist	www.maine.gov/pfr/professionallicensing/professions.htm
RN/Advanced Practice/Professional	www.pfr.maine.gov/ALMSOnline/ALMSQuery
Securities Broker-Dealer/Agent	www.finra.org/Investors/ToolsCalculators/BrokerCheck/
Social Worker	www.maine.gov/pfr/professionallicensing/professions.htm
Soil Scientist	www.maine.gov/pfr/professionallicensing/professions.htm
Speech Pathologist/Audiologist	www.maine.gov/pfr/professionallicensing/professions.htm
Surplus Lines Company	http://pfr.informe.org/almsonline/almsquery
Utilization Review Entity	www.maine.gov/pfr/insurance/
Veterinarian/Veterinary Technician	www.maine.gov/pfr/professionallicensing/professions.htm

State and Local Courts

State Court Structure: A **Superior Court** – the court of general jurisdiction – is located in each of Maine's sixteen counties, except for Aroostook County which has two Superior Courts. Both Superior and District Courts handle misdemeanor and felony cases, with jury trials being held in Superior Court only. The District Court hears both civil and criminal and always sits without a jury.

The **District Court** hears both civil and criminal and always sits without a jury. Within the District Court is the Family Division, which hears all divorce and family matters, including child support and paternity cases. The District Court also hears child protection cases, and serves as Maine's juvenile court. Actions for protection from abuse or harassment, mental health, small claims cases, and money judgments are filed in the District Court. Traffic violations are processed primarily through a centralized Violations Bureau, part of the District Court system. Prior to year 2001, District Courts accepted civil cases involving claims less than $30,000. Now, District Courts have jurisdiction concurrent with that of the Superior Court for all civil actions, except cases vested in the Superior Court by statute.

Probate Courts are part of the county's court system, not the state system. Although the Probate Court may be housed with other state courts, the court is generally on a different phone system and calls may not be transferred.

Appellate Courts: The website www.courts.state.me.us offers access to Maine Supreme Court opinions and administrative orders, but not all documents are available online.

Statewide Court Online Access: The state court system does not offer online access to trial court records. Some county level courts are online through a private vendor.

Search probate records free at https://www.maineprobate.net/index.html. Images are $2.00 each if not registered; $1.00 each if you subscribe.

Note: No individual Maine courts offer online access, other than to probate records as described above.

Recorders, Assessors, and Other Sites of Note

Recording Office Organization: 16 counties, 18 recording offices. The recording officer is the County Register of Deeds. Counties maintain a general index of all transactions recorded. Aroostook and Oxford Counties each have 2 recording offices. There are no county assessors; each town and city has its own.

Statewide or Multi-Jurisdiction Access: There is no statewide system, however a number of counties offer access. Some counties outsource via vendors.

- MaineLandRecords.com provides real property official records free at some counties, for at fee at others, at https://www.mainelandrecords.com/. Commercial/Monthly subscriptions available for full data, also a $3.00 per doc pay-per access for members, or a free index search. Participating county jurisdictions are: Cumberland, Knox, Oxford East, Oxford West, Piscataquis, Somerset, Waldo, and Washington.
- A vendor provides assessor property records, usually free, at www.vgsi.com/vision/Applications/ParcelData/ME/Home.aspx. A list of the participating cities and towns is found at the web page. Note this URL will give you the main site to VISION Government Solutions and then you must click on each individual town for the data. The ensuing URL begins with data.visionappraisal.com for each town. These are the sites listed below.

County Sites:

Androscoggin County ***Real Estate, Deed, Lien, All Documents Records*** http://androscoggindeeds.com Access the Registry index by subscription for a $350.00 annual fee. Indexes go back to 1854. For info and sign-up, contact Registry of Deeds at 207-753-2500. Search for free at http://androscoggindeeds.com/ALIS/WW400R.PGM. Index goes back to 1854; images to 1900 but images cannot be printed. **$$$**

Property, Taxation City of Auburn tax assessor data is free at http://avgis.org/auburnparcelmapping/auburnparcelmapper-p.htm. Also, property assessment data free at http://auburnme.patriotproperties.com/default.asp.

Aroostook County (Northern District) ***Real Estate, Deed, Lien, Judgment Records*** www.aroostook.me.us/index.php?option=com_content&view=article&id=60&Itemid=216 Remote access via a commercial online system has been replaced by a subscription internet-based system. Data on the internet system includes deeds, mortgages, liens, judgment, and land recording generally. Records go back to 1969. Subscription fee is $100 for North District, $100 for South. For more info and signup, see www.aroostookdeedsnorth.com/ then click on Access Information button on left side of page. **$$$**

Aroostook County (Southern District) ***Recorded Documents*** www.aroostook.me.us/departments/deeds.html Remote access via a commercial online system has been replaced by a subscription internet-based system. Data on the internet system includes deeds, mortgages, liens, judgment, and land recording generally. Records go back to 1985. Subscription fee is $100 for South and North Districts. For more info and signup, see www.aroostookdeedssouth.com/ (south) or www.aroostookdeedsnorth.com/ (north) then click on Access Information button on left side of page. **$$$**

Property, Taxation Access to GIS/mapping for free at http://webmap.jws.com/taxmap/viewer.aspx?JWSCONFIG=ME_Houlton.

Cumberland County ***Recorded Documents*** www.cumberlandcounty.org/Deeds/ Searching and viewing for free at https://me.uslandrecords.com/ME/Cumberland/default.aspx?AspxAutoDetectCookieSupport=1. For commercial users the charge is $.50 per page to copy and a $50.00 per month subscription fee. Plans may be printed/downloaded for $.50 per copy. Any other copies are available for $5.00 each by calling the Registry at 207-871-8389 x3. **$$$**

Property, Taxation Access to Cumberland online database for free at http://data.visionappraisal.com/CumberlandME/DEFAULT.asp. Also, access to property tax and personal property info for the Town of Falmouth, ME free at https://falmouthme.munisselfservice.com/citizens/default.aspx. For Cape Elizabeth go to www.capeelizabeth.com/services/land_use/maps/assessors_maps/home.shtml.

Franklin County ***Real Estate, Deed, Lien, Judgment, UCC Records*** www.franklincountydeedsme.com Access to recorders data index is free at www.franklincountydeedsme.com/. Land index goes back to 1984; images go back to part of 1985 (in process). For full access and to print documents, registration and fees are required. **$$$**

Hancock County ***Recorded Documents*** www.hancockcountydeeds.com/ Access to the county registry of deeds database at www.registryofdeeds.com/. Fee is $.50 per page is required to view full-size, printable pages. For info see website, www.hancockcountydeeds.com/. Also, City of Ellsworth real estate data look-up is free at www.mygovnow.com/ellsci/Invision/assessing/index.htm. Look-up by name or plot. Also, another free search appears at www.hancockcountymaineregistryofdeeds.com/public.htm. **$$$**

Property, Taxation Access to Mount Desert assessor's database for free at http://data.visionappraisal.com/MountDesertME/DEFAULT.asp. Also, access Ellsworth property data free at www.mygovnow.com/ellsci/Invision/assessing/index.htm or download from http://cityofellsworthme.org/files/reweb.txt.

Kennebec County ***Recorded Documents*** https://gov.propertyinfo.com/ME-kennebec/ Register free and search recorder index free at https://gov.propertyinfo.com/ME-kennebec/. Fee for images by subscription or pay-per-view. **$$$**

Property, Taxation Access Winslow Town Property database free at http://data.visionappraisal.com/WinslowME/DEFAULT.asp. The Town of Waterville Assessor's data is free at http://data.visionappraisal.com/WatervilleME/. Also, search City of Augusta assessor database at http://data.visionappraisal.com/AugustaME/DEFAULT.asp. Rquires free registration for all three towns.

Knox County ***Recorded Documents*** www.knoxcountymaine.gov/index.asp?Type=B_BASIC&SEC={F52A773D-3C3C-4657-AB9C-D49F67E6D3F9} Search property records at https://i2a.uslandrecords.com/ME/Knox/. Indexes are available from 1966 to present. Document images are available from 1966 to present; fees for images are $.50 per page. Monthly subscribers will be charged $35.00 per month. **$$$**

Property, Taxation Search Camden, Rockland, Rockport, and South Thomaston town assessors data at www.visionappraisal.com/databases/maine/index.htm.

Lincoln County ***Recorded Documents*** https://www.lincolncomeregofdeeds.com/ Search Register of Deeds indices and images back to 1954 for free at https://www.lincolncomeregofdeeds.com/. Must register to use.

Property, Taxation Search Town of Boothbay property data free at http://data.visionappraisal.com/BoothbayME/DEFAULT.asp.

Oxford County East ***Recorded Documents*** www.oxfordcounty.org/deeds-east.php Search recording records for the Eastern portion of the county for free at https://i2a.uslandrecords.com/ME/OxfordEast/. $.50 per page. Monthly subscribers will be charged $50.00 per month subscription fee. **$$$**

Oxford County West ***Recorded Documents*** www.oxfordcounty.org/deeds-west.php Recording records for the Western portion of the county for free are available, see https://i2a.uslandrecords.com/ME/OxfordWest/. Images are available back to 4/85. Monthly subscribers will be charged $50.00 per month subscription fee. **$$$**

Penobscot County ***Real Estate, Deed Records*** https://penobscotdeeds.com/ Search the Register of Deeds index back to 1967 and images back to 1967 for free at https://penobscotdeeds.com/. A fee is charged for copies. **$$$**

Property, Taxation Search the City of Old Town real estate database for free at www.old-town.me.us/assessor/rev.asp.

Piscataquis County ***Recorded Documents*** www.piscataquis.us/Pages/deeds.html Search free on Register of Deeds site at https://i2a.uslandrecords.com/ME/Piscataquis/. Printing or downloading fees for commercial users-$.50 per page; monthly subscribers will be charged $50.00 per month subscription fee. **$$$**

Sagadahoc County ***Recorded Documents*** http://sagcounty.com/sag_deeds.html Register of Deeds records are online for a $300.00 per year fee ($35.00 monthly; $85.00 quarter) plus $.50 per page to copy. Records go back to 1962 on Grantor/Grantee index. Images go back to 1965. For info and registration, go to www.sagadahocdeedsme.com/ or call the Register of Deeds. **$$$**

Property, Taxation Search records on the City of Bath Assessor database free at http://assessdb.cityofbath.com/parcel.list.php. Search Topsham assessor property records free at http://data.visionappraisal.com/TopshamME/DEFAULT.asp.

Somerset County ***Recorded Documents*** www.somersetcounty-me.org/ Access real estate records free at https://i2a.uslandrecords.com/ME/Somerset/. Registration required for all users. Records goes back to 1956. $.50 per page or can subscribe and pay monthly fee of $35.00 plus $.50 per page. **$$$**

Waldo County ***Recorded Documents*** www.waldocountyme.gov/rod/index.html Access real estate records by subscription at https://i2a.uslandrecords.com/ME/Waldo/. Index back to 1981, images back to 1800's. $.50 fee per page. **$$$**

Washington County ***Recorded Documents*** www.washingtoncountymaine.com/ Access to land deed's records go to https://i2a.uslandrecords.com/ME/Washington/. Searching and document viewing is free, printing and/or downloading will incur charges. Index and images from 1972 to present; survey plan index and images from 1994 to present. **$$$**

York County ***Real Estate, Deed, Mortgage, Assignment, Discharges, Foreclosure Records*** https://gov.propertyinfo.com/ME-York/ Search Register of Deeds records at https://gov.propertyinfo.com/ME-York/. Register then search basic index free; purchase copies of documents for $.50 per page that you print out on your own printers. Credit card purchases only. Search parameters are the same online as they are in the registry office. Online research only goes back to January, 1966 thru the present. **$$$**

Property, Taxation Access to Berwick, Cornish, Eliot, Kennebunkport, Kittery, Ogunquit, Saco, Wells, and York Town assessors data is free at http://data.visionappraisal.com/YorkME/DEFAULT.asp.

Maryland

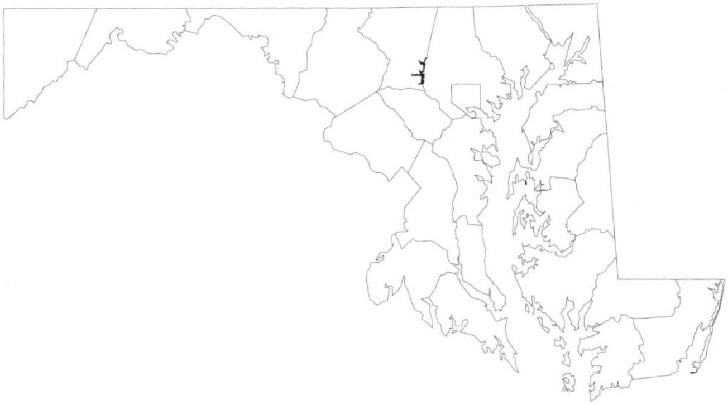

Capital: Annapolis
Anne Arundel County
Time Zone: EST
Population: 5,884,563,344
# of Counties: 23

Useful State Links

Website: www.maryland.gov
Governor: www.gov.state.md.us
Attorney General: www.oag.state.md.us
State Archives: http://msa.maryland.gov/
State Statutes and Codes: http://mgaleg.maryland.gov
Legislative Bill Search: h http://mgaleg.maryland.gov
Unclaimed Funds: https://interactive.marylandtaxes.com/Individuals/Unclaim/default.aspx

State Public Record Agencies

Sexual Offender Registry

Criminal Justice Information System, PO Box 32708, www.socem.info/ Online access is free at www.socem.info/. Search by name or ZIP Code. An interactive map is also available. *Other Options:* A printout is available of partial or complete SOR. Request must be in writing,

Incarceration Records

DPS and Correctional Services, Maryland Division of Corrections, www.dpscs.state.md.us Search inmates online at www.dpscs.state.md.us/onlineservs/oil/. The Locator may not list some short sentenced inmates who, although committed to the Commissioner of Correction, are in fact housed at Division of Pretrial and Detention Services facilities.

Corporation, LP, LLP, LLC, Fictitious Name, Trade Name

Department of Assessments and Taxation, Charter Corporate Division, www.dat.state.md.us Search for corporate name and trade name records for free at the main website (see above); also includes real estate statewide (cannot search by name) and UCC records. A Certificate of Good Standing is available online at https://sdatcert1.resiusa.org/certificate_net/ for the $40.00 fee. Certificates of Status are not available for trade names, name reservations, and sole proprietorships. **$$$** *Other Options:* This agency will release information in a bulk output format through a contactor. Obtain prices, formats, production schedules, etc. from Specprint, Inc. Contact Mr. Joe Jenkins of Specprint, Inc. at 410- 561-9600.

Trademarks/Servicemarks

Secretary of State, Trademarks Division, www.marylandsos.gov/Registrations/Trademarks/Trademarks.aspx Online searching is available atwww.marylandsos.gov/Registrations/Trademarks/TMSearch.aspx. Search can be by keyword in the description field, the service or product, the owner, the classification, or the mark name or keyword in the mark name. The site also offers application forms to register, renew, or assign trade and service marks, and general info about registration. *Other Options:* A computer printout of all marks registered, renewed or assigned within a 3 month period is available for $.05 per trademark.

Uniform Commercial Code

UCC Division-Taxpayer's Services, Department of Assessments & Taxation, http://sdatcert3.resiusa.org/ucc-charter/ The Internet site above or http://sdatcert3.resiusa.org/ucc-charter/ offers free access to UCC index information. Also, there is a related site offering access to real property data for the whole state at www.dat.state.md.us/. *Other Options:* The agency has available for sale copies of public release master data files including corporation, real estate, and UCC. In addition, they can produce customized files on paper or disk. Visit the website for more information.

Sales Tax Registrations

Taxpayer Services, Revenue Administration Division, www.marylandtaxes.com/taxes.asp Using the web, one can determine if a MD sales tax account number is valid. See https://interactive.marylandtaxes.com/Business/VerifyExempt/User/Home.aspx.

Vital Records

Department of Health, Division of Vital Records, http://dhmh.maryland.gov/vsa/SitePages/Home.aspx Records may be ordered from a designated vendor at www.vitalchek.com. Use of credit card is required and additional $7.00 fee required. **$$$**

Workers' Compensation Records

Workers' Compensation Commission, www.wcc.state.md.us Free access is provided and there is a more in-depth service available for a fee. The free Public Information is found at www.wcc.state.md.us/WFMS/public_inquiry.html. The free access is at Request for online hook-up must be in writing on letterhead. There is no search fee, but programming fees must be paid in advance. The system is open 24 hours a day to only in-state accounts. Write to the Commission at address above, care of Information Technology Division, or at 410-864-5170. **$$$** *Other Options:* This agency will sell its entire database depending on the use of the purchaser. Intended use must be validated and approved. Contact the commission for further information.

Driver Records

MVA, Driver Records Unit, Rm 145, www.mva.maryland.gov Effective May 1, 2012, the Maryland Motor Vehicle Administration began partnering with NICUSA regarding the access of driver and vehicle records previously accessed through MVA's subscription services (DARS, LMS, etc.). The fee is $12.00 per record for either interactive or batch access. There is a $95.00 subscription fee (which was waived for existing subscribers to DARS). For more information go to https://www.egov.maryland.gov/register/ or call 888-963-3468. **$$$** *Other Options:* Drivers may view their own record online at https://secure.marylandmva.com/emvaservices/VRR/DrRecord_Entry.asp?sku=drrecord after obtaining a PIN. Also, a License Monitoring System (LMS) is available to employers, call 888-963-3468.

Vehicle Ownership & Registration

Motor Vehicle Administration, Data Management, www.mva.maryland.gov/ Effective May 1, 2012, the Maryland Motor Vehicle Administration began partnering with NICUSA regarding the access of vehicle records previously accessed through MVA's subscription services (DARS, LMS, etc.). The fee is $12.00 per record for either interactive or batch access. There is a $95.00 subscription fee (which was waived for existing subscribers to DARS). For more information go to https://www.egov.maryland.gov/register/ or call 888-963-3468. **$$$**

Voter Registration, Campaign Finance, PACs

State Board of Elections, www.elections.state.md.us Search the campaign finance database and disclosure of expenditures and contributions at www.elections.state.md.us/campaign_finance/index.html. Search PAC data at https://campaignfinancemd.us/Public/ViewCommittees. Note that lobbyists are managed by a different agency - see http://ethics.gov.state.md.us/listing.htm.

Occupational Licensing Boards

Accountant-CPA............ www.dllr.state.md.us/pq/
Acupuncturist............ https://mdbnc.dhmh.md.gov/ACUPTVerification/default.aspx
Architect............ https://www.dllr.state.md.us/cgi-bin/ElectronicLicensing/OP_search/OP_search.cgi?calling_app=AR::AR_qselect
Architectural Partnership/Corp............ www.dllr.state.md.us/pq/
Attorney............ www.courts.state.md.us/cpf/attylist.html
Audiologist............ https://mdbnc.dhmh.md.gov/AUDVerification/Default.aspx
Barber............ https://www.dllr.state.md.us/cgi-bin/ElectronicLicensing/OP_search/OP_search.cgi?calling_app=BAR::BAR_qselect
Business, Any Licensed............ www.kellysolutions.com/md/Business/index.htm
Carrier Vehicle............ http://webapp.psc.state.md.us/intranet/transport/GetCarrier_new.cfm
Charity............ www.sos.state.md.us/Charity/SearchCharity.aspx
Chiropractor/Chiropractic Assist............ https://mdbnc.dhmh.md.gov/chiroverification/default.aspx
Condominium/Timeshare............ www.sos.state.md.us/OrganizRegistration.aspx
Contractor............ https://www.dllr.state.md.us/cgi-bin/ElectronicLicensing/OP_search/OP_search.cgi?calling_app=HIC::HIC_qselect
Cosmetologist............ https://www.dllr.state.md.us/cgi-bin/ElectronicLicensing/verR5/ver1.cgi?unit=22
Day Care Provider............ www.checkccmd.org/
Dietitian/Nutritionist............ https://mdbnc.dhmh.md.gov/dietVerification/Default.aspx
Driver For Hire............ http://webapp.psc.state.md.us/Intranet/Transport/ForHireDriver_new.cfm
Election............ www.elections.state.md.us/
Electrician, Master............ www.dllr.state.md.us/pq/
Electrologist............ http://167.102.241.39/verification/Search.aspx
Engineer, Examining............ www.dllr.state.md.us/pq/

Engineer, Professional .... www.dllr.state.md.us/pq/
Esthetician... https://www.dllr.state.md.us/cgi-bin/ElectronicLicensing/verR5/ver1.cgi?unit=22
Extradition/Requisition .... www.sos.state.md.us/Services/Extradit.aspx
For Hire Carrier Suspended .... http://webapp.psc.state.md.us/Intranet/Transport/ForHireSuspendedCarriers_new.cfm
Forester... www.dllr.state.md.us/pq/
Fund Raising Counsel................................. www.sos.state.md.us/Charity/SearchCharity.aspx
Funeral Director/Establishment.................... https://mdbnc.dhmh.md.gov/mortverification/default.aspx
Gem Dealer... www.dllr.state.md.us/pq/
Hearing Aid Dispenser .... https://mdbnc.dhmh.md.gov/AUDVerification/Default.aspx
Home Improvement Contractor.................... www.dllr.state.md.us/pq/
Home Improvement Salesperson .....https://www.dllr.state.md.us/cgi-bin/ElectronicLicensing/OP_search/OP_search.cgi?calling_app=HIC::HIC_qselect
Home Inspector... www.dllr.state.md.us/pq/
Horse Stable, 5 or more www.marylandhorseindustry.org/Stables10.htm
HVACR Contractor....................................... www.dllr.state.md.us/pq/
Insurance Agent .... https://sbs-md.naic.org/Lion-Web/jsp/sbsreports/AgentLookup.jsp
Interior Designer.. www.dllr.state.md.us/pq/
Landscape Architect/Land Surveyor .... www.dllr.state.md.us/pq/
Lobbyist/Employer....................................... http://ethics.gov.state.md.us/listing.htm
Manicurist/Nail Technician .... https://www.dllr.state.md.us/cgi-bin/ElectronicLicensing/verR5/ver1.cgi?unit=22
Massage Therapist....................................... https://mdbnc.dhmh.md.gov/chiroverification/default.aspx
Mortician/Embalmer .... https://mdbnc.dhmh.md.gov/mortverification/default.aspx
Notary Public... www.sos.state.md.us/Notary/NotarySearch.aspx
Nurse-RN/LPN/Aide http://167.102.241.39/verification/Search.aspx
Nursery, Plant .... www.mda.state.md.us/plants-pests/plant_protection_weed_mgmt/nurseries_plant_dealers/
Nursing Home Administrator........................ https://mdbnc.dhmh.md.gov/NHAVerification/Default.aspx
Nursing Occupation..................................... http://167.102.241.39/verification/Search.aspx
Occupational Therapist/Assistant .... https://maryland.mylicense.com/mdbotverif/
Optometrist... https://mdbnc.dhmh.md.gov/optverification/default.aspx
Pardon/Commutation .... www.sos.state.md.us/Services/Pardons.aspx
Pawnbroker .... www.dllr.state.md.us/pq/
Pesticide Applicator/Operator/Consultant.... www.mda.state.md.us/plants-pests/Pages/pesticide_db.aspx
Pesticide Business/Dealer .... www.mda.state.md.us/plants-pests/Pages/pesticide_db.aspx
Pharmacist/Establishments......................... http://dhmh.maryland.gov/pharmacy/SitePages/verifications.aspx
Physical Therapist/Assistant .... https://mdbnc.dhmh.md.gov/bptverification/default.aspx
Physician/Medical Doctor............................ https://www.mbp.state.md.us/bpqapp/
Plant Broker/Dealer..................................... www.mda.state.md.us/plants-pests/plant_protection_weed_mgmt/nurseries_plant_dealers/
Plumber... www.dllr.state.md.us/pq/
Podiatrist .... https://encrypt.emdhealthchoice.org/searchable/main.action
Polygraph Examiner/School/Sales.............. www.mdpolygraph.org/info.htm
Precious Metal & Gem Dealer .... www.dllr.state.md.us/pq/
Psychologist.. https://mdbnc.dhmh.md.gov/psychVerification/Default.aspx
Real Estate Agent/Broker https://www.dllr.state.md.us/cgi-bin/ElectronicLicensing/RE/certification/RECertification1.cgi
Real Estate Appraiser .... www.dllr.state.md.us/pq/
Social Worker.. https://mdbnc.dhmh.md.gov/bsweverification/default.aspx
Special Police/Railroad Police .... www.sos.state.md.us/Services/Police.aspx
Speech & Language Pathologists................ https://mdbnc.dhmh.md.gov/AUDVerification/Default.aspx
Subcontractor..................................https://www.dllr.state.md.us/cgi-bin/ElectronicLicensing/OP_search/OP_search.cgi?calling_app=HIC::HIC_qselect
Taxicab.. http://webapp.psc.state.md.us/Intranet/Transport/TaxicabDriver_new.cfm
Transportation Permit Holder .... http://webapp.psc.state.md.us/Intranet/Transport/GetPermitList_new.cfm

State and Local Courts

State Court Structure: **Circuit Courts** generally handle the State's major civil cases and more serious criminal matters, along with juvenile cases, family matters such as divorce, and most appeals from the District Court, orphans' courts and administrative agencies. The Circuit Courts also can hear cases from the District Court (civil or criminal) in which one of the parties has requested a jury trial, under certain circumstances.

The **District Court** hears both civil and criminal cases involving claims up to $30,000, and has exclusive jurisdiction over peace order cases and landlord/tenant, replevin (recovery of goods claimed to be wrongfully taken or detained), and other civil cases involving amounts at or less than $5,000. The District Court also handles motor vehicle/boating violations and other misdemeanors and limited felonies, although the circuit courts share jurisdiction if the penalties authorized are three years or more in prison, a fine of $2,500 or more, or both. Both trial courts can hear domestic violence cases.

Orphans' Courts handle wills, estates, and other probate matters. In addition, they have jurisdiction—along with the circuit courts—to appoint guardians of the person, and to protect the estates of un-emancipated minors (minors who remain under parental authority).

The Circuit Court handles **probate** in only Montgomery and Harford counties. In other counties, probate is handled by the **Orphan's Court**. The clerk is called the **Register of Wills** and is a county, not a court, function.

Note there is a Baltimore County and the City of Baltimore; each has its own courts.

Appellate Courts: The Maryland Court of Appeals is the highest court in the state (commonly called the Supreme Court in other states). The Court of Special Appeals is Maryland's intermediate appellate court and generally considers any reviewable judgment, decree, order, or other action of the circuit and orphans' courts. The web page www.mdcourts.gov gives access to opinions.

Statewide Court Online Access: All courts participate in the systems described below.

- See http://casesearch.courts.state.md.us/inquiry/inquiry-index.jsp for a free search of dockets of the trial courts, including civil, traffic and criminal. A search of civil or criminal includes all District and Circuit courts in the state - but a search of liens and judgments do not include District Courts and Circuit Court for Prince George's County.
    - Note the DOB is shown on some but not all dockets. Records are updated daily, but case information from Montgomery and Prince George's counties usually lag one additional day. All case information may be searched by party name or case number. The amount of historical information may vary by county based on when an automated case management system was deployed in that county and how the system has evolved. There is a disclaimer: "This site reflects the electronic record of the cases presented and may not always reflect the information maintained within the official case file. The data may not be reliable in the sense that further action may occur in the case that would affect the record."
- Bulk subscription data of civil record information from the District Courts can be requested for an annual and monthly fee - see www.courts.state.md.us/district/forms/acct/dca107.pdf. Reportedly, plans are underway for subscribing parties to access statewide Case Search bulk data and data extracts through a standards-based interface in XML format. Also, there is an Attorney Calendar Service that displays information related to an attorney's trial and hearing schedule such as case number, attorney name, trial or hearing date, defendant name, time, room, etc.
- A free statewide or single county docket search of the database of Register of Wills records is offered at http://jportal.mdcourts.gov/willsandtrusts/index.jsf. One may search by Decedent, Guardian, Interested Party, Minor, or Personal Representative. Records from the Register of Wills of all counties go back to at least 1998.

Counties with Sites Not Mentioned Above:

Montgomery County

Circuit Court www.montgomerycountymd.gov/ciatmpl.asp?url=/content/circuitcourt/index.asp
The daily calendar is free at www.montgomerycountymd.gov/mc/judicial/circuit/docket.html.

Recorders, Assessors, and Other Sites of Note

Recording Office Organization: 23 counties and one independent city; 24 recording offices. **The recording officer is the Clerk of the Circuit Court.** Baltimore City has a recording office separate from the County of Baltimore. All tax liens are filed with the county Clerk of Circuit Court.

Statewide or Multi-Jurisdiction Access: There are number of web pages that provide recorded land instruments and/or real property tax and assessor record data for all Maryland counties. Several are government sites, several are vendors. These sites are shown below and are followed by the handful of unique county sites.

- The State Dept. of Planning offers MDPropertyview with property maps/parcels and assessments via the web or by CD-ROM.Visit http://planning.maryland.gov/OurProducts/PropertyMapProducts/FinderOnlineProduct.shtml. Registration required, there is no name searching.
- See an experimental Digital Image Retrieval System for Land Record Indices at www.mdlandrec.net. The Maryland Judiciary, the 24 elected Maryland Court Clerks, and Maryland State Archives joined in partnership to provide this up-to-date access to all verified land record instruments in Maryland. This service is currently being provided free to all those interested in testing the system.
- Search property records data free at http://sdatcert3.resiusa.org/rp_rewrite/. There is no name searching. Search by county, all counies included.
- Search property tax records at www.taxrecords.com.
- The State Archives has a very usual web service site. Land survey, condominium, and survey plats are available free by county at http://msa.maryland.gov/megafile/msa/stagser/s1500/s1529/html/0000.html.

Counties with Sites Not Mentioned Above:

Baltimore City ***Property, Taxation Records*** Search tax assessments at http://sdatcert3.resiusa.org/rp_rewrite/. No name searching. Search state held archival property records at http://msa.maryland.gov/megafile/msa/stagser/s1500/s1529/html/0000.html. Search property tax and ownership at http://cityservices.baltimorecity.gov/realproperty/default.aspx.

Caroline County ***Property, Taxation Records*** Access to property tax free at www.carolinemd.org/governmt/taxoffice/tax_db/ptax_search.html.

Charles County ***Property, Taxation Records*** Access to property tax data is free at http://www.charlescountymd.gov/fas/treasury/treasury.

Montgomery County ***Property, Taxation Records*** Access to the assessor's property tax account database is free at https://www6.montgomerycountymd.gov/apps/tax/index.asp.

Prince George's County ***Property, Taxation Records*** Search the Treasurer's property tax inquiry system at http://taxinquiry.princegeorgescountymd.gov/.

Massachusetts

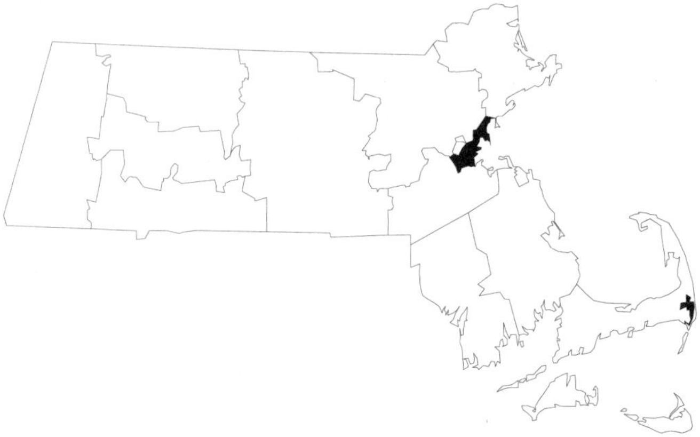

Capital: Boston
Suffolk County
Time Zone: EST
Population: 6,646,144
# of Counties: 14

Useful State Links

Website: www.mass.gov/portal
Governor: www.mass.gov/governor
Attorney General: www.mass.gov/ago
State Archives: www.sec.state.ma.us/arc/
State Statutes and Codes: www.malegislature.gov/Laws/GeneralLaw
Legislative Bill Search: www.malegislature.gov
Unclaimed Funds: http://abpweb.tre.state.ma.us/abp/frmNewSrch.aspx

State Public Record Agencies

Criminal Records

MA Dept of Criminal Justice, Information Services, www.mass.gov/eopss/agencies/dcjis/ The online system known as iCORI provides access to criminal offender record information. All accounts must be approved and registered. The data provided is entered and maintained by the Office of the Commissioner of Probation and is not supported by any type of biometric identifier, including fingerprints. This system requires use of a credit card. Note the agency recently stopped taking business checks. The Open Access record is $50.00, Personal is $25.00; Standard Request is $25.00. **$$$**

Sexual Offender Registry

Sex Offender Registry Board, www.mass.gov/eopss/agencies/sorb/ Search free from home page link for Level 3 sex offenders. To obtain a list of offenders in a geographical area (County, City or Postal code) enter information in that field only. You may also obtain a list of Level3 offenders who are not in compliance.

Incarceration Records

MA Executive Office of Public Safety& Security, Department of Corrections, www.mass.gov/eopss/agencies/doc/ No online search for inmates is offered by this agency; however the agency promotes a private company with free web access to DOC offenders at https://www.vinelink.com/vinelink/siteInfoAction.do?siteId=20000. DOC most wanted is at www.mass.gov/eopss/law-enforce-and-cj/prisons/doc-most-wanted/

Corporation, LLP, LP, LLC, Trademarks/Servicemarks,

Secretary of the Commonwealth, Corporation Division, www.sec.state.ma.us/cor/coridx.htm There are a number of free searches form the home page including: trademark, corporate database, corporate rejected filings, UCCs, and liens. *Other Options:* Bulk sale on CD is available.

Uniform Commercial Code

UCC Division, Secretary of the Commonwealth, www.sec.state.ma.us/cor/corpweb/corucc/uccmain.htm There is free access to record index from http://corp.sec.state.ma.us/uccfiling/uccSearch/Default.aspx. Search by name, organization or file number. *Other Options:* CDs may be purchased.

Sales Tax Registrations

Revenue Department - Customer Srv. Bureau, Sales Tax Registrations, www.mass.gov/dor/ Verify a Sales Tax Resale Certificate at https://wfb.dor.state.ma.us/webfile/business/Public/WebForms/STR/VerifyCertificate.aspx.

Vital Certificates

Registry of Vital Records and Statistics, www.mass.gov/eohhs/gov/departments/dph/programs/health-stats/vitals/ Orders can be placed via a state designated vendor. Go to www.vitalchek.com. Extra fees are involved. **$$$**

Workers' Compensation Records

Keeper of Records, Department of Industrial Accidents, www.mass.gov/lwd/workers-compensation/ Outside parties legally entitled to access may view database. There is an online insurance inquiry as well for account holders. The links are very lengthy, use the home page above. Email questions to Info2@massmail.state.ma.us.

Driver Records-Registry

Registry of Motor Vehicles, Court Records Department, www.massrmv.com/ High volume accounts, approved accounts may purchase record for $8.00 per record.The driver license number is needed for input. Records are generally available in batch mode (afternoon requests ready early the next morning) or within minutes interactive. Call the above number for further details. Also the public may order an unattested record in PDF format for $8.00, or order an attested (certified) record to be mailed for $20.00. The record is only mailed to the address shown on the license-holder's DL. Use of a credit card is required. One may view or order a record on another as long as complete information is disclosed about the requesters. See https://secure.rmv.state.ma.us/DrvRecords/intro.aspx A free License/Permit and ID Inquiry is at https://secure.rmv.state.ma.us/LicInquiry/intro.aspx. No personal information is displayed. **$$$** *Other Options:* The RMV offers a Driver Verification System (DVS). DVS is a web based application that allows companies, cities, towns, state agencies and authorities to track the license statuses of their employees. Email dvs@state.ma.us or call 617-351-9521.

Driver Records-Insurance

Merit Rating Board, Attn: Detailed Driving History Records, www.massrmv.com/MeritRatingBoard.aspx An online service is available to authorized insurance companies and agents to view driving records maintained by the MRB. This service is available through the RMV Uninsured Motorist System (www.mass.gov/rmv/ums). The information is used to adjust automobile insurance rates. Per statute, this method is not available to the general public. **$$$**

Vehicle Ownership & Registration

Registry of Motor Vehicles, Document Control, www.massrmv.com/ The Title/Lien Inquiry Transaction is for vehicle owners and lienholders to track a title, to verify lienholder accuracy, or to ensure a title has been sent to the appropriate party. Visit https://secure.rmv.state.ma.us/TitleLookup/intro.aspx. The Registration Inquiry Transaction works in a similar manner. Requesters must have the vehicle's registration plate type and registration number as printed on the vehicle registration card. Visit https://secure.rmv.state.ma.us/RegInquiry/intro.aspx. Both systems display no personal information. $$$ *Other Options:* Bulk retrieval media is available for permitted commercial vendors, exclusive of bulk marketing and solicitation purposes which is not permitted.

Campaign Finance, Donations, Expenditures, PACs

Office of Campaign & Political Finance, One Ashburton Place, http://ocpf.cloudapp.net/ Search for and find reports for campaign finance, donations, expenditures, and PACs from links at http://ocpf.cloudapp.net/.

Occupational Licensing Boards

Accountant-CPA.. http://license.reg.state.ma.us/pubLic/licque.asp?query=license&color=red&board=PA
Adjuster, Fire Loss .... http://agentfinder.doi.state.ma.us/Home.aspx?AspxAutoDetectCookieSupport=1
Adoption Center .... www.eec.state.ma.us/ChildCareSearch/AdoptFoster.aspx
Aesthetician.. http://license.reg.state.ma.us/pubLic/licque.asp?query=license&color=red&board=HD
Alarm Installer/Burglar/Fire .... http://license.reg.state.ma.us/pubLic/licque.asp?query=license&color=red&board=EL
Alcoholism/Drug Facility/Program .... http://db.state.ma.us/dph/bsas/search.asp
Ambulance Service .... http://db.state.ma.us/dph/amb/amb_search.asp
Amusement Device Inspector .... http://elicense.chs.state.ma.us/Verification/Search.aspx
Appraiser, MVR Damage .... http://agentfinder.doi.state.ma.us/Home.aspx?AspxAutoDetectCookieSupport=1
Architect .... http://license.reg.state.ma.us/public/licque.asp?color=red&Board=AR
Asbestos Training Providers .... www.mass.gov/lwd/labor-standards/asbestos-program/license-lists/
Asbestos/Lead Abatement Vocation .... www.mass.gov/lwd/labor-standards/asbestos-program/license-lists/
Athletic Trainer .... http://license.reg.state.ma.us/pubLic/licque.asp?query=license&color=red&board=AH
Attorney .... http://massbbo.org/bbolookup.php
Audiologist.. http://license.reg.state.ma.us/pubLic/licque.asp?query=license&color=red&board=SP
Automobile Repair Shop .... www.aib.org/ContentPages/Public/RepairGlass.aspx
Automobile Sales Financer .... www.mass.gov/Eoca/docs/dob/mvlist.xls
Bank & Savings Institution .... http://license.dob.state.ma.us/licenseelist.asp
Bank, Cooperative....................................... http://license.dob.state.ma.us/licenseelist.asp

Barber/Barber Shop .... http://license.reg.state.ma.us/public/licque.asp?color=red&Board=BR
Brokerage Firm .... www.finra.org/Investors/ToolsCalculators/BrokerCheck/index.htm
Bus/Motor Coach Driver.............................. www.env.state.ma.us/DPU_FileRoom/frmTransportationSP.aspx
Check Casher .... www.mass.gov/Eoca/docs/dob/cclist.xls
Check Casher/Seller .... http://license.dob.state.ma.us/licenseelist.asp
Chiropractor .... http://license.reg.state.ma.us/public/licque.asp?color=red&Board=CH
Collection Agency .... http://license.dob.state.ma.us/licenseelist.asp
Consumer Credit Grantor............................ http://license.dob.state.ma.us/licenseelist.asp
Cosmetologist/Manicurist/Aesthetician .... http://license.reg.state.ma.us/pubLic/licque.asp?query=license&color=red&board=HD
Credit Union .... http://license.dob.state.ma.us/licenseelist.asp
Debt Collector .... www.mass.gov/Eoca/docs/dob/dclist.xls
Electrician... http://license.reg.state.ma.us/public/licque.asp?color=red&Board=EL
Electrologist... http://license.reg.state.ma.us/public/licque.asp?color=red&Board=ET
Elevator Operator/Construction/Maintenance.....http://elicense.chs.state.ma.us/Verification/Search.aspx
Embalmer.. http://license.reg.state.ma.us/public/licque.asp?color=red&Board=EM
Emergency Medical Technician .... http://db.state.ma.us/dph/emtcert/cert_search.asp
Employment Agency, Placing/Temp .... www.mass.gov/lwd/docs/dos/ea/ea-licensed.pdf
EMS Training Institution..www.mass.gov/eohhs/gov/departments/dph/programs/hcq/oems/emt-training-inst/public-health-oems-training-institutions.html
Engineer.. http://license.reg.state.ma.us/pubLic/licque.asp?query=license&color=red&board=EN
Engineers/Fireman School.......................... http://elicense.chs.state.ma.us/Verification/Search.aspx
Family Child Care Provider .... www.eec.state.ma.us/ChildCareSearch/CCRR.aspx
Finfishing, Commercial .... www.mass.gov/dfwele/dmf/
Fire Sprinkler Contractor/Fitter.................... http://elicense.chs.state.ma.us/Verification/Search.aspx
Fireman, 1st/2nd Class/Engineer................ http://elicense.chs.state.ma.us/Verification/Search.aspx
Foreign Transmittal Agency .... http://license.dob.state.ma.us/licenseelist.asp
Foster Care Provider.................................. www.eec.state.ma.us/ChildCareSearch/AdoptFoster.aspx
Funeral Director .... http://license.reg.state.ma.us/public/licque.asp?color=red&Board=EM
Fur Buyer .... www.mass.gov/dfwele/dfw/
Gas Fitter .... http://license.reg.state.ma.us/pubLic/licque.asp?query=license&color=red&board=PL
Health Insurer.. http://agentfinder.doi.state.ma.us/Home.aspx?AspxAutoDetectCookieSupport=1
Health Profession, Allied .... http://license.reg.state.ma.us/pubLic/licque.asp?query=license&color=red&board=AH
HMO.. http://agentfinder.doi.state.ma.us/Home.aspx?AspxAutoDetectCookieSupport=1
Hoisting Machinery Operator .... http://elicense.chs.state.ma.us/Verification/Search.aspx
Home Health Care Provider........................ www.mass.gov/lwd/docs/dos/ea/ea-licensed.pdf
Home Improvement Contractor.................... http://services.oca.state.ma.us/hic/licenseelist.aspx
Home Inspector... http://license.reg.state.ma.us/public/licque.asp?color=red&Board=HI
Insurance Advisor/Adjuster .... http://agentfinder.doi.state.ma.us/Home.aspx?AspxAutoDetectCookieSupport=1
Insurance Agent/Broker.................http://agentfinder.doi.state.ma.us/(X(1)S(yahwgn551kjiteekih4q4i3u))/Home.aspx?AspxAutoDetectCookieSupport=1
Insurance Premium Financer....................... http://license.dob.state.ma.us/licenseelist.asp
Insurance, Domestic/Foreign Firm.............. http://agentfinder.doi.state.ma.us/Home.aspx?AspxAutoDetectCookieSupport=1
Investment Advisor...................................... www.finra.org/Investors/ToolsCalculators/BrokerCheck/index.htm
Land Surveyor... http://license.reg.state.ma.us/pubLic/licque.asp?query=license&color=red&board=EN
Landscape Architect .... http://license.reg.state.ma.us/pubLic/licque.asp?color=red&Board=LA
Lead Inspector .... www.mass.gov/lwd/labor-standards/asbestos-program/license-lists/
Loan Company, Small/Servicer .... www.nmlsconsumeraccess.org/
Lobbyist/Lobbyist Employer .... www.sec.state.ma.us/lobbyist/LobbyistSearch/PublicSearch.asp?action=P
Lobstering .... www.mass.gov/dfwele/dmf/
Mammography Radiologic Technol'gist....... http://db.state.ma.us/dph/Radtechs/
Manicurist.. http://license.reg.state.ma.us/pubLic/licque.asp?query=license&color=red&board=HD
Marriage & Family Therapist....................... http://license.reg.state.ma.us/pubLic/licque.asp?query=personal&color=red&board=MH
Mental Health Counselor .... http://license.reg.state.ma.us/pubLic/licque.asp?query=personal&color=red&board=MH
Mental Health/Human Svcs Pro, Allied........ http://license.reg.state.ma.us/pubLic/licque.asp?query=personal&color=red&board=MH
Mortgage Broker/Lender............................. www.nmlsconsumeraccess.org/
Motor Vehicle Sales Financer...................... http://license.dob.state.ma.us/licenseelist.asp
Nuclear Plant Engineer/Oper'tor .... http://elicense.chs.state.ma.us/Verification/Search.aspx

Nursing Home	www.mass.gov/eohhs/docs/dph/quality/healthcare/healthcare-facilities.xls
Occupational Therapist/Assistant	http://license.reg.state.ma.us/pubLic/licque.asp?query=license&color=red&board=AH
Oil Burner Technician/Contr.	http://elicense.chs.state.ma.us/Verification/Search.aspx
Optician/Dispensing	http://license.reg.state.ma.us/public/licque.asp?color=red&Board=OP
Optometrist	http://license.reg.state.ma.us/public/licque.asp?color=red&Board=OP
Out-Patient Rehabilitation Facility	www.mass.gov/eohhs/docs/dph/quality/healthcare/healthcare-facilities.xls
P&C Insurance Agency	http://agentfinder.doi.state.ma.us/Home.aspx?AspxAutoDetectCookieSupport=1
Pesticide Applicator/Dealer	www.mass.gov/agr/pesticides/licensing/exams/exam_pass.htm
Physical Therapist/Assistant	http://license.reg.state.ma.us/pubLic/licque.asp?query=license&color=red&board=AH
Physician Assistant	https://checkalicense.hhs.state.ma.us/
Physician/Medical Doctor	http://profiles.ehs.state.ma.us/Profiles/Pages/FindAPhysician.aspx
Pipefitter/School	http://elicense.chs.state.ma.us/Verification/Search.aspx
Plumber	http://license.reg.state.ma.us/pubLic/licque.asp?query=license&color=red&board=PL
Podiatrist	http://license.reg.state.ma.us/public/licque.asp?color=red&Board=PD
Psychologist, Educational	http://license.reg.state.ma.us/public/licque.asp?color=red&Board=PY
Radiation Therapy/Radiologic Tech	http://db.state.ma.us/dph/Radtechs/
Radio & TV Repair Technician	http://license.reg.state.ma.us/public/licque.asp?color=red&Board=TV
Radiographer	http://db.state.ma.us/dph/Radtechs/
Radiologic Technologist	http://webapps.ehs.state.ma.us/radtechs/default.aspx
Real Estate Agent/Broker/Sales	http://license.reg.state.ma.us/public/licque.asp?color=red&Board=RE
Real Estate Appraiser	http://license.reg.state.ma.us/public/licque.asp?color=red&Board=RA
Refrigeration Technician School/Contractor	http://elicense.chs.state.ma.us/Verification/Search.aspx
Rehabilitation Therapist	http://license.reg.state.ma.us/pubLic/licque.asp?query=personal&color=red&board=MH
Rescue Shelters	www.mass.gov/agr/animalhealth/ApprovedEntities.htm
Residential Care, Youth	www.eec.state.ma.us/ChildCareSearch/RPMap.aspx
Retail Installment Financer	http://license.dob.state.ma.us/licenseelist.asp
Sales Finance Company	www.mass.gov/Eoca/docs/dob/mvlist.xls
Sanitarian	http://license.reg.state.ma.us/pubLic/licque.asp?color=red&Board=SA
School Bus	www.env.state.ma.us/DPU_FileRoom/frmTransportationSP.aspx
Seafood Dealer	www.mass.gov/dfwele/dmf/
Securities Agent/Broker/Dealer	www.finra.org/Investors/ToolsCalculators/BrokerCheck/index.htm
Shellfishing, Commercial	www.mass.gov/dfwele/dmf/
Social Worker	http://license.reg.state.ma.us/public/licque.asp?color=red&Board=SW
Speech-Language Pathologist	http://license.reg.state.ma.us/pubLic/licque.asp?query=license&color=red&board=SP
Sprinkler Fitting School	http://elicense.chs.state.ma.us/Verification/Search.aspx
Surplus Lines Broker	http://agentfinder.doi.state.ma.us/Home.aspx?AspxAutoDetectCookieSupport=1
Taxidermist	www.mass.gov/dfwele/dfw/
Theatrical Booking Agent	http://elicense.chs.state.ma.us/Verification/Search.aspx
Ticket Reseller	http://elicense.chs.state.ma.us/Verification/Search.aspx
Trapping	www.mass.gov/dfwele/dfw/
Trauma Center	www.facs.org/trauma/verified.html
Trust Company	http://license.dob.state.ma.us/licenseelist.asp
Veterinarian	http://license.reg.state.ma.us/public/licque.asp?color=red&Board=VT
Water Supply Facility Operator	http://license.reg.state.ma.us/pubLic/licque.asp?color=red&Board=DW

State and Local Courts

State Court Structure: The Massachusetts Trial Court is organized by "Departments" and within each department there are "Divisions." The **Superior Court** has concurrent civil jurisdiction with the **District** and **Boston Municipal Court** departments; however, most plaintiffs seeking damages of $25,000 or less file in the District, the **Boston Municipal Court**, or the **Housing Court**. District, Boston Municipal, and Housing Court departments resolve small claims matters which are $7,500 or less.

Criminal jurisdiction in the District and Boston Municipal Court departments extend to all city and town ordinances, all misdemeanors, all felonies punishable by a sentence up to five years, as well as other specifically enumerated felonies carrying greater potential penalties.

Eviction cases may be filed at a county District Court or at the regional "**Housing Court**." A case may be moved from a District Court to a Housing Court, but never the reverse. Housing Courts also hear misdemeanor *Code Violation* cases and prelims for these. There are six Housing Court Regions - Boston (Suffolk County), Worcester (Worcester County and 5 towns from Middlesex and Norfolk), Southeast (Plymouth and Bristol Counties), Northeast (Essex County and parts of Middlesex County), and Western (Berkshire, Franklin, Hampden and Hampshire Counties). The Southeast Housing Court has three branches - Brockton, Fall River, and New Bedford.

There is one **Probate and Family Court** per county, but several counties have additional full sessions and satellite office locations – including Essex, Bristol Middlesex, and Plymouth.

Appellate Courts: Appellate Courts and Supreme Court opinions are available at http://massreports.com/.

Statewide Court Online Access: There is a statewide system.

- Online access to **superior court civil case** information is provided on the statewide Trial Courts Information Center website at www.ma-trialcourts.org/tcic/welcome.jsp. The system provides an index by party names. No DOBs are shown.
- One may also search the **criminal record** index, but only if the case docket number is provided - there is no name search. Site is updated daily. Registration is required, but there is no fee. For more information, contact Marie Zollo at marie.zollo@jud.state.ma.us.

Note: No individual Massachusetts courts offer online access, other than as described above.

Recorders, Assessors, and Other Sites of Note

Recording Office Organization: 14 counties, 21 recording offices. Berkshire and Bristol counties each have three recording offices. Essex, Middlesex, and Worcester counties each have two recording offices. Note there are cities/towns bearing the same name as a county: Barnstable, Essex, Franklin, Hampden, Nantucket, Norfolk, Plymouth, and Worcester.

Federal tax liens on personal property are filed with the U.S. District Court in Boston as well as with the towns/cities. State tax liens on personal property are filed with the Town/City Clerk or the Tax Collector. All tax liens against real estate are filed with the county Register of Deeds.

Statewide or Multi-Jurisdiction Access: All counties offer access to recorded documents. And quite a few towns and several counties offer online access to assessor records for no charge, often via a vendor. The key vendors are listed below.

- Private vendor Vision Government Solutions provides assessor property records, for free, at www.vgsi.com/vision/Applications/ParcelData/Home.aspx. There are approximately 77 participating jurisdictions.
- Private vendor CSC provides assessor property records free at http://csc-ma.us/PROPAPP/Opening.do?subAction=NewSearch&town=AllCommunities. There are approximately 54 participating jurisdictions.
- Another vendor providing online property records searching from assessor data is Patriot Properties at www.patriotproperties.com/. They provide access to land records at approximately 78 Massachusetts cities and towns.

County Sites:

Towns and cities that offer online access are listed under their county location.

Barnstable County ***Recorded Documents*** www.barnstabledeeds.org/ Access to County records is free at https://72.8.52.132/ALIS/WW400R.HTM. Search for free, but to print requires a $50 annual fee. Records date back to 1940. Lending agency data is available. **$$$**

Property, Taxation Access to real estate assessment search site for free at www.town.barnstable.ma.us/assessing/propertydisplay13.asp.

Barnstable Town ***Property, Taxation*** Access town assessor records free at www.town.barnstable.ma.us/assessing/propertydisplay13.asp.

Bourne Town ***Property, Taxation*** Access to property taxes free go to www.assessedvalues.com/index.zhtml?jurcode=36.

Brewster Town ***Property, Taxation*** Access to assessors' property data at www.assessedvalues.com/index.zhtml?jurcode=41.

Chatham Town ***Property, Taxation*** Free access to assessor database at www.mapsonline.net/chathamma/web_assessor/search.php#sid=b789b3d2cfac1dd51e944197f7b3d9ee.

Dennis Town ***Property, Taxation*** Access to assessor property records is free at www.assessedvalues.com/index.zhtml?jurcode=75.

Eastham Town ***Property, Taxation*** Assessor's online database of property card data is free at www.assessedvalues.com/index.zhtml?jurcode=86.

Falmouth Town ***Property, Taxation*** Access property data free at http://falmouth.patriotproperties.com/default.asp.

Mashpee Town ***Property, Taxation*** Search Town of Mashpee Assessor database free at www.assessedvalues.com/index.zhtml?jurcode=172,

Orleans Town ***Property, Taxation*** Search current assessment data free at www.assessedvalues.com/search.zhtml?jurcode=224. Also, access to GIS/mapping free at http://gis1.cdm.com/fl/orleansma/main.html.

Provincetown Town ***Property, Taxation*** Access to property record cards for free at www.provincetown-ma.gov/index.aspx?NID=220. Access to GIS/mapping free at www.provincetown-ma.gov/index.aspx?NID=161.

Sandwich Town ***Property, Taxation*** Access to GIS/mapping free at www.mapgeo.com/sandwichma/.

Truro Town ***Property, Taxation*** Access to Assessor's database for free at www.assessedvalues.com/INDEX.ZHTML?JURCODE=300.

Wellfleet Town ***Property, Taxation*** Access to property assessment records for free at www.assessedvalues.com/index.zhtml?jurcode=318. Also, access to GIS/mapping for free at www.wellfleetma.org/Public_Documents/WellfleetMA_Departments/assessors/assessors_atlas.

Yarmouth Town ***Property, Taxation*** Records on the Assessor's database are free at http://gis.vgsi.com/YarmouthMA/.

Berkshire County (Middle District) ***Recorded Documents*** www.berkshiremiddledeeds.com/ Access land records for free at www.masslandrecords.com/BerkMiddle/.

Berkshire County (Northern District) ***Recorded Documents*** www.sec.state.ma.us/rod/rodbrknth/brknthidx.htm Also, access land records for free at www.masslandrecords.com/BerkNorth/. Recorded land name search dates from 5/18/72 to current.

Berkshire County (Southern District) ***Recorded Documents*** www.sec.state.ma.us/rod/rodbrksth/brksthidx.htm Access to Southern District Recorder's records is free at www.masslandrecords.com/BerkSouth/; Registered land date back to 1908. Searchable indices include recorded land, plans (back to 1847). Lending agency data available. Also, search Register of Deeds Records for all Berkshire districts free at www.masslandrecords.com/. Click on appropriate Division on map.

Adams Town ***Property, Taxation*** Access to parcel searches free at http://csc-ma.us/PROPAPP/Opening.do?subAction=NewSearch&town=AllCommunities.

Alford Town ***Recorded Documents*** http://townofalford.org/category/town-clerk/ Access to recorded documents for a fee at http://csc-ma.us/. **$$$**

Property, Taxation Access assessor rolls and property sales free at http://csc-ma.us/PROPAPP/Opening.do?subAction=NewSearch&town=AllCommunities. No name searches.

Becket Town ***Property, Taxation*** Access to parcels for free at Access to parcels for free at http://csc-ma.us/PROPAPP/Opening.do?subAction=NewSearch&town=AllCommunities. No name searches. Also, access to Assessor maps free at www.townofbecket.org/Public_Documents/BecketMA_Maps/.

Egremont Town ***Property, Taxation*** Access assessor rolls and property sales free at http://csc-ma.us/PROPAPP/Opening.do?subAction=NewSearch&town=AllCommunities.

Great Barrington Town ***Property, Taxation*** Access assessor rolls and property sales free at http://csc-ma.us/PROPAPP/Opening.do?subAction=NewSearch&town=AllCommunities.

Hinsdale Town ***Property, Taxation*** Access assessor rolls and property sales free at http://csc-ma.us/PROPAPP/Opening.do?subAction=NewSearch&town=AllCommunities.

Lee Town ***Property, Taxation*** Access assessor rolls and property sales free at http://csc-ma.us/PROPAPP/Opening.do?subAction=NewSearch&town=AllCommunities.

Lenox Town ***Property, Taxation*** Access and search assessor's data free at www.assessedvalues.com/search.zhtml?jurcode=152.

Middlefield Town ***Property, Taxation*** Access assessor rolls and property sales free at http://csc-ma.us/PROPAPP/Opening.do?subAction=NewSearch&town=AllCommunities.

Monterey Town *Property, Taxation* Access to GIS/mapping free at www.caigisonline.com/MontereyMA/.

Otis Town *Property, Taxation* Search town assessor database at http://data.visionappraisal.com/OtisMA/DEFAULT.asp.

Peru Town *Property, Taxation* Access assessor rolls and property sales free at http://csc-ma.us/PROPAPP/Opening.do?subAction=NewSearch&town=AllCommunities. No name searches.

Richmond Town *Property, Taxation* Access assessor rolls and property sales free at http://csc-ma.us/PROPAPP/Opening.do?subAction=NewSearch&town=AllCommunities.

Sheffield Town *Property, Taxation* Access assessor rolls and property sales free at http://csc-ma.us/PROPAPP/Opening.do?subAction=NewSearch&town=AllCommunities.

Stockbridge Town *Property, Taxation* Access to GIS/mapping free at www.caigisonline.com/StockbridgeMA/.

Washington Town *Property, Taxation* Access to assessor rolls and property sales is free at http://csc-ma.us/PROPAPP/Opening.do?subAction=NewSearch&town=AllCommunities.

West Stockbridge Town *Property, Taxation* Access assessor rolls and property sales free at http://csc-ma.us/PROPAPP/Opening.do?subAction=NewSearch&town=AllCommunities. No name searches.

Williamstown Town *Property, Taxation* Access to parcel data for free to go http://csc-ma.us/PROPAPP/Opening.do?subAction=NewSearch&town=AllCommunities.

Windsor Town *Property, Taxation* Access assessor rolls and property sales free at http://csc-ma.us/PROPAPP/Opening.do?subAction=NewSearch&town=AllCommunities.

Bristol County (Northern District) *Recorded Documents* www.tauntondeeds.com Access recorded real property searches at www.tauntondeeds.com/Default.aspx. There is an advanced image search as well.
Property, Taxation Access to Assessor's database free at http://data.visionappraisal.com/TauntonMA/DEFAULT.asp.

Bristol County (Fall River District) *Recorded Documents, Death Records* Access registry documents at https://www.fallriverdeeds.com/. Search index free - click on Free Search - but a subscription is required for pay-per views of images, $1.00 per page, maximum of $5.00 per doc. Another access point is http://74.8.243.132/MLR-i2_PreLive/. For add'l online search see Bristol County Southern District. Indexes are 1982 to present. **$$$**
Property, Taxation Access to property assessment data for free at http://fallriver.patriotproperties.com/default.asp.

Attleboro City *Property, Taxation* Property data available free at www.nereval.com/OnlineDatabases.aspx.

Berkley Town *Property, Taxation* Access to parcel search for free at http://csc-ma.us/PROPAPP/Opening.do?subAction=NewSearch&town=AllCommunities.

Dartmouth Town *Property, Taxation* Search the town assessor database at http://data.visionappraisal.com/DartmouthMA/DEFAULT.asp.

Dighton Town *Property, Taxation* Access assessor rolls and property sales free at http://csc-ma.us/PROPAPP/Opening.do?subAction=NewSearch&town=AllCommunities.

Easton Town *Vital Records* www.easton.ma.us/Directory/townclerk/TownClerk.htm Access to Family Vital Records from 1725-1843 for free at www.easton.ma.us/Directory/townclerk/1725-1843%20Family%20Book%20Indexed.pdf.
Property, Taxation Search the town assessor database at http://data.visionappraisal.com/EastonMA/DEFAULT.asp.

Fairhaven Town *Property, Taxation* Access to the property assessment data for free at http://fairhaven.patriotproperties.com/default.asp.

Fall River City *Property, Taxation* Access property data free at http://fallriver.patriotproperties.com/default.asp.

Freetown Town *Property, Taxation* Access property data free at http://assessedvalues.com/search.zhtml?jurcode=102.

New Bedford City *Property, Taxation* Access to the assessor property database is free at www.newbedford-ma.gov/Assessors/RealProperty/RealpropertyLookup.cfm.

North Attleborough Town *Property, Taxation* Search the town assessor database at http://data.visionappraisal.com/NorthAttleboroMA/DEFAULT.asp.

Raynham Town *Property, Taxation* Access the Online Property Viewer free at www.mapgeo.com/raynhamma/. Also, access to property data to be available free on a private site at www.nereval.com/OnlineDatabases.aspx.

Seekonk Town *Property, Taxation* Access to parcels and property sales for free http://csc-ma.us/PROPAPP/Opening.do?subAction=NewSearch&town=AllCommunities. No name searches.

Somerset Town ***Property, Taxation*** Access assessor rolls and property sales free at http://csc-ma.us/PROPAPP/Opening.do?subAction=NewSearch&town=AllCommunities.

Swansea Town ***Property, Taxation*** Access assessor property data free at http://data.visionappraisal.com/swanseaMA/DEFAULT.asp. Also, access to Assessor's maps free at http://346swa.wycliffe.hostingrails.com/site/department/21.

Taunton City ***Property, Taxation*** Access assessor data free at http://data.visionappraisal.com/TauntonMA/DEFAULT.asp.

Westport Town ***Property, Taxation*** Access to GIS/mapping for free at www.mapgeo.com/westportma/.

Dukes County ***Recorded Documents*** http://dukescounty.org/Pages/DukesCountyMA_Deeds/index Access to Registry of Deeds data is free at www.masslandrecords.com/Dukes/.

Property, Taxation Access to database for free at http://dukescounty.org/Pages/DukesCountyMA_Deeds/assessors.

Edgartown Town ***Property, Taxation*** Search the Town assessor's database at http://data.visionappraisal.com/EdgartownMA/DEFAULT.asp. Also, free access to GIS/mapping at www.edgartown-ma.us/cms/index.php?option=com_docman&task=cat_view&gid=71&Itemid=518.

Essex County (Northern District) ***Recorded Documents*** www.sec.state.ma.us/rod/rodnrthessex/nrthessexidx.htm Search the recorder database for free at http://72.72.82.242/alis/ww400r. Also see Andover Town and Essex County Southern District.

Essex County (Southern District) ***Recorded Documents*** www.salemdeeds.com Records on the Essex County South Registry of Deeds database are free at www.salemdeeds.com/. Click on "Search Deeds online". Images start 1/3/1983; Grantor/Grantee index goes back to 1/1984. Search by grantee/grantor, town & date, street, or book & page. Also, search the recorder database for free at www.lawrencedeeds.com/dsSearch.asp. Also see Andover Town and Essex County Northern District. Also, access land records for free at www.masslandrecords.com/malr/index.htm; click Bristol-Fall River under "Select a County."

Aquinnah Town ***Property, Taxation*** GIS mapping is offered at www.caigisonline.com/AquinnahMA/.

Gosnold Town ***Property, Taxation*** Access to property assessment search for free at http://data.visionappraisal.com/GosnoldMA/.

Tisbury Town ***Property, Taxation*** Access to GIS/mapping free at www.caigisonline.com/tisburyma/.

West Tisbury Town ***Property, Taxation*** Access assessor data at http://data.visionappraisal.com/WestTisburyMA/DEFAULT.asp. Also, access to GIS/mapping free at www.caigisonline.com/West_TisburyMA/.

Amesbury Town ***Property, Taxation*** Search the town assessor data at http://data.visionappraisal.com/AmesburyMA/DEFAULT.asp. Also, access toe the Assessor's maps 1-111 free at www.amesburyma.gov/government.cfm?subpage=157942.

Andover Town ***Property, Taxation*** Property tax records on the Assessor's database are free at http://andoverma.gov/assessedvalues/ but no name searching.

Beverly City ***Property, Taxation*** Access city property data free at http://beverly.patriotproperties.com/default.asp. Access to GIS/mapping free at www.mapgeo.com/BeverlyMA/.

Boxford Town ***Property, Taxation*** Access to online database for free at http://data.visionappraisal.com/BoxfordMA/DEFAULT.asp.

Danvers Town ***Property, Taxation*** Access property data free at http://danvers.patriotproperties.com/default.asp. Also, access to GIS/mapping free at www.danvers.govoffice.com/index.asp?Type=B_BASIC&SEC={02FAF51E-E3E9-4D86-90E6-05D068FE7A83}.

Town of Essex ***Property, Taxation*** Access to property assessment data free at http://essex.patriotproperties.com/default.asp.

Georgetown Town ***Property, Taxation*** Free access to assessor database at http://data.visionappraisal.com/GeorgetownMA/DEFAULT.asp. Registration required.

Gloucester City ***Property, Taxation*** Access to property assessment search for free at http://data.visionappraisal.com/GloucesterMA/DEFAULT.asp.

Groveland Town ***Property, Taxation*** Access to the property assessment data free at http://groveland.patriotproperties.com/default.asp.

Hamilton Town ***Property, Taxation*** Assessor records available at http://data.visionappraisal.com/HamiltonMA/DEFAULT.asp. Real Estate Recording records located at Essex County.

Haverhill City ***Property, Taxation*** Access property data free at http://haverhill.patriotproperties.com/default.asp.

Ipswich Town ***Property, Taxation*** Access property data free at http://ipswich.patriotproperties.com/default.asp. Also, access to GIS/mapping free at www.ipswichma.gov/index.php?option=com_content&view=article&id=325&Itemid=295.

Lawrence City ***Property, Taxation*** Access assessor data free at http://data.visionappraisal.com/LawrenceMA/DEFAULT.asp.

Lynn City ***Property, Taxation*** Access property data free at http://lynn.patriotproperties.com/default.asp.

Lynnfield Town ***Property, Taxation*** Access property data free at http://lynnfield.patriotproperties.com/default.asp.

Manchester-by-the-Sea Town ***Property, Taxation*** Search the property assessment data at http://manchester.patriotproperties.com/default.asp.

Marblehead Town ***Property, Taxation*** Access property data free at http://marblehead.patriotproperties.com/default.asp.

Merrimac Town ***Property, Taxation*** Access to property assessment data for free at http://merrimac.patriotproperties.com/default.asp. Also, access to Assessor's maps free at www.merrimac01860.info/Pages/MerrimacMA_BComm/BOA/forms.

Middleton Town ***Property, Taxation*** Access to property assessment data free at http://middleton.patriotproperties.com/default.asp.

Nahant Town ***Property, Taxation*** Access property data free at http://nahant.patriotproperties.com/default.asp.

Newbury Town ***Property, Taxation*** Access property tax data free at http://newbury.patriotproperties.com/default.asp.

Newburyport City ***Property, Taxation*** Search the city assessor database at http://data.visionappraisal.com/NewBURYPORTMA/DEFAULT.asp.

North Andover Town ***Property, Taxation*** Free access to assessor rolls and property sales at http://csc-ma.us/PROPAPP/Opening.do?subAction=NewSearch&town=AllCommunities.

Peabody City ***Property, Taxation*** Access property data free at http://host.appgeo.com/PeabodyMA/

Rockport Town ***Property, Taxation*** Access GIS/mapping for free at www.townofrockport.com/cfml/special.cfm?page=maps.

Rowley Town ***Property, Taxation*** Search the town assessor data at http://data.visionappraisal.com/RowleyMA/DEFAULT.asp. Free registration for full data.

Salem City ***Property, Taxation*** Search property data by location or parcel ID for free at http://salem.patriotproperties.com/default.asp. Also, access to GIS/mapping free at www.salem.com/Pages/SalemMA_WebDocs/maps.

Salisbury Town ***Property, Taxation*** Access property data free at http://salisbury.patriotproperties.com/default.asp.

Saugus Town ***Property, Taxation*** Access to GIS/mapping for free at www.saugus-ma.gov/Pages/SaugusMA_Assessor/plates/. Also, access assessor rolls and property sales free at http://csc-ma.us/PROPAPP/Opening.do?subAction=NewSearch&town=AllCommunities. No name searches.

Swampscott Town ***Property, Taxation*** Access to GIS/mapping for free at http://ags.cdm.com/fl/swampscottma/. Also, access to property assessment data free at http://swampscott.patriotproperties.com/default.asp.

Topsfield Town ***Property, Taxation*** Access Assessor data free at http://data.visionappraisal.com/TopsfieldMA/DEFAULT.asp. Free registration required.

West Newbury Town ***Property, Taxation*** Access to property assessment data free at http://westnewbury.patriotproperties.com/default.asp.

Franklin County ***Recorded Documents*** www.sec.state.ma.us/rod/rodfranklin/franklinidx.htm Access to Registry of Deeds data is free at www.masslandrecords.com/Franklin/.
Property, Taxation Access to The Town of Franklin real property assessment data for free at http://franklin.patriotproperties.com/default.asp.

Ashland Town ***Recorded Documents*** www.ashlandmass.com/ashland/offices-departments/town-clerk-office Access to recorded documents for a fee at http://csc-ma.us/. $$$
Property, Taxation Also, access to property and sales database for free at http://csc-ma.us/PROPAPP/Opening.do?subAction=NewSearch&town=AllCommunities. No name searches.

Bernardston Town ***Property, Taxation*** Access assessor rolls and property sales free at http://csc-ma.us/PROPAPP/Opening.do?subAction=NewSearch&town=AllCommunities.

Charlemont Town ***Property, Taxation*** Access assessor rolls and property sales free at http://csc-ma.us/PROPAPP/Opening.do?subAction=NewSearch&town=AllCommunities.

Deerfield Town ***Property, Taxation*** Free access to property data found at http://deerfield.patriotproperties.com/default.asp. Also, access to GIS/mapping free at www.caigisonline.com/DeerfieldMA/.

Erving Town ***Property, Taxation*** Access to Assessor's maps for free at www.erving-ma.org/forms/2/109-assessors-maps.

Franklin Town ***Property, Taxation*** Access property data free at http://franklin.patriotproperties.com/default.asp.

Gill Town ***Property, Taxation*** Access property data free at http://gill.patriotproperties.com/default.asp.

Greenfield Town ***Property, Taxation*** Access to property information website free at http://greenfield.patriotproperties.com/default.asp.

Monroe Town ***Property, Taxation*** Access assessor rolls and property sales free at http://csc-ma.us/PROPAPP/Opening.do?subAction=NewSearch&town=AllCommunities.

Montague Town ***Property, Taxation*** Access property and assessment data free at http://montague.patriotproperties.com/default.asp.

Orange Town ***Property, Taxation*** Access to property assessment data for free at http://orange.patriotproperties.com/default.asp. Also, access to GIS/mapping for free at www.caigisonline.com/orangema/.

Shelburne Town ***Property, Taxation*** Access assessor rolls and property sales free at http://csc-ma.us/PROPAPP/Opening.do?subAction=NewSearch&town=AllCommunities.

Shutesbury Town ***Property, Taxation*** Access to assessments for 2009 for free at www.shutesbury.org/assessor/

Warwick Town ***Property, Taxation*** Access to assessor rolls and property sales is free at http://csc-ma.us/PROPAPP/Opening.do?subAction=NewSearch&town=AllCommunities.

Wendell Town ***Property, Taxation*** Access to assessor rolls and property sales is free at http://csc-ma.us/PROPAPP/Opening.do?subAction=NewSearch&town=AllCommunities.

Hampden County ***Recorded Documents*** www.registryofdeeds.co.hampden.ma.us/ Access to the county index of land records is free or via subscription at http://204.213.242.147/. Images can be viewed free, but cannot be printed unless you subscribe and become a remote access customer. Copies can be printed at no charge. Records go back to 1956. Lending agency info is available. Searchable indexes are unregistered land site, and registered land site. **$$$**

Property, Taxation Assessor records available at http://data.visionappraisal.com/HampdenMA/DEFAULT.asp. Registration is required.

Agawam Town ***Property, Taxation*** Access Property Assessment Data free at http://agawam.patriotproperties.com/default.asp. Also, access to GIS/mapping free at http://107.20.209.214/agawamma_public/default.html.

Blandford Town ***Property, Taxation*** Access to property assessment data for free at http://blandford.patriotproperties.com/default.asp.

Brimfield Town ***Property, Taxation*** Access property data free at http://brimfield.patriotproperties.com/default.asp.

Chester Town ***Property, Taxation*** Access assessor rolls and property sales free at http://csc-ma.us/PROPAPP/Opening.do?subAction=NewSearch&town=AllCommunities.

Chicopee City ***Property, Taxation*** To view the FY 2012 values in street order or real estate date free at https://www.chicopeema.gov/page.php?id=23.

East Longmeadow Town ***Property, Taxation*** Access to the property assessment data for free at http://eastlongmeadow.patriotproperties.com/default.asp.

Granville Town ***Property, Taxation*** Access to the Assessors database free at www.assessedvalues2.com/index.aspx?jurcode=112.

Holland Town ***Property, Taxation*** Access assessor data free at http://data.visionappraisal.com/HollandMA/DEFAULT.asp.

Longmeadow Town ***Property, Taxation*** Access to tax records is at http://data.visionappraisal.com/LONGMEADOWMA/DEFAULT.asp.

Palmer Town ***Property, Taxation*** Search town assessor database at http://data.visionappraisal.com/PalmerMA/DEFAULT.asp.

Russell Town ***Property, Taxation*** Access to assessed values free at www.townofrussell.us/assessors.html. Click on list by owner, by map or by location.

Southwick Town ***Property, Taxation*** Search the town assessor database at http://data.visionappraisal.com/SouthwickMA/DEFAULT.asp.

Springfield City ***Recorded Documents*** www3.springfield-ma.gov/cos/index.php?id=788 Search city properties/owners with tax liens free at www3.springfield-ma.gov/finance/taxtitle/.

Property, Taxation Access to city assessor property valuations is free at www3.springfield-ma.gov/finance/assessors/. Also, search the city GIS-mapping site for property data at www2.springfieldcityhall.com/gis/viewer.htm but no name searching.

Tolland Town ***Property, Taxation*** Access property data in pdf format free at www.tolland-ma.gov/Public_Documents/TollandMA_Assessor/property_lookup. Also, access assessor rolls and property sales free at http://csc-ma.us/PROPAPP/Opening.do?subAction=NewSearch&town=AllCommunities. No name searches.

West Springfield Town ***Property, Taxation*** Search the town assessor database at http://data.visionappraisal.com/WestSpringfieldMA/DEFAULT.asp. Free registration required.

Westfield City ***Property, Taxation*** Assessor records can be found free for Westfield City at http://data.visionappraisal.com/WestfieldMA/DEFAULT.asp.

Wilbraham Town ***Property, Taxation*** Access to GIS/mapping for free at http://107.20.209.214/WilbrahamMA_public/default.html. Search the town assessor data at http://data.visionappraisal.com/Wilbrahamma/DEFAULT.asp.

Hampshire County ***Recorded Documents*** www.sec.state.ma.us/sec/rod/rodhamp/hampidx.htm Access to records for free at www.sec.state.ma.us/sec/rod/rodhamp/hampidx.htm; index back to 1948, images back to 1786. Also, Registry of Deeds records are searchable at www.masslandrecords.com/Hampshire/; images go back to 1786, index back to 1948. **$$$**

Property, Taxation Access to property evaluation searches for free at www.northamptonassessor.us/.

Amherst Town Clerk ***Property, Taxation*** The town has a GIS-mapping site but no name searching, free at http://gis.amherstma.gov/apps/assessment/. No name searches.

Belchertown Town ***Property, Taxation*** Access property data free at http://belchertown.patriotproperties.com/default.asp.

Chesterfield Town ***Property, Taxation*** Access to Assessor's online database free at www.assessedvalues.com/search.zhtml?jurcode=60. Also, access to GIS/mapping for free at www.townofchesterfieldma.com/Files/parcels/parcels.html.

Cummington Town ***Property, Taxation*** Access to GIS/mapping for free at www.cummington-ma.gov/Maps.php. Also, access parcels for free at http://csc-ma.us/PROPAPP/Opening.do?subAction=NewSearch&town=AllCommunities.

Easthampton City ***Property, Taxation*** Property assessment searching is at www.easthampton.org/pages.php?which_page=parcel_search. Also, access to GIS/mapping for free at www.caigisonline.com/EasthamptonMA/.

Hatfield Town ***Property, Taxation*** Access to Assessor data for free at www.mainstreetmaps.com/MA/Hatfield/. Also, access to Assessor's database free at http://hatfield.patriotproperties.com/default.asp.

Huntington Town ***Property, Taxation*** Access to parcel search for free at http://66.152.242.251/Huntington/ParcelSearch.aspx. Also, access to GIS/mapping for free at www.caigisonline.com/HuntingtonMA/.

Northampton City ***Property, Taxation*** Access to property evaluation information for free at www.northamptonassessor.us/

South Hadley Town ***Property, Taxation*** Access to GIS/mapping for free at www.southhadley.org/Pages/SouthHadleyMA_Assessors/mapparcel

Southampton Town ***Property, Taxation*** Access assessor property data in spreadsheet format free at www.town.southampton.ma.us/dbcc/files/SOUTHAMPTON%20FY2008%20ASSESSED%20VALUES.xls

Westhampton Town ***Property, Taxation*** Access assessor rolls and property sales free at http://csc-ma.us/PROPAPP/Opening.do?subAction=NewSearch&town=AllCommunities. No name searches.

Williamsburg Town ***Property, Taxation*** Access assessor rolls and property sales free at http://csc-ma.us/PROPAPP/Opening.do?subAction=NewSearch&town=AllCommunities.

Worthington Town ***Property, Taxation*** Access to property assessment data free at http://worthington.patriotproperties.com/default.asp.

Middlesex County (Southern District) ***Recorded Documents*** www.sec.state.ma.us/rod/rodmidsth/midsthidx.htm Access to Register of Deeds data is free www.masslandrecords.com/MiddlesexSouth/.

Middlesex County (Northern District) ***Recorded Documents*** www.lowelldeeds.com/ Access Register of Deeds data free at www.masslandrecords.com/MiddlesexNorth/.

Acton Town ***Property, Taxation*** Access to GIS/mapping for free at http://host.appgeo.com/ActonMA/.

Arlington Town ***Property, Taxation*** Search the town assessor database free at http://arlingtonma.us/property/select.pl.

Ashby Town ***Recorded Documents*** www.ci.ashby.ma.us/clerk/clerk.html Access to recorded documents for a fee at http://csc-ma.us/. **$$$**

Property, Taxation Access assessor rolls and property sales free at http://csc-ma.us/PROPAPP/Opening.do?subAction=NewSearch&town=AllCommunities. No name searches. Also, access to parcel maps for free at www.ci.ashby.ma.us/assessors/maplink.html.

Ayer Town ***Recorded Documents*** www.ayer.ma.us/Pages/AyerMA_Clerk/index Access to recorded documents for a fee at http://csc-ma.us/. **$$$**
Property, Taxation Access to parcels for free at http://csc-ma.us/PROPAPP/Opening.do?subAction=NewSearch&town=AllCommunities. No name searches. Also, access to GIS/mapping free at www.ayer.ma.us/Pages/AyerMA_Assessor/maps/maps.

Bedford Town ***Property, Taxation*** Access property data free at http://bedford.patriotproperties.com/default.asp.

Billerica Town ***Property, Taxation*** Access property data free at http://billerica.patriotproperties.com/default.asp. No name searching. Access to GIS/mapping free at www.billericadpw.org/gis_taxmaps.asp.

Boxborough Town ***Property, Taxation*** Access to Assessor's maps free at www.town.boxborough.ma.us/boxborough/AssessorsMaps.html.

Burlington Town ***Property, Taxation*** Access property data free at http://burlington.patriotproperties.com/default.asp.

Cambridge City ***Property, Taxation*** Search city assessor database at www2.cambridgema.gov/fiscalaffairs/PropertySearch.cfm.

Chelmsford Town ***Property, Taxation*** Search town assessor database at http://data.visionappraisal.com/ChelmsfordMA/DEFAULT.asp.

Concord Town ***Property, Taxation*** Search the city assessor database at http://data.visionappraisal.com/ChelseaMA/DEFAULT.asp.

Dracut Town ***Property, Taxation*** Search the town assessor database at http://gis.vgsi.com/dracutma/.

Dunstable Town ***Property, Taxation*** Access to Assessor's maps for free at http://dunstable-ma.gov/Pages/DunstableMA_Bcomm/BOA/maps.pdf.

Everett City ***Property, Taxation*** Access to the property assessment data for free at http://everett.patriotproperties.com/.

Framingham Town ***Property, Taxation*** Access assessor rolls and property sales free at http://csc-ma.us/PROPAPP/Opening.do?subAction=NewSearch&town=AllCommunities.

Groton Town ***Property, Taxation*** Access to GIS/mapping for free at www.mapgeo.com/GrotonMA/. Also, access to assessors online database from free go to http://data.visionappraisal.com/GrotonMA/DEFAULT.asp.

Holliston Town ***Property, Taxation*** Access assessor rolls and property sales free at http://csc-ma.us/PROPAPP/Opening.do?subAction=NewSearch&town=AllCommunities.

Hopkinton Town ***Property, Taxation*** Access Board of Assessors maps free at www.hopkinton.org/assessor/listing.htm; no name searching. Also, access to property assessment data for free at http://hopkinton.patriotproperties.com/default.asp.

Hudson Town ***Property, Taxation*** Access assessor records free at http://data.visionappraisal.com/HudsonMA/DEFAULT.asp. Also, access GIS/mapping for free at www.townofhudson.org/public_documents/HudsonMA_GIS/Requests.

Lexington Town ***Property, Taxation*** Access assessor data free at http://data.visionappraisal.com/LexingtonMA/DEFAULT.asp.

Lincoln Town ***Property, Taxation*** Access to 2013 assessments free at www.lincolntown.org/Adobe%20Acrobat%20Files/Assessors/2012_0919_Assessor_FY13AssessmentList.pdf.

Littleton Town ***Property, Taxation*** Access to Assessor's Maps for free at www.littletonma.org/content/53/1044/97/5904/default.aspx. Also, access to the property assessment data free at http://littleton.patriotproperties.com/default.asp.

Lowell City ***Property, Taxation*** Access property assessment data free at www.lowellma.gov/services/gis/.

Malden City ***Property, Taxation*** Access to assessment/Property tax, parcel and property sale information for free at http://malden.patriotproperties.com/default.asp.

Marlborough City ***Property, Taxation*** Search the city assessor data at http://data.visionappraisal.com/MarlboroughMA/DEFAULT.asp.

Maynard Town ***Property, Taxation*** Access to property assessment data free at http://maynard.patriotproperties.com/default.asp.

Medford City ***Property, Taxation*** Search the city assessor database at http://data.visionappraisal.com/MedfordMA/DEFAULT.asp.

Melrose City ***Property, Taxation*** Access property data free at http://melrose.patriotproperties.com/default.asp.

Natick Town ***Property, Taxation*** Search town assessments free at www.natickma.org/assess/assessinfo.asp. Includes name searches.

Newton City ***Property, Taxation*** Records on the City of Newton Fiscal 2003 assessment database are free at http://assessing.newtonma.gov/NewtonMAWebApp/. Data represents market value as of January of current year.

North Reading Town ***Property, Taxation*** Access assessor rolls and property sales free at http://csc-ma.us/PROPAPP/Opening.do?subAction=NewSearch&town=AllCommunities. No name searches.

Pepperell Town ***Property, Taxation*** Access to property assessment data free at http://pepperell.patriotproperties.com/default.asp.

Reading Town ***Property, Taxation*** Records on the Town of Reading Assessor database are free at http://csc-ma.us/PROPAPP/Opening.do?subAction=NewSearch&town=AllCommunities. No name searches.

Sherborn Town ***Property, Taxation*** Access to town maps free at www.sherbornma.org/Pages/SherbornMA_Assessor/2010mapstable.

Shirley Town ***Property, Taxation*** Access to parcel data for free at http://shirley.patriotproperties.com/default.asp.

Somerville City ***Property, Taxation*** Search the city assessor database at http://data.visionappraisal.com/SomervilleMA/DEFAULT.asp. Also, access to the town maps for free at www.somervillema.gov/departments/finance/assessing/maps.

Stoneham Town ***Property, Taxation*** Access to property assessment data for free at http://stoneham.patriotproperties.com/default.asp.

Stow Town Clerk ***Property, Taxation*** Free access to the Assessor's database at http://stow.univers-clt.com/. No name searches. Free access to 2012 property maps at www.stow-ma.gov/Pages/StowMA_Assessor/Stow%20Property%20Maps%202012/.

Sudbury Town ***Property, Taxation*** Access to the property valuations list for current year is free at www.town.sudbury.ma.us/services/department_home.asp?dept=Assessors. No name searching on this address index list.

Tewksbury Town ***Property, Taxation*** Search lists of yearly tax assessments free at www.tewksbury.net/Pages/TewksburyMA_Assessor/2008. Also, access Assessor data free at http://data.visionappraisal.com/TewksburyMA/DEFAULT.asp.

Townsend Town ***Property, Taxation*** Access to Assessor's database free at http://realprop.townsend.ma.us/realform.htm.

Tyngsborough Town ***Property, Taxation*** Access to property assessment date free at http://tyngsborough.patriotproperties.com/default.asp.

Wakefield Town ***Property, Taxation*** Access to property assessment data free at http://wakefield.patriotproperties.com/default.asp.

Waltham City ***Property, Taxation*** Access to property assessment data free at http://waltham.patriotproperties.com/default.asp.

Watertown Town ***Property, Taxation*** Access to property assessment data for free at http://watertown.patriotproperties.com/default.asp.

Wayland Town ***Property, Taxation*** Access assessor property records free at http://data.visionappraisal.com/WaylandMA/DEFAULT.asp.

Westford Town ***Voter Registration Records*** www.westfordma.gov/pages/government/towndepartments/WestfordMA_clerk/index
Check voter registration verification free at https://data.westfordma.gov/voter/.
Property, Taxation Access the town online offerings - property, GIS-mapping for free at www.westfordma.gov/pages/onlineservices/gis. Also, access to parcel look-up free at www.westfordma.gov/Pages/Government/TownDepartments/WestfordMA_MapsGIS/ parcellookup. Also, access to property assessment data free at http://westford.patriotproperties.com/default.asp.

Weston Town ***Property, Taxation*** Access to GIS/mapping free at www.mapsonline.net/westonma/index.html.

Wilmington Town ***Property, Taxation*** Access to Assessors online database for free at http://data.visionappraisal.com/WilmingtonMA/DEFAULT.asp.

Winchester Town ***Property, Taxation*** Access to property assessment data free at http://winchester.patriotproperties.com/default.asp.

Woburn City ***Property, Taxation*** Search the city assessor data at http://data.visionappraisal.com/WoburnMA/DEFAULT.asp.

Nantucket County ***Recorded Documents*** www.masslandrecords.com/Nantucket/ Access land records for free at www.masslandrecords.com/Nantucket/.
Property, Taxation Access to Assessors database for free at http://data.visionappraisal.com/NantucketMA/DEFAULT.asp.

Nantucket Town ***Property, Taxation*** Access property data free at http://data.visionappraisal.com/NantucketMA/DEFAULT.asp.

Norfolk County ***Recorded Documents*** www.norfolkdeeds.org Access to county online records is on two levels, both accessible via http://research.norfolkdeeds.org/ALIS/WW400R.PGM. You may search images and indices free, however, to print requires a subscription; $100 per year plus $1.00 per page. Land records go back to 1900; images to 1793. Land court records go back to 9/1984, with images back to 1901. **$$$**
Property, Taxation Access to Assessors database for free at http://data.visionappraisal.com/DedhamMA/DEFAULT.asp.

Avon Town ***Property, Taxation*** Access to online database for free at http://data.visionappraisal.com/AvonMA/DEFAULT.asp.

Bellingham Town ***Property, Taxation*** Access property data free at http://bellingham.patriotproperties.com/.

Braintree Town ***Property, Taxation*** Access property data free at http://braintree.patriotproperties.com/default.asp?br=exp&vr=6.

Brookline Town ***Property, Taxation*** Records on the Town of Brookline Assessors database are free at www.brooklinema.gov/assessors/propertylookup1.asp.

Canton Town ***Property, Taxation*** Access assessed value data at www.town.canton.ma.us/assessors/assessors.htm. No name searching; search by address only.

Cohasset Town ***Property, Taxation*** Access property data free at http://cohasset.patriotproperties.com/default.asp.

Dedham Town ***Property, Taxation*** Property records on the Assessor's database are free at http://data.visionappraisal.com/DedhamMA/DEFAULT.asp. Does not require a username & password, simply click on link. Also, search the GIS mapping site for owner and property data free at http://gis.dedham-ma.gov/.

Dover Town ***Property, Taxation*** Access to the assessor property values data is free at www.doverma.org/town-government/town-offices/assessor/. Have tables for 2009 and 2010.

Holbrook Town ***Property, Taxation*** Access property data free at http://holbrook.patriotproperties.com/default.asp.

Medfield Town ***Recorded Documents*** www.town.medfield.net/index.cfm/page/Town-Clerk/pid/21441 Access to recorded documents for a fee at http://csc-ma.us/. **$$$**

Property, Taxation Access town property data free at http://medfield.patriotproperties.com/default.asp?br=exp&vr=6.

Medway Town ***Property, Taxation*** Access town assessor database free at www.assessedvalues.com/index.zhtml?jurcode=177. Also, Parcel Maps available free via the link on the Assessor webpage. Also, access to property assessment data free at http://medway.patriotproperties.com/default.asp.

Milton Town ***Property, Taxation*** Access to real property assessment data free at http://milton.patriotproperties.com/default.asp.

Needham Town ***Property, Taxation*** Access assessor rolls and property sales free at http://csc-ma.us/PROPAPP/Opening.do?subAction=NewSearch&town=AllCommunities.

Norfolk Town ***Property, Taxation*** Access to town property data is free at http://data.visionappraisal.com/NorfolkMA/DEFAULT.asp.

Quincy City ***Property, Taxation*** Access assessor property data free at http://data.visionappraisal.com/QuincyMA/DEFAULT.asp.

Randolph Town ***Property, Taxation*** Access assessor property data free at http://gis.vgsi.com/RandolphMA/. Also, access to GIS/mapping free at www.mapgeo.com/RandolphMA/.

Sharon Town ***Property, Taxation*** Search the town assessor data at http://data.visionappraisal.com/RowleyMA/DEFAULT.asp. Also, access to GIS/mapping free at www.mainstreetmaps.com/MA/Sharon/.

Stoughton Town ***Property, Taxation*** Access to property assessment data for free at http://stoughton.patriotproperties.com/default.asp.

Walpole Town ***Property, Taxation*** Search the town assessor database at http://data.visionappraisal.com/WalpoleMA/DEFAULT.asp.

Wellesley Town ***Property, Taxation*** Property tax records on the Assessor's database are free at http://wellesleyma.virtualtownhall.net/Pages/WellesleyMA_Assessor/index. Click on Assessment Information at left of page.

Westwood Town ***Property, Taxation*** Search the town assessor data at http://data.visionappraisal.com/WestwoodMA/DEFAULT.asp.

Weymouth Town ***Property, Taxation*** Access to property data is free at www.weymouth.ma.us/propview/.

Wrentham Town ***Property, Taxation*** Access to the Assessor's database for free at www.assessedvalues.com/index.zhtml?jurcode=350.

Plymouth County ***Recorded Documents*** http://plymouthdeeds.org/ Access to Titleview at http://titleview.org/plymouthdeeds/ requires registration. There is a usage charge of $30.00 per month, plus $1.00 per image page, but guests may do index searches for free, but no image printing. Indices date back to 1945. Access is by dial-up or internet. For info call 508-830-9284. **$$$**

Abington Town ***Property, Taxation*** Search town assessor database at http://data.visionappraisal.com/AbingtonMA/DEFAULT.asp.

Bridgewater Town ***Property, Taxation*** Access property data free on the GIS-mapping site at www.bridgewaterma.org/gisviewer/Index.cfm. No name searching.

Brockton City ***Property, Taxation*** Access to the Assessors database for free at www.brockton.ma.us/Online/AssessorsDB.aspx.

Duxbury Town ***Property, Taxation*** Access to the Towns property information free at http://gis.vgsi.com/DuxburyMA/.

East Bridgewater Town ***Property, Taxation*** Access to Assessor's online database free at www.assessedvalues.com/index.zhtml?jurcode=83.

Halifax Town ***Property, Taxation*** Assessor property records free at www.visionappraisal.com/ coming soon.

Hanover Town ***Property, Taxation*** Assessor records available at http://data.visionappraisal.com/HanoverMA/DEFAULT.asp.

Hanson Town ***Property, Taxation*** Access property records free on the GIS-mapping site at http://gis.virtualtownhall.net/hanson/index.htm; no name searching.

Hingham Town ***Property, Taxation*** Access to the assessor online database free at http://data.visionappraisal.com/HinghamMA/DEFAULT.asp.

Hull Town ***Property, Taxation*** Access to property assessment data free at http://hull.patriotproperties.com/default.asp?br=exp&vr=6.

Kingston Town ***Property, Taxation*** Access assessor records free at http://data.visionappraisal.com/KingstonMA/DEFAULT.asp.

Lakeville Town ***Property, Taxation*** Access assessor data free at http://data.visionappraisal.com/LakevilleMA/DEFAULT.asp.

Marion Town ***Property, Taxation*** Search town assessor data at http://data.visionappraisal.com/MarionMA/DEFAULT.asp.

Marshfield Town ***Property, Taxation*** Search town assessor database at http://marshfield.patriotproperties.com/default.asp.

Mattapoisett Town ***Property, Taxation*** Access to GIS/mapping for free at www.mapgeo.com/mattapoisettma/.

Middleborough Town ***Property, Taxation*** Search town assessor database at http://data.visionappraisal.com/MiddleboroMA/DEFAULT.asp. Also, free access to the monthly sales found at http://middleboroughcom.vps1.dependable-hosting.com/assessors/index.html.

Norwell Town ***Property, Taxation*** Access assessor property data free at http://data.visionappraisal.com/NorwellMA/DEFAULT.asp.

Pembroke Town ***Property, Taxation*** Access assessor data free at http://pembroke.patriotproperties.com/default.asp.

Plymouth Town ***Property, Taxation*** Access property data free at http://plymouth.patriotproperties.com/default.asp.

Rochester Town ***Property, Taxation*** Assessor property records free at http://data.visionappraisal.com/RochesterMA/DEFAULT.asp.

Rockland Town ***Property, Taxation*** Access to assessment listings for free at www.nereval.com/OnlineDatabases.aspx.

Scituate Town ***Property, Taxation*** Search the Assessor property data for free at www.town.scituate.ma.us/assessor/index.html. Click on "Town of Scituate Property Assessment Data as of…"

Wareham Town ***Property, Taxation*** Search town assessor database at http://data.visionappraisal.com/WarehamMA/DEFAULT.asp. Also, access to GIS-mapping information for free at http://gis.virtualtownhall.net/wareham_new/index.asp

West Bridgewater Town ***Property, Taxation*** To access records free at http://westbridgewater.patriotproperties.com/default.asp.

Whitman Town ***Property, Taxation*** Access to property assessment data free at http://whitman.patriotproperties.com/default.asp.

Suffolk County ***Recorded Documents*** www.suffolkdeeds.com Records on the County Registry of Deeds database are free at www.masslandrecords.com/Suffolk/.
Property, Taxation Search Boston assessor property records free at www.cityofboston.gov/assessing/search/. City property taxes also available, but no name searching.

Boston City ***Property, Taxation*** Records on the City of Boston Assessor database are free at www.cityofboston.gov/assessing/search/. Also, property tax bill and payment is searchable by parcel number for free at www.cityofboston.gov/assessing/paysearch.asp.

Chelsea City ***Property, Taxation*** Search the city assessor database at http://data.visionappraisal.com/ChelseaMA/DEFAULT.asp. Also, access to GIS/mapping free at www.ci.chelsea.ma.us/Public_Documents/ChelseaMA_IT/gis.

Revere City ***Property, Taxation*** Access property data free at http://revere.patriotproperties.com/default.asp.

Winthrop Town ***Property, Taxation*** Access to Assessors online database for free at http://gis.vgsi.com/winthropma/.

Worcester County (Northern District) ***Recorded Documents*** www.sec.state.ma.us/rod/rodnw/nwidx.htm Access to Registry of Deeds is free at http://74.8.243.133/. Scroll down left column then click 'Click here to access…' Small fee to copy or certify documents. Land index back to 1956; images to 1868. **$$$**

Worcester County (South Worcester District) ***Recorded Documents*** www.worcesterdeeds.com/ Access to the Register of Deeds database is free at www.masslandrecords.com/Worcester/.

Athol Town ***Property, Taxation*** Access to GIS/mapping free at www.caigisonline.com/atholma/.

Auburn Town ***Property, Taxation*** Access to Real Estate tax lookup free at www.mapsonline.net/auburnma/tax_collector/search.php#sid=ccc0a8016dd46806dfdd8fa9273c8330.

Blackstone Town ***Property, Taxation*** Access property data free at http://data.visionappraisal.com/BlackstoneMA/DEFAULT.asp. Also, access to GIS/mapping free at http://host.appgeo.com/BlackstoneMA/.

Bolton Town ***Property, Taxation*** Access property record cards for free at http://csc-ma.us/PROPAPP/Opening.do?subAction=NewSearch&town=AllCommunities. Also, access to Assessor maps free at www.townofbolton.com/pages/BoltonMA_Assessors/Assessor%20MAPS.

Boylston Town ***Property, Taxation*** Access to maps for free at www.boylston-ma.gov/Pages/BoylstonMA_Assessors/index

Brookfield Town ***Property, Taxation*** Access parcels for free at http://csc-ma.us/PROPAPP/Opening.do?subAction=NewSearch&town=AllCommunities.

Charlton Town ***Property, Taxation*** Access property data free at http://charlton.patriotproperties.com/default.asp. Also, access to GIS/mapping free at www.townofcharlton.net/assessors.htm#AssessorsMaps.

Dudley Town ***Property, Taxation*** Search the town assessor database at http://data.visionappraisal.com/DudleyMA/DEFAULT.asp. Also, access to zoning maps free at www.dudleyma.gov/ZoningMap.pdf.

East Brookfield Town ***Property, Taxation*** Access assessor rolls and property sales free at http://csc-ma.us/PROPAPP/Opening.do?subAction=NewSearch&town=AllCommunities.

Fitchburg City ***Property, Taxation*** Access property data free at http://fitchburg.patriotproperties.com/default.asp.

Gardner City ***Property, Taxation*** Search the city assessor data at http://data.visionappraisal.com/GardnerMA/DEFAULT.asp.

Grafton Town ***Property, Taxation*** Access to GIS/mapping for free at www.grafton-ma.gov/Public_Documents/GraftonMA_Assessor/Assessors%20Maps/. Also, access to parcel search free at http://csc-ma.us/PROPAPP/Opening.do?subAction=NewSearch&town=AllCommunities.

Hardwick Town ***Property, Taxation*** Access assessor rolls and property sales free at http://csc-ma.us/PROPAPP/Opening.do?subAction=NewSearch&town=AllCommunities. Also, access to GIS/mapping free at www.townofhardwick.com/assessorsmaps1.html.

Harvard Town ***Property, Taxation*** Search town assessor database at http://data.visionappraisal.com/HarvardMA/DEFAULT.asp. Free registration required.

Holden Town ***Property, Taxation*** Search the Town assessor's database free at http://data.visionappraisal.com/HoldenMA/DEFAULT.asp.

Hopedale Town ***Property, Taxation*** Access town assessment data free at http://hopedale.patriotproperties.com/default.asp.

Hubbardston Town ***Property, Taxation*** Access assessor data free at http://data.visionappraisal.com/HubbardstonMA/DEFAULT.asp.

Lancaster Town ***Property, Taxation*** Access to GIS/mapping for free at www.ci.lancaster.ma.us/Pages/LancasterMA_BComm/AssessorMap2011/. Access assessor rolls and property sales free at http://csc-ma.us/PROPAPP/Opening.do?subAction=NewSearch&town=AllCommunities.

Leicester Town ***Property, Taxation*** Access property data free at http://leicester.patriotproperties.com/default.asp.

Leominster City ***Property, Taxation*** Search the assessor's maps for free to go www.leominster-ma.gov/assessors_department_maps.htm. Also, access to GIS/mapping/property cards free at http://eis.woodardcurran.com/leominster/.

Lunenburg Town ***Property, Taxation*** Access assessor rolls and property sales free at http://csc-ma.us/PROPAPP/Opening.do?subAction=NewSearch&town=AllCommunities.

Mendon Town ***Property, Taxation*** Access to property cards for free at www.mendonma.gov/TownGovernment/BoardsandCommittees/BoardofAssessors/PropertyCards.aspx.

Milford Town ***Property, Taxation*** Access property data free at http://milford.patriotproperties.com/default.asp.

Millbury Town ***Property, Taxation*** Access to the town tax assessor info is free at http://data.visionappraisal.com/MillburyMA/DEFAULT.asp.

Millville Town ***Property, Taxation*** Access to property assessment data free at http://millville.patriotproperties.com/default.asp.

New Braintree Town ***Property, Taxation*** Access assessor rolls and property sales free at http://csc-ma.us/PROPAPP/Opening.do?subAction=NewSearch&town=AllCommunities.

North Brookfield Town ***Property, Taxation*** Access assessor rolls and property sales free at http://csc-ma.us/PROPAPP/Opening.do?subAction=NewSearch&town=AllCommunities.

Northborough Town ***Property, Taxation*** Access assessor rolls and property sales free at http://csc-ma.us/PROPAPP/Opening.do?subAction=NewSearch&town=AllCommunities.

Northbridge Town ***Property, Taxation*** Access to alphabetical street listing for free at www.northbridgemass.org/sites/northbridgema/files/file/file/northbridgevalues4.pdf.

Oxford Town ***Property, Taxation*** Search the property assessments byname or address from a link at www.town.oxford.ma.us/Pages/OxfordMA_Assessor/index.

Paxton Town ***Property, Taxation*** Search town assessor database at http://data.visionappraisal.com/PaxtonMA/DEFAULT.asp.

Phillipston Town ***Property, Taxation*** Access to Assessors property data free at www.caigisonline.com/phillipstonma/.

Princeton Town ***Property, Taxation*** GIS/mapping available for free at http://town.princeton.ma.us/Pages/PrincetonMA_Assessors/Maps.

Royalston Town ***Property, Taxation*** Access assessor rolls and property sales free at http://csc-ma.us/PROPAPP/Opening.do?subAction=NewSearch&town=AllCommunities. No name searches.

Shrewsbury Town ***Property, Taxation*** Search the town assessor data at http://data.visionappraisal.com/RowleyMA/DEFAULT.asp.

Southborough Town ***Property, Taxation*** Access assessor rolls and property sales free at http://csc-ma.us/PROPAPP/Opening.do?subAction=NewSearch&town=AllCommunities. No name searches.

Southbridge Town ***Property, Taxation*** Access assessor data free with registration at http://data.visionappraisal.com/SouthbridgeMA/DEFAULT.asp.

Sturbridge Town ***Property, Taxation*** Access assessor property data free with registration at http://data.visionappraisal.com/SturbridgeMA/DEFAULT.asp. Also, access to tax maps free at www.town.sturbridge.ma.us/public_documents/sturbridgema_assessor/Tax_Maps/.

Sutton Town ***Property, Taxation*** Access assessor property data free at http://data.visionappraisal.com/suttonMA/DEFAULT.asp.

Templeton Town ***Property, Taxation*** Access to GIS/mapping free at www.caigisonline.com/templetonma/.

Upton Town ***Property, Taxation*** Access to tax maps free at www.upton.ma.us/Pages/UptonMA_BComm/Assessor/Assessormaps/.

Uxbridge Town ***Property, Taxation*** Access to assessor rolls and property sales is free at http://csc-ma.us/PROPAPP/Opening.do?subAction=NewSearch&town=AllCommunities. Search maps by owner's name or address at www.caigisonline.com/UxbridgeMA/.

Webster Town ***Property, Taxation*** Access to GIS/mapping free at www.mapgeo.com/websterma/.

West Boylston Town ***Property, Taxation*** Access to GIS/mapping free at www.westboylston-ma.gov/Pages/WBoylstonMA_WebDocs/gis.

West Brookfield Town ***Property, Taxation*** Access assessor rolls and property sales free at http://csc-ma.us/PROPAPP/Opening.do?subAction=NewSearch&town=AllCommunities. No name searches.

Westborough Town ***Property, Taxation*** Access to property assessment data free at http://westborough.patriotproperties.com/default.asp.

Worcester City ***Property, Taxation*** Online access to the City Real Estate Tax/CML database is free at www.worcesterma.gov/e-services/search-public-records/real-estate-tax-cml. Also, assessor property records free at http://data.visionappraisal.com/WorcesterMA/DEFAULT.asp. Also, access to online GIS/mapping free at www.ci.worcester.ma.us/finance/technical-services/gis/online-maps

Michigan

Capital: Lansing
Ingham County

Time Zone: EST

Four NW Michigan counties are in the CST:

They are: Dickinson, Gogebic, Iron, Menominee.

Population: 9,883,360

# of Counties: 83

Useful State Links

Website: www.michigan.gov

Governor: www.michigan.gov/gov

Attorney General: www.michigan.gov/ag

State Archives: www.michigan.gov/dnr/0,1607,7-153-54463_19313---,00.html

State Statutes and Codes: www.legislature.mi.gov

Legislative Bill Search: www.legislature.mi.gov

Unclaimed Funds: www.michigan.gov/treasury/0,1607,7-121-44435---,00.html

State Public Record Agencies

Criminal Records

Michigan State Police, Criminal History Section, Criminal Justice Information Center, www.michigan.gov/cjic Online access is available. All felonies and serious misdemeanors that are punishable by over 93 days are required to be reported to ICHAT by the state repository by law enforcement agencies, prosecutors, and courts in all 83 Michigan counties. Register at http://apps.michigan.gov/ICHAT/Home.aspx. Fee is $10.00 per name. Call 517-241-0606. Also, you are allowed up to three variations on one name search. Suppressed records and warrant information are not available through ICHAT. Use of a MasterCard, Discover or VISA is required. This is the only method available for a non-fingerprint search. **$$$**

Sexual Offender Registry

Michigan State Police, SOR Section, www.mipsor.state.mi.us One may search the registry at the website, there is no charge. Data includes an offender's registerable offense, his/her photo (if available), physical description, offender's last reported address, if offender is attending and/or employed at a post secondary school and any aliases Email questions to PSORS@Michigan.gov.

Incarceration Records

Michigan Department of Corrections, Central Records Office, www.michigan.gov/corrections The online access found at www.state.mi.us/mdoc/asp/otis2.html has many search criteria capabilities. There is also a DOC Most Wanted list at www.state.mi.us/mdoc/MostWanted/MostWanted.asp. *Other Options:* Bulk sales of database information is available.

Corporation, LLC, LP, LLP, Assumed Name

Department of Energy, Labor & Economic Growth, Bureau of Commercial Services - Corp Div, http://michigan.gov/corporations At the main website, search by company name or file number for records of domestic corporations, limited liability companies, limited partnerships and of foreign corporations, and limited partnerships qualified to transact business in the state. Click on Business Entity Search or go to www.dleg.state.mi.us/bcs_corp/sr_corp.asp. *Other Options:* The database is for sale by contract.

Trademarks/Servicemarks

Dept of labor & Economic Growth, Commercial Svcs - Trademarks & Service Marks, www.michigan.gov/lara/0,4601,7-154-35299_61343_35413_35431---,00.html Download files of trademarks and services marks at www.dleg.state.mi.us/dms/results.asp?docowner=BCSC&doccat=Mark&Search=Search. One file is A-L, the other M-Z.

Uniform Commercial Code, Federal & State Tax Liens

MI Department of State, UCC Section, http://apps.michigan.gov/UCC/Home.aspx At http://apps.michigan.gov/UCC/Home.aspx, for a free name search click on Conducting a Debtor Name Quick Search. No login is needed. Also, documents may be ordered for a fee. Registration is required. A credit card is necessary unless the requester has an established billing account. **$$$** *Other Options:* A monthly subscription service is available for the bulk purchase of UCC filings on microfilm. The fee is $50 or actual cost, whichever is greater. Call 517-322-1144 for additional information.

Vital Records

Department of Health, Vital Records Requests, www.michigan.gov/mdch Records can be ordered from the web site, credit card is required. Processing time is 2 weeks. **$$$**

Workers' Compensation Records

Department of Labor & Economic Dev., Workers' Compensation Agency, www.michigan.gov/wca Go to the website and follow the links to see if an employer has coverage. The site does not allow searching by employee name.

Driver Records

Department of State, Record Lookup Unit, www.michigan.gov/sos Online ordering is available on an interactive or batch basis. The system is open 7 days a week. Ordering is by DL or name and DOB. An account must be established and billing is monthly. Fee is $7.00 per record. A $25,000 surety bond is required. Also, the agency offers an activity notification service for employers who register their drivers. Account holders may also access vehicle and watercraft records. For more information on either program, call 517-322-6281 or visit the web. **$$$** *Other Options:* The state offers the license file for bulk purchase to approved requesters. Customized runs are $64 per thousand records; complete database can be purchased for $16 per thousand. A $25,000 surety bond is required. Call 517-322-1042.

Vehicle, Vessel Ownership & Registration

Department of State, Record Lookup Unit, www.michigan.gov/sos Online searching via the Internet is single inquiry and requires a VIN or plate number (no name searches). An account is required with a $25,000 surety bond. Fee is $7.00 per record. For more information, call 517-322-6281. The program is called Direct Access and details are found on the web. A unique service offered is the Repeat Offender Inquiry. This web search function allows dealers and others to learn if a vehicle purchaser is ineligible for license plates and subject to registration denial under Michigan's Repeat Offender Law. Search results state if the purchaser is eligible, not eligible, or if not on file. The web site is https://services.sos.state.mi.us/RepeatOffender/Inquiry.aspx. **$$$** *Other Options:* Michigan offers bulk retrieval from the VIN and plate database. A written request letter, stating purpose, must be submitted and approved. A $25,000 surety bond is required upon approval. Please call 517-322-1042.

Accident Reports

Department of State Police, Criminal Justice Information Center, www.michigan.gov/msp/0,1607,7-123-1593_24055-35982--,00.html Records may be viewed and printed from the Traffic Crash Purchasing System at http://mdotjboss.state.mi.us/TCPS/login/welcome.jsp. The fee is $10.00, a credit card must be used unless billing arrangements are made. Reports are not mailed.. Records are available going back 10 years. For specific questions email CrashPurchaseTCPS@michigan.gov. **$$$**

Voter Registration, Campaign Finance, Lobbyists, PACs

Secretary of State, Bureau of Elections, www.michigan.gov/sos/1,1607,7-127-1633---,00.html Single name voter registration searches are to https://webapps.sos.state.mi.us/mivote/votersearch.aspx. Must have first and last name, birth month and year and residential zip code. Campaign finance disclosures and lobbyist disclosures are available from links at www.michigan.gov/sos/1,1607,7-127-1633---,00.html. Search lobbyists from a different Division at http://miboecfr.nicusa.com/cgi-bin/cfr/lobby_srch.cgi. *Other Options:* The agency will sell district, statewide or customized subsets of the voter registration database on CD. Fees are usually $22.25, depending on data requested.

GED Certificates

Workforce Development Agency, Div of Education & Career Success - GED Testing, www.michigan.gov/adulteducation Will accept e-mail requests with a scanned signature.

Occupational Licensing Boards

Accountant-CPA.. www.dleg.state.mi.us/verify.htm
Adoption Agency/Child Placing Agency....... www.michigan.gov/dhs/0,1607,7-124-5455_27716_27721---,00.html
Aircraft Dealer.. www.michigan.gov/documents/aero/DEALERLISTFORWEB_MAY_10_321513_7.pdf
Alarm System Service................................ https://www2.dleg.state.mi.us/colaLicVerify/
Ambulance Attendant................................. www7.dleg.state.mi.us/free/
Amusement Ride.. www.dleg.state.mi.us/verify.htm
Appraiser, Real Estate/Gen/Residential...... www.dleg.state.mi.us/verify.htm
Aquaculture Operation............................... www.michigan.gov/documents/mda/mda_aquaculture_192478_7.pdf

Architect	www.dleg.state.mi.us/verify.htm
Asbestos Accreditation, Individ'l	www.dleg.state.mi.us/asbestos_program/sr_individual.asp
Asbestos Contractor	www.dleg.state.mi.us/asbestos_program/sr_contractor.asp
Asbestos Training Provider	www.dleg.state.mi.us/asbestos_program/sr_tcp.asp
Atmosphere Storage Operator	www.michigan.gov/mdard/0,4610,7-125-1569_16993_19105-46661--,00.html
Attorney, State Bar	www.michbar.org/memberdirectory/
Auto Dealer/Mech'/Repair Facility	www.michigan.gov/sos/0,1607,7-127-1640_14837-51047--,00.html
Bank & Trust Company	www.michigan.gov/statelicensesearch
Barber	www.dleg.state.mi.us/verify.htm
Barber Shop/School	www.dleg.state.mi.us/verify.htm
Boxing/Wrestling Occupation	www.dleg.state.mi.us/verify.htm
Builder, Residential	www.dleg.state.mi.us/verify.htm
Camp, Child/Adult Foster Care	www.dleg.state.mi.us/brs_afc/sr_afc.asp
Carnival	www.dleg.state.mi.us/verify.htm
Casino Interest Personnel/Firm	http://miboecfr.nicusa.com/cgi-bin/cfr/casino_srch.cgi
Cemetery	www.dleg.state.mi.us/verify.htm
Check Seller	www.michigan.gov/difs/0,5269,7-303-13251_13257---,00.html
Child Care Family/Group/Center	www.michigan.gov/dhs/0,4562,7-124-5529_49572---,00.html
Child Care Institution/Facility, Court Operated	www.dleg.state.mi.us/brs_cwl/sr_cwl.asp
Chiropractor	www7.dleg.state.mi.us/free/
Collection Manager	www.dleg.state.mi.us/verify.htm
Community Planner	www.dleg.state.mi.us/verify.htm
Community Planner (Mfg. Home)	https://www2.dleg.state.mi.us/colaLicVerify/
Consumer Financial Service	www.michigan.gov/difs/0,5269,7-303-13251_13257---,00.html
Contractor, Residential	www.dleg.state.mi.us/verify.htm
Cosmetologist	www.dleg.state.mi.us/verify.htm
Cosmetology Shop/School	www.dleg.state.mi.us/verify.htm
Counselor	www7.dleg.state.mi.us/free/
Credit Card Issuer	www.michigan.gov/difs/0,5269,7-303-13251_13257---,00.html
Credit Union	www.michigan.gov/statelicensesearch
Debt Management	www.michigan.gov/difs/0,5269,7-303-13251_13257---,00.html
Debt Management Firm	www.dleg.state.mi.us/fis/ind_srch/ConsumerFinance/Search.asp
Dentist/Dental Assistant/Hygienist	www7.dleg.state.mi.us/free/
Election Campaign Finance Comm'tee	http://miboecfr.nicusa.com/cgi-bin/cfr/mi_com.cgi
Election Candidate Committee	http://miboecfr.nicusa.com/cgi-bin/cfr/can_search.cgi
Emergency Medical Personnel	www7.dleg.state.mi.us/free/
Employment Agency, fee only	www.dleg.state.mi.us/verify.htm
EMT Advanced/Specialist/Instructor	www7.dleg.state.mi.us/free/
Engineer	www.dleg.state.mi.us/verify.htm
Flight School	www.michigan.gov/documents/AERO_Flight_Schools_Aug_2005_134972_7.pdf
Forester	www.dleg.state.mi.us/verify.htm
Funeral Home/Salesperson	www.dleg.state.mi.us/verify.htm
Funeral, Prepaid Contract Regis	www.dleg.state.mi.us/verify.htm
Grain Dealer/Trucker	www.michigan.gov/mdard/0,4610,7-125-1569_16993_16996---,00.html
Health Facility/Laboratory	www7.dleg.state.mi.us/free/
Hearing Aid Dealer	www.dleg.state.mi.us/verify.htm
HMO	www.michigan.gov/difs/0,5269,7-303-13251_13262---,00.html
Insurance Adjuster	www.michigan.gov/difs/0,5269,7-303-13251_13262---,00.html
Insurance Agent/Counsel/Solicit/Admin.	www.michigan.gov/difs/0,5269,7-303-13251_13262---,00.html
Insurance Counselor/Solicitor	www.dleg.state.mi.us/fis/ind_srch/ins_agnt/insurance_agent_criteria.asp
Insurance-related Entity	www.michigan.gov/difs/0,5269,7-303-13251_13262---,00.html
Investment Adviser/Firm	http://adviserinfo.sec.gov/(S(4fggs545p2sc4zai2xunvw55))/IAPD/Content/Search/iapd_Search.aspx
Landscape Architect	www.dleg.state.mi.us/verify.htm
Liquor Dist/Whlse/Mfg	www2.dleg.state.mi.us/llist/
Liquor Finance Division	www2.dleg.state.mi.us/llist/

Liquor Hearings & Appeals	www2.dleg.state.mi.us/llist/
Liquor License/Licensing Director	www2.dleg.state.mi.us/llist/
Living Care Facility	www.michigan.gov/documents/cis_ofis_lclist_25541_7.pdf
Loan Originator	www.michigan.gov/difs/0,5269,7-303-13251_13257---,00.html
Lobbyist/Lobbyist Agent	http://miboecfr.nicusa.com/cgi-bin/cfr/lobby_srch.cgi
Long Term Care Company	www.michigan.gov/difs/0,5269,7-303-13251_13262---,00.html
Mammography Facility	www7.dleg.state.mi.us/free/
Marriage & Family Therapist	www7.dleg.state.mi.us/free/
Medical First Responder	www7.dleg.state.mi.us/free/
Mortgage Licensee	www.michigan.gov/difs/0,5269,7-303-13251_13257---,00.html
Mortuary Science	www.dleg.state.mi.us/verify.htm
Motor Vehicle Loan Seller/Financer	www.michigan.gov/difs/0,5269,7-303-13251_13257---,00.html
Notary Public	http://services.sos.state.mi.us/notarysearch/
Nurse/Aide	www7.dleg.state.mi.us/free/
Nursery Dealer/Grower	www.mda.state.mi.us/license/
Nursing Home	www.dleg.state.mi.us/bhs_car/sr_car.asp
Nursing Home Administrator	www7.dleg.state.mi.us/free/
Ocularist	www.dleg.state.mi.us/verify.htm
Optometrist	www7.dleg.state.mi.us/free/
Osteopathic Physician	www7.dleg.state.mi.us/free/
Paramedic	www7.dleg.state.mi.us/free/
Personnel Agency	https://www2.dleg.state.mi.us/colaLicVerify/
Pesticide Application Business	www.michigan.gov/mdard/0,4610,7-125-1569_16988_35288-11993--,00.html
Pharmacist	www7.dleg.state.mi.us/free/
Physical Therapist	www7.dleg.state.mi.us/free/
Physician/Medical Doctor/Assistant	www7.dleg.state.mi.us/free/
Podiatrist	www7.dleg.state.mi.us/free/
Political Action Committee	http://miboecfr.nicusa.com/cgi-bin/cfr/pac_search.cgi
Political Party Committee	http://miboecfr.nicusa.com/cgi-bin/cfr/mi_com.cgi?com_type=PPY
Polygraph Examiner	www.dleg.state.mi.us/verify.htm
Potato Dealer	www.michigan.gov/mdard/0,4610,7-125-1566_1733_2321-11149--,00.html
Premium Finance Company	www.michigan.gov/difs/0,5269,7-303-13251_13257---,00.html
Private Investigator/Detective	https://www2.dleg.state.mi.us/colaLicVerify/
Private Security/Secur'y arrest author'y	https://www2.dleg.state.mi.us/colaLicVerify/
Psychologist	www7.dleg.state.mi.us/free/
Real Estate Agent/Broker/Seller	www.dleg.state.mi.us/verify.htm
Regulatory Loan Licensee	www.michigan.gov/difs/0,5269,7-303-13251_13257---,00.html
Sanitarian	www7.dleg.state.mi.us/free/
Savings Bank	www.michigan.gov/statelicensesearch
Securities Agent/Broker/Dealer	www.finra.org/Investors/ToolsCalculators/BrokerCheck/index.htm
Security Agency	https://www2.dleg.state.mi.us/colaLicVerify/
Security Alarm Installer	https://www2.dleg.state.mi.us/colaLicVerify/
Security Guard, Private	https://www2.dleg.state.mi.us/colaLicVerify/
Social Worker	www7.dleg.state.mi.us/free/
Surety Company	www.michigan.gov/difs/0,5269,7-303-13251_13262---,00.html
Surplus Line Broker	www.michigan.gov/difs/0,5269,7-303-13251_13262---,00.html
Surveyor, Professional	www.dleg.state.mi.us/verify.htm
Teacher	https://mdoe.state.mi.us/MOECS/PublicCredentialSearch.aspx
Third-Party Administrator	www.michigan.gov/difs/0,5269,7-303-13251_13262---,00.html
Veterinarian/Veterinary Technician	www7.dleg.state.mi.us/free/
Weights & Measures Person/Agency	www.mda.state.mi.us/service/

For **Boilermaker/Boiler Installer/Repairer, Electrician (various types), Mechanical Construction** , and **Plumber** see:
https://www.velocityhall.com/accela/velohall/index.cfm?CITY=MICHIGANLICENSES&STATE=MICHIGAN&CFID=836999&CFTOKEN=98745934&j

State and Local Courts

State Court Structure: The **Circuit Court** is the court of general jurisdiction. In general, the Circuit Court handles all civil cases with claims of more than $25,000 and all felony criminal cases (cases where the accused, if found guilty, could be sent to prison). The **Family Division** of Circuit Court handles all cases regarding divorce, paternity, adoptions, personal protection actions, emancipation of minors, treatment and testing of infectious disease, safe delivery of newborns, name changes, juvenile offenses, and child abuse and neglect. In addition, the Circuit Court hears cases appealed from the other trial courts or from administrative agencies.

The **District Court** handles most traffic violations, civil cases with claims up to $25,000, landlord-tenant matters, most traffic tickets, and all misdemeanor criminal cases (generally, cases where the guilty, cannot be sentenced to more than one year in jail). Small claims cases are heard by a division of the District Court.

Four municipalities have chosen to retain a **Municipal Court** rather than create a District Court. The Municipal Courts have limited powers and are located in Grosse Pointe, Grosse Pointe Farms, Grosse Pointe Park, and Grosse Point Shores/Grosse Pointe Woods.

The **Probate Court** handles wills, administers estates and trusts, appoints guardians and conservators, and orders treatment for mentally ill and developmentally disabled persons. There is a **Court of Claims** in Lansing that is a function of the 30th Circuit Court with jurisdiction over claims against the state of Michigan.

Appellate Courts: Court of Appeals opinions are free online to view at http://courts.mi.gov/opinions_orders/Pages/default.aspx. Subscribe to free email updates of appellate opinions at http://courts.mi.gov/opinions_orders/subscribe-to-opinions-and-orders/pages/default.aspx.

Statewide Court Online Access: There is no statewide program offered for online access. However there are at least 50 local courts with onlien access. Several counties (Barry, Berrien, Iron, Isabella, Lake, and Washtenaw) plus courts in the 46th Judicial Circuit are participating in a *Demonstration Pilot* project designed to streamline court services and consolidate case management. Note that these courts may refer to themselves as County Trial Courts.

County Sites:

Antrim County

13th Circuit Court www.antrimcounty.org/circuitcourt.asp

Civil: Access to a record index is at http://online.co.grand-traverse.mi.us/iprod/clerk/cccivil.html . *Criminal:* Access to criminal record index is found at http://online.co.grand-traverse.mi.us/iprod/clerk/cccriminal.html.

86th District Court www.co.grand-traverse.mi.us/courts/86th_District_Court.htm

Civil: Access to a list of cases is found at http://districtcourt.co.grand-traverse.mi.us/c86_cases/. *Criminal:* same

Bay County

18th Circuit Court www.baycountycourts.com/

Civil: Access the county court records for free at from home page or http://12.221.137.17/c74/c74_cases.php. Calendar of scheduled cases at home page. *Criminal:* same

74th District Court www.baycountycourts.com/

Civil: Access the county court records for free at http://12.221.137.17/c74/c74_cases.php. Calendar of scheduled cases at http://12.221.137.17/c74/c74_calendar.php. *Criminal:* Access the county courts' records for free at http://12.221.137.17/c74/c74_cases.php. Calendar of scheduled cases at http://12.221.137.17/c74/c74_calendar.php.

Calhoun County

37th Circuit Court www.calhouncountymi.gov/government/circuit_court/

Civil: Search civil case index and many related county records at https://mcc.co.calhoun.mi.us/. *Criminal:* Search criminal case index at https://mcc.co.calhoun.mi.us/.

Cheboygan County

89th District Court www.cheboygancounty.net/89th_district_court/

Civil: Court dispositions are searchable at http://216.109.207.51:81/c89_cases/. Calendars are at the home page. *Criminal:* same

Crawford County

46th Circuit Court - All Divisions in Crawford www.Circuit46.org

Civil: Access to civl and probate case records (closed cases for 90 days only) is free at www.circuit46.org/Crawford/c46c_cases.php. *Criminal:* same

Genesee County

7th Circuit Court www.gc4me.com/departments/circuit_court_7th/index.php

Civil: Online access to court records is free at www.gc4me.com/departments/circuit_court_7th/online_records.php. *Criminal:* same

67th District Court www.gc4me.com/departments/district_court/index/index.php

Civil: Online access to court records is free www.co.genesee.mi.us/cgi-bin/gweb.exe?mode=7800&sessionname=genpool. *Criminal:* Online access to court records is free www.co.genesee.mi.us/cgi-bin/gweb.exe?mode=7800&sessionname=genpool. Also includes traffic.

68th District Court www.68thdistrictcourt.com/

Civil: Enter a name or case number at http://records.68thdistrictcourt.com/roawebinq/default.aspx. *Criminal:* same

Grand Traverse County

13th Circuit Court www.13thcircuitcourt.org/

Civil: Search civil records free at http://online.co.grand-traverse.mi.us/iprod/clerk/cccivil.html . 1964 through 1985 contain only index information. 1986 to present include case information and register of actions. Database updated nightly. *Criminal:* Access to a record index is found at http://online.co.grand-traverse.mi.us/iprod/clerk/cccriminal.html.

86th District Court www.co.grand-traverse.mi.us/courts.htm

Civil: Access to a list of cases is found at http://districtcourt.co.grand-traverse.mi.us/c86_cases/. A second site is at http://online.co.grand-traverse.mi.us/iprod/clerk/cccivil.html *Criminal:* same

Ingham County

30th Circuit Court www.ingham.org/cc/circuit.htm

Civil: Access court records and schedules at https://courts.ingham.org/. Schedules search free; record search is not; register or search by credit card, $11 fee per name and $2.50 for each Register of Action viewed. Cases go back to 1986. Search by case number free at https://courts.ingham.org/CourtRecordSearch/searchByCase.do. Note this search is NOT countywide. **$$$** *Criminal:* same **$$$**

54 A District Court www.lansingmi.gov/court/

Civil: The court has a link to online records at https://secure.courts.michigan.gov/jis/, but this site may be severely limited. At times it is unavailable. *Criminal:* The court has a link to online records at https://secure.courts.michigan.gov/jis/, but this site may be severly limited. At times it is unavailable.

54 B District Court www.cityofeastlansing.com/Home/Departments/54BDistrictCourt/

Civil: Access court records is online for part of the county, but not records from this court. See https://courts.ingham.org/. *Criminal:* Access to criminal records online is for other courts in this county, but not this court, is at https://courts.ingham.org/.

55th District Court http://dc.ingham.org/

Civil: Access court records and schedules at http://dc.ingham.org/OnlineServices.aspx. Schedules search free; record search is not; register or search by credit card, $10.00 fee per name plus $2.50 for each Register of Action. Cases go back to 1991. Search by case number free at https://courts.ingham.org/CourtRecordSearch/searchByCase.do. A new site may have records back to 2009 at https://secure.courts.michigan.gov/jis/?court=MASON. The site is not always available. **$$$** *Criminal:* same **$$$**

Jackson County

4th Circuit Court www.co.jackson.mi.us/county_courts/CNP.asp

Civil: Access court records free at http://173.241.216.100/c12/c12_cases.php. *Criminal:* same

12th District Court www.d12.com/county_courts/d12/index.asp

Civil: Access court records free at www.d12.com/county_courts/d12/court_records.asp. *Criminal:* same

Kalkaska County

46th Circuit Court www.circuit46.org/Kalkaska/c46k_home.html

Civil: Online access to court case records (open or closed cases for 90 days only) is free at www.circuit46.org/Kalkaska/c46k_cases.php. *Criminal:* same

87-B District Court www.Circuit46.org

Civil: Online access to limited index of court records is free at www.circuit46.org/Kalkaska/c46k_cases.php. *Criminal:* same

Kent County

17th Circuit Court www.accesskent.com/Courts/17thcc/default.htm

Civil: Search for $6.00 per name at https://www.accesskent.com/CourtNameSearch/. DOB not required but credit card is for record found. Also, search hearings schedule free at https://www.accesskent.com/CCHearing/ **$$$** *Criminal:* Search for $6.00 per name at https://www.accesskent.com/CourtNameSearch/. DOB and credit card required for results. Also, search for accident reports at $3.00 per name at https://www.accesskent.com/AccidentReports/ **$$$**

61st District Court - Grand Rapids www.grcourt.org/

Civil: Search online at www.grcourt.org/CourtPayments/. *Criminal:* Search at www.grcourt.org/CourtPayments/.

Leelanau County

13th Circuit Court www.leelanau.cc/coclerk.asp

Civil: Access to a record index is at http://online.co.grand-traverse.mi.us/iprod/clerk/cccivil.html . Family court records also included. Search by name or case number. *Criminal:* Access to a record index is found at http://online.co.grand-traverse.mi.us/iprod/clerk/cccriminal.html. Search by name or case number to 1981.

86th District Court www.co.grand-traverse.mi.us/courts/86th_District_Court.htm

Civil: Access to a list of cases is found at http://districtcourt.co.grand-traverse.mi.us/c86_cases/. A second site is at http://online.co.grand-traverse.mi.us/iprod/clerk/cccivil.html *Criminal:* same

Livingston County

44th Circuit Court http://co.livingston.mi.us/CircuitCourtClerk/

Civil: Access civil name index and abbreviated case summary online free or by more detailed data subscription at https://www.livingstonlive.org/CourtRecordValidation/. The subscription fee is $6.00 for the verification and $2.50 for an abbreviated summary. Search cases for the 53rd District, 44th Circuit Court, Juvenile & Family Courts. **$$$** *Criminal:* Access criminal name index and abbreviated case summary back to 1997 free or more detailed by subscription at https://www.livingstonlive.org/CourtRecordValidation/; a DOB is required to search. The subscription fee is $6.00 for the verification and $2.50 for an abbreviated summary. **$$$**

53 A District Court http://co.livingston.mi.us/DistrictCourt/

Civil: Access civil records after registration or by subscription at https://www.livingstonlive.org/CourtRecordValidation/. $6.00 fee for each name and court searched; $2.50 for each summary or case history. Search cases for the 53rd District, 44th Circuit Court, Juvenile & Family Courts. **$$$** *Criminal:* Access criminal records back to 1997 after registration or by subscription at https://www.livingstonlive.org/CourtRecordValidation/ but a DOB is required to search on the free access. $6.00 fee for each name and court searched; $2.50 for each summary or case history. **$$$**

53 B District Court http://co.livingston.mi.us/DistrictCourt/

Civil: Access civil records after registration or by subscription at https://www.livingstonlive.org/CourtRecordValidation/. Search cases for the 53rd District, 44th Circuit Court, Juvenile & Family Courts. *Criminal:* Access criminal records back to 1997 after registration or by subscription at https://www.livingstonlive.org/CourtRecordValidation/ but a DOB is required to search on the free access.

Macomb County

16th Circuit Court www.macombcountymi.gov/clerksoffice/

Civil: Civil online access is the same as criminal, see below. Online records include divorces. *Criminal:* Access Circuit Court index for free at http://macombcountymi.gov/pa/. From this site one may order document copies. **$$$**

38th District Court - Eastpointe www.macombcountymi.gov/district_court/court38.htm

Civil: Access case name look-ups free at https://secure.courts.michigan.gov/jis/ *Criminal:* Access case name look-ups at https://secure.courts.michigan.gov/jis/

Marquette County

25th Circuit Court www.co.marquette.mi.us/departments/courts/circuit_court/index.htm

Civil: The county partners with a vendor to provide docket entries, name searches, divorce judgments for a fee at http://orders.paymentsolutions.lexisnexis.com/mi/marquetteco/. **$$$** *Criminal:* The county partners with a vendor to provide dockey entries and name searches for a fee at http://orders.paymentsolutions.lexisnexis.com/mi/marquetteco/. **$$$**

Midland County

42nd Circuit Court http://co.midland.mi.us/departments/home.php?id=4

Civil: Search court calendars free at http://co.midland.mi.us/court_calendar.php. *Criminal:* same

75th District Court - Criminal Division

Criminal: Search court calendars free at http://co.midland.mi.us/court_calendar.php.

Muskegon County

14th Circuit Court

Civil: There is a subscription based online record search at https://www.muskegongov.org/MCCircuitSearch/. The fee for each name searched is $6.00 and $2.50 for each Register of Action viewed. **$$$** *Criminal:* same **$$$**

Oakland County

6th Circuit Court www.oakgov.com/courts/

Civil: Register of Actions free at www.oakgov.com/clerkrod/pages/courtexplorer.aspx. Order document copies online, note there is an additional enhanced access fee starting at $2.50, and can be higher with more volume. **$$$** *Criminal:* Register of Actions free at www.oakgov.com/clerkrod/pages/courtexplorer.aspx. Order document copies online, note there is an additional enhanced access fee starting at $2.50, and can be higher with more volume. **$$$**

50th District Court - Pontiac Criminal Division www.50thdistrictcourt.com/Pages/default.aspx

Criminal: This court recently converted to a new Case Management System with online access. Criminal records prior to 2005 may not be available online. See https://secure.courts.michigan.gov/jis/.

50th District Court - Pontiac Civil Division www.50thdistrictcourt.com/Pages/default.aspx
Civil: This court recently converted to a new Case Management System with online access. Civil records prior to 2005 may not be available online. See https://secure.courts.michigan.gov/jis/.

52nd District All Courts www.oakgov.com/courts/dc52div1/Pages/default.aspx
Civil: This court recently converted to a new Case Management System with online access. Civil records prior to 2011 may not be available online. See https://secure.courts.michigan.gov/jis/. *Criminal:* This court recently converted to a new Case Management System with online access. Criminal records prior to 2011 may not be available online. See https://secure.courts.michigan.gov/jis/.

Otsego County

46th Circuit Trial Court - District Court www.circuit46.org
Civil: Online access to limited index (generally only open cases) is free at www.circuit46.org/Otsego/c46g_home.html. *Criminal:* Access to onlinelimited index (generally only open cases) is free at www.circuit46.org/Otsego/c46g_home.html. There are limitations, this system is not meant to be used for background checks, it is supplemental only.

Ottawa County

20th Circuit Court www.miottawa.org/Courts/20thcircuit/
Civil: A fee-service is offered at https://www.miottawa.org/CourtRecordLookup/. One may set-up an account. Search by name or case numbers. There is a $12 cost for each name searched and a $2.50 cost for each case history or summary viewed. **$$$** *Criminal:* A fee-service is offered at https://www.miottawa.org/CourtRecordLookup/. One may set-up an account. Search by name or case numbers. Includes traffic. **$$$**

58th District All Courts www.miottawa.org/Courts/58thDistrict/
Civil: A fee-service is offered at https://www.miottawa.org/CourtRecordLookup/. One may set-up an account. Search by name or case numbers. There is a $12 cost for each name searched and a $2.50 cost for each case history or summary viewed. **$$$** *Criminal:* A fee-service is offered at https://www.miottawa.org/CourtRecordLookup/. One may set-up an account. Search by name or case numbers. Includes traffic. **$$$**

Saginaw County

10th Circuit Court www.saginawcounty.com/CircuitCourt.aspx?AspxAutoDetectCookieSupport=1
Civil: Search civil records from 2000 forward online free at www.saginawcounty.com/Clerk/Court/CivilRecords.aspx *Criminal:* Search criminal records online free at www.saginawcounty.com/Clerk/Court/CriminalRecords.aspx. Records shown are from 2000 to present.

St. Clair County

31st Circuit Court www.stclaircounty.org/Offices/courts/
Civil: A index of records can be viewed at www.stclaircounty.org/Offices/courts/circuit/records.asp. *Criminal:* Records index can be viewed at www.stclaircounty.org/Offices/courts/circuit/records.asp.

72nd District Court www.stclaircounty.org/Offices/courts/
Civil: Access court case index free at www.stclaircounty.org/DCS/search.aspx. *Criminal:* same

Washtenaw County

15th District Court - Criminal Division www.a2gov.org/services/OtherServices/15D/Pages/default.aspx
Criminal: Access court records free at www.a2gov.org/services/OtherServices/15D/Pages/OnlineCaseSearch.aspx. Includes cases files on or after 08/05/2006. Older cases are found at https://secure.a2gov.org/15darchive/login.asp.

15th District Court - Civil Division www.a2gov.org/services/OtherServices/15D/Pages/default.aspx
Civil: Access court records free at www.a2gov.org/services/OtherServices/15D/Pages/OnlineCaseSearch.aspx. Includes cases filed on or after 08/05/2006. Older cases available at https://secure.a2gov.org/15darchive/login.asp.

14A-1 District All Courts http://14adistrictcourt.org/locations/14a-1
Civil: Dockets and calendars are searchable at www.14adistrictcourt.org/cases. *Criminal:* same

Wayne County

3rd Circuit Court - Criminal Div https://www.3rdcc.org/
Criminal: Free access to the criminal docket at https://cmspublic.3rdcc.org/default.aspx.

3rd Circuit Court - Civil Div https://www.3rdcc.org/
Civil: Free access to the docket index at https://cmspublic.3rdcc.org/default.aspx.

33rd District Court www.d33.courts.mi.gov/
Civil: Docket information is offered at www.d33.courts.mi.gov/jisdocket/jisdocket.aspx, searchable by name. attorney, judge or case number. *Criminal:* same

Recorders, Assessors, and Other Sites of Note

Recording Office Organization: 83 counties, 83 recording offices. The recording officer is the County Register of Deeds. Federal and state tax liens on personal property of businesses are filed with the Secretary of State. Other federal and state tax liens are filed with the Register of Deeds.

Statewide or Multi-Jurisdiction Access: There is no statewide online access to recorded documents or tax assessor data, but a number of counties offer free access.

- The site at www.dleg.state.mi.us/platmaps/sr_subs.asp provides free access to digital images - with print capability - of the plats and related documents of land subdivisions in the State of Michigan's construction plat files. Search by location or subdivision. Covers all 83 counties. These sites are not shown in the profiles below.
- Access local property record data at over 640 Michigan jurisdictions (towns, townships, cities, etc.) at https://is.bsasoftware.com/bsa.is/SelectUnit.aspx. Many are found in the county list but it is suggested you visit the vendor site for the complete list and updates. For most locations, index searching is free. Tax information searches may also be available. Some units charge a small convenience fee to view records. A business account allows you to perform lookups without paying up-front; monthly billing is available.
- Access property data and GIS-maps free via a vendor Maps inDeed at https://mapsindeed.com - 10 counties are particiapting: Alpena, Calhoun, Cass, Genessee, Mason, Montmorency, Menonimee, Oceana, Osceola, Van Buren and more to be added.

County Sites:

Alcona County ***Recorded Documents***
http://public.alconacountymi.com/index.php?option=com_content&view=section&id=9&Itemid=79 Access records for a fee at https://mi.uslandrecords.com/milr/MilrApp/index.jsp. **$$$**

Allegan County ***Property, Taxation*** Search index by name or address at https://is.bsasoftware.com/bsa.is/SelectUnit.aspx. The site includes Cities of Otsego, Plainwell, Douglas, and Saugatuck Township. Search tax index or foreclosures by name or address at www.allegancounty.org/Government/TR/TaxSearch.asp?pt= OR https://is.bsasoftware.com/bsa.is/SelectUnit.aspx including Cities of Otsego, Plainwell, Wayland, Douglas, and Saugatuck Township.

Alpena County ***Property, Taxation*** Search the assessor property tax data free at www.alpena.mi.govern.com/parcelquery.php. Access property tax data and GIS-maps for a fee at https://mapsindeed.com/michigan/alpena-county.**$$$**

Antrim County ***Grantor/Grantee, Deed, Mortgage, Lien, Misc Records*** www.antrimcounty.org/rod.asp Access to land records for a fee at https://mi.uslandrecords.com/milr/controller;jsessionid=4E14EDDD34DB3DCF00E3D079B40A1B8A. Records from 1/1/93 to present. **$$$**
Property, Taxation Search parcel data information free at www.antrimcounty.org/parcelsearch.asp.

Arenac County ***Recorded Documents*** www.arenaccountygov.com/register_of_deeds/ Access to public records available at https://rodweb.arenaccountygov.com/LandShark/login.jsp?url=https%3A%2F%2Frodweb.arenaccountygov.com%2FLandShark%2Fsearchname.jsp. User name and password are both PUBLIC, please remember this is case sensitive. **$$$**

Baraga County ***Recorded Documents*** www.baragacounty.org/government/county-clerk-register-of-deeds/ To access to records for a fee at https://is.bsasoftware.com/BSA.IS/default.aspx. Must register. **$$$**

Barry County ***Real Estate, Deed, Lien, Mortgage, Judgment, Vital Records*** www.barrycounty.org/county-departments/register-of-deeds/ Access recorded Indexes back to 1989 free at www.barrycounty.org/online-services/register-of-deeds-image-search/. Pre 1993 images being added. Also, search Vital Records data free at http://internal.barrycounty.org:8081/clerk/web/.
Property, Taxation Access to county parcel data is free at www.barrycounty.org/online-services/parcel-search/. County property Index is from 12/95 to 12/2005; assessment rolls should not be used for a title search or legal description.

Bay County ***Real Estate, Deed, Lien Records*** www.baycounty-mi.gov/ROD/ Access the register's land records data after registration, login with username and password at www.baycounty-mi.gov/ROD/. Index goes back to 1985; images now available with copy cost and $5.00 login fee.
Property, Taxation Access county property tax data for free at https://is.bsasoftware.com/bsa.is/SelectUnit.aspx. Do a general property search free at https://is.bsasoftware.com/bsa.is/AssessingServices/ServiceAssessingSearch.aspx?i=1&appid=0&unit=685. Also, search residential sales, interactive map. Also, access tax data for City of Essexville and Hampton Township at https://is.bsasoftware.com/bsa.is/SelectUnit.aspx.

Benzie County ***Real Estate, Deed, Lien, Parcel Records*** www.benzieco.net/dept_register_of_deeds.htm The agency sends requesters to the Laredo system. Fees are based on a flat rate by usage ranging from $50 to $250 per month. The same vendor offers the Tapestry program with a $5.95 search fee and copies for $.50 per page. You can pay as you go with a credit card or be billed monthly with a $25.00 monthly minimum. Visit at www.fidlar.com or call 800-747-4600 at ext 271 or 324. **$$$**

Property, Taxation Access to parcel search and mapping for free at www.liaa.ws/benzieco/.

Berrien County ***Real Estate, Deed, Records*** http://berriencounty.org/RegisterofDeeds Access to records from register of deeds free at http://regofdeeds.berriencounty.org/.

Property, Taxation Access to information on real estate properties, see http://berriencounty.org/inside.php?action=property_listing_search&dept=8. GIS data is at http://beacon.schneidercorp.com/. Access to City of Niles property data is free with registration at https://is.bsasoftware.com/bsa.is/SelectUnit.aspx.

Branch County ***Real Estate, Deed, Lien Records*** www.countyofbranch.com/departments/26 Recorder land data by subscription on either the Laredo system using subscription and fees or the Tapestry2 System using credit card, https://tapestry.fidlar.com/Tapestry2/Default.aspx. $5.95 search; $1.00 per image. Index and images go back to 1/1/1994. **$$$**

Property, Taxation Access City of Coldwater and Township of Coldwater property tax and special assessments free after registration at https://is.bsasoftware.com/bsa.is/SelectUnit.aspx.

Calhoun County ***Real Estate, Grantor/Grantee, Deed, Lien, Parcel Records*** www.co.calhoun.mi.us/ Access the recorder's Land Records Index free back to 1/3/1966 at http://rod.co.calhoun.mi.us/indexsearch.html.

Property, Taxation Access to data for Cities of Albion, Battle Creek, Marshall, Springfield and Townships of Marshall, Newton, and Sheridan is free with registration at https://is.bsasoftware.com/bsa.is/SelectUnit.aspx. Also, access property tax data and GIS-maps for a fee at https://mapsindeed.com/.

Cass County ***Real Estate, Grantor/Grantee, Deed Records*** www.casscountymi.org Access to recorded records free at https://index.casscountymi.org/recorder/web/. Search documents recorded from 11/1/93 to present.

Property, Taxation Access county property tax records free at www.cass.mi.govern.com/parcelquery.php. Also access to GIS-mapping for free at http://maps.casscountymi.org/ Also, access property tax data and GIS-maps for a fee at https://mapsindeed.com/.

Charlevoix County ***Real Estate, Deed Records*** www.charlevoixcounty.org/rod.asp Register of Deeds records to view are free back to 1/1/84 at http://12.150.40.69/rodweb/. Copies fees are $1.05 per page. **$$$**

Property, Taxation Access the assessor's basic property data or property tax payment free at www.charlevoixcounty.org/propertysearch.asp. Also, access county and Township of Evangeline tax data free with registration at https://is.bsasoftware.com/bsa.is/SelectUnit.aspx. Index search is free but registration is required to view and print documents for $2.00 each.

Cheboygan County ***Real Estate Records*** www.cheboygancounty.net/cheboygan-county-clerkregister-o/ Access to land records free at https://clerk.cheboygancounty.net:4430/landweb.dll/EXEC. Guest login for images only. Must subscribe for more detailed information. **$$$**

Property, Taxation Access to assessor property index is free at www.cheboyganequalization.com/.

Chippewa County ***Recorded Documents*** www.chippewacountymi.gov/rod.html Access to limited records index free at www.chippewacountymi.gov/rod_online_searching.html. Indexes available from 2/1/78 to present. No online viewing of documents available.

Property, Taxation Access to parcel records for free at http://mi-chippewa-equalization.governmax.com/collectmax/collect30.asp.

Clinton County ***Real Estate, Deed, Judgment, Lien Records*** www.clinton-county.org/Government/RegisterofDeeds.aspx Register to search free on the recorders database at www.clinton-county.org/OnlineServices.aspx. Username and password is required. Copies of documents online can be purchased with a credit card for $1.25 per page.

Property, Taxation Access DeWitt, Eagle, Victor, and Watertown tax data, utility bills, and assessments free with registration at https://is.bsasoftware.com/bsa.is/SelectUnit.aspx. Property data available at http://maps.clinton-county.org/ClintonCountyCX/Disclaimer.htm, no name searching.

Crawford County ***Property, Taxation*** Access to property and land records for free got to https://is.bsasoftware.com/bsa.is/AssessingServices/ServiceAssessingSearch.aspx?i=1&appid=0&unit=466.

Dickinson County ***Property, Taxation*** Access City of Iron Mountain land and property tax data free with registration at https://is.bsasoftware.com/bsa.is/SelectUnit.aspx.

Eaton County ***Deed, Mortgage, Plat Records*** www.eatoncounty.org/index.php/departments/register-of-deeds Access to records free at https://portal2.recordfusion.com/countyweb/login.do?countyname=Eaton. No fee to access index (under login as guest), however to view image thumbnails and print images must open account and pay. **$$$**

Property, Taxation Search access property and tax data for Cities of Charlotte, Eaton Rapids, Grand Ledge, and Townships of Carmel and Delta for free at https://is.bsasoftware.com/bsa.is/SelectUnit.aspx. Images are $2.00 each. Includes access to delinquent tax data.**$$$**

Emmet County ***Real Estate, Deed, Lien Records*** www.emmetcounty.org/registerofdeeds/ Access recorder land records for free if you login as Public User at http://apps1.emmetcounty.org:8080/Recorder/web/newUser.jsp. Also, full online access to view and print images is available for $1.03 per page, payable via credit card/PayPal. **$$$**

Property, Taxation Access assessor property records free at www.emmetcounty.org/property-search-68/. Also, access county property tax, land, animal licenses, and delinquent taxes free with registration at https://is.bsasoftware.com/bsa.is/SelectUnit.aspx.

Genesee County ***Recorded Documents, Marriage, Death Records*** www.gc4me.com/departments/register_of_deeds/index/index.php Access to Register of Deeds database is free at www.co.genesee.mi.us/rod/. But to view documents back to 10/2000, there is a fee, and user ID and password required. Also, online access to the county clerk's marriage (back to 1963) and death (back to 1930) indexes are free at www.co.genesee.mi.us/vitalrec/. Also, access to records for free to go https://co.genesee.mi.us/pax/. Must purchase copies and can do that through PayPal.

Property, Taxation Search property index at www.co.genesee.mi.us/tax/tax.html. Also, access property tax data and GIS-maps for a fee at https://mapsindeed.com/. Also, access property data for the county and for Cities of Burton, Linden and townships of Fenton, Davison, Grand Blanc, and Vienna free with registration at https://is.bsasoftware.com/bsa.is/SelectUnit.aspx.

Gladwin County ***Recorded Documents*** www.gladwinco.com Access to subscription service contact Ann Manning at 989-426-7551. **$$$**

Property, Taxation Access City of Gladwin property data free with registration at https://is.bsasoftware.com/bsa.is/SelectUnit.aspx. Also, access to land records portal for free at https://www.fetchgis.com/gladwinlrp/appauth/GladwinLRP.html#.

Grand Traverse County ***Real Estate, Deed, Tax Lien, Judgment, Assumed Name, Construction Permit, Marriage, Death*** www.co.grand-traverse.mi.us/departments/Register_of_Deeds.htm Recorder's document index search back to 1986 is free at www.co.grand-traverse.mi.us/services/online_records.htm. Images require fee; pay by credit card. Deaths go back to 1867; marriages to 1853. Also, recording data by sub on Laredo system or Tapestry credit card system at http://tapestry.fidlar.com; $5.95 search; $.50 per image back to 1986. Also, access tax & special assessments free at https://is.bsasoftware.com/bsa.is/. **$$$**

Property, Taxation Access property tax and special assessments free at https://is.bsasoftware.com/bsa.is/SelectUnit.aspx.

Gratiot County ***Property, Taxation*** Free access to GIS/mapping is found at www.fetchgis.com/gratiotweb/rma/GratiotMapViewer.html#.

Hillsdale County ***Recorded Documents*** http://co.hillsdale.mi.us/index.php/deeds Access to the recorder's index is free but images available only by sub. Records go back to 9/1984 and more being added. Fee is $300.00 for recorder, or $50.00 for just the assessor's equalization records. Copies included. Call recorder for signup. The office does allow credit card purchases online in addition to sub. Also, access to recorders index is free via a private firm at https://portal1.recordfusion.com/countyweb/login.do?countyname=Hillsdale. Search free as Guest; registration and fees for full data. Fees to view images. Also, access to Michigan UCC online service go to https://apps.michigan.gov/UCC/Home.aspx. Debtor name quick search is free, More detail information with a subscription. **$$$**

Property, Taxation Search parcels free at www.hillsdalecounty.info/parcelsearch.asp, no name searching. Also, access City of Hillsdale tax records free with registration at https://is.bsasoftware.com/bsa.is/SelectUnit.aspx. Map searching is available at www.hillsdalecounty.info/mapspage0002.asp. See County Register of Deeds section for subscription info for county assessment data.

Houghton County ***Real Estate, Deed, Lien, Mortgage, Plat Records*** www.houghtoncounty.net/directory-hcdeeds.shtml The agency sends requesters to the Laredo system. Fees are based on a flat rate by usage ranging from $50 to $250 per month. The same vendor offers the Tapestry program with a $5.95 search fee and copies for $.50 per page. You can pay as you go with a credit card or be billed monthly with a $25.00 monthly minimum. Visit at www.fidlar.com or call 800-747-4600 at ext 271 or 324. **$$$**

Property, Taxation Access to land records search for free at http://fidlar.houghtoncounty.net/websense/default.aspx.

Huron County ***Property, Taxation*** Access to records for a fee at https://is.bsasoftware.com/BSA.IS/default.aspx.**$$$**

Ingham County ***Real Estate, Grantor/Grantee, Deed, Marriage, Fictitious Name Records*** http://rd.ingham.org/ Access the Register of Deeds online database for a fee, there are 3 ways to access-1. AVA - https://ava.fidlar.com/michigan/ingham/ava (this information is delayed for 30 days), images are available for $1.10 per page; 2. Tapestry - https://tapestry.fidlar.com/Tapestry2/Default.aspx, Fee is $5.95 per search, copies of images are $1.00 per page; and 3. Laredo - www.fidlar.com/, subscription plan rates plus images are $1.00 per page. **$$$**

Property, Taxation Access land, tax, utility records and more free with registration for Cities of East Lansing, Lansing, Leslie, Mason and townships of Aurelius, Lansing, Vevay, and Village of Stockbridge at https://is.bsasoftware.com/bsa.is/SelectUnit.aspx. Also, access to GIS/mapping free at http://ingham-equalization.rsgis.msu.edu/.

Ionia County ***Real Estate, Deed, Judgment, Lien, Will, Death Records*** www.ioniacounty.org/register-of-deeds/default.aspx Access recorder records free at https://portal2.recordfusion.com/countyweb/login.do?countyname=Ionia. Login as "guest" for free name search. More detailed must register with fees. **$$$**

Property, Taxation Access county property data and GIS/mapping free at www.ioniacounty.org/online-services.aspx. Also, access City of Belding and Ionia City and Lyons Town land and property records free with registration at https://is.bsasoftware.com/bsa.is/SelectUnit.aspx. Use www.ioniacounty.org/ under the heading "online parcel information" to search tax records online.

Iosco County ***Real Estate Records*** www.iosco.net Subscription available by contacting Bonita Coyle, 989-362-2021. **$$$**

Property, Taxation Three jurisdictions are available free at https://is.bsasoftware.com/bsa.is/SelectUnit.aspx - City of East Tawas, and Oscoda, Plainfield, and Baldwin Townships.

Isabella County ***Real Estate, Grantor/Grantee, Deed, Lien, Mortgage, UCC Records*** www.isabellacounty.org/deeds/ Access recorder land data back to 1940 on ACS at https://mi.uslandrecords.com/milr/MilrApp/index.jsp. Index only. Fees involved. **$$$**

Property, Taxation Access to City of Mt Pleasant property and tax data is free with registration at https://is.bsasoftware.com/bsa.is/SelectUnit.aspx.

Jackson County ***Real Estate, Grantor/Grantee, Deed, Lien, Divorce Judgment, Death, UCC Records*** www.co.jackson.mi.us/rod/ Search recorded documents at https://portal2.recordfusion.com/countyweb/login.do?countyname=Jackson with a fee for add'l services. **$$$**

Property, Taxation Access property, tax and land data for the county and City of Jackson and townships of Columbia and Rives for free with registration at https://is.bsasoftware.com/bsa.is/SelectUnit.aspx. Search for Columbia utility bills as well. Also, search GIS-mapping site for property free at www.co.jackson.mi.us/departments/equalization/jackson_county_gis/map_gallery.asp. Search tax sale data free at www.jacksoncountytaxsale.com/.

Kalamazoo County ***Recorded Deeds, Vital Records*** www.kalcounty.com Access to public records go to https://clerkregister.kalcounty.com:8443/eaglerecorder/web/. The public search allows users to search the index only; images are not available. Once you are registered, you may purchase single documents by credit card for $1.00 per page. Also, there is a free vital records search at https://clerkregister.kalcounty.com:8444/eagleclerk/web/login.jsp. **$$$**

Property, Taxation Access property assessor data free at www.kalcounty.com/equalization/parcel_search.php. Access property, land, and tax data for Cities of Kalamazoo, Parchment, Portage and the townships of Alamo, Brady, Comstock, Kalamazoo, Oshtemo, Pavilion, Ross , Schoolcraft, and Wakeshma free with registration at https://is.bsasoftware.com/bsa.is/SelectUnit.aspx. Search treasurer's delinquent taxes free at https://is.bsasoftware.com/bsa.is/default.aspx. GiS at www.kalcounty.com/planning/gis.htm.

Kalkaska County ***Deed, Judgment, Plat, UCC Records*** www.kalkaskacounty.net/regdeeds.asp Access to records go to https://tapestry.fidlar.com/Tapestry2/Default.aspx. Infrequent users fee-$5.95 search fee plus $1.00 print; frequent users contact JoAnn DeGraaf for details and monthly subscriptions. **$$$**

Property, Taxation Access to property search for free at www.kalkaskacounty.net/propertysearch.asp. Also, access to GIS/mapping for free to go www.kalkaskacounty.net/mapindex.asp.

Kent County ***Recorded Documents, Fictitious Name Records*** www.accesskent.com/Departments/RegisterofDeeds/ Access Kent deeds index free at https://www.accesskent.com/deeds/. Fee for document $2.00 per page plus a $.50 convenience fee. Search and purchase accident reports $3.00 at https://www.accesskent.com/AccidentReports/. Search fictitious business names free at https://www.accesskent.com/BusinessNames/. **$$$**

Property, Taxation Access to property search for free at https://www.accesskent.com/Property/.**$$$**

Lake County ***Property, Taxation*** Access to property and land searches for free at https://is.bsasoftware.com/bsa.is/Login.aspx?ReturnUrl=%2fbsa.is%2fdefault.aspx. Must register with user name and password.

Lapeer County ***Real Estate, Deed, Lien, Judgment Records*** www.county.lapeer.org/Deeds/index.html Access recorder index free by name by clicking on "Guest Login" at http://207.72.70.14/scripts/landweb.html. Registration and fees required for full search. Pop-up blocker must be off. No images online. Indexes available from 9/10/1836 thru present. **$$$**

Property, Taxation Access property, land and tax data for Cities of Lapeer and Imlay, and townships of Almont, Imlay, Mayfield for free with registration at https://is.bsasoftware.com/bsa.is/SelectUnit.aspx. Also has special assessment records for City of Lapeer.

Leelanau County ***Real Estate, Deed, Lien, Mortgage, Judgment Records*** www.leelanau.cc Access the recorders database of indexes free at www.leelanau.cc/RODSearch.asp. Records go back past 1980 but may be subject to errors and omissions. Subscription service for full data and images; $1.25 per page. **$$$**

Property, Taxation Access assessor property data free at www.leelanau.cc/PropertySearch.asp. https://is.bsasoftware.com/BSA.IS/default.aspx

Lenawee County ***Deeds, Mortgages, Land Contracts, Liens, Affidavits, Etc. Records*** www.lenawee.mi.us/departments/register-of-deeds Access recorder records free at https://portal2.recordfusion.com/countyweb/login.do?countyname=Lenawee. Login as "guest" for free name search. More detailed must register with fees. **$$$**

Property, Taxation Search assessing/property data free at https://is.bsasoftware.com/bsa.is/SelectUnit.aspx. Also, access to City of Tecumseh data including animal licensing is free with registration at https://is.bsasoftware.com/bsa.is/SelectUnit.aspx.

Livingston County ***Real Estate, Deed, Lien, Death Records*** www.co.livingston.mi.us/RegisterofDeeds/ Web access to county records back to 1984 available to occasional users; a dedicated line is available for professionals for $1200 fee. Annual fee for occasional use- $400. Records date back to 1984. Lending agency data available. See https://www.livingstonlive.org/Deeds/ or contact IT Dept at 517-548-3230. Also, search the county death indices to 1948 for free at www.livgenmi.com/deathlisting.htm. **$$$**

Property, Taxation Access property, tax, and other civil data for Cities of Brighton, Howell, and Townships of Brighton, Handy, Hartland, Putnam free with registration at https://is.bsasoftware.com/bsa.is/SelectUnit.aspx. Includes Village of Fowler property tax data. Also, access property data at https://www.livingstonlive.org/Property/.

Mackinac County ***Property, Taxation*** Access to property and land searches for free at https://is.bsasoftware.com/bsa.is/Login.aspx?ReturnUrl=%2fBSA.IS%2fdefault.aspx. Must register with user name and password.

Macomb County ***Real Estate, Deed, Business Registration Records*** http://macombcountymi.gov/clerksoffice/index.asp Land records database found at http://hosted.acsgrm.com/cgibin/homepage?County=8025. Free registration for password and user name. Subscription by month or purchase on pay-per-view basis. Also, county recorder index and images (back to 1818) from a private source at www.courthousedirect.com/. Fees/registration required. **$$$**

Property, Taxation 13 cities' and towns' property, tax, and certain other civil records are free with registration at https://is.bsasoftware.com/bsa.is/SelectUnit.aspx.

Manistee County ***Recorded Documents*** www.manisteecountymi.gov/index.php?option=com_content&view=article&id=53&Itemid=92 Access to records for a fee at https://tapestry.fidlar.com/Tapestry2/Default.aspx. **$$$**

Property, Taxation Access property records free at www.liaa.org/manisteeparcels/propertysearch.asp.

Marquette County ***Real Estate, Deed, Lien Records*** www.co.marquette.mi.us/departments/register_of_deeds/index.htm A free land records search is at http://67.212.214.84/DirectSearch/Default.aspx. Also, the agency sends requesters to the Tapestry program with a $5.95 search fee and copies for $.50 per page. You can pay as you go with a credit card or be billed monthly with a $25.00 monthly minimum. Visit at www.fidlar.com or call 800-747-4600 at ext 271 or 324. **$$$**

Property, Taxation Access building records free with registration at https://is.bsasoftware.com/BSA.IS/default.aspx.

Mason County ***Real Estate, Deed, Lien Records*** www.masoncounty.net/ 3 options available to search county Register database at www.masoncounty.net/content.aspx?Page=Online%20Services&departmentID=10. Search the Websense index free; other two require registration and fees. The agency sends requesters to the Laredo system. Fees are based on a flat rate by usage ranging from $75 to $400 per month. The same vendor offers the Tapestry program with a $5.95 search fee and copies for $1.00 per page. You can pay as you go with a credit card or be billed monthly with a $25.00 monthly minimum. Visit at www.fidlar.com or call 800-747-4600 at ext 271 or 324. **$$$**

Property, Taxation Access county property data at www.liaa.org/masonparcels/propertysearch.asp. Also, access property tax data and GIS-maps for a fee at https://mapsindeed.com/. Access to City of Ludington parcels and tax data is free with registration at https://is.bsasoftware.com/bsa.is/SelectUnit.aspx. Ditto for Hamlin Township property, and ditto for Pere Marquette Township property and utility bills.

Mecosta County ***Recorded Documents, Oil and Gas Records*** www.co.mecosta.mi.us/deeds.asp Access to land records free at https://mi.uslandrecords.com/milr/MilrApp/index.jsp. Records are available from 1968 to present.

Property, Taxation Access county property, land, and tax data index free with registration at https://is.bsasoftware.com/bsa.is/SelectUnit.aspx. May charge fees to view images. Data includes City of Big Rapids and Animal License, Special Assessments, Delinquent Taxes.

Menominee County ***Real Estate, Deed Records*** www.menomineecounty.com/ Access to land records is free at www.menomineecounty.com/online_services/category_general/ then click on County Land Records. Search is free - use "Guest Login." Document images available online, credit card accepted. Tax certification checks for Warranty Deeds, and land contracts for $1.00 need to be made payable to the Monominee County Treasurer. Subscriptions available for full data. **$$$**

Property, Taxation Access property tax and land data for City of Menominee and Township of Menominee free with registration at https://is.bsasoftware.com/bsa.is/SelectUnit.aspx. Also, access property tax data and GIS-maps for a fee at https://mapsindeed.com/.

Midland County ***Recorded Documents*** www.co.midland.mi.us/departments/home.php?id=25 Access to records free at http://webapps.co.midland.mi.us/countyweb/login.do?countyname=Midland. No fee to access index (under login as guest), however to view image thumbnails and print images must open account and pay. **$$$**

Property, Taxation Access the county and City of Midland property data free with registration at https://is.bsasoftware.com/bsa.is/SelectUnit.aspx. County access via www.co.midland.mi.us/ also includes delinquent tax and animal license data.

Missaukee County ***Property, Taxation*** Access to records for free at https://is.bsasoftware.com/BSA.IS/default.aspx.

Monroe County ***Real Estate, Deed, Lien, Fictitious Name Records*** www.co.monroe.mi.us//government/departments_offices/clerks/register_of_deeds.html The agency sends requesters to the Laredo system. Fees are based on a flat rate by usage ranging from $75 to $400 per month. There is also a non-refundable application fee of $75.00. The same vendor offers the Tapestry program with a $5.75 search fee and copies for $.50 per page. Visit at www.fidlar.com or call 800-747-4600 at ext 271 or 324. Access fictitious business names free at https://www.co.monroe.mi.us/egov/searchdbanames.aspx. **$$$**

Property, Taxation Access assessment database land index and county tax bill and delinquent tax date free with registration at https://is.bsasoftware.com/bsa.is/SelectUnit.aspx. Printing full record card of property requires credit card payment.

Montcalm County ***Real Estate, Deed, Lien Records*** Access to recorders index is free via a private firm at https://portal1.recordfusion.com/countyweb/login.do?countyname=Montcalm. Search free as Guest; registration and fees for full data or images. **$$$**

Property, Taxation Assessor parcel data is free at http://parcels.montcalm.org/. Also, search tax roll and tax sale data free at www.co.whatcom.wa.us/treasurer/index.jsp. Access to Cities of Greenville property, tax, and land data is free with registration at https://is.bsasoftware.com/bsa.is/SelectUnit.aspx.

Montmorency County ***Property, Taxation*** To view land records free at https://www.fetchgis.com/montlrp/appauth/MontLRP.html#. To get further information on property must register and pay fees. Also, access property tax data and GIS-maps for a fee at https://mapsindeed.com/.**$$$**

Muskegon County ***Real Estate, Grantor/Grantee, Deed, Mortgage, Lien Records*** www.co.muskegon.mi.us/deeds/ Login as Great, password Muskegon, to search recorder land records free at www.co.muskegon.mi.us/deeds/record_search.htm. Registration and fees apply in access images. **$$$**

Property, Taxation Access to the GIS/mapping for free at www.muskegoncountygis.com/ Access the county genealogical death index system for free at www.co.muskegon.mi.us/clerk/websearch.cfm. Records 1867-1965.

Newaygo County ***Recorded Documents*** www.countyofnewaygo.com/ROD/RODHome.htm Access the county land records search system free at http://rod.countyofnewaygo.com/landweb.dll/EXEC. Login as Guest. Subscription required for full access, $500 monthly plus $1 per page. **$$$**

Property, Taxation Search property data free on the GIS-mapping site at http://gis.countyofnewaygo.com/MapViews/Public%5FV2/Newaygo/viewer.htm but no name searching. A subscription version offering various options is available, call 231-689-7281 or see Also, access City of Fremont land/property data free with registration at https://is.bsasoftware.com/bsa.is/SelectUnit.aspx.

Oakland County ***Business Name, Assumed Name Records*** www.oakgov.com/clerkrod/Pages/default.aspx Search fictitious/assumed names for a fee at www.oakgov.com/clerkrod/vital_records/Pages/dba.aspx. **$$$**

Property, Taxation Access to Oakland property data is by subscription, available monthly or per use. For info or sign-up, visit www.oakgov.com/accessok/Pages/default.aspx or call Information Services at 248-858-0861. Search Rochester Hills tax assessor data at www.rochesterhills.org/index.aspx?NID=134. No name searching. Also access 8 municipalities land, property tax records and more free at https://is.bsasoftware.com/bsa.is/SelectUnit.aspx.**$$$**

Oceana County ***Real Estate, Deed Records*** www.oceana.mi.us/register_of_deeds/ Access the record index for a fee at http://grm.thomsonreuters.com/. **$$$**

Property, Taxation Access property tax and land records for Hart Township for free with registration at https://is.bsasoftware.com/bsa.is/SelectUnit.aspx. Also, access property tax data and GIS-maps for a fee at https://mapsindeed.com/.

Ogemaw County ***Property, Taxation*** Access assessor equalization data free at http://ogemaw.mi.govern.com/parcelquery.php. Also, access property data free at http://ogemawgis.com/parcelquery/website/.

Osceola County ***Property, Taxation*** Access property tax data and GIS-maps for a fee at https://mapsindeed.com/.

Oscoda County ***Real Estate, Deed, Lien, UCC, Mortgage, Plat, Judgment Records*** www.oscodacountymi.com/Register%20of%20Deeds.htm The agency sends requesters to the Laredo system. Fees are based on a flat rate by usage ranging from $50 to $250 per month. The same vendor offers the Tapestry program with a $5.95 search fee and copies for $.50 per page. You can pay as you go with a credit card or be billed monthly with a $25.00 monthly minimum. Visit at www.fidlar.com or call 800-747-4600 at ext 271 or 324. Also, access record documents index free at http://65.111.217.227/DirectSearch/Default.aspx. **$$$**

Property, Taxation Access to Equalization records for free at www.oscodacountymi.com/Equalization.htm.

Otsego County ***Recorded Documents*** www.otsegocountymi.gov/register-of-deeds-34/ Access to records free at http://rod.otsegocountymi.gov/Landweb.dll/EXEC. Indexes available from 3/5/1864 to present.

Property, Taxation Search property and assessment data on the Equalization Dept search site at www.otsegocountymi.gov/property-search--27/.

Ottawa County ***Recorded Documents*** www.miottawa.org/ Search property data free at https://www.miottawa.org/Property/noLogin.do; fee may apply to view docs. Also, search land records at https://tapestry.fidlar.com/Tapestry2/LoggedOut.aspx with payment by search and image with credit card or account. **$$$**

Property, Taxation Access Treasurer and Equalization tax records free at https://www.miottawa.org/Property/noLogin.do but a fee applies to view docs; purchase by subscription or with credit card.

Presque Isle County ***Property, Taxation*** Search property tax data free at www.presqueisle.mi.govern.com/parcelquery.php.

Roscommon County ***Recorded Documents*** www.roscommoncounty.net/county-departments/register-of-deeds Access land recorded index free at https://mi.uslandrecords.com/milr/MilrApp/index.jsp. Select Roscommon.

Saginaw County ***Real Estate, Grantor/Grantee, Deed, Assumed Business Name, Marriage, Death, Election Records*** www.saginawcounty.com/Rod/Default.aspx Search the Register of Deeds index at www.saginawcounty.com/Rod/RODSimpleSearch.aspx. Access county clerks assumed names, marriages, death free at www.saginawcounty.com/Clerk/Search.aspx. Vital statistic records go back to 1995. **$$$**

Property, Taxation Search equalization board tax records at www.saginawcounty.com/Apps/Equal/PropertySearch.aspx. Also, a general property and sales search on the GIS site is free at www.saginawcounty.com/OnlineServices.aspx.

St. Clair County ***Real Estate, Deed, Lien, Death Records*** www.stclaircounty.org/Offices/register_of_deeds/ Access register of deeds database free at http://publicdeeds.stclaircounty.org/.

Property, Taxation Search tax equalization data free at www.stclaircounty.org/offices/equalization/search.aspx. Also, land data may be available at http://gis.stclaircounty.org/landmanagement/ on the map site. Also, access land and property tax data for Cities of Algonac, Marysville, St Clair also Townships of Clay, Cottleville, East China, and Ira for free with registration at https://is.bsasoftware.com/bsa.is/SelectUnit.aspx.

St. Joseph County ***Property, Taxation*** Search parcel records for free at www.stjosephcountymi.org/taxsearch/default.asp. Also offered is a subscription service with additional features. Also, property tax and delinquent tax data and City of Sturgis land data for free with registration at https://is.bsasoftware.com/bsa.is/SelectUnit.aspx.

Sanilac County ***Recorded Documents (Index Only) Records*** www.sanilaccounty.net/PublicPages/Entity.aspx?ID=220 Access to records free at www.sanilaccounty.net/PublicPages/Entity.aspx?ID=220. Indexes available from 5/24/1801 to present.

Property, Taxation Access to parcel information for free at www.sanilaccounty.net/PublicPages/Parcels.aspx. Also, access county land and property tax records free with registration at https://is.bsasoftware.com/bsa.is/SelectUnit.aspx. Access Argyle Township and Moore Township property records for free there also.**$$$**

Shiawassee County ***Recorded Documents*** https://counties2.recordfusion.com/ShiawasseeMI/website/index.htm Access to public records go to https://portal2.recordfusion.com/countyweb/login.do?countyname=Shiawassee. Can login as guest, for more detailed information can sign in for a fee for subscription. **$$$**

Property, Taxation Access land and property tax data for Cities of Laingsburg and Perry, and Caledonia Township for free with registration at https://is.bsasoftware.com/bsa.is/SelectUnit.aspx. Also at this site is property tax data for Venice Township.

Tuscola County ***Recorded Documents*** www.tuscolacounty.org/deeds/ Access to the recorder's index for free at www.landaccess.com/.

Property, Taxation Search property tax data free or by account at https://is.bsasoftware.com/BSA.IS/default.aspx. Some unites charge a small convenience fee to view records. Signing up for a Business Account will allow you to perform lookups without paying up-front. You will be billed monthly for the lookups you perform.

Van Buren County ***Property, Taxation*** Access City/Township of South Haven property tax, land, and special assessment data for free with registration at https://is.bsasoftware.com/bsa.is/SelectUnit.aspx. Also includes property records for Townships of Antwerp and Paw Paw. Also, access to property tax searches free at www.vanburen.mi.govern.com/parcelquery.php. Also, access property tax data and GIS-maps for a fee at https://mapsindeed.com/.

Washtenaw County ***Real Estate, Deed, Lien, Judgment, Death, Marriage, Business Name Records*** www.ewashtenaw.org/government/clerk_register Access a menu of searchable databases at www.ewashtenaw.org/online. $1.00 fee for real estate images from Register of Deeds search page; click on Deeds Document Search. **$$$**

Property, Taxation Search land and property tax data and more for Cities of Ann Arbor, Chelsea, Milan, Saline, Ypsilanti, and townships of Ann Arbor, Augusta, Bridgewater, Dexter, Lodi, Pittsfield, Superior, Webster, York, Ypsilanti and Village of Dexter for free with registration at https://is.bsasoftware.com/bsa.is/SelectUnit.aspx. Also, for Property/Parcel Lookup free at https://secure.ewashtenaw.org/ecommerce/property/pStart.do.

Wayne County ***Real Estate, Deed, Judgment, Lien, Assumed Name Records*** www.waynecounty.com/deeds.htm Search county recorder land records database for free back to '86 at www.waynecountylandrecords.com/. A full data on-demand svc and a business svc available for a fee, call 313-967-6857 for info/sign-up or see above website. Access to unclaimed property free at www.michigan.gov/treasury/0,1607,7-121-44435-7924--,00.html. **$$$**

Property, Taxation Property and tax data and more for 16 municipalities free at https://is.bsasoftware.com/bsa.is/SelectUnit.aspx. Dearborn property Assessment data free at http://addlapps.cityofdearborn.org/dbnassessor/. No name searching.

Wexford County ***Real Estate Records*** www.wexfordcounty.org/Services/RegisterofDeeds/tabid/4275/Default.aspx Access to recorded documents for a fee at https://mi.uslandrecords.com/milr/. Records available from 1/82 to present. **$$$**

Property, Taxation Access the land parcel and Assessment roll site free at www.liaa.info/wexford/propertysearch.asp.

Reminder:

The site at www.dleg.state.mi.us/platmaps/sr_subs.asp provides free access to digital images - with print capability - of the plats and related documents of land subdivisions in the State of Michigan's construction plat files. Search by location or subdivision. Covers all 83 counties. These sites are not shown in the profiles above.

Minnesota

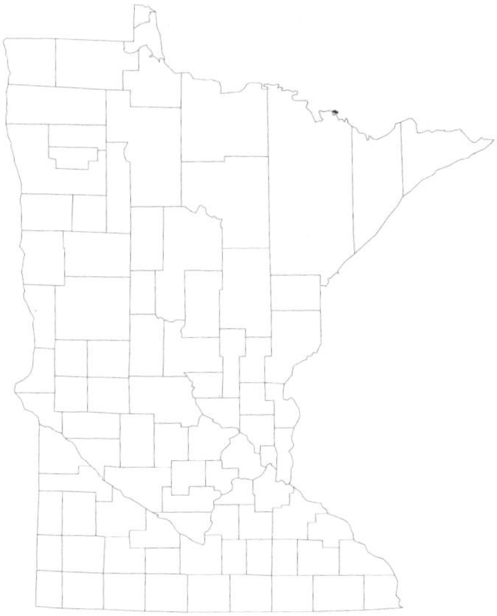

Capital: St. Paul
Ramsey County
Time Zone: CST
Population: 5,379,139
# of Counties: 87

Useful State Links

Website: www.mn.gov/portal/
Governor: http://mn.gov/governor/
Attorney General: www.ag.state.mn.us
State Archives: www.mnhs.org
State Statutes and Codes: https://www.revisor.mn.gov/pubs/
Legislative Bill Search: www.leg.state.mn.us/leg/legis.aspx
Bill Monitoring: www.house.leg.state.mn.us/leg/billsublogin.asp
Unclaimed Funds: http://mn.gov/commerce/

State Public Record Agencies

Criminal Records

Bureau of Criminal Apprehension, MNJIS - Criminal History Access Unit, https://dps.mn.gov/divisions/bca/Pages/default.aspx The agency distinguishes the free online search as a Background Check, and the pay service as a Criminal History. Access to the public criminal history record (15 year, no consent) is available free at https://dps.mn.gov/divisions/bca/Pages/background-checks.aspx. Search for Methamphetamine offenders at https://mor.state.mn.us/MorOffenderSearch.aspx. *Other Options:* A public database is available on CD-ROM. Monthly updates can be purchased. Data is in ASCII format and is raw data. Fee is $40.00

Sexual Offender Registry

Bureau of Criminal Apprehension, Minnesota Predatory Offender Program, https://por.state.mn.us/ Offenders and non-compliant offender if 16 or older may be searched at https://por.state.mn.us/OffenderSearch.aspx. Risk level 3 search available at DOC site www.doc.state.mn.us/level3/Search.asp.

Incarceration Records

Minnesota Department of Corrections, Records Management Unit, www.corr.state.mn.us Search at the web to retrieve public information about adult offenders who have been committed to the Commissioner of Corrections, and who are still under our jurisdiction (i.e. in prison, or released from prison and still under supervision). Search by name, with or without DOB, or by OID number at http://info.doc.state.mn.us/publicviewer/main.asp. Also, there is a separate search for Level 3 offender/predatory information.

Corporation, LLC, LP, Assumed Name, Trademarks/Servicemarks

Business Services, Secretary of State, www.sos.state.mn.us/ Go to http://mblsportal.sos.state.mn.us/ for free look-ups of business names and corporation files. Information includes Registered Office Address and Agent/CEO and PPPB address when applicable and Name Availability Searches Online orders or copies and Good Standing certificates are available for $10.00 fee. Good Standing Certs purchased online are downloaded immediately and copy orders are mailed out. Go to www.sos.state.mn.us/index.aspx?page=350 to locate lists of entities statutorily dissolved for not filing a renewal. **$$$** *Other Options:* Information can be purchased in bulk format. Call for more information.

Uniform Commercial Code, Federal & State Tax Liens

UCC Division, Secretary of State, www.sos.state.mn.us/index.aspx?page=89 There is a free look-up by filing number available from the website. A fee is charged for a name search. A comprehensive commercial program called Direct Access is available 24 hours. There is an annual subscription fee of

$75.00 per year, plus $5.00 per debtor name. Call 651-296-2803 for more information. **$$$** *Other Options:* This agency will provide information in bulk form on CD. Call 651-296-2803 or 877-551-6767 for more information.

Sales Tax Registrations

Minnesota Revenue Dept, Sale and Use Tax, www.revenue.state.mn.us/Pages/default.aspx Email requests are accepted at salesuse.tax@state.mn.us.

Birth Certificates

Minnesota Department of Health, Vital Records, www.health.state.mn.us/divs/chs/osr/birth.html Search for a marriage certificate fee at www.mncounty.com/Modules/Certificates/Marriage/Default.aspx but not all counties are on the MOMS system yet. Also, search the Birth Certificates Index free from 1900 to 1934 at http://people.mnhs.org/bci/Search.cfm?bhcp=1. *Other Options:* Bulk lists and files of information, if public record, are available on paper and in electronic format. Call Cheri Denardo at 651-201-5970 for details.

Death Records

Minnesota Department of Health, Vital Records, www.health.state.mn.us/divs/chs/osr/death.html No official online access available from this agency. However the State Historical Society offers a free Death Certificate Search at http://people.mnhs.org/dci/Search.cfm?bhcp=1. Records are from 1906 to 1996. *Other Options:* Bulk lists and files of information, if public record, are available on paper and in electronic format. Call Cheri Denardo at 651-201-5970 for details.

Workers' Compensation Records

Labor & Industry Department, Workers Compensation Division - File Review, www.dli.mn.gov/WorkComp.asp Copies of decision decided by the Minnesota Workers' Compensation Court of Appeals (WCCA) can be found at www.workerscomp.state.mn.us/.

Driver Records

Driver & Vehicle Services, Records Section, www.mndriveinfo.org Online access costs $1.25 per record. Online inquiries can be processed either as interactive or as batch files (overnight) 24 hours a day, 7 days a week. Requesters operate from a "bank." Records are accessed by either DL number or full name and DOB. Call Data Services at 651-297-5352 for more information. A free view of a DL status report is found at the home page above. The DL# is needed, no personal information is released. **$$$** *Other Options:* Minnesota will sell its entire database of driving record information with monthly updates per DPPA guidelines. Customized request sorts are available. Fees vary by type with programming and computer time and are quite reasonable.

Vehicle Ownership & Registration

Driver & Vehicle Services, Vehicle Record Requests, www.dps.state.mn.us/dvs/index.html Online access costs $5.00 per record. There is an additional monthly charge for dial-in access. The system, the same as described for driving record requests, is open 24/7. Search by name, plate, VIN or title number. Lien holder information is included. Users, who must qualify per DPPA, will receive address information. Call Records & Management Information 651-297-5352 for more information. Also, to obtain a renewal status report on a plate go to https://dutchelm.dps.state.mn.us/dvsinfo/mainframepublic.asp. Need the plate number and the last four digits of the VIN. **$$$**

Campaign Finance, Disclosures., PACs, Lobbyists

Campaign Finance & Public Disclosure, 190 Centennial Office Building, www.cfboard.state.mn.us/ A myriad of searchable database are available from links at www.cfboard.state.mn.us/. Search contributions and expenditures for candidates and PACs. Also search lobbyists and the associations that hire them by lobbyist or association name.

Voter Registration

Secretary of State-Election Division, Voter Registration Lists, www.sos.state.mn.us/index.aspx?page=4 Check voter registration status at https://mnvotes.sos.state.mn.us/VoterStatus.aspx. *Other Options:* The order form for ordering lists is found at www.sos.state.mn.us/index.aspx?page=893. Email questions to listrequest.sos@state.mn.us.

Occupational Licensing Boards

Abstractor/Abstractor Company .... www.commerce.state.mn.us/LicenseLookupMain.html
Accountant Firm .... www.boa.state.mn.us/Licensing/Find-Cpa-Firm.aspx
Accountant-CPA .... www.boa.state.mn.us/Licensing/Find-Cpa.aspx
Acupuncturist .... www.docboard.org/mn/df/mndf.htm
Adjuster .... www.commerce.state.mn.us/LicenseLookupMain.html
Alcohol/Drug Counselor .... https://www.hlb.state.mn.us/BBHTOnline/DesktopModules/ServiceForm.aspx?svid=37&mid=178
Ambulance Service/Personnel .... www.emsrb.state.mn.us/
Appraiser/Appraisal Mgmt Co .... www.commerce.state.mn.us/LicenseLookupMain.html
Architect .... http://mn.gov/aelslag/roster.html

Asbestos Contractor/Worker	www.health.state.mn.us/divs/eh/asbestos/contactus.html
Athletic Trainer	www.docboard.org/mn/df/mndf.htm
Attorney	www.mncourts.gov/mars/default.aspx
Bingo Operation	www.gcb.state.mn.us/ConductBingo.htm
Boiler Inspector	www.doli.state.mn.us/CCLD/BoilerInspectors.asp
Bondsman (Insurance)	www.commerce.state.mn.us/LicenseLookupMain.html
Buildiing Code Jurisdiction Directory	http://workplace.doli.state.mn.us/jurisdiction/
Building Contractor, Residen'l	www.commerce.state.mn.us/LicenseLookupMain.html
Campground Membership Agent	www.commerce.state.mn.us/LicenseLookupMain.html
Chemical & Mental Health	http://licensinglookup.dhs.state.mn.us/
Child Care Facility	http://licensinglookup.dhs.state.mn.us/
Children's Service	http://licensinglookup.dhs.state.mn.us/
Chiropractor	https://www.hlb.state.mn.us/chi/PublicAccess/search.asp
Collection Agency	www.commerce.state.mn.us/LicenseLookupMain.html
Consumer Credit/Payday Lender	www.commerce.state.mn.us/LicenseLookupMain.html
Contractor/Remodeler, Resid'l	www.commerce.state.mn.us/LicenseLookupMain.html
Controlled Substance	https://www.hlb.state.mn.us/mnbop/glsuiteweb/homeframe.aspx
Cosmetologist/Cosmetology Instr'r/School	https://www.hlb.state.mn.us/mnbce/glsuiteweb/clients/mnboc/public/License_Verifications.aspx
Credit Union	www.commerce.state.mn.us/LicenseLookupMain.html
Crematory	www.health.state.mn.us/divs/hpsc/mortsci/mortsciselect.cfm
Currency Exchange	www.commerce.state.mn.us/LicenseLookupMain.html
Debt Collector	www.commerce.state.mn.us/LicenseLookupMain.html
Debt Prorate Company	www.commerce.state.mn.us/LicenseLookupMain.html
Dentist/Dental Assistant/Hygienist	https://www.hlb.state.mn.us/mnbod/glsuiteweb/homeframe.aspx
Dietitian	www.dieteticsnutritionboard.state.mn.us/Default.aspx?tabid=1001
Drug Mfg/Whlse/Dist	https://www.hlb.state.mn.us/mnbop/glsuiteweb/homeframe.aspx
Electrical Contractor	https://secure.doli.state.mn.us/lookup/licensing.aspx
Electrical Inspector	www.dli.mn.gov/CCLD/ElectricalInspect.asp
Electrical Technology System Contractor	https://secure.doli.state.mn.us/lookup/licensing.aspx
Electrician	https://secure.doli.state.mn.us/lookup/licensing.aspx
Electronic Gaming	www.gcb.state.mn.us/PDF_Files/Electronic%20Games%20Sites.pdf
Elevator Contractor	https://secure.doli.state.mn.us/lookup/licensing.aspx
Emergency Medical Technician	www.emsrb.state.mn.us/
EMS Examiner	www.emsrb.state.mn.us/examiner.asp?p=s
Engineer	http://mn.gov/aelslag/roster.html
Esthetician	www.commerce.state.mn.us/LicenseLookupMain.html
Food Manager	www.health.state.mn.us/divs/eh/food/fmc/fmgr_query.cfm
Foster Care Program	http://licensinglookup.dhs.state.mn.us/
Funeral Director/Establishment	www.health.state.mn.us/divs/hpsc/mortsci/mortsciselect.cfm
Gambling Equipment Distributor	www.gcb.state.mn.us/ListDist.htm
Gambling Organizations	www.gcb.state.mn.us/PDF_Files/ListOrgAlpha.pdf
Geologist	http://mn.gov/aelslag/roster.html
Grain Licensing	www2.mda.state.mn.us/webapp/lis/default.jsp
Hearing Aid Dispenser	https://pqc.health.state.mn.us/hopVerify/loginAction.do
Insurance Agent/Seller/Agency	www.commerce.state.mn.us/LicenseLookupMain.html
Interior Designer	http://mn.gov/aelslag/roster.html
Landscape Architect	http://mn.gov/aelslag/roster.html
Lawyer, Discipline	http://lprb.mncourts.gov/Pages/Default.aspx
Lender, Small	www.commerce.state.mn.us/LicenseLookupMain.html
Liquor Store, On-sale Retail/Municipal	https://app.dps.mn.gov/age/
Livestock Dealer/Market/Weigher	www2.mda.state.mn.us/webapp/lis/default.jsp
Loan Company	www.commerce.state.mn.us/LicenseLookupMain.html
Lobbyist	www.cfboard.state.mn.us/lob_lists.html
Lottery Retailer	www.mnlottery.com/news__info/lottery_retailers_by_city/
Managing General Agent	www.commerce.state.mn.us/LicenseLookupMain.html

Manicurist	www.commerce.state.mn.us/LicenseLookupMain.html
Manufactured Home Installer	www.dli.mn.gov/CCLD/ManufacturedLicenseDealer.asp
Manufactured Home Mfg/Dealer	www.dli.mn.gov/CCLD/ManufacturedLicenseDealer.asp
Manufactured Structures Section	www.dli.mn.gov/CCLD/ManufacturedLicenseDealer.asp
Marriage & Family Therapist	www.bmft.state.mn.us/search.asp
Medical Gas Mfg/Whlse/Dist	https://www.hlb.state.mn.us/mnbop/glsuiteweb/homeframe.aspx
Medical Professional Firm	www.docboard.org/mn/df/mndf.htm
Mental Health, Chem'l Depend'cy Prof	http://licensinglookup.dhs.state.mn.us/
Midwife	www.docboard.org/mn/df/mndf.htm
Mortician	www.health.state.mn.us/divs/hpsc/mortsci/mortsciselect.cfm
Motor Vehicle Financer	www.commerce.state.mn.us/LicenseLookupMain.html
Notary Public	www.commerce.state.mn.us/LicenseLookupMain.html
Nurse-LPN/RN	https://www.hlb.state.mn.us/mbn/Portal/DesktopDefault.aspx?tabindex=0&tabid=41
Nursing Home Administrator	https://www.hlb.state.mn.us/sblmONLINE/public/default.aspx
Nutritionist	www.dieteticsnutritionboard.state.mn.us/Default.aspx?tabid=1001
Occupational Therapist/Assistant	https://pqc.health.state.mn.us/hopVerify/loginAction.do
Optometrist	www.optometryboard.state.mn.us/Default.aspx?tabid=799
Pesticide Applicator Company	www.mda.state.mn.us/licensing/license-lookup.aspx
Pesticide Applicator, Private	www2.mda.state.mn.us/webapp/PrivApp/default.jsp
Pharmaceutical Technician	https://www.hlb.state.mn.us/mnbop/glsuiteweb/homeframe.aspx
Pharmacist/Pharmacy	https://www.hlb.state.mn.us/mnbop/glsuiteweb/homeframe.aspx
Physician/Medical Doctor/Assistant	www.docboard.org/mn/df/mndf.htm
Podiatrist	https://www.hlb.state.mn.us/sblmonline/public/default.aspx
Political Action Committee	www.cfboard.state.mn.us/campfin/pcfatoz.html
Political Candidate	www.cfboard.state.mn.us/cand_lists.html
Preceptor	https://www.hlb.state.mn.us/mnbop/glsuiteweb/homeframe.aspx
Private Investigator	www.dps.state.mn.us/pdb/License_Holders.htm
Re-Insurance Intermediary	www.commerce.state.mn.us/LicenseLookupMain.html
Real Estate Agent/Broker/Dealer	www.commerce.state.mn.us/LicenseLookupMain.html
Respiratory Care Practitioner	www.docboard.org/mn/df/mndf.htm
Sanitarian	www.health.state.mn.us/divs/eh/san/sani_query.cfm
Securities Salesperson/Inves't Advisor	www.commerce.state.mn.us/LicenseLookupMain.html
Security Agent/Protective Agent	www.dps.state.mn.us/pdb/License_Holders.htm
Social Worker	https://www.hlb.state.mn.us/BOSW/Online/DesktopModules/ServiceForm.aspx?svid=21&mid=164
Soil Scientist	http://mn.gov/aelslag/roster.html
Speech-Language Audiologist/Pathologist	https://pqc.health.state.mn.us/hopVerify/loginAction.do
Surgeon	www.docboard.org/mn/df/mndf.htm
Surveyor, Land	http://mn.gov/aelslag/roster.html
Teacher	http://education.state.mn.us/MDE/EdExc/Licen/TeachLicLook/index.html
Telemedicine	www.docboard.org/mn/df/mndf.htm
Thrift/Industrial Loan Company	www.commerce.state.mn.us/LicenseLookupMain.html
Undergr'nd Storage Tank Contr./Supvr.	www.pca.state.mn.us/index.php/view-document.html?gid=15373
Veterinarian	www.vetmed.state.mn.us/default.aspx?tabid=801
Water Well Contractor	http://mdh-agua.health.state.mn.us/cwi/cwiViewer.htm
X-Ray Supplier	www.health.state.mn.us/divs/eh/radiation/xray/servproviders/spvendoral.pdf

State and Local Courts

State Court Structure: There are 97 District Courts (some counties gave divisional courts) comprising 10 judicial districts. The limit for small claims is $7500 unless the case involves a consumer credit transaction then the limit is $4000. There are eleven **Tribal Courts** that have jurisdiction on tribal land.

Appellate Courts: One may view Opions at www.mncourts.gov.

Statewide Court Online Access: All courts participate in the system described below.

- Minnesota offers the Trial Court Public Access (MPA) of searchinh statewide or by county. Records available include criminal, civil, family, and probate. Searches can be performed using a case number or by name. See http://pa.courts.state.mn.us/default.aspx.
- However searchers should first know there are a number of caveats, especially for cirminal record searches. Certain publicly-accessible case records or data fields found at the courthouse cannot be viewed online. For example, comment fields for all case types are not available online but are available at the courthouse. Party street address and name searches on criminal, traffic, and petty misdemeanor pre-conviction case records are not accessible online, but are at the courthouse. A criminal/traffic/petty search excludes all Hennepin County and Ramsey County payable citations except: 1) those that result in a court appearance; and 2) Ramsey DNR payable citations. Also, Party street address and name searches on criminal pre-conviction case records are publicly accessible and available at the courthouse, but not online. The federal Violence Against Women Act (VAWA) prevents the state from displaying harassment and domestic abuse case records online, but these convictions are available at the courthouse. Online users are not notified when such public data is restricted from online viewing.
- The bottom line is the public access terminals found at the courthouses display additional data the online system and are still the most accurate searching locations. The online system is best as a supplemental search when true due dilligence is needed.

Note: No individual Minnesota courts offer online access, other than as described above.

Recorders, Assessors, and Other Sites of Note

Recording Office Organization: 87 counties, 87 recording offices. The recording officer is the County Recorder. Federal and state tax liens on personal property of businesses are filed with the Secretary of State. Other federal and state tax liens are filed with the County Recorder.

Statewide or Multi-Jurisdiction Access: There is no statewide system but a number of counties offer web access to assessor data and recorded deeds.

Also an endorsed vendor works with quite a few counties. Access recorder land data by subscription on the Tapestry System. One can either use a credit card and pay $5.95 per image or take advantage of a subcription with a flat rate. See the site at https://tapestry.fidlar.com for details. Approximately 14 participating counties.

County Sites:

Aitkin County ***Property, Taxation*** Access property data free at http://gisweb.co.aitkin.mn.us/wf2_aitkinpublic/Default.aspx. To access more detailed building information, including dimensions and sales report generating capability, a subscription to WebFusion is required. Call 218-927-7327 for more information.**$$$**

Anoka County ***Property, Taxation*** Access property data at https://prtinfo.co.anoka.mn.us:443/(bixyr1ryehkdp555jdukdu45)/search.aspx. Also, GIS/mapping records for free at http://ww2.anokacounty.us/v4_gis/default.aspx.

Becker County ***Recorded Documents*** www.co.becker.mn.us/dept/recorder/default.aspx Access for iDoc database for online real estate for a fee at www.co.becker.mn.us/dept/recorder/default.aspxFee is $25.00 per month, view only; $50.00 per month, unlimited access and copies. There is a $50.00 set-up fee for either option. Must sign-up and pay before use. Records available index+image: 1986. **$$$**

Property, Taxation Access to the assessor property data is free at http://gis-server.co.becker.mn.us/link/jsfe/index.aspx. Also, search plat images free at www.co.becker.mn.us/dept/recorder/plats_online.aspx.

Beltrami County ***Recorded Documents*** www.co.beltrami.mn.us Access to records for a fee at https://tapestry.fidlar.com/Tapestry2/Default.aspx. Contact 309-794-3283 or kylec@fidlar.com for subscription information. Search fee is $5.95 each, printed images $.50 each unless otherwise noted. **$$$**

Property, Taxation Access to GIS/mapping for free at www.co.beltrami.mn.us/Departments/AuditorTreasurer/Taxpayer_Services.html.

Benton County ***Recorded Documents*** www.co.benton.mn.us/County_Recorder/index.php Access to plats available for free at www.co.benton.mn.us/County_Recorder/Plats.php. Recorded land records for a fee at http://landshark.co.benton.mn.us/LandShark/login.jsp. **$$$**

Property, Taxation Free search of Auditor property tax data at http://benton.visualgov.com/ParcelSearch.aspx but no name searching. Also, access to property records free at http://qpublic.net/mn/benton/. Also, access to GIS/mapping for free at www.co.benton.mn.us/GIS/index.php.

Big Stone County ***Property, Taxation*** Access to sales listing for free at www.bigstonecounty.org/assessor/sales.vbhtml.

Blue Earth County ***Recorded Documents*** www.co.blue-earth.mn.us Access to records for a fee at https://tapestry.fidlar.com/Tapestry2/Default.aspx. Contact 309-794-3283 or kylec@fidlar.com for subscription information. Search fee is $5.95 each, printed images $.50 each unless otherwise noted. **$$$**

Property, Taxation Access to the property data search database is free at http://mn-blueearth.manatron.com/. Also, you may search at www.blueearth.minnesotaassessors.com/. No name searching at either site, but a subscription service is available at the latter.**$$$**

Brown County ***Recorded Documents*** www.co.brown.mn.us/departmentslink/recorders-office Access to records in subscription contact Betti Kamolz, Recorder at 507-233-6653. **$$$**

Property, Taxation Access to GIS/mapping for free at www.co.brown.mn.us/gis-a-property-info.

Carver County ***Recorded Documents*** www.co.carver.mn.us Access to recorded land records available by subscription at http://landshark.co.carver.mn.us/LandShark/login.jsp. No fee to search, fee for images. Fee schedule is online under fees. **$$$**

Property, Taxation Access property and tax roll data free at http://mn-carver.manatron.com/Tabs/TaxSearch.aspx but no name searching. Also search the GIS-mapping site free at www.co.carver.mn.us/departments/admin/IS/gis_mapping_applications.asp.

Cass County ***Property, Taxation*** Access property data at www.co.cass.mn.us/cassmnpublicreports/taxsearch/search.aspx but no name searching. View GIS-mapping data free at www.co.cass.mn.us/maps/map_home.html.

Chippewa County ***Property, Taxation*** Access property tax records free at www.co.chippewa.mn.us/taxdisclaim.htm but no name searching.

Chisago County ***Recorded Documents*** www.co.chisago.mn.us/government/recorder/ Access to the recorder's real property data back to 1988 is by subscription with LandShark, see http://24.56.144.170/wf2_chisagopublic/Default.aspx. No fee to search, fee for images. **$$$**

Property, Taxation Search the treasurer's property search site at http://24.56.144.170/chisago_tax/ for free. Also, access parcel data at the GIS-mapping site after disclaimer at http://24.56.144.170/wf2_chisagopublic/Default.aspx, but no name searching.

Clay County ***Recorded Documents*** www.co.clay.mn.us/Depts/Recorder/Recorder.htm Access to records for a fee at https://tapestry.fidlar.com/Tapestry2/Default.aspx. Contact 309-794-3283 or kylec@fidlar.com for subscription information. Search fee is $5.95 each, printed images $.50 each unless otherwise noted. Also, plats and corner certificates online free at www.co.clay.mn.us/depts/recorder/laredo/rerrol.htm **$$$**

Property, Taxation Search property data for City of Moorhead and Clay County free at www.co.clay.mn.us/AboutUs/CCPrSear.htm. Also, access to GIS/mapping free at www.co.clay.mn.us/Depts/GIS/GIS.htm.

Clearwater County ***Property, Taxation*** Access to GIS mapping/E911 Rural Addressing System for free at http://webster.co.clearwater.mn.us/website/clearwaterpublic/Default.aspx.

Cook County ***Property, Taxation*** Access Cook County property and assessment data free at www.co.cook.mn.us/index.php/property-information.

Cottonwood County ***Recorded Documents*** www.co.cottonwood.mn.us/countyrecorder.html Access to records for a fee at https://tapestry.fidlar.com/Tapestry2/Default.aspx. Contact 309-794-3283 or kylec@fidlar.com for subscription information. Search fee is $5.95 each, printed images $.50 each unless otherwise noted. **$$$**

Crow Wing County ***Recorded Documents*** http://crowwing.us/index.aspx?nid=197 Access to recorder data is available by subscription, $50.00 per month and $.25 per image. Email the County Recorder at kathyl@co.crow-wing.mn.us for info and signup, or login at http://erecord.co.crow-wing.mn.us/LandShark/login.jsp. **$$$**

Property, Taxation Access to GIS/mapping for free at http://crowwing.us/index.aspx?nid=186

Dakota County ***Recorded Documents*** www.co.dakota.mn.us/HomeProperty/Recording/Pages/default.aspx Access to recorded documents requires a subscription and an escrow account set up with Property Taxation & Records. Fee is $100/month and $0.50/image viewed. To obtain a Login ID and Password, contact 651-438-4355. **$$$**

Property, Taxation Search foreclosure data free by address at www.co.dakota.mn.us/HomeProperty/Foreclosed/Pages/ForeclosureSearch.aspx.

Dodge County ***Property, Taxation*** Access to property tax records is free at http://secure.co.dodge.mn.us/dodgeCounty/.

Douglas County ***Recorded Documents*** www.co.douglas.mn.us Access to database for a fee at www.landshark.co.douglas.mn.us/LandShark/login.jsp?url=http%3A%2F%2F **$$$**

Property, Taxation Look-up assessor property tax data free at http://morris.state.mn.us/tax/. Also, access GIS/mapping for free at http://douglas.houstoneng.com/.

Faribault County ***Recorded Documents*** www.faribaultcountyrecorder.com/ Access to records for a fee at https://tapestry.fidlar.com/Tapestry2/Default.aspx. Contact 309-794-3283 or kylec@fidlar.com for subscription information. Search fee is $5.95 each, printed images $.50 each unless otherwise noted. **$$$**

Fillmore County ***Property, Taxation*** Access to public viewing on GIS/mapping free at www.co.fillmore.mn.us/gis.html, subscription available for more detailed information for a fee at same site.**$$$**

Freeborn County ***Property, Taxation*** Online access to property records is available at http://beacon.schneidercorp.com/Application.aspx?AppID=333&LayerID=3791&PageTypeID=2&PageID=2400&Q=1253517675&KeyValue=030320081.

Goodhue County ***Recorded Documents*** www.co.goodhue.mn.us/Departments/recorder/index.aspx Access to recorder's land records is by subscription through LandShark at www.co.goodhue.mn.us/Departments/recorder/LandShark.aspx. Fees- $50.00 setup, $.25 per doc viewed. Username, and password required. **$$$**

Property, Taxation Access property and sales data free at www.co.goodhue.mn.us/goodhuecountyrecap/ but no name searching. Also, search GIS/mapping for free at www.co.goodhue.mn.us/departments/LANDUSE/surveyor/platsmainpage.aspx. Also, forfeited land list at www.co.goodhue.mn.us/departments/auditortreasurer/ForfeitedLandList.aspx.

Grant County ***Recorded Documents*** Access to records for a fee at https://tapestry.fidlar.com/Tapestry2/Default.aspx. Contact 309-794-3283 or kylec@fidlar.com for subscription information. Search fee is $5.95 each, printed images $.50 each unless otherwise noted. **$$$**

Property, Taxation Look-up assessor property tax data free at http://morris.state.mn.us/tax/.

Hennepin County ***Recorded Documents*** http://www.hennepin.us/portal/site/HennepinUS Access to Hennepin County online records requires a $35 annual fee with a charge of $5 per hour from 7AM-7PM, or $4.15 per hour at other times. Records date back to 1988. Only lending agency data is available. An Automated phone system is also available; 612-348-3011. **$$$**

Property, Taxation Search parcel property tax records on county Property Information Search database free at www16.co.hennepin.mn.us/pins/.

Houston County ***Recorded Documents*** www.houstoncounty.govoffice2.com/index.asp?Type=B_BASIC&SEC={4DBF015F-1AD9-4B6C-A4C2-2C3089CCC334} Online access by subscription to records starting in 1991 forward. Contact the Recorder's Office. **$$$**

Property, Taxation Online access to property records is available at http://beacon.schneidercorp.com/.**$$$**

Hubbard County ***Property, Taxation*** Access property tax data free at www.co.hubbard.mn.us/wf2_hubbardpublic/Default.aspx.

Isanti County ***Property, Taxation*** Search assessor property and tax data free at http://isanti.visualgov.com/ no name searching. Access monthly sales sheets by Town for free at www.co.isanti.mn.us/assessdept.html#Monthly_Sales_Sheets. Access property data free on the GIS-mapping site at http://209.139.208.16/mapguide/isanti/, but no name searching.

Itasca County ***Recorded Documents*** www.co.itasca.mn.us/Home/Departments/Recorders/Pages/default.aspx The agency sends requesters to the Idoc system. Fees are based on a flat rate by usage ranging from $8.00 to $500 per month. You pay as you go with a credit card. Visit at https://www.idocmarket.com/ **$$$**

Property, Taxation Access property and parcel data free from a private company at www.parcelinfo.com/index.php.

Kanabec County ***Recorded Documents*** www.kanabeccounty.org/index.asp Access to to records on LandShark is available for a fee. Contact Rhonda or Lisa at 320-679-6466. **$$$**

Property, Taxation Online access to property records is available at www.qpublic.net/mn/kanabec/.

Kandiyohi County ***Recorded Documents*** www.co.kandiyohi.mn.us Access to records for a fee at https://tapestry.fidlar.com/Tapestry2/Default.aspx. Contact 309-794-3283 or kylec@fidlar.com for subscription information. Search fee is $5.95 each, printed images $.50 each unless otherwise noted. **$$$**

Property, Taxation Look-up assessor property tax data free at http://morris.state.mn.us/tax/disclaimer.asp?cid=34. Also, access to GIS/mapping free at http://gis.co.kandiyohi.mn.us/GIS/about.htm.

Koochiching County ***Property, Taxation*** Access to property and parcel data is free from a private company at www.parcelinfo.com/.

Lac qui Parle County ***Recorded Documents*** www.lqpco.com/recorder.php Access to online access for index and images of recorded documents for a fee contact Josh Amland at 320-598-3724. fee is $30.00 per month of unlimited access at this time. **$$$**

Lake County ***Property, Taxation*** Access property data free at www.parcelinfo.com/main.php; click on Lake County Users Click Here.

Lake of the Woods County ***Property, Taxation*** Access to GIS/mapping for free at http://oak.co.lake-of-the-woods.mn.us/lakeofthewoodspublic/Default.aspx.

Le Sueur County Recorder ***Recorded Documents*** www.co.le-sueur.mn.us/Recorder.html Access to recorder's land records back to 5/1/1991 is by subscription through LandShark at http://156.99.35.20/LandShark/login.jsp. Fees of $50.00 installation, $2.00 per doc viewed, $50.00 per month, username and password required. **$$$**

Lincoln County ***Recorded Documents*** www.lincolncounty-mn.us/Departments/Recorder.htm Access to records for a fee at https://tapestry.fidlar.com/Tapestry2/Default.aspx. Contact 309-794-3283 or kylec@fidlar.com for subscription information. Search fee is $5.95 each, printed images $.50 each unless otherwise noted. **$$$**

Lyon County ***Recorded Documents*** www.lyonco.org Access to records for a fee at https://tapestry.fidlar.com/Tapestry2/Default.aspx. Contact 309-794-3283 or kylec@fidlar.com for subscription information. Search fee is $5.95 each, printed images $.50 each unless otherwise noted. **$$$**

Property, Taxation Look-up assessor property tax data free at http://morris.state.mn.us/tax/tax.asp.

McLeod County ***Recorded Documents*** www.co.mcleod.mn.us/mcleodco.cfm?pageID=25&sub=yes Access recorder data by subscription at http://landshark.co.mcleod.mn.us/LandShark/login.jsp. Set-up $50 plus $50.00 per month, plus $2.00 per image. **$$$**

Property, Taxation Access to property records and tax information for free at www.co.mcleod.mn.us/. Check property taxes and delinquent taxes online at www.co.mcleod.mn.us/. Info goes back to 1993.

Marshall County ***Property, Taxation*** Look-up assessor property tax data free at http://morris.state.mn.us/tax/.

Martin County ***Recorded Documents*** www.co.martin.mn.us/index.php/government/recorder Access to records for a fee at https://tapestry.fidlar.com/Tapestry2/Default.aspx. Contact 309-794-3283 or kylec@fidlar.com for subscription information. Search fee is $5.95 each, printed images $.50 each unless otherwise noted. **$$$**

Property, Taxation Online access to property records and GIS/mapping are available at http://beacon.schneidercorp.com/.**$$$**

Meeker County ***Property, Taxation*** Look-up assessor property tax data free at http://morris.state.mn.us/tax/disclaimer.asp?cid=47.

Mille Lacs County ***Recorded Documents*** http://www.co.mille-lacs.mn.us/ Access to LandShark for a fee at http://136.234.73.242/LandShark/login.jsp. **$$$**

Property, Taxation Look-up assessor property tax data free at http://morris.state.mn.us/tax/.

Morrison County ***Recorded Documents*** www.co.morrison.mn.us/index.asp Access is via Landshark subscription 2-user service; $50 setup fee; several monthly service plans; first doc image free then $.25 per downloaded page. Info and signup at directly with Bunny or Eileen at 320-632-0145 or 0146. Visit http://landshark.co.morrison.mn.us/LandShark/login.jsp - tract index by legal disc. back to 1897, images start at 245403 6/1/72. **$$$**

Property, Taxation Search for property data on a GIS-mapping site free at http://beacon.schneidercorp.com/.

Mower County ***Recorded Documents*** www.co.mower.mn.us/Recorder.htm Access to records for a fee at https://tapestry.fidlar.com/Tapestry2/Default.aspx. Contact 309-794-3283 or kylec@fidlar.com for subscription information. Search fee is $5.95 each, printed images $.50 each unless otherwise noted. **$$$**

Property, Taxation Search property assessor data free at www.mower.minnesotaassessors.com/. No name searching for free, but a sub service is available which does.

Murray County ***Property, Taxation*** Access to property tax search for free at http://morris.state.mn.us/tax/

Nicollet County ***Recorded Documents*** www.co.nicollet.mn.us/index.asp Access to LandShark for a fee at https://landshark.co.nicollet.mn.us/LandShark/login.jsp **$$$**

Property, Taxation Access to property information for free at www.nicollet.minnesotaassessors.com/.

Nobles County ***Property, Taxation*** Look-up assessor property tax data free at http://morris.state.mn.us/tax/.

Norman County ***Property, Taxation*** Look-up assessor property tax data free at http://morris.state.mn.us/tax/disclaimer.asp?cid=54.

Olmsted County ***Recorded Documents*** www.co.olmsted.mn.us/prl/Pages/default.aspx Recording office land records information by subscription via Landshark at http://landshark.co.olmsted.mn.us/LandShark/login.jsp. Yearly or monthly signup required, plus escrow account for usage. Occasional user option now available. See website or contact Wendy at 507-328-7634. **$$$**

Property, Taxation Property records and GIS-map data is available free at https://webapp.co.olmsted.mn.us/propertytax/Site/Default.aspx

Otter Tail County ***Recorded Documents*** www.co.otter-tail.mn.us Access recorder office real estate data by a LandShark subscription at www.co.otter-tail.mn.us/LandShark/login.jsp. User name and login required. Call recorder office for details and sign-up **$$$**

Property, Taxation Search property tax data at www.co.otter-tail.mn.us/taxes/. Parcel searching or map searching only.

Polk County ***Recorded Documents*** www.co.polk.mn.us/list_departments/recordersOffice/index.aspx To search records at just this county, the agency sends requesters to the IDOC Market system Fees are based on a flat rate by usage ranging from $50 to $125 per month. Coverage for multiple counties is offered by the IDOC Market program from the same vendor. There is a $6.00 fee per pass and copies can be generated for $.50 per page. You can pay as you go with a credit card. Visit at https://www.idocmarket.com/ for more information. **$$$**

Pope County ***Recorded Documents*** www.co.pope.mn.us/recorder.php Access to records for a fee at https://tapestry.fidlar.com/Tapestry2/Default.aspx. Contact 309-794-3283 or kylec@fidlar.com for subscription information. Search fee is $5.95 each, printed images $.50 each unless otherwise noted. **$$$**

Property, Taxation Look-up assessor property tax data free at http://morris.state.mn.us/tax/disclaimer.asp?cid=61. Also, access to county property/parcel data is free at http://morris.state.mn.us/tax/.

Ramsey County ***Recorded Documents*** www.co.ramsey.mn.us/prr/recorder/index.htm This agency's extensive search product including recorded documents is available by subscription; see http://rrinfo.co.ramsey.mn.us/public/document/index.asp. **$$$**

Property, Taxation Search the property assessment rolls free at http://rrinfo.co.ramsey.mn.us/public/characteristic/index.aspx but no name searching.

Redwood County ***Property, Taxation*** Look-up assessor property tax data free at http://morris.state.mn.us/tax/.

Renville County ***Property, Taxation*** Look-up assessor property tax data free at http://morris.state.mn.us/tax/.

Rice County ***Recorded Documents*** www.co.rice.mn.us/departments/recorder Access to LandShark database for a fee at http://landshark.co.rice.mn.us/LandShark/login.jsp. Must register with user name and password. **$$$**
Property, Taxation Search assessor property data free on the GIS system at http://beacon.schneidercorp.com/ but no name searching.**$$$**

Rock County ***Recorded Documents*** www.co.rock.mn.us Access to records for a fee at https://tapestry.fidlar.com/Tapestry2/Default.aspx. Contact 309-794-3283 or kylec@fidlar.com for subscription information. Search fee is $5.95 each, printed images $.50 each unless otherwise noted. **$$$**
Property, Taxation Look-up assessor property tax data free at http://morris.state.mn.us/tax/disclaimer_value.asp?cid=67. Also, access to GIS/mapping free at http://rock.houstoneng.com/rock/rock.html.

Roseau County ***Property, Taxation*** Access to GIS/mapping for free at http://gis.co.roseau.mn.us/link/jsfe/index.aspx.

St. Louis County ***Recorded Documents*** www.stlouiscountymn.gov/LANDPROPERTY/RealEstateRecording.aspx Access the recorder database by subscription. Fee is $126 monthly and includes assessment records. Contact the Auditor or Recorder office for sign up, or visit the Recorder office website and click on Online Contract. **$$$**
Property, Taxation Access auditor tax records for tax professionals database by subscription. Fee is $120 monthly. For info or sign-up, contact Pam Palen at 218-726-2380 or email to palenp@co.st-louis.mn.us. Also, search auditor info for free at www.stlouiscountymn.gov/GOVERNMENT/DepartmentsAgencies/Auditor.aspx. Also, search the City of Duluth property assessor data free at www.duluthmn.gov/assessor/search/index.cfm.**$$$**

Scott County ***Recorded Documents*** www.co.scott.mn.us/Pages/DepartmentDetail.aspx?LID=14 Access to land records free at www.co.scott.mn.us/PropertyGISLand/LandRecords/Pages/LandRecords.aspx. Also, access to the images, or print copies, of multiple recorded documents or certificates of title for a monthly fee go to https://scottcountypropertyportal.com/us/mn/scott/default.pmpx.
Property, Taxation Search assessor and a variety of other property data free at www2.co.scott.mn.us/stellent/idcplg/records/pxs?IdcService=SC_PROPERTYTAX_HOME but no name searching. Search the county property databases free by link at www.co.scott.mn.us/wps/portal/ScottCounty/. There is also a free online document subscription service and GIS mapping.

Sherburne County ***Recorded Records*** www.co.sherburne.mn.us Call Holly or Samantha for information on their online access. **$$$**
Property, Taxation Property records from the county tax assessor database are free at http://beacon.schneidercorp.com/?site=SherburneCountyMN. However, to perform a name search, you must subscribe; fee is $25.00 setup and $300.00 per year.**$$$**

Sibley County ***Recorded Documents*** www.co.sibley.mn.us/recorder/index.html Access to Sibley County Land Records from Aug. 1994 to present, by Landshark. Access fees for LandShark are $50 installation, $50 per month and $2 per document viewed. **$$$**

Stearns County ***Recorded Documents*** www.co.stearns.mn.us/Government/CountyDepartments/RecordersOffice Access to land records for a fee at www.co.stearns.mn.us/OnlineServices/LandRecordsSearch. **$$$**

Steele County ***Recorded Documents*** www.co.steele.mn.us Access to records for a fee at https://tapestry.fidlar.com/Tapestry2/Default.aspx. Contact 309-794-3283 or kylec@fidlar.com for subscription information. Search fee is $5.95 each, printed images $.50 each unless otherwise noted. **$$$**
Property, Taxation Search parcel data, sales, and GIS-mapping site free at www.co.steele.mn.us/tax_information/index.html.

Stevens County ***Property, Taxation*** Look-up assessor property tax data free at http://morris.state.mn.us/tax/.

Swift County ***Property, Taxation*** Access parcel data by address, ID, or book/page for free at http://morris.state.mn.us/tax/.

Todd County ***Recorded Documents*** www.co.todd.mn.us/departments/recorder/recorder_frontpage_panel Access to recorder's records for a fee at Landshark. Contact Cheryl Perish at 320-732-4459 or cheryl.perish@co.todd.mn.us. **$$$**
Property, Taxation Access property data on the GIS-mapping site free at www.co.todd.mn.us/departments/gis_land_services/gis_land_services_frontpage_panel. Also, look-up assessor property/parcel tax data and free at http://morris.state.mn.us/tax/. Search buildings at www.co.todd.mn.us/TODDCOUNTY/propertyinfo0012.asp.

Traverse County ***Property, Taxation*** Access to assessor records for free at http://morris.state.mn.us/tax/disclaimer_value.asp?cid=78.

Wabasha County ***Property, Taxation*** Access property searches for free at www.co.wabasha.mn.us/index.php/property-search.

Wadena County ***Recorded Documents*** www.co.wadena.mn.us/county_directory/recorder/recorder.htm Access to parcel database free at http://206.145.187.205/tax/disclaimer.asp?cid=80. Access to LandShark by subscription. Contact Recorders office to set up account or go to www.co.wadena.mn.us/. **$$$**
Property, Taxation Search tax parcels free at www.co.wadena.mn.us/website/wadenapublic/main.php, but no name searching.

Waseca County ***Recorded Documents*** www.co.waseca.mn.us/index.aspx?nid=131 With registration, username and password you may access recording data on LandShark system at http://landshark.co.waseca.mn.us/LandShark/login.jsp. Fee is $50.00 per month, plus copy fee for images. **$$$**

Property, Taxation Access to GIS/mapping free at http://gis.co.waseca.mn.us/wasecapublic/Default.aspx.

Washington County ***Recorded Documents*** www.co.washington.mn.us Access to county tract records requires a $50.00 set up fee and $50.00 monthly fee; abstract images go back to 1/1984; Torrens images to 1/1984; tracts to 1984. UCC and Torrens cert. data is not on this system. **$$$**

Watonwan County ***Property, Taxation*** Free access to recorded documents at http://beacon.schneidercorp.com/?site=watonwancountymn.

Wilkin County ***Property, Taxation*** Access parcel data free at http://morris.state.mn.us/tax/disclaimer_value.asp?cid=84 but no name searching.

Winona County ***Recorded Documents*** www.co.winona.mn.us/se3bin/clientgenie.cgi Access to recorded sales free at www.co.winona.mn.us/se3bin/clientgenie.cgi.

Property, Taxation Access to property records for free at www.qpublic.net/mn/winona/.

Wright County ***Recorded Documents*** www.co.wright.mn.us/department/recorder/ Access to Land Title database is free at https://landshark.co.wright.mn.us/LandShark/login.jsp?url=https%3A%2F%2Flandshark.co.wright.mn.us%2FLandShark%2Fsearchname.jsp. No images. Data & images available with LandShark remote access, fee based.

Property, Taxation Search the property tax database for free at www.co.wright.mn.us/department/audtreas/proptax/default.asp.

Yellow Medicine County ***Property, Taxation*** Look-up assessor property tax data free at http://morris.state.mn.us/tax/disclaimer.asp?cid=87.

Mississippi

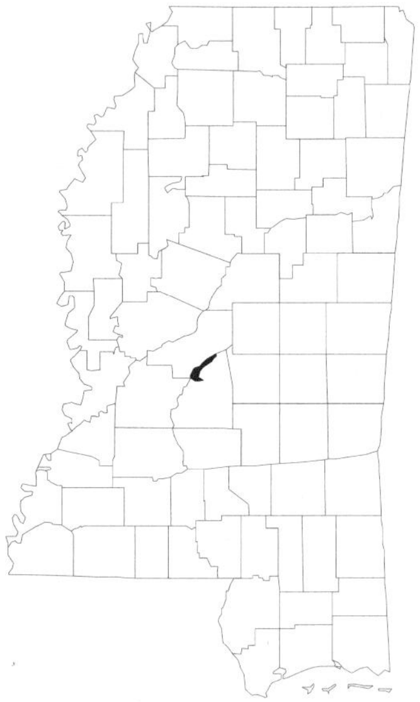

Capital: Jackson
Hinds County
Time Zone: CST
Population: 2,984,926
# of Counties: 82

Useful State Links

Website: www.ms.gov/home
Governor: www.governorbryant.com/
Attorney General: www.ago.state.ms.us
State Archives: www.mdah.state.ms.us
State Statutes and Codes: www.sos.state.ms.us/ed_pubs/mscode/
Legislative Bill Search: http://billstatus.ls.state.ms.us/
Unclaimed Funds: www.treasury.state.ms.us

State Public Record Agencies

Sexual Offender Registry

DPS- MS Bureau of Investigation, Sex Offender Registration, http://state.sor.dps.ms.gov/ The state Sex Offender Registry can be accessed at the website. Search by last name, city, county, or ZIP Code.

Incarceration Records

Mississippi Department of Corrections, Records Department, www.mdoc.state.ms.us Search online by name only from the website. Click on Inmate Search. Also, search the Parole Board records (click on Parole Board and follow instructions).

Corporation, LP, LLP, LLC, Trademarks/Servicemarks

Secretary of State, Business Services, www.sos.ms.gov/ A variety of online search services are available at https://business.sos.state.ms.us/corp/soskb/csearch.asp. There is no fee to view records, including officers and registered agents. A Good Standing can be ordered. Download images for no charge. Also, search securities companies, charities, fundraisers, and pre-needs registered with the state at www.sos.ms.gov/securities_and_charities_securities_search.aspx. *Other Options:* The Data Division offers bulk release of information on an annual subscription basis ($1500). Monthly subscription to list of new corporations and new qualifications is $25.00.

Uniform Commercial Code, Federal & State Tax Liens

Secretary of State, Business Services - UCC, www.sos.ms.gov/business_services_ucc.aspx Free searching for UCC debtors is at www.sos.ms.gov/business_services_ucc2.aspx for basic search. For more detailed searches, one must sign up for the UCC subscription service. **$$$** *Other Options:* A monthly list of farm liens is available for purchase.

Vital Records

State Department of Health, Vital Statistics & Records, www.msdh.ms.gov/phs/ Orders can be placed via a state designated vendor. Go to www.vitalchek.com. Extra fees are involved. **$$$**

Workers' Compensation Records

Workers Compensation Commission, www.mwcc.state.ms.us The First Report of Injury, proof of coverage by an employer, and other documents are available via the web. There is no fee, but users mat need to register for some services.

Driver Records

Department of Public Safety, Driver Services, www.dps.state.ms.us/driver-services/ In 2012, the processing of electronic driving record requests was taken over by Mississippi Interactive (MSI), an affiliate of NIC. This is in concert with the new state portal for Mississippi. The fee is $14.00 per record. All requesters are required to be initially approved by the DPS and must sign a subscription agreement with MS.gov. There is an annual $95 subscription fee for new accounts. Billing is monthly. At present there are no details about this service on the web page, but details will be added. Interested new subscribers should contact the MSI at 877-290-9487. **$$$**

Vehicle Ownership & Registration

Department of Revenue, Motor Vehicle Licensing Bureau, www.dor.ms.gov/mvl/main.html Internet access to vehicle records is available to approved, DPPA compliant entities. Accounts must pay an annual $100 registration fee, record search fees are the same as listed above. Access is via the web. **$$$** *Other Options:* Mississippi offers some standardized files as well as some customization for bulk requesters of VIN and registration information. For more information, contact MLVB at the address listed above.

Accident Reports

Safety Responsibility, Accident Records, www.dps.state.ms.us/online-collision-reports/ Persons legally eligible to obtain a copy of the report can do so online by visiting http://reportbeam.com. Select "Purchase a Report" under the "Public Access" tab. The fee is $20.00. Reports are available from local law enforcement and from the Highway Patrol. **$$$**

Vessel Ownership & Registration

Wildlife, Fisheries, & Parks Dept, Boating Registration, www.mdwfp.com/license/boating-registration.aspx One may do a search at the registration renewal site https://www.ms.gov/gf/boating/index.jsp. There is no name searching; both the MI Number and Serial (HIN) must be input. *Other Options:* This agency makes records available electronically and on printed lists. Fees vary.

Voter Registration, Campaign Finance, Lobbyists

Secretary of State, Elections Division, www.sos.ms.gov/elections.aspx Campaign finance reports are at www.sos.ms.gov/elections3.aspx. A lobbyist and client search is at www.sos.ms.gov/elec/portal/msel/page/search/portal.aspx. A PAC list is at www.sos.ms.gov/links/elections/home/tab1/PACReport_100610.pdf. *Other Options:* Voter registration lists are available for purchase. Call for details.

Occupational Licensing Boards

Accountant-CPA/Active Firm .... www.msbpa.ms.gov/Pages/Home.aspx
Alcoholic Beverage Retailer........................ www.dor.ms.gov/abc/wholesaleretailpackagestore.html
Architect/Landscape Architect .... www.archbd.state.ms.us/main_find_licensee.html
Asbestos Contractor/Insp/Supv/Worker....... http://opc.deq.state.ms.us/report_asbestos_el.aspx
Asbestos Project Designer/Planner .... http://opc.deq.state.ms.us/report_asbestos_el.aspx
Attorney/Attorney Firm .... www.msbar.org/lawyerdirectory.php
Audiologist... https://apps.msdh.ms.gov/licreviews/index.aspx
Bank .... www.dbcf.state.ms.us/documents/banking/mslist.pdf
Beauty School .... www.msbc.state.ms.us/msbc/Cosmetology.nsf
Child Care Facility .... www.msdh.state.ms.us/msdhsite/_static/30,332,183,438.html
Chiropractor .... www.msbce.ms.gov/msbce/msbce.nsf/Search?OpenForm
Contractor, Commercial/Residential .... www.msboc.us/OnlineServices/CheckLicenseRequest.html
Counselor, Professional .... https://dsitspe01.its.state.ms.us/lpc/roster.nsf/webpage/lpc_2?editdocument
Dental Hygienist/Radiologist .... www.dentalboard.ms.gov/msbde/msbdesearch.nsf/WebStart?OpenFOrm
Dentist .... www.dentalboard.ms.gov/msbde/msbdesearch.nsf/WebStart?OpenFOrm
Engineer... www.pepls.state.ms.us/pepls/web.nsf/webpages/LN_LV_PAGE_LV?OpenDocument
Funeral Director/Service Practitioner .... https://www.msbfs.ms.gov/licenseverification.asp
Funeral Home/Establishment....................... https://www.msbfs.ms.gov/licenseverification.asp
Funeral Pre-Need Contractor...................... www.sos.ms.gov/links/reg_enf/funeral/active_providers.pdf
Geologist www.msbrpg.ms.gov/MSBRPG%20Documents/rpg.htm
Health Facility.. http://msdh.ms.gov/msdhsite/_static/resources/4662.pdf
Home Inspector... http://appserver.mrec.ms.gov/findlicensee.asp
Insurance Agent/Solicitor/Advisor .... www.mid.ms.gov/licapp/download_list.aspx
Insurance/Domestic Insurance Company .... www.mid.ms.gov/licapp/download_list.aspx
Lobbyist.. www.sos.state.ms.us/elections/Lobbying/Lobbyist_Dir.asp
Marriage & Family Therapist....................... www.swmft.ms.gov/swmft/Roster.nsf/webpage/Therapist_1?editdocument

Notary Public .... www.sos.ms.gov/page.aspx?s=2&s1=1&s2=5
Nurse-LPN/RN .... https://www.ms.gov/msbn/inquiry_disclaimer.do
Nursing Home Administrator .... www.bnha.state.ms.us/msbnha/roster.nsf/webpage/bnha_1?editDocument
Optometrist .... www.msbo.ms.gov/msbo/OptoRoster.nsf/webpage/Opto_1?editdocument
Osteopathic Physician .... https://www.ms.gov/medical_licensure/renewal/verificationSearch.jsp
Pawn Shop/Pawnbroker .... www.dbcf.state.ms.us/documents/lists/pawnbroker.pdf
Pharmacist/Pharmacy/Intern/Technician ..... http://msphrweb.starsystemlive.com/star/portal/msphr/page/LicenseLookup/portal.aspx
Physician/Medical Doctor .... https://www.ms.gov/medical_licensure/renewal/verificationSearch.jsp
Podiatrist .... https://www.ms.gov/medical_licensure/renewal/verificationSearch.jsp
Polygraph Examiner .... http://webcache.googleusercontent.com/search?q=cache:www.polygraphplace.com/docs/c-15-s-Mississippi-examiners.html
Psychologist .... www.psychologyboard.state.ms.us/msbp/roster.nsf/webpage/psych_1?editdocument
Real Estate Agent/Seller/Broker .... http://appserver.mrec.ms.gov/findlicensee.asp
Real Estate Appraiser .... http://appserver.mrec.ms.gov/findappraiser.asp
Social Worker .... www.swmft.ms.gov/swmft/Roster.nsf/webpage/Therapist_1?editdocument
Speech-Language Pathologist .... https://apps.msdh.ms.gov/licreviews/index.aspx
Surveyor, Land .... www.pepls.state.ms.us/pepls/web.nsf/webpages/LN_LV_PAGE_LV?OpenDocument
Teacher .... https://sso.mde.ms.gov/Login/Login.aspx

State and Local Courts

State Court Structure: **Circuit Courts** hear felony criminal prosecutions and civil lawsuits.

Chancery Courts have jurisdiction over matters involving equity; domestic matters including adoptions, custody disputes and divorces; guardianships; sanity hearings; probate, wills; and challenges to constitutionality of state laws. Land records are filed in Chancery Court. Chancery Courts have jurisdiction over juvenile matters in counties which have no County Court.

County Courts have exclusive jurisdiction over eminent domain proceedings and juvenile matters, among other things. In counties which have a County Court, a County Court judge also serves as the Youth Court judge. County Courts share jurisdiction with Circuit and Chancery Courts in some civil matters. The jurisdictional limit of County Courts is up to $200,000, The traditional limit is $75,000 max for a County Court, but this is not adhered to at all counties. County Courts may handle non-capital felony cases transferred from Circuit Court. County Courts have concurrent jurisdiction with Justice Courts in all matters, civil and criminal.

Justice Courts have jurisdiction over small claims civil cases involving amounts of $3,500 or less, misdemeanor criminal cases and any traffic offense that occurs outside a municipality

Civil cases under $3,500 are usually found in Justice Courts as filing fees are less there than at Circuit Courts. Jasper County added a 2nd Justice Court in 5/2008; it is located in City of Paulding. Since July 2008, there is a $3,500 case limit (formerly $2,500) for both civil and small claims cases at the Justice Courts. Circuit and County Courts are usually combined, except in Harrison County.

Municipal Courts have jurisdiction over misdemeanor crimes, municipal ordinances and city traffic violations.

Drug Courts are special courts which address crimes committed by persons addicted to drugs or alcohol. **Youth Courts** generally deal with matters in involving abuse and neglect of juveniles, as well as offenses committed by juveniles.

Appellate Courts: The website at http://courts.ms.gov offers searching of the MS Supreme Court and Court of Appeals Decisions and dockets.

Statewide Court Online Access: Mississippi is in the midst of implementing the Mississippi Electronic Courts System (MEC). The MEC system is a comprehensive case management system that allows courts to maintain electronic case files and offer electronic filing over the Internet. Access to the filing segment of MEC **is only available to attorneys registered with MEC** and authorized users. For details visit http://courts.ms.gov/mec/mec.html.

Otherwise, there are only a handful of courts offering online access to the public, as whown below.

Adams County

Circuit & County Court www.adamscountyms.net/index.php

Civil: The Circuit Court Case and Judgment Roll Information is $25/monthly or $275/yearly. A user account and subscription is required to use this service at www.deltacomputersystems.com/MS/MS01/ **$$$** *Criminal:* same as civil **$$$**

Clay County
Chancery Court www.desotocountyms.gov/index.aspx?nid=116

Probate, Civil Land, Divorce, Family: A private company permits online access to civil records; go to www.recordsusa.com or call Rob at 888-633-4748 x17 for info and demo. **$$$**

De Soto County
Circuit Court www.desotocountyms.gov/index.aspx?nid=116

Civil: Search docket information, records and judgments at www.deltacomputersystems.com/ms/ms17/index.html. Fee is $30 monthly or $360 annually. **$$$** *Criminal:* same **$$$**

George County
Chancery Court

Probate, Civil Land, Divorce, Family: A private company permits online access to civil records; go to www.recordsusa.com or call Rob at 888-633-4748 x17 for info and demo. **$$$**

Harrison County
Circuit & County Courts - Both Districts http://co.harrison.ms.us/elected/circuitclerk

Civil: Access to Judicial District judgments are free at http://co.harrison.ms.us/elected/circuitclerk/jroll/. Search current court dockets free by date at http://co.harrison.ms.us/dockets/. *Criminal:* Search current court dockets free by date at http://co.harrison.ms.us/dockets/.

Hinds County
Circuit & County Courts - Both Districts www.co.hinds.ms.us/pgs/index.asp

Civil: Access the clerk's judgment rolls free at www.co.hinds.ms.us/pgs/apps/jridx_query.asp. *Criminal:*

Jackson County
Circuit Court www.co.jackson.ms.us/DS/CircuitCourt.html

Civil: Access to only Circuit Court monthly dockets is free at www.co.jackson.ms.us/courts/circuit-court/Docket.aspx *Criminal:* Online access to criminal dockets is the same as civil

Jones County
Circuit & County Court – Both Districts www.co.jones.ms.us

Civil: Access the circuit court judgment roll free at www.deltacomputersystems.com/MS/MS34/INDEX.HTML.

Leflore County
Circuit & County Court

Civil: A private company permits online access to civil records; go to www.recordsusa.com or call Rob at 888-633-4748 x17 for info and demo. **$$$**

Lowndes County
Circuit & County Court

Civil: Online access is via a designated vendor, the fee is $30 monthly fee or an $360 annual fee. Circuit Court civil cases and the Judgment Roll are available from 1993 to pre4sent are included - images from 2008. Marriage licenses are available for 1991. **$$$** *Criminal:* Online access is via a designated vendor, the fee is $30 monthly fee or an $360 annual fee. Circuit Court criminal cases from 1993 to pre4sent are included - images from September 2008. **$$$**

Oktibbeha County
Circuit Court www.oktibbehacountyms.org/?q=node/78

Civil: Access the county civil circuit records and judgment roll per subscription account at www.deltacomputersystems.com/MS/MS53/INDEX.HTML. Fee is $25 monthly or $275 annual. **$$$** *Criminal:* same as civil.

Pike County
Circuit & County Court www.co.pike.ms.us/

Civil: Search the judgment roll free at www.co.pike.ms.us/jrlinkquerym.html, The civil index is available by subscription at www.co.pike.ms.us/mclinkquerycc.html. Fee is either $25 monthly or $275 annually. **$$$** *Criminal:* same as civil

Recorders, Assessors, and Other Sites of Note

Recording Office Organization: 82 counties, 92 recording offices. The recording officers are Chancery Clerk for most recorded documents. Ten counties have two separate recording offices - Bolivar, Carroll, Chickasaw, Harrison, Hinds, Jasper, Jones, Panola, Tallahatchie, and Yalobusha. Federal tax liens on personal property of businesses are filed with the Secretary of State. Federal tax liens on personal property of individuals are filed with the county Chancery Clerk. State tax liens on personal property are filed with the county Clerk of Circuit Court. State tax liens on real property are filed with the Chancery Clerk.

Statewide or Multi-Jurisdiction Access: A limited number of counties offer online access to records; there is no statewide system except for the Secretary of State's UCC access.

One vendor is worthy of mention. Access a variety of county information including property tax data free on Delta's PropertyLink System at www.deltacomputersystems.com/search.html. Approximate amount of participating counties: 38.

County Sites:

Adams County ***Recorded Documents*** www.adamscountyms.net/elected-officials/chancery-clerk/ Access judgment rolls and marriage records for a fee at www.deltacomputersystems.com/MS/MS01/INDEX.HTML. Subscription fees are $25/monthly or $275/yearly. **$$$**

Property, Taxation Assess assessor property and map data free at www.emapsplus.com/MSAdams/maps/.

Alcorn County ***Property, Taxation*** Access to real property taxes and appraisal is free at www.deltacomputersystems.com/MS/MS02/INDEX.HTML.

Benton County ***Property, Taxation*** Access to deeds and records free at www.deltacomputersystems.com/MS/MS05/INDEX.HTML. Unofficial copies of scanned records are $1.50 per page. From 1994-present.

Chickasaw County (Both Districts) ***Recorded Documents*** www.chickasawcoms.com/ Access to records for a fee at www.deltacomputersystems.com/MS/MS09/index_chancery.html. Must subscribe and fees are $30/monthly or $360/annually. Records from 2008 to present with images. **$$$**

Clarke County ***Property, Taxation*** Access to property taxes and appraisal free at www.deltacomputersystems.com/MS/MS12/INDEX.HTML.

Copiah County ***Property, Taxation*** Access to Court Calendar free at www.deltacomputersystems.com/ms/ms15/index.html.

Covington County ***Property, Taxation*** Access to real property tax and appraisal for a fee at www.deltacomputersystems.com/ms/ms16/index.html. Must subscribe and fees are $25/monthly or $275/annually.**$$$**

De Soto County ***Recorded Documents*** www.desotoms.info Access to Chancery Clerk grantor/grantee index is available at www.desotoms.info/; click on "Chancery Clerk." For voter registration data, click on Circuit Clerk and then Voter Registration tab. Also available, county board and planning commission minutes. For courts and marriages, click on Circuit Clerk. Access to Judgment rolls for a fee go to www.deltacomputersystems.com/ms/ms17/index.html. Fee is $30.00 monthly or $360 per year. Must subscribe. **$$$**

Property, Taxation Access to GIS/mapping for free from home page.

Forrest County ***Property, Taxation*** Access property tax or appraisal records free at www.deltacomputersystems.com/MS/MS18/INDEX.HTML.

George County ***Real Estate, Deed Records*** A private company permits online access by subscription; go to www.recordsusa.com/ or call Rob at 888-633-4748 x17 for info and demo. **$$$**

Property, Taxation Access to property taxes and appraisal free at www.deltacomputersystems.com/MS/MS20/INDEX.HTML.

Greene County ***Property, Taxation*** Access to property taxes and appraisal records free at www.deltacomputersystems.com/MS/MS21/INDEX.HTML.

Grenada County ***Property, Taxation*** Search assessor real property and tax sale free at www.tscmaps.com/mg/ms/grenada/index.asp but no name searching.

Hancock County ***Property, Taxation*** Access property data free through the GIS-mapping site owner search page free at www.geoportalmaps.com/atlas/hancock/. Search parcel data generally on the mapping site free www.mstc.state.ms.us/.

Harrison County (Both Districts) ***Recorded Documents*** http://co.harrison.ms.us/elected/chanceryclerk/ Access general instruments,recorded land records, and marriage records at at http://co.harrison.ms.us/services. ***Property, Taxation*** Access property tax data free at http://co.harrison.ms.us/elected/taxassessor/landroll and at http://deltacomputersystems.com/MS/MS24DELTA/plinkquerym.html.

Hinds County (Both Districts) ***Real Estate, Grantor/Grantee, Deed, Lien, Judgment Records*** www.co.hinds.ms.us/pgs/elected/chanceryclerk.asp Access a list of free search databases at http://www.co.hinds.ms.us/pgs/apps/gindex.asp. Choose to search general index, land roll, judgments, acreage, subdivision, condominiums.The Judgment Roll is at www.co.hinds.ms.us/pgs/apps/jridx_query.asp.

Property, Taxation Search the assessor land rolls for free also judgments, acreage, condos, and subdivisions free at http://www.co.hinds.ms.us/pgs/apps/landroll_query.asp. A property tax list can be saerched at http://www.co.hinds.ms.us/pgs/apps/tax_sale_query.asp.

Holmes County ***Recorded Documents*** Access recorded land records at http://www.recordsusa.com/.

Jackson County ***Recorded Documents*** www.co.jackson.ms.us/officials/chancery-clerk/ Access to Chancery Court cases go to www.deltacomputersystems.com/MS/MS30/MCLINKQUERYCH.HTML.

Property, Taxation Access to real property tax data for free at www.deltacomputersystems.com/MS/MS30/INDEX.HTML.

Jones County ***Judgment Records*** www.co.jones.ms.us/chancery.php Access county judgment roll free at www.deltacomputersystems.com/MS/MS34/JRLINKQUERYM.HTML.

Property, Taxation County appraisal and tax records are available by subscription at www.deltacomputersystems.com/MS/MS34/INDEX.HTML for $25.00 monthly or $275.00 annually.**$$$**

Kemper County ***Property, Taxation*** Access to land roll taxes free at www.mstc.state.ms.us/LandrollTPN/?countyName=Kemper&year=07

Lafayette County ***Recorded Documents*** www.lafayettecoms.com/HTML/Main.html?Chancery%20Clerk%20Page Access to a multitude of records free at www.deltacomputersystems.com/MS/MS36/INDEX.HTML.

Property, Taxation Also, access to property taxes and appraisal is free at www.deltacomputersystems.com/MS/MS36/INDEX.HTML.

Lamar County ***Property, Taxation*** Access to property data and GIS/mapping is free at www.deltacomputersystems.com/MS/MS37/INDEX.HTML.

Lauderdale County ***Property, Taxation*** Access property data free at www.deltacomputersystems.com/MS/MS38/INDEX.HTML.

Lawrence County ***Property, Taxation*** Search appraisal, Real Property Tax, and tax sales lists free at www.tscmaps.com/mg/ms/lawrence/index.asp.

Lee County ***Property, Taxation*** Access is to property records is free at www.deltacomputersystems.com/MS/MS41/INDEX.HTML.

Leflore County ***Recorded Judgments, Marriage Records*** Access judgment rolls and marriage records from a vendor. Fees inolved. See http://www.recordsusa.com/

Lincoln County ***Recorded Documents*** Access to county deed records is free at www.deltacomputersystems.com/MS/MS43/INDEX.HTML. Requires a user ID and login.

Lowndes County ***Recorded Documents*** A subscription service is found at www.deltacomputersystems.com/MS/MS44/index_chancery.html. The fee is either $30 per month or $360 per years. Records are available 2002 to present. Also, another subscription site is available at http://www.recordsusa.com. **$$$**

Property, Taxation Access property assessor data free at www.lowndesassessor.com/mappage.asp. Also, access to property tax link for free at www.deltacomputersystems.com/MS/MS44/INDEX.HTML.

Madison County ***Recorded Documents*** www.madison-co.com/elected-offices/chancery-clerk/index.php Access the Chancery clerks recorded land records free at www.madison-co.com/elected-offices/chancery-clerk/. Other databases available. Also, search at www.madison-co.com/online_services/index.php for Federal Lien, Chancery Ct, Plat, Covenant, and more.

Property, Taxation Access Land Roll data free at www.madison-co.com/elected_offices/tax_assessor/real_property_search.php. Also, search personal property tax data free at www.madison-co.com/elected_offices/tax_assessor/personal-property-tax-roll.php.

Marion County ***Recorded Documents*** www.chancery10.com/countymarion.php Access county records free at www.deltacomputersystems.com/MS/MS46/INDEX.HTML. Recorder index goes back to 5/1997; no images.

Property, Taxation Access property data free at www.deltacomputersystems.com/MS/MS46/INDEX.HTML.

Marshall County ***Property, Taxation*** Access to property tax records and real property appraisal for free at www.deltacomputersystems.com/MS/MS47/INDEX.HTML.

Monroe County ***Property, Taxation*** Access property records free on the mapping site at www.tscmaps.com/mg/ms/monroe/index.asp.

Neshoba County ***Property, Taxation*** Access to property data is free at www.deltacomputersystems.com/MS/MS50/INDEX.HTML. Also, access to property rolls free at www.dor.ms.gov/inquiry.html?dept=PropertyTax.

Oktibbeha County ***Recorded Documents*** www.oktibbehachanceryclerk.com/index.php Search county information at www.oktibbehachanceryclerk.com/online-search/index.php. Must have username and password. Also, search the marriage index and Judgments roll for free at www.deltacomputersystems.com/MS/MS53/INDEX.HTML. **$$$**

Property, Taxation Online access to property records, appraisals, tax sale lists free at www.tscmaps.com/mg/ms/oktibbeha/index.asp. Also, assess the Land Redemption database free at www.deltacomputersystems.com/MS/MS53/INDEX.HTML.

Pearl River County ***Property, Taxation*** Access to property data is free at www.deltacomputersystems.com/MS/MS55/INDEX.HTML.

Perry County ***Property, Taxation*** Access property and personal property and appraisal data free at www.deltacomputersystems.com/MS/MS56/INDEX.HTML.

Pike County ***Recorded Documents*** www.co.pike.ms.us/chanceryclerk.html Access to county Deeds & Records is free at www.co.pike.ms.us/mclinkquerych.html.

Property, Taxation Search property assessor and tax records free at www.co.pike.ms.us/plinkquery.html.

Rankin County ***Property, Taxation*** Records on the county Land Roll database are free at www.rankincounty.org/TA/LandRollDB.asp. Also, access to property tax data for free at www.deltacomputersystems.com/MS/MS61/plinkquerym.html.

Scott County ***Records*** Access to online records, contact Paul at Syscon (205) 758-2000 x8107 or paul.sellers@syscon0nline.com. **$$$**
Property, Taxation Access assessor and appraiser property data free at www.deltacomputersystems.com/MS/MS62/INDEX.HTML.

Smith County ***Property, Taxation*** Access to property tax and appraisal for a fee at www.deltacomputersystems.com/MS/MS65/INDEX.HTML. Fees are $25 monthly or $275 annually.**$$$**

Stone County ***Property, Taxation*** Access property tax records free at www.deltacomputersystems.com/MS/MS66/INDEX.HTML.

Tate County ***Property, Taxation*** Access real property data for free at http://cdms.datasysmgt.com/dsmh/WWREALH1.

Tippah County ***Property, Taxation*** Access to property taxes and appraisal for a fee at www.deltacomputersystems.com/MS/MS70/INDEX.HTML. Fee is $25.00 monthly or $275.00 annually.**$$$**

Tunica County ***Property, Taxation*** Access to parcel/mapping for free at www.tunicamaps.com/mappage.asp.

Union County ***Property, Taxation***
Access property tax records and appraisals for free at www.deltacomputersystems.com/MS/MS73/INDEX.HTML.

Walthall County ***Property, Taxation*** Access to property rolls for free at www.dor.ms.gov/taxareas/property/main.html.

Warren County ***Property, Taxation*** Access is free at www.deltacomputersystems.com/MS/MS75/INDEX.HTML.

Washington County ***Property, Taxation***
Access to property taxes and appraisal for free at www.deltacomputersystems.com/MS/MS76/INDEX.HTML.

Wayne County ***Property, Taxation***
Access property tax and appraisal data free at www.deltacomputersystems.com/MS/MS77/INDEX.HTML.

Adair County ***Property, Taxation*** Access to parcel search for free at http://adair.missouriassessors.com/search.php.

Missouri

Capital: Jefferson City
Cole County
Time Zone: CST
Population: 6,021,998
# of Counties: 114

Useful State Links

Website: www.mo.gov
Governor: http://governor.mo.gov
Attorney General: http://governor.mo.gov/
State Archives: www.sos.mo.gov/archives/Default.asp
State Statutes and Codes: www.moga.mo.gov/statutesearch/
Legislative Bill Search: www.house.mo.gov/billcentral.aspx
Unclaimed Funds: www.treasurer.mo.gov/content/find-your-property

State Public Record Agencies

Criminal Records

Missouri State Highway Patrol, Criminal Justice Information Srvs Division, www.mshp.dps.missouri.gov/MSHPWeb/Root/index.html Online access and retrieval is available at https://www.machs.mshp.dps.mo.gov/MACHSFP/home.html. An account must be first created and use of a credit card is required. The same $10.00 fee applies plus a 'convenience fee' for each transaction. This fee is $1.00 for 1 to 3 records, when more than 3 records are ordered, a sliding scale is used which will vary from 3% to 2.6%. Once an account is created, users may submit the name, date of birth, and/or social security number of a person. Requesters receive all Missouri open record criminal history information related to the individual - meaning convictions, arrests within 30 days, pending charges and suspended imposition of sentences during probation. All completed records are emailed in a PDF format to the user's account, usually within seconds unless further research is need to determine a disposition. Data includes felonies, misdemeanors, and selected municipal ordinance violations. **$$$** *Other Options:* Bulk/multiple requests can be submitted on diskette; prior arrangement and agency approval required. Responses are printed out, checked for accuracy and returned; however they cannot be returned on diskette. Alias or maiden names require separate search.

Sexual Offender Registry

Missouri State Highway Patrol, Sexual Offender Registry, www.mshp.dps.mo.gov/CJ38/search.jsp The name index can be searched at the website, by name, county or ZIP Code. The web page also gives links lists to the county sheriffs who have online access. *Other Options:* Look at bottom of disclaimer page for access to Excel spreadsheet.

Incarceration Records

Missouri Department of Corrections, Offender Inquiry, http://doc.mo.gov/ Inmate searching is offered at https://web.mo.gov/doc/offSearchWeb/. Includes including probationers and parolees not previously excluded.

Corporation, LLC, LP, Fictitious/Assumed Name, Trademarks/Servicemarks

Secretary of State, Corporation Services, www.sos.mo.gov/business/corporations/ Search free online at https://www.sos.mo.gov/BusinessEntity/soskb/csearch.asp. The corporate name, the agent name or the charter number is required to search. The site indicates the currency of the data. Many business entity type searches are available. Also, with an established account one may order copies and certified documents online. Use of a credit card is required. *Other Options:* Bulk listings are available for a fee, call for details.

Uniform Commercial Code

UCC Division, Attn: Records, www.sos.mo.gov/ucc/ The web address is https://bsd.sos.mo.gov/. Must register with User ID and Password, but no fees to register. Passwords will expire 90 days after creation. You will receive a reminder via your email 10 days in advance for your password expiration date. There are no fees. *Other Options:* The agency will release information for bulk purchase, call for procedures and pricing.

Vital Records

Department of Health & Senior Svcs, Bureau of Vital Records, http://health.mo.gov/data/vitalrecords/index.php Orders may be placed online at www.vitalchek.com. Records prior to 1910 are available by county at www.sos.mo.gov/archives/resources/birthdeath/. **$$$**

Workers' Compensation Records

Labor & Industrial Relations Department, Workers Compensation Division, www.labor.mo.gov/DWC/ Online access is available to claimants using a pre-assigned PIN. Appeal decisions is shown to public at www.labor.mo.gov/LIRC/Forms/WC_Decisions/. To check if an employer has coverage, visit www.labor.mo.gov/DWC/tool/wc_cov_ver.asp.

Driver Records

Department of Revenue, Motor Vehicle and Driver Licensing, http://dor.mo.gov/drivers/ Electronic access is different in MO compared to other states. Two methods are offered. Fees are not based on a per record basis, but instead on a batch or file purchase basis. The fee is $52.00 per batch, regardless of the number of requests included. There are set-up fees involved for state programmer's time. If requests are sent by 2AM, results can be picked up at 6AM same day. Also, approved users or vendors may purchase the entire file for drivers and histories (for $2035) and then purchase daily or monthly updates. For further information, call 573-526-3669 or e-mail dlrecords@dor.mo.gov. Requests for driver records may be e-mailed to dlrecords@dor.mo.gov. Customer's request must include all credit card information (type, number, expiration date, etc.) in order for the request to be processed. **$$$** *Other Options:* If requests are sent by 2AM, results can be picked up at 6AM same day.

Vehicle, Vessel Ownership & Registration

Department of Revenue, Motor Vehicle and Driver Licensing Div, http://dor.mo.gov/motorv/ Online record searches are available to registered entities who have a DPPA security access code issued by the Department. The fee is $.0382 per record and is automatically withdrawn through the requestor's ACH account. Access is via the Internet. Visit the web page for more information. **$$$** *Other Options:* Missouri has an extensive range of records and information available on electronic format or labels or paper. Besides offering license, vehicle, title, dealer, and marine records, specific public report data is also available.

Accident Reports

Missouri State Highway Patrol, Traffic Records Division, www.mshp.dps.missouri.gov/MSHPWeb/PatrolDivisions/TFD/index.html Information on accidents investigated by the Highway Patrol for the most recent 29 days only is found at www.mshp.dps.mo.gov/HP68/search.jsp. Records cannot be e-mailed. *Other Options:* Some crash reconstruction reports may be available via CD, depending on date of crash. CD includes photos and other attachments.

Campaign Finance, Disclosure, Lobbyists, PACs

Missouri Ethics Commission, Division of Elections, www.mec.mo.gov/Ethics/Generalinfo/Generalinfo.aspx A number of searches are available at www.mec.mo.gov/Ethics/GeneralInfo/GeneralInfo.aspx. View campaign finance reports, view lobbyist reports, search contribution and expenditures for candidates.

Occupational Licensing Boards

Accountant-CPA/Firm .... https://renew.pr.mo.gov/licensee-search.asp
Acupuncturist .... https://renew.pr.mo.gov/licensee-search.asp
Anesthesia Permit, Dental .... https://renew.pr.mo.gov/licensee-search.asp
Announcer, Athletic Event/Ring .... https://renew.pr.mo.gov/licensee-search.asp
Architect .... https://renew.pr.mo.gov/licensee-search.asp
Athletic Event/Physician/Timekeeper .... https://renew.pr.mo.gov/licensee-search.asp
Athletic Trainer .... https://renew.pr.mo.gov/licensee-search.asp
Attorney .... http://members.mobar.org/members/LawyerSearch/GSSearch.aspx
Audiologist .... https://renew.pr.mo.gov/licensee-search.asp
Bail Bond Agents .... https://sbs-mo.naic.org/Lion-Web/jsp/sbsreports/AgentLookup.jsp
Barber/Barber Shop/Instructor/School .... https://renew.pr.mo.gov/licensee-search.asp
Body Piercer/Brander/Branding Estab .... https://renew.pr.mo.gov/licensee-search.asp
Boxer/Boxing Professional .... https://renew.pr.mo.gov/licensee-search.asp
Cemetery .... https://renew.pr.mo.gov/licensee-search.asp

Child Care Facility	https://webapp01.dhss.mo.gov/childcaresearch/searchengine.aspx
Chiropractor	https://renew.pr.mo.gov/licensee-search.asp
Cosmetologist/School/Instructor/Shop	https://renew.pr.mo.gov/licensee-search.asp
Counselor, Professional/Trainee	https://renew.pr.mo.gov/licensee-search.asp
Dentist, Dental Hygienist/Specialist	https://renew.pr.mo.gov/licensee-search.asp
Drug Distributor	https://renew.pr.mo.gov/licensee-search.asp
DSGA Permit/Site Certificate	https://renew.pr.mo.gov/licensee-search.asp
ECS Permit/Site Certificate	https://renew.pr.mo.gov/licensee-search.asp
Embalmer	https://renew.pr.mo.gov/licensee-search.asp
Engineer	https://renew.pr.mo.gov/licensee-search.asp
Esthetician/Manicurist	https://renew.pr.mo.gov/licensee-search.asp
Funeral Director/Establishment,Misc	https://renew.pr.mo.gov/licensee-search.asp
General Anesthesia Permit	https://renew.pr.mo.gov/licensee-search.asp
Geologist/Registrant in Training	https://renew.pr.mo.gov/licensee-search.asp
Hearing Instrument Specialist	https://renew.pr.mo.gov/licensee-search.asp
Insurance Agent/Broker	https://sbs-mo.naic.org/Lion-Web/jsp/sbsreports/AgentLookup.jsp
Insurance Consultant, Chiropractic	https://renew.pr.mo.gov/licensee-search.asp
Interior Designer	https://renew.pr.mo.gov/licensee-search.asp
Interpreter for the Deaf	https://renew.pr.mo.gov/licensee-search.asp
Landscape Architect	https://renew.pr.mo.gov/licensee-search.asp
Lobbyist Report	www.mec.mo.gov/Ethics/Lobbying/LobElecReports.aspx
Marital & Family Therapist	https://renew.pr.mo.gov/licensee-search.asp
Martial Artist/Martial Art Occupation	https://renew.pr.mo.gov/licensee-search.asp
Massage Therapist/Business	https://renew.pr.mo.gov/licensee-search.asp
Midwife	https://renew.pr.mo.gov/licensee-search.asp
Notary Public	www.sos.mo.gov/Notary/NotarySearch/NotarySearch.aspx
Nurse-RN/LPN/PA	https://renew.pr.mo.gov/licensee-search.asp
Nursing Home Administrator	http://health.mo.gov/information/boards/bnha/pdf/administrators.pdf
Nursing School	https://renew.pr.mo.gov/licensee-search.asp
Occupation'l Therapist/Therapist Ass't	https://renew.pr.mo.gov/licensee-search.asp
Optometrist	https://renew.pr.mo.gov/licensee-search.asp
Osteopathic Physician	https://renew.pr.mo.gov/licensee-search.asp
Parenteral Conscious Sedation	https://renew.pr.mo.gov/licensee-search.asp
PCS Permit/Site Certificate	https://renew.pr.mo.gov/licensee-search.asp
Perfusionist	https://renew.pr.mo.gov/licensee-search.asp
Pesticide Applicator/Technician	www.kellysolutions.com/MO/Applicators/index.asp
Pesticide Dealer/Registered	www.kellysolutions.com/MO/Dealers/index.asp
Pharmacist/Pharmacy/Intern/Technician	https://renew.pr.mo.gov/licensee-search.asp
Physical Therapist/Assistant	https://renew.pr.mo.gov/licensee-search.asp
Physician/Medical Doctor/Assistant	https://renew.pr.mo.gov/licensee-search.asp
Podiatrist/Ankle Specialist	https://renew.pr.mo.gov/licensee-search.asp
Private Investigator/Agency/Branch/Trainer	https://renew.pr.mo.gov/licensee-search.asp
Private Investigator/Fire Investigator Discipline Licensees	http://pr.mo.gov/pi-discipline.asp
Psychologist	https://renew.pr.mo.gov/licensee-search.asp
Real Estate Agent/Seller/Broker/Partner	https://renew.pr.mo.gov/licensee-search.asp
Real Estate Appraiser	https://renew.pr.mo.gov/licensee-search.asp
Respiratory Care Practitioner	https://renew.pr.mo.gov/licensee-search.asp
School Nurse	https://renew.pr.mo.gov/licensee-search.asp
Social Worker, Baccalaureate/Clinical	https://renew.pr.mo.gov/licensee-search.asp
Speech-Language Pathologist	https://renew.pr.mo.gov/licensee-search.asp
Surveyor, Land	https://renew.pr.mo.gov/licensee-search.asp
Tattoo Artist/Establishment	https://renew.pr.mo.gov/licensee-search.asp
Teacher	https://k12apps.dese.mo.gov/webapps/tcertsearch/tc_search1.asp
Veterinarian/Veterinary Tech/Facility	https://renew.pr.mo.gov/licensee-search.asp
Wrestler/Wrestling Professional	https://renew.pr.mo.gov/licensee-search.asp

State and Local Courts

State Court Structure: The **Circuit Courts** are the primary trial courts in Missouri, and they have general jurisdiction over almost all civil and criminal matters. Each circuit court consists of divisions including associate circuit, small claims, municipal, criminal, family, probate and juvenile. The type of case determines the division to which a particular case is assigned.

At one time, every county had an **Associate Circuit Court**. Over the past few years the Associate Courts has been consolidated into the Circuit Court, with the Associate Court beginning a division of the Circuit Court. Since 01/01/2010, all Associate Courts are supposedly absorbed into the Circuit Court as Divisions. Herein we have segregated the Associate Courts when record keeping, fees and phone numbers indicated are completely comingled with the Circuit Court.

The **Municipal Court** has original jurisdiction on municipal ordinance violations.

- **Appellate Courts:** At www.courts.mo.gov/page.jsp?id=12086&dist=Opinions one mat\y search Supreme Court and Appellate Court Oinions.

Statewide Court Online Access: All courts participate in the system described below.

- Available at https://www.courts.mo.gov/casenet/base/welcome.do is Missouri CaseNet, an online system for access to civil, paternity, adult & child protection, and criminal docket data. The system includes all Circuit Courts, City of St. Louis, the Eastern, Western, and Southern Appellate Courts, the Supreme Court, and Fine Collection Center. Cases can be searched case number, filing date, or litigant name. A number of Municipal Courts also participate. CaseNet search results show full name and address, but usually only the year of birth (click on Parties and Attorneys at case result page). Note the following statement found at the web page: "The information available on Case.net is provided as a service and is not considered an official court record." However, the CaseNet system is what the county court house public access terminals show on their screens. It is generally thought that a search on the online version of CaseNet is equivalent to a search of the public access terminal at the courthouse. The advantage of being at the courthouse is one can look at case files to try and determine the true identity since CaseNet does not provide the full DOB.
- Since June 29, 2012, final judgment documents on domestic relations cases are longer available on Casenet. Not all courts have electronic documents available, only those using the Document Management System (DMS) within the Judicial Information System (JIS). If a document is available for viewing and printing it shows as a blue hyperlink on the screen.
- Note some individual courts offer access to probate records outside of CaseNet, and are listed bel.ow.

County Sites Other Than the Statewide Casenet Mentioned Above:

Butler County

Consolidated Circuit Court www.courts.mo.gov/page.jsp?id=1650

Online access to probate records is free at www.16thcircuit.org/publicaccess.asp. This includes private process servers, jury verdicts, criminal traffic, and criminal sureties.

Carter County

Combined Circuit Court www.courts.mo.gov/page.jsp?id=1652

Online access to probate records is free at www.16thcircuit.org/publicaccess.asp. This includes private process servers, jury verdicts, criminal traffic, and criminal sureties.

Clay County

Consolidated Circuit Court www.circuit7.net

View probate records data at www.16thcircuit.org/Depts/PRB/prb_inquiry.asp. This includes private process servers, jury verdicts, criminal traffic, and criminal sureties.

Cole County

Consolidated Circuit Court www.courts.mo.gov/page.jsp?id=1905

Online access to probate records is free at www.16thcircuit.org/publicaccess.asp. This includes private process servers, jury verdicts, criminal traffic, and criminal sureties.

Dunklin County

Consolidated Circuit Court www.courts.mo.gov/page.jsp?id=1647

Online access to probate records is free at www.16thcircuit.org/publicaccess.asp. This includes private process servers, jury verdicts, criminal traffic, and criminal sureties.

Hickory County
Circuit Court www.positech.net/~dcourt/
Access probate records at www.16thcircuit.org/publicaccess.asp.

Jackson County
Circuit Court - Criminal Division www.16thcircuit.org
Online access to probate records is free at www.16thcircuit.org/Depts/PRB/prb_inquiry.asp?dept=prb. This includes private process servers, jury verdicts, criminal traffic, and criminal sureties.

Jefferson County
Circuit Court - Civil Division www.courts.mo.gov/page.jsp?id=1620
Online access to probate records is free at www.16thcircuit.org/Depts/PRB/prb_inquiry.asp?dept=prb. This includes private process servers, jury verdicts, criminal traffic, and criminal sureties.

Pettis County
Circuit Court - Civil www.courts.mo.gov/page.jsp?id=1615
Online access to probate records is free at www.16thcircuit.org/publicaccess.asp. This includes private process servers, jury verdicts, criminal traffic, and criminal sureties.

Shelby County
Consolidated Circuit Court www.courts.mo.gov/page.jsp?id=1667
Online access to probate records is free at www.16thcircuit.org/publicaccess.asp. This includes private process servers, jury verdicts, criminal traffic, and criminal sureties.

St. Francois County
Circuit Court - Division I & II www.courts.mo.gov/page.jsp?id=1626
Online access to probate records is free at www.16thcircuit.org/publicaccess.asp. This includes private process servers, jury verdicts, criminal traffic, and criminal sureties.

St. Louis County and St. Louis City
Circuit Court of St. Louis County - Civil www.stlouisco.com/circuitcourt
Online access to probate records is free at www.16thcircuit.org/publicaccess.asp. This includes private process servers, jury verdicts, criminal traffic, and criminal sureties.

Ste. Genevieve County
Circuit Court www.courts.mo.gov/page.jsp?id=1625
Online access to probate records is free at www.16thcircuit.org/publicaccess.asp. This includes private process servers, jury verdicts, criminal traffic, and criminal sureties.

Sullivan County
Consolidated Circuit Court www.courts.mo.gov/page.jsp?id=1576
Online access to probate records is free at www.16thcircuit.org/publicaccess.asp. This includes private process servers, jury verdicts, criminal traffic, and criminal sureties.

Reminder:

There is a free, government-based statewide system that serivces all counties. See beginning of this section for details on https://www.courts.mo.gov/casenet/base/welcome.do.

Recorders, Assessors, and Other Sites of Note

Recording Office Organization: 114 counties and one independent city; 115 recording offices. The recording officer is the Recorder of Deeds. The City of St. Louis has its own recording office. Watch for ZIP Codes that may be City of St. Louis or County of St. Louis. All federal and state tax liens are filed with the county Recorder of Deeds. Tax liens are usually indexed together.

Statewide or Multi-Jurisdiction Access: A number of counties offer online access to records; there is no statewide system except for the Secretary of State's UCC access. Also there are two vendors of note that operate in a number of counties.

- Access recorder land data for various counties by subscription from an endorsed vender. The Tapestry system is found at https://tapestry.fidlar.com/Tapestry2/Search.aspx. Fees are based either on a $5.95 per search or ongoing custmners can set up a flat rate plus a slight per minute if usage is surpassed.
- Search assessor GIS property data from 9 jurisdictions for a fee on the GIS system at http://beacon.schneidercorp.com/ with registration and username required.

County Sites:

Adair County ***Property, Taxation*** Access to parcel search for free at http://adair.missouriassessors.com/search.php.

Audrain County ***Recorded Documents*** http://audraincounty.org/county-offices/157-2/ Access to records for a fee at https://tapestry.fidlar.com/Tapestry2/Default.aspx. Contact 309-794-3283 or kylec@fidlar.com for subscription information. Search fee is $5.95 each, printed images $.50 each unless otherwise noted. **$$$**

Property, Taxation Search assessor property data for a fee on the GIS system at http://beacon.schneidercorp.com. Registration and username required. At the default website, choose Missouri then Audrain County, then register.**$$$**

Barry County ***Recorded Documents*** http://barrycorecorder.com/ Access to records for a fee at https://cotthosting.com/moportal/User/Login.aspx?ReturnUrl=%2fmoportal%2fIndex.aspx. **$$$**

Bates County ***Recorded Documents*** http://batescounty.net/recorder.php Access to records for a fee at http://mo830.cichosting.com/. (Must subscribe to services in order to view instruments and to be able to make copies. Contact recorder's office for details. **$$$**

Property, Taxation Access to GIS/mapping for free at https://bates.integritygis.com/.

Benton County ***Property, Taxation*** Access to GIS/mapping free at https://benton.integritygis.com/.

Boone County ***Recorded Documents*** www.showmeboone.com/RECORDER/ Access to the recorder database is free at www.showmeboone.com/recorder/.

Property, Taxation Assessor data is free at www.showmeboone.com/ASSESSOR/. Free registration and password required.

Buchanan County ***Recorded Documents*** www.co.buchanan.mo.us/offices/recorder/index.html Access the recorder database for a fee at www.co.buchanan.mo.us/offices/recorder/online.html. Fee for database is $250.00 per month by contract agreement. Now also have for occasional user agreement $.25 per minute. **$$$**

Property, Taxation Search the GIS-mapping site for property data free at https://buchanan.integritygis.com/ but no name searching.

Callaway County ***Recorded Documents*** http://callawaycounty.org/recorder/ Access to records for a fee at http://68.188.14.30/imagesearch/. **$$$**

Camden County ***Property, Taxation*** Access to the 2012 Tax Sale List free at www.camdenmo.org/TaxSale/taxsale.txt. Also, access to the 2012 Tax Sale GIS/mapping free at https://camden.integritygis.com/?xmin=1424211&xmax=1712276&ymin=697992&ymax=910123.

Cape Girardeau County ***Recorded Documents*** www.capecounty.us/Recorder/Recorders%20Office.aspx Access to records for a fee at https://tapestry.fidlar.com/Tapestry2/Default.aspx. Contact 309-794-3283 or kylec@fidlar.com for subscription information. Search fee is $5.95 each, printed images $.50 each unless otherwise noted. **$$$**

Cass County ***Recorded Documents*** www.casscounty.com/recorder/webaccessr.html Access to index searches are free, to view and copy images, contact Marilyn Morris at 816-380-8168 to set-up account. Fees are $150.00 per month or $.10 per minute. Go to www.casscounty.com/recorder/webaccessr.html for information regarding accessing records and to set up an account. **$$$**

Property, Taxation Search assessor property data for a fee on the GIS system at http://beacon.schneidercorp.com. Registration and username required. At the default website, choose Missouri then Cass County, then register.

Cedar County ***Recorded Documents*** http://cedarcountymo.gov/recorder.html Access to records for free at http://cedarmo.icounty.com/iRecordWeb2.0/Login.aspx. The "GUEST" user provides access to the data, but does not allow you to view document images. Images are from a paid subscription. Contact 417-276-6700 x6 for subscription information. **$$$**

Christian County ***Recorded Documents*** www.christiancountymo.gov/recorder.htm Access the recording office records free at http://landrecords.christiancountymo.gov/. Real estate, marriage records go back to 10/1994; tax liens to 1/3/2000. Username and password is Public.

Property, Taxation Search on the tax payment lookup at www.christiancountycollector.com/christian-payment.php.**$$$**

Clay County ***Recorded Documents*** https://www.claycountymo.gov/recorder Access to the recorder's database is free at http://recorder.claycogov.com/pages/online_access.asp. Overall index goes back to 7/1986; images back to 1986. Real estate only UCCs back to 1986. No images for marriages, discharges, just data.

Property, Taxation Access assessor property records free at http://gisweb.claycogov.com/realEstate/realEstate.jsp but no name searching. Also, access real estate records from Collector's Office free at https://collector.claycountymo.gov/ascend/(cowatc55rk03xq55fpwy0iz0)/search.aspx. Also, search county property manually on the GIS-mapping site free at http://gisweb.claycogov.com/gis/viewer.htm.

Cole County ***Property, Taxation*** Access property and other mapping data for a fee at www.midmogis.com/colesl/.**$$$**

Cooper County ***Recorded Documents*** www.mo-river.net/Government/coopercounty_gov.htm Access to records for a fee at https://tapestry.fidlar.com/Tapestry2/Default.aspx. Contact 309-794-3283 or kylec@fidlar.com for subscription information. Search fee is $5.95 each, printed images $.50 each unless otherwise noted. **$$$**

De Kalb County ***Property, Taxation*** Search assessor property data for a fee on the GIS system at http://beacon.schneidercorp.com. Registration and username required. At the default website, choose Missouri then De Kalb County, then register.**$$$**

Franklin County ***Recorded Documents*** www.franklinmo.org Access to records for a fee at https://tapestry.fidlar.com/Tapestry2/Default.aspx. Contact 309-794-3283 or kylec@fidlar.com for subscription information. Search fee is $5.95 each, printed images $.50 each unless otherwise noted. **$$$**

Property, Taxation Access to Assessor records for free at www.franklinmo.net/Assessor/Default.aspx.

Gasconade County ***Recorded Documents*** Access to records for a fee at https://tapestry.fidlar.com/Tapestry2/Default.aspx. Contact 309-794-3283 or kylec@fidlar.com for subscription information. Search fee is $5.95 each, printed images $.50 each unless otherwise noted. **$$$**

Greene County ***Recorded Documents*** www.greenecountymo.org Search the recorder database for free at www.greenecountymo.org/recorder/realsearch.php. Search tax liens at www.greenecountymo.org/recorder/taxliensearch.php.

Property, Taxation Search assessor property data for a fee on the GIS system at http://beacon.schneidercorp.com. Registration and username required. At the default website, choose Missouri then Greene County, then register.**$$$**

Hickory County ***Recorded Documents*** Access to records for a fee at https://tapestry.fidlar.com/Tapestry2/Default.aspx. Contact 309-794-3283 or kylec@fidlar.com for subscription information. Search fee is $5.95 each, printed images $.50 each unless otherwise noted. **$$$**

Howell County ***Recorded Documents*** Access to records for a fee at https://tapestry.fidlar.com/Tapestry2/Default.aspx. Contact 309-794-3283 or kylec@fidlar.com for subscription information. Search fee is $5.95 each, printed images $.50 each unless otherwise noted. **$$$**

Jackson County (Kansas City) ***Recorded Documents*** www.jacksongov.org/content/3310/3356/default.aspx Search the recorder records database for free atwww.jacksongov.org/content/3310/3356/3575/default.aspx. Also, access recording office land data at www.etitlesearch.com/; registration required, fee based on usage. **$$$**

Property, Taxation Search real estate sales, tax payments, parcel info at www.jacksongov.org/content/3271/3635/default.aspx. Search property tax and ownership at https://ascendweb.jacksongov.org/ascend/(1qxstkjilfrguge52brxm4mq)/search.aspx.

Jasper County ***Property, Taxation*** Search assessor property data for a fee on the GIS system at http://beacon.schneidercorp.com. Registration and username required. At the default website, choose Missouri then Jasper County, then register.**$$$**

Jefferson County ***Recorded Documents*** www.jeffcomo.org Access recording office land data at www.etitlesearch.com/; registration required, fee based on usage; call 870-856-3055 for info. Also, access to records for a fee at https://tapestry.fidlar.com/Tapestry2/Default.aspx. Contact 309-794-3283 or kylec@fidlar.com forsubscription information. Search fee is $5.95 each, pringed images $.50 each unless otherwise noted. **$$$**

Property, Taxation Search assessor property data for free at www.jcao.org/.

Johnson County ***Recorded Documents*** http://jocorecorder.com/ Access to recorder records for a fee at http://search.jocorecorder.com/irecordclient/login.aspx. Must sign a contract for subscription. **$$$**

Laclede County ***Recorded Documents (index only), Marriage Records*** http://lacledecountymissouri.org/recorder/ Access to recorders documents indexes is free at http://lacledecountymissouri.org/index.php?page=free-on-line-search. Images available with a pre-paid subscription. **$$$**

Property, Taxation Access to real estate/property look-up for a fee at http://lacledemo.civictoolbox.com/. Must fill out user form and be issued user-name and password.**$$$**

Lafayette County ***Recorded Documents*** Access to records for a fee at https://tapestry.fidlar.com/Tapestry2/Default.aspx. Contact 309-794-3283 or kylec@fidlar.com for subscription information. Search fee is $5.95 each, printed images $.50 each unless otherwise noted. **$$$**

Lawrence County ***Recorded Documents*** Access to ndexes ise free, images are with subscription, go to https://cotthosting.com/moportal/User/Login.aspx?ReturnUrl=%2fmoportal%2fIndex.aspx.. Index dates and images available from 1/4/88 to current.

Property, Taxation Access to GIS/mapping for free at https://lawrence.integritygis.com/.

Lincoln County ***Recorded Documents*** https://gov.propertyinfo.com/mo-lincoln/ Access recording real estate and UCC records after registering at https://gov.propertyinfo.com/mo-lincoln/. Click on New To This Site to register. Index search is free; there is a fee to purchase documents; credit cards accepted. Real estate records index goes back to 1/1/1988; Tax liens back to 10/1/2001. Also, access to Recorder of Deeds portal for a fee go to https://cotthosting.com/moportal/User/Login.aspx?ReturnUrl=%2fmoportal%2fIndex.aspx. Online index books (deeds) from 1819-1987, (right of ways) from 1927-1947. Can sign-in as a guest but info is limited. **$$$**

Property, Taxation For free parcel searches go to https://lincoln.integritygis.com/. Also, access to Assessor's database free at http://lincoln.missouriassessors.com/ppSearch.php.

Linn County ***Recorded Documents*** Access to records for a fee at https://tapestry.fidlar.com/Tapestry2/Default.aspx. Contact 309-794-3283 or kylec@fidlar.com for subscription information. Search fee is $5.95 each, printed images $.50 each unless otherwise noted. **$$$**

Livingston County ***Recorded Documents*** www.livingstoncountymo.com Access to images of recorded documents for free (short-term day passes) go to https://www.idocmarket.com/. Subscriptions available for more detailed information. **$$$**

McDonald County ***Recorded Documents*** www.mcdonaldcountygov.com/depts/recorder.php Access to indexes and images of records for a fee at https://cotthosting.com/moportal/User/Login.aspx?ReturnUrl=%2fmoportal%2fIndex.aspx. Deeds from 1988, current, mortgages from 1998 to present, (survey, military and marriage-index only no images). Guest index search only for free. **$$$**

Property, Taxation Access to GIS/mapping for free at http://mcdonald.villagis.net/.

Macon County ***Recorded Documents*** http://maconcountymo.com/Government/RecorderofDeeds/tabid/83/language/en-US/Default.aspx Access to records for a fee at https://tapestry.fidlar.com/Tapestry2/Default.aspx. Contact 309-794-3283 or kylec@fidlar.com for subscription information. Search fee is $5.95 each, printed images $.50 each unless otherwise noted. **$$$**

Maries County ***Recorded Documents*** For subscription service call Mark Bushmann for more information. **$$$**

Marion County ***Recorded Documents*** Access to records for a fee at https://tapestry.fidlar.com/Tapestry2/Default.aspx. Contact 309-794-3283 or kylec@fidlar.com for subscription information. Search fee is $5.95 each, printed images $.50 each unless otherwise noted. **$$$**

Miller County ***Property, Taxation*** Access to GIS/mapping for free at www.millercomogis.com/miller/.**$$$**

Mississippi County ***Recorded Documents*** www.misscomo.net/countyofficeindex/recorderofdeeds.html Access land records at http://etitlesearch.com. You can do a name search; choose from $200.00 monthly subscription or per click account. **$$$**

Monroe County ***Recorded Documents*** www.parismo.net/recorder.htm Access to records for a fee at https://tapestry.fidlar.com/Tapestry2/Default.aspx. Contact 309-794-3283 or kylec@fidlar.com for subscription information. Search fee is $5.95 each, printed images $.50 each unless otherwise noted. **$$$**

New Madrid County ***Recorded Documents*** Land records may be available at http://etitlesearch.com. You can do a name search; choose from $200.00 monthly subscription or per click account. **$$$**

Newton County ***Recorded Documents, Vital Records*** www.ncrecorder.org Search the index free at http://search.ncrecorder.org/resolution/. Use "guest" for userID and password.

Property, Taxation Access to property records free at http://newtoncountyassessor.com/onlinepers/perspin.php. Must have OL number (located on the left side of your address label).

Nodaway County ***Recorded Documents*** www.nodawaycountymo.com/content/view/37/49/ Access to Recorder documents for free at http://search.nodawaycountyrecorder.com/iRecordWeb2.0/Login.aspx. Guest access for searching online indexes is offered. For images must register.

Pemiscot County ***Recorded Documents*** Access land records at http://etitlesearch.com. You can do a name search; choose from $200.00 monthly subscription or per click account. **$$$**

Perry County ***Recorded Documents*** www.perrycountymo.us/index.aspx?nid=76 Access to records for a fee at https://tapestry.fidlar.com/Tapestry2/Default.aspx. Contact 309-794-3283 or kylec@fidlar.com for subscription information. Search fee is $5.95 each, printed images $.50 each unless otherwise noted. **$$$**

Property, Taxation Access to property search information go to www.perry.missouriassessors.com/. Basic search free, more detailed search for a yearly fee. Contact office for more information.**$$$**

Pettis County ***Recorded Documents*** www.pettiscomo.com/rec.html Access to records for a fee at https://tapestry.fidlar.com/Tapestry2/Default.aspx. Contact 309-794-3283 or kylec@fidlar.com for subscription information. Search fee is $5.95 each, printed images $.50 each unless otherwise noted. **$$$**

Property, Taxation Search assessor property data for a fee on the GIS system at http://beacon.schneidercorp.com. Registration and username required. At the default website, choose Missouri then Pettis County, then register.**$$$**

Phelps County ***Recorded Documents*** www.phelpscounty.org/recorder/recorder.htm Access to records for a fee at https://tapestry.fidlar.com/Tapestry2/Default.aspx. Contact 309-794-3283 or kylec@fidlar.com for subscription information. Search fee is $5.95 each, printed images $.50 each unless otherwise noted. **$$$**

Property, Taxation Access to GIS/mapping for free at www.phelpscounty.org/assessor/index.html. Must have Microsoft Silverlight. Can install from this website.

Pike County ***Recorded Documents*** Access to records for a fee at https://tapestry.fidlar.com/Tapestry2/Default.aspx. Contact 309-794-3283 or kylec@fidlar.com for subscription information. Search fee is $5.95 each, printed images $.50 each unless otherwise noted. **$$$**

Property, Taxation Search assessor property data for a fee on the GIS system at http://beacon.schneidercorp.com. Registration and username required. At the default website, choose Missouri then Pike County, then register.**$$$**

Platte County ***Recorded Documents*** www.co.platte.mo.us/county_offices_departments/recorder.html To access recorder's indexes online, complete the online deed form and a password will be issued to you; no fee at this time.

Property, Taxation Assessor data available free at http://maps.co.platte.mo.us/. Also, access the Collector's tax payments data free at www.plattecountycollector.com/platte-payment.php but parcel ID or account number required.

Putnam County ***Property, Taxation*** Free parcel search at http://putnam.missouriassessors.com/search.php?mode=search.

Randolph County ***Recorded Documents*** www.randolphcounty-mo.com/recorder-of-deeds/ Access to records for free at http://randolphmo.icounty.com/iRecordWeb2.0/Login.aspx. Must register for use. Images are for a fee. Call 660-277-4718 for more information. **$$$**

Property, Taxation Access to property search free at www.rcao.com/namesearch.php.

Ray County ***Property, Taxation*** Free assessor parcel search at http://ray.missouriassessors.com/search.php?mode=search.

St. Charles County ***Property, Taxation*** Access recorder records free at http://scharles.landrecordsonline.com/. Search index free; images - $1.00 per page. Property assessment data is free at http://assessor.sccmo.org/assessor/index.php?option=com_assessordb&Itemid=49. No name searching.

St. Francois County ***Recorded Documents*** www.sfcgov.org Access to records for a fee at https://tapestry.fidlar.com/Tapestry2/Default.aspx. Contact 309-794-3283 or kylec@fidlar.com for subscription information. Search fee is $5.95 each, printed images $.50 each unless otherwise noted. **$$$**

Property, Taxation Access property assessor data free at www.sfcassessor.org/parcel_search.html.

St. Louis City ***Recorded Documents*** http://stlouis-mo.gov/government/departments/recorder-deeds.cfm Access to records for a fee at https://tapestry.fidlar.com/Tapestry2/Default.aspx. Contact 309-794-3283 or kylec@fidlar.com for subscription information. Search fee is $5.95 each, printed images $.50 each unless otherwise noted. **$$$**

Property, Taxation Access the mapping site free at http://maps.stlouisco.com/propertyview/. Also, access address and property search data for free at http://stlouis-mo.gov/data/address-search/index.cfm. Search personal property by account number, address, or name at http://revenue.stlouisco.com/Collection/ppInfo/. Assessor property data for a fee on the GIS system at http://beacon.schneidercorp.com. Registration and username required. At the default website, choose City of Wildwood, then register.

St. Louis County ***Recorded Documents*** http://stlouisco.com/YourGovernment/CountyDepartments/Revenue/RecorderofDeedsDivision.aspx Access to records for a fee at https://tapestry.fidlar.com/Tapestry2/Default.aspx. Contact 309-794-3283 or kylec@fidlar.com for subscription information. Search fee is $5.95 each, printed images $.50 each unless otherwise noted. **$$$**

Property, Taxation Access county property data free at http://revenue.stlouisco.com/ias/. Search personal property tax data free at http://revenue.stlouisco.com/Collection/ppInfo/.

Saline County ***Recorded Documents*** www.deeds.com/recording/missouri/saline/ Access to records for a fee at https://tapestry.fidlar.com/Tapestry2/Default.aspx. Contact 309-794-3283 or kylec@fidlar.com for subscription information. Search fee is $5.95 each, printed images $.50 each unless otherwise noted. **$$$**

Scott County ***Recorded Documents*** Access recording land data at www.etitlesearch.com; registration required, fee based on usage. **$$$**

Property, Taxation Access to GIS/mapping for free at www.semogis.com/flexviewers/Scott/.

Stoddard County ***Recorded Documents*** Access to record images free at http://stoddardmo.icounty.com/iRecordWeb2.0/Login.aspx. Paid subscription is also available for more detailed information. Records from 1993 to present. **$$$**

Stone County ***Recorded Documents*** www.stoneco-mo.us/Recorder.htm Access to recorder data is free through land access.com at https://www.uslandrecords.com/molr/MolrApp/index.jsp.

Property, Taxation Access property data from the GIS interactive map at https://stone.integritygis.com/.

Taney County Recorder ***Recorded Documents*** www.co.taney.mo.us/cgi-bin/County/index.cgi?department=18 Access to records for a fee at https://tapestry.fidlar.com/Tapestry2/Default.aspx. Contact 309-794-3283 or kylec@fidlar.com for subscription information. Search fee is $5.95 each, printed images $.50 each unless otherwise noted. **$$$**

Property, Taxation Search assessor property data for a fee on the GIS system at http://beacon.schneidercorp.com. Registration and username required. At the default website, choose Missouri then Taney County, then register.

Vernon County ***Property, Taxation*** Personal property search is free at www.vernon.missouriassessors.com/search.php?mode=search

Warren County ***Recorded Documents*** Access to records for a fee at https://tapestry.fidlar.com/Tapestry2/Default.aspx. Contact 309-794-3283 or kylec@fidlar.com for subscription information. Search fee is $5.95 each, printed images $.50 each unless otherwise noted. **$$$**

Webster County ***Recorded Documents*** www.webstercountymo.gov/pages/recorders_office Access to recorded data is by subscription; $200.00 per month. Get info and register through the recorder's office. **$$$**

Property, Taxation Access to GIS/mapping go to www.webstercountymo.gov/pages/assessors_office.Click on free version or Subscribers for more detailed mapping. To subscribe contact the Assessors Office at above number or jjones@webstercountymo.gov.**$$$**

Montana

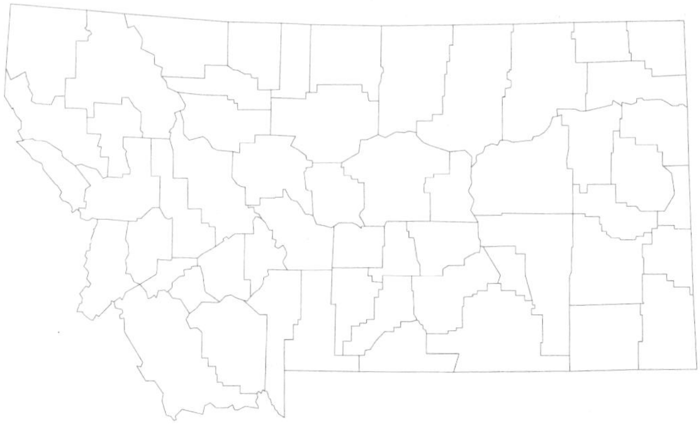

Capital: Helena
Lewis and Clark County
Time Zone: MST
Population: 1,005,141
# of Counties: 56

Useful State Links

Website: http://mt.gov/
Governor: http://governor.mt.gov/
Attorney General: https://doj.mt.gov/agooffice
State Archives: http://montanahistoricalsociety.org/default.asp
State Statutes and Codes: http://leg.mt.gov/css/mtcode_const/default.asp
Legislative Bill Search: http://leg.mt.gov/css/bills/default.asp
Unclaimed Funds: http://revenue.mt.gov/forbusinesses/unclaimed_property/owners_unclaimed_property/default.mcpx

State Public Record Agencies

Criminal Records

Department of Justice, Criminal Records, https://doj.mt.gov/ Access is available for "public users" or "registered users" at https://app.mt.gov/choprs/. Fee is $11.50 per record. Registered users must pay a $75 annual fee and have access to other data. Search using the name and DOB. The SSN is helpful but not required. Results include up to 4 aliases, dispositions, detentions, sentences, and correctional status. **$$$**

Sexual Offender Registry

Sexual or Violent Offender Registration Unit, Division of Criminal Investigation, http://svcalt.mt.gov/svor/search.asp The state sexual offender list is available at the website. You may search by offender name; by city, county or zip code; or by offender type. You may also search for offenders within a certain radius of a specific street address. The percent sign (%) may be used as a wildcard character in the Last Name field to represent one or more other characters. *Other Options:* The entire database may no longer be purchased nor updated.

Incarceration Records

Montana Department of Corrections, Directors Office, www.cor.mt.gov/default.mcpx Search current or former inmates on the ConWeb system at https://app.mt.gov/conweb/. Search by ID# or by name. A list of parole violators at large is found at https://app.mt.gov/cgi-bin/boppviolator/boppviolator.cgi. *Other Options:* Entire offender database is available for purchase; call Discovering Montana, 406-449-3468. Academic or social researchers can acquire the same database for no charge.

Corporation, LLC, LP, Fictitious/Assumed Name, Trademarks/Servicemarks

Business Services Division, Secretary of State, http://sos.mt.gov/ Visit https://app.mt.gov/bes/ for free searches of MT business entities. Certified copies may be ordered online at https://app.mt.gov/ccop/ for $10.00 using a credit card. There is a commercial service for finding registered principles. One must have an account. Visit https://app.mt.gov/rps/. **$$$** *Other Options:* One may purchase a download a customized list of new business entities. Various ways to customize a list and fees are found at https://app.mt.gov/cgi-bin/corprecords/corprecords.cgi.

Uniform Commercial Code, Federal Tax Liens

Business Services Division, Secretary of State, Rm 260, www.sos.mt.gov A web-based subscription service provides information about all active liens filed with the office. To use the service you need to establish an account with Discovering Montana for a fee of $25 per month. See https://app.mt.gov/uccs/. Accounts may view active lien information and also perform and print unlimited certified search certificates. Bulk downloads are available for $1,000 per month. Contact Discovering Montana at 101 N Rodney #3, Helena MT 59601, or call 866-449-3468, or visit their website at http://mt.gov/default.asp. **$$$** *Other Options:* Registered users may receive farm bill filings lists on a monthly basis for $5.00 per category on paper or microfiche. A CD-Rom for all Farm Products is available for $20.00.

Birth Certificates, Death Records

Montana Department of Health, Vital Records, https://dphhs.mt.gov/certificates/ordercertificates.shtml Orders can be placed at https://mtvr.cdc.nicusa.com/CDC.VitalRecords.Web.Mt/wizard/Start.aspx, add $3.00 per record. Or via a state designated vendor at www.vitalchek.com. Extra fees are involved. **$$$**

Driver Records

Motor Vehicle Division, Driver's Services, https://doj.mt.gov/driving/ There are two methods offered, one for Public User requests and a subscription service. The fee is $7.25. The Public Access results do not offer address information. For registered subscribers, an agreement must be signed and there is an annual $100.00 registration fee. Services online also include a License Status Conviction Activity batch or monitoring search, at a reduced price. For more about online services visit https://app.mt.gov/dojdrs/ or call 406-449-3468. **$$$** *Other Options:* Under the LSCA program, approved requesters may submit a monthly list of names, at $.15 per name. If there is conviction activity within the past 30 days, the requester is sent a driving record for the $.25 fee.

Vehicle, Vessel Ownership & Registration

Department of Justice, Title and Registration Bureau, https://doj.mt.gov/driving/vehicle-title-and-registration/ Both "Public User" and Registered User" interfaces are offered . See https://app.mt.gov/dojvs for the Public Users., which is for MT citizens or users with an occasional need to know the ownership history of a pre-owned car. Sensitive information, such as the SSN or home address is not released. A $5.00 fee applies and a credit card must be used. The Registered User system is for ongoing registered accounts approved by the Motor Vehicle Division. The Registered User system is for ongoing registered accounts approved by the Motor Vehicle Division. The fee is $2.25 per search. There is an annual $100.00 registration fee for 10 users. Depending on the level of authority granted, the following is available: Vehicle Information, License Plate Information, Vehicle Owner Information, Lien History, Title History and Registration Information. **$$$** *Other Options:* Bulk or batch ordering of registration information is available on tape, disk, or paper. The user must fill out a specific form, which gives the user the capability of customization. For further information, contact the Registrar at address above.

Campaign Finance, Lobbyist

Commissioner of Politcial Practices, http://sos.mt.gov/Elections/ Search for a lobbyist and principal at https://app.mt.gov/cgi-bin/camptrack/lobbysearch/lobbySearch.cgi. Search and download campaign data at https://app.mt.gov/ccrs/index/index.html. This includes contributions and expenditures. Search committee reports at http://campaignreport.mt.gov/forms/committeesearch.jsp. A number of searches on complaints and opinions are available from the home page.

Voter Registration

Secretary of State, Elections and Government Srvs, http://sos.mt.gov/Elections/ Access voter registration records at http://app.mt.gov/voterfile/select_criteria.html. Records can be purchased for non-commercial use only. **$$$** *Other Options:* This agency database or customized portions can be purchased on disk or CD-ROM for $200 or less. Fee to purchase entire database is $1,000 or $5,000 for subscription with updates. For more information, call 406-449-2468 ext 228.

Occupational Licensing Boards

Accountant-CPA/LPA.................................. https://ebiz.mt.gov/pol/
Acupuncturist .... https://app.mt.gov/lookup/
Adoption Agency... www.dphhs.mt.gov/cfsd/adoption/privateadoptionagencies.shtml
Alarm Response Runner............................. https://ebiz.mt.gov/pol/
Architect .... https://ebiz.mt.gov/pol/
Asbestos Contractor/Supvr/Supplier............ http://svc.mt.gov/deq/asbestosaccred/
Asbestos Inspector/Worker.......................... http://svc.mt.gov/deq/asbestosaccred/
Asbestos Project Designer/Planner .... http://svc.mt.gov/deq/asbestosaccred/
Athletic Event/Event Timekeeper................. https://ebiz.mt.gov/pol/
Attorney .... https://m360.montanabar.org/frontend/search.aspx?cs=22
Audiologist... https://ebiz.mt.gov/pol/
Barber/Barber Shop/Instruct'r .... https://ebiz.mt.gov/pol/
Boxer/Boxing Prof/Mgr/Promoter/Judge ...... https://ebiz.mt.gov/pol/
Cemetery, Privately Owned .... https://ebiz.mt.gov/pol/
Chemical Dependency Counselor .... http://bsd.dli.mt.gov/license/bsd_boards/lac_board/board_page.asp
Child Care Provider..................................... http://ccubs-sanswrite.hhs.mt.gov/MontanaPublic/ProviderSearch.aspx
Chiropractor .... https://ebiz.mt.gov/pol/
Clinical Social Worker .... https://ebiz.mt.gov/pol/
Construction Blaster.................................... https://buildingpermits.mt.gov/Licenses/licenses.aspx

Cosmetologist/Cosmetol'y Instr/Sch'l	https://ebiz.mt.gov/pol/
CP Installer/Designer	http://nris.mt.gov/deq/remsitequery/default.aspx?qt=ust
Crematory/Crematory Oper/Tech	https://ebiz.mt.gov/pol/
Day Care Center	www.dphhs.mt.gov/qad/licensure/childcarefacilitylicensingregistration.shtml
Dentist/Dental Assistant/Hygienist	https://ebiz.mt.gov/pol/
Denturist	https://ebiz.mt.gov/pol/
Discount Card Companies	www.sao.mt.gov
Drug Registration, Dangerous	https://ebiz.mt.gov/pol/
Drug Wholesaler	https://ebiz.mt.gov/pol/
Electrician	https://ebiz.mt.gov/pol/
Electrologist/Esthetician/Manicurist	https://ebiz.mt.gov/pol/
Emergency Medical Technician	https://app.mt.gov/lookup/
Engineer	https://ebiz.mt.gov/pol/
Euthanasia Agency/ Technician	https://ebiz.mt.gov/pol/
Firearms Instructor	https://ebiz.mt.gov/pol/
Funeral Director	https://ebiz.mt.gov/pol/
Group Home, Youth	www.dphhs.mt.gov/qad/youthgrouphomes/youthgrouphomes.pdf
Hearing Aid Dispenser	https://ebiz.mt.gov/pol/
Insurance Adjuster/Producer	http://svc.mt.gov/csi/apps/sas/query.aspx
Land Surveyor	https://ebiz.mt.gov/pol/
Landscape Architect	https://ebiz.mt.gov/pol/
Living Trust Seller	www.sao.mt.gov
Lobbyist/Lobbying Principal	https://app.mt.gov/cgi-bin/camptrack/lobbysearch/lobbySearch.cgi
Midwife, Apprentice	https://ebiz.mt.gov/pol/
Monitoring Well Installer	http://nris.mt.gov/deq/remsitequery/default.aspx?qt=ust
Mortuary/Mortician	https://ebiz.mt.gov/pol/
Multi-level Marketing Company	www.sao.mt.gov
Naturopathic Physician	https://ebiz.mt.gov/pol/
Nurse Anesthetist/Clinical Specialist	https://ebiz.mt.gov/pol/
Nurse-RN/LPN/PA	https://ebiz.mt.gov/pol/
Nutritionist	https://app.mt.gov/lookup/
Occupational Therapist	https://ebiz.mt.gov/pol/
Optometrist	https://ebiz.mt.gov/pol/
Osteopathic Physician	https://app.mt.gov/lookup/
Outfitter/Guide, Hunting/Fishing	https://ebiz.mt.gov/pol/
Pesticide Applicator/Dealer	http://services.agr.mt.gov/Pesticide_Applicators/
Pharmacist	https://ebiz.mt.gov/pol/
Physical Therapist/Assistant	https://ebiz.mt.gov/pol/
Physician//Medical Doctor/Assistant	https://app.mt.gov/lookup/
Plumber	https://ebiz.mt.gov/pol/
Podiatrist	https://app.mt.gov/lookup/
Private Investigator/Trainee	https://ebiz.mt.gov/pol/
Private Placement Offering	www.sao.mt.gov
Private Security Guard	https://ebiz.mt.gov/pol/
Process Server	https://ebiz.mt.gov/pol/
Property Manager	https://ebiz.mt.gov/pol/
Psychologist	https://app.mt.gov/lookup/
Radiologic Technologist	https://ebiz.mt.gov/pol/
Real Estate Agent/Broker/Sales	https://ebiz.mt.gov/pol/
Real Estate Appraiser/Trainee	https://ebiz.mt.gov/pol/
Referee	https://ebiz.mt.gov/pol/
Resident Manager	https://ebiz.mt.gov/pol/
Respiratory Care Practitioner	https://ebiz.mt.gov/pol/
Securities Broker/Seller	www.finra.org/Investors/ToolsCalculators/BrokerCheck/
Security Alarm Installer/Company	https://ebiz.mt.gov/pol/

Security Org, Proprietary .... https://ebiz.mt.gov/pol/
Social Worker, LSW .... https://ebiz.mt.gov/pol/
Speech Pathologist .... https://ebiz.mt.gov/pol/
Telephone, Customer-Owned, Coin .... www.sao.mt.gov
Timeshare Broker/Salesperson .... https://ebiz.mt.gov/pol/
Underground Tank Inspector/Intal/Remover http://nris.mt.gov/deq/remsitequery/default.aspx?qt=ust
Variable Annuities Seller .... www.sao.mt.gov
Veterinarian .... https://ebiz.mt.gov/pol/
Wrestler .... https://ebiz.mt.gov/pol/
X-Ray Technician .... https://ebiz.mt.gov/pol/

State and Local Courts

State Court Structure: The **District Courts,** the courts of general jurisdiction, handle all felony cases and probate cases, most civil cases at law and in equity, and other special actions and proceedings.

The courts of limited jurisdiction are **Justice Courts**, **City Courts** and **Municipal Courts**. Although the jurisdiction of these courts differs slightly, collectively they address cases involving misdemeanor offenses, civil cases for amounts up to $12,000, small claims valued up to $7,000, landlord/tenant disputes, local ordinances, forcible entry and detainer, protection orders, certain issues involving juveniles, and other matters. Some Justice Courts and City Courts have consolidated.

Note - Effective July 1, 2011, the District Court's minimum civil limit amount was raised from $7,000 to $12,000; the lower courts maximum from $7,000 to $12,000; small claims from 3,000 to $7,000, and City Court jurisdiction on certain matters from increased from $5,000 to $9,500.

There is also a **Water Court** and a **Workers' Compensation Court** in Montana.

Appellate Courts: Supreme Court opinions, orders, and recently filed briefs may be found at http://searchcourts.mt.gov.

Statewide Court Online Access: There is no statewide access to docket information from the trial courts. Several courts respond to email requests, but none offer online access to records.

The state does have an exsiting centralized case management system and is working towards implmenting an e-filing system sometime in the future.

Recorders, Assessors, and Other Sites of Note

Recording Office Organization: 57 counties, 56 recording offices. Yellowstone National Park is considered a county but is not included as a filing location. The recording officer is the County Clerk and Recorder, and Clerk of District Court for state tax liens. Federal tax liens on personal property of businesses are filed with the Secretary of State. Other federal tax liens are filed with the county Clerk and Recorder.

Statewide or Multi-Jurisdiction Access: There is no statewide search for recorded documents at the county level, but there is a state site mentioned below. An increasing number of counties also outsource data via a vendor for a fee.

- **All counties** participate in a free search for a Montana property owner by name and county on the Montana Cadastral Mapping Project GIS mapping database at http://svc.mt.gov/msl/mtcadastral/.

County Sites - Other Than the Free State Site Mentioned Above:

Carbon County ***Property, Taxation*** Access to county tax search free at http://209.137.229.213/bmsrdl/tax_search.php?customer_id=454.

Cascade County ***Real Estate, Deed, GIS/Mapping Records*** http://departments.cascadecountymt.gov/clerkandrecorder Recording office land data available at http://clerkrecorder.co.cascade.mt.us/Recorder/web/; registration and fees required. Also, access to GIS/mapping free at www.co.cascade.mt.us/?p=departament&ido=92. **$$$**

Deer Lodge County ***Property, Taxation*** Access to GIS/mapping free at www.anacondadeerlodge.mt.gov/super/gis.aspx.

Flathead County ***Real Estate, Grantor/Grantee, Deed, Mortgage, Lien, Judgment Records*** http://flathead.mt.gov/clerk_recorder/ Access recorded lard records by subscribing to the idoc system at http://flathead.mt.gov/clerk_recorder/idoc.php. Annual fee is $180.00; contact the Clerk and Recorder's office for info and signup, or visit the web. **$$$**

Gallatin County ***Real Estate, Deed Records*** www.gallatin.mt.gov/Public_Documents/gallatincomt_clerk/clerk Access to records free at https://eagleweb.gallatin.mt.gov/recorder/web/. Searches are free but individual images must be purchased. Also can subscribe to full image access for $200.00 a year. **$$$**

Property, Taxation Search property data on the GIS-mapping site free at http://webapps.gallatin.mt.gov/mappers/.

Judith Basin County ***Real Estate, Deed Records*** Recording office land data to be available at a later date at www.etitlesearch.com/; registration and fees required. **$$$**

Lake County ***Real Estate, Deed, Map, Survey Records*** www.lakecounty-mt.org/clerkrecorder/index.html Real estate doc images, COS's, maps, and surveys can be downloaded free from the ftp site at ftp://lakecounty-mt.org. Folders by type and month.

Property, Taxation Access the Web Tax System at www.lakecounty-mt.org/ but password is required. Search treasurer's tax payment list after registration at www.mtcounty.com/bmsrdl/tax_pay_search.php?customer_id=321.

Lewis and Clark County ***Recorded Documents*** https://www.lccountymt.gov/clerk-and-recorder.html Search Grantor/Grantee index and recorder records free at https://eagle-web.co.lewis-clark.mt.us/recorder/web/. Public users can search recorded documents without images, must subscript is you want images. Includes document imaging via subscription online service. Records go back approximately to the end of 1999. **$$$**

Lincoln County ***Recorded Documents*** www.lincolncountymt.us/clerkandrecorder/index.html Access to online documents for a fee at www.lincolncountymt.us/clerkandrecorder/onlinesearch.html. **$$$**

Property, Taxation Access to tax search free at www.mtcounty.com/bmsrdl/tax_search.php?customer_id=188.

Madison County ***Recorded Documents*** www.madison.mt.gov/departments/clerk_recorder/clerk_recorder.asp Access to tax records free at http://blkmtn.madison.mt.gov/scripts/xworks.exe.

Mineral County ***Recorded Documents*** www.co.mineral.mt.us/departments/Clerk_Recorder.aspx Recording office land data to be available at a later date at www.etitlesearch.com/; registration and fees required. **$$$**

Missoula County ***Real Estate, Deed Records*** www.co.missoula.mt.us/clerkrec/ Recording office land data to be available at a later date at www.etitlesearch.com; registration and fees required. **$$$**

Property, Taxation Access the county property data system free at www.co.missoula.mt.us/owner/. Property search by Address, Tax ID, Geocode, Map. Records search by Tax ID, Geocode, Book/Page. No name searching.

Musselshell County ***Recorded Documents*** Access to parcel searches free at http://svc.mt.gov/msl/mtcadastral/.

Park County ***Real Estate, Grantor/Grantee, Deed, Lien Records*** www.parkcounty.org/site/1cr.html Access to document searches at www.parkcounty.org/idoc/. The computer document indexing begins from January 1, 1989. **$$$**

Property, Taxation Access to tax records free at www.parkcounty.org/parkwebtax/.

Ravalli County ***Recorded Documents*** http://rc.mt.gov/clerkrecorder/default.mcpx Access property tax and recorded document info at http://rc.mt.gov/OnlineServices/default.mcpx. Signed Access Authorization Memo with the County required; must pay the annual fee, either $120 yearly for companies of 5 or less, or $400 for large companies. Call IT office for info and sign-up at 406-375-6700. First time users pay an add'l one time fee of $25.00. Check website for 1/2 years and other fees. **$$$**

Sanders County ***Recorded Records*** www.sanderscounty.mt.gov/Pages/ClerkRecorder.html Access to tax, document indexing and plat maps free at www.mtcounty.com/bmsrdl/doc_search.php?customer_id=220.

Valley County ***Property, Taxation*** Access to county tax search free at www.mtcounty.com/bmsrdl/tax_search.php?customer_id=113.

Yellowstone County ***Real Estate, Grantor/Grantee, Deed, Lien, Mortgage Records*** www.co.yellowstone.mt.gov/clerk/ Access county clerk & recorder documents free at www.co.yellowstone.mt.gov/clerk/. Click on Free Service Search or you may register and login for full data for a fee. **$$$**

Property, Taxation Access tax assessor records free at www.co.yellowstone.mt.gov/assessor/index.asp.

Reminder:

All counties participate in a free search for a Montana property owner by name and county on the Montana Cadastral Mapping Project GIS mapping database at http://svc.mt.gov/msl/mtcadastral/.

Nebraska

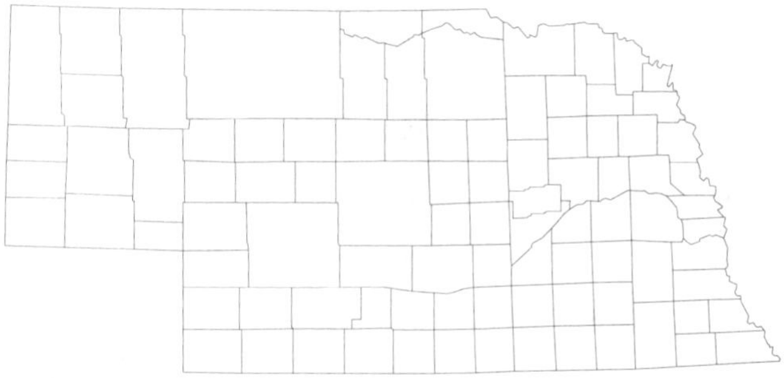

Capital: Lincoln
Lancaster County

Time Zone: CST

Nebraska's nineteen western-most counties are MST. They are: Arthur, Banner, Box Butte, Chase, Cherry, Cheyenne, Dawes, Deuel, Dundy, Garden, Grant, Hooker, Keith, Kimball, Morrill, Perkins, Scotts Bluff, Sheridan, Sioux.

Population: 1,885,525

# of Counties: 93

Useful State Links

Website: www.nebraska.gov/

Governor: www.governor.nebraska.gov/

Attorney General: www.ago.ne.gov

State Archives: www.nebraskahistory.org

State Statutes and Codes: http://uniweb.legislature.ne.gov/

Legislative Bill Search: http://uniweb.legislature.ne.gov/

Bill Monitoring: www.nebraska.gov/billtracker/

Unclaimed Funds: www.treasurer.org/index.asp

State Public Record Agencies

Sexual Offender Registry

Nebraska State Patrol, Sexual Offender Registry, https://sor.nebraska.gov/ Three different types of searches are available at https://sor.nebraska.gov/. The records may be searched by either ZIP Code, last name, first name, city, or county. Search or review the entire list of names.

Incarceration Records

Nebraska Department of Correctional Services, Central Records Office, www.corrections.nebraska.gov Click on Inmate Records at the website for a search of inmates incarcerated after 1977.

Corporation, LLC, LP, Trade Names, Trademarks/Servicemarks

Secretary of State, Corporation Division, www.sos.state.ne.us/business/corp_serv/ There are two levels of service. The free lookup at https://www.nebraska.gov/sos/corp/corpsearch.cgi?nav=search provides general information to obtain information on the status of corporations and other business entities registered in this state. The state has designated Nebraska.gov (800-747-8177) to facilitate online retrieval of records. This access to records requires fees and the lookup can be accessed from the same webpage. A Letter of Good Standing is $6.50 Also, search securities companies registered with the state at www.ndbf.ne.gov/searches/securities.shtml. **$$$** *Other Options:* Nebraska.gov has the capability of offering database purchases.

Uniform Commercial Code, Federal & State Tax Liens

UCC Division, Secretary of State, Rm 1301, www.sos.state.ne.us/business/ucc/ Access is outsourced to Nebraska.gov To set an account, go to www.nebraska.gov/subscriber/index.html. The system is available 24 hours daily. There is an annual $50.00 fee in addition to charges to view records. Call 800-747-8177 for more information. **$$$** *Other Options:* Check with Nebrask@ Online for bulk purchase via UCC/EFS, there is a per record rate of $2.00 for the first 1,000 records then a flat rate afterward. Also, by debt location the rate is $15 per 1000 records.

Sales Tax Registrations

Revenue Department, Taxpayer Assistance, www.revenue.ne.gov/salestax.html Summaries of court cases are displayed at www.revenue.ne.gov/legal/court_cases/court.html. *Other Options:* Bulk data on registered businesses and new businesses is available for purchase.

Vital Records

Health and Human Services System, Vital Statistics Section, http://dhhs.ne.gov/publichealth/Pages/vital_records.aspx Records may be ordered online the web page. For Internet requests, fax to 402-471-8230 the indicating name(s) on the record(s) requested and the Internet confirmation number. Fees start at $11.00. **$$$**

Workers' Compensation Records

Workers' Compensation Court, www.wcc.ne.gov This is for requesting records, not viewing online. Record requests may be made at https://www.nebraska.gov/WC/records.phtml. Unless specifically requested, responses will be limited to first and subsequent reports filed within the last five (5) years. First reports will include the original report of injury and the current status of the report if updated information has been filed. Same fee schedule above applies. **$$$** *Other Options:* Request for bulk access are considered. Send request to Su Perk Davis at address listed.

Driver Records

Department of Motor Vehicles, Driver & Vehicle Records Division, www.dmv.ne.gov/ Nebraska outsources all electronic record requests to Nebraska.gov at www.nebraska.gov/subscribe.phtml or call 402- 471-7810 The system is interactive and open 24 hours a day, 7 days a week. Fee is $3.00 per record. There is an annual fee of $50.00 and a $.12 per minute connect fee or no connect fee if through the Internet. An online status check is offered at https://www.nebraska.gov/dmv/reinstatements/client.cgi. Enter the full name, dob and either the DL or SSN. There is no fee. **$$$** *Other Options:* Bulk requesters must be authorized by state officials. Purpose of the request and subsequent usage are reviewed. For information, call 402-471-3885.

Vehicle Title & Registration, Vessel Title

Department of Motor Vehicles, Driver & Vehicle Records Division, www.dmv.ne.gov/ Electronic access is through Nebraska.gov at www.nebraska.gov/subscribe.phtml. There is an annual $50.00 up fee addition to the $1.00 per record fee. The system is open 24 hours a day, 7 days a week. Call 800-747-8177 for more information. Title Status, lien notation confirmation and brand information may be obtained at no fee using the Vehicle identification number (VIN), go to www.clickdmv.ne.gov and select Title Inquiry. **$$$** *Other Options:* Bulk requesters must be authorized by state officials. Purpose of the request and subsequent usage are reviewed. For more information, call 402-471-3885

Campaign Finance, Lobbyists, Conflicts of Interest

NE Accountability and Disclosure Commission, PO Box 95086, http://nadc.nol.org/ View campaign filings at http://nadc.nol.org/ccdb/search.cgi. A list of registered PACs is at http://nadc.nol.org/cf/active_pacs.html. View lobbyists reports at http://nebraskalegislature.gov/lobbyist/view/. To obtain actual copies of documents which were not filed in electronic format, please email lobby@leg.ne.gov. *Other Options:* Current law dictates the database can only be sold for political purposes and not for commercial purposes. A statewide CD can be purchased for $500.

Voter Registration

Secretary of State, Elections Division-Records, www.sos.ne.gov/dyindex.html A voter registration status link is found at https://www.votercheck.necvr.ne.gov/. *Other Options:* Current law dictates the database can only be sold for political purposes and not for commercial purposes. A statewide CD can be purchased for $500.

Occupational Licensing Boards

Abstrator/Abstractor Company.................... www.abe.state.ne.us/local/license_search.phtml
Accountant-CPA.. www.nbpa.ne.gov/search/
Adult Day Care... www.nebraska.gov/LISSearch/search.cgi
Alarm, Fire/Installer.................................... www.nebraska.gov/sed/search/index.cgi
Alcohol/Drug Tester .... www.nebraska.gov/LISSearch/search.cgi
Animal Technician....................................... www.nebraska.gov/LISSearch/search.cgi
Architect .... www.ea.ne.gov/search/search.php
Asbestos Worker/Supvr .... www.nebraska.gov/LISSearch/search.cgi
Asbestos-Related Occupation .... www.nebraska.gov/LISSearch/search.cgi
Assisted Living Facility................................ www.nebraska.gov/LISSearch/search.cgi
Athletic Event, Contestant/Judge/Manager . www.athcomm.state.ne.us/certificationcourses.html
Athletic Event, Physician, Timekeeper......... www.athcomm.state.ne.us/certificationcourses.html
Athletic Trainer .... www.nebraska.gov/LISSearch/search.cgi
Attorney .... www.nebar.com/displaycommon.cfm?an=1&subarticlenbr=151
Audiologist.. www.nebraska.gov/LISSearch/search.cgi
Bank .... www.ndbf.ne.gov/searches/fisearch.shtml
Boxer... www.athcomm.state.ne.us/certificationcourses.html
Check Seller.. www.ndbf.ne.gov/searches/fisearch.shtml
Child Care Center/Child Caring/Placing Agency..........www.nebraska.gov/LISSearch/search.cgi

Chiropractor .... www.nebraska.gov/LISSearch/search.cgi
Club, Amateur .... www.athcomm.state.ne.us/certificationcourses.html
Collection Agency www.sos.ne.gov/licensing/collection/pdf/Collection%20Agencies%20Nov2010.pdf
Contractor Registration .... http://dol.nebraska.gov/center.cfm?PRICAT=2&SUBCAT=5H
Cosmetologist/Nail Care/Salon/School .... www.nebraska.gov/LISSearch/search.cgi
Credit Union .... www.ndbf.ne.gov/searches/fisearch.shtml
Debt Management Agency .... www.sos.state.ne.us/licensing/debt.html
Delayed Deposit Service............................. www.ndbf.ne.gov/searches/fisearch.shtml
Dental Hygienist/Anesthesia Permit............ www.nebraska.gov/LISSearch/search.cgi
Dentist .... www.nebraska.gov/LISSearch/search.cgi
Developmentally Disabled/Mentally Retarded Care Service..........www.nebraska.gov/LISSearch/search.cgi
Drug Distributor, Wholesale .... www.nebraska.gov/LISSearch/search.cgi
Drug Wholesale Facility .... www.nebraska.gov/LISSearch/search.cgi
Electrician, Sign/Heating & Cooling .... www.nebraska.gov/sed/search/index.cgi
Electrician/Apprentice .... www.nebraska.gov/sed/search/index.cgi
Electrologist/Electrology Facility .... www.nebraska.gov/LISSearch/search.cgi
Embalmer.. www.nebraska.gov/LISSearch/search.cgi
Emergency Medical Care Facility .... www.nebraska.gov/LISSearch/search.cgi
Engineer.. www.ea.ne.gov/search/search.php
Environmental Health Specialist .... www.nebraska.gov/LISSearch/search.cgi
Esthetician/Esthetician Establishment .... www.nebraska.gov/LISSearch/search.cgi
Fund Transmission...................................... www.ndbf.ne.gov/searches/fisearch.shtml
Funeral Director/Establishment................... www.nebraska.gov/LISSearch/search.cgi
Geologist .... www.geology.state.ne.us/pdf/roster.pdf
Health Clinic .... www.nebraska.gov/LISSearch/search.cgi
Hearing Aid Dispenser/Fitter....................... www.nebraska.gov/LISSearch/search.cgi
Home Health Agency .... www.nebraska.gov/LISSearch/search.cgi
Hospice .... www.nebraska.gov/LISSearch/search.cgi
Hospital .... www.nebraska.gov/LISSearch/search.cgi
Insurance Agency/Agent/Broker/Prod.......... www.doi.nebraska.gov/appointments/search/search.htm
Insurance Company/Consultant.................. www.doi.nebraska.gov/appointments/search/search.htm
Intermediate Care Facility (Retarded).......... www.nebraska.gov/LISSearch/search.cgi
Interpreter for the Deaf................................ www.ncdhh.ne.gov/pdf/InterpreterLicense3.22.13.pdf
Investment Advisor/Advisor Rep................. www.ndbf.ne.gov/searches/fisearch.shtml
Labor/Delivery Service/Clinic .... www.nebraska.gov/LISSearch/search.cgi
Laboratory .... www.nebraska.gov/LISSearch/search.cgi
Landscape Architect .... www.landarch.state.ne.us/registrants.pdf
Lead Abatement Worker, etc .... www.nebraska.gov/LISSearch/search.cgi
Liquor Retailers/ Whlse/Shipper .... www.lcc.ne.gov/license_search/licsearch.cgi
Lobbyist... www.nebraskalegislature.gov/reports/lobby.php
Local Anesthesia Certification..................... www.nebraska.gov/LISSearch/search.cgi
Long Term Care Center .... www.nebraska.gov/LISSearch/search.cgi
Marriage & Family Therapist....................... www.nebraska.gov/LISSearch/search.cgi
Massage Establishment/Therapy School..... www.nebraska.gov/LISSearch/search.cgi
Matchmaker .... www.athcomm.state.ne.us/certificationcourses.html
Mental Health Center .... www.nebraska.gov/LISSearch/search.cgi
Nurse-RN/LPN .... www.nebraska.gov/LISSearch/search.cgi
Nursing Home/Administrator....................... www.nebraska.gov/LISSearch/search.cgi
Nutrition Therapy, Medical .... www.nebraska.gov/LISSearch/search.cgi
Occupational Therapist .... www.nebraska.gov/LISSearch/search.cgi
Optometrist.. www.nebraska.gov/LISSearch/search.cgi
Osteopathic Physician .... www.nebraska.gov/LISSearch/search.cgi
Pesticide Applicator/Dealer......................... www.kellysolutions.com/ne/
Pharmacist/Pharmacy/Pharmacy................ www.nebraska.gov/LISSearch/search.cgi
Physical Therapist....................................... www.nebraska.gov/LISSearch/search.cgi

Physician/Medical Doctor/Assistant	www.nebraska.gov/LISSearch/search.cgi
Podiatrist	www.nebraska.gov/LISSearch/search.cgi
Polygraph Examiner, Private/Public	www.sos.state.ne.us/licensing/poly_menu.html
Preschool	www.nebraska.gov/LISSearch/search.cgi
Private Investigator/Agency	www.sos.ne.gov/licensing/private_eye/index.html
Psychologist	www.nebraska.gov/LISSearch/search.cgi
Radiographer	www.nebraska.gov/LISSearch/search.cgi
Radon Mitigation Specialist/Technician	www.nebraska.gov/LISSearch/search.cgi
Real Estate Agent/Seller/Broker	www.nrec.ne.gov/licinfodb/index.cgi
Real Estate Appraiser	www.appraiser.ne.gov/appraiser_listing.html
Referee	www.athcomm.state.ne.us/certificationcourses.html
Rehabilitation Agency	www.nebraska.gov/LISSearch/search.cgi
Respiratory Care Practitioner	www.nebraska.gov/LISSearch/search.cgi
Respite Care Service	www.nebraska.gov/LISSearch/search.cgi
Sales Finance Company	www.ndbf.ne.gov/searches/fisearch.shtml
Saving & Loan	www.ndbf.ne.gov/searches/fisearch.shtml
Seconds, Athletic Event	www.athcomm.state.ne.us/certificationcourses.html
Securities Agent/Broker/Dealer	www.ndbf.ne.gov/searches/fisearch.shtml
Social Worker	www.nebraska.gov/LISSearch/search.cgi
Speech-Language Pathologist	www.nebraska.gov/LISSearch/search.cgi
Substance Abuse Treatment Center	www.nebraska.gov/LISSearch/search.cgi
Surplus Lines Seller	www.doi.nebraska.gov/appointments/search/search.htm
Surveyor, Land	www.nbels.nebraska.gov/lsalpha.html
Swimming Pool Operator	www.nebraska.gov/LISSearch/search.cgi
Teacher	http://datacenter.education.ne.gov/nclblookup/main.aspx
Trust Company	www.ndbf.ne.gov/searches/fisearch.shtml
Veterinarian/Veterinary Technician	www.nebraska.gov/LISSearch/search.cgi
Voice Stress Examiner/Analyzer	www.sos.state.ne.us/licensing/poly_menu.html
Water Operator	www.nebraska.gov/LISSearch/search.cgi
Water Treatment Plant Operator	www.nebraska.gov/LISSearch/search.cgi
Well Driller/Pump Installer	www.nebraska.gov/LISSearch/search.cgi
Wrestler/Wrestling/Boxing Matches	www.athcomm.state.ne.us/certificationcourses.html
X-Ray Equipment (Portable)	www.nebraska.gov/LISSearch/search.cgi

State and Local Courts

State Court Structure: **District Courts** have original jurisdiction in all felony cases, equity cases, domestic relations cases, and civil cases where the amount in controversy involves more than $52,000. District Courts also have appellate jurisdiction in certain matters arising out of County Courts.

County Courts have original jurisdiction in probate matters, violations of city or village ordinances, juvenile court matters without a separate juvenile court, adoptions, preliminary hearings in felony cases, and eminent domain proceedings. The County Courts have concurrent jurisdiction in civil matters when the amount in controversy is $52,000 or less, criminal matters classified as misdemeanors or infractions, some domestic relations matters, and paternity actions. Nearly all misdemeanor cases are tried in the County Courts. As a rule of thumb, only District Courts can enter a sentence which incarcerates a defendant for more than one year.

County Courts have juvenile jurisdiction in all but 3 counties. Douglas, Lancaster, and Sarpy counties have separate **Juvenile Courts**. Also, there is a separate Workers' Compensation Court – see www.wcc.ne.gov.

Appellate Courts: Opinions are available from http://court.nol.org/opinions under *Quick Links*.

Statewide Court Online Access: All courts participate in the system described below.

- An online access subscription service is available for all Nebraska County Courts and all District Courts. Douglas County District Court was the last county added in April 2011. Case details, all party listings, payments, and actions taken for criminal, civil, probate, juvenile, and traffic are available. District Courts and County Courts must be searched separately. The system starts with a name search and resulting list gives full DOB. Both convictions and pending cases are available in the criminal search.

The fee for a onetime search using a credit card is $15.00. Ongoing users may register with Nebraska.gov and have an account that also gives access to other records. There is a start-up/annual fee for $50.00. For court record access the fee is $1.00 per record or a flat rate of $300.00 per month. Go to www.nebraska.gov/faqs/justice or call 402-471-7810 for more information.

Other Sites (not mentioned above):

Platte County

District Court www.plattecounty.net/district.htm

Court Calendar for month available at www.plattecounty.net/district/calendar.htm.

Recorders, Assessors, and Other Sites of Note

Recording Office Organization: 93 counties, 109 recording offices. The recording officers are County Clerk (UCCs and some state tax liens) and Register of Deeds (real estate and most tax liens). Most counties have a combined Clerk/Register office that is designated as "County Clerk" for our purposes. Still, in combined offices, the Register of Deeds is frequently a different person from the County Clerk. Sixteen counties have separate offices for real estate recording and UCC filing - Adams, Cass, Dakota, Dawson, Dodge, Douglas, Gage, Hall, Lancaster, Lincoln, Madison, Otoe, Platte, Sarpy, Saunders, and Scotts Bluff. Most federal and state tax liens are filed with the County Register of Deeds. Some state tax liens on personal property are filed with the County Clerk. Some federal tax liens on individuals are filed at the Sec. of State's office.

Statewide or Multi-Jurisdiction Access: There is no statewide access, but almost all Nebraska counties are represented online in some manner. Many also offer some degree of access to property tax information, gis-mapping, or assessor data. Access real estate or personal property data for free for over 50 counties at www.nebraskataxesonline.us. At least 10 of the counties also offer access to the tax apprisial data.

County Sites:

Adams County ***Recorded Documents*** www.adamscounty.org/index.php/9-uncategorised/84 Access to records free at http://deeds.adamscounty.org:8085/DeedSifter/Disclaimer.aspx?ReturnUrl=%2fDeedsifter%2fDefault.aspx.

Property, Taxation Records Access to property tax search for free at www.nebraskataxesonline.us/. Click on Adams County. Also, access to property tax for free at http://assessor.adamscounty.org/Appraisal/PublicAccess/. Also, access to GIS/mapping free at http://gis.adamscounty.org/map/.

Antelope County ***Property, Taxation Records*** Access to property search for free at www.antelope.assessor.gisworkshop.com/

Boone County ***Property, Taxation Records*** Access to property tax search for free at www.nebraskataxesonline.us/. Click on Boone County.

Box Butte County ***Property, Taxation Records*** Access to property tax search for free at www.nebraskataxesonline.us/. Click on Box Butte County. Also, access to property search info free at http://boxbutte.assessor.gisworkshop.com/.

Buffalo County ***Property, Taxation Records*** Access to property tax search for free at www.nebraskataxesonline.us/. Click on Buffalo County.

Burt County ***Recorded Documents*** www.burtcounty.ne.gov/clerk.html The agency has made arrangements with www.nebraskadeedsonline.us/ to provide an online search to recorded deeds. The subscriber fee is $20.00 per month per county. **$$$**

Property, Taxation Records Access to property tax search for free at www.nebraskataxesonline.us/. Click on Burt County.

Butler County ***Property, Taxation Records*** Search assessor property data on the GIS site free at http://butler.gisworkshop.com/.

Cass County Clerk ***Property, Taxation Records*** Access to GIS/mapping for free at http://cass.gisworkshop.com/.

Cass County Register of Deeds ***Property, Taxation Records*** Access GIS and Assessor data free at http://gis-srv.cassne.org/CassIMSPublic/index.html. Also, access property data free at www.nebraskataxesonline.us/search.aspx?county=Cass.

Cedar County ***Property, Taxation Records*** Access to property tax search for free at www.nebraskataxesonline.us/. Click on Cedar County.

Chase County ***Property, Taxation Records*** Access to property tax search for free at www.nebraskataxesonline.us/. Click on Chase County.

Cherry County ***Property, Taxation Records*** Access to GIS/mapping free at www.cherry.gisworkshop.com/.

Clay County ***Property, Taxation Records*** Access to property tax search for free at www.nebraskataxesonline.us/. Click on Clay County.

Colfax County ***Recorded Documents*** www.colfaxne.com/webpages/clerk/clerk.html Access to deeds online at www.nebraskadeedsonline.us/, then select a county. Index is free, but images are $20.00 per person, per county, per month plus applicable sales tax. **$$$**
Property, Taxation Records Access to taxes for free go to www.nebraskataxesonline.us/search.aspx?county=Colfax.

Cuming County ***Recorded Documents*** http://cumingcounty.ne.gov/government/clerk-2/ Access to records for a fee at www.nebraskadeedsonline.us/search.aspx?county=24. Can try with free pass before buying. **$$$**
Property, Taxation Records Access to property tax search for free at www.nebraskataxesonline.us/. Click on Cuming County.

Custer County ***Property, Taxation Records*** Access to TaxSifter Parcel search free at http://custerne.taxsifter.com/taxsifter/disclaimer.asp.

Dakota County Clerk ***Property, Taxation Records*** Access to property search free at www.dakotarealproperty.nebraska.gov/Appraisal/PublicAccess/.

Dawes County ***Recorded Documents*** www.dawes-county.com/county-offices/clerk.html The agency has made arrangements with www.nebraskadeedsonline.us/ to provide an online search to recorded deeds. The subscriber fee is $20.00 per month per county. **$$$**
Property, Taxation Records Access to property tax search for free at www.nebraskataxesonline.us/. Click on Dawes County. Also, access to GIS/mapping free at http://dawes.assessor.gisworkshop.com/. This is also a link for the home page, but it does not always work (www.dawes-county.com/county-offices/assessor/property-info.html).

Dawson County Clerk ***Property, Taxation Records*** Access to property tax search for free at www.nebraskataxesonline.us/search.aspx?county=Dawson.

Dawson County Register of Deeds ***Property, Taxation Records*** Access to property tax search for free at www.nebraskataxesonline.us/. Click on Dawson County.

Deuel County ***Property, Taxation Records*** Access to property tax search for free at www.nebraskataxesonline.us/. Click on Deuel County.

Dodge County Register of Deeds ***Property, Taxation Records*** Access assessor records free at www.dodgerealproperty.nebraska.gov/Appraisal/PublicAccess/.

Douglas County Clerk ***Property, Taxation Records*** Search property tax online payments database free at http://webapps.dotcomm.org:8080/TreasTax/ but no name searching. Also, access to property tax records and GIS/mapping free at http://douglascone.wgxtreme.com/.

Douglas County Register of Deeds ***Marriage Records*** www.dcregisterofdeeds.org/ Search the clerk/comptroller marriage database free at www.douglascountyclerk.org/marriage-licenses/marriagelicensesearch.
Property, Taxation Records Assessor to the county assessor property valuation lookup is free at http://douglasne.mapping-online.com/DouglasCoNe/static/valuation.jsp. Also search the treasurer's property tax data free at http://webapps.dotcomm.org:8080/TreasTax/ but no name searching.

Dundy County ***Property, Taxation Records*** Access to property tax search for free at www.nebraskataxesonline.us/. Click on Dundy County.

Fillmore County ***Property, Taxation Records*** Access to GIS/mapping for free at http://fillmore.assessor.gisworkshop.com/ Also, access to property tax search free at www.nebraskataxesonline.us/. Click on Fillmore County.

Franklin County ***Property, Taxation Records*** Access to property tax search for free at www.nebraskataxesonline.us/. Click on Franklin County.

Frontier County ***Recorded Documents*** www.co.frontier.ne.us Access to deeds online go to www.nebraskadeedsonline.us/, then select a county. Index is free, but images are pay-$20.00 per person, per county, per month plus applicable sales tax. **$$$**
Property, Taxation Records Access to basic property assessor data is available free at http://frontier.gisworkshop.com. A subscription is required for full data including sales, photos, history, buildings for $200 per year. Also, access to property tax search free at www.nebraskataxesonline.us/. Click on Frontier County.**$$$**

Furnas County ***Property, Taxation Records*** Access to property tax search for free at www.nebraskataxesonline.us/. Click on Fumas County.

Gage County Clerk ***Recorded Documents*** www.gagecountynebraska.us/webpages/clerk/clerk.html The agency has made arrangements with www.nebraskadeedsonline.us/ to provide an online search to recorded deeds. The subscriber fee is $20.00 per month per county. **$$$**
Property, Taxation Records Access assessor property data free at www.nebraskataxesonline.us/search.aspx?county=Gage.

Gage County Register of Deeds ***Recorded Documents*** www.gagecountynebraska.us/webpages/rod/register_of_deeds.html Access to deeds online go to www.nebraskadeedsonline.us/, then select a county. Index is free, but images are pay-$20.00 per person, per county, per county, per month plus applicable sales tax. **$$$**
Property, Taxation Records Access to property tax search for free at www.nebraskataxesonline.us/. Click on Gage County.. Also, access property data via the county Assessor GIS service free at http://gage.assessor.gisworkshop.com/

Garden County *Property, Taxation Records* Access to property tax search for free at www.nebraskataxesonline.us/. Click on Garden County.

Garfield County *Property, Taxation Records* Access parcel records free at http://garfield.pat.gisworkshop.com/.

Gosper County *Property, Taxation Records* Access to property tax search for free at www.nebraskataxesonline.us/. Click on Gosper County.

Greeley County *Property, Taxation Records* Access to property tax search for free at www.nebraskataxesonline.us/. Click on Greeley County. Also access parcel records free at www.nebraskaassessorsonline.us/search.aspx?county=Greeley.

Hall County Clerk *Recorded Documents* www.hcgi.org/content.lasso?page=6070 Access register of deeds real estate data free at http://deeds.hallcountyne.gov/.
Property, Taxation Records Access to GIS/mapping for free at http://gisweb.grand-island.com/mapsifter7/

Hall County Register of Deeds *Recorded Documents* www.hallcountyne.gov/content.lasso?page=6089 Access to the county Register of Deeds Document Search is free at http://grandislandne.map.beehere.net//.
Property, Taxation Records Access property data free at http://grandislandne.map.beehere.net//.

Hamilton County *Property, Taxation Records* Access to property tax search for free at www.nebraskataxesonline.us/. Click on Hamilton County. Also, access parcel records free at http://hamilton.gisworkshop.com/.

Harlan County *Property, Taxation Records* Access parcel records free at www.harlanrealproperty.nebraska.gov/Appraisal/PublicAccess/.

Hayes County *Property, Taxation Records* Access to property search for free at www.hayes.assessor.gisworkshop.com/.

Register of Deeds *Property, Taxation Records* Access parcel records free at www.hitchcockrealproperty.nebraska.gov/Appraisal/PublicAccess/. There is a state search atwww.nebraskataxesonline.us/. Click on Hitchcock County.

Howard County *Property, Taxation Records* Access to GIS/mapping for free at http://howard.assessor.gisworkshop.com/.

Jefferson County *Property, Taxation Records* Access to property tax search for free at www.nebraskataxesonline.us/search.aspx?county=Jefferso.

Johnson County *Property, Taxation Records* Access property data free at http://johnson.assessor.gisworkshop.com/. Also, access to property tax search for free at www.nebraskataxesonline.us/.

Kearney County *Property, Taxation Records* Access property data and parcel records free at http://kearney.gisworkshop.com/.

Keith County *Recorded Documents* www.keithcountyne.gov Access to deeds online go to www.nebraskadeedsonline.us/, then select a county. Index is free, but images are pay-$20.00 per person, per county, per month plus applicable sales tax. **$$$**
Property, Taxation Records Access to property tax search for free at www.nebraskataxesonline.us/. Click on Keith County. Also access parcel records free at www.co.keith.ne.us/assessor.html.

Keya Paha County *Property, Taxation Records* Access to GIS/mapping free at http://keyapaha.gisworkshop.com/#.

Kimball County *Property, Taxation Records* Access to property tax search for free at www.nebraskataxesonline.us/. Click on Kimball County.

Knox County Clerk *Property, Taxation Records* Access to GIS/mapping for free at www.knox.assessor.gisworkshop.com/. Also, access to property tax search for free at www.nebraskataxesonline.us/. Click on Knox County.

Lancaster County Clerk *Marriage, Building Permit Records* http://lancaster.ne.gov/clerk/index.htm Search Lincoln Document Management records site free at www.lincoln.ne.gov/asp/city/clerk/docman.asp. See also Register of Deeds. Search county marriages at http://lancaster.ne.gov/clerk/marrsrch.htm; building permits- www.lincoln.ne.gov/city/build/bldgsrv/permits.htm.
Property, Taxation Records Access parcel records at http://orion.lancaster.ne.gov/Appraisal/PublicAccess/. Also, search treasurer' property info at www.lincoln.ne.gov/cnty/treas/property.htm. Also, access to GIS/mapping free at http://lancaster.ne.gov/assessor/GIS.htm.

Lancaster County Register of Deeds *Recorded Documents* http://deeds.lincoln.ne.gov/recorder/web/login.jsp Search register of deeds Grantor/Grantee index free at http://deeds.lincoln.ne.gov/recorder/web/login.jsp. Use Public Login or you may register. See also County Clerk for other databases online.
Property, Taxation Records Access to property information for free at http://lancaster.ne.gov/treasurer/property.htm.

Lincoln County Clerk *Property, Taxation Records* Access to property tax search for free at www.nebraskataxesonline.us/search.aspx?county=Lincoln. Also, access to GIS/mapping free at at http://lincoln.gisworkshop.com/.

Lincoln County Register of Deeds *Property, Taxation Records* Access to property tax search for free at www.nebraskataxesonline.us/. Click on Lincoln County. Access to GIS/mapping free at http://lincoln.gisworkshop.com/.

Madison County Clerk ***Property, Taxation Records*** Access to property tax search for free at www.nebraskataxesonline.us/. Click on Madison County.

Madison County Register of Deeds ***Property, Taxation Records*** Access to property tax search for free at www.nebraskataxesonline.us/. Click on Madison County. Also access assessor records free at http://madison.gisworkshop.com/.

Merrick County ***Recorded Documents*** www.merrickcounty.ne.gov/clerk.html Access to deeds online go to www.nebraskadeedsonline.us/, then select a county. Index is free, but images are pay-$20.00 per person, per county, per month plus applicable sales tax. **$$$**
Property, Taxation Records Access to property tax search for free at www.nebraskataxesonline.us/. Click on Merrick County.

Morrill County ***Property, Taxation Records*** Access to property tax search for free at www.nebraskataxesonline.us/. Click on Morrill County.

Nance County ***Property, Taxation Records*** Access to property tax search for free at www.nebraskataxesonline.us/. Click on Nance County.

Nemaha County ***Property, Taxation Records*** Access to property tax search for free at www.nebraskataxesonline.us/. Click on Nemaha County. Also, access to GIS/mapping free at www.nemaha.assessor.gisworkshop.com/.

Otoe County Register of Deeds ***Property, Taxation Records*** Access to property tax search for free at www.nebraskataxesonline.us/. Click on Otoe County. Also, to access property search and mapping for free at www.otoe.deeds.gisworkshop.com/.

Otoe County Clerk ***Property, Taxation Records*** Access to GIS/mapping free at records for free at www.otoe.gisworkshop.com/.

Pawnee County ***Recorded Documents*** www.co.pawnee.ne.us/clerk.html Access to deeds online go to www.nebraskadeedsonline.us/, then select a county. Index is free, but images are pay-$20.00 per person, per county, per month plus applicable sales tax. **$$$**
Property, Taxation Records Access to property tax search for free at www.nebraskataxesonline.us/. Click on Pawnee County.

Perkins County ***Property, Taxation Records*** Access to property searches for free at www.perkins.gisworkshop.com/. Also, access to property tax search for free at www.nebraskataxesonline.us/. Click on Perkins County.

Phelps County ***Recorded Documents*** www.phelpsgov.org/webpages/clerk/clerk.html Search recorded deeds at http://phelpsdeeds.gisworkshop.com/.
Property, Taxation Records Access to property tax search for free at www.nebraskataxesonline.us/. Click on Phelps County. Also, access to records for free at http://phelps.gisworkshop.com/.

Pierce County ***Property, Taxation Records*** Access to property records free at http://pierce.assessor.gisworkshop.com/.

Platte County Clerk ***Property, Taxation Records*** Access to GIS/mapping for free at http://platte.assessor.gisworkshop.com/

Platte County ***Property, Taxation Records*** Access the GIS/mapping at http://platte.assessor.gisworkshop.com/. Access to property tax search for free at www.nebraskataxesonline.us/. Click on Platte County.

Polk County ***Property, Taxation Records*** Search property and mapping free at http://polk.gisworkshop.com/. Access the treasurer county tax record search free at http://polk.treasurer.gisworkshop.com/.

Red Willow County ***Recorded Documents*** www.co.red-willow.ne.us/clerk.html Access to online records go to www.nebraskadeedsonline.us/. Click on Red Willow County. Free records include: grantor/grantee and legal descriptions. Actual Register of Deeds scanned documents from the courthouse are available on a subscription basis for a fee of $20 per person, per county, per month plus any applicable sales tax. **$$$**
Property, Taxation Records Search auditor's county property data on the gis-mapping site free at http://redwillow.gisworkshop.com. Also, access to property tax search for free at www.nebraskataxesonline.us/. Click on Red Willow County.

Richardson County Clerk/Register of Deeds ***Property, Taxation Records*** Access to property search for free at www.richardson.assessor.gisworkshop.com/. Access to property tax search for free at www.nebraskataxesonline.us/.

Rock County ***Property, Taxation Records*** Access to property search and mapping for free at http://rock.assessor.gisworkshop.com/

Saline County ***Property, Taxation Records*** Access property data free at http://saline.assessor.gisworkshop.com/. Also, access to property tax search for free at www.nebraskataxesonline.us/. Click on Saline County.

Sarpy County Clerk ***Property, Taxation Records*** Access to GIS/mapping for free at http://maps.sarpy.com/sims20/.

Sarpy County Register of Deeds ***Recorded Documents*** www.sarpy.com/deeds/ Search the historical grantor/grantee index 1857-1990 free at www.sarpy.com/rodggi/.
Property, Taxation Records A simple property search is available free at www.sarpy.com/sarpyproperty/ but no name searching. A premium subscription service built based on your needs is available starting at $240 per year and goes higher; see contract at www.sarpy.com/oldterra/SarpyContract.pdf. Also, register to accept tax sales lists at www.sarpy.com/taxsale/.**$$$**

Saunders County ***Property, Taxation Records*** Access to assessor database for free at www.saundersrealproperty.nebraska.gov/Appraisal/PublicAccess/.

Saunders County Register of Deeds ***Property, Taxation Records*** Access assessment data on the GIS-mapping site free at http://saunders.pat.gisworkshop.com/. Also, access to property tax search for free at www.nebraskataxesonline.us/. Click on Saunders County.

Scotts Bluff County Clerk ***Recorded Documents*** www.scottsbluffcounty.org/register-deeds/deeds.html Access recorded documents from www.scottsbluffcounty.org/register-deeds/deeds.html.

Property, Taxation Records Access real estate or personal property data free at www.nebraskataxesonline.us/search.aspx?county=Scotts.

Scotts Bluff Register of Deeds ***Recorded Documents*** www.scottsbluffcounty.org/register-deeds/deeds.html Access to records free at http://deedsonline.scottsbluffcounty.org/DeedSifter/Disclaimer.aspx?ReturnUrl=%2fdeedsifter%2fdefault.aspx.

Property, Taxation Records Access to property tax search for free at www.nebraskataxesonline.us/. Click on Scotts Bluff County. Also, access to TaxSifter Parcel Search free at http://scottsbluffne.taxsifter.com/taxsifter/T-Parcelsearch.asp

Seward County ***Property, Taxation Records*** Free access to property tax searches at www.nebraskataxesonline.us/. Click on Seward County. Also, search parcel records free at http://seward.gisworkshop.com/.

Sherman County ***Property, Taxation Records*** Access to parcel records free at http://sherman.assessor.gisworkshop.com/.

Stanton County ***Recorded Documents*** www.co.stanton.ne.us Access to deeds online go to www.nebraskadeedsonline.us/, then select a county. Index is free, but images are pay-$20.00 per person, per county, per month plus applicable sales tax. **$$$**

Property, Taxation Records Access to property tax search for free at www.nebraskataxesonline.us/. Click on Stanton County.

Thayer County ***Property, Taxation Records*** Access to property tax search for free at www.nebraskataxesonline.us/search.aspx?county=Thayer.

Thurston County ***Property, Taxation Records*** Access to property tax search for free at www.nebraskataxesonline.us/. Click on Thurston County.

Valley County ***Property, Taxation Records*** To get on the Unclaimed property Division list from Treasurer's Office go to www.treasurer.state.ne.us/up/upMailList.asp. They send quarterly email newsletters. Also, access to GIS/mapping free at www.valley.gisworkshop.com/.

Washington County ***Recorded Documents*** www.co.washington.ne.us/deeds.html Access to deeds online go to www.nebraskadeedsonline.us/, then select a county. Index is free, but images are pay-$20.00 per person, per county, per month plus applicable sales tax. Contact MIPS, Inc at 402-434-5685. **$$$**

Wayne County Clerk ***Property, Taxation Records*** Access to property tax search for free at www.nebraskataxesonline.us/. Click on Wayne County. Search the sheriff's sales list free at www.waynecountyne.org/index.aspx?nid=128.

Webster County ***Recorded Documents*** www.co.webster.ne.us Access to deeds online go to www.nebraskadeedsonline.us/, then select a county. Index is free, but images are pay-$20.00 per person, per county, per month plus applicable sales tax. **$$$**

Property, Taxation Records Access to property tax search for free at www.nebraskataxesonline.us/. Click on Webster County.

Wheeler County ***Property, Taxation Records*** Access to property tax search for free at www.nebraskataxesonline.us/. Click on Wheeler County.

York County ***Property, Taxation Records*** Access to property search for free at http://york.assessor.gisworkshop.com/.

Nevada

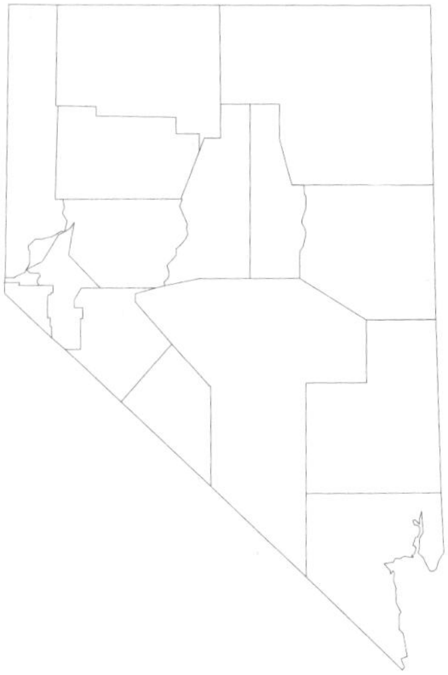

Capital: Carson City
Carson City County
Time Zone: PST
Population: 2,758,931
# of Counties: 17

Useful State Links

Website: www.nv.gov
Governor: http://gov.state.nv
Attorney General: http://ag.nv.gov/
State Archives: http://nsla.nevadaculture.org//index.php
State Statutes and Codes: www.leg.state.nv.us/NRS/
Legislative Bill Search: www.leg.state.nv.us
Bill Monitoring: https://www.leg.state.nv.us
Unclaimed Funds: https://nevadatreasurer.gov/UnclaimedProperty.htm

State Public Record Agencies

S Sexual Offender Registry

Records and Techmology Division, Sex Offender Registry, www.nvsexoffenders.gov Note: Per state law (NRS 179B.270), a search of this free public database online CANNOT be used for employment purposes. Information available on the website is extensive, including aliases, photograph (where available), conviction information, and latest registered address. Search by name, ZIP Code, or license plate number. There is no fee. Information is provided for sex offenders with a risk assessment score of a TIER Level 3 or TIER Level 2.

Incarceration Records

Nevada Department of Corrections, Attn: Records, www.doc.nv.gov Offender Tracking System, searchable by the public at www.doc.nv.gov/notis/search.php, provides information on current and released inmates. Click on Download Information to download text files of offender information suitable for importing into other programs. Several sort options are provided.

Corporation, LP, LLC

Secretary of State, Records, www.nvsos.gov Online access is offered on the Internet site for no charge. You can search by corporate name, resident agent, corporate officers, or by file number. To broaden the search, enter only the main name without entity suffixes (Inc, LLC, LP etc.) Also, good standing certificates can be ordered online - no add'l search fee. Email search requests are encouraged, copies@sos.nv.gov. Note that most orders may be emailed back if email is provided. *Other Options:* Reports and data downloads available - Foreign Corporation lists, Non-Profits, for example - under the Online Services tab at the website; fees vary.

Trademarks/Servicemarks

Secretary of State, Corporate Expedite Office, www.nvsos.gov/index.aspx?page=246 Search marks at http://nvsos.gov/sosentitysearch/. While this may look like a business entity search, it will bring up marks. Look on the document number; SM is servicemark; TM is trademark.

Uniform Commercial Code, Federal & State Tax Liens

UCC Division, Secretary of State, http://nvsos.gov/index.aspx?page=155 After registration, searching is available at https://esos.state.nv.us/NVUCC/user/login.asp. To receive documents the fee is $30.00, an order form may be downloaded. A full commercial system is also available. **$$$** *Other Options:* Bulk purchase services are available. Go to https://nvsos.gov/SOSWebAccountManager/Login.aspx and sing in. Must have an account with email and password.

Birth Certificates, Death Records

Nevada Department of Health, Office of Vital Statistics, www.health.nv.gov/ Online ordering available from state designated vendor at www.vitalchek.com. **$$$**

Driver Records

Department of Motor Vehicles, Records Section, www.dmvnv.com/ The state has an FTP type online system available for high volume users. All files received by 5:30 PM are processed and returned at 6:30 PM. Fee is $7.00 per record. Call 775-684-4702 for details. Also, a batch processing system has recently be added for higher volume accounts. Only three-year histories are available online. A person may order his or her own record at online. Go to https://dmvapp.nv.gov/dmv/dl/OL_DH/Drvr_Usr_Info.aspx. The fee is $7.00. **$$$**

Vehicle Ownership & Registration

Department of Motor Vehicles, Motor Vehicle Record Section, www.dmvnv.com A registration status inquiry is at https://dmvapp.nv.gov/dmv/vr/vr_dev/VR_reg/VR_Reg_Default.aspx. The license plate number and last four digits of the VIN are required to display the registration information. There is no fee. *Other Options:* Database is available for sale to permissible users under DPPA at costs varying from $500 to $2,500.

Voter Registration, Campaign Finance, PACs

Secretary of State, Elections Division, http://nvsos.gov/index.aspx?page=3 A names search, single inquiry is offered. Either the last four digits of the SSN or the DL number of the subject must be entered. Access to the statewide list is also available online at http://nvsos.gov/index.aspx?page=332. First, create an online web account. Then submit the Official Request for List of Registered Voters form. This submission must be made by made, fax or in person. Upon acceptance (which can take 7 days), the requester is notified by email. Then the approved requester may download online. View registered PACs at http://nvsos.gov/index.aspx?page=111. View campaign finance reports at www.nvsos.gov/SOSCandidateServices/AnonymousAccess/CEFDSearch/Candidate.aspx. *Other Options:* Bulk access of voter registration is available for purchase in electronic format. See the web page listed above for details.

Occupational Licensing Boards

Accountant-CPA/Accountancy-Audotor....... www.nvaccountancy.com/search.fx
Adult Day Care/Group Care........................ http://dhhs.nv.gov/Health/hcqc/healthfacilitiesquery/
Alcohol & Drug Abuse Center/Counselor..... http://dhhs.nv.gov/Health/hcqc/healthfacilitiesquery/
Ambulatory Surgery Ctr (Pharm) .... https://pharmacy.bop.nv.gov/datamart/mainMenu.do;jsessionid=87743A7F52A1D430E87CB401C314C5A8
Architect .... http://nsbaidrd.state.nv.us/?page=7
Attorney... www.nvbar.org/find-a-lawyer
Audiologist.. www.nvaud-sp.org/license/
Automobile/Vehicle Garage, Rebuilder........ https://dmvapp.nv.gov/DMV/OBL/Business_Reports/Pages/BusinessLicenses.aspx
Automobile/Vehicle Mfg'r/Transporter.......... https://dmvapp.nv.gov/DMV/OBL/Business_Reports/Pages/BusinessLicenses.aspx
Automobile/Vehicle Wrecker/Salvage Pool . https://dmvapp.nv.gov/DMV/OBL/Business_Reports/Pages/BusinessLicenses.aspx
Bank .... http://fid.state.nv.us/New_Banks.htm
Body Shop.. https://dmvapp.nv.gov/DMV/OBL/Business_Reports/Pages/BusinessLicenses.aspx
Building Mover .... www.nvcontractorsboard.com/#fragment-14
Carpentry Contractor .... www.nvcontractorsboard.com/#fragment-14
Check Casher .... http://fid.state.nv.us/New_Qry_CkCashLicensee.asp
Chiropractor .... https://nvbochiro.glsuite.us/GLSuiteWeb/Clients/NVBOChiro/Public/Licensee/LicenseeSearch.aspx
Clinical Laboratory Technologist................. http://dhhs.nv.gov/Health/hcqc/healthpersonnelquery/
Collection Agency .... http://fid.state.nv.us/New_Qry_CollectionAgency.asp
Concrete Contractor................................... www.nvcontractorsboard.com/#fragment-14
Contractor, General.................................... www.nvcontractorsboard.com/#fragment-14
Cosmetology School .... http://cosmetology.nv.gov/Forms/SchoolList.pdf
Court Reporter, Certified............................. http://crptr.nv.gov/consumer/License_Verification/
Credit Union .... http://fid.state.nv.us/New_CreditUnions.htm
Debt Adjuster .... https://fid.online.nv.gov/datamart/selLicType.do?type=name
Deferred Deposit Company .... http://fid.state.nv.us/New_Qry_CkCashLicensee.asp
Denied/Unsuitable Gaming Individual.......... http://gaming.nv.gov/index.aspx?page=76
Dentist/Dental Hygienist.............................. www.nvdentalboard.nv.gov/Verification.htm
Director (Medical Laboratory) .... http://dhhs.nv.gov/Health/hcqc/healthpersonnelquery/

Driving School/DUI School	https://dmvapp.nv.gov/DMV/OBL/Business_Reports/Pages/BusinessLicenses.aspx
Drug Wholesaler/Dist/Mfg	https://pharmacy.bop.nv.gov/datamart/mainMenu.do;jsessionid=87743A7F52A1D430E87CB401C314C5A8
Electrical Contractor	www.nvcontractorsboard.com/#fragment-14
Elevator/Conveyor	www.nvcontractorsboard.com/#fragment-14
Emergency Medical Service Nurse	www.nursingboard.state.nv.us/Verification/index.html
Engineer	www.nvboe.org/rosters/
Engineering, General	www.nvcontractorsboard.com/#fragment-14
Euthanasia Technician (Animal)	https://pharmacy.bop.nv.gov/datamart/mainMenu.do;jsessionid=87743A7F52A1D430E87CB401C314C5A8
Euthanasia/Animal Technician	https://www.nvvetboard.us/glsuiteweb/clients/nvbov/public/LicenseeList.aspx
Fencing	www.nvcontractorsboard.com/#fragment-14
Fire Protection Contractor	www.nvcontractorsboard.com/#fragment-14
Floor/Tile/Carpet Layer	www.nvcontractorsboard.com/#fragment-14
Gas Fitter	www.nvcontractorsboard.com/#fragment-14
GCB Most-Wanted & Banned List	http://gaming.nv.gov/index.aspx?page=76
Glazier Contractor	www.nvcontractorsboard.com/#fragment-14
Hearing Aid Specialist	http://hearingaidboard.nv.gov/HearingAidSpecialistRoster.pdf
Heating & Air Conditioning Mechanic	www.nvcontractorsboard.com/#fragment-14
Home Health Agency	http://dhhs.nv.gov/Health/hcqc/healthfacilitiesquery/
Home Inspector	www.inspectordatabase.com/state.php?statecode=NV
Homeopathic Physician/Assistant	http://nvbhme.org/licensees.html
Homeopathic Practitioner, Advanced	http://nvbhme.org/licensees.html
Hospice	http://dhhs.nv.gov/Health/hcqc/healthfacilitiesquery/
Hospital	http://dhhs.nv.gov/Health/hcqc/healthfacilitiesquery/
Hospital Pharmacy-Institutional	https://pharmacy.bop.nv.gov/datamart/mainMenu.do;jsessionid=87743A7F52A1D430E87CB401C314C5A8
Installment Loan Company	http://fid.state.nv.us/New_Qry_InstLoanLicensee.asp
Insulation Installer Contractor	www.nvcontractorsboard.com/#fragment-14
Interior Designer	http://nsbaidrd.state.nv.us/?page=7
Intermediate Care Facility (Retarded)	http://dhhs.nv.gov/Health/hcqc/healthfacilitiesquery/
Intermedical Care Facility	http://dhhs.nv.gov/Health/hcqc/healthfacilitiesquery/
Laboratory Assist/Blood Gas Assist	http://dhhs.nv.gov/Health/hcqc/healthpersonnelquery/
Laboratory, Medical	http://dhhs.nv.gov/Health/hcqc/healthpersonnelquery/
Landscape Architect	http://nsbla.state.nv.us/Licensed.htm
Landscape Contractor	www.nvcontractorsboard.com/#fragment-14
Lobbyist	www.leg.state.nv.us/AppCF/lobbyist/
Mason	www.nvcontractorsboard.com/#fragment-14
Medical Device-Equipment or Gas	https://pharmacy.bop.nv.gov/datamart/mainMenu.do;jsessionid=87743A7F52A1D430E87CB401C314C5A8
Medical Doctor, Disciplinary Action	http://medboard.nv.gov/Verification/
Medical Technician	http://dhhs.nv.gov/Health/hcqc/healthpersonnelquery/
Money Transmitter Agent/Company	http://fid.state.nv.us/New_Qry_MT-Lic.asp
Narcotic Treatment Center	https://pharmacy.bop.nv.gov/datamart/mainMenu.do;jsessionid=87743A7F52A1D430E87CB401C314C5A8
Nurse Anesthetist	www.nursingboard.state.nv.us/Verification/index.html
Nurse-Adv'd Practitioner (Pharm)	https://pharmacy.bop.nv.gov/datamart/mainMenu.do;jsessionid=87743A7F52A1D430E87CB401C314C5A8
Nurse/Adverse Action Report	www.nursingboard.state.nv.us/dactions/
Nurse/RN/LPN/Advanced Practice/Aide	www.nursingboard.state.nv.us/Verification/index.html
Nursing Care Facility/Nursing Facility	http://dhhs.nv.gov/Health/hcqc/healthfacilitiesquery/
Nursing Pool Operator	http://dhhs.nv.gov/Health/hcqc/healthfacilitiesquery/
Occupational Therapist/Assistant	http://nvot.org/services/licensure
Optometrist	http://optometry.nv.gov/Qry-LicenseeInfoForm1.asp
Oriental Medical Doctor (OMD)	http://oriental_medicine.state.nv.us/qry-licensees_name.asp
Osteopathic Physician/Assistant	http://license.k3systems.com/LicensingPublic/app?page=licenseeSearch&service=page
Painter/Paper Hanger	www.nvcontractorsboard.com/#fragment-14
Pest Control Applicator/Company	http://agri.nv.gov/Plant/PEST/Licensed_Pest_Control_Companies/
Pesticide, Restricted Use	http://npirspublic.ceris.purdue.edu/state/state_menu.aspx?state=IN
Pharmacist/Pharmaceutical Tech	https://pharmacy.bop.nv.gov/datamart/mainMenu.do;jsessionid=87743A7F52A1D430E87CB401C314C5A8
Pharmacy/Pharmacy Practitioner	https://pharmacy.bop.nv.gov/datamart/mainMenu.do;jsessionid=87743A7F52A1D430E87CB401C314C5A8

Physical Therapist/Assistant	http://ptboard.nv.gov/PT-verif-index.htm
Physician Assistant (Pharm)	https://pharmacy.bop.nv.gov/datamart/mainMenu.do;jsessionid=87743A7F52A1D430E87CB401C314C5A8
Physician/Medical Doctor/Assistant	http://medboard.nv.gov/Verification/
Plasterer/Drywall Installer/Lather	www.nvcontractorsboard.com/#fragment-14
Playground Builder	www.nvcontractorsboard.com/#fragment-14
Plumber	www.nvcontractorsboard.com/#fragment-14
Podiatrist	http://podiatry.state.nv.us/Licensees.htm
Prison Pharmacy	https://pharmacy.bop.nv.gov/datamart/mainMenu.do;jsessionid=87743A7F52A1D430E87CB401C314C5A8
Pump Installer	www.nvcontractorsboard.com/#fragment-14
Real Estate Pre-Licensing Schools	http://red.state.nv.us/Forms/502.pdf
Refractory/Firebrick Contractor	www.nvcontractorsboard.com/#fragment-14
Residential Designer	http://nsbaidrd.state.nv.us/?page=7
Respiratory Care Practitioner	http://medboard.nv.gov/Verification/
Roofer	www.nvcontractorsboard.com/#fragment-14
Sewerage Contractor	www.nvcontractorsboard.com/#fragment-14
Sheet Metal Fabricator	www.nvcontractorsboard.com/#fragment-14
Siding Installer	www.nvcontractorsboard.com/#fragment-14
Sign Erector	www.nvcontractorsboard.com/#fragment-14
Social Worker	http://socwork.nv.gov/Lookup_Menu.htm
Solar Contractor	www.nvcontractorsboard.com/#fragment-14
Speech Pathologist	www.nvaud-sp.org/license/
Steel Contractor	www.nvcontractorsboard.com/#fragment-14
Surgical Center, Ambulatory	http://dhhs.nv.gov/Health/hcqc/healthfacilitiesquery/
Surveyor, Land	www.nvboe.org/rosters/
Tank Installer, Pressure/Storage	www.nvcontractorsboard.com/#fragment-14
Taxi Wraps	http://taxi.nv.gov/About_Us/ALL/Taxi_Wraps/Taxi_Wraps/
Teacher	http://nvteachersearch.doe.nv.gov/
Thrift Company	https://fid.online.nv.gov/datamart/selLicType.do?type=name
Traffic Safety School	https://dmvapp.nv.gov/DMV/OBL/Business_Reports/Pages/BusinessLicenses.aspx
Trust Company	https://fid.online.nv.gov/datamart/selLicType.do?type=name
Vehicle Broker/Dealer	https://dmvapp.nv.gov/DMV/OBL/Business_Reports/Pages/BusinessLicenses.aspx
Veterinarian/Facility	https://www.nvvetboard.us/glsuiteweb/clients/nvbov/public/LicenseeList.aspx
Water Well Driller	http://water.nv.gov/data/drillers/
Well Driller	www.nvcontractorsboard.com/#fragment-14
Well Driller/Monitor	http://water.nv.gov/data/drillers/
Wrecker/Demolisher	www.nvcontractorsboard.com/#fragment-14

State and Local Courts

State Court Structure: Note that Nevada does NOT have a unified court system.

The **District Courts** are the courts of general jurisdiction. Probate is handled by the District Courts, as are divorce records. The judges also hear appeals from Justice and Municipal Court cases.

The **Justice Courts** are generally named for the township of jurisdiction. Due to their small populations, some townships no longer have Justice Courts. The Justice Courts handle misdemeanor crime and traffic matters, small claims disputes, evictions, and other civil matters less than $10,000, the maximum amount for Small Claims increased from $5,000 to $7,500 in July 2011. The Justices of the Peace also preside over felony and gross misdemeanor arraignments and conduct preliminary hearings to determine if sufficient evidence exists to hold criminals for trial at District Court.

The **Municipal Courts** manage cases involving violations of traffic and misdemeanor ordinances that occur within the city limits of incorporated municipalities. Generally they do not oversee civil matters.

Appellate Courts: The Supreme Court website found at www.nevadajudiciary.us gives access to opinions.

Statewide Court Online Access: Only Clark and Washoe counties offer online access to the public. A statewide court automation system is in the process of being implemented.

Clark County

8th Judicial District Court http://www.clarkcountycourts.us/

Civil: Case records are searchable free at https://www.clarkcountycourts.us/Anonymous/default.aspx. Search by case number or party name or attorney. A wealth of data is available including calendars, but few personal identifiers. Online access to probate cases filed prior to 01/01/2009 are found at http://courtgate.coca.co.clark.nv.us/DistrictCourt/asp/CaseNo.asp. Otherwise use site above. *Criminal:* Online access to criminal cases filed prior to 01/01/2009 are found at http://courtgate.coca.co.clark.nv.us/DistrictCourt/asp/CaseNo.asp.

All Township Justice Court http://www.clarkcountycourts.us

Civil: Access the county Justice Courts docket at http://www.clarkcountycourts.us/CaseLookupLinks.htm. Search calendars from that site also. *Criminal:* Access the county Justice Courts docket at http://cvpublicaccess.co.clark.nv.us/pa/. Includes traffic citations.

Washoe County

2nd Judicial District Court http://www.washoecourts.com

Civil: Two options are available at http://www.washoecourts.com/index.cfm?page=caseinquiryMain. One option (CourtConnect) allows a name search, the other options requires a case number. *Criminal:* Same as civil. Per the discliamer, this site does not offer an official search; searches performed are informational only. Not suggested as the sole search for FCRA related needs.

Recorders, Assessors, and Other Sites of Note

Recording Office Organization: 16 counties and one independent city; 17 recording offices. The recording officer is the County Recorder. Carson City has a separate filing office. Federal tax liens on personal property of businesses are filed with the Secretary of State. Federal tax liens on personal property of individuals are filed with the County Recorder. Although not called state tax liens, employment withholding judgments have the same effect and are filed with the County Recorder.

Statewide or Multi-Jurisdiction Access: There is no statewide access, but a number of counties provide access to searchable databases online.

County Sites:

Carson City ***Real Estate, Deed, Marriage, Vital Statistic Records*** www.carson.org/index.aspx?page=86 Most all recordings are indexed online at www.carson.org/Index.aspx?page=155. Images available. Use the pull-down menu. Search limited documents for free at www.ccapps.org/cgi-bin/dmw200.

Property, Taxation Records Access assessor data of parcels and secured property free at www.ccapps.org/cgi-bin/asw100. Find Carson city parcel maps searchable by parcel number at www.carson.org/Index.aspx?page=59.

Churchill County ***Real Estate, Grantor/Grantee, Deed, Judgment, UCC, Lien Records*** www.churchillcounty.org/index.aspx?nid=168 Access recorder records at www.churchillcounty.org/index.aspx?NID=215. Documents 2000 and forward can be viewed, all maps can be viewed.

Property, Taxation Records Access assessor property records free at www.churchillcounty.org/index.aspx?nid=88.

Clark County ***Recorded Documents, Marriage Records*** www.clarkcountynv.gov/depts/recorder/pages/default.aspx Access to the Recorder's real estate records free at https://recorder.co.clark.nv.us/RecorderEcommerce/ but no images. Can purchase a document for a fee. Also, access to fictitious firm filing free at http://sandgate.co.clark.nv.us:8498/clarkcounty/clerk/clerkSearch.html. Biz license-http://sandgate.co.clark.nv.us/businessLicense/businessSearch/blindex.asp. Voter Reg- www.clarkcountynv.gov/depts/election/pages/default.aspx. **$$$**

Property, Taxation Records Property records, assessor maps, manufactured housing, road documents, and business personal property on the county Assessor database are free at www.clarkcountynv.gov/depts/assessor/pages/recordsearch.aspx. Property-GIS at http://gisgate.co.clark.nv.us/openweb/. Must install Microsoft Silverlight to use this site.

Douglas County ***Recorded Documents, Voter Registration, Building Permit Records*** www.douglascountynv.gov/index.aspx?NID=66 Access recorded documents index back thru 1983 free at http://rdb.co.douglas.nv.us/docsearch/index.cfm. Indexed online from 1/1/83 to present.

Property, Taxation Records Parcel records on the Assessor's database are free at http://adb.co.douglas.nv.us/parcel/new3/indexi.cfm. Also, download maps at http://adb.co.douglas.nv.us/maps/index.cfm. Also, the clerk/treasurer property tax database is free at http://cltr.co.douglas.nv.us/database/treasurers/.

Elko County ***Real Estate, Deed, Marriage, Filed Map Records*** www.elkocountynv.net//departments/recorder/index.html Access to the recorder database including marriages is free at www.elkocountynv.net/recorder.htm. Recording records go back to 1984. All documents back to 1996 are viewable and/or printable. Maps go back to 1869.

Property, Taxation Records Access to the assessor database including personal property and sales records is free at www.elkocountynv.net//assessor1/public_records.html.

Esmeralda County ***Property, Taxation Records*** Access the Assessor's Sales Data Inquiry free at http://www.esmeraldacountynv.net:1401/cgi-bin/asw300.

Eureka County ***Recorded Documents Records*** www.co.eureka.nv.us/audit/auditor01.htm Access to document inquiry free at http://eurekacounty.net:1403/cgi-bin/diw200.

Property, Taxation Records Search the assessor property data at http://eurekacounty.net:1401/cgi-bin/asw100. Search the treasurer's secured property tax roll at http://eurekacounty.net:1401/cgi-bin/tcw100.

Humboldt County ***Recorded Documents*** Access to record indexes only free at http://12.198.104.85/. Must call office for copies of documents. Must sign in with user name of Public (upper case P) and the password public (lower case p). Due to redaction laws, no images are available at this time.

Property, Taxation Records Access assessor property records free at www.hcnv.us:1401/cgi-bin/aswmenu.

Lander County ***Property, Taxation Records*** Access real property tax, personal property, and sales free at www.landercounty.org:1401/cgi-bin/aswmenu. Also, access to plat maps free at www.landercounty.org:1401/maps/LANDER_INDEX_MAP.pdf.

Lincoln County ***Property, Taxation Records*** Access to GIS/mapping for free at http://maps.gnomon.com/website/WMR_Lincoln/

Lyon County ***Real Estate, Deed, UCC, Map Records*** www.lyon-county.org/index.aspx?nid=108 Access recorder records free at www.lyon-county.org/index.aspx?nid=110; images go back to 1/2001.

Property, Taxation Records Search assessor data at www1.lyon-county.org:403/cgi-bin/aswmenu.

Mineral County ***Real Estate, Misc Records*** www.mineralcountynv.org/index.php/recorer-auditor Access to document inquiry free at www.mineralcountynv.us:1401/cgi-bin/diw200.

Nye County ***Grantor/Grantee Records*** www.nyecounty.net/ Access to records free at www.tylerworksasp.com/nyecounty/web/splash.jsp. Some images are available prior to 1986. Also access to recorder database free at http://nye.nv.countygovernmentrecords.com/nyecounty/web/. Index available from 1/1/86 to present.

Property, Taxation Records Search property assessor data free at http://asdb.co.nye.nv.us:1401/cgi-bin/asw100. Access secured tax data sheets free at www.nyecounty.net/.

Pershing County ***Property, Taxation Records*** Access to Assessor data for free at http://pershingcounty.net/index.php/Online-Property-Records.html.

Storey County ***Real Estate, Deeds, Judgment Records*** www.storeycounty.org/recorder/ Access to records free at www.storeycounty.org/recorder/adsrecorder.asp. Images available from 071/01/1998 to date.

Property, Taxation Records Search assessor's assessment roll free at www.storeycounty.org/assessor/search_new.asp.

Washoe County ***Recorded Documents, Voter Registration Records*** www.washoecounty.us/recorder Access grantor/grantee index free at www.washoecounty.us/recorder/icris.washoecounty.us; a $1.00 per page fee for documents. Data from 11/19/1991 to present, images from 8/16/1999 to present. **$$$**

Property, Taxation Records Access property tax data at www.washoecounty.us/assessor/cama/index.php. Download property sales 2002-2013 data free at www.washoecounty.us/assessor/SalesRpt.htm. Also, search aircraft, business property, mobile home data free at www.washoecounty.us/assessor/index.htm. Click on Search Our Data.

White Pine County ***Property, Taxation Records*** A property search is offered by the Treasurer at www.whitepinecountytreasurer.org:1401/cgi-bin/aswmenu.

Carson City ***Real Estate, Deed, Marriage, Vital Statistic Records*** www.carson.org/index.aspx?page=86 Most all recordings are indexed online at www.carson.org/Index.aspx?page=155. Images available. Use the pull-down menu. Search limited documents for free at www.ccapps.org/cgi-bin/dmw200.

Property, Taxation Records Access assessor data of parcels and secured property free at www.ccapps.org/cgi-bin/asw100. Find Carson city parcel maps searchable by parcel number at www.carson.org/Index.aspx?page=59.

New Hampshire

Capital: Concord
MerrimackCounty
Time Zone: EST
Population: 1,320,718
# of Counties: 10

Useful State Links

Website: www.nh.gov/
Governor: www.governor.nh.gov/
Attorney General: http://doj.nh.gov
State Archives: http://sos.nh.gov/arch_rec_mgmt.aspx
State Statutes and Codes: http://gencourt.state.nh.us/rsa/html/indexes/default.html
Legislative Bill Search: http://gencourt.state.nh.us/index/
Unclaimed Funds: www.nh.gov/treasury/Divisions/AP/APsearch2.htm

State Public Record Agencies

Sexual Offender Registry

Division of State Police, Special Investigations Unit-SOR, www4.egov.nh.gov/nsor/search.aspx The web site at www4.egov.nh.gov/nsor/search.aspx gives access to the NH Registration of Criminal Offenders. There are disclaimers as this information may not reflect all sexual offender acts. There is also a Warrants Non-compliant Criminal Offenders search at www4.egov.nh.gov/nsor/Warrant.aspx. Persons accessing the warrants database are cautioned that this database contains information about the FIRST offense for which the sex offender/offender against children was registered.

Incarceration Records

New Hampshire Department of Corrections, Offender Records Office, www.nh.gov/nhdoc/ An inmate locator is available on their web page. The inmate locator displays the offender's current controlling sentence and does not show concurrent sentences also being served or consecutive sentences that have yet to be served.

Corporation, LP, LLP, LLC, Trademarks/Servicemarks, Trade Names

Secretary of State, Corporation Division, http://sos.nh.gov/Corp_Div.aspx A free business name lookup is available at the website. Results include a wealth of information including registered agent. Documents filed after 12/2004 and some older documents have been imaged and are also available in the entity's Filed Documents. *Other Options:* Monthly lists of corporations, LLCs, or trade names are $50 per month or $500 for last 12 months. . A list of all non-profits on file is available for $250.00.

Uniform Commercial Code, Federal & State Tax Liens

UCC Division, Secretary of State, http://sos.nh.gov/ucc.aspx Visit https://corp.sos.nh.gov/ for commercial online access to records. Accounts may be established using either automated clearing house (ACH) debit account or credit card. The fee is $27.00 plus a $2.00 handling fee per debtor name on a pay as you go basis, or for a $5,000 subscription fee receive unlimited online searches for one full year. Users can apply for an ACH (Automated Clearing House) account to be used as a payment option for filings or search. **$$$**

Vital Records

Department of State, Bureau of Vital Records, http://sos.nh.gov/vital_records.aspx Records may be ordered online from www.vitalchek.com (see expedited services). The Division's web page offers access to statistical data. You can also produce data reports in a spreadsheet format. **$$$**

Workers' Compensation Records

Labor Department, Workers Compensation Division, www.nh.gov/labor/workers-comp/ Verification of employer coverage is found at https://www.ewccv.com/cvs/

Driver Records

Department of Motor Vehicles, Driving Records, www.nh.gov/safety/divisions/dmv/ Electronic online access and FTP (file transfer protocol) are both offered for approved commercial accounts. Search by license number, or by name and DOB. Fee is $12.00 per record. The minimum daily order requirement is fifty requests. If more information is required, call 603-227-4050. **$$$**

Voter Registration, Campaign Finance, PACs

Secretary of State, Election Division, http://sos.nh.gov/Elections.aspx View information of campaign finance and PACs at http://cfs.sos.nh.gov/cfs/public/default.aspx. View what individuals have contributed.

Occupational Licensing Boards

Accountant-CPA/Firm .... www.nh.gov/jtboard/boarosters.htm
Acupuncturist .... www.nh.gov/acupuncture/licensees.htm
Architect https://nhlicenses2.nh.gov/cgi-bin/professional/nhprof/search.pl
Attorney Discipline System .... http://nhattyreg.org/search.php
Auctioneer .... www.sos.nh.gov/auctioneers/Licensees.htm
Bank, Cooperative .... www.nh.gov/banking/bank-cu-trust/documents/bank.xls
Bank/Holding Company .... www.nh.gov/banking/bank-cu-trust/documents/bank.xls
Banking Service Unit .... www.nh.gov/banking/bank-cu-trust/documents/bank.xls
Barber/Cosmetologist Licensed Schools ..... www.nh.gov/cosmet/schools/index.htm
Cash Dispenser Machine, Non-bank .... www.nh.gov/banking/consumer-credit/non-bank-cash-disp-machines.htm
Child Care Facility .... http://childcaresearch.dhhs.nh.gov/Mylicense%20Verification/Search.aspx?facility=Y
Court Reporter https://nhlicenses2.nh.gov/cgi-bin/professional/nhprof/search.pl
Credit Union .... www.nh.gov/banking/bank-cu-trust/documents/credit-union.xls
Debt Adjuster .... www.nh.gov/banking/consumer-credit/documents/list-debt-adjuster.xls
Dentist/Dental Hygienist https://nhlicenses.nh.gov/MyLicense%20Verification/
Drug Wholesaler/Manufacturer .... www.nh.gov/pharmacy/licensing/verification.htm
Electrician, High/Medium Volt/Trainee https://nhlicenses.nh.gov/MyLicense%20Verification/
Electrician, Master/Journeyman/Apprentice https://nhlicenses.nh.gov/MyLicense%20Verification/
Embalmer .... www.nh.gov/funeral/documents/embalmers-funeral-directors.pdf
Embalmer, Apprentice .... www.nh.gov/funeral/documents/apprentice-embalmers.pdf
Engineer https://nhlicenses2.nh.gov/cgi-bin/professional/nhprof/search.pl
Forester https://nhlicenses2.nh.gov/cgi-bin/professional/nhprof/search.pl
Funeral Director .... www.nh.gov/funeral/documents/embalmers-funeral-directors.pdf
Geologist https://nhlicenses2.nh.gov/cgi-bin/professional/nhprof/search.pl
Insurance Agent/Broker .... https://sbs-nh.naic.org/Lion-Web/jsp/sbsreports/AgentLookup.jsp
Liquor Keg Shipper, Direct .... https://nhlicenses.nh.gov/MyLicense%20Verification/Search.aspx?facility=Y
Liquor Product/Store .... www.nh.gov/liquor/pllicen.shtml
Loan Production Office .... www.nh.gov/banking/consumer-credit/documents/list-small.xls
Lobbyist .... http://sos.nh.gov/lobby.aspx
Marital/Family Mediator .... www.nh.gov/family-mediator/mediators/index.htm
Marriage & Family Therapist https://nhlicenses.nh.gov/MyLicense%20Verification/
Mental Health Counselor, Clinical https://nhlicenses.nh.gov/MyLicense%20Verification/
Midwife .... www.nhmidwives.org/find.html
Mortgage Banker/Broker/Servicer .... www.nh.gov/banking/consumer-credit/documents/list-banker-broker.xls
Motor Vehicle Financer/Sales Finance .... www.nh.gov/banking/consumer-credit/documents/list-sales.xls
Motor Vehicle Retailer .... www.nh.gov/banking/consumer-credit/documents/list-retail.xls
Nurse-LPN/Practical/Advanced/Assistant https://nhlicenses.nh.gov/MyLicense%20Verification/
Optometrist .... www.arbo.org/index.php?action=findanoptometrist
Pastoral Psychotherapist https://nhlicenses.nh.gov/MyLicense%20Verification/

Pharmacist .... www.nh.gov/pharmacy/licensing/verification.htm
Pharmacy/Technician/Mail Order................ www.nh.gov/pharmacy/licensing/verification.htm
Physician/Medical Doctor/Assistant............ www4.egov.nh.gov/medicineboard/
Plumber... https://nhlicenses.nh.gov/MyLicense%20Verification/
Psychologist... https://nhlicenses.nh.gov/MyLicense%20Verification/
Public Health Clinic .... www.nh.gov/pharmacy/licensing/verification.htm
Real Estate Agent/Seller/Broker/Firm.......... https://nhlicenses.nh.gov/MyLicense%20Verification/
Real Estate Appraiser.................................. https://nhlicenses2.nh.gov/cgi-bin/professional/nhprof/search.pl
Savings Bank .... www.nh.gov/banking/bank-cu-trust/documents/bank.xls
Scientist, Natural/Wetlands.......................... https://nhlicenses2.nh.gov/cgi-bin/professional/nhprof/search.pl
Small Loan Lender....................................... www.nh.gov/banking/consumer-credit/documents/list-small.xls
Social Worker, Clinical https://nhlicenses.nh.gov/MyLicense%20Verification/
Surveyor, Land... https://nhlicenses2.nh.gov/cgi-bin/professional/nhprof/search.pl
Trust Company... www.nh.gov/banking/bank-cu-trust/documents/trust.xls
Verbatim Court Reporter............................. https://nhlicenses2.nh.gov/cgi-bin/professional/nhprof/search.pl
Veterinary Medicine https://nhlicenses.nh.gov/MyLicense%20Verification/

State and Local Courts

State Court Structure: The **Superior Court** is the court of General Jurisdiction and has jurisdiction over a wide variety of cases, including criminal, domestic relations, and civil cases, and provides the only forum in this state for trial by jury. Felony cases include Class A misdemeanors. The Superior Court has exclusive jurisdiction over cases in which the damage claims exceed $25,000.

Effective July 1, 2011, a new **Circuit Court** system was established that consolidated the then existing 32 **District Courts**, 10 **Probate Courts**, and 25 **Family Courts**. Under the new rules, each county now has a Circuit Court with three Divisions: District, Family and Probate. All the current District Court locations remained open. In Cheshire County, the marital division continues to operate as part of the Cheshire County Superior Court. In all other counties, the Circuit Court Family Division operates at the same locations as before.

To view which town is associated with which court jurisdiction, use the toll found at www.courts.state.nh.us/courtlocations/index.htm.

Probate cases are filed in the Circuit Court located at the county seat.

Appellate Courts: For Slip Opinions from the Supreme Court visit www.courts.state.nh.us/supreme/opinions/index.htm.

Statewide Court Online Access: There is no statewide access available for trial court record.

Note: No individual New Hampshire courts offer online access.

Recorders, Assessors, and Other Sites of Note

Recording Office Organization: New Hampshire has 10 recording offices. There are 233 cities/town which previously handled the filing of UCCs. The recording officers are Register of Deeds (for real estate only) and Town/City Clerk (for UCCs). Be careful to distinguish the following names that are identical for both a town/city and a county - Grafton, Hillsborough, Merrimack, Strafford, and Sullivan. The following unincorporated towns do not have a Town Clerk, so all liens are located at the corresponding county: Cambridge (Coos), Dicksville (Coos), Green's Grant (Coos), Hale's Location (Carroll), Millsfield (Coos), and Wentworth's Location (Coos). New Hampshire is in the Eastern Time Zone (EST).

Real estate transactions recorded at the county level; property taxes are handled at the town/city level. Federal and state tax liens on personal property of businesses are filed with the Secretary of State. Other federal and state tax liens on personal property are filed with the Town/City Clerk. Federal and state tax liens on real property are filed with the county Register of Deeds.

Statewide or Multi-Jurisdiction Access: Property data is readily available online for a growing number of jurisdictions, usually inexpensively through a vendor.

- A links list to the web pages of New Hampshire Counties Registry of Deeds is at www.nhdeeds.com.

- A private vendor has placed assessor records from a number of towns on the internet, visit www.vgsi.com/vision/Applications/ParcelData/NH/Home.aspx. Access varies, some allow free index searches, some require registration, and a few may charge for access. There are over 35 participating jurisdictions.
- A vendor at http://data.avitarassociates.com/logon.aspx?ReturnUrl=%2fDefault.aspx offers Property Card data for over 100 municipalities. Three fee structures are offered, ranging from $25 for one town for one month to $500 for all towns for one year.

County Sites (County Recorder, Followed by Towns with Online Access in that County):

Belknap County ***Recorded Documents Records*** www.nhdeeds.com/belknap/BeHome.html Access to county register of deeds data is free at www.nhdeeds.com/belknap/BeDisclaimer.html. Online records go back to 1765. To establish an account for copies of documents from the internet, go to www.nhdeeds.com/belknap/BeCopyAcct.html. Fees are $2.00 per page from Internet, $3.00 per page faxed. **$$$**

Property, Taxation Records Access to GIS/mapping for the City of Laconia free at www.caigisonline.com/LaconiaNH/.

Alton Town ***Property, Taxation Records*** Search the assessor database at http://data.visionappraisal.com/AltonNH/DEFAULT.asp.

Barnstead Town ***Property, Taxation Records*** Access assessor data by subscription at http://data.avitarassociates.com/logon.aspx?ReturnUrl=%2fDefault.aspx. Fees range from $25 per month (1 town) to $500 per year (all towns).**$$$**

Gilford Town ***Property, Taxation Records*** Access assessor and other town online documents free at www.eb2gov.com/scripts/eb2gov.dll/townlaunch?towncode=110. Must register to use.

Gilmanton Town ***Property, Taxation Records*** Access assessor data by subscription at http://data.avitarassociates.com/logon.aspx?ReturnUrl=%2fDefault.aspx. Fees range from $25 per month (1 town) to $500 per year (all towns).**$$$**

Laconia City ***Property, Taxation Records*** Records on the town assessor database are online at http://data.visionappraisal.com/LaconiaNH/DEFAULT.asp. Free registration is required for full access.

Meredith Town ***Recorded Documents Records*** http://meredithnh.org/Joomla/index.php/town-departments/meredith-town-clerk Access to recorded documents free at www.nhdeeds.com/belknap/BeHome.html.

Property, Taxation Records Access to Belknap County Registry of Deeds records is at www.nhdeeds.com/. Also, search town assessor database free at http://data.visionappraisal.com/LaconiaNH/DEFAULT.asp. Also, access to tax maps free at http://meredithnh.org/Joomla/index.php/tax-maps.

New Hampton Town ***Property, Taxation Records*** Access assessment lists free at www.new-hampton.nh.us/newhampton/assessmentlists.asp.

Sanbornton Town ***Property, Taxation Records*** Access to tax maps and property record maps free at www.sanborntonnh.org/Interactive%20maps/Property%20Record%20Master%20Pages/PRMP%20TML/PR%20Home.htm.

Tilton Town ***Property, Taxation Records*** Access assessor data by subscription at http://data.avitarassociates.com/logon.aspx?ReturnUrl=%2fDefault.aspx. Fees range from $25 per month (1 town) to $500 per year (all towns).**$$$**

Carroll County

Albany Town ***Property, Taxation Records*** Access assessor data by subscription at http://data.avitarassociates.com/logon.aspx?ReturnUrl=%2fDefault.aspx. Fees range from $25 per month (1 town) to $500 per year (all towns).**$$$**

Effingham Town ***Property, Taxation Records*** Access assessor data by subscription at http://data.avitarassociates.com/logon.aspx?ReturnUrl=%2fDefault.aspx. Fees range from $25 per month (1 town) to $500 per year (all towns).**$$$**

Hart's Location Town ***Property, Taxation Records*** Access assessor data by subscription at http://data.avitarassociates.com/logon.aspx?ReturnUrl=%2fDefault.aspx. Fees range from $25 per month (1 town) to $500 per year (all towns). Also, town maps for free at www.hartslocation.com/.**$$$**

Madison Town ***Property, Taxation Records*** Access assessor data by subscription at http://data.avitarassociates.com/logon.aspx?ReturnUrl=%2fDefault.aspx. Fees range from $25 per month (1 town) to $500 per year (all towns). Access to GIS/mapping free at http://208.88.76.81/mapguide2011/fusion/templates/mapguide/TerraMap/index.html?ApplicationDefinition=Library%3a%2f%2fMadison Online%2fNew Folder%2fAerial.ApplicationDefinition.**$$$**

Moultonborough Town ***Property, Taxation Records*** Search town assessor database at http://data.visionappraisal.com/MoultonboroughNH/DEFAULT.asp.

Ossipee Town ***Property, Taxation Records*** Access to GIS/mapping free at www.caigisonline.com/ossipeenh/.

Tuftonboro Town ***Property, Taxation Records*** Access assessor data by subscription at http://data.avitarassociates.com/logon.aspx?ReturnUrl=%2fDefault.aspx. Fees range from $25 per month (1 town) to $500 per year (all towns).**$$$**

Wakefield Town ***Property, Taxation Records*** Access assessor data by subscription at http://data.avitarassociates.com/logon.aspx?ReturnUrl=%2fDefault.aspx. Fees range from $25 per month (1 town) to $500 per year (all towns).**$$$**

Wolfeboro Town ***Property, Taxation Records*** Access assessor data by subscription at http://data.avitarassociates.com/logon.aspx?ReturnUrl=%2fDefault.aspx. Fees range from $25 per month (1 town) to $500 per year (all towns).**$$$**

Cheshire County ***Real Estate, Deed, Mortgage, Lien Records*** http://nhdeeds.com/cheshire/ChHome.html Access to county register of deeds data is free at www.nhdeeds.com/cheshire/ChDisclaimer.html. Online records go back to 1975.

Alstead Town ***Property, Taxation Records*** Access assessor data by subscription at http://data.avitarassociates.com/logon.aspx?ReturnUrl=%2fDefault.aspx. Fees range from $25 per month (1 town) to $500 per year (all towns).**$$$**

Dublin Town ***Property, Taxation Records*** Access assessor data by subscription at http://data.avitarassociates.com/logon.aspx?ReturnUrl=%2fDefault.aspx. Fees range from $25 per month (1 town) to $500 per year (all towns).**$$$**

Fitzwilliam Town ***Property, Taxation Records*** Access assessor data by subscription at http://data.avitarassociates.com/logon.aspx?ReturnUrl=%2fDefault.aspx. Fees range from $25 per month (1 town) to $500 per year (all towns).**$$$**

Gilsum Town ***Property, Taxation Records*** Access assessor data by subscription at http://data.avitarassociates.com/logon.aspx?ReturnUrl=%2fDefault.aspx. Fees range from $25 per month (1 town) to $500 per year (all towns).**$$$**

Harrisville Town ***Property, Taxation Records*** Access assessor data by subscription at http://data.avitarassociates.com/logon.aspx?ReturnUrl=%2fDefault.aspx. Fees range from $25 per month (1 town) to $500 per year (all towns).**$$$**

Hinsdale Town ***Property, Taxation Records*** Access to assessor database for free at http://data.visionappraisal.com/HinsdaleNH/DEFAULT.asp.

Keene City ***Property, Taxation Records*** Online access to property values at www.ci.keene.nh.us/services/property-value-look.

Marlow Town ***Property, Taxation Records*** Access to town property maps free at www.marlownewhampshire.org/town-property-maps.php.

Nelson Town ***Property, Taxation Records*** Access assessor data by subscription at http://data.avitarassociates.com/logon.aspx?ReturnUrl=%2fDefault.aspx. Fees range from $25 per month (1 town) to $500 per year (all towns).**$$$**

Richmond Town ***Property, Taxation Records*** Access assessor data by subscription at http://data.avitarassociates.com/logon.aspx?ReturnUrl=%2fDefault.aspx. Fees range from $25 per month (1 town) to $500 per year (all towns).**$$$**

Rindge Town ***Property, Taxation Records*** Search town assessor database at http://data.visionappraisal.com/RindgeNH/DEFAULT.asp.

Roxbury Town ***Property, Taxation Records*** Access assessor data by subscription at http://data.avitarassociates.com/logon.aspx?ReturnUrl=%2fDefault.aspx. Fees range from $25 per month (1 town) to $500 per year (all towns).**$$$**

Sullivan Town ***Property, Taxation Records*** Access assessor data by subscription at http://data.avitarassociates.com/logon.aspx?ReturnUrl=%2fDefault.aspx. Fees range from $25 per month (1 town) to $500 per year (all towns).**$$$**

Surry Town ***Property, Taxation Records*** Access assessor data by subscription at http://data.avitarassociates.com/logon.aspx?ReturnUrl=%2fDefault.aspx. Fees range from $25 per month (1 town) to $500 per year (all towns).**$$$**

Swanzey Town ***Property, Taxation Records*** Access assessor data at http://data.visionappraisal.com/SwanzeyNH/DEFAULT.asp. Free registration for full data.

Walpole Town ***Property, Taxation Records*** Access assessor data by subscription at http://data.avitarassociates.com/logon.aspx?ReturnUrl=%2fDefault.aspx. Fees range from $25 per month (1 town) to $500 per year (all towns).**$$$**

Westmoreland Town ***Property, Taxation Records*** Access assessor data by subscription at http://data.avitarassociates.com/logon.aspx?ReturnUrl=%2fDefault.aspx. Fees range from $25 per month (1 town) to $500 per year (all towns).**$$$**

Winchester Town ***Property, Taxation Records*** Access assessor data by subscription at http://data.avitarassociates.com/logon.aspx?ReturnUrl=%2fDefault.aspx. Fees range from $25 per month (1 town) to $500 per year (all towns).**$$$**

Coos County ***Recorded Documents Records*** www.nhdeeds.com/coos/CoHome.html Access to county register of deeds data is free at www.nhdeeds.com/coos/CoIndex.html.

Berlin City ***Property, Taxation Records*** Access assessor data by subscription at http://data.avitarassociates.com/logon.aspx?ReturnUrl=%2fDefault.aspx. Fees range from $25 per month (1 town) to $500 per year (all towns).**$$$**

Clarksville Town ***Property, Taxation Records*** Access assessor data by subscription at http://data.avitarassociates.com/logon.aspx?ReturnUrl=%2fDefault.aspx. Fees range from $25 per month (1 town) to $500 per year (all towns).**$$$**

Colebrook Town ***Property, Taxation Records*** Access assessor property card data by subscription at www.avitarofneinc.com or call 603-798-4419. Annual subscription fee is $150 per Town.**$$$**

Columbia Town ***Property, Taxation Records*** Access assessor data by subscription at http://data.avitarassociates.com/logon.aspx?ReturnUrl=%2fDefault.aspx. Fees range from $25 per month (1 town) to $500 per year (all towns).**$$$**

Dummer Town ***Property, Taxation Records*** Access assessor data by subscription at http://data.avitarassociates.com/logon.aspx?ReturnUrl=%2fDefault.aspx. Fees range from $25 per month (1 town) to $500 per year (all towns).**$$$**

Gorham Town ***Property, Taxation Records*** Access to Assessor's database free at http://data.visionappraisal.com/GorhamNH/DEFAULT.asp.

Milan Town ***Property, Taxation Records*** Access assessor data by subscription at http://data.avitarassociates.com/logon.aspx?ReturnUrl=%2fDefault.aspx. Fees range from $25 per month (1 town) to $500 per year (all towns).**$$$**

Pittsburg Town ***Property, Taxation Records*** Access assessor data by subscription at http://data.avitarassociates.com/logon.aspx?ReturnUrl=%2fDefault.aspx. Fees range from $25 per month (1 town) to $500 per year (all towns).**$$$**

Shelburne Town ***Property, Taxation Records*** Access assessor data by subscription at http://data.avitarassociates.com/logon.aspx?ReturnUrl=%2fDefault.aspx. Fees range from $25 per month (1 town) to $500 per year (all towns).**$$$**

Stark Town ***Property, Taxation Records*** Access assessor data by subscription at http://data.avitarassociates.com/logon.aspx?ReturnUrl=%2fDefault.aspx. Fees range from $25 per month (1 town) to $500 per year (all towns).**$$$**

Stewartstown Town ***Property, Taxation Records*** Access assessor data by subscription at http://data.avitarassociates.com/logon.aspx?ReturnUrl=%2fDefault.aspx. Fees range from $25 per month (1 town) to $500 per year (all towns).**$$$**

Stratford Town ***Property, Taxation Records*** Access assessor data by subscription at http://data.avitarassociates.com/logon.aspx?ReturnUrl=%2fDefault.aspx. Fees range from $25 per month (1 town) to $500 per year (all towns).**$$$**

Grafton County ***Real Estate, Deed, Lien, Mortgage Records*** www.nhdeeds.com/grafton/GrHome.html Access to county register of deeds data is free at www.nhdeeds.com/grafton/GrIndex.html. A subscription may be required to print images. Access to the County dial-up service requires a $50.00 set up fee and $1.00 per page charge. Lending agency data is available. A fax-back service is available, need to have payment before they fax out whether in or out of state. For info, call 603-787-6921. **$$$**

Alexandria Town ***Property, Taxation Records*** Access assessor data by subscription at http://data.avitarassociates.com/logon.aspx?ReturnUrl=%2fDefault.aspx. Fees range from $25 per month (1 town) to $500 per year (all towns).**$$$**

Ashland Town ***Property, Taxation Records*** Access to GIS/mapping for free at www.ashland.nh.gov/.

Bridgewater Town ***Property, Taxation Records*** Access to GIS/mapping for free at www.bridgewater-nh.com/offices-departments/assessor

Bristol Town ***Property, Taxation Records*** Access assessor data by subscription at http://data.avitarassociates.com/logon.aspx?ReturnUrl=%2fDefault.aspx. Fees range from $25 per month (1 town) to $500 per year (all towns).**$$$**

Canaan Town ***Property, Taxation Records*** Access assessor data by subscription at http://data.avitarassociates.com/logon.aspx?ReturnUrl=%2fDefault.aspx. Fees range from $25 per month (1 town) to $500 per year (all towns). Town of Orange is included in the Town of Canaan records.**$$$**

Dorchester Town ***Property, Taxation Records*** Access assessor data by subscription at http://data.avitarassociates.com/logon.aspx?ReturnUrl=%2fDefault.aspx. Fees range from $25 per month (1 town) to $500 per year (all towns).**$$$**

Ellsworth Town ***Property, Taxation Records*** Access assessor data by subscription at http://data.avitarassociates.com/logon.aspx?ReturnUrl=%2fDefault.aspx. Fees range from $25 per month (1 town) to $500 per year (all towns).**$$$**

Enfield Town ***Property, Taxation Records*** Assessor data is free at www.visionappraisal.com/databases/nh/.

Franconia Town ***Property, Taxation Records*** Access assessor data by subscription at http://data.avitarassociates.com/logon.aspx?ReturnUrl=%2fDefault.aspx. Fees range from $25 per month (1 town) to $500 per year (all towns).**$$$**

Grafton Town ***Property, Taxation Records*** Access assessor data by subscription at http://data.avitarassociates.com/logon.aspx?ReturnUrl=%2fDefault.aspx. Fees range from $25 per month (1 town) to $500 per year (all towns).**$$$**

Groton Town ***Property, Taxation Records*** Access assessor data by subscription at http://data.avitarassociates.com/logon.aspx?ReturnUrl=%2fDefault.aspx. Fees range from $25 per month (1 town) to $500 per year (all towns).**$$$**

Hanover Town ***Property, Taxation Records*** Access current assessment data free at www.hanovernh.org/Pages/HanoverNH_Assessing/current.

Haverhill Town ***Property, Taxation Records*** Access to new property values for 2011 for free at http://haverhill-nh.com/2011%20Property%20Values0001.pdf.

Hebron Town ***Property, Taxation Records*** Access assessor data by subscription at http://data.avitarassociates.com/logon.aspx?ReturnUrl=%2fDefault.aspx. Fees range from $25 per month (1 town) to $500 per year (all towns).**$$$**

Holderness Town ***Property, Taxation Records*** Property assessment data at www.holderness-nh.gov/Public_Documents/HoldernessNH_Assessor/assessments

Landaff Town ***Property, Taxation Records*** Access assessor data by subscription at http://data.avitarassociates.com/logon.aspx?ReturnUrl=%2fDefault.aspx. Fees range from $25 per month (1 town) to $500 per year (all towns).**$$$**

Lebanon City ***Property, Taxation Records*** Access to property assessment data for free at http://lebanonnh.patriotproperties.com/default.asp?br=exp&vr=6. Search interactive GIS maps free at http://ims.lebcity.com/.

Lincoln Town ***Property, Taxation Records*** Free access to GIS/mapping found at www.caigisonline.com/lincolnnh/.

Lisbon Town ***Property, Taxation Records*** Access assessor data by subscription at http://data.avitarassociates.com/logon.aspx?ReturnUrl=%2fDefault.aspx. Fees range from $25 per month (1 town) to $500 per year (all towns).**$$$**

Littleton Town ***Property, Taxation Records*** Access to Parcel maps and online maps for free at www.townoflittleton.org/assessment.php

Lyman Town ***Property, Taxation Records*** Access assessor data by subscription at http://data.avitarassociates.com/logon.aspx?ReturnUrl=%2fDefault.aspx. Fees range from $25 per month (1 town) to $500 per year (all towns).**$$$**

Monroe Town ***Property, Taxation Records*** Access assessor data by subscription at http://data.avitarassociates.com/logon.aspx?ReturnUrl=%2fDefault.aspx. Fees range from $25 per month (1 town) to $500 per year (all towns).**$$$**

Orford Town ***Property, Taxation Records*** Access assessor data by subscription at http://data.avitarassociates.com/logon.aspx?ReturnUrl=%2fDefault.aspx. Fees range from $25 per month (1 town) to $500 per year (all towns).**$$$**

Piermont Town ***Property, Taxation Records*** Access assessor data by subscription at http://data.avitarassociates.com/logon.aspx?ReturnUrl=%2fDefault.aspx. Fees range from $25 per month (1 town) to $500 per year (all towns).**$$$**

Rumney Town ***Property, Taxation Records*** Access assessor data by subscription at http://data.avitarassociates.com/logon.aspx?ReturnUrl=%2fDefault.aspx. Fees range from $25 per month (1 town) to $500 per year (all towns).**$$$**

Sugar Hill Town ***Property, Taxation Records*** Access assessor property data free at http://data.visionappraisal.com coming soon.

Thornton Town ***Property, Taxation Records*** Access assessor data by subscription at http://data.avitarassociates.com/logon.aspx?ReturnUrl=%2fDefault.aspx. Fees range from $25 per month (1 town) to $500 per year (all towns).**$$$**

Warren Town ***Property, Taxation Records*** Access assessor data by subscription at http://data.avitarassociates.com/logon.aspx?ReturnUrl=%2fDefault.aspx. Fees range from $25 per month (1 town) to $500 per year (all towns).**$$$**

Waterville Valley Town ***Property, Taxation Records*** Access assessor data by subscription at http://data.avitarassociates.com/logon.aspx?ReturnUrl=%2fDefault.aspx. Fees range from $25 per month (1 town) to $500 per year (all towns).**$$$**

Wentworth Town ***Property, Taxation Records*** Access assessor data by subscription at http://data.avitarassociates.com/logon.aspx?ReturnUrl=%2fDefault.aspx. Fees range from $25 per month (1 town) to $500 per year (all towns).**$$$**

Hillsborough County

Real Estate, Grantor/Grantee, Deed, Mortgage, Lien Records www.nhdeeds.com/hillsborough/HiHome.html
Access to county register of deeds data is free at www.nhdeeds.com/hillsborough/HiDisclaimer.html. Online records go back to 1966.
Property, Taxation Records Access assessor data by subscription at http://data.avitarassociates.com/logon.aspx?ReturnUrl=%2fDefault.aspx. Fees range from $25 per month (1 town) to $500 per year (all towns).**$$$**

Amherst Town ***Property, Taxation Records*** Records on the town assessor database are free at http://data.visionappraisal.com/AmherstNH/DEFAULT.asp.

Antrim Town ***Property, Taxation Records*** Access to property cards, tax maps and zoning maps for free at www.antrimnh.org/Pages/index.

Bedford Town ***Property, Taxation Records*** Access assessor data at http://data.visionappraisal.com/BedfordNH/DEFAULT.asp. Free registration for full data.

Bennington Town ***Property, Taxation Records*** Access assessor data by subscription at http://data.avitarassociates.com/logon.aspx?ReturnUrl=%2fDefault.aspx. Fees range from $25 per month (1 town) to $500 per year (all towns).**$$$**

Brookline Town ***Property, Taxation Records*** Access assessor data by subscription at http://data.avitarassociates.com/logon.aspx?ReturnUrl=%2fDefault.aspx. Fees range from $25 per month (1 town) to $500 per year (all towns).**$$$**

Deering Town ***Property, Taxation Records*** Access assessor data by subscription at http://data.avitarassociates.com/logon.aspx?ReturnUrl=%2fDefault.aspx. Fees range from $25 per month (1 town) to $500 per year (all towns).**$$$**

Francestown Town ***Property, Taxation Records*** Access assessor data by subscription at http://data.avitarassociates.com/logon.aspx?ReturnUrl=%2fDefault.aspx. Fees range from $25 per month (1 town) to $500 per year (all towns).**$$$**

Goffstown Town ***Property, Taxation Records*** Access to the Assessors online database for free at http://data.visionappraisal.com/goffstownnh/DEFAULT.asp.

Greenfield Town ***Property, Taxation Records*** Access assessor data by subscription at http://data.avitarassociates.com/logon.aspx?ReturnUrl=%2fDefault.aspx. Fees range from $25 per month (1 town) to $500 per year (all towns).**$$$**

Greenville Town ***Property, Taxation Records*** Access assessor data by subscription at http://data.avitarassociates.com/logon.aspx?ReturnUrl=%2fDefault.aspx. Fees range from $25 per month (1 town) to $500 per year (all towns).**$$$**

Hancock Town ***Property, Taxation Records*** Access to expanded owner index sorted by owner name list for free form home page www.hancocknh.org/Tax/Tax.htm. Also, access assessor data by subscription at http://data.avitarassociates.com/logon.aspx?ReturnUrl=%2fDefault.aspx. Fees range from $25 per month (1 town) to $500 per year (all towns).**$$$**

Hillsborough Town ***Property, Taxation Records*** Access assessor data and property cards by subscription from private company at www.avitarofneinc.com/online.html.**$$$**

Hollis Town ***Property, Taxation Records*** Access assessor data free at http://data.visionappraisal.com/HollisNH/DEFAULT.asp.

Hudson Town ***Property, Taxation Records*** Access property data free at http://hudsonnh.patriotproperties.com.

Litchfield Town ***Property, Taxation Records*** Access assessor data by subscription at http://data.avitarassociates.com/logon.aspx?ReturnUrl=%2fDefault.aspx. Fees range from $25 per month (1 town) to $500 per year (all towns).**$$$**

Manchester City ***Property, Taxation Records*** Search Property data on the GIS-mapping and Tax Collector account sites free at http://208.82.76.123/pubgis/ but no name searching. Also, search city assessor database free at http://data.visionappraisal.com/ManchesterNH/DEFAULT.asp.

Mason Town ***Property, Taxation Records*** Access to tax maps free at www.mason-nh.org/. Click on "Documents Page". Scroll down to bottom of page for the maps.

Merrimack Town ***Property, Taxation Records*** Access assessor data by subscription at http://data.avitarassociates.com/logon.aspx?ReturnUrl=%2fDefault.aspx. Fees range from $25 per month (1 town) to $500 per year (all towns).**$$$**

Nashua City ***Property, Taxation Records*** Search the City Assessor database of property, GIS-mapping, sales histories for free at www.ci.nashua.nh.us/CityGovernment/Departments/Assessing/tabid/440/Default.aspx

New Boston Town ***Property, Taxation Records*** Access assessor data by subscription at http://data.avitarassociates.com/logon.aspx?ReturnUrl=%2fDefault.aspx. Fees range from $25 per month (1 town) to $500 per year (all towns).**$$$**

New Ipswich Town ***Property, Taxation Records*** Access assessor data by subscription at http://data.avitarassociates.com/logon.aspx?ReturnUrl=%2fDefault.aspx. Fees range from $25 per month (1 town) to $500 per year (all towns).**$$$**

Pelham Town ***Property, Taxation Records*** Search town assessor database at http://data.visionappraisal.com/PelhamNH/DEFAULT.asp. Free registration for full data.

Peterborough Town ***Property, Taxation Records*** Access to Assessor database for free at http://peterborough.ias-clt.com/parcel.list.php. Also, access to GIS/mapping free at www.townofpeterborough.com/index.asp?Type=B_BASIC&SEC={276B89D7-E39D-45DD-929E-87985F2BFAFF}.

Sharon Town ***Property, Taxation Records*** Access assessor data by subscription at http://data.avitarassociates.com/logon.aspx?ReturnUrl=%2fDefault.aspx. Fees range from $25 per month (1 town) to $500 per year (all towns).**$$$**

Temple Town ***Property, Taxation Records*** Access assessor data by subscription at http://data.avitarassociates.com/logon.aspx?ReturnUrl=%2fDefault.aspx. Fees range from $25 per month (1 town) to $500 per year (all towns).**$$$**

Weare Town ***Property, Taxation Records*** Access assessor data by subscription at http://data.avitarassociates.com/logon.aspx?ReturnUrl=%2fDefault.aspx. Fees range from $25 per month (1 town) to $500 per year (all towns).**$$$**

Windsor Town ***Property, Taxation Records*** Access assessor data by subscription at http://data.avitarassociates.com/logon.aspx?ReturnUrl=%2fDefault.aspx. Fees range from $25 per month (1 town) to $500 per year (all towns).**$$$**

Merrimack County ***Real Estate, Grantor/Grantee, Deed Records*** https://gov.propertyinfo.com/NH-Merrimack/ Access records on the county Registry of Deeds index for a fee at https://gov.propertyinfo.com/NH-Merrimack/. Must register. **$$$**

Allenstown Town ***Property, Taxation Records*** Access to Town Assessments for free at www.allenstown.org/townweb/BOS-MIN/Posted-Documents/Assessing/Assessments/ from 2000 to 2008.

Andover Town ***Property, Taxation Records*** Access assessor data by subscription at http://data.avitarassociates.com/logon.aspx?ReturnUrl=%2fDefault.aspx. Fees range from $25 per month (1 town) to $500 per year (all towns). Also, tax bill payment and invoices available at https://nhtaxkiosk.com/Default.aspx?KIOSKID=ANDOVER for free.**$$$**

Boscawen Town ***Real Estate, Grantor/Grantee, Deed Records*** Access records on the county Registry of Deeds index for free after registration; images require subscription at www.merrimackcounty.nh.us.landata.com. **$$$**
Property, Taxation Records Access assessor data by subscription at http://data.avitarassociates.com/logon.aspx?ReturnUrl=%2fDefault.aspx. Fees range from $25 per month (1 town) to $500 per year (all towns).**$$$**

Bow Town ***Property, Taxation Records*** Records on the town assessor database are free at http://data.visionappraisal.com/BowNH/DEFAULT.asp. Registration is required to view full data.**$$$**

Bradford Town ***Property, Taxation Records*** Access assessor data by subscription at http://data.avitarassociates.com/logon.aspx?ReturnUrl=%2fDefault.aspx. Fees range from $25 per month (1 town) to $500 per year (all towns).**$$$**

Canterbury Town ***Property, Taxation Records*** Access assessor data by subscription at http://data.avitarassociates.com/logon.aspx?ReturnUrl=%2fDefault.aspx. Fees range from $25 per month (1 town) to $500 per year (all towns).**$$$**

Chichester Town ***Property, Taxation Records*** Access assessor data by subscription at http://data.avitarassociates.com/logon.aspx?ReturnUrl=%2fDefault.aspx. Fees range from $25 per month (1 town) to $500 per year (all towns).**$$$**

Concord City ***Property, Taxation Records*** Records on the city assessor database are free at http://data.visionappraisal.com/ConcordNH/DEFAULT.asp.

Epsom Town ***Property, Taxation Records*** Access assessor data by subscription at http://data.avitarassociates.com/logon.aspx?ReturnUrl=%2fDefault.aspx. Fees range from $25 per month (1 town) to $500 per year (all towns).**$$$**

Franklin City ***Property, Taxation Records*** Access to tax maps free at www.franklinnh.org/Pages/FranklinNH_PlanZoning/TaxMapsDoc.

Hill Town ***Property, Taxation Records*** Access assessor data by subscription at http://data.avitarassociates.com/logon.aspx?ReturnUrl=%2fDefault.aspx. Fees range from $25 per month (1 town) to $500 per year (all towns).**$$$**

Hooksett Town ***Property, Taxation Records*** Access to assessor database records for free at http://data.visionappraisal.com/HooksettNH/DEFAULT.ASP.

Hopkinton Town ***Property, Taxation Records*** Access to GIS/mapping for free at www.caigisonline.com/hopkintonnh/.

Loudon Town ***Property, Taxation Records*** Access assessor data by subscription at http://data.avitarassociates.com/logon.aspx?ReturnUrl=%2fDefault.aspx. Fees range from $25 per month (1 town) to $500 per year (all towns).**$$$**

Northfield Town ***Property, Taxation Records*** Access assessor data by subscription at http://data.avitarassociates.com/logon.aspx?ReturnUrl=%2fDefault.aspx. Fees range from $25 per month (1 town) to $500 per year (all towns).**$$$**

Pembroke Town ***Property, Taxation Records*** Access assessor data free at http://data.visionappraisal.com/PembrokeNH/DEFAULT.asp.

Pittsfield Town ***Property, Taxation Records*** Access assessor data by subscription at http://data.avitarassociates.com/logon.aspx?ReturnUrl=%2fDefault.aspx. Fees range from $25 per month (1 town) to $500 per year (all towns).**$$$**

Salisbury Town ***Property, Taxation Records*** Access to town maps free at www.salisburynh.org/pages/planning_board/town_maps.html.

Webster Town ***Property, Taxation Records*** Access to property tax searches free at https://www.nhtaxkiosk.com/?KIOSKID=WEBSTER.

Wilmot Town ***Property, Taxation Records*** Access assessor data by subscription at http://data.avitarassociates.com/logon.aspx?ReturnUrl=%2fDefault.aspx. Fees range from $25 per month (1 town) to $500 per year (all towns).**$$$**

Rockingham County ***Recorded Documents Records*** www.nhdeeds.com/rockingham/RoHome.html Access to the register of deeds database is free at www.nhdeeds.com/rockingham/RoDisclaimer.html. Index goes back to 1629; search by book and page numbers.

Atkinson Town ***Property, Taxation Records*** Access assessor data by subscription at http://data.avitarassociates.com/logon.aspx?ReturnUrl=%2fDefault.aspx. Fees range from $25 per month (1 town) to $500 per year (all towns). Also, access to GIS/mapping free at www.town-atkinsonnh.com/assessor.html, at bottom of page.**$$$**

Auburn Town ***Property, Taxation Records*** Access assessor data by subscription at http://data.avitarassociates.com/logon.aspx?ReturnUrl=%2fDefault.aspx. Fees range from $25 per month (1 town) to $500 per year (all towns).**$$$**

Chester Town ***Property, Taxation Records*** Search town assessor database free at http://data.visionappraisal.com/ChesterNH/DEFAULT.asp.

Danville Town ***Property, Taxation Records*** Access assessor data by subscription at http://data.avitarassociates.com/logon.aspx?ReturnUrl=%2fDefault.aspx. Fees range from $25 per month (1 town) to $500 per year (all towns).**$$$**

Deerfield Town ***Property, Taxation Records*** Access assessor data by subscription at http://data.avitarassociates.com/logon.aspx?ReturnUrl=%2fDefault.aspx. Fees range from $25 per month (1 town) to $500 per year (all towns).**$$$**

Derry Town ***Property, Taxation Records*** Access Derry Town assessor database free at http://data.visionappraisal.com/DerryNH/.

East Kingston Town ***Property, Taxation Records*** Access assessor data by subscription at http://data.avitarassociates.com/logon.aspx?ReturnUrl=%2fDefault.aspx. Fees range from $25 per month (1 town) to $500 per year (all towns).**$$$**

Epping Town ***Property, Taxation Records*** Search the assessor database at http://data.visionappraisal.com/EppingNH/.

Exeter Town ***Property, Taxation Records*** Access assessor property data free at www.visionappraisal.com/databases/.

Fremont Town ***Property, Taxation Records*** Search town assessor database at http://data.visionappraisal.com/FremontNH/DEFAULT.asp.

Greenland Town ***Property, Taxation Records*** Access is via a private company at http://data.visionappraisal.com/GreenlandNH/DEFAULT.asp. Free registration is required to view full data.

Hampstead Town ***Property, Taxation Records*** Access to expanded owner index sorted by parcel location for free at www.hampsteadnh.us/Pages/HampsteadNH_Assessing/address.pdf. Email questions to Townclerk@hampsteadnh.us.

Hampton Town ***Property, Taxation Records*** Access town property assessor database free at www.visionappraisal.com/databases/.

Londonderry Town ***Property, Taxation Records*** Access property data free at http://londonderrynh.patriotproperties.com/default.asp. Also, access to GIS/mapping free at www.londonderrynh.org/Pages/LondonderryNH_Assessing/Maps/Index.

New Castle Town ***Property, Taxation Records*** Access assessor data by subscription at http://data.avitarassociates.com/logon.aspx?ReturnUrl=%2fDefault.aspx. Fees range from $25 per month (1 town) to $500 per year (all towns).**$$$**

Newfields Town ***Property, Taxation Records*** Access assessor data by subscription at http://data.avitarassociates.com/logon.aspx?ReturnUrl=%2fDefault.aspx. Fees range from $25 per month (1 town) to $500 per year (all towns).**$$$**

Newmarket Town ***Property, Taxation Records*** Access is free via a private company at http://data.visionappraisal.com/NewmarketNH/DEFAULT.asp.

Newton Town ***Property, Taxation Records*** Access assessor data by subscription at http://data.avitarassociates.com/logon.aspx?ReturnUrl=%2fDefault.aspx. Fees range from $25 per month (1 town) to $500 per year (all towns).**$$$**

North Hampton Town ***Property, Taxation Records*** Access to property assessor data is at http://data.visionappraisal.com/NorthHamptonNH/DEFAULT.asp.

Northwood Town ***Property, Taxation Records*** Access assessor data by subscription at http://data.avitarassociates.com/logon.aspx?ReturnUrl=%2fDefault.aspx. Fees range from $25 per month (1 town) to $500 per year (all towns).**$$$**

Nottingham Town ***Property, Taxation Records*** Access assessor data by subscription at http://data.avitarassociates.com/logon.aspx?ReturnUrl=%2fDefault.aspx. Fees range from $25 per month (1 town) to $500 per year (all towns).**$$$**

Plaistow Town ***Property, Taxation Records*** Property owner list free at www.plaistow.com/Pages/PlaistowNH_Assessor/index and click on Current Year Property Owner List. Also, mapping and property interface is being developed; check www.plaistow.com/Pages/PlaistowNH_WebDocs/maps

Portsmouth City ***Property, Taxation Records*** Search the Portsmouth Assessed Property Values database free at www.portsmouthnh.com/realestate//

Raymond Town ***Property, Taxation Records*** Search the town assessor database at http://data.visionappraisal.com/RaymondME/DEFAULT.asp. Free registration required to view full data.

Rye Town ***Property, Taxation Records*** Access is via a private company at http://data.visionappraisal.com/RyeNH/DEFAULT.asp. Free registration is required to view full data.

Salem Town ***Property, Taxation Records*** Records from the town database are free at http://data.visionappraisal.com/SalemNH/DEFAULT.asp.

Seabrook Town ***Property, Taxation Records*** Access to tax maps free at www.seabrooknh.org/Pages/SeabrookNH_Assessing/maps.

South Hampton Town ***Property, Taxation Records*** Access assessor data by subscription at http://data.avitarassociates.com/logon.aspx?ReturnUrl=%2fDefault.aspx. Fees range from $25 per month (1 town) to $500 per year (all towns).**$$$**

Stratham Town ***Property, Taxation Records*** Access assessor data by subscription at http://data.avitarassociates.com/logon.aspx?ReturnUrl=%2fDefault.aspx. Fees range from $25 per month (1 town) to $500 per year (all towns).**$$$**

Windham Town ***Property, Taxation Records*** Access lists of parcels, sales data and GIS info for free at www.windhamnewhampshire.com/updated/assessing.htm

Strafford County ***Real Estate, Grantor/Grantee, Deed, Mortgage, Lien Records*** www.nhdeeds.com/strafford/StHome.html Access to county register of deeds data is free at http://nhdeeds.com/strafford/StDisclaimer.html. Online records go back to 1921.

Barrington Town ***Property, Taxation Records*** Access to GIS/mapping free at www.caigisonline.com/BarringtonNH/Default.aspx?Splash=True. Also, access assessor data by subscription at http://data.avitarassociates.com/logon.aspx?ReturnUrl=%2fDefault.aspx. Fees range from $25 per month (1 town) to $500 per year (all towns).**$$$**

Durham Town ***Property, Taxation Records*** Assessor data is free at http://data.visionappraisal.com/DurhamNH/DEFAULT.asp.

Lee Town ***Property, Taxation Records*** Access assessor data by subscription at http://data.avitarassociates.com/logon.aspx?ReturnUrl=%2fDefault.aspx. Fees range from $25 per month (1 town) to $500 per year (all towns). Access to tax maps free at http://leenh.virtualtownhall.net/Pages/LeeNH_Assessor/maps.**$$$**

Madbury Town ***Property, Taxation Records*** Access assessor data by subscription at http://data.avitarassociates.com/logon.aspx?ReturnUrl=%2fDefault.aspx. Fees range from $25 per month (1 town) to $500 per year (all towns).**$$$**

Middleton Town ***Property, Taxation Records*** Access assessor data by subscription at http://data.avitarassociates.com/logon.aspx?ReturnUrl=%2fDefault.aspx. Fees range from $25 per month (1 town) to $500 per year (all towns).**$$$**

Milton Town ***Property, Taxation Records*** Access assessor data by subscription at http://data.avitarassociates.com/logon.aspx?ReturnUrl=%2fDefault.aspx. Fees range from $25 per month (1 town) to $500 per year (all towns).**$$$**

New Durham Town ***Property, Taxation Records*** Access assessor data free at http://data.visionappraisal.com/NewDurhamNH/DEFAULT.asp.

Rochester City ***Property, Taxation Records*** Access property data free at http://rochesternh.patriotproperties.com/default.asp.

Rollinsford Town ***Property, Taxation Records*** Access assessor data by subscription at http://data.avitarassociates.com/logon.aspx?ReturnUrl=%2fDefault.aspx. Fees range from $25 per month (1 town) to $500 per year (all towns).**$$$**

Strafford Town ***Property, Taxation Records*** Search property data free at http://data.visionappraisal.com/StraffordNH/. Also, access to the tax map index free at http://strafford.nh.gov/index.php?option=com_content&task=view&id=72&Itemid=1.

Sullivan County ***Recorded Documents Records*** www.nhdeeds.com/sullivan/SuHome.html Access to the county Register of Deeds database is free at www.nhdeeds.com/sullivan/SuDisclaimer.html.

Acworth Town ***Recorded Documents Records*** http://homepages.sover.net/~townoff/TownClerkInfo.htm Access to the county Register of Deeds database is free at www.nhdeeds.com/sullivan/SuHome.html.

Charlestown Town ***Real Estate, Grantor/Grantee, Deed, Lien Records*** Access to the county Register of Deeds database is free at www.nhdeeds.com/sullivan/start.htm.
Property, Taxation Records Search town assessor database free at http://data.visionappraisal.com/CharlestownNH/DEFAULT.asp.

Claremont City ***Real Estate, Grantor/Grantee, Deed, Lien Records*** www.claremontnh.com/ Access to the county Register of Deeds database is free at www.nhdeeds.com/sullivan/start.htm.

Cornish Town ***Real Estate, Grantor/Grantee, Deed, Lien Records*** www.cornishnh.net Access to the county Register of Deeds database is free at www.nhdeeds.com/sullivan/start.htm.

Croydon Town ***Real Estate, Grantor/Grantee, Deed, Lien Records*** Access to the county Register of Deeds database is free at www.nhdeeds.com/sullivan/start.htm.

Property, Taxation Records Access assessor data by subscription at http://data.avitarassociates.com/logon.aspx?ReturnUrl=%2fDefault.aspx. Fees range from $25 per month (1 town) to $500 per year (all towns).**$$$**

Goshen Town ***Real Estate, Grantor/Grantee, Deed, Lien Records*** www.goshennh.org/townclerk.html Access to the county Register of Deeds database is free at www.nhdeeds.com/sullivan/start.htm.

Grantham Town ***Recorded Documents Records*** http://granthamnh.net Access to the county Register of Deeds database is free at www.nhdeeds.com/sullivan/start.htm.

Property, Taxation Records Search town assessor database free at http://data.visionappraisal.com/GranthamNH/DEFAULT.asp.

Langdon Town ***Real Estate, Grantor/Grantee, Deed, Lien Records*** http://langdonnh.org/town_clerk.htm Access to the county Register of Deeds database is free at www.nhdeeds.com/sullivan/start.htm.

Lempster Town ***Real Estate, Grantor/Grantee, Deed, Lien Records*** www.lempsternh.org Access to the county Register of Deeds database is free at www.nhdeeds.com/sullivan/start.htm.

Property, Taxation Records Access assessor data by subscription at http://data.avitarassociates.com/logon.aspx?ReturnUrl=%2fDefault.aspx. Fees range from $25 per month (1 town) to $500 per year (all towns).**$$$**

Newport Town ***Real Estate, Grantor/Grantee, Deed, Lien Records*** www.newportnh.net/ Access to the county Register of Deeds database is free at www.nhdeeds.com/sullivan/start.htm.

Property, Taxation Records Access assessor data by subscription at http://data.avitarassociates.com/logon.aspx?ReturnUrl=%2fDefault.aspx. Fees range from $25 per month (1 town) to $500 per year (all towns).**$$$**

Plainfield Town ***Real Estate, Grantor/Grantee, Deed, Lien Records*** www.plainfieldnh.org Access to the county Register of Deeds database is free at www.nhdeeds.com/sullivan/start.htm.

Springfield Town ***Real Estate, Grantor/Grantee, Deed, Lien Records*** www.springfieldnh.net Access to the county Register of Deeds database is free at www.nhdeeds.com/sullivan/start.htm.

Property, Taxation Records Access assessor data by subscription at http://data.avitarassociates.com/logon.aspx?ReturnUrl=%2fDefault.aspx. Fees range from $25 per month (1 town) to $500 per year (all towns).**$$$**

Sunapee Town ***Real Estate, Grantor/Grantee, Deed, Lien Records*** www.town.sunapee.nh.us/Pages/index Access to the county Register of Deeds database is free at www.nhdeeds.com/sullivan/start.htm.

Unity Town ***Real Estate, Grantor/Grantee, Deed, Lien Records*** Access to the county Register of Deeds database is free at www.nhdeeds.com/sullivan/start.htm.

Washington Town ***Real Estate, Grantor/Grantee, Deed, Lien Records*** www.washingtonnh.org Access to the county Register of Deeds database is free at www.nhdeeds.com/sullivan/start.htm.

Property, Taxation Records Access assessor data by subscription at http://data.avitarassociates.com/logon.aspx?ReturnUrl=%2fDefault.aspx. Fees range from $25 per month (1 town) to $500 per year (all towns).**$$$**

New Jersey

Capital: Trenton
Mercer County
Time Zone: EST
Population: 8,864,590
# of Counties: 21

Useful State Links

Website: www.state.nj.us
Governor: www.state.nj.us/governor
Attorney General: www.state.nj.us/lps
State Archives: www.state.nj.us/state/darm/index.html
State Statutes and Codes: www.njleg.state.nj.us
Legislative Bill Search: www.njleg.state.nj.us
Bill Monitoring: www.njleg.state.nj.us/bills/BillsSubscriptionLogin.asp
Unclaimed Funds: http://webdb.state.nj.us/treasury/taxation/unclaimsrch.htm

State Public Record Agencies

Sexual Offender Registry

Division of State Police, Sexual Offender Registry, www.njsp.org Data can be searched online at the website. Click on NJ Sex Offender Registry. There are a variety of searches available including geographic, individual, advanced, and fugitives,

Incarceration Records

New Jersey Department of Corrections, ATTN: Correspondence Unit, http://njdoc.gov/pages/index.shtml Extensive search capabilities are offered from the website; click on "Offender Search Engine" or visit https://www6.state.nj.us/DOC_Inmate/inmatefinder?i=I. Offenders on Work Release, Furlough, or in a Halfway House are not necessarily reflected as such in their profile. Also, search offenders and inmates on a private site free at https://www.vinelink.com/vinelink/siteInfoAction.do?siteId=29017.

Corporation, LLC, LP, Fictitious Name

Division of Revenue, Corporate Records, www.nj.gov/treasury/revenue/ A number of different searches are offered at www.nj.gov/treasury/revenue/. Available searches include trademarks and trade names. There is no fee to browse the site to locate a name; however fees are involved for copies or status reports. Reports are mailed. Also, search securities agency enforcement actions at www.njsecurities.gov/bosdisc.htm. (This is provided by a different agency.) **$$$**

Trademarks/Servicemarks

Department of Treasury, Trademark Division, www.nj.gov/treasury/revenue/ Search trademarks and trade names at www.nj.gov/treasury/revenue/. Search by Status Report of view Lists.

Uniform Commercial Code

NJ Dept of Revenue, UCC Unit, www.nj.gov/treasury/revenue/ The site at https://www.njportal.com/UCC/ gives several search options for UCC records, including certified and non-certified. Same fees as above apply, but add $5.00 for a portal for searches or $.20 per page for copies. **$$$** *Other Options:* Bulk record downloads may also be purchased at https://www.njportal.com/UCC/.

Vital Records

Department of Health & Senior Svcs, Bureau of Vital Statistics, www.state.nj.us/health/vital/index.shtml Order online from www.state.nj.us/health/vital/expedited. Pay with credit card, there is additional processing fee of $5, online authentication fee of $5 (non-refundable) and $30 shipping fee via UPS carrier. **$$$**

Divorce Records

Clerk of Superior Court, Records Center, www.judiciary.state.nj.us Access is available from a statewide system at www.judiciary.state.nj.us/superior/eap_main.htm. Case information available includes a list of documents filed, orders entered, proceedings scheduled, motion dispositions, list of litigants and their status (e.g., active, defaulted, settled), and associated attorneys. Subscribers can look up information by docket number, judgment number or party name. **$$$**

Workers' Compensation Records

Labor Department, Division of Workers Compensation, http://lwd.state.nj.us/labor/wc/wc_index.html COURTS on-line is a secure Internet website that provides authorized subscribers access to the Division's database for review of cases in which they are a party. Possible subscribers include: Insurance Carrier/Law Firms; Court Reporting Firms; and WC Forensic Experts (Physicians). See http://lwd.dol.state.nj.us/labor/wc/egov/col/courts2_index.html. **$$$**

Driver Records

Motor Vehicle Commission, Driver History Abstract Unit, www.state.nj.us/mvc/ The commercial access system is called CAIR. Visit www.state.nj.us/mvcbiz/Records/CAIR.htm. The system is only available to those with a permissible use such as insurance companies, bus and truck companies, and highway/parking authorities. Both batch (SFT) and individual modes are offered. Records can only be accessed by using a driver license number, which will provide a five-year driver history abstract (there is no name only searching offered). Account holders may also obtain a License Status check for $2.00. NJ drivers may order their own record online at www.state.nj.us/mvc/Licenses/driver_history_page.htm. A user account must be opened first. The fee is $15.00 per record plus a $.75 service fee per record. **$$$**

Vehicle, Vessel Ownership & Registration

Motor Vehicle Commission, Office of Communication, www.state.nj.us/mvc/ Online access is available for insurance companies, bus and truck companies, highway/parking authorities, and approved vendors. Vehicle record inquiries can only be made by submitting a VIN or plate number - not by name. The VIN number will produce the mileage, mileage status, owner/lien holder names and addresses and lessee information if the vehicle is leased. The license plate number will provide the owner's name, address, vehicle information, leased vehicle status. If using the Ownership History option (only available to insurance companies), the New Jersey VIN data will also be provided. The fee for a registration or title record including ownership history is $12.00 per record. For details visit www.state.nj.us/mvcbiz/Records/CAIR.htm. **$$$**

Accident Reports

New Jersey State Police, CJRB - Traffic, www.njsp.org Online access to accidents reports is available via a state designated vendor - www.buycrash.com. The site does not indicate the fee, but it is probably similar to the fee the state charges. **$$$**

Voter Registration, Contributions. PACS, Lobbyists

Dept of State, Division of Elections, http://nj.gov/state/elections/index.html Search contributions to candidates and PACs at www.elec.state.nj.us/publicinformation/searchdatabase.htm, an advanced search is also offered at www.elec.state.nj.us/ELECReport/AdvancedSearch.aspx. *Other Options:* Since September 2006, bulk purchase is of voter registration records are available for political purposes.

GED Certificates

GED Testing Program, NJ Dept. of Education, www.state.nj.us/education/students/ged/ Through the E-Transcripts process examinees can access their records at any time from the web as well as give permission to third parties and employers to verify a transcript - but only with an Access Code provided by the NJ DOE. GED graduates since April 1, 2007 can find their access code at the bottom center of their diplomas. Graduates prior to April 1, 2007 can obtain an access code by submitting a written request to the Department of Education's Office of GED Testing, along with proof of identity, or may request a code in person with proper ID.

Occupational Licensing Boards

Accountant Sponsor .... www.state.nj.us/lps/ca/accountancy/cesponsor.pdf
Accountant-CPA/Firm/Municipal .... https://newjersey.mylicense.com/verification/Search.aspx?facility=Y
Acupuncturist .... https://newjersey.mylicense.com/verification/Search.aspx?facility=Y
Alcohol/Drug Counselor .... https://newjersey.mylicense.com/verification/Search.aspx?facility=Y
Animal Control Officer .... www.state.nj.us/health/cd/izdp/revoked.shtml
Animal Facility .... www.state.nj.us/health/animalwelfare/lic_facilities.shtml

Appraiser, Real Estate/Gen/Residential ...... https://newjersey.mylicense.com/verification/Search.aspx?facility=Y
Appraiser/Apprentice, Real Estate .... https://newjersey.mylicense.com/verification/Search.aspx?facility=Y
Architect .... https://newjersey.mylicense.com/verification/Search.aspx?facility=Y
Athletic Trainer .... https://newjersey.mylicense.com/verification/Search.aspx?facility=N
Attorney www.judiciary.state.nj.us/cpf/ineliglist01242011.pdf
Audiologist .... https://newjersey.mylicense.com/verification/Search.aspx?facility=Y
Barber/Shop .... https://newjersey.mylicense.com/verification/Search.aspx?facility=Y
Candidate Report .... www.elec.state.nj.us/ELECReport/StandardSearch.aspx
Cemetery/Salesperson .... https://newjersey.mylicense.com/verification/Search.aspx?facility=Y
Certificate of Authorization .... https://newjersey.mylicense.com/verification/Search.aspx?facility=Y
Charity .... www.njconsumeraffairs.gov/charity/chardir.htm
Check Casher/Seller .... https://www16.state.nj.us/DOBI_LicSearch/bnkSearch.jsp
Chiropractor .... https://newjersey.mylicense.com/verification/
Contributor, Political .... www.elec.state.nj.us/ELECReport/contribStandardSearch.aspx
Cosmetologist/Hairstylist/Beautician/Shop .. https://newjersey.mylicense.com/verification/Search.aspx?facility=Y
Counselor, Professional .... https://newjersey.mylicense.com/verification/Search.aspx?facility=Y
Court Reporter .... https://newjersey.mylicense.com/verification/Search.aspx?facility=Y
Debt Adjuster .... https://www16.state.nj.us/DOBI_LicSearch/bnkSearch.jsp
Dental Assistant/Hygienist .... https://newjersey.mylicense.com/verification/Search.aspx?facility=Y
Dentist .... https://newjersey.mylicense.com/verification/Search.aspx?facility=Y
Electrical Contractor .... https://newjersey.mylicense.com/verification/Search.aspx?facility=Y
Embalmer .... https://newjersey.mylicense.com/verification/Search.aspx?facility=Y
Emergency Medical Svc Provider .... www.state.nj.us/health/ems/services.shtml
Employment Agency .... www.state.nj.us/lps/ca/ocp/agency.pdf
Engineer/Survey Company .... https://newjersey.mylicense.com/verification/Search.aspx?facility=Y
Funeral Practitioner/Home .... https://newjersey.mylicense.com/verification/Search.aspx?facility=Y
Health Care Service Agency .... www.state.nj.us/lps/ca/ocp/agency.pdf
Health Spa .... https://newjersey.mylicense.com/verification/Search.aspx?facility=Y
Hearing Aid Dispenser/Fitter .... https://newjersey.mylicense.com/verification/Search.aspx?facility=Y
Home Health Aide .... https://newjersey.mylicense.com/verification/
Home Inspector .... www.njconsumeraffairs.gov/hiac/hi_services.htm
Home Repair Contractor/Seller .... https://www16.state.nj.us/DOBI_LicSearch/bnkSearch.jsp
Insurance Agent/Public Adjuster .... https://www16.state.nj.us/DOBI_LicSearch/insSearch.jsp
Insurance Carrier .... www.state.nj.us/dobi/data/inscomp.htm
Interior Design .... https://newjersey.mylicense.com/verification/Search.aspx?facility=Y
Lab Director, Bio-Analytical .... https://newjersey.mylicense.com/verification/Search.aspx?facility=N
Landfill .... www.nj.gov/dep/dshw/lrm/landfill.htm
Landscape Architect .... https://newjersey.mylicense.com/verification/Search.aspx?facility=Y
Lender, Consumer .... https://www16.state.nj.us/DOBI_LicSearch/bnkSearch.jsp
Lobbyist .... www.elec.state.nj.us/PublicInformation/GAA_Annual.htm
Manicurist/Manicurist Shop .... https://newjersey.mylicense.com/verification/Search.aspx?facility=Y
Marriage/Family Counselor .... https://newjersey.mylicense.com/verification/Search.aspx?facility=Y
Medical Waste Generator .... www.nj.gov/dep/dshw/hwr/medwaste.htm
Midwife .... https://newjersey.mylicense.com/verification/Search.aspx?facility=N
Modeling & Talent Agency .... www.state.nj.us/lps/ca/ocp/agency.pdf
Money Transmitter .... https://www16.state.nj.us/DOBI_LicSearch/bnkSearch.jsp
Mortgage (2nd) Lender .... https://www16.state.nj.us/DOBI_LicSearch/bnkSearch.jsp
Mortician .... https://newjersey.mylicense.com/verification/Search.aspx?facility=Y
Mover .... https://newjersey.mylicense.com/verification/
Nuclear Medicine Technologist .... http://datamine2.state.nj.us/DEP_OPRA/OpraMain/categories?category=Radiologic%20Technologists
Nurse-Advance Practice .... https://newjersey.mylicense.com/verification/
Nurse-LPN/RN .... https://newjersey.mylicense.com/verification/
Nursing Home Administrator .... https://www.asisvcs.com/services/registry/search_generic.asp?CPCat=0231STATEREG
Nursing Registry Svc .... www.state.nj.us/lps/ca/ocp/agency.pdf
Occupational Therapist/Assistant .... https://newjersey.mylicense.com/verification/Search.aspx?facility=N

Optician/Ophthalmic Technician/Dispenser. https://newjersey.mylicense.com/verification/Search.aspx?facility=Y
Optometrist .... https://newjersey.mylicense.com/verification/Search.aspx?facility=Y
Orthopedist .... https://newjersey.mylicense.com/verification/Search.aspx?facility=N
Orthotist/Prosthetist .... https://newjersey.mylicense.com/verification/Search.aspx?facility=Y
Pawnbroker .... https://www16.state.nj.us/DOBI_LicSearch/bnkSearch.jsp
Pest Management (IPM) School .... www.nj.gov/dep/enforcement/pcp/ipm-contacts.htm
Pharmacist/Pharmacy .... https://newjersey.mylicense.com/verification/Search.aspx?facility=Y
Physical Therapist/Assistant .... https://newjersey.mylicense.com/verification/Search.aspx?facility=Y
Physician/Medical Doctor/Assistant .... https://newjersey.mylicense.com/verification/Search.aspx?facility=N
Planner, Professional .... https://newjersey.mylicense.com/verification/Search.aspx?facility=Y
Plumber/Master Plumber .... https://newjersey.mylicense.com/verification/Search.aspx?facility=Y
Podiatrist .... https://newjersey.mylicense.com/verification/Search.aspx?facility=N
Psychologist .... https://newjersey.mylicense.com/verification/Search.aspx?facility=Y
Radiation Machine Registration .... http://datamine2.state.nj.us/DEP_OPRA/OpraMain/categories?category=Radiologic%20Technologists
Radiation Technologist/Therapist .... http://datamine2.state.nj.us/DEP_OPRA/OpraMain/categories?category=Radiologic%20Technologists
Radon Tester/Businesses www.nj.gov/dep/rpp/radon/CERTMES2.HTM
Real Estate Agent/Broker/Seller .... https://www16.state.nj.us/DOBI_LicSearch/recSearch.jsp
Real Estate School/ Instructor .... www.state.nj.us/cgi-bin/dobi/urs/schlist.pl
Recycle Coordinator .... www.nj.gov/dep/dshw/
Recycling Facility .... www.nj.gov/dep/dshw/lrm/classbsch.htm
Respiratory Therapist .... https://newjersey.mylicense.com/verification/Search.aspx?facility=Y
Security Agencies, Licensed .... www.njsp.org/info/pdf/pdet/010312_actagency.pdf
Skin Care Specialist/Shop .... https://newjersey.mylicense.com/verification/Search.aspx?facility=Y
Social Worker .... https://newjersey.mylicense.com/verification/Search.aspx?facility=Y
Speech-Language Pathologist .... https://newjersey.mylicense.com/verification/Search.aspx?facility=Y
Surveyor, Land .... https://newjersey.mylicense.com/verification/Search.aspx?facility=Y
Temporary Help Agency .... www.state.nj.us/lps/ca/ocp/agency.pdf
Tree Expert .... www.state.nj.us/dep/parksandforests/forest/community/cte.html
Veterinarian .... https://newjersey.mylicense.com/verification/Search.aspx?facility=Y
Viatical Settlement Broker .... https://www16.state.nj.us/DOBI_LicSearch/insSearch.jsp
Warehouseman .... https://newjersey.mylicense.com/verification/
Waste Company .... www.nj.gov/dep/dshw/
X-Ray Equipment .... http://datamine2.state.nj.us/DEP_OPRA/OpraMain/categories?category=Radiologic%20Technologists

State and Local Courts

State Court Structure: Each **Superior Court** has 3 divisions; Civil, Criminal, and Family. Search requests should be addressed separately to each division. Criminal cases are those in which a defendant stands accused of a serious crime, such as assault, theft, robbery, fraud, or murder. These indictable crimes consist of 4th, 3rd, 2nd and 1st Degree charges. Civil cases in which the amount in controversy exceeds $15,000 are heard in the Civil Division of Superior Court.

Cases in which the amounts in controversy are between $3,000 and $15,000 are heard in the Special Civil Part of the Civil Division. Those in which the amounts in controversy are less than $3,000 also are heard in the Special Civil Part and are known as Small Claims cases.

Civil cases in which monetary damages are not being sought are heard in the General Equity Division of Superior Court. General Equity judges handle non-jury cases such as those involving trade secrets, labor matters, foreclosures and other disputes in which court relief, often in the form of restraining orders, is sought on an emergency basis.

Family related cases, such as those involving divorce, domestic violence, juvenile delinquency, child support, foster-care placements and termination of parental rights, are heard by the Family Division.

Probate can be handled by either the **Surrogates' Courts** or by the Chancery Division, Probate Part of the Superior Court.

More About Criminal Records: New Jersey is unique. NJ courts use the term "indictable offense" instead of felony. These offenses are called as such because the accused has the right to have his case presented to a grand jury. These matters are heard in the Superior Court and if a trial ensues, it is trial by jury. Less serious offenses are called "disorderly persons offenses." These offenses are similar to misdemeanors and encompass a wide array of lower level criminal offenses such as shoplifting (if under $200), disorderly conduct, simple assault, etc.

Appellate Courts: Opinions from the Supreme or Appellate Court are viewable from www.judiciary.state.nj.us – click on *Opinions*.

Statewide Court Online Access: All courts participate in the systems described below.

- A limited information system of criminal records - PROMIS/Gavel - has public access at https://njcourts.judiciary.state.nj.us/web10/ExternalPGPA/. This is a supplemental search that does not contain all criminal case files, espcially those from the lower courts. Note there is a strong disclaimer - the data is for informational purposes only. A study by a NJ Private Investigator showed excessive data lacking.
- A free statewide access service (ACMS Public Access) to civil cases is available at http://njcourts.judiciary.state.nj.us/web1/ACMSPA/. One may search by name or docket number. If a name search is performed, it is name only - no personal identifiers are shown except an address on docket. There is a strong disclaimer that states "The Judiciary provides this information as a public service and makes no warranties, either expressed or implied, regarding accuracy, reliability, currency, completeness, or suitability for any particular purpose."
- Search civil judgments and liens at http://njcourts.judiciary.state.nj.us/web11/JudgmentWeb/jsp/judgmentCaptcha.faces.
- Also, the agency offers a much more robust program, called the Electronic Access Program, to civil case docket and summary information from four separate state information systems. Included are the Automated Case Management Systems (ACMS) (mentioned above), the Civil Judgment and Order Docket, the Family Automated Case Tracking System (FACTS), and the Automated Traffic System (ATS). The fee is $1.00 per minute. Subscribers receive only a screen view; the ability to perform downloads or data extraction (screen-scraping) is not offered. This information is in 'real-time'. When a new case or document is entered by court personnel, the information is immediately available to the public for viewing. For more information and enrollment forms see the page at www.judiciary.state.nj.us/superior/eap_main.htm.
- The Judiciary's civil motion calendar and schedule is searchable at www.judiciary.state.nj.us/calendars.htm. The database includes all Superior Court Motion calendars for the Civil Division (Law-Civil Part, Special Civil Part and Chancery-General Equity), and proceeding information for a six-week period (two weeks prior to the current date and four weeks following the current date).

Note: No individual New Jersey courts offer online access, other than as described above.

Recorders, Assessors, and Other Sites of Note

Recording Office Organization: 21 counties, 21 recording offices. The recording officer title varies depending upon the county, either the Register of Deeds or the County Clerk. The Clerk of Circuit Court records the equivalent of some state's tax liens. All federal tax liens are filed with the County Clerk/Register of Deeds and are indexed separately from all other liens. State tax liens comprise two categories - certificates of debt are filed with the Clerk of Superior Court (some, called docketed judgments are filed specifically with the Trenton court), and warrants of execution are filed with the County Clerk/Register of Deeds.

Statewide or Multi-Jurisdiction Access: There is no statewide access to recorded documents from the government sites. A few counties offer public searching through their official websites, but much of New Jersey is serviced by private vendors.

Two vendors provide access to property and assessor records for all counties:

- A statewide database of property tax records can be accessed at http://taxrecords.com. This is a free index search, but fees involved for deeper searches. See http://imac.taxrecords.com/login/signup.html?url=ww w.taxrecords.com.
- Access property assessment data free at http://tax1.co.monmouth.nj.us/cgi-bin/prc6.cgi?menu=index&ms_user=glou&passwd=. This is a backdoor and may eventually go away.

County Sites Other Than the Two Vendors Mentioned Above

Atlantic County ***Recorded Documents*** www.atlanticcountyclerk.org Access to public record index for free at www.atlanticcountyclerk.org/onlinesearch.htm or http://24.246.110.8/or_web1/disclaim.asp. Note the online system may not be as accurate and current as indices at the courthouse which allows for more name variations or may not include maps, tax sales, constr. liens, Lis Pendens, or surrogate records.

Burlington County ***Recorded Documents*** www.co.burlington.nj.us/Pages/ViewDepartment.aspx?did=2 Access to recorded property records for free at http://press.co.burlington.nj.us/PRESS/Index.aspx.

Cape May County ***Recorded Documents*** www.capemaycountygov.net/Cit-e-Access/webpage.cfm?TID=5&TPID=417 Property records for Cape May county are free to view online at http://50.195.106.200/ALIS/WW400R.PGM. To print, registration and login is required. $1.00 per page copy and/or $10.00 certification fees apply to documents. Online documents go back to 1996, images to 2000. For assistance, telephone 609-465-1010. **$$$**

Gloucester County ***Recorded Documents*** www.co.gloucester.nj.us/depts/c/cclerk/default.asp Access recording office land records free for individual verification at http://i2e.uslandrecords.com/Gloucester_PreLive/(X(1)S(t2r1yyaemstpi2znwsyjamu1))/Default.aspx?AspxAutoDetectCookieSupport=1

Mercer County ***Recorded Documents*** http://nj.gov/counties/mercer/officials/clerk/ Also, access to property searches free at https://records.mercercounty.org/RecordsNG_Search/. Non registered user gets view of full index, view of 1st 2 pages. Registered user get fill index, view of all pages of doc, password required, fee based subscription. **$$$**

Middlesex County ***Recorded Documents*** www.co.middlesex.nj.us/countyclerk/index.asp Access the county public access system index free at https://mcrecords.co.middlesex.nj.us/records/index.jsp. Printing clean copies of document images is a paid service. **$$$**

Monmouth County ***Recorded Documents*** http://co.monmouth.nj.us/page.aspx?ID=125 Access county clerk deed and mortgage data free at http://oprs.co.monmouth.nj.us/Oprs/clerk/ClerkHome.aspx?op=basic. Deeds-1876 to present; Most other documents 1996 to present. Full access to Recorder of Deeds is by subscription at www.landex.com/remote/. Index goes back to 1930; images to 10/1996. **$$$**
Property, Taxation Records Search GIS Taxview free at http://oprs.co.monmouth.nj.us/oprs/External.aspx?iId=7.

Morris County ***Recorded Documents*** www.morriscountyclerk.org/ Access the county clerk's records free at http://mcclerkweb.co.morris.nj.us/or_wb1/or_sch_1.asp or at http://63.119.46.22/or_wb1/default.asp.
Property, Taxation Records Search assessor/treasurer property tax data free at http://mcweb1.co.morris.nj.us/TaxBoard/SearchTR.jsp.

Ocean County ***Recorded Documents*** www.oceancountyclerk.com Land records on the County Clerk database are free at www.oceancountyclerk.com/search.htm. Search by parties, document or instrument type. This online system includes maps, tax sales, construction liens and Lis Pendens. Also, another direct site is at http://sng.co.ocean.nj.us/searchapplication/.

Passaic County ***Recorded Documents*** www.passaiccountynj.org/Index.aspx?NID=131 The county recording index online is at http://records.passaiccountynj.org/press/indexPassaic.aspx. **$$$**

Somerset County ***Recorded Documents*** www.co.somerset.nj.us/clerk/index.htm Access to the County Clerk's recordings database is free at http://64.206.95.6/. Free index of deeds, mortgages, federal liens, trade names, assignments, releases, discharges-perm indexes; images from 1/1/77 to present. UCCs are not included. All maps from 1800. Also, see online notes in state summary at beginning of section.
Property, Taxation Records The agency sends people to this vendor: www.vitalgov.net/public.asp. Also, see online notes in state summary.

Sussex County ***Recorded Documents*** www.sussexcountyclerk.com Access recorder records back to 1/1964 free at http://sussex.landrecordsonline.com/. Also, see online notes in state summary at beginning of section.

Union County ***Recorded Documents*** http://ucnj.org/government/county-clerk/ Search recorded real estate related documents at https://clerk.ucnj.org/UCPA/DocIndex. Index goes from 6/1977 to present. Images from 1/1986 to present.

Reminder:

Two vendors provide access to property and assessor records for all counties.

A statewide database of property tax records can be accessed at http://taxrecords.com. This is a free index search, but fees involved for deeper searches. See http://imac.taxrecords.com/login/signup.html?url=ww w.taxrecords.com.

Access property assessment data free at http://tax1.co.monmouth.nj.us/cgi-bin/prc6.cgi?menu=index&ms_user=glou&passwd=. This is a backdoor and may eventually go away.

New Mexico

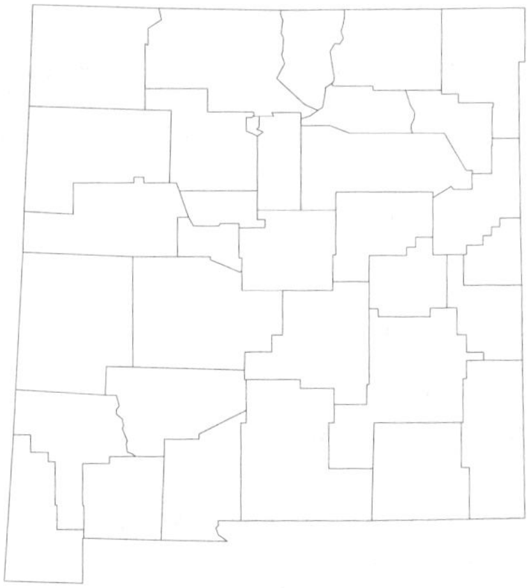

Capital: Santa Fe
Santa Fe County
Time Zone: MST
Population: 2,085,538
# of Counties: 33

Useful State Links

Website: www.newmexico.gov/
Governor: www.governor.state.nm.us
Attorney General: www.nmag.gov/
State Archives: www.nmcpr.state.nm.us
State Statutes and Codes: www.conwaygreene.com/NewMexico.htm
Legislative Bill Search: http://nmlegis.gov/lcs/BillFinder.aspx
Unclaimed Funds: www.tax.newmexico.gov/Online-Services/Pages/Unclaimed-Property-Search.aspx

State Public Record Agencies

Sexual Offender Registry

Department of Public Safety, Records Bureau, www.nmsexoffender.dps.state.nm.us The website offers a variety of search methods including by name, county, city, and ZIP Code. The site also offers a complete state list, also an absconder list.

Incarceration Records

New Mexico Corrections Department, Records Bureau, http://corrections.state.nm.us To search at the website, you must first click on Offender Information, then on Offender Search.

Corporation, LLC Records

New Mexico Public Regulation Commission, Corporations Bureau, www.nmprc.state.nm.us/cb.htm There is no charge to view records at the Internet site, http://web.prc.newmexico.gov/Corplookup/(S(iakcfnrpnogl5tcvks4j1wo4))/ CorpSearch. aspx. Records can be searched by company name or by director name.

Uniform Commercial Code

UCC Division, Secretary of State, www.sos.state.nm.us/Business_Services/UCC_Overview.aspx The website https://secure.sos.state.nm.us/UCC/soskb/SearchStandardRA9.asp permits searching by name, organization, or file number. The site also provides the ability to order copies of filings, including via email. *Other Options:* Microfilm and images (from 7/99) on disk may be purchased.

Birth Certificates

Department of Health, Bureau of Vital Records, http://vitalrecordsnm.org/ Records can be ordered at www.vitalrecordsnm.org/vitalrecords.shtml via a state designated vendor. This is considered expedited service. **$$$**

Death Records

Department of Health, Bureau of Vital Records, www.health.state.nm.us Records can be ordered at www.vitalrecordsnm.org/vitalrecords.shtml via a state designated vendor. This is considered expedited service. This is also a look-up at www.usgwarchives.net/nm/deaths.htm for deaths 1899 to 1940. **$$$**

Driver Records

Motor Vehicle Division, Driver Services Bureau, www.mvd.newmexico.gov/ The New Mexico MVD contracts with New Mexico Interactive to provide all electronic media requests of driver license histories, title, registration and lien searches. Records are available to subscribers that meet federal and state standards. The annual subscription fee is $75 for up to 10 users. The fee for a driving record is $6.50, a non-hit result incurs a fee. Both single inquiry and batch modes are available for driving records. Monthly billing is provided. For more information call New Mexico Interactive at 877-660-3468 or visit the Online Services section at www.mvd.newmexico.gov/Online-Services/subscriber. Visit www.nmcourts.gov/dwi.html for a free DUI Offender History search. This is not an official record and may not contain all court records. Nm drivers may order their own record online for $6.63 form the home page above. **$$$** *Other Options:* New Mexico Interactive provides a driver monitoring program for approved subscribers. A monthly fee per driver is charged and if activity occurs, then a driving record is automatically ordered. Call 877-660-3468 for details.

Vehicle, Vessel Ownership & Registration

Motor Vehicle Division, Vehicle Services Bureau, www.mvd.newmexico.gov/ The New Mexico MVD contracts with New Mexico Interactive to provide all electronic media requests of title, registration and lien searches, as well as driving records. Records are available to subscribers that meet federal and state standards. The annual subscription fee is $75 for up to 10 users. The fee is $4.95 per record. Records must be accessed by VIN or plate number - no name searching is provided. Monthly billing is provided. For more information call New Mexico Interactive at 877-660-3468 or visit the Online Services section at www.mvd.newmexico.gov/Online-Services/subscriber-services.html#motor. **$$$** *Other Options:* Bulk requests for vehicle or ownership information must be approved by the Director's office. Once a sale is made, further resale is prohibited.

Voter Registration, Campaign Finance, PACs, Lobbyists

Secretary of State, Bureau of Elections, www.sos.state.nm.us/Elections_Data/ A registrant verification is provided at https://voterview.state.nm.us/VoterView/RegistrantSearch.do. Results give zip code of registrant and polling place. View public information on PACS and campaign finance at https://cfis.state.nm.us/media/Reports.aspx.

Occupational Licensing Boards

Accountant-CPA	http://rldverification.rld.state.nm.us/Verification/
Acupuncturist	www.rld.state.nm.us/boards/Look_Up_A_License.aspx
Alcohol Server	http://rldverification.rld.state.nm.us/Verification/
Announcer, Athletic Event/Ring	http://rldverification.rld.state.nm.us/Verification/
Architect	http://nmbea.org/People/Architect_Roster/index.html
Armored Car Company	www.rld.state.nm.us/boards/Look_Up_A_License.aspx
Art Therapist	www.rld.state.nm.us/boards/Look_Up_A_License.aspx
Athletic Promoter/Matchmaker	http://rldverification.rld.state.nm.us/Verification/
Athletic Trainer	www.rld.state.nm.us/boards/Look_Up_A_License.aspx
Audiologist	www.rld.state.nm.us/boards/Look_Up_A_License.aspx
Bank	http://rldverification.rld.state.nm.us/Verification/Search.aspx?facility=Y
Barber	www.rld.state.nm.us/boards/Look_Up_A_License.aspx
Bingo/Raffle, Non-profit	www.nmgcb.org/bingoandraffle/BINGOCONTACTS.pdf
Boiler Operator Journeyman	http://public.psiexams.com/index_login.jsp
Booking Agent	http://rldverification.rld.state.nm.us/Verification/
Boxer/Manager/Judge/Timekeeper	http://rldverification.rld.state.nm.us/Verification/
Cemetery, Endow'd/Perpet'l Care	http://rldverification.rld.state.nm.us/Verification/Search.aspx?facility=Y
Certified Court Reporter	www.nmcra.com/Default.aspx?pageId=376021
Chiropractor	www.rld.state.nm.us/boards/Look_Up_A_License.aspx
Clinical Nurse Specialist	https://www.bon.state.nm.us/lookup.html
Collection Agency/Manager	http://rldverification.rld.state.nm.us/Verification/Search.aspx?facility=Y
Consumer Credit Grantor/Loaner	http://rldverification.rld.state.nm.us/Verification/Search.aspx?facility=Y
Contractor	www.public.psiexams.com/search.jsp
Cosmetologist	www.rld.state.nm.us/boards/Look_Up_A_License.aspx
Counseling/Therapy Practice	www.rld.state.nm.us/boards/Look_Up_A_License.aspx
Court Reporting Schools	www.nmcra.com/Default.aspx?pageId=399048
Credit Union	http://rldverification.rld.state.nm.us/Verification/Search.aspx?facility=Y
Crematory	http://rldverification.rld.state.nm.us/Verification/
Dental Assistant/Hysienist	www.rld.state.nm.us/boards/Look_Up_A_License.aspx
Dentist	www.rld.state.nm.us/boards/Look_Up_A_License.aspx
Dietitian/Nutritionist	www.rld.state.nm.us/boards/Look_Up_A_License.aspx
Direct Disposer/FSI (Funerary)	http://rldverification.rld.state.nm.us/Verification/
Dispens'g Physician Cont'd Substance	www.rld.state.nm.us/boards/Look_Up_A_License.aspx
Electrologist	www.rld.state.nm.us/boards/Look_Up_A_License.aspx

Electrophysician .... www.rld.state.nm.us/boards/Look_Up_A_License.aspx
Emergency Medical Technician www.nmems.org/documents/EMTLicenseListforwebReport05102010.pdf
Engineer .... www.sblpes.state.nm.us/PEPSBoard/PEPSBoard.jsp
Esthetician .... www.rld.state.nm.us/boards/Look_Up_A_License.aspx
Funeral Home/Director/Practitioner .... http://rldverification.rld.state.nm.us/Verification/
Gambling, Non-Profit.................................. http://rldverification.rld.state.nm.us/Verification/
Hearing Aid Specialist .... www.rld.state.nm.us/boards/Look_Up_A_License.aspx
Hemodialysis Technician .... https://www.bon.state.nm.us/lookup.html
Insurance Agent/Producer .... www.nmprc.state.nm.us/insurance/producer-search.html
Interior Designer.. www.rld.state.nm.us/boards/Look_Up_A_License.aspx
Journeyman Contractor .... www.public.psiexams.com/search.jsp
Landscape Architect .... http://rldverification.rld.state.nm.us/Verification/
Liquor Distributor.. http://rldverification.rld.state.nm.us/Verification/
Loan Company, Small................................ http://rldverification.rld.state.nm.us/Verification/Search.aspx?facility=Y
Lobbist/Lobbying Organization .... www.sos.state.nm.us/Lobbyist_Information/
LPG Gas License .... www.public.psiexams.com/search.jsp
Manicurist.. www.rld.state.nm.us/boards/Look_Up_A_License.aspx
Manufactured Housing - Various .... www.rld.state.nm.us/Verify_a_License.aspx
Marriage & Family Therapist........................ www.rld.state.nm.us/boards/Look_Up_A_License.aspx
Martial Arts Contest.................................... http://rldverification.rld.state.nm.us/Verification/
Massage Therapist/Instr/Practitioner .... http://rldverification.rld.state.nm.us/Verification/
Massage Therapy School .... http://rldverification.rld.state.nm.us/Verification/Search.aspx?facility=Y
Medical Researcher/ Facility....................... www.rld.state.nm.us/boards/Look_Up_A_License.aspx
Medical Wholesale Company .... www.rld.state.nm.us/boards/Look_Up_A_License.aspx
Medication Aide.. https://www.bon.state.nm.us/lookup.html
Mental Health Counselor .... www.rld.state.nm.us/boards/Look_Up_A_License.aspx
Midwife .... http://nmhealth.org/PHD/midwife_roster.shtml
Money Order Agent/Firm/Exempts .... http://rldverification.rld.state.nm.us/Verification/Search.aspx?facility=Y
Mortgage Firm/Loan Broker/Branch............ http://rldverification.rld.state.nm.us/Verification/Search.aspx?facility=Y
Motor Vehicle Sales Financer .... http://rldverification.rld.state.nm.us/Verification/Search.aspx?facility=Y
Nurse-LPN/RN/Anesthetist/Practitioner .... https://www.bon.state.nm.us/lookup.html
Nursing Home Administrator/Facility........... www.rld.state.nm.us/boards/Look_Up_A_License.aspx
Occupational Therapist/Assistant .... www.rld.state.nm.us/boards/Look_Up_A_License.aspx
Optometrist.. http://rldverification.rld.state.nm.us/Verification/
Oriental Medicine Doctor .... www.rld.state.nm.us/boards/Look_Up_A_License.aspx
Osteopathic Physician/Assistant................. www.rld.state.nm.us/boards/Look_Up_A_License.aspx
Pharmacist, Pharmacy................................ www.rld.state.nm.us/boards/Look_Up_A_License.aspx
Pharmacy, Non-Residential .... www.rld.state.nm.us/boards/Look_Up_A_License.aspx
Physical Therapist/Assistant....................... www.rld.state.nm.us/boards/Look_Up_A_License.aspx
Physician/Medical Doctor/Assistant .... www.docboard.org/nm/
Podiatrist .... www.rld.state.nm.us/boards/Look_Up_A_License.aspx
Polygraph Examiner.................................... www.rld.state.nm.us/boards/Look_Up_A_License.aspx
Private Investigator .... www.rld.state.nm.us/boards/Look_Up_A_License.aspx
Psychologist/Associate .... www.rld.state.nm.us/boards/Look_Up_A_License.aspx
Radiation Therapy Technologist .... www.nmenv.state.nm.us/nmrcb/documents/web.pdf
Radiologic Technologist............................. www.nmenv.state.nm.us/nmrcb/documents/web.pdf
Real Estate Agent/Seller/Broker .... www.rld.state.nm.us/boards/Look_Up_A_License.aspx
Real Estate Appraiser .... www.rld.state.nm.us/boards/Look_Up_A_License.aspx
Referee .... http://rldverification.rld.state.nm.us/Verification/
Respiratory Care Therapist......................... www.rld.state.nm.us/boards/Look_Up_A_License.aspx
Savings & Loan .... http://rldverification.rld.state.nm.us/Verification/Search.aspx?facility=Y
Securities Broker/Dealer/Sales Rep/Division Agent.......www.finra.org/Investors/ToolsCalculators/BrokerCheck/
Security Dog Company .... www.rld.state.nm.us/boards/Look_Up_A_License.aspx
Security Guard/Company............................ www.rld.state.nm.us/boards/Look_Up_A_License.aspx
Social Worker (LBSW, LI, LM)/Provisional .. www.rld.state.nm.us/boards/Look_Up_A_License.aspx

Speech-Language Pathologist.................... www.rld.state.nm.us/boards/Look_Up_A_License.aspx
Substance Abuse Counselor/Intern .... www.rld.state.nm.us/boards/Look_Up_A_License.aspx
Surveyor, Land... www.sblpes.state.nm.us/PEPSBoard/PEPSBoard.jsp
Teacher.. http://164.64.166.19/LicenInq/search.asp
Trust Company... http://rldverification.rld.state.nm.us/Verification/Search.aspx?facility=Y
Veterinarian/Veterinary Technician............. www.nmbvm.org/index.php?option=com_sobi2&sobi2Task=search&Itemid=181
Veterinary Facility....................................... www.nmbvm.org/index.php?option=com_sobi2&sobi2Task=search&Itemid=182
Wrestler.. http://rldverification.rld.state.nm.us/Verification/

State and Local Courts

State Court Structure: The **District Courts** hear felony, civil, tort, contract, real property rights, estate, exclusive domestic relations, mental health. They handle appeals for administrative agencies and lower courts, miscellaneous civil jurisdiction; and misdemeanors.

The **Magistrate Court** handles tort, contract, landlord/tenant rights, civil, ($0-10,000); small claims, felony preliminary hearings; misdemeanor, DWI/DUI and other traffic violations.

Municipal Courts handle petty misdemeanors, DWI/DUI, traffic violations, and other municipal ordinance violations. The **Bernalillo Metropolitan Court** has jurisdiction in cases up to $10,000.

County Clerks hold the case files for "informal" or "uncontested" probate cases seen by the Probate Judge. The District Courts hold case files for "formal" or "contested" probate cases.

Appellate Courts: Supreme Court opinions may be researched at http://coa.nmcourts.gov.

Statewide Court Online Access: All District Courts participate in the system described below.

- The page at www.nmcourts.gov/caselookup/app offers free access to District Courts and Magistrate Courts case information statewide except Bernalillo Metropolitan Court (see below). There is also a separate look-up for DWI Reports and DWI Offenders. Municipal Court data is limited to criminal Domestic Violence and DWI historic convictions from September 1, 1991 forward. In general, the other records are available from June 1997 forward. The search is inclusive of all counties participating. Search by name & DL and/or DOB, and by county and type of case or by case number. Case lookup does not display the full date of birth, it displays only the year of birth. In addition, driver's license numbers are not displayed on records. A disclaimer reads: "Use of this site for any purpose other than viewing individual electronic court records, or attempts to download multiple records per transaction, are strictly prohibited."
- There is also a DWI Reports site at www.nmcourts.gov/dwi.php. Search by name.

County Sites (Other than the two state sites mentioned above):

Bernalillo County

Metropolitan Court www.metrocourt.state.nm.us

Civil: Access Metropolitan court civil records online at www.metrocourt.state.nm.us. *Criminal:* Search Metro Court criminal case records free at www.metrocourt.state.nm.us. The DWI data is available at www2.nmcourts.gov/caselookup/app

Cibola County - Sandoval County - Valencia County

13th Judicial District Court www.13districtcourt.com

Civil: Case lookup from 1997 forward is free at www.nmcourts.gov. Also, view all civil jury verdicts in the 13th Judicial District Court free back to 1995 at www.13districtcourt.com/verdict/jury_verdict_intro.php. Case Lookup rarely displays any part of the DOB. In addition, driver's license numbers are no longer displayed on any records. *Criminal:* Online access to criminal records is free at www.nmcourts.gov. Case Lookup no longer displays the full date of birth, it displays only the year of birth. In addition, driver's license numbers are no longer displayed on any records.

Recorders, Assessors, and Other Sites of Note

Recording Office Organization: 33 counties, 33 recording offices. The recording officer is the County Clerk. Most New Mexico counties maintain both a grantor/grantee index and a miscellaneous index. All federal and state tax liens are filed with the County Clerk. Financing statements are filed at the state level except for real estate related collateral which are filed with the County Clerk.

Statewide or Multi-Jurisdiction Access: **None.** A handful of counties offer online access but there is no statewide system.

Bernalillo County ***Recorded Documents*** http://www.bernco.gov/clerk/ Search recorders data and Grantor/Grantee index free at http://eagleweb.bernco.gov:8080/recorder/web/. Free registration but small charge for copies. Records from 1978 to present. **$$$**

Property, Taxation Records Search assessor records at http://www.bernco.gov/property-tax-search-disclaimer/.

Chaves County ***Property, Taxation Records*** Access to property records for free at http://eagleweb.co.chaves.nm.us:8080/assessor/taxweb/.

Cibola County ***Recorded Documents*** http://www.co.cibola.nm.us/clerk.html Access to recorded documents go to http://cibola.tylerworksasp.com/cibola/web/login.jsp?submit=I+Acknowledge. Has public login for documents without images. Must register for a fee for more advanced records. **$$$**

Curry County ***Recorded Documents*** http://www.currycounty.org/elected-offices/clerks-office/ Access to records free at http://lookup.currycounty.org:8080/clerk.aspx?source=clerk.

Property, Taxation Records Access to property records for free at http://lookup.currycounty.org:8080/assessor.aspx?source=assessor.

Dona Ana County ***Recorded Documents*** http://www.donaanacounty.org/clerk/ Access to county database (search and view document recording information) free at http://records.donaanacounty.org/countyweb/login.do?countyname=DonaAna. Must login with user ID and password. Also access indexs of recorded documents at http://donaanacounty.org/clerk/docs/.

Property, Taxation Records Access assessor index free at http://www2.donaanacounty.org/search/realprop.php. Access property data free on the GIS-mapping site at http://gis.co.dona-ana.nm.us/advparcels/viewer.htm. No name searching. Use the black circle with the 'I' in it to show parcel data.**$$$**

Eddy County ***Property, Taxation Records*** Access to records and maps free at http://liveweb.co.eddy.nm.us/.

Lea County ***Property, Taxation Records*** Access to maps of county for a fee at http://www.emapsplus.com/. Must sign-up and purchase a subscription to a county.**$$$**

Lincoln County ***Property, Taxation Records*** Access to the assessor property records is free at http://www.lincolncountynm.net/new_county_offices/assessor/database_access.php. Registration, software, username and password is required. Follow prompts at website.

Los Alamos County ***Recorded Documents*** http://www.losalamosnm.us/clerk/Pages/default.aspx Access to recorded data at https://portal1.recordfusion.com/countyweb/login.do?countyname=LosAlamos username/password required or login free as Guest. **$$$**

Otero County ***Recorded Documents*** http://www.co.otero.nm.us/Clerk/clerk.htm Access to the county documents go to http://occlerk.co.otero.nm.us/AppXtender/Login.aspx. Must register by contacting the clerk's office at above number. **$$$**

Property, Taxation Records Search the treasurer's tax data inquiry site free at http://ocwebserver2.co.otero.nm.us:81/webtaxinq/default.asp?action=taxdatainq. Also, access to property data free at http://ocwebserver2.co.otero.nm.us:81/webpropinq/default.asp?action=stats. Also, access to GIS/mapping free at http://ocwebserver2.co.otero.nm.us/website/index.htm.

Sandoval County ***Property, Taxation Records*** Access assessor property data free at http://etweb.sandovalcountynm.gov/Assessor/web/.

San Juan County ***Recorded Documents, Marriage, Probate*** http://www.sjcclerk.net./ Access to records for free to go https://portal2.recordfusion.com/countyweb/login.do?countyname=SanJuan. Recorded documents back to 9/16/1983, marriage records back to 1887, probate records back to 1887 and plats and surveys back to 1890. No fee to access index (under login as guest), however to veiw image thumbnails and print images put open account and pay. **$$$**

Property, Taxation Records Access to county property tax data is free at http://www.sjcassessor.net/search.asp.

Santa Fe County ***Recorded Documents*** http://www.santafecountynm.gov/clerk Access to recorder's grantor/grantee index available by subscription on the WEBXtender Document Imaging System. $36.00 setup fee and $25.00 monthly fee. There is a $7.00 per hour usage fee and $.50 per printer page. **$$$**

Property, Taxation Records Access to county property data for free at http://www.santafecountynm.gov/assessor/appraisal_tax_information.**$$$**

Sierra County ***Recorded Documents*** http://www.sierracountynm.gov/department/138752-clerk Access to recorded documents free at http://liveweb.sierracountynm.gov/clerk.aspx?source=clerk.

Property, Taxation Records Access to records free at http://liveweb.sierracountynm.gov/assessor.aspx?source=assessor.

Taos County ***Property, Taxation Records*** Access to records for free at http://lookup.taoscounty.org/assessor.aspx?source=assessor. Also, access to GIS/mapping free at http://lookup.taoscounty.org/assessor.aspx?source=assessor.

Valencia County ***Recorded Documents , Probate Records*** http://www.co.valencia.nm.us/departments/clerk/County_Clerk.html Access to records free at http://publiclookup.co.valencia.nm.us/clerk.aspx?source=clerk.

Property, Taxation Records Access to GIS/mapping for free at http://www.co.valencia.nm.us/departments/gis/GIS.html.

New York

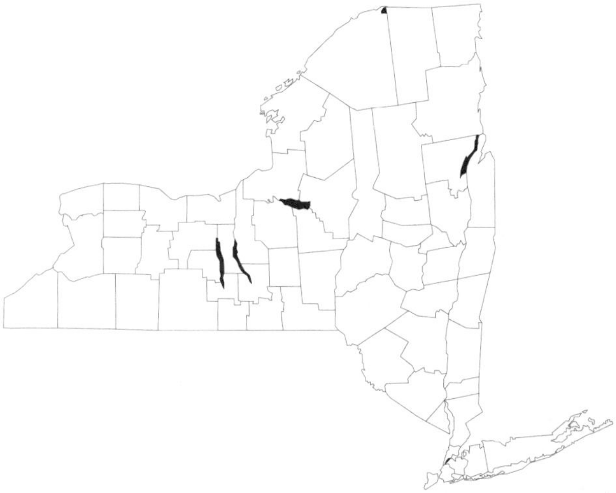

Capital: Albany
AlbanyCounty
Time Zone: EST
Population: 19,570,261
# of Counties: 62

Useful State Links

Website: www.ny.gov
Governor: www.governor.ny.gov
Attorney General: www.oag.state.ny.us
State Archives: www.archives.nysed.gov/aindex.shtml
State Statutes & Codes: http://public.leginfo.state.ny.us/menugetf.cgi?COMMONQUERY=LAWS
Legislative Bill Search: http://public.leginfo.state.ny.us/menuf.cgi
Unclaimed Funds: www.osc.state.ny.us/ouf/index.htm

State Public Record Agencies

Sexual Offender Registry

Sex Offender Registry, Alfred E. Smith Building, www.criminaljustice.state.ny.us/nsor/index.htm The sex offender registry of level 2 and 3 can be searched at www.criminaljustice.state.ny.us/SomsSUBDirectory/search_index.jsp. Search by last name, or ZIP, or by county. If an offender is not be listed on this site, information about the offender is available through DCJS at 800-262-3257.

Incarceration Records

New York Department of Correctional Services, Building 2 - Central Files, www.doccs.ny.gov/ Computerized inmate information is available from the Inmate Lookup at http://nysdoccslookup.doccs.ny.gov/kinqw00 or follow "inmate lookup" link at main site. Records go back to early 1970s. To acquire inmate DIN number, you may call 518-457-5000. The site is open, in general, from Mon. thru Sat. 2:00 a.m.-11:00 p.m. & Sun. 4:00 a.m. thru 11:00 p.m. which has state DOC data but not data from all counties.

Corporation, LP, LLC, LLP

Division of Corporations, Dept. of State, One Commerce Plaza, www.dos.ny.gov/corps/ A commercial account can be set up for direct access. Fee is $.75 per transaction through a draw down account. There is an extensive amount of information available including historical information. Also, the Division's corporate and business entity DB for not-for-profit corporations, LPs, LLCs, and LLPs may be accessed without charge at www.dos.ny.gov/corps/bus_entity_search.html. Searches of assumed names used by corporations, LLCs or LPs must be made manually. Note general partnerships, sole proprietorships and limited liability partnerships file an assumed name certificate directly with the county clerk. Search the child support warrant notice system at www.dos.ny.gov/corps/child_support_search.html. **$$$** *Other Options:* One may submit an email search request to corporations@dos.state.ny.us. Search the child support warrant notice system at

Uniform Commercial Code, Federal & State Tax Liens

Department of State, UCC Unit - Records, www.dos.ny.gov/corps/uccforms.html Free access is available at http://appext20.dos.ny.gov/pls/ucc_public/web_search.main_frame. Search financing statements and federal tax lien notices by debtor name, or secured party name, or by filing number and date. Please note that UCC Images indicated as *N/A are unavailable on the website. There are two other searchable databases from the home page - the State Child Support Enforcement Warrant Notice System and the State Tax Warrant Notice System. *Other Options:* A UCC image subscription via the web is offered for $300 per month. Images are downloaded in TIFF format. Filings available 5 business days after filing and remain downloadable for 30 days. Call 518-486-5049.

Sales Tax Registrations

NY Dept of Taxation & Finance, Records Access - WA Harriman Campus, www.tax.ny.gov/bus/ A registered sales tax look-up is offered at https://www7b.tax.ny.gov/TIVL/tivlStart.

Vital Records - Outside New York City

Vital Records Section, Certification Unit, www.health.ny.gov/vital_records/ Online ordering is available via an approved third party vendor, go to www.vitalchek.com. **$$$**

Birth Certificate - In New York City, Death Records

Department of Health, Bureau of Vital Records, www.nyc.gov/html/doh/html/services/vr.shtml Records may be requested via www.vitalchek.com. Use of credit card is required. **$$$**

Workers' Compensation Records

NY Workers' Compensation Board, Office of General Counsel, www.wcb.ny.gov/ Email requests accepted . - officeofgeneralcounsel@wcb.state.ny.gov. This is considered a FOIL request. See www.wcb.state.ny.us/content/main/wclaws/FoilPPPL.jsp. Search if an employers has coverage at www.wcb.ny.gov/content/ebiz/icempcovsearch/icempcovsearch_overview.jsp. **$$$**

Driver Records

Department of Motor Vehicles, MV-15 Processing, www.dmv.ny.gov NY has implemented a "Dial-In Display" system which enables customers to obtain data online 24 hours a day. An application and pre-paid escrow account are required. The fee is $7.00 per record. For more information, visit www.dmv.ny.gov/dialin.htm. Also, drivers may request their own DMV records at www.dmv.ny.gov/driverabstract; however, records are returned by mail and the fee is $10.00. **$$$** *Other Options:* This agency offers a program to employers whereby the agency will notify the employers when a change posts to an employee's record. To find out about the "LENS" program, visit www.dmv.ny.gov/LENS/.

Vehicle, Vessel Ownership & Registration

Department of Motor Vehicles, MV-15 Processing, www.dmv.ny.gov/ New York offers plate, VIN and ownership data through the same network discussed in the Driving Records Section. The system is interactive and open 24 hours a day. The fee is $7.00 per record. All accounts must be approved, requesters must follow DPPA guidelines. Call 518-474-4293 or visit www.dmv.ny.gov/dialin.htm for more information. A free title/lien status check is offered at www.dmv.ny.gov/titlestat/. The VIN is needed, this is not a name search. A free insurance status check is at www.dmv.ny.gov/insStatus/, but a control number is needed. **$$$** *Other Options:* DMV awards contracts for the sale of access to bulk of registration and ownership files to third party vendors, via a competitive bidding process. Stringent rules apply. For details, contact the DMV by email at DataServices@dmv.ny.gov.

Accident Reports

NYS - DMV, MV-198C processing, www.dmv.ny.gov/dmvfaqs.htm Online access is available to eligible requesters. There is a $7.00 search fee and a $15.00 report fee. There is no charge to simply view a list of accidents for a date and county. Available records go back 4 years. Reports can be viewed and printed. Visit www.dmv.ny.gov/AIS/default.html. **$$$**

Campaign Finance, Voter Registration

State Board of Elections, Public Information Officer, www.elections.ny.gov/ View campaign finance reports at www.elections.ny.gov/CFViewReports.html. This database contains all financial disclosure reports filed with NYSBOE from July of 1999 to the present. Opinions from the Campaign Ethics Center is at www.nycourts.gov/ip/jcec/.

Occupational Licensing Boards

Accountant-CPA.. www.op.nysed.gov/opsearches.htm#nme
Acupuncturist/Acupuncture Assis't.............. www.op.nysed.gov/opsearches.htm#nme
Addiction Counselor.................................... www.oasas.state.ny.us/credentialingVerification/verification/home.cfm
Addiction Treatment Center......................... www.oasas.ny.gov/atc/directory.cfm
Adoption Agency... www.ocfs.state.ny.us/adopt/agcymenu.asp
Adult Care Medical Facility .... www.health.ny.gov/facilities/adult_care/
Adult Care Suspended List.......................... www.health.ny.gov/facilities/adult_care/memorandum.htm
Alarm Installer-Fire/Security........................ http://appext9.dos.ny.gov/lcns_public/chk_load
Alcohol/Substance Abuse Counselor........... www.oasas.state.ny.us/credentialingVerification/verification/home.cfm
Alcohol/Substance Abuse Provider............. www.oasas.state.ny.us/credentialingVerification/verification/home.cfm
Apartment Mgr/Vendor/Agent/Info Vendor... http://appext9.dos.ny.gov/lcns_public/chk_load
Apartment Sharing Manager........................ http://appext9.dos.ny.gov/lcns_public/chk_load
Appearance Enhancement Firm/Prof........... http://appext9.dos.ny.gov/lcns_public/chk_load

Architect	www.op.nysed.gov/opsearches.htm#nme
Armored Car/Car Carrier/Guard	http://appext9.dos.ny.gov/lcns_public/chk_load
Athlete Agent	http://appext9.dos.ny.gov/lcns_public/chk_load
Athletic Trainer	www.op.nysed.gov/opsearches.htm#nme
Attorney	http://iapps.courts.state.ny.us/attorney/AttorneySearch
Audiologist	www.op.nysed.gov/opsearches.htm#nme
Backflow Prev't'n Device Tester	www.health.ny.gov/environmental/water/drinking/cross/backflow_testers/index.htm
Bail Bond Agent	https://myportal.dfs.ny.gov/web/guest-applications/bail-bonds-search
Bail Enforcement Agent	http://appext9.dos.ny.gov/lcns_public/chk_load
BarberApprentice//Barber Shop	http://appext9.dos.ny.gov/lcns_public/chk_load
Bedding Manufacturing	http://appext9.dos.ny.gov/lcns_public/chk_load
Budget Planner, Banking-related	www.dfs.ny.gov/about/whowesupervise/sibudget.htm
Building Permit	https://appsext7.dos.ny.gov/nydos/selSearchType.do
Casino Employee	www.gaming.ny.gov/
Charitable Gaming	www.gaming.ny.gov/
Charity, Registered	www.charitiesnys.com/RegistrySearch/search_charities.jsp
Check Casher	www.dfs.ny.gov/about/whowesupervise/sicheckc.htm
Chemical Dependence Operation	www.oasas.state.ny.us/credentialingVerification/verification/home.cfm
Chiropractor	www.op.nysed.gov/opsearches.htm#nme
Cigarette/Tobacco Tax Agent	www8.tax.ny.gov/CGTX/cgtxHome
Cigarette/Tobacco Whlse/Retailer	www8.tax.ny.gov/CGTX/cgtxHome
Coin Processor	https://appsext7.dos.ny.gov/nydos/selSearchType.do
Cosmetologist/Nail Technologist/Esthetics	http://appext9.dos.ny.gov/lcns_public/chk_load
Day Care Center	http://it.ocfs.ny.gov/ccfs_facilitysearch/
Day Care, Farm Worker (ABCD)	www.agriculture.ny.gov/programs/childdev.html
DEC Permit Application	www.dec.ny.gov/
Dental Hygienist/Dental Assistant	www.op.nysed.gov/opsearches.htm#nme
Dentist	www.op.nysed.gov/opsearches.htm#nme
Dietitian	www.op.nysed.gov/opsearches.htm#nme
Dispatch Facility- Alarm/Sec/Fire	http://appext9.dos.ny.gov/lcns_public/chk_load
Electrician-Master	https://appsext7.dos.ny.gov/nydos/selSearchType.do
Engineer	www.op.nysed.gov/opsearches.htm#nme
Environmental Permit	www.dec.ny.gov/
Family/Group Day Care	http://it.ocfs.ny.gov/ccfs_facilitysearch/
Farm Product Dealers	www.agriculture.ny.gov/AP/LicFarmProdDealersList.asp
Farm Products Dealer	www.agriculture.ny.gov/programs/apsf.html
Games of Chance Registration	https://appsext7.dos.ny.gov/nydos/selSearchType.do
Guard/Patrol/Guard Dog Agency	http://appext9.dos.ny.gov/lcns_public/chk_load
Health Club	https://appsext7.dos.ny.gov/nydos/selSearchType.do
Hearing Aid Dealer/Business	http://appext9.dos.ny.gov/lcns_public/chk_load
Home Inspector	http://appext9.dos.ny.gov/lcns_public/chk_load
Hospice	http://homecare.nyhealth.gov/
Hospital	www.health.ny.gov/facilities/hospital/index.htm
Hotel/Motel Name Certificate	https://appsext7.dos.ny.gov/nydos/selSearchType.do
Insurance Adjuster/Appraiser	www.dfs.ny.gov/insurance/abindx.htm
Insurance Agent/Consultant/Broker	www.dfs.ny.gov/insurance/abindx.htm
Insurance Company	https://myportal.dfs.ny.gov/web/guest-applications/ins.-company-search
Interior Designer	www.op.nysed.gov/opsearches.htm#nme
Juvenile Detention Facility	www.ocfs.state.ny.us/main/rehab/regionalListing.asp
Kosher Food	www.agriculture.ny.gov/kosher/search.aspx
Landscape Architect	www.op.nysed.gov/opsearches.htm#nme
Lender, Licensed	www.dfs.ny.gov/about/whowesupervise/silicend.htm
Lobbyist/Client/Public Corporation	www.nyc.gov/lobbyistsearch/
Mammography Facility	www.accessdata.fda.gov/scripts/cdrh/cfdocs/cfMQSA/mqsa.cfm
Massage Therapist	www.op.nysed.gov/opsearches.htm#nme

Medicaid Long-Term Care Service	www.health.ny.gov/health_care/managed_care/mltc/mltcplans.htm
Medical Disciplinary Action	http://w3.health.state.ny.us/opmc/factions.nsf
Medical Examiner-Independent	www.wcb.ny.gov/content/main/hcpp/ListofAuthIMENYC.jsp
Mental Health Facility	www.omh.ny.gov/omhweb/aboutomh/omh_facility.html
Midwife	www.op.nysed.gov/opsearches.htm#nme
Minority/Woman-owned Business	www.empire.state.ny.us/MWBE/NewMWBEs.html
Money Transmitter	www.dfs.ny.gov/about/whowesupervise/simoneyt.htm
Notary Public	http://appext9.dos.ny.gov/lcns_public/chk_load
Nurse-LPN/RPN	www.op.nysed.gov/opsearches.htm#nme
Nursery/Plant Dealer/Greenhouse	www.agriculture.ny.gov/nurseryDealers.html
Nurses Aide	https://registry.prometric.com/registry/public
Nursing Home	www.health.ny.gov/facilities/nursing/
Nursing Home Administrator	www.health.ny.gov/professionals/nursing_home_administrator/licensed_nha/master_lnha.htm
Nutritionist	www.op.nysed.gov/opsearches.htm#nme
Occupational Therapist/Assistant	www.op.nysed.gov/opsearches.htm#nme
Off-Track Betting	www.gaming.ny.gov/
Ophthalmic Dispenser	www.op.nysed.gov/opsearches.htm#nme
Optometrist	www.op.nysed.gov/opsearches.htm#nme
Pesticide, Bus., Commercial Applicator	www.dec.ny.gov/docs/materials_minerals_pdf/appweb.pdf
Pet Cemetery/Crematory	https://appsext7.dos.ny.gov/nydos/selSearchType.do
Pet Dealer	www.agriculture.ny.gov/petdealer/PetDealerExtract.asp
Pharmacist	www.op.nysed.gov/opsearches.htm#nme
Physician/Medical Doctor/Assistant	www.op.nysed.gov/opsearches.htm#nme
Podiatrist	www.op.nysed.gov/opsearches.htm#nme
Premium Finance Company	www.dfs.ny.gov/about/whowesupervise/sipremfi.htm
Private Investigator	http://appext9.dos.ny.gov/lcns_public/chk_load
Psychologist	www.op.nysed.gov/opsearches.htm#nme
Racetrack, Racing Occupation	www.gaming.ny.gov/
Radiologic Technologist	www.health.ny.gov/professionals/doctors/radiological/
Radiologic Technology School	www.health.ny.gov/professionals/doctors/radiological/schlist2.htm
Radon Testing Lab	www.wadsworth.org/labcert/elap/radon.html
Railroad/Steamboat Policeman	https://appsext7.dos.ny.gov/nydos/selSearchType.do
Real Estate Agent/Broker/Office	https://appsext7.dos.ny.gov/nydos/selSearchType.do
Real Estate Appraiser	http://appext9.dos.ny.gov/lcns_public/chk_load
Real Estate Appraiser School	https://appsext7.dos.ny.gov/nydos/selSearchType.do
Respiratory Therapist/Therapy Tech	www.op.nysed.gov/opsearches.htm#nme
Sales Finance Company	www.dfs.ny.gov/about/whowesupervise/sisalesf.htm
Security Guard	http://appext9.dos.ny.gov/lcns_public/chk_load
Social Worker	www.op.nysed.gov/opsearches.htm#nme
Speech Pathologist/Audiologist	www.op.nysed.gov/opsearches.htm#nme
State Telecommunication Contractor	www.ogs.state.ny.us/purchase/telecomContracts.asp
Surveyor-Land	www.op.nysed.gov/opsearches.htm#nme
Teacher	http://eservices.nysed.gov/teach/certhelp/CpPersonSearchExternal.jsp?trgAction=INQUIRY
Telemarketer Business	http://appext9.dos.ny.gov/lcns_public/chk_load
Trading Stamp Registration	https://appsext7.dos.ny.gov/nydos/selSearchType.do
Uniform Procedures Act Permit	www.dec.ny.gov/permits/6081.html
Upholster & Bedding Industry	http://appext9.dos.ny.gov/lcns_public/chk_load
Vendor, New York City	http://slnx-prd-web.nyc.gov/cfb/cfbSearch.nyc?method=search
Veteran - Skilled Nursing Home	www.nysvets.org/
Veterinarian/Veterinary Technician	www.op.nysed.gov/opsearches.htm#nme
Water Processing Facility, Bulk	www.health.ny.gov/environmental/water/drinking/bulk_bottle/bulkwter.htm
Water Supply Permit	www.dec.ny.gov/
Water Treatment Plant Operator	www.health.ny.gov/environmental/water/drinking/operate/operate.htm
Waxing Establishment/Operator/Tech	http://appext9.dos.ny.gov/lcns_public/chk_load
Workers Comp Appr'v'd Health Provid'r	www.wcb.ny.gov:8765/query.html?qt=Approved+Health+Providers+licensing&Submit=Search

State and Local Courts

State Court Structure: **Supreme and County Courts** are the highest trial courts in the state, equivalent to what may be called circuit or district in other states. New York's Supreme and County Courts may be administered together or separately. When separate, there is a clerk for each. Supreme and/or County Courts are not appeals courts. Supreme Courts handle civil cases – usually civil cases over $25,000 – but there are many exceptions. The County Courts handle felony cases and, in many counties, these County Courts also handle misdemeanors. The New York City Courts are structured differently.

For non-NYC courts (called Upstate Courts), **City Courts** handle misdemeanors and civil case claims up to $15,000, small claims, and eviction cases. Not all counties have City Courts, thus cases there fall to the Supreme and County Courts for civil and criminal respectively, or, in many counties, to the small **Town and Village Courts**, which can number in the dozens within a county.

Probate is handled by **Surrogate Courts**. Surrogate Courts may also hear Domestic Relations cases in some counties.

In **New York City**, the Supreme Court is the trial court with unlimited jurisdiction. The Civil Court of the City of New York has jurisdiction on civil matters up to $25,000. The Criminal Court of the City of New York has jurisdiction over misdemeanors and minor violations. The Family Court hears matters involving children and families. Probate is handled by the Surrogate's Court.

In the five boroughs of New York City the courts records are administered directly by the state **OCA – Office of Court Administration.**

Appellate Courts: The Court of Appeals is the state's highest court. The next step down is the four Appellate Divisions of the Supreme Court, one in each of the State's four Judicial Departments. Find decisions at www.nycourts.gov/decisions/index.shtml.

Statewide Court Online Access: There are a number of statewide systems - see below.

- The OCA offers online access to criminal records. Requesters must apply for an account. There is a weekly minimum of searches required. This is not an interactive system - the search results are sent via email. Call the OCA at 212-428-2916 or visit www.nycourts.gov/apps/chrs/ for details on how to set up an account.
- A state search site at http://iapps.courts.state.ny.us/webcivil/ecourtsMain provides five resources, but know there limitations. The links accessible from this site works best as a **supplemental resource**. The site limitations are based on search logic issues. For example, when searching the civil index, the search index apparently only contains the name of the first defendant. Thus if there are multiple defendants, the site cannot be relied upon as being equivalent to an on-site search. The five resources are as follows:
    - **WebCrims** provides pending criminal case data in 13 local and all Supreme Courts. **WebFamily** provides information on active Family Court cases in all 62 counties of New York State and Integrated Domestic Violence (IDV) Court cases in those counties with IDV Courts. **WebCivil Supreme** contains information on both Active and Disposed Civil Supreme Court cases in all 62 counties of New York State. The **WebCivil Local link** gives access civil case data from 60+ City Courts and several County Courts. **WebHousing** offers information on pending Landlord Tenant cases in the Housing Part of New York City Civil Court (Bronx, Kings, New York, Queens and Richmond) as well as the Buffalo City Court in Erie County. There is also a case tracking service called eTrack.
- Search http://decisions.courts.state.ny.us/search/query3.asp for **Supreme Court Civil and Criminal decisions**, dating back to 2001. Civil Cases are from the following counties: Allegany, Bronx, Broome, Cattaraugus, Chautauqua, Cortland, Delaware, Erie, Kings, Livingston, Madison, Monroe, Nassau, New York, Niagara, Oneida, Onondaga, Ontario, Orange, Putnam, Queens, Richmond, Schuyler, Seneca, Steuben, Suffolk, Westchester and Wyoming Counties. Criminal Cases are from the following counties: Albany, Bronx, Broome, Cattaraugus, Cayuga, Chautauqua, Chemung, Delaware, Erie, Kings, Monroe, Nassau, New York, Oneida, Onondaga, Ontario, Orange, Oswego, Queens, Richmond, Seneca, Suffolk, and Wayne Counties.

Other County Sites Not Mentioned Above:

Bronx County

Supreme Court - www.courts.state.ny.us/courts/12jd/

Civil & Crimina: Access docket data free on the law case search at www.bronxcountyclerkinfo.com/law/UI/Admin/login.aspx and sign in as guest.

Broome County

County Clerk www.gobcclerk.com

Civil: Lookup judgment index free at www.gobcclerk.com/cgi/Official_Search_Types.html/input; records go back to 1987.

Erie County

County Clerk www.erie.gov/depts/government/clerk/civil_criminal.phtml

Civil: Online access to the county clerk's database of recorded civil judgments is free at http://ecclerk.erie.gov. Records go back to 01/93.

Madison County

County Clerk www.madisoncounty.ny.gov/

Civil: The fee for unlimited access to the Madison County Land/Court Records website includes an account activation fee of $50.00 and an additional $600 per quarter, payable in advance. See www.searchiqs.com/madison.html. **$$$** *Criminal:* same as civil.

Monroe County

County Clerk www.monroecounty.gov/clerk-index.php

Civil: Online access to judgments and some other court documents is free online at www.monroe.ny.us.landata.com/. The index goes back to 06/09/93. Images on judgment gooes back to 6/1993, and earlier film images are being added. Registration is required, there are no fees.

Putnam County

County Clerk www.putnamcountyny.com/countyclerk/index.htm

Civil: Access to the clerk's records index (but not images except judgments) is via subscription service at www2.landaccess.com/cgibin/homepage?County=8002. Pay per use ($5.00 to view doc) or $100 per month plan available. **$$$**

Rockland County

County Clerk www.rocklandcountyclerk.com

Online access to county clerk index is free at www.rocklandcountyclerk.com/court_records.html. Online includes civil judgments, real estate records, tax warrants. Call 845-638-5221 for info. Index includes criminal records back to 1982. Free registration required.

Westchester County

County Clerk www.westchesterclerk.com

Civil: Access civil cases on the county clerk database search site back to 2002 at https://wro.westchesterclerk.com/Login/Login.aspx?ReturnUrl=%2fdefault.aspx. Data includes liens, judgments, tax warrants, foreclosures, Divorces (no images). *Criminal:* same as civil.

Recorders, Assessors, and Other Sites of Note

Recording Office Organization: 62 counties, 62 recording offices. Recording officer is the County Clerk except in the counties of Bronx, Kings, New York, and Queens where the recording officer is the New York City Register. Federal tax liens on personal property of businesses are filed with the Secretary of State and are usually indexed with UCC records. Other federal tax liens are filed with the County Clerk. State tax liens are filed with the County Clerk and placed on a master list - called state tax warrants - available from the Secretary of State. State tax liens are usually indexed with other miscellaneous liens and judgments.

Statewide or Multi-Jurisdiction Access: Many counties and towns offer free internet access to assessor records. Recording records are more likely to require registration and password; many also require a fee. Below are several notable sites.

- The New York City Register offers free access to all borough's real estate records (including Staten Island) on the ACRIS system at http://a836-acris.nyc.gov/Scripts/Coverpage.dll/index. Search by name, address, doc type, or legal description.
- New York Citty's Dept of Finance Property Assessment Rolls are free at http://nycprop.nyc.gov/nycproperty/nynav/jsp/selectbbl.jsp but no name searching.
- Use https://www.taxlookup.net to review localized property tax records free for limited communities in 40 or so counties.

County Sites:

Albany County ***Real Estate, Deed, Mortgage Records*** www.albanycounty.com/clerk/ Access deeds and mortgages free at https://access.albanycounty.com/clerk/deedsandmortgages/.

Property, Taxation A private company offers property assessment data online at www.accuriz.com/index.aspx. Also search Town of Guilderland property data free at https://www.taxlookup.net.

Allegany County ***Real Estate, Deeds, Mortgage Records*** www.alleganyco.com/default.asp?show=btn_county_clerk Access to records for a fee at www.searchiqs.com/allegany.html. **$$$**

Property, Taxation Access to land records, GIS/mapping and Tax maps for free at http://allegany.sdgnys.com/index.aspx.

Bronx County (Borough) ***Real Estate, Deed, Lien, Judgment, UCC, Mortgage, Assumed Name Records*** www.nyc.gov/html/records/home.html Recording data from City Register is free at http://a836-acris.nyc.gov/Scripts/Coverpage.dll/index. Also, for deeper financial data back 10 years, subscribe to the NYC Dept of Finance dial-up system; fee-$250 monthly and $5.00 per item. Info/signup- call Richard Reskin 718-935-6523. NYC's Dept of Finance offers daily downloads for borough-wide transactions of UCCs, Fed lien, deeds, real estate at www.nyc.gov/html/dof/html/home/home.shtml. **$$$**

Property, Taxation Property tax and ownership is at http://webapps.nyc.gov:8084/cics/fin2/find001i? and http://nycprop.nyc.gov/nycproperty/nynav/jsp/selectbbl.jsp. Also, a private company offers property assessment data online at www.accuriz.com/index.aspx. See tax claim property sales at www.xspand.com/investors/realestate_sale/index.aspx.

Broome County ***Real Estate, Deed, Mortgage, Real Estate, Lien, Judgment Records*** www.gobcclerk.com Search the clerk's indexes free at www.gobcclerk.com/Broome.html?goPage=www.gobcclerk.com/cgi/Official_Search_Types.html/input. Online miscellaneous and lien records go back to 1989, deeds & mortgages go back to 1963, court records (civil and criminal) from 1985 tp present.

Property, Taxation A private company offers property assessment data online at www.accuriz.com/index.aspx. Also search City of Binghamton and Towns of Chenango, Conklin, Dickinson, Fenton, Kirkwood, Maine, Union, Vestal, and Windsor property tax data free at https://www.taxlookup.net. City allows name searching; Town does not.

Cattaraugus County ***Property, Taxation*** Search for property info on the interactive map at http://maps.cattco.org/parcel_disclaimer.php. To name search, select to search without the map. Also, a private company offers property assessment data at www.accuriz.com/index.aspx.

Cayuga County ***Recorded Documents*** http://co.cayuga.ny.us/clerk/ Search mortgages & deeds at https://www.nylandrecords.com/nylr/controller. Subscription fee is $440 per year or $40 per month, $5.00 per image, plus a one time usage fee, credit cards accepted. Index goes back to 1972; images back to 1980. **$$$**

Property, Taxation Search tax data, rolls, current sales, tax maps, final assessments free at www.cayugacounty.us/realproperty/index.html#.**$$$**

Chautauqua County ***Recorded Documents*** www.co.chautauqua.ny.us/departments/clerk/Pages/default.aspx Access to records for a fee at www.searchiqs.com/nycha/. Must register for subscription. **$$$**

Property, Taxation Access property data free on the GIS-mapping site at www.chautauquagis.com/.

Chemung County ***Property, Taxation*** Search the treasurer's property tax data at http://chemung.sdgnys.com/index.aspx. Username and password is required for deeper data.**$$$**

Chenango County ***Real Estate Records*** www.co.chenango.ny.us/clerk/ Access to records search for a fee at https://cotthosting.com/nychenango/User/Login.aspx?ReturnUrl=%2fnychenango%2findex.aspx. Must have a user ID and password. **$$$**

Property, Taxation A private company offers property assessment data online at www.accuriz.com/index.aspx for a fee.**$$$**

Clinton County ***Property, Taxation*** Access to the Public Access site is at http://clinton.sdgnys.com/index.aspx. Enhanced data for a fee, includes property taxes, tax maps and photos of parcels, call Tammy 518-565-4763 or Martine at 518-565-4762.**$$$**

Cortland County ***Real Estate, Deed, Mortgage, Judgment, UCC, Lien Records*** www.cortland-co.org/cc/ Online access for free at www.searchiqs.com/ gives judgments and other county clerk records. Deeds may be searched online from 1808 to 1992 on Infodex option.

Property, Taxation A private company offers property assessment data online at www.accuriz.com/index.aspx. Also, property data is available by $40 per month subscription at www.cortland-co.org/rpts/Imagemate.htm.**$$$**

Delaware County ***Property, Taxation*** A private company offers property assessment data online at www.accuriz.com/index.aspx.**$$$**

Dutchess County ***Recorded Documents*** www.co.dutchess.ny.us/CountyGov/Departments/CountyClerk/CCindex.htm Access to records free at www.co.dutchess.ny.us/CountyGov/Departments/CountyClerk/12976.htm.

Property, Taxation Search the county tax roll at http://geoaccess.co.dutchess.ny.us/parcelaccess/. Search the Town of East Fishkill property tax roll data free at https://www.taxlookup.net.

Erie County ***Real Estate, Deed, Mortgage, UCC, Judgment Records*** www2.erie.gov/clerk/index.php?q=online-records Access to the county clerk's database index and images is at http://ecclerk.erie.gov/recordsng_web/. View index free. $5.00 fee to view full documents; a $250 initial escrow account required. **$$$**

Property, Taxation Parcel data is free at www.erie.gov/ecrpts/webprop.asp. Also, a private company offers property assessments at www.accuriz.com/index.aspx. Also, a private company that sells county tax claim property, view list free at www.xspand.com/investors/realestate_sale/index.aspx.**$$$**

Essex County ***Property, Taxation*** Parcel data, tax rolls, and available free at www.co.essex.ny.us/realproperty.asp. Also, a private company offers property assessment data online at www.accuriz.com/index.aspx. A property tax search is at www.co.essex.ny.us/Treasurer/PropertyLookup.aspx?SearchReason=TaxSearch.

Franklin County ***Recorded Documents*** http://franklincony.org/content/Departments/View/4? Access to records for a fee at www.searchiqs.com/franklin.html. **$$$**

Property, Taxation Access to real property and GIS/mapping for free at http://franklin.sdgnys.com/index.aspx.

Fulton County ***Property, Taxation*** Access tax assessor data at http://74.39.247.67/imo/index.aspx and assessment rolls at www.fultoncountyny.gov/index.php?word=departments/rolls.htm.

Genesee County ***Property, Taxation*** Access to real property information for free at www.oarsystem.com/ny/geneseecounty/default.asp. A private company offers property assessment data online at www.accuriz.com/index.aspx.**$$$**

Greene County ***Property, Taxation*** Access to the Web Map for free at http://gis.greenegovernment.com/giswebmap/. Also, access Town of Catskill GIS property data free at http://mapgears.mapsonline.net/catskillny/.

Hamilton County ***Property, Taxation*** A private company offers property assessment data online at www.accuriz.com/index.aspx. Also, access to GIS/mapping free at www.hamcomaps.net/#.**$$$**

Herkimer County ***Property, Taxation*** A private company offers property assessment data online at www.accuriz.com/index.aspx. Also, search City of Little Falls property data free at https://www.taxlookup.net. Access to tax searches free at http://herkimercounty.sdgnys.com/index.aspx.**$$$**

Jefferson County ***Property, Taxation*** Property assessment data offered online for free at http://jefferson.sdgnys.com/index.aspx. For more in depth records you must register. Also, a private company offers property assessment data online at www.accuriz.com/index.aspx. Also, access to GIS/mapping free at www.jeffcountymaps.com/.**$$$**

Kings County (Brooklyn Borough) ***Real Estate, Deed, Lien, Judgment, UCC, Mortgage Records*** www.nyc.gov/html/kcpa/html/home/home.shtml Recording data from the City Register free at http://a836-acris.nyc.gov/Scripts/Coverpage.dll/index. Also, for deeper financial data back 10 years, subscribe to the NYC Dept of Finance dial-up system; fee-$250 monthly and $5.00 per item. For info/signup, call Richard Reskin 718-935-6523. **$$$**

Property, Taxation Property tax and ownership is at http://webapps.nyc.gov:8084/cics/fin2/find001i? and http://nycprop.nyc.gov/nycproperty/nynav/jsp/selectbbl.jsp. Also, a private company offers property assessment data online at www.accuriz.com/index.aspx. Tax claim sales are atwww.xspand.com/investors/realestate_sale/index.aspx.

Lewis County ***Real Estate Records*** http://lewiscountyny.org/content/Departments/View/24? Real property search free at http://lewiscountyny.org/content/RealProperty.

Property, Taxation A private company offers property assessment data online at www.accuriz.com/index.aspx.**$$$**

Livingston County ***Real Estate, Deed Records*** www.co.livingston.state.ny.us/clerk.htm Access to recorded data at https://portal2.recordfusion.com/countyweb/login.do?countyname=Livingston. Username/password required or logon free at Guest. **$$$**

Property, Taxation Access to real property tax services free at http://depot.livingstoncounty.us/rptx/rpsonlg2.pgm.

Madison County ***Recorded Documents*** www.madisoncounty.ny.gov/county-clerk/madison-county-clerk Access to records for a fee at www.accuriz.com/index.aspx/madison.html. **$$$**

Property, Taxation A private company offers property assessment data online at www.accuriz.com/index.aspx.**$$$**

Monroe County ***Real Estate, Deed, Lien, Judgment, UCC, Voter Registration Roll Records*** www.monroecounty.gov/clerk-index.php Access the county clerk database at https://gov.propertyinfo.com/NY-Monroe/. Index search is free but must register first. Fee for printing of images. Also, access voter registration roll free at https://www.monroecounty.gov/apps/voterapp.php. **$$$**

Property, Taxation Search the County Real Property Portal at www.monroecounty.gov/apps/propertyapp.php. Also, a private company offers property assessment data online at www.accuriz.com/index.aspx. Also search Town of Penfield property data free at https://www.taxlookup.net.

Montgomery County ***Property, Taxation*** A private company offers property assessment data online at www.accuriz.com/index.aspx. Also, access property data via the GIS-mapping site free at http://ranger.co.montgomery.ny.us/IMO/index.aspx.**$$$**

Nassau County ***Property, Taxation*** Access to the county assessor tax data for free at www.nassaucountyny.gov/mynassauproperty/main.jsp. No name searching, must search by address or lot and parcel number. Also, access to property reports is through a private company at www.courthousedirect.com. Fee for data.**$$$**

New York County ***Recorded Documents*** www.nyc.gov/html/records/home.html Recording data from the City Register are free at http://a836-acris.nyc.gov/Scripts/Coverpage.dll/index. Also, for deeper financial data back 10 years, subscribe to the NYC Dept of Finance dial-up system; fee-$250 monthly and $5.00 per item. For info/signup, call Rich Reskin 718-935-6523. **$$$**

Property, Taxation Property tax and ownership is at http://webapps.nyc.gov:8084/cics/fin2/find001i? and http://nycprop.nyc.gov/nycproperty/nynav/jsp/selectbbl.jsp. Also, a private company sells county tax claim property, view list free at www.xspand.com/investors/realestate_sale/index.aspx.**$$$**

Niagara County ***Recorded Documents*** www.niagaracounty.com/Departments/CountyClerk.aspx Access to county records for a fee at www.searchiqs.com/niagara.html. **$$$**

Oneida County ***Recorded Documents (Land Indexes Only) Records*** http://ocgov.net/countyclerk Access to public records call IQS Inc for free password (315-463-1400). Also, access to records for a fee go to www.searchiqs.com/oneida.html. **$$$**

Property, Taxation A private company offers property assessment data online at www.accuriz.com/index.aspx.**$$$**

Onondaga County ***Grantor/Grantee Records*** www.ongov.net/clerk/index.html Access to records free at http://psi.ongov.net/PublicClerk/Search/Name.jsp. Images are not available at this time. For a copy of your document mail a self addressed stamped envelope and $.65 per page or $1.30 per document minimum.

Property, Taxation Search for property data free on the GIS-mapping page at www.maphost.com/syracuse-onondaga/main.asp. Access county property data free at www.ongov.net/rpts/index.html, includes access to City of Syracuse property data. Also, search Town of Tully tax roll free at www.taxlookup.net/search.aspx?jurisdiction=tully&year=2010.

Ontario County ***Real Estate, Deed Records*** www.co.ontario.ny.us/index.aspx?nid=102 Access to recorded data at https://counties2.recordfusion.com/countyweb/login.do?countyname=Ontario. Username/password required or login free at Guest. **$$$**

Property, Taxation A private company offers property assessment data online at www.accuriz.com/index.aspx. Also, City of Canandaigua property, assessment, and sales lists in pdf format available free at www.canandaiguanewyork.gov/index.asp?Type=B_BASIC&SEC={27669D54-CE6F-4445-9CED-0861BE56EFA0}.

Orange County ***Property, Taxation*** Real Property Tax Assessment Information is available free at http://propertydata.orangecountygov.com/imate/index.aspx. Registration and fees apply for fuller data. Also, search GIS-mapping site data at http://ocgis.orangecountygov.com/.**$$$**

Orleans County ***Property, Taxation*** A private company offers property assessment data online at http://orleans.sdgnys.com/index.aspx.**$$$**

Oswego County ***Real Estate, Deed, Mortgage Records*** www.co.oswego.ny.us/clerk.shtml Access county clerk records 1963 to present at http://72.43.24.100/. Username and password required. You may email sales@InfoQuickSolutions.com for a free trial account or for info, or call Info Quick Solutions at 800-320-2617. Also, access to records for a fee go to www.searchiqs.com/oswego.html. **$$$**

Property, Taxation Access tax roll data for Towns of Sandy Creek, Schroeppel, and Scriba free at www.taxlookup.net/#Oswego.

Otsego County ***Recorded Documents*** www.otsegocounty.com/depts/clk/ Access to public records free at www.searchiqs.com/. Must register before using.

Property, Taxation Search the county real property lookup free at http://imo.otsegocounty.com/index.aspx. A private company offers property assessment data online at www.accuriz.com/index.aspx.**$$$**

Putnam County ***Real Estate, Deed, UCC, Lien Records*** www.putnamcountyny.com Recorder records are accessible by subscription through a private online service at http://hosted.acsgrm.com/cgibin/homepage?County=8002. Registration is required; pay per use ($5.00 to view doc) or $100 monthly plan available. **$$$**

Queens County (Borough) ***Real Estate, Deed, Lien, Judgment, UCC, Mortgage Records*** www.queensbp.org/ Recording data from the City Register are free at http://a836-acris.nyc.gov/Scripts/Coverpage.dll/index. Also, for deeper financial data back 10 years, subscribe to the NYC Dept of Finance dial-up system; fee-$250 monthly and $5.00 per item. For info/signup, call Richard Reskin 718-935-6523. **$$$**

Property, Taxation Property tax and ownership is at http://webapps.nyc.gov:8084/cics/fin2/find001i? and http://nycprop.nyc.gov/nycproperty/nynav/jsp/selectbbl.jsp. Tax claim sales are atwww.xspand.com/investors/realestate_sale/index.aspx.

Rensselaer County ***Real Estate, Deed, Lien Records*** www.rensco.com/departments_countyclerk.asp Search real estate deeds and liens at www.nylandrecords.com. Click on Rennselaer. Registration required. Commercial users can subscribe for $25.00 per month and $.25 per search; Personal users can purchase documents for $5.00 each, no monthly fee. **$$$**

Richmond County (Staten Island Borough) ***Real Estate, Deed, Lien, Judgment, UCC, Mortgage Records*** Recording data from the City Register are free at http://a836-acris.nyc.gov/Scripts/Coverpage.dll/index. Also, for deeper financial data back 10 years, subscribe to the NYC Dept of Finance dial-up system; fee-$250 monthly and $5.00 per item. For info/signup, call Richard Reskin 718-935-6523. **$$$**

Property, Taxation Property tax and ownership is at http://webapps.nyc.gov:8084/cics/fin2/find001i? and http://nycprop.nyc.gov/nycproperty/nynav/jsp/selectbbl.jsp. See tax claim property sales at www.xspand.com/investors/realestate_sale/index.aspx.

Rockland County ***Real Estate, Deed, Judgment, Lien, Mortgage, Misc Records*** www.rocklandcountyclerk.com/ Access to most land records free at https://search.rocklandcountyclerk.com/External/User/Login.aspx?ReturnUrl=%2fexternal%2flndex.aspx. Can print copies at no charge but will contain a large "Unofficial Copy" watermark. If you wish to print documents without watermark must register for an account and printing will be charged at $.50 per page. **$$$**

Property, Taxation A private company offers property assessment data online at www.accuriz.com/index.aspx. Also, access to GIS/mapping free at https://geopower.jws.com/rockland/.**$$$**

St. Lawrence County ***Property, Taxation*** County assessor rolls available at www.co.st-lawrence.ny.us/Departments/RealProperty/#. Search Towns of Brasher, Canton, Clare, Clifton, Colton, DeKalb, Depeyster, Edwards, Fine, Fowler, Gouverneur, Hammond, Hermon, Hopkinton, Lawrence, Lisbon, Louisville, Macomb, Madrid, Massena, Morristown, Norfolk, Oswegatchie, Parishville, Piercefield, Pierrepont, Pitcairn, Potsdam, Rossie, Russell, Stockholm, Waddington property data free at https://www.taxlookup.net. 14 Villages also available.

Saratoga County ***Records Records*** www.saratogacountyny.gov/departments.asp?did=144 Access to online records free at www.saratogacountyny.gov/departments.asp?did=144. Go to bottom of page and click on Online records application. Must apply online and get password.

Property, Taxation A private company offers property assessment data online at www.accuriz.com/index.aspx. Also, access the assessment database free at www.saratogacountyny.gov/subpage.asp?pageid=234.**$$$**

Schenectady County ***Real Estate, Deed, Mortgage, Lien, UCC Records*** www.schenectadycounty.com/FullStory.aspx?m=47&amid=2070 Access county land records back to 1996 free at http://landrecords.schenectadycounty.com. Also, access the county clerk court and land indexes via www.landex.com/webstore/jsp/cart/DocumentSearch.jsp. Full access to records is by subscription at www.landex.com/remote/. The land records index goes back to 1984; courts indexes back to 1988. Images go back to 12/1999. **$$$**

Schoharie County ***DEED, Mortgage, Judgment, Civil, Criminal, Misc Records*** www.schohariecounty-ny.gov/CountyWebSite/CountyClerk/countyclerkservice.html Access to records free at www.schohariecounty-ny.gov/remote/OpeningScreen?menuItem=43

Property, Taxation A private company offers property assessment data online at www.accuriz.com/index.aspx. Also, search property tax data free at www.schohariecounty-ny.gov/CountyWebSite/findTaxInformation.html.

Schuyler County ***Property, Taxation*** Access to land records for free at http://schuyler.sdgnys.com/index.aspx. Guests may search free; registration and fees required for images, etc.**$$$**

Seneca County ***Property, Taxation*** A private company offers property assessment data online at www.accuriz.com/index.aspx.**$$$**

Steuben County ***Property, Taxation*** Search Steuben County assessment rolls free online at www.steubencony.org/Pages.asp?PGID=40. Search Town of Erwin Real Property Assessment Roll free online at www.erwinny.org/ertxsrch.htm.

Suffolk County ***Real Estate, Grantor/Grantee, Deed, Mortgage, Lien, Judgment, Corporation, Business Name Records*** www.suffolkcountyny.gov/departments/countyclerk.aspx Access county land records, business names, and limited civil court records free at https://kiosk.suffolkcountyny.gov/KioskWeb/Notifications.aspx. Land records is index only. Search the county corporation database free at http://clerk.co.suffolk.ny.us/buscerts/corpsearch.aspx.

Property, Taxation The Areis Real Property subscription service is available, call 631-852-1550. View county accidents and details free at http://gis.co.suffolk.ny.us/website/accident/viewer.htm.**$$$**

Sullivan County ***Property, Taxation*** The agency has an agreement for property assessment data to be provided at http://webapps.co.sullivan.ny.us/IMO/index.aspx. Assseesment Roll by town are provided at http://co.sullivan.ny.us/Departments/RealPropertyTaxServices/tabid/3319/Default.aspx. Private companies offer property assessment data online at www.accuriz.com/index.aspx and at https://www.taxlookup.net.**$$$**

Tioga County ***Property, Taxation*** Search Town of Owego property data free at https://www.taxlookup.net.

Tompkins County ***Property, Taxation*** Access to property records on ImageMate system at www.tompkins-co.org/assessment/online.html has 2 levels: basic free and a registration/password fee-based full system. Free version has no name searching. Fee service is $20 monthly or $200 per year. For info or registration for the latter, email assessment@tompkins-co.org. Also, a private company offers property assessment data online at www.accuriz.com/index.aspx.**$$$**

Ulster County ***Real Estate, Deed, Lien, Mortgage, Voter Registration Records*** www.co.ulster.ny.us Access to County records for a fee at https://www.nylandrecords.com/nylr/controller;jsessionid=B659AEC3BF793BBBE681C10013C1393E. Land Records date back to 1984. Includes county court records back to 1987. **$$$**

Property, Taxation A private company offers property assessment data at www.accuriz.com/index.aspx. Also, access to county maps free at www.ulstercountyny.gov/maps/ulsterco.html.**$$$**

Warren County ***Property, Taxation*** A private company offers property assessment data online at www.accuriz.com/index.aspx.**$$$**

Washington County ***Recorded Documents*** www.co.washington.ny.us/Departments/cclerk/clk1.htm Access to records for a fee at https://www.nylandrecords.com/nylr/NylrApp/index.jsp. **$$$**

Property, Taxation Access to GIS/mapping for free at http://gis.co.washington.ny.us/webmap/index.htm.

Wayne County ***Property, Taxation*** Access tax property data free at www.co.wayne.ny.us/RPT-TaxSearch/default.aspx.

Westchester County ***Recorded Documents*** www.westchesterclerk.com/ Access to the clerk's recorded documents and liens is free at https://wro.westchesterclerk.com/Login/Login.aspx?ReturnUrl=%2fdefault.aspx. There is also an advanced search that features images for a fee; registration is required. Data available also includes registrations of corporations, foreclosures, and divorces. **$$$**

Property, Taxation Access GIS/mapping, land records, trades licenses and legal records for free at http://pender-rod.inttek.net/. Must sign up for User ID and password. Access Sleepy Hollow Village tax roll data free at www.taxlookup.net/ and click on Westchester County; no name searching.

Wyoming County ***Recorded Documents*** www.wyomingco.net Recorder index is accessible free through a private online service at http://hosted.acsgrm.com/cgibin/homepage?County=8008. This is a subscription service, fees and registration may be required. **$$$**

Property, Taxation A private company offers property assessment data online at www.accuriz.com/index.aspx. Search by owner or address.**$$$**

Yates County ***Property, Taxation*** A private company offers property assessment data online at www.accuriz.com/index.aspx.**$$$**

North Carolina

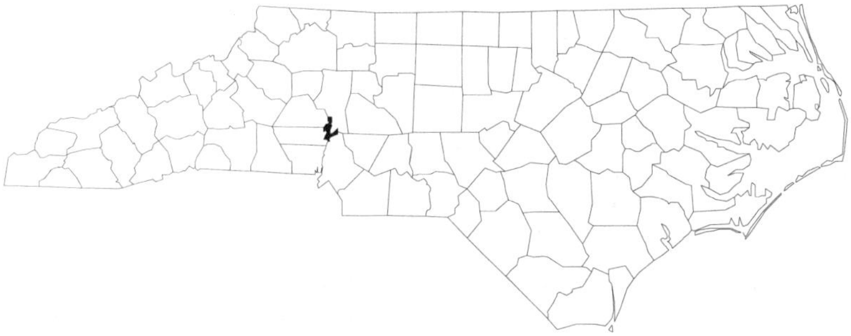

Capital: Raleigh
Wake County
Time Zone: EST
Population: 9,752,053
# of Counties: 100

Useful State Links

Website: www.ncgov.com
Governor: www.governor.state.nc.us
Attorney General: www.ncdoj.gov/
State Archives: www.history.ncdcr.gov/
State Statutes and Codes: www.ncleg.net/gascripts/Statutes/Statutes.asp
Legislative Bill Search: www.ncleg.net
Unclaimed Funds: https://www.nctreasurer.com/Claim-Your-Cash/Claim-Your-NC_Cash/Pages/Search.aspx

State Public Record Agencies

Sexual Offender Registry

State Bureau of Investigation, Criminal Information & Ident Sect - SOR Unit, http://sexoffender.ncdoj.gov/ Search Level 3 records at the website. Search by name or geographic region. *Other Options:* Agency can provide data on CD-Rom.

Incarceration Records

North Carolina Department of Public Safety, Incarceration Records, www.doc.state.nc.us The web access allows searching by name or ID number for public information on inmates, probationers, or parolees since 1972. http://webapps6.doc.state.nc.us/opi/offendersearch.do?method=view.

Corporation, LP, LLC, Trademarks/Servicemarks

Secretary of State, Corporations Division, www.secretary.state.nc.us/corporations/ The website offers a free search of status, corporate documents, and search by registered agent. Search trademarks at www.secretary.state.nc.us/trademrk/search.aspx. Copies may be ordered online. A free verification page is offered at https://www.secretary.state.nc.us/verification/thepage.aspx, search by certificate or authority number. *Other Options:* This agency makes database information available for purchase via an FTP site. Contact Don Beckett at 919-807-2203 for details.

Uniform Commercial Code, Federal Tax Liens

UCC Division, Secretary of State, www.secretary.state.nc.us/UCC/ A free search is offered at www.secretary.state.nc.us/UCC/FilingSearch.aspx. Search by debtor name or filing number. *Other Options:* The UCC or tax lien database can be purchased on an annual basis via an FTP site. For more information, call 919-807-2219.

Sales Tax Registrations

Revenue Department, Sales & Use Tax Division, www.dornc.com/ Delinquent debtors are shown on the web at www.dor.state.nc.us/collect/delinquent.html. Three different tax registries can be viewed at www.dornc.com/taxes/sales/.

Vital Records

Center for Health Statistics, Vital Records Branch, http://vitalrecords.nc.gov/ Online ordering is available using a credit card via a state-designated vendor at www.vitalchek.com. Additional fees are incurred for using a credit card and delivery. **$$$**

Workers' Compensation Records

NC Industrial Commission, Worker's Comp Records, www.ic.nc.gov/ The N.C. Industrial Commission provides public access to half a dozen full-text searchable databases via Livelink from www.ic.nc.gov/database.html. In the Username: box, type public in all lowercase letters and click the Log-in button. There is no password. The site allows citizens to access Full Commission, Deputy Commissioner, and state appellate court decisions about workers' compensation and tort cases.

Driver Records

Division of Motor Vehicles, Driver License Records, www.ncdot.gov/dmv/driver/ There are two systems. A commercial system is offered for approved, ongoing requesters. Records are $8.00 each. A minimum $500 security deposit is required. Call 919-861-3062 for details. NC drivers or requesters who attest to a valid reason for the request per DPPA may obtain records at https://edmv-dr.dot.state.nc.us/drivingrecords/drivingrecords. Requesters must first apply for a PIN. Non-certified records may be viewed and printed. fees are $8.00 uncertified or $11.00 if certified. Certified records, if ordered, are not viewable but are mailed within three days. **$$$**

Voter Registration, Lobbyists, Campaign Finance

State Board of Elections, www.ncsbe.gov/ Online access to voter registration records is available free at https://www.ncsbe.gov/VoterLookup.aspx. A DOB is needed for best results. One may also have results emailed. Also, the agency has an FTP site available for requesters. See ftp://www.sboe.state.nc.us. Search campaign finance and lobbyists at www.ncsbe.gov/content.aspx?id=22. *Other Options:* Most records are sold in CD format, FTP or sent via email. The maximum fee is $25.00, subject to change if more than 2 CDs used.. Request forms are available at the webpage. This is the most prompt access to records, other than in person.

Accountant-CPA/Firm .... http://nccpaboard.gov/welcome/search-the-database/
Acupuncturist .... www.ncalb.com/search.php
Alarm Installer............................www.ncdoj.com/About-DOJ/Law-Enforcement-Training-and-Standards/Alarm-System-Licensing/Active-Licensees.aspx
Alarm System Business .... www.ncdoj.com/getdoc/9e7cbf2a-3a98-4f74-bb35-a47865159614/Burglar-Alarm-Business-(1).aspx
Amusement Device .... www.nclabor.com/elevator/elevator.htm
Anesthesiologist Assistant .... wwwapps.ncmedboard.org/Clients/NCBOM/Public/LicenseeInformationSearch.aspx
Anesthetist Nurse....................................... https://ncbon.com/LicenseVerification/Search.aspx
Architect .... www.membersbase.com/ncbarch/public/lic/searchdb.asp
Architect/Architectural Firm......................... www.membersbase.com/ncbarch/public/firms/searchdb.asp
Armored Car..........................www.ncdoj.com/About-DOJ/Law-Enforcement-Training-and-Standards/Private-Protective-Services/Active-Licensees.aspx
Athletic Trainer... www.ncbate.org/search.php
Attorney Disciplinary Actions .... www.ncbar.com/discipline/
Auctioneer Disciplinary Action .... www.ncalb.org/discActions.cfm
Auctioneer/Auctioneer Appren/Company..... www.ncalb.org/search.cfm
Bail Bond Runner....................................... https://sbs-nc.naic.org/Lion-Web/jsp/sbsreports/AgentLookup.jsp
Bank .... https://www.nccob.org/Online/brts/BanksAndTrusts.aspx
Bank Branch... https://www.nccob.org/Online/brts/BankBranchSearch.aspx
Barber School .... www.ncbarbers.com/homepages/Schools.aspx
Beauty Shop/Salon .... https://www.nccosmeticarts.com/userman/UserAccounts/Login.aspx?ReturnUrl=/onlineservices/
Bodywork Therapist .... www.bmbt.org/pages/License_Status.html
Boiler/Pressure Vessel Inspector................ www.nclabor.com/boiler/boiler.htm
Building Inspector....................................... https://sbs-nc.naic.org/Lion-Web/jsp/sbsreports/AgentLookup.jsp
Cemetery.. http://nccemetery.com/north-carolina-cemeteries/
Certification Schools .... www.ncwater.org/pws/ncwtfocb_cert/approved_school.htm
Charitable/Sponsor Organization................ www.secretary.state.nc.us/csl/Search.aspx
Check Casher .... https://www.nccob.org/Online/CCS/CompanyListing.aspx
Chiropractor .... http://ncchiroboard.com/
Clinical Nurse Specialist .... https://ncbon.com/LicenseVerification/Search.aspx
Clinical Pharmacist Practitioner .... wwwapps.ncmedboard.org/Clients/NCBOM/Public/LicenseeInformationSearch.aspx
Clinical Social Worker................................ www.ncswboard.org/
Consumer Financer.................................... https://www.nccob.org/online/CFS/CFSCompanyListing.aspx
Contractor, General.................................... www.nclbgc.org/lic_fr.html
Cosmetologist Instruct/Appren/Practit'r........ https://www.nccosmeticarts.com/userman/UserAccounts/Login.aspx?ReturnUrl=/onlineservices/
Cosmetology Disciplinary Action................. https://www.nccosmeticarts.com/userman/UserAccounts/Login.aspx?ReturnUrl=/onlineservices/
Counselor, Professional.............................. www.ncblpc.org/Verify.php
Courier Service.......................www.ncdoj.com/About-DOJ/Law-Enforcement-Training-and-Standards/Private-Protective-Services/Active-Licensees.aspx

Crematory .... www.ncbfs.org/directory.html
Dentist/Dental Hygienist.............................. www.ncdentalboard.org/ncdbe_search.asp
DME-Rx Device.. www.ncbop.org/ncbop_verification.htm
Electrical Contractor/Inspector.................... http://lookup.ncbeec.org/
Electronic Countermeasures...www.ncdoj.com/About-DOJ/Law-Enforcement-Training-and-Standards/Private-Protective-Services/Active-Licensees.aspx
Elevator Inspector .... www.nclabor.com/elevator/elevator.htm
Engineer/Land Surveyor/Firm .... https://www.membersbase.com/ncbels-vs/public/searchdb.asp
Esthetician Instruc./Appren/Practition'r .... https://www.nccosmeticarts.com/userman/UserAccounts/Login.aspx?ReturnUrl=/onlineservices/
Family Therapist.. www.nclmft.org/public_resources/verify_a_licensee/
Fire Sprinkler Contractor/Inspection Contr/Maintenance Tech.............http://onlineweb.nclicensing.org/Lookup/LicenseLookup.aspx
Firearms Trainer.....................www.ncdoj.com/About-DOJ/Law-Enforcement-Training-and-Standards/Private-Protective-Services/Active-Licensees.aspx
Forester... www.ncbrf.org/list.htm
Fund Raiser Consultant/Solicitor .... www.secretary.state.nc.us/csl/Search.aspx
Funeral Director/Service/Chapel................. www.ncbfs.org/directory.html
Funeral Education Studied.......................... www.ncbfs.org/list.html
Funeral Home, Transport, Trainee.............. www.ncbfs.org/directory.html
Geologist... www.ncblg.org/licensees.html
Guard Dog Srv........................www.ncdoj.com/About-DOJ/Law-Enforcement-Training-and-Standards/Private-Protective-Services/Active-Licensees.aspx
Hearing Aid Dispenser/Fitter....................... www.nchalb.org/ceu.php
Heating Contractor...................................... http://onlineweb.nclicensing.org/Lookup/LicenseLookup.aspx
HMO.. http://infoportal.ncdoi.net/cmp_lookup.jsp
Home Inspector... https://apps.ncdoi.net/f?p=135:126
Insurance Agent.. https://sbs-nc.naic.org/Lion-Web/jsp/sbsreports/AgentLookup.jsp
Insurance Company.................................... https://sbs-nc.naic.org/Lion-Web/jsp/sbsreports/CompanySearchLookup.jsp
Landscape Architect .... www.ncbola.org/architect_directory.lasso
Lobbyist... www.secretary.state.nc.us/lobbyists/directory.aspx
Manicurist Instruct/Appren/Practitioner........ https://www.nccosmeticarts.com/userman/UserAccounts/Login.aspx?ReturnUrl=/onlineservices/
Manuf'd Housing Retailer/Mfg/Contr/Seller/Qualifier.........www.ncdoi.com/OSFM/Manufactured_Building.aspx
Marriage & Family Therapist....................... www.nclmft.org/public_resources/verify_a_licensee/
Massage Therapist..................................... www.bmbt.org/pages/License_Status.html
Midwife .... https://ncbon.com/LicenseVerification/Search.aspx
Money Transmitter .... https://www.nccob.org/Online/MTS/MTSCompanyListing.aspx
Nurse-LPN/Practitioner/Aide....................... https://ncbon.com/LicenseVerification/Search.aspx
Nursing Home Administrator....................... www.ncbenha.org/searchdb.asp
Occupational Therapist/Therapy Assist .... www.ncbot.org/OTpages/license_verification.html
Optometrist... http://web1.ncoptometry.org/verify.aspx
Osteopathic Physician .... wwwapps.ncmedboard.org/Clients/NCBOM/Public/LicenseeInformationSearch.aspx
Pesticide Applicator/Dealer/Consultant........ www.ncagr.gov/aspzine/str-pest/pesticides/data/advsearch.asp
Pharmacist .... www.ncbop.org/ncbop_verification.htm
Pharmacy/Physician Pharmacy/Technician. www.ncbop.org/ncbop_verification.htm
Physical Therapist/Assistant....................... https://www.ncptboard.org/OnlineServices/Secure/VerifyTherapist/VerifyTherapist.php
Physician Assistant .... wwwapps.ncmedboard.org/Clients/NCBOM/Public/LicenseeInformationSearch.aspx
Plumber... http://onlineweb.nclicensing.org/Lookup/LicenseLookup.aspx
Podiatrist .... www.ncbpe.org/content/search-podiatrist
Polygraph Examiner.............www.ncdoj.com/About-DOJ/Law-Enforcement-Training-and-Standards/Private-Protective-Services/Active-Licensees.aspx
Private Investigator...............www.ncdoj.com/About-DOJ/Law-Enforcement-Training-and-Standards/Private-Protective-Services/Active-Licensees.aspx
Psychological Associate .... www.ncpsychologyboard.org/search.htm
Psychologist.. www.ncpsychologyboard.org/search.htm
Real Estate Agent/Broker/Dealer................ www.members-base.com/ncrec/oecgi3.exe/O4W_LIC_SEARCH
Real Estate Firm .... www.members-base.com/ncrec/oecgi3.exe/O4W_FIRM_SEARCH
Reg. Tax Refund Loan Facilitator .... https://www.nccob.org/online/RALS/RALSCompanyListing.aspx

Sanitarian .... www.ncrehs.com/rsboard-old/rsweb/directory/directory.htm
Security Guard & Patrol...........www.ncdoj.com/About-DOJ/Law-Enforcement-Training-and-Standards/Private-Protective-Services/Active-Licensees.aspx
Social Worker/Manager .... www.ncswboard.org/

Soil Scientist.. www.ncblss.org/directory.html
Speech Pathologist/Audiologist .... www.ncboeslpa.org/search_members.asp
Therapist, Bodywork-Massage .... www.bmbt.org/pages/License_Status.html
Trust Company.. https://www.nccob.org/Online/BRTS/TrustLicensees.aspx

State and Local Courts

State Court Structure: All felony criminal cases, civil cases involving more than $10,000 and misdemeanor and infraction appeals from District Court are tried in the **Superior Court**.

District Courts handle civil, misdemeanors and infractions, juvenile and magistrate. Civil cases include divorce, custody, child support and cases involving less than $10,000 or small claims ($5,000 or less). A **Magistrate** is a judicial officer of the District Court and the Magistrate presides over Small Claims Court and evictions. The principal relief sought in Small Claims Court is money, the recovery of specific personal property, or summary ejectment (eviction).

Uncontested Probate is handled by County Clerks.

Appellate Courts: Appellate and Supreme Court opinions are at www.aoc.state.nc.us/www/public/html/opinions.htm

Statewide Court Online Access: All courts participate in the systems described below.

- The state AOC provides ongoing, high volume requesters and vendors with portions of electronic criminal and civil records on an ongoing basis pursuant to a licensing agreement. A Daily Criminal access is supplied. However starting in 2011, the case dispositions were removed from the extract. Users must now access a secondary source - known as the Green Screen - to find the case details. The Green Screen is a cumbersome system using technology from the 1970's. The requirement to using the Green Screen has increased the turnaround time and fees charged by vendors. To obtain cost and connectivity information contact the NCAOC Remote Public Access team at 919-890-2220 or via email at rpa@nccourts.org. For a list of the participating vendors visit the web at http://www.nccourts.org/Citizens/GoToCourt/Documents/cbccompanies.pdf.
- There are several other limited North Carolina online services that are free. Search current civil and criminal court calendars at www1.aoc.state.nc.us/www/calendars.html. Search the District and Superior Court Query system for current criminal defendants at www1.aoc.state.nc.us/www/calendars/CriminalQuery.html. At this site there are also queries for Impaired Driving, Citations, and Current Civil and Criminal Calendars.
- Also, note an eFiling Pilot Program is operational in Chowan, Davidson, and Wake counties.

Note: No individual North Carolina courts offer online access beyond the systems mentioned above.

Recorders, Assessors, and Other Sites of Note

Recording Office Organization: 100 counties, 100 recording offices. The recording officer is the Register of Deeds but for tax liens the officer is the Clerk of Superior Court. Federal tax liens on personal property of businesses are filed with the Secretary of State. Other federal and all state tax liens are filed with the county Clerk of Superior Court. Oddly, even tax liens on real property are also filed with the Clerk of Superior Court, not with the Register of Deeds.

Statewide or Multi-Jurisdiction Access: A growing number of counties offer free access to assessor and real estate records. Some county websites are provided by private vendors, but overal presence of vendor-sponsored searching among North Carolina counties is limited.

Alamance County ***Recorded Documents, Birth, Death, Marriage Records*** www.alamance-nc.com/d/register-of-deeds.html Access the recorded document database free at http://cotthosting.com/ncalamance/User/Login.aspx?ReturnUrl=%2fncalamance%2fLandRecords%2fprotected%2fSrchSimpleName.aspx. Must register.
Property, Taxation Records Property tax, parcel data and GIS/mapping are available free at www.alamance-nc.com/d/gis.html.

Alexander County ***Recorded Documents*** www.alexandercountync.gov/rod/ Access recorder land records free for residents at http://cotthosting.com/ncalexander/LandRecords/protected/SrchSimpleName.aspx. Also, access to county records for a fee go to https://www.countygovernmentrecords.com/. Must register. **$$$**

Property, Taxation Records Access parcel data free on the GIS/mapping site a http://maps.co.alexander.nc.us/. Real property index and records available free at www.alexandercountync.gov/index/online_services.php. Searchproperty tax records at http://alexander.ustaxdata.com/

Alleghany County ***Recorded Documents*** www.alleghanycounty-nc.gov/index.php?option=com_content&view=article&id=79&Itemid=92 Access to the Register of Deeds database is free at http://24.172.15.58/Opening.asp. All Deed images are online back thru 1859 to current. Real property indexes available 1859 to present week.

Property, Taxation Records Search for property data on a GIS mapping site at http://arcgis.webgis.net/nc/Alleghany/.

Anson County ***Recorded Documents*** www.co.anson.nc.us/content/index.php?deeds Access to land records free at www.ansonncrod.org/. Have access to both full system and imaging system only. Deeds from 8/1/89 to present only.

Property, Taxation Records Search the county Online Tax Inquiry System free at www.co.anson.nc.us/pubcgi/taxinq/. Tax collections search at www.co.anson.nc.us/pubcgi/colinq/.

Ashe County ***Recorded Documents*** http://ashecountygov.info/?page_id=196 Access to the register of deeds real estate data is free at www.ashencrod.org/Opening.asp. Full index goes back to 1/1995; images to 1/1934.

Property, Taxation Records Access to records on the county Tax Parcel Information System is free at http://ashegis.ashecountygov.com/webgis/.

Avery County ***Recorded Documents*** www.averydeeds.com/ Search the recorders database free at http://search.averydeeds.com/.

Property, Taxation Records Access to property data is free on the GIS mapping site at http://arcims.webgis.net/nc/avery/. To name search click Quick Search.

Bertie County ***Recorded Documents*** www.co.bertie.nc.us/departments/rod/rod.html Access real property data back to 1/1/1983 free at http://bertie-rod.inttek.net/ after registration.

Property, Taxation Records Access property records through gis-mapping system free at www.co.bertie.nc.us/departments/tm/GISD.html.

Bladen County ***Recorded Documents*** www.bladenncrod.org/ Access to register of deeds site at www.bladenncrod.org/opening.asp; search comprehensive index or direct images.

Property, Taxation Records Search the GIS-mapping site for property info free at http://web2.mobile311.com/bladen/.**$$$**

Brunswick County ***Recorded Documents*** http://rod.brunsco.net Access to the recorder database is free at http://rod.brunsco.net. Free registration, logon and password are required. Records are updated daily.

Property, Taxation Records Search the tax administration data for real property or vehicle for free at http://tax.brunsco.net/itsnet/.

Buncombe County ***Recorded Documents*** www.buncombecounty.org/governing/depts/RegisterDeeds/ Access to county Register of Deeds records is free at http://registerofdeeds.buncombecounty.org/external/LandRecords/protected/v4/SrchName.aspx. Includes marriages, deaths, deeds.

Property, Taxation Records County assessor tax records are free at www.buncombetax.org/Default.aspx. Also, GIS property search available at www.buncombecounty.org/Governing/Depts/GIS/Disclaimer.aspx. Also, search tax property sales free at www.buncombecounty.org/Governing/Depts/Tax/LegalDivision_Owned.aspx.

Burke County ***Recorded Documents, Marriage, Birth, Death (Index only], Assumed Names Records*** www.co.burke.nc.us/index.asp?Type=B_BASIC&SEC={8CED9168-4924-4719-B08C-94B1F3E730E0} Access to public records free at https://rod.burkenc.org/.

Property, Taxation Records Access to property data is free on the GIS mapping site at http://arcgis.webgis.net/nc/Burke/.

Cabarrus County ***Recorded Documents*** www.cabarrusncrod.org/Opening.asp Access to the recorder records is free at www.cabarrusncrod.org/Opening.asp by two methods: full system or image-only system. Land records & images back to 1792.

Property, Taxation Records Search tax appraisal cards by name free at http://onlineservices.cabarruscounty.us/Tax/TaxAppraisalCard/. Also, search land records of all kinds including GIS free on the ClaRIS system at www.cabarruscounty.us/Pages/default.aspx.

Caldwell County ***Recorded Documents*** www.caldwellrod.org/ Access register of deeds recording data with images back to 1930 free at http://rod.caldwellcountync.org/resolution/User/Login.aspx?ReturnUrl=/resolution/default.aspx.

Property, Taxation Records Access to GIS/mapping for free at www.caldwellcountync.org/caldwell-county-nc-departments/information-technology/geographic-information-system-gis/caldwell-map-viewer/

Camden County ***Recorded Documents*** www.camdencountync.gov/departments/register-of-deeds Access to records free at http://cotthosting.com/nccamden/LandRecords/protected/SrchSimpleName.aspx. Land conveyances are available by name from 5/3/99. Also, access to county records for a fee go to https://www.countygovernmentrecords.com/. Must register. **$$$**

Property, Taxation Records Search property records on the gis-mapping system free at http://67.239.151.203/gomaps/.

Carteret County ***Recorded Documents*** www.carteretcountygov.org/Register-of-Deeds.aspx Access to Register of Deeds database for free at http://deeds.carteretcounty.com/.

Property, Taxation Records Search tax parcel cards free at http://web2.mobile311.com/Carteretsearch/default.aspx.

Caswell County ***Recorded Documents*** www.caswellcountync.gov/resources/rod.htm Search recorded deeds at www.caswellrod.net/ and click Search Online. Images are shown.

Property, Taxation Records Access to property data is free on the GIS mapping site at http://arcgis.webgis.net/nc/Caswell/.

Catawba County ***Recorded Documents*** www.catawbacountync.gov/depts/regdeed/default.asp Also, search Register of Deeds records free at www.catawbarod.org/Opening.asp. Land index goes back to 1955; images to 9/30/1959.

Property, Taxation Records Search the Catawba County GIS Map Server database free at www.gis.catawba.nc.us/website/Parcel/parcel_main.asp. Search property tax bill data free at www.catawbacountync.gov/Tax/billsearch.asp. Also, access real estate reports at www.gis.catawba.nc.us/nomap/parcel_search.asp.

Chatham County ***Recorded Documents*** www.chathamnc.org/Index.aspx?page=905 Access land records free at www.chathamncrod.org/Opening.asp. Land Record Index Data back to 1771; UCC data goes back to 2008.

Property, Taxation Records Access property data and tax records free at http://ustaxdata.com/nc/chatham/Search.cfm.

Cherokee County ***Recorded Documents*** www.cherokeecounty-nc.gov/index.aspx?page=137 Access to land records and imaging free at www.cherokeencrod.org/. Images go back to 07/1999, index back to 1993.

Chowan County ***Property, Taxation Records*** Access property tax records free at http://208.27.112.94/paas/. Double click on Parcels. Search property data on the GIS-mapping site free at www.chowancountygis.com/mapguide/chowangis/.

Clay County ***Recorded Documents*** www.clayconc.com/services/details.php?id=25 Access to property and deeds indexes and images is via a private company at www.titlesearcher.com/. Fee/registration required. Deeds go back to 1/1999; indices back to 1/1/94; images to 8/22/2003. **$$$**

Cleveland County ***Recorded Documents*** www.clevelandcounty.com/ccmain/ Also, access to county records for a fee at https://www.countygovernmentrecords.com/. Must register. **$$$**

Property, Taxation Records Access property records free on the GIS-mapping site at http://quicksearch.webgis.net/search.php?site=nc_cleveland_co. Access to property data is free on the GIS mapping site at http://arcgis.webgis.net/nc/Cleveland/.

Columbus County ***Recorded Documents*** http://columbusdeeds.com/ Access to the Recorder's database is free at http://search.columbusdeeds.com/.

Property, Taxation Records Access property tax data free at http://webtax.columbusco.org/viewer.htm.

Craven County ***Recorded Documents*** www.cravencounty.com/departments/reg.cfm Search register of deeds free at www.co.craven.nc.us/departments/reg/regwwwdisclaimer.cfm. Real estate 1995-present; Corporations 2002-3/2007; Births/Deaths 1914-2007; UCCs 1999-2001; older real estate 1984-1994; marriages 1964-present.

Property, Taxation Records Access to assessor and property data is free at www.cravencounty.com/departments/tax/property.cfm.

Cumberland County ***Recorded Documents*** www.ccrod.org Search two systems free at www.ccrodinternet.org/Opening.asp. The land records index data dated from 1754 t0 1976 (scanned index books) and images from Book 1 (1754) to Book 2083 (2/68).

Property, Taxation Records Assessor real estate search is free at http://mainfr.co.cumberland.nc.us/. Also, search property data free on the GIS mapping site at http://152.31.99.8/.

Currituck County ***Recorded Documents*** www.co.currituck.nc.us/Register-of-Deeds.cfm Access to land recorded documents is free at www.courthousecomputersystems.com/currituoknc/.

Property, Taxation Records Search property, sales, assessor data and more free at www.co.currituck.nc.us/Real-Estate-Searches.cfm. Also, name search for parcel ownership data free on the GIS-mapping site at www.co.currituck.nc.us/Interactive-Online-MappingDup2.cfm.

Dare County ***Recorded Documents*** www.darenc.com/depts/Deeds/index.htm Recording office records are free at http://eglweb.darenc.com/recorder/web/. Images available and indexes verified only from 12/13/99 forward. Indexes prior to 12/13/99 copied directly from COTT tape and are not verified. Also, a land transfer search is free at www.darenc.com/public/LT/LTsearch.asp.

Property, Taxation Records County assessor records free at www.darenc.com/public/TaxInqOwner.asp. Search property data on the GIS-mapping site free at www.darenc.com/public/gis.htm but no name searching.

Davidson County ***Recorded Documents*** www.co.davidson.nc.us/ROD/ Access recorders database free at http://davidsoncorod.org/. **$$$**

Property, Taxation Records Records on the county Tax Dept database are free at www.co.davidson.nc.us/taxnet/. Search for property info on the GIS mapping site for free at http://webgis.co.davidson.nc.us/website/davidsongis/viewer.htm.

Davie County ***Recorded Documents*** www.daviecountync.gov/index.aspx?nid=98 Access Register of Deeds site at www.daviencrod.org/. Land records go back to 1993. Accessed in three different ways - Full System, Imaging System Only, or Scanned Index Books.

Property, Taxation Records Access to county property data on the GIS-mapping site is free at http://maps.co.davie.nc.us/ITSNet/.

Duplin County ***Recorded Documents, Marriage, Death, Notary, Military Discharge Records*** http://rod.duplincounty.org/ Access to the Register's multiple databases is free at http://rod.duplincounty.org/. Vital stats and discharges are index only.

Property, Taxation Records Access assessment data on real estate and personal property free at http://duplintax.duplincounty.org/. Also, access to GIS/mapping for free at http://gis.duplincountync.com/.

Durham County ***Recorded Documents*** http://dconc.gov/index.aspx?page=455&redirect=1 Access the Register of Deeds database free at http://rodweb.co.durham.nc.us/.

Property, Taxation Records Search property records and tax bills free at www.ustaxdata.com/nc/durham/durhamtaxsearch.cfm. Search GIS mapping site free athttp://gisweb.durhamnc.gov/sp/index.cfm.

Edgecombe County ***Recorded Documents*** www.edgecombecountync.gov/rod/rod.aspx Access the recorder's database free at http://76.7.71.236/external/User/Login.aspx?ReturnUrl=%2fexternal%2findex.aspx. RE index goes back to 1973, financing statements 1993 to 2005.

Property, Taxation Records Access to county property data is free at http://206.107.103.195/paas/default.htm.

Forsyth County ***Recorded Documents*** www.co.forsyth.nc.us/ROD/ Access online record lookup for free at www.forsythdeeds.com/index.php. Search voter registration records free at https://www.ncsbe.gov/VoterLookup.aspx?Feature=voterinfo. Also, access to property and deeds indexes and images is via a private company at www.titlesearcher.com/. Fee/registration required; monthly and per day access available. Deeds and indices go back to 1849; images to 1973. **$$$**

Property, Taxation Records Access assessor records on Geo-Data free- www.co.forsyth.nc.us/Tax/geodata.aspx. Click "Launch Geo-Data Explorer." Search tax bills free- www.co.forsyth.nc.us/Tax/. Tax Admin tax bill svc free at www.co.forsyth.nc.us/taxbill.aspx. Also, assessment data for City of Winston-Salem available free at www.cwsonline.org/assessments/.

Franklin County ***Recorded Documents*** www.franklincountync.us/services/register-of-deeds Access to recording records index free at http://deeds.co.franklin.nc.us/External/User/Login.aspx?ReturnUrl=%2fExternal%2fLandRecords%2fprotected%2fSrchSimpleName.aspx.

Property, Taxation Records Access to tax data on the county spatial data explorer database is free at www.franklincountytax.us/Main/Home.aspx or at parcel search page at www.franklincountytax.us/Search/GenericSearch.aspx?mode=OWNER. Also, access to tax records free at www.franklincountytax.us/Search/GenericSearch.aspx?mode=OWNER. Also, access to GIS/mapping free at http://maps.roktech.net/franklintax/#.

Gaston County ***Recorded Documents*** www.gastongov.com/departments/register-of-deeds Access to recorded documents is free at http://207.235.60.108/external/LandRecords/protected/SrchSimpleName.aspx. Indexes prior to 1960 are now online.

Property, Taxation Records Access to GIS/mapping for free at http://egov1.co.gaston.nc.us/website/ParcelDataSite/WelcomePage.html.

Gates County ***Recorded Documents*** www.gatesrod.net/ Access to county records for a fee at https://www.countygovernmentrecords.com/. Must register. Also, access to recorded documents free at www.gatesrod.net/. **$$$**

Property, Taxation Records Access to GIS/mapping free at www.gatescountygis.com/.

Graham County ***Recorded Documents*** www.grahamcounty.org/grahamcounty_departments_registrar.html Access the consolidated real property database back to 1/1995 free at http://cotthosting.com/ncgraham/LandRecords/protected/SrchSimpleName.aspx. Also search pre-1995 real estate 7/1/1978 to 12/31/1994.

Property, Taxation Records Access to real estate search for free at http://taxsearch.grahamcounty.org/.

Granville County ***Recorded Documents*** www.granvillenc.govoffice2.com/index.asp?Type=B_BASIC&SEC={065B3E1D-52CB-458F-AEE3-1895B88124A0} Access recorders index free at www.granvillecountydeeds.org/External/LandRecords/protected/SrchSimpleName.aspx.

Property, Taxation Records Access to GIS/mapping records free at www.granvillegis.org/. Must register to log-in.

Greene County ***Property, Taxation Records*** Access to GIS/mapping data for free at www.co.greene.nc.us/gisdownload.aspx.

Guilford County ***Recorded Documents, Vital Records Records*** http://countyweb.co.guilford.nc.us/rod-homepage Access to county databases is free at www.co.guilford.nc.us/services/index.html. Vital statistic records after registration and login at http://66.162.203.229/vital/login.php. Also, access to register records free at http://66.162.203.229/guilfordNameSearch.php. Also, access to register of deeds online records system for free go to http://rdlxweb.co.guilford.nc.us/guilfordNameSearch.php.

Property, Taxation Records Search for property data free on the GIS-mapping site at http://gisweb02.co.guilford.nc.us/guilford/default.htm. Also, name search tax data free at http://taxweb.co.guilford.nc.us/CamaPublicAccess/.

Halifax County ***Recorded Documents*** www.halifaxnc.com/index.php?option=com_content&view=article&id=68&Itemid=66 Access to the Register's land records is at http://65.254.204.43/external/User/Login.aspx?bSkipAutoGuest=true.

Property, Taxation Records Search assessor property tax records free at http://qpublic.net/nc/halifax/.

Harnett County ***Recorded Documents*** http://rod.harnett.org County real estate and property tax data is free at http://rod.harnett.org. Search Births, Deaths, Marriages, UCCs and official public records.

Property, Taxation Records Access property tax records free at http://tax.harnett.org/pws10/main/billing/default.aspx.

Haywood County ***Recorded Documents*** http://rodweb.haywoodnc.net/ Records on the Register of Deeds database are free at http://search.haywooddeeds.com/. Real estate records from 01/01/86 to present.

Property, Taxation Records Access property tax records and GIS mapping free at http://public.haywoodnc.net/. Also, search for property data on the GIS-mapping site for free at http://maps.haywoodnc.net/.

Henderson County ***Recorded Documents*** www.hendersoncountync.org/depts/deeds.html Access to recorded documents free at www.courthousecomputersystems.com/hendersonnc/. Index records are from 1979 to present (images forthcoming).

Property, Taxation Records Look-up tax bills free at http://taxinfo.hendersoncountync.org/main/billing/default.aspx. Access the GIS mapping system free at http://henderson.roktech.net/ParcelMap/.

Hertford County ***Recorded Documents*** www.hertfordrod.net/ Access recorded land data free at http://216.27.81.171/hertfordnc/disclaimer.asp.

Hoke County ***Recorded Documents*** www.hokencrod.org Access recorder data for free at www.hokencrod.org/Opening.asp. Land records index goes back to 7/1992; images back to 12/1994.

Property, Taxation Records Access property data on GIS mapping site free at http://hoke2.connectgis.com/Disclaimer.aspx?ReturnUrl=%2fDisclaimer.aspx.

Hyde County ***Recorded Documents*** www.hydecountync.gov/departments/register_of_deeds.php Access to county records for a fee at https://www.countygovernmentrecords.com/. Must register. **$$$**

Property, Taxation Records Access to GIS/mapping for free at www.hydecountygis.com/mapguide/hydegis/.

Iredell County ***Recorded Documents*** www.co.iredell.nc.us/Departments/RegDeeds/ Access recorder records at https://rodweb2.co.iredell.nc.us/esearch/User/Login.aspx?ReturnUrl=/esearch/Default.aspx. Can register as a new user or can also click on as a guest. **$$$**

Property, Taxation Records Search property appraisal cards free at www.co.iredell.nc.us/apprcard/.

Jackson County ***Recorded Documents*** www.jacksonnc.org/register-of-deeds.html Access to records for free at http://deeds.jacksonnc.org/External/LandRecords/protected/SrchSimpleName.aspx.

Property, Taxation Records Search assessor and property data free at http://maps.jacksonnc.org/gomapsags/#.

Johnston County ***Recorded Documents*** www.johnstonnc.com/rod2/ Access to Register's indexes is free at http://152.31.96.7/NC/Johnston/Welcome. Land records go back to 1789; UCCs back to 7/2001.

Property, Taxation Records Access property records free at www.johnstonnc.com/newtaxpay/BasicSearch.aspx.

Jones County ***Recorded Documents*** www.jonescountync.gov/index.asp?SEC=E1C244F1-2CC1-4306-9304-E7B2A3615402&Type=B_BASIC Access to records free at http://cotthosting.com/ncjones/LandRecords/protected/SrchSimpleName.aspx. Also, access to county records for a fee go to https://www.countygovernmentrecords.com/. Must register. **$$$**

Property, Taxation Records Access to GIS/mapping for free at www.jonescountygis.com/.

Lee County ***Recorded Documents*** www.leecountync.gov/Departments/RegisterofDeeds.aspx Access Register of Deeds index and images free at www.leencrod.org/Opening.asp. Land record index goes back to 1985; images to 1908-1984, and all plat images.

Property, Taxation Records Access sales data and maps free at www.leecountync.gov/Departments/GISStrategicServices/tabid/124/Default.aspx.

Lenoir County ***Recorded Documents Records*** www.co.lenoir.nc.us/registerofdeeds.html Access land records index back to 1976 at http://cottweb.co.lenoir.nc.us/external/User/Login.aspx?ReturnUrl=%2fexternal%2fLandRecords%2fprotected%2fSrchSimpleName.aspx.

Property, Taxation Records Access property taxes free at www.lenoircountytaxes.com/. Also, access to GIS/mapping free at http://lenoir.connectgis.com/Default/Default.aspx.

Lincoln County ***Recorded Documents*** www.lincolncounty.org/index.aspx?nid=133 Access tax, property, and recording data for free at www.lincolncounty.org/index.aspx?NID=509. Grantor/Grantee indices go back to 1993. Images go back to Book 186. Search either of the 2 databases There is also a comparable properties search utility.

Property, Taxation Records Access to the county GIS Land System is free at http://207.4.172.206/website/lcproperty2/viewer.htm.

McDowell County ***Recorded Documents*** www.mcdowellgov.com Access to property and deeds indexes and images is via a private company at www.titlesearcher.com. Fee/registration required; see state introduction. Free 7 day demo for 1st time users. **$$$**

Property, Taxation Records Access GIS property data free at www.mcdowellcountygis.com/mapguide/mcdowellgis/.

Macon County ***Recorded Records, Map Records*** www.maconncdeeds.com/ Access deed images back to book 6 free and selected other recording types free at http://search.maconncdeeds.com/.

Property, Taxation Records Access property tax records and land records for free at www.maconnctax.com/ (old from 2010 back) and new (8/2010 to present). Also, access to GIS/mapping free athttp://gis2.maconnc.org/www2/gis/.

Madison County ***Recorded Documents*** http://madisonrod.net/ Access real property records free at http://nc.countygovernmentrecords.com/login.php.

Property, Taxation Records Access to property data for free atwww.madcotax.com/.

Martin County ***Recorded Documents*** www.martincountyncgov.com/deeds Access to database free at www.martinrod.org/. Three ways to access-Full System, Imaging System Only & Scanned Index Books.
Property, Taxation Records Access to GIS/mapping for free at www.martincountygis.com/.

Mecklenburg County ***Recorded Documents*** www.meckrodindex.com/ Access to records free at http://meckrod.manatron.com/. Also, access real estate from 1763 to 2/1990 for free at http://meckrodindex.com/oldindexsearch.php.
Property, Taxation Records Access to the assessors records for real estate, personal property, and tax bills are free at http://meckcama.co.mecklenburg.nc.us/relookup/. Search property ownership and data free on the GIS site at http://polaris.mecklenburgcountync.gov/website/redesign/viewer.htm.

Mitchell County ***Recorded Documents*** www.mitchellcounty.org/departments/registerofdeeds.html Access to county records free at http://search.mitchelldeeds.com/.

Montgomery County ***Recorded Documents*** www.montgomeryrod.net/ Access to recorders real estate data is free at www.montgomeryrod.net/.
Property, Taxation Records Search property records free on the GIS mapping site at http://arcims.webgis.net/nc/montgomery/.

Moore County ***Recorded Documents*** http://rod.moorecountync.gov Find a menu of search choices for recordings, land records at http://rod.moorecountync.gov. No images are available online of birth & death records.
Property, Taxation Records Access property and tax data free at http://webapps.moorecountync.gov/rpl/index.asp.

Nash County ***Recorded Documents*** www.co.nash.nc.us/index.aspx?nid=243 Search real estate and UCCs free back to 1970 free at www.deeds.co.nash.nc.us/eSearch/LandRecords/protected/SrchSimpleName.aspx.
Property, Taxation Records Access to tax records for free at http://taxdata.nashcountync.gov/Main/Home.aspx. Also, access to GIS/mapping free at http://gis.co.nash.nc.us/connectgis/nash/.

New Hanover County ***Recorded Documents*** http://srvrodweb.nhcgov.com/localization/menu.asp Access to the Register of Deeds database is free at http://srvrodweb.nhcgov.com. Subscription svc also available. **$$$**
Property, Taxation Records Access to the real estate tax database is free at http://etax.nhcgov.com/Search/Disclaimer2.aspx?. Also, access property data on the GIS-mappings site at www.nhcgov.com/Pages/GISData.aspx.

Northampton County ***Property, Taxation Records*** Access to GIS/mapping for free at http://gis.northamptonnc.com/

Onslow County ***Recorded Documents, Birth, Death, Marriage Records*** www.onslowcountync.gov/Register/ Access recorder office index data free at https://deeds.onslowcountync.gov/external/LandRecords/protected/v4/SrchName.aspx. Consolidated real estate goes back to 1/01/95, births 01/01/64-4/30/12, deaths 01/01/82-12/31/11, marriages back to 01/01/62, UCCs back to 1/01/95, conveyances 01/01/77-12/31/94.
Property, Taxation Records Access to property data is free at http://maps2.roktech.net/onslow/. Also, access to property records free at http://property.onslowcountync.gov/Search/Disclaimer2.aspx?FromUrl=../Search/GenericSearch.aspx?mode=owner.

Orange County ***Recorded Documents*** www.orangecountync.gov/deeds/index.asp Access to records database free at http://roam.orangecountync.gov/orange/.
Property, Taxation Records Access to property records on the GIS mapping site is free at http://server2.co.orange.nc.us/OrangeNCGIS/default.aspx.

Pamlico County ***Recorded Documents*** www.co.pamlico.nc.us/register-of-deeds.aspx Access to county records for a fee at https://www.countygovernmentrecords.com/. Must register. Also, access to register of deeds records free at http://cotthosting.com/ncpamlicoexternal/LandRecords/protected/SrchSimpleName.aspx. Index searches available from 6/1/88 to present (starting with Book 253 Page 132). **$$$**
Property, Taxation Records Search the GIS-mapping site for property data free at www.pamlicocountygis.com/mapguide/pamlicogis/.

Pasquotank County ***Recorded Documents*** www.pasquotankrod.net/ Access to database free at www.pasquotankrod.net/.
Property, Taxation Records Search assessor database at www.co.pasquotank.nc.us/GIS/taxsearch.cfm. Search Sales histories free at www.co.pasquotank.nc.us/GIS/salessearch.cfm..

Pender County ***Recorded Documents*** www.pendercountync.gov/Government/Departments/RegisterofDeeds.aspx Access recorder data free with registration at http://pender-rod.inttek.net/.
Property, Taxation Records Property records are available for free at www.pendercountync.gov/OnlineServices/OnLineTaxInformation.aspx.

Perquimans County ***Recorded Documents*** www.co.perquimans.nc.us/departments/register-of-deeds.html Access to county records for a fee at https://www.countygovernmentrecords.com/. Must register. **$$$**
Property, Taxation Records Access property assessor, tax, property card and GIS data free at www.co.perquimans.nc.us/taxcards/index.php.

Person County ***Real Estate, Grantor/Grantee, Deed Records*** www.personrod.net Access to county real estate records is free at http://216.27.81.171/personncnw/application.asp?resize=true.

Pitt County ***Recorded Documents*** www.pittcountync.gov/depts/regdeeds/ Access recorder land data for free at http://regdeeds.pittcountync.gov/External/User/Login.aspx?ReturnUrl=%2fExternal%2fLandRecords%2fprotected%2fSrchQuickName.aspx.

Property, Taxation Records Online access to property records is available at http://gis2.pittcountync.gov/opis/. Also, view overdue tax accounts at www.pittcountync.gov/depts/taxadmin/apps/foreclosure/.

Polk County ***Recorded Documents*** www.polknc.org/departments/registrardeeds/index.php Access to county records free at http://cotthosting.com/ncpolkexternal/LandRecords/protected/SrchSimpleName.aspx.

Property, Taxation Records Access to GIS/mapping for free at http://gis.polknc.org/GoMaps/

Randolph County ***Recorded Documents*** www.randrod.com Real Estate records and plats at www.randrod.com/officialrecords.html after registration. **$$$**

Property, Taxation Records Access the county GIS database free at www.co.randolph.nc.us/gis.htm.htm. Access property owners/property data, liens, and foreclosure lists free at www.co.randolph.nc.us/tax/default.htm.

Richmond County ***Recorded Documents*** www.richmondrod.net/ Access Register of Deeds land records free at www.richmondrod.net/.

Robeson County ***Recorded Documents*** http://rod.co.robeson.nc.us Access to recorder data is free at http://robeson.bislandrecords.com/. Also, access to property and deeds indexes and images is via a private company at www.titlesearcher.com/. Fee/registration required. Deeds and images go back to 1787; Indices back to 1787. **$$$**

Property, Taxation Records Access assessor property records free at www.ustaxdata.com/nc/robeson/robesonsearch.cfm.

Rockingham County ***Recorded Documents*** www.registerofdeeds.info/ Access to Register of Deeds database is free at www.courthousecomputersystems.com/RockinghamNC/. Land indexes 1996 to present. Paper index (in the office only) contains official index information from 1787 to 1995.

Property, Taxation Records Access to Tax Admin. property data (1996 forward) also tax bills are free at www.ustaxdata.com/nc/rockingham/RockinghamSearch.cfm. Also, search property data free at the GIS/mapping site at http://arcgis.webgis.net/nc/Rockingham/.

Rowan County ***Recorded Documents*** www.rowancountync.gov/GOVERNMENT/Departments/RegisterOfDeeds.aspx Access to the Register of Deeds land records database after registration at http://rod.rowancountync.gov/external/User/Login.aspx?ReturnUrl=%2fexternal%2findex.aspx. Records go back to 1975; financing statements back to 1993; deed images back to 1975. **$$$**

Property, Taxation Records Access to the county GIS mapping site is free at http://rowan.connectgis.com/Default/Default.aspx. Also, there is a tax inquiry quick search at www.co.rowan.nc.us/taxinq/name/default.asp. More tax and property data available http://rowan.ustaxdata.com/.

Rutherford County ***Recorded Documents, Birth, Death, Marriage Records*** http://rutherfordcountync.gov/registerofdeeds Access property data free at http://208.90.175.25/External/LandRecords/protected/SrchSimpleName.aspx. RE goes back to 1974; births 1991 to 2006; Deaths and marriages back to 1994/1995.

Property, Taxation Records Access to GIS/mapping for free at http://arcgis.webgis.net/nc/Rutherford/.

Sampson County ***Recorded Documents*** www.sampsonrod.org Access to county Register of Deeds land data is free at www.sampsonrod.org/Opening.asp. Index goes back to 1962.

Scotland County ***Recorded Documents*** www.scotlandcounty.org/register-of-deeds-1.aspx Access ROD real estate records and also financing statements from 1999 to 2/2004 free at http://rod.scotlandcounty.org/external/LandRecords/protected/SrchSimpleName.aspx.

Property, Taxation Records Access to online taxes for free to go www.scotlandcountytaxes.com/taxSearch. Access to GIS/mapping for free at http://38.124.248.92/ConnectGIS_v6/Map.aspx?p=Laurinburg.

Stanly County ***Recorded Documents*** www.stanlyrod.net/ Access the Register of Deeds index back to 1841 at www.stanlyrod.net/.

Property, Taxation Records Access property data on the GIS search free at www.stanlycountync.gov/real-property-assessments/.

Stokes County ***Recorded Documents*** www.co.stokes.nc.us/deeds/ Access to the Register of Deeds Remote Access site is free at www.stokescorod.org/Opening.asp. Land records go back to 1787, images to 1787; UCCs back to 1994.

Property, Taxation Records Access to property info on the GIS mapping site is free at www.stokescountync.gov/.

Surry County ***Recorded Documents*** www.co.surry.nc.us/Departments/RegisterOfDeeds/RegisterOfDeeds.htm Access recording index free at www.co.surry.nc.us/Departments/RegisterOfDeeds/RecordSearch.htm. Real property index goes back to 1/1980; financing statements 1989-6/30/2001; plats are 1/1980 to present. Must purchase a subscription to see images. Annual fee of $120.00 provides unlimited copying and viewing of Real Estate index data and images. **$$$**

Property, Taxation Records Access property tax data free at http://arcgis.webgis.net/nc/Surry/.

Swain County ***Recorded Documents*** www.swaincorod.org/ Access to recorder land data is free at www.swaincorod.org/. There is a full system and an image only system. Land Record Indexing data goes back to 1/1995; images back to 8/1979.

Property, Taxation Records Access to parcel and land information for free at www.qpublic.net/nc/swain/.

Transylvania County ***Recorded Documents*** www.transylvaniacounty.org/register-of-deeds Access real estate records at www.titlesearcher.com/. Registration and username required. Images are viewable back to 12/30/2003; deeds and indices back to 1/3/1973. **$$$**

Property, Taxation Records Access full or partial property data free on the GIS site at http://arcgis.webgis.net/nc/Transylvania/.

Tyrrell County ***Recorded Documents*** www.tyrrellrod.net/ Access to county records for a fee at www.tyrrellrod.net/. Must register. Also, access to county records for a fee go to https://www.countygovernmentrecords.com/. Must register. **$$$**

Union County ***Recorded Documents*** www.unioncountync.us/Departments/RegisterofDeeds.aspx Access to recorder land records is free at www.unionconcrod.org/Opening.asp; index and images go back to 6/21/1993.

Property, Taxation Records Access to records for free at http://union.ustaxdata.com/Search.cfm.

Vance County ***Recorded Documents*** http://vancencrod.org/ Access to Register records free at http://vancencrod.org/Opening.asp.

Property, Taxation Records Access to real estate property search for free at www.ustaxdata.com/nc/vance/vancepolicy.cfm/.

Wake County ***Recorded Documents*** https://rod.wakegov.com/ Access Register of Deeds database free at http://services.wakegov.com/BOOKSweb/GenExtSearch.aspx. Records go back to 1885.

Property, Taxation Records Free real estate property and tax bill search is at http://services.wakegov.com/realestate/search.asp. Also, download individual town property data free at www.wakegov.com/tax/downloads/default.htm.

Warren County ***Recorded Documents*** www.warrenrod.org/ Access to remote access site free at www.warrenrod.org/opening.asp.

Property, Taxation Records Access to GIS/mapping data for free at http://maps2.roktech.net/warren/.

Washington County ***Recorded Documents*** www.washingtonrod.net/ Access to county records for a fee at www.washingtonrod.net/. www.washingtonrod.net **$$$**

Property, Taxation Records Search assessor property and building record cards free at http://taxweb.washconc.org/.

Watauga County ***Recorded Documents*** www.wataugacounty.org/main/App_Pages/Dept/Deeds/home.aspx Access to Register of Deeds database is free at http://72.15.246.181/wataugand/.

Property, Taxation Records Access to county tax search data is free at www.wataugacounty.org/ias/Search/Disclaimer2.aspx?FromUrl=../search/commonsearch.aspx?mode=owner.

Wayne County ***Recorded Documents*** www.waynegov.com/domain/41 Access to the registers CRP, financing statement, and real estate databases is free at http://rod.waynegov.com/Resolution/LandRecords/protected/SrchSimpleName.aspx. Real Estate includes records from 1969-1994; beginning 1995 all real estate records are indexed under CRP. Birth and Death records go back to 1995; marriages back to 1997. Plats are online beginning 1982.

Property, Taxation Records Access property records free at http://realestate.waynegov.com/ITSNet/.

Wilkes County ***Property, Taxation Records*** Free access to property data of the GIS-mapping site at http://74.114.71.51/wilkesweb/wilkes.html. Also, free access to the real estate property taxes database found at https://tax.wilkescounty.net/MSS/citizens/RealEstate/Default.aspx?mode=new.

Wilson County ***Recorded Documents*** www.wilson-co.com/index.aspx?nid=167 Access the Register of Deeds search site for free at http://rod.wilson-co.com/External/LandRecords/protected/v4/SrchName.aspx.

Property, Taxation Records Records on the county Geo-link property tax database are free at www.wilson-co.com/index.aspx?NID=229.

Yadkin County ***Recorded Documents*** www.yadkincountync.gov/index.aspx?nid=83 Access recorder's land records free at www.yadkincorod.org/Opening.asp. Index goes back to 1/1/1993. Land Record Imaging Data back to Volume 0210 8/24/1978 through Volume 0790 page 76 6/20/2006. Search either the full system or the imaging system.

Property, Taxation Records Search property tax date free at www.ustaxdata.com/nc/yadkin/.

Yancey County ***Recorded Documents*** http://yanceycountync.gov/departments/register-of-deeds Access to county records for a fee at www.yanceyrod.com/NorthCarolinaRecorder/web/. Must register. **$$$**

Property, Taxation Records Access to real/personal tax scroll for free at http://yanceycountync.gov/images/stories/pdf/2011_Real_Personal_Tax_Scroll.pdf.

North Dakota

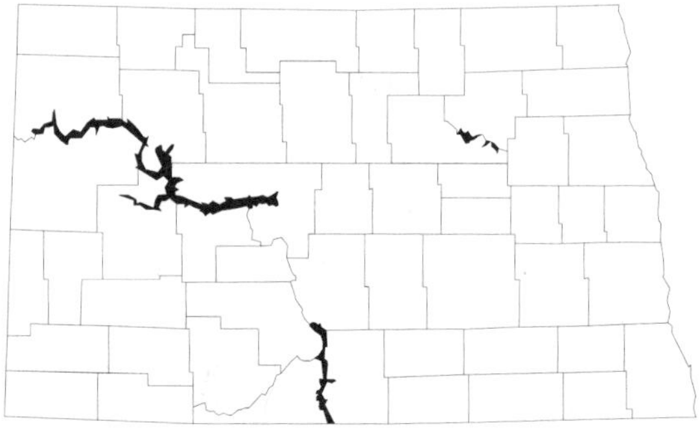

Capital: Bismarck
Burleigh County

Time Zone: The southwestern area of North Dakota (west and south of the Missouri River) is in Mountain Time Zone. The remainder of the state is in the Central Time Zone.

Population: 699,628

# of Counties: 53

Useful State Links

Website: www.nd.gov/

Governor: www.governor.state.nd.us

Attorney General: www.ag.state.nd.us

State Archives: http://history.nd.gov/archives/

State Statutes and Codes: www.legis.nd.gov/information/statutes/cent-code.html

Legislative Bill Search: www.legis.nd.gov/

Unclaimed Funds: www.land.nd.gov/UnclaimedProperty/

State Public Record Agencies

Sexual Offender Registry

Bureau of Criminal Investigation, SOR Unit, www.sexoffender.nd.gov/ Access is available from the website. Information on all offenders with a registration requirement (including moderate and low risk offenders) can be downloaded. See 'Printable List of All Offenders' at www.sexoffender.nd.gov/PublicListing.aspx.

Incarceration Records

Department of Corrections and Rehabilitation, Records Clerk, www.nd.gov/docr/ A free lookup service of current inmates is at www.nd.gov/docr/search/. Search by last name, index screen shows full name and DOB. Results screen gives picture, estimated release date, and facility.

Corporation, LLC, LP, LLP, Trademarks/Servicemarks, Fictitious/Assumed Name

Secretary of State, Business Information/Registration, www.nd.gov/sos/businessserv/ The Secretary of State's registered business database may be viewed at https://apps.nd.gov/sc/busnsrch/busnSearch.htm for no charge. Documents are not available online. Records include corporations, limited liability companies, limited partnerships, limited liability partnerships, limited liability limited partnerships, partnership fictitious names, trade names, trademarks, and real estate investment trusts. The database includes all active records and records inactivated within past twelve months. Access by the first few words of a business name, a significant word in a business name, or by the record ID number assigned. If questions, email sosbir@nd.gov. Also, search securities industry professionals database free at www.nd.gov/securities/industry-registration. *Other Options:* This agency provides a database purchase program. Cost is $35.00 per database and processing fees vary for type of media.

Uniform Commercial Code, Federal & State Tax Liens

UCC Division, Secretary of State, www.nd.gov/sos/businessserv/centralindex/index.html Access to the Central Indexing System provides both filing and online searching. There is an annual subscription $150 fee and a one-time $50.00 registration fee. The UCC-11 search fee (normally $7.00) applies, but documents will not be certified. Searches include UCC-11 information listing and farm product searches. **$$$** *Other Options:* The agency offers bulk access via FTP or paper copy. Call for details.

Sales Tax Registrations

Office of State Tax Commissioner, Sales & Special Taxes Division, www.nd.gov/tax/salesanduse/ A permit number may be verified online at www.nd.gov/tax/salesanduse/permitinquiry/. System indicates valid permit registered to company name.

Birth Certificates

ND Department of Health, Vital Records, http://ndhealth.gov/vital/ Records may be ordered online from the Internet site or from vitalchek.com. Records are not returned online. **$$$**

Death Records

ND Department of Health, Vital Records, http://ndhealth.gov/vital/ Search the Public Death Index free at https://secure.apps.state.nd.us/doh/certificates/deathCertSearch.htm. Deaths within the past 12 months do not appear. Also, records may be ordered online from the Internet site or from vitalchek.com. Records are not returned online. **$$$**

Workers' Compensation Records

Workforce Safety & Insurance, Workers' Compensation Records, www.workforcesafety.com A claim look-up is available at https://www.workforcesafety.com/WSI/external/onlineservices/claimlookup.aspx. Must provide an injured worker's (SSN), Claim Number, or Name and DOB, and the injury date to retrieve claim verification information. Am employer search is offered at https://www.workforcesafety.com/online-services/employersearch/.

Driver Records

Department of Transportation, Driver License Division, www.dot.nd.gov There are two systems. Ongoing, approved commercial accounts may request records with personal information via a commercial system. There is a minimum of 100 requests per month. For more information, call 701-328-4790. Also, from home page above one may view and print a limited record. The fee is $3.00 per record and a use of a credit card is required. The limited record does not include total points or convictions more than three years old, violations less than three points, or any crash information. No documents will be sent via mail. A free DL status check is found at https://apps.nd.gov/dot/dlts/dlos/requeststatus.htm; access by DL number. **$$$**

Vessel Ownership & Registration

North Dakota Game & Fish Department, Boat Registration Records, http://gf.nd.gov There is a free public inquiry system at https://apps.nd.gov/gnf/onlineservices/lic/public/online/main.htm. Click on "Watercraft Registration and Renewals" to find registration number, or click on "Find Watercraft Safety Number" for that search. Requests may be submitted by email - ndgf@nd.gov. *Other Options:* Am electronic list is available of all registered vessels.

Voter Registration

Secretary of State, Elections Division, www.nd.gov/sos/electvote/ Search campaign disclosure reports at www.nd.gov/sos/campfinance/. Search lobbyists at www.nd.gov/sos/lobbylegislate/lobbying/reg-mnu.html.

GED Certificates

Department of Public Instruction, GED Testing - CKEN-11, www.dpi.state.nd.us/adulted/index.shtm One may request records via email at JMarcellais@nd.gov. There is no fee, unless a transcript is ordered.

Occupational Licensing Boards

Abstractor/Abstractor Company .... www.governor.nd.gov/boards/bcpublicsearch.asp?searchtype=member
Adoption Agency .... www.nd.gov/dhs/services/childfamily/adoption/agencies.html
Alcoholic Beverage Control .... www.ag.nd.gov/Licensing/LicenseHolders/LicenseHolders.htm
Amusement Device, Coin-Op .... www.ag.nd.gov/Licensing/LicenseHolders/LicenseHolders.htm
Architect .... www.ndsba.net/?id=221&page=Active+License+Query
Asbestos Contractor .... www.ndhealth.gov/AQ/IAQ/ASB/Contractors.pdf
Attorney .... www.ndcourts.gov/court/lawyers/index/frameset.htm
Bank, Commercial .... www.nd.gov/dfi/regulate/reg/regulated.asp
Charitable Solicitation .... www.nd.gov/sos/forms/pdf/charorg.pdf
Chiropractor .... http://ndsbce.org/doctor-search/
Collection Agency .... www.nd.gov/dfi/regulate/reg/regulated.asp
Consumer Finance Company .... www.nd.gov/dfi/regulate/reg/regulated.asp
Contractor/General Contractor .... https://apps.nd.gov/sc/busnsrch/busnSearch.htm
Cosmetology School .... www.ndcosmetology.com/home/index.php?option=com_content&view=section&layout=blog&id=2&Itemid=4
Counselor, Professional .... www.ndbce.org/PDFs/counselor-list.pdf

Credit Union .... www.nd.gov/dfi/regulate/reg/regulated.asp
Debt Collector .... www.nd.gov/dfi/regulate/reg/regulated.asp
Deferred Presentment Provider .... www.nd.gov/dfi/regulate/reg/regulated.asp
Dental Assistant/Hygienist .... https://secure.ebigpicture.com/ndbode/renewals/verify.asp
Dentist .... https://secure.ebigpicture.com/ndbode/renewals/verify.asp
Dietitian/Nutritionist .... www.ndbodp.com/verify.html
Disapproved Medical School .... https://www.ndbomex.org/practitioners/physicians/newapp/disapprovedMedSchools.asp
Drug Mfg/Wholesaler .... https://www.nodakpharmacy.com/verify.asp
Electrical Contractor.................................. https://www.ndseb.com/?id=69
Electrician/Apprentice .... https://www.ndseb.com/?id=69
Engineer... http://ndpelsboard.org/?id=48
Fireworks, Wholesale/Distributor .... www.ag.nd.gov/Licensing/LicenseHolders/LicenseHolders.htm
Funeral Home .... www.ndfda.org/joomla/index.php?option=com_sobi2&Itemid=20
Gaming/Distributor/Manufacturer................ www.ag.nd.gov/Licensing/LicenseHolders/LicenseHolders.htm
Home Inspector.. www.nd.gov/sos/forms/pdf/home-inspectors.pdf
Insurance Agency/Agent/Broker .... www.nd.gov/ndins/find/
Investment Advisor...................................... www.nd.gov/securities/node/5498
Land Surveyor... http://ndpelsboard.org/?id=48
Livestock Agent/Dealer .... www.nd.gov/ndda/Programs/Livestock/Livestock.html
Livestock Auction Market .... www.nd.gov/ndda/Programs/Livestock/Livestock.html
Lobbyist.. www.nd.gov/sos/lobbylegislate/lobbying/reg-mnu.html
Medication Assistant .... https://www.ndbon.org/verify_renew/verify_default.asp
Money Broker Firm...................................... www.nd.gov/dfi/regulate/reg/regulated.asp
Nurse-LPN/RN/Assistant .... https://www.ndbon.org/verify_renew/verify_default.asp
Nursing Home Administrator....................... www.ndnha.org/Admin%20List.pdf
Nutritionist .... www.ndbodp.com/verify.html
Oil and Gas Broker...................................... https://www.dmr.nd.gov/oilgas/findwellsvw.asp
Oil/Gas Well .... https://www.dmr.nd.gov/oilgas/confidential.asp
Optometrist... www.ndsbopt.org/directory/
Osteopathic Physician .... https://www.ndbomex.org/public/find_verify/verify.asp
Pharmacist .... https://www.nodakpharmacy.com/verify.asp
Pharmacy/Technician/Intern .... https://www.nodakpharmacy.com/verify.asp
Physical Therapist/Assistant....................... https://www.ndbpt.org/verify.asp
Physician/Medical Doctor/Assistant............ https://www.ndbomex.org/public/find_verify/verify.asp
Podiatrist .... www.ndpodiatryboard.org/indexframes.html
Private Investigator/Agency .... www.nd.gov/pisb/holders.html
Real Estate Agent/Broker .... www.realestatend.org/?id=42
Respiratory Care Practitioner...................... https://secure.ebigpicture.com/ndsbrc/renewals/verify.asp
Sale of Check.. www.nd.gov/dfi/regulate/reg/regulated.asp
Securities Agent/Dealer www.nd.gov/securities/node/5498
Security Provider/Company .... www.nd.gov/pisb/holders.html
Social Worker.. http://secure.ebigpicture.com/ndbswe/live/public.asp
Soil Classifier .... www.ndsu.edu/pubweb/soils/BRPSCND/brpscnd_roster.html
Speech-Language Patholog't/Audiologist.... www.governor.nd.gov/boards/bcpublicsearch.asp?searchtype=member
Tobacco, Retail/Wholesale .... www.ag.nd.gov/Licensing/LicenseHolders/LicenseHolders.htm
Transient Merchant .... www.ag.nd.gov/Licensing/LicenseHolders/LicenseHolders.htm
Trust Company.. www.nd.gov/dfi/regulate/reg/regulated.asp
Veterinarian/Veterinary Technician............. www.ndbvme.org/
Water Well Driller/Pump & Pitless Unit www.swc.state.nd.us/4DLink2/4dcgi/contractsearchform/Map%20and%20Data%20Resources
Well Contractor, Monitoring www.swc.state.nd.us/4DLink2/4dcgi/contractsearchform/Map%20and%20Data%20Resources

State and Local Courts

State Court Structure: The **District Courts** have general jurisdiction over criminal, civil, and juvenile matters. At one time there were County Courts, but these courts merged with the District Courts statewide in 1995. These older County Court records are held by the 53 District Court Clerks in the 7 judicial districts.

Municipal Courts in North Dakota have jurisdiction for all violations of traffic and municipal ordinances, with some exceptions.

Appellate Courts: One may search North Dakota Supreme Court dockets and opinions at www.ndcourts.gov. Search by docket number, party name, or anything else that may appear in the text. Records are from 1982 forward. Email notification of new opinions is also available.

Statewide Court Online Access: All courts participate in the system described below.

- All District Courts and fourteen Muncipal Courts participate on an online access system for court record index data, including civil, criminal, probate, traffic, family case files as well as judgments. The web page is found at http://publicsearch.ndcourts.gov/. There are a variety of searches, including by name, case number, attorney, and date filed. Results will provide year of birth for criminal (or entire DOB is entered as part of search), but not for civil, family or judgments. Data throughput varies by each county; most counties go back at least 7 years. Some counties have data included from as early as 1991 and beyond; other counties that have been added in 2003 will have data for only the most recent cases. The system alos incluides access to a number of municipal courts including those in Bismarck, Devils Lake, Dickinson, Grafton, Jamestown, Lincoln, Mandan, Minot, Valley City, Rolla, Wahpeton, West Fargo, and Williston. Data is current through the end of the previous business day.
- Caution is urged:
  - Note the site disclaimer: "The information provided on and obtained from this site does not constitute the official record of the Court. This information is provided as a service to the general public. Any user of this information is hereby advised that it is being provided 'as is'. Further, the site warns name searches are not relaiable. The information provided may be subject to errors or omissions. Visitors to this site agree that the Court is not liable for errors or omissions of any of the information provided." (see www.ndcourts.gov/publicsearch/counties.aspx).

Other Sites (not mentioned above):

Cass County

East Central Judicial District Court

Probate: Search probate records from the 1870s to 1951 online at http://library.ndsu.edu/db/probate/. There is no fee.

Recorders, Assessors, and Other Sites of Note

Recording Office Organization: 53 counties, 53 recording offices. The recording officer is the County Recorder. Federal tax liens on personal property of businesses are filed with the Secretary of State. Other federal and all state tax liens are filed with the County Recorder. Some counties automatically include business federal tax liens as part of a UCC search because they appear on the statewide database. However, be careful - federal tax liens on individuals may only be in the county lien books and not on the statewide system.

Statewide or Multi-Jurisdiction Access: A large amount of property and deed data is available online, most through the statewide Recorders Information Network website mentioned below.

- The North Dakota Recorders Information Network (NDRIN) is an electronic central repository representing all of the North Dakota counties. The network offers Internet access to records, indices, and images. There is a $25 monthly usage fee, and a $1.00 charge per page printed. Register or request information via the website at www.ndrin.com.
- Property tax data is available from 16 counties at www.ndpropertytax.com.

Other Sites (not mentioned above as part of the NDRIN):

Barnes County ***Property, Taxation Records*** Tax lien sale list free at www.co.barnes.nd.us/dept/aud/. Link at bottom of page. Access records at www.ndpropertytax.com/.

Billings County ***Property, Taxation Records*** Access to tax inquiry for free at www.billingscountynd.gov/taxinquire.txt.

Burleigh County ***Property, Taxation Records*** Access to treasurer and auditor property data is free at www.co.burleigh.nd.us/property-information/. No name searching. Access records at www.ndpropertytax.com/.

Cass County ***Property, Taxation Records*** Access the treasurer's property tax data free at https://extranet.casscountynd.gov/depts/treasurer/proptax/app/Default.aspx#Search but no name searching. Also, search data free at the Parcel Information site at http://fargoparcels.com/ but no name searching. Access records at www.ndpropertytax.com/.

Dunn County ***Property, Taxation Records*** Access to county tax information is free at www.ndpropertytax.com/.

Grand Forks County ***Property, Taxation Records*** Access to GIS, property and document searches for free at www.gfcounty.nd.gov/?q=node/58. Access records at www.ndpropertytax.com/.

La Moure County ***Property, Taxation Records*** Access records at www.ndpropertytax.com/.

McKenzie County ***Property, Taxation Records*** Access records at www.ndpropertytax.com/.

McLean County ***Property, Taxation Records*** Access records at www.ndpropertytax.com/.

Morton County ***Property, Taxation Records*** Access records at www.ndpropertytax.com/.

Mountrail County ***Property, Taxation Records*** Access records at www.ndpropertytax.com/.

Pembina County ***Property, Taxation Records*** Access records at www.ndpropertytax.com/.

Ransom County ***Property, Taxation Records*** Access records at www.ndpropertytax.com/.

Sargent County ***Property, Taxation Records*** Access records at www.ndpropertytax.com/.

Stutsman County ***Property, Taxation Records*** Access records at www.ndpropertytax.com/.

Traill County ***Property, Taxation Records*** Free access to property sales or GIS/mapping found at www.co.traill.nd.us/template.cfm?d=6.

Williams County ***Property, Taxation Records*** Access to county tax data is free at www.williamsnd.com/tax/search/. Also, access to property tax records for free at www.williamsnd.com/Tax.aspx. Access records at www.ndpropertytax.com/.

Reminder:

The North Dakota Recorders Information Network (NDRIN) is an electronic central repository representing all of the North Dakota counties. The network offers Internet access to records, indices, and images. There is a $25 monthly usage fee, and a $1.00 charge per page printed. Register or request information via the website at www.ndrin.com.

Ohio

Capital: Columbus
Franklin County
Time Zone: EST
Population: 11,544,225
# of Counties: 88

Useful State Links

Website: www.ohio.gov
Governor: http://governor.ohio.gov
Attorney General: www.ohioattorneygeneral.gov/
State Archives: http://ww2.ohiohistory.org/resource/statearc/
State Statues and Code: www.legislature.state.oh.us/search.cfm
Legislative Bill Search: www.legislature.state.oh.us/search.cfm
Unclaimed Funds: www.com.ohio.gov/unfd/TreasureHunt.aspx

State Public Record Agencies

Criminal Records

Ohio Bureau of Investigation, Civilian Background Section, www.ohioattorneygeneral.gov/Business/Services-for-Business/Webcheck Civilian Background Checks (WebCheck) is a web-based system for all in-state record requests. Results are NOT returned via the Internet. Agencies can send fingerprint images and other data via the Internet using a single digit fingerprint scanner and a driver's license magnetic strip reader. Hardware costs are involved. The search fee is $22.00 per fingerprint record. **$$$**

Sexual Offender Registry

Sexual Offender Services, Dept. of Rehabilitation and Correction, http://drc.ohio.gov/web/sexoffenderprogram.html Search www.icrimewatch.net/index.php?AgencyID=55149&disc=. Users can search by offender name, zip code, county and / or school district.

Incarceration Records

Ohio Department of Rehabilitation and Correction, Bureau of Records Management, www.drc.ohio.gov/ From the website, in the Select a Destination box, select Offender Search or see www.drc.ohio.gov/OffenderSearch/Search.aspx. You can search by name, geographic location, or inmate number. The Offender Search includes all offenders currently incarcerated or under some type of Department supervision (parole, post-release control, or transitional control). Search Parole Violators at large at www.drc.ohio.gov/pval/ParoleViolators.aspx.

Corporation, LLC, LP, Fictitious/Trade Name, Trademarks/Servicemarks

Secretary of State, Business Services, www.sos.state.oh.us/SOS/Businesses.aspx The agency provides free Internet searching for business and corporation records from the home page. A Good Standing can be ordered. Validation is available for $5.00. Also, not from this agency, but search securities exemption filings free at https://www.comapps.ohio.gov/secu/secu_apps/offering/offering.aspx, and securities enforcement orders by year at https://www.comapps.ohio.gov/secu/secu_apps/FinalOrders/. **$$$** *Other Options:* This agency makes the database available for purchase, call for details.

Uniform Commercial Code

UCC Records, Secretary of State, www.sos.state.oh.us/SOS/Businesses/UCC.aspx The Internet site offers free online access to records. Search by debtor, secured party, or financing statement number. *Other Options:* The complete database is available on electronic media with weekly updates. Call for current pricing.

Birth Certificates

Ohio Department of Health, Office of Vital Statistics, www.odh.ohio.gov Records can be ordered from state's site at http://publicapps.odh.ohio.gov/orderbirthcertificate/. A credit card is needed. **$$$**

Death Records

Ohio Department of Health, Office of Vital Statistics, www.odh.ohio.gov The Ohio Historical Society Death Certificate Index Searchable Database at http://ohsweb.ohiohistory.org/death//index.cfm/ permits searching by name, county, index. Data is available from 1913 to 1944 only. Records can be ordered from a state-designated vendor - see expedited service below. **$$$**

Workers' Compensation Records

Bureau of Workers Compensation, Customer Contact Center - Records Mgr, www.ohiobwc.com/Default.aspx Injured workers, injured worker designees, representatives and managed care organizations (MCOs) can view a list of all claims associated with a given SSN, but are limited to viewing only the claims with which they are associated. Employers, their representatives or designees, and managed care organizations can view a list of all claims associated to their BWC policy number. Medical providers can view all claims associated with any given SSN. Access is through the website listed above. *Other Options:* Bulk data is released to approved accounts; however, the legal department must approve requesters. The agency has general information available on a website.

Driver Records

Bureau of Motor Vehicles, Record Requests, www.ohiobmv.com Anyone can order a record on another, if permission has been granted, at https://www.oplates.com/. Also, using prepaid is suggested for requesters who order 100 or more motor vehicle reports per day in batch mode. The DL# or SSN and name are needed when ordering. Fee is $5.00 per record. For more information, call Fiscal Svrs at 614-752-2091. Also, Ohio drivers may view an unofficial copy of their record at www.ohiobmv.com/abstract.stm. There is no fee for a two year uncertified record. The BMV offers a free status check of an auto dealer. Go to https://ext.dps.state.oh.us/BMVOnlineServices.Public/DealerSearch.aspx. **$$$**

Vehicle Ownership & Registration

Bureau of Motor Vehicles, Motor Vehicle Title Records, www.ohiobmv.com Three searchers are offered for Prepaid accounts - seehttp://bmv.ohio.gov/fiscal_prepaid_accounts.stm. Ohio offers online access through AAMVA. All requesters must comply with a contractual agreement prior to release of data, which complies with DPPA regulations. Fee is same as mentioned above. Call 614-752-7598 for more information. The web offers free access to title records for vehicles and watercraft. No personal information is released. Search by title number or ID. Also search at https://www.dps.state.oh.us/atps/. **$$$** *Other Options:* Bulk records are available for purchase, per DPPA guidelines.

Accident Reports

Department of Public Safety, OSHP Central Records, 1st Fl, http://statepatrol.ohio.gov/crash.stm Crash reports purchased online will be sent to your e-mail within 24 hours. Crash photographs purchased online will be sent on CD by mail. Online crash reports are available for crashes 5 years to present. Search is www.statepatrol.ohio.gov/crash.htm. Reports must be purchased for $4.00 using a credit card. **$$$**

Vessel Ownership & Registration

DNR-Division of Watercraft, Titles and Registration, www.dnr.state.oh.us/Watercraft/tabid/2062/Default.aspx A free title inquiry is available at https://ext.dps.state.oh.us/BMVOnlineServices.Public/TitleSearch.aspx. Note this is through another agency, but people are directed to this site from the DNR site. The title information available from this web page is obtained from Ohio county title offices. Records are from 1993 forward. This provides owner name only, no personal information.

Voter Registration, Campaign Finance, PACs

Secretary of State, Elections Division, www.sos.state.oh.us Search campaign finance reports at www.sos.state.oh.us/SOS/CampaignFinance/Search.aspx. To see what personal financial disclosures are made, see www.sos.state.oh.us/SOS/CampaignFinance/pfdisclosure.aspx. Search PACs at www2.sos.state.oh.us/pls/cfonline/f?p=119:1:0:::::. *Other Options:* Voter Reg. Records may obtained on disk in a text format. No customization is possible, only the entire database is released. For more information, contact Robin Fields.

GED Certificates

GED Transcript Office, Priority Processing, www.education.ohio.gov Only available for students, must have a SAFE account and valid Ohio DL or ID. **$$$**

Occupational Licensing Boards

Accountant-CPA/PA/Firm .... https://license.ohio.gov/lookup/default.asp
Acupuncturist .... https://license.ohio.gov/lookup/default.asp?division=78
Anesthesiologist Assistant .... https://license.ohio.gov/lookup/default.asp?division=78

Architect	https://license.ohio.gov/lookup/default.asp
Athlete Agent	www.aco.ohio.gov/LinkClick.aspx?fileticket=Sfl849JRJJ8%3d&tabid=85
Athletic Trainer	http://otptat.ohio.gov/LicenseVerification.aspx
Attorney, State	www.supremecourt.ohio.gov/AttySvcs/AttyReg/Public_AttorneyInformation.asp
Backflow Prev Assembly Insp	https://www.comapps.ohio.gov/dic/dico_apps/bdcc/CertifiedBackFlowTesters/
Bank	https://elicense2-secure.com.ohio.gov/
Barber/Instructor/Shop/School	https://license.ohio.gov/lookup/default.asp?division=87
Boiler Contractor	https://www.comapps.ohio.gov/dic/dico_apps/boil/boiler_contractors/Default.aspx
Boiler Inspector/Operator	https://www.comapps.ohio.gov/dic/dico_apps/boil/boiler_contractors/Default.aspx
Boxer/Boxing Professional	www.aco.ohio.gov/LinkClick.aspx?fileticket=Ecq3TFsglyQ%3d&tabid=100
Cemetery	http://com.ohio.gov/eLicense.aspx
Check Cashing/Lending Service	https://elicense2-secure.com.ohio.gov/
Child Care Type A or B House	www.odjfs.state.oh.us/cdc/query.asp
Child Day Care Facility	www.odjfs.state.oh.us/cdc/query.asp
Chiropractor	https://license.ohio.gov/lookup/default.asp?division=90
Clinical Nurse Specialist	https://license.ohio.gov/lookup/default.asp?division=86
Consumer Finance Company	https://elicense2-secure.com.ohio.gov/
Contractor	www.com.ohio.gov/dico/
Cosmetic Therapist	https://license.ohio.gov/lookup/default.asp?division=78
Cosmetologist/Cosmetolog't, Instructor	https://license.ohio.gov/lookup/default.asp
Counselor	https://license.ohio.gov/lookup/default.asp?division=97
Day Camp, Children's	www.odjfs.state.oh.us/cdc/query.asp
Dental Assistant Radiologist/Hygienist	https://license.ohio.gov/lookup/default.asp?division=95
Dentist	https://license.ohio.gov/lookup/default.asp?division=95
Dialysis Technician	https://license.ohio.gov/lookup/default.asp?division=86
Dietitian	https://license.ohio.gov/lookup/default.asp?division=85
Drug Wholesaler/Distributor	https://license.ohio.gov/lookup/default.asp?division=96
Electrical Safety Inspector/Trainee	https://www.comapps.ohio.gov/dic/dico_apps/bbst/ElectricalSafetyInspectors/
Electrician	www.com.ohio.gov/dico/
Elevator Inspector	https://www.comapps.ohio.gov/dic/dico_apps/elev/elev_lookup/Default.aspx
Embalmer/Embalming Facility	https://license.ohio.gov/lookup/default.asp?division=85
Emergency Medical Agency	www.publicsafety.ohio.gov/links/ems_agengy_list11.xls
Emergency Medical Technician	https://www.dps.state.oh.us/certrenewal/Verification.aspx
Engineer	https://license.ohio.gov/lookup/default.asp?division=100
Engineering/Surveying Company	https://license.ohio.gov/lookup/default.asp?division=100
Esthetician/Managing Esthetician	https://license.ohio.gov/lookup/default.asp
Fire Extinguisher (Portable) Inspector	www.com.ohio.gov/OnlineServices.aspx
Fire Extinguisher Equipm't Inspector	www.com.ohio.gov/OnlineServices.aspx
Fire Protection System Designer	https://www.comapps.ohio.gov/dic/dico_apps/bbst/FireProtectionSystemDesigners/
Foreign Real Estate Property	http://com.ohio.gov/eLicense.aspx
Funeral Director	https://license.ohio.gov/lookup/default.asp?division=85
Heating/Refrigeration (HVAC)	www.com.ohio.gov/dico/
Hydronic-related Occupation	www.com.ohio.gov/dico/
Insurance Agent/Agency	https://gateway.insurance.ohio.gov/UI/ODI.Agent.Public.UI/AgentLocator.mvc/DisplaySearch
Landscape Architect	https://license.ohio.gov/lookup/default.asp
Legislative Agent/Agent Employer	www2.jlec-olig.state.oh.us/olac/
Liquor Distributor	www.com.ohio.gov/liqr/
Liquor License	www.com.ohio.gov/liqr/rpts/phone.txt
Liquor License Cancellation	www.com.ohio.gov/liqr/PermitsActive.aspx
Liquor Permit	www.com.ohio.gov/liqr/PermitsActive.aspx
Liquor Store	https://www.comapps.ohio.gov/liqr/liqr_apps/PermitLookup/
Lobbyist/Lobbyist Employer	www2.jlec-olig.state.oh.us/olac/
Lottery Retailer	www.ohiolottery.com/Find-A-Retailer.aspx
Manicuring/Esthetician Instructor	https://license.ohio.gov/lookup/default.asp
Manicurist/Managing Manicurist	https://license.ohio.gov/lookup/default.asp

Marriage and Family Therapist	https://license.ohio.gov/lookup/default.asp?division=97
Massage Therapist	https://license.ohio.gov/lookup/default.asp?division=78
Mechanotherapist	https://license.ohio.gov/lookup/default.asp?division=78
Midwife	https://license.ohio.gov/lookup/default.asp?division=86
Milk Hauler	www.agri.ohio.gov/dairy/DairySearchIndex.aspx?type=mh
Milk Tester/Sampler	www.agri.ohio.gov/divs/dairy/DairySearchIndex.aspx?type=wst
Mixed Martial Arts Amateur	www.aco.ohio.gov/LinkClick.aspx?fileticket=NEhyr7hgVV0%3d&tabid=101
Mixed Martial Arts Professional	www.aco.ohio.gov/LinkClick.aspx?fileticket=nwRiRJYKcKU%3d&tabid=102
Mortgage Broker	https://elicense2-secure.com.ohio.gov/
Naprapath	https://license.ohio.gov/lookup/default.asp?division=78
Notary Public	www2.sos.state.oh.us/pls/notary/f?p=246:1:1696483662868702::::
Nurse-RN/LPN/Anesthetist/Practitionier	https://license.ohio.gov/lookup/default.asp?division=86
Occupational Therapist/Assistant	http://otptat.ohio.gov/LicenseVerification.aspx
Ocularist/Ocularist Apprentice	https://license.ohio.gov/lookup/default.asp?division=80
Optical Dispenser	https://license.ohio.gov/lookup/default.asp?division=80
Optician/Optician Apprentice	https://license.ohio.gov/lookup/default.asp?division=80
Optometrist/ Diagnostic/Therapeutic	https://license.ohio.gov/lookup/default.asp?division=91
Osteopathic Physician	https://license.ohio.gov/lookup/default.asp?division=78
Pawnbroker	https://elicense2-secure.com.ohio.gov/
Pesticide Applicator Business	www.agri.ohio.gov/apps/odaprs/pestfert-PRS-index.aspx#tog
Pesticide Applicator/Operator/Dealer	www.agri.ohio.gov/apps/odaprs/pestfert-PRS-index.aspx#tog
Pesticide Limited Comm' l Applicator	www.agri.ohio.gov/apps/odaprs/pestfert-PRS-index.aspx#tog
Pharmacist	https://license.ohio.gov/lookup/default.asp?division=96
Pharmacy/Pharmacy Dispensary	https://license.ohio.gov/lookup/default.asp?division=96
Physical Therapist/Assistant	http://otptat.ohio.gov/LicenseVerification.aspx
Physician/Medical Doctor/Assistant	https://license.ohio.gov/lookup/default.asp?division=78
Plumber	www.com.ohio.gov/dico/
Plumbing Inspector	https://www.comapps.ohio.gov/dic/dico_apps/bdcc/PlumbingInspectorCertification/
Podiatrist	https://license.ohio.gov/lookup/default.asp?division=78
Polygraph Examiner	www.ohiopolygraph.org/members.asp
Precious Metals Dealer	https://elicense2-secure.com.ohio.gov/
Premium Finance Company	https://elicense2-secure.com.ohio.gov/
Prescriptive Authority	https://license.ohio.gov/lookup/default.asp?division=86
Pressure Piping Inspector	www.com.ohio.gov/dico/
Private Investigator	https://www.dps.state.oh.us/ALRS/ProviderSearch.aspx
Psychologist	https://license.ohio.gov/lookup/default.asp?division=83
Real Estate Agent/Seller/Broker	http://com.ohio.gov/eLicense.aspx
Real Estate Appraiser	http://com.ohio.gov/eLicense.aspx
Respiratory Therapist/Student	https://license.ohio.gov/lookup/default.asp
Savings & Loan Association	https://elicense2-secure.com.ohio.gov/
Savings Bank	https://elicense2-secure.com.ohio.gov/
School Psychologist	https://license.ohio.gov/lookup/default.asp?division=83
Securities Filing	https://www.comapps.ohio.gov/secu/secu_apps/offering/
Securities Salesperson/Dealer	https://www.comapps.ohio.gov/secu/secu_apps/recordrequest/
Security Guard	https://www.dps.state.oh.us/ALRS/ProviderSearch.aspx
Social Worker	https://license.ohio.gov/lookup/default.asp?division=97
Speech Pathologist/Audiologist/Aide	https://license.ohio.gov/lookup/default.asp?division=84
Sprinkler Equipment Inspector	www.com.ohio.gov/dico/
Sprinkler Inspector	www.com.ohio.gov/OnlineServices.aspx
Steam Engineer	https://www.comapps.ohio.gov/dic/dico_apps/boil/boiler_contractors/Default.aspx
Surveyor, Land	https://license.ohio.gov/lookup/default.asp?division=100
Veterinarian/Veterinary Tech	https://license.ohio.gov/lookup/default.asp?division=88

State and Local Courts

State Court Structure: The **Court of Common Pleas** is the general jurisdiction court with separate divisions including General, Domestic Relations, Juvenile and Probate. Per the Supreme Court web page, the General Division has original jurisdiction in all criminal felony cases and in all civil cases in which the amount in controversy is more than $15,000. However, the Administrative Director's Office advises the Common Pleas can hear civil cases for $501 or more.

County and **Municipal Courts** handle virtually the same subject matter with some minor operational differences. Both have the authority to conduct preliminary hearings in felony cases, both have jurisdiction over traffic and non-traffic misdemeanors and, and have limited civil jurisdiction in which the amount of money in dispute does not exceed $15,000.

Mayor's Courts are not a part of the judicial branch of Ohio government and are not courts of record. A person convicted in a Mayor's Court may appeal the conviction to the Municipal or County court having jurisdiction within the municipal corporation. Ohio and Louisiana are the only two states that allow the mayors of municipal corporations to preside over a court.

The **Court of Claims** has original jurisdiction to hear and determine all civil actions filed against the state of Ohio and its agencies.

Appellate Courts: Appellate and Supreme Court opinions may be researched from the Supreme Court website at www.supremecourtofohio.gov

Statewide Court Online Access: Quite a few individual Common Pleas, County and Municipal courts offer online access. There is no statewide access. However the Supreme Court of Ohio is in the process of implementing the Ohio Court Network (OCN) for users from the court and justice systems. **There is no public access to OCN at this time**. This system will include court case docket information from all courts of record, including criminal, civil and traffic records.

County Sites:

Allen County

Common Pleas Court www.allencountyohio.com/commonpleas/ccom.php

Civil: Access civil records including judgment liens free at www.allencountyohio.com/clerkofcourts/cle_disclaimer.php. *Criminal:* Online access to index is free at www.allencountyohio.com/clerkofcourts/cle_disclaimer.php. Records go back to 12/1/1988.

Lima Municipal Court www.cityhall.lima.oh.us/index.aspx?NID=100

Civil: Search index information at http://connection.limamunicipalcourt.org/awc/Court/Default.aspx. Direct email search requests to limamuni@wcoil.com *Criminal:* same

Ashland County

Common Pleas Court www.ashlandcounty.org/clerkofcourts/

Civil: Access records at www.ashlandcountycpcourt.org. *Criminal:* same

Ashland Municipal Court www.ashlandmunicourt.com/

Civil: Search the docket index for free at http://web01.civicacmi.com/Ashland/Court/. Search by either plaintiff or defendant. *Criminal:* Search the criminal and traffic docket index for free at http://web01.civicacmi.com/Ashland/Court/.

Ashtabula County

Common Pleas Court http://courts.co.ashtabula.oh.us/

Civil: Access to index is free at http://courts.co.ashtabula.oh.us/eservices/home.page.2. *Criminal:* same

County Court Eastern Division http://courts.co.ashtabula.oh.us/eastern_county_court.htm

Civil: Access to records are free at http://courts.co.ashtabula.oh.us/pa.htm. *Criminal:* same

County Court Western Division http://courts.co.ashtabula.oh.us/western_county_court.htm

Civil: Access records free at http://courts.co.ashtabula.oh.us/pa.htm. *Criminal:* same

Ashtabula Municipal Court www.ashtabulamunicipalcourt.com/

Civil: Online access to civil court cases are free at www.ashtabulamunicourt.com/searchdocket.asp. *Criminal:* Online access to case information, including traffic, is free at www.ashtabulamunicourt.com/searchdocket.asp.

Athens County

Common Pleas Court www.co.athensoh.org/Common_Pleas_Court.html

Civil: Online access to CP court records are free at http://coc.athensoh.org/pa/. *Criminal:* same

Athens Municipal Court www.ci.athens.oh.us/index.aspx?NID=108

Civil: Search by name or case number at http://docket.webxsol.com/athens/index.html . Records available from 1992. *Criminal:* same

Auglaize County

Common Pleas Court www2.auglaizecounty.org/courts/common-pleas

Civil: Access civil records back to 2/2000 free at www.auglaizecounty.org/pa/. *Criminal:* Access criminal records back to 2/2000 free at www.auglaizecounty.org/pa/. **$$$**

Auglaize County Municipal Court www2.auglaizecounty.org/courts/municipal

Civil: Access civil and small claims court records back to 4/1/1994 free at www.auglaizecounty.org/pa/. *Criminal:* Access criminal and traffic records back to 10/1/1993 free at www.auglaizecounty.org/pa/. DOB shows sometimes.

Belmont County

County Courts - All Divisions www.belmontcountycourts.com/

Civil: View the docket index at http://eaccess.belmontcountycourts.com/eservices_w/home.page.3. There is no fee. *Criminal:* same

Brown County

Common Pleas Court www.browncountyohio.gov/index.php/clerk-of-courts46

Civil: Search court records free at www.browncountyclerkofcourts.org/Search/. *Criminal:* same

County Municipal Court www.browncountycourt.org

Civil: Access to records are free at www.browncountycourt.org/search.html. Online criminal search results do not include address and DOB. *Criminal:* same Online criminal search results include address and DOB.

Butler County

Common Pleas Court www.butlercountyclerk.org

Civil: Online access to Probate Court records is free at http://66.117.197.22/index.cfm?page=courtRecords. Search the Estate or Guardianship databases. Civil is no longer online.

Hamilton Municipal Court www.hamiltonmunicipalcourt.org

Civil: Search record access free at http://hamiltonmunicipalcourt.org/connect/court/. *Criminal:* Search records free at http://hamiltonmunicipalcourt.org/connect/court/.

Fairfield Municipal Court www.fairfield-city.org/municipalcourt/index.cfm

Civil: Search records online back to 1988 free at www.fairfield-city.org/courtrecords/municipal-court-records.cfm. *Criminal:* same

Middletown Municipal Court www.cityofmiddletown.org/court/

Civil: Index to the civil docket is at http://court.cityofmiddletown.org/connection/court/index.xsp. *Criminal:* Search criminal and traffic records back to early 1990s and court schedules free at http://court.cityofmiddletown.org/connection/court/index.xsp. Online records go back to 1990.

Champaign County

Champaign County Municipal Court www.champaigncountymunicipalcourt.com

Civil & Criminal: Access court records back to 1992 free at www.champaigncountymunicipalcourt.com/Docket.aspx includes civil, criminal and traffic.

Clark County

Common Pleas Court www.clarkcountyohio.gov/index.aspx?nid=93

Civil: Online access to clerk's record index is free at www.clarkcountyohio.gov/index.aspx?NID=314. *Criminal:* same

Clark County Municipal Court www.clerkofcourts.municipal.co.clark.oh.us/

Civil: Online access to case information is free at www.clerkofcourts.municipal.co.clark.oh.us/. Images available back to 4/15/06. Online records go back to 3/90. *Criminal:* same

Clermont County

Common Pleas Court www.clermontclerk.org/Case_Access.htm

Civil: Online access to civil records is the same as criminal, see following. *Criminal:* Online access to court records is free at www.clermontclerk.org/Case_Access.htm. Online records go back to 1/1987. Includes later Municipal Court records.

Clermont County Municipal Court www.clermontclerk.org

Civil: Access to court records is the same as criminal. *Criminal:* Access to court records is free at www.clermontclerk.org/Case_Access.htm. Online records go back to 5/1/1996.

Clinton County

Clinton County Municipal Court www.clintonmunicourt.org

Civil: Search court records online at www.clintonmunicourt.org/search.html. *Criminal:* same

Columbiana County

Common Pleas Court www.ccclerk.org

Civil: Access all county court index and docket records free at www.ccclerk.org/case_access.htm. Includes probate. *Criminal:* Access all county court index and docket records free at www.ccclerk.org/case_access.htm.

Municipal Court www.ccclerk.org/the_courts.htm
Civil: Access all county court index and docket records free at www.ccclerk.org/case_access.htm. *Criminal:* same

East Liverpool Municipal Court www.elcourt.org/
Civil: Access all county court index and docket records free at www.ccclerk.org/pa/paELIVER.urd/pamw6500.display. *Criminal:* same

Coshocton County

Common Pleas Court www.coshoctoncounty.net
Civil: Search civil and domestic relations cases back to 01/01/1999 at http://eaccess.coshoctoncounty.net/eservices/home.page. General identifiers given, but does not include DOB. *Criminal:* Search criminal cases back to 01/01/1999 at http://eaccess.coshoctoncounty.net/eservices/home.page. General identifiers given, but does not include DOB.

Coshocton Municipal Court www.coshoctonmunicipalcourt.com
Civil: Online access to civil records is at the website. Search by name, case number, attorney, date. *Criminal:* Online access to the criminal record index is at the website. Search by name, case number, attorney, date.

Crawford County

Common Pleas Court www.crawfordcocpcourt.org/
Civil: Online access to Common Pleas court records is free at www.crawford-co.org/Clerk/default.html and click on \"Internet Inquiry.\" Data is updated nightly. *Criminal:* same as civil.

Cuyahoga County

Common Pleas Court - General Division http://cp.cuyahogacounty.us/internet/index.aspx
Civil: Online access to Common Please civil courts; click on Civil Case Dockets at http://cpdocket.cp.cuyahogacounty.us. Access Probate index at http://probate.cuyahogacounty.us/pa/. *Criminal:* Online access to criminal records dockets is free at http://cpdocket.cp.cuyahogacounty.us.

Cleveland Municipal Court http://clevelandmunicipalcourt.org/home.html
Civil: See http://clevelandmunicipalcourt.org/cvdisclaimer.html for docket information. There are limited personal identifiers to view. *Criminal:* See http://clevelandmunicipalcourt.org/cvdisclaimer.html for docket information. The data is incomplete and should not be relied upon for a full background search. There are limited personal identifiers to view as well.

Bedford Municipal Court www.bedfordmuni.org/
Civil: Access index to court records at www.bedfordmuni.org/info.asp?pageId=5. Click on Case Information. *Criminal:* Access index to court records at www.bedfordmuni.org/info.asp?pageId=5. Click on Case Information.

East Cleveland Municipal Court www.eccourt.com/
Civil: Non-official court record data can be access for free at http://caseinfo.eccourt.com/. *Criminal:* same

Cleveland Heights Municipal Court www.clevelandheightscourt.com
Civil: Search Muni civil (to $15,000) docket records from the home page. Search by name or case number. *Criminal:* Search Muni misdemeanor docket records from the home page. Search by name or case number.

Berea Municipal Court www.bereamunicourt.org/
Civil: Search docket information at hwww.bedfordmuni.org/info.asp?pageId=5. *Criminal:* Search docket info at www.bedfordmuni.org/info.asp?pageId=5.

Euclid Municipal Court www.cityofeuclid.com/community/court
Civil: Docket index and daily docket lists of civil cases available at www.cityofeuclid.com/community/court/HearingDocketsandCaseInformation. *Criminal:* Docket index and daily docket lists of misdemeanor and traffic cases are available at www.cityofeuclid.com/community/court/HearingDocketsandCaseInformation.

Garfield Heights Municipal Court www.ghmc.org
Civil: Online access is limited to dockets; search by name, date or case number at http://docket.ghmc.org. *Criminal:* same

Lakewood Municipal Court www.lakewoodcourtoh.com
Civil: Search dockets at www.lakewoodcourtoh.com/casesearch.html. *Criminal:* Seaach dockets at www.lakewoodcourtoh.com/casesearch.html. Includes traffic.

Lyndhurst Municipal Court www.lyndhurstmunicipalcourt.org/
Civil: Access court records free at www.lyndhurstmunicipalcourt.org/. Click on Case Search. *Criminal:* Access court records free at www.lyndhurstmunicipalcourt.org/. Click on Case Search.

Parma Municipal Court www.parmamunicourt.org/
Civil: Access to the court dockets index is available free at www.parmamunicourt.org/info.asp?pageId=5. *Criminal:* Access to criminal docket at www.parmamunicourt.org/info.asp?pageId=5. Note that the site disclaimer states that there can be a 24 delay and that this site does not provide the official court record.

Rocky River Municipal Court www.rrcourt.net
Civil: Public access to record index at https://rrcourt.net/pa/pa.htm. *Criminal:* Access record index free at https://rrcourt.net/pa/pa.htm.

Shaker Heights Municipal Court www.shakerheightscourt.org/home/
Civil: Search case records and dockets at www.shakerheightscourt.org/home/. *Criminal:* same

South Euclid Municipal Court www.southeuclidcourt.com/
Civil: Search case records and dockets at /www.southeuclidcourt.com/record_search.php /. *Criminal:* same

Darke County

Common Pleas Court www.darkecourts.com/
Civil: Free online access to the docket at www.darkecourts.com/. Includes judgments and divorce. Includes access to records from Darke County Municipal Court. *Criminal:* Free online access to the docket at www.darkecourts.com/. Includes access to records from Darke County Municipal Court, such as traffic.

County Municipal Court www.darkecourts.com/
Civil: Records available at http://69.34.179.131/eservices/home.page.2. *Criminal:* same

Delaware County

Common Pleas Court www.delawarecountyclerk.org
Civil: Access to court records is free at www.delawarecountyclerk.org. Probate court index from 1852 to 1920 is free at www.midohio.net/dchsdcgs/probate.html. *Criminal:* Access to court records is free at www.delawarecountyclerk.org. Search the sheriff's county database of sex offenders, deadbeat parents, and most wanted list for free at www.delawarecountysheriff.com.

Delaware Municipal Court www.delawareohio.net/MunicipalCourt/CourtHome/default.aspx
Civil: Municipal courts records are at www.delawareohio.net/MunicipalCourt/CourtHome/default.aspx *Criminal:* Misdemeanor and traffic case records are free at www.delawareohio.net/MunicipalCourt/CourtHome/default.aspx.

Erie County

Sandusky Municipal Court www.sanduskymunicipalcourt.org/
Civil: Access Muni court records free at www.sanduskymunicipalcourt.org/search.shtml. *Criminal:* same

Vermilion Municipal Court www.vermilionmunicipalcourt.org
Civil: Online access to Municipal court records at www.vermilionmunicipalcourt.org/search.shtml. *Criminal:* Online access to municipal court records is at www.vermilionmunicipalcourt.org/search.shtml

Fairfield County

Common Pleas Court www.fairfieldcountyclerk.com
Civil: Online access to County Clerk's court records database is free at http://courtview.co.fairfield.oh.us/eservices/home.page. *Criminal:* same

Fairfield County Municipal Court www.fcmcourt.org
Civil: Search civil case info online at http://12.49.195.19/cvsearch.shtml. *Criminal:* Search criminal and traffic at http://12.49.195.19/trsearch.shtml.

Fayette County

Common Pleas Court www.fayette-co-oh.com/Commplea/index.html
Civil: Search docket information free at http://cp.onlinedockets.com/fayettecp/case_dockets/search.aspx. Search by name or case number. Includes access to wills and estates, marriage licenses and divorces. *Criminal:* Search docket info free at http://cp.onlinedockets.com/fayettecp/case_dockets/search.aspx. Includes appeals from Muni court.

Municipal Court http://70.61.249.71/
Civil: Search record index free at http://70.62.185.171/search.shtml. *Criminal:* same

Franklin County

Common Pleas Court www.fccourts.org/gen/WebFront.nsf//wp/Home?open
Civil: Access records 3AM-11PM at http://fcdcfcjs.co.franklin.oh.us/CaseInformationOnline/ and includes domestic relations cases. The searchable online record index for court records often does not provide identifiers for civil and domestic case searches. *Criminal:* Access records 3AM-11PM at http://fcdcfcjs.co.franklin.oh.us/CaseInformationOnline/. Most online index lists show the DOB, but not all.

Franklin County Municipal Court - Criminal Division www.fcmcclerk.com
Criminal: Criminal and traffic records from the Clerk of Court Courtview database free online at www.fcmcclerk.com/case/. Search by name, dates, ticket, address or case numbers.

Franklin County Municipal Court - Civil Division www.fcmcclerk.com
Civil: Records from the Clerk of Court CourtView database is free online at www.fcmcclerk.com/case/. Search by name or case number.

Fulton County

Common Pleas Court www.fultoncountyoh.com
Civil: Access an index of civil case records at http://pa.fultoncountyoh.com/pa/. **$$$** *Criminal:* Access the criminal record index at http://pa.fultoncountyoh.com/pa/.

County Court Western District www.fultoncountyoh.com
Civil: Access court records back to 1995 free at www.fultoncountyoh.com/pa/. *Criminal:* same as civil

County Court Eastern District www.fultoncountyoh.com/
Civil: Access court records back to 1995 free at www.fultoncountyoh.com/pa/. *Criminal:* same as civil.

Gallia County

Common Pleas Court - Gallia County Courthouse www.gallianet.net/index.php/gallia-county/criminal-justice-departments/clerk-of-courts
Civil: Access the docket index at http://eaccess.gallianet.net/eservices/home.page. Includes judgments and divorce. *Criminal:* Access the docket index at http://eaccess.gallianet.net/eservices/home.page. Includes criminal and domestic violence. and

Gallipolis Municipal Court www.cityofgallipolis.com/judicial_system/municipal_court.php
Civil: Search the record index at http://173.249.134.245/searchMC.shtml. Results show address. *Criminal:* same as civil.

Geauga County

Common Pleas Court www.geaugacourts.org/
Civil: Search court record index free from the home page. Click on type of court then court records. Online records go back to 1990. Includes domestic cases. *Criminal:* Search court record index free from the home page. Click on type of court then court records. Includes traffic.

Chardon Municipal Court http://co.geauga.oh.us/MuniCourt/Home.aspx
Civil: Search court record index free at http://municourt.co.geauga.oh.us/eservices/home.page.2. *Criminal:* same

Greene County

Common Pleas Court www.co.greene.oh.us/index.aspx?nid=402
Civil: Online access to clerk of court records is free at http://courts.co.greene.oh.us/eservices/home.page.2. Search by name or case number. Also, search probate cases free at http://apps.co.greene.oh.us/probate/casesearch.aspx. *Criminal:* same as civil.

Xenia Municipal Court www.ci.xenia.oh.us/index.php?page=municipal-court
Civil: Online access to Municipal Court records free at www.ci.xenia.oh.us/index.php?page=public-access. *Criminal:* same

Fairborn Municipal Court www.fairbornmunicipalcourt.us/
Civil: Website offers free online access to civil, misdemeanor and traffic records from home page. *Criminal:* Online access same as civil for traffic and misdemeanor.

Guernsey County

Common Pleas Court www.guernseycounty.org/cms/?q=clerkofcourts
Civil: Access case index data free at http://74.218.3.68/eservices/home.page.4. Judge calendars also available online. *Criminal:* same

Cambridge Municipal Court www.cambridgeoh.org/cms/court
Civil: Access Muni Court records free at http://webconnect03.civicacmi.com/cambridge/court/. *Criminal:* same

Hamilton County

Common Pleas Court www.courtclerk.org
Civil: Records and calendars from the court clerk are free at www.courtclerk.org/namesearch.asp. Online civil index goes back to 1991. Also, search probate records free at www.probatect.org/case_search/casesearch.asp. *Criminal:* Online access to criminal record docket is at www.courtclerk.org/queries.asp. Online criminal index goes back to 1986. Also, there is a subscription service for document access but this appears to be for attorneys only.

Hancock County

Common Pleas Court http://cp.co.hancock.oh.us/
Civil: Search records online back to 1985 at http://pa.co.hancock.oh.us/pa/. *Criminal:* same

Findlay Municipal Court https://findlaymunicourt.com/municourt/
Civil: Search civil records online at https://findlaymunicourt.com/municourt/searchcivildocket.asp?pageId=71/. *Criminal:* Search traffic and civil cases at https://findlaymunicourt.com/municourt/searchdocket.asp?pageId=32.

Hardin County

Common Pleas Court www.hardincourts.com/
Civil: Online access to the civil docket is available at www.hardincourts.com/CLSite/search.dis.shtml. *Criminal:* Online access to the criminal docket is offered at www.hardincourts.com/CLSite/search.dis.shtml.

Highland County

Common Pleas Court www.hccpc.org/
Civil: Search the index online at http://70.61.138.206/eservices/app/home.page.2. *Criminal:* same

Hillsboro Municipal Court www.hillsboroohio.net/municipal%20court.html
Civil: Online access is same as criminal, see below. *Criminal:* Online access is free at http://24.123.13.34/.

Hocking County

Common Pleas Court www.hockingcountycommonpleascourt.com/index.htm
Civil: Access the court case index free at www.court.co.hocking.oh.us/cgi-bin/db2www.pgm/cpq.mbr/main. *Criminal:* same

Hocking County Municipal Court www.hockingcountymunicipalcourt.com
Civil: Access civil records free at www.hockingcountymunicipalcourt.com/search.shtml. Shows case number, docket entry, charge, case type. *Criminal:* Access criminal records free at www.hockingcountymunicipalcourt.com/search.shtml. Shows case number, docket entry, charge, case type.

Huron County

Common Pleas Court www.huroncountyclerk.com
Civil: Search court dockets and public records free at the website www.huroncountyclerk.com/html/case_search.html Civil results on internet do not include DOB. *Criminal:* Search court dockets and public records free at the website www.huroncountyclerk.com/html/case_search.html.

Norwalk Municipal Court www.norwalkmunicourt.com
Civil: Access records free at www.norwalkmunicourt.com/search.htm. *Criminal:* same

Jackson County

Common Pleas Court www.jcclerk.com/
Civil: Search the docket by name or case number at http://173.249.140.218/pa/. *Criminal:* same

Jackson County Municipal Court www.jacksoncountymunicipalcourt.com/
Civil: Search record index free at www.jacksoncountymunicipalcourt.com/Search/. *Criminal:* Search the record index at www.jacksoncountymunicipalcourt.com/Search/.

Jefferson County

Common Pleas Court www.jeffersoncountyoh.com/
Civil: Access court index free at www.jeffersoncountyoh.com/CountyCourts/CommonPleas.aspx. No birthdates shown. *Criminal:* same

All County Courst www.jeffersoncountyoh.com/
Civil: Search court case index free at www.jeffersoncountyoh.com/CountyCourts/ClerkofCourts/tabid/156/Default.aspx. *Criminal:* same

Steubenville Municipal Court www.cityofsteubenville.us/court/
Civil: Online access to the docket index is at http://webconnect03.civicacmi.com/steubenvilleMC/court/. *Criminal:* Online access to the criminal and traffic docket index is at http://webconnect03.civicacmi.com/steubenvilleMC/court/.

Knox County

Common Pleas Court
Civil: Search court index, dockets, calendars free online at www.coc.co.knox.oh.us/pa/. Search by name or case number. *Criminal:* same

Mount Vernon Municipal Court www.mountvernonmunicipalcourt.org
Civil: Access to the clerk's civil records are free at http://mountvernonmunicipalcourt.org/connection/court/index.xsp. *Criminal:* Access to the clerk's criminal and traffic records are free at http://mountvernonmunicipalcourt.org/connection/court/index.xsp.

Lake County

Common Pleas Court www.lakecountyohio.org
Civil: Online access to court records, dockets, and quick index, including probate records, is free at https://phoenix.lakecountyohio.gov/pa/. *Criminal:* Online access to court records and dockets is free at https://phoenix.lakecountyohio.gov/pa/.

Painesville Municipal Court www.pmcourt.com
Civil: Free online access to index at www.pmcourt.com/search.shtml. *Criminal:* same

Mentor Municipal Court www.mentormunicipalcourt.org/
Civil: Record searches at www.mentormunicipalcourt.org/search.shtml. The initial docket list does not show identifiers, but click on the case number to find identifiers. *Criminal:* same as civil.

Willoughby Municipal Court www.willoughbycourt.com
Civil: Access the court's case lookup plus schedules free at www.willoughbycourt.com/connection/court/. *Criminal:* Access the court's case lookup plus bench warrants and schedules free at www.willoughbycourt.com/connection/court/.

Lawrence County

Common Pleas Court www.lawrenceclerk.com/
Civil: Online access to civil records is free at www.lawrenceclerk.com/. *Criminal:* Online access to criminal records is free at www.lawrenceclerk.com/

Lawrence County Municipal Court www.lawcomunicourt.com/
Civil: Click on \"Record Search\" at the web page for a search of the record index. *Criminal:* same

Licking County

Common Pleas Court www.lcounty.com/clerkofcourts/
Civil: County clerk's office offers free Internet access to current records at www.lcounty.com/eservices/home.page.2. *Criminal:* same

Licking County Municipal Court www.lcmunicipalcourt.com
Civil: Online access to Municipal Court record docket is free at http://70.61.248.70/connection/court/. Results include addresses. *Criminal:* same

Logan County

Common Pleas Court http://co.logan.oh.us/clerkofcourts/
Civil: A supplemental free search is offered at http://caserecords.co.logan.oh.us/eservices/home.page. "Case Status" field may not reflect actual case status. *Criminal:* same

Lorain County

Common Pleas Court www.loraincounty.com/clerk/
Civil: Free access to indices and dockets for common please court cases at http://cp.onlinedockets.com/loraincp/case_dockets/search.aspx. Access probate records at www.loraincounty.com/probate/search.shtml. *Criminal:* same

Lorain Municipal Court www.cityoflorain.org/municipal_court/
Civil: Access municipal court records free at www.cityoflorain.org/municipal_court/public_access. Search by name, date, case number or license number. *Criminal:* same

Elyria Municipal Court www.elyriamunicourt.org
Civil: Search at the Internet site, also you can request information by email to civil@elyriamunicourt.org. *Criminal:* Search misdemeanor and traffic records back to 1992 at the website, also send email requests to crtr@elyriamunicourt.org.

Avon Lake Municipal Court www.avonlakecourt.com/
Civil: Search docket index by name or case number at www.avonlakecourt.com/search.php. *Criminal:* Search docket index by name, case number or ticket number at www.avonlakecourt.com/search.php.

Oberlin Municipal Court www.oberlinmunicipalcourt.org
Civil: Access case information free online at www.oberlinmunicipalcourt.org/public.htm. Search by a variety of ways. *Criminal:* same

Vermilion Municipal Court www.vermilionmunicipalcourt.org
Civil: Online access to Municipal court records at www.vermilionmunicipalcourt.org/search.shtml. *Criminal:* Online access to municipal court records is at www.vermilionmunicipalcourt.org/search.shtml

Lucas County

Common Pleas Court www.co.lucas.oh.us/index.aspx?nid=83
Civil: Online access to clerk of courts dockets is free at www.co.lucas.oh.us/index.aspx?NID=99. Online records go back to 9/1997. Search probate records at www.lucas-co-probate-ct.org/. *Criminal:* Online access to clerk of courts dockets is free at www.co.lucas.oh.us/index.aspx?NID=99. Online record go back to 9/1997. Search sex offenders at www.lucascountysheriff.org/sheriff/disclaimer.asp.

Toledo Municipal Court www.tmc-clerk.com/
Civil: Dockets are online at www.tmc-clerk.com/caseinformation/civilcase/. Direct email requests to tmc-clerk@noris.org *Criminal:* Dockets are online at www.tmc-clerk.com/caseinformation/criminaltraffic/. Direct email requests to tmc-clerk@noris.org.

Maumee Municipal Court www.maumee.org/municipal/default.htm
Civil: Online access to web court system database is free at www.maumee.org/municipal/caseinfo.htm. *Criminal:* same, includes traffic.

Oregon Municipal Court www.oregonohio.org/View_Court_Records.html
Civil: Direct email civil search requests to court@ci.oregon.oh.us. Search court cases and schedules free at www.oregonohio.org/View_Court_Records.html. *Criminal:* same as civil.

Sylvania Municipal Court www.sylvaniacourt.com
Civil: Online access free at http://courtsvr.sylvaniacourt.com/. *Criminal:* same

Madison County

Common Pleas Court http://co.madison.oh.us/commonpleas/
Civil: Search probate records (but no civil records) at http://207.58.255.212/. *Criminal:*

Madison County Municipal Court http://207.58.255.213/
Civil: Access civil case record free at http://207.58.255.213/search.shtml. Shows case number, docket entry, charge, case type. *Criminal:* Access criminal case record free at http://207.58.255.213/search.shtml. Shows case number, docket entry, charge, case type. Includes traffic.

Mahoning County

Common Pleas Court www.mahoningcountyoh.gov/tabid/810/default.aspx
Civil: For online access, see criminal section. Judgments can be printed off the internet. *Criminal:* Access integrated justice system cases back to 1995 free at http://courts.mahoningcountyoh.gov/. Attorney searching also available.

All County Courts www.mahoningcountyoh.gov/tabid/810/default.aspx
Civil: For online access, see criminal section. *Criminal:* Access integrated justice system cases back to 1995 free at http://courts.mahoningcountyoh.gov/. Attorney searching also available.

Struthers Municipal Court www.cityofstruthers.com/court.aspx
Civil: Access court records at http://74.219.105.102/searchMC.shtml - records go back to 1996. *Criminal:* same

Youngstown Municipal Court www.youngstownmuniclerk.com/
Civil: Access cases record data back to 1998 free at www.youngstownmunicipalcourt.com/eservices/app/home.page.2. Search by name, case number, attorney or ticket number. *Criminal:* same

Marion County

Common Pleas Court http://mcoprx.co.marion.oh.us/
Civil: Court record access free at http://mcoprx.co.marion.oh.us/clerk/index.php?option=com_content&task=view&id=13&Itemid=27. *Criminal:* same

Marion Municipal Court www.marionmunicipalcourt.org
Civil: Online record searching available at www.marionmunicipalcourt.org/search.php. *Criminal:* same

Medina County

Common Pleas Court www.clerk.medinaco.org/
Civil: Online access is the same as criminal, see below. *Criminal:* Search court documents, motion dockets, sexual predator judgments and court notices at the web page.

Medina Municipal Court www.medinamunicipalcourt.org
Civil: Access the online Civil Case Lookup free from home page or go direct to http://24.144.216.42/connection/court/index.xsp. *Criminal:* Access the online Criminal and Traffic Case Lookup free from home page or go direct to http://24.144.216.42/connection/court/index.xsp.

Wadsworth Municipal Court www.wadsworthmunicipalcourt.com/
Civil: Access civil case lookups and case queries free at www.wadsworthmunicipalcourt.com/municipal-court/search-records.html. *Criminal:* Online access to criminal case and traffic lookups and case queries is the same as civil, see above.

Meigs County

Common Pleas Court www.meigscountyclerkofcourts.com/
Civil: The courts' docket information is searchable at www.meigscountyclerkofcourts.com/courtview_online_records.htm. *Criminal:* same

Meigs County Court
Civil: Access civil records free at http://docket.webxsol.com/meigs/index.html. *Criminal:* same as civil.

Mercer County

Common Pleas Court www.mercercountyohio.org/clerk/
Civil: Online access for the public available from the home page. *Criminal:* Online access available for the public from the home page.

Miami County

Miami County Municipal Court www.co.miami.oh.us/muni/index.htm
Civil: Online access to records is free at www.co.miami.oh.us/pa/index.htm. *Criminal:* same

Monroe County

Common Pleas Court www.monroecountyohio.com/countyoffices/clerkofcourts.html
Criminal: Search records from November 2012 forward at http://12.165.45.120/

Montgomery County

Common Pleas Court www.clerk.co.montgomery.oh.us/
Civil: Online access to the Courts countywide PRO system is free at www.clerk.co.montgomery.oh.us/legal/records.cfm. Access probate and guardianship record info free at www.mcohio.org/government/probate/prodcfm/casesearchg.cfm. *Criminal:* same

Municipal Court - Western Division www.mccountycourts.org/Courts/Index.aspx?COURTID=1
Civil: Search countywide records online at www.clerk.co.montgomery.oh.us/. *Criminal:* same

Municipal Court - Eastern Division www.mccountycourts.org/Courts/Index.aspx?COURTID=2
Civil: Search countywide records online at www.clerk.co.montgomery.oh.us/. *Criminal:* same

Dayton Municipal Court - Criminal Division www.daytonmunicipalcourt.org
Criminal: Online access to municipal court record search is free at www.wejis.com/pa/Search.cfm; includes traffic.

Dayton Municipal Court - Civil Division www.daytonmunicipalcourt.org
Civil: Online access to civil Municipal court case summary is free at www.wejis.com/PA/CvSearch.cfm. Search by plaintiff, defendant, attorney name or filing date. There is a separate field if company is used. No personal identifiers shown.

Kettering Municipal Court www.ketteringmunicipalcourt.com
Civil: Access case lookups free from a vendor at http://caselookup.ketteringmunicipalcourt.com/awc/Court/Default.aspx. There is a disclaimer that the court does not warrant the accuracy of the data. *Criminal:* same

Miamisburg Municipal Court www.miamisburgcourts.com
Civil: Access case lookup options and case schedules for free at http://64.56.106.117/connection/court/. *Criminal:* same

Vandalia Municipal Court www.vandaliacourt.com
Civil: Search records, including traffic, at http://docket.vandaliacourt.com/. *Criminal:* same

Morrow County

Municipal Court www.morrowcountymunict.org/
Criminal: Search upcoming or historical criminal and traffic case records at www.morrowcountymunict.org/.

Muskingum County

Common Pleas Court www.muskingumcounty.org/clerkofcourts.shtm
Civil: Online access to court records is available at http://clerkofcourts.muskingumcounty.org/PA/. Records indexed back to 1994. *Criminal:* same

County Court www.muskingumcountycourt.org
Civil: Access to county court records is free at www.muskingumcountycourt.org/recordSearch.php. *Criminal:* same

Zanesville Municipal Court www.coz.org/municipal_court.cfm
Civil: Online access free at http://74.219.84.227/searchMC.shtml *Criminal:* Same and includes traffic.

Ottawa County

Common Pleas Court www.ottawacocpcourt.com
Civil: Record search and dockets free at http://198.101.52.132/search.shtml. *Criminal:* same

Ottawa County Municipal Court www.ottawacountymunicipalcourt.com
Civil: Search record index is at www.ottawacountymunicipalcourt.com/search.php. Includes small claims. *Criminal:* Same, includes traffic.

Paulding County

County Court www.pauldingcountycourt.com
Civil: Access to civil records is free at www.pauldingcountycourt.com/Search/index.shtml. *Criminal:* same as civil.

Perry County

Perry County Court www.perrycountycourt.com
Civil: Access court record index free at www.perrycountycourt.com/Search/. *Criminal:* same

Pickaway County

Common Pleas Court www.pickawaycountycpcourt.org
Civil: Search docket information at www.pickawaycountycpcourt.org. *Criminal:* same

Circleville Municipal Court www.circlevillecourt.com
Civil: Search online at www.circlevillecourt.com/AccessCourtRecords.asp. *Criminal:* Search at www.circlevillecourt.com/AccessCourtRecords.asp.

Pike County

Pike County Court www.pikecountycourt.org/
Civil: Search the index by name, case number or date at www.pikecountycourt.org/search.shtml. Results give full identifiers. *Criminal:* Same, includes traffic.

Portage County

Common Pleas Court www.co.portage.oh.us/clerkofcourts.htm
Civil: For online records from 1977 forward, go to www.co.portage.oh.us/courtsearch.htm. Case number provided. *Criminal:* For index from 1977 forward or images 06/2005 forward, go to www.co.portage.oh.us/courtsearch.htm. Direct questions about online access to Kathy Gray at 330-297-3648.

Portage County Municipal Court - Ravenna www.co.portage.oh.us
Civil: Search records back to 1992 free at www.co.portage.oh.us/courtsearch.htm. *Criminal:* Search records back to 1992 free at www.co.portage.oh.us/courtsearch.htm. Direct questions about online access to Cindy W. at 330-297-5654.

Portage Municipal Court - Kent Branch www.co.portage.oh.us
Civil: Online records from 1992 forward at www.co.portage.oh.us/. *Criminal:* Records from 1992 forward at www.co.portage.oh.us/. Direct questions about online access to Robyn Godfrey at 330-296-2530.

Preble County

Common Pleas Court www.preblecountyohio.net/
Civil: Access to court records and calendars free at www.preblecountyohio.net/. *Criminal:* same

Eaton Municipal Court www.eatonmunicipalcourt.com

Civil: Search by name or case number free at www.eatonmunicipalcourt.com/docket/index.html. Records go back to 1989. *Criminal:* Search by name or case number free at www.eatonmunicipalcourt.com/docket/index.html. Computerized records begin in 1992 for online civil, criminal and traffic cases.

Putnam County

Common Pleas Court www.putnamcountyohio.gov/

Civil: Online access is free at www.putnamcountycourtsohio.com/Common.urd/pamw6500.display. *Criminal:* same

Putnam County Municipal Court www.putnamcountyohio.gov/

Civil: Online access is free at www.putnamcountycourtsohio.com/crtv.urd/pamw6500.display. *Criminal:* same

Richland County

Common Pleas Court http://richlandcourtsoh.us/

Civil: Access to civil records is at http://richlandcourtsoh.us/pa/. Most cases prior to 1990 are not shown. *Criminal:* Access to criminal dockets at http://richlandcourtsoh.us/pa/. Most cases prior to 1990 are not shown.

Mansfield Municipal Court www.ci.mansfield.oh.us/index.php/departments/municipal-court

Civil: Online access at http://ci.mansfield.oh.us/index.php?option=com_content&view=article&id=378 for records from 1992 forward. *Criminal:* Online access at hhttp://ci.mansfield.oh.us/index.php?option=com_content&view=article&id=378 for records from 1992 forward.

Ross County

Common Pleas Court www.co.ross.oh.us/ClerkOfCourts/

Civil: Search records back to 11/89 at www.co.ross.oh.us/ClerkOfCourts/. *Criminal:* same

Chillicothe Municipal Court www.chillicothemunicipalcourt.org

Civil: Search docket information at www.chillicothemunicipalcourt.org/Search/. Search by name or case number. *Criminal:* Search docket info at www.chillicothemunicipalcourt.org/Search/. Search by name or case number. Search traffic by ticket number.

Sandusky County

Common Pleas Court www.sandusky-county.com/index.php?page=common-pleas-court

Civil: Access the civil dockets at www.sandusky-county.org/Clerk/Disclaimer/All/default.asp. Search by name or case number. *Criminal:* Access misdemeanor traffic and criminal data free at www.sandusky-county.org/Clerk/Disclaimer/All/default.asp.

All County Courts www.sandusky-county.com/index.php?page=county-courts

Civil: Access civil docket online at www.sandusky-county.org/Clerk/Disclaimer/All/default.asp. *Criminal:* Access misdemeanor traffic and criminal data free at www.sandusky-county.org/Clerk/Disclaimer/All/default.asp.

Scioto County

Common Pleas Court www.sciotocountycpcourt.org/eservices/

Civil: Online access to civil records back to 1/1986 is free at www.sciotocountycpcourt.org/eservices/home.page.2. Search by court calendar, quick index, general index or docket sheet. *Criminal:* Online access to criminal record index back to 1/1986 is free at www.sciotocountycpcourt.org/eservices/home.page.2. Search by court calendar, quick index, general index or docket sheet.

Portsmouth Municipal Court www.pmcourt.org

Civil: Access is free at www.pmcourt.org/disc.html. *Criminal:* Access criminal records online free at www.pmcourt.org/disc.html.

Seneca County

Common Pleas Court www.senecacocourts.org/

Civil: Search dockets online at www.senecaco.org/clerk/default.html. Click on Internet Inquiry. *Criminal:* same

Tiffin Municipal Court www.tiffinmunicipalcourt.org/

Civil: Access records free at www.tiffinmunicipalcourt.org/search.shtml. *Criminal:* same

Fostoria Municipal Court www.fostoriamunicipalcourt.com/

Civil: Search the index by name or case number at www.fostoriamunicipalcourt.com/search.shtml. The DOB is generally not shown for civil records. *Criminal:* Search the index by name, ticket number, or case number at www.fostoriamunicipalcourt.com/search.shtml. The DOB generally does show for criminal records and traffic tickets.

Shelby County

Common Pleas Court http://co.shelby.oh.us/clerkofcourts/

Civil: Free online search of docket index is at http://co.shelby.oh.us/clerkofcourts/recordsearch.asp. *Criminal:* same

Stark County

Common Pleas Court - Civil Division www.starkclerk.org

Civil: Online access to the county online case docket database is free at www.starkcourt.org/docket/index.html. Search by name or case number. There is an advanced search as well.

Common Pleas Court - Criminal Division www.starkclerk.org
Criminal: Online access to county case docket database is free at www.starkcjis.org/docket/main.html. Search by name, case number. Will accept requests by email at crim.clerk@co.stark.oh.us

Canton Municipal Court www.cantoncourt.org/Forms/Default.aspx
Civil: Search docket information at www.cantoncourt.org/Forms/OnlineDocket.aspx or www.starkcjis.org/docket/main.html. *Criminal:* Search docket info at www.starkcjis.org/docket/main.html. Includes search of traffic records.

Massillon Municipal Court www.massilloncourt.org
Civil: Search the Online Case Docket of the Massillon Court at www.starkcjis.org/docket/main.html. *Criminal:* Search the Online Case Docket of the Massillon Court at www.starkcjis.org/docket/main.html. Includes traffic and misdemeanor records.

Alliance Municipal Court www.alliancecourt.org/
Civil: Search the Online Case Docket of the Alliance Court at www.starkcountycjis.org/cjis2/docket/main.html. *Criminal:* Search the Online Case Docket of the Alliance Court at www.starkcountycjis.org/cjis2/docket/main.html includes traffic and misdemeanor records.

Summit County

Common Pleas Court www.cpclerk.co.summit.oh.us/welcome.asp
Civil: Access to county clerk of courts records is free at www.cpclerk.co.summit.oh.us. Click on \"Record Search.\" Access to probate records at http://summitohioprobate.com/pa/pa.urd/pamw6500*display. *Criminal:* same

Akron Municipal Court http://courts.ci.akron.oh.us
Civil: Online access to court records and schedules is free at http://courts.ci.akron.oh.us/disclaimer.htm. *Criminal:* same

Barberton Municipal Court www.cityofbarberton.com/clerkofcourts/doc_home.html
Civil: Online records for Barberton, Green, Norton, Franklin, Clinton, Copley and Coventry are free at http://74.62.106.19/. Includes civil and small claims. *Criminal:* Online records for Barberton, Green, Norton, Franklin, Clinton, Copley and Coventry are free at http://74.62.106.19/. Includes traffic and cirminal.

Stow Municipal Court www.stowmunicourt.com.
Civil: Court docket information is free at www.stowmunicourt.com/docket.htm. *Criminal:* Court docket information is free at www.stowmunicourt.com/docket.htm

Trumbull County

Common Pleas Court http://clerk.co.trumbull.oh.us/
Civil: Online access to court records is free at http://courts.co.trumbull.oh.us/eservices/home.page.2. Records go back to May, 1996. Includes divorce. Online access to probate court records is free at www.trumbullprobate.org/paccessfront.htm. *Criminal:* Online access to criminal records is at http://courts.co.trumbull.oh.us/pa.urd/pamw6500.display.

Warren Municipal Court http://warren.org/city_departments/municipal_court
Civil: Access to the docket is free at http://records.warrenmuni.us/warren/search.do. There is a 24 hour delay after filings and actions until the record is posted. *Criminal:* Access to the docket is free at http://records.warrenmuni.us/warren/search.do. There is a 24 hour delay after filings and actions until the record is posted. Includes traffic cases.

Girard Municipal Court www.girardmunicipalcourt.com/
Civil: Access available at www.girardmunicipalcourt.com. Click on public access. *Criminal:* same

Niles Municipal Court www.nilesmunicipalcourt.com/
Civil: Access the index free at www.nilesmunicipalcourt.com/recordSearch.php. *Criminal:* Access the index free at www.nilesmunicipalcourt.com/recordSearch.php. Inlcudes traffic.

Newton Falls Municipal Court www.newtonfallscourt.com
Civil: Search record index free at www.newtonfallscourt.com/Search/. *Criminal:* same Online results include violation, hearing info and disposition.

Tuscarawas County

Common Pleas Court www.co.tuscarawas.oh.us
Civil: Search dockets online at http://general.clerkweb.co.tuscarawas.oh.us/eservices/home.page. *Criminal:* Search dockets online at http://general.clerkweb.co.tuscarawas.oh.us/eservices/home.page. Can view docket only, no images may be printed.

County Court www.tusccourtsouthern.com/
Civil: Search records free at http://66.219.135.176/ *Criminal:* Search records free at http://66.219.135.176/. Warrants are also available on the court website.

New Philadelphia Municipal Court www.npmunicipalcourt.org
Civil: A record search of the index is available at www.npmunicipalcourt.org/search.php. Search by name or case number. *Criminal:* A record search of the index is aviilable at www.npmunicipalcourt.org/search.php. Search by name, case number, or ticket number.

Union County

Common Pleas Court www.co.union.oh.us/GD/Templates/Pages/UC/UCDetail.aspx?page=416

Civil: Online access to the court clerk's public records and index is free the home page. Records go back to 1/1990, older records added as accessed. Images go back to 1/2002. *Criminal:* same as civil.

Marysville Municipal Court http://municourt.co.union.oh.us/

Civil: The record index may be searched for free at http://municourt.co.union.oh.us/recordSearch.php. Search by name, case number or ticket number. *Criminal:* The record index may be searched for free at http://municourt.co.union.oh.us/recordSearch.php. Search by name, case number or ticket number.

Van Wert County

Common Pleas Court www.vwcommonpleas.org

Civil: Court calendars available online. Access to civil records for free at http://eservices.vanwertcounty.org/eservices/home.page.3. Records back to 5/1998 *Criminal:* Court calendar available online. Access to criminal records for free at http://eservices.vanwertcounty.org/eservices/home.page.3. Records back to 5/1998

Vinton County

Common Pleas Court

Civil: Civil records available at http://vintonco.com/clerk-of-courts/. *Criminal:* Criminal records available at http://vintonco.com/clerk-of-courts/.

Warren County

Common Pleas Court www.co.warren.oh.us/clerkofcourt/legal/index.aspx

Civil: Access to court records is free at http://countycourt.co.warren.oh.us/pa/. *Criminal:* same

Lebanon Municipal Court http://court.lebanonohio.gov/

Civil: Search by name or case number at http://court.lebanonohio.gov/search.shtml. Results show address. **$$$** *Criminal:* Search by name or case number at http://court.lebanonohio.gov/search.shtml. Results show DOB and address.

County Court www.co.warren.oh.us/countycourt/

Civil: Search court records on the CourtView system free at http://countycourt.co.warren.oh.us/pa/. Online records go back to 1990; no DOBs on civil results. *Criminal:* Search court records on the CourtView system free at http://countycourt.co.warren.oh.us/pa/. Online records go back to 1990..

Franklin Municipal Court www.franklinmunicourt.com/

Civil: Free access to the docket index at http://eaccess.franklinohio.org/eservices/home.page.2. Includes small claims. *Criminal:* Free access to the docket index at http://eaccess.franklinohio.org/eservices/home.page.2. Includes traffic.

Mason Municipal Court www.masonmunicipalcourt.org

Civil: Online access to court records is free at http://courtconnect.masonmunicipalcourt.org/connection/court/. *Criminal:* same

Washington County

Marietta Municipal Court www.mariettacourt.com

Civil: Online access to from 1992 of court dockets is free at www.mariettacourt.com/search.shtml. *Criminal:* same

Wayne County

Common Pleas Court www.wayneohio.org/

Civil: Online access same as criminal, see below, probate index included.. *Criminal:* Online access free at www.waynecourts.org/disclaimer.

Wayne County Municipal Court Clerk www.waynecourts.org/

Civil: Online access is same as criminal, see below. *Criminal:* Online access free at www.waynecourts.org/disclaimer.

Williams County

Common Pleas Court www.co.williams.oh.us/

Civil: Public search index available at www.co.williams.oh.us/. Choose Clerk of Courts tab, then public search. Searchers are to search on-line first, or they may do public search in the office as well. If website is down, you should fax over the search request. If data of birth of social needed to verify, fax or call. Records from 4/1988 to present. *Criminal:* Public search index available at www.co.williams.oh.us/. Choose Clerk of Courts tab, then public search. Searchers are to search on-line first, or they may do public search in the office as well. If website is down, you should fax over the search request. If data of birth of social needed to verify, fax or call. Records from 4/1988 to current.

Bryan Municipal Court www.bryanmunicipalcourt.com

Civil: Muni Ct data available free at http://casesearch.bryanmunicipalcourt.com/. *Criminal:* same

Wood County

Common Pleas Court http://clerkofcourt.co.wood.oh.us/

Civil: Access court index free at http://pub.clerkofcourt.co.wood.oh.us/eservices/home.page.3. *Criminal:* same

Perrysburg Municipal Court www.perrysburgcourt.com

Civil: Online access to court records is free at www.perrysburgcourt.com/disc.html. *Criminal:* same

Bowling Green Municipal Court www.bgcourt.org
Civil: Access is free to civil records at http://bgcourtweb.bgohio.org/connection/court/. *Criminal:* Free access to criminal and traffic records from http://bgcourtweb.bgohio.org/connection/court/.

Wyandot County

Common Pleas Court www.co.wyandot.oh.us/clerk/index.html
Civil: Click on \"Common Pleas Inquiry\" from web page to view record index. *Criminal:* Click on \"Common Pleas Inquiry\" at web page to view record index.

Upper Sandusky Municipal Court https://www.uppermunicourt.com/
Civil: A free search is provided at https://www.uppermunicourt.com/search.shtml. Generally the docket entry shows the address and DOB but the SSN is kept confidential. *Criminal:* same

Recorders, Assessors, and Other Sites of Note

Recording Office Organization: 88 counties, 88 recording offices. The recording officer is the County Recorder. State tax liens are managed by the Clerk of Common Pleas Court. Federal tax liens are filed in the "Official Records" of each county. All federal tax liens are filed with the County Recorder where the property is located. All state tax liens are filed with the Clerk of Common Pleas Court.

Statewide or Multi-Jurisdiction Access: While there is no statewide resource, many Ohio counties offer internet access to assessor/real estate data, usually for free. One vendor is mentioned below.

- Access to at least 30 Ohio county recorders' deeds, land, and UCC records is free at www.landaccess.com. **Participating counties:** Athens, Auglaize, Belmont, Brown, Carroll, Champaign, Clark, Clermont, Coshocton, Defiance, Delaware, Fairfield, Fayette, Fulton, Hancock, Henry, Highland, Hocking, Madison, Mahoning, Paulding, Perry, Pickaway, Pike, Richland, Ross, Seneca, Van Wert, Washington, Williams.

County Sites:

Adams County ***Property, Taxation Records*** Access the treasurer and auditor property tax data free at www.adamscountyauditor.org/Cookies.aspx.

Allen County ***Recorded Documents*** www.co.allen.oh.us/rec.php Access recorder index and images free after registration, username and password at http://recorder.allencountyohio.com/ext/logon.asp. Contact the recorder for sign-up or get user agreement info at www.co.allen.oh.us/rec.php.
Property, Taxation Records Access to the auditor property data is free at http://oh-allen-auditor.governmaxa.com/propertymax/rover30.asp.

Ashland County ***Property, Taxation Records*** Access property records and sales on the Auditor's database free at www.ashlandcoauditor.org/propertymax/rover30.asp?sid=A613F3CEC6DF4DE195770BA1D014F2FA.

Ashtabula County ***Recorded Documents*** www.co.ashtabula.oh.us Search real estate data back to 1/1984 at http://cotthosting.com/ohashtabula/LandRecords/protected/SrchQuickName.aspx.
Property, Taxation Records Property records on the county Auditor's database are free at http://ashtabulaoh-auditor.ddti.net/Cookies.aspx.

Athens County ***Recorded Documents*** www.co.athensoh.org/Recorder.html Access to county land and UCC records is free at www.landaccess.com/sites/oh/disclaimer.php?county=athens. Records go back to 1/1981.
Property, Taxation Records Search the auditor's property data by name form home page at www.athenscountyauditor.org/. Also, access to GIS/mapping free at www.athenscountyauditor.org/.

Auglaize County ***Real Estate, Deed, Lien, UCC Records*** Search recorder data free at www.landaccess.com/sites/oh/disclaimer.php?county=auglaize.
Property, Taxation Records Look-up assessor property tax data free at www.auglaizeauditor.ddti.net/.

Belmont County ***Real Estate, Deed, Mortgage Records*** www.belmontcountyohio.org/recorder/index.html Access to recorder deed data is free at www.landaccess.com/sites/oh/disclaimer.php?county=belmont.
Property, Taxation Records Online access to property records free at www.belmontcountyohio.org/auditor.htm. Also, search auditor records at http://belmontpropertymax.governmaxa.com/propertymax/rover30.asp.

Brown County ***Recorded Documents*** www.ohiorecorders.com/brown.html Access to record indexes free at https://www.uslandrecords.com/ohlr

Property, Taxation Records Visit www.browncountygis.com/PUBLIC-MAP/PUBLICMAP.HTM for parcel information and maps. Also, access to property search data free at http://brownauditor.ddti.net/

Butler County ***Real Estate, Deed, UCC, Voter Registration, Vendor Records*** www.butlercountyohio.org/recorder/ Access recorded documents free at www.butlercountyohio.org/recorder/index.cfm?page=regLand_search; no images available. Can sign in as guest or get UserID and Password account. Also, county voter records are at www.butlercountyelections.org/index.cfm?page=voterSearch. Also, search county vendors lists free at www.butlercountyauditor.org/index.cfm?page=vl_search. **$$$**

Property, Taxation Records Search auditor property records free at http://propertysearch.butlercountyohio.org/butler/Main/Home.aspx. Search tax bills/payments by name free at https://epay.butlercountyohio.org/payment/portal.exe. The sheriff's tax sale list is at www.butlersheriff.org/.

Carroll County ***Real Estate, Deed Records*** www.carrollcountyohio.us/recorder.html Free access to recorded documents back to 1/1990 at www.landaccess.com/sites/oh/carroll/index.php.

Property, Taxation Records Access to the Auditor's property data is free at http://50.54.8.162/. Also includes Dog Tag Search.

Champaign County ***Real Estate Tax Records*** www.co.champaign.oh.us/auditor/ Access to land access free at www.landaccess.com/sites/oh/disclaimer.php?county=champaign.

Property, Taxation Records Online access to property records is free at http://champaignoh.ddti.net/. From 2003 to 2008. Also, access to GIS/mapping free at www.co.champaign.oh.us/engineer/Who_We_Are/GIS/gis.htm.

Clark County ***Real Estate, Deed, UCC Records*** www.landaccess.com Access to county land and UCC records is free at www.landaccess.com/sites/oh/disclaimer.php?county=clark. Records go back to 1/1988.

Property, Taxation Records Access to property records and GIS/mapping for free at www.gis.co.clark.oh.us/.

Clermont County ***Real Estate, Deed, UCC, Property Records*** http://recorder.clermontcountyohio.gov/ Access to the recorder's property, deed, and UCC records back to 1993 at www.landaccess.com/sites/oh/disclaimer.php?county=clermont.

Property, Taxation Records Records from the auditor's county property database are free at www.clermontauditorrealestate.org/search/commonsearch.aspx?mode=owner.

Clinton County ***Deed, Finance Statement, Records, Plats, Voter Registration Records*** http://co.clinton.oh.us/government/recorder/ Access to recorder records free at http://cotthosting.com/ohclinton/. Check names to see if registered to vote free at www.voterfind.com/public/ohclinton/pages/vtrlookup.asp.

Property, Taxation Records Access the Auditor's property database including weekly sales for free at http://clintonoh.ddti.net/. Access deed references alphabetically by name at www.clintoncountyohgis.org/DeedReferences.htm.

Columbiana County ***Recorded Documents*** www.columbianacountyrecorder.org/ Access the recorder index of official records back to 1993 and financing statements (index only) back to 3/1995 free at www.ccclerk.org/external/LandRecords/protected/SrchQuickName.aspx.

Property, Taxation Records Access property records and tax sale land on the Auditor's database free at www.columbianacntyauditor.org/propertymax/rover30.asp.

Coshocton County ***Real Estate, Deed, UCC, GIS-mapping, Birth, Death Records*** www.coshoctoncounty.net/agency/recorder/ Search the county 's system at http://eaccess.coshoctoncounty.net/eservices/home.page. Access to county land and UCC records is free at www.landaccess.com/sites/oh/disclaimer.php?county=coshocton. Images not available. Also, access to GIS-mapping and deeds for free at www.coshoctoncounty.net/agency/taxmap/GISfiles.php.

Property, Taxation Records Search property tax records for free at www.coshcoauditor.org/Main/Home.aspx; click on "Property Search."

Crawford County ***Property, Taxation Records*** Access the auditor database of property search or sales search for free at www.crawfordauditor.info/. Access to GIS-mapping for free at http://gis.crawford-co.org/giswebsite/.

Cuyahoga County ***Real Estate, Deed, Lien, Marriage, Death Records*** http://recorder.cuyahogacounty.us/ Access the Recorders database free at http://recorder.cuyahogacounty.us/searchs/generalsearchs.aspx. Also, access to the Property Alert System for a fee go to http://recorder.cuyahogacounty.us/Members/Login.aspx?ReturnUrl=%2fmembers%2fnotific. This permits the subscriber to identify and monitor activity pertaining to parcels of land which have been identified as being of some interest to the user. **$$$**

Property, Taxation Records Search the auditor property tax database free at http://fiscalofficer.cuyahogacounty.us/en-US/REPI.aspx. Also, a private company sells county tax claim property, view list free at www.xspand.com/investors/realestate_sale/index.aspx.

Darke County ***Property, Taxation Records*** Property and property tax records on the Darke County database are free at www.darkecountyrealestate.org/Cookies.aspx.

Defiance County ***Real Estate Records*** www.defiance-county.com/recorder/index.php Free access to land records found at www.landaccess.com/sites/oh/disclaimer.php?county=defiance.

Property, Taxation Records Free access to auditor real estate data found at http://defiance.ddti.net/.

Delaware County ***Property, Taxation Records*** Access to auditor's property and sales data is free at www.delawarecountyauditor.org/propertymax/rover30.asp?.

Erie County ***Recorded Records*** www.erie-county-ohio.net/recorder/ Free access to indexes at http://erecorder.eriecounty.oh.gov/oncoreweb/. Online records date back to 9/1990 and deeds only back to 3/1987. Only plat images are currently available on this website.

Property, Taxation Records Free access to the auditor property database including weekly sales at http://erie.iviewauditor.com/Map.aspx.

Fairfield County ***Real Estate, Deed, UCC Records*** www.co.fairfield.oh.us Access to county land and UCC records is free at www.landaccess.com/sites/oh/disclaimer.php?county=fairfield.

Property, Taxation Records Access to the Auditor's property and sales database is free at http://realestate.co.fairfield.oh.us/. Also, access to the sheriff's real estate sale list at www.sheriff.fairfield.oh.us/.

Fayette County ***Real Estate, Deed, Lien Records*** www.fayette-co-oh.com Access to recorders index database is free at www.landaccess.com/sites/oh/disclaimer.php?county=fayette.

Property, Taxation Records Access the auditor's database for property data at http://fayettepropertymax.governmax.com/propertymax/rover30.asp.

Franklin County ***Real Estate, Deed Records*** www.franklincountyohio.gov/recorder/ Access to the recorded data is free at http://recorderweb.co.franklin.oh.us/Rec/default.asp.

Property, Taxation Records Auditor's property data is at http://franklin.governmaxa.com/propertymax/rover30.asp. Access auditor's GIS-data site with property lookup, history and more free at www.franklincountyauditor.com/your-property. Various databases from county e-services at www.franklincountyohio.gov/fc/.**$$$**

Fulton County ***Real Estate, Deed, UCC Records*** www.fultoncountyoh.com/index.aspx?nid=274 Access to property, deed, and UCC records is to be free at www.landaccess.com/sites/oh/disclaimer.php?county=fulton.

Property, Taxation Records Search auditor property data and weekly sales free at http://fultonoh-auditor.ddti.net/. Search by name, address or parcel number.

Gallia County ***Property, Taxation Records*** Property records on the county auditor real estate database are free at http://galliaauditor.ddti.net. Click on "attributes" for property data; click on "sales" to search by real estate attributes. Also, property and GIS-mapping data free at http://galliacountygis.org/index.aspx.

Geauga County ***Property, Taxation Records*** Search the Auditor's property database at www.auditor.co.geauga.oh.us/.

Greene County ***Recorded Documents, Marriage Records*** www.co.greene.oh.us/index.aspx?nid=473 Access to the recorders index is free at http://apps.co.greene.oh.us/recorder/disclaimer.aspx. Indexed from 1984 to present and some internet images are available from 1997 to present. Also, Search marriages free at http://apps.co.greene.oh.us/probate/marriagesearch.aspx.

Property, Taxation Records Access to GIS/mapping for free at http://gis.co.greene.oh.us/gismap/map.asp. Also, access to auditor data free at http://apps.co.greene.oh.us/auditor/ureca/default.aspx.

Guernsey County ***Recorded Documents*** www.guernseycounty.org/cms/?q=recorder Access to court-related records free at http://74.218.3.68/eservices/home.page.2.

Property, Taxation Records Access to property search for free at http://guernseycountyauditor.org/Cookies.aspx.

Hamilton County ***Real Estate, Deed, Lien, Mortgage, UCC, Marriage, Military Discharge, Partnership, Subdivision Records*** http://recordersoffice.hamilton-co.org Access to recorder land records is free at http://recordersoffice.hamilton-co.org/hcro-pdi/index.jsp. Search the marriage license database at www.probatect.org/case_search/mlsearch.asp. Also, search probate records back to 1/2000 at www.probatect.org/case_search/casesearch.asp.

Property, Taxation Records Access to the auditor's tax records database is free at www.hamiltoncountyauditor.org/retax_menu_taxsummaries.asp. Assess to property search data free at www.hamiltoncountyauditor.org/realestateii/ROVER30.ASP.

Hancock County Recorder ***Real Estate, Deed, UCC Records*** http://co.hancock.oh.us/recorder/recorder.htm Access to recorder records is free at www.landaccess.com/sites/oh/disclaimer.php?county=hancock. Index goes back to 1986; images from 1/1/86 to present - 12/4/90 will be added at a later date.

Property, Taxation Records Search the auditor's property database free at http://hancock.iviewauditor.com/Disclaimer.aspx?Redirect=%2fSearch.aspx&CheckForCookies=Yes. No name searching.

Hardin County ***Property, Taxation Records*** Access property records from the auditor's database free at http://realestate.co.hardin.oh.us/cgi-bin/db2www.pgm/req.mbr/main?nuser=15:19:42&midf=&midn=. Also, search property data on the GIS-mapping site at www.hcgis.com/.

Henry County ***Recorded Documents*** www.henrycountyohio.com Access recorder data free at www.landaccess.com/sites/oh/disclaimer.php?county=henry.

Property, Taxation Records Access and search property data free at www.co.henry.oh.us/index.php. Also, search sheriff sales list for free at www.henrycountysheriff.com/.

Highland County ***Real Estate, Deed, UCC Records*** www.co.highland.oh.us/Department%20Home%20Pages/Recorder.html Access to recorders database is free at www.landaccess.com/sites/oh/disclaimer.php?county=highland.

Property, Taxation Records Access and search property data free at http://highlandpropertymax.governmaxa.com/propertymax/rover30.asp. Click on "start your search" to begin. Search auditor's tax and sales data for free at www.co.highland.oh.us/.

Hocking County ***Real Estate Records*** www.co.hocking.oh.us/recorder/ Access to county real estate search free at www.realestate.co.hocking.oh.us/cgi-bin/db2www.pgm/req.mbr/main?nuser=14:54:21&midf=&midn=. Also, record searchable at www.landaccess.com/sites/oh/disclaimer.php?county=ohhocking.

Property, Taxation Records Access to county real estate assessor data for free at www.realestate.co.hocking.oh.us/cgi-bin/db2www.pgm/req.mbr/main?nuser=14:54:21&midf=&midn=.

Holmes County ***Property, Taxation Records*** Access the auditor's property data and sales free at www.holmescountyauditor.org/.

Huron County ***Real Estate, Deed, Lien, UCC Records*** www.huroncountyrecorder.org/ Search the recorder's land records free at www.huroncountyrecorder.org/. Index online from 1992 to present.

Property, Taxation Records Access to the auditor data and property sales is free at www.huroncountyauditor.org/.

Jackson County ***Property, Taxation Records*** Access property and sales data free at www.jacksoncountyauditor.org/ and click on Start Search.

Jefferson County ***Real Estate, Parcel, Voter Registration Records*** Access to real estate records free at www.jeffersoncountyoh.com/OnLineServices/RealEstateSearch/tabid/199/Default.aspx. Also, search voter names free at www.voterfind.com/public/ohjefferson/pages/vtrlookup.asp. Access the sheriff, treasurer, and auditor foreclosure sales lists free at www.jeffersoncountysheriff.com/sales.html.

Property, Taxation Records Access to the county auditor property data is free at http://public.jeffersoncountyoh.com/realtax/(X(1)S(h5zxfr45x2tage451v3wc43z))/MasterFrame.aspx?AspxAutoDetectCookieSupport=1. Also, download real estate data from the auditor's database free at http://public.jeffersoncountyoh.com/tax/realdown.htm. Also, access to GIS/mapping free at www.jeffersoncountyoh.com/OnLineServices/OnLineGISRealEstatePlats.aspx.

Knox County ***Recorded Documents*** www.co.knox.oh.us/offices/recorder/ Access index records free at www.recorder.co.knox.oh.us/external/LandRecords/protected/SrchQuickName.aspx.

Property, Taxation Records Online access to property records is available at www.knoxcountyauditor.org/Cookies.aspx.

Lake County ***Real Estate, Deed, Lien, UCC (indexes only) Records*** www.lakecountyohio.gov/Default.aspx?alias=www.lakecountyohio.gov/recorder Access the Recorder's Document Index free at www.lakecountyohio.gov/RS2009/Search.aspx/Search.aspx/Search.aspx. Records go back to 1986. UCCs are index only. Images of documents not available.

Property, Taxation Records Access to the treasurer and auditor's real estate databases is free at www.lake.iviewauditor.com/.

Lawrence County ***Deed, Mortgage, Liens, Misc Records*** www.lawrencecountyohiorecorder.org Access to records free at www.lawrencecountyohiorecorder.org/record_search.htm. Deeds 1982 to present, mortgages 1968 to present, leases, liens and misc 1981 to present, financing statement 1989 to present.

Property, Taxation Records Search the auditor's data free at www.lawrencecountyauditor.org/.

Licking County ***Real Estate, Deed, Lien Records*** www.lcounty.com/rec/ Access to the recorders database is free at www.lcounty.com/recordings/. Records with images go back to 1984.

Property, Taxation Records Access the Assessor's county property database free at www.lcounty.com/OnTrac/.

Logan County ***Real Estate, Deed, Lien, Grantor/Grantee Records*** www.co.logan.oh.us/recorder/index.html Access to the recorders database is free at http://landrecords.co.logan.oh.us/. Treasurer's delinquent property tax lists free at www.co.logan.oh.us/Treasurer/Delinquent_Real.htm.

Property, Taxation Records Records on the County Auditor's database are free at http://realestate.co.logan.oh.us/. Also, search the sheriff's sales lists at www.logansheriff.com/index.php?option=com_content&view=article&id=154&Itemid=55.

Lorain County ***Real Estate, Deed, Lien Records*** www.loraincounty.com/recorder/ Access the recorder records free at http://162.39.12.36/External/User/Login.aspx?ReturnUrl=%2fexternal%2findex.aspx. Can sign in as a guest or make an account.

Property, Taxation Records Access property records and sales on the County Auditor's database for free at http://oh-lorain-auditor.governmaxa.com/propertymax/rover30.asp. Search sheriff sales lists for free at www.loraincountysheriff.com/.

Lucas County ***Real Estate, Deed Records*** www.co.lucas.oh.us/index.aspx?nid=675 Access to recorder real estate records is free with registration at http://apps.co.lucas.oh.us/rec/logon.asp.

Property, Taxation Records Property records on the County Auditor's Real Estate Information System (AREIS) database are free at www.co.lucas.oh.us/index.aspx?nid=377.

Madison County ***Real Estate, Deed, UCC Records*** www.ohiorecorders.com/madison.html Access recorder's office records free at www.landaccess.com/sites/oh/disclaimer.php?county=madison.

Property, Taxation Records Access records on the County Auditor's database free at http://madisonoh.ddti.net/.

Mahoning County ***Recorded Documents*** www.mahoningcountyoh.gov/tabid/795/default.aspx Access to recorder's property, deed, and UCC records is to be free at www.co.madison.oh.us/436/41301.html. Records go back to 1985. Also, access to land records free at www.landaccess.com/sites/oh/disclaimer.php?county=mahoning.

Property, Taxation Records Property tax records on the Auditor's database are free at http://ohmahoningpropertymax.governmaxa.com/propertymax/rover30.asp. Also, access property data free on the GIS site at http://gis.mahoningcountyoh.gov/.

Marion County ***Recorded Documents (Indexes only) Records*** http://mcoprx.co.marion.oh.us/recorder/ Access the recorders index at http://recorder.co.marion.oh.us/LandRecords/protected/SrchQuickName.aspx. Official records go back to 1983; UCCs to 1990; plats back to 1820.

Property, Taxation Records Access to the county auditor real estate database is free at http://realestate.co.marion.oh.us/cgi-bin/db2www.pgm/req.mbr/main?nuser=09:17:50&midf=&midn=. Also, access the sheriff sales list free at http://mcoprx.co.marion.oh.us/sheriff/index.php?option=com_content&task=view&id=93&Itemid=64.

Medina County ***Recorded Documents*** www.recorder.co.medina.oh.us Access to indexes 1983 to present on the recorder database is free at www.recorder.co.medina.oh.us/fcquery.htm.

Property, Taxation Records Access property records, dog tags, and unclaimed funds on the Medina County Auditor database free at www.medinacountyauditor.org/allsearches.htm. Sheriff's county tax sale list is at www.medinacountyauditor.org/shersale/.

Meigs County ***Property, Taxation Records*** Access to Auditor database free from the home page www.meigscountyauditor.org/.

Mercer County ***Real Estate, Deed, Lien, Mortgage, Judgment, UCC Records*** www.mercercountyohio.org/recorder/ Access recorder data free at www2.mercercountyohio.org/oncoreweb42/

Property, Taxation Records Access property records on County Auditor Real Estate database free at www2.mercercountyohio.org/auditor/ParcelSearch/.

Miami County ***Recorded Documents*** www.miamicountyrecorder.org/ All public documents on record my be viewed free-of-charge at www.miamicountyrecorder.org/search.php. A fee is charged for the copies. Records from 1807 to present. **$$$**

Property, Taxation Records Access auditor data free at www.miamicountyauditor.org/.

Monroe County ***Property, Taxation Records*** A commercial subscription program is available from the Auditor's office at http://monroecountyauditor.org. Call first to register, 740-472-0873; $15 fee per month fee applies.**$$$**

Montgomery County ***Real Estate, Deed, Lien, Veterans Gravesites Records*** www.mcohio.org/government/recorder/index.html Access to the recorders data is free at http://public.mcrecorder.org/External/User/Login.aspx?ReturnUrl=%2fexternal%2findex.aspx.

Property, Taxation Records Search auditor's property data and GIS-data free at www.mcrealestate.org/Main/Home.aspx. Property tax records on the county treasurer tax information database are free at www.mctreas.org/. Also, search auditor's trade name and vendor license free at www.mcauditor.org/VEN_list.cfm?letter=D. Also, search sheriff sales at www.co.montgomery.oh.us/Sheriff/.

Morgan County ***Property, Taxation Records*** Access the auditor property data free at http://morgancountyauditor.org. Also, search the Engineer website for tax map property data free at www.morgancoengineer.com/. Click on Tax Maps.

Morrow County ***Property, Taxation Records*** Access to the county auditor database is free at http://auditor.co.morrow.oh.us/Cookies.aspx. Includes property sales data.

Muskingum County ***Recorded Documents*** http://recorder.muskingumcounty.org/ Access the recorders database free at http://cotthosting.com/ohmuskingum/LandRecords/protected/SrchQuickName.aspx. Deeds back to 1977, Mortgages-1976, Liens & Misc-1975, Military Discharges back to 1865, Leases-1981, Plat-1800 and UCC's-1993. Effective 4/1/11, if you want to search records before the above dates, you will need to click on the "Historical Indexes" tab. Also, the sheriff's site provides sale lists and sex offender data at www.ohiomuskingumsheriff.org/.

Property, Taxation Records Records on the county auditor database are free at www.muskingumcountyauditor.org/. Parcel data and GIS-mapping free at www.muskingumcountyauditor.org/Cookies.aspx. Also, the sheriff's site provides sale lists at www.ohiomuskingumsheriff.org/.

Ottawa County ***Property, Taxation Records*** Access to the auditor's property database including sales is free at www.ottawacountyauditor.org/Cookies.aspx.

Paulding County ***Real Estate, Deed, Lien, UCC Records*** Access recorder data free at www.landaccess.com/sites/oh/disclaimer.php?county=paulding.

Property, Taxation Records Access to land searches for free at www.pauldingcountyauditor.com/Cookies.aspx.

Perry County ***Recorded Documents (Indexes Only) Records*** www.ohiorecorders.com/perry.html Access to record indexes free at https://www.uslandrecords.com/ohlr

Property, Taxation Records Access to property search records for free at www.perrycountyauditor.us/Disclaimer.aspx?Redirect=%2fSearch.aspx.

Pickaway County ***Real Estate, Deed, UCC Records*** www.pickaway.org/ Search recorder data free at www.landaccess.com/sites/oh/disclaimer.php?county=pickaway.

Property, Taxation Records Access to the county auditor property data is http://pickaway.iviewauditor.com/Cookies.aspx.

Pike County ***Real Estate, Deed, Lien, UCC Records*** www.ohiorecorders.com/pike.html Access to the recorder's database is free at www.landaccess.com/sites/oh/disclaimer.php?county=pike.

Property, Taxation Records Access auditor databases free at www.pike-co.org/ including assessments, parcels, sales, personal property, dog tags, GIS-mapping. Search sheriff sales lists at http://wp2.pikecosheriff.com/?cat=12.

Portage County ***Recorded Records*** www.co.portage.oh.us/recorder.htm Access to various records free at www.co.portage.oh.us/recorder.htm. Index is from 1995-present and documents from 2001 to present. Also has an index from 1979-1994 (deeds, POA and easements).

Property, Taxation Records Access to the auditor's property records and sales is free at www.portagecountyauditor.org/. Access to the sheriff's property sales list is free at www.co.portage.oh.us/sheriffsales.htm.

Preble County ***Property, Taxation Records*** Property records on the County Auditor's database are free at www.preblecountyauditor.org/.

Putnam County ***Recorded Documents*** www.putnamcountyrecorder.com Access to real estate, property tax indexes back to 1993 go to www.putnamcountyrecorder.com/putnam_county_recorders_search.htm. Images not viewable on this site. If you want to purchase a copy, must contact the Recorders office. **$$$**

Property, Taxation Records Access to real estate for free at http://co.putnam.oh.us/cgi-bin/db2www.pgm/req.mbr/main?nuser=14:34:19&midf=&midn=. Also, access to GIS/mapping free at www.putnamcountygis.com/.

Richland County ***Real Estate, Deed, Mortgage, etc Records*** www.richlandcountyoh.us/Recorder/Recorder.html Access county land records free at www.landaccess.com/. Records go back to 4/1989.

Property, Taxation Records Property records from the County Auditor database are free at www.richlandcountyauditor.org/Main/Home.aspx. Also, search the sheriff sales lists for free at www.sheriffrichlandcounty.com/.

Ross County ***Real Estate, Deed, UCC Records*** www.co.ross.oh.us Access to county land, recording and UCC records is free at www.landaccess.com. Deed images online back to 1/1974, other images available online back to 10/10/95.

Property, Taxation Records Access to the auditor's property and sales data is free at www.co.ross.oh.us/Auditor/.

Sandusky County ***Property, Taxation Records*** Access to county auditor and treasurer property data is free at http://ohsanduskypropertymax.governmaxa.com/propertymax/rover30.asp. Click on "Property Search" and choose to search by name.

Scioto County ***Property, Taxation Records*** Access to the auditor's property data is free at www.sciotocountyauditor.org/propertymax/rover30.asp; click on Property Search.

Seneca County ***Recorded Documents*** www.landaccess.com Recorder RE data is accessible at www.landaccess.com/sites/oh/disclaimer.php?county=ohseneca.

Property, Taxation Records Access to land records for free at www.senecacountyauditor.org/Cookies.aspx.

Shelby County ***Property, Taxation Records*** Access to property search data for free at http://206.51.148.202/cama/.

Stark County ***Recorded Documents*** www.co.stark.oh.us/internet/HOME.DisplayPage?v_page=recorder Access the recorder's database free after registration at http://app.recorder.co.stark.oh.us/Recorder_Disclaimer.htm. Chose simple, advanced or instrument search. View historical (civil war and back) documents at www.co.stark.oh.us/internet/docs/recorder/frame.htm.

Property, Taxation Records Search auditor's property data free at www.auditor.co.stark.oh.us/PropertySearch/. Also, a weekly delinquent taxpayers list is at www.starktaxes.com/list.cgi. Access to sheriff sales lists are at http://webapp.co.stark.oh.us/sheriff_sales/.

Summit County ***Recorded Documents*** https://fiscaloffice.summitoh.net/ Access to records free at https://fiscaloffice.summitoh.net/.

Property, Taxation Records Access tax map data from the county fiscal officer for free at https://fiscaloffice.summitoh.net/index.php/geographic-information. Also property appraisal, images and tax data are on this site. Also, search property tax bill and appraisal records free at https://fiscaloffice.summitoh.net/index.php/property-tax-search. Also, search sheriff tax sale list free at www.co.summit.oh.us/sheriff/sales.htm.

Trumbull County ***Real Estate, Deed, Mortgage, Lien Records*** http://recorder.co.trumbull.oh.us/ Access the recorder's database free at http://records.co.trumbull.oh.us/.

Property, Taxation Records Search auditor property tax data free at http://property.co.trumbull.oh.us/. Also, search the Sheriff sales/land sales list free at http://sheriff.co.trumbull.oh.us/sheriffsale.htm

Tuscarawas County ***Property, Taxation Records*** County real estate records are free at www.co.tuscarawas.oh.us/tusca208/LandRover.asp. The auditor's delinquent tax list is updated in September.

Union County ***Real Estate, Deed, Lien, Mortgage, Judgment, UCC Records*** www.co.union.oh.us/GD/Templates/Pages/UC/UCDetail.aspx?page=61 Search recorded documents at www.co.union.oh.us/GD/Templates/Pages/UC/UCCrumbTrail.aspx?page=70.

Property, Taxation Records Access to the Auditors tax assessment/property records database & the appraiser property information database is free at www2.co.union.oh.us/parcelSearch/parcelSearch.aspx/ or www.co.union.oh.us/GD/Templates/Pages/UC/UCDetail.aspx?page=301. Also search property via the GIS mapping site at www3.co.union.oh.us/website/pub_webgis/viewer.htm. Also, search the treasurers' list of delinquent taxpayers at www3.co.union.oh.us/treasurer/Default.aspx.

Van Wert County ***Real Estate, Deed, UCC Records*** www.vanwertcounty.org/recorder/ Access to county land and UCC records is free at www.landaccess.com. Index go back to 1/1994, copies of documents back to 1/94; earlier records being added.

Property, Taxation Records Online access to property records free at www.co.vanwert.oh.us/

Warren County ***Recorded Documents (Index Only) Records*** www.co.warren.oh.us/recorder/ Access Recorders records free back to 1979 at www.co.warren.oh.us/recorder/.

Property, Taxation Records Access to the auditor Property Search database is free at www.co.warren.oh.us/auditor/property_search/index.htm. An advanced search is available at www.co.warren.oh.us/auditor/property_search/advsrch.asp. This will allow you to research properties using multiple search criteria of your choise. Also, search sheriff sales records free at www.wcsooh.org/search/shfentry.htm.

Washington County ***Recorded Documents*** www.washingtongov.org/index.aspx?NID=324 Access to records is free at www.landaccess.com/sites/oh/disclaimer.php?county=washington.

Property, Taxation Records Access to the county auditor's property search database is free at www.washingtoncountyauditor.us/Cookies.aspx.

Wayne County ***Property, Taxation Records*** Access to the auditor's property and sales data is free at www.waynecountyauditor.org/. Click on Search. The late taxpayer list appears on the treasurer's website at http://waynecountytreasurer.org/LateTaxpayers.aspx.

Williams County ***Real Estate, Deed, Lien, UCC Records*** www.co.williams.oh.us/Recorder/wms_co_recorder_home.htm Search recorder records free at www.landaccess.com/sites/oh/disclaimer.php?county=williams.

Property, Taxation Records Access to the auditor's property data and sales is free at http://williamsoh.ddti.net/.

Wood County ***Recorded Documents (indexes only) Records*** www.co.wood.oh.us/recorder/ Access to indexes free at www.co.wood.oh.us/recorder/search_indices_online.html.

Property, Taxation Records Access to the auditor's property data is free at http://auditor.co.wood.oh.us/. No name searching. Also, search the treasurer's tax data for free at http://woodtaxcollector.governmax.com/collectmax/collect30.asp?

Oklahoma

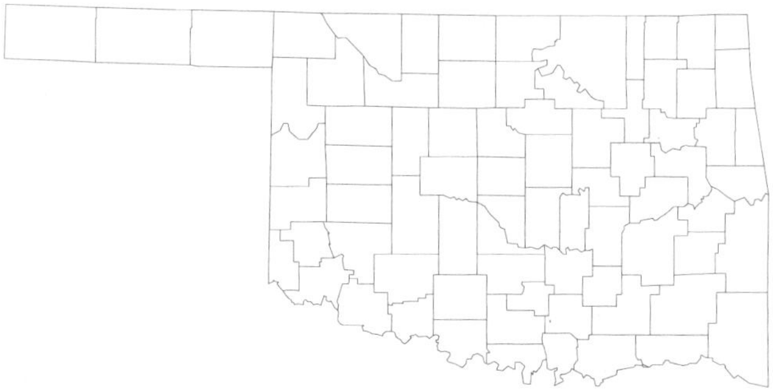

Capital: Oklahoma City
Oklahoma County
Time Zone: CST
Population: 3,814,820
# of Counties: 77

Useful State Links

Website: www.ok.gov/
Governor: www.ok.gov/governor/
Attorney General: www.oag.state.ok.us
State Archives: www.odl.state.ok.us
State Statutes and Codes: /www.oklegislature.gov/osStatuesTitle.aspx
Legislative Bill Search: www.oklegislature.gov/
Bill Monitoring: www.oklegislature.gov/AdvancedSearchForm.aspx /
Unclaimed Funds: https://www.ok.gov/unclaimed/

State Public Record Agencies

Criminal Records

OK State Bureau of Investigation, Criminal History Reporting, www.ok.gov/osbi/ The agency provides the ACHS - Automated Criminal History System. $15.00 fee applies. See www.ok.gov/osbi/Criminal_History/Automated_Criminal_History_System/index.html. Applications are only accepted for companies who currently conduct at least 50 record checks a month. For questions on establishing an account, contact Carol Kinser at 405-879-2653 or carol.kinser@osbi.ok.gov. There is a User's manual found at www.ok.gov/osbi/documents/ACHS%20User%20Manual.pdf. **$$$**

Sexual Offender Registry

Oklahoma Department of Corrections, Sex Offender Registry, www.doc.state.ok.us/index.htm Searching is available from the website at http://sors.doc.state.ok.us/svor/f?p=106:1:. There are a number of search options. A parole status search is available at http://gov.ok.gov/parole/parole_lookup.php. *Other Options:* Database and bulk purchases can be requested from the IT department. Call for pricing and media.

Incarceration Records

Oklahoma Department of Corrections, Offender Records, www.doc.state.ok.us At the main website, click on Offender Information or visit www.doc.state.ok.us/offenders/offenders.htm. The online system is not available between 3:15 AM to 3:20 AM Monday through Friday, and 3:15 AM to 7:00 AM Saturdays for system maintenance.

Corporation, LLC, LP, LLP, Trade Name, Fictitious Name, Trademark

Secretary of State, Business Records Department, https://www.sos.ok.gov/Default.aspx Visit https://www.sos.ok.gov/corp/corpInquiryFind.aspx for free searches on business entities. Search trademarks at https://www.sos.ok.gov/trademarks/default.aspx. Customers may also order and receive status certificates as well as certified and plain copies. Fees vary, see the web page for details. There is a list of domestic LLCs. Also, search securities brokers/investment advisors at www.securities.ok.gov/_private/DB_Query/IA_Query/IA_Search_Form.asp. Also securities firms at www.securities.ok.gov/_private/DB_Query/Licensing/IA_Search_FOI.asp. **$$$**

Uniform Commercial Code

UCC Central Filing Office, Oklahoma County Clerk, http://countyclerk.oklahomacounty.org/registrar-of-deeds/ucc Records of all UCC financing statements may be viewed free at http://countyclerk.oklahomacounty.org/registrar-of-deeds/rod-search. Search by debtor or secured party. The site gives a disclaimer stating there may be a significant delay between the filing of the record and availability to a requester on this site. Neither certified searches nor record requests are accepted at the web page. *Other Options:* The entire database is available on microfilm or computer tapes. The initial history is $500 with $50 per update. Images are available for $.04 per image.

Sales Tax Registrations

Taxpayer Assistance, Sales Tax Registration Records, www.tax.ok.gov/bustax.html A free tax permit look-up service is provided at www.oktax.onenet.net/permitlookup/. *Other Options:* Current sales tax permit holders are permitted to purchase the sales tax database on microfiche or disk. Monthly updates are available. Call for fees.

Birth, Death Records

State Department of Health, Vital Records Service, www.ok.gov/health/Birth_and_Death_Certificates/index.html Online ordering is available via a designated vendor - www.vitalchek. Their web page gives details - one may also order by phone. Additional fees are involved, use of a credit card is required. **$$$**

Driver Records

MVR Desk, Records Management Division, www.dps.state.ok.us/recm/ Electronic access is available for qualified, approved users through www.ok.gov. This is a batch mode process with plans for interactive service in the future. The $27.50 record fee includes a $2.50 service fee. There is an annual $75.00 subscription fee upon approval. Search by either the DL# or by the name, and DOB and gender. The full record fee applies for a no record found. For more information, call 800-955-3468 or visit https://www.ok.gov/idlr/index.php. **$$$**

Vehicle, Vessel Ownership & Registration

Oklahoma Tax Commission, Motor Vehicle Division, Attn: Research, www.tax.ok.gov/motveh.html Oklahoma offers an Insurance Verification online. The site allows one to verify compulsory liability insurance coverage on privately-owned vehicle insured by a personal policy of vehicle insurance It does not verify coverage for a vehicle covered by a commercial policy. The request must include the VIN and Policy Number. Visit www.ok.gov/redirect.php?link_id=716. *Other Options:* Oklahoma does not offer bulk delivery of vehicle and ownership information except for purposes such as vehicle recall.

Campaign Finance

Okalhoma Ethics Commission, 2300 N. Lincoln Blvd Rm. B-5, www.ok.gov/oec/ Search a myriad of financial information at www.ok.gov/ethics/public/index.php. Also, opinions and investigations can be searched from the home page.

Occupational Licensing Boards

Accountant-CPA/Firm .... https://lic.ok.gov/PublicPortal/OAB/FindCPA.jsp
Alarm Firm/Employee................................. www.ok.gov/odol/Workforce_Protection/Alarm_&_Locksmith_/index.html
Animal Technician....................................... https://www.ok.gov/okvetboard/renewal/search.php
Architect/Architectural Firm......................... https://www.ok.gov/architects/licensee_search.php
Athletic Trainer/Apprentice.......................... www.okmedicalboard.org/search
Attorney... www.oklahomafindalawyer.com/FindALawyer
Audiologist.. www.ok.gov/obespa/Licensee_Verification/index.html
Bail Bondsman.. https://sbs-ok.naic.org/Lion-Web/jsp/sbsreports/AgentLookup.jsp
Bank... www.ok.gov/banking/Bank_Listing.html
Barber School.........www.ok.gov/health/Protective_Health/Occupational_Licensing_Division/Barber_Licensing_Program/Licensed_Barber_Schools.html
Beauty School.. www.state.ok.us/~cosmo/schools.html
Chiropractor .... www.ok.gov/chiropracticboard/Disciplined_Chiropractors/index.html
Counselor LPC/MLFT/LBP .... www.ok.gov/health/Protective_Health/Professional_Counselor_Licensing_Division/License_Verification.html
Credit Services Organization .... www.ok.gov/okdocc/License_Rosters/index.html
Credit Union .... www.ok.gov/banking/Credit_Union_Listing.html
Dental Laboratory....................................... www.ok.gov/dentistry/Licenses/index.html
Dentist/Dental Assistant/Hygienist.............. www.ok.gov/dentistry/Licenses/index.html
Dietitian/Provisional Dietitian .... www.okmedicalboard.org/search
Electrologist.. www.okmedicalboard.org/search
Embalmer... www.okfuneral.com/licenseverification.htm
Engineer... https://www.ok.gov/pels/search/search.php
Funeral Director/Home............................... www.okfuneral.com/licenseverification.htm
Health Spa .... www.ok.gov/okdocc/License_Rosters/index.html
Home Inspector.. http://cibverify.ok.gov/

Insurance Adjuster .... https://sbs-ok.naic.org/Lion-Web/jsp/sbsreports/AgentLookup.jsp
Insurance Agent/Representative.................. https://www.sircon.com/ComplianceExpress/Inquiry/consumerInquiry.do?nonSscrb=Y
Insurance Company .... https://sbs-ok.naic.org/Lion-Web/jsp/sbsreports/CompanySearchLookup.jsp
Insurance Consultant .... https://sbs-ok.naic.org/Lion-Web/jsp/sbsreports/AgentLookup.jsp
Investment Adviser/Rep.............................. www.securities.ok.gov/_private/DB_Query/IA_Query/IA_Search_Form.asp
Landscape Architect .... https://www.ok.gov/architects/licensee_search.php
Lobbyist... www.ok.gov/oec/Lobbyist_Reporting/
LPG-Liquefied Petrol. Dealer/Mfg./Mgr........ www.oklpgas.org/search/index.php
Midwife .... https://www.ok.gov/nursing/verify/index.php
Money Order Agent/Company .... www.ok.gov/banking/Money_Order_Licensee_Listing.html
Mortgage Broker .... www.ok.gov/okdocc/License_Rosters/index.html
Notary Public... https://www.sos.ok.gov/notary/search.aspx
Nurse Anesthetist-Certified Registered........ https://www.ok.gov/nursing/verify/index.php
Nurse Practitioner-Adv'd Registered............ https://www.ok.gov/nursing/verify/index.php
Nurse-RN/LPN/Specialist-Clinical................ https://www.ok.gov/nursing/verify/index.php
Nursery, Plant .... www.oda.state.ok.us/forms/cps/cps-nursdir.pdf
Occupational Therapist/Assistant .... www.okmedicalboard.org/search
Optometrist.. www.arbo.org/index.php?action=findanoptometrist
Orthotist/Prosthetist .... www.okmedicalboard.org/search
Osteopathic Physician .... www.docboard.org/ok/df/oksearch.htm
Pawnbroker .... www.ok.gov/okdocc/License_Rosters/index.html
Pedorthist.. www.okmedicalboard.org/search
Perfusionist .... www.okmedicalboard.org/search
Pesticide Applicator/Dealer......................... http://kellysolutions.com/ok/
Pesticide Certification/Registration .... http://kellysolutions.com/ok/
Pharmacist/Pharmacy Intern/Technician ..... http://lv.pharmacy.state.ok.us/osbpinquire/RegSearch.asp
Pharmacy .... http://lv.pharmacy.state.ok.us/osbpinquire/PhrmcySearch.asp
Pharmacy Facility.. http://lv.pharmacy.state.ok.us/osbpinquire/FacilitySearch.asp
Physical Therapist/Assistant....................... www.okmedicalboard.org/search
Physician/Medical Doctor/Assistant............ www.okmedicalboard.org/search
Podiatrist .... www.okpodiatrists.org/search
Precious Metals & Gem Dealer................... www.ok.gov/okdocc/License_Rosters/index.html
Private Investigator/Agency .... www.opia.com/find_a_pi/default.asp
Prosthetist .... www.okmedicalboard.org/search
Psychologist.. https://www.ok.gov/OSBEP/_app/search/index.php
Real Estate Agent/Broker/Sales/Corp/Partnership........ https://www.ok.gov/OREC/licensee_lookup/lookup.php
Real Estate Appraisers Training Providers.. www.ok.gov/oid/documents/List%20of%20Initial%20Providers.pdf
Registrants Performing Audits/GAS............ https://lic.ok.gov/PublicPortal/OAB/FindCPA.jsp
Rent to Own Dealer..................................... www.ok.gov/okdocc/License_Rosters/index.html
Residential Child Care Facility .... http://childcarefind.okdhs.org/childcarefind/
Respiratory Care Practitioner....................... www.okmedicalboard.org/search
Savings & Loan Association .... www.ok.gov/banking/Savings_&_Loan_Listing.html
Securities Broker/Dealer .... www.securities.ok.gov/_private/DB_Query/IA_Query/IA_Search_Form.asp
Social Worker... www.osblsw.state.ok.us/licensee_search.php
Speech Pathologist .... www.ok.gov/obespa/Licensee_Verification/index.html
Surveyor, Land... https://www.ok.gov/pels/search/search.php
Trust Company... www.ok.gov/banking/Trust_Company_Listing.html
Veterinarian/Technician .... https://www.ok.gov/okvetboard/renewal/search.php

State and Local Courts

State Court Structure: The **District Court** is the trial court and hears all cases except traffic and ordinance matters. There are 77 District Courts in 26 judicial districts. The Court in Creek County has three Divisions, the Court in Seminole County has two Divisions.

Cities with populations in excess of 200,000 (Oklahoma City and Tulsa) have a criminal **Municipal Courts of Record**. Cities with less than 200,000 do not have such courts.

There is also an **Oklahoma Workers' Compensation Court**.

Appellate Courts: See www.ok.gov/redirect.php?link_id=345 for information about the Appellate Courts and online access to opinions.

Statewide Court Online Access: There are two sites that provide access to trial court records. All counties have access except Cimarron.

- 1) Free Internet access to docket information is available for District Courts in 13 counties and for all Appellate courts at www.oscn.net. Both civil and criminal docket information is available for the counties involved. The participating counties, referred to as the OCIS Counties, are: Adair, Canadian, Cleveland, Comanche, Ellis, Garfield, Logan, Oklahoma, Payne, Pushmataha, Roger Mills, Rogers, and Tulsa. Also one may search the Oklahoma Supreme Court Network from this website. A disclaimer states: "The information on this page is NOT an official record. Do not rely on the correctness or completeness of this information. Verify all information with the official record keeper."
- 2) The Oklahoma District Court Records site at www1.odcr.com offers both a basic and an advanced subscription search service. This service (provided by a designated third party) includes a search of the OSCN counties above and of the rest of the county district court in the state EXCEPT Cimarron County. The subscription to the Advanced Tools feature is $5.00 per month. This includes advanced search for date of birth, street address, city-state-zip, outstanding warrants filter, offense or cause, and case closed date range, case and party monitoring, and search history. Also, the site provides a Court Image Access service for $50 per month which includes unlimited access to court images, view scanned court documents, and download and print full case filings. HOWEVER, this last service is only available to attorneys. The OBA# must be provided.
- Case information is available in bulk format for downloading to computer. For information, call the Administrative Offices of the Court at 405-556-9300.

Note: No individual Oklahoma courts offer online access, other than as described above.

Recorders, Assessors, and Other Sites of Note

Recording Office Organization: 77 counties, 77 recording offices. The recording officer is the County Clerk. Federal tax liens on personal property of businesses are filed with the County Clerk of Oklahoma County, which is the central filing office for the state. Other federal and all state tax liens are filed with the County Clerk. Usually state and federal tax liens on personal property are filed in separate indexes, state liens on businesses or individuals usually in the real estate index.

Statewide or Multi-Jurisdiction Access: There is a wide variety of data available from the counties direct and also from designated vendors. Plus there are a number of vendors who have purchased property data and plat maps and have set up their own proprietary access product and systems.

- A private company provides oklahoma public land records free online at http://okcountyrecords.com/search.php for over 60 counties. Search by name, legal description, instrument number or type, also subdivision, plat number, and by date range.
- A great links list to Oklahoma's treasurer offices that offer free online access to parcel and property tax data for research is at www.okcountytreasurers.com.

Two vendors offer both free and subscription services to tax assess data. See http://oklahoma.usassessor.com or www.countyassessor.info/freeaccess/free_login.aspx. Since these sites are applicable to all counties, and for the sake of avoiding redundancy, these sites are not shown on each of the profiles below.

County Sites:

Adair County ***Property, Taxation*** After registration you may search assessment data free temporarily at www.pvplus.com/freeaccess/free_login.aspx.

Beaver County ***Real Estate, Deed, Judgment, Lien Records*** http://beaver.okcounties.org/ Access to land and court records free at http://beaver.okcounties.org/. Data and image ranges from 5/98 to present.

Property, Taxation Access treasurer property records free at http://beaver.okcountytreasurers.com/.

Beckham County ***Recorded Documents*** http://beckham.okcounties.org/officials/officialpage.aspx?officerid=6 Recording records available free online at http://okcountyrecords.com/search.php?County=005.

Property, Taxation Access treasurer property data free at http://beckham.okcountytreasurers.com/.

Blaine County ***Real Estate, Grantor/Grantee, Deed, Lien, Judgment, Fictitious Name Records*** Recording records available free at www1.odcr.com/search.php.

Bryan County ***Recorded Documents*** Access to records free at http://okcountyrecords.com/search.php?county=007. Fees for printing. **$$$**

Property, Taxation Access treasurer property data free at http://bryan.okcountytreasurers.com/.

Caddo County ***Property, Taxation*** Access treasurer property data free at http://caddo.okcountytreasurers.com/.

Canadian County ***Real Estate, Grantor/Grantee, Deed, Lien, Judgment Records*** www.canadiancounty.org/index.aspx?nid=119 Access to recorders database is free http://search.cogov.net/okcana/. If you want to download images, contact clerk's office for user name and password at 405-295-6122/6124/6123.

Property, Taxation Access treasurer property data free at www.tmconsulting.us.com/visitor/visitor_taxroll.php?cnty=Canadian.

Carter County ***All Recorded Documents*** www.brightok.net/cartercounty/countyclerk.html Recorded records available free at http://okcountyrecords.com/search.php.

Property, Taxation Search the county assessor database for free at www.cartercountyassessor.org/search.asp.

Cherokee County ***Real Estate, Grantor/Grantee, Deed, Lien, Judgment, Fictitious Name Records*** www.tax.ok.gov/advalcount/cherokee.html Recording records available free at http://okcountyrecords.com/search.php.

Choctaw County ***Real Estate, Grantor/Grantee, Deed, Lien, Judgment, Fictitious Name Records*** Access land records index free at http://okcountyrecords.com/search.php. **$$$**

Property, Taxation See notes at beginning of section. With registration you may search assessment data free temporarily at www.pvplus.com/freeaccess/free_login.aspx.

Cimarron County ***Real Estate, Deeds, Lien Records*** Access to land records free at http://okcountyrecords.com/search.php?county=013. Data and image ranges from 9/10 to present.

Cleveland County ***Real Estate, Deed, Lien, Judgment, UCC, Fictitious Name Records*** www.clevelandcountycourtclerk.com/ Access to the Clerk Index is free at http://search.cogov.net/okclev/default.asp. Includes access to various liens, Real Estate, UCCs.

Property, Taxation Access to property records is free at www.clevelandcountyassessor.us/. Also, access treasurer property data free at http://ok-cleveland-treasurer.governmax.com/collectmax/collect30.asp.

Coal County ***Real Estate, Deed, Lien, Judgment, Misc Records*** Access to public records free at http://okcountyrecords.com/search.php?county=015. Data range and image range from 12/98 to present.

Comanche County ***Recorded Documents*** http://comanchecounty.us/index.php?option=com_content&view=article&id=56&Itemid=221 Access land records index free at http://okcountyrecords.com/search.php?county=016. Data and image ranges from 11/88 to present.

Property, Taxation Access treasurer property and tax data free at www.tmconsulting.us.com/visitor/visitor_taxroll.php?cnty=Comanche.

Cotton County ***Real Estate, Grantor/Grantee, Deed, Lien, Judgment, Fictitious Name Records*** Access land records index free at http://okcountyrecords.com/search.php.

Craig County ***Recorded Documents, Fictitious Name Records*** www.county-clerk.net/countyclerk.asp?state=Oklahoma&county=Craig Recording records available free at http://okcountyrecords.com/search.php. Data range from Dec, 2008 to Dec 27, 2011.

Property, Taxation Access treasurer property data free at www.tmconsulting.us.com/visitor/visitor_home.php?cnty=Craig.

Creek County ***Recorded Documents*** www.creekcountyonline.com/county_clerk.htm Access land records index free at http://okcountyrecords.com/search.php?county=019. Date range from June, 1997 to present, image range the same.

Property, Taxation Access treasurer property data free at www.tmconsulting.us.com/visitor/visitor_taxroll.php?cnty=Creek.

Custer County ***Recorded Documents, Fictitious Name Records*** http://custer.okcounties.org/index.aspx Recording records available free at http://okcountyrecords.com/search.php.

Property, Taxation Access to assessor records for free at http://custer.okcountyassessors.org/. Also, access treasurer property data free at www.tmconsulting.us.com/visitor/visitor_home.php?cnty=Custer.

Delaware County ***Real Estate, Grantor/Grantee, Deed, Lien, Judgment, Fictitious Name Records*** www.delawareclerk.org Access land records index free at http://okcountyrecords.com/search.php?County=021. Subscription required for images; $10.00 per month. **$$$**

Dewey County ***Property, Taxation*** Access to assessor data may be available at www.pvplus.com/freeaccess/free_login.aspx. Registration required. Subscription and fees for full access.

Ellis County ***Real Estate, Deed, Misc Records*** Access to land records free at http://okcountyrecords.com/search.php?county=023.

Garfield County ***Property, Taxation*** Access assessor parcel data for free at http://cadata.garfieldcountyassessor.com/search.stm.

Garvin County ***Real Estate, Grantor/Grantee, Deed, Lien, Judgment, Fictitious Name Records*** Recording records available free at http://okcountyrecords.com/search.php.

Property, Taxation Access treasurer property data free at http://garvin.okcountytreasurers.com/.

Grady County ***Real Estate, Grantor/Grantee, Deed, Lien, Judgment, Fictitious Name Records*** www.gradycountyok.com/drupal/clerk Recording records available free at http://okcountyrecords.com/search.php.

Property, Taxation Access assessor records free at http://grady.okcountyassessors.org/. Also, access treasurer property data free at http://grady.okcountytreasurers.com/.

Grant County ***Real Estate, Deed, Lien, Judgment, Misc Records*** www.grantcountyok.com/county_clerk.html Access to public land records free at http://okcountyrecords.com/search.php?county=027. Data range and image range from 12/02 to present.

Greer County ***Property, Taxation*** Access treasurer property data free at http://greer.okcountytreasurers.com/.

Jackson County ***Property, Taxation*** Access to parcel, treasurer and property tax data free at http://jackson.okcountytreasurers.com/.

Jefferson County ***Recorded Documents*** www.jeffcoinfo.org/Courts.html Access to records free at http://okcountyrecords.com/search.php?county=034.

Property, Taxation Access to the tax roll records at http://jefferson.okcountytreasurers.com/.

Johnston County ***Real Estate, Grantor/Grantee, Deed, Lien, Judgment, Fictitious Name Records*** Records available free at http://okcountyrecords.com/search.php?County=035.

Property, Taxation Access treasurer property data free at http://johnston.okcountytreasurers.com/.

Kay County ***Real Estate, Grantor/Grantee, Deed, Lien, Judgment, Fictitious Name Records*** www.courthouse.kay.ok.us/coclerk.html Recording records available free at http://okcountyrecords.com/search.php.

Property, Taxation The assessor office has a subscription to property data; fee is $10.00 per month. A basic index search is to be available. Call 580-362-2565 for details. Access the treasurer tax lookup page free at www.courthouse.kay.ok.us/kcaaboutus.htm.

Kingfisher County ***Recorded Documents*** Access to record indexes free at http://okcountyrecords.com/search.php?county=037. If you need more detailed information, must register with a fee. Data range from 1/92 to present; image range from 10/92 to present. **$$$**

Latimer County ***Real Estate, Deed Records*** www.tax.ok.gov/advalcount/latimer.html Access to land records free at http://okcountyrecords.com/search.php?county=039.

Property, Taxation Access treasurer property data free at http://latimer.okcountytreasurers.com/.

Le Flore County ***Real Estate, Grantor/Grantee, Deed, Lien, Judgment, Fictitious Name Records*** Access land records index free at http://okcountyrecords.com/search.php?county=040. **$$$**

Property, Taxation Also, access treasurer property data free at http://leflore.okcountytreasurers.com/.

Lincoln County ***Real Estate, Deed, Lien, Judgment, Misc Records*** Access to public land records free at http://okcountyrecords.com/search.php?county=041. Data range and image range from 1/94 to present.

Property, Taxation Access treasurer property data free at www.tmconsulting.us.com/visitor/visitor_home.php?cnty=Lincoln.

Logan County ***Recorded Documents*** http://okcountyrecords.com/index.php Assess recorded data free at http://okcountyrecords.com/search.php?county=042. Images available from 1994 to current. Can not print, call office to request copies.

Property, Taxation Access assessor property records free at http://eland.logancounty-ok.org/display.php. Also, access treasurer property data free at www.tmconsulting.us.com/visitor/visitor_home.php?cnty=Logan.

Love County ***Real Estate, Grantor/Grantee, Deed, Lien, Judgment, Fictitious Name Records*** www.love.okcounties.org/officials/officialpage.aspx?officerid=6 Recording records available free at http://okcountyrecords.com/search.php. Also, access to court records and land records free at www.love.okcounties.org/.

Property, Taxation Access to Assessor records for free at http://love.okcountyassessors.org/. Also, access treasurer property data free at http://love.okcountytreasurers.com/.

McClain County ***Recorded Documents*** www.okcountyrecords.com Access to land records free at http://okcountyrecords.com/search.php?county=044. Data range 5/94 to present day. Image range 5/94 to present day.

Property, Taxation Search the tax roll inquiry site free at www.tmconsulting.us.com/visitor/visitor_home.php?cnty=McClain.

McCurtain County ***Recorded Documents*** Records available free at http://okcountyrecords.com/search.php?County=045.

Property, Taxation Access treasurer property data free at www.tmconsulting.us.com/visitor/visitor_home.php?cnty=mccurtain.

McIntosh County ***Real Estate Records*** Access to land records free at http://okcountyrecords.com/search.php.

Major County ***Real Estate, Grantor/Grantee, Deed, Lien, Judgment, Fictitious Name Records*** Recording records available free at http://okcountyrecords.com/search.php.

Marshall County ***Real Estate, Grantor/Grantee, Deed, Lien, Judgment, Fictitious Name Records*** www.marshall.okcounties.org/officials/officialpage.aspx?officerid=6 Recording records available free at http://okcountyrecords.com/search.php.

Property, Taxation Access treasurer property data free at http://marshall.okcountytreasurers.com/.

Mayes County ***Real Estate Records*** www.mayes.okcounties.org/officials/officialpage.aspx?officerid=6 Access to county records free at http://okcountyrecords.com/search.php?county=049. Data range and image range- 3/85 to present.

Property, Taxation Access treasurer property data free at www.tmconsulting.us.com/visitor/visitor_home.php?cnty=Mayes.

Murray County ***Recorded Records Records*** Access to recorded records free at http://okcountyrecords.com/search.php?county=050. Data and image range from 8/1989 to present.

Property, Taxation With registration you may search assessment data free temporarily at www.pvplus.com/freeaccess/free_login.aspx. Subscription fees required. Also, access to property searches free at http://murray.oklahoma.usassessor.com/.

Muskogee County ***Real Estate, Grantor/Grantee, Deed, Lien, Judgment, Fictitious Name Records*** Recording records available free at http://okcountyrecords.com/search.php. Also, access to public records free at http://okcountyrecords.com/search.php?county=051. Data and images from 12/97 -present.

Property, Taxation Access treasurer property data free at www.tmconsulting.us.com/visitor/visitor_home.php?cnty=Muskogee.

Noble County ***Real Estate, Grantor/Grantee, Deed, Lien, Judgment, Fictitious Name Records*** www.perryok.org/countyinfo.html Recording records available free at http://okcountyrecords.com/search.php.

Nowata County ***Land Records Records*** Access to land records free at http://okcountyrecords.com

Okfuskee County ***Real Estate Records*** Access to land records free at http://okcountyrecords.com/. Images available by subscription to Kellpro at 888-535-5776.

Oklahoma County ***Real Estate, Grantor/Grantee, Deed, UCC Records*** http://countyclerk.oklahomacounty.org/ Search the register of deeds index at http://clerkpi.oklahomacounty.org/. Images, index and printing available. Search the register of deeds index at http://countyclerk.oklahomacounty.org/.

Property, Taxation Assessor and property data on county assessor database is free at www.oklahomacounty.org/assessor/disclaim.htm. Also, search the treasurer's property info at www.oklahomacounty.org/treasurer/.

Okmulgee County ***Real Estate, Tax Liens Records*** www.okcountyrecords.com Access to land records for free to go http://okcountyrecords.com/. Click on Okmulgee County. Data range from 12/94 to present, image range from 7/04 to present..

Property, Taxation Access is free for basic info from a private company at www.pvplus.com/freeaccess/register.aspx - free registration is required. Can upgrade account to include advances searches for a fee.

Osage County ***Real Estate, Grantor/Grantee, Deed, Lien, Judgment, Fictitious Name Records*** Recording records index available free at http://okcountyrecords.com/search.php. No images online.

Ottawa County ***Real Estate, Grantor/Grantee, Deed, Lien, Judgment, Fictitious Name Records*** www.ottawa.okcounties.org/ Recording records available free at http://okcountyrecords.com/search.php?county=058.

Property, Taxation Access to property data is through a subscription with a private company, visit www.pvplus.com/. Fee is $10.00 per month per county. Also, access treasurer property data free at http://ottawa.okcountytreasurers.com/.

Pawnee County ***Real Estate, Liens, Plats Records*** Access to records free at http://okcountyrecords.com/. Click on Pawnee County. Data range from 9/94 to present.

Property, Taxation Access treasurer property data free at http://pawnee.okcountytreasurers.com/.

Payne County ***Real Estate, Grantor/Grantee, Deed, Lien, Judgment, Fictitious Name Records*** http://okcountyrecords.com/search.php?county=060 Access land records index free at http://okcountyrecords.com/search.php?county=060. Index and details only; data range - 5/72 to present, images range - 1/2000 to present. **$$$**

Property, Taxation Access treasurer property data free at www.tmconsulting.us.com/visitor/visitor_home.php?cnty=Payne. Also, access to land records free at www.paynecounty.org/assessor/index.php. Free public access, for subscription - fee is $25.00 per month.

Pittsburg County ***Real Estate, Grantor/Grantee, Deed, Lien, Judgment, Fictitious Name Records*** Recording records available free at http://okcountyrecords.com/search.php.

Pontotoc County ***Recorded Documents*** http://okcountyrecords.com/ Access recorder's index free at http://okcountyrecords.com/search.php?county=062. Data range from 1/93 to present, image range from 11/99 to present. Images must be purchased, must register with clerk first. **$$$**

Property, Taxation Access treasurer property data free at http://pontotoc.okcountytreasurers.com/.

Pottawatomie County ***Real Estate, Deed, Tract Records*** Access property data and free at www.landaccess.com/sites/ok/pottawatomie/index.php?okpottawatomie.

Roger Mills County ***GIS, Property Records*** Access to property records and GIS records free at www.oklahomacounty.org/assessor/disclaim.htm. Also, access to land records free at http://okcountyrecords.com/search.php?county=065. Data range and image range is from 9/93 to present.

Rogers County ***Recorded Documents*** www.rogerscounty.org Recording records available free at http://okcountyrecords.com/search.php. Also, access land records at http://etitlesearch.com; for registration and subscription, call 888-535-5776. **$$$**

Property, Taxation Access to the assessor database is free at www.rogerscounty.org/assessor/search_records.htm. Also, search the treasurers tax database free at www.tmconsulting.us.com/visitor/visitor_taxroll.php?cnty=Rogers.

Seminole County ***Recorded Documents*** Access to records for free go to http://okcountyrecords.com. Data ranges from 7/94 to 2/4/13, image range from 5/2000 to 2/4/13.

Sequoyah County ***Real Estate Records*** Access to public land records free at http://okcountyrecords.com/search.php?county=068.

Property, Taxation A free property tax search is at http://sequoyah.oklahoma.usassessor.com/Shared/base/LiteSearch/Search.php.

Stephens County ***Recorded Documents*** www.okcountyrecords.com Access land records index free at http://okcountyrecords.com/search.php. Data range from 6/92-present.

Property, Taxation Access treasurer property data free at http://stephens.okcountytreasurers.com/.

Tillman County ***Real Estate, Mortgage, Tax Lien, Misc Records*** www.tillmancounty.org Access to public land records free at http://okcountyrecords.com/search.php?county=071. Data and image range- 1/04 to present.

Property, Taxation Access treasurer property data free at http://tillman.okcountytreasurers.com/.

Tulsa County ***Real Estate, Deed, Property Records*** www.tulsacounty.org/TulsaCounty/dynamic.aspx?id=720 Access to Tulsa County's Land Records System requires an approved user agreement, username and password, see https://lrmis.tulsacounty.org/. Monthly access fee is $30.00. Records go back to 1979. For info or signup, call 918-596-5206 or email LRMIShelp@tulsacounty.org. **$$$**

Property, Taxation Access to Tulsa County's Land Records System requires an agreement, username and password, and fees, see https://lrmis.tulsacounty.org/.

Wagoner County ***Real Estate, Grantor/Grantee, Deed, Lien, Judgment Records*** www.ok.gov/wagonercounty/Elected_Officials/County_Clerk/index.html Access recorders official records free at www.edoctecinc.com/. There may be a 2 week to 1 month lag time. Also, access to land records free at http://24.173.220.138/wagoner/HomePage.aspx?ID=Wagoner County. **$$$**

Property, Taxation Access treasurer property tax data free at www.tmconsulting.us.com/visitor/visitor_taxroll.php?cnty=Wagoner. Also, access to plats free at www.wagonerassessor.com/sectionplats.html.

Washington County ***Recorded Documents*** www.countycourthouse.org/Default.aspx Access to the recorders database is free at http://okcountyrecords.com/search.php?county=074. Data range from 5/94 to present, image range from 6/95 to present.

Property, Taxation Access treasurer property tax and parcel date free at www.tmconsulting.us.com/visitor/visitor_taxroll.php?cnty=Washington.

Woods County ***Property, Taxation*** Access treasurer property data free at http://woods.okcountytreasurers.com/.

Woodward County ***Real Estate, Grantor/Grantee, Deed, Lien, Judgment, Fictitious Name Records*** http://woodwardcounty.org/9322.html Recording records index available free at http://okcountyrecords.com/search.php but cannot view documents.

Reminder:

Two vendors offer both free and subscription services to tax assess data.
See http://oklahoma.usassessor.com or www.countyassessor.info/freeaccess/free_login.aspx.
Since these sites are applicable to all counties, and for the sake of avoiding redundancy, these sites are not shown on each of the profiles above.

Oregon

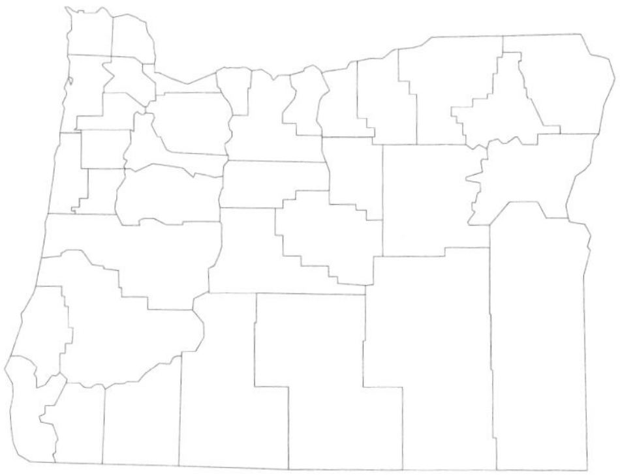

Capital: Salem
Marion County
Time Zone: PST
Population: 3,899,353
# of Counties: 36

Useful State Links

Website: www.oregon.gov
Governor: www.oregon.gov/gov/pages/index.aspx /
Attorney General: www.doj.state.or.us
State Archives: http://arcweb.sos.state.or.us
State Statutes and Codes: www.leg.state.or.us/ors/home.htm
Legislative Bill Search: www.leg.state.or.us/bills_laws/
Unclaimed Funds: /www.oregon.gov/DSL/UP/Pages/index.aspx

State Public Record Agencies

Criminal Records

Oregon State Police, Unit 11, Identification Services Section, www.oregon.gov/OSP/ID/pages/index.aspx A web based site is available for requesting and receiving criminal records is offered for registered users or the public. Results are posted as "No Record" or "In Process" ("In Process" means a record will be mailed in 14 days). Use the "open records" link to get into the proper site. Fee is $10.00 per record. See https://xn.osp.state.or.us/openrec/. **$$$**

Sexual Offender Registry

Oregon State Police, SOR Unit, www.oregon.gov/OSP/SOR/Pages/index.aspx Visit http://sexoffenders.oregon.gov/ for online searching of sex offenders who have been designated as Predatory. A mapping function is also offered. Be cautioned that the address and some of the information provided is information provided by the registrant and may not reflect the current residence, status, or other information regarding an offender. *Other Options:* Lists by city or ZIP can usually be requested for no fee, a statewide list be purchased for $85.00.

Incarceration Records

Oregon Department of Corrections, Offender Information & Sentence Computation, www.oregon.gov/doc An Offender Search is offered at http://docpub.state.or.us/OOS/intro.jsf. The site also lists contacts for each penitentiary or correction institution. The agency web page promotes a private company offering free web access at https://www.vinelink.com/vinelink/siteInfoAction.do?siteId=38000; includes state, DOC, and most county jails. A Corrections Most Wanted list in the pull down menu box. Use imate.info@doc.state.or.us to request by email. *Other Options:* Bulk sale of information is available. Contact ITS - Information Technology Services.

Corporation, LP, LLC, Trademarks/Servicemarks, Fictitious/Assumed Name

Corporation Division, Public Service Building, www.filinginoregon.com There is free access at http://egov.sos.state.or.us/br/pkg_web_name_srch_inq.login for business registry information. Search by name or business registry number. Displays active and inactive records. There are several other related searches available. Search for consumer complaints on OR businesses at https://justice.oregon.gov/complaints/. Also, search a list of active trademarks at https://data.oregon.gov/Business/Active-Trademark-Registrations/ny3n-dx3v. *Other Options:* New business lists downloadable at www.filinginoregon.com/pages/business_registry/info_center/publications/bus_stats.html.

Uniform Commercial Code, Federal & State Tax Liens

UCC Division, Attn: Records, www.filinginoregon.com/pages/ucc/index.html Search the web page for information on UCC secured transactions, as well as Farm Product notices, IRS Tax Liens, Agricultural searches Liens, Agricultural Produce Liens, Grain Producer's Liens, Revenue Warrants and Employment Warrants. See https://secure.sos.state.or.us/ucc/searchHome.action. There are three search tabs to choose from. The Farm Products

Registration and master List is available at www.filinginoregon.com/pages/ucc/farm/index.html. Online access to UCC images is available for filings after July 1, 2007. *Other Options:* Filing lists are available online at www.filinginoregon.com/pages/ucc/ucc-data-lists.html.

Vital Records

Department of Human Services, Vital Records, http://public.health.oregon.gov/Pages/Home.aspx Order records online at www.vitalchek.com, the state's designated vendor. There is an additional $16.50 service fee per "group of 5 records. **$$$**

Workers' Compensation Records

Department of Consumer & Business Svcs, Workers Compensation Division, www.cbs.state.or.us/external/wcd/ Search of employers by WCD# with coverage or that have coverage ending soon is found at www.oregonwcd.org/compliance/ecu/empcoverage.html.Companies with 10 or fewer employees not listed. Search by employer name at Search by employer name at www4.cbs.state.or.us/ex/wcd/employer/ Search by claims number or by employer's claim number at www4.cbs.state.or.us/ex/imd/reports/rpt/index.cfm?ProgID=CE8039. *Other Options:* State is allowed to deliver data in other forms to parties that qualify under ORS 192.502(19).

Driver Records

Driver and Motor Vehicle Services, Record Section, www.oregondmv.com The Oregon DMV offers a Real-Time Driving Record Service (RADR) that allows qualified customers to access Oregon driving records via a real time connection through AAMVA. Records are $2.00 each, including employment, non-employment, and court records. However, a one-time set-up fee of $2,500 is required. Qualified Requestors must meet technical requirements, sign an agreement, and establish a Record Inquiry Account. For more information, contact the Records Policy Unit at 503-945-8905 or 503-945-8906. NOTE: Effective late May or early June 2012. the local NIC affiliate will be the designated DMV source to provide electronic driving records to approved entities. The fee for an electronic driving record will be $9.68. **$$$** *Other Options:* The agency offers an automated "flag program" that informs customers of activity on a name list, for approved account holders only. Call the Automated Reporting Service at 503-945-5427 for more information.

Vehicle Ownership & Registration

Driver and Motor Vehicle Services, Record Section, www.oregondmv.com Online ordering form option of records is available, but only for approved account holders. The fillable form may be downloaded from the web page. Records are returned by fax or mail, per requester's instructions. Fees range from $1.50 to $22.50 depending on type of record needed. **$$$** *Other Options:* Bulk lists available via FTP to qualified accounts. Call 503-945-8906 for more information.

Voter Registration, Campaign Finance, PACs

Secretary of State, Elections Division, http://oregonvotes.org/ Access to campaign finance and PAC info is free at http://oregonvotes.org/pages/cand/index.html,

GED Certificates

Dept of Community Colleges/ Workforce Development, Oregon GED Program, www.oregon.gov/CCWD/Pages/ged/index.aspx For records from 2002 forward, online access is available with the access code provided by the testing center to the GED recipient..

Occupational Licensing Boards

Accountant-CPA/Firm .... http://boahost.com/egovlicsearch.lasso
Acupuncturist .... www.oregon.gov/OMB/Pages/search.aspx
Animal Euthanasia Technician/Facility .... https://hrlb.oregon.gov/ovmeb/licenseelookup/
Animal Feed (Livestock) .... www.oregon.gov/ODA/Pages/license.aspx
Animal Food Processor .... www.oregon.gov/ODA/Pages/license.aspx
Appraisal Management Companies .... www.cbs.state.or.us/external/dfcs/online.html
Architect/Architectural Firm .... http://orbae.com/search-licensees/
Athletic Trainer .... https://elite.hlo.state.or.us/elitepublic/LPRBrowser.aspx
Attorney .... www.osbar.org/members/membersearch_start.asp
Audiologist .... https://hrlb.oregon.gov/bspa/licenseelookup/
Auditor-Municipal .... http://boahost.com/egovlicsearch.lasso
Bakery .... http://oda.state.or.us/dbs/licenses/search.lasso?&division=fsd
Bank/Registered Agent .... www.cbs.state.or.us/external/dfcs/online.html
Barber .... https://elite.hlo.state.or.us/elitepublic/LPRBrowser.aspx
Body Piercer .... https://elite.hlo.state.or.us/elitepublic/LPRBrowser.aspx
Boilermaker .... www4.cbs.state.or.us/ex/all/mylicsearch/index.cfm?fuseaction=search.show_search_name&group_id=30
Brand (Livestock)/Brand Inspector .... www.oregon.gov/ODA/Pages/license.aspx
Cemetery .... www.oregon.gov/MortCem/Pages/License_Directory_link_created_2004_07_08.aspx

Check/Money Order Seller........................... www.cbs.state.or.us/external/dfcs/online.html
Chiropractor/Chiropractic Assistant .... http://obce.alcsoftware.com/liclookup.php
Christmas Tree Grower............................... http://oda.state.or.us/dbs/licenses/search.lasso?&division=nursery
Collection Agency .... www.cbs.state.or.us/external/dfcs/online.html
Construction Contractor/Subcontr............... https://ccbed.ccb.state.or.us/ccb_frames/consumer_info/
Consumer Finance Company .... www.cbs.state.or.us/external/dfcs/online.html
Cosmetologist/Hair Stylist/Hairdresser .... https://elite.hlo.state.or.us/elitepublic/LPRBrowser.aspx
Counselor, Professional.............................. https://hrlb.oregon.gov/oblpct/licenseelookup/index.asp
Credit Service Organization .... www.cbs.state.or.us/external/dfcs/online.html
Credit Union .... www.cbs.state.or.us/external/dfcs/online.html
Crematorium .... www.oregon.gov/MortCem/Pages/License_Directory_link_created_2004_07_08.aspx
Dairy Establishment .... http://oda.state.or.us/dbs/licenses/search.lasso?&division=fsd
Debt Consolidating Agency.......................... www.cbs.state.or.us/external/dfcs/online.html
Dental Hygienist/Specialist .... http://obd.oregonlookups.com/
Dentist .... http://obd.oregonlookups.com/
Denture Technologist.................................. https://elite.hlo.state.or.us/elitepublic/LPRBrowser.aspx
Denturist.. https://elite.hlo.state.or.us/elitepublic/LPRBrowser.aspx
Diagnostic Radiologic Technologist............. https://hrlb.oregon.gov/OBMI/LicenseeLookup/index.asp
Dietitian .... https://elite.hlo.state.or.us/elitepublic/LPRBrowser.aspx
Digital Signature Authority .... www.cbs.state.or.us/external/dfcs/online.html
Direct Entry Midwife .... https://elite.hlo.state.or.us/elitepublic/LPRBrowser.aspx
Drug Manufacturer/Wholesaler.................... https://obop.oregon.gov/LicenseeLookup/
Drug Outlet, Over-the-Counter..................... https://obop.oregon.gov/LicenseeLookup/
Egg Handler/Breaker .... http://oda.state.or.us/dbs/licenses/search.lasso?&division=fsd
Electrician... www4.cbs.state.or.us/ex/all/mylicsearch/index.cfm?fuseaction=search.show_search_name&group_id=30
Electrologist/Facial Technician/Technologisthttps://elite.hlo.state.or.us/elitepublic/LPRBrowser.aspx
Electrology Instructor/School .... https://elite.hlo.state.or.us/elitepublic/LPRBrowser.aspx
Elevator Journeyman, Limited .... www4.cbs.state.or.us/ex/all/mylicsearch/index.cfm?fuseaction=search.show_search_name&group_id=30
Embalmer/Embalmer Apprentice .... www.oregon.gov/MortCem/Pages/License_Directory_link_created_2004_07_08.aspx
Endowment Care .... www.cbs.state.or.us/external/dfcs/online.html
Engineer.. www.oregon.gov/Osbeels/Pages/Search_License.aspx
Environmental Health Specialist .... https://elite.hlo.state.or.us/elitepublic/LPRBrowser.aspx
Escrow Agent/Agency................................. https://orea.elicense.irondata.com/Lookup/LicenseLookup.aspx
Farm/Forest Labor Contractor .... http://licenseinfo.oregon.gov/index.cfm?fuseaction=holder_search
Fertilizer/Mineral/Lime Registrant .... http://oda.state.or.us/dbs/licenses/search.lasso?&division=pest
Florist .... http://oda.state.or.us/dbs/licenses/search.lasso?&division=nursery
Food Establishment, Retail .... http://oda.state.or.us/dbs/licenses/search.lasso?&division=fsd
Food Exporter/Processing Facility .... http://oda.state.or.us/dbs/licenses/search.lasso?&division=fsd
Food Producer/Distributor........................... http://oda.state.or.us/dbs/licenses/search.lasso?&division=fsd
Food Storage Facility .... http://oda.state.or.us/dbs/licenses/search.lasso?&division=fsd
Frozen Desert-Related Industry.................. http://oda.state.or.us/dbs/licenses/search.lasso?&division=fsd
Funeral Plan, Prearranged.......................... www.cbs.state.or.us/external/dfcs/online.html
Funeral Service Practitioner/Apprentice/Establishment www.oregon.gov/MortCem/Pages/License_Directory_link_created_2004_07_08.aspx
Geologist, Engineering................................ www.oregon.gov/OSBGE/Pages/registrants.aspx
Greenhouse Grower-Herbaceous Plant....... http://oda.state.or.us/dbs/licenses/search.lasso?&division=nursery
Hair Salon .... https://elite.hlo.state.or.us/elitepublic/LPRBrowser.aspx
Hearing Aid Dealer/Dispenser .... https://elite.hlo.state.or.us/elitepublic/LPRBrowser.aspx
Hearing Aid Specialist................................. https://elite.hlo.state.or.us/elitepublic/LPRBrowser.aspx
Home Inspector... http://licenseinfo.oregon.gov/index.cfm?fuseaction=holder_search
Immediate Disposition Company .... www.oregon.gov/MortCem/Pages/License_Directory_link_created_2004_07_08.aspx
Insurance Adjuster/Agent/Consultant .... https://sbs-or.naic.org/Lion-Web/jsp/sbsreports/AgentLookup.jsp
Insurance Company.................................... https://sbs-or.naic.org/Lion-Web/jsp/sbsreports/CompanySearchLookup.jsp
Interpreter, Legal... http://courts.oregon.gov/OJD/docs/OSCA/cpsd/InterpreterServices/CertifiedInterpreterRoster.pdf
Investment Advisor...................................... www.cbs.state.or.us/external/dfcs/securities.html
Landscape Architect .... www.oregon.gov/landarch/pdfs/CurrentLARegistrants.pdf

Landscape Business	http://licenseinfo.oregon.gov/index.cfm?fuseaction=holder_search
Landscaper	http://oda.state.or.us/dbs/licenses/search.lasso?&division=nursery
Liquor Store	www.oregon.gov/OLCC/LIQUORSTORES/Pages/index.aspx
Livestock-Related Business	www.oregon.gov/ODA/Pages/license.aspx
Lobbyist/Political Candidate Statement	www.oregon.gov/OGEC/Pages/public_records.aspx
Manicurist/Nail Technician	https://elite.hlo.state.or.us/elitepublic/LPRBrowser.aspx
Manufactured Housing Construction	www4.cbs.state.or.us/ex/all/mylicsearch/index.cfm?fuseaction=search.show_search_name&group_id=30
Manufactured Structures Dealer	www.cbs.state.or.us/external/dfcs/online.html
Marriage & Family Therapist	https://hrlb.oregon.gov/oblpct/licenseelookup/index.asp
Massage Therapist	https://hrlb.oregon.gov/obmt/licenseelookup/
Measuring Device	http://oda.state.or.us/dbs/search.lasso#msd
Milk Hauler/Milk Stabilizer/Handler	http://oda.state.or.us/dbs/licenses/search.lasso?&division=fsd
Money Transmitter	www.cbs.state.or.us/external/dfcs/online.html
Mortgage Banker/Broker/Lender	www.cbs.state.or.us/external/dfcs/online.html
Motor Fuel Quality	http://oda.state.or.us/dbs/search.lasso#msd
Naturopathic Physician	https://hrlb.oregon.gov/OBNM/licenseelookup/
Non-Alcoholic Beverage Plant	http://oda.state.or.us/dbs/licenses/search.lasso?&division=fsd
Notary Public	www.filinginoregon.com/pages/notary/search/find_notary/index.html
Nurse-LPN/Assistant	http://osbn.oregon.gov/OSBNVerification/Default.aspx
Nursery Dealer	http://oda.state.or.us/dbs/licenses/search.lasso?&division=nursery
Nursery Stock/Native Plant Collector	http://oda.state.or.us/dbs/licenses/search.lasso?&division=nursery
Nursing Home Administrator	https://elite.hlo.state.or.us/elitepublic/LPRBrowser.aspx
Occupational Therapist/Assistant	https://hrlb.oregon.gov/otlb/licenseelookup/
Optometrist	www.oregonobo.org/doctorinfo.htm
Oral Pathology Endorsement	https://elite.hlo.state.or.us/elitepublic/LPRBrowser.aspx
Oregon Product	www.oregon.gov/ODA/Pages/license.aspx
Osteopathic Physician/Surgeon	www.oregon.gov/OMB/Pages/search.aspx
Pawnbroker	www.cbs.state.or.us/external/dfcs/online.html
Permanent Color Technician	https://elite.hlo.state.or.us/elitepublic/LPRBrowser.aspx
Pesticide Applicator/Dealer/Consultant/Trainee	http://oda.state.or.us/dbs/licenses/search.lasso?&division=pest
Pesticide Product	http://oda.state.or.us/dbs/pest_productsL2K/search.lasso
Pharmacy/Pharmacist	https://obop.oregon.gov/LicenseeLookup/
Physical Therapist/Assistant	https://hrlb.oregon.gov/ptlb/licenseelookup/
Physician/Medical Doctor/Surgeon/Assistant	www.oregon.gov/OMB/Pages/search.aspx
Plumber	www4.cbs.state.or.us/ex/all/mylicsearch/index.cfm?fuseaction=search.show_search_name&group_id=30
Podiatrist	www.oregon.gov/OMB/Pages/search.aspx
Polygraph Examiner	www.oregon.gov/DPSST/Pages/sc/Polygraph.aspx
Polygraph Schools	www.polygraph.org/section/training/apa-accredited-polygraph-schools
Private Investigator/Instructor/Business	www.oregon.gov/DPSST/PS/docs/PIContactInfo.pdf
Property Manager	https://orea.elicense.irondata.com/Lookup/LicenseLookup.aspx
Psychologist/Associate	http://obpe.alcsoftware.com/liclookup.php
Pump Installation Contr, Limited	www.cbs.state.or.us/bcd/licensing.html
Radiologic Technologist Ltd Permit	https://hrlb.oregon.gov/OBMI/LicenseeLookup/index.asp
Radiologic Therapy Technologist	https://hrlb.oregon.gov/OBMI/LicenseeLookup/index.asp
Real Estate Agent/Seller/Broker	https://orea.elicense.irondata.com/Lookup/LicenseLookup.aspx
Real Estate Appraiser	http://oregonaclb.org/aclb_prod/index.php?option=com_wrapper&view=wrapper&Itemid=94
Real Estate Branch Office	https://orea.elicense.irondata.com/Lookup/LicenseLookup.aspx
Refrigerated Plant	http://oda.state.or.us/dbs/licenses/search.lasso?&division=fsd
Respiratory Care Practitioner	https://elite.hlo.state.or.us/elitepublic/LPRBrowser.aspx
Respiratory Therapist	https://elite.hlo.state.or.us/elitepublic/LPRBrowser.aspx
Savings & Loan Association	www.cbs.state.or.us/external/dfcs/online.html
Securities Broker/Dealer/Seller	www.cbs.state.or.us/external/dfcs/securities.html
Shellfish-related Industry	http://oda.state.or.us/dbs/licenses/search.lasso?&division=fsd
Sign Contractor, Limited	www.cbs.state.or.us/bcd/licensing.html
Slaughterhouse	http://oda.state.or.us/dbs/licenses/search.lasso?&division=fsd

Social Worker, Clinical, Licensed	https://hrlb.oregon.gov/BLSW/LicenseeLookup/index.asp
Special Qualifications Corporation	www.cbs.state.or.us/external/dfcs/online.html
Speech Language Pathologist/Assistant	https://hrlb.oregon.gov/bspa/licenseelookup/
Surveyor, Land	www.oregon.gov/Osbeels/Pages/Search_License.aspx
Tattoo Artist	https://elite.hlo.state.or.us/elitepublic/LPRBrowser.aspx
Tax Consultant/Preparer/Business	http://apps.oregon.gov/Application/OBTPSearch
Teacher/Charter School Teacher	www.tspc.state.or.us/lookup_query.asp?op=9&id=0
Therapeutic Radiologic Technologist	https://hrlb.oregon.gov/OBMI/LicenseeLookup/index.asp
Transaction Verification	http://oda.state.or.us/dbs/search.lasso#msd
Trust Company	www.cbs.state.or.us/external/dfcs/online.html
Veterinarian/Technician	https://hrlb.oregon.gov/ovmeb/licenseelookup/
Veterinary Clinic/Product, Livestock	http://oda.state.or.us/dbs/licenses/search.lasso?&division=vet_products
Waste Water System Operator	www.deq.state.or.us/wq/opcert/stpcertoperqry.asp
Water Rights Examiner	www.oregon.gov/Osbeels/Pages/Search_License.aspx
Weighing Device	http://oda.state.or.us/dbs/search.lasso#msd

State and Local Courts

State Court Structure: **Circuit Courts** have original jurisdiction in all civil and criminal matters within the state, including probate, juvenile, and some traffic matters, as well as civil and criminal jury trials. The Small Claims limit is $5,000. The Clerk of Court is the record custodian.

The majority of **Municipal Court** cases involve traffic and ordinance matters.

Probate filing is a function of the Circuit Court; however, each county has a **Register in Probate** who maintains and manages the probate, guardianship, and mental health records.

The **Oregon Tax Court** has exclusive jurisdiction to hear tax appeals including personal income tax, property tax, corporate excise tax, timber tax, local budget law and property tax limitations. There are 2 divisions: Magistrate Division and Regular Division.

Appellate Courts: Appellate opinions are found at www.publications.ojd.state.or.us.

Statewide Court Online Access: All courts participate in the system described below.

- OJIN is the acronym for the online program provides court case information from Circuit Courts in all 36 counties in the state. It allows one to search for civil, small claims, tax, domestic, and criminal cases. The search mechanism allows single county or statewide searching for either civil or criminal cases. Note OJIN does not provide records from Municipal or County Courts. Also Circuit cases that are confidential and protected statutorily are not available to the public. There is a one-time setup fee of $295.00 plus a monthly usage fee per user based on the type of search, if printed, and time of day. The minimum monthly usage is $10.00. Note that OJIN information is provided in real time from the Oregon Judicial Department database. Although OJIN provides a disclaimer statement (*The information does not constitute the official record. The official record of the court is located at the court site where the case was filed.*), OJIN displays the same data as displayed on public access terminals at the courts. The onsite terminals use OJIN.

  See http://courts.oregon.gov/OJD/OnlineServices/OJIN/getstarted.page? or call 800-858-9658.

Editor's Note: The Oregon Judicial Department is working towards migrating the online platform from OJIN to a designated vendor (Odyssey). The purpose is to create a more modern, user-friendly environment for record access, compared to the OJIN command line based system.

Note: No individual Oregon courts offer online access, other as described above.

Recorders, Assessors, and Other Sites of Note

Recording Office Organization: 36 counties, 36 recording offices. The recording officer is the County Clerk. All federal and state tax liens on personal property are filed with the Secretary of State. Other federal and state tax liens are filed with the County Clerk. Government agencies file 'warrants' that represent liens for unpaid taxes and other state fees. Certain warrants are filed with the Sec. of State such as those related to income tax and hazardous waste and are included in a UCC search. Other warrants are filed at the county level, such as those relating to employment taxes.

Statewide or Multi-Jurisdiction Access: A number of counties offer internet access to assessor records; a few counties offer access to recorded documents.

The ORMAP Tax Viewing System at www.ormap.net/ provides GIS maps for free for ALL Counties. Search by county, then by address. While there is no name searching and maps are pdfs arranged in folders (and you may zoom in to a map location), this is a step towards owner identification.

This site is applicable to all counties. For the sake of avoiding redundancy it is not shown on the profiles below.

County Sites:

Baker County ***Real Estate, Deeds Records*** www.bakercounty.org/clerks/clerks.html Access to index searches free at www2.bakercounty.org/webclerks2/Index_Search.jsp.

Property, Taxation Records Access to the assessor property database is free at www2.bakercounty.org/webproperty/Assessor_Search.html

Benton County ***Property, Taxation Records*** Assessor has a number of searches at www.co.benton.or.us/assess/property_search.php. Also, view property data/mapping for free at http://www.co.benton.or.us/maps/bentonmaps.php.

Clackamas County ***Property, Taxation Records*** Assessment and tax rolls available from the home page. GIS at https://gis.oregonmetro.gov/metromap/.

Clatsop County ***Property, Taxation Records*** Access to property data/maps for free at http://maps.co.clatsop.or.us/applications/login.asp.

Crook County ***Property, Taxation Records*** Access property data free on the GIS-mapping site at http://gis.co.crook.or.us/ but no name searching.

Curry County ***Recorded Documents*** www.co.curry.or.us/Clerk/index.html Access to subscription service contact Becky Ross at 541-247-3295. **$$$**

Property, Taxation Records Access to GIS/mapping for free at http://gis.co.curry.or.us/imf/imf.jsp?site=external. Also, access to the Assessor's maps free at http://gis.co.curry.or.us/gis/AssessorMap/index.html.

Deschutes County ***Real Estate, Deed, Mortgage, Lien Records*** www.deschutes.org/Clerks-Office.aspx Search real estate, deeds, mortgages, liens on the clerk's recording system web inquiry for free at http://recordings.co.deschutes.or.us/search.asp. Index and images go back to 1985

Property, Taxation Records View records on the Assessor Inquiry System site at www.deschutes.org/Assessors-Office/DIAL-Search-Form.aspx. There is also business property searching. Access property tax map records on the Lava system free at http://lava.deschutes.org/gisapps/index.cfm, but no name searching.

Douglas County ***Recorded Documents*** www.co.douglas.or.us/clerk/ Access to online subscription, contact Carol Engels at 541-440-4320. Index back to 1993, Images back to 1971. **$$$**

Property, Taxation Records Access to the assessor property data and sales is free at www.co.douglas.or.us/puboaa/puboaa_search.asp. Access to property sales is free at www.co.douglas.or.us/puboaa/ressales.asp.

Harney County ***Recorded Documents*** www.co.harney.or.us/countyclerk.html Access to records free at www.co.harney.or.us/records_research.html. Deed records are indexed back to 1950; Mortgage, Lien and Probate records are indexed back to 1984. All indexed records are current through today.

Hood River County ***Property, Taxation Records*** Access to WebMap online parcel viewer free at www.co.hood-river.or.us/index.asp?Type=B_BASIC&SEC={282D7000-DA1E-411C-9620-6B27BB917C50}.

Jackson County Clerk ***Recorded Documents*** www.co.jackson.or.us/SectionIndex.asp?SectionID=8 Access to all images for copy, must subscribe. Email is helmancd@jacksoncounty.org or call 541-774-6129. **$$$**

Property, Taxation Records Access GIS/mapping for free at www.smartmap.org/portal/.

Jefferson County ***Property, Taxation Records*** Access assessor property and tax data free at http://199.48.41.18/AandTWebQuery/.

Josephine County ***Real Estate, Deed, Lien, Judgment Records*** www.co.josephine.or.us/SectionIndex.asp?SectionID=110 Access to recording office index and documents is by subscription; fee is $35 per month plus $45.00 set up fee, minimum 3 months. Contact Art at the recording office for signup, username and password. **$$$**

Property, Taxation Records Access property via the Map Book Viewer free at www.co.josephine.or.us/Page.asp?NavID=921 but no name searching. Also, search property data on the LION system free at http://68.185.2.151/website/pumaweb/ but no name searching.

Klamath County ***Property, Taxation Records*** Search tax property sales annual list free at www.co.klamath.or.us/PropertySales/index.html. Also, access to Assessor's Data for a fee at www.co.klamath.or.us:8008/.**$$$**

Lane County ***Recorded Documents*** www.lanecounty.org/Departments/CAO/Operations/CountyClerk/pages/default.aspx Access recorded land data on the Reg. Land Information Database RLID by subscription. Visit www.rlid.org/ or call Eric at 541-682-4338 for info/signup. Initiation fee is $200; monthly access fee is $80.00. **$$$**

Property, Taxation Records Access property and sales data on the Reg. Land Information Database RLID by subscription. Visit www.rlid.org/ or call Eric at 541-682-4338 for info/signup. Initiation fee is $200; monthly access fee is $80.00. Property records on the County Tax Map site are free at http://apps.lanecounty.org:80//TaxStatement/Search.aspx. No name searching. **$$$**

Lincoln County ***Property, Taxation Records*** Access limited property info via the County Map Site free at www.co.lincoln.or.us/assessor/maps.html but no name searching. Download the free viewer and search by Township. Map pdfs also available

Linn County ***Property, Taxation Records*** Tax assessor rolls and sales may be viewed at www.co.linn.or.us/assessorshomep/assessor.htm. Also, search property via the ELLA Maps site free at www.co.linn.or.us/assessorshomep/maps.htm.

Malheur County ***Real Estate, Deed, Misc. Records*** www.malheurco.org Access to records free at http://info.malheurco.org/recording/Search.asp.

Property, Taxation Records Search assessment data free at http://assessor.malheurco.org/.

Marion County ***Property, Taxation Records*** Access assessor property data via the GIS-mapping pages at http://gis.co.marion.or.us/gisdownload/disclaimer.aspx. Also, property search for free at http://apps.co.marion.or.us/PropertyRecords/. Search free on the Mapper page at http://gis.co.marion.or.us/MYCIMA/ but no name searching.

Multnomah County ***Property, Taxation Records*** Search assessor maps at http://web.multco.us/assessment-taxation/maps. Find property tax data at www.multcoproptax.org/. GIS at https://gis.oregonmetro.gov/metromap/. Also, search property info at Catbird subscription site; fee is $150 setup plus a monthly fee equaling $.25 per page viewed. For info/signup, call 503-988-3345.**$$$**

Polk County ***Recorded Documents*** www.co.polk.or.us/clerk Access to images are available on computer back to 1840. Only images back to 1983 are indexed. Contact office to sign up. Fee is $20.00 per year. **$$$**

Property, Taxation Records Access property data free at http://apps.co.polk.or.us/webmap/source/login.asp and click on Agree and Accept, then click on Search on left hand side, then choose Tax Lots. Search by name, address, etc. Also, search for assessor maps for free at http://apps.co.polk.or.us/AandTMapSearch/mapsearch.htm but no name searching.

Tillamook County ***Real Estate, Deed, Lien, Judgment Records*** www.co.tillamook.or.us/gov/clerk/default.htm Access to recorded document index free at www.co.tillamook.or.us/gov/clerk/recinq/Login.asp; use username "public" and password "inquiry." Viewing document images is not available online.

Property, Taxation Records Assessment and taxation records on the County Property database are free at www.co.tillamook.or.us/Documents/Search/query.asp. Search by property ID number or by name in the general query. Also, search for property info on the GIS-mapping service site at www.co.tillamook.or.us/gov/A&T/parcelmaps.htm.

Union County ***Property, Taxation Records*** Access property tax data free at www.union-county.org/assessor_search.html.

Wasco County ***Property, Taxation Records*** The GIS-mapping services offers custom designed and also pre-packaged property data products, including the assessor data CD-rom for $300. Other online access through private companies.**$$$**

Washington County ***Property, Taxation Records*** Records on County GIS Intermap database are free at http://washims.co.washington.or.us/gis/ but no name searching. Also, GIS at https://gis.oregonmetro.gov/metromap/.

Yamhill County ***Property, Taxation Records*** Search assessor property data free at www.co.yamhill.or.us/taxinfo/PropSearch.aspx. No name searching. Also, access maps via the statewide mapping site free at www.co.yamhill.or.us/gis/gis.asp. Limited property data from the county surveyor is free at www.co.yamhill.or.us/surveyor/.

Pennsylvania

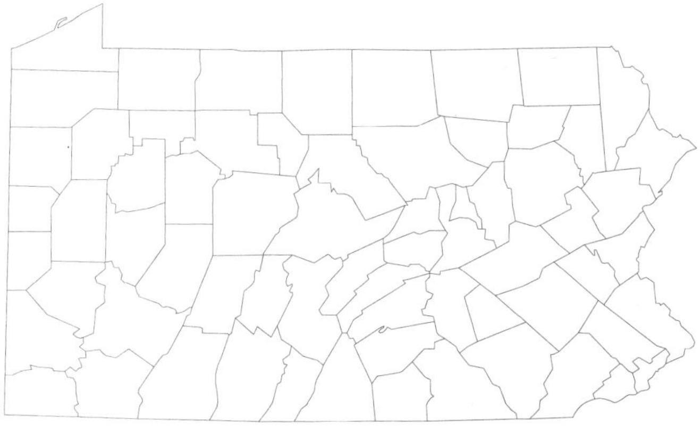

Capital: Harrisburg
Dauphin County
Time Zone: EST
Population: 12,763,536
# of Counties: 67

Useful State Links

Website: www.pa.gov
Governor: www.governor.state.pa.us
Attorney General: www.attorneygeneral.gov
State Archives: www.phmc.state.pa.us
State Statutes and Codes: www.legis.state.pa.us/cfdocs/legis/LI/Public/cons_index.cfm
Legislative Bill Search: www.legis.state.pa.us/cfdocs/legis/home/session.cfm
Unclaimed Funds: www.patreasury.org/unclaimedProperty.html

State Public Record Agencies

Criminal Records

State Police, Central Repository -164, www.psp.state.pa.us/portal/server.pt/community/psp/4451 Record check requests are available for approved agencies through the Internet on the Pennsylvania Access to Criminal History (PATCH). This is a commercial system with a $10.00 fee per name. Go to https://epatch.state.pa.us/Home.jsp. There are registered users. No new accounts are being added, but anyone can order on an individual basis using a credit card. It can take three weeks for a response. This site refers users to the state court site for dispositions on some offenses. Eighty-five percent of the time, "No Record" certificates are returned immediately. But note it can take three weeks for a response. This site refers users to the state court site for dispositions on some offense. **$$$**

Sexual Offender Registry

State Police Bureau of Records and Ident., Megan's Law Unit, www.pameganslaw.state.pa.us Limited information on all registered sex offenders can be viewed online from the webpage. Complete address information is listed for all active offenders. Upon opening the offender's record, you are provided tabs to click on access details such as alias, address, offense, vehicle, and physical characteristics information.

Incarceration Records

Pennsylvania Department of Corrections, Population Mgmt and Central Office, www.cor.state.pa.us At the website, click on Inmate Locator for information about each inmate currently under the jurisdiction of the Department of Corrections. The site indicates where an inmate is housed, race, date of birth, marital status and other items. The Inmate Locator contains information only on inmates currently residing in a state correctional institution. Note that the program is designed for use with I. Explorer. It may not function properly when using other browsers, such as Mozilla Firefox.

Corporation, LP, LLC, LLP, Trademarks/Servicemarks, Fictitious/Assumed Name

Bureau of Corporations & Charitable Organizations, Department of State, www.dos.state.pa.us/portal/server.pt/community/corporations/12457 There is free general searching by entity name or number from https://www.corporations.state.pa.us/corp/soskb/csearch.asp?corpsNav=|. Searching by name provides a list of entities whose name starts with the search name entered. Users can click on any one entity in the list displayed to get more detailed information regarding that entity. Also, search Securities Commission enforcement actions database at https://www.secure.psc.state.pa.us/releases/Members/index.cfm. *Other Options:* The entire database of Image data is available for purchase. There is a $5,000 start fee and an annual fee of $12,000. Also, Business Lists may be purchased for $.25 per name. Contact Web Services.

Uniform Commercial Code

UCC Division, Department of State, www.dos.state.pa.us/ https://www.corporations.state.pa.us/ucc/soskb/SearchStandardRA9.asp allows a search of UCC-1 financing statements filed with the Corporation Bureau by debtor name or financing statement number; a list of financing statements is displayed.

The site also allows a search of financing statement records filed with the Corporation Bureau by financing statement number. Note that this database is usually current within three days. For best search results for filings indexed under a specific business or individual name, please use the "Non-Standard RA9" tab, mark the "Starting With" option and change "Lapse Status" to read "All." *Other Options:* UCC information is available in bulk via various formats. Call the number above for details.

Birth, Death Records

PA Department of Health, Division of Vital Records, www.portal.state.pa.us/portal/server.pt/community/birth_and_death_certificates/11596 Records may be requested online via a vendor - www.vitalchek. Extra fees applicable. **$$$**

Driver Records

Department of Transportation, Driver Record Services, www.dmv.state.pa.us The online system is available to high volume requesters for three or ten-year records. Fee is $5.00 per record. The driver's license number and first two letters of the last name are required. High volume vendors who represent end-users cannot transmit results via the web unless process and end-user is pre-approved. The resale of records by vendors to other vendors is generally forbidden. Call 717-705-1051 for more information about establishing an account. Also, PA licensed drivers may order their own record from the web page using a credit card. **$$$**

Voter Registration, Campaign Finance

Board of Commissions, Elections, & Leg., Voter Registration, www.dos.state.pa.us/portal/server.pt/community/voting_and__elections/12363 A request for a list is available from the web. Click on Voting & Elections and then click on the Request for Voter Lists on the left side. Not for use for commercial purposes. Campaign finance reports can be searched at https://www.campaignfinanceonline.state.pa.us/pages/CFReportSearch.aspx. *Other Options:* A CD of the entire state or by county can be purchased for $20.00 per disk. Be sure to ask for Voter Registration or go to www.dos.state.pa.us/elections/lib/elections/057request_for_voter_lists/requestvoterlists.pdf for form.

Occupational Licensing Boards

Accountant-CPA/Firm .... www.licensepa.state.pa.us/
Acupuncturist .... www.licensepa.state.pa.us/
Amphetamine Program .... www.licensepa.state.pa.us/
Anesthesia Permit, Dental .... www.licensepa.state.pa.us/
Animal Health Technician .... www.licensepa.state.pa.us/
Appraiser, Real Estate/Gen/Residential ...... www.licensepa.state.pa.us/
Appraiser/Broker .... www.licensepa.state.pa.us/
Architect/Architectural Firm .... www.licensepa.state.pa.us/
Athletic Agent .... www.sac.state.pa.us/Pages/RegisteredAthleticAgents.aspx
Athletic Trainer .... www.licensepa.state.pa.us/
Attorney .... www.padisciplinaryboard.org/look-up/pa-attorney-search.php
Auctioneer Company/House .... www.licensepa.state.pa.us/
Auctioneer, Real Estate .... www.licensepa.state.pa.us/
Audiologist .... www.licensepa.state.pa.us/
Bank .... www2.fdic.gov/idasp/main_bankfind.asp
Barber/School/Teacher/Shop/Manager .... www.licensepa.state.pa.us/
Bondsman, Professional http://apps02.ins.state.pa.us/producer/ilist1.asp
Builder/Owner, Real Estate .... www.licensepa.state.pa.us/
Campaign Finance Report .... https://www.campaignfinanceonline.state.pa.us/pages/CFReportSearch.aspx
Campground Membership Seller .... www.licensepa.state.pa.us/
Cemetery Broker/Seller/Regis. .... www.licensepa.state.pa.us/
Check Casher .... www.banking.state.pa.us/portal/server.pt/community/consumer_information/14322
Child Day Care Facility .... http://listserv.dpw.state.pa.us/ocd-pa-child-care-certification.html
Chiropractor .... www.licensepa.state.pa.us/
Cosmetologist/Cosmetician .... www.licensepa.state.pa.us/
Cosmetology Teacher/School/Manicurist Shop...........www.licensepa.state.pa.us/
Counselor, Professional .... www.licensepa.state.pa.us/
Credit Union .... http://researchcu.ncua.gov/Views/FindCreditUnions.aspx
Dental Assistant, Expanded Function/Hygienist..........www.licensepa.state.pa.us/
Dentist .... www.licensepa.state.pa.us/
Dietitian/Nutritionist LDN .... www.licensepa.state.pa.us/

Emergency Medical Technician	https://ems.health.state.pa.us/emsportal/
Engineer	www.licensepa.state.pa.us/
Evaluator, Appraisal	www.licensepa.state.pa.us/
Funeral Director/Supervisor/Establishment	www.licensepa.state.pa.us/
Geologist	www.licensepa.state.pa.us/
Hearing Aid Fitter/Fitter Apprentice/Dealer	www.licensepa.state.pa.us/
Hearing Examiner	www.licensepa.state.pa.us/
Insurance Agent/Company	http://apps02.ins.state.pa.us/producer/ilist1.asp
Landscape Architect	www.licensepa.state.pa.us/
Liquor Distributor/Retailer/Whlse	www.lcbapps.lcb.state.pa.us/webapp/Agency/SearchCenter/PublicLicenseeSearchDefault.asp
Lobbyist/Lobbying Firm/Principal	https://www.palobbyingservices.state.pa.us/
Manicurist	www.licensepa.state.pa.us/
Marriage & Family Therapist	www.licensepa.state.pa.us/
Midwife	www.licensepa.state.pa.us/
Mortgage Banker/Broker/Limited Broker	www.nmlsconsumeraccess.org/
Mortgage Loan Correspondent	www.nmlsconsumeraccess.org/
Mortgage (accelerat'd) Paym't Provider	www.nmlsconsumeraccess.org/
Notary Public	https://www.notaries.state.pa.us/Pages/NotarySearch.aspx
Nuclear Medicine Technologist	www.licensepa.state.pa.us/
Nurse	www.licensepa.state.pa.us/
Nurses Aide	https://www.pulseportal.com/
Nursing Home	http://app2.health.state.pa.us/commonpoc/nhlocatorNS4.asp
Nursing Home Administrator	www.licensepa.state.pa.us/
Occupational Therapist/Assistant	www.licensepa.state.pa.us/
Optometrist	www.licensepa.state.pa.us/
Osteopathic Acupuncturist	www.licensepa.state.pa.us/
Osteopathic Physician/Surgeon/Assistant	www.licensepa.state.pa.us/
Osteopathic Respiratory Care	www.licensepa.state.pa.us/
Pesticide Applicator/Technician	https://www.paplants.state.pa.us/PesticideApplicator/ApplicatorExternalSearch.aspx
Pharmacist/Pharmacy	www.licensepa.state.pa.us/
Physical Therapist/Assistant	www.licensepa.state.pa.us/
Physician/Medical Doctor/Assistant	www.licensepa.state.pa.us/
Pilot, Navigational	www.licensepa.state.pa.us/
Podiatrist	www.licensepa.state.pa.us/
Political Contributor/Committee	https://www.campaignfinanceonline.state.pa.us/pages/CFReportSearch.aspx
Political Finance Statement	https://www.palobbyingservices.state.pa.us/
Psychologist	www.licensepa.state.pa.us/
Public Adjuster/ Solicitor	http://apps02.ins.state.pa.us/producer/ilist1.asp
Radiation Therapy Technician	www.licensepa.state.pa.us/
Radiologic Auxiliary, Chiropractic	www.licensepa.state.pa.us/
Radiologic Technologist	www.licensepa.state.pa.us/
Real Estate Agent/Broker/Sales/School	www.licensepa.state.pa.us/
Real Estate Appraiser	www.licensepa.state.pa.us/
Rental Listing Referral Agent	www.licensepa.state.pa.us/
Respiratory Care Practitioner	www.licensepa.state.pa.us/
Social Worker	www.licensepa.state.pa.us/
Speech-Language Pathologist	www.licensepa.state.pa.us/
Surplus Lines Broker	http://apps02.ins.state.pa.us/producer/ilist1.asp
Surveyor, Land	www.licensepa.state.pa.us/
Teacher	https://www.tcs.ed.state.pa.us/
Therapist, Drugless	www.licensepa.state.pa.us/
Timeshare Salesperson	www.licensepa.state.pa.us/
Title Insurance	http://apps02.ins.state.pa.us/producer/ilist1.asp
Used Vehicle Lot	www.licensepa.state.pa.us/
Vehicle Auction	www.licensepa.state.pa.us/

Vehicle Dealer/Mfg'r/Dist/Salesperson .... www.licensepa.state.pa.us/
Veterinarian/Veterinary Techn'c'n .... www.licensepa.state.pa.us/
Viatical Settlement Broker............................ http://apps02.ins.state.pa.us/producer/ilist1.asp

State and Local Courts

State Court Structure: The **Courts of Common Pleas** are the general trial courts, with jurisdiction over both civil and criminal matters and appellate jurisdiction over matters disposed of by the special courts. Note that the **civil records clerk** of the Court of Common Pleas is called the **Prothonotary**. The Prothonotary is elected by the county and is not a state employee. But Allegheny County (Pittsburgh) civil records are an exception - in 2008, a Dept. of Court Records Civil/Family Division was created and civil records were removed from the Prothonotary Office. The Superior Court is a Court of Appeals. Probate is handled by the Register of Wills.

The **Philadelphia Municipal Court** is a Court of Record and hears felony cases. Philadelphia also has its own Traffic Court. The **Pittsburgh Municipal Court** is not a court of record, but does have criminal, traffic, and non-traffic divisions.

The **Magisterial District Justice Courts**, which are designated as "special courts," also handle civil cases up to $8,000. These courts are in all counties except Philadelphia. Small claims cases are usually handled by the Magisterial District Justice Courts; however, all small claims are recorded with the other civil records through the Prothonotary Section of the Court of Common Pleas, which then holds the records. Thus it is not necessary to check with each Magisterial District Court, but rather to check with the county Prothonotary.

Appellate Courts: View opinions and docket at www.pacourts.us/courts/supreme-court/court-opinions/.

Statewide Court Online Access: There are a number of multi-jurisdictional online resources.

- The Pennsylvania Judiciary Web Portal at http://ujsportal.pacourts.us/ provides:
  1. ***The Public Web Docket Sheets*** access to search, view and print the docket sheets for Pennsylvania's Appellate Courts, Criminal Courts of Common Pleas, Magisterial District Courts and the Philadelphia Municipal Court. In addition, a Court Summary Information report is available for Criminal Courts of Common Pleas and Philadelphia Municipal Court cases. This service does not provide name searches, user must have the case file number.
  2. ***The Secure Web Docket Sheet*** option provides access to search, view and print docket sheets that contain additional content not accessible for public viewing, for Pennsylvania's Criminal Courts of Common Pleas, Magisterial District Courts and the Philadelphia Municipal Court. In addition, secure Court Summary Information, Case Accounting and Pre-Sentence Summary reports are available for Criminal Courts of Common Pleas and Philadelphia Municipal Court cases. A secure login is required to access this service.
  3. Other search services available from this web page includes access to court calendars and an eServices – a specialized access system only available to users with a secure login. Approval for this service must be granted by a county clerk of court or district court administrator – access is not available direct to the general public.

  For more information, call the Help Desk at 877-227-2672.

  A word of caution – Professional researchers have indicated certain discrepancies in the Pennsylvania Judiciary Web Portal systems. The UJS dockets may lack sentencing information, have incomplete gradings, no mention of violation of probations, and alias' are not always listed. Also, per local researchers, there are instances when some records can have incomplete or missing terms of probation or amended charges.
- 30 PA counties use the Infocon County Access System to provide a commercial direct dial-up access to county public records, most provide court record information and some include probate. There is a $25.00 base set-up fee plus a minimum $25.00 per month with a $1.10 fee per minute. For information, call Infocon at 814-472-6066 or visit www.infoconcountyaccess.com.
- A vendor at www.landex.com/remote provides access to the index and to some file images for Register of Will records from twelve counties. Fees are involved. Participating counties include: Armstrong, Blair, Bradford, Clearfield, Columbia, Luzerne, Monroe, Perry, Sullivan, Susquehanna, Tioga, and York.

Since all courts participate in the Public Web Docket Sheets and Secure Web Docket Sheets, this redundant information is omitted. Please see the explanations above.

Allegheny County

Court of Common Pleas - Civil www.alleghenycounty.us/civil/index.aspx

Civil: Search civil cases after registration at https://dcr.alleghenycounty.us/. Credit card payment or drawn down account; fee is $.15 per search during office hours, $.10 if not. Search civil opinions at www.alleghenycourts.us/search/default.aspx?source=opinions_civil. **$$$**

Armstrong County

Court of Common Pleas - Civil www.co.armstrong.pa.us/departments/elected-officials/proth-coc

Civil: Online access is by subscription from private company-Infocon at www.infoconcountyaccess.com, 814-472-6066. See note in court summary section for fees. Images are not available; only the index. **$$$**

Probate (Register of Wills): Online access available by subscription from private company; Landex - http://landex.com/, 717-274-5890. Images are available from 2010 (May) to present. **$$$**

Beaver County

Court of Common Pleas - Civil www.beavercountypa.gov/courts/courts-common-pleas

Civil: Online access to civil records is by subscription from private company-Infocon at www.infoconcountyaccess.com, 814-472-6066. Register of Wills data is also provided. A link is at the court's home page. Also at the court's home page is a link to naturalization records. **$$$**

Court of Common Pleas - Criminal www.beavercountypa.gov/courts/courts-common-pleas

Criminal: Images are available by subscription from private company-Infocon at www.infoconcountyaccess.com, 814-472-6066. **$$$**

Bedford County

Court of Common Pleas - Criminal/Civil

Civil& Probate (Register of Wills): Online access is by subscription from private company-Infocon at www.infoconcountyaccess.com, 814-472-6066. See note in court summary section. Probate also available. Images are available. **$$$** *Criminal:* Access is by subscription from private company-Infocon at www.infoconcountyaccess.com, 814-472-6066. See note at beginning of section.

Berks County

Court of Common Pleas - Civil www.co.berks.pa.us/prothonotary/site/default.asp

Civil: The Prothonotary has a remote system to access dockets from 2002 forward. Subscription fee is $300 per year. For information, call 610-478-6970. **$$$**

Blair County

Court of Common Pleas - Criminal/Civil

Civil: Online access is by subscription from private company-Infocon at www.infoconcountyaccess.com, 814-472-6066. See note in court summary section. Includes probate. Images are not available. **$$$** *Criminal:* Access is by subscription from private company-Infocon at www.infoconcountyaccess.com, 814-472-6066. See note at beginning of section.

Bradford County

Court of Common Pleas - Probate www.bradfordcountypa.org/Courts/

Online access is by subscription from private company-Infocon at www.infoconcountyaccess.com, 814-472-6066. **$$$**

Bucks County

Court of Common Pleas - Civil www.buckscounty.org/courts/CourtInfo/CommonPleas.aspx

Civil: Access case searches for the Prothonotary Office and Family Court (excluding Support), please use the web link: http://propublic.co.bucks.pa.us/PSI/Viewer/Search.aspx. Civil case documents can be accessed on line for a fee ($1.00 convenience fee and $.10 per page). See www.buckscounty.org/government/departments/PublicAccess/ProthonotaryInstructions.pdf. No Family Court documents are available online. **$$$**

Butler County

Court of Common Pleas - Civil www.co.butler.pa.us

Civil: Online access is by subscription from a private company - Infocon at www.infoconcountyaccess.com, 814-472-6066. See note in court summary section. Images are available. **$$$** *Criminal:* Search dockets online free at http://ujsportal.pacourts.us/DocketSheets/CP.aspx back to 1988 for complete index. Also, online access to the index is by subscription from private company-Infocon at www.infoconcountyaccess.com, 814-472-6066. See note in court summary section for fees. **$$$**

Cambria County

Court of Common Pleas www.co.cambria.pa.us/prothonotary.aspx

Civil: Access to civil index is available by subscription at Infocon.com; Signup online or get details at 814-472-6066. Images are not available. **$$$**

Probate(Register of Wills): Online access is by subscription from private company-Infocon at www.infoconcountyaccess.com, 814-472-6066.

Carbon County

Court of Common Pleas www.carboncourts.com

Civil: Online access to the clerk of courts docket records is free at www.carboncourts.com/pubacc.htm, includes probate. Registration required. *Criminal:* Online access to clerk of courts docket records is free at www.carboncourts.com/pubacc.htm. Registration required. **$$$**

Chester County

Court of Common Pleas - Civil www.chesco.org/index.aspx?NID=1333

Civil: Internet access to county records including court records requires a sign-up and credit card payment. Application fee: $50. There is a $10.00 per month minimum (no charge for no activity); and $.10 each transaction beyond 100. Sign-up and/or logon at http://epin.chesco.org/. **$$$**

Clarion County

Court of Common Pleas - Civil www.co.clarion.pa.us/

Civil & Probate(Register of Wills): Online access is by subscription from private company-Infocon at www.infoconcountyaccess.com, 814-472-6066. See note in court summary section. Images are not available. **$$$**

Clearfield County

Register of Wills - Probate www.clearfieldco.org

Access to data is by subscription at www.landex.com/remote/. **$$$**

Clinton County

Court of Common Pleas - Criminal/Civil www.clintoncountypa.com/departments/court_services/prothonotary/

Civil & Probate: Online access is by subscription from private company-Infocon at www.infoconcountyaccess.com, 814-472-6066. See note in court summary section for fees. Images are available. **$$$** *Criminal:* Internet access to court records is by subscription from a private company-Infocon at www.ic-access.com, 814-472-6066. See note at beginning of section. **$$$**

Columbia County

Register of Wills - Probate http://columbiapa.org/courts/

Access to data is by subscription at www.landex.com/remote/.cketSheets/CP.aspx back to 1991. $$$

Crawford County

Court of Common Pleas - Civil www.crawfordcountypa.net

Civil: Online access to Prothonotary records and Register of Wills is by subscription from private company-Infocon at www.infoconcountyaccess.com, 814-472-6066. See note in court summary section. Images not shown. **$$$**

Cumberland County

Court of Common Pleas - Civil www.ccpa.net/index.asp?nid=121

Civil: Online access available by subscription from private company-Infocon at www.infoconcountyaccess.com, 814-472-6066. See Summary of State Court System for more details. Images are available. Also, searchable civil records by docket # at www.ccpa.net/index.aspx?NID=3805. **$$$**

Dauphin County

Court of Common Pleas - Civil www.dauphincounty.org/government/Court-Departments/Pages/default.aspx

Civil: Access civil cases back to 11/2001, suits (1992-10/31/2001) and judgments back to 1983 free at www.dauphinc.org/onlineservices/public/header.asp.

Delaware County

Court of Common Pleas - Criminal/Civil www.co.delaware.pa.us

Civil: Online access to court civil records free (may begin charging in near future) at http://w01.co.delaware.pa.us/pa/publicaccess.asp. Search online by document type, document number, etc.

Erie County

Court of Common Pleas - Civil www.eriecountygov.org/

Civil & Probate (Register of Wills): Online access is by subscription from private company-Infocon at www.infoconcountyaccess.com, 814-472-6066. See note in court summary section. Images are available. **$$$**

Fayette County

Court of Common Pleas - Civil

Civil: Internet access to court records is by subscription from a private company-Infocon at www.infoconcountyaccess.com/, 814-472-6066. See Summary of State Court System for more details. Images are available. **$$$**

Forest County

Court of Common Pleas www.warrenforestcourt.org/

Civil: Online access available by subscription from private company-Infocon at www.infoconcountyaccess.com, 814-472-6066. See Summary of State Court System for more details. Images are available from 2006. **$$$**

Franklin County

Court of Common Pleas - Civil www.franklincountypa.gov/Pages/CourtOffices.aspx

Civil: Access index by subscription from private company-Infocon at www.infoconcountyaccess.com, 814-472-6066. See Summary of State Court System for more details. Images are not available. **$$$**

Probate(Register of Wills): Online access available by subscription from private company-Infocon at www.infoconcountyaccess.com, 814-472-6066. See note at beginning of section. Images are not available. **$$$**

Fulton County

Court of Common Pleas - Criminal/Civil www.co.fulton.pa.us/court-common-pleas.php

Civil: Online access available by subscription from private company-Infocon at www.infoconcountyaccess.com, 814-472-6066. See Summary of State Court System for more details. Images are available. Images are not available. **$$$**

Huntingdon County

Court of Common Pleas - Criminal/Civil

Civil: Online access is by subscription from private company-Infocon at www.infoconcountyaccess.com, 814-472-6066. See note in court summary section. Images not shown. **$$$**

Indiana County

Court of Common Pleas - Criminal/Civil www.countyofindiana.org/courts

Civil: Online access is by subscription from private company-Infocon at www.infoconcountyaccess.com, 814-472-6066. See note in court summary section. Images not shown. **$$$**

Jefferson County

Court of Common Pleas - Criminal/Civil

Civil: Online access is by subscription from private company-Infocon at www.infoconcountyaccess.com, 814-472-6066. See note in court summary section. Images not shown. **$$$**

Register of Wills - Probate

$10.00 per name-search fee; $1.00 per page copy fee. Online access is by subscription from private company-Infocon at www.infoconcountyaccess.com, 814-472-6066. See note in court summary section. **$$$**

Juniata County

Register of Wills - Probate www.co.juniata.pa.us/

Online access available by subscription from private company-Infocon at www.infoconcountyaccess.com, 814-472-6066. **$$$**

Lackawanna County

Court of Common Pleas - Civil www.lackawannacounty.org/index.php/judiciary

Civil: See www.lpa-homes.org/LPA_Applications.htm for access to the docket index from 2003 for the Civil and Family Court Divisions, including Register of Wills, Orphans' Court and Marriage Licenses.

Lancaster County

Court of Common Pleas - Civil www.co.lancaster.pa.us/courts/site/default.asp

Civil: Access to the Prothonotary's civil court records is free at http://gisweb1.co.lancaster.pa.us/bannerwebimg/. Also, historical court case schedules are free at www.co.lancaster.pa.us, click on "Court Calendar Archives." Includes Register, Treasurer, and other courthouse record data. Results include addresses. Call Kathy Harris at 717-299-8252 for info.

Probate (Register of Wills) Access probate back to 1933 and marriage records back to 1948 free at http://paperless.co.lancaster.pa.us/viewerportal.

Lawrence County

Court of Common Pleas - Criminal/Civil www.co.lawrence.pa.us

Civil: Online access is by subscription from private company-Infocon at www.infoconcountyaccess.com, 814-472-6066. See note in court summary section. Images shown. **$$$** *Criminal:* same as civil

Lehigh County

Court of Common Pleas - Civil www.lccpa.org/civil/

Civil: Access to the county online system requires $300.00 annual usage fee. Search by name or case number. Call Lehigh Cty Fiscal Office at 610-782-3112 for more information. **$$$**

Probate (Register of Wills: Online access to Wills: call Lehigh Cty Computer Svcs Dept at 610-782-3286 for info.

Luzerne County

Court of Common Pleas - Civil www.luzernecounty.org/county/row_offices/prothonotary

Civil: Civil record index may be viewed free online at http://civilrecords.luzernecounty.org/psi/Viewer/Search.aspx. Copies of judgments are also viewable for this site.

Probate (Register of Wills): Access to data is by subscription at www.landex.com/remote/. **$$$**

McKean County

Court of Common Pleas - Criminal/Civil

Civil: Online access is by subscription from private company-Infocon at www.infoconcountyaccess.com, 814-472-6066. Monthly usage fee and per minute fees apply. **$$$** *Criminal:*same as civil

Mercer County

Court of Common Pleas - Civil www.mcc.co.mercer.pa.us

Civil: Online access is by subscription from private company-Infocon at www.infoconcountyaccess.com, 814-472-6066. See note in court summary section. Images not shown. **$$$**

Mifflin County

Court of Common Pleas - Criminal/Civil www.co.mifflin.pa.us/CourtOffice/Pages/CRT_main_pg.aspx

Civil: Online access is by subscription from private company-Infocon at www.infoconcountyaccess.com, 814-472-6066. See note in court summary section. Images not shown. Court calendar available at main website. **$$$**

Probate (Register of Wills): Online access available by subscription from private company-Infocon at www.infoconcountyaccess.com, 814-472-6066. Some images not shown, but not all. **$$$**

Monroe County

Court of Common Pleas - Civil

Civil: Online access is by subscription from private company-Infocon at www.infoconcountyaccess.com, 814-472-6066. See note in court summary section. Images not shown. **$$$**

Probate (Register of Wills): Access to data is by subscription at www.landex.com/remote/. **$$$**

Montgomery County

Court of Common Pleas - Civil www.montcopa.org/index.aspx?nid=97

Civil: Search court and other record indices free from Prothonotary at http://webapp.montcopa.org/PSI/Viewer/Search.aspx?c=CaseSearch. This includes active and purged civil cases, also active probate cases, also calendars. Landlord/tenant actions are found at the local District Court level. A list of judges is found at www.montcopa.org/index.aspx?nid=186.

Register of Wills - Probate

Search active cases at http://webapp.montcopa.org/PSI/Viewer/Search.aspx?c=CaseSearch. The Office is also agent for the Commonwealth in the collection of inheritance taxes.

Montour County

Court of Common Pleas - Criminal/Civil www.montourco.org/Pages/Prothonotary.aspx

Civil: Online access is by subscription from private company-Infocon at www.infoconcountyaccess.com, 814-472-6066. See note in court summary section. Images not shown. **$$$** *Criminal:* Online access is by subscription from private company-Infocon at www.infoconcountyaccess.com, 814-472-6066. See note in court summary section. Images not shown. Record date back to 8/25/2005, no images.. **$$$**

Register of Wills - Probate

Online access available by subscription from private company-Infocon at www.infoconcountyaccess.com, 814-472-6066. Will index 1850 to present at www.montourco.org/RegisterRecorder/Pages/WillIndex1850toPresent.aspx. **$$$**

Northampton County

Court of Common Pleas - Civil www.nccpa.org

Civil: Search calendars and schedules for free at www.nccpa.org/schedule.html. Opinions and judgments may be available.

Court of Common Pleas - Criminal www.nccpa.org/

Criminal: Search calendars and schedules for free online at www.nccpa.org/cals. Court opinions are available also at this site.

Perry County

Court of Common Pleas - Criminal/Civil www.perryco.org/Dept/Courts/Prothonotary_ClerkOfCourts/Pages/ProthonotaryAndClerkOfCourts.aspx

Civil: Recorded judgments are on the County Recorder web page. *Criminal:* Search dockets online free at http://ujsportal.pacourts.us/DocketSheets/CP.aspx back to 1975.

Probate (Register of Wills): Access to data is by subscription at www.landex.com/remote/. **$$$**

Philadelphia County

Court of Common Pleas - Civil www.courts.phila.gov/common-pleas/

Civil: Access to 1st Judicial District Civil Trial records is free at www.courts.phila.gov/casesearch/. Search by name, judgment and docket info.

Municipal Criminal Trial Division www.courts.phila.gov/municipal/

Criminal: Search dockets online free at www.courts.phila.gov/casesearch/ back to 1968.

Municipal Court - Civil http://fjd.phila.gov

Civil: Access Muni court dockets online free at http://fjdclaims.phila.gov/phmuni/login.do or you may register for a username and password.

Marriage: Search marriage records free back to 1995 at http://secureprod.phila.gov/wills/marriagesearch.aspx. For marriage records call 215-686-2234.

Pike County

Court of Common Pleas www.pikepa.org

Civil: Online access is by subscription from private company-Infocon at www.infoconcountyaccess.com, 814-472-6066. See note in court summary section. Images shown. **$$$** *Criminal:* Internet access to court records is by subscription from a private company-Infocon at www.infoconcountyaccess.com, 814-472-6066. See note at beginning of section. Images shown. **$$$**

Probate (Register of Wills): Online access available by subscription from private company-Infocon at www.infoconcountyaccess.com, 814-472-6066 **$$$**

Potter County

Court of Common Pleas www.pottercountypa.net/prothonotary_court.php

Civil: Online access is by subscription from private company-Infocon at www.infoconcountyaccess.com, 814-472-6066. See note in court summary section. Images shown. **$$$** *Probate (Register of Wills):* Online access available by subscription from private company-Infocon at www.infoconcountyaccess.com, 814-472-6066

Schuylkill County

Court of Common Pleas - Civil www.co.schuylkill.pa.us

Civil: Access civil court records and judgments free at www.co.schuylkill.pa.us/info/Civil/Inquiry/Search.csp.

Register of Wills: For a marriage index for free go to www.co.schuylkill.pa.us/Offices/RegisterOfWills/index.asp. Also at this court are birth and death records from 1893-1905.

Somerset County

Court of Common Pleas - Civil www.co.somerset.pa.us

Civil: Court calendars (no names) and daily schedules free at www.co.somerset.pa.us. Also, judgments may appear on the Landex system at www.landex.com/remote/ - registration and password required. Court calendars free at www.co.somerset.pa.us/courtcalendar/ but no name searching. Recorded judgements are filed by the Prothonotary, and are online for a fee at www.infoconcountyaccess.com. **$$$**

Court of Common Pleas - Criminal www.co.somerset.pa.us

Criminal: Search dockets online free at http://ujsportal.pacourts.us/DocketSheets/CP.aspx back to 1990. Court calendars free at www.co.somerset.pa.us/courtcalendar/ but no name searching.

Sullivan County

Register of Wills - Probate

The Register of Wills has access to data is by subscription at www.landex.com/remote/. **$$$**

Susquehanna County

Court of Common Pleas - Civil www.susquehannacountyclerkofcourts.com/

Civil: Online access is by subscription from private company-Infocon at www.infoconcountyaccess.com, 814-472-6066. See note in court summary section. Images not shown. **$$$**

Register of Wills - Probate

The Register of Wills has access to data is by subscription at www.landex.com/remote/. **$$$**

Tioga County

Register of Wills - Probate

Online access to wills is available through a private company at www.landex.com/remote/. Fee is $.20 per minute and $.50 per fax page. Images and wills go back to 2/1999. **$$$**

Venango County

Court of Common Pleas - Criminal/Civil www.co.venango.pa.us

Civil: Online access is by subscription from private company-Infocon at www.infoconcountyaccess.com, 814-472-6066. See note in court summary section for fees. Images are available. **$$$**

Warren County

Court of Common Pleas - Criminal/Civil www.warrenforestcourt.org/

Civil: Online access is by subscription from private company-Infocon at www.infoconcountyaccess.com, 814-472-6066. See note in court summary section for fees. Images are not available; only the index. **$$$**

Washington County

Court of Common Pleas - www.co.washington.pa.us

Civil: Access to Prothonotary civil records including also orphans court is by subscription; enroll form at www.co.washington.pa.us/downloadpage.aspx?menuDept=28. Also, records (**including probate & criminal**) available on Common Pleas Ct database at www.co.washington.pa.us/wccourtdocuments/code/login.asp. Registration, username, and password required. **$$$**

Westmoreland County

Court of Common Pleas www.co.westmoreland.pa.us/index.aspx?nid=528

Access civil court dockets back to 1985 free at http://westmorelandweb400.us:8088/EGSPublicAccess.htm. Also, search Register of Wills and marriages free back to 1986. Access to full remote online system has $100 setup (no set-up if accessed via Internet) plus $20 monthly minimum. System includes civil, criminal, Prothonotary indexes and recorder data. For info, call 724-830-3874, or click on "e-services" at website. **$$$**

York County

Court of Common Pleas - Civil http://yorkcountypa.gov/courts-criminal-justice/court-courtrelated-offices/prothonotary.html

Civil: A civil case search is offered online, but the exact site depends on the users software. See http://yorkcountypa.gov/courts-criminal-justice/court-courtrelated-offices/prothonotary/civil-case-search.html. Documents filed on May 8, 2008 and thereafter are available as scanned images.

Probate (Register of Wills): Access to data is by subscription at www.landex.com/remote/. **$$$**

Reminder

The following programs are also available for all courts at http://ujsportal.pacourts.us/

The Public Web Docket Sheets access to search, view and print the docket sheets for Pennsylvania's Appellate Courts, Criminal Courts of Common Pleas, Magisterial District Courts and the Philadelphia Municipal Court. In addition, a Court Summary Information report is available for Criminal Courts of Common Pleas and Philadelphia Municipal Court cases. This service does not provide name searches; user must have the case file number.

The Secure Web Docket Sheet option provides access to search, view and print docket sheets that contain additional content not accessible for public viewing, for Pennsylvania's Criminal Courts of Common Pleas, Magisterial District Courts and the Philadelphia Municipal Court. In addition, secure Court Summary Information, Case Accounting and Pre-Sentence Summary reports are available for Criminal Courts of Common Pleas and Philadelphia Municipal Court cases. A secure login is required to access this service.

There are cautions - please review the front text for this section.

Recorders, Assessors, and Other Sites of Note

Recording Office Organization: 67 counties, 67 recording offices and 134 UCC filing offices. Each county has two different recording offices. One is the Prothonotary - Pennsylvania's term for "clerk" - who accepted UCC and tax lien filings until July 1, 2001. The other is the Recorder of Deeds who maintains real estate records. All federal and state tax liens on personal property and on real property are filed with the Prothonotary. Usually, tax liens on personal property are filed in the judgment index of the Prothonotary.

Statewide or Multi-Jurisdiction Access: A number of counties provide web access to recorded documents and to assessor data. Many counties use the services of a designated vendor, generally either Infocon or Landex. The profiles below indicate when county uses a vendor. Below is a further explanation.

- The Infocon County Access System is a cooperative fee-based subscriber service that provides access to certain public records contained in participating County databases. Infocon provides internet (and formerly offered a direct dial-up access) to recorded record information (and often add'l data) for over 40 Pennsylvania counties. Visit www.infoconcountyaccess.com.
- Access records from the recording indexes of 27 counties via a private vendor free at www.landex.com/webstore/jsp/cart/DocumentSearch.jsp. Full access to Recorder of Deeds (and in most counties Wills and Orphans Court, and sometimes assessor data) is by subscription at www.landex.com/remote/. Fees start as low is $.10 per page view, $.50 per fax page. Fees and services vary by county; most information you need is readily available on the website.

County Sites:

Adams County ***Recorded Documents*** www.adamscounty.us/CountyOffices/ElectedOfficials/RegisterRecorder.aspx Access to public records for a fee at https://adamscountyparecorder.com/external/User/Login.aspx?ReturnUrl=%2fexternal%2fIndex.aspx. **$$$**

Property, Taxation Records Access to GIS/mapping for free at http://173.163.156.193/Freeance/Client/PublicKiosk1/index.html?appconfig=test_kiosk.

Allegheny County ***Recorded Documents*** www.county.allegheny.pa.us/re/ Access Recorder's Index for a fee at https://pa_allegheny.uslandrecords.com/palr/. Commercial draw down account copy fee is $.50 per page. **$$$**

Property, Taxation Records Access to Allegheny County real estate database is free at www2.county.allegheny.pa.us/realestate/Default.aspx.

Armstrong County ***Recorded Documents*** Access is through a private company to land records for a fee at www.landex.com/webstore/jsp/cart/DocumentSearch.jsp. Online and images from 1805 to present. Fees are $.10 per minute/$.05 per page viewed. Includes Orphan Court, Recorder of Deeds, Register of Wills images. Also, a private company offers online access to recorded documents and many Prothonotary records. Call Infocon at 814-472-6066, www.infoconcountyaccess.com. **$$$**

Beaver County ***Recorded Documents*** www.beavercountypa.gov/recorder-deeds Access to the Recorder's database is free at www.beavercountypa.gov/recorder-deeds/recorder-deeds-online-search. Images from 1957 to present. Also, a private company offers online access to recorded documents and many Prothonotary records. Call Infocon at 814-472-6066, www.infoconcountyaccess.com. **$$$**

Property, Taxation Records Access property search for free at www.beavercountypa.gov/property-search.

Bedford County ***Recorded Documents*** http://registerrecorder.webs.com/ The Prothonotary sends online requesters for a fee to http://infoconcountyaccess.com/. **$$$**

Berks County ***Recorded Documents*** www.co.berks.pa.us/recorder Access recorder's records index and images at https://portal2.recordfusion.com/countyweb/login.do?countyname=Berks. Must register before using. Indexes for deeds recorded prior to 1959 and satisfied mortgages recorded prior to 1969, use the electronic Russell Index books. All indexes since 1752 via traditional search or computerized index books for all deeds, mortgages and misc documents including images.

Property, Taxation Records Access parcel records free at http://ema.countyofberks.com/Parcel_Search/presentation/chameleon/search.asp.

Blair County ***Recorded Documents*** www.blaircountyrecorder.com Also, access to land records for a fee at www.landex.com/webstore/jsp/cart/DocumentSearch.jsp. Online and images of deeds and mortgages from 1976 to present, miscellaneous online from 1990 to present, images from 2005 to present. Fees are $.10 per minute/$.05 per page viewed. Also, limited access is via a private company; call Infocon at 814-472-6066 or www.infoconcountyaccess.com/. Includes Recorder of Deeds and Register of Wills indexes. **$$$**

Property, Taxation Records A private company sells county tax claim property, view list free at www.xspand.com/investors/realestate_sale/index.aspx.

Bradford County ***Recorded Documents*** www.bradfordcountypa.org Access to land records for a fee at www.landex.com/webstore/jsp/cart/DocumentSearch.jsp. Online and images of Recorder of Deeds from 1945 to 1950 and 1970 to present, marriages from 1885 to 1907 and 1994 to present. Fees are $.20 per minute. **$$$**

Property, Taxation Records Access to property records and GIS/mapping free at www.bradfordappraiser.com/GIS/Search_F.asp.

Bucks County ***Recorded Documents*** www.buckscounty.org/government/rowOfficers/RecorderofDeeds/index.aspx Access to land records for a fee at www.landex.com/webstore/jsp/cart/DocumentSearch.jsp. Online and all other documents from 1980 to present, mortgages from 1968 to present. Fees $.20 per minute. **$$$**

Property, Taxation Records Access Prothonotary records free at http://propublic.co.bucks.pa.us/PSI/Viewer/Search.aspx?c=CaseSearch&panel=CaseNumber.

Butler County ***Recorded Documents*** www.co.butler.pa.us/butler/cwp/view.asp?a=1494&q=571959&butlerNav=|33534|33544| Access deeds records free at www.co.butler.pa.us/recorder/. Also access probate court estate and guardianship records free at http://66.117.197.22/index.cfm?page=home. At bottom of webpage, click on the type of \"lookup\" you want. Also, a private company offers online access to recorded documents and many Prothonotary records. Call Infocon at 814-472-6066, www.infoconcountyaccess.com. **$$$**

Cambria County ***Recorded Documents*** www.co.cambria.pa.us/recorder-of-deeds-office.aspx A private company offers online access to most Prothonotary records. Call Infocon at 814-472-6066, www.infoconcountyaccess.com. **$$$**

Property, Taxation Records Access to GIS/mapping for free at http://gis.co.cambria.pa.us/publicgis1/.

Cameron County ***Recorded Documents*** www.cameroncountypa.com/Cameron_County_Prothonotary.htm Access to land records for a fee at www.landex.com/webstore/jsp/cart/DocumentSearch.jsp. **$$$**

Carbon County ***Recorded Documents*** www.carboncounty.com/deeds.htm Access to land records for a fee at www.landex.com/webstore/jsp/cart/DocumentSearch.jsp. Online from 1988 to present, images from 1994 to present. Fees $.10 per minute/$.05 per page viewed. County Prothonotary, Register of Wills, and Clerk of Courts by remote public access; instructions and registration at www.carboncourts.com/disclaimer-prothy-public.html. **$$$**

Property, Taxation Records Access assessor property data free at www.carboncounty.com/records.htm.

Centre County ***Recorded Documents*** http://centrecountypa.gov/index.aspx?NID=418 Access recorded data on the WEB IA subscription system from 1800 forward; fee is $10.00 set-up plus $.06 per click or other per click plan. This replaces the old dial-up system. See http://webia.co.centre.pa.us/login.asp. **$$$**

Property, Taxation Records Assessment data on the WEB IA subscription system; registration and per page fees apply; see http://webia.co.centre.pa.us/login.asp.**$$$**

Chester County ***Recorded Documents*** www.chesco.org/index.aspx?nid=169 Search Recorder of Deeds records free at http://dsf.chesco.org/recorder/cwp/view.asp?A=1519&Q=606686. Also, full countywide records including court records requires a sign-up and credit card payment. Signup and info at https://epin.chesco.org/Main/PinAgreement.aspx. Also, genealogical and older vital statistics are free at http://dsf.chesco.org/archives/site/default.asp. Also, full countywide records including court records requires a sign-up and credit card payment. Application fee is $50 with $10.00/month minimum; no charge for no activity; $.10 each transaction beyond 100. Sign-up and logon at http://epin.chesco.org. **$$$**

Property, Taxation Records Assessment data available by subscription at http://epin.chesco.org.**$$$**

Clarion County ***Recorded Documents*** www.co.clarion.pa.us/government/register-and-recorders-office.html Access is through a private company. For info, call Infocon at 814-472-6066 or www.infoconcountyaccess.com/. Includes images for Recorder, Register of Wills, and Orphans court. Also, a private company offers online access to recorded documents and many Prothonotary records. Call Infocon at 814-472-6066, www.infoconcountyaccess.com. **$$$**

Clearfield County ***Recorded Documents*** www.clearfieldco.org Access to land records for a fee at www.landex.com/webstore/jsp/cart/DocumentSearch.jsp. Online and images for Recorder of Deeds from 1986 to present. Fees $.10 per minute/$.05 per page viewed. **$$$**

Property, Taxation Records Assessors county tax sale list is updated weekly at http://it.clearfieldco.org/default.asp. Must have username and password.

Clinton County ***Recorded Documents*** www.clintoncountypa.com/departments/county_departments/register_recorder/recorder_of_deeds.shtml A private company offers online access to most recorded documents and many Prothonotary records. Call Infocon at 814-472-6066, www.infoconcountyaccess.com. **$$$**

Property, Taxation Records Access to gis-mapping property and assessment data is free at http://gismapping.clintoncountypa.com/Mapping_Pilot/.

Columbia County ***Recorded Documents*** www.columbiapa.org/registerrecorder/index.php Access to land records for a fee at www.landex.com/webstore/jsp/cart/DocumentSearch.jsp. Online and images for Recorder of Deeds from 1974 to present. Fees $.20 per minute. **$$$**

Property, Taxation Records Access to gis-mapping is free at http://gis.columbiapa.org/mapsonline/default.aspx.

Crawford County ***Recorded Documents*** www.crawfordcountypa.net/ Access available via a private company. For info call Infocom at 814-472-6066 or www.infoconcountyaccess.com/. Includes images for Recorder, Register of Wills, Orphans Court, Prothonotary. **$$$**

Property, Taxation Records Access to GIS/mapping free at www.crawfordcountypa.net:81/911addmap/gisdisclaimer.htm.

Cumberland County ***Recorded Documents*** www.ccpa.net/index.aspx?nid=123 Access to land records for a fee at www.landex.com/webstore/jsp/cart/DocumentSearch.jsp. Online for Recorder of Deeds from 1973 to present. Images for Recorder of Deeds from 1993 to present. Fees $.10 per minute/$.05 per page viewed. Also, civil dockets (judgments, etc.) available free at http://records.ccpa.net/weblink_public/Browse.aspx?dbid=8. Also, a private company offers online access to recorded documents and many Prothonotary records. Call Infocon at 814-472-6066, www.infoconcountyaccess.com. **$$$**

Property, Taxation Records Access to the property assessment data is free at www.ccpa.net/index.aspx?NID=2295. No name searching. Access property data on the GIS-mapping site free at http://gis.ccpa.net/PropertyMapper/. Search delinquent tax index at http://taxdb.ccpa.net/delinquent/default.asp but no name searching. Tax Sale data at www.ccpa.net/index.aspx?nid=2675.

Dauphin County ***Recorded Documents*** www.dauphincounty.org/government/Publicly-Elected-Officials/Recorder-of-Deeds/Pages/default.aspx Access the register's land records database free at www.dauphincounty.org/government/Publicly-Elected-Officials/Recorder-of-Deeds/Pages/default.aspx. Indexes and images from 1979 to present.

Property, Taxation Records Access to the GIS/mapping data for free is available at www.dauphincounty.org/government/About-the-County/County-Offices/Information-Technology/GIS/Pages/Interactive-Map.aspx.**$$$**

Delaware County ***Recorded Documents*** www.co.delaware.pa.us/depts/recorder.html Access to the public access system is free at www.co.delaware.pa.us/depts/recorder.html. Also, records available at http://w01.co.delaware.pa.us/pa/publicaccess.asp. Other public records included in this URL.

Property, Taxation Records Access to Real Estate and Assessment for free at http://w01.co.delaware.pa.us/pa/publicaccess.asp?real.x=71&real.y=50.

Erie County ***Recorded Documents*** www.eriecountygov.org A private company offers online access to marriage licenses and recorded deeds. Most Prothonotary records also included. Call Infocon at 814-472-6066, www.infoconcountyaccess.com. **$$$**

Property, Taxation Records Access property records data free at www.eriecountygov.org/government/assessment/parcelsearch.aspx, no name searching. Also, full data for real estate professionals is available by subscription, click on \"sign in\" and follow the menu for details. Also, you may purchase judicial and/or sheriff sale property sale lists for $10.00 each, see www.eriecountygov.org/government/taxclaim/default.aspx.**$$$**

Fayette County ***Recorded Documents*** www.co.fayette.pa.us/deeds/Pages/default.aspx A private company offers online access to most Prothonotary records. Call Infocon at 814-472-6066, www.infoconcountyaccess.com. Also, access to land records for the state free at https://pa.uslandrecords.com/palr_new/PalrApp/index.jsp. Select Fayette County. This is an index only from 1975 to present. **$$$**

Property, Taxation Records Access to property assessments is free at www.fayetteproperty.org/assessor/Main/Home.aspx. Also, access to property auction sales for 2012 free at www.co.fayette.pa.us/assessment/Documents/2012_County_Auction_Sale.pdf.

Forest County ***Recorded Documents*** www.co.forest.pa.us A private company offers online access to recorded documents and most Prothonotary records. Call Infocon at 814-472-6066, www.infoconcountyaccess.com. **$$$**

Franklin County ***Recorded Documents*** www.co.franklin.pa.us/Pages/RegisterRecordersOffice.aspx Access to land records for a fee at www.landex.com/webstore/jsp/cart/DocumentSearch.jsp. Online and images for Deeds from 1962 to present, online for mortgages from 1785 to present, images for mortgage from 1960 to present. All other land record data for both online and images from 1962 to present. Fees are $.10 per minute/$.05 per page viewed. Also, a private company offers online access to recorded documents and many Prothonotary records. Call Infocon at 814-472-6066, www.infoconcountyaccess.com. **$$$**

Fulton County ***Recorded Documents*** www.co.fulton.pa.us/prothonotary.php A private company offers online access to most Prothonotary records. Call Infocon at 814-472-6066, www.infoconcountyaccess.com. **$$$**

Property, Taxation Records Access to GIS/mapping free at http://gis.co.fulton.pa.us/. Must register. At this same site you can also search assessment information for a fee.**$$$**

Greene County ***Recorded Documents*** www.co.greene.pa.us/secured/gc2/depts/lo/rr/rr.htm Access real estate records index back to 1950 free at https://pa.uslandrecords.com/palr_new/PalrApp/index.jsp. Subscription required for full access; view document for $.50 per page, max $5.00 per doc. **$$$**

Huntingdon County ***Recorded Documents*** http://huntingdoncounty.net/Pages/RegisterandRecorder.aspx A private company offers online access to most Prothonotary records. Call Infocon at 814-472-6066, www.infoconcountyaccess.com. **$$$**

Indiana County ***Recorded Documents*** www.countyofindiana.org Access is available by subscription at http://regrec.countyofindiana.org/countyweb/login.jsp?countyname=Indiana/ but you may login as Guest and search free. **$$$**

Jefferson County ***Recorded Documents*** A private company offers online access to most Prothonotary records. Call Infocon at 814-472-6066, www.infoconcountyaccess.com. **$$$**

Juniata County ***Recorded Documents*** www.co.juniata.pa.us/elected-officials/recorder-deeds/ A private company offers online access to most Prothonotary records. Call Infocon at 814-472-6066, www.infoconcountyaccess.com. Access to land records for a fee at www.landex.com/webstore/jsp/cart/DocumentSearch.jsp. **$$$**

Lackawanna County ***Recorded Documents*** www.lackawannacounty.org/viewDepartment.aspx?DeptID=9 Access the index free at www.landex.com/webstore/jsp/cart/DocumentSearch.jsp. Full access to Recorder of Deeds and Wills and Orphans Court is by subscription at www.landex.com/remote/. Index and images go back to 8/1994. Also, access to Recorder of Deeds public records free at www.searchiqs.com/palac/. **$$$**

Property, Taxation Records Access property data free at http://ao.lackawannacounty.org/agreed.php.

Lancaster County ***Recorded Documents*** www.lancasterdeeds.com/ Access to deeds, UCCs and other recordings is free after registration at http://searchdocs.lancasterdeeds.com/countyweb/login.jsp?countyname=Lancaster. Also, search probate, death and marriage records free at http://paperless.co.lancaster.pa.us/viewerportal/.

Property, Taxation Records Three different online access services are available for tax assessment, GIS, and property sales search at http://www.co.lancaster.pa.us/lanco/cwp/view.asp?a=565&q=608310&lancoNav=|&lancoNav_GID=998. Sheriff sales list at www.co.lancaster.pa.us/sheriffs/cwp/view.asp?a=3&q=620112&sheriffsNav=|.

Lawrence County ***Recorded Documents*** www.co.lawrence.pa.us Access to Recorder of Deeds records free at https://portal1.recordfusion.com/countyweb/login.do?countyname=Lawrence. Must log in with username and password. Also, a private company offers online access to recorded documents and many Prothonotary records. Call Infocon at 814-472-6066, www.infoconcountyaccess.com.

Property, Taxation Records Search property records after free registration at https://portal1.recordfusion.com/countyweb/login.do?countyname=LawrenceAssessor. Must register with use username and password.

Lebanon County ***Recorded Documents*** www.lebcounty.org/Recorder_of_Deeds/Pages/home.aspx Access to land records for a fee at www.landex.com/webstore/jsp/cart/DocumentSearch.jsp. Online Deeds from 1933 to present, images from 1956 to present. Online mortgages from 1933 to present, images from 1992 to present. Misc for both online and images from 1969 to present. Fees $.10 per minute/$.05 per page viewed. **$$$**

Property, Taxation Records Access property data by subscription at www.courthouseonline.com/MyProperty.asp. Sub fee $9.95 3-days, up to $275 per year. A free view available if you have control number and password from tax notice or are registered.**$$$**

Lehigh County ***Recorded Documents*** www.lehighcounty.org/Departments/ClerkofJudicialRecords/tabid/327/Default.aspx County's full-access internet pay system initial cost is $300.00 per year. For signup info, call the Fiscal Office at 610-782-3112. Also, at www.lehighcounty.org/, the County Grants database is searched free (click on Services); free registration required. **$$$**

Property, Taxation Records Access to Assessor records for free at www.lehighcounty.org/Departments/Assessment/SearchRecords/tabid/315/Default.aspx.

Lehigh County ***Recorded Documents*** www.lehighcounty.org Access to the county's full-access internet pay system 1s $318.00 a year initial cost. Call Lehigh County Computer Svcs Dept at 610-782-3286 for signup or info. Also, subscribe to view naturalization, property tax, assessment, tax records for a fee at www.lehighcounty.org/public/public.cfm. Court records, marriages, and Register of Wills records and land records and images from 1812 to 1983 online by subscription at www.lehighcounty.org/public/public.cfm?doc=ody_home.cfm. Also, access to land records for a fee go to www.landex.com/webstore/jsp/cart/DocumentSearch.jsp. Both online and images for land data from 1984 to present. Fees $.10 per minute/$.05 per page viewed. **$$$**

Property, Taxation Records Access assessor property data free at www.lehighcounty.org/Departments/Assessment/SearchRecords/tabid/315/Default.aspx, but no name searching. Also, view sheriff's tax sales lists free at www.lehighcounty.org/Departments/SheriffsOffice/SheriffSale/tabid/554/Default.aspx.

Luzerne County ***Recorded Documents*** www.luzernecounty.org/county/row_offices/recorder_of_deeds Access to land records for a fee at www.landex.com/webstore/jsp/cart/DocumentSearch.jsp. Online for Recorder of Deeds from 9/1990 to present, images from 1968 to present. Fees $.10 per minute/$.05 per page viewed. Also, access to recorded liens and judgments free at http://civilrecords.luzernecounty.org/psi/Viewer/Search.aspx?oq=Yz1DYXNlU2VhcmNoJnBhbmVsPUFsbA%3d%3d. **$$$**

Property, Taxation Records Access data by subscription at www.courthouseonline.com/MyProperty.asp. $9.95 3-day, up to $275 per year. Get free view with control number & password from tax notice-registration.**$$$**

Lycoming County ***Recorded Documents*** www.assessorsoffice.net/countyappraisal.asp?state=Pennsylvania&county=Lycoming A private company offers online access to most Prothonotary records. Call Infocon at 814-472-6066, www.infoconcountyaccess.com. **$$$**

Property, Taxation Records Access property data by subscription at www.courthouseonline.com/MyProperty.asp. Sub fee $9.95 3-days, up to $275 per year. A free view available if you have control number and password from tax notice or are registered.**$$$**

McKean County ***Recorded Documents*** www.mckeancountypa.org/Departments/Recorder_Of_Deeds/Index.aspx Access to land records for a fee at www.landex.com/webstore/jsp/cart/DocumentSearch.jsp. Both online and images for land records from 1973 to present, online misc from 1973 to present. Fees $.10 per minute/$.05 per page viewed. Also, a private company offers online access to recorded documents and many Prothonotary records. Call Infocon at 814-472-6066, www.infoconcountyaccess.com. **$$$**

Mercer County ***Recorded Documents*** http://mcc.co.mercer.pa.us/Recorders/default.htm Access to records for a fee at https://recorder.mcc.co.mercer.pa.us/User/Login.aspx?ReturnUrl=%2fIndex.aspx. Can sign in as a guest or account sign-in. Search dog ownership database for free at www.mcc.co.mercer.pa.us/DogOwnerSearch/default.htm but no name search. Also, a private company offers online access to recorded documents and many Prothonotary records. Call Infocon at 814-472-6066, www.infoconcountyaccess.com. **$$$**

Mifflin County ***Recorded Documents*** www.co.mifflin.pa.us/RegisterandRecorder/Pages/REG_main_pg.aspx Access is via a private company; call Infocon at 814-472-6066 or www.infoconcountyaccess.com; recorder back to 1993, probate, orphans and marriages back to 2000; images soon to be available for Recorder records, indexes for others. **$$$**

Property, Taxation Records Access to GIS/mapping for free at www.co.mifflin.pa.us/GIS/Pages/GISDataAgreement.aspx.

Monroe County ***Recorded Documents*** www.co.monroe.pa.us/planning_records/cwp/view.asp?a=1549&q=605419 Access to land records for a fee at www.landex.com/webstore/jsp/cart/DocumentSearch.jsp. Online land index from 1930 to present, land images from 1958 to present. Online map index from 1919 to present, map imaged from 1982 to present. Fees $.10 per minute/$.05 per page viewed. Also, a private company offers online access to recorded documents and many Prothonotary records. Call Infocon at 814-472-6066, www.infoconcountyaccess.com. **$$$**

Montgomery County ***Recorded Documents*** www.montcopa.org/index.aspx?nid=353 Recorder of Deeds records are at http://rodviewer.montcopa.org/countyweb/login.jsp?countyname=Montgomery. Login as Guest or subscribe. Records date back to 1990. Lending agency and Prothonotary data on system. Certified online copies are $10.50. Also, access to Marriage licenses for free go to http://webapp.montcopa.org/PSI/Viewer/Search.aspx?oq=Yz1DYXNlU2VhcmNo. **$$$**

Property, Taxation Records Search property records free at http://propertyrecords.montcopa.org/Main/home.aspx. Also, search parcels and court data at http://webapp.montcopa.org/PSI/Viewer/Search.aspx?oq=Yz1DYXNlU2VhcmNoJnBhbmVsPUNhc2VOdW1iZXI%3d. Also, a private company sells county tax claim property, view list free at www.xspand.com/investors/realestate_sale/index.aspx.

Montour County ***Recorded Documents, Marriage Records*** www.montourco.org/RegisterRecorder/Pages/RegisterRecorder.aspx Access to Recorder of Deeds data is by subscription from a private company, visit www.infoconcountyaccess.com/. Also includes Register of Wills, Prothonotary, Clerk of Courts. Also, access to the index of wills free at www.montourco.org/RegisterRecorder/Lists/Index%20Of%20Wills/AllItems.aspx. **$$$**

Northampton County ***Recorded Documents*** www.northamptoncounty.org/northampton/site/default.asp Access to land records for a fee at www.landex.com/webstore/jsp/cart/DocumentSearch.jsp. Both online and images for deeds from 12/1985 to present. Both mortgages from 9/1963 to present and misc from 11/1958 to present. Online maps from 1993 to present, images from 1/2003 to present. Fees $.20 per minute. **$$$**

Property, Taxation Records Access to assessor's property records data is free at www.ncpub.org/Main/Home.aspx.

Northumberland County ***Recorded Documents*** Access to land records for a fee at www.landex.com/webstore/jsp/cart/DocumentSearch.jsp. Online for land records from 1928 to present, images from 1903 to present. Marriage licensed for online from 1950 to present, images from 1946 to present. Fees $.20 per minute. **$$$**

Perry County ***Recorded Documents*** Access to land records for a fee at www.landex.com/webstore/jsp/cart/DocumentSearch.jsp. Online for Recorder of Deeds from 1906 to present, images from 1820 to present. Both for marriage licensed from 1885 to present. Online estates from 1820 to present (remote only). Fees $.10 per minute/$.05 per page viewed. **$$$**

Property, Taxation Records Access property data by subscription at www.courthouseonline.com/MyProperty.asp. Sub fee $9.95 3-days, up to $275 per year. A free view available if you have control number and password from tax notice or are registered.

Philadelphia County ***Recorded Documents*** www.phila.gov/Records/index.html Name search recorder data for a fee at http://philadox.phila.gov/picris/splash.jsp; registration required; $15.00 for (1) hour, $40.00 for (1) 24-hour day, $60.00 for (1) 7-day week, $125.00 for

(1) full month. $750 per year. Images go back to 1974, index to 1957. Assess to Prothonotary records is free at http://fjdweb2.phila.gov/fjd1/repl1/zk_fjd_public_qry_00.zp_main_idx.html. Also, includes judgments and liens on behalf of governmental entities. **$$$**

Property, Taxation Records Search property assessment data for free at http://opa.phila.gov/opa.apps/Search/Disclaimer/disclaimer.aspx?url=search. No name searching. Also, search Board of Revision of Taxes records for free at http://brtweb.phila.gov/index.aspx. No name searching.

Pike County ***Recorded Documents*** www.pikepa.org/recdeed.html A private company offers online access to most Prothonotary records. Call Infocon at 814-472-6066, www.infoconcountyaccess.com. **$$$**

Property, Taxation Records Access parcel data and GIS/mapping for free at www.pikegis.org/pike/disclaimer.htm.

Potter County ***Recorded Documents*** www.pottercountypa.net/register_deeds.php A private company offers online access to most Prothonotary records. Call Infocon at 814-472-6066, www.infoconcountyaccess.com. Also, access to land records for a fee go to www.landex.com/webstore/jsp/cart/DocumentSearch.jsp. Online data from 1997 to present. Iimages from 2003 to present. Fees $.10 per minute/$.05 per page viewed. **$$$**

Schuylkill County ***Recorded Documents*** www.co.schuylkill.pa.us/Offices/RecorderOfDeeds/RecorderOfDeeds.asp Search marriage dockets free at www.co.schuylkill.pa.us/info/Offices/Archives/MarriageDockets.csp. Also, judgments on civil court files at www.co.schuylkill.pa.us/info/Civil/Inquiry/Search.csp.

Property, Taxation Records Access items for the sheriff sale free at www.co.schuylkill.pa.us/Offices/Sheriff/Sale.asp. Click on your choice at the left of the page.

Snyder County ***Property, Taxation Records*** Access to GIS/mapping for free at www.snydercounty.org/Depts/GIS/Pages/GIS.aspx.

Somerset County ***Recorded Documents*** www.co.somerset.pa.us Access property records by monthly subscription; $35.00 start-up fee plus $10.00 per month. For info or signup, call Cindy or John at 814-445-1536. Provide your email, company info and check. System to provide images and comparable sales. Access to land records for a fee go to www.landex.com/webstore/jsp/cart/DocumentSearch.jsp. Online and images for Recorder of Deeds from 1985 to present. Fees $.20 per minute. Access to real estate records at www.co.somerset.pa.us/pages/realestatehome.asp. Also, access to complaints/pleadings, judgments/liens, miscellaneous actions, scanned images on certain cases for a fee go to www.infoconcountyaccess.com/. **$$$**

Property, Taxation Records Access property data free at www.co.somerset.pa.us/realestatesearch.asp?agree=1.

Sullivan County ***Recorded Documents*** www.sullivancounty-pa.us Access to land records for a fee at www.landex.com/webstore/jsp/cart/DocumentSearch.jsp. Online for Recorder of Deeds from 1980 to present, images from 1847 to present. Fees $.10 per minute/$.05 per page viewed. **$$$**

Susquehanna County ***Recorded Documents*** www.susqco.com/subsites/gov/pages/govhome.htm Access to land records for a fee at www.landex.com/webstore/jsp/cart/DocumentSearch.jsp. Online and images for land data from 1974 to present. Both for marriage from 1977 to present. Fees $.10 per minute/$.05 per page viewed. Also, a private company offers online access to recorded documents and many Prothonotary records. Call Infocon at 814-472-6066, www.infoconcountyaccess.com. **$$$**

Property, Taxation Records Access property data by subscription at www.courthouseonline.com/MyProperty.asp. Sub fee $9.95 3-days, up to $275 per year. A free view available if you have control number and password from tax notice or are registered.**$$$**

Tioga County ***Recorded Documents*** www.tiogacountypa.us/Departments/Register_Recorder/Pages/RegisterofWills_RecorderofDeeds_ClerkofOrphans%27Court.aspx Access to land records for a fee at www.landex.com/webstore/jsp/cart/DocumentSearch.jsp. Online for Recorder of Deeds Index from 1977 to present, images from 1806 to present. Fees $.20 per minute. **$$$**

Property, Taxation Records Access property data by subscription at www.courthouseonline.com/MyProperty.asp. Sub fee $9.95 3-days, up to $275 per year. A free view available if you have control number and password from tax notice or are registered. Sheriff sales lists also available free online at www.tiogacountypa.us/Departments/Sheriff%27s_Office/Pages/SheriffSales.aspx.**$$$**

Union County ***Recorded Documents*** www.unionco.org Access to Register of Deeds land records for a fee at https://pa.uslandrecords.com/palr_new/PalrApp/index.jsp. Online records go back to 1/1962. **$$$**

Property, Taxation Records Access to GIS/mapping for free at www.unioncountypa.org/residents/government/land/assessment/. Also, access to land records for a fee for the images at https://pa.uslandrecords.com/palr_new/PalrApp/index.jsp. Fees are $.50 per page with maximum charge of $5.00 per document.**$$$**

Venango County ***Property, Taxation Records*** Access property data by subscription at www.courthouseonline.com/MyProperty.asp. Subscription fee $9.95 3-days, up to $374.95 per year. A free view available if you have control number and password from tax notice. Also, access to GIS/mapping free at http://gis.venangopa.us/parcelviewer/default.aspx**$$$**

Warren County ***Recorded Documents*** www.warrencountypa.net/current/depts.php?name=Register%20-%20Recorder A private company offers online access to most Prothonotary records. Call Infocon at 814-472-6066, www.infoconcountyaccess.com. **$$$**

Washington County ***Recorded Documents*** www.co.washington.pa.us Access to land records for a fee at www.landex.com/webstore/jsp/cart/DocumentSearch.jsp. All land related documents in the Recorder of Deeds office are from 1781 to present. Fees $.10 per minute/$.05 per page viewed. Also, access to online subscription information call Steve Tkach. **$$$**

Property, Taxation Records Access treasurer real estate tax data free at http://washcounty.info/wcmtp/tri.asp.

Wayne County ***Property, Taxation Records*** Search assessor property data free at http://taxpub.co.wayne.pa.us/Main.asp.

Westmoreland County ***Recorded Documents*** www.co.westmoreland.pa.us/index.aspx?nid=146 Register's old fee-based system has been replaced by a free, searchable site at www.wcdeeds.us/dts/default.asp. Choose simple, advanced, or instrument search.

Property, Taxation Records A variety of county records are accessible online from www.co.westmoreland.pa.us/index.aspx?NID=1572. Subscription services from http://pa-westmorelandcounty.civicplus.com/index.aspx?nid=1041. Property tax, estate search, and marriage license search from http://westmorelandweb400.us:8088/EGSPublicAccess.htm.**$$$**

York County ***Recorded Documents*** https://yorkcountypa.gov/property-taxes/recorder-of-deeds.html Access to land records for a fee at www.landex.com/webstore/jsp/cart/DocumentSearch.jsp. Online and images for Recorder of Deeds from 1981 to present. Fees $.20 per minute. Access to records for free at www.yorkcountypa.gov, select department directory, select Prothonotary, click on civil case search, read instructions 3/4 down the page. **$$$**

Property, Taxation Records Access to GIS/mapping for free at http://gis.york-county.org/.

Rhode Island

Capital: Providence
Providence County
Time Zone: EST
Population: 1,050,292
# of Counties: 5

Useful State Links

Website: www.ri.gov/
Governor: www.governor.state.ri.us
Attorney General: www.riag.ri.gov
State Archives: http://sos.ri.gov/archives/
State Statutes and Codes: http://webserver.rilin.state.ri.us/Statutes/Statutes.html
Legislative Bill Search: http://webserver.rilin.state.ri.us/legislation/
Unclaimed Funds: www.treasury.ri.gov/unclaimedproperty/

State Public Record Agencies

Sexual Offender Registry

Sex Offender Community Notification Unit, www.paroleboard.ri.gov/ Website information about a sex offender is available to the public only if the Sex Offender Board of Review has classified the offender as a Level 3, or as a Level 2 as of January 1, 2006. Go to www.paroleboard.ri.gov/sexoffender/agree.php. Also, search by town or ZIP.

Incarceration Records

Rhode Island Department of Corrections, Records, www.doc.ri.gov/index.php A free DOC search is available at www.doc.ri.gov/inmate_search/index.php. The database only has inmates currently incarcerated and there is a 24 hour lag time on updates.

Corporation, LLC, LP, LLP, Fictitious Name

Secretary of State, Corporations Division, http://sos.ri.gov/ At the web, search filings for active and inactive Rhode Island and foreign business corporations, non-profit corporations, limited partnerships, limited liability companies, and limited liability partnerships. Weekly listings of new corporations are also available. There is no fee. A variety of certifications can also be requested, fees involved. Online filing is available for corporations, LLCs and LPs. *Other Options:* Various databases may be downloaded or purchased on CD. Call for pricing.

Trademarks/Servicemarks

Secretary of State, Trademark Section, http://sos.ri.gov/ Search the trademark/servicemark database at http://ucc.state.ri.us/trademarks/trademarksearch.asp.

Uniform Commercial Code

UCC Section, Secretary of State, http://sos.ri.gov/business/ucc/ View debtor names in the Pubic Search Index at http://sos.ri.gov/business/ucc/database/. One may also search by file number or business organization. Rhode Island's UCC Public Search Index allows its users to search using both Standard Search Logic and Non-Standard Search Logic. *Other Options:* Bulk data can be purchased by request. Call for details.

Sales Tax Registrations

Taxation Division, Sales & Use Tax Office, www.tax.state.ri.us View administrative decisions by this office at www.tax.state.ri.us/AdministrativeDecisions/. Search by Tax Type or Decision Number.

Driver Records

Division of Motor Vehicles, Driving Record Clerk, Operator Control, www.dmv.ri.gov Driving records are available in two manners. From the home page above, anyone may request a record online, pay the $20.00 service fee with a credit card and the record will be mailed to the address shown on the DL. This record does not contain the driver's address or SSN. The driver name. DOB and license number must be submitted. Ongoing requesters who qualify to receive records with personal information may obtain a subscription account for interactive service. The same record fee applies. For more information about becoming a subscriber visit www.ri.gov/subscriber/. **$$$**

Vehicle Ownership & Registration

Division of Motor Vehicles, Vehicle Records, www.dmv.ri.gov This application allows RI.gov subscribers to access title records currently on file with the Rhode Island Division of Motor Vehicles. The record presented is the most recent record on file with the Division of Motor Vehicles. Historical records must be obtained in person or by mail. The total fee for this service is $53.30. For more information on becoming a subscriber call 401-831-8099 x230 or visit www.ri.gov/subscriber. **$$$** *Other Options:* Bulk retrieval of vehicle and ownership information is limited to statistical purposes.

Accident Reports

Rhode Island State Police, Accident Reports, www.risp.ri.gov/ The agency has outsourced online record requests to a vendor at www.getcrashreports.com/. Search by name or by any number of factors. Fee is $20.00. Records include reports from at least 32 cities/towns in Rhode Island. The site works well, provides detailed information, but lacks upfront details on costs and record throughput. One must basically to go through the order process to find these details. There is a subscription program for ongoing requesters, but no details given until the third step in the order process. **$$$**

Voter Registration. Campaign Finance PACs

Secretary of State, Elections Division, www.sos.ri.gov A specific look-up or verification of voter registration is available at http://sos.ri.gov/vic/. The name, DOB and town is needed. The search shows voter preferences. Also, one may make requests by email at elections@sos.ri.gov. Search candidate, PAC, and committee filed reports at www.elections.ri.gov/finance/publicinfo/. *Other Options:* The web offers voter lists sales statewide on paper ($700) or CD ($25). Customized lists are also available. Click on Voter Registration List at the home page.

Occupational Licensing Boards

Accountant Firm .... www.dbr.state.ri.us/documents/divisions/accountancy/Licensed_Public_Accounting_Firms.pdf
Accountant-CPA, PA .... www.dbr.state.ri.us/documents/divisions/accountancy/LicensedCPAsandPAs.pdf
Acupuncturist .... https://healthri.mylicense.com/Verification/
Alarm Agent/Company .... www.dlt.ri.gov/profregsonline/PROLentree.aspx
Ambulatory Care Facility .... https://healthri.mylicense.com/Verification/
Asbestos Worker .... https://healthri.mylicense.com/Verification/
Assisted Living Facility/Admin .... https://healthri.mylicense.com/Verification/
Athletic Trainer .... https://healthri.mylicense.com/Verification/
Attorney .... http://rijrs.courts.ri.gov/rijrs/attorney.do
Auctioneer .... www.dbr.state.ri.us/documents/divisions/commlicensing/auctioneering/auct-Licensee_List.pdf
Audiologist .... www.health.ri.gov/licenses/healthcare/index.php
Automobile Body Shop .... www.dbr.state.ri.us/documents/divisions/commlicensing/autobody/Auto_Body_Shop_-_Licensee_List.pdf
Automobile Glass Installer .... www.dbr.state.ri.us/documents/divisions/commlicensing/autoglass/Auto_Glass_-_Licensee_List.pdf
Automobile Wrecker .... www.dbr.state.ri.us/documents/divisions/commlicensing/autowrecking/Auto_Wrecking_-_Licensee_List.pdf
Barber/Barber Instructor/Ship .... www.health.ri.gov/licenses/healthcare/index.php
Birth Center .... https://healthri.mylicense.com/Verification/
Blood Test Screener .... https://healthri.mylicense.com/Verification/
Business Filing/Annual Report .... http://sos.ri.gov/publicinfo/lobbying/
Charter School .... www.ride.ri.gov
Chemical Dependency Clinical Spvr/Prof/Adv .... www.ribccdp.com/LISTS.html
Chiropractor .... https://healthri.mylicense.com/Verification/
Clinical Lab Scientist/Technician/Cytogenetic .... https://healthri.mylicense.com/Verification/Search.aspx
Contractor, Resid'l Building .... www.crb.state.ri.us/search.php
Contractor, Watch List .... www.crb.state.ri.us/watchlist.php
Controlled Substance Wholesaler .... https://healthri.mylicense.com/Verification/
Cosmetologist/Cosmetology Instructor .... www.health.ri.gov/licenses/healthcare/index.php
Counselor in Training .... www.ribccdp.com/LISTS.html
Criminal Justice Professional .... www.ribccdp.com/LISTS.html

Day Care, Children	www.dcyf.state.ri.us/day_care_provider.php
Dentist/Dental Hygienist	https://healthri.mylicense.com/Verification/
Dietitian/Nutritionist	https://healthri.mylicense.com/Verification/
Electrician	www.dlt.ri.gov/profregsonline/PROLentree.aspx
Electrologist	https://healthri.mylicense.com/Verification/
Embalmer	https://healthri.mylicense.com/Verification/
Emergency Care Facility	https://healthri.mylicense.com/Verification/
Emergency Med Technician/Service	https://healthri.mylicense.com/Verification/
Esthetician/Manicurist/Shop	www.health.ri.gov/licenses/healthcare/index.php
Funeral Director	https://healthri.mylicense.com/Verification/
Hazardous Waste Transporter	www.dem.ri.gov/programs/benviron/waste/transpor/index.htm
Health Club	www.dbr.state.ri.us/documents/divisions/commlicensing/mobile/MobileHomesParksList.pdf
Hearing Aid Dispenser	https://healthri.mylicense.com/Verification/
Hoisting Engineer	www.dlt.ri.gov/profregsonline/PROLentree.aspx
Home Nursing Care Provider	https://healthri.mylicense.com/Verification/
Hospice Provider	https://healthri.mylicense.com/Verification/
Hospital	https://healthri.mylicense.com/Verification/
Hypodermic Dispenser	https://healthri.mylicense.com/Verification/
Insurance Broker/Producer/Agent	www.dbr.ri.gov/divisions/insurance/licensed.php
Interpreter for the Deaf	https://healthri.mylicense.com/Verification/
Investment Advisor	www.adviserinfo.sec.gov/IAPD/Content/Search/iapd_Search.aspx
Laboratory/Medical	https://healthri.mylicense.com/Verification/
Lobbyist Registration	http://sos.ri.gov/publicinfo/lobbying/
Marriage & Family Therapist	https://healthri.mylicense.com/Verification/
Massage Therapist	https://healthri.mylicense.com/Verification/
Medical Waste Transporter	www.dem.ri.gov/programs/benviron/waste/transpor/index.htm
Midwife	https://healthri.mylicense.com/Verification/
Mobile Home Park	www.dbr.state.ri.us/documents/divisions/commlicensing/mobile/MobileHomesParksList.pdf
Mortgage Broker	www.dbr.state.ri.us/documents/divisions/banking/program_operations/List_of_Licensees.pdf
Notary Public	http://ucc.state.ri.us/notarysearch/onlinesearch.asp
Nurse-LPN/Aide	https://healthri.mylicense.com/Verification/
Nursing Home Administrator	https://healthri.mylicense.com/Verification/
Nursing Service	https://healthri.mylicense.com/Verification/
Occupational Therapist	https://healthri.mylicense.com/Verification/
Open Meeting	http://sos.ri.gov/publicinfo/openmeetings/
Optician	https://healthri.mylicense.com/Verification/
Optometrist	https://healthri.mylicense.com/Verification/
Outpatient Rehabilitation	https://healthri.mylicense.com/Verification/
Pharmacist/Pharmacy/Technician	https://healthri.mylicense.com/Verification/
Phlebotomy Station	https://healthri.mylicense.com/Verification/
Physical Therapist/Assistant	https://healthri.mylicense.com/Verification/
Physician/Medical Doctor/Assistant	https://healthri.mylicense.com/Verification/
Physicians Controlled Substance	https://healthri.mylicense.com/Verification/
Pipefitter	www.dlt.ri.gov/profregsonline/PROLentree.aspx
Plumber/Master Plumber/Journey'n	www.dlt.ri.gov/profregsonline/PROLentree.aspx
Podiatrist	https://healthri.mylicense.com/Verification/
Prevention Specialist/Supvr/Advanced	www.ribccdp.com/LISTS.html
Prosthetist	https://healthri.mylicense.com/Verification/
Psychologist	https://healthri.mylicense.com/Verification/
Radiation Therapist	https://healthri.mylicense.com/Verification/
Radiographer	https://healthri.mylicense.com/Verification/
Real Estate Agent/Seller	www.dbr.state.ri.us/pdf_forms/RE-Real%20Estate%20Salespersons.pdf
Real Estate Appraiser	www.dbr.state.ri.us/pdf_forms/RE-Real%20Estate%20Appraisers.pdf
Real Estate Broker	www.dbr.state.ri.us/pdf_forms/RE-Real%20Estate%20Brokers.pdf
Residential Care Facility	https://healthri.mylicense.com/Verification/

Respiratory Care Practitioner	https://healthri.mylicense.com/Verification/
Roofer, Commercial	www.crb.state.ri.us/search.php
Salvage Yard	www.dbr.state.ri.us/documents/divisions/commlicensing/autowrecking/Auto_Wrecking_-_Licensee_List.pdf
Sanitarian	https://healthri.mylicense.com/Verification/
Securities Broker/Dealer/Seller	www.finra.org/Investors/ToolsCalculators/BrokerCheck/p085698
Septic Transporter	www.dem.ri.gov/programs/benviron/waste/transpor/index.htm
Social Worker	https://healthri.mylicense.com/Verification/
Speech/Language Pathologist	https://healthri.mylicense.com/Verification/
Student Assistance Counselor	www.ribccdp.com/LISTS.html
Tanning Facility	https://healthri.mylicense.com/Verification/
Tattoo Artist	https://healthri.mylicense.com/Verification/
Telecommunications Technician	www.dlt.ri.gov/profregsonline/PROLentree.aspx
Upholstery/Bedding Mfg	www.dbr.state.ri.us/documents/divisions/commlicensing/upholstery/Upholstery-Licensee_List.pdf
Veterinarian	https://healthri.mylicense.com/Verification/
X-Ray Equipment (Portable)/Facility	https://healthri.mylicense.com/Verification/

State and Local Courts

State Court Structure: The **Superior Court** has original jurisdiction in all felony proceedings, in civil cases where the amount in controversy exceeds $10,000, and in equity matters. The court has concurrent jurisdiction with the District Court in civil matters when the amount in controversy is between $5,000 and $10,000.

The **District Court** has exclusive jurisdiction of all civil actions at law wherein the amount in controversy is under $5,000. The District Court handles arraignments for felony and misdemeanor cases. Misdemeanor cases are punishable for up to one year in prison and fines are not to exceed $1,000. There are no jury trials heard in District Court.

Rhode Island has five counties but only four **Superior/District Court Locations**— 2nd-Newport, 3rd-Kent, 4th-Washington, and 6th-Providence/Bristol Districts. Bristol and Providence counties are completely merged at the Providence location. 26 of the 39 cities and towns in Rhode Island have **Municipal Courts**. In general, Municipal Courts oversee traffic, ordinance, housing and zoning violations, but not every court has authority in all areas. The Municipal Courts do not hear cases involving state criminal laws nor are they administrated by the State Court Administrator's Office. For more information on municipalities, see www.muni-info.ri.gov.

Probate is handled by the Town Clerk at the 39 cities and towns, not at the Superior or District courts. The contact information is shown herein.

Civil traffic violations will be heard either at a Municipal Court or at the **Traffic Tribunal which** has original jurisdiction over civil traffic offenses committed in Rhode Island, including breathalyzer refusals. Reach the Traffic Tribunal at 401-275-2700.

Appellate Courts: Supreme Court and Appellate opinions are available from the judicial home page at www.courts.ri.gov

Statewide Court Online Access: All courts participate in the system described below.

- The Rhode Island Judiciary offers free access to an index of county criminal cases statewide at http://courtconnect.courts.state.ri.us. Access to civil records is not available (regardless of what drop down box says).
- There are a couple of cautions. The online site is known to show cases that were sealed or were supposed to be removed. Only the year of birth is shown on results. And the site provides a very strong disclaimer. The disclaimer specifically states the following regarding background checks or employment screening:

  > "This website is provided as an informational service only and does not constitute and should not be relied upon as an official record and/or schedule of the court. Since the full date of birth and other personally identifying information is not included in this service, the information contained herein shall not be relied upon to confirm a person's identity or a person's criminal record for any purpose including, but not limited to, background checks or employment."

- The disclaimer also states that the court employees will not confirm case content referenced for the Web service by telephone. There is no statewide access to other types of court records, including civil, family or probate.

Note: No individual Rhode Island court offers online access, other than as described above.

Recorders, Assessors, and Other Sites of Note

Recording Office Organization: 5 counties and 39 towns, 39 recording offices. There is **no county recording** in this state. All recording is done at the city/town level. Be aware that three sites bear the same name as their respective counties. Therefore, the recordings within the counties of Bristol, Newport, and Providence can relate to property located in cities/towns other than the individual cities of Bristol, Newport, and Providence. The recording officers are the Town/City Clerks. The Town/City Clerk usually also serves as Recorder of Deeds. All federal and state tax liens on personal property and on real property are filed with the Recorder of Deeds.

Statewide or Multi-Jurisdiction Access: A few jurisdictions provide online searching although access, generally, is provided by vendor companies. Searching is almost always free; there are a few exceptions. Two

- Gis mapping and property appraisal data is provided by a vendor for a number of towns on the Internet; visit www.vgsi.com/vision/Applications/ParcelData/RI/Home.aspx. Note this URL will give you the main site to VISION Government Solutions and then you must click on each individual town for the data. The ensuing URL begins with data.visionappraisal.com for each town.

County Sites:

Bristol County

Barrington Town ***Property, Taxation Records*** Access to GIS/mapping for free at www.mainstreetmaps.com/RI/Barrington/.

Bristol Town ***Property, Taxation Records*** Access property data on a private site at www.clipboardinc.com/bristolsearchpage.html.

Warren Town ***Real Estate Records*** www.townofwarren-ri.gov/departmentsaz/townclerk.html Access to record viewing free at https://i2b.uslandrecords.com/Warren/Default.aspx?AspxAutoDetectCookieSupport=1. Printing and/or downloading will incur charges. **$$$**
Property, Taxation Records Access property and assessor data free on the private site at www.nereval.com/OnlineDatabases.aspx. Also, plat records are available free at www.townofwarren-ri.gov/documentlibraries/platmaps.html.

Kent County

Coventry Town ***Property, Taxation Records*** Property data is listed on a private site at www.nereval.com/SearchInfo.aspx?town=Coventry.

East Greenwich Town ***Voter Registration Records*** www.eastgreenwichri.com Access to voter registration free at http://sos.ri.gov/vic/.
Property, Taxation Records Access property data on a private site at www.nereval.com/OnlineDatabases.aspx.

Warwick City ***Property, Taxation Records*** Access to property searches found at http://data.visionappraisal.com/WarwickRI/DEFAULT.asp.

West Greenwich Town ***Property, Taxation Records*** Access property data free at www.crcpropertyinfo.com/crcdb/westgreenwich.htm.

Newport County

Jamestown Town ***Property, Taxation Records*** Plat Map data for free at www.jamestownri.net/pw/gis/platmaps.html. Also, access to Assessor's online database free at http://data.visionappraisal.com/JamestownRI/DEFAULT.asp.

Little Compton Town ***Property, Taxation Records*** Access assessor property data free at http://data.visionappraisal.com/LittleComptonRI/DEFAULT.asp.

Middletown Town ***Real Estate, Grantor/Grantee Records*** www.middletownri.com/ Access to records for free at https://i2b.uslandrecords.com/Middletown/(X(1)S(hrutx1vyu5vxy0n2qagnggf1))/Default.aspx?AspxAutoDetectCookieSupport=1. Printing or downloading will incur charges. **$$$**
Property, Taxation Records Records on the town assessor database are online at http://data.visionappraisal.com/MiddletownRI/DEFAULT.asp.

Newport City ***Property, Taxation Records*** Access is via a private company at http://data.visionappraisal.com/NewportRI/DEFAULT.asp.

Portsmouth Town ***Recorded Documents Records*** www.portsmouthri.com/clerk/ Access to records found at https://i2b.uslandrecords.com/Portsmouth/Default.aspx?AspxAutoDetectCookieSupport=1. Searching and document viewing are provided as a free service. Printing and/or downloading will incur charges. **$$$**

Property, Taxation Records Search town assessor database at http://data.visionappraisal.com/PortsmouthRI/DEFAULT.asp.

Tiverton Town ***Recorded Records Records*** www.tiverton.ri.gov/government/townclerk.html Access to record viewing free at https://i2b.uslandrecords.com/RI/Tiverton/Default.aspx?AspxAutoDetectCookieSupport=1. For images and printing a fee is charged. Information regarding fees on above site. Records go back to 1/1/84. **$$$**

Property, Taxation Records Access tax rolls and tax bills free at www.tiverton.ri.gov/government/assessor.html. Also search free at www.crcpropertyinfo.com/crcdb/tiverton.htm.

Providence County

Burrillville Town ***Recorded Documents Records*** www.burrillville.org/Public_Documents/BurrillvilleRI_Clerk/clerk Access to recorded documents free at www.burrillville.org/Public_Documents/BurrillvilleRI_Clerk/landevidence. Document index from 1977 to present; images from 12/87 to present. There is a fee for printing or downloading. **$$$**

Property, Taxation Records Access to property records is free at www.crcpropertyinfo.com/crcdb/burrillville.htm. Also, access to GIS/mapping free at www.mainstreetmaps.com/RI/Burrillville/.

Central Falls City ***Property, Taxation Records*** Access to city property data is free at http://data.visionappraisal.com/CentralFallsRI/. Does not require username & password, simply click on link. Also, search property data free at www.nereval.com/OnlineDatabases.aspx.

Cranston City ***Property, Taxation Records*** Records on the city assessor database are online at http://data.visionappraisal.com/CranstonRI/DEFAULT.asp. Free registration is required for full data. Also, access to 2012 tax roll and Assessor maps free at www.cranstonri.com/taxfiles2012.php or at http://gis.cranstonri.org/assessor_flex/.

Cumberland Town ***Property, Taxation Records*** Access to property data is free at www.crcpropertyinfo.com/crcdb/search.asp?lcUserName=cumberland&lcUserPass=freepass&lcTownName=cumberland.

East Providence City ***Property, Taxation Records*** Access to Town property data is free at http://data.visionappraisal.com/EastProvidenceRI/DEFAULT.asp.

Foster Town ***Property, Taxation Records*** Access property data free at www.crcpropertyinfo.com/crcdb/foster.htm.

Glocester Town ***Real Estate, Grantor/Grantee Records*** www.glocesterri.org/townclerk.htm Access to land records free at https://i2b.uslandrecords.com/RI/Glocester/(X(1)S(hb3o50ngfv2qzp45zqjohk55))/Default.aspx?AspxAutoDetectCookieSupport=1. Indexes available from 8/1965 to present; images available from 9/2002 to present. Fees for Commercial users, pay=per access members/search and search results printing. **$$$**

Property, Taxation Records Access property data free at www.glocesterri.org/taxassessor.htm. Also, access to Assessor's maps 1-20 for free at www.glocesterri.org/taxassessor.htm#gis.

Johnston Town ***Property, Taxation Records*** Access to Town property data is free at http://data.visionappraisal.com/JohnstonRI/DEFAULT.asp.

Lincoln Town ***Property, Taxation Records*** Property data free at www.crcpropertyinfo.com/crcdb/lincoln.htm.

North Providence Town ***Property, Taxation Records*** Access property data on a private site at www.nereval.com/OnlineDatabases.aspx.

North Smithfield Town ***Property, Taxation Records*** Access is via a private company at http://data.visionappraisal.com/NorthSmithfieldRI/DEFAULT.asp.

Pawtucket City ***Recorded Documents Records*** www.pawtucketri.com Access real estate data free at http://72.248.180.6/alis/ww400r.pgm. Online indices go back to 1970.

Property, Taxation Records Search the assessor database free at http://data.visionappraisal.com/PawtucketRI/DEFAULT.asp.

Providence City ***Property, Taxation Records*** Search the assessor database free at http://gis.vgsi.com/providenceri/. Property tax card data available free at http://providence.ias-clt.com/parcel.list.php.

Scituate Town ***Property, Taxation Records*** Access to town property data is free at www.crcpropertyinfo.com/crcdb/scituate.htm.

Smithfield Town ***Property, Taxation Records*** Access to town property data is free at http://data.visionappraisal.com/SmithfieldRI/DEFAULT.asp. Tax Rolls and tax bills are also free online at https://www.opaldata.net/VGSITaxRolls/PublicMain.aspx?MunID=SmithfieldTown&VGSIMenu=ON.

Woonsocket City ***Property, Taxation Records*** Access assessor data free at http://data.visionappraisal.com/WoonsocketRI/DEFAULT.asp. Also, access to GIS/mapping free at http://ceo.fando.com/Woonsocket/

Washington County

Charlestown Town *Recorded Documents Records* http://www.charlestownri.org

Property, Taxation Records Search town assessor database at http://data.visionappraisal.com/CharlestownRI/DEFAULT.asp. Searching and document viewing for free at https://i2b.uslandrecords.com/charlestown/(X(1)S(bgwcejarwbfowy45j5emdp2p))/Default.aspx?AspxAutoDetectCookieSupport=1. There is a fee for printing and/or downloading.

Exeter Town *Property, Taxation Records*

Access property data free at www.crcpropertyinfo.com/crcdb/exeter.htm. Access to real estate tax collection data is by subscription from a private company at www.opaldata.net/OnlineTax/.

Hopkinton Town *Property, Taxation Records*

Access to town property data is free at www.hopkintonri.org/Assessor.htm, Also, access property data free at www.crcpropertyinfo.com/crcdb/hopkinton.htm.

Narragansett Town *Recorded Documents Records* www.narragansettri.gov/index.aspx?nid=331

Access to recorded land records free at https://i2b.uslandrecords.com/Narragansett/Default.aspx?AspxAutoDetectCookieSupport=1.

Property, Taxation Records Access to assessors online database for free at http://data.visionappraisal.com/NarragansettRI/DEFAULT.asp.

New Shoreham, Town of *Property, Taxation Records*

Access to Town property data is free at http://data.visionappraisal.com/NewShorehamRI/DEFAULT.asp.

North Kingstown Town *Property, Taxation Records*

Access is via a private company at http://data.visionappraisal.com/NorthKingstownRI/DEFAULT.asp.

Richmond Town *Property, Taxation Records*

Search town assessor database at http://data.visionappraisal.com/RichmondRI/DEFAULT.asp.

South Kingstown Town *Real Estate, Deed, Lien, Mortgage, Judgment Records* www.southkingstownri.com

Access town real estate data free at http://70.168.204.238/ALIS/WW400R.HTM. Land indexes go back to 1975 and images go back to Oct, 1979; complete excluding maps. Land indexes only go back to 1980; More to be added. Registration required for full data. **$$$**

Property, Taxation Records Access to the property values database is free at www.southkingstownri.com/taxroll/. Also, assess to Town property data is free at http://data.visionappraisal.com/SouthKingstownRI/DEFAULT.asp.

Westerly Town *Recorded Documents Records* www.westerly.govoffice.com/index.asp?

Access to records free at https://i2b.uslandrecords.com/westerly/Default.aspx. Index and document images back to 1909.

Property, Taxation Records Access town property assessment data free at http://data.visionappraisal.com/WesterlyRI/DEFAULT.asp. Also, access prior tax rolls and tax bills free at www.westerly.govoffice.com/index.asp and click on "Land Records Online." Also, access to GIS/mapping free at http://ags2.cdm.com/fl/westerlyri/main.html.

South Carolina

Capital: Columbia
Richland County
Time Zone: EST
Population: 4,723,723
# of Counties: 46

Useful State Links

Website: www.sc.gov
Governor: www.governor.sc.gov/
Attorney General: www.scattorneygeneral.org
State Archives: http://scdah.sc.gov/
State Statutes and Codes: www.scstatehouse.gov/research.php
Legislative Bill Search: www.scstatehouse.gov
Unclaimed Funds: www.treasurer.sc.gov/palmetto_payback_unclaimed_property/Pages/default.aspx

State Public Record Agencies

Criminal Records

South Carolina Law Enforcement Division (SLED), Criminal Records Section, www.sled.sc.gov/ SLED offers commercial access to criminal record history from 1960 forward on the website. Fees are $25.00 per screening or $8.00 if for a charitable organization. Credit card ordering accepted. Visit the website for details. Documentation of charitable status is required **$$$**

Sexual Offender Registry

Sex Offender Registry, c/o SLED, www.communitynotification.com/cap_main.php?office=54575 Access is available from the website. Search by name, address including ZIP Code, county or city, or by email/Internet. A complete, viewable list of all offenders is shown, with pictures and addresses.

Incarceration Records

Department of Corrections, Inmate Records Branch, www.doc.sc.gov/pubweb/ The Inmate Search on the Internet is found at www.doc.sc.gov/pubweb/InmateSearchDisclaimer.jsp, or click on Inmate search at the main website.

Corporation, LP, LLP, LLC, Trademarks/Servicemarks

Corporation Division, 1205 Pendleton Street, www.sos.sc.gov/ One may search business filings and a database of registered charities from the home page. The database provides access to basic filing information about any entity filed with the office. Registered agents' names and addresses, dates of business filings and types of filings are all available. The database is updated every 48 hours.

Uniform Commercial Code

UCC Division, Secretary of State, www.scsos.com One may do a "free search" to find a filing number, but the fee kicks in to view the documents. A pay system to index of records is at https://ucconline.sc.gov/UCCFiling/UCCMainPage.aspx. Search by debtor name or number. Records are generally current within 48 hours. The fee is $10.00 per search using a credit card. Frequent requesters may obtain a subscription account and be billed. Transactions over $100, increase by $2.25 for each additional $100. Transactions over $100, increasing by $2.25 for each additional $100. There is a $75 annual fee. See https://ucconline.sc.gov/UCCFiling/SubscriptionServices.aspx. **$$$**

Vital Records

South Carolina DHEC, Vital Records, www.scdhec.gov/administration/vr/ Order from state-designated vendor - www.vitalchek.com. See expedited services. **$$$**

Workers' Compensation Records

Workers Compensation Commission, Claims Dept, www.wcc.sc.gov/Pages/default.aspx ECase Status provides with electronic access to workers' compensation cases. Public information for cases on appeal is available to site visitors, and parties to a claim may register to access confidential case status information. See https://wccprogress.sc.gov/wccprod.wsc/onlinereports.html.

Driver License Information, Driver Records

Department of Motor Vehicles, Driver Records Section, www.scdmvonline.com/DMVNew/default.aspx Commercial records are available from the portal https://dmvdhr.sc.gov/DriverHistoryRecords/Interactive/CDBLogin.aspx. Authorized businesses must establish an account through a formal approval and acceptance process. The fee is $7.25 per record and a $75.00 annual fee is required. Members have access to additional online services. For more information about setting up an account, call 803-771-0131 or email support@sc-egov.com. For no fee, at https://www.scdmvonline.com/DMVpublic/trans/DRecPoints.aspx one may view a driver license status. The status includes points history. The DL, SSN and DOB are needed. Also, SC drivers may purchase their own record after viewing at https://www.scdmvonline.com/dmvpublic/trans/DrvRecWarn.aspx. A certified copy is mailed for $6.00. **$$$**

Campaign Finance, Lobbyists, Ethics Violations

State Ethics Commission, 5000 Thurmond Mall, Suite 250, www.scvotes.org/ Search by candidate or by contributor at https://ssl.sc.gov/Ethics/. Search reports at http://apps.sc.gov/PublicReporting/Index.aspx. The State Ethics Commission levies late filing penalties, and enforcement fines against violators. A list is viewable at http://ethics.sc.gov/Debtors/Pages/index.aspx. Search lobbyists and reporting at http://apps.sc.gov/LobbyingActivity/LAIndex.aspx.

Voter Registration

State Election Commission, Records, www.scvotes.org/ Intended to check your own registration, free verification is offered at https://info.scvotes.sc.gov/eng/voterinquiry/VoterInformationRequest.aspx?PageMode=VoterInfon. When checking information, must provide the name, county and date of birth exactly as registered. *Other Options:* Lists, labels, diskettes, and electronic media are available with a variety of sort features. The minimum charge varies from $75 to $160 depending on the media.

GED Certificates

Office fo Adult Educations, GED Testing Office, http://ed.sc.gov/agency/programs-services/92/ One may order an unofficial copy through GED Wizard at https://secure.gedwizard.com/. Students may order a copy of a GED transcript or diploma at www.ed.sc.gov/apps/ged/. The DOB and last four digits of SSN is required. Use of a credit card is required. Fee is $10.OO for document to be delivered by mail, $5.00 if by fax. **$$$**

Occupational Licensing Boards

Accountant-CPA/PA.................................... https://verify.llronline.com/LicLookup/?Aspx
Acupuncturist.. www.llr.state.sc.us/POL/Medical/index.asp?file=licensure.htm
Agricultural Dealer/Handler.......................... www.kellysolutions.com/SC/handlers/showall.asp
Airport Professional/Contact........................ www.scaeronautics.com/directorySearch.asp
Animal Health Technician............................ https://verify.llronline.com/LicLookup/?Aspx
Architect/Architectural Partnership/Corp...... https://verify.llronline.com/LicLookup/LookupMain.aspx
Attorney... www.scbar.org/MemberResources/MemberDirectory.aspx
Auctioneer/Auctioneer Apprentice/Company https://verify.llronline.com/LicLookup/?Aspx
Audiologist.. https://verify.llronline.com/LicLookup/?Aspx
Aviation Facility... www.scaeronautics.com/AirportList.asp
Barber Instructor/School............................. https://verify.llronline.com/LicLookup/?Aspx
Barber/Barber Apprentice........................... https://verify.llronline.com/LicLookup/?Aspx
Bodywork Therapist.................................... https://verify.llronline.com/LicLookup/?Aspx
Building Inspector/Official........................... https://verify.llronline.com/LicLookup/?Aspx
Burglar Alarm Contractor............................ https://verify.llronline.com/LicLookup/?Aspx
Chiropractor.. https://verify.llronline.com/LicLookup/?Aspx
Contact Lens License.................................. https://verify.llronline.com/LicLookup/?Aspx
Contractor, General/Mechanical................. https://verify.llronline.com/LicLookup/?Aspx
Contractor, Specialty Resid'l....................... https://verify.llronline.com/LicLookup/?Aspx
Cosmetologist/Instructor/School................. https://verify.llronline.com/LicLookup/?Aspx
Counselor, Professional/Intern.................... https://verify.llronline.com/LicLookup/?Aspx
Dental Hygienist/Specialist/Technician........ https://verify.llronline.com/LicLookup/?Aspx
Dentist... https://verify.llronline.com/LicLookup/?Aspx
Embalmer.. https://verify.llronline.com/LicLookup/?Aspx

Emergency Medical Technician	www.scdhec.gov/health/ems/CertStatus.htm
Engineer	https://verify.llronline.com/LicLookup/?Aspx
Esthetician/Manicurist/Nail Technician	https://verify.llronline.com/LicLookup/?Aspx
Ethics Debtors	http://ethics.sc.gov/Debtors/Pages/index.aspx
Forester	https://verify.llronline.com/LicLookup/?Aspx
Funeral Director/Home	https://verify.llronline.com/LicLookup/?Aspx
Geologist	https://verify.llronline.com/LicLookup/?Aspx
Hair Care Master Specialist	https://verify.llronline.com/LicLookup/?Aspx
Home Builder, Residential	https://verify.llronline.com/LicLookup/?Aspx
Home Inspector	https://verify.llronline.com/LicLookup/?Aspx
Inspector, Bldg/Housing/Mech/Elec/Plumb	https://verify.llronline.com/LicLookup/?Aspx
Landscape Architect	https://verify.llronline.com/LicLookup/?Aspx
Lobbyist/Principal	http://apps.sc.gov/LobbyingActivity/LAIndex.aspx
Manicure Assistant	https://verify.llronline.com/LicLookup/?Aspx
Manufact'd House Seller/Install/Repair	https://verify.llronline.com/LicLookup/?Aspx
Manufactured House Mfg/Dealer/Rep	https://verify.llronline.com/LicLookup/?Aspx
Marriage & Family Therapist/Intern/Spvr	https://verify.llronline.com/LicLookup/?Aspx
Massage Therapist	https://verify.llronline.com/LicLookup/?Aspx
Notary Public	www.scsos.com/Notaries_and_Apostilles/Notary_Search
Nurse-RN/LPN	https://verify.llronline.com/LicLookup/?Aspx
Nursing Home Administrator	https://verify.llronline.com/LicLookup/?Aspx
Occupational Therapist/Assistant	https://verify.llronline.com/LicLookup/?Aspx
Optician/Apprentice	https://verify.llronline.com/LicLookup/?Aspx
Optometrist	https://verify.llronline.com/LicLookup/?Aspx
Osteopathic Physician	www.llr.state.sc.us/POL/Medical/index.asp?file=licensure.htm
Pesticide Registration	www.kellysolutions.com/clemson/pesticides/pesticideindex.asp
Pharmacist/Pharmacy Technician	https://verify.llronline.com/LicLookup/?Aspx
Pharmacy/Drug Outlet	https://verify.llronline.com/LicLookup/?Aspx
Physical Therapist/Therapist Asst	https://verify.llronline.com/LicLookup/?Aspx
Physician/Medical Doctor/Assistant	www.llr.state.sc.us/POL/Medical/index.asp?file=licensure.htm
Plans Examiner, Building	https://verify.llronline.com/LicLookup/?Aspx
Podiatrist	https://verify.llronline.com/LicLookup/?Aspx
Produce Whlse Dealer	www.kellysolutions.com/SC/handlers/showall.asp
Psycho-Educational Specialist	https://verify.llronline.com/LicLookup/?Aspx
Psychologist	https://verify.llronline.com/LicLookup/?Aspx
Real Estate Appraiser	https://verify.llronline.com/LicLookup/?Aspx
Residential Care, Community	https://verify.llronline.com/LicLookup/?Aspx
Respiratory Care Practitioner	www.llr.state.sc.us/POL/Medical/index.asp?file=licensure.htm
Shampoo Assistant	https://verify.llronline.com/LicLookup/?Aspx
Social Worker	https://verify.llronline.com/LicLookup/?Aspx
Soil Classifier	https://verify.llronline.com/LicLookup/?Aspx
Speech-Language Pathologist	https://verify.llronline.com/LicLookup/?Aspx
Sprinkler Systems Contractor	https://verify.llronline.com/LicLookup/?Aspx
Surveyor, Land	https://verify.llronline.com/LicLookup/?Aspx
Veterinarian	https://verify.llronline.com/LicLookup/?Aspx
Wholesaler/Shipper (Food)	www.kellysolutions.com/SC/handlers/showall.asp

State and Local Courts

State Court Structure: The **Circuit Court** is the state's court of general jurisdiction. It has a civil court called the **Court of Common Pleas**, and a criminal court called the **Court of General Sessions**. In addition to its general trial jurisdiction, the Circuit Court has limited appellate jurisdiction over appeals from the Probate Court, Magistrate's Court, and Municipal Court. Masters-In-Equity have jurisdiction in matters referred to them by the Circuit Courts.

Magistrate Courts (also known as **Summary Courts**) generally have criminal trial jurisdiction over all offenses subject to the penalty of a fine, as set by statute, but generally, not exceeding $500.00 or imprisonment not exceeding 30 days, or both. In addition, they are responsible for setting bail, conducting preliminary hearings, and issuing arrest and search warrants. Magistrates have civil jurisdiction when the amount does not exceed $7,500.

Municipal Courts have jurisdiction over cases arising under ordinances of the municipality, and over all offenses which are subject to a fine not exceeding $500.00 or imprisonment not exceeding 30 days, or both, and which occur within the municipality. In addition Municipal Courts may hear cases transferred from General Sessions when the penalty for which does not exceed one year imprisonment or a fine of $5,000, or both.

Probate Courts have jurisdiction over marriage licenses, estates, guardianships of incompetents, conservatorships of estates of minors and incompetents, minor settlements under $25,000 and involuntary commitments to institutions for mentally ill and/or chemically dependent persons.

The **Family Court** has exclusive jurisdiction over all matters involving domestic or family relationships.

Appellate Courts: Opinions from the Supreme Court and Court of Appeals are viewable from the web page at www.sccourts.org.

Statewide Court Online Access: The web page at www.sccourts.org/caseSearch/ gives individual county links for a case record search. All counties participate. But the search is available on a per-county look-up; there is no statewide single search. Reportedly, the search is equivalent to a search at the court location using the on-site public access terminal.

Many of these county online search sites give users an initial choice between searching for records from a Circuit Court or Summary Court. It is worth noting that a number of local record researchers indicate that not all Summary (Magistrate) Courts' records are online. Also, searchers indicate there are instances when Summary records may be missing cases, sentence details, probation updates/violations.

County Sites:

Abbeville County

Circuit Court www.abbevillecountysc.com/clerkcourt.aspx

Civil: Online access to the index for both the Circuit and Summary courts at http://publicindex.sccourts.org/abbeville/publicindex/. *Criminal:* same as civil.

Aiken County

Circuit Court www.aikencountysc.gov/DspOfc.cfm?qOfcID=COCCV

Civil: Access the record index at http://publicindex.sccourts.org/aiken/publicindex/. *Criminal:*same as civil.

Allendale County

Circuit Court

Civil: Search the index at http://publicindex.sccourts.org/allendale/publicindex/. *Criminal:*same as civil.

Anderson County

Circuit Court www.judicial.state.sc.us/index.cfm

Civil: Access the record index at www.andersoncountysc.org/web/scjdweb/publicindex/. *Criminal:* Access to criminal case details at www.andersoncountysc.org/web/scjdweb/publicindex/.

Bamberg County

Circuit Court

Civil: Free access to the Circuit and Summary Courts' record index at http://publicindex.sccourts.org/bamberg/publicindex/. *Criminal:*same as civil.

Barnwell County

Circuit Court

Civil: Record docket online at http://publicindex.sccourts.org/barnwell/publicindex/. Includes General Sessions records. *Criminal:* Record docket online at http://publicindex.sccourts.org/barnwell/publicindex/.

Beaufort County

Circuit Court www.bcgov.net/

Civil: Access to public case index and court dockets for free go to http://publicindex.sccourts.org/beaufort/publicindex/. *Criminal:*same as civil.

Berkeley County

Circuit Court www.berkeleycountysc.gov/

Civil: A case index search is offered at http://courts.berkeleycountysc.gov/publicindex/. *Criminal:*same as civil.

Calhoun County

Circuit Court

Civil: Search the index at http://publicindex.sccourts.org/calhoun/publicindex/. *Criminal:*same as civil.

Charleston County

Circuit Court www3.charlestoncounty.org

Civil: Civil case details 1988 forward, also judgments and lis pendens are free at www3.charlestoncounty.org/connect. Online document images go back to 1/1/1999. Also accessible via www.sccourts.org/casesearch/. *Criminal:* Access to criminal case details from 04/92 forward free at www3.charlestoncounty.org/connect. Search by name or case number. Also accessible via www.sccourts.org/casesearch/.

Cherokee County

Circuit Court

Civil: Civil case details online at http://publicindex.sccourts.org/cherokee/publicindex/. *Criminal:* Access case details online at http://publicindex.sccourts.org/cherokee/publicindex/.

Chester County

Circuit Court www.chestersc.org

Civil: Search the index at http://publicindex.sccourts.org/chester/publicindex/. *Criminal:*same as civil.

Chesterfield County

Circuit Court

Civil: Access the docket index for free at http://publicindex.sccourts.org/chesterfield/publicindex/. *Criminal:*same as civil.

Clarendon County

Circuit Court

Civil: Civil case details free on state system at http://publicindex.sccourts.org/clarendon/publicindex/. *Criminal:* Access case details free at http://publicindex.sccourts.org/clarendon/publicindex/.

Colleton County

Circuit Court www.colletoncounty.org/

Civil: Online access to the index is at http://publicindex.sccourts.org/colleton/publicindex/. *Criminal:*same as civil.

Darlington County

Circuit Court www.darcosc.com/ClerkofCourt/

Civil: Access the docket index at http://publicindex.sccourts.org/darlington/publicindex/. *Criminal:*same as civil.

Dillon County

Circuit Court

Civil: Access online index at http://publicindex.sccourts.org/dillon/publicindex/. However, judgments of the Circuit Court only go back to Feb 2010. *Criminal:* Access online index at http://publicindex.sccourts.org/dillon/publicindex/.

Dorchester County

Circuit Court www.dorchestercounty.net/

Civil: Access case index free at http://publicindex.sccourts.org/dorchester/publicindex/. *Criminal:*same as civil.

Edgefield County

Circuit Court www.edgefieldcounty.sc.gov/

Civil: Civil case details free at http://publicindex.sccourts.org/edgefield/publicindex/. Also search pending cases free at http://publicindex.sccourts.org/edgefield/courtrosters/PendingCases.aspx. *Criminal:* same as civil.

Fairfield County

Circuit Court

Civil: A case index search if found at http://publicindex.sccourts.org/fairfield/publicindex/. *Criminal:*same as civil.

Florence County

Circuit Court http://florenceco.org/elected-offices/clerk-of-court/

Civil: Search judgments back to 1994 at www.sccourts.org/caseSearch/. *Criminal:* Access crim records from 1995 forward at www.sccourts.org/caseSearch/.

Georgetown County

Circuit Court

Civil: Access the court dockets free at http://publicindex.sccourts.org/georgetown/publicindex/ Also, access court rosters at http://publicindex.sccourts.org/georgetown/courtrosters/. *Criminal:* Access the court dockets free at http://publicindex.sccourts.org/georgetown/publicindex/.

Greenville County

Circuit Court www.greenvillecounty.org

Civil: Family Court and civil index at www.greenvillecounty.org/scjd/publicindex/disclaim23.asp. *Criminal:* same as civil.

Greenwood County

Circuit Court

Civil: Online access to the docket index is at http://198.206.194.114/greenwood/publicindex/. *Criminal:*same as civil.

Hampton County

Circuit Court

Civil: Search the index free at http://publicindex.sccourts.org/hampton/publicindex/. *Criminal:*same as civil.

Horry County

Circuit Court www.horrycounty.org/hcgPortal.asp

Civil: Civil case details free at http://publicindex.sccourts.org/horry/courtrosters/. *Criminal:* Criminal docket access online is free at http://publicindex.sccourts.org/horry/courtrosters/. County bookings are at http://sheriff.horrycounty.org/Detention/DailyBookingsandReleases.aspx.

Jasper County

Circuit Court www.jaspercourt.org/

Civil: Civil case details and dockets free at http://publicindex.sccourts.org/Jasper/publicindex/. *Criminal:* same as civil.

Kershaw County

Circuit Court

Civil: Online access to the docket index is at www.sccourts.org/caseSearch/. *Criminal:*same as civil.

Lancaster County

Circuit Court

Civil: Online access to the docket index is at www.sccourts.org/caseSearch/. *Criminal:*same as civil.

Laurens County

Circuit Court

Civil: Online access to the docket index for the Circuit and Summary Courts at http://publicindex.sccourts.org/laurens/publicindex/. *Criminal:* Online access to the docket index is at http://publicindex.sccourts.org/laurens/publicindex/.

Lee County

Circuit Court

Civil: Access to civil index for free at http://publicindex.sccourts.org/lee/publicindex/. *Criminal:* same as civil.

Lexington County

Circuit Court www.lex-co.sc.gov/departments/DeptAH/clerkofcourt/Pages/default.aspx

Civil: Search record index free at http://cms.lex-co.com/scjdweb/publicindex/. *Criminal:* Search the record index at http://cms.lex-co.com/scjdweb/publicindex/. Online records prior to 1994 may include missing/incorrect IDs, wrong charge codes, and be missing some cases, also sentence details, probation updates/violations.

Marion County

Circuit Court

Civil: A free name index search is at http://publicindex.sccourts.org/marion/publicindex/. *Criminal:*same as civil.

Marlboro County

Circuit Court

Civil: Free access to the docket index at http://publicindex.sccourts.org/marlboro/publicindex/. Includes search for civil judgments. *Criminal:* Free access to the docket index at http://publicindex.sccourts.org/marlboro/publicindex/. Search by name or case number.

McCormick County

Circuit Court www.mccormickcountysc.org/mccormick_county_clerk.php

Civil: A free index search is at http://publicindex.sccourts.org/mccormick/publicindex/. *Criminal:*same as civil.

Newberry County

Circuit Court www.newberrycounty.net/clerk/index.html

Civil: Access the docket index from the Circuit and Summary Courts at http://publicindex.sccourts.org/newberry/publicindex/. *Criminal:*same as civil.

Oconee County

Circuit Court www.oconeesc.com/

Civil: Search the index free at http://publicindex.sccourts.org/oconee/publicindex/. *Criminal:*same as civil.

Walhalla Magistrate (Summary) Court
Civil: The index is searchable at http://publicindex.sccourts.org/oconee/publicindex/. *Criminal:*same as civil.

Orangeburg County
Circuit Court www.orangeburgcounty.org/
Civil: Online access to the docket index is at www.sccourts.org/caseSearch/. *Criminal:*same as civil.

Pickens County
Circuit Court www.co.pickens.sc.us
Civil: Civil case details free at http://publicindex.sccourts.org/pickens/publicindex/. *Criminal:* same as civil.

Richland County
Circuit Court www.richlandonline.com/departments/clerkofcourt/
Civil: Limited civil case details free at www4.rcgov.us/publicindex/default.aspx. Limited court rosters online at www.richlandonline.com/departments/clerkofcourt/courtroster.asp; search by date. *Criminal:* Limited access case details free at www4.rcgov.us/publicindex/default.aspx. Access limited court rosters at www.richlandonline.com/departments/clerkofcourt/courtroster.asp; search by date.

Saluda County
Circuit Court
Civil: Search the case record index at http://publicindex.sccourts.org/saluda/publicindex/. Includes access to civil judgments. *Criminal:* Search the case record index at http://publicindex.sccourts.org/saluda/publicindex/. Search by name or case number.

Spartanburg County
Circuit Court www.spartanburgcounty.org/govt/depts/coc/index.htm
Civil: Civil case details free at http://192.146.148.40/publicindex/. *Criminal:* Access case details free at http://192.146.148.40/publicindex/.

Sumter County
Circuit Court www.sumtercountysc.org
Civil: Civil record index is at www.sumtercountysc.org/?q=online-service/judicial-court-records-search. Family court case details online at the website. *Criminal:* Access criminal record index is at www.sumtercountysc.org/?q=online-service/judicial-court-records-search.

Union County
Circuit Court www.countyofunion.org
Civil: Search the case index free at http://publicindex.sccourts.org/union/publicindex/. Also includes search of civil judgments. *Criminal:* Search the case index free at http://publicindex.sccourts.org/union/publicindex/. Search by name or case number.

Williamsburg County
Circuit Court www.williamsburgcounty.sc.gov
Civil: Search record index free at http://publicindex.sccourts.org/williamsburg/publicindex/. *Criminal:*same as civil.

York County
General Sessons www.yorkcountygov.com/departments/clerkCourt/COC-GeneralSessions
Criminal: Access case details free at http://publicindex.sccourts.org/york/publicindex/disclaimer.aspx Also. search current court dockets free at http://scsolicitor16.org/GeneralSessions/CourtDocket.

Circuit Court - Common Pleas www.yorkcountygov.com/departments/clerkCourt/COC-CommonPleas
Civil: Access case details free at http://publicindex.sccourts.org/york/publicindex/disclaimer.aspx. Also. search current court dockets free at http://scsolicitor16.org/GeneralSessions/CourtDocket.

Recorders, Assessors, and Other Sites of Note

Recording Office Organization: 46 counties, 46 recording offices. South Carolina is divided into 46 recorder districts with an elected or appointed Recorder or Clerk responsible for each office. The recording officer is either the Register of Mesne Conveyances or Clerk of Court; this varies by county. Documents related to the ownership of real estate within the county are recorded at either the Recorder of Deeds Office, or the Clerk of Courts Office depending on the county.All federal and state tax liens on personal property and on real property are filed with the Register of Mesne Conveyances or Clerk of Court.

Statewide or Multi-Jurisdiction Access: There is no statewide system but a quite number of counties offer free record data via their websites.

Abbeville County ***Property, Taxation Records*** Assess to GIS/mapping for free at http://gis.abbevillecountysc.com/abbeville/default.htm

Aiken County ***Recorded Documents, Comparable Sale Records*** www.aikencountysc.gov/DspDept.cfm?qDeptID=RMC Access to the county e-services are free at www.aikencountysc.gov/eGovDisclaimer1.cfm but not all modules allow name searching. For full data and name searching, must register and currently no charge. Registration and password required for Property Cards and Comparable Sales. Also, access to property and deeds indexes and images is via a private company at www.titlesearcher.com. Fee/registration required. Deeds and index goes back to 1/1982; images back to 6/13/2005. Also a vendor provides subscription data at www.titlesearcher.com/countyHomepages.php?state=SC. **$$$**

Property, Taxation Records Search assessor property data free at https://cxap2.aikencountysc.gov/EGSV2Aiken/egsreal/rpSearch.jsp;jsessionid=721C9173F091BC30ABD5A54ACBBC4D83. For more detailed information you can subscribe for a fee.**$$$**

Allendale County ***Real Estate, Grantor/Grantee, Deed, Mortgage, Lien Records*** http://allendalecounty.com/ Access to recorders data is free via a private firm at https://portal2.recordfusion.com/countyweb/login.do?countyname=Allendale. Login as Guest to search free. Judgments found in the Clerk of Courts office.

Anderson County ***Real Estate, Deed Records*** www.andersoncountysc.org/web/register_00.asp Access to the county ACPASS super search site is free at http://acpass.andersoncountysc.org.

Property, Taxation Records Access to GIS/mapping or on-line mapping system free at www.andersoncountysc.org/web/GIS_Atlas.asp. Access property tax and vehicle tax and other data free at http://acpass.andersoncountysc.org/welcome.shtml.

Bamberg County ***Property, Taxation Records*** Access to property records and GIS/mapping for free at www.qpublic.net/sc/bamberg/.

Barnwell County ***Property, Taxation Records*** Access to Assessor records for free at www.qpublic.net/sc/barnwell/.

Beaufort County ***Recorded Documents*** www.bcgov.net/departments/Real-Property-Services/register-of-deeds/index.php Access to recorded documents free at http://rodweb.bcgov.net/nvtest/.

Property, Taxation Records Search assessor data free at http://sc-beaufort-county.governmax.com/svc/default.asp?sid=A69E6D90AC6548BABFC9F28E1A81D26D.

Berkeley County ***Recorded Documents*** www.berkeleycountysc.gov/dept/registerofdeeds/ Access real estate data at www.sclandrecords.com/sclr/controller. Recorded dates from 1/1/1991 to present. Images only. Must contact office for certified copies.

Property, Taxation Records Search assessor data free at www.berkeleycountysc.gov/main/eserv.asp?linkID=e. Search personal property and vehicle tax data also at this site.

Calhoun County ***Recorded Documents*** www.judicial.state.sc.us/clerksCourt/clerk.cfm?countyno=9 Access to property and deeds indexes and images is via a private company at www.titlesearcher.com. Fee/registration required. Images and indices go back to 8/2004. **$$$**

Property, Taxation Records Access to the Assessor's data by parcel number or owner name free at http://egs-appserver1.lylesdata.com:8080/EGSV3Calhoun/RPSearch.do.

Charleston County ***Recorded Documents, Marriage, Probate, Business License Records*** www.charlestoncounty.org/Departments/RMC/index.htm Access RMC recording data free at www2.charlestoncounty.org - land records/images go back to 2/1997. Search court judgments- www3.charlestoncounty.org/connect?ref=MIE. Marriages- www3.charlestoncounty.org/connect/LU_GROUP_2?ref=Marriage. Search probate, wills, guardianships free- www3.charlestoncounty.org/connect/LU_GROUP_2?ref=Conserv. Business licenses- www3.charlestoncounty.org/surfer/group3?s=b.

Property, Taxation Records Access auditor & treasurer's tax system free at http://taxweb.charlestoncounty.org. Access the county's GIS mapping database of property records free at http://gisweb.charlestoncounty.org.

Cherokee County ***Recorded Deeds Records*** www.cherokeecountysc.com/id39.html View recorded deeds for free at https://www.sclandrecords.com/sclr_sc025/.

Chesterfield County ***Recorded Deeds Records*** www.chesterfieldcountysc.com/secondary.aspx?pageID=111 View recorded land deeds for free at https://www.sclandrecords.com/sclr_sc025/.

Clarendon County ***Property, Taxation Records*** Access to public records free at www.qpublic.net/sc/clarendon/index.html.

Colleton County ***Property, Taxation Records*** Access property and vehicle tax data free at http://sc-colleton-county.governmax.com/svc/default.asp?sid=53EB5F78D5044B628583D69CA6863444.

Darlington County ***Recorded Documents*** www.darcosc.com/ClerkOfCourt/ Access to records free at http://rod.darcosc.com/External/LandRecords/protected/SrchSimpleName.aspx.

Property, Taxation Records Access property records free at www.qpublic.net/sc/darlington/search.html. Lookup tax records at www.darcosc.com/OnlineTaxes/.

Dillon County ***Judgment, Civil, Tax Records*** http://dilloncounty.sc.gov/Departments/clerkofcourt/Pages/default.aspx Access to records from Circuit and Summary Courts free at http://publicindex.sccourts.org/dillon/publicindex/.

Dorchester County ***Real Estate, Deed Records*** www.dorchestercounty.net Access to Register of Deeds real estate records is free at www.dorchestercounty.net/index.aspx?page=299.

Property, Taxation Records Search tax and property records free on the GIS-mapping site at http://gisweb.dorchestercounty.net/imap/.

Edgefield County ***Recorded Deeds, Grantor/Grantee, Liens Records*** www.edgefieldcounty.sc.gov/Pages/Home.aspx Access county land record index and images free at http://publicindex.sccourts.org/edgefield/PUBLICINDEX/. View recorded deeds at https://www.sclandrecords.com/sclr_sc025/.

Property, Taxation Records Access property assessor data free at www.edgefieldcountysc.com/search.aspx.

Fairfield County ***Property, Taxation Records*** Search property/GIS data free at www.emapsplus.com/scfairfield/maps/.

Florence County ***Real Estate, Grantor/Grantee, Deed, Lien, Judgment Records*** http://florenceco.org/elected-offices/clerk-of-court/ Access recorder data free at http://web.florenceco.org/cgi-bin/coc/coc.cgi.

Property, Taxation Records Access property tax records free at http://web.florenceco.org/cgi-bin/ta/tax-inq.cgi. Also, access vehicle tax records free at http://web.florenceco.org/cgi-bin/ta/vehinq.cgi.

Georgetown County ***Recorded Documents*** www.georgetowncountysc.org Access to records free at www.landaccess.com/sites/sc/disclaimer.php?county=scgeorgetown.

Property, Taxation Records Access to property data on the GIS-mapping site is free at www.georgetowncountysc.org/gis/default.html.

Greenville County ***Recorded Documents*** www.greenvillecounty.org/rod/ Search the Register of Deeds database free at www.greenvillecounty.org/rod/searchrecords.asp. Have a search records prior to 1985 and a search records after 1985.

Property, Taxation Records Search the property tax and vehicles data at www.greenvillecounty.org/appsas400/votaxqry/. Also, search real estate data at www.greenvillecounty.org/vrealpr24/clrealprop.asp. No name searching.

Greenwood County ***Real Estate, Grantor/Grantee, Deed, Mortgage Federal & State Tax Liens, Judgment Records*** www.greenwoodsc.gov/countywebsite/index.aspx?page=138 Document search for free at www.greenwoodsc.gov/docsearch/default.aspx

Property, Taxation Records Access to GIS/mapping free at www.greenwoodsc.gov/GreenwoodSL/.

Hampton County ***Recorded Deeds, Liens, Plats, Mortgages, Other Recorded Records*** www.hamptoncountysc.org/index.aspx?nid=11 View recorded deeds at https://www.sclandrecords.com/sclr_sc025/. Access to public records index free at http://publicindex.sccourts.org/hampton/publicindex/.

Property, Taxation Records Access to Appraiser property records for free at http://qpublic5.qpublic.net/sc_search.php?county=sc_hampton.

Horry County ***Real Estate, Deed, Liens, Recorded Judgments Records*** www.horrycounty.org/hcgPortal.asp Access the recorded documents free at www.horrycounty.org/idx_rod.asp.

Property, Taxation Records Search the land records database free at www.horrycounty.org/gateway/disclaimer/idx_real.html.

Jasper County ***Real Estate, Grantor/Grantee, Deed, Mortgage, Lien Records*** www.jaspercountysc.org/secondary.aspx?pageID=62 Access to recorders data is free via a private firm at https://portal1.recordfusion.com/countyweb/login.do?countyname=Jasper. Logon as Guest to search free. Judgments found in the Clerk of Courts office.

Kershaw County ***Recorded Deeds Records*** www.kershaw.sc.gov/Index.aspx?page=148 View recorded deeds https://www.sclandrecords.com/sclr_sc025/.

Property, Taxation Records Access to property/vehicle tax for free at www.kershawcountysctax.com/.

Lancaster County ***Recorded Documents*** www.mylancastersc.org/index.asp?Type=B_BASIC&SEC={1AE29148-C09A-487D-983C-47A02BC9D737} Access to property and deeds indexes and images is via a private company at www.titlesearcher.com/. Fee/registration required. Indices and images go back to 8/27/2002. **$$$**

Property, Taxation Records Access property records data free at www.qpublic.net/sc/lancaster/search.html.

Laurens County ***Real Estate, Deed, Treasurer Records*** www.laurenscountysctaxes.com/secondary.aspx?pageID=150 Access to property and deeds indexes and images is via a private company at www.titlesearcher.com. Fee/registration required. Deed records go back to 7/1991; indices back to 6/1/1996; images to 8/26/2006. **$$$**

Property, Taxation Records Access property data free at www.laurenscountysctaxes.com/secondary.aspx?pageID=139. Also, access to property tax searches free at www.laurenscountysctaxes.com/secondary.aspx?pageID=175.

Lexington County ***Recorded Documents*** www.lex-co.sc.gov/onlineservices/Pages/RODOnlineServices.aspx Access Register of Deeds records free at www.lex-co.sc.gov/onlineservices/Pages/RODOnlineServices.aspx.

Property, Taxation Records Access property and tax data free at www.lex-co.sc.gov/departments/DeptAH/PGIS/Pages/default.aspx. Property tax is found at www.lex-co.com/PCSearch/tb001-pg.asp.

McCormick County ***Property, Taxation Records*** Access to GIS/mapping for free at http://thinkopengis.mccormick.sc.wthtechnology.com/.

Marlboro County ***Property, Taxation Records*** Access to property tax information for free at www.marlborocountytax.com/search.aspx.

Newberry County ***Property, Taxation Records*** Access to assessor database is free at http://68.156.95.36/webpronewberry/open.htm. Access to auditor's property data is free at www.newberrycounty.net/auditor/Index.html. Access to auditor and treasurer property tax data is free at www.newberrycountysctaxes.com/.

Oconee County ***Recorded Documents*** www.oconeesc.com/Departments/KZ/RegisterofDeeds.aspx Access recorder's index search free at http://deeds.oconeesc.com/External/LandRecords/protected/SrchQuickName.aspx.

Property, Taxation Records Free access county parcel data found at http://arcserver2.oconeesc.com/ParcelViewer/default.aspx. Also, free access to property records at www.qpublic.net/sc/oconee/search2.html.

Orangeburg County ***Real Estate, Deed, Mortgage, UCC, Plat Records*** www.orangeburgscrod.org/Opening.asp Access free deeds, mortgages and plat records back to 1989 at www.orangeburgscrod.org/Opening.asp.

Property, Taxation Records Access to county property tax records is free at http://sc-orangeburg-assessor.governmax.com/propertymax/rover30.asp?sid=07544F662DD64AB49267AE2C4D48969E.

Pickens County ***Real Estate, Deed, Lien, Mortgage, UCC, Plat Records*** www.co.pickens.sc.us/deeds/default.aspx Access the recorders database back to 12/1/1986 free at http://67.32.48.38/oncoreweb/.

Property, Taxation Records A variety of search choices are offered at www.pickensassessor.org including owners name. parcel number, sales list and mailing addresses.

Richland County ***Recorded Documents, Marriage, Estates Records*** www.richlandonline.com/departments/rod/index.asp Search register of deeds free at www.richlandonline.com/services/rodsearch.asp; no name searching. Also, search marriages free at www.richlandonline.com/services/marriagelicense.asp. Search estate records from 1983 (probate related) at www.richlandonline.com/Services/EstatesInquiry2.asp. Also, Subscription Management System for a fee at https://www4.rcgov.us/SMS_External/Login.aspx?AspxAutoDetectCookieSupport=1 **$$$**

Property, Taxation Records Search assessments at www.richlandonline.com/services/assessorsearch/assessorsearch.asp; no name searching. Access to county property data is free at www.richlandmaps.com/.

Spartanburg County ***Recorded Liens, Real Estate, Deed, UCC, Plat, Charter Records*** www.spartanburgcounty.org/govt/depts/regdeed/index.htm Access recording data free at www.spartanburgcounty.org/rmsdmsclient/index.asp. Images being added daily. Currently, the system has a limited number of images available; however, new images are being added daily.

Property, Taxation Records Access property tax data free at http://qpublic.net/sc/spartanburg/search.html. GIS Mapping is offered at www.spartanburgcounty.org/govt/depts/gis/index.htm.

Sumter County ***Recorded Documents*** www.sumtercountysc.org/?q=department/register-deeds-0 Search county data free at www.sumtercountysc.org:8080/EGSV2SMTR/RODSearch.do.

Property, Taxation Records Search assessment data and property cards free at www.sumtercountysc.org:8080/EGSV2SMTR/PCSearch.do. Also, access to GIS/mapping free at http://svr4.sumtercountysc.org/Sumter_County_Property_Map/.

Williamsburg County ***Property, Taxation Records*** Access to GIS/mapping free at http://williamsburg.sc.wthgis.com/.

York County ***Property, Taxation Records*** Access to the county GIS/mapping for free atwww.yorkcountygov.com/departments/mis/GIS/OnlineMappingApplications/EasyGISSearch. Also, the assessors sales report free at www.yorkcountygov.com/departments/assessor/AssessorsSalesReport. Also, search tax records free at http://onlinetaxes.yorkcountygov.com/taxes.

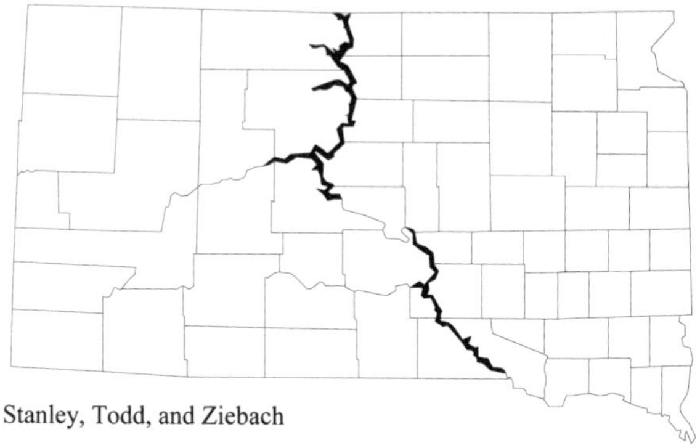

South Dakota

Capital: Pierre
Hughes County

Time Zone: CST

South Dakota's eighteen western-most counties are MST:
They are: Bennett, Butte, Corson, Custer, Dewey, Fall River, Haakon, Harding, Jackson, Lawrence, Meade, Mellette, Pennington, Perkins, Shannon, Stanley, Todd, and Ziebach

Population: 833,354

# of Counties: 66

Useful State Links

Website: www.sd.gov
Governor: http://sd.gov/governor
Attorney General: http://atg.sd.gov
State Archives: http://history.sd.gov
State Statutes and Codes: http://legis.state.sd.us/mylrc/index.aspx
Legislative Bill Search: http://legis.state.sd.us/statutes/index.aspx
Bill Monitoring: http://legis.state.sd.us/mylrc/index.aspx
Unclaimed Funds: www.sdtreasurer.gov/unclaimedproperty

State Public Record Agencies

Sexual Offender Registry

Division of Criminal Investigation, Identification Section - SOR Unit, https://sor.sd.gov/default.aspx Searching is available from the website. One may search by name, map, or neighborhood. There is a search option to include incarcerated offenders.

Corporation, LP, LLC, Trademarks/Servicemarks

Corporation Division, Secretary of State, http://sdsos.gov/Business/Default.aspx Search the Secretary of State Corporations Div. Database free at http://sdsos.gov/Business/Search.aspx. One may also search commercial registered agents from this site. Trademark searches may be requested via e-mail at trademark@state.sd.us. The Secretary of State offers a Fictitious Name Registration search at https://apps.sd.gov/Applications/st08bnrs/secure/ASPX/BNRS_Search.aspx. *Other Options:* FTP downloads are available for purchase.

Uniform Commercial Code, Federal Tax Liens

UCC Division, Secretary of State, http://sdsos.gov/content/viewcontent.aspx?cat=corporations&pg=/corporations/ucc.shtm Dakota Fast File is the filing and searching service available from the home page. This commercial service requires registration and a $120.00 fee per year. Certified search and printing is offered. Also, other requesters may ask that a document be returned by email, there is an additional $5.00 fee. **$$$** *Other Options:* FTP downloads are available for purchase.

Vital Records

South Dakota Department of Health, Vital Records, http://doh.sd.gov/VitalRecords/ Records may be ordered online at the website via a state supported vendor. You can order recent (less than 100 years) birth records at the website, for a fee. You can search free at http://apps.sd.gov/applications/PH14Over100BirthRec/index.aspx for birth records over 100 years old. **$$$**

Driver Records

Dept of Public Safety, Driver Licensing Program, http://dps.sd.gov/licensing/driver_licensing/default.aspx The system is open for batch requests 24 hours a day. There is a minimum of 250 requests daily. It generally takes 10 minutes to process a batch. The current fee is $5.00 per records and there are some start-up costs. For more information, call 605-773-6883. **$$$** *Other Options:* Lists are available to the insurance industry.

Voter Registration, Campaign Finance, PACs

Secretary of State, Elections Division, http://sdsos.gov/Elections/Default.aspx An advanced search for campaign finance matters is found at https://sdsos.gov/CampaignFinance/CFSearch.aspx. This includes donations by PACs. Also the webpage has a list of various files available for purchase on CD or paper. For example, statewide CD is $2,500, statewide printed list is $5,500. Data may be purchased by county or legislative district.

Occupational Licensing Boards

911 Telecommunicator http://dci.sd.gov/LawEnforcementTraining/911BasicTelecommunicatorCertification.aspx
Abstractor/Abstractor Company .... http://dlr.sd.gov/bdcomm/abstracters/roster.aspx
Accountant-CPA/Firm .... http://apps.sd.gov/applications/ld01DOL/Template/main.aspx?templateid=15
Alcoholic Beverage Distributor www.state.sd.us/drr2/propspectax/alcohol/licenses/licenses.htm
Ambulance Service .... http://dps.sd.gov/emergency_services/emergency_medical_services/ambulance_service_directories.aspx
Animal Feed Seller/Producer .... http://sdda.sd.gov/farming-ranching-agribusiness/feed-animal-remedy-program/default.aspx
Animal Remedy (medicine/drug) .... http://sdda.sd.gov/farming-ranching-agribusiness/feed-animal-remedy-program/default.aspx
Architect/Landscape .... https://apps.sd.gov/applications/ld17btp/takehomeexam/(S(dxrzmoyvdgpncaxn3t5znqog))/FirmRoster.aspx
Asbestos Service Company/Worker .... http://denr.sd.gov/des/wm/asb/Documents/AsbestosServices.pdf
Athletic Trainer .... https://login.sdbmoe.gov/Public/Services/VerificationSearch
Auctioneer .... https://sdrec.sd.gov/registration/licenseelist.aspx
Audiologist .... http://doh.sd.gov/boards/audiology/roster.aspx
Bail Bond Agent .... http://dlr.sd.gov/insurance/license_inquiry_service_intro.aspx
Bank .... http://dlr.sd.gov/banking/banks.aspx
Barber .... http://dlr.sd.gov/bdcomm/barber/barberpdfs/rosterofbarbers.pdf
Barber Shop .... http://dlr.sd.gov/bdcomm/barber/barberpdfs/rosterofbarbershops.pdf
Beauty Shop/Nail/Beauth Salon .... http://dlr.sd.gov/bdcomm/cosmet/ccverification/
Canine Team .... http://dci.sd.gov/LawEnforcementTraining/CanineTeamCertification.aspx
Chiropractor .... www.sdchiropractors.com/search.php
Chiropractor Disciplinary Action Reports .... http://doh.sd.gov/Boards/chiropractic/Discipline.aspx
Clinical Nurse Specialist .... https://ifmc.sd.gov/lookup.php
Cosmetologist/Instructor/Salon .... http://dlr.sd.gov/bdcomm/cosmet/ccverification/
Cosmetology Schools .... http://dlr.sd.gov/bdcomm/cosmet/ccschools.aspx
Counselor http://dss.sd.gov/behavioralhealthservices/docs/CounselorsMarriageFamily/BCEWEBLIST05.10.2013.pdf
Court/Shorthand Reporter www.southdakotacourtreporters.org/2.html
Crematory .... http://doh.sd.gov/Boards/FuneralBoard/Roster.aspx
Dentist, Dental Hygienist/Assistant .... https://www.sdboardofdentistry.com/verify.asp
Dietitian/Nutritionist .... https://login.sdbmoe.gov/Public/Services/VerificationSearch
Driller, Oil and Gas Supervisor .... http://denr.sd.gov/des/og/welldata.aspx
Electrical Inspector .... http://dlr.sd.gov/bdcomm/electric/ecinspections.aspx
Embalmer .... http://doh.sd.gov/Boards/FuneralBoard/Roster.aspx
Emergency Medical Technician/Paramedic. https://login.sdbmoe.gov/Public/Services/VerificationSearch
Engineer/ Petroleum Environmen'l .... https://apps.sd.gov/applications/ld17btp/takehomeexam/(S(dxrzmoyvdgpncaxn3t5znqog))/FirmRoster.aspx
Esthetician/Manicurist/Nail Technician .... http://dlr.sd.gov/bdcomm/cosmet/ccverification/
Fertilizer .... http://sdda.sd.gov/farming-ranching-agribusiness/fertilizer-program/default.aspx
Funeral Director/Establishment .... http://doh.sd.gov/Boards/FuneralBoard/Roster.aspx
Gaming Manufacturer .... http://gaming.sd.gov/LicensedMfgDistributors.aspx
Health Insurer .... http://dlr.sd.gov/insurance/license_inquiry_service_intro.aspx
Hearing Aid Dispenser .... http://doh.sd.gov/boards/audiology/roster.aspx
Home Inspector .... https://sdrec.sd.gov/registration/licenseelist.aspx
Insurance Agent, Company .... http://dlr.sd.gov/insurance/license_inquiry_service_intro.aspx
Insurer of Health/Re-Insurer, Accredited/Qualified .... http://dlr.sd.gov/insurance/license_inquiry_service_intro.aspx
Investment Advisor/Firm .... www.adviserinfo.sec.gov/(S(lto1ii0alerchaz455qv2mwt))/IAPD/Content/Search/iapd_Search.aspx
Landfill .... http://denr.sd.gov/des/wm/asb/asbhomepage.aspx
Law Enforcement Officer .... http://dci.sd.gov/LawEnforcementTraining/BasicOfficerCertification.aspx
Lobbyist http://apps.sd.gov/applications/ST12ODRS/
Marriage & Family Therapist http://dss.sd.gov/behavioralhealthservices/docs/CounselorsMarriageFamily/BCEWEBLIST05.10.2013.pdf

Midwife .... https://ifmc.sd.gov/lookup.php
Money Lender .... http://dlr.sd.gov/banking/money_lenders/documents/money_lender_licensee_list.pdf
Money Order BusinessMoney Transmitters. http://dlr.sd.gov/banking/money_transmitters/documents/money_transmitter_licensee_list.pdf
Mortgage Broker/Lender .... www.nmlsconsumeraccess.org/
Notary .... http://apps.sd.gov/applications/ST12ODRS/aspx/frmNotaryViewlist.aspx?cmd=resetall
Nurse-RN/LPN/Aide Certified/Anesthetist.... https://ifmc.sd.gov/lookup.php
Nursing Facility Administrator .... http://doh.sd.gov/Boards/NursingFacility/PDF/LicenseeList.pdf
Occupational Therapist/Assistant .... https://login.sdbmoe.gov/Public/Services/VerificationSearch
Oil & Gas Driller Senior Geologist .... http://denr.sd.gov/des/og/welldata.aspx
Optometrist .... http://doh.sd.gov/Boards/Optometry/PDF/LicenseVerification.pdf
Osteopathic Physician .... https://login.sdbmoe.gov/Public/Services/VerificationSearch
Pesticide Applicator/Dealer .... http://sdda.sd.gov/farming-ranching-agribusiness/pesticide-program/default.aspx
Pet Health Insurer .... http://dlr.sd.gov/insurance/license_inquiry_service_intro.aspx
Petrol. Release Assessor/Remediator .... https://apps.sd.gov/applications/ld17btp/takehomeexam/(S(dxrzmoyvdgpncaxn3t5znqog))/FirmRoster.aspx
Physical Therapist/Assistant .... https://login.sdbmoe.gov/Public/Services/VerificationSearch
Physician/Medical Doctor/Assistant .... https://login.sdbmoe.gov/Public/Services/VerificationSearch
Podiatrist .... http://doh.sd.gov/boards/podiatry/PDF/roster.pdf
Polygraph Examiner .... http://dci.sd.gov/LawEnforcementTraining/PolygraphLicensingPage.aspx
Property Manager .... https://sdrec.sd.gov/registration/licenseelist.aspx
Psychologist http://dss.sd.gov/behavioralhealthservices/docs/Psychologists/SDLicensedPsychologists4-2-13.pdf
Radiology (Dental) .... https://www.sdboardofdentistry.com/verify.asp
Real Estate Agent/Seller/Broker/Firm .... https://sdrec.sd.gov/registration/licenseelist.aspx
Respiratory Care Practitioner .... https://login.sdbmoe.gov/Public/Services/VerificationSearch
Securities Agent/Broker/Dealer .... www.finra.org/Investors/ToolsCalculators/BrokerCheck/index.htm
Septic Tank Installer .... http://denr.sd.gov/des/sw/SepticInstallers.aspx
Social Worker http://dss.sd.gov/behavioralhealthservices/docs/SocialWorkers/SDLicensedSocialWorkers4-2-13.pdf
Storage Tank, Above/Below Ground .... http://denr.sd.gov/des/gw/tanks/ust_ast_definition.aspx
Surveyor, Land .... https://apps.sd.gov/applications/ld17btp/takehomeexam/(S(dxrzmoyvdgpncaxn3t5znqog))/FirmRoster.aspx
Timeshare Real Estate, Registered Project. https://sdrec.sd.gov/registration/licenseelist.aspx
Tobacco Wholesaler www.state.sd.us/drr2/propspectax/tobacco/manufacturer.htm
Trust Company .... http://dlr.sd.gov/banking/trusts/documents/state_chartered_trust_companies.pdf
Waste Water System Operator .... http://denr.sd.gov/des/dw/PDF/operator.pdf
Waste Water Treatm't Plant Operator .... http://denr.sd.gov/des/wm/hw/hwcontractors.aspx
Water Distributor/Treatment Operator .... http://denr.sd.gov/des/wm/hw/hwcontractors.aspx
Weapon, Concealed .... http://sdsos.gov/content/viewcontent.aspx?cat=adminservices&pg=/adminservices/concealedpistolpermits.shtm
Well Driller .... http://denr.sd.gov/des/wr/dbdrillerlist.aspx

State and Local Courts

State Court Structure: The **Circuit Courts** are the general trial courts of the Unified Judicial System (UJS). These courts have original jurisdiction in all civil and criminal cases. **Magistrate Courts** operate under the authority and supervision of the Circuit Courts, and assist in processing preliminary hearings for felony cases, hear minor criminal cases, municipal ordinance violations, and hear uncontested civil and small claims cases under $12,000. Circuit Courts also have jurisdiction over appeals from **Magistrate Court** decisions. There are 66 counties, but 63 courts. Circuit cases for Buffalo County are handled at the Brule County Circuit Court. Circuit cases for Shannon County are handled by the Fall River County Circuit Court. Circuit cases for Todd County are handled by the Tripp County Circuit Court. The state re-aligned their circuits from 8 to 7 effective June, 2000.

Appellate Courts: There is not a Court of Appeals in South Dakota. The Supreme Court calendar, opinions, rules and archived oral arguments may be searched from the judicial website www.sdjudicial.com.

Statewide Court Online Access: All courts participate in the system described below.

- A web search is offered by the UJS (Unified Judicial System) for all active money judgments and inactive civil money judgments from 04/19/2004 forward. This service includes a search of both the Circuit and Magistrate Courts. Case document images are not provided. This online system does not provide probate or criminal information. Charges for searches are $4.00 per name or date range search. There is an additional $1.00 charge to access the judgment docket. The system works off a pre-paid deposit using a credit card, so the system deducts from your balance. Users may also obtain unlimited access to system, including bulk downloading of civil money judgment information, by subscribing on a monthly or yearly basis. Contact the UJS Help Desk, State Court Administrator's Office, 500 E. Capitol Avenue, Pierre, SD 57501. Case document images are not provided. See https://apps.sd.gov/applications/judgmentquery/login.aspx.

- Historical bulk data on civil money judgments filed in South Dakota dating back twenty years on active judgments and back to April 19, 2004 on inactive judgments may be obtained by contacting the State Court Administrator's Office Pursuant to SDCL 16-2-29.6, the cost for accessing this historical database is $3,000. This data is provided on a DVD in XML format.
- Use of SD court records, including the UJS's Electronic Civil Money Judgment System mentioned above, is governed by SDCL 1-27-1, SD's open records law and SDCL ch. 15-15A, SD's Court Records law. Reselling or redistributing lists of information from this database or from the paper court records is prohibited by law as a Class 2 misdemeanor.

Note: No individual South Dakota court offers online access, other than as described above.

Recorders, Assessors, and Other Sites of Note

Recording Office Organization: 66 counties, 66 recording offices. The recording officer is the Register of Deeds. Federal tax liens on personal property of businesses are filed with the Secretary of State. Other federal and state tax liens are filed with the county Register of Deeds. Most counties will perform tax lien searches.

Statewide or Multi-Jurisdiction Access: There is no statewide system and no counties offerr access to recorded documents. However some counties access to assess data, some by subscrption via a vendor.

County Sites:

Brookings County ***Property, Taxation Records*** Access to GIS/mapping for free at http://beacon.schneidercorp.com/?site=BrookingsCountySD If questions, email jdragseth@brookingscountysd.gov.

Brown County ***Property, Taxation Records*** Search assessor property data for free on the GIS system at http://beacon.schneidercorp.com/?site=BrownCountySD.

Brule County ***Property, Taxation Records*** Access to GIS/mapping for free at www.districtiii.org/gis/interactive_mapping.php.

Clay County ***Property, Taxation Records*** Search assessor property data for free on the GIS system at http://beacon.schneidercorp.com

Corson County ***Property, Taxation Records*** Search assessor property data for free on GIS system at http://beacon.schneidercorp.com/

Custer County ***Property, Taxation Records*** Search assessor property data for free on the GIS system at http://beacon.schneidercorp.com/.

Lake County ***Property, Taxation Records*** Search assessor property data for free on the GIS system at http://beacon.schneidercorp.com/

Lawrence County ***Property, Taxation Records*** Access to GIS/mapping for Deedwood, Spearfish and the County for free at www2.lawrence.sd.us:45500/webGIS/GIShome.html

McCook County ***Property, Taxation Records*** Access assessor property data for free on the GIS system at http://beacon.schneidercorp.com/.

Minnehaha County ***Property, Taxation Records*** Access to the county property tax database is free at www.minnehahacounty.org/property_tax/. No name searching at this time.

Moody County ***Property, Taxation Records*** Search assessor property data for free on the GIS system at http://beacon.schneidercorp.com/.

Pennington County Register of Deeds ***Property, Taxation Records*** Access to the county property tax database is free at http://209.159.193.156/appraisal/publicaccess/.

Spink County ***Property, Taxation Records*** Search assessor property data for free on GIS system at http://beacon.schneidercorp.com/

Union County ***Property, Taxation Records*** Search assessor property data for free on the GIS system at http://beacon.schneidercorp.com/.

Yankton County ***Property, Taxation Records*** Search assessor property data for free on the GIS system at http://beacon.schneidercorp.com/.

Tennessee

Capital: Nashville
Davidson County

Time Zone: CST

Tennessee's twenty-nine eastern-most counties are EST.
They are: Anderson, Blount, Bradley, Campbell, Carter, Claiborne, Cocke, Grainger, Greene, Hamilton, Hancock, Hawkins, Jefferson, Johnson, Knox, Loudon, McMinn, Meigs, Monroe, Morgan, Polk, Rhea, Roane, Scott, Sevier, Sullivan, Unicoi, Union, Washington.

Population: 6,456,243

# of Counties: 95

Useful State Links

Website: www.tennessee.gov

Governor: www.tn.gov/governor

Attorney General: www.tn.gov/attorneygeneral

State Archives: www.tennessee.gov/tsla

State Statutes and Codes: www.lexisnexis.com/hottopics/tncode

Legislative Bill Search: www.legislature.state.tn.us

Unclaimed Funds: www.treasury.state.tn.us/unclaim

State Public Record Agencies

Criminal Records

Tennessee Bureau of Investigation, TN Open Records Information Svcs, www.tbi.state.tn.us Records may be requested online via email from the website, but this is not an interactive service. Records must still manually searched and will take several days. A $29.00 fee is charged. See https://www.tbibackgrounds.com/toris/. **$$$**

Sexual Offender Registry

Tennessee Bureau of Investigation, Sexual Offender Registry, www.tbi.tn.gov/sex_ofender_reg/sex_ofender_reg.shtml Search sexual offenders at www.tbi.tn.gov/sorint/SOMainpg.aspx by last name, city, county or ZIP Code. One may also search for missing children, and people placed on parole who reside in Tennessee. A search by map is offered at http://tnmap.state.tn.us/sor/.

Incarceration Records

Dept of Corrections-ATTN: PIO/FOIL, Rachel Jackson Building, Ground Fl, www.state.tn.us/correction/ Extensive search capabilities are offered from https://apps.tn.gov/foil/foil_index.jsp. *Other Options:* A CD-Rom is available with only public information from current offender database; nominal fee; contact the Planning & Research Division.

Corporation, LLC, LP, LLP, Fictitious Name, Assumed Name

TN Sec of State: Corporation Filing Unit, William R Snodgrass Tower, www.tn.gov/sos/bus_svc/index.htm There is a free online search at http://tnbear.tn.gov/Ecommerce/NameAvailability.aspx for name availability and at http://tnbear.tn.gov/ECommerce/FilingSearch.aspx for business records. This gives online access to over 4,000,000 records relating to corporations, limited liability companies, limited partnerships and limited liability partnerships formed or registered in Tennessee. Also, search securities department enforcement actions at http://tn.gov/commerce/securities/enfaction.shtml#. *Other Options:* Some data can be purchased in bulk or list format. Call 615-253-4015 for more details.

Trademarks/Servicemarks, Trade Names

Sec. of State - Trademarks Unit, Willima R Snodgrass Tower - 6th Fl, www.tn.gov/sos/bus_svc/trademarks.htm The Internet provides a record search of TN Trademarks, newest records are 3 days old. Search free at www.tn.gov/sos/bus_svc/TrademarkSearch.htm. *Other Options:* The agency will provide a file update every three months for $1.00 per page. Requests must be in writing.

Uniform Commercial Code

Dept of State - UCC Division, William R Snodgrass Tower, www.tn.gov/sos/bus_svc/ucc.htm Free access to general, limited information at www.tn.gov/sos/bus_svc/UccSearch.htm. Search by debtor name or file number. Images are not available. A disclaimer mentions that this data may not be reflective of an official search per TN statutes. The UCC database is updated between 7:30AM and 11AM (CST). During the update process, secured party information may not be available and/or related UCC document information may not be accurately reflected for a UCC1 filing.

Birth, Marriage, Divorce Records

Tennessee Department of Health, Office of Vital Records, http://health.state.tn.us/vr/index.htm Records may be ordered from the designated vendor - www.vitalchek.com. Extra fees involved. **$$$**

Death Records

Tennessee Department of Health, Office of Vital Records, http://health.state.tn.us/vr/index.htm Records may be ordered from the designated vendor - www.vitalchek.com. Extra fees involved. The Cleveland (Tennessee) Public Library staff and volunteers published the 1914-1933 statewide death records at www.tn.gov/tsla/history/vital/tndeath.htm. Note that the records of children under two years of age have been omitted from this project. **$$$**

Driver Records

Dept. of Safety, Financial Responsibility Section, Attn: Driving Records, www.tn.gov/safety/dlmain.shtml Driving records are available to subscribers, signup at www.tennesseeanytime.org. There is a $75 registration fee. Records are available 24 hours daily on an interactive basis. Records are $7.00 each. Suggested only for ongoing users. Companies retrieving more than 500 records per month can use a "batch" process in which multiple license numbers can be searched and the results are returned in one file. Call 1-866-886-3468 for more information. Subscribers may also obtain a DL status check online for a fee of $1.25. **$$$** *Other Options:* Bulk retrieval is available for high volume users. Purchase of the DL file is available for approved requesters. Call Information Systems at 615-251-5322.

Vehicle Ownership & Registration

Vehicle Services Division, Records, www.tn.gov/revenue/vehicle/ Online access is available for approved subscribers at www.tennesseeanytime.org/ivtr. This is the same subscription system used to pull driving records. The $75.00 annual fee includes 10 users. IVTR allows subscribers to retrieve vehicle, title, and registration information for vehicles registered in Tennessee. Search with license plate or VIN. The fee is $2.00 per search. All subscribers must be approved per state law and guidelines of DPPA. There is a free search for temporary vehicle liens (270 days or less) on the web site for the Secretary of State. Search by debtor last name or VIN at http://tn.gov/sos/bus_svc/MotorVehicleSearch.htm. **$$$**

Campaign Finance, PACs, Lobbyists

Bureau of Ethics and Campaign Finance, 404 James Robertson Parkway, Suite 104, www.state.tn.us/sos/election/index.htm The web page at www.tn.gov/tref/cand/cand.htm offers various drop down box searches for campaign finance reports, PAC information, and lobbyist registrations.

Occupational Licensing Boards

Accountant-CPA/Firm .... http://verify.tn.gov/
Aerial Applicators/Private Applicators .... http://agriculture.state.tn.us/
Alarm Contractor .... http://verify.tn.gov/
Architect .... http://verify.tn.gov/
Athletic Trainer .... http://health.state.tn.us/licensure/
Attorney .... www.tbpr.org/Consumers/FindALawyer.aspx
Attorney - Disciplinary Actions .... www.tbpr.org/NewsAndPublications/Releases/
Auctioneer/Auction Company .... http://verify.tn.gov/
Audiologist .... http://health.state.tn.us/licensure/
Barber Shop/Barber School .... http://verify.tn.gov/
Barber/Barber Technician .... http://verify.tn.gov/
Boxing/Racing Personnel .... http://verify.tn.gov/
Candidates .... https://apps.tn.gov/tncamp-app/public/cpsearch.htm
Chiropractor/Chiropractic Assist .... http://health.state.tn.us/licensure/
Clinical Lab Technician/Personnel .... http://health.state.tn.us/Licensure/default.aspx
Collection Agent/Manager .... http://verify.tn.gov/

Contractor .... http://verify.tn.gov/
Cosmetologist/Shop/School .... http://verify.tn.gov/
Counselor, Alcohol & Drug Abuse .... http://health.state.tn.us/licensure/
Counselor, Associate/Professional .... http://health.state.tn.us/licensure/
Dentist/Dental Hygienst/Assistant .... http://health.state.tn.us/licensure/
Dietitian/Nutritionist .... http://health.state.tn.us/licensure/
Electrologist .... http://health.state.tn.us/licensure/
Electrology Instructor/School .... http://health.state.tn.us/licensure/
Elevator Inspector .... http://tennessee.gov/labor-wfd/elevatorsinsp.html
Embalmer .... http://verify.tn.gov/
Emergency Med Personnel/Dispatch/Service http://health.state.tn.us/licensure/
Engineer .... http://verify.tn.gov/
First Responder EMS .... http://health.state.tn.us/licensure/
Funeral & Burial Director/Apprentice .... http://verify.tn.gov/
Funeral & Burial Est/Cemetery .... http://verify.tn.gov/
Geologist .... http://verify.tn.gov/
Hearing Aid Dispenser .... http://health.state.tn.us/licensure/
Home Improvement .... http://verify.tn.gov/
Home Inspector .... http://verify.tn.gov/
Insurance Agent/Firm/Education Provider ... http://verify.tn.gov/
Interior Designer .... http://verify.tn.gov/
Laboratory Personnel, Medical .... http://health.state.tn.us/Licensure/default.aspx
Landscape Architect/Architect Firm .... http://verify.tn.gov/
Lobbyist .... https://apps.tn.gov/ilobbysearch-app/search.htm
Manicurist/Shampoo Technician .... http://verify.tn.gov/
Marriage & Family Therapist .... http://health.state.tn.us/licensure/
Massage Therapist/Establishment .... http://health.state.tn.us/licensure/
Medical Disciplinary Tracking .... https://health.state.tn.us/AbuseRegistry/default.aspx
Midwife .... http://health.state.tn.us/Licensure/default.aspx
Motor Vehicle Dealer/Salesperson/Auction . http://verify.tn.gov/
Notary Public .... http://state.tn.us/sos/bus_svc/iets1/ieny/PglenySearch.jsp
Nurse-RN/LPN .... http://health.state.tn.us/Licensure/default.aspx
Nursery Plant Dealer .... http://agriculture.state.tn.us/
Nurses Aide .... http://health.state.tn.us/Licensure/default.aspx
Nursing Home Administrator .... http://health.state.tn.us/licensure/
Occupational Therapist/Assistant .... http://health.state.tn.us/licensure/
Optician, Dispensing .... http://health.state.tn.us/licensure/
Optometrist .... http://health.state.tn.us/licensure/
Orthopedic Physician Assistant .... http://health.state.tn.us/Licensure/default.aspx
Osteopathic Physician .... http://health.state.tn.us/Licensure/default.aspx
Pastoral Therapist, Clinical .... http://health.state.tn.us/licensure/
Personnel Leasing .... http://verify.tn.gov/
Pesticide Applicator/Dealer/Training School http://agriculture.state.tn.us/
Pharmacist/Pharmacy/Researcher .... http://verify.tn.gov/
Physical Therapist/Assistant .... http://health.state.tn.us/Licensure/default.aspx
Physician/Medical Doctor/Assistant .... http://health.state.tn.us/Licensure/default.aspx
Podiatrist .... http://health.state.tn.us/licensure/
Polygraph Examiner .... http://verify.tn.gov/
Private Investigator/Agency .... http://verify.tn.gov/
Private Security Guard .... http://verify.tn.gov/
Psychologist/Psychological Examiner .... http://health.state.tn.us/licensure/
Racetrack .... http://verify.tn.gov/
Radiologic Assistant .... http://health.state.tn.us/licensure/
Radiologic Technician, American .... http://health.state.tn.us/Licensure/default.aspx
Real Estate Agent/Broker/Sales/Firm .... http://verify.tn.gov/

Real Estate Appraiser	http://verify.tn.gov/
Respiratory Care Therapist/Tech./Asst.	http://health.state.tn.us/Licensure/default.aspx
Securities Agent/Broker/Dealer	www.state.tn.us/securities/index.shtml
Security Guard/Company/Trainer	http://verify.tn.gov/
Social Worker, Master/Clinical	http://health.state.tn.us/licensure/
Speech Pathologist	http://health.state.tn.us/licensure/
Surveyor, Land	http://verify.tn.gov/
Timeshare Agent	http://verify.tn.gov/
Veterinarian/Animal Euthanasia Technician	http://health.state.tn.us/licensure/
Water Treatment Plant Operator	http://tn.gov/environment/fleming/docs/certification.pdf
Worker/Handlers/Registered Dealers	http://agriculture.state.tn.us/
X-Ray Technician	http://health.state.tn.us/Licensure/default.aspx

State and Local Courts

State Court Structure: **Circuit Courts** hear civil and criminal cases and appeals of decisions from City, Juvenile, Municipal and General Sessions Courts. The jurisdiction of Circuit Courts often overlaps with that of the Chancery Courts.

Criminal cases are tried in Circuit Court except in districts with separate **Criminal Courts. These courts were established by the** General Assembly in counties with heavy caseloads. Criminal Courts exist in 13 of the 31 districts and hear felony cases and misdemeanor appeals from the lower courts.

Chancery Courts handle a variety of issues including lawsuits, contract disputes, application for injunctions and name changes. A number of matters, such as divorces, adoptions, and workers' compensation, can be heard in either Chancery or Circuit court.

General Sessions Court jurisdiction varies from county to county based on state laws and private acts. But every county is served by this court of limited jurisdiction. Civil jurisdiction is restricted to specific monetary limits and types of actions. Criminal jurisdiction is limited to preliminary hearings in felony cases and to most misdemeanor cases. Combining of Circuit Court and General Sessions Courts in smaller population counties often occurs.

Each **Juvenile & Family Court**, with the exception of Bristol and Johnson City, is county-based and administered with at least one juvenile court located in each of the state's 95 counties. There are 98 courts, but 17 are designated "Private Act" Juvenile Courts while the remaining 81are General Sessions Courts with juvenile jurisdiction.

Appellate Courts: Appellate Court opinions are found at www.tncourts.gov/media/case-resources.

Statewide Court Online Access: A limited number of counties offer online access to court records. There is no statewide access system other than the access to Supreme and Appellate Court mentioned above.

County Sites:

Carter County

1st District Circuit, Criminal & General Sessions Court www.cartercountytn.gov/government/officials/circuitcourtclerk.html

Civil: General Session Dockets are shown online at www.cartercountycircuitcourt.com/gensessions.asp. Data is shown by day in a PDF format. *Criminal:* Criminal Court Dockets are shown online at www.cartercountycircuitcourt.com/circuitcriminal.asp. Data is shown by day in a PDF format.

Davidson County

Circuit Court http://circuitclerk.nashville.gov/

Civil: Access filed cases online on CaseLink at http://circuitclerk.nashville.gov/caselink/; $35.00 per month fee required plus username, password. Email Caselink@Nashville.Gov for signup or add'l info. The type of case information accessible through CaseLink is: style of the case (plaintiff vs. defendant), pleadings filed, court dates, judgments, addresses, representing attorneys, service of process, and history of payments. **$$$**

20th District Criminal Court http://ccc.nashville.gov

Criminal: Access Davidson County Criminal Court Clerk database and current session dockets at http://ccc.nashville.gov/portal/page/portal/ccc/caseSearch/caseSearchPublic/caseSearchPublicForms/.

General Sessions Court http://circuitclerk.nashville.gov/sessions/

Civil: Access filed cases online on CaseLink at http://caselink.nashville.gov/; $35.00 per month fee required, plus username and password. Email Caselink@Nashville.Gov for signup or add'l info. The type of case information accessible through CaseLink is: style of the case (plaintiff vs. defendant), pleadings filed, court dates, judgments, addresses, representing attorneys, service of process, and history of payments. **$$$**

Hamilton County

11th District Civil Court www.hamiltontn.gov/courts/

Civil: Online access to current court dockets are free at www.hamiltontn.gov/courts/Default.aspx.

Chancery Court www.hamiltontn.gov/courts/Default.aspx

Civil: Chancery motion dockets are online at www.hamiltontn.gov/courts/Chancery/dockets/default.aspx

11th District General Sessions Court www.hamiltontn.gov/courts/sessions/

Civil: Online access to current (7 days) court dockets is free on the web. Search dispositions and calendars free at http://cjusgeneralsessions.hamiltontn.gov/appfolder/GS_Web_Calendar.aspx.

11th District Criminal Court www.hamiltontn.gov/courts/

Criminal: Search court's disposition records and court dates free at http://cjuscriminal.hamiltontn.gov/AppFolder/CC_Web_Calendar.aspx and records go back to 1989. Also, online access to current court dockets is free at web page.

Jefferson County

4th District Circuit & General Sessions Court www.jeffersoncountytn.gov/

Civil: Records are not online, but a PDF list of the daily docket schedule for at least 7 days appears at www.jefferson.mytncourts.com/. *Criminal:* Records are not online, but a PDF list of the daily docket schedule for at least 7 days appears at www.jefferson.mytncourts.com/45201dlydocket.pdf.

Knox County

Circuit Court www.knoxcounty.org/circuit/index.php

Civil: Current dockets are found at www.knoxcounty.org/circuit/docket.php. There is no access to historical documents.

Putnam County

13th District Circuit & General Sessions Court www.dockets.putnamco.org

Civil: Current docket information available at the website. There is no historical data. *Criminal:* same

Shelby County

Circuit Court http://circuitcourt.shelbycountytn.gov/

Civil: Search clerk's circuit court records for free at the website or at http://circuitdata.shelbycountytn.gov/crweb/ck_public_qry_main.cp_main_idx.

30th District Criminal Court www.shelbycountytn.gov/index.aspx?nid=224

Criminal: Search the criminal court records for free at http://jssi.shelbycountytn.gov/.

General Sessions - Civil http://gs4.shelbycountytn.gov/gscvinq/gscv_civilhome

Civil: Search case history for free at http://gs4.shelbycountytn.gov/gscvinq/gscv_caseinquirieshome.

General Sessions - Criminal http://gs4.shelbycountytn.gov/gscvinq/gscr_criminaldivision

Criminal: Search criminal court records free at http://jssi.shelbycountytn.gov/.

Chancery Court www.shelbycountytn.gov/index.aspx?nid=222

Civil: Search court records for free at http://chancerydata.shelbycountytn.gov/chweb/ck_public_qry_main.cp_main_idx. Note the disclaimer, the court will not guarantee or warrant the correctness, completeness, currentness or utility for any general or specific purpose of the data made available through the access of this site.

White County

13th District Circuit & General Sessions Court www.whiteccc.com/

Civil: Current case dockets available free at www.whiteccc.com/ but no historical data. *Criminal:* same

Recorders, Assessors, and Other Sites of Note

Recording Office Organization: 95 counties, 96 recording offices. The recording officer is the Register of Deeds. Sullivan County has two recording offices. All federal tax liens are filed with the county Register of Deeds. State tax liens are filed with the Secretary of State or the Register of Deeds.

Statewide or Multi-Jurisdiction Access: Land records for a county are most-likely on one or more private vendor search sites; assessments on the statewide system and are free.

- The State Comptroller of the Treasury Real Estate Assessment Database can be searched free at www.assessment.state.tn.us/. Select a county then search by name, property address or parcel ID for real property information. All Tennessee counties except Davidson, Hamilton, Knox, Shelby, participate.
- Also, www.tnrealestate.com offers free and fee services for real estate information for all Tennessee counties.

- Online access to a number of county' property and deeds indexes and images is available via a private company at www.titlesearcher.com/countyHomepages.php?state=TN. Registration, login, and monthly $35 fee per county required, plus a one-time $20.00 set up fee. A $5 per day plan is also available. There are over 50 participating counties.
- Also, online access to a large group of county property, deeds, judgment, liens, and UCCs is available via a private company at www.ustitlesearch.net/ or call 615-223-5420. Registration, login, and monthly $25 fee required, plus $50 set up fee. Use DEMO as your username to sample the system. There are over 36 participating counties.

County Sites:

Anderson County ***Recorded Documents*** www.andersondeeds.com/ Access property and deeds indexes/images at www.titlesearcher.com/countyHomepages.php?state=TN. Must register with user name and password. Fees vary by county and type of record. **$$$**

Property, Taxation Records Assessment data on state comptroller system is free at www.assessment.state.tn.us/SelectCounty.asp?map=true&SelectCounty=030.

Bedford County ***Recorded Documents*** Access property and deeds indexes/images at www.titlesearcher.com/countyHomepages.php?state=TN. Must register with user name and password. Fees vary by county and type of record. **$$$**

Property, Taxation Records Assessment data on state comptroller system is free at www.assessment.state.tn.us/SelectCounty.asp?map=true&SelectCounty=030.

Benton County ***Property, Taxation Records*** Assessment data on state comptroller system is free at www.assessment.state.tn.us/SelectCounty.asp?map=true&SelectCounty=030.

Bledsoe County ***Recorded Documents*** www.ctas.tennessee.edu/gml-ctas.nsf/CountyOfficialsNewWeb/640A1AADC9896F6F85256AF70058D010?OpenDocument Access property and deeds indexes/images at www.titlesearcher.com/countyHomepages.php?state=TN. Must register with user name and password. Fees vary by county and type of record. **$$$**

Property, Taxation Records Assessment data on state comptroller system is free at www.assessment.state.tn.us/SelectCounty.asp?map=true&SelectCounty=030.

Blount County ***Property, Taxation Records*** Assessment data on state comptroller system is free at www.assessment.state.tn.us/SelectCounty.asp?map=true&SelectCounty=030.

Bradley County ***Recorded Documents*** www.bradleyco.net/registerofdeedshome.aspx Access property and deeds indexes/images at www.titlesearcher.com/countyHomepages.php?state=TN. Must register with user name and password. Fees vary by county and type of record. **$$$**

Property, Taxation Records Assessment data on state comptroller system is free at www.assessment.state.tn.us/SelectCounty.asp?map=true&SelectCounty=030.

Campbell County ***Recorded Documents*** Access property and deeds indexes/images at www.titlesearcher.com/countyHomepages.php?state=TN. Must register with user name and password. Fees vary by county and type of record. **$$$**

Property, Taxation Records Assessment data on state comptroller system is free at www.assessment.state.tn.us/SelectCounty.asp?map=true&SelectCounty=030.

Cannon County ***Real Estate, Deed, Judgment, Lien, UCC Records*** Access real estate records at www1.ustitlesearch.net/, registration/fee required; also see state introduction. **$$$**

Property, Taxation Records Assessment data on state comptroller system is free at www.assessment.state.tn.us/SelectCounty.asp?map=true&SelectCounty=030.

Carroll County ***Real Estate, Deed, Judgment, Lien, UCC Records*** Access real estate indexes and images at www1.ustitlesearch.net/. Registration/monthly fee required. Also, see state introduction. **$$$**

Property, Taxation Records Assessment data on state comptroller system is free at www.assessment.state.tn.us/SelectCounty.asp?map=true&SelectCounty=030.

Carter County ***Recorded Documents*** www.cartercountytn.gov/government/officials/registerofdeeds.html Access property and deeds indexes/images at www.titlesearcher.com/countyHomepages.php?state=TN. Must register with user name and password. Fees vary by county and type of record. **$$$**

Property, Taxation Records Assessment data on state comptroller system is free at www.assessment.state.tn.us/SelectCounty.asp?map=true&SelectCounty=030.

Cheatham County ***Real Estate, Deed, Judgment, Lien, UCC Records*** http://cheathamcountytn.gov Access real estate indexes/images at www1.ustitlesearch.net/; registration/monthly fee required. Also see state introduction. **$$$**

Property, Taxation Records Assessment data on state comptroller system is free at www.assessment.state.tn.us/SelectCounty.asp?map=true&SelectCounty=030.

Chester County ***Recorded Documents*** http://chestercountytn.org/county_offices/index.html#register Access real estate indexes/images at www1.ustitlesearch.net/; registration/monthly fee required. Also see state introduction. **$$$**
Property, Taxation Records Assessment data on state comptroller system is free at www.assessment.state.tn.us/SelectCounty.asp?map=true&SelectCounty=030.

Claiborne County ***Recorded Documents*** Access property and deeds indexes/images at www.titlesearcher.com/countyHomepages.php?state=TN. Must register with user name and password. Fees vary by county and type of record. **$$$**
Property, Taxation Records Assessment data on state comptroller system is free at www.assessment.state.tn.us/SelectCounty.asp?map=true&SelectCounty=030.

Clay County ***Recorded Documents*** Access property and deeds indexes/images at www.titlesearcher.com/countyHomepages.php?state=TN. Must register with user name and password. Fees vary by county and type of record. **$$$**
Property, Taxation Records Assessment data on state comptroller system is free at www.assessment.state.tn.us/SelectCounty.asp?map=true&SelectCounty=030.

Cocke County ***Recorded Documents*** Access property and deeds indexes/images at www.titlesearcher.com/countyHomepages.php?state=TN. Must register with user name and password. Fees vary by county and type of record. **$$$**
Property, Taxation Records Assessment data on state comptroller system is free at www.assessment.state.tn.us/SelectCounty.asp?map=true&SelectCounty=030.

Coffee County ***Recorded Documents*** www.coffeecountytn.org/government/elected_offices/register_of_deeds/index.html Access property and deeds indexes/images at www.titlesearcher.com/countyHomepages.php?state=TN. Must register with user name and password. Fees vary by county and type of record. **$$$**
Property, Taxation Records Assessment data on state comptroller system is free at www.assessment.state.tn.us/SelectCounty.asp?map=true&SelectCounty=030. Also, access to GIS/mapping free at www.waalex.com/webgis/coff_gismap.html.

Crockett County ***Real Estate, Deed, Judgment, Lien, UCC Records*** Access real estate indexes/images at www1.ustitlesearch.net/; registration/monthly fee required. Also, see state introduction. **$$$**
Property, Taxation Records Assessment data on state comptroller system is free at www.assessment.state.tn.us/SelectCounty.asp?map=true&SelectCounty=030.

Cumberland County ***Recorded Documents*** http://cumberlandcountytn.gov/register-of-deeds/ Access property and deeds indexes/images at www.titlesearcher.com/countyHomepages.php?state=TN. Must register with user name and password. Fees vary by county and type of record. **$$$**
Property, Taxation Records Assessment data on state comptroller system is at www.assessment.state.tn.us/SelectCounty.asp?map=true&SelectCounty=030.

Davidson County ***Recorded Documents*** www.nashville.gov/Register-of-Deeds.aspx The records of the Davidson County Register of Deeds office are available on line by subscription. Subscription rates are $ 100.00 per month by check, or $ 75.00 per month through Automatic Withdrawal. Images are available. Call Charles Synder. See www.nashville.gov/rod/internet_svc_desc.asp. **$$$**
Property, Taxation Records Search county assessments free at www.padctn.com/propertywebprodata.htm. Click on property Webpro data link. Also, access to GIS/mapping is free at http://maps.nashville.gov/HomePage/index.html.

Decatur County ***Recorded Documents*** Access property and deeds indexes/images at www.titlesearcher.com/countyHomepages.php?state=TN. Must register with user name and password. Fees vary by county and type of record. **$$$**
Property, Taxation Records Assessment data on state comptroller system is free at www.assessment.state.tn.us/SelectCounty.asp?map=true&SelectCounty=030.

DeKalb County ***Property, Taxation Records*** Assessment data on state comptroller system is free at www.assessment.state.tn.us/SelectCounty.asp?map=true&SelectCounty=030.

Dickson County ***Property, Taxation Records*** Assessment data on state comptroller system is free at www.assessment.state.tn.us/SelectCounty.asp?map=true&SelectCounty=030.

Dyer County ***Real Estate, Deed, Judgment, Lien, UCC Records*** Access real estate indexes/images at www1.ustitlesearch.net/; registration/monthly fee required. Also see state introduction. **$$$**
Property, Taxation Records Assessment data on state comptroller system is free at www.assessment.state.tn.us/SelectCounty.asp?map=true&SelectCounty=030.

Fayette County ***Recorded Documents*** www.fayettetn.us/CountyDepts/Register.htm Access property and deeds indexes/images at www.titlesearcher.com/countyHomepages.php?state=TN. Must register with user name and password. Fees vary by county and type of record. **$$$**
Property, Taxation Records Assessment data on state comptroller system is free at www.assessment.state.tn.us/SelectCounty.asp?map=true&SelectCounty=030.

Fentress County ***Recorded Documents*** Access property and deeds indexes/images at www.titlesearcher.com/countyHomepages.php?state=TN. Must register with user name and password. Fees vary by county and type of record. **$$$**
Property, Taxation Records Assessment data on state comptroller system is free at www.assessment.state.tn.us/SelectCounty.asp?map=true&SelectCounty=030.

Franklin County ***Recorded Documents*** Access property and deeds indexes/images at www.titlesearcher.com/countyHomepages.php?state=TN. Must register with user name and password. Fees vary by county and type of record. **$$$**
Property, Taxation Records Assessment data on state comptroller system is free at www.assessment.state.tn.us/SelectCounty.asp?map=true&SelectCounty=030.

Gibson County ***Real Estate, Deed, Judgment, Lien, UCC Records*** Access real estate indexes/images at www1.ustitlesearch.net/; registration/monthly fee required. Also see state introduction. **$$$**
Property, Taxation Records Assessment data on state comptroller system is free at www.assessment.state.tn.us/SelectCounty.asp?map=true&SelectCounty=030.

Giles County ***Recorded Documents*** www.gilescounty-tn.us/CountyOfficials.aspx Access property and deeds indexes/images at www.titlesearcher.com/countyHomepages.php?state=TN. Must register with user name and password. Fees vary by county and type of record. **$$$**
Property, Taxation Records Assessment data on state comptroller system is free at www.assessment.state.tn.us/SelectCounty.asp?map=true&SelectCounty=030.

Grainger County ***Recorded Documents*** Access property and deeds indexes/images at www.titlesearcher.com/countyHomepages.php?state=TN. Must register with user name and password. Fees vary by county and type of record. **$$$**
Property, Taxation Records Assessment data on state comptroller system is free at www.assessment.state.tn.us/SelectCounty.asp?map=true&SelectCounty=030.

Greene County ***Recorded Documents*** www.greenecountytngov.com/e_registerofdeeds.php Access property and deeds indexes/images at www.titlesearcher.com/countyHomepages.php?state=TN. Must register with user name and password. Fees vary by county and type of record. In 1999 the Register's office implemented a computer imaging system. Once documents are saved into the data base they can be viewed by the public in deed room or via the web. **$$$**
Property, Taxation Records Assessment data on state comptroller system is free at www.assessment.state.tn.us/SelectCounty.asp?map=true&SelectCounty=030.

Grundy County ***Property, Taxation Records*** Assessment data on state comptroller system is free at www.assessment.state.tn.us/SelectCounty.asp?map=true&SelectCounty=030.

Hamblen County ***Recorded Documents*** www.hamblencountygovernment.us/county_commission/register_of_deeds.html Access property and deeds indexes/images at www.titlesearcher.com/countyHomepages.php?state=TN. Must register with user name and password. Fees vary by county and type of record. **$$$**
Property, Taxation Records Assessment data on state comptroller system is free at www.assessment.state.tn.us/SelectCounty.asp?map=true&SelectCounty=032.

Hamilton County ***Real Estate, Deed Records*** www.hamiltontn.gov/register/ County Register of Deeds subscription service is $50 per month and $1.00 per fax page. Search by name, address, or book & page. For info, call 423-209-6560; or visit www.hamiltontn.gov/Register/. Credit cards accepted. **$$$**
Property, Taxation Records Property assessor records are free at http://assessor.hamiltontn.gov/PropertyInquiry/InquiryHome/PropertySearch.aspx. Search property taxes at www.hamiltontn.gov/trustee/default.aspx. Also, search City of Chattanooga property tax database at http://propertytax.chattanooga.gov.

Hancock County ***Real Estate, Deed, Judgment, Lien, UCC Records*** Access real estate indexes/images at www1.ustitlesearch.net/; registration/monthly fee required. Also see state introduction. **$$$**
Property, Taxation Records Assessment data on state comptroller system is free at www.assessment.state.tn.us/SelectCounty.asp.

Hardeman County ***Real Estate, Deed, Judgment, Lien, UCC Records*** http://hardemancountytn.com/government/hardeman-county/registers-office.php Access real estate indexes/images at www1.ustitlesearch.net/; registration/monthly fee required. Also see state introduction. **$$$**
Property, Taxation Records Assessment data on state comptroller system is free at www.assessment.state.tn.us/SelectCounty.asp?map=true&SelectCounty=030.

Hardin County ***Real Estate, Deed, Judgment, Lien, UCC Records*** www.ctas.tennessee.edu/gml-ctas.nsf/CountyOfficialsNewWeb/3DE1E98DEA1DAB1E85256AF70058BB3E?OpenDocument Access real estate indexes/images at www1.ustitlesearch.net/; registration/monthly fee required. Also see state introduction. **$$$**
Property, Taxation Records Assessment data on state comptroller system is free at www.assessment.state.tn.us/SelectCounty.asp?map=true&SelectCounty=030.

Hawkins County ***Recorded Documents*** www.hawkinscountytn.gov/index.php?option=com_content&view=article&id=26&Itemid=38 Access property and deeds indexes/images at www.titlesearcher.com/countyHomepages.php?state=TN. Must register with user name and password. Fees vary by county and type of record. **$$$**

Property, Taxation Records Assessment data on state comptroller system is free at www.assessment.state.tn.us/SelectCounty.asp?map=true&SelectCounty=030.

Haywood County ***Real Estate, Deed Records*** Access real estate indexes/images at www1.ustitlesearch.net/; registration/monthly fee required. Also see state introduction. **$$$**

Property, Taxation Records Assessment data on state comptroller system is free at www.assessment.state.tn.us/SelectCounty.asp?map=true&SelectCounty=030.

Henderson County ***Real Estate, Deed, Judgment, Lien, UCC Records*** Access real estate indexes/images at www1.ustitlesearch.net/; registration/monthly fee required. Also see state introduction. **$$$**

Property, Taxation Records Assessment data on state comptroller system is free at www.assessment.state.tn.us/SelectCounty.asp?map=true&SelectCounty=030.

Henry County ***Real Estate, Deed, Judgment, Lien, UCC Records*** www.henryco.com/offices/registerofdeeds.htm Access real estate indexes/images at www1.ustitlesearch.net/; registration/monthly fee required. Also see state introduction. **$$$**

Property, Taxation Records Assessment data on state comptroller system is free at www.assessment.state.tn.us/SelectCounty.asp?map=true&SelectCounty=030.

Hickman County ***Recorded Documents*** Access property and deeds indexes/images at www.titlesearcher.com/countyHomepages.php?state=TN. Must register with user name and password. Fees vary by county and type of record. **$$$**

Property, Taxation Records Assessment data on state comptroller system is free at www.assessment.state.tn.us/SelectCounty.asp?map=true&SelectCounty=030.

Houston County ***Real Estate, Deed, Judgment, Lien, UCC Records*** www.houstoncochamber.com/news.php?viewStory=76 Access real estate indexes/images at www1.ustitlesearch.net/; registration/monthly fee required. Also see state introduction. **$$$**

Property, Taxation Records Assessment data on state comptroller system is free at www.assessment.state.tn.us/SelectCounty.asp?map=true&SelectCounty=030.

Humphreys County ***Recorded Documents*** www.humphreystn.com/register_of_deeds/index.html Access property and deeds indexes/images at www.titlesearcher.com/countyHomepages.php?state=TN. Must register with user name and password. Fees vary by county and type of record. **$$$**

Property, Taxation Records Assessment data on state comptroller system is free at www.assessment.state.tn.us/SelectCounty.asp?map=true&SelectCounty=030.

Jackson County ***Recorded Documents*** www.jacksonco.com/register-of-deeds.htm Access property and deeds indexes/images at www.titlesearcher.com/countyHomepages.php?state=TN. Must register with user name and password. Fees vary by county and type of record. **$$$**

Property, Taxation Records Assessment data on state comptroller system is free at www.assessment.state.tn.us/SelectCounty.asp?map=true&SelectCounty=030.

Jefferson County ***Recorded Documents*** www.jeffersoncountytn.gov/businesses/register-of-deeds/ Access property and deeds indexes/images at www.titlesearcher.com/countyHomepages.php?state=TN. Must register with user name and password. Fees vary by county and type of record. **$$$**

Property, Taxation Records Assessment data on state comptroller system is free at URL www.assessment.state.tn.us/SelectCounty.asp?map=true&SelectCounty=030.

Johnson County ***Recorded Documents*** http://johnsoncountytnchamber.org/?attachment_id=15 Access property and deeds indexes/images at www.titlesearcher.com/countyHomepages.php?state=TN. Must register with user name and password. Fees vary by county and type of record. **$$$**

Property, Taxation Records Assessment data on state comptroller system is free at www.assessment.state.tn.us/SelectCounty.asp?map=true&SelectCounty=030.

Knox County ***Recorded Documents*** www.knoxcounty.org/register/ For online subscription for recorded document records call Rose Browing at 865-215-3535. Reportedly the online index of recorded documents may be missing information on older records. **$$$**

Property, Taxation Records Search the property tax rolls for free at https://www.knoxcounty.org/apps/tax_search/index.php. Search assessor records at http://tn-knox-assessor.publicaccessnow.com/Welcome.aspx. A comparison look-up is at http://tn-knox-assessor.publicaccessnow.com/PropertyLookup.aspx.

Lake County ***Real Estate, Deed, Judgment, Lien, UCC Records*** Access real estate indexes/images at www1.ustitlesearch.net/; registration/monthly fee required. Also see state introduction. **$$$**

Property, Taxation Records Assessment data on state comptroller system is free at www.assessment.state.tn.us/SelectCounty.asp?map=true&SelectCounty=030.

Lauderdale County ***Real Estate, Deed, Judgment, Lien, UCC Records*** Access real estate indexes/images at www1.ustitlesearch.net/; registration/monthly fee required. Also see state introduction. **$$$**
Property, Taxation Records Assessment data on state comptroller system is free at www.assessment.state.tn.us/SelectCounty.asp?map=true&SelectCounty=030.

Lawrence County ***Recorded Documents*** www.lawrencecountytn.gov/Departments/register-of-deeds Access property and deeds indexes/images at www.titlesearcher.com/countyHomepages.php?state=TN. Must register with user name and password. Fees vary by county and type of record. **$$$**
Property, Taxation Records Assessment data on state comptroller system is free at www.assessment.state.tn.us/SelectCounty.asp?map=true&SelectCounty=030. Access to GIS/mapping free at http://tnmap.state.tn.us/Assessment/.

Lewis County ***Recorded Documents*** http://lewiscountytn.com/Register%20of%20Deeds.html Access real estate indexes/images at www1.ustitlesearch.net/; registration/monthly fee required. Also see state introduction. **$$$**
Property, Taxation Records Assessment data on state comptroller system is free at www.assessment.state.tn.us/SelectCounty.asp?map=true&SelectCounty=030.

Lincoln County ***Recorded Documents*** www.lincolncountytngov.com/officials.html Access property and deeds indexes/images at www.titlesearcher.com/countyHomepages.php?state=TN. Must register with user name and password. Fees vary by county and type of record. **$$$**
Property, Taxation Records Assessment data on state comptroller system is free at www.assessment.state.tn.us/. Also, search property/GIS data free at www.emapsplus.com/TNLincoln/maps/.

Loudon County ***Recorded Documents*** Access property and deeds indexes/images at www.titlesearcher.com/countyHomepages.php?state=TN. Must register with user name and password. Fees vary by county and type of record. **$$$**
Property, Taxation Records Assessment data on state comptroller system is free at www.assessment.state.tn.us/SelectCounty.asp?map=true&SelectCounty=030.

McMinn County ***Real Estate, Deed, Judgment, Lien, UCC Records*** http://mcminncountytn.gov/register_of_deeds/register_of_deeds.html Access real estate indexes/images back to 9/1999 at www1.ustitlesearch.net/; registration/monthly fee required. Also see state introduction. **$$$**
Property, Taxation Records Assessment data on state comptroller system is free at www.assessment.state.tn.us/SelectCounty.asp?map=true&SelectCounty=030. Also, access to parcel and maps data free at http://tn.mcminn.geopowered.com/.

McNairy County ***Recorded Documents*** www.mcnairycountytn.com/register_of_deeds.htm Access real estate indexes/images at www1.ustitlesearch.net/; registration/monthly fee required. Also see state introduction. **$$$**
Property, Taxation Records Assessment data on state comptroller system is free at www.assessment.state.tn.us/SelectCounty.asp?map=true&SelectCounty=030.

Macon County ***Recorded Documents*** www.maconcountytn.com/register_of_deeds.htm Access property and deeds indexes/images at www.titlesearcher.com/countyHomepages.php?state=TN. Must register with user name and password. Fees vary by county and type of record. **$$$**
Property, Taxation Records Assessment data on state comptroller system is free at www.assessment.state.tn.us/SelectCounty.asp?map=true&SelectCounty=030.

Madison County ***Recorded Documents*** www.co.madison.tn.us/index.aspx?nid=118 Access property and deeds indexes/images at www.titlesearcher.com/countyHomepages.php?state=TN. Must register with user name and password. Fees vary by county and type of record. **$$$**
Property, Taxation Records Assessment data on state comptroller system is free at www.assessment.state.tn.us/SelectCounty.asp?map=true&SelectCounty=030.

Marion County ***Recorded Documents*** Access property and deeds indexes/images at www.titlesearcher.com/countyHomepages.php?state=TN. Must register with user name and password. Fees vary by county and type of record. **$$$**
Property, Taxation Records Assessment data on state comptroller system is free at www.assessment.state.tn.us/SelectCounty.asp?map=true&SelectCounty=030.

Marshall County ***Property, Taxation Records*** Assessment data on state comptroller system is free at www.assessment.state.tn.us/SelectCounty.asp?map=true&SelectCounty=030.

Maury County ***Recorded Documents*** Access property and deeds indexes/images at www.titlesearcher.com/countyHomepages.php?state=TN. Must register with user name and password. Fees vary by county and type of record. **$$$**
Property, Taxation Records Assessment data on state comptroller system is free at www.assessment.state.tn.us/. Also, search property/GIS data free at www.emapsplus.com/TNMaury/maps/.

Meigs County ***Real Estate, Deed Records*** Access real estate indexes/images at www1.ustitlesearch.net/; registration/monthly fee required. Also see state introduction. **$$$**
Property, Taxation Records Assessment data on state comptroller system is free at www.assessment.state.tn.us/SelectCounty.asp?map=true&SelectCounty=030.

Monroe County ***Recorded Documents*** Access property and deeds indexes/images at www.titlesearcher.com/countyHomepages.php?state=TN. Must register with user name and password. Fees vary by county and type of record. **$$$**
Property, Taxation Records Assessment data on state comptroller system is free at www.assessment.state.tn.us/SelectCounty.asp?map=true&SelectCounty=030.

Montgomery County ***Real Estate, Deed, Judgment, Lien, UCC Records*** www.mcgtn.org/deeds Access real estate indexes/images at www1.ustitlesearch.net/; registration/monthly fee required. Also see state introduction. **$$$**
Property, Taxation Records Assessment data on state comptroller system is free at www.assessment.state.tn.us/SelectCounty.asp?map=true&SelectCounty=030.

Moore County ***Recorded Documents*** www.ctas.tennessee.edu/gml-ctas.nsf/CountyOfficialsNewWeb/0CB2127ECFF460A186257724006A8285?OpenDocument Access property and deeds indexes/images at www.titlesearcher.com/countyHomepages.php?state=TN. Must register with user name and password. Fees vary by county and type of record. **$$$**
Property, Taxation Records Assessment data on state comptroller system is free at www.assessment.state.tn.us/SelectCounty.asp?map=true&SelectCounty=030.

Morgan County ***Recorded Documents*** Access real estate indexes/images at www1.ustitlesearch.net/; registration/monthly fee required. Also see state introduction. **$$$**
Property, Taxation Records Assessment data on state comptroller system is free at www.assessment.state.tn.us/SelectCounty.asp?map=true&SelectCounty=030.

Obion County ***Property, Taxation Records*** Assessment data on state comptroller system is free at www.assessment.state.tn.us/SelectCounty.asp?map=true&SelectCounty=030.

Overton County ***Real Estate, Deed Records*** www.overtoncountytn.com/index.php?option=com_content&task=view&id=11&Itemid=16 Access real estate indexes/images at www1.ustitlesearch.net/; registration/monthly fee required. Also see state introduction. **$$$**
Property, Taxation Records Assessment data on state comptroller system is free at www.assessment.state.tn.us/SelectCounty.asp?map=true&SelectCounty=030.

Perry County ***Recorded Documents*** Access property and deeds indexes/images at www.titlesearcher.com/countyHomepages.php?state=TN. Must register with user name and password. Fees vary by county and type of record. **$$$**
Property, Taxation Records Assessment data on state comptroller system is free at www.assessment.state.tn.us/SelectCounty.asp?map=true&SelectCounty=030.

Pickett County ***Recorded Documents*** www.lethamccurdy.com/index.html Access property and deeds indexes/images at www.titlesearcher.com/countyHomepages.php?state=TN. Must register with user name and password. Fees vary by county and type of record. **$$$**
Property, Taxation Records Assessment data on state comptroller system is free at www.assessment.state.tn.us/SelectCounty.asp?map=true&SelectCounty=030.

Polk County ***Recorded Documents*** www.polkgovernment.com/register-of-deeds Access property and deeds indexes/images at www.titlesearcher.com/countyHomepages.php?state=TN. Must register with user name and password. Fees vary by county and type of record. **$$$**
Property, Taxation Records Assessment data on state comptroller system is free at www.assessment.state.tn.us/SelectCounty.asp?map=true&SelectCounty=030.

Putnam County ***Real Estate, Deed, Judgment, Lien, UCC Records*** www.putnamcountytn.gov/index.php?p=departments&s=register Access real estate indexes/images at www1.ustitlesearch.net/; registration/monthly fee required. **$$$**
Property, Taxation Records Assessment data on state comptroller system is free at www.assessment.state.tn.us/. Also, search property/GIS data free at www.emapsplus.com/TNputnam/maps/. Also see state introduction.

Rhea County ***Recorded Documents*** Access property and deeds indexes/images at www.titlesearcher.com/countyHomepages.php?state=TN. Must register with user name and password. Fees vary by county and type of record. **$$$**
Property, Taxation Records Assessment data on state comptroller system is free at www.assessment.state.tn.us/SelectCounty.asp?map=true&SelectCounty=030.

Roane County ***Recorded Documents*** www.roanegov.org/index.html Access property and deeds indexes/images at www.titlesearcher.com/countyHomepages.php?state=TN. Must register with user name and password. Fees vary by county and type of record. **$$$**
Property, Taxation Records Assessment data on state comptroller system is free at www.assessment.state.tn.us/SelectCounty.asp?map=true&SelectCounty=030. Access to parcel search and maps free at http://tn.roane.geopowered.com/.

Robertson County ***Recorded Documents*** Access real estate indexes/images at www.ustitlesearch.net/; registration/monthly fee required. Also see state introduction. **$$$**
Property, Taxation Records Assessment data on state comptroller system is free at www.assessment.state.tn.us/SelectCounty.asp?map=true&SelectCounty=030.

Rutherford County ***Real Estate, Deed, Judgment, Lien, UCC Records*** www.rutherfordcountytn.gov/dept/register.htm Access real estate indexes/images at www1.ustitlesearch.net/; registration/monthly fee required. To subscribe call 615-223-1823. Also see state introduction. **$$$**
Property, Taxation Records Access to property data for free at www.rutherfordcounty.org/assessor/Default.htm. Also, access to GIS/mapping free at http://maps.rutherfordcounty.org/Freeance/Client/PublicAccess1/index.html?appconfig=Rutherford2.

Scott County ***Property, Taxation Records*** Assessment data on state comptroller system is free at www.assessment.state.tn.us/SelectCounty.asp?map=true&SelectCounty=030.

Sequatchie County ***Recorded Documents*** www.sequatchiecounty-tn.gov/ Access property and deeds indexes/images at www.titlesearcher.com/countyHomepages.php?state=TN. Must register with user name and password. Fees vary by county and type of record. **$$$**
Property, Taxation Records Assessment data on state comptroller system is free at www.assessment.state.tn.us/SelectCounty.asp?map=true&SelectCounty=001.

Sevier County ***Recorded Documents*** www.seviercountytn.gov/index.php?option=com_content&view=article&id=26&Itemid=38 Access property and deeds indexes/images at www.titlesearcher.com/countyHomepages.php?state=TN. Must register with user name and password. Fees vary by county and type of record. **$$$**
Property, Taxation Records Assessment data on state comptroller system is free at www.assessment.state.tn.us/SelectCounty.asp?map=true&SelectCounty=030.

Shelby County ***Recorded Documents*** http://register.shelby.tn.us/ Access the Register of Deeds database free at http://register.shelby.tn.us/index.php. Partial indexes and images go back to 1986; full to 12/2001. Also, access property and deeds indexes/images at www.titlesearcher.com/countyHomepages.php?state=TN. Must register with user name and password. Fees vary by county and type of record. **$$$**
Property, Taxation Records Access property assessor data free at www.assessor.shelby.tn.us/content.aspx. Also, access to personal property search free at www.assessor.shelby.tn.us/Accept.aspx.

Smith County ***Recorded Documents*** Access property and deeds indexes/images at www.titlesearcher.com/countyHomepages.php?state=TN. Must register with user name and password. Fees vary by county and type of record. **$$$**
Property, Taxation Records Assessment data on state comptroller system is free at www.assessment.state.tn.us/SelectCounty.asp?map=true&SelectCounty=030.

Stewart County ***Recorded Documents*** www.stewartcogov.com/elected_officials/elected_officials.html Access real estate indexes/images at www1.ustitlesearch.net/; registration/monthly fee required. Also see state introduction. **$$$**
Property, Taxation Records Assessment data on state comptroller system is free at www.assessment.state.tn.us/SelectCounty.asp?map=true&SelectCounty=030.

Sullivan County (Blountville Office) ***Recorded Documents*** www.sullivancountytn.gov/node/19 Access property and deeds indexes/images at www.titlesearcher.com/countyHomepages.php?state=TN. Must register with user name and password. Fees vary by county and type of record. **$$$**
Property, Taxation Records Assessment data on state comptroller system is free at www.assessment.state.tn.us/SelectCounty.asp?map=true&SelectCounty=030.

Sullivan County (Bristol Office) ***Recorded Documents*** Access property and deeds indexes/images at www.titlesearcher.com/countyHomepages.php?state=TN. Must register with user name and password. Fees vary by county and type of record. **$$$**
Property, Taxation Records Office closed. Records in Bountville, TN office.

Sumner County ***Recorded Documents*** www.deeds.sumnercounty.org Access real estate indexes and deed images back to 1787 and /images back to 10/22/1989 at www.ustitlesearch.net/; registration/monthly fee required. Deeds of Trust back to 1972. Also see state introduction. **$$$**
Property, Taxation Records Assessment data on state comptroller system is free at www.assessment.state.tn.us/SelectCounty.asp?map=true&SelectCounty=030. Also, search property data free on the GIS site at http://tn.sumner.geopowered.com.

Tipton County ***Property, Taxation Records*** Assessment data on state comptroller system is free at www.assessment.state.tn.us/SelectCounty.asp.

Trousdale County ***Real Estate, Deed, Judgment, Lien, UCC Records*** Access real estate indexes/images back to 10/22/1989 at www1.ustitlesearch.net/; registration/monthly fee required. Also see state introduction. **$$$**
Property, Taxation Records Assessment data on state comptroller system is free at www.assessment.state.tn.us/SelectCounty.asp?map=true&SelectCounty=030.

Unicoi County ***Recorded Documents*** www.unicoicountytn.gov/ Access property and deeds indexes/images at www.titlesearcher.com/countyHomepages.php?state=TN. Must register with user name and password. Fees vary by county and type of record. **$$$**

Union County ***Recorded Documents*** www.unioncountytn.com/register_of_deeds/registerofdeeds.htm Access property and deeds indexes/images at www.titlesearcher.com/countyHomepages.php?state=TN. Must register with user name and password. Fees vary by county and type of record. **$$$**

Property, Taxation Records Access assessment data on the state comptroller system free at www.assessment.state.tn.us/SelectCounty.asp?map=true&SelectCounty=030.

Van Buren County ***Recorded Documents*** www.ctas.tennessee.edu/gml-ctas.nsf/CountyOfficialsNewWeb/A5802D5034B2B8C186257728006D02C5?OpenDocument Access property and deeds indexes/images at www.titlesearcher.com/countyHomepages.php?state=TN. Must register with user name and password. Fees vary by county and type of record. **$$$**
Property, Taxation Records Assessment data on state comptroller system is free at www.assessment.state.tn.us/SelectCounty.asp?map=true&SelectCounty=030.

Warren County ***Real Estate, Deed, Judgment, Lien, UCC Records*** www.warrencountytn.gov/deeds.asp Access real estate indexes/images at www1.ustitlesearch.net/; registration/monthly fee required. Also see state introduction. **$$$**
Property, Taxation Records Assessment data on state comptroller system is free at www.assessment.state.tn.us/SelectCounty.asp?map=true&SelectCounty=030.

Washington County ***Recorded Documents*** www.washingtoncountytn.org/government/register_of_deeds Access property and deeds indexes/images at www.titlesearcher.com/countyHomepages.php?state=TN. Must register with user name and password. Fees vary by county and type of record. **$$$**
Property, Taxation Records Assessment data on state comptroller system is free at www.assessment.state.tn.us/.

Wayne County ***Property, Taxation Records*** Assessment data on state comptroller system is free at www.assessment.state.tn.us/SelectCounty.asp?map=true&SelectCounty=030.

Weakley County ***Recorded Documents*** www.weakleycountytn.gov/registerofdeeds.html Access property and deeds indexes/images at www.titlesearcher.com/countyHomepages.php?state=TN. Must register with user name and password. Fees vary by county and type of record. **$$$**
Property, Taxation Records Assessment data on state comptroller system is free at www.assessment.state.tn.us/SelectCounty.asp?map=true&SelectCounty=030.

White County ***Recorded Documents*** www.ctas.tennessee.edu/gml-ctas.nsf/CountyOfficialsNewWeb/E2BAE5D762D053B485256AF70058D03D?OpenDocument Access property and deeds indexes/images at www.titlesearcher.com/countyHomepages.php?state=TN. Must register with user name and password. Fees vary by county and type of record. **$$$**
Property, Taxation Records Assessment data on state comptroller system is free at www.assessment.state.tn.us/SelectCounty.asp?map=true&SelectCounty=030.

Williamson County ***Recorded Documents*** www.williamsoncounty-tn.gov/index.aspx?nid=61 Access to the Professional Access database by subscription is a $50 per month fee. Info and sign-up at http://williamson-tn.org/co_gov/profacc.htm. Also,access property and deeds indexes/images at www.titlesearcher.com/countyHomepages.php?state=TN. Must register with user name and password. Fees vary by county and type of record. **$$$**
Property, Taxation Records Assessment data on state comptroller system is free at www.assessment.state.tn.us/SelectCounty.asp?map=true&SelectCounty=030. Also, access to property search data free go to http://inigo.williamson-tn.org/assessor/.

Wilson County ***Recorded Documents*** www.wilsondeeds.com Access to the Register of Deeds database requires a $10 registration fee and $25.00 per month usage fee at www.wilsondeeds.com/. Includes indices back to 1925; images back to 1992. Also, access property and deeds indexes/images at www.titlesearcher.com/countyHomepages.php?state=TN. Must register with user name and password. Fees vary by county and type of record. **$$$**
Property, Taxation Records Assessment data on state comptroller system is free at www.assessment.state.tn.us/SelectCounty.asp?map=true&SelectCounty=030.

Texas

Capital: Austin
Travis County
Time Zone: CST
Texas' two most western ounties are in MST:
They are El paso and Hudspeth.
Population: 26,059,203
# of Counties: 254

Useful State Links

Website: www.texas.gov
Governor: www.governor.state.tx.us
Attorney General: www.oag.state.tx.us
State Archives: https://www.tsl.state.tx.us/
State Statutes and Codes: www.capitol.state.tx.us/
or search at www.statutes.legis.state.tx.us/
Legislative Bill Search and Monitoring: www.legis.state.tx.us/Search/BillSearch.aspx
or if you know the number www.legis.state.tx.us/BillLookup/BillNumber.aspx
Unclaimed Funds: https://txcpa.cpa.state.tx.us/up/Search.jsp

State Public Record Agencies

Criminal Records

DPS - Access & Dissemination Bureau, Crime Records Service, https://records.txdps.state.tx.us/DpsWebsite/Index.aspx The Texas Department of Public Safety offers two websites for accessing criminal records. The Public site at https://records.txdps.state.tx.us. Public requesters may use a credit card and establish an account to pre-purchase credits. The fee established by the Department (Sec. 411.135(b)) is $3.15 per request plus a $.57 handling fee. The other site is strictly for eligible entities authorized by law. See https://secure.txdps.state.tx.us/DpsWebsite/Index.aspx. These checks are instantaneous and provide convictions and deferred adjudications only. **$$$**

Sexual Offender Registry

Dept of Public Safety, Sex Offender Registration, https://records.txdps.state.tx.us/SexOffender/PublicSite/Index.aspx Sex offender data is available at the web page. There is no charge for a sex offender search. Search by name or city/ZIP or by map. The Department of Public Safety has a notification system that allows the public to subscribe to e-mail notifications regarding database changes relating to registered sex offenders. The signup is available at this site. Also, one may download the offender database from the web page. The data is updated twice a week and is available at no charge to users.

Incarceration Records

Texas Department of Criminal Justice, Bureau of Classification and Records, www.tdcj.state.tx.us Name searching is available from this agency at http://offender.tdcj.state.tx.us/POSdb2/index.jsp. You may also send an email search request to exec.services@tdcj.state.tx.us.

Corporation, LLC, LP, Fictitious/Assumed Name, Trademarks/Servicemarks

Secretary of State, Corporation Section, www.sos.state.tx.us Corporate and other TX Sec of State data is available via SOSDirect on the Web; visit www.sos.state.tx.us/corp/sosda/index.shtml. Printing and certifying capabilities available. Web access is available 24 hours daily. There is a $1.00 fee for each record searched. Filing procedures and forms are available from the website. Also, of note (but from another agencies) one may search securities dept enforcement actions- www.ssb.state.tx.us/Enforcement/Recent_Enforcement_Actions.php. **$$$** *Other Options:* The agency makes portions of its database available for purchase. Call 512-463-5589 for more information.

Uniform Commercial Code, Federal Tax Liens

UCC Section, Secretary of State, www.sos.state.tx.us/ucc/index.shtml UCC and other Texas Secretary of State data is available via SOSDirect on the Web at www.sos.state.tx.us/corp/sosda/index.shtml. UCC records are $1.00 per search, with printing $1.00 per page and certifying $15.00. General information and forms can also be found at the website. **$$$** *Other Options:* This agency offers the database for sale, contact the Information Services Dept at 512-463-5609 for further details.

Sales Tax Registrations

Comptroller of Public Accounts, Sales Tax Permits, www.window.state.tx.us/taxinfo/sales/ This office provides a taxable entity search at https://ourcpa.cpa.state.tx.us/coa/Index.html. There is no fee. Send email requests to open.records@cpa.state.tx.us. *Other Options:* Sales tax registration lists are available to download as ftp files.

Birth Certificates

Department of State Health Svcs, Bureau of Vital Statistics, www.dshs.state.tx.us/vs/default.shtm Records may be ordered online at www.dshs.state.tx.us/vs/default.shtm. **$$$** *Other Options:* Birth Indexes from 1926-1995 are available on CD-Rom and microfiche.

Death Records

Department of State Health Svcs, Bureau of Vital Statistics, www.dshs.state.tx.us/vs/default.shtm Records may be ordered online at www.dshs.state.tx.us/vs/default.shtm. Death records from 1964 thru 1998 may be viewed at http://vitals.rootsweb.ancestry.com/tx/death/search.cgi. **$$$** *Other Options:* Death indices from 1964-1998 are available on CD-Rom and microfiche.

Marriage Certificates

Department of State Health Svcs, Bureau of Vital Statistics, www.dshs.state.tx.us/vs/default.shtm Records may be ordered online at www.dshs.state.tx.us/vs/default.shtm. The department provides marriage data commercially on CD-rom at www.dshs.state.tx.us/vs/marriagedivorce/mindex.shtm, or you may download each year of the marriage index for free, from 1966 to 2008. Also, marriage records for 1966 to 2008 are available through a private company website at www.genlookups.com/texas_marriages/. **$$$**

Divorce Records

Department of State Health Svcs, Bureau of Vital Statistics, www.dshs.state.tx.us/vs/default.shtm Records may be ordered online at www.dshs.state.tx.us/vs/default.shtm. The department provides divorce data commercially on CD-rom at www.dshs.state.tx.us/vs/marriagedivorce/dindex.shtm, or you may download each year of the divorce index for free, from 1968 to 2008. Also, a private company website at www.genlookups.com/texas_divorces/ offers records from 1968 to 2008. **$$$**

Workers' Compensation Records

Texas Department of Insurance - Worker's Comp, 7551 Metro Center Dr, #100, www.tdi.texas.gov/wc/indexwc.html The website gives administrative decisions for cases back to 1991and also permits searching for employers with coverage. The company look-up is at https://apps.tdi.state.tx.us/pcci/pcci_search.jsp or at www.tdi.texas.gov/wc/employer/coverage.html.

Driver Records

Department of Public Safety, License and Records Service, www.dps.texas.gov/DriverLicense/ Access is limited to only high volume users who have a permissible use and sign an agreement. The fee is $6.50 for a three-year Type 2 record and $7.50 for a complete Type 3 record. Both batch and interactive modes are available. Fees vary from $4.50 to $22.00, depending on type of record and if certified. Call 512-424-2600 to receive a copy of the license agreement. Fees vary from $4.50 to $22.00, depending on type of record and if certified. The state also offers access to TX license holders to request their own record at the web page. **$$$** *Other Options:* Bulk data is available in electronic format for approved requesters. Weekly updates are available. The file does not include driver history data.

Vehicle Ownership & Registration

TX Department of Motor Vehicles, Titles and Registration, www.txdmv.gov The Technology Support Branch offers a web inquiry system for immediate VIN and plate look ups. A $200 deposit is required, there is a $23.00 charge per month and $.12 fee per inquiry. Searching by name or owner is not permitted. For more information, contact Technology Support. Also, the TxDMV provides access to various databases for use by the public to search for Motor Carrier records, such as registration, complaints, safety, and DPS records. See www.dmv.tx.gov/motor_carrier/records_tracking.htm. **$$$** *Other Options:* The TxDMV Technology Support Branch offers CD and FTP retrieval of VIN and plate numbers (but not by name) to eligible organizations under signed contract. Fees are based on the cost of a "computer run" and on a small fee per record.

Crash Reports

Texas Department of Transportation, Crash Records Section, www.txdot.gov/driver/laws/crash-reports.html While not associated with this agency, quite a number of city and town police departments are hooked up with a vendor who supplies online ordering. See www.buycrash.com. **$$$**

Vessel Ownership & Registration

Parks & Wildlife Dept, www.tpwd.state.tx.us/fishboat/boat/ Online search of current ownership information is offered at https://apps.tpwd.state.tx.us/tora/jump.jsf. Requester must certify that the Texas Parks Wildlife vessel/boat and/or outboard motor record information obtained will be used for lawful purposes. This inquiry provides the current owner/lienholder name(s), address(es), vessel/boat, and/or outboard motor description. This data is updated daily. *Other Options:* Records are released in bulk format; however, requesters are screened for lawful purpose. The agency requires a copy of any item mailed or distributed as a result of purchase. Media includes tape, labels, and printed lists.

Campaign Finance, PACs, Lobbyists

Texas Ethics Commission, P. O. Box 12070, www.ethics.state.tx.us/ Filing information is offered for candidates, lobbyists, PACs, political parties at www.ethics.state.tx.us/index.html. Delinquent filer lists are at www.ethics.state.tx.us/dfs/delinquent_filers.htm. Campaign finance reports and lobby reports are at www.ethics.state.tx.us/main/search.htm.

GED Certificates

Texas Education Agency, GED Unit, www.texged.com The agency has a excellent verification search at https://bass.tea.state.tx.us/Tea.GEDi.Web/Forms/CertificateSearch.aspx. Search by SSN or TEA assigned ID and DOB or by name (maiden) and DOB. Records go back to 1994. One may order a certificate to be sent to an employer.

Occupational Licensing Boards

Academic Alternative Program Providers .... www.tcleose.state.tx.us/content/training_providers_academic.cfm
Academy Training Providers........................ www.tcleose.state.tx.us/content/training_providers_academy.cfm
Accountant-CPA/Firm .... www.tsbpa.state.tx.us/general/database-search.html
Acupuncturist .... http://reg.tmb.state.tx.us/OnLineVerif/Phys_NoticeVerif.asp?
Air Condition'g/Refrigeration Contr. .... www.license.state.tx.us/LicenseSearch/
Alarm Installer/Firm/Seller/Security Instructor.....www.txdps.state.tx.us/rsd/psb/company/company_search.aspx
Alcoholic Beverage Dist/Mfg/Retailer........... www.tabc.state.tx.us/public_inquiry/index.asp
Alcoholic Beverage Permit........................... www.tabc.state.tx.us/public_inquiry/index.asp
Architect .... www.tbae.state.tx.us/PublicInformation/FindDesignProfessional
Architectural Barrier .... www.license.state.tx.us/LicenseSearch/
Asbestos Consultant/Inspector .... www.dshs.state.tx.us/asbestos/locate.shtm
Asbestos Contractor/Worker........................ www.dshs.state.tx.us/asbestos/locate.shtm
Asbestos Mgmt Planner/Air Monitor Tech ... www.dshs.state.tx.us/asbestos/locate.shtm
Athletic Agent.. www.sos.state.tx.us/statdoc/index.shtml
Athletic Trainer... www.dshs.state.tx.us/at/at_roster.shtm
Attorney.. www.texasbar.com/am/template.cfm?section=home
Auctioneer .... www.license.state.tx.us/LicenseSearch/
Audiologist/Assistant.................................. www.dshs.state.tx.us/plc/default.shtm
Automobile Club.. www.sos.state.tx.us/statdoc/index.shtml
Bank Agency, Foreign................................. www.banking.state.tx.us/supreglic_ent.asp
Bank, State Chartered .... www.banking.state.tx.us/supreglic_ent.asp
Barber Student/School/Shop .... www.license.state.tx.us/LicenseSearch/
Boiler Inspector/Installer .... www.license.state.tx.us/LicenseSearch/
Boxing/Combative Sports Event .... www.license.state.tx.us/LicenseSearch/
Business Opportunity Offering .... www.sos.state.tx.us/statdoc/index.shtml
Career Counselor.. www.license.state.tx.us/LicenseSearch/
Chemical Dependency Counselor .... www.dshs.state.tx.us/lcdc/lcdc_search.shtm
Child Care Facility/Admin..........https://www.dfps.state.tx.us/Child_Care/Search_Texas_Child_Care/CCLNET/Source/CPA/ppSearchTXChildCare2.aspx
Child Care Operation................https://www.dfps.state.tx.us/Child_Care/Search_Texas_Child_Care/CCLNET/Source/CPA/ppSearchTXChildCare2.aspx
Child Support Agency, Private .... www.banking.state.tx.us/supreglic_ent.asp
Chiropractic Radiologic Technologist........... https://www.tbce.state.tx.us/verify_menu.html
Chiropractor/Facility .... https://www.tbce.state.tx.us/verify_menu.html
Code Enforcement Officer .... www.dshs.state.tx.us/op/op_roster.shtm
Contact Lens Dispenser.............................. www.dshs.state.tx.us/contactlens/cl_roster.shtm
Cosmetologist/Shop/Salon/Schools............. www.license.state.tx.us/LicenseSearch/licfile.asp
Counselor, Professional/Supervisor............ www.dshs.state.tx.us/counselor/lpc_rosters.shtm

Courier Company .... www.txdps.state.tx.us/rsd/psb/company/company_search.aspx
Court Reporting Firm.................................. www.crcb.state.tx.us/csr-crf-list.asp
Court/Shorthand Reporter........................... www.crcb.state.tx.us/csr-crf-list.asp
Credit Service Organization .... www.sos.state.tx.us/statdoc/index.shtml
Currency Exchange.................................... www.banking.state.tx.us/supreglic_ent.asp
Day Care Center/Residential.....https://www.dfps.state.tx.us/Child_Care/Search_Texas_Child_Care/CCLNET/Source/CPA/ppSearchTXChildCare2.aspx
Deaf Service Provider .... www.dars.state.tx.us/dhhs/list.shtml
Dental Assistant/Hygienist/Laboratory .... www.tsbde.state.tx.us/index.php?option=com_content&task=section&id=6&Itemid=38
Dentist .... www.tsbde.state.tx.us/index.php?option=com_content&task=section&id=6&Itemid=38
Dietitian .... www.dshs.state.tx.us/plc/default.shtm
ECA.. www.dshs.state.tx.us/emstraumasystems/NewCert.shtm
Elevator/Escalator .... www.license.state.tx.us/LicenseSearch/
Emergency Medical Technician .... www.dshs.state.tx.us/emstraumasystems/NewCert.shtm
Engineer/Firm... http://engineers.texas.gov/downloads.htm
Family Home Day Care............https://www.dfps.state.tx.us/Child_Care/Search_Texas_Child_Care/CCLNET/Source/CPA/ppSearchTXChildCare2.aspx
Fire Alarm System Contractor..................... www.tdi.texas.gov/fire/fmli.html
Fire Extinguisher Contractor .... www.tdi.texas.gov/fire/fmli.html
Fire Inspector/Investigator .... www.tcfp.texas.gov/certification/certification_verification.asp
Fire Protection Sprinkler Contr.................... www.tdi.texas.gov/fire/fmli.html
Fire Suppression Specialist .... www.tcfp.texas.gov/certification/certification_verification.asp
Firearm Instructor....................................... www.txdps.state.tx.us/rsd/psb/company/company_search.aspx
Firefighter .... www.tcfp.texas.gov/certification/certification_verification.asp
Fireworks Display.. www.tdi.texas.gov/fire/fmli.html
Funeral Prepaid Permit Holder .... www.banking.state.tx.us/supreglic_ent.asp
Guard Dog Company .... www.txdps.state.tx.us/rsd/psb/company/company_search.aspx
Health Spa .... www.sos.state.tx.us/statdoc/index.shtml
Hearing Instrument Dispenser/Fitter .... www.dshs.state.tx.us/plc/default.shtm
Home Equity & 2nd Mortgage Lender.......... www.occc.state.tx.us/pages/searches.html
Home Inspector.. www.trec.state.tx.us/inspector/inspector_search_by_city.asp
Industrialized Housing................................. www.license.state.tx.us/LicenseSearch/
Insurance Adjuster .... https://txapps.texas.gov/NASApp/tdi/TdiARManager
Insurance Agency/Agent/Company .... https://txapps.texas.gov/NASApp/tdi/TdiARManager
Interior Designer.. www.tbae.state.tx.us/PublicInformation/FindDesignProfessional
Interpreter for the Deaf............................... www.dars.state.tx.us/dhhs/beiterpsearch.shtml
Investment Advisor..................................... www.ssb.state.tx.us/public/CertificateSearch.php
Landscape Architect .... www.tbae.state.tx.us/PublicInformation/FindDesignProfessional
Lead Abatement Project Designer .... www.dshs.state.tx.us/elp/locate.shtm
Lead Abatement Worker/Supervisor........... www.dshs.state.tx.us/elp/locate.shtm
Lead Firm .... www.dshs.state.tx.us/elp/locate.shtm
Lead Risk Assessor/Inspector .... www.dshs.state.tx.us/elp/locate.shtm
Lead Training Program Provider................. www.dshs.state.tx.us/elp/locate.shtm
Loan Company.. www.occc.state.tx.us/pages/searches.html
Loan Officer.. www.sml.texas.gov:8080/licenseeDownload/
Lobbyist.. www.ethics.state.tx.us/main/search.htm
Manicurist... www.license.state.tx.us/LicenseSearch/licfile.asp
Manicurist/Manicurist Shop .... www.license.state.tx.us/LicenseSearch/
Marriage & Family Therapist....................... www.dshs.state.tx.us/mft/mft_search.shtm
Massage Therapist...................................... www.dshs.state.tx.us/massage/mt_rosters.shtm
Massage Therapy School/Instructor/Establishment.......www.dshs.state.tx.us/massage/mt_rosters.shtm
Medical Physicist... www.dshs.state.tx.us/mp/mp_roster.shtm
Medical Specialty (Doctor) .... http://reg.tmb.state.tx.us/OnLineVerif/Phys_NoticeVerif.asp?
Medication Aide... www.dads.state.tx.us/providers/NF/credentialing/sanctions/index.cfm
Money Service Business............................. www.banking.state.tx.us/supreglic_ent.asp
Mortgage Banker/Broker............................. www.sml.texas.gov:8080/licenseeDownload/
Motor Vehicle Sales Finance Firm .... www.occc.state.tx.us/pages/searches.html

Notary Public	https://direct.sos.state.tx.us/notaries/NotarySearch.asp
Nurse/Advanced Practice	www.bon.state.tx.us/olv/verification.html
Nurse/RN/Vocational	www.bon.state.tx.us/olv/verification.html
Nurses Aide	www.dads.state.tx.us/providers/NF/credentialing/sanctions/index.cfm
Nursing Home Administrator/Facility	www.dads.state.tx.us/providers/NF/credentialing/sanctions/index.cfm
Occupation'l/Physical Therapy Facility	www.ptot.texas.gov/license-verification
Occupational Therapist/Assistant	www.ptot.texas.gov/license-verification
Optician	www.dshs.state.tx.us/optician/opt_roster.shtm
Optometrist	www.tob.state.tx.us/varifyinfo.htm
Orthotics & Prosthetics Facility	www.dshs.state.tx.us/op/op_roster.shtm
Orthotist/Prosthetist	www.dshs.state.tx.us/op/op_rost.pdf
Paramedic	www.dshs.state.tx.us/emstraumasystems/NewCert.shtm
Pawn Shop	www.occc.state.tx.us/pages/searches.html
Perfusionist	www.dshs.state.tx.us/perfusionist/pf_roster.shtm
Perpetual Care Cemetery	www.banking.state.tx.us/supreglic_ent.asp
Personal Employment Service	www.license.state.tx.us/LicenseSearch/
Pharmacist/Intern	www.tsbp.state.tx.us/dbsearch/default.asp
Pharmacy/Technician	www.tsbp.state.tx.us/dbsearch/default.asp
Physical Therapist/Assistant	www.ptot.texas.gov/license-verification
Physician/Medical Doctor/Assistant	http://reg.tmb.state.tx.us/OnLineVerif/Phys_NoticeVerif.asp?
Plumber Master/Journeyman/Inspector	https://licensing.hpc.state.tx.us/datamart/selSearchType.do?from=loginPage
Podiatrist	www.foot.state.tx.us/verifications.htm
Political Action Committee List	www.ethics.state.tx.us/dfs/paclists.htm
Political Contributor	www.ethics.state.tx.us/main/search.htm
Polygraph Examiner	www.license.state.tx.us/LicenseSearch/
Private Business Letter of Authority	www.txdps.state.tx.us/rsd/psb/company/company_search.aspx
Private Investigator	www.txdps.state.tx.us/rsd/psb/company/company_search.aspx
Property Tax Consultant	www.license.state.tx.us/LicenseSearch/
Psychological Associate	https://licensing.hpc.state.tx.us/datamart/selSearchType.do?from=loginPage
Psychologist	https://licensing.hpc.state.tx.us/datamart/selSearchType.do?from=loginPage
Psychologist, Provisional	https://licensing.hpc.state.tx.us/datamart/selSearchType.do?from=loginPage
Public Safety Org, Promoter Solicitat'n	www.sos.state.tx.us/statdoc/index.shtml
Radiology Technician	www.dshs.state.tx.us/mrt/mrt_roster.shtm
Real Estate Agent/Broker/Sales/Inspector	www.trec.state.tx.us/newsandpublic/licenseeLookup/
Real Estate Appraiser	www.talcb.state.tx.us/appraisers/Appraiser_Search.asp
Representative Office-Foreign Bank	www.banking.state.tx.us/supreglic_ent.asp
Respiratory Care Practitioner	www.dshs.state.tx.us/respiratory/rc_search.shtm
Sanitarian	www.dshs.state.tx.us/plc/default.shtm
Savings & Loan Association	www.sml.texas.gov:8080/licenseeDownload/
Savings Bank	www.sml.texas.gov:8080/licenseeDownload/
School Psychology Specialist	www.tsbep.state.tx.us/files/agencydocs/2009_Roster.pdf
Securities Agent/Seller	www.ssb.state.tx.us/public/NoticeFillerSearch.php
Securities Broker/Dealer	www.ssb.state.tx.us/public/CertificateSearch.php
Security Agency, Private	www.txdps.state.tx.us/rsd/psb/company/company_search.aspx
Security Agent/Service/Seller	www.txdps.state.tx.us/rsd/psb/company/company_search.aspx
Service Contract Provider	www.license.state.tx.us/LicenseSearch/
Social Worker	www.dshs.state.tx.us/socialwork/sw_rosters.shtm
Speech-Language Pathologist	www.dshs.state.tx.us/plc/default.shtm
Staff Leasing	www.license.state.tx.us/LicenseSearch/
STAP Vendor	http://stap.puc.state.tx.us/stapc/StapVendorReport.aspx
Surveyor, Land/State Land/Out-of-TX	https://licensing.hpc.state.tx.us/datamart/mainMenu.do
Talent Agency	www.license.state.tx.us/LicenseSearch/
Tax Appraisal Professional	www.license.state.tx.us/LicenseSearch/
Teacher	https://secure.sbec.state.tx.us/SBECONLINE/virtcert.asp
Telephone Solicitation	www.sos.state.tx.us/statdoc/index.shtml

Temporary Common Worker .... www.license.state.tx.us/LicenseSearch/
Training Providers .... www.tcleose.state.tx.us/content/training_providers_contract.cfm
Transportation Service Provider .... www.license.state.tx.us/LicenseSearch/
Trust Company.. www.banking.state.tx.us/supreglic_ent.asp
Underground Storage Tank Installer........... www2.tceq.texas.gov/lic_dpa/index.cfm
Vehicle Protection Provider......................... www.license.state.tx.us/LicenseSearch/
Veterans Organization Solicitation.............. www.sos.state.tx.us/statdoc/index.shtml
Veterinarian.. www.tbvme.state.tx.us/verify.php
Water Well & Pump Installer .... www.license.state.tx.us/LicenseSearch/
Weather Modification Service .... www.license.state.tx.us/LicenseSearch/
Wig Specialist... www.license.state.tx.us/LicenseSearch/licfile.asp

State and Local Courts

State Court Structure: Generally, Texas **District Courts** have general civil jurisdiction and exclusive felony jurisdiction, along with typical variations such as contested probate and divorce. There are 360 Districts fully within one county and 96 Districts within more than one county. There can be multiple Districts and multiple District Courts in one courthouse. But the record keeping is organized by county and there is only one searchable database per courthouse. Therefore the profiles of the District Courts are herein organized by county.

The **County Court** structure consists of two forms of courts - **Constitutional** and **At Law**. The Constitutional upper civil claim limit is $10,000 while the At Law upper limit is $100,000 and some jurisdictions are higher. County Courts have original jurisdiction for misdemeanors with fines greater than $500 or jail sentences. Within the county the District Court or County Court can handles **evictions.** In 69 counties, one individual serves as both the District Clerk and County Clerk.

Justice Courts handle misdemeanors where the fine is less than $500 and no jail sentences.

Probate is handled in **Probate Court** in the ten largest counties and in the County Court elsewhere. The County Clerk is responsible for these records in every county.

A PDF file of the addresses and phone numbers of the 920 **Municipal Courts** is found at www.courts.state.tx.us/pubs/JudicialDirectory/MNCourts.pdf.

Appellate Courts: Case records of the Supreme Court can be searched at www.supreme.courts.state.tx.us. Appellate Court case information is searchable free at the website of each Appellate Court, reached online from www.courts.state.tx.us/courts/coa.asp. Court of Criminal Appeals opinions are found at www.cca.courts.state.tx.us.

Statewide Court Online Access: There is no statewide portal of case records. However, at press time over 35% of the courts offer online access. At least 150 local courts provide online access to civil records and at least 155 to criminal records. At least half of the counties involved use a designated vendor – www.idocket.com.

County Sites:

Angelina County

District Court www.angelinacounty.net

Civil: A free search of the docket is at http://public.angelinacounty.net/default.aspx. Records go back to 1996. If you are not sure of the spelling of the name, enter at least 3 initials and an asterisk. The site includes all civil, family and probate records in the county, including the County Court and JP. *Criminal:* Same as civil. The site includes all criminal, jail and law enforcement records in the county, including the County Court and JP.

County Court www.angelinacounty.net

Civil: A free search of the docket is at http://public.angelinacounty.net/. Records go back to 1996. If you are not sure of the spelling of the name, enter at least 3 initials and an asterisk. The site includes all civil, family and probate records in the county, including the County Court and JP. Also, a vendor offers a subscription account at http://idocket.com/homepage2.htm. Civil to 11/30/1996; probate to 1/31/1995. **$$$** *Criminal:* Online access to the criminal dockets is free at http://public.angelinacounty.net/default.aspx. Includes jail and law enforcement records. If you are not sure of the spelling of the name, enter at least 3 initials and an asterick. The site includes all criminal, jail and law enforcement records in the county, including the County Court and JP. Also, a vendor offers a subscription account at http://idocket.com/homepage2.htm. Misdemeanors to 12/31/1983. **$$$**

Aransas County

District Court www.aransascountytx.gov/districtclerk/

Civil: Online case access at www.idocket.com; registration and password required. Civil and family law records (no probate) go back to 01/01/2001. One free name search permitted a day, otherwise subscription required. **$$$** *Criminal:* Online index to 01/01/1960 at www.idocket.com; registration and password required. One free name search permitted a day, otherwise subscription required. **$$$**

County Court at Law www.aransascountytx.gov/clerk/

Civil: Online case access at www.idocket.com; registration and password required. Civil and family law records, probate, go back to 01/01/2001. One free name search permitted a day, otherwise subscription required. **$$$** *Criminal:* Online index to 01/01/1971 at www.idocket.com; registration and password required. One free name search permitted a day, otherwise subscription required. **$$$**

Bandera County

District Court www.banderacounty.org/departments/district_clerk.htm

Civil: Civil case information is free at www.idocket.com. Registration and password required. Records go back to 12/31/1990. One free name search permitted a day, otherwise subscription required. **$$$** *Criminal:* Felony record index access is through www.idocket.com; registration and password required; records go back to 12/31/1990. One free name search permitted a day, otherwise subscription required. **$$$**

County Court www.banderacounty.org/departments/county_clerk.htm

Civil: Online access to dockets is through www.idocket.com; registration and password required. Civil cases from 1/1994; probate from 1/1991.One free name search permitted a day, otherwise subscription required. **$$$** *Criminal:* Online access to dockets is through www.idocket.com; registration and password required. Misdemeanor cases from 1/1992. One free name search permitted a day, otherwise subscription required. **$$$**

Bastrop County

District & County Courts www.co.bastrop.tx.us/site/content/districtclerk

Civil: Search online docket at www.co.bastrop.tx.us:8080/default.aspx. *Criminal:* same

Bee County

District Court www.co.bee.tx.us/default.aspx?Bee_County/District.Clerk

Civil: Online access is at www.idocket.com; registration and password required. A fee service; only one free name search per day. Records may go back to 12/31/1987. **$$$** *Criminal:* Felony case record access at www.idocket.com; registration and password required. A fee service; only one free name search a day. Records may go back to 12/31/1994. **$$$**

Bell County

District Court www.bellcountytx.com/county_government/district_courts/index.php

Civil: Access the current civil docket data at www.bellcountytx.com/county_government/district_courts/27th_district_court/court_dockets.php. The data is in PDF format. *Criminal:* Same as civil.

Bexar County

District Court - Central Records http://gov.bexar.org/dc/

Civil: Access to the remote online system back to 1980 requires $100 setup fee, plus a $25 monthly fee, plus inquiry fees. Call BCIT for info at 210-335-0202. Also, search civil litigants free at https://apps.bexar.org/dklitsearch/search.aspx. Civil and family law record access at www.idocket.com; registration and password required. A fee service; only one free name search a day. Records go back to 01/01/1980. **$$$** *Criminal:* A free search is offered at http://gov.bexar.org/dc/dcrecords.html. Data is in Excel sheet, updated first Fri of month. Also, felony record access at www.idocket.com; registration and password required. A fee service; only one free name search a day. Access to the remote online system back to 1980 requires $100 setup fee, plus a $25 monthly fee, plus inquiry fees. Call BCIT for info at 210-335-0202. **$$$**

County Court - Criminal http://gov.bexar.org/dc/Criminal.html

Criminal: Access to the criminal online system requires $100 setup fee, plus a $25 monthly fee, plus inquiry fees. Call Alma Flores at 210-335-0202 for more information. **$$$**

Brazoria County

District Court www.brazoria-county.com/dclerk/

Civil: Access civil record docket free at their Judicial Record Search site at www.brazoria-county.com/dclerk/. Access index and docs back to 6/1/1987 at www.idocket.com; registration and password required. This is a fee service; only one free name search per day. *Criminal:* Access criminal record docket free at their Judicial Record Search site at www.brazoria-county.com/dclerk/.

County Court www.brazoria-county.com

Civil: Access index and docs back to 1/1/1986 at www.idocket.com; registration and password required. This is a fee service; only one free name search per day. Fee must be prepaid before faxing in a search request. **$$$** *Same as civil.* **$$$**

Brazos County

District Court www.brazoscountytx.gov/index.aspx?nid=135

Civil: Civil case index and hearing index available at http://justiceweb.co.brazos.tx.us/judicialsearch/. *Criminal:* Same as civil

County Court www.brazoscountytx.gov/index.aspx?nid=126

Civil: Dockets available at http://justiceweb.co.brazos.tx.us/. *Criminal:* Crimianl docket index available http://justiceweb.co.brazos.tx.us/.

Brooks County

District Court www.co.brooks.tx.us/default.aspx?Brooks_County/District.Clerk

Civil: Civil case index and doc online at www.idocket.com. Records go back to 12/31/1993. One free name search permitted a day, otherwise subscription required. **$$$** *Criminal:* Same as civil **$$$**

County Court www.co.brooks.tx.us/default.aspx?Brooks_County/County.Clerk

Criminal: Access misdemeanor case info back to 12/31/94 at www.idocket.com; registration and password required. This is a fee service; only one free name search per day. **$$$**

Brown County

County Court www.browncountytx.org

Civil: Access civil and probate index and docs back to 1/1/1987 at www.idocket.com; registration and password required. This is a fee service; only one free name search per day. **$$$** *Criminal:* Access index and docs back to 1/1/1987 at www.idocket.com; registration and password required. This is a fee service; only one free name search per day. **$$$**

Burnet County

District Court www.burnetcountytexas.org/

Civil: For online access go to www.burnetcountytexas.org/default.aspx?name=dclerk.home and click on Burnet County Online Court Records Search. Login Required: user id - visitor, password - visitor. *Criminal:* Signup for email notifications of criminal dockets at www.dcourt.org/_attys/dockets.htm. Online access to the criminal record docket at www.burnetcountytexas.org/default.aspx?name=dclerk.home and click on Burnet County Online Court Records Search. Login Required: user id - visitor, password - visitor. The site also offers \"Law Enforcement\" records which includes a wide variety of incident types.

County Court

Civil: Search civil, family and probate cases at http://pubody.burnetcountytexas.org/Login.aspx?ReturnUrl=%2fdefault.aspx. Use \"visitor\" as both user ID and password. *Criminal:* Search criminal cases free at http://pubody.burnetcountytexas.org/Login.aspx?ReturnUrl=%2fdefault.aspx. Use \"visitor\" as both user ID and password. The site also offers \"Law Enforcement\" records which includes a variety of incident types.

Calhoun County

District Court

Civil: Access case records at www.idocket.com; registration and password required. A fee service; only one free name search per day. Records go back to 01/01/1998. **$$$** *Criminal:* Access case records including probate at www.idocket.com; registration and password required. A fee service; only one free name search per day. Records go back to 01/01/1999. **$$$**

County Court At Law

Civil: Access index and images online at http://idocket.com/homepage2.htm. Registration required. One free name search permitted a day, otherwise subscription required. Records go back to 01/01/2006. **$$$** *Criminal:* Access index and images online at http://idocket.com/homepage2.htm. Registration required. One free name search permitted a day, otherwise subscription required. Records go back to 01/01/1992. **$$$**

Callahan County

District Court www.callahancounty.org/

Civil: Access case records back to 12/31/2001 including probate at www.idocket.com; registration and password required. A fee service; only one free name search per day. **$$$** *Criminal:* same **$$$**

Cameron County

District Court

Civil: Online access to cases is at www.idocket.com; registration and password required. A fee service; only one free name search per day. **$$$** *Criminal:* Same as civil. Records may go back to 12/31/1988. **$$$**

County Court No. 1, 2 & 3 www.co.cameron.tx.us/courts_at_law/index.htm

Civil: Access case records back to 12/01/93 including probate at www.idocket.com; registration and password required. A fee service; only one free name search per day. **$$$** *Criminal:* Same as civil

Chambers County

District Clerk www.co.chambers.tx.us/default.aspx?name=district.clerk

Civil: Search online after registering free for login and password at www.texasonlinerecords.com/clerk/?office_id=7 Access records back to 01/011900 including family law at www.idocket.com; registration and password required. A fee service; only one free name search per day. **$$$** *Criminal:* same as civil, felonies back to 12/31/1870 on idocket.

Cherokee County

District Court http://co.cherokee.tx.us/ips/cms/

Civil: Case record access at www.idocket.com; registration and password required. A fee service; only one free name search a day. Records may go back to 01/01/92. **$$$** *Criminal:* same **$$$**

Clay County

County Court www.co.clay.tx.us/

Civil: Civil index and many images back to 1/1/2007 and probate to 03/01/2005 are online at www.idocket.com. One free name search permitted a day, otherwise subscription required. *Criminal:* Misdemeanor index and images back to 03/01/2003 at www.idocket.com. One free name search permitted a day, otherwise subscription required.

Coleman County

County Court www.co.coleman.tx.us

Civil: Access case records and dockets at www.idocket.com; registration and password required. Is a fee service; only one free name search a day. Civil and probate records go back to 4/1/2011. **$$$** *Criminal:* Access case records and dockets at www.idocket.com; registration and password required. Is a fee service; only one free name search a day.Misdemeanor records go back to 01/01/94. **$$$**

Collin County

District Clerk www.co.collin.tx.us/district_courts/index.jsp

Civil: Name and case look up is at http://apps.collincountytx.gov/cccasesearch/. There is also a commercial system- see county courts. Call Lisa Zoski at 972-548-4503 for subscription info. *Criminal:* Name and case look up is at http://apps.collincountytx.gov/cccasesearch/. Search case schedules for free at www.co.collin.tx.us/ShowScheduleSearchServlet.

County Court At Law www.collincountytexas.gov

Civil: Online access to dockets is free at http://apps.collincountytx.gov/cccasesearch/. *Criminal:* Online access to dcokets is free at http://apps.collincountytx.gov/cccasesearch/. Record displayed back to 2000.

Comal County

County Court at Law www.comalcounty.net

Civil: Online access county judicial records free at www.co.comal.tx.us/recordsearch.htm. Search by either party name. *Criminal:* Online access county criminal judicial records free at www.co.comal.tx.us/recordsearch.htm.

District Court www.co.comal.tx.us/DC.htm

Civil: Online access county judicial records free at www.co.comal.tx.us/recordsearch.htm. Search by either party name. *Criminal:* Online access county criminal judicial records free at www.co.comal.tx.us/recordsearch.htm. Data includes date filed, disposed, offense, warrant status and attorney.

Coryell County

District Court www.coryellcounty.org/district_clerk.html

Civil: Case record access at www.idocket.com; registration and password required. A fee service; only one free name search a day. Records may go back to 01/01/99. **$$$** *Criminal:* same **$$$**

County Court www.coryellcounty.org

Civil: Case record access at www.idocket.com; registration and password required. A fee service; only one free name search a day. Records may go back to 01/01/94. **$$$** *Criminal:* same **$$$**

Dallas County

District Court - Criminal www.dallascounty.org

Criminal: Search is at www.dallascounty.org/criminalBackgroundSearch/. Criminal index includes DOB. There is no fee unless a record is viewed, but many records can be viewed for free. Dallas County Jail look-up is free at www.dallascounty.org/jaillookup.

District Court - Civil www.dallascourts.com/forms/lstCourts.asp?division=cvd

Civil: Search district civil and family case index free at www.dallascounty.org/public_access.php. Cases go back to early 1960s. **$$$**

County Court - Civil www.dallascounty.org

Civil: Search civil judgment index at www.dallascounty.org/public_access.php. No fee unless a record is viewed. Access case records and dockets at www.idocket.com; registration and password required. Is a fee service; only one free name search a day. Civil records go back to 01/01/63. **$$$**

County Court - Misdemeanor www.dallascounty.org

Criminal: www.dallascounty.org/criminalBackgroundSearch/. Criminal index includes DOB. There is no fee unless a record is viewed but most records viewed for free. Email questions to DCRecordscriminal@dallascounty.org. Dallas County Jail look-up is free at www.dallascounty.org/jaillookup/. **$$$**

Denton County

District Court http://dentoncounty.com/dept/main.asp?Dept=26

Civil: Search civil records free at http://justice.dentoncounty.com. Search by name or cause number. *Criminal:* Criminal searches are free at http://justice.dentoncounty.com. Records go back to 1990 forward. Access also includes sheriff bond and jail records.

County Court http://dentoncounty.com/deptall.asp

Civil: Online access civil court records free at http://justice.dentoncounty.com/CivilSearch/civfrmd.htm. *Criminal:* Online access county criminal records free at http://justice.dentoncounty.com/CrimSearch/crimfrmd.htm. Jail, bond, and parole records are also available at http://justice.dentoncounty.com. Search for registered sex offenders by ZIP Code at http://sheriff.dentoncounty.com/sex_offenders/default.htm.

Eastland County

County Court

Criminal: Access case records and dockets at www.idocket.com; registration and password required. Is a fee service; only one free name search a day. Misdemeanor records go back to 5/1/1987; probate records go back to 12/01/1870. **$$$**

Ector County

District Court

Civil: Case record access at www.idocket.com; registration and password required. A fee service; only one free name search a day. Records may go back to 12/31/94, includes fmaily law but not probate. **$$$** *Criminal:* same **$$$**

El Paso County

District Court www.epcounty.com/districtclerk/

Civil: Online access to civil court records is free at www.epcounty.com/publicsearch/CivilRecords/CivilRecSearchForm.aspx. Also, access index and images at www.idocket.com; registration and password required; online civil records go back to 12/31/1986. *Criminal:* Online access to criminal court active records is free at www.epcounty.com/publicrecords/criminalrecords/CriminalRecordSearch.aspx. Also, online access index and images at www.idocket.com; registration and password required; online records go back to 12/31/1986.

County Court www.co.el-paso.tx.us

Civil: Online access to civil court records is free at www.co.el-paso.tx.us/JIMSSearch/CivilRecordsearch.asp. Also, search vital records and recordings. Also, access index and images at www.idocket.com; registration and password required. Civil records go back to 12/31/1986, probate to 12/31/1989. *Criminal:* Online access to misdemeanor criminal records is at www.co.el-paso.tx.us/JIMSSearch/CriminalRecordsearch.asp. Also, access index and images at www.idocket.com; registration and password required. Misdemeanor records go back to 12/31/1986.

Erath County

District Court http://co.erath.tx.us/districtclerk.html

Civil: Access to District Clerk records requires registration, login and password; signup online at www.texasonlinerecords.com/clerk/?office_id=22. *Criminal:* same

County Court

Civil: Access to County Court records requires registration, login and password; signup online at www.texasonlinerecords.com/clerk/?office_id=21. *Criminal:* same

Fannin County

District Court www.co.fannin.tx.us/default.aspx?Fannin_County/District.Court

Civil: Access to civil, probate and family court dockets at http://71.97.114.198/default.aspx. *Criminal:* Online access to criminal docket records at http://71.97.114.198/default.aspx.

County Court www.co.fannin.tx.us/default.aspx?Fannin_County/County.Clerk

Civil: Access to civil, probate and family court dockets at http://71.97.114.198/default.aspx. *Criminal:* Online access to criminal docket records at http://71.97.114.198/default.aspx.

Floyd County

District Court

Civil: Online case access is through www.idocket.com; registration and password required. Records go back to 10/1/2005. One free name search permitted a day, otherwise subscription required. **$$$** *Criminal:* same **$$$**

County Court

Civil: Online case access is through www.idocket.com; registration and password required. Records go back to 1/1/2010. One free name search permitted a day, otherwise subscription required. **$$$** *Criminal:* Online case access is through www.idocket.com; registration and password required. Records go back to 1/1/2003. One free name search permitted a day, otherwise subscription required. **$$$**

Fort Bend County

District Court www.fortbendcountytx.gov/index.aspx?page=176

Civil: Search civil, probate and divorce index at http://tylerpaw.co.fort-bend.tx.us/default.aspx. Partial DOBs shown. *Criminal:* Search criminal records free at http://tylerpaw.co.fort-bend.tx.us/default.aspx. Partial DOBs shown.

County Court www.fortbendcountytx.gov/index.aspx?page=147

Civil: Search civil, probate and divorce index at http://tylerpaw.co.fort-bend.tx.us/default.aspx. Partial DOBs shown. *Criminal:* Online access to misdemeanor and felony index is at http://tylerpaw.co.fort-bend.tx.us/default.aspx. Searches records from 1982 forward.

Freestone County

County Court

Civil: Access case records and dockets at www.idocket.com; registration and password required. Is a fee service; only one free name search a day. Civil and probate records go back to 12/31/2000. **$$$** *Criminal:* Access case records and dockets at www.idocket.com; registration and password required. Is a fee service; only one free name search a day. Records go back to 12/31/2000. **$$$**

Galveston County

District Court www2.co.galveston.tx.us/District_Clerk/

Civil: Online access to judge's daily calendars is free at www2.co.galveston.tx.us/District_Clerk/courts.htm. *Criminal:* Online access to Judge's daily calendars is free at www2.co.galveston.tx.us/District_Clerk/courts.htm.

County Court www2.co.galveston.tx.us/County_Clerk/

Civil: Online access is at http://ccweb.co.galveston.tx.us/. Generally records go back to 1995. *Criminal:* Online access is at http://ccweb.co.galveston.tx.us/. Index search is free. Generally records go back to 1995.

Gillespie County

County Court www.gillespiecounty.org/

Civil: The civil, family and probate index is free online at https://odysseypa.tylerhost.net/Gillespie/default.aspx. *Criminal:* The county court crimianl index is free online at https://odysseypa.tylerhost.net/Gillespie/default.aspx. This includes records from the Sheriff's office. The site is fairly new, the number of years included in a search is not many.

Grayson County

District Court www.co.grayson.tx.us/default.aspx?name=dclk.home

Civil: Access to judicial records is free at http://24.117.89.66:3007/default.aspx. *Criminal:* same

County Court www.co.grayson.tx.us/default.aspx?name=cclk.home

Civil: Online access to civil and probate records free at http://24.117.89.66:3007/default.aspx. *Criminal:* same as civil.

Gregg County

District Court www.co.gregg.tx.us/government/courts.asp

Civil: Online access to county judicial records is free at www.co.gregg.tx.us/judsrch.htm. Search by name, cause number, status. *Criminal:* same

County Court www.co.gregg.tx.us/government/county_courts/countyclerk.asp

Civil: Online access to county judicial records is free at www.co.gregg.tx.us/judsrch.htm. Search by name, cause number, or status. *Criminal:* same

Guadalupe County

District Court www.co.guadalupe.tx.us/guadalupe2010/home.php?content=dist_Clerk

Civil: Access to court records and hearings is available free at http://judicial.co.guadalupe.tx.us/default.aspx. The calendar is searchable from the home page. *Criminal:* Access to court records and hearings is available free at http://judicial.co.guadalupe.tx.us/default.aspx. Search sheriff's jail and bond records also. Dockets go back to 01/1970.

County Court www.co.guadalupe.tx.us/guadalupe2010/home.php?content=co_clerk

Civil: Access to court records and hearings is available free at http://judicial.co.guadalupe.tx.us/default.aspx. *Criminal:* Access to court records and hearings is available free at http://judicial.co.guadalupe.tx.us/default.aspx. Also search sheriff's jail and bond records.

Hale County

District Court www.242ndcourt.com

Civil: Access docket data from 01/1990 online at www.idocket.com; registration and password required. A fee service; only one free name search per day. **$$$** *Criminal:* same **$$$**

County Court

Civil: Online access is through www.idocket.com; registration and password required. Civil and probate data back to 01/1991. One free name search permitted a day, otherwise subscription required. **$$$** *Criminal:* same as civil **$$$**

Harris County

District Court www.hcdistrictclerk.com/Common/Default.aspx

Civil: First, an online county case lookup service is free at www.cclerk.hctx.net/applications/websearch/Civil.aspx or http://apps.jims.hctx.net/courts/. Online records go back to 10/1989. A docket search is at www.hcdistrictclerk.com/eDocs/Public/Search.aspx. Qualified subscribers may access records for a fee at http://home.jims.hctx.net/WebServices.aspx. Search civil dockets free at http://apps.jims.hctx.net/courts/. **$$$** *Criminal:* Online criminal index case lookup is at www.hcdistrictclerk.com/Edocs/Public/Search.aspx?BGCheckTab=1. No county's records, or Justice of the Peace or other Municipalities Class C Misdemeanors are included. A general docket search is at www.hcdistrictclerk.com/Edocs/Public/Search.aspx?dockettab=1. Qualified subscribers may access records for a fee at http://home.jims.hctx.net/WebServices.aspx. **$$$**

County Court www.cclerk.hctx.net

Civil: Online access is free at www.cclerk.hctx.net. System includes civil data search and county civil settings inquiry and other county clerk functions. For further information, visit the website or call 713-755-6421. Also, civil case online access back to 12/31/1997 at www.idocket.com; registration and password required. A fee service; only one free name search a day. **$$$**

Harrison County

District Court www.co.harrison.tx.us

Civil: Current docket information is available at the web page. Click on 71st District Court, then on Criminal Docket Information. *Criminal:* same

Hays County

District Court www.co.hays.tx.us/index.php/justice-system-courts/district-clerk/

Civil: Search by name, case number or attorney from home page or at www.co.hays.tx.us/index.php/justice-system-courts/district-clerk/records-search/. Also, online access is through www.idocket.com; registration and password required. Case records go back to 12/31/1986. One free name search permitted a day, otherwise subscription required. **$$$** *Criminal:* same **$$$**

County Court www.co.hays.tx.us

Civil: Search the docket index free from the home page, click on Public Record Search. Search by name or case number. Includes civil, family and probate cases. Index includes DOB, address on docket. Online access is through www.idocket.com; registration and password required. Includes probate. Case records from 01/88. One free name search permitted a day, otherwise subscription required. Includes DOB **$$$** *Criminal:* Search the docket index free from the home page, click on Public Record Search. Search by name or case number. Index includes DOB, address on docket. Misdemeanor records online access is through www.idocket.com; registration and password required. Case records go back to 12/31/1987. One free name search permitted a day, otherwise subscription required. **$$$**

Henderson County

District Court www.co.henderson.tx.us/default.aspx?Henderson_County/District.Clerk

Civil: Search the index at www.co.henderson.tx.us/default.aspx?henderson_county/judicial.recordssearch. *Criminal:* Search the index at www.co.henderson.tx.us/default.aspx?henderson_county/judicial.recordssearch. Includes separate search of jail records and bond records.

County Court www.co.henderson.tx.us/

Civil: Search the index at www.co.henderson.tx.us/ips/cms/JudicialRecordsSearch.html. *Criminal:* same

Hidalgo County

District Court www.co.hidalgo.tx.us/index.aspx?nid=192

Civil: Online case access is through www.idocket.com; registration and password required. Records go back to 12/31/1986. One free name search permitted a day, otherwise subscription required. Interestingly, the court claims it is not providing data to Idocket, but the District Courts located in this county show on the Idocket menu. **$$$** *Criminal:* same **$$$**

County Court www.co.hidalgo.tx.us/index.aspx?NID=243

Civil: Online case access is through www.idocket.com; registration and password required. Civil and probate records go back to 12/31/1986. One free name search permitted a day, otherwise subscription required. **$$$** *Criminal:* Misdemeanor case records access is through www.idocket.com; registration and password required. Records go back to 12/31/1991. One free name search permitted a day, otherwise subscription required. **$$$**

Hill County

District Court & County Court at Law www.co.hill.tx.us

Civil: Online case access is through www.idocket.com. One search a day is free; subscription required for more. Records go back to 12/31/1990. **$$$** *Criminal:* Criminal case access is through www.idocket.com; registration and password required. Records go back to 12/31/1990. One free name search permitted a day, otherwise subscription required. **$$$**

Hockley County

District Court

Civil: One may search the docket index online at www.texasonlinerecords.com/clerk/?office_id=9. There is no fee, but access requires a password. Search civil or probate by name or case number. Online results do not give identifiers. *Criminal:* One may search the criminal docket index online at www.texasonlinerecords.com/clerk/?office_id=9. There is no fee, but access requires a password. Online results give DOB.

Hood County

County Court & County Court at Law http://tx-hoodcounty.civicplus.com/index.aspx?NID=211

Civil: The civil index is found at http://tx-hoodcounty.civicplus.com/index.aspx?NID=679. Records go back to 1995. Search by name and by either plaintiff or defendant.. The probate index is found at http://tx-hoodcounty.civicplus.com/index.aspx?NID=678. Records are grouped into three segments. *Criminal:* Search the criminal index by year (back to 1995) at http://tx-hoodcounty.civicplus.com/index.aspx?NID=677.

Hopkins County

District Court

Civil: Access civil case index online at www.idocket.com; registration and password required. A fee service; only one free name search a day. **$$$** *Criminal:* same as civil.

County Court www.hopkinscountytx.org/

Civil: Search county court index free after registering for login and password at www.hopkinscountyonline.net/countyclerk/. Online case access at www.idocket.com; registration and password required. Civil records go back to 05/01/1989, probate to 1/1/1985. One free name search permitted a day, otherwise subscription required. **$$$** *Criminal:* same Online case access at www.idocket.com; registration and password required. Misdemeanor records go back to 05/01/1985. One free name search permitted a day, otherwise subscription required. **$$$**

Houston County

District Court www.co.houston.tx.us/ips/cms/districtcourt/districtClerk.html

Civil: Access case records and dockets at www.idocket.com; registration and password required. Is a fee service; only one free name search a day. Civil and family law records go back to 01/01/96. **$$$** *Criminal:* Access case records and dockets at www.idocket.com; registration and password required. Is a fee service; only one free name search a day. Records go back to 01/01/97. **$$$**

Howard County

District Court

Civil: Online case access is available by subscription at www.idocket.com including civil (no probate) back to 10/01/1951. One free name search permitted a day, otherwise subscription required. **$$$** *Criminal:* Online case access is available by subscription at www.idocket.com including felony back to 10/01/1990. One free name search permitted a day, otherwise subscription required. **$$$**

Hunt County

County Court #1 and #2 www.huntcounty.net/

Civil: Online case access is through www.idocket.com; registration and password required. Records go back to 1/1/1986, probate back to 1/1840. One free name search permitted a day, otherwise subscription required. **$$$** *Criminal:* Online case access is through www.idocket.com; registration and password required. Records go back to 1/1/1987. One free name search permitted a day, otherwise subscription required.

Hutchinson County

District Court http://hutchinsoncountyonline.com/district-court/

Civil: Online case access is available by subscription at www.idocket.com including civil (no probate) back to 1/1/1990. One free name search permitted a day, otherwise subscription required. **$$$** *Criminal:* Online case access is available by subscription at www.idocket.com including criminal back to 1/1/1989. One free name search permitted a day, otherwise subscription required. **$$$**

Jack County

District Court www.jackcounty.org/districtclerk.html

Civil: Access index online at http://idocket.com/homepage2.htm. Registration required. Civil records back to 1/1/58, Family Law to 1/1/95. One free name search permitted a day, otherwise subscription required. **$$$** *Criminal:* Access index online at http://idocket.com/homepage2.htm. Registration required. Criminal records back to 1/1/58, One free name search permitted a day, otherwise subscription required

County Court

Civil: Online case access is available by subscription at www.idocket.com including civil and probate back to 1/2000. One free name search permitted a day, otherwise subscription required. **$$$** *Criminal:* Online misdemeanor case access is available by subscription at www.idocket.com including criminal back to 1/1999. One free name search permitted a day, otherwise subscription required. **$$$**

Jefferson County

District Court www.co.jefferson.tx.us/dclerk/dc_home.htm

Civil: Online access to the civil records index at www.co.jefferson.tx.us/dclerk/civil_index/main.htm. Search by year by defendant or plaintiff by year 1985 to present. Index goes back to 1995; images back to 12/1998. There is also a Domestic Index. Access case records and dockets at www.idocket.com; registration and password required. Is a fee service; only one free name search a day. Civil records go back to 01/01/87. *Criminal:* Online access to criminal records index is at www.co.jefferson.tx.us/dclerk/criminal_index/main.htm. Search by name by year 1981 to present.

County Court www.co.jefferson.tx.us/cclerk/clerk.htm

Civil: Search county clerk's civil index free at http://jeffersontxclerk.manatron.com. Index goes back to 1995; images back to 12/1998. $1.00 per page to obtain online docs, plus a $2.50 processing fee. Court reports it is adding additional records in 2011. *Criminal:* Access to Class A&B and C Misdemeanor that are appealed indexes back to 1982 are free at http://jeffersontxclerk.manatron.com/. $1.00 per page to obtain online docs with a $2.50 processing fee. Add'l criminal records being added.

Jim Wells County

District Court www.co.jim-wells.tx.us/default.aspx?Jim-Wells_County/District.Clerk

Criminal: Online case access is available by subscription at www.idocket.com including felony back to 05/05/1982. One free name search permitted a day, otherwise subscription required. **$$$**

Johnson County

District Court www.johnsoncountytx.org

Civil: Access index and images online at www.idocket.com; registration and password required. A fee service; only one free name search per day. Records go back to 11/10/1989. Images available. Also search at http://ira.johnsoncountytx.org/. **$$$** *Criminal:* same Also search at http://ira.johnsoncountytx.org/ **$$$**

County Court www.johnsoncountytx.org

Civil: Access index and images online at http://idocket.com/homepage2.htm. Registration required. Civil records back to 12/31/85, probate to 01/01/1918. One free name search permitted a day, otherwise subscription required. Also search at http://ira.johnsoncountytx.org/. **$$$** *Criminal:* Access misdemeanor index and images online at http://idocket.com/homepage2.htm. Registration required. Records back to 12/31/88. One free name search permitted a day, otherwise subscription required. **$$$**

Kaufman County

District Court www.kaufmancounty.net/dc.html

Civil: Access court record index for civil and family free at http://12.14.175.53/default.aspx. Online court records do not always show all identifiers. *Criminal:* Access criminal court record index free at http://12.14.175.53/default.aspx. Online court records do not always show complete dispositions.

County Court www.kaufmancountyclerk.com/

Civil: Access court record index for civil and probate free at http://12.14.175.23/default.aspx. Online court records do not always show all identifiers. *Criminal:* Access criminal court record index free at http://12.14.175.23/default.aspx. Online court records do not always show complete dispositions.

Kerr County

District Court www.co.kerr.tx.us/dclerk/districtclerk.html

Civil: Search all court indexes also jail and bond indexes free at http://public.co.kerr.tx.us/CaseManagement/PublicAccess/default.aspx. *Criminal:* same

County Court & County Court at Law www.co.kerr.tx.us/

Civil: For online access, see criminal section, below. *Criminal:* Search all court records also jail and bond records free at http://public.co.kerr.tx.us/CaseManagement/PublicAccess/default.aspx.

Kleberg County

District & County Court at Law

Civil: Online access is at www.idocket.com; registration and password required. A fee service, only one free name search per day. Records go back to 1/1992. **$$$** *Criminal:* Online case access is at www.idocket.com; registration and password required. A fee service; only one free name search per day. Records go back to 12/31/1995. **$$$**

County Court - Criminal www.co.kleberg.tx.us

Criminal: Online case access at www.idocket.com; registration and password required. A fee service; only one free name search per day. Records go back to 1/1/1983. **$$$**

Lamar County

District Court www.co.lamar.tx.us

Civil: Access to county judicial records is free at www.co.lamar.tx.us/. Search by either party name. *Criminal:* Access to county judicial records is free online at www.co.lamar.tx.us. Search by defendant name.

County Court www.co.lamar.tx.us

Civil: Access to county judicial records is free at http://68.89.102.225/. Search by either party name. *Criminal:* Access to county judicial records is free online at www.co.lamar.tx.us. Search by defendant name.

Liberty County

District Court www.co.liberty.tx.us

Civil: A docket name search is offered at www.texasonlinerecords.com/clerk/?office_id=10. Must register before usage. Probate records available as well. *Criminal:* A docket name search is offered at www.texasonlinerecords.com/clerk/?office_id=10. Must register before usage.

Lubbock County

District Court www.co.lubbock.tx.us/department/?fDD=11-0

Criminal: The court offers a subscription service to criminal records. The application is found at www.co.lubbock.tx.us/egov/docs/1294749845_585784.pdf. Access excludes images prior to May 2007. **$$$**

County Courts www.co.lubbock.tx.us/judiciary/

Criminal: The court offers a subscription service to records. The application is at www.co.lubbock.tx.us/egov/docs/1294749845_585784.pdf. Interestingly the application asks the subscriber to check which the user group he/she belongs to, but left out the biggest user group of criminal records. **$$$**

Maverick County

District Court

Civil: Access cases online back to 11/1994 at www.idocket.com; registration and password required. A fee service; only one free name search per day. **$$$** *Criminal:* Access felony cases back to 8/1/1995 at www.idocket.com; registration and password required. A fee service; only one free name search per day. **$$$**

County Court www.co.maverick.tx.us

Civil: Access cases online back to 1/2006 at www.idocket.com; registration and password required. A fee service; only one free name search per day. **$$$** *Criminal:* Access misdemeanor cases back to 1/1999 at www.idocket.com; registration and password required. A fee service; only one free name search per day. **$$$**

McLennan County

District Court www.co.mclennan.tx.us/distclerk/index.aspx

Civil: Online index and image access is through http://idocket.com/homepage2.htm; registration, password and fees required. Records go back to 1/1955; no probate. One free name search permitted a day, otherwise subscription required. **$$$** *Criminal:* Online index and image access is through www.idocket.com; registration and password required. Felony records go back to 1/1981. One free name search permitted a day, otherwise subscription required. **$$$**

Medina County

District Court www.medinacountytexas.org/default.aspx?Medina_County/District.Clerk

Civil: Online index and image access is through http://idocket.com/homepage2.htm; registration, password and fees required. Records go back to 01/01/1990; no probate. One free name search permitted a day, otherwise subscription required. **$$$** *Criminal:* Online index and image access is through http://idocket.com/homepage2.htm; registration, password and fees required. Records go back to 01/01/1990. One free name search permitted a day, otherwise subscription required. **$$$**

Midland County

District Court www.co.midland.tx.us/departments/dc/Pages/default.aspx

Civil: Online access to district clerk database is by subscription. Registration and password required; Fee is $120 per year plus $.10 per image. Contact the clerk for access restrictions. **$$$** *Criminal:* same **$$$**

Mitchell County

County Court

Civil: Access to dockets is free at www.edoctecinc.com, data is within 24 hours of being current. *Criminal:* same

Montgomery County

County Court www.mctx.org/dept/departments_c/county_clerk/index.html

Civil: Search the civil docket and probate docket online at http://ccinternet.mctx.org/php/menu/menu-public.php. 14-day daily dockets free at the main website. *Criminal:* Search the county clerk's misdemeanor records free at http://ccinternet.mctx.org/php/menu/menu-public.php. Online search results also give physical features. Also, 14-day daily dockets free at the main website. Access misdemeanor cases online at www.idocket.com; registration and password required. A fee service. Records go back to 12/31/1989.

Morris County

District Court

Civil: Access case records and dockets at www.idocket.com; registration and password required. Is a fee service; only one free name search a day. Civil and family law records go back to 06/01/2001. **$$$** *Criminal:* same as civil **$$$**

County Court

Criminal: Access case records and dockets at www.idocket.com; registration and password required. Is a fee service; only one free name search a day. Records go back to 06/01/2001. **$$$**

Nacogdoches County

District Court

Civil: Online case access is available by subscription at www.idocket.com including civil and family back to 12/31/1986. One free name search permitted a day, otherwise subscription required. **$$$** *Criminal:* same as civil. **$$$**

County Court www.co.nacogdoches.tx.us

Civil: Online case access is available by subscription at www.idocket.com including civil and probate back to 12/31/1986. One free name search permitted a day, otherwise subscription required. **$$$** *Criminal:* Online case access is available by subscription at www.idocket.com; online records go back to 12/31/1986. One free name search permitted a day, otherwise subscription required. **$$$**

Navarro County

District Court www.co.navarro.tx.us/

Civil: Online civil case access is through www.idocket.com. Records go back to 12/31/1990. One free name search permitted a day, otherwise subscription required. **$$$** *Criminal:* Online criminal case access is through www.idocket.com; registration and password required. Records go back to 12/31/1990. One free name search permitted a day, otherwise subscription required. **$$$**

County Court www.co.navarro.tx.us

Civil: Online civil case access is through www.idocket.com. One free name search permitted a day, otherwise subscription required. **$$$** *Criminal:* same as civil

Nueces County

District & County Court www.co.nueces.tx.us/districtclerk/

Civil: Online access to civil District & County Court records are free at www.co.nueces.tx.us/districtclerk/. Click on Civil/Criminal Case Search, register, then search by name, company, or cause number. *Criminal:* Online access to criminal District & County Court records are free at www.co.nueces.tx.us/districtclerk/. Click on Civil/Criminal Case Search, register, then search by name, SID number, or cause number.

Ochiltree County

District Court

Civil: Online index and image access is through http://idocket.com/homepage2.htm; registration, password and fees required. Civil and Family records go back to 01/01/1948. One free name search permitted a day, otherwise subscription required. **$$$** *Criminal:* Online index and image access is through http://idocket.com/homepage2.htm; registration, password and fees required. Records go back to 01/01/2002. One free name search permitted a day, otherwise subscription required. **$$$**

County Court

Civil: Online index and image access is through http://idocket.com/homepage2.htm; registration, password and fees required. Records go back to 01/01/1992, probate to 01/01/1996. One free name search permitted a day, otherwise subscription required. **$$$** *Criminal:* Online index and image access is through http://idocket.com/homepage2.htm; registration, password and fees required. Records go back to 01/01/1983. One free name search permitted a day, otherwise subscription required. **$$$**

Oldham County

District & County Court

Civil: Online case access is through www.idocket.com; registration and password required. Records go back to 3/1998, probate to 2/1996. Civil County cases to 3/1/1998, civil District cases to 03/01/1994. One free name search permitted a day, otherwise subscription required. **$$$** *Criminal:* Online case access is through www.idocket.com; registration and password required. Misdemeanor records go back to 1/1993, felony to 1/1992. One free name search permitted a day, otherwise subscription required. **$$$**

Orange County

County Court www.co.orange.tx.us

Civil: View court documents online. Go to home page, click on Departments, then click on county clerk. Please read instructions. No name searching, must have case number to access the record. All probate is online. Scanned cycle is online. *Criminal:* Search misdemeanor warrants free at www.co.orange.tx.us/Misdomeanor%20Warrants.htm. Also, search misdemeanor records to 2005 by case number online from home page.

Panola County

District Court & County Court at Law www.co.panola.tx.us/

Civil: Access to civil records is free at http://odysseypa.tylerhost.net/Panola/default.aspx. *Criminal:* Access to criminal records is free at http://odysseypa.tylerhost.net/Panola/default.aspx.

Parker County

District Court www.parkercountytx.com

Civil: Access to court records is free at www.parkercountytx.com. Online civil records go back to 1/2003. Civil results include party names, case type, atty. *Criminal:* Access to criminal records and sheriff inmates and bonds search is free at www.parkercountytx.com. Online criminal records go back to 7/88. Online results include atty, offense, disposition.

County Court www.parkercountytx.com

Civil: Online access to civil is same as criminal, see below. *Criminal:* Online access is free at www.parkercountytx.com. Search the sheriff bond and jail lists here also.

Parmer County

District Court

Civil: Online case access is through www.idocket.com; registration and password required. Records go back to 12/31/1995. One free name search permitted a day, otherwise subscription required. **$$$** *Criminal:* same **$$$**

Polk County

County Court

Civil: Civil case information is free at www.idocket.com. Registration and password required. One free name search permitted a day, otherwise subscription required. **$$$** *Criminal:* Criminal case information is free at www.idocket.com. Registration and password required. One free name search permitted a day, otherwise subscription required. **$$$**

Potter County

District Court www.co.potter.tx.us/districtclerk/

Civil: Civil index and images back to 1988 at www.idocket.com. One free name search permitted a day, otherwise subscription required. **$$$** *Criminal:* Felony cases online at www.idocket.com. Felonies go back to 1/1989. One free name search permitted a day, otherwise subscription required. **$$$**

County Court & County Courts at Law 1 & 2 www.co.potter.tx.us/countyclerk/index.html

Civil: Online case access is through www.idocket.com; registration and password required. Records go back to 9/1/1987, probate back to 1/1886. One free name search permitted a day, otherwise subscription required. **$$$** *Criminal:* Misdemeanor cases online at www.idocket.com. Misdemeanors go back to 1/1991. One free name search permitted a day, otherwise subscription required. **$$$**

Rains County

District Court www.co.rains.tx.us

Civil: Civil index at www.co.rains.tx.us/default.aspx?Rains_County/District.Clerk. Records from 1/1/03-3/31/13. *Criminal:* Criminal index at www.co.rains.tx.us/default.aspx?Rains_County/District.Clerk. Records from 1/1/03-3/31/13.

Randall County

District Courts www.randallcounty.org/cclerk/

Civil: Civil case information at www.idocket.com. Records from 12/31/84. Subscription required. **$$$** *Criminal:* Felony cases online at Idocket at http://idocket.com/counties.htm. Is a fee service. Felony records go back to 1/1992. Subscription required. **$$$**

County Court www.randallcounty.org/cclerk/

Civil: Civil case information at www.idocket.com. Records go back to 1/2000; probate back to 9/11/1969. One free name search permitted a day, otherwise subscription required. Direct email records requests to countyclerk@randallcounty.org. **$$$** *Criminal:* Misdemeanor cases online at Idocket at http://idocket.com/counties.htm. Misd. records go back to 1/1985. One free name search permitted a day, otherwise subscription required. **$$$**

Refugio County

District Court

Civil: Access cases back to 1/1994 at www.idocket.com; registration and password required. A fee service; only one free name search per day. **$$$**

County Court

Civil: Access cases back to 1/1994 at www.idocket.com; registration and password required. A fee service; only one free name search per day. **$$$** *Criminal:* Access misdemeanor cases back to 1/1991 at www.idocket.com; registration and password required. A fee service; only one free name search per day. **$$$**

Rockwall County

District Court www.rockwallcountytexas.com

Civil: Online access is same as criminal, see below. *Criminal:* Online access is free at http://trueauto.rockwallcountytexas.com/judicialsearch/. Search sheriff bond and jail lists too. Online court records only go back 7 years; some dismissals/deferred cases are not online.

County Court at Law www.rockwallcountytexas.com/index.asp?nid=77

Civil: Online access is same as criminal, see below. *Criminal:* Online access is free at http://trueauto.rockwallcountytexas.com/judicialsearch/. Search sheriff bond and jail lists too. Online court records only go back 7 years; some dismissals/deferred cases are not online.

San Patricio County

District Court www.co.san-patricio.tx.us

Civil: Access civil cases online back to 11/1992 at www.idocket.com; registration and password required. One free name search permitted a day, otherwise subscription required. **$$$** *Criminal:* Online access to felony cases back to 1/1994 at www.idocket.com; registration and password required. One free name search permitted a day, otherwise subscription required. **$$$**

County Court www.co.san-patricio.tx.us

Civil: Access civil cases including probate online back to 1/1997 at www.idocket.com; registration and password required. One free name search permitted a day, otherwise subscription required. **$$$** *Criminal:* Online access to Misd. cases back to 1/1994 at www.idocket.com; registration and password required. One free name search permitted a day, otherwise subscription required. **$$$**

Shelby County

County Court http://cc.co.shelby.tx.us/

Civil: Access court index free at http://cc.co.shelby.tx.us/. *Criminal:* Access court records free at http://cc.co.shelby.tx.us/.

Smith County

District Court www.smith-county.com/Courts/DistrictCourt/Default.aspx

Civil: Access court indexes and sheriff's jail and bond data free at http://judicial.smith-county.com/judsrch.asp. Access current docket information - by the District Court - at www.smith-county.com/Courts/DistrictCourt/Default.aspx. *Criminal:* hsitorical court record data is forund at http://judicial.smith-county.com/judsrch.asp.

County Court at Law 1, 2, 3 www.smith-county.com/Courts/CountyCourt/Default.aspx

Civil: Access court and probate indexes and sheriff's jail and bond data free at http://judicial.smith-county.com/judsrch.asp. *Criminal:* same

Starr County

District & County Court www.co.starr.tx.us/ips/cms/districtcourt/

Civil: Access index and images online at www.idocket.com; registration and password required. A fee service; only one free name search per day. Records go back to 01/2003. Probate is not online. **$$$** *Criminal:* Access felony index and images online at www.idocket.com; registration and password required. A fee service; only one free name search per day. Felony records go back to 1/2003, misdemeanors to 12/31/1996. **$$$**

County Court

Criminal: Online access is at www.idocket.com; registration and password required. A fee service; only one free name search per day. Records go back to 12/31/96.

Tarrant County

District Court www.tarrantcounty.com/ecourts/site/default.asp

Civil: Access to the remote online system requires $50 setup fee and $35.00 monthly with add'l month prepaid; for 1 to 5 users; fees increase with more users. Call 817-884-1345 for info and signup. Note that certified copies cannot be ordered online. **$$$** *Criminal:* same **$$$**

County Court - Criminal www.tarrantcounty.com/ecourts/site/default.asp

Criminal: Access to the remote online system requires $50 setup fee and $35.00 monthly with add'l month prepaid; this is for 1 to 5 users. Fees increase with more users. The District Court records are on this system also. Call 817-884-1345 for more information. **$$$**

Titus County

District Court www.co.titus.tx.us/

Civil: Access case records and dockets at www.idocket.com; registration and password required. Is a fee service; only one free name search a day. Civil and family law records go back to 12/01/1955. **$$$** *Criminal:* Same as civil. Records go back to 12/01/1965. **$$$**

County Court www.co.titus.tx.us/

Civil: Access to court records from www.tituscountyonline.net/clerk/. Must be registered. Also gives vital record index from home page, click on County Clerk then Index Search. *Criminal:* Access to court records from www.tituscountyonline.net/clerk/. Must be registered.

Tom Green County

District Court www.co.tom-green.tx.us/distclrk/

Civil: Online access to civil case records back to 1994 is online at http://odysseypa.co.tom-green.tx.us/default.aspx. Search by name, case number. Access case records and dockets at www.idocket.com; registration and password required. Is a fee service; only one free name search a day. Civil records go back to 04/04/92. **$$$** *Criminal:* Online access to criminal case records back to 1994 at http://odysseypa.co.tom-green.tx.us/default.aspx. Search by name, case number. Access case records and dockets at www.idocket.com; registration and password required. Is a fee service; only one free name search a day. Civil records go back to 01/01/94. **$$$**

County Court www.co.tom-green.tx.us/ips/cms/countyoffices/CountyClerk/

Civil: Online access to civil records from1994 is free at http://odysseypa.co.tom-green.tx.us/. Access case records and dockets at www.idocket.com; registration and password required. Is a fee service; only one free name search a day. Civil records go back to 01/01/94. *Criminal:* Online access to criminal records from 1994 is free at http://odysseypa.co.tom-green.tx.us/. Access case records and dockets at www.idocket.com; registration and password required. Is a fee service; only one free name search a day. Records go back to 01/01/94.

Travis County

District & County Courts

Criminal: Online access through www.idocket.com; registration and password required. Records date back to 11/01/2004. One free name search permitted a day, otherwise subscription required. Current docket information is available at www.co.travis.tx.us/courts/files/dockets/dockets_criminal.asp. **$$$**

District & County Courts www.co.travis.tx.us/courts/civil/default.asp

Civil: Current docket information is available at www.co.travis.tx.us/courts/files/dockets/dockets_Civil.asp. Online case access is through www.idocket.com; registration and password required. Records date back to 12/01/2005 for civil and family law. One free name search permitted a day, otherwise subscription required. **$$$**

Trinity County

County Court www.co.trinity.tx.us/ips/cms/County_Court/

Civil: Online case access is through www.idocket.com; registration and password required. One free name search permitted a day, otherwise subscription required. **$$$** *Criminal:* same **$$$**

Tyler County

County Court

Civil: Access case records and dockets at www.idocket.com; registration and password required. Is a fee service; only one free name search a day. Records go back to 12/31/90. **$$$** *Criminal:* same **$$$**

Upshur County

District & County Courts www.countyofupshur.com

Civil: Access court records and hearings free at www.countyofupshur.com/judicialsearch/. *Criminal:* same

Upton County

District & County Court www.co.upton.tx.us

Civil: Access case records and dockets at www.idocket.com; registration and password required. Is a fee service; only one free name search a day. *Criminal:* same **$$$**

Val Verde County

District Court www.valverdecounty.org/District_Clerk.html

Civil: Access civil cases and family law (no probate) at www.idocket.com; registration and password required. A fee service; only one free name search per day. Records go back to 12/31/89. **$$$** *Criminal:* same as civil. Felonies go back to 12/31/93. **$$$**

Victoria County

District Court www.vctx.org/

Civil: Online index and images at www.idocket.com; registration and password required. Records go back to 12/31/1993. One free name search permitted a day, otherwise subscription required. Images available. **$$$** *Criminal:* Access felony index and images at www.idocket.com; registration and password required. Records go back to 12/31/1993. One free name search permitted a day, otherwise subscription required. **$$$**

County Court www.vctx.org

Civil: Online case access at www.idocket.com; registration and password required. Civil records go back to 12/31/1991; probate to 6/31//1991. One free name search permitted a day, otherwise subscription required. **$$$** *Criminal:* Access Misd. cases online at www.idocket.com; registration and password required. Records go back to 12/31/1989. One free name search permitted a day, otherwise subscription required. **$$$**

Walker County

District Court www.co.walker.tx.us/department/?fDD=9-0

Civil: Online access to case summary data at http://odysseypa.tylerhost.net/Walker/default.aspx. Includes civil, family, and probate. *Criminal:* Online access to case summary data at http://odysseypa.tylerhost.net/Walker/default.aspx.

County Court www.co.walker.tx.us/department/index.php?fDD=5-0

Civil: Online access to case summary data at http://odysseypa.tylerhost.net/Walker/default.aspx. Includes civil, family, and probate. *Criminal:* Online access to case summary data at http://odysseypa.tylerhost.net/Walker/default.aspx. The site alos provides access to jail records, jail bond records, and law enforcement incident records.

Waller County

District Court http://ww2.co.waller.tx.us/district_clerk.html

Civil: Online case access at www.idocket.com; registration and password required. Civil records (no probate) go back to 01/01/2000. One free name search permitted a day, otherwise subscription required. **$$$** *Criminal:* Online case access at www.idocket.com; registration and password required. Felony records (no misdemeanor) go back to 01/01/1998. One free name search permitted a day, otherwise subscription required. **$$$**

County Court http://ww2.co.waller.tx.us/

Civil: Access to civil records at http://odysseypa.tylerhost.net/Waller/default.aspx. *Criminal:* same as civil.

Washington County

District Court www.co.washington.tx.us

Civil: Online case access at www.idocket.com. Dockets from 12/30/1988. One search a day is free; subscription required for more. **$$$** *Criminal:* Access felony cases at www.idocket.com. Dockets from 12/30/1988. One search a day is free; subscription required for more. **$$$**

County Court

Civil: Online case access at www.idocket.com; registration and password required. Civil records go back to 12/31/85; probate to 12/31/68. One free name search permitted a day, otherwise subscription required. **$$$** *Criminal:* Access Misd. cases at www.idocket.com; registration and password required. Misdemeanor records back to 12/31/1985. One free name search permitted a day, otherwise subscription required. **$$$**

Webb County

District Court www.webbcountytx.gov

Civil: Online case access at www.idocket.com; registration and password required. Civil records (no probate) go back to 12/31/1988. One free name search permitted a day, otherwise subscription required. **$$$** *Criminal:* Online felony cases at www.idocket.com; registration and password required. Felonies go back to 12/31/1988. One free name search permitted a day, otherwise subscription required. **$$$**

County Court www.webbcountytx.gov/

Civil: Online case access at www.idocket.com; registration and password required. Civil records and probate go back to 12/31/1989. One free name search permitted a day, otherwise subscription required. *Criminal:* Online case access at www.idocket.com; registration and password required. Misdemeanor index goes back to 12/31/1989. One free name search permitted a day, otherwise subscription required. Also, an online search is for traffic warrants is at www.webbcountytx.gov/warrant-lookup/Search.aspx. **$$$**

Wharton County

County Court

Civil: Access case records including probate at www.idocket.com; registration and password required. A fee service; only one free name search per day. **$$$** *Criminal:* same **$$$**

Willacy County

District Court

Civil: Access civil and family law cases back to 01/01/1990 at www.idocket.com; registration and password required. A fee service; only one free name search per day. **$$$** *Criminal:* Access cases back to 01/01/1989 at www.idocket.com; registration and password required. A fee service; only one free name search per day. **$$$**

County Court

Civil: Access civil case index back to 01/01/1989 at www.idocket.com; registration and password required. A fee service; only one free name search per day. **$$$** *Criminal:* Access misdemeanor case index back to 01/01/1990 at www.idocket.com; registration and password required. A fee service; only one free name search per day. **$$$**

Williamson County

District Court www.wilco.org/default.aspx?tabid=448

Civil: Search the civil docket index at http://judicialrecords.wilco.org/default.aspx. Search by case number, party, or attorney. *Criminal:* Search the criminal docket index at http://judicialrecords.wilco.org/default.aspx. Search by case number, party, or attorney.

County Court www.wilco.org/CountyDepartments/CountyCourts/tabid/235/language/en-US/Default.aspx

Civil: Access to civil and probate court records countywide available for free at http://judicialrecords.wilco.org/default.aspx. *Criminal:* Access to criminal case records countywide available for free at http://judicialrecords.wilco.org/default.aspx. Jail and jail bonsd records also available.

Wise County

County Court at Law www.co.wise.tx.us/cc/

Civil: There is a case look-up from the home page - Click on \"Court Department.\"

Wood County

District Court http://judicial.co.wood.tx.us

Civil: Search civil case index at http://judicial.co.wood.tx.us/CivilSearch/civfrmd.asp. *Criminal:* Search criminal case index at http://judicial.co.wood.tx.us/CrimSearch/crimfrmd.asp.

County Court www.mywoodcounty.com/

Civil: Search all courts free at http://judicial.co.wood.tx.us/. *Criminal:* Search all courts and Sheriff bond and inmate lists free at http://judicial.co.wood.tx.us/.

Yoakum County

District Court www.co.yoakum.tx.us

Civil: Access civil cases (but not probate) at www.idocket.com; registration and password required. A fee service; only one free name search per day. Civil and Family Law cases go back to 12/31/1980. **$$$** *Criminal:* Access criminal docket at www.idocket.com; registration and password required. A fee service; only one free name search per day. Felony case information goes back to 12/31/1980. **$$$**

Young County

District Court www.co.young.tx.us/ips/cms/index.html

Civil: Access civil cases except probate at www.idocket.com; registration and password required. A fee service; only one free name search per day. Civil cases go back to 3/1/1998. **$$$** *Criminal:* Access felony cases at www.idocket.com; registration and password required. A fee service; only one free name search per day. Records go back to 3/1/1998. **$$$**

County Court

Civil: Access civil cases except probate at www.idocket.com; registration and password required. A fee service; only one free name search per day. Civil and probate cases go back to 1/1/1992 *Criminal:* Access civil cases except probate at www.idocket.com; registration and password required. A fee service; only one free name search per day. Misdemeanor cases go back to 1/1/1992.

Zapata County

County Court

Civil: Access civil cases except probate at www.idocket.com; registration and password required. A fee service; only one free name search per day. **$$$** *Criminal:* same

Recorders, Assessors, and Other Sites of Note

Recording Office Organization: 254 counties, 254 recording offices. The recording officer is the County Clerk. Federal tax liens on personal property of businesses are filed with the Secretary of State. Other federal and all state tax liens are filed with the County Clerk.

Statewide or Multi-Jurisdiction Access: Numerous counties offer online access to assessor and recorded document data via vendors summarized below.

- A search at the State Archives' TRAIL website at https://www.tsl.state.tx.us/trail/index.html lets you locate information from over 170 Texas state agency web servers. A good place to link to county appraisal districts is http://appraisaldistrict.net/ where you can click through all the county appraisers, many with free searching.
- There is plenty of competition in Texas among vendors offering online access to assessor and recorded document data. Below are some of the more prominent vendors with wide coverage:
  - Search for documents recorded in the County Clerk's office in a number of Texas counties at https://countygovernmentrecords.com/texas/web/login.jsp?submit=Enter. Users of this site must register and pay a fee to conduct document searches.
  - www.taxnetusa.com - offers appraisal district and property appraisal records for all Texas counties. Also, delinquent tax data is available for about half of the participating counties. Free searches as well as online subscriptions services using a sliding fee scale, or purchase bulk data download, are available. Visit the website or call 877-652-2707. To search free at the TaxNetUSA site, click on the "county" and fill out the top portion.
  - www.titlex.com - offers recording office records in county grantor/grantee indices - including real estate, deeds, liens, judgments records and more - for at least 102 Texas counties. In order to search, view, and print records you

must first purchase Tokens. Tokens are $.25 and to view is four, to print is four more. You may pay by credit card and open or add to your account.

- The site at https://www.texaslandrecords.com/txlr/TxlrApp/index.jsp - offers a free land index search for 53 or more Texas counties. Subscribers may print and view document images. A flat rate membership fee is also offered.
- View property tax data free on the True Automation site for 100+ Texas counties at http://trueautomation.com.

Individual County Sites:

These Profiles do NOT include the Vendor Sites Mentioned Above. We suggest to visit these vendor sites and determine which one(s) might work best for you.

Anderson County ***Property, Taxation Records*** Access to property tax data for free at www.andersoncad.net/search.php?searchType=name.

Andrews County ***Property, Taxation Records*** Access to property search options for free at www.andrewscountytax.com/taxSearch.

Angelina County ***Recorded Documents, Probate Records*** www.angelinacounty.net/departments/cc Search grantor/grantee index free at https://texaslandrecords.com/txlr/TxlrApp/index.jsp. Registration and fees required for full data. Search probate records back to 1996 at http://idocket.com/countycourt.htm. Probate records are at the County Court but accessible through the County Clerks Office. Also see note at beginning of section for add'l property data. **$$$**

Property, Taxation Records Access appraisal district data free at www.angelinacad.org/property-search. Also, access assessment records at www.txcountydata.com/.

Aransas County ***Probate Records*** www.aransascountytx.gov/clerk/ Search probate records at http://idocket.com/countycourt.htm. Probate records are at the County Court but accessible through the County Clerks Office. **$$$**

Property, Taxation Records Access dated appraiser and property tax data at www.aransascad.org/Appraisal/PublicAccess/. Also, property tax inquiries can be made via www.txcountydata.com/selectCounty.asp. Other online access through private companies.**$$$**

Atascosa County ***Real Estate, Grantor/Grantee, Judgment, Deed, Lien Records*** Access recording records free at www.titlex.com/; select Atascosa County. Also, see note at beginning of section.

Austin County ***Recorded Documents Records*** www.austincounty.com/default.aspx?Austin_County/County.Clerk Access recording records free at www.titlex.com; select Austin county. Records range is 8/1997 to 9/2005. Also, see note at beginning of section for add'l property data.

Property, Taxation Records Search property records for free at http://austincad.net/search.php?searchType=name. Also, property tax inquiries can be made via www.txcountydata.com/selectCounty.asp.

Bandera County ***Recorded Documents, Probate Records*** www.banderacounty.org Search grantor/grantee index free at https://texaslandrecords.com/txlr/TxlrApp/index.jsp. Registration and fees required for full data. Also, to search probate records for a fee go to http://idocket.com/countycourt.htm. Probate records are at the County Court but accessible through the County Clerks Office. **$$$**

Property, Taxation Records Access to Appraisal District records is free at http://propaccess.banderaproptax.org/clientdb/?cid=1. Search Tax Collector data a www.banderacounty.org/departments/tax.htm.

Bastrop County ***Real Estate, Grantor/Grantee, Deed, Judgment, Lien, UCC, Marriage Records*** www.co.bastrop.tx.us/site/content/countyclerk Access county clerk public access page for recorded documents free at www.cc.co.bastrop.tx.us/. Also, access recording records free at www.titlex.com; select Bastrop county. Record range is 3/2001 to 8/31/2001.

Property, Taxation Records Access to tax office records is free at www.bastroptac.com/Appraisal/PublicAccess/. Also, property tax inquiries can be made via www.txcountydata.com/selectCounty.asp. Also, see note at beginning of section.

Bee County ***Recorded Documents Records*** www.co.bee.tx.us/default.aspx?Bee_County/County.Clerk Search grantor/grantee index free at https://texaslandrecords.com/txlr/TxlrApp/index.jsp. Registration and fees required for full data. **$$$**

Property, Taxation Records Access property records free at www.beecad.org/.

Bell County ***Recorded Documents Records*** www.bellcountytx.com/county_government/county_clerk/index.php Search grantor/grantee index free at https://texaslandrecords.com/txlr/TxlrApp/index.jsp. Registration and fees required for full data. **$$$**

Property, Taxation Records Search property and parcel data free at http://propaccess.bellcad.org/clientdb/?cid=1.

Bexar County Clerk's Office ***Recorded Documents Records*** https://gov.propertyinfo.com/TX-Bexar/ Access to the County Clerk database is free after free registration at https://gov.propertyinfo.com/TX-Bexar/. Includes land records, deeds, UCCs, assumed names and foreclosure notices, and more.

Property, Taxation Records Access the county Central Appraisal District database free at www.bcad.org/ClientDB/PropertySearch.aspx?cid=1.

Bosque County ***Recorded Documents Records*** www.bosquecounty.us/office_of_bosque_county_clerk.htm Search grantor/grantee index free at https://texaslandrecords.com/txlr/TxlrApp/index.jsp. Registration and fees required for full data. **$$$**

Property, Taxation Records Access property records at www.txcountydata.com/county.asp?County=018. Other online access through private companies.**$$$**

Bowie County ***Property, Taxation Records*** Access to Appraisal District's Appraisal Roll data is free at www.bowiecad.org/?404=Y.

Brazoria County ***Recorded Documents, Probate Records*** www.brazoriacountyclerk.net/recorder/content/ Access recording records free at www.titlex.com; select Brazoria county. Records range from 3/2001 to 4/2007. Also, see note at beginning of section for add'l property data. Also, search probate records for a fee at http://idocket.com/countycourt.htm. Probate records are at the County Court but accessible through the County Clerks Office. **$$$**

Property, Taxation Records Access to the county Central Appraisal District database is free at www.brazoriacad.org/. Click on \"appraisal roll.\" Also, property tax inquiries can be made at www.txcountydata.com/selectCounty.asp.

Brazos County ***Recorded Documents Records*** www.brazoscountytx.gov/index.aspx?nid=114 Search grantor/grantee index free at https://texaslandrecords.com/txlr/TxlrApp/index.jsp. Registration and fees required for full data. **$$$**

Property, Taxation Records Access to County Appraisal District data is free at https://propaccess.trueautomation.com/clientdb/?cid=65. Also, property tax inquiries can be made via www.txcountydata.com/selectCounty.asp. Also, see notes at beginning of section.

Brewster County ***Recorded Documents Records*** https://gov.propertyinfo.com/TX-Brewster/Default.aspx Access to document images and index information for a fee at https://gov.propertyinfo.com/TX-Brewster/ **$$$**

Property, Taxation Records Free access to property search data and GIS/mapping available at www.brewstercotad.org/mapsparcel.htm.

Brooks County ***Recorded Documents Records*** www.co.brooks.tx.us/default.aspx?Brooks_County/County.Clerk Access recording office land data at www.etitlesearch.com; registration required, fee based on usage. Also, to search probate records and judgment records go to http://idocket.com/countycourt.htm. Probate records are at the County Court but accessible through the County Clerks Office. **$$$**

Property, Taxation Records Access to property tax searches for free at https://propaccess.trueautomation.com/clientdb/?cid=34.

Brown County ***Probate Records*** www.browncountytx.org/default.aspx?Brown_County/County.Clerk Search probate records for a fee at http://idocket.com/countycourt.htm. Probate records are at the County Court but accessible through the County Clerks Office. **$$$**

Property, Taxation Records Access to Appraisal District records is free at http://clientdb.trueautomation.com/clientdb/main.asp?id=30. Other online access through private companies.

Burleson County ***Recorded Documents Records*** www.co.burleson.tx.us/index.php?page_name=County+Clerk&page_id=18&id=6 Search grantor/grantee index free at https://texaslandrecords.com/txlr/TxlrApp/index.jsp. Registration and fees required for full data. **$$$**

Burnet County ***Recorded Documents Records*** www.burnetcountytexas.org/default.aspx?name=cclerk.home Access recording records free at www.titlex.com; select Burnett county. Records range from 1/1998 to 11/2001. Also, see note at beginning of section.

Property, Taxation Records Property tax inquiries can be made at https://propaccess.trueautomation.com/clientdb/?cid=85.**$$$**

Caldwell County ***Property, Taxation Records*** Access the county Appraisal District database now free at www.txcountydata.com/. Also, see online notes in state summary at beginning of section.

Calhoun County ***Recorded Documents, Probate Records*** www.calhouncotx.org/cclerk.html Access recording records free at via a vendor at www.titlex.com; select Calhoun county; login and password required. Records range up to 9/2003. Also, search probate records for a fee at http://idocket.com/countycourt.htm. Probate records are at the County Court but accessible through the County Clerks Office. **$$$**

Property, Taxation Records Access Appraisal District records free at https://propaccess.trueautomation.com/clientdb/?cid=83.

Callahan County ***Property, Taxation Records*** Access to records from the appraisal district and the collections offices free at http://isouthwestdata.com/corp/.

Cameron County ***Recorded Documents, Probate Records*** www.co.cameron.tx.us/countyclerk/index.htm Search grantor/grantee index free at https://texaslandrecords.com/txlr/TxlrApp/index.jsp. Registration and fees required for full data. Also, access probate records for a fee at http://idocket.com/countycourt.htm. Probate records are at the County Court but accessible through the County Clerks Office. Also, see note at beginning of section for add'l property data. **$$$**

Carson County ***Recorded Documents Records*** www.co.carson.tx.us/default.aspx?Carson_County/County.Clerk Access to county records for a fee at https://countygovernmentrecords.com/texas/web/login.jsp?submit=Enter. Must register. **$$$**

Cass County ***Property, Taxation Records*** Access to property records is free at https://propaccess.trueautomation.com/clientdb/?cid=3.

Chambers County ***Recorded Documents Records*** www.co.chambers.tx.us/default.aspx?name=county.clerk Access county clerk's real property records free after registering for a login name and password at www.texasonlinerecords.com/realproperty/?office_id=3.

Property, Taxation Records Search the appraiser property tax database for free at www.chamberscad.org/. Also, see note at beginning of section.

Cherokee County ***Recorded Documents Records*** Search grantor/grantee index free at https://texaslandrecords.com/txlr/TxlrApp/index.jsp. Registration and fees required for full data. **$$$**

Property, Taxation Records Search the Cherokee CAD database for free at https://propaccess.trueautomation.com/clientdb/?cid=61.

Clay County ***Probate Records*** www.co.clay.tx.us/default.aspx?Clay_County/County.Clerk Search probate records for a fee at http://idocket.com/countycourt.htm. Probate records are at the County Court but accessible through the County Clerks Office. **$$$**

Property, Taxation Records Access property tax records free at www.claycad.org/. Also, see note at beginning of section.

Cochran County ***Recorded Documents Records*** http://co.cochran.tx.us/default.aspx?Cochran_County/County.Clerk Search grantor/grantee index free at https://texaslandrecords.com/txlr/TxlrApp/index.jsp. Registration and fees required for full data. **$$$**

Coleman County ***Recorded Documents Records*** www.co.coleman.tx.us/default.aspx?Coleman_County/County.Clerk Search grantor/grantee index free at https://texaslandrecords.com/txlr/TxlrApp/index.jsp. Registration and fees required for full data. Also, search probate records for a fee at http://idocket.com/countycourt.htm. Probate records are at the County Court but accessible through the County Clerks Office. **$$$**

Collin County ***Recorded Documents, Vital Records Records*** www.co.collin.tx.us Access to the county clerk Deeds database is free at http://countyclerkrecords.co.collin.tx.us/webinquiry/. Also, see note at beginning of section for more property data.

Property, Taxation Records Search the Appraiser's property tax and business property database free at www.collincad.org/propertysearch. Also, search the tax assessor and collector look up free at www.co.collin.tx.us/tax_assessor/taxstmt_search.jsp.

Colorado County ***Recorded Documents Records*** www.co.colorado.tx.us/default.aspx?Colorado_County/County.Clerk Access recording records free at www.titlex.com; select Colorado county. Records range is 5/1997 to 9/2001. For more land data, see note at beginning of section.

Property, Taxation Records For property search go to www.coloradocad.org/ and click on property search. Also, see note at beginning of section.

Comal County ***Property, Taxation Records*** Search property tax data free at http://taxweb.co.comal.tx.us/clientdb/?cid=1.

Cooke County ***Recorded Documents Records*** www.co.cooke.tx.us/ips/cms/countyoffices/countyClerk.html Search grantor/grantee index free at https://texaslandrecords.com/txlr/TxlrApp/index.jsp. Registration and fees required for full data. **$$$**

Coryell County ***Probate Records*** www.coryellcounty.org/county_clerk.html Search probate records for a fee at http://idocket.com/countycourt.htm. Probate records are at the County Court but accessible through the County Clerks Office. **$$$**

Crane County ***Real Estate, Grantor/Grantee, Deed, Lien, Birth, Death, Marriage Records*** www.co.crane.tx.us Search official records after choosing county at www.edoctecinc.com/ for a fee. If records are Unofficial, you search or copy them freely; if not Unofficial, a $1.00 per page fee applies. **$$$**

Dallas County ***Recorded Documents, Marriage, Assumed Name Records*** www.dallascounty.org/department/countyclerk/countyclerk.php Search most records for a fee at http://roamdallaspropertyrecords.com/ailis/search.do. Must register for subscription. Name search recorded documents for deeds, marriages, assumed names, and UCCs back to 1964. Viewing and printing documents are free. Also, access County Voter Registration Records free at www.dallascountyvotes.org/voter-information/voter-lookup/. Shows if registered and precinct. **$$$**

Property, Taxation Records Access Central Appraisal District data free at www.dallascad.org/SearchOwner.aspx.

Dawson County ***Property, Taxation Records*** Access to real estate roll, mineral roll and property taxes for free at www.dawsoncad.org - click on \"search our data.\"

Denton County ***Recorded Documents Records*** www.dentoncounty.com/dept/ccl.htm Search grantor/grantee index free at https://texaslandrecords.com/txlr/TxlrApp/index.jsp. Registration and fees required for full data. Also, search voter registration rolls free at https://elections.dentoncounty.com/goVR.asp?Dept=82&Link=292. **$$$**

Property, Taxation Records Property tax inquiries and property searches for free can be made at www.dentoncad.com/.

De Witt County ***Property, Taxation Records*** Access appraisal district property data free at www.dewittcad.org/ and click on Search our data. Also, access assessor tax payment data free at www.dewittcountyonline.net/tax/disclaim.faces.

Dimmit County ***Property, Taxation Records*** Access to property searches for free at https://propaccess.trueautomation.com/clientdb/?cid=29.

Duval County ***Recorded Documents Records*** http://courthouse.duval-county.net/defaultIE.htm Search grantor/grantee index free at https://texaslandrecords.com/txlr/TxlrApp/index.jsp. Registration and fees required for full data. **$$$**

Eastland County ***Recorded Documents Records*** www.eastlandcountytexas.com/co-clerk/index.htm Access to county records for a fee at https://countygovernmentrecords.com/texas/web/login.jsp?submit=Enter. Must register. Also, search probate records for a fee at http://idocket.com/countycourt.htm. Probate records are at the County Court but accessible through the County Clerks Office. **$$$**

Ector County ***Recorded Documents Records*** www.co.ector.tx.us Access to county records for a fee at https://countygovernmentrecords.com/texas/web/login.jsp?submit=Enter. Must register. **$$$**

Property, Taxation Records Search appraisal district property data and personal property free at www.ectorcad.org/.

Edwards County ***Recorded Documents Records*** Search grantor/grantee index free at https://texaslandrecords.com/txlr/TxlrApp/index.jsp. Registration and fees required for full data.

Ellis County ***Property, Taxation Records*** Search the property appraiser database for free at www.elliscad.org/. Access to property tax information for a fee at https://actweb.acttax.com/act_webdev/ellis/index.jsp.

El Paso County ***Recorded Documents, Probate Records*** www.epcounty.com/clerk/ Search official records including recordings, vital statistics and property free at www.epcounty.com/ publicrecords/officialpublicrecords/OfficialPublicRecordSearch.aspx, also marriages at www.epcounty.com/publicrecords/marriagerecords/ MarriageRecordSearch.aspx. Also, to search probate records for a fee go to http://idocket.com/countycourt.htm. Search assumed names free at www.epcounty.com/publicrecords/assumednames/AssumedNameRecordSearch.aspx. For county births and deaths search www.epcounty.com/publicrecords/birthrecords/BirthRecordSearch.aspx; OR www.epcounty.com/publicrecords/deathrecords/DeathRecordSearch.aspx. **$$$**

Property, Taxation Records Search property tax data free at www.epcad.org/clientdb/?cid=1.

Erath County ***Recorded Documents Records*** http://co.erath.tx.us/countyclerk.html Access to county records for a fee at https://countygovernmentrecords.com/texas/web/login.jsp?submit=Enter. Must register. **$$$**

Property, Taxation Records Find appraisal district data free at http://isouthwestdata.com/corp/. Also, search tax office records free at www.texaspayments.com/072000/. Also, see note at beginning of section.

Falls County ***Property, Taxation Records*** Access to Appraisal District records free at http://isouthwestdata.com/corp/.

Fannin County ***Recorded Documents Records*** www.co.fannin.tx.us/default.aspx?Fannin_County/County.Clerk Search grantor/grantee index free at https://texaslandrecords.com/txlr/TxlrApp/index.jsp. Registration and fees required for full data. **$$$**

Floyd County ***Probate Records*** www.floydcountytexas.us/ Search probate records for a fee at http://idocket.com/countycourt.htm. Probate records are at the County Court but accessible through the County Clerks Office. **$$$**

Property, Taxation Records Find appraisal district data free at http://isouthwestdata.com/corp/.

Fort Bend County ***Recorded Documents, Marriage, Death, Birth Records*** www.co.fort-bend.tx.us/index.aspx?page=107 Recorded records, property records, marriage, and divorce can be searched for free at http://ccweb.co.fort-bend.tx.us/RealEstate/SearchEntry.aspx. Also, see note at beginning of section. **$$$**

Property, Taxation Records Access appraisal records free at www.fbcad.org/Appraisal/PublicAccess/. Also, property tax inquiries can be made free at https://actweb.acttax.com/act_webdev/fbc/index.jsp.

Franklin County ***Recorded Documents Records*** www.co.franklin.tx.us/default.aspx?Franklin_County/County.Clerk Access to county records for a fee at https://countygovernmentrecords.com/texas/web/login.jsp?submit=Enter. Must register. **$$$**

Property, Taxation Records Access to property data is free at www.franklincad.com/. Click on Search Our Data. Also, see note at beginning of section.

Freestone County ***Recorded Documents, Probate Records*** www.co.freestone.tx.us/default.aspx?Freestone_County/County.Clerk Search grantor/grantee index free at https://texaslandrecords.com/txlr/TxlrApp/index.jsp. Registration and fees required for full data. Also, search probate records for a fee at http://idocket.com/countycourt.htm. Probate records are at the County Court but accessible through the County Clerks Office. **$$$**

Property, Taxation Records Access to Appraiser's property data is free at www.freestonecad.org/. Click on Search Our Data.

Galveston County ***Recorded Documents Records*** www.co.galveston.tx.us/County_Clerk/ Several sources exist. Access the county online official records index free at http://ccweb.co.galveston.tx.us/. Also, a Grantor/Grantee index free at www.titlex.com; select Galveston County; records go back to 1/1965. Also, see note at beginning of section.

Property, Taxation Records Search Central Appraisal Dist. database free at www.galvestoncad.org/Appraisal/PublicAccess/. For info, call 409-766-5115.

Gillespie County ***Recorded Documents, Birth, Death, Marriage Records*** www.gillespiecounty.org/default.aspx?name=county_clerk Free access to public records found at www.gillespiecounty.org/default.aspx?name=records_search.

Property, Taxation Records Access Appraiser property data free at https://propaccess.trueautomation.com/clientDB/?cid=52. Also, make Property tax inquiries at www.txcountydata.com/selectCounty.asp. Other online access through private companies.

Goliad County ***Recorded Documents Records*** www.co.goliad.tx.us/default.aspx?Goliad_County/County.Clerk Search grantor/grantee index free at https://texaslandrecords.com/txlr/TxlrApp/index.jsp. Registration and fees required for full data. **$$$**

Grayson County ***Recorded Documents Records*** www.co.grayson.tx.us/default.aspx?name=cclk.home Search grantor/grantee index free at https://texaslandrecords.com/txlr/TxlrApp/index.jsp. Registration and fees required for full data. Access recording records free at www.titlex.com/; select Grayson county. **$$$**

Property, Taxation Records Search appraiser property data free at www.taxnetusa.com/texas/grayson/. Also, property assessment & tax data free at http://24.117.89.66:3005/Appraisal/PublicAccess/.

Gregg County ***Recorded Documents, Vital Statistic Records*** www.co.gregg.tx.us Access to the County Clerk's Official Public Records database is free to view at www.co.gregg.tx.us/A2WebUI/. Fee to copy documents. Also, access recording records free at www.titlex.com; select Gregg county. Records range is 4/1977 to 5/2005. Also, see note at beginning of section. **$$$**

Property, Taxation Records Search property tax records for a fee at https://actweb.acttax.com/act_webdev/gregg/index.jsp. Credit cards accepted. Also, property tax inquiries can be made at https://propaccess.trueautomation.com/clientdb/?cid=38.**$$$**

Grimes County ***Recorded Documents Records*** www.co.grimes.tx.us/default.aspx?Grimes_County/County.Clerk Search grantor/grantee index free at https://texaslandrecords.com/txlr/TxlrApp/index.jsp. Registration and fees required for full data. **$$$**
Property, Taxation Records Access property appraisal data free at http://67.76.234.90/Appraisal/PublicAccess/. Other online access through private companies.

Guadalupe County ***Probate, Guardianship Records*** www.co.guadalupe.tx.us/guadalupe2010/home.php?content=co_clerk Access to probate and guardianship records for free at http://judicial.co.guadalupe.tx.us/default.aspx.
Property, Taxation Records Search appraisal roll, parcel tax data free at www.co.guadalupe.tx.us/Appraisal/PublicAccess/.

Hale County ***Recorded Documents, Probate Records*** Access to county records for a fee at https://countygovernmentrecords.com/texas/web/login.jsp?submit=Enter. Must register. Also, search probate records for a fee at http://idocket.com/countycourt.htm. Probate records are at the County Court but accessible through the County Clerks Office. **$$$**

Hardin County ***Property, Taxation Records*** Access to tax/property records for free at www.tax.cagi.com/#/TaxOfficeSearch?cc=C100.

Harris County ***Real Estate, Grantor/Grantee, Lien, Judgment, Appraiser, Voter, UCC, Assumed Name, Vital Statistic Records*** www.cclerk.hctx.net Access to Assumed Name records, UCC filings, vital statistic, and Real Property are at www.cclerk.hctx.net/applications/websearch/. County Court Civil, marriage and informal marriage records also available. Also, access recording records free at www.titlex.com; select Harris county. Search voter registrations free at www.tax.co.harris.tx.us/Voter/voterintro.aspx.
Property, Taxation Records Appraiser records are at www.hcad.org/Records/. Search tax assessor data free at www.tax.co.harris.tx.us/property/current/currentsearch.aspx. Search delinquents at www.tax.co.harris.tx.us/Property/deltax/currentsearch.aspx.

Harrison County ***Recorded Documents Records*** www.co.harrison.tx.us/ Access to county records for a fee at https://countygovernmentrecords.com/texas/web/login.jsp?submit=Enter. Must register. **$$$**
Property, Taxation Records Find appraisal district data and tax collection office data free at http://isouthwestdata.com/corp/

Hartley County ***Property, Taxation Records*** Find appraisal district data and collection office data free at http://isouthwestdata.com/corp/.

Hays County ***Recorded Documents, Probate Records*** www.co.hays.tx.us/index.php/government/county-clerk/ Search grantor/grantee index free at https://texaslandrecords.com/txlr/TxlrApp/index.jsp. Registration and fees required for full data. Access probate records back to 1997 for a fee at http://idocket.com/countycourt.htm. Probate records are at the County Court but accessible through the County Clerks Office. **$$$**
Property, Taxation Records Access mapping data free at www.hayscad.com/interactivemap/. Access tax collector property data free at http://hayscountytax.com/taxes. Also, see notes at beginning of section for add'l property data.

Henderson County ***Recorded Documents Records*** http://co.henderson.tx.us/default.aspx?Henderson_County/County.Clerk Access to county records for a fee at https://countygovernmentrecords.com/texas/web/login.jsp?submit=Enter. Must register. **$$$**
Property, Taxation Records Access to tax records for free at www.hendersoncountyonline.net/tax/disclaim.faces. Also, access to the appraisal district records free at http://isouthwestdata.com/corp/.

Hidalgo County ***Recorded Documents Records*** www.co.hidalgo.tx.us/index.aspx?NID=161 Search grantor/grantee index free at https://texaslandrecords.com/txlr/TxlrApp/index.jsp. Registration and fees required for full data. Also, search probate records for a fee at http://idocket.com/countycourt.htm. Probate records are at the County Court but accessible through the County Clerks Office. **$$$**
Property, Taxation Records Search appraiser property records free at https://actweb.acttax.com/act_webdev/hidalgo/index.jsp.

Hill County ***Recorded Documents Records*** Access to county records for a fee at https://countygovernmentrecords.com/texas/web/login.jsp?submit=Enter. Must register. Also, see note at beginning of section. **$$$**
Property, Taxation Records Access appraisal district property records free at www.hillcad.org/in/reportshome.php.

Hockley County ***Recorded Documents Records*** www.co.hockley.tx.us/default.aspx?Hockley_County/County.Clerk Search grantor/grantee index free at https://texaslandrecords.com/txlr/TxlrApp/index.jsp. Registration and fees required for full data. **$$$**
Property, Taxation Records Access property records free at https://propaccess.trueautomation.com/clientdb/?cid=59.

Hood County ***Recorded Documents Records*** www.co.hood.tx.us Access to county records for a fee at https://countygovernmentrecords.com/texas/web/login.jsp?submit=Enter. Must register. **$$$**
Property, Taxation Records Access to appraisal district data and collection office data for free at http://isouthwestdata.com/corp/. Add'l online access through private companies.

Hopkins County ***Recorded Documents, Probate Records*** www.hopkinscountytexas.org/county-clerk/ Access real property records free after registering for login and password at www.hopkinscountyonline.net/countyclerk/. Also, search probate records for a fee at http://idocket.com/countycourt.htm. Probate records are at the County Court but accessible through the County Clerks Office. **$$$**
Property, Taxation Records Access to appraisal district data free at http://isouthwestdata.com/corp/.

Houston County ***Real Estate, Deed, Official Records*** www.co.houston.tx.us Search official records after choosing county at www.edoctecinc.com/. All records are unofficial, you search freely; $1.00 per page fee applies for copies. For details and signup, contact clerk or Michelle Haas at 800-578-7746. **$$$**
Property, Taxation Records Access to property tax records is free at www.houstoncad.org/.

Howard County ***Recorded Documents Records*** www.co.howard.tx.us/default.aspx?Howard_County/County.Clerk Access to county records for a fee at https://countygovernmentrecords.com/texas/web/login.jsp?submit=Enter. Must register. **$$$**
Property, Taxation Records Access to tax records for free at http://tax.cagi.com/#/TaxOfficeSearch?cc=A114.

Hunt County ***Recorded Documents, Probate Records*** www.huntcounty.net Access to county records for a fee at https://countygovernmentrecords.com/texas/web/login.jsp?submit=Enter. Must register. Also, search probate records for a fee at http://idocket.com/countycourt.htm. Probate records are at the County Court but accessible through the County Clerks Office. **$$$**
Property, Taxation Records Access property tax data and sheriff sales data free at www.hctax.info/. Also see notes at beginning of section for add'l property data.

Hutchinson County ***Recorded Documents Records*** www.co.hutchinson.tx.us/ips/cms/countyoffices/countyClerk.html Search grantor/grantee index free at https://texaslandrecords.com/txlr/TxlrApp/index.jsp. Registration and fees required for full data. **$$$**
Property, Taxation Records Access to property tax data is free at www.hutchinsoncad.org/. Access to property appraisal and assessment searches free at http://69.92.87.82/appraisal/publicaccess/.

Jack County ***Probate Records*** www.jackcounty.org/clerk/ Search probate records for a fee at http://idocket.com/countycourt.htm. Probate records are at the County Court but accessible through the County Clerks Office. **$$$**

Jackson County ***Real Estate, Grantor/Grantee, Deed, Lien, Judgment Records*** www.co.jackson.tx.us Access recording records free at www.titlex.com; select Jackson county. Records range is 1/1993 to 9/2004. Also, see note at beginning of section. Also, property tax inquiries can be made at www.txcountydata.com/selectCounty.asp.
Property, Taxation Records Access appraiser property records free at www.jacksoncad.org/#!__disclamer. Also, property tax inquiries can be made at www.txcountydata.com/selectCounty.asp.

Jasper County ***Recorded Documents Records*** www.co.jasper.tx.us/default.aspx?Jasper_County/County.Clerk Access to county records for a fee at https://countygovernmentrecords.com/texas/web/login.jsp?submit=Enter. Must register. **$$$**
Property, Taxation Records Access to property tax free at www.jaspercotxtax.com/Appraisal/PublicAccess/.

Jefferson County ***Probate, Civil, Criminal, Real Estate, Deed, Lien, Judgment, Marriage, UCC, Assumed Name Records*** www.co.jefferson.tx.us Access the recorder database free at http://jeffersontxclerk.manatron.com/. Recording index goes back to 1983; images to 1983. Marriages go back to 1995; UCCs to 7/2001. Also, see note at beginning of section.
Property, Taxation Records Access property tax records free at http://propaccess.jcad.org/clientdb/?cid=1.

Jim Hogg County ***Real Estate, Deed Records*** Access recording office land data at www.etitlesearch.com; registration required, fee based on usage. **$$$**

Jim Wells County ***Recorded Documents Records*** www.co.jim-wells.tx.us/default.aspx?Jim-Wells_County/County.Clerk Access recording office land data at www.etitlesearch.com; registration required, fee based on usage. Also, search grantor/grantee index free at https://texaslandrecords.com/txlr/TxlrApp/index.jsp. Registration and fees required for full data. **$$$**

Johnson County Court ***Probate Records*** www.johnsoncountytx.org/departments/countyclerk/ Search probate records for a fee at http://idocket.com/countycourt.htm. Records go back to 1980s. Probate records are at the County Court but accessible through the County Clerks Office. **$$$**
Property, Taxation Records Records from the County Appraiser are free at www.johnsoncountytaxoffice.org/accountSearch.asp or at Taxnet site at www.johnsoncountytaxoffice.org/.

Jones County ***Property, Taxation Records*** Access property tax records free at www.jonescad.org/ and click on Search Our Data.

Karnes County ***Recorded Documents Records*** www.co.karnes.tx.us/default.aspx?Karnes_County/County.Clerk Search grantor/grantee index free at https://texaslandrecords.com/txlr/TxlrApp/index.jsp. Registration and fees required for full data. **$$$**

Kaufman County ***Recorded Documents Records*** www.kaufmancountyclerk.com Search grantor/grantee index and images free at https://www.texaslandrecords.com/txlr/TxlrApp/index.jsp. Access to county records for a fee go to https://countygovernmentrecords.com/texas/web/login.jsp?submit=Enter. Must register. Also, see note at beginning of section. **$$$**
Property, Taxation Records Access to maps for free at http://12.14.175.35/website/KaufmanCounty/viewer.htm.

Kendall County ***Recorded Documents Records*** www.co.kendall.tx.us/default.aspx?Kendall_County/County.Clerk Access to land records free at https://gov.propertyinfo.com/TX-Kendall/. Must register before being allowed to search. Also, access recording records free at www.titlex.com; select Kendall county. Also see note at beginning of section.

Kerr County ***Recorded Documents, Marriage Records*** www.co.kerr.tx.us/ Access to recorder land data at www.edoctecinc.com/. Registration and login required. **$$$**

Property, Taxation Records Access appraiser's property records free at http://public.co.kerr.tx.us:8088/Appraisal/PublicAccess/. Also, see note at beginning of section. Also, access to property records free at https://propaccess.trueautomation.com/clientdb/?cid=35.

Kleberg County ***Property, Taxation Records*** Access to county appraisal rolls and property data is free at www.klebergcad.org/search_appr.php.

Knox County ***Recorded Documents Records*** Access recording records free at www.titlex.com/; select Knox county; login and password required. **$$$**

Property, Taxation Records Access to appraisal district and collection office data free at http://isouthwestdata.com/corp/.

Lamar County ***Recorded Documents Records*** www.co.lamar.tx.us/default.aspx?Lamar_County/County.Clerk Access to county records for a fee at https://countygovernmentrecords.com/texas/web/login.jsp?submit=Enter. Must register. **$$$**

Lamb County ***Recorded Documents Records*** www.co.lamb.tx.us/default.aspx?Lamb_County/County.Clerk Search grantor/grantee index free at https://texaslandrecords.com/txlr/TxlrApp/index.jsp. Registration and fees required for full data. **$$$**

La Salle County ***Property, Taxation Records*** Access property tax data free at https://propaccess.trueautomation.com/clientdb/?cid=23. Search tax sales lists free at http://tax.acttax.com/pls/sales/property_taxsales_pkg.search_page?PI_STATE=TX and chose Struck Off as sales type.

Lee County ***Property, Taxation Records*** Access Appraisal District records free at https://propaccess.trueautomation.com/clientdb/?cid=75.

Leon County ***Recorded Documents Records*** Search grantor/grantee index free at https://texaslandrecords.com/txlr/TxlrApp/index.jsp. Registration and fees required for full data. **$$$**

Liberty County ***Recorded Documents Records*** www.co.liberty.tx.us/default.aspx?Liberty_County/County.Clerk Access to record lists free at http://countyclerk.co.liberty.tx.us/.

Property, Taxation Records Access to property tax sales for free at http://tax.acttax.com/pls/sales/property_taxsales_pkg.search_page?PI_STATE=TX.

Limestone County ***Recorded Documents Records*** www.co.limestone.tx.us/default.aspx?Limestone_County/County.Clerk Search grantor/grantee index free at https://texaslandrecords.com/txlr/TxlrApp/index.jsp. Registration and fees required for full data. Fee is $1.00 per record to print. **$$$**

Property, Taxation Records Access appraiser's property data free at www.limestonetexas-tax.com/Appraisal/PublicAccess/.

Lipscomb County ***Property, Taxation Records*** Find appraisal district and collection offices data for free at http://isouthwestdata.com/corp/.

Live Oak County ***Recorded Documents Records*** www.co.live-oak.tx.us/default.aspx?Live-Oak_County/County.Clerk Search grantor/grantee index free at https://texaslandrecords.com/txlr/TxlrApp/index.jsp. Registration and fees required for full data. **$$$**

Llano County ***Recorded Documents Records*** www.co.llano.tx.us/default.aspx?Llano_County/County.Clerk Access to a property search free at https://propaccess.trueautomation.com/clientdb/?cid=11.

Property, Taxation Records Search tax collecting office data free by selecting county at http://isouthwestdata.com/corp/.

Loving County ***Recorded Records Records*** Access to county records for a fee at https://countygovernmentrecords.com/texas/web/login.jsp?submit=Enter. Must register. **$$$**

Lubbock County ***Real Estate, Grantor/Grantee, Deed, Assumed Name, Marriage Records*** www.co.lubbock.tx.us/department/?fDD=2-0 Access to index only of records free at http://opr.co.lubbock.tx.us.

Property, Taxation Records Search the property appraiser database for free at www.lubbockcad.org/Appraisal/PublicAccess/.

McLennan County ***Recorded Documents Records*** www.co.mclennan.tx.us/cclerk/index.aspx Access recording records free at www.titlex.com; select McLennan county. Records range from 1/1996 to 12/2002. Also, see note at beginning of section. Also, access land records at http://etitlesearch.com. You can do a name search; choose from $50.00 monthly subscription or per-click account. Also, see note at beginning of section. **$$$**

Property, Taxation Records Search real estate appraisal records at www.mclennancad.org/ or at https://propaccess.trueautomation.com/clientDB/?cid=20. Property Tax balance information free at https://actweb.acttax.com/act_webdev/mclennan/index.jsp.

Madison County ***Recorded Documents Records*** www.co.madison.tx.us/default.aspx?Madison_County/County.Clerk Search grantor/grantee index free at https://www.texaslandrecords.com/txlr/TxlrApp/index.jsp. Registration and fees required for full data. **$$$**

Property, Taxation Records Access to property data for free at https://propaccess.trueautomation.com/clientdb/?cid=49.

Marion County ***Recorded Documents Records*** Access recording records free at www.titlex.com; select Marion county. Also, search grantor/grantee index free at https://texaslandrecords.com/txlr/TxlrApp/index.jsp. Registration and fees required for full data. **$$$**
Property, Taxation Records Access property tax records free at www.marioncad.org/. Click on Search Our Data.

Martin County ***Property, Taxation Records*** Access to property data is free at www.martincad.org/

Mason County ***Property, Taxation Records*** Access to property data searches free at www.masoncad.org/, click on \"Search Our Data.\"

Matagorda County ***Recorded Documents Records*** www.co.matagorda.tx.us/default.aspx?Matagorda_County/County.Clerk Search grantor/grantee index free at https://texaslandrecords.com/txlr/TxlrApp/index.jsp. Registration and fees required for full data. **$$$**
Property, Taxation Records Access to Appraisal District records is free at https://propaccess.trueautomation.com/clientdb/?cid=72.

Maverick County ***Recorded Documents Records*** https://www.gov.propertyinfo.com/tx-maverick/ Access to land record indexes free at https://gov.propertyinfo.com/tx-maverick/#. Must register first. Also available for a fee are the images. **$$$**

Medina County ***Recorded Documents Records*** www.medinacountytexas.org/default.aspx?Medina_County/County.Clerk Access to records for free at http://odysseypa.tylerhost.net/Medina/default.aspx. Access to county records for a fee go to https://countygovernmentrecords.com/texas/web/login.jsp?submit=Enter. Must register. **$$$**
Property, Taxation Records Access to tax rolls for free at www.medinacountytx.org/Appraisal/PublicAccess/.

Midland County ***Recorded Documents Records*** www.co.midland.tx.us/departments/cc/Pages/default.aspx Access grantor/grantee index free at https://texaslandrecords.com/txlr/TxlrApp/index.jsp. Registration and fees required for full data. Any judgment, lien records, etc, that contain SSNs will not be online; search at office. **$$$**
Property, Taxation Records Access property tax data free at www.co.midland.tx.us/departments/tax/Pages/Property.aspx. Also, find appraisal district and collecting office data free at http://isouthwestdata.com/corp/.

Milam County ***Recorded Documents Records*** www.milamcounty.net/countyclerk.html Access recording records free at www.titlex.com/; select Milam county. Records range is 5/2000 to 8/2001. Also, see note at beginning of section. Also, search grantor/grantee index free at https://texaslandrecords.com/txlr/TxlrApp/index.jsp. Registration and fees required for full data. **$$$**
Property, Taxation Records Search appraisal district data free at www.txcountydata.com/county.asp?County=166. Also see note at beginning of section.

Mills County ***Property, Taxation Records*** Find appraisal district and collection offices data free at http://isouthwestdata.com/corp/.

Mitchell County ***Land, Deed, Lien, Marriage, Death, Probate Records*** Search official records after choosing county at www.edoctecinc.com/. If records are stamped Unofficial, you can copy them freely; Official, a $1.00 per page fee applies. For details and signup, contact Edoc Tec at 800-578-7746. **$$$**
Property, Taxation Records Access to real property searches for free found at www.mitchellcad.org/.

Montague County ***Property, Taxation Records*** Find appraisal district and collection offices data free at http://isouthwestdata.com/corp/.

Montgomery County ***Recorded Documents, Probate Records*** www.co.montgomery.tx.us Access recording records free at www.titlex.com/; select Montgomery county. Records go back to 1/1966. Similar index search may also be performed free at www.courthousedirect.com/IndexSearches.aspx. Registration and password required for full data. Also, search probate for a fee at http://idocket.com/countycourt.htm. Probate records are at the County Court but accessible through the County Clerks Office. Also, access to the county online records for free go to https://gov.propertyinfo.com/TX-Montgomery/. Registration and login required. Images from 1980 to present. **$$$**
Property, Taxation Records Access property appraiser data free at www.mcad-tx.org/html/records.html.

Moore County ***Property, Taxation Records*** Free access to property data is found at https://propaccess.trueautomation.com/clientdb/?cid=9.

Morris County ***Recorded Documents Records*** www.co.morris.tx.us/default.aspx?Morris_County/County.Clerk Access to county records for a fee at https://countygovernmentrecords.com/texas/web/login.jsp?submit=Enter. Must register. **$$$**
Property, Taxation Records Find appraisal district data free at http://isouthwestdata.com/corp/.

Nacogdoches County ***Recorded Documents, Probate Records*** www.co.nacogdoches.tx.us Search grantor/grantee index free at https://texaslandrecords.com/txlr/TxlrApp/index.jsp. Registration and fees required for full data. Also, search probate records for a fee at http://idocket.com/countycourt.htm. Probate records are at the County Court but accessible through the County Clerks Office. **$$$**
Property, Taxation Records Access property tax data free at www.nacocad.org/. Click on Search Our Data.

Navarro County ***Recorded Documents Records*** www.co.navarro.tx.us/default.aspx?Navarro_County/County.Clerk Search grantor/grantee index free at https://texaslandrecords.com/txlr/TxlrApp/index.jsp. Land records from 1985 to present. Registration and fees required for full data. **$$$**
Property, Taxation Records Access to property tax balance for free at http://actweb.acttax.com/act_webdev/navarro/index.jsp.

Nueces County ***Real Estate, Grantor/Grantee, Deed, Judgment, Lien Records*** www.co.nueces.tx.us/countyclerk/ Access to county clerk recording records (indexes for free) is free after registration at https://gov.propertyinfo.com/tx-nueces/; subscription service (gives you unlimited view of index data) also available, $50 monthly.

Property, Taxation Records Access County Appraiser records free at www.ncadistrict.com/ and click on Property to choose search mode. Also, see notes at beginning of section. Also, access to finding your property tax balance free at https://actweb.acttax.com/act_webdev/nueces/index.jsp.

Ochiltree County Clerk ***Probate Records*** www.co.ochiltree.tx.us/default.aspx?Ochiltree_County/County.Clerk Search probate records for a fee at http://idocket.com/countycourt.htm. Probate records are at the County Court but accessible through the County Clerks Office. **$$$**

Oldham County ***Probate Records*** www.co.oldham.tx.us/default.aspx?Oldham_County/County.Clerk Search probate records for a fee at http://idocket.com/countycourt.htm. Probate records are at the County Court but accessible through the County Clerks Office. **$$$**

Orange County ***Recorded Documents Records*** www.co.orange.tx.us/ Access to online records free at www.co.orange.tx.us/. The Criminal and Civil documents in this index are from 2005 to present. The Probate documents are from 1850's to present.

Property, Taxation Records Access to the county appraisal district records is free at the county site directly at www.orangecad.net/Appraisal/PublicAccess/.

Palo Pinto County ***Recorded Documents Records*** www.co.palo-pinto.tx.us/default.aspx?Palo-Pinto_County/County.Clerk Access to county records for a fee at https://countygovernmentrecords.com/texas/web/login.jsp?submit=Enter. Must register. **$$$**

Property, Taxation Records Access to appraisers property and collection offices data free at http://isouthwestdata.com/corp/.

Panola County ***Recorded Documents Records*** www.co.panola.tx.us/default.aspx?Panola_County/County.Clerk Access recording records free at www.titlex.com; select Panola county. Search grantor/grantee index free at https://texaslandrecords.com/txlr/TxlrApp/index.jsp. Registration and fees required for full data. **$$$**

Parker County ***Recorded Documents Records*** www.co.parker.tx.us/ips/cms/countyoffices/countyClerk.html Access to county records for a fee at https://countygovernmentrecords.com/texas/web/login.jsp?submit=Enter. Must register. **$$$**

Property, Taxation Records Find appraisal district and collecting offices data free at http://isouthwestdata.com/corp/.

Pecos County ***Recorded Documents Records*** www.co.pecos.tx.us/index.php?option=com_contact&task=view&contact_id=11&Itemid=30 Access to county records for a fee at https://countygovernmentrecords.com/texas/web/login.jsp?submit=Enter. Must register. **$$$**

Property, Taxation Records Access to property data is free at www.pecoscad.org/. Click on Search Our Data.

Polk County ***Recorded Documents, Probate Records*** www.co.polk.tx.us/default.aspx?Polk_County/County.Clerk Access to County Clerk's data is by subscription at www.co.polk.tx.us/ips/cms/countyoffices/countyClerk.html. Username and password required. Also, search probate records for a fee at http://idocket.com/countycourt.htm. Probate records are at the County Court but accessible through the County Clerks Office. **$$$**

Property, Taxation Records Access to tax records for free at http://mytax.eztaxonline.net/polk/tax/faces/search.jsp.

Potter County ***Recorded Documents, Probate Records*** www.co.potter.tx.us/countyclerk/index.html Access recording records at www.titlex.com/; select Potter county for a fee. Also, search grantor/grantee index free at https://texaslandrecords.com/txlr/TxlrApp/index.jsp. Registration and fees required for full data. Also, search probate records for a fee at http://idocket.com/countycourt.htm. Probate records are at the County Court but accessible through the County Clerks Office. Also, access to county records for a fee go to https://countygovernmentrecords.com/texas/web/login.jsp?submit=Enter. Must register. **$$$**

Property, Taxation Records Records on the Potter-Randall Appraisal District database are free at www.prad.org/. Records periodically updated; for current tax info call Potter- 806-342-2600 or Randall- 806-665-6287.

Randall County ***Recorded Documents, Probate Records*** www.randallcounty.org/cclerk/default.htm Access to county records for a fee at https://countygovernmentrecords.com/texas/web/login.jsp?submit=Enter. Must register. Also, search probate records for a fee at http://idocket.com/countycourt.htm. Probate records are at the County Court but accessible through the County Clerks Office. **$$$**

Property, Taxation Records Randall County appraisal and personal property records are combined online with Potter County; see Potter County for access info or visit www.prad.org/. Randall County sheriff sales records are combined online with Potter County; see Potter County for access info or www.prad.org/

Reagan County ***Real Estate, Grantor/Grantee, Divorce Records*** www.county-clerk.net/countyclerk.asp?state=Texas&county=Reagan See note at beginning of section.

Real County ***Recorded Documents Records*** www.co.real.tx.us/default.aspx?Real_County/County.Clerk Free access to property searched found at www.trueautomation.com/index.php/Property_Search. Choose Real County.

Property, Taxation Records Free access to property searches found at www.trueautomation.com/. Click on Real CAD.

Reeves County ***Property, Taxation Records*** Access to appraisal districts and collection offices data free at http://isouthwestdata.com/corp/.

Refugio County ***Property, Taxation Records*** Access property data free at www.refugiocad.org/. Click on Search Our Data.

Robertson County ***Recorded Documents Records*** Access recording records free at www.titlex.com/; select Robertson county. Also, search grantor/grantee index free at https://texaslandrecords.com/txlr/TxlrApp/index.jsp. Registration and fees required for full data. **$$$**

Rockwall County ***Recorded Documents, Vital Records Records*** www.rockwallcountytexas.com/index.asp?nid=108 Search grantor/grantee index free at https://texaslandrecords.com/txlr/TxlrApp/index.jsp. Registration and fees required for full data. **$$$**

Runnels County ***Property, Taxation Records*** Find appraisal district and collection offices data free at http://isouthwestdata.com/corp/.

Rusk County ***Recorded Documents Records*** www.co.rusk.tx.us/default.aspx?Rusk_County/County.Clerk Search grantor/grantee index free at https://texaslandrecords.com/txlr/TxlrApp/index.jsp. Registration and fees required for full data. **$$$**

Property, Taxation Records Access property data free at www.ruskcad.org/. Click on Search Our Data.

San Augustine County ***Recorded Documents Records*** www.co.san-augustine.tx.us/countyClerk.html Search grantor/grantee index free at https://texaslandrecords.com/txlr/TxlrApp/index.jsp. Registration and fees required for full data. **$$$**

San Patricio County ***Probate Records*** www.co.san-patricio.tx.us/default.aspx?San-Patricio_County/County.Clerk Search probate records for a fee at http://idocket.com/countycourt.htm. Probate records are at the County Court but accessible through the County Clerks Office. **$$$**

Property, Taxation Records Access to property tax balance for a fee at https://actweb.acttax.com/act_webdev/sanpatricio/index.jsp.**$$$**

Scurry County ***Recorded Documents Records*** www.co.scurry.tx.us/default.aspx?Scurry_County/County.Clerk Search grantor/grantee index free at https://texaslandrecords.com/txlr/TxlrApp/index.jsp. Registration and fees required for full data. **$$$**

Shelby County ***Recorded Documents, Marriage, Probate Records*** http://cc.co.shelby.tx.us/ Access to record indexes free at http://cc.co.shelby.tx.us/. Probate index on this URL.

Property, Taxation Records Access to property data for free at https://propaccess.trueautomation.com/clientdb/?cid=73.

Smith County ***Recorded Documents Records*** www.smith-county.com Search grantor/grantee index free at https://texaslandrecords.com/txlr/TxlrApp/index.jsp. Registration and fees required for full data. **$$$**

Property, Taxation Records Access to county appraisal district records is free at www.smithcountymapsite.org/. Also, access property data on the GIS-mapping site free at www.smithcad.org/scadarc/viewer_temp.htm. Also, see note at beginning of section.

Somervell County ***Property, Taxation Records*** Access to appraisal district and collection offices data free at http://isouthwestdata.com/corp/.

Stephens County ***Recorded Documents Records*** www.co.stephens.tx.us/default.aspx?Stephens_County/County.Clerk Access to county records for a fee at https://countygovernmentrecords.com/texas/web/login.jsp?submit=Enter. Must register. **$$$**

Property, Taxation Records Find appraisal district and collection offices data free at http://isouthwestdata.com/corp/.

Tarrant County ***Recorded Documents Records*** www.tarrantcounty.com/eCountyClerk/site/default.asp Search real estate index for free at https://ccanthem.co.tarrant.tx.us/RealEstate/SearchEntry.aspx.

Property, Taxation Records Access Appraisal District Property data free at www.tad.org/Datasearch/datasearch.cfm. Access assessor's accounts search for tax data free at http://taxoffice.tarrantcounty.com/AccountSearch.asp. Access City of Grapevine and Coffeyville tax office free at www.texaspayments.com/validate.asp.

Taylor County ***Recorded Documents, Vital Records Records*** http://taylorcountytexas.org/index.aspx?nid=120 Search grantor/grantee index free at https://texaslandrecords.com/txlr/TxlrApp/index.jsp. Registration and fees required for full data. **$$$**

Property, Taxation Records Access Appraisal District records free at https://propaccess.trueautomation.com/clientdb/?cid=32. Also, search the treasurer's database of unclaimed property free at www.taylorcountytexas.org/unclaime.html.

Titus County ***Recorded Documents Records*** www.co.titus.tx.us/ Access to real property records go to www.texasonlinerecords.com/realproperty/?office_id=1. Must register before using. Also, access to public records go to www.tituscountyonline.net/clerk/. Must also register before using. Also, access to county records for a fee go to https://countygovernmentrecords.com/texas/web/login.jsp?submit=Enter. Must register. **$$$**

Tom Green County ***Recorded Documents, Marriage, Fictitious Name, (Birth, Death-Index Only), Records*** www.co.tom-green.tx.us/ips/cms/countyoffices/CountyClerk/ Access official public records including vital stats and fictitious names free at http://countyclerk.tomgreencountytx.gov/. Also, access recording records free at www.titlex.com; select Tom Green County. Also, access to county records for a fee go to https://countygovernmentrecords.com/texas/web/login.jsp?submit=Enter. Must register. **$$$**

Property, Taxation Records Access to appraisal district and collection offices data for free at http://isouthwestdata.com/corp/.

Travis County ***Real Estate, Grantor/Grantee, Deed, UCC, Marriage, Voter Registration Records*** www.co.travis.tx.us/county_clerk/default.asp Access to recorders official records is free at http://deed.co.travis.tx.us/localization/BrowserTest.aspx?mode=2.

Property, Taxation Records Access the Central Appraisal District database free at www.traviscad.org/property_search.html. Also search business personal property. Also, you may search on the county tax payment system at www.traviscountytax.org/showSearchMain.do.

Upshur County ***Real Estate, Grantor/Grantee, Deed, Lien, Judgment, Marriage, Birth, Death, Probate Records*** www.countyofupshur.com/Departments/County%20Clerk.htm Access County Clerks' OPR and other recorder records including civil and probate free

at http://countyofupshur.com:8001/ucc/default.asp. Also, access recording records free at www.titlex.com; select Upshur county. Also, see note at beginning of section.
Property, Taxation Records To view property information for free at www.trueautomation.com/.

Upton County ***Recorded Documents Records*** www.co.upton.tx.us/default.aspx?Upton_County/County.Clerk Search grantor/grantee index free at https://texaslandrecords.com/txlr/TxlrApp/index.jsp. Registration and fees required for full data. **$$$**

Val Verde County ***Recorded Documents Records*** www.valverdecounty.org/ Search grantor/grantee index free at https://texaslandrecords.com/txlr/TxlrApp/index.jsp. Registration and fees required for full data. **$$$**

Van Zandt County ***Recorded Documents Records*** www.vanzandtcounty.org/default.aspx?Van-Zandt_County/County.Clerk Access to county records for a fee at https://countygovernmentrecords.com/texas/web/login.jsp?submit=Enter. Must register. Also, access recording records 1/1971 to current free at www.titlex.com; select Van Zandt county. Registration required; pay by tokens. Also, see note at beginning of section. **$$$**
Property, Taxation Records Find appraisal districts and collection offices data for free at http://isouthwestdata.com/corp/.

Victoria County ***Recorded Documents, Probate Records*** www.vctx.org/index.php?option=com_content&view=article&id=66&Itemid=29 Access recording records free at www.titlex.com/; select Victoria county. Records range is 1/1964 to 5/26/2005 only. Also, search probate records for a fee at http://idocket.com/countycourt.htm. Probate records are at the County Court but accessible through the County Clerks Office. **$$$**
Property, Taxation Records Access to property assessment and tax information free at http://orion.vctx.org/appraisal/publicaccess/. Access to appraisal district records is free at www.victoriacad.org/.

Walker County ***Recorded Documents Records*** www.co.walker.tx.us/department/index.php?fDD=5-0 Search grantor/grantee index free at https://texaslandrecords.com/txlr/TxlrApp/index.jsp. Registration and fees required for full data. **$$$**

Ward County ***Recorded Documents Records*** www.co.ward.tx.us/default.aspx?Ward_County/County.Clerk Access to county records for a fee at https://countygovernmentrecords.com/texas/web/login.jsp?submit=Enter. Must register. **$$$**

Washington County ***Recorded Documents, Probate, Vital Records, Military Discharge Records*** www.co.washington.tx.us Access recording records for a fee at www.titlex.com/, Select Washington county. Records go back to 1950. Also, search probate records for a fee at http://idocket.com/countycourt.htm. Probate records are at the County Court but accessible through the County Clerks office. Also, search official records after choosing county at www.edoctecinc.com/. If records are Unofficial, you search or copy them free; if not Unofficial, a $1.00 per page fee applies. For details and signup, contact clerk or Jerry Anderson at 800-578-7746. **$$$**
Property, Taxation Records Access appraisal district property records free at www.washingtoncad.org/Appraisal/PublicAccess/.

Webb County ***Recorded Documents, Probate Records*** www.webbcounty.com/CountyClerk/ Access recorded documents for a fee at http://acclaimweb.webbcountytx.gov/county/webbportal. Also, search probate records for a fee at http://idocket.com/countycourt.htm. Probate records are at the County Court but accessible through the County Clerks Office. **$$$**
Property, Taxation Records Search the county Central Appraisal District database at www.webbcountytax.com/faces/search.jsp.

Wharton County ***Recorded Documents, Probate Records*** www.co.wharton.tx.us Access recording records free at www.titlex.com/; select Wharton county. Records go up to 11/2003. Registration, login and password required to search. Also, access to the county eSearch website go to www.co.wharton.tx.us, then county offices, then county clerk, then to real properties records online click here. There is a fee for this subscription and you must have a user ID and password. Also, search probate records for a fee at http://idocket.com/countycourt.htm. Probate records are at the County Court but accessible through the County Clerks office. **$$$**

Wheeler County ***Property, Taxation Records*** Find tax collection office data free at http://isouthwestdata.com/corp/.

Wichita County ***Recorded Documents Records*** www.co.wichita.tx.us/county.html Search grantor/grantee index free at https://texaslandrecords.com/txlr/TxlrApp/index.jsp. Registration and fees required for full data. Also, see note at beginning of section. **$$$**
Property, Taxation Records Access to county appraisal district records is free at http://propaccess.wadtx.com/clientdb/?cid=1. Also, see online notes in state summary at beginning of section.

Wilbarger County ***Recorded Documents Records*** www.co.wilbarger.tx.us/CountyClerk.htm Search grantor/grantee index free at https://texaslandrecords.com/txlr/TxlrApp/index.jsp. Registration and fees required for full data. **$$$**
Property, Taxation Records Access to property data is free at www.wilbargerappraisal.org/. Click on Search Our Data. Also see note at beginning of section.

Willacy County ***Recorded Documents, Probate Records*** http://co.willacy.tx.us/default.aspx?Willacy_County/County.Clerk Access recording records at www.titlex.com; select Willacy county. Record range is 8/1998 to 1/2004. Also, search probate records for a fee at http://idocket.com/countycourt.htm. Probate records are at the County Court but accessible through the County Clerks Office. **$$$**
Property, Taxation Records Assessor data available from a private company; see note at beginning of section.**$$$**

Williamson County ***Real Estate, Grantor/Grantee, Deed, Lien, Judgment, UCC, Records*** www.wilco.org/CountyDepartments/CountyClerk/tabid/230/language/en-US/Default.aspx Access to recorded documents, liens, certain vital records at https://deed.wilco.org/. A vendor provides free access to recorded real estate records at www.titlex.com; select Williamson county. Records go back to 5/1999.

Property, Taxation Records Access the appraiser database free at www.wcad.org/property-search. Also, see note in the state summary section.

Wilson County ***Recorded Documents Records*** www.co.wilson.tx.us/default.aspx?Wilson_County/County.Clerk Search grantor/grantee index free at https://texaslandrecords.com/txlr/TxlrApp/index.jsp. Registration and fees required for full data. **$$$**

Property, Taxation Records Assessor data available from a private company; see note at beginning of section.**$$$**

Winkler County ***Recorded Documents Records*** Access to county records for a fee at https://countygovernmentrecords.com/texas/web/login.jsp?submit=Enter. Must register. **$$$**

Wise County ***Recorded Documents Records*** www.co.wise.tx.us/CC/ Search grantor/grantee index free at https://texaslandrecords.com/txlr/TxlrApp/index.jsp. Registration and fees required for full data. Also, access to county records for a fee go to https://countygovernmentrecords.com/texas/web/login.jsp?submit=Enter. Must register. **$$$**

Property, Taxation Records Find appraisal district and collection offices data free at http://isouthwestdata.com/corp/.

Wood County ***Recorded Documents Records*** www.mywoodcounty.com/default.aspx?name=countyclerk Access to county records for a fee at https://countygovernmentrecords.com/texas/web/login.jsp?submit=Enter. Must register. **$$$**

Property, Taxation Records Search property tax records free at www.woodcountytax.com/taxSearch.

Yoakum County ***Recorded Documents Records*** www.co.yoakum.tx.us/default.aspx?Yoakum_County/County.Clerk Access to county records for a fee at https://countygovernmentrecords.com/texas/web/login.jsp?submit=Enter. Must register. **$$$**

Property, Taxation Records Access to assessment/property search data for free at www.trueautomation.com/.

Young County ***Recorded Documents, Probate Records*** www.co.young.tx.us/ips/cms/countyoffices/countyClerk.html Indexes available at www.co.young.tx.us/ips/cms/countyoffices/countyClerk.html. Must register. Also, search probate records for a fee at http://idocket.com/countycourt.htm. Probate records are at the County Court but accessible through the County Clerks Office. **$$$**

Property, Taxation Records Access to property data is free at www.youngcad.org/. Click on Search Our Data.

Zapata County ***Recorded Documents Records*** www.co.zapata.tx.us/default.aspx?Zapata_County/County.Clerk Access recording office land data at www.etitlesearch.com/; registration required, fee based on usage. Also, search grantor/grantee index free at https://texaslandrecords.com/txlr/TxlrApp/index.jsp. Registration and fees required for full data. **$$$**
om; registration required, fee based on usage. **$$$**

Reminder...

Numerous vendors offer online access to assessor and recorded document data for a number of counties. The vendors awere not shown on the county profile. via vendors summarized below.

- Search for documents recorded in the County Clerk's office in 32 Texas counties at https://countygovernmentrecords.com/texas/web/login.jsp?submit=Enter. Users of this site must register and pay a fee to conduct document searches.
- www.taxnetusa.com - offers appraisal district and property appraisal records for all Texas counties. Also, delinquent tax data is available for about half of the participating counties. Free searches as well as online subscriptions services using a sliding fee scale, or purchase bulk data download, are available. Visit the website or call 877-652-2707. To search free at the TaxNetUSA site, click on the "county" and fill out the top portion.
- www.titlex.com - offers recording office records in county grantor/grantee indices - including real estate, deeds, liens, judgments records and more - for 102 Texas counties. In order to search, view, and print records you must first purchase Tokens. Tokens are $.25 and to view is four, to print is four more. You may pay by credit card and open or add to your account.
- The site at https://www.texaslandrecords.com/txlr/TxlrApp/index.jsp - offers a free land index search for 53 Texas counties. Subscribers may print and view document images. A flat rate membership fee is also offered.
- View property tax data free on the True Automation site for 100+ Texas counties at http://trueautomation.com.

Utah

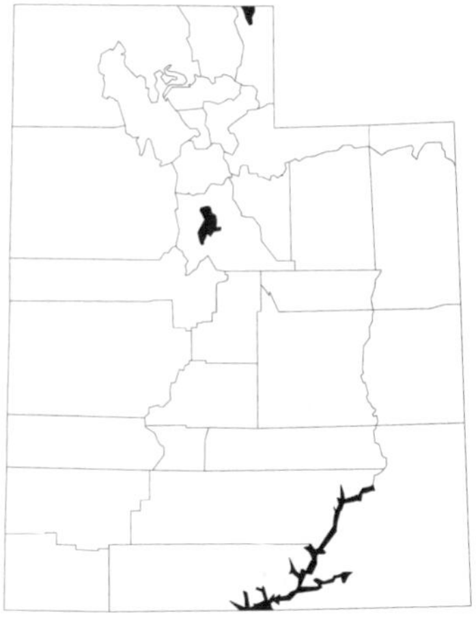

Capital: Salt Lake City
Salt Lake County
Time Zone: MST
Population: 2,855,287
# of Counties: 29

Useful State Links

Website: www.utah.gov
Governor: www.utah.gov/governor/index.html
Attorney General: http://attorneygeneral.utah.gov
State Archives: http://archives.utah.gov/index.html
State Statutes and Codes: http://le.utah.gov/Documents/code_const.htm
Legislative Bill Search: http://le.utah.gov/Documents/bills.htm
Bill Monitoring: http://le.utah.gov/asp/billtrack/track.asp
Unclaimed Funds: https://www.up.utah.gov/UP_Start.asp

State Public Record Agencies

Sexual Offender Registry

Sex Offenders Registration Program, http://corrections.utah.gov/index.php/services/sex-offender-registry.html The Registry may be searched from the Search link at the web page per a program called SONAR. Records are searchable by name, city or geographic area, county, or ZIP Code. The information released includes photos, descriptions, addresses, vehicles, offenses, and targets. One can also search by specific area please register for email alerts.

Incarceration Records

Utah Department of Corrections, Records Bureau, http://corrections.utah.gov An offender search is provided at http://corrections.utah.gov/index.php/services/offender-search.html. Search by name or offender number. The site includes information on only current inmates; historical data is not available.

Corporation, LLC, LP, Fictitious/Assumed Name, Trademarks/Servicemarks

Commerce Department, Division of Corporations and Commercial Code, www.corporations.utah.gov/ A number of search options, including business entity, principle, Certificate of Existence is available at www.utah.gov/services/business.html?type=citizen. Basic information (name, address, agent) is free. Also a subscription service is offered with expanded data. The website also offers an Unclaimed Property search page. Also, search securities professions database free at www.securities.utah.gov/investors/before_verify.html. **$$$** *Other Options:* State allows e-mail access for orders of Certification of Existence at orders@utah.gov

Uniform Commercial Code

Department of Commerce, UCC Division, http://corporations.utah.gov/ UCC uncertified records are available free online at https://secure.utah.gov/uccsearch/uccs. Search by debtor individual name or organization, or by filing number. Certified searches may also be ordered for $12.00 per search. To receive certified searches, you may be a registered user or use a credit card. The website gives details. Note for subscribers there is a $70 annual registration fee which includes 10 user logins. Email requests are accepted at orders@br.state.ut.us. **$$$** *Other Options:* Records are available on CD-ROM. Suggest writing or faxing.

Birth Certificates

Department of Health, Office of Vital Records & Statistics, http://health.utah.gov/vitalrecords/ Orders can be placed online via the agency's Silver system. See https://silver.health.utah.gov/birthinfo.html. Fee is $18.00, certificate is mailed is 7-10 days. Orders can also be placed via a state approved vendor. Go to www.vitalchek.com. Extra fees are involved. See expedited service. **$$$**

Death Records

Department of Health, Office of Vital Records & Statistics, http://health.utah.gov/vitalrecords/ A Death Certificate index search for records 1904-1960 is found at http://archives.utah.gov/research/indexes/20842.htm. Orders can be placed online via the agency's Silver system. See https://silver.health.utah.gov/birthinfo.html. Fee is $18.00, certificate is mailed is 7-10 days. Orders can also be placed via a state approved vendor. Go to www.vitalchek.com. Extra fees are involved. See expedited service. **$$$** *Other Options:* Search the state's Cemetery and Burials database for free at http://history.utah.gov/apps/burials/execute/searchburials.

Marriage Certificates

Department of Health, Office of Vital Records & Statistics, http://health.utah.gov/vitalrecords/ Orders can be placed online via the agency's Silver system. See https://silver.health.utah.gov/birthinfo.html. Fee is $18.00, certificate is mailed is 7-10 days. Orders can also be placed via a state approved vendor. Go to www.vitalchek.com. Extra fees are involved. See expedited service. **$$$**

Divorce Records

Department of Health, Office of Vital Records & Statistics, http://health.utah.gov/vitalrecords/ Orders can be placed online via the agency's Silver system. See https://silver.health.utah.gov/birthinfo.html. Fee is $18.00, certificate is mailed is 7-10 days. Orders can also be placed via a state approved vendor. Go to www.vitalchek.com. Extra fees are involved. See expedited service. **$$$**

Driver Records

Department of Public Safety, Driver License Division, Customer Service Section, http://publicsafety.utah.gov/dld/ riving records are available to eligible organizations through the eUtah. The system is available 24 hours daily. The fee per driving record is $9.00. There is an annual $75.00 subscription fee which includes access for 10 users. Eligible organizations may subscribe by visiting www.utah.gov/registration/ or call 801-983-0275. Subscribers may also use the Address Verification service. This is for insurance organizations to check for uninsured drivers residing at the same address as current policyholders. Fee is $5.00. Also, drivers may secure their own record online at https://secure.utah.gov/mvr-personal/public/index.html. Use of a credit card is required AND the billing address of the credit card must match the address the Division has on file for the driver. **$$$** *Other Options:* Utah offers a monitoring notification program to insurance companies. Fee is $.12 per driver, plus must pay the subscription fee mentioned above plus if activity, an MVR is automatically generate and must be purchased. See www.utah.gov/registration.

Vehicle, Vessel Ownership & Registration

State Tax Commission, Motor Vehicle Division Records Section, http://dmv.utah.gov The "Title, Lien and Motor Vehicle Information Service (TLRIS) is offered to qualified requesters. There is a $75 annual fee PLUS one must be a subscriber to the online system at www.utah.gov/registration/. That fee is also $75 per year. The record fee is $2.00 per record accessed. **$$$** *Other Options:* Bulk requests are available for approved entities. Submit all requests in writing.

Accident Reports

Driver's License Division, Accident Reports Section, http://publicsafety.utah.gov/dld/ Eligible requesters may order the electronically and instantly receive it at https://secure.utah.gov/accidentreport/index.html. The fee is $7.50. **$$$** *Other Options:* The Utah Highway patrol will sell the complete accident file to qualified parties. Visit http://publicsafety.utah.gov/highwaypatrol/index.html. The fee is $5.00 for 1 to 10 pages and $25.00 for 11 to 50 pages.

Voter Registration, Campaign Finance, Lobbyists

Elections - Office of Lt Governor, PO Box 142325, http://elections.utah.gov Campaign finance repots and PAC disclosures are searchable from http://elections.utah.gov/campaign-finance. Also lobbyists data is shown at https://secure.utah.gov/lobbyist/lobb. Overall financial disclosures are shown at http://disclosures.utah.gov/. This includes those of lobbyists.

Occupational Licensing Boards

Accountant Firm .... https://secure.utah.gov/llv/search/index.html
Acupuncturist .... https://secure.utah.gov/llv/search/index.html
ADRP/Arbitrator/Negotiator .... https://secure.utah.gov/llv/search/index.html
Architect .... https://secure.utah.gov/llv/search/index.html
Athletic Agent .... https://secure.utah.gov/llv/search/index.html
Bank .... www.dfi.utah.gov/Banks.htm
Bedding/Upholst'y Mfg/Whlse/Dealer .... http://webapp.ag.utah.gov/LicenseLookup/

Beekeeper.. http://webapp.ag.utah.gov/LicenseLookup/
Brand Inspector.. http://webapp.ag.utah.gov/LicenseLookup/
Building Inspector, Combo or Ltd................ https://secure.utah.gov/llv/search/index.html
Burglar Alarm Firm/Agent/Temp .... https://secure.utah.gov/llv/search/index.html
Check Cashier/Payday Lender .... www.dfi.utah.gov/ckcash.htm
Chiropractic Physician/or/Temp .... https://secure.utah.gov/llv/search/index.html
Consumer Lender .... www.dfi.utah.gov/consumer.htm
Contractor-All .... https://secure.utah.gov/llv/search/index.html
Control'd Substance Precurs'r Dist/Prch...... https://secure.utah.gov/llv/search/index.html
Cosmetology/Barber/School/Instruct .... https://secure.utah.gov/llv/search/index.html
Counselor, Professional/Trainee/Intern .... https://secure.utah.gov/llv/search/index.html
Court Reporter, Shorthand/Voice................ https://secure.utah.gov/llv/search/index.html
Credit Union .... www.dfi.utah.gov/CreditUn.htm
Deception Detection Examiner/Intern .... https://secure.utah.gov/llv/search/index.html
Dental Hygienist/Local Anesthesia .... https://secure.utah.gov/llv/search/index.html
Dentist.. https://secure.utah.gov/llv/search/index.html
Dentist w/ Anesthesia Class I-IV................. https://secure.utah.gov/llv/search/index.html
Dietitian, Certified or Temporary................. https://secure.utah.gov/llv/search/index.html
Egg & Poultry Inspector .... http://webapp.ag.utah.gov/LicenseLookup/
Electrician, Appren./Journey'n/Master .... https://secure.utah.gov/llv/search/index.html
Electrician, Resid'l/Journeym'n/Master .... https://secure.utah.gov/llv/search/index.html
Electrologist Instructor/School .... https://secure.utah.gov/llv/search/index.html
Engineer/Land Surveyor/Structural Professional...........https://secure.utah.gov/llv/search/index.html
Enviro'l Health Scientist/or/in-training .... https://secure.utah.gov/llv/search/index.html
Escrow Agent... www.dfi.utah.gov/escrow.htm
Esthetician Master/Instructor/School .... https://secure.utah.gov/llv/search/index.html
Factory Built Housing Dealer .... https://secure.utah.gov/llv/search/index.html
Feed... http://webapp.ag.utah.gov/LicenseLookup/
Food & Dairy Inspector .... http://webapp.ag.utah.gov/LicenseLookup/
Funeral Service Director/Apprentice/Establishment........https://secure.utah.gov/llv/search/index.html
Genetic Counselor/Temp Counselor............ https://secure.utah.gov/llv/search/index.html
Geologist.. https://secure.utah.gov/llv/search/index.html
Grain & Seed.. http://webapp.ag.utah.gov/LicenseLookup/
Health Facility Administrator/Temp .... https://secure.utah.gov/llv/search/index.html
Hearing Instrument Specialist/Intern............ https://secure.utah.gov/llv/search/index.html
Holding Company.. www.dfi.utah.gov/HCSList.htm
Industrial Banks.. www.dfi.utah.gov/industbk.htm
Insurance Agent/Broker/Adjusters/Consultants..............https://secure.utah.gov/cas/search?page=index
Insurance Establishment............................. https://secure.utah.gov/cas/search?page=index
Interpreter for the Deaf................................ https://aslterpsutah.org/terpsdb/index.php
Landscape Architect .... https://secure.utah.gov/llv/search/index.html
Liquor Store (Retail Liquor License) .... http://abc.utah.gov/about/liquor_stores.html
Lobbyist/Lobbyist Report .... http://elections.utah.gov/lobbyists
Marriage/Family Therapist/Temporary......... https://secure.utah.gov/llv/search/index.html
Massage Therapist/Apprentice .... https://secure.utah.gov/llv/search/index.html
Meat Inspector .... http://webapp.ag.utah.gov/LicenseLookup/
Midwife... https://secure.utah.gov/llv/search/index.html
Mortgage Broker, Residential .... https://secure.utah.gov/rer/relv/search.html
Mortgage Loan Service............................... www.dfi.utah.gov/mortgage.htm
Nail Technician/Instructor/School .... https://secure.utah.gov/llv/search/index.html
Naturopath .... https://secure.utah.gov/llv/search/index.html
Naturopathic Physician .... https://secure.utah.gov/llv/search/index.html
Nurse/Controlled Substance .... https://secure.utah.gov/llv/search/index.html
Nurse/LPN/RN/Practical .... https://secure.utah.gov/llv/search/index.html
Occupational Therapist/Assist Temp .... https://secure.utah.gov/llv/search/index.html

Optometrist/Cont'd Subst./Diagnostic	https://secure.utah.gov/llv/search/index.html
Osteo Phys'n/Surg'n/Cont'd Substance	https://secure.utah.gov/llv/search/index.html
Pesticide Dealer/Applicator	www.kellysolutions.com/UT/pesticideindex.htm
Pharmac't/Intern/Tech./Contr'd Substance	https://secure.utah.gov/llv/search/index.html
Pharmacy Class A-E	https://secure.utah.gov/llv/search/index.html
Physical Therapist	https://secure.utah.gov/llv/search/index.html
Physician/Surgeon, Cont'd Substance/Assistant	https://secure.utah.gov/llv/search/index.html
Plumber Apprentice/Journeyman	https://secure.utah.gov/llv/search/index.html
Podiatric Physic'n/Control'd Substance	https://secure.utah.gov/llv/search/index.html
Political Candidate	http://elections.utah.gov/campaign-finance
Polygraph Examiner	www.polygraphplace.com/docs/c-15-s-Utah-examiners.html
Pre-Need Provider/Sales Agent	https://secure.utah.gov/llv/search/index.html
Probation Provider/Private	https://secure.utah.gov/llv/search/index.html
Psychologist/Resident/Temporary	https://secure.utah.gov/llv/search/index.html
Radiology Practical Technician	https://secure.utah.gov/llv/search/index.html
Radiology Technologist/or/Temp	https://secure.utah.gov/llv/search/index.html
Real Estate Agent/Broker/Company	https://secure.utah.gov/rer/relv/search.html
Real Estate Appraiser	https://secure.utah.gov/rer/relv/search.html
Recreational Therapist/master/Spec'l'st	https://secure.utah.gov/llv/search/index.html
Respiratory Care Practitioner	https://secure.utah.gov/llv/search/index.html
Savings & Loan	www.dfi.utah.gov/sls.htm
Security Company/Officer, Private	https://secure.utah.gov/llv/search/index.html
Social Worker-Clinical/Certified	https://secure.utah.gov/llv/search/index.html
Speech Pathologist/Audiologist	https://secure.utah.gov/llv/search/index.html
Substance Abuse Counselor/Temp	https://secure.utah.gov/llv/search/index.html
Third Party Payment Issuer	www.dfi.utah.gov/montrans.htm
Title Lender	www.dfi.utah.gov/titlelen.htm
Trust Company	www.dfi.utah.gov/trslist.htm
Upholst'r/Upholstery Mfg/Whlse/Dealer	http://webapp.ag.utah.gov/LicenseLookup/
Veterinarian/Vet Intern/cont'l substance	https://secure.utah.gov/llv/search/index.html
Weights & Measures	http://webapp.ag.utah.gov/LicenseLookup/
Wine Store	www.alcbev.state.ut.us/Stores/wine_stores.html

State and Local Courts

State Court Structure: The **District Court** has original jurisdiction for all civil cases, all criminal felonies, certain misdemeanors, domestic relations cases such as divorces, child custody and support, adoption, and probate.

Justice Courts, established by counties and municipalities, deal with class B and C misdemeanors, violations of ordinances, small claims, and infractions committed within their territorial jurisdiction.

Appellate Courts: Opinions, dockets and calendars are viewable at www.utcourts.gov/courts/sup/.

Statewide Court Online Access: All courts participate in the system described below.

Case information from all Utah District Court locations and 43 Justice Courts is available online through XChange. Recently the case information from Justice Courts became available on this system, although the data throughput dates may vary. Fees include a $25.00 registration fee and $30.00 per month fee which includes 200 searches. Each additional search is billed at $.10 per search. The search provides a summary of the docket index; case files and copies are not available. Information about XChange and the subscription agreement can be found at www.utcourts.gov/records or call 801-578-3850. Effective April 2012, certain civil court actions are now private. These actions include divorce, separate maintenance, grandparent visitation, temporary separation, adjudication of marriage, civil stalking, guardianship, conservatorship, cohabitant abuse, custody and support(UCCJEA), (UIFSA), and paternity. The case history with minute entries of public hearings; judgments; orders and decrees; and letters of appointment remain public unless made private by judicial order.

Record access to XChange is considered to be equivalent to an on-site search using the public access terminals in those courts which provide the terminals.

Note: No individual Utah courts offer online access, other than as described above.

Recorders, Assessors, and Other Sites of Note

Recording Office Organization: 29 counties, 29 recording offices. The recording officers are the County Recorder for real estate and the Clerk of District Court for state tax liens. All federal tax liens are filed with the County Recorder. All state tax liens are filed with Clerk of District Court, many of which have online access and most all will perform searches

Statewide or Multi-Jurisdiction Access: An excellent **statewide search site** is of all counties is provided by the Utah County Government at www.utahcounty.gov/LandRecords/Index.asp. Search for many types of records, including recorded documents, property evaulations, by name, property address or parcel. There is also a delinquent tax search. One may also pull document images of recorded documents if the document number is given.

Individual County Sites (Statewide Site Above Not Shown on Profiles):

Box Elder County ***Recorded Documents*** www.boxeldercounty.org/recorder.htm Access to county recordings data is available free for indexed data only at http://erecord.boxeldercounty.org/eaglesoftware/taxweb/. Click on Public Login. Can purchase single documents by credit card for $1.50 per document or have the option to purchase a one or three month subscription. Must register first.

Property, Taxation Records Access to GIS/mapping for free at www.boxeldercounty.org/gismaps.htm.

Cache County ***Recorded Documents*** www.cachecounty.org/recorder/ Access to recording records is via subscription at www.landlight.com/. Choose from 3 subscription plans; short free trial is offered. Grantor/Grantee Index goes back to 10/1980; Abstracts to 7/1984; images to 12/1992. Call 435-787-9003 for more info on online access. $$$

Property, Taxation Records A subscription service is available at www.landlight.com/ for assessor records. Also, access to GIS/mapping free at http://maps.cachecounty.org/.**$$$**

Carbon County ***Recorded Documents*** www.carbon.utah.gov/recorder/ Access to images of recorded documents and plats free at www.carbon.utah.gov/recorder/.

Davis County ***Recorded Documents*** www.co.davis.ut.us/recorder/default.cfm Access to the recorder's land records database requires written registration and $25.00 per month fee plus $.10 per transaction. Records go back to 1981. For info and sign-up go to https://dc-webpub.daviscountyutah.gov/apps/redi_web/ or call 801-451-3347. **$$$**

Property, Taxation Records Search property and tax data free at www.co.davis.ut.us/recorder/property_search/property_search.cfm.

Duchesne County ***Recorded Documents*** http://duchesne.utah.gov/government/recorder.html

Emery County ***Recorded Documents*** www.emerycounty.com/recorder/index.htm Access plat map data by parcel ID number or location on county map free at www.emerycounty.com/recorder/needa_plat.htm.

Iron County ***Recorded Documents*** www.ironcounty.net/departments/Recorder/ Access to online search database free at http://eagleweb.ironcounty.net/eaglesoftware/web/. See index of documents recorded not images.

Kane County ***Recorded Documents*** http://kane.utah.gov Access county property records (indexes only) free at http://eagleweb.kane.utah.gov/eaglesoftware/web/login.jsp

Property, Taxation Records Access property data free at http://eagleweb.kane.utah.gov/eaglesoftware/taxweb/search.jsp but no name searching.

Morgan County ***Recorded Documents*** www.morgan-county.net/CountyDepartments/CountyRecorder/tabid/96/Default.aspx Access to records for a fee-$1,000 Itime fee, $250.00 per 1/4 plus cost for copies. Contact office for information. **$$$**

Rich County ***Recorded Documents*** www.richcountyut.org/recorder.html Access to ownership plats and final subdivision plats free at www.richcountyut.org/property.html.

Property, Taxation Records Access current tax sale data at http://richcountyut.org/documents/delinquent_taxes.htm. Check main website for other record types to be added. Also, access to plats/subdivisions free at www.richcountyut.org/property.html.

Salt Lake County ***Recorded Documents*** www.slcorecorder.org/SLCR/Home.aspx Access to recording office records is by subscription; minimum $150 sign-up, $25.00 monthly, plus $.02 per screen view or image. Tax maps $1.00, Subdivision maps $2.00 per page. Add'l info at http://slcorecorder.siredocs.com/RecHome/SiteOverview.aspx or phone 801-468-3013 x2 for signup. Check an address on voter registration rolls free at https://secure.slco.org/cl/elections/index.cfm. **$$$**

Property, Taxation Records Name search assessor records free at http://assessor.slco.org/cfml/Query/query2.cfm. Also, search parcel data at http://maps.slco.org/website/assessor/public_parcelviewer/viewer.htm but no name searching.

Sevier County ***Recorded Documents*** www.sevierutah.net/index.aspx?nid=102 Access to recorder's database index of data is available with free login at http://qdocs.sevierutah.net/recorder/web/login.jsp. No images available.

Property, Taxation Records Assessor data and sales included in recorder document search lookup with free login at http://qdocs.sevierutah.net/recorder/web/login.jsp.

Summit County ***Recorded Documents*** www.summitcounty.org/recorder/ Access the county Document search page free at http://property.summitcounty.org/eaglesoftware/web/login.jsp?submit=Enter. For free search use username public and password public.

Property, Taxation Records Access property data free at http://property.summitcounty.org/eaglesoftware/web/.

Tooele County ***Recorded Documents*** www.co.tooele.ut.us/recorder.htm Access to public records for a fee at https://geodata.tooelecountyonline.org/. **$$$**

Property, Taxation Records Access the property information database free at www.co.tooele.ut.us/taxinfo.html.

Uintah County ***Recorded Documents*** www.co.uintah.ut.us/recorder/rec.php Access to property searches free at www.co.uintah.ut.us/recorder/rec.php. Also subscription access information available for more in-depth searches also at www.co.uintah.ut.us/recorder/rec.php. For fees, visit www.co.uintah.ut.us/recorder/internetagreement.pdf. There is a plan for low volumen and high volume users. **$$$**

Property, Taxation Records Access assessor property data free by name at www.co.uintah.ut.us/recorder/ownerqueryform.php. Search by address at www.co.uintah.ut.us/recorder/addrqueryform.php.The resulting screen shows tax assessment data

Wasatch County ***Recorded Documents*** www.co.wasatch.ut.us/departments/property_tax_services/recorder.aspx Access to a limited grantor/grantee index (entry#, book & page/date/KOI). Also, surveys & subdivisions http://beta.co.wasatch.ut.us/sirepub/docs.aspx. Documents from 1973 to present are accessible. Grantor/Grantee data back to 5/20/2002.

Property, Taxation Records Access to property tax look-up for free at www.co.wasatch.ut.us/on-line_services/property_tax_system_lookup.aspx.

Washington County ***Recorded Documents*** www.washco.utah.gov/ Access recorder data free at http://eweb.washco.utah.gov/recorder/web/login.jsp.

Property, Taxation Records Search GIS property data free at http://maps.washco.utah.gov/imf/imf.jsp?site=washco_main and click on Locate but no name searching. Access the treasurer's property tax data free at www.washco.utah.gov/treasurer/AccountQuery.php, but no name searching.

Weber County ***Recorded Documents*** www1.co.weber.ut.us/rs/recorder/index.php Access recorder's ownership and dedicated plats data free at www.co.weber.ut.us/ded_plats.php.

Property, Taxation Records Property records on the County Parcel Search site are free at www.co.weber.ut.us/psearch/. Also, access Abstract Title Registrations for a monthly fee at www.co.weber.ut.us/recorder/abstract_title_reg.php. Multiple GIS-mapping aps available free at www.co.weber.ut.us/gis/?content=interactive. **$$$**

Reminder:

An excellent **statewide search site** of all counties is provided by the Utah County Government at www.utahcounty.gov/LandRecords/Index.asp.

Search for many types of records, including recorded documents, property evaulations, by name, property address or parcel. There is also a delinquent tax search. One may also pull document images of recorded documents if the document number is given.

Vermont

Capital: Montpelier
Washington County
Time Zone: EST
Population: 626,011
# of Counties: 14

Useful State Links

Website: http://vermont.gov/portal
Governor: http://governor.vermont.gov
Attorney General: www.atg.state.vt.us
State Archives: http://vermont-archives.org
State Statutes and Codes: www.leg.state.vt.us/statutesMain.cfm
Legislative Bill Search: www.leg.state.vt.us/statutesMain.cfm
Unclaimed Funds: www.vermonttreasurer.gov/unclaimed-property

State Public Record Agencies

Criminal Records

Criminal Record Check Section, Vermont Criminal Information Center, http://vcic.vermont.gov/ Access to District Court criminal records is at https://secure.vermont.gov/DPS/criminalrecords/. Search by name and DOB. One may use a credit or billing is available to subscribers to Vermont.gov. The fee is $30.00 per record. Results are immediate and can be printed. A validation service is also offered, but records are not certified. Search results report the date of conviction, charge, sentence and venue. It won't show the original charge filed, or give information about the circumstances of the crime. A free online validation service is offered. Disclosure of the contents of the conviction report to anyone other than the subject of the record or properly designated employees of any agency with a documented need to know the contents of the record is prohibited. **$$$** *Other Options:* Any Criminal Conviction Record purchased through this service can be verified through the Vermont Criminal Information Center at no cost by entering the validation code through the Online Validation Service.

Sexual Offender Registry

State Repository, Vermont Criminal Information Center, http://vcic.vermont.gov/sex_offender Search free online at www.communitynotification.com/cap_office_disclaimer.php?office=55275. There is a disclaimer that states "This service does not contain the names of all the registered sex offenders in Vermont." The requestor must also acknowledge a statement which specifies the conditions under which the registry information is being released.

Incarceration Records

Vermont Department of Corrections, Inmate Information Request, www.doc.state.vt.us The website provides an Incarcerated Offender Locator to ascertain where an inmate is located. Click at the top of main page, or go directly to http://doc.vermont.gov/offender-locator/ Search results give name, DOB, location and case worker. This is not designed to provide complete inmate records nor is it a database of all inmates past and present in the system.

Corporation, LLC, LLP, LP, L3C, Trade Name, Trademarks/Servicemarks

Secretary of State, Corporation Division, www.sec.state.vt.us/corps/index.htm Information on Corporate and trademark records can be accessed from the Internet for no fee. For the corporation name search, go to www.sec.state.vt.us/seek/database.htm#2. Many records, included corporation, UCC, trademark, trade name, and name look-ups are available. Also, search securities investment professionals free at www.dfr.vermont.gov/securities/securities-division. *Other Options:* There is an option on the web to download the entire corporation (and trade name) database.

Uniform Commercial Code

UCC Division, Secretary of State, www.sec.state.vt.us/tutor/dobiz/ucc/ucchome.htm UCC searches available free at www.sec.state.vt.us/seek/ucc_seek.htm. Search by debtor or business name. *Other Options:* The database may be downloaded from the web. The data file is in a self extracting, IBM compatible, generic dbf format. Also the last 30 days of images may be downloaded in a ZIP format.

Vital Records

Reference & Research, Vital Records - Archives, http://vermont-archives.org/research/genealogy/vitals/ Email requests for informational copies to archives@sec.state.vt.us. **$$$**

Workers' Compensation Records

Department of Labor, Workers Compensation Division, www.labor.vermont.gov/ Hearing decisions, by year, are found at www.labor.vermont.gov/InfoCenter/Decisions/tabid/127/Default.aspx. Also provided is a list of employers with penalties assessed.

Driver Records, Driver License Information

Department of Motor Vehicles, DI - Records Unit, http://dmv.vermont.gov/ Record access is available to approved requesters as a premium service from Vermont.gov. The fee is $15.00 per record; a $75.00 annual subscription fee is also required. Single inquiry and batch mode are both available. The system is open 24 hours a day, 7 days a week (except for file maintenance periods). Only the license number is needed when ordering, the system does not ask for the name and DOB. All information concerning the forms and how to become a subscriber is found at https://secure.vermont.gov/DMV/mvr/help/. Contact Vermont Information Consortium directly at 802-229-4171. **$$$** *Other Options:* This agency will sell its license file to approved requesters for non-commercial use, but customization is not available.

Voter Registration, Campaign Finance, PACs, Lobbyists

Secretary of State, Election Division, http://vermont-elections.org/soshome.htm View campaign finance reports at http://vermont-elections.org/elections1/campaign_finance.html. Search lobbyist data at http://vermont-elections.org/elections1/lobbyist.html.

Occupational Licensing Boards

Accountant Firm .... https://secure.vtprofessionals.org/Lookup/LicenseLookup.aspx
Acupuncturist .... https://secure.vtprofessionals.org/Lookup/LicenseLookup.aspx
Anesthesiologist Assistant .... https://webmail.vdh.state.vt.us/CAVU/Lookup/LicenseLookup.aspx
Architect .... https://secure.vtprofessionals.org/Lookup/LicenseLookup.aspx
Asbestos Contractor/Worker/Labs/Company .... http://healthvermont.gov/enviro/asbestos/documents/asbestos_consult_contractor_list.pdf
Athlete Agents www.sos.ne.gov/licensing/ahtlete/AA%20Dec2010.pdf
Athletic Trainer .... https://secure.vtprofessionals.org/Lookup/LicenseLookup.aspx
Auctioneer .... https://secure.vtprofessionals.org/Lookup/LicenseLookup.aspx
Bank .... www.dfr.vermont.gov/banking/verify-license
Barber .... https://secure.vtprofessionals.org/Lookup/LicenseLookup.aspx
Body Piercer/Tattooist .... https://secure.vtprofessionals.org/Lookup/LicenseLookup.aspx
Boiler & Pressure Vessel Inspectors http://firesafety.vermont.gov/sites/firesafety/files/pdf/License%20%26%20TQP/License/BoilerInspectors.pdf
Boxing Manager/Promoter .... https://secure.vtprofessionals.org/Lookup/LicenseLookup.aspx
Boxing Professional .... https://secure.vtprofessionals.org/Lookup/LicenseLookup.aspx
Caterers .... http://liquorcontrol.vermont.gov/downloads
Chemical Suppression TQP Cert .... http://firesafety.vermont.gov/building_trades
Chimney Sweep TQP Cert .... http://firesafety.vermont.gov/building_trades
Chiropractor .... https://secure.vtprofessionals.org/Lookup/LicenseLookup.aspx
Cosmetologist .... https://secure.vtprofessionals.org/Lookup/LicenseLookup.aspx
Credit Union .... www.dfr.vermont.gov/banking/find-company
Crematory .... https://secure.vtprofessionals.org/Lookup/LicenseLookup.aspx
Dental Assistant/Hygienist .... https://secure.vtprofessionals.org/Lookup/LicenseLookup.aspx
Dentist .... https://secure.vtprofessionals.org/Lookup/LicenseLookup.aspx
Dietitian .... https://secure.vtprofessionals.org/Lookup/LicenseLookup.aspx
Electrician .... http://firesafety.vermont.gov/building_trades
Electrologist .... https://secure.vtprofessionals.org/Lookup/LicenseLookup.aspx
Elevator Inspector/Mechanic .... http://firesafety.vermont.gov/building_trades
Embalmer .... https://secure.vtprofessionals.org/Lookup/LicenseLookup.aspx
Engineer .... https://secure.vtprofessionals.org/Lookup/LicenseLookup.aspx

Esthetician	https://secure.vtprofessionals.org/Lookup/LicenseLookup.aspx
Fire Alarm System Instal'r/Dealer	http://firesafety.vermont.gov/building_trades
Fire Sprinkler System Design/Installer	http://firesafety.vermont.gov/building_trades
Funeral Director	https://secure.vtprofessionals.org/Lookup/LicenseLookup.aspx
Hearing Aid Dispenser	https://secure.vtprofessionals.org/Lookup/LicenseLookup.aspx
Investment Advisor	www.dfr.vermont.gov/securities/investor/find-registered-professional
Land Surveyor	https://secure.vtprofessionals.org/Lookup/LicenseLookup.aspx
Landscape Architect	https://secure.vtprofessionals.org/Lookup/LicenseLookup.aspx
Lead Abatement Contractor/Worker/Labs/Company	http://healthvermont.gov/enviro/lead/documents/lead_consult_contractor_list.pdf
Lift Mechanic	http://firesafety.vermont.gov/building_trades
Liquor, Retail/Wholesale	http://liquorcontrol.vermont.gov/downloads
Lobbyist Gift	http://vermont-elections.org/elections1/lobbyist.html
Lobbyist/Employer/Firm	http://vermont-elections.org/elections1/lobbyist.html
LPG/Propane Installer	http://firesafety.vermont.gov/building_trades
Manicurist	https://secure.vtprofessionals.org/Lookup/LicenseLookup.aspx
Marriage & Family Therapist	https://secure.vtprofessionals.org/Lookup/LicenseLookup.aspx
Meat Inspection Laboratory	www.vermontagriculture.com/fscp/meatInspection/index.html
Mental Health Counselor, Clinical	https://secure.vtprofessionals.org/Lookup/LicenseLookup.aspx
Midwife	https://secure.vtprofessionals.org/Lookup/LicenseLookup.aspx
Mortgage Company/Professional	www.dfr.vermont.gov/banking/verify-license
Motor Vehicle Racing	https://secure.vtprofessionals.org/Lookup/LicenseLookup.aspx
Natural Gas System Installer	http://firesafety.vermont.gov/building_trades
Naturopath	https://secure.vtprofessionals.org/Lookup/LicenseLookup.aspx
Notary Public	https://secure.vtprofessionals.org/Lookup/LicenseLookup.aspx
Nurse/Nurse Practitioner/LNA	https://secure.vtprofessionals.org/Lookup/LicenseLookup.aspx
Nursing Home Administrator	https://secure.vtprofessionals.org/Lookup/LicenseLookup.aspx
Occupational Therapist	https://secure.vtprofessionals.org/Lookup/LicenseLookup.aspx
Oil Burning Equipment Installer	http://firesafety.vermont.gov/building_trades
Optician	https://secure.vtprofessionals.org/Lookup/LicenseLookup.aspx
Optometrist	https://secure.vtprofessionals.org/Lookup/LicenseLookup.aspx
Osteopathic Physician	https://secure.vtprofessionals.org/Lookup/LicenseLookup.aspx
Pharmacist/Pharmacy	https://secure.vtprofessionals.org/Lookup/LicenseLookup.aspx
Physical Therapist/Assistant	https://secure.vtprofessionals.org/Lookup/LicenseLookup.aspx
Physician/Medical Doctor/Surgeon/Asst	https://webmail.vdh.state.vt.us/CAVU/Lookup/LicenseLookup.aspx
Plumber	http://firesafety.vermont.gov/building_trades
Podiatrist	https://webmail.vdh.state.vt.us/CAVU/Lookup/LicenseLookup.aspx
Private Investigator	https://secure.vtprofessionals.org/Lookup/LicenseLookup.aspx
Psychoanalyst	https://secure.vtprofessionals.org/Lookup/LicenseLookup.aspx
Psychologist/Psychotherapist	https://secure.vtprofessionals.org/Lookup/LicenseLookup.aspx
Radiation Tech	https://secure.vtprofessionals.org/Lookup/LicenseLookup.aspx
Real Estate Agent/Broker/Seller	https://secure.vtprofessionals.org/Lookup/LicenseLookup.aspx
Real Estate Appraiser	https://secure.vtprofessionals.org/Lookup/LicenseLookup.aspx
Respiratory Therapy	https://secure.vtprofessionals.org/Lookup/LicenseLookup.aspx
Security Guard	https://secure.vtprofessionals.org/Lookup/LicenseLookup.aspx
Social Worker	https://secure.vtprofessionals.org/Lookup/LicenseLookup.aspx
Tattooist	https://secure.vtprofessionals.org/Lookup/LicenseLookup.aspx
Teacher	http://education.vermont.gov/new/html/licensing/disciplinary.html
Veterinarian	https://secure.vtprofessionals.org/Lookup/LicenseLookup.aspx
Waste Water Treatm't Plant Operator	www.vtwaterquality.org/ww/docs/OpCert/WW_Operator_List.pdf

State and Local Courts

State Court Structure: The Superior Court has five Divisions: **Criminal, Civil, Family, Probate**, and **Environmental**. The Civil Division of the Superior Court hears predominantly civil, tort, real estate, and small claims cases. On rare occasion it hears criminal cases, but the Criminal Division of the Superior Court hears predominantly criminal cases, but will also hear some civil suspension cases, fish and wildlife violations, and appeals from the Judicial Bureau. Specialty courts include Probate Division Courts and Family Division Courts. The Environmental Division hears municipal land use enforcement cases and enforcement actions brought by states natural resources agencies.

In Vermont, the **Judicial Bureau** has jurisdiction over traffic, municipal ordinances, and Fish and Game violations, minors in possession, and hazing.

Appellate Courts: Supreme Court opinions are available from www.vermontjudiciary.org (click on *Legal Information*) and are also maintained by the Vermont Department of Libraries at http://dol.state.vt.us.

Statewide Court Online Access:

- Vermont Courts Online provides access to civil and small claim cases and court calendar information from 12 of the 14 county Superior Courts. Access is not offered for Chittenden (which has its own system) and Franklin. Go to https://secure.vermont.gov/vtcdas/user. Records are in real-time mode. There is a $12.50 activation fee plus a fee of $.50 per case for look-up after the 1st 5 cases. A disclaimer states "The information obtained from *VTCourtsOnLine* is not guaranteed to be complete or accurate."
- A great source of Vermont legal decisions including those made by Judiciary Boards is found at http://libraries.vermont.gov/law.
- See a list of Probate Court locations at www.vermontjudiciary.org/courts/probate/probateinfo/index.htm.

Addison County

Superior Court Civil Division www.vermontjudiciary.org
Civil: Access civil and small claims case records by web subscription, $12.50 activation plus $.50 per page; registration info at https://secure.vermont.gov/vtcdas/user. Also, click on Calendars by Date and County to view calendars free. **$$$**
Superior Court Criminal Division www.vermontjudiciary.org/GTC/criminal/default.aspx
Criminal: Click on Calendars by Date and County at https://secure.vermont.gov/vtcdas/user.

Bennington County

Superior Court Civil Division http://vermontjudiciary.org/default.aspx
Civil: Access civil and small claims case records by web subscription, $12.50 activation plus $.50 per page; registration info at https://secure.vermont.gov/vtcdas/user. Also, click on Calendars by Date and County to view calendars free. **$$$**
Superior Court Criminal Division www.vermontjudiciary.org
Criminal: Click on Calendars by Date and County at https://secure.vermont.gov/vtcdas/user.

Caledonia County

Superior Court Civil Division www.vermontjudiciary.org
Civil: Access civil and small claims case records by web subscription, $12.50 activation plus $.50 per page; registration info at https://secure.vermont.gov/vtcdas/user. Also, click on Calendars by Date and County to view calendars free. **$$$**
Superior Court Criminal Division http://vermontjudiciary.org/default.aspx
Criminal: Click on Calendars by Date and County at https://secure.vermont.gov/vtcdas/user.

Chittenden County

Superior Court Civil Division www.vermontjudiciary.org/GTC/civil/default.aspx
Civil: Access case information free from 01/01/2012 forward at https://secure.vermont.gov/vtcdas/user. This court's home page also directs users to find prior records at www.chittendensuperiorcourt.com/index.htm, but this site is often down.
Superior Court Criminal Division www.vermontjudiciary.org/GTC/criminal/default.aspx
Criminal: Click on Calendars by Date and County at https://secure.vermont.gov/vtcdas/user.

Essex County

Superior Court www.vermontjudiciary.org
Civil: Access case records by internet subscription, $12.50 activation plus $.50 per page; registration info at https://secure.vermont.gov/vtcdas/user. Also, click on Calendars by Date and County to view calendars free. **$$$** *Criminal:* Click on Calendars by Date and County at https://secure.vermont.gov/vtcdas/user.

Franklin County

Superior Court Criminal Division http://vermontjudiciary.org/default.aspx
Criminal: Click on Calendars by Date and County at https://secure.vermont.gov/vtcdas/user.

Grand Isle County

Superior Court www.vermontjudiciary.org

Civil: Access case records by internet subscription, $12.50 activation plus $.50 per page; registration info at https://secure.vermont.gov/vtcdas/user. Also, click on Calendars by Date and County to view calendars free. **$$$** *Criminal:* Click on Calendars by Date and County at https://secure.vermont.gov/vtcdas/user.

Lamoille County

Superior Court Civil Division www.vermontjudiciary.org

Civil: Access civil and small claims case records by web subscription, $12.50 activation plus $.50 per page; registration info at https://secure.vermont.gov/vtcdas/user. Also, click on Calendars by Date and County to view calendars free. **$$$**

Superior Court Criminal Division www.vermontjudiciary.org

Criminal: Click on Calendars by Date and County at https://secure.vermont.gov/vtcdas/user.

Orange County

Superior Court www.vermontjudiciary.org

Civil: Access case records by internet subscription, $12.50 activation plus $.50 per page; registration info at https://secure.vermont.gov/vtcdas/user. Also, click on Calendars by Date and County to view calendars free. **$$$** *Criminal:* Click on Calendars by Date and County at https://secure.vermont.gov/vtcdas/user.

Orleans County

Superior Court Civil Division www.vermontjudiciary.org

Civil: Access civil and small claims case records by web subscription, $12.50 activation plus $.50 per page; registration info at https://secure.vermont.gov/vtcdas/user. Also, click on Calendars by Date and County to view calendars free. **$$$**

Superior Court Criminal Division www.vermontjudiciary.org

Criminal: Click on Calendars by Date and County at https://secure.vermont.gov/vtcdas/user.

Rutland County

Superior Court Civil Division www.vermontjudiciary.org

Civil: Access civil and small claims case records by web subscription, $12.50 activation plus $.50 per page; registration info at https://secure.vermont.gov/vtcdas/user. Also, click on Calendars by Date and County to view calendars free. **$$$**

Superior Court Criminal Division http://vermontjudiciary.org/default.aspx

Criminal: Click on Calendars by Date and County at https://secure.vermont.gov/vtcdas/user.

Washington County

Superior Court Civil Division www.vermontjudiciary.org

Civil: Access civil and small claims case records by web subscription, $12.50 activation plus $.50 per page; registration info at https://secure.vermont.gov/vtcdas/user. Also, click on Calendars by Date and County to view calendars free. **$$$**

Superior Court Criminal Division www.vermontjudiciary.org

Criminal: Click on Calendars by Date and County at https://secure.vermont.gov/vtcdas/user.

Windham County

Superior Court Civil Division http://vermontjudiciary.org/default.aspx

Civil: Access civil and small claims case records by web subscription, $12.50 activation plus $.50 per page; registration info at https://secure.vermont.gov/vtcdas/user. Also, click on Calendars by Date and County to view calendars free. **$$$**

Superior Court Criminal Division www.vermontjudiciary.org

Criminal: Click on Calendars by Date and County at https://secure.vermont.gov/vtcdas/user.

Windsor County

Superior Court Civil Division www.vermontjudiciary.org

Civil: Access civil and small claims case records by web subscription, $12.50 activation plus $.50 per page; registration info at https://secure.vermont.gov/vtcdas/user. Also, click on Calendars by Date and County to view calendars free. **$$$**

Superior Court Criminal Division www.vermontjudiciary.org/default.aspx

Criminal: Click on Calendars by Date and County at https://secure.vermont.gov/vtcdas/user.

Recorders, Assessors, and Other Sites of Note

Recording Office Organization: Vermont has 14 counties and 246 towns/cities which have 246 recording offices. There is **no county recording** in this state. All recording is done at the city/town level. Many towns are so small that their mailing addresses are in different towns. 4 towns had the same names as cities - Barre, Newport, Rutland, and St. Albans. 11 cities or towns bear the same name as a Vermont county - Addison, Bennington, Chittenden, Essex, Franklin, Grand Isle, Orange, Rutland, Washington, Windham, and Windsor. All federal and state tax liens on personal property and on real property are filed with the Town/City Clerk in the lien/attachment book and indexed in real estate records.

Statewide or Multi-Jurisdiction Access: There is no statewide online access to recorded documents or assessor data. However a growing number of towns have contracted out online services to usually offer property assessment records or property cards.

Local Sites Organized by County:

Addison County

Ferrisburgh Town ***Property, Taxation Records*** Access to parcel listing for free at www.ferrisburghvt.org/index.asp?Type=B_BASIC&SEC={F73BEED9-246C-44F8-ABE5-DF6ED550EAD7}.

Hancock Town ***Property, Taxation Records*** Access to GIS/mapping free at www.trorc.org/maps_ha.html.

Lincoln Town ***Property, Taxation Records*** The Town Grand List is available from the Listers at the Assessor office.**$$$**

Middlebury Town ***Recorded Documents*** www.middlebury.govoffice.com Access to town indexes free at https://vermont-townclerks-records.com. For images you must subscribe for a fee. **$$$**

Bennington County

Bennington Town ***Property, Taxation Records*** Access to the Grand List search program is free at www.bennington.com/government/grandlist/index.html. No name searching at this time; site is under construction and data is incomplete.

Dorset Town ***Recorded Documents*** www.dorsetvt.org/clerk.php Access to town indexes free at https://vermont-townclerks-records.com. For images you must subscribe for a fee. **$$$**

Manchester Town Clerk ***Property, Taxation Records*** Access to property values, by address at http://manchester-vt.gov/properties.

Caledonia County

Barnet Town ***Property, Taxation Records*** Access to the Grand List for free at www.kevaco.com/BarnetVT/documents/BARNET2011GRANDLIST.xls.

Chittenden County

Burlington City ***Recorded Documents*** www.burlingtonvt.gov/CT/ Access to town indexes free at https://vermont-townclerks-records.com. For images you must subscribe for a fee. **$$$**

Property, Taxation Records Access to city property tax data is free at www.burlingtonvt.gov/Assessor/Property-Database/Property-Database-Search/.

Colchester Town ***Property, Taxation Records*** Access to appraisal data and GIS/mapping for free at www.vgsi.com/vision/Applications/ParcelData/VT/Home.aspx.e.aspx

Essex Town ***Property, Taxation Records*** Access to tax/parcel maps for free at www.essex.org/index.asp?Type=B_LIST&SEC={B8AF3EEC-F98B-4423-9C11-FC7E889BEF3B}.

Killington Town ***Recorded Documents*** www.killingtontown.com/index.asp?Type=B_BASIC&SEC={CDDD41E8-D7DF-4229-ABFC-206C0F335173} Access to town indexes free at https://vermont-townclerks-records.com. For images you must subscribe for a fee. **$$$**

Williston Town ***Property, Taxation Records*** Access to the Grand List Property Info - 2012 free at http://willistonvt.govoffice3.com/vertical/Sites/%7BF506B13C-605B-4878-8062-87E5927E49F0%7D/uploads/GRAND_LIST_PROPERTY_INFORMATION_2012(1).pdf.

Essex County

Guildhall Town *Property, Taxation Records*
Access to GIS/mapping for free at www.guildhallvt.org/tax-map.html.

Franklin County

Enosburgh Town *Property, Taxation Records*
Access to GIS/mapping for free at http://enosburghvermont.org/Maps/TownMap.php.

Fairfax Town *Recorded Records Records*
www.vtgrandpa.com/ This is an individual site for property transfers, births, deaths, marriages and zoning permits for free at burialswww.vtgrandpa.com/fhs/fxtwnhap.html

Franklin Town *Property, Taxation Records*
Access to GIS/mapping for free at www.emapsplus.com/alfranklin/maps/.

St. Albans City *Recorded Documents*
www.stalbansvt.com Access to town indexes free at https://vermont-townclerks-records.com. For images you must subscribe for a fee. **$$$**

Lamoille County

Elmore Town *Property, Taxation Records*
Access to the 2012 Grand List free at www.elmorevt.org/town/listers/index.php.

Orange County

Randolph Town *Recorded Documents*
http://randolphvt.govoffice2.com/index.asp?Type=B_BASIC&SEC={C5BB9C85-ACEE-48F8-B611-B83D5247EDBC} Access to town indexes free at https://vermont-townclerks-records.com. For images you must subscribe for a fee. **$$$**

Thetford Town *Recorded Documents*
www.thetfordvermont.us/departments/clerk-office/ Access to records at http://cotthosting.com/vtportal/User/Login.aspx?ReturnUrl=%2fvtportal%2fIndex.aspx. Town index is free, as a subscriber, unlimited access to indexes and images for a fee. **$$$**

Orleans County

Barton Town *Recorded Documents*
www.townofbarton.com/ Access to recorded records free at www.townofbarton.com/viewing-our-records. Records are from 1/2010 to 3/13. Also included are property tax transfer requests listed by date of receipt from 12/2009 to 1/2013.

Property, Taxation Records Delinquent tax lists may be viewed at www.townofbarton.com/delinquent-taxes.

Craftsbury Town *Property, Taxation Records*
Access to 2012 Grand List or mappings free at www.townofcraftsbury.com/gov/listers.shtml.

Morgan Town *Property, Taxation Records*
Access to property maps for free at http://town.morgan-vt.org/pm/propmap.htm.

Newport City *Property, Taxation Records*
Access to Newport City assessor data is free at http://data.visionappraisal.com/newportvt/DEFAULT.asp.

Newport Town *Property, Taxation Records*
Access to appraisal data and GIS/mapping for free at www.vgsi.com/vision/Applications/ParcelData/VT/Home.aspx.vt/.

Rutland County

Brandon Town *Recorded Documents*
http://townofbrandon.com/departments/town-clerk/ Access to town indexes free at https://vermont-townclerks-records.com. For images you must subscribe for a fee. **$$$**

Castleton Town *Property, Taxation Records*
Access to the 2010/2011 Grand List for free at http://castletonvermont.org/wp-content/uploads/2011/12/2010grandlist.pdf

Clarendon Town *Recorded Documents*
www.clarendonvt.org/index.html Access to town indexes free at https://vermont-townclerks-records.com. For images you must subscribe for a fee. **$$$**

Pittsford Town *Recorded Documents*
http://pittsfordvermont.com/departments/town-clerk/ Access to town indexes free at https://vermont-townclerks-records.com. For images you must subscribe for a fee. **$$$**

Poultney Town *Recorded Documents*
www.poultneyvt.com/chamber-of-commerce/town-government-directory/town-clerk/ Access to town indexes free at https://vermont-townclerks-records.com. For images you must subscribe for a fee. **$$$**

Rutland City *Recorded Documents*
www.rutlandcity.com/index.asp?Type=B_BASIC&SEC={D0A4D01D-5919-4903-AAE4-0CC130FF2E49} Access to town indexes free at https://vermont-townclerks-records.com. For images you must subscribe for a fee. **$$$**

West Rutland Town *Recorded Documents*
www.westrutlandtown.com/tdtownclerk.php Access to town indexes free at http://cotthosting.com/vtportal/User/Login.aspx. For images you must subscribe for a fee. **$$$**

Washington County

Calais Town ***Recorded Documents*** www.calaisvermont.gov Access to town indexes free at https://vermont-townclerks-records.com. For images you must subscribe for a fee. **$$$**

Marshfield Town ***Recorded Documents (Indexes Only)*** www.town.marshfield.vt.us/index.asp?Type=B_BASIC&SEC={3F2E8902-9DD3-4DA0-99BD-2D9FA8315BBB} Access to town indexes free at http://cotthosting.com/vtportal/User/Login.aspx. Images are only accessible at the Town Clerk's Office.

Montpelier City ***Property, Taxation Records*** Access to records/GIS/mapping for free at www.montpelier-vt.org/department/69/Assessor.html?id=xEN9egGr.

Warren Town ***Property, Taxation Records*** Access to property transfer tax returns for free at www.warrenvt.org/depts/clerk.htm. Click on 2004-Present or 2003-1999 at bottom of page.

Windham County

Brattleboro Town ***Property, Taxation Records*** Access to Grand List by Owner or Location for free at www.brattleboro.org/index.asp?Type=B_BASIC&SEC={034F3706-09C4-4E46-AA89-1FF70573060B}&DE={361FA9C8-08F1-4DF1-9561-6E284AA54D8A}.

Halifax Town ***Property, Taxation Records*** Send questions to townclerk@halifaxvermont.com

Jamaica Town ***Recorded Documents*** www.jamaicavermont.org/index.php?option=com_content&view=article&id=21&Itemid=55 Access to records for a fee at https://i2d.uslandrecords.com/vt/jamaica/. **$$$**

Marlboro Town ***Property, Taxation Records*** Access to maps for free at http://marlboro.vt.us/old/maps.htm.

Newfane Town ***Recorded Documents*** http://newfanevt.com/ Access to town indexes free at https://vermont-townclerks-records.com. For images you must subscribe for a fee. **$$$**

Stratton Town ***Property, Taxation Records*** Access to appraisal data and GIS/mapping for free at www.vgsi.com/vision/Applications/ParcelData/VT/Home.aspx.

Westminster Town ***Property, Taxation Records*** Access to GIS/mapping for free at www.westminstervt.org/index.asp?Type=B_BASIC&SEC={46765053-9BEE-4DD0-8A28-01AF3752806B}. Also, access to the Grand List free at www.westminstervt.org/vertical/sites/%7BA171D8D5-AAF9-44F2-8E0E-B30695F0816B%7D/uploads/GRAND_LIST_2011_FOR_WEB_2.pdf.

Wilmington Town ***Property, Taxation Records*** The Grand List is available as a pdf at www.wilmingtonvermont.us/index.asp?Type=B_BASIC&SEC={D29D8978-A87B-4F53-9925-D964D479F8F9}.

Windsor County

Bridgewater Town ***Property, Taxation Records*** Access to appraisal data and GIS/mapping for free at www.vgsi.com/vision/Applications/ParcelData/VT/Home.aspx.

Hartford Town ***Property, Taxation Records*** Access to appraisal data and GIS/mapping for free at www.vgsi.com/vision/Applications/ParcelData/VT/Home.aspx.

Norwich Town ***Recorded Documents*** http://norwich.vt.us/town-clerk/ Access to town indexes free at https://vermont-townclerks-records.com. For images you must subscribe for a fee. **$$$**
Property, Taxation Records Assess to grand list report (parcel info) for free at http://norwich.vt.us/wp-content/uploads/2012/10/2012GL.pdf.

Town of Woodstock ***Property, Taxation Records*** Access to the Lister's Grand Lists and Sales List is available free at www.townofwoodstock.org/Town_of_Woodstock_VT_Grand_List.aspx.

Virginia

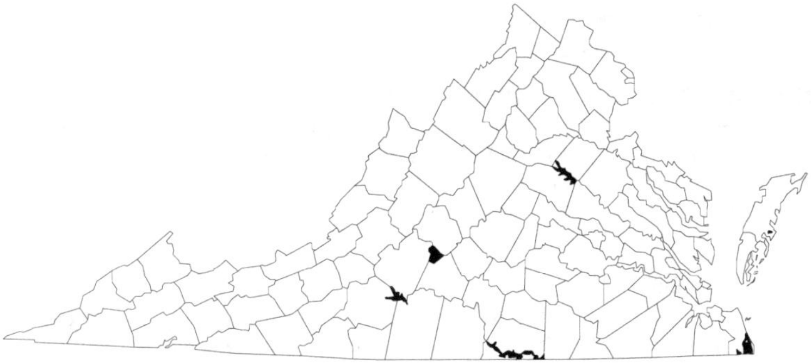

Capital: Richmond
Richmond City County
Time Zone: EST
Population: 8,185,867
# of Counties: 95

Useful State Links

Website: www.virginia.gov/cmsportal3/
Governor: www.governor.virginia.gov
Attorney General: www.oag.state.va.us
State Archives: www.lva.virginia.gov/
State Statutes and Codes: http://leg1.state.va.us/000/src.htm
Legislative Bill Search: http://virginiageneralassembly.gov/
Bill Monitoring: http://virginiageneralassembly.gov/
Unclaimed Funds: http://www.trs.virginia.gov

State Public Record Agencies

Criminal Records

Virginia State Police, CCRE, www.vsp.state.va.us Certain entities, including screening companies, can apply for online access via the NCJI System, but it is ONLY available to IN-STATE accounts. NCJI allows requesters to receive notice of clean records faster (48 hours). If hits, record is mailed. The SP-167 release form must be kept on file and showable if audited. Fees are same as manual submission-$15.00 per record or $20.00 SOR record search. Username and password required. There is a minimum usage requirement of 10 requests per month. Turnaround time is 24-72 hours. See www.vsp.state.va.us/CJIS_NCJI.shtm. **$$$**

Sexual Offender Registry

Virginia State Police, Sex Offender and Crimes Against Minors Registry, http://sex-offender.vsp.virginia.gov/sor/ Search by name, city, county or ZIP Code, or from a map at a link at the home page. There is also a search for Wanted Sex Offenders.

Incarceration Records

Virginia Department of Corrections, Records Unit, www.vadoc.virginia.gov/ Visit www.vadoc.virginia.gov/offenders/locator/index.cfm to do a name search or to locate a current offender. Searcher must have either the inmates' Department of Corrections' seven digit (new) or six digit (old) identification number or search by exact last name and at least the first 2 initials of the first name. Note this disclaimer: This system is not designed to provide complete offender records nor is it a database of all offenders past and present in our system. A DOC wanted/fugitives list is found at www.vadoc.virginia.gov/offenders/wanted/fugitive.shtm.

Corporation, LLC, LP, Fictitious Name, Business Trust Records

State Corporation Commission, Clerks Office, www.scc.virginia.gov/clk/bussrch.aspx A business entity search is at www.scc.virginia.gov/clk/bussrch.aspx. The Clerk's Information System (CIS), an electronic database, also contains general information on file for Virginia and foreign corporations, limited liability companies, limited partnerships, and business trusts. https://sccefile.scc.virginia.gov/ also access to filings, but not as robust as the above. Visit http://docket.scc.virginia.gov/vaprod/main.asp for SCC Case File Docket Search to review status of cases and public filings. Also, search securities companies, agents, and franchises registered with the state at www.scc.virginia.gov/srf/index.aspx. *Other Options:* The database is available for bulk purchase. Monthly downloads are available with a signed agreement. Monthly fees are generally $150. Call for details.

Trademarks, Service Marks

State Corporation Commission, Virginia Securities Division, www.scc.virginia.gov/srf/bus/tmsm.aspx Searching Trademarks and Service Marks are available at www.scc.virginia.gov/srf/bus/tmsm.aspx.

Uniform Commercial Code, Federal Tax Liens

UCC Division, State Corporation Commission, www.scc.virginia.gov/clk/uccsrch.aspx Their electronic access system is called the Clerk's Information System (CIS) and is available free at www.scc.virginia.gov/clk/uccsrch.aspx. Images of UCC filings and tax liens are not available for electronic or online viewing. Collateral information is not available in CIS but can be obtained if a search is ordered and the associated fee paid. **$$$** *Other Options:* The database is available for bulk purchase. Monthly downloads are available with a signed agreement. Monthly fee is $150 for UCC and federal lien data or $300 for the lien data plus business entity data. Call for details.

Vital Records

State Health Department, Office of Vital Records, www.vdh.virginia.gov/vital_Records/index.htm One may process a request online through an independent company that the Virginia Division of Vital Records has partnered with: VitalChek.com. Additional fee apply. **$$$**

Workers' Compensation Records

Workers' Compensation Commission, www.workcomp.virginia.gov/ Some records, including Judicial Opinions, can be obtained online. There is no name searching option. The Opinions link is www.workcomp.virginia.gov/portal/vwc-website/OnlineServices/JudicialOpinions.

Driver Records

Department of Motor Vehicles, Customer Records Work Center, Rm 514, www.dmvnow.com The DMV must approve all customers. Visit www.dmvnow.com to Request an Information Use Application. There is a $25.00 application fee valid for two years for new accounts and the search fee is $7.00 per record Either a five year insurance record or seven year employment record can be ordered. The system is open 24/7 and is Internet-based. The driver's address is provided as part of the record. The driver license number or name, date of birth and sex are needed to search. Billing is monthly. **$$$** *Other Options:* The agency offers a Voluntary Monitoring program and a mandatory Driving Record Monitoring Programs for employers of commercial drivers. Call 804-497-7155 for details.

Vehicle Ownership & Registration

Department of Motor Vehicles, Vehicle Records, Cust Work Center, Rm 514, www.dmvnow.com The online system, managed by the Virginia Interactive, open 24 hours daily. There is an annual $95.00 administration fee and records are $7.00 each. All accounts must be approved by both the DMV and Virginia Interactive. Call 804-786-4718 to request an information use agreement application. The URL is www.virginiainteractive.org/cmsportal2/ Also, a $12.00 vehicle verification search is for prospective vehicle buyers is available at https://www.dmv.virginia.gov/dmvnet/ppi/intro.asp. **$$$** *Other Options:* Bulk release of vehicle or ownership information is not available except for statistical and vehicle recall purposes.

Vessel Ownership & Registration

Dept of Game & Inland Fisheries, Boat Registration and Titling, www.dgif.virginia.gov The VA boat registration database may be searched on the web at www.virginiainteractive.org/cmsportal2/. There are two options, one for commercial use, and for non-commercial use. Both require a subscription, which is $95.00 a year and record fees are incurred. Additional services are provided. **$$$** *Other Options:* CDs with data may be provided to approved requesters. A fee may be required, depending on extent of request.

Voter Registration, Campaign Finance, PACs

State Board of Elections, www.sbe.virginia.gov/cms/ One may verify registration ones one registration status at the web page, but cannot search for another's status. View campaign finance reports for free at http://cfreports.sbe.virginia.gov/. This includes PACs. *Other Options:* Voter data output is available on CD (CSV files), computer printout or on ready made labels.

Occupational Licensing Boards

Accountant-CPA https://secure1.boa.virginia.gov/Verification/
Accountant-CPA Firm .... https://secure1.boa.virginia.gov/Verification/Search.aspx?facility=Y
Acupuncturist .... https://secure01.virginiainteractive.org/dhp/cgi-bin/search_publicdb.cgi
Alcoholic Beverage Distributor .... www.abc.virginia.gov/licenseesearch/welcome.do
Athletic Trainer .... https://secure01.virginiainteractive.org/dhp/cgi-bin/search_publicdb.cgi
Attorney/Attorney Assoc .... www.vsb.org/attorney/attSearch.asp?S=D
Audiologist .... https://secure01.virginiainteractive.org/dhp/cgi-bin/search_publicdb.cgi
Bank .... www.scc.virginia.gov/bfi/reg_inst/banks.pdf
Check Casher .... www.scc.virginia.gov/bfi/reg_inst/check.pdf
Chiropractor .... https://secure01.virginiainteractive.org/dhp/cgi-bin/search_publicdb.cgi

Clinical Nurse Specialist	https://secure01.virginiainteractive.org/dhp/cgi-bin/search_publicdb.cgi
Consumer Finance Comapnys	www.scc.virginia.gov/bfi/reg_inst/sav.pdf
Cosmetic Procedure Certification	https://secure01.virginiainteractive.org/dhp/cgi-bin/search_publicdb.cgi
Counselor, Professional	https://secure01.virginiainteractive.org/dhp/cgi-bin/search_publicdb.cgi
Credit Counseling Agencies	www.scc.virginia.gov/bfi/reg_inst/credit.pdf
Credit Union	www.scc.virginia.gov/bfi/reg_inst/check.pdf
Crematory	https://secure01.virginiainteractive.org/dhp/cgi-bin/search_publicdb.cgi
Dental Hygienist	https://secure01.virginiainteractive.org/dhp/cgi-bin/search_publicdb.cgi
Dentist	https://secure01.virginiainteractive.org/dhp/cgi-bin/search_publicdb.cgi
Embalmer	https://secure01.virginiainteractive.org/dhp/cgi-bin/search_publicdb.cgi
Funeral Director/Establ./Trainee/Service Provider	https://secure01.virginiainteractive.org/dhp/cgi-bin/search_publicdb.cgi
Humane Society	https://secure01.virginiainteractive.org/dhp/cgi-bin/search_publicdb.cgi
Insurance Agent/Agency/Company	www.scc.virginia.gov/boi/ConsumerInquiry/default.aspx
Investment Advisor/Advisor Agency	www.scc.virginia.gov/srf/index.aspx
Lobbyist	https://solutions.virginia.gov/Lobbyist/Reports/Database
Marriage & Family Therapist	https://secure01.virginiainteractive.org/dhp/cgi-bin/search_publicdb.cgi
Massage Therapist	https://secure01.virginiainteractive.org/dhp/cgi-bin/search_publicdb.cgi
Medical Equipment Supplier	https://secure01.virginiainteractive.org/dhp/cgi-bin/search_publicdb.cgi
Medical Wholesaler/Mfg	https://secure01.virginiainteractive.org/dhp/cgi-bin/search_publicdb.cgi
Money Transmitter	www.scc.virginia.gov/bfi/reg_inst/trans.pdf
Mortgage Lender/Broker	www.scc.virginia.gov/bfi/reg_inst/mort.pdf
Mortgage Loan Originators	www.nmlsconsumeraccess.org/
Motor VehicleTtitle Lenders	www.scc.virginia.gov/bfi/reg_inst/title.pdf
Nurse-LPN/RN/Aide	https://secure01.virginiainteractive.org/dhp/cgi-bin/search_publicdb.cgi
Nursing Home Administrator	https://secure01.virginiainteractive.org/dhp/cgi-bin/search_publicdb.cgi
Occupational Therapist	https://secure01.virginiainteractive.org/dhp/cgi-bin/search_publicdb.cgi
Optometrist	https://secure01.virginiainteractive.org/dhp/cgi-bin/search_publicdb.cgi
Oral/Maxillofacial Surgeon	https://secure01.virginiainteractive.org/dhp/cgi-bin/search_publicdb.cgi
Osteopathic Physician	https://secure01.virginiainteractive.org/dhp/cgi-bin/search_publicdb.cgi
Payday Lender	www.scc.virginia.gov/bfi/reg_inst/pay.aspx
Pesticide Applicat'r/Firm (Commercial)	www.vdacs.virginia.gov/pesticides/pdffiles/reports-applicators.pdf
Pesticide Applicator (Private)	www.vdacs.virginia.gov/pesticides/pdffiles/reports-private.pdf
Pharmacist/Pharmacy	https://secure01.virginiainteractive.org/dhp/cgi-bin/search_publicdb.cgi
Physical Therapist	https://secure01.virginiainteractive.org/dhp/cgi-bin/search_publicdb.cgi
Physician/Medical Doctor/Assistant	https://secure01.virginiainteractive.org/dhp/cgi-bin/search_publicdb.cgi
Podiatrist	https://secure01.virginiainteractive.org/dhp/cgi-bin/search_publicdb.cgi
Prescriptive Authorization	https://secure01.virginiainteractive.org/dhp/cgi-bin/search_publicdb.cgi
Private Investigator	https://www.dcjs.virginia.gov/ps/directory/rocs/?facility=y
Psychologist at School	https://secure01.virginiainteractive.org/dhp/cgi-bin/search_publicdb.cgi
Psychologist, Clinical/Applied	https://secure01.virginiainteractive.org/dhp/cgi-bin/search_publicdb.cgi
Psychology School	https://secure01.virginiainteractive.org/dhp/cgi-bin/search_publicdb.cgi
Radiologic Technologist-limited	https://secure01.virginiainteractive.org/dhp/cgi-bin/search_publicdb.cgi
Rehabilitation Provider	https://secure01.virginiainteractive.org/dhp/cgi-bin/search_publicdb.cgi
Respiratory Care Practitioner	https://secure01.virginiainteractive.org/dhp/cgi-bin/search_publicdb.cgi
Savings Institution	www.scc.virginia.gov/bfi/reg_inst/sav.pdf
School Guidance Counselor	https://p1pe.doe.virginia.gov/tinfo/
School Library Media Specialist	https://p1pe.doe.virginia.gov/tinfo/
School Principal/Superintendent	https://p1pe.doe.virginia.gov/tinfo/
Securities Broker/Brokerage/Dealer/Dealer Agent	www.scc.virginia.gov/srf/index.aspx
Security Business Services	https://www.dcjs.virginia.gov/ps/directory/rocs/?facility=y
Security Canine Handler	https://www.dcjs.virginia.gov/ps/directory/rocs/?facility=y
Security Officer, Unarmed/Armed	https://www.dcjs.virginia.gov/ps/directory/rocs/?facility=y
Security Technic'n (electronic security)	https://www.dcjs.virginia.gov/ps/directory/rocs/?facility=y
Social Worker, Clinical/Registered	https://secure01.virginiainteractive.org/dhp/cgi-bin/search_publicdb.cgi
Special Conservator of the Peace	https://www.dcjs.virginia.gov/ps/directory/rocs/?facility=y

Speech Pathologist at School .... https://secure01.virginiainteractive.org/dhp/cgi-bin/search_publicdb.cgi
Speech Pathologist/Audiologist .... https://secure01.virginiainteractive.org/dhp/cgi-bin/search_publicdb.cgi
Substance Abuse Counselor .... https://secure01.virginiainteractive.org/dhp/cgi-bin/search_publicdb.cgi
Substance Abuse Treatm't Practitioner .... https://secure01.virginiainteractive.org/dhp/cgi-bin/search_publicdb.cgi
Teacher https://p1pe.doe.virginia.gov/tinfo/
Training Schools .... https://www.dcjs.virginia.gov/ps/directory/rocs/?facility=y
Trust Companies... www.scc.virginia.gov/bfi/reg_inst/trust.aspx
Unarmed Security Officer/Courier................ https://www.dcjs.virginia.gov/ps/directory/rocs/?facility=y
University Limited Medical License............. https://secure01.virginiainteractive.org/dhp/cgi-bin/search_publicdb.cgi
Veterinarian/Veterinary Technician/Facility . https://secure01.virginiainteractive.org/dhp/cgi-bin/search_publicdb.cgi
Warehouser, Medical .... https://secure01.virginiainteractive.org/dhp/cgi-bin/search_publicdb.cgi

State and Local Courts

State Court Structure: The **Circuit Court** handles felonies, all civil cases with claims of more than $25,000 but it shares authority with the General District court to hear matters involving claims between $4,500 and $25,000. The Circuit Court also handles family matters including divorce. There is a Circuit Court in each city and county in Virginia.

The **General District Court** decides all offenses involving ordinances laws, and by-laws of the county or city where it is located and all misdemeanors under state law, and small claims ($4,500 or less). A misdemeanor is any charge that carries a penalty of no more than one year in jail or a fine of up to $2,500, or both. Please note that a District can comprise a county or a city.

As stated, records of civil action from $4,500 to $25,000 can be at either the Circuit Court or District Court as either can have jurisdiction. Thus it is necessary to check both record locations as there is no concurrent database or index.

Fifteen independent cities share the Clerk of Circuit Court with the county (but have separate District Courts) - Bedford, Covington (Alleghany County), Emporia (Greenville County), Fairfax, Falls Church (Arlington or Fairfax County), Franklin (Southhampton County), Galax (Carroll County), Harrisonburg (Rockingham County), Lexington (Rockbridge County), Manassas and Manassas Park (Prince William County), Norton (Wise County), Poquoson (York County), South Boston (Halifax County), and Williamsburg (James City County).

Magistrate Offices issue various types of processes such as arrest warrants, summonses, bonds, search warrants, subpoenas, and certain civil warrants. Magistrates may also conduct bail hearings.

Appellate Courts: One may view opinos and case information at www.courts.state.va.us.

Statewide Court Online Access: There is one online system for the Circuit Courts Court case records, one for the District Courts, and an older system for recorded documents at the Circuit Courts which can include civil judgments. Plus a new emerging system for obtaining certified document is in place for a limited number of jurisdictions. Each court type and each county or county equivalent must be searched separately.

1. At http://wasdmz2.courts.state.va.us/CJISWeb/circuit.html the case docket index may be searched for all of the Circuit Courts except Chesterfield, Fairfax (which has its own system), Henrico, and King and Queen counties. Henrico and Chesterfield are two of the biggest counties in the state.
2. **All General District Courts are searchable** at this site: http://epwsgdp1.courts.state.va.us/gdcourts/captchaVerification.do?landing=landing.

The above two free online systems usually include partial DOBs in criminal results; civil results sometimes include addresses.

3. At least nine Circuit Courts now are connected with a service offered by www.Clerkepass.com to view or obtain certified documents and non-certified documents. There is no name searching. A "User" can request and view Certified as well as Non-Certified documents. A "View" can only view Certified documents ordered by other users but cannot request any documents. A "Guest User" is a User who can request documents without registering with ClerkePass.com. The web page states it will charge a CAF (customized access fee) plus the existing court fees. The fees are detailed at the individual court URLs for this site.

County Sites (Profiles do not include the statewide sites mentioned in #1 and #2 above):

(Be sure to visit www.courts.state.va.us/)

Alexandria City

18th Circuit Court www.alexandriava.gov/clerkofcourt/

Civil: There is limited free online access to civil docket information from 1/01/1983, and a subscription service ($500 per year or $50 per month) to full data including images. Visit https://secure.alexandriava.gov/ajis/index.php. **$$$** *Criminal:* Online access to criminal record index is free, access to images require a subscription (either $500 a year or $0 a month). Data available back to 7/01/1987. **$$$**

Carroll County

27th Circuit Court www.courts.state.va.us/courts/circuit.html

Civil: Certified or non-certified documents may be ordered online at https://www.clerkepass.com/Carroll/. There are added fees which depend on the type of document ordered. **$$$** *Criminal:* same **$$$**

Fairfax County

19th Circuit Court www.fairfaxcounty.gov/courts/circuit/

Civil: Access to current court case indexes is via CPAN subscription; call 703-246-2366 IT Dept. or see www.fairfaxcounty.gov/courts/circuit/cpan.htm to apply. Fee is $50.00 per month per user. Also, daily and Friday's Motion dockets are available free at www.fairfaxcounty.gov/circuitcourtdocket/. **$$$** *Criminal:* Access to current court case indexes is via CPAN subscription; call 703-246-2366 IT Dept. or see www.fairfaxcounty.gov/courts/circuit/cpan.htm to apply. Fee is $50.00 per month per user, flat rate. The Daily and Friday's Motion dockets are available free at www.fairfaxcounty.gov/circuitcourtdocket/. **$$$**

Loudoun County

20th Circuit Court www.loudoun.gov/Default.aspx?tabid=798

Civil: Search free by name or case number at www.courts.state.va.us/. Results show address of subject and the day and month of birth, but not year. Also, docket lists are free at www.loudoun.gov/Default.aspx?tabid=318&fmpath=/Dockets. *Criminal:* Search free by name only or by case number at www.courts.state.va.us/. Results show address of subject and the day and month of birth, but not year. Also, docket lists are online free at www.loudoun.gov/Default.aspx?tabid=318&fmpath=/Dockets. \

King George County

15th Circuit Court www.courts.state.va.us/courts/circuit/King_George/home.html

Civil: Certified documents may be ordered online at https://www.clerkepass.com/KingGeorge/. There is a total fee of $1.00 per document Plus $.50 a page, plus shipping. **$$$** *Criminal:* same

Pulaski County

Circuit Court www.courts.state.va.us/courts/circuit/pulaski/home.html

Civil: Online access to court records is $300 annual fee http://records.pulaskicircuitcourt.com/icris/splash.jsp. Registration required; search by name, document type or number. Also certified or non-certified documents may be ordered online at http://clerkepass.com/pulaski/. There are added fees which depend on the type of document ordered. Search free by name only or by case number at www.courts.state.va.us/. Results show address of subject and the day and month of birth, but not year. **$$$** *Criminal:* same **$$$**

Rockingham County

26th Circuit Court www.courts.state.va.us/courts/circuit.html

Civil: Certified or non-certified documents may be ordered online at https://www.clerkepass.com/rockingham/. There are added fees which depend on the type of document ordered. **$$$** *Criminal:* same

Scott County

Circuit Court www.courts.state.va.us/courts/circuit.html

Civil: Certified or non-certified documents may be ordered online at https://www.clerkepass.com/scott/. There are added fees which depend on the type of document ordered. **$$$** *Criminal:* same

Smyth County

County Circuit Court www.courts.state.va.us/courts/circuit/smyth/home.html

Civil: Certified or non-certified documents may be ordered online at https://www.clerkepass.com/Smyth/. There are added fees which depend on the type of document ordered. **$$$** *Criminal:* Same as civil

Suffolk City

Suffolk 5th Circuit Court www.courts.state.va.us/courts/circuit.html

Civil: Certified or non-certified documents may be ordered online at https://www.clerkepass.com/suffolk/. There are added fees which depend on the type of document ordered. **$$$** *Criminal:*same as civil

Washington County

Circuit Court www.courts.state.va.us/courts/circuit/Washington/home.html

Civil: Certified or non-certified documents may be ordered online at https://www.clerkepass.com/WashingtonCircuit/. There are added fees which depend on the type of document ordered. **$$$** *Criminal:* same **$$$**

Wise County

30th Circuit Court www.courts.state.va.us/courts/circuit/wise/home.html

Civil: SAccess court indexes and images via www.courtbar.org. Records go back to June, 2000. Certified or non-certified documents may be ordered online at https://www.clerkepass.com/wise/. There are added fees which depend on the type of document ordered. *Criminal:* same as civil.

Recorders, Assessors, and Other Sites of Note

Recording Office Organization: 95 counties and 41 independent cities; 123 recording offices. The recording officer is the Clerk of Circuit Court. Sixteen independent cities share the Clerk of Circuit Court with the county – Bedford; Covington and Clifton Forge (Alleghany County); Emporia (Greenville County); Fairfax; Falls Church (Arlington or Fairfax County); Franklin (Southhampton County); Galax (Carroll County); Harrisonburg (Rockingham County); Lexington (Rockbridge County); Manassas and Manassas Park (Prince William County); Norton (Wise County); Poquoson (York County); South Boston (Halifax County); and Williamsburg (James City County).

Charles City and James City are counties, not cities. The City of Franklin is not in Franklin County. The City of Richmond is not in Richmond County. The City of Roanoke is not in Roanoke County.

Federal tax liens on personal property of businesses are filed with the State Corporation Commission. Other federal and all state tax liens are filed with the county Clerk of Circuit Court.

Statewide or Multi-Jurisdiction Access: A number of Virginia counties and cities provide free access to real estate related information via the Internet.

- A vendor offers online tax assessor data with both free and/or subscription to over 40 jurisdictions as shown in the profiles below. See www.vamanet.com/cgi-bin/HOME.
- Plus the state's Records Management System provides its Secure Remote Access System at https://risweb.courts.state.va.us/index.html for participating recording offices through Clerk of the Circuit Court. This is a subscription system. Records available include deeds, marriage licenses, judgments, and will. Each local Circuit Court Clerk's office must be contacted for requirements, fees, and log-in.

County Sites:

Virginia Counties (Virginia Cities listed as separate section after the Counties)

Accomack County ***Real Estate, Grantor/Grantee, Deed, Mortgage, Lien, Judgment, Marriage, Will Records***
www.co.accomack.va.us/departments/clerk-of-circuit-court Access recorder's index by subscription service. Call 877-658-6018 x2111 to apply or visit the home page. There is a$50 monthly fee. **$$$**

Property, Taxation Records Access parcel assessment value data free atwww.co.accomack.va.us/departments/real-estate-assessment/real-estate-land-book-2012.

Albemarle County ***Real Estate, Deed, Lien, Judgment, UCC Records*** www.courts.state.va.us/courts/circuit/Albemarle/home.html
Access to clerk's recorded index available by subscription; fee- $600 per year per user or $1200 for corporate 4-user sub. Does not include vital records. Land records go back to 1957. Contact clerk Debra Shipp at 434-972-4083. **$$$**

Property, Taxation Records Search assessor data free at http://albemarlevapropertymax.governmaxa.com/propertymax/rover30.asp; search free by parcel, owner name, address, sales. Also, search parcel data on GIS-mapping site free at http://gisweb.albemarle.org/GISWeb/Welcome.aspx. Also, search zoning notices free at www.albemarle.org/upload/images/webapps/zoning/.

Alleghany County ***Recorded Documents Records*** www.courts.state.va.us/courts/circuit/alleghany/home.html Subscription available for $50.00 per month. Contact Carol Davis. **$$$**
Property, Taxation Records Access City of Covington property data free at www.vamanet.com/cgi-bin/HOME. Access Alleghany County data free also at www.vamanet.com/cgi-bin/HOME. Also, access to GIS-mapping free at http://alleghany.mapsdirect.net/default.aspx.

Amelia County ***Real Estate, Deed Records*** www.ameliacova.com/department/view/12/ Access real estate recording records by subscription only, contact Clerk of Circuit Court for information. **$$$**
Property, Taxation Records Search for property card and assessment data free at www.ameliacountyrealestate.com/.

Amherst County ***Documents, Deeds, Judgment Records*** http://courts.state.va.us Access to private subscription service contact Roy Mayo at 434-946-9321. Also, access to clerks records free at https://landrecords.countyofamherst.com/. Must have UserID and Password. **$$$**
Property, Taxation Records Access data free at www.vamanet.com/cgi-bin/HOME.

Appomattox County ***Real Estate Records*** www.courts.state.va.us/courts/circuit/Appomattox/home.html Access to land records for a fee at https://lto.landsystems.com/LTOonline/logon.aspx?ReturnUrl=%2fLTOOnline%2fdefault.aspx. An application must be completed and approval granted to receive access. **$$$**

Arlington County ***Property, Taxation Records*** Property records on the County assessor database are free at www.arlingtonva.us/departments/realestate/reassessments/scripts/dreadefault.asp. Includes trade name search. Also, access Falls Church City property data free on the GIS-mapping site at http://property.fallschurchva.gov/public/ieprop.htm but no name searching.

Augusta County ***Real Estate Records*** www.courts.state.va.us/ For subscription service information contact Carol Brydge at 540-245-5321. **$$$**
Property, Taxation Records Click on Augusta County to search property data for free at www.vamanet.com/cgi-bin/HOME.

Bath County ***Property, Taxation Records*** Access current assessment info and sales by VamaNet subscription at www.vamanet.com/cgi-bin/HOME. Fee is $35 per month or $300 per year with discounts for multiple localities, regions.**$$$**

Bedford County ***Real Estate Records*** www.bedfordva.gov/ Access to real estate records free at www.co.bedford.va.us/Realestate/default.asp.
Property, Taxation Records Real estate records on the Bedford County GIS site are free at www.co.bedford.va.us/Res/GIS/index.asp; however, no name searching at this time. Also access via www.onlinegis.net/VaBedford/. Click on Display Map then Search. Also, access City of Bedford property info on the GIS site free at http://bedfordgis.bedfordva.gov/bedfordcity/search.asp?skipopen=1.

Bland County ***Property, Taxation Records*** Access current assessment info and sales by VamaNet subscription at www.vamanet.com/cgi-bin/HOME. Fee is $35 per month or $300 per year with discounts for multiple localities, regions.**$$$**

Botetourt County ***Property, Taxation Records*** Access property data free at www.onlinegis.net/VaBotetourt/asp/controlVersion.asp. Click on Display Map then Search, no name searching.

Brunswick County ***Real Estate, Deed, Judgment, Will, Marriage Records*** www.brunswickco.com/co_clerk.asp Access to Circuit Court Records Search System is by subscription at www.courts.state.va.us/rmsweb/. $300 per year, username and password required, signup with local Circuit Court Clerk. **$$$**

Buchanan County ***Real Estate, Grantor/Grantee, Deed, Lien, Judgment, UCC, Marriage, Wills, Fictitious Name, Court Orders Records*** www.courts.state.va.us/courts/circuit/Buchanan/home.html Access to the recorder's database is available by subscription, registration and password required; $50.00 per month. Contact clerk's office for signup and info. Data goes back to 1991. Deeds index will go back to 1976. **$$$**

Campbell County ***Property, Taxation Records*** Access county property data from Dept of Real Estate and Mapping free at http://campbellvapropertymax.governmaxa.com/propertymax/rover30.asp?. Also, search at http://gis.co.campbell.va.us/campbellims/default.aspx. Also, search property by name on the county GIS-mapping site at http://gis.co.campbell.va.us/campbellims/default.aspx. Login as guest; registration required for full data. Click on 'Find' to search.

Caroline County ***Property, Taxation Records*** Click on Caroline County to search property records for free at www.vamanet.com/cgi-bin/HOME.

Carroll County ***Real Estate, Deed, Judgment, UCC, Will, Plat Records*** www.courts.state.va.us/courts/circuit/carroll/home.html Access to Carroll county property data indexes and images is a $25 monthly fee. Username and password required; signup through Clerk of Circuit Court, 276-730-3070. Land index and images go back to 1842; plats to 2002. **$$$**
Property, Taxation Records Access Town of Hillsville property data on the gis-mapping site at http://arcgis.webgis.net/va/hillsville/.

Charles City County ***Property, Taxation Records*** View property cards free at www.charlescitycountyrealestate.com/.

Chesterfield County ***Real Estate Records*** www.chesterfield.gov Access to land records for a fee at https://www.ccclandrecords.org/Opening.asp. Must have a user name and password for this subscription service. **$$$**

Property, Taxation Records Search the real estate assessment data free at www.chesterfield.gov/eServices/RealEstateAssessments/RealEstate.aspx?id=11063.

Clarke County ***Real Estate, Grantor/Grantee, Deed, Judgment Records*** www.clarkevacocc.org With username and password you may access recorder's land records at www.clarkevacocc.org/. Includes deed books back to 1836. Set up account online; fee is $25.00 per month. **$$$**
Property, Taxation Records Access current assessment info and sales by VamaNet subscription at www.vamanet.com/cgi-bin/HOME. Fee is $35 per month or $300 per year with discounts for multiple localities, regions.**$$$**

Culpeper County ***Recorded Documents Records*** http://web.culpepercounty.gov/CountyGovernment/CircuitCourt.aspx Access to subscription records for a fee of $600.00 per year available. Contact Janice J Corbin, Clerk at 540-727-3438. **$$$**
Property, Taxation Records Access property data free at www.onlinegis.net/VaCulpeper/asp/controlVersion.asp. No name searching. Also, view property tax estimator free at http://web.culpepercounty.gov/eServices/TaxEstimator.aspx. Also, access current assessment info and sales by VamaNet subscription at www.vamanet.com/cgi-bin/HOME. Fee is $35 per month or $300 per year with discounts for multiple localities, regions.**$$$**

Cumberland County ***Recorded Documents Records*** www.courts.state.va.us/courts/circuit/cumberland/home.html County deed and land records available by subscription from private company at http://grm.thomsonreuters.com/. **$$$**
Property, Taxation Records Access to property values data for free at www.cumberlandcountyvalues.com/.

Dickenson County ***Recorded Documents Records*** www.dickensonva.org/index.aspx?nid=112 Access to records free at www.dickensonva.org/index.aspx?NID=289.

Dinwiddie County ***Recorded Documents Records*** www.dinwiddieva.us/index.aspx?nid=153 Online Index/Images from 1833 to present in subscription service. Contact clerk's office for information. Also, access to parcel viewer free at http://dinwiddie.mapsdirect.net/. **$$$**
Property, Taxation Records Access current assessment info and sales by VamaNet subscription at www.vamanet.com/cgi-bin/HOME. Fee is $35 per month or $300 per year with discounts for multiple localities, regions.**$$$**

Essex County ***Recorder Documents Records*** www.essex-virginia.org Subscription service available. Records go back to 2006 only. $50.00 per month, must be paid 6 months at a time. Contact Clerk for more information. **$$$**
Property, Taxation Records Search the treasurer's site free at www.essex-virginia.org/taxes.htm. RE taxes free at https://county.essex-va.org/applications/trapps/REIindex.htm. Also, access assessment info and sales by VamaNet subscription at www.vamanet.com/cgi-bin/HOME. Fee-$35/month or $300/year with discounts for multiple localities.**$$$**

Fairfax County ***Recorded Documents Records*** www.fairfaxcounty.gov/courts/circuit/ A subscriber-based internet service that allows users to access recorded documents found at www.fairfaxcounty.gov/courts/circuit/cpan.htm (known as CPAN). **$$$**
Property, Taxation Records Records on the Dept. of Tax Administration RE Assessment database are free at http://icare.fairfaxcounty.gov/search/commonsearch.aspx?mode=address. Also, the list of auction properties is free at www.fairfaxcounty.gov/dta/auction.htm. Also, search City Assessments for free at http://va-fairfax-assessment.governmax.com/propertymax/rover30.asp but no name searching.

Fauquier County ***Recorded Documents Records*** www.fauquiercounty.gov Real estate data may be available by subscription, $600.00 annual only fee; call Records room at 540-422-8110. **$$$**
Property, Taxation Records Search for property data and deed book info for free on the gis-mapping site at http://65.222.163.24/viewerexternal/. Also, Search Town of Warrenton property index free at http://quicksearch.webgis.net/search.php?site=va_warrenton. Search property data free via the email response form at www.fauquiercounty.gov/government/departments/commrev/index.cfm?action=realestatetaxform.

Floyd County ***Property, Taxation Records*** Access the property assessment search page free at http://egov.efile.com/floyd/Search.asp. Also, access to GIS/mapping free at www.floydcova.org/webgis/.

Fluvanna County ***Property, Taxation Records*** Click on Fluvanna County to search property data for free at www.vamanet.com/cgi-bin/HOME. Access property data free at www.onlinegis.net/VaFluvanna/. Click on Display Map then Search, no name searching.

Franklin County ***Recorded Documents Records*** www.franklincountyva.gov/franklin-county-courts Online subscription service available by contacting Teresa J Brown, Clerk and 540-483-3065. Records available through secure remote assess. **$$$**
Property, Taxation Records Access property data free at http://arcgis.webgis.net/va/Franklin/. Also, search delinquent tax data free at www.franklincountyva.gov/resources/tax-rates-and-delinquents. Also, access current assessment info and sales by VamaNet subscription at www.vamanet.com/cgi-bin/HOME. Fee is $35 per month or $300 per year with discounts for multiple localities, regions.

Frederick County ***Real Estate, Deed, Mortgage, Lien Records*** www.winfredclerk.com Access to the County Records management System is by subscription; base fee is $500 per year for 3 users. Contact Debby Payne in the Circuit Court Clerk's office for info. **$$$**
Property, Taxation Records Access current assessment info and sales by VamaNet subscription at www.vamanet.com/cgi-bin/HOME. Fee is $35 per month or $300 per year with discounts for multiple localities, regions. Also, access parcel data on the GIS-mapping site free at http://gis.co.frederick.va.us/Freeance/Client/PublicAccess1/Index.html?appconfig=GISMap.**$$$**

Giles County ***Recorded Documents, Marriage Records*** www.gilescounty.org/clerk-of-court/index.htm Access land records and deeds on subscription service ILS; call 804-786-5511 to apply; $50 monthly fee. **$$$**

Property, Taxation Records Click on Giles County to search for property records for free at www.vamanet.com/cgi-bin/HOME. Search property info on the county GIS site for free at http://arcgis.webgis.net/va/Giles/.

Gloucester County ***Property, Taxation Records*** Access to Real Estate assessment data for free at www.gloucesterva.info/RealEstateAssessment/tabid/623/Default.aspx Also, access current assessment info and sales by VamaNet subscription at www.vamanet.com/cgi-bin/HOME. Fee is $35 per month or $300 per year with discounts for multiple localities, regions.**$$$**

Goochland County ***Property, Taxation Records*** Click on Goochland County to search property data for free at www.vamanet.com/cgi-bin/HOME. Also, access to GIS/mapping free at www.co.goochland.va.us/Departments/Departments(GZ)/GIS/GISDisclaimer.aspx.

Grayson County ***Recorded Documents Records*** www.graysoncountyva.com/ Online access is available for a monthly fee of $25.00 per month. Contact--Susan M Herrington, Clerk or Debbie Hensley, DC. **$$$**

Property, Taxation Records Access the Real Estate Tax Search page free at http://graysongovernment.com/realestatetax/. Also, access property data free at http://arcgis.webgis.net/va/Grayson/. Also, access current assessment info and sales by VamaNet subscription at www.vamanet.com/cgi-bin/HOME. Fee is $35 per month or $300 per year with discounts for multiple localities, regions.**$$$**

Greene County ***Deeds, Judgment Records*** www.gcva.us/dpts/cort/clerk.htm Can subscribe for a fee of $600.00 per year for internet access to indexes-Deed 1/1/86 to present, Images 9/1/2006 to present, and Judgments 9/1/06 to present. Contact Marie C Durrer, Clerk at 434-985-5208. **$$$**

Property, Taxation Records Access real estate and parcel data free at www.onlinegis.net/VaGreene/. Click on Display Map then Search, no name searching.

Greensville County ***Property, Taxation Records*** Access current assessment info and sales by VamaNet subscription at www.vamanet.com/cgi-bin/HOME. Fee is $35 per month or $300 per year with discounts for multiple localities, regions.**$$$**

Hanover County ***Deed, Judgments, Wills, Financing Statements Records*** www.co.hanover.va.us/circuitct/default.htm Access to Secure Remote Assess records for a fee at http://hanover.landrecordsonline.com/. Must apply for subscription. **$$$**

Property, Taxation Records Access the parcel search function of the GIS site free at www.hanovercountygis.org/hanover/ but no name searching.

Henrico County ***Real Estate, Deed, Judgment Records*** www.co.henrico.va.us/clerk/ County deed and land records available by subscription from private company at www.landsystems.com/. **$$$**

Henry County ***Recorded Documents Records*** www.courts.state.va.us/courts/circuit/henry/home.html Online access available via secure remote access with paid subscription for $50.00 per month or $500.00 per year.. Contact the Clerks office at above phone number. **$$$**

Property, Taxation Records The Henry County and Martinsville GIS site has many searching capabilities at http://gis.co.henry.va.us/.

Highland County ***Recorded Documents Records*** www.courts.state.va.us/courts/circuit/highland/home.html For subscription information contact Lois Ralston, Clerk at 540-468-2447. **$$$**

Isle of Wight County ***Recorded Documents Records*** www.co.isle-of-wight.va.us/ Access to recorder land records is by subscription; fee is $50.00 per month; online deed records go back to 1914, judgments to 1991. Contact Wanda Wills at 757-365-6233 for registration and info. **$$$**

Property, Taxation Records Access property data via the GIS-mapping site free at http://isleofwight.interactivegis.com/. Must register to use. There is a guest sign-in with limited use. Also, access current assessment info and sales by VamaNet subscription at www.vamanet.com/cgi-bin/HOME. Fee is $35 per month or $300 per year with discounts for multiple localities, regions.**$$$**

James City County ***Recorded Documents Records*** www.jamescitycountyva.gov/courts/index.html Access to records for a fee contact Gretchen Bifillipo at 757-564-2242 for forms to fill out. **$$$**

Property, Taxation Records Access assessment data free at http://property.jccegov.com/parcelviewer/. Search City of Williamsburg property assessor data free at http://williamsburg.sc.wthgis.com/. At map, click on find to search.

King and Queen County ***Land Records Records*** www.kingandqueenco.net/html/Govt/circct.html Secure remote access to land records available by subscription. Contact Deborah F Longest, Clerk for details. **$$$**

King George County ***Recorded Documents Records*** www.king-george.va.us/county-offices/circuit-court/circuit-court.php Subscription available-contact Jessica Jackson, Deputy Clerk at 540-775-3322. **$$$**

Property, Taxation Records Access property data free at www.onlinegis.net/VaKingGeorge/asp/controlVersion.asp. Also, access current assessment info and sales by VamaNet subscription at www.vamanet.com/cgi-bin/HOME. Fee is $35 per month or $300 per year with discounts for multiple localities, regions.**$$$**

King William County ***Property, Taxation Records*** Access to property cards for free at https://e-services.kingwilliamcounty.us/applications/txapps/index.htm.

Lancaster County ***Property, Taxation Records*** Click on Lancaster County to search property data for free at www.vamanet.com/cgi-bin/HOME. Also, access parcel data free on the GIS-mapping site free at www.lancova.com/GIS/disclaimer.asp.

Lee County ***Real Estate, Deed, Lien, Judgment, Will, Marriage, UCC Records*** Access to the recorder's database is available by subscription, registration and password required; $50 per month or $500 per year. Contact clerk's office for registration form. Deeds go back to 11/20/40, judgments and wills from 3/3/1794 to present, marriages from 1/5/1933 to present, financing statements to 1/1995. **$$$**

Loudoun County ***Real Estate, Deed, Will, Estate, Judgment, Plat, UCC Records*** www.loudoun.gov/index.aspx?NID=98 Access to recorders land records of deeds, wills, judgment, plats and UCCs is available by subscription, see Land Records at www.loudoun.gov.clerk. Fee is $300 per year per user; deeds go back to 1893, wills 1928 judgments 1985, UCCs 1996. Also, access to online index archives free at www.loudoun.gov/Default.aspx?tabid=2010. **$$$**

Property, Taxation Records Search the property assessor data for free at http://reparcelasmt.loudoun.gov/Search/Disclaimer.aspx?FromUrl=../search/commonsearch.aspx?mode=address. No name searching; search by address, number, or ID only. Access property data on the GIS-mapping site free at http://logis.loudoun.gov/weblogis/ but no name searching.

Louisa County ***Records Records*** www.louisacounty.com/LCconst/courts.htm Online access is available for a fee of $600 per year. Contact the Clerk for more information. **$$$**

Property, Taxation Records Search property and person property tax data for free at https://louweb.louisa.org/Applications/web/default.htm. Also, search property on the GIS-mapping site free at http://louisagis.timmons.com/. Click on Search. Also, access data free at www.vamanet.com/cgi-bin/HOME.

Madison County ***Recorded Documents Records*** Contact for Remote Access Service-Liz Smith at 540-948-6888. **$$$**

Property, Taxation Records Access data free at www.vamanet.com/cgi-bin/HOME.

Mathews County ***Property, Taxation Records*** Access to land records for free at www.emapsplus.com/vamathews/maps/.

Mecklenburg County ***Property, Taxation Records*** Access to land files for free at www.mecklenburgva.com/govt/LB_DL.html.

Middlesex County ***Property, Taxation Records*** Access current assessment info and sales by VamaNet subscription at www.vamanet.com/cgi-bin/HOME. Fee is $35 per month or $300 per year with discounts for multiple localities, regions. Also, access to property record card search free at https://websrv-vmw.dmz.co.middlesex.va.us/applications/TXApps/PropCardsIndex.htm.**$$$**

Montgomery County ***Real Estate, Deed Records*** www.montgomerycountyva.gov/content/1144/100/197/default.aspx Land record access via subscription service Manatron Inc; call 804-786-5511 to apply. **$$$**

Property, Taxation Records Search county property index free at http://quicksearch.webgis.net/search.php?site=va_montgomery. Also, access to the county Parcel Search Gateway database is free at www.montgomerycountyva.gov/content/1146/98/123/2476.aspx. Records on the Town of Blacksburg GIS site are free at http://arcgis.webgis.net/va/blacksburg/. Also, access to Real Estate Assessment Card Search free at http://parcelsearch.montva.com/.

Nelson County ***Property, Taxation Records*** Access to GIS/mapping for free at www.nelsoncountygis.org/.

New Kent County ***Property, Taxation Records*** Access to New Kent county assessor records is free at http://data.visionappraisal.com/NewKentCountyVA/DEFAULT.asp. Register free for full data.

Northampton County ***Real Estate, Deeds Records*** www.co.northampton.va.us/gov/clerkofcourt.html Access to land records for a fee at www.courts.state.va.us/rmsweb/. **$$$**

Northumberland County ***Land Records Records*** www.co.northumberland.va.us/ Access to land title records for a fee at https://lto.landsystems.com/LTOonline/NewUser.aspx to register. Must register before using. **$$$**

Property, Taxation Records Access Land Book data free at www.co.northumberland.va.us/NH-land-book.htm.

Orange County ***Property, Taxation Records*** Access property data free at www.onlinegis.net/VaOrange/. Click on Display Map then Search, no name searching. Also, access current assessment info and sales by VamaNet subscription at www.vamanet.com/cgi-bin/HOME. Fee is $35 per month or $300 per year with discounts for multiple localities, regions.**$$$**

Page County ***Recorded Documents Records*** www.pagecounty.virginia.gov/index.php?option=content&task=view&id=247 Access to records for a fee at http://grm.thomsonreuters.com/. **$$$**

Property, Taxation Records Access current assessment info and sales by VamaNet subscription at www.vamanet.com/cgi-bin/HOME. Fee is $35 per month or $300 per year with discounts for multiple localities, regions.**$$$**

Patrick County ***Property, Taxation Records*** Access property data free at www.patrick.interactivegis.com/. Must register.

Pittsylvania County ***Property, Taxation Records*** Search parcel information free at www.pittgov.org/GIS_Disclaimer.htm.

Powhatan County ***Real Estate, Grantor/Grantee, Deed, Mortgage, Lien, Judgment, Marriage, Will Records*** www.powhatanva.gov/ Access recorder's index by subscription service ILS; call 877-658-6018 x2111 to apply. **$$$**

Property, Taxation Records Access current assessment info and sales by VamaNet subscription at www.vamanet.com/cgi-bin/HOME. Fee is $35 per month or $300 per year with discounts for multiple localities, regions. Also, search assessment and reassessment data free at www.powhatancountyrealestate.com/.**$$$**

Prince William County ***Recorded Documents, Marriage Records*** www.pwcgov.org/government/courts/circuit/Pages/default.aspx
Access to the clerk's exhaustive database is available by subscription; fee is $300 per quarter. Login in https://www3.pwcgov.org/panet/logon.asp. Most records go back to mid-1980's; deeds back to 1918. **$$$**

Property, Taxation Records Records on the county Property Assessment Information database are free at www04a.pwcgov.org/realestate/LandRover.asp but no name searching. Also, City of Manassas Park Commissioner of the Revenue's real estate assessment data is at http://data.visionappraisal.com/ManassasVA/DEFAULT.asp.

Pulaski County ***Recorded documents Records*** www.courts.state.va.us/courts/circuit/Pulaski/home.html The county participates in a subscription service offered at https://risweb.courts.state.va.us/. The Clerk prefers that all interested parties contact the office for an account name and password. **$$$**

Property, Taxation Records Access to the county GIS mapping info for a fee at www.netgis.pulaskicountyva.gov/pulaski/. Annual fee of $250.00 to access the netGIS information containing parcel owner names and addresses.**$$$**

Rappahannock County ***Recorded Documents Records*** Record access is by subscription through Clerk's Office. Fee-$600.00 per year. **$$$**

Property, Taxation Records Access current assessment info and sales by VamaNet subscription at www.vamanet.com/cgi-bin/HOME. Fee is $35 per month or $300 per year with discounts for multiple localities, regions.**$$$**

Richmond County ***Real Estate, Deed, Lien Records*** www.co.richmond.va.us Access recorders land data by subscription at https://lto.landsystems.com/LTOonline/logon.aspx?ReturnUrl=%2fLTOonline%2fdefault.aspx. Individual account- $50.00 per month; 5-user business account- $200 per month. **$$$**

Property, Taxation Records Search county parcel data on the GIS-mapping site free at www.onlinegis.net/VaRichmond/.

Roanoke County ***Real Estate, Deeds, Judgment, Marriage Records*** www.roanokecountyva.gov/index.aspx?nid=26 Access to Records Management System for a fee at www.courts.state.va.us/rmsweb/. Contact clerk's office for signup information. **$$$**

Property, Taxation Records Access to property data is free on the county GIS mapping site at http://imsweb.roanokecountyva.gov/GIS/Roanoke2/.

Rockbridge County ***Recorded Documents Records*** www.courts.state.va.us/courts/circuit/Rockbridge/home.html Access by paid subscription only. $50.00 per month subscription fee payable 6 months in advance. Contact Clerk for more information. **$$$**

Property, Taxation Records Access county records on the GIS-mapping site free at http://quicksearch.webgis.net/search.php?site=va_rockbridge. Also, access City of Lexington property data free at www.vamanet.com/cgi-bin/MAPSRCHPGM?LOCAL=LEX. Also, access county current assessment info and sales by VamaNet subscription at www.vamanet.com/cgi-bin/HOME. Fee is $35 per month or $300 per year with discounts for multiple localities, regions.**$$$**

Rockingham County ***Recorded Documents Records*** www.rockinghamcountyva.gov/index.aspx?nid=173 Access to real property by subscription at https://www.uslandrecords.com/uslr/UslrApp/index.jsp. **$$$**

Property, Taxation Records Access to real estate assessment records at http://rockingham.gisbrowser.com/home.cfm.

Russell County ***Real Estate, Deed Records*** County deed and land records available by subscription from private company at www.landsystems.com/. **$$$**

Property, Taxation Records Access current assessment info and sales by VamaNet subscription at www.vamanet.com/cgi-bin/HOME. Fee is $35 per month or $300 per year with discounts for multiple localities, regions.**$$$**

Scott County ***Lien, Judgment, UCC, Marriage, Fictitious Name Records*** www.courts.state.va.us/courts/circuit/scott/home.html
Access recorder's data by subscription; signup at clerk's office. **$$$**

Property, Taxation Records Access current assessment info and sales by VamaNet subscription at www.vamanet.com/cgi-bin/HOME. Fee is $35 per month or $300 per year with discounts for multiple localities, regions. Find property records at www.loopnet.com/sitemap/property-records/Virginia/Scott-County/.**$$$**

Shenandoah County ***Real Estate, Grantor/Grantor, Deed, Judgment, UCC, Marriage, Will Records***
www.courts.state.va.us/courts/circuit/shenandoah/home.html Recorded data available by subscription with images back to 1999 and earlier being added. Fee is $50.00 per month or $500.00 per year, contact Sarona Irvin 540-459-6153 in clerk's office. **$$$**

Property, Taxation Records Access current assessment info and sales by VamaNet subscription at www.vamanet.com/cgi-bin/HOME. Fee is $35 per month or $300 per year with discounts for multiple localities, regions. Also, access tax payment histories free at https://204.111.80.202/applications/trapps/index.htm. Also, access parcel data on the GIS-mapping site free at www.shenandoahgis.org/ and click on Find to name search.**$$$**

Smyth County ***Recorded Documents Records*** www.courts.state.va.us/courts/circuit/smyth/home.html For subscription service contact Shirley Blevins. **$$$**

Property, Taxation Records Access current assessment info and sales by VamaNet subscription at www.vamanet.com/cgi-bin/HOME. Fee is $35 per month or $300 per year with discounts for multiple localities, regions. Also, search county property index free at http://quicksearch.webgis.net/search.php?site=va_smyth.**$$$**

Southampton County ***Recorded Records Records*** www.southamptoncounty.org/Clerk-of-the-Court.aspx For subscription service contact person is Richard Francis, Clerk or Heather Simmons, DC **$$$**

Property, Taxation Records Click on Southampton County to search property data for free at www.vamanet.com/cgi-bin/HOME. Also, county GIS tax map data is free at www.onlinegis.net/VaSouthampton/asp/controlVersion.asp.

Spotsylvania County ***Real Estate, Deed, Lien Records*** www.spotsylvania.va.us/content/2614/147/2740/161/default.aspx Access the recorder's recording index and images by subscription; fee is $150.00 per quarter; contact Land Recording Desk at 540-507-7615 at the clerk's office. Also, online http://en.landsystems.com/index.php. **$$$**

Property, Taxation Records Access to property assessment found at www.spotsylvania.va.us/content/2614/147/2740/165/151/1915.aspx, GIS/mapping for free at www.spotsylvania.va.us/content/2614/147/2740/165/151/default.aspx.

Stafford County ***Recorder Documents Records*** http://co.stafford.va.us/index.aspx?NID=760 Access to remote access site for a fee at www.staffordcocc.org/. Must have username and password. Contact Clerk's office for information. **$$$**

Property, Taxation Records Personal Property and RE Lookup free at http://taxpaid.stafford.va.us/. Access property data free at http://staffordvapropertymax.governmaxa.com/propertymax/rover30.asp but no name searching.

Surry County ***Land Records, Deed, Judgment, Liens Records*** www.surryvacocc.org/Opening.asp Access to Circuit Court Records Search System is by subscription at www.surryvacocc.org/Opening.asp. $600.00 per year payable $50 per month, username and password required. **$$$**

Property, Taxation Records Access to GIS/mapping for free at http://surry.mapsdirect.net/.

Sussex County ***Property, Taxation Records*** Access to assessor property records is free at www.sussexcountyproperty.com/.

Tazewell County ***Real Estate Records*** www.tazewellcounty.org/CCClerk.html Access to online records by subscription contact--Tammy Allison, Chief Deputy Clerk at 276-988-1221. **$$$**

Property, Taxation Records Click on Tazewell County to search property data for free at www.vamanet.com/cgi-bin/HOME.

Warren County Circuit Court ***Real Estate, Deed, Land, Lien, Will, UCC Records*** www.warrencountyva.net/index.php?option=com_workforce&view=department&id=3&Itemid=70 Access the Clerk's data on the web for a fee; username and password required. For a fee username and password contact Jennifer Sims at 540-635-2435 or at jsims@courts.state.va.us. Images go back to 1994. **$$$**

Property, Taxation Records Access current assessment info and sales by VamaNet subscription at www.vamanet.com/cgi-bin/HOME. Fee is $35 per month or $300 per year with discounts for multiple localities, regions.**$$$**

Washington County ***Property, Taxation Records*** Access current assessment info and sales by VamaNet subscription at www.vamanet.com/cgi-bin/HOME. Fee is $35 per month or $300 per year with discounts for multiple localities, regions.**$$$**

Westmoreland County ***Recorded Documents Records*** www.westmoreland-county.org/index.php?p=govt&c=countyCourts Access to subscription records for a fee of $600.00 per year available. Contact G J Chatham at 804-493-0108. Must come to the office to receive a password. **$$$**

Property, Taxation Records Access real estate tax payment database free at https://eservices.westmoreland-county.org/applications/trapps/REIindex.htm. Also, search property card records free at https://eservices.westmoreland-county.org/applications/txapps/index.htm. Also, search utility payment records free at https://eservices.westmoreland-county.org/applications/trapps/UTIindex.htm.

Wise County ***Recorded Documents Records*** www.courtbar.org Access recording office records at see https://egov.mixnet.com/courts/ccwise2000/login.asp. For full access fee is $600 annually. This fee service includes index and images, court orders, land documents from 1970 and links to RE tax assessments, 50-year RE, tax maps, plat maps, delinquent taxes, permit images, probate, marriage, judgment liens for 20 years, and more. UCC-1 indices for past 5 years. Online records include City of Norton. **$$$**

Property, Taxation Records Property data is at www.wise-assessor.org/assessor/web/. Must register to login. Also, search county parcel data free at http://quicksearch.webgis.net/search.php?site=va_wise.**$$$**

Wythe County ***Real Estate, Deed, Mortgage, Will, UCC, Marriage, Gen Misc., Judgment Records*** www.wytheco.org/index.php/departments/clerk-of-circuit-court.html Access to recording index and judgments records is by subscription; $25.00 registration fee for username and password, also $25.00 per transaction fee. Contact the clerk office for signup. **$$$**

Property, Taxation Records Access current assessment info and sales by VamaNet subscription at www.vamanet.com/cgi-bin/HOME. Fee is $35 per month or $300 per year with discounts for multiple localities, regions. Also, search the GIS site free at http://wythe.interactivegis.com/wythe/index.php but no name searching.**$$$**

York County ***Recorded Documents Records*** www.yorkcounty.gov/Default.aspx?alias=www.yorkcounty.gov/circuitcourt Subscription information found at www.yorkcounty.gov/Default.aspx?tabid=2616. Must apply and sign subscriber agreement. **$$$**

Property, Taxation Records Records from the County Property Search site are free at http://maps.yorkcounty.gov/PropertyInfo/default.aspx.

Virginia Cities - Administered As Counties

Alexandria City ***Recorded Deeds Records*** http://alexandriava.gov/clerkofcourt/ Land Records (Deeds) with images, since Jan. 2, 1970 is available for $500 per year or $50 per month. See https://secure.alexandriava.gov/ajis/index.php. **$$$**

Property, Taxation Records Access to city real estate assessments is free at http://realestate.alexandriava.gov/ but no name searching. Search property free at the GIS-mapping site at http://gis.alexandriava.gov/parcelviewernet/viewer.htm but no name searching.

Bristol City ***Recorded Records Records*** www.courts.state.va.us/courts/circuit/Bristol/home.html For remote access, contact Terry G Rohr, Clerk at 276-645-7328. Images back to 2000 only. **$$$**

Property, Taxation Records Access data free at www.vamanet.com/cgi-bin/HOME.

Buena Vista City ***Real Estate, Deed, Judgment Records*** Access to subscription database for a fee contact Clerk at above number. **$$$**

Property, Taxation Records Access current assessment info and sales by VamaNet subscription at www.vamanet.com/cgi-bin/HOME. Fee is $35 per month or $300 per year with discounts for multiple localities, regions.**$$$**

Charlottesville City ***Property, Taxation Records*** Access to GIS/mapping free at http://gisweb.charlottesville.org/GISViewer/Account/Logon.

Chesapeake City ***Recorded Documents Records*** www.cityofchesapeake.net/Government/City-Departments/Courts-and-Judicial-Offices/circuit-court-clerk.htm? Access to records for a fee at www.chesapeakeccland.org/. **$$$**

Property, Taxation Records Access to property data for free at www.cityofchesapeake.net/Government/City-Departments/Departments/Real-Estate-Assessor/app.htm.

Colonial Heights City ***Recorded Documents Records*** www.colonialheightsva.gov/index.aspx?nid=86 Access to a subscription service for records contact Nancy Wood at 520-9364. **$$$**

Property, Taxation Records Access real estate property and assessor records free atwww.crsdata.com/classic/ps/propertysearch.asp.

Danville City ***Recorded Documents Records*** www.danville-va.gov/index.aspx?nid=496 Access to internet excess to records management contact-Clerk's office. Fee is $150.00 quarterly and an application is required. **$$$**

Property, Taxation Records Access to Danville City assessor online records is free at http://gis.danville-va.gov/GISPortal/. Also, access to GIS/mapping free at www.discoverdanvillesites.com/.

Falls Church City ***Property, Taxation Records*** Access city property data free on the GIS-mapping site at http://property.fallschurchva.gov/ParcelViewer/ but no name searching.

Fredericksburg City ***Recorded Documents Records*** www.fredericksburgva.gov/Departments/CircuitCourt/index.aspx?id=66 Access to Circuit Court Records Search System is by subscription at http://208.210.219.102/cgi-bin/p/rms.cgi. Includes images for other selected jurisdictions; username and password required, signup with local Circuit Ct Clerk. **$$$**

Property, Taxation Records Access current assessment info and sales by VamaNet subscription at www.vamanet.com/cgi-bin/HOME. Contact for fees. Also, access to GIS/mapping free at http://gis.fredericksburgva.gov/parcelViewer/.**$$$**

Hampton City ***Recorded Documents Records*** www.hampton.gov/va_courts.html Access to recorded documents is via the state subscription system. This system includes real estate, judgments, financing statements, etc. Application must be filed and approved by the Clerk of Court - fee is $50.00 per month prorated to 10/1 or $600.00 per year; for registration and info call 757-727-6297. Also, search for limited judgment case records on the state court website at www.courts.state.va.us/caseinfo/home.html. **$$$**

Property, Taxation Records Access City Real Estate Information free at http://webgis.hampton.gov/sites/ParcelViewer/Account/Logon. Search property transfer pdf lists free at www.hampton.gov/index.aspx?NID=2148.

Hopewell City ***Recorded Documents Records*** www.hopewellva.gov/data/publish/court_services.shtml A subscription service is available to in-state users only. The fee is $600 per year per a signed contractual agreement. Contact the Clerk's Office for details. **$$$**

Lynchburg City ***Property, Taxation Records*** Access to parcel searches free at http://mapviewer.lynchburgva.gov/parcelviewer/default.aspx

Martinsville City ***Real Estate, Deed, Judgment, Will, Marriage, Delinquent Tax Records*** www.martinsville-va.gov/Circuit-Court-Clerk.html Access to Circuit clerk records is at www.ci.martinsville.va.us/Circuitclerk/subscription_page.htm. Fee is $50.00 per month, or you may search at a rate of $1 per doc. For info, call office of Ashby Pritchett at 276-403-5106 or visit website. **$$$**

Property, Taxation Records Access to GIS/mapping for free at http://gis.co.henry.va.us/.

Newport News City ***Real Estate Recordings Records*** www.courts.state.va.us/courts/circuit/Newport_News/home.html Visit www.courts.state.va.us/rmsweb/ for remote access to land records including both indices and images. This is a subscription based service that runs $500 per year. **$$$**

Property, Taxation Records Access to the City's \"Real Estate on the Web\" database is free at www.nngov.com/assessor/resources/reis. Search by address or parcel number; new \"advanced search\" may include name searching. Search for property data free on the gis-mapping site at http://gis.nngov.com/gis/(S(gahbjl4524delfimgq3ftl55))/Default.aspx. No name searching.

Norfolk City ***Real Estate, Deed, Judgment, Lien, Will, Marriage Records*** http://icourt.info/ Access to Circuit Court Records Search System is by subscription at http://208.210.219.102/cgi-bin/p/rms.cgi. Includes images for other selected jurisdictions; $1200 per year, username and password required, signup with local Circuit Ct Clerk. **$$$**

Property, Taxation Records The City of Norfolk Real Estate Property Assessment database data is free at http://norfolkair.norfolk.gov/norfolkair/.

Norton City ***Property, Taxation Records*** Access current assessment info and sales by VamaNet subscription at www.vamanet.com/cgi-bin/HOME. Fee is $35 per month or $300 per year with discounts for multiple localities, regions.**$$$**

Petersburg City ***Property, Taxation Records*** Access to real estate records for free at www.petersburg-va.org/assessor/index.asp.

Portsmouth City ***Real Estate Records*** www.portsmouthva.gov Subscription service at $600.00 per year. Contact Cynthia Morrison at 757-393-8160. **$$$**

Property, Taxation Records Access to property records is free at www.portsmouthva.gov/assessor/data/. No name searching. Access the treasurer's Real Estate Receivable Data free at www.portsmouthva.gov/treasurer/data/, but no name searching. Also, search GIS-mapping site for parcel data free at www.portsmouthva.gov/website/portsweb2_in.aspx. Use map tools to identify parcel data.

Radford City ***Property, Taxation Records*** Access City property card info for a fee at http://208.88.162.36/inVizeDA/login.aspx?ReturnUrl=%2finVizeDA%2finVizeDA.aspx.**$$$**

Richmond City ***Property, Taxation Records*** Search the city's Property & Real Estate Assessment data for free at http://eservices.ci.richmond.va.us/applications/propertysearch/. City's Property & Real Estate Assessment data for free at http://map.richmondgov.com/parcel/.

Roanoke City ***Deeds, Marriage, Judgment Records*** www.roanokeva.gov/WebMgmt/ywbase61b.nsf/CurrentBaseLink/N254MHW7086JCRTEN Access to certain land records available by subscription only. Contact Clerk of Circuit court. Minimum subscription of 1 year at $50 per month ($600) required. **$$$**

Property, Taxation Records Access to property data is free on the City GIS website at http://gis.roanokeva.gov/text.htm.

Staunton City ***Property, Taxation Records*** Access property tax data on the City GIS site free at http://gis1.ci.staunton.va.us:8086/freeance/client/publicaccess1/index.html?appconfig=masterpublicaccess.

Suffolk City ***Recorded Documents Records*** www.suffolkva.us/citygovt/co/clerk-of-the-circuit-court Access to land record indexes for free to go https://suffolk.amcad.com/. Get indexes for free, images you must register and pay a fee. **$$$**

Property, Taxation Records Access property assessment data free at www.suffolkva.us/realest/Search_Real_Estate_3.html, but no name searching.

Virginia Beach City ***Recorded Documents, Marriage Records*** www.vbgov.com/government/departments/courts/circuit-court-clerks-office/Pages/default.aspx Access the Clerk of Circuit Court database free at www.vblandrecords.com/index.aspx. The second method of access will be via a $50 per month Monthly Subscription using credit card. For credit card account, call 866-793-6505. Direct general questions to Emilie Inman at 757-385-4462. Also, browse document archives free at http://edocs.vbgov.com/weblink/Browse.aspx. **$$$**

Property, Taxation Records Search the assessor database for free at http://va-virginiabeach-realestate.governmax.com/ but no name searching.

Waynesboro City ***Real Estate Records*** To access paid subscription, contact Clerk of Court for inquires to remote access to land records. **$$$**

Property, Taxation Records Access current assessment info and sales by VamaNet subscription at www.vamanet.com/cgi-bin/HOME. Fee is $35 per month or $300 per year with discounts for multiple localities, regions.**$$$**

Winchester City ***Real Estate, Deed, Mortgage, Lien Records*** www.winfredclerk.com Access to the County Records management System is by subscription; base fee is $500 per year for 3 users. Contact Debby Payne in the Winchester County Circuit Court Clerk's office for info. **$$$**

Property, Taxation Records Access current assessment info and sales by VamaNet subscription at www.vamanet.com/cgi-bin/HOME. Fee is $35 per month or $300 per year with discounts for multiple localities, regions. Also, access surrounding Frederick County parcel data on the GIS-mapping site free at http://gis.co.frederick.va.us/ and click on Parcel Mapping Service.**$$$**

Reminder:

Virginia Cities are listed as separate section, after the Counties.

Washington

Capital: Olympia
Thurston County
Time Zone: PST
Population: 6,897,012
# of Counties: 39

Useful State Links

Website: http://access.wa.gov
Governor: www.governor.wa.gov
Attorney General: www.atg.wa.gov
State Archives: www.sos.wa.gov/archives/Default.aspx
State Statutes and Codes: www.leg.wa.gov/LawsAndAgencyRules/Pages/default.aspx
Legislative Bill Search: http://apps.leg.wa.gov/billinfo/
Bill Monitoring: www.leg.wa.gov/pages/home.aspx
Unclaimed Funds: http://ucp.dor.wa.gov/

State Public Record Agencies

Criminal Records

Washington State Patrol, Identification and Criminal History Section, www.wsp.wa.gov/crime/crimhist.htm WSP offers access through a system called WATCH, which can be accessed from their website. The fee per name search is $10.00. The exact DOB and exact spelling of the name are required. Credit cards are accepted online. Add $10.00 for notarize seal (fax requests accepted for these). To set up a WATCH account, call 360-534-2000 or email watch.help@wsp.wa.gov. Non-profits can request a fee-exempt account. WATCH stands for Washington Access To Criminal History. **$$$** *Other Options:* See the State Court Administrator's office for information about their criminal records database (JIS-Link).

Sexual Offender Registry

Washington State Patrol, SOR, www.wsp.wa.gov/ In cooperation with the Washington Assoc. of Sheriffs and Police Chiefs, free online access to Level II and Level III sexual offenders is available at www.icrimewatch.net/washington.php. *Other Options:* The website provides a printable list of all offenders, but page by page.

Incarceration Records

Washington Department of Corrections, Public Disclosure Unirt, www.doc.wa.gov "Find an Offender" is free at www.doc.wa.gov/offenderinfo/default.aspx. Search by name or DOC number. *Other Options:* Data is available by subscription for bulk users; for information, contact the Contracts Office at 360-725-8363.

Corporation, Trademarks/Servicemarks, LP, LLC Records

Secretary of State, Corporations Division, www.sos.wa.gov/corps/Default.aspx Free searching of corporation registrations is at www.sos.wa.gov/corps/corps_search.aspx. Information is updated daily. Also, search securities companies registered with the state and other financial institutions free at http://dfi.wa.gov/about/records-index-licensing-registration.htm. *Other Options:* Bulk purchase is offered with prices starting at $75.00.

Trade Names

Master License Service, Department of Licensing, www.dol.wa.gov The web page give the ability to check trade name ability, assuming the business name listed is the trade name. *Other Options:* Records can be purchased on cartridges or 9 track tapes. Information includes date of registration, owner name, state ID numbers, and cancel date if cancelled. Call same number and ask for Jody Miller.

Uniform Commercial Code, Federal Tax Liens

Department of Licensing, UCC Records, www.dol.wa.gov/business/UCC/ For online access, go to https://fortress.wa.gov/dol/ucc. There is no search fee for name search or by file number. Fee is $15.00 if copies are mailed. **$$$** *Other Options:* The database may be purchased via FTP.

Sales Tax Registrations

Department of Revenue, Taxpayer Services, http://dor.wa.gov/Content/Home/Default.aspx The agency provides a state business records database with free access on the Internet at http://dor.wa.gov/content/doingbusiness/registermybusiness/brd/. Look-ups are by owner names, DBAs, tax reporting numbers, and reseller permit numbers. Results show a myriad of data.

Vital Records

Department of Health, Center for Health Statistics, www.doh.wa.gov/LicensesPermitsandCertificates/BirthDeathMarriageandDivorce.aspx Records may requested from www.Vitalchek.com, a state-endorsed vendor. **$$$** *Other Options:* The Digital Archives, launched in 2004, contains various periods for marriages, death, birth, military, naturalization, institution, and various historical records at www.digitalarchives.wa.gov/default.aspx.

Workers' Compensation Records

Labor and Industries, Public Records Unit, www.lni.wa.gov/ClaimsIns/default.asp Claim information is accessible to authorized users at www.lni.wa.gov/orli/logon.asp. Claims inactive for 18+ months or crime victims claims are not in the Claim & Account Center. *Other Options:* Many claim files are available on CD. Records may not be available include file records received before June 16, 1994. For more info call 360-902-5556.

Driver Records

Department of Licensing, Driver Record Section, www.dol.wa.gov FTP retrieval is offered for high volume requesters, minimum of 2,000 requests per month. Requesters must be approved and sign a contract. Call Data Sales Management at 360-902-3851. Contract holders may also participate in a notification program (monitoring and notification of activity on a record), but strictly used for only insurance company needs. There is a secondary online check for status of a driver license, permit or ID card free at https://fortress.wa.gov/dol/dolprod/dsdDriverStatusDisplay/. Online access is available for drivers to obtain their own driving records at https://fortress.wa.gov/dol/dolprod/dsdiadr/. Use of a credit card is required. Record is shown as PDF. **$$$**

Vehicle, Vessel Ownership & Registration

Department of Licensing, Public Disclosure Unit, www.dol.wa.gov/vehicleregistration/ This Internet Vehicle/Vessel Information Processing System is a commercial subscription service and all accounts must be pre-approved. A $25.00 deposit is required and there is a fee per hit. **$$$** *Other Options:* Large bulk lists cannot be released for any commercial purposes. Lists are released to non-profit entities and for statistical purposes.

Accident Reports

State Patrol, Collision Records Section, www.wsp.wa.gov/publications/collision.htm Purchase a collision report online at https://fortress.wa.gov/wsp/wrecr/WSPCRS/Search.aspx. **$$$**

Campaign Finance

Public Disclosure Commission, 711 Capitol WAY #206, www.sos.wa.gov/elections/Default.aspx All searches can be made at www.pdc.wa.gov/MvcQuerySystem. This includes campaign finance, lobbyists, and PACs. Email questions to pdc@pdc.wa.gov.

Occupational Licensing Boards

Accountant Firm .... www.cpaboard.wa.gov/LicenseeSearchApp/default.aspx?querytype=Firm
Accountant-CPA .... www.cpaboard.wa.gov/LicenseeSearchApp/default.aspx
Acupuncturist .... https://fortress.wa.gov/doh/providercredentialsearch/
Adult Family Home .... https://fortress.wa.gov/dshs/adsaapps/lookup/AFHPubLookup.aspx
Animal Technician .... https://fortress.wa.gov/doh/providercredentialsearch/
Announcer, Athletic Event/Ring .... https://fortress.wa.gov/dol/dolprod/bpdLicenseQuery/
Applicator, Pesticide, Private/Commercial ... http://agr.wa.gov/pestfert/LicensingEd/Search/default.aspx
Architect/Architectural Corp .... https://fortress.wa.gov/dol/dolprod/bpdLicenseQuery/
Athl' Judge/Timekeeper/Physician .... https://fortress.wa.gov/dol/dolprod/bpdLicenseQuery/
Athlete, Professional/Inspector .... https://fortress.wa.gov/dol/dolprod/bpdLicenseQuery/
Athletic Mgr/Promot'r/Matchmaker .... https://fortress.wa.gov/dol/dolprod/bpdLicenseQuery/
Attorney .... www.mywsba.org/Default.aspx?tabid=177
Audiologist .... https://fortress.wa.gov/doh/providercredentialsearch/
Bail Bond Agent/Agency .... https://fortress.wa.gov/dol/dolprod/bpdLicenseQuery/
Bail Bond Recovery Agent .... https://fortress.wa.gov/dol/dolprod/bpdLicenseQuery/
Bank .... www.dfi.wa.gov/banks/commercial_banks.htm

Barber	https://fortress.wa.gov/dol/dolprod/bpdLicenseQuery/
Barber Instructor/School/Shop/Mobile	https://fortress.wa.gov/dol/dolprod/bpdLicenseQuery/
Boarding Home	https://fortress.wa.gov/dshs/adsaapps/lookup/BHPubLookup.aspx
Boiler Inspector	www.lni.wa.gov/TradesLicensing/Boilers/Inspectors/default.asp
Boxer	https://fortress.wa.gov/dol/dolprod/bpdLicenseQuery/
Bulk Hauler	www.dol.wa.gov/listoflicenses.html
Business Opportunity Offering	https://fortress.wa.gov/dfi/licenselu/dfi/licenseLU/LicenseLLU.aspx
Cemetery	https://fortress.wa.gov/dol/dolprod/bpdLicenseQuery/
Cemetery Certificate of Authority	https://fortress.wa.gov/dol/dolprod/bpdLicenseQuery/
Cemetery Prearrangem't Seller	https://fortress.wa.gov/dol/dolprod/bpdLicenseQuery/
Certificate of Removal Registr'n	https://fortress.wa.gov/dol/dolprod/bpdLicenseQuery/
Charitable Gift Annuity	www.insurance.wa.gov/consumertoolkit/search.aspx
Check Casher/Seller	https://fortress.wa.gov/dfi/licenselu/dfi/licenseLU/LicenseLLU.aspx
Child Care Provider/Facility	www.childcarenet.org/families/your-search
Chiropractor	https://fortress.wa.gov/doh/providercredentialsearch/
Cigarette Retailer/Vender/Whlse	www.dol.wa.gov/listoflicenses.html
Collection Agency	www.dol.wa.gov/listoflicenses.html
Consumer Loan Company	https://fortress.wa.gov/dfi/licenselu/dfi/licenseLU/LicenseLLU.aspx
Contractor, Construction	https://fortress.wa.gov/lni/bbip/
Contractor, General, Company	https://fortress.wa.gov/lni/bbip/
Contractor, General, Individual	www.dol.wa.gov/listoflicenses.html
Contributor, Political	http://web.pdc.wa.gov/MvcQuerySystem
Cosmetologist	https://fortress.wa.gov/dol/dolprod/bpdLicenseQuery/
Cosmetology Instructor/School/Shop	https://fortress.wa.gov/dol/dolprod/bpdLicenseQuery/
Counselor	https://fortress.wa.gov/doh/providercredentialsearch/
Cremated Remains Dispositor	https://fortress.wa.gov/dol/dolprod/bpdLicenseQuery/
Crematory	https://fortress.wa.gov/dol/dolprod/bpdLicenseQuery/
Currency Exchange	https://fortress.wa.gov/dfi/licenselu/dfi/licenseLU/LicenseLLU.aspx
Dental Hygienist	https://fortress.wa.gov/doh/providercredentialsearch/
Dentist	https://fortress.wa.gov/doh/providercredentialsearch/
Dietitian	https://fortress.wa.gov/doh/providercredentialsearch/
Domestic Insurance Carrier	www.insurance.wa.gov/consumertoolkit/search.aspx
Egg Handler/Dealer	www.dol.wa.gov/listoflicenses.html
Electrical Contractor/Administrator	https://fortress.wa.gov/lni/bbip/
Electrician	https://fortress.wa.gov/lni/bbip/
Elevator Contractor/Mechanic	https://fortress.wa.gov/lni/bbip/
Embalmer/Intern	https://fortress.wa.gov/dol/dolprod/bpdLicenseQuery/
Emergency Medical Technician	https://fortress.wa.gov/doh/providercredentialsearch/
Employment Agency	www.dol.wa.gov/listoflicenses.html
Employment Directory Service	www.dol.wa.gov/listoflicenses.html
Engineer	https://fortress.wa.gov/dol/dolprod/bpdLicenseQuery/
Engineering Geologist	https://fortress.wa.gov/dol/dolprod/bpdLicenseQuery/
Engineering/Land Surveying Firm	https://fortress.wa.gov/dol/dolprod/bpdLicenseQuery/
Escrow Company/Officer	https://fortress.wa.gov/dfi/licenselu/dfi/licenseLU/LicenseLLU.aspx
Esthetician/Esthetician Instructor/Salon	https://fortress.wa.gov/dol/dolprod/bpdLicenseQuery/
Feedlot	http://agr.wa.gov/FoodAnimal/Livestock/LicensedCertifiedFeedlotsPublicMarkets.aspx
Fertilizer Distributor, Bulk	www.dol.wa.gov/listoflicenses.html
Fishing/Hunting License Dealer	http://wdfw.wa.gov/licensing/vendors/
Franchise	https://fortress.wa.gov/dfi/licenselu/dfi/licenseLU/LicenseLLU.aspx
Funeral Director/Intern	https://fortress.wa.gov/dol/dolprod/bpdLicenseQuery/
Funeral Establishment/Branch	https://fortress.wa.gov/dol/dolprod/bpdLicenseQuery/
Funeral Prearrangement Contract	https://fortress.wa.gov/dol/dolprod/bpdLicenseQuery/
Gaming Operation	www.wsgc.wa.gov/search/emp_lic_search.asp
Gaming-related Occupation	www.wsgc.wa.gov/search/emp_lic_search.asp
Geologist	https://fortress.wa.gov/dol/dolprod/bpdLicenseQuery/

Healthcare Service Company	www.insurance.wa.gov/consumertoolkit/search.aspx
Hearing Instrument Fitter/Dispenser	https://fortress.wa.gov/doh/providercredentialsearch/
HMO	www.insurance.wa.gov/consumertoolkit/search.aspx
Home Health Care Agency	https://fortress.wa.gov/doh/providercredentialsearch/
Hydrogeologist	https://fortress.wa.gov/dol/dolprod/bpdLicenseQuery/
Hypnotherapist	https://fortress.wa.gov/doh/providercredentialsearch/
Insurance Agent/Broker	www.insurance.wa.gov/consumertoolkit/search.aspx
Insurance Broker, Resident/Non-Resi.	www.insurance.wa.gov/consumertoolkit/search.aspx
Insurance Company	www.insurance.wa.gov/consumertoolkit/search.aspx
Insurance Corporation, Resident	www.insurance.wa.gov/consumertoolkit/search.aspx
Investment Advisor	https://fortress.wa.gov/dfi/licenselu/dfi/licenseLU/LicenseLLU.aspx
Kickboxer	https://fortress.wa.gov/dol/dolprod/bpdLicenseQuery/
Land Surveyor/Surveyor-in-Training	https://fortress.wa.gov/dol/dolprod/bpdLicenseQuery/
Landscape Architect	https://fortress.wa.gov/dol/dolprod/bpdLicenseQuery/
Liquor License New Apps, Approvals & Discontinuances	www.liq.wa.gov/lcbservices/LicensingInfo/EntireStateWeb.asp
Livestock Market	http://agr.wa.gov/FoodAnimal/Livestock/LicensedCertifiedFeedlotsPublicMarkets.aspx
Lobbyist/Lobbyist Report	http://web.pdc.wa.gov/MvcQuerySystem
Lottery Retailer	www.dol.wa.gov/listoflicenses.html
Manicurist/Manicurist Instructor/Salon	https://fortress.wa.gov/dol/dolprod/bpdLicenseQuery/
Manufactured Home Dealer	www.dol.wa.gov/listoflicenses.html
Marriage & Family Therapist	https://fortress.wa.gov/doh/providercredentialsearch/
Massage Therapist	https://fortress.wa.gov/doh/providercredentialsearch/
Medical Gas Plumber	https://fortress.wa.gov/lni/bbip/
Mental Health Counselor	https://fortress.wa.gov/doh/providercredentialsearch/
Midwife	https://fortress.wa.gov/doh/providercredentialsearch/
Minor Worker	www.dol.wa.gov/listoflicenses.html
Mobile Home/Travel Trailer Dealer	www.dol.wa.gov/listoflicenses.html
Money Transmitter	https://fortress.wa.gov/dfi/licenselu/dfi/licenseLU/LicenseLLU.aspx
Mortgage Broker	https://fortress.wa.gov/dfi/licenselu/dfi/licenseLU/LicenseLLU.aspx
Naturopathic Physician	https://fortress.wa.gov/doh/providercredentialsearch/
Nurse-LPN/Aide	https://fortress.wa.gov/doh/providercredentialsearch/
Nursery Retailer/Whlse	www.dol.wa.gov/listoflicenses.html
Nursing Home	https://fortress.wa.gov/dshs/adsaapps/lookup/NHPubLookup.aspx
Nursing Home Administrator	https://fortress.wa.gov/doh/providercredentialsearch/
Occupational Therapist	https://fortress.wa.gov/doh/providercredentialsearch/
Ocularist	https://fortress.wa.gov/doh/providercredentialsearch/
Optician	https://fortress.wa.gov/doh/providercredentialsearch/
Optometrist	https://fortress.wa.gov/doh/providercredentialsearch/
Osteopathic Physician	https://fortress.wa.gov/doh/providercredentialsearch/
Payday Lender	https://fortress.wa.gov/dfi/licenselu/dfi/licenseLU/LicenseLLU.aspx
Pest Control Operator/Consul't, Public	http://agr.wa.gov/PestFert/LicensingEd/Search/default.aspx
Pesticide Dealer/Manager	http://agr.wa.gov/PestFert/LicensingEd/Search/default.aspx
Pesticide Demo & Research Applicator	http://agr.wa.gov/PestFert/LicensingEd/Search/default.aspx
Pesticide Operator/Applicator	http://agr.wa.gov/PestFert/LicensingEd/Search/default.aspx
Pesticide Private Application	http://agr.wa.gov/PestFert/LicensingEd/Search/default.aspx
Pharmacist/Pharmacy Technician	https://fortress.wa.gov/doh/providercredentialsearch/
Physical Therapist	https://fortress.wa.gov/doh/providercredentialsearch/
Physician/Medical Doctor/Assistant	https://fortress.wa.gov/doh/providercredentialsearch/
Pilot, Marine, Commercial	www.pilotage.wa.gov/documents/Licensedpilots.PDF
Plumber	https://fortress.wa.gov/lni/bbip/
Podiatrist	https://fortress.wa.gov/doh/providercredentialsearch/
Political Candidate	http://web.pdc.wa.gov/MvcQuerySystem
Political Committee	http://web.pdc.wa.gov/MvcQuerySystem
Private Investigator/Agency/Trainer	https://fortress.wa.gov/dol/dolprod/bpdLicenseQuery/
Psychologist	https://fortress.wa.gov/doh/providercredentialsearch/

Purchasing Group (Insurance)...................... www.insurance.wa.gov/consumertoolkit/search.aspx
Radiologic Technologist.............................. https://fortress.wa.gov/doh/providercredentialsearch/
Real Estate Agent/Seller/Broker .... https://fortress.wa.gov/dol/dolprod/bpdLicenseQuery/
Real Estate Appraiser .... https://fortress.wa.gov/dol/dolprod/bpdLicenseQuery/
Real Estate LLC, LLP, Corp, etc................. www.dol.wa.gov/listoflicenses.html
Referee (Athletic) .... https://fortress.wa.gov/dol/dolprod/bpdLicenseQuery/
Rental Car .... www.dol.wa.gov/listoflicenses.html
Respiratory Therapist.................................. https://fortress.wa.gov/doh/providercredentialsearch/
Risk Retention Group.................................. www.insurance.wa.gov/consumertoolkit/search.aspx
Savings & Loan/Savings Bank..................... www.dfi.wa.gov/banks/commercial_banks.htm
Scrap Processor.. www.dol.wa.gov/listoflicenses.html
Security Guard, Private .... https://fortress.wa.gov/dol/dolprod/bpdLicenseQuery/
Security Guard/Agency .... https://fortress.wa.gov/dol/dolprod/bpdLicenseQuery/
Seed Dealer .... www.dol.wa.gov/listoflicenses.html
Service Contract Provider (Ins).................... www.insurance.wa.gov/consumertoolkit/search.aspx
Sex Offender Treatment Provider................ https://fortress.wa.gov/doh/providercredentialsearch/
Shopkeeper (non-prescription drug)............ www.dol.wa.gov/listoflicenses.html
Snowmobile Dealer..................................... www.dol.wa.gov/listoflicenses.html
Social Worker.. https://fortress.wa.gov/doh/providercredentialsearch/
Speech-Language Pathologist..................... https://fortress.wa.gov/doh/providercredentialsearch/
Structural Pest Inspector............................. http://agr.wa.gov/pestfert/LicensingEd/Search/default.aspx
Telephone Solicitor .... www.dol.wa.gov/listoflicenses.html
Tow Truck Operator .... www.dol.wa.gov/listoflicenses.html
Trust Company.. www.dfi.wa.gov/banks/trusts.htm
Underground Storage Tank .... www.dol.wa.gov/listoflicenses.html
Vehicle Dealer/Manufacturer .... www.dol.wa.gov/listoflicenses.html
Vehicle for Hire.. www.dol.wa.gov/listoflicenses.html
Vehicle Sales/Disposal .... www.dol.wa.gov/listoflicenses.html
Vehicle Transporter..................................... www.dol.wa.gov/listoflicenses.html
Vessel Dealer.. www.dol.wa.gov/listoflicenses.html
Veterinarian/Veterinary Medical Clerk .... https://fortress.wa.gov/doh/providercredentialsearch/
Viatical Settlement Provider......................... www.insurance.wa.gov/consumertoolkit/search.aspx
Waste Tire Site Owner/Carrier..................... www.dol.wa.gov/listoflicenses.html
Wastewater System Designer/Inspect......... https://fortress.wa.gov/dol/dolprod/bpdLicenseQuery/
Whitewater River Outfitter............................ www.dol.wa.gov/listoflicenses.html
Wrecker... www.dol.wa.gov/listoflicenses.html
Wrestler... https://fortress.wa.gov/dol/dolprod/bpdLicenseQuery/
X-Ray Technician.. https://fortress.wa.gov/doh/providercredentialsearch/

State and Local Courts

State Court Structure: **Superior Court** is the court of general jurisdiction, and has exclusive jurisdiction for felony matters, real property rights, domestic relations, estate, mental illness, juvenile, and civil cases over $50,000. The Superior Courts also hear appeals from courts of limited jurisdiction.

District Courts have concurrent jurisdiction with superior courts over misdemeanor and gross misdemeanor violations, and civil cases under $75,000. District Courts have exclusive jurisdiction over small claims and infractions. Criminal jurisdiction over misdemeanors, gross misdemeanors, and criminal traffic cases. The maximum penalty for gross misdemeanors is one year in jail and a $5,000 fine. The maximum penalty for misdemeanors is 90 days in jail and a $1,000 fine.

Municipal Courts have concurrent jurisdiction with Superior Courts over misdemeanor and gross misdemeanor violations and have exclusive jurisdiction over infractions. Cities electing not to establish a Municipal Court may contract with the District Court for services. Many Municipal Courts combine their record keeping with a District Court housed in the same building..

Appellate Courts: Supreme and Appellate opinions are at www.courts.wa.gov/appellate_trial_courts.

Statewide Court Online Access: All courts participate in the first 2 systems described below.

1. For detailed case docket data, the AOC provides the Judicial Information System's subscription service called JIS-Link. JIS-Link, provides access to all counties and court levels. One may search a single county or statewide for criminal searches; however, searching for civil records is by single county only. Civil cases include small claims, domestic violence, vehicle impounds, name changes, anti-harassment petitions, and lien foreclosures vehicle impounds, and property damages.

   The JIS subscription includes access to SCOMIS (the case management system) and ACORDS (appellate courts data). SCOMIS enables the superior court to record parties and legal instruments filed in superior court cases, to set cases on court calendars, and to enter case judgments and final dispositions. It is important to note that when a SCOMIS case number is found in the JIS application, detail level of the case may need to be viewed within the appropriate SCOMIS court display.

   The throughput date for JIS is normally back to 1994 or 1995 for JIS, the dates vary from 1979 to 1993 for SCOMIS. The subscription fees include a one-time $100.00 per site, a transaction fee of $.065. There is a $6.00 per month minimum charge. Visit www.courts.wa.gov/jislink or call 360-357-3365.
2. There is also a limited, free look-up of docket information at http://dw.courts.wa.gov/. Search by name or case number. The index is of cases filed in the municipal, district, superior, and appellate courts of the state of Washington. The outcome is not shown, but a link to a summary of the judgment does appear. The index will point where the official or complete court record is housed. No identifiers are shown. The search is by Municipal and District cases or by Superior cases or by Appellate cases.
3. At present 17 Superior Courts are connecting with a third party service offered by www.Clerkepass.com/ to view or obtain certified documents and non-certified documents. There is no name searching. A "User" can request and view Certified as well as Non-Certified documents. A "View" can only view Certified documents ordered by other users but cannot request any documents. A "Guest User" is a User who can request documents without registering with ClerkePass.com. The web page states it will charge a CAF (customized access fee) plus the existing court fees. The fees are detailed at the individual court URLs for this site. The 17 Superior Courts are located in these counties: Chelan, Clark, Douglas, Franklin, Grant, Island, Jefferson, Kitsap, Kittitas, Klickitat, Mason, Okanogan, Pend Oreille, Skagit, Skamania, Stevens, and Walla Walla.

Courts with Onlne Sites Not Part of Statewide Systems #1 and #2 Mentioned Above

Chelan County

Superior Court www.co.chelan.wa.us/scc/scc_main.htm

Civil & Criminal:: Certified or non-certified documents may be ordered online at https://www.clerkepass.com/Chelan/. There are added fees which depend on the type of document ordered. No name searching here. **$$$**

Clark County

Superior Court www.clark.wa.gov/courts/superior/index.html

Civi & Criminal: Daily dockets are at www.clark.wa.gov/courts/superior/docket.html. Search by name or case number. Also, certified or non-certified documents may be ordered online at https://www.clerkepass.com/Clark/. There are added fees which depend on the type of document ordered. No name searching here. **$$$**

District Court www.clark.wa.gov/courts/district/index.html

Civil & Criminal: Daily dockets are at www.clark.wa.gov/courts/district/docket.html l.

Douglas County

Civil & Criminal: Certified or non-certified documents may be ordered online at https://www.clerkepass.com/Douglas/. There are added fees which depend on the type of document ordered. No name searching here. **$$$**

Franklin County

Superior Court www.co.franklin.wa.us/clerk/

Civil & Criminal: Order a document for a fee (no name searching) at www.clerkepass.com. **$$$**

Grant County

Superior Court www.grantcountyweb.us/clerk/index.htm

Civil & Criminal: Certified or non-certified documents may be ordered online at https://www.clerkepass.com/Grant/. There are added fees which depend on the type of document ordered. No name searching here. **$$$**

Island County

Superior Court www.islandcounty.net/clerk/

Civil & Criminal: Certified or non-certified documents may be ordered online at https://www.clerkepass.com/Island/. There are added fees which depend on the type of document ordered. No name searching here. **$$$**

Jefferson County

Superior Court www.co.jefferson.wa.us/supcourt/

Civil & Criminal: Certified or non-certified documents may be ordered online at https://www.clerkepass.com/jefferson/. There are added fees which depend on the type of document ordered. No name searching here. **$$$**

King County

All Superior Courts www.kingcounty.gov/courts/Clerk.aspx

Civl & Criminal: Order court documents online at http://dja-eweb.kingcounty.gov/records/. Registration and fees involved. **$$$**

Kitsap County

Superior Court www.kitsapgov.com/clerk/

Civil & Criminal: Certified or non-certified documents may be ordered online at https://www.clerkepass.com/kitsap/. There are added fees which depend on the type of document ordered. No name searching here. **$$$**

Kittitas County

Superior Court www.co.kittitas.wa.us/clerk/

Civil & Criminal: Certified or non-certified documents may be ordered online at https://www.clerkepass.com/kittitas/. There are added fees which depend on the type of document ordered. No name searching here. **$$$**

Klickitat County

Superior Court www.klickitatcounty.org/

Civil & Criminal: Certified or non-certified documents may be ordered online at https://www.clerkepass.com/Klickitat/. There are added fees which depend on the type of document ordered. No name searching here. **$$$**

Mason County

Superior Court www.co.mason.wa.us/clerk/index.php

Civil & Criminal: Certified or non-certified documents may be ordered online at https://www.clerkepass.com/mason/. There are added fees which depend on the type of document ordered. No name searching here. **$$$**

Okanogan County

Superior Court http://okanogancounty.org/superiorcourt/

Civil & Criminal: Certified or non-certified documents may be ordered online at https://www.clerkepass.com/Okanogan/. There are added fees which depend on the type of document ordered. No name searching here. **$$$**

Pend Oreille County

Superior Court www.pendoreilleco.org/county/superior.asp

Civil & Criminal: Certified or non-certified documents may be ordered online at https://www.clerkepass.com/PendOreille/. There are added fees which depend on the type of document ordered. No name searching here.

Skagit County

Superior Court www.skagitcounty.net/Common/asp/default.asp?d=Clerk&c=General&p=main.htm

Civil & Criminal: Certified or non-certified documents may be ordered online at https://www.clerkepass.com/Skagit/. There are added fees which depend on the type of document ordered. No name searching here. **$$$**

Skamania County

Superior Court www.courts.wa.gov/court_dir/orgs/289.html

Civil & Criminal: Certified or non-certified documents may be ordered online at https://www.clerkepass.com/Skamania/. There are added fees which depend on the type of document ordered. No name searching here. **$$$**

Stevens County

Superior Court

Civil & Criminal: Certified or non-certified documents may be ordered online at https://www.clerkepass.com/Stephens/. There are added fees which depend on the type of document ordered. No name searching here. **$$$**

Walla Walla County

Superior Court www.co.walla-walla.wa.us/

Civil & Criminal: Certified or non-certified documents may be ordered online at https://www.clerkepass.com/WallaWalla/. There are added fees which depend on the type of document ordered. No name searching here. **$$$** *Criminal:* same **$$$**

Recorders, Assessors, and Other Sites of Note

Recording Office Organization: 39 counties, 39 recording offices. The recording officer is the County Auditor. County records are usually combined in a Grantor/Grantee index. All federal tax liens are filed with the Department of Licensing. All state tax liens are filed with the County Auditor.

Statewide or Multi-Jurisdiction Access: There is no statewide access to recorded documents or assesor data. But a number of counties offer online access.

County Sites:

Adams County ***Property, Taxation Records*** Access to county property tax and sales records, and inmate records is free at http://adamswa.taxsifter.com/Disclaimer.aspx.

Benton County ***Recorded Documents*** www.co.benton.wa.us/pview.aspx?id=1358&catID=45 Access to grantor/grantee index, parcels and recordings back to 1/1/85. **$$$**

Property, Taxation Records Access to Benton County assessor data is free at http://bentonpropertymax.governmaxa.com/propertymax/rover30.asp. Search by parcel ID#, address or map; no name searching.

Chelan County ***Recorded Documents, Marriage Records*** www.co.chelan.wa.us/ad/default.asp Access to Oncore Web searches free at http://63.135.55.89/oncoreweb/Search.aspx. Index from 1974 forward. All images available back to county inception.

Property, Taxation Records Access parcel data free on the GIS-mapping and access to property and tax information for free at www.co.chelan.wa.us/as/property_tax_disclaimer.htm. Search historical plats and images free at www.co.chelan.wa.us/assessor/mapping/historicalplats_disclaimer.htm.

Clallam County ***Recorded Documents*** www.clallam.net/ Access to recording records free at http://vpn.clallam.net:8080/recorder/web/login.jsp.

Property, Taxation Records Access to assessor property data is free at http://websrv8.clallam.net/propertyaccess/?cid=0. Auditor property maps are also downloadable at www.clallam.net/RealEstate/html/recorded_maps.htm. Add'l property maps at www.clallam.net/Map/.

Clark County ***Recorded Documents*** www.co.clark.wa.us/auditor/recording/ Access County GIS database online free at http://gis.clark.wa.gov/applications/gishome/auditor/index.cfm.

Property, Taxation Records Search maps online for property data at http://gis.clark.wa.gov/imf/imf.jsp?site=mapsonline. No name searching. Search property tax sales data free at www.co.clark.wa.us/treasurer/salesinfo.html. Search treasurer property data free at www.co.clark.wa.us/treasurer/property/index.html but no name search.

Columbia County ***Property, Taxation Records*** Access to property search data for free at http://65.101.117.251/PropertyAccess/PropertySearch.aspx?cid=0.

Cowlitz County ***Recorded Documents, Birth, Death, Marriage Records*** www.co.cowlitz.wa.us/Index.aspx?NID=126 Access Auditor and recorded documents free at http://apps.co.cowlitz.wa.us/cowlitzapps/cowlitzauditorpublicrecords/(S(mqj1qmryrmkhll45chhand55))/default.aspx.

Property, Taxation Records Access Assessor property records free at www.cowlitzinfo.net/applications/cowlitzassessorparcelsearch/.

Douglas County ***Recorded Documents*** www.douglascountywa.net Access to records free at www.douglascountywa.net/oncoreweb/search.aspx. Records go back to 1972.

Property, Taxation Records Access to the County Parcel Search including taxes, plats and parcels is free at http://douglaswa.taxsifter.com/taxsifter/disclaimer.asp.

Ferry County ***Property, Taxation Records*** Access property data on the TaxSifter database free at http://ferrywa.taxsifter.com/Disclaimer.aspx.

Franklin County ***Recorded Documents , Marriage Records*** www.co.franklin.wa.us/auditor/ Access to records free at http://auditor.co.franklin.wa.us/oncoreweb/.

Property, Taxation Records Search for assessor property data and map search for free at www.co.franklin.wa.us/assessor/.

Grant County ***Recorded Documents*** www.co.grant.wa.us/Auditor/index.htm Access to document index only free at http://eagleweb.grantcountyweb.com/grantrecorder/eagleweb/.

Property, Taxation Records Access assessor data on the GIS-mapping site free at http://grantwa.mapsifter.com/Disclaimer.aspx?ReturnUrl=%2fdefault.aspx.

Grays Harbor County ***Recorded Documents*** www.co.grays-harbor.wa.us Access docket information for judgments at www.co.grays-harbor.wa.us/info/clerk/docket/index.asp.

Property, Taxation Records Access to the county Parcel Database is free at http://bentonpropertymax.governmaxa.com/propertymax/rover30.asp. Search by parcel ID#, address, legal description, but no name searching.

Island County ***Recorded Documents*** https://wei.sos.wa.gov/county/island/en/pages/default.aspx Access to recorded database index free at http://auditor.islandcounty.net/recorder/web/. Must register. The images are not free-$100.00 per month.
Property, Taxation Records Access county property tax data free at www.islandcounty.net/guestlogin.html.

Jefferson County ***Recorded Documents*** www.co.jefferson.wa.us/auditor/Default.asp Access the \"Recorded Document Search\" database at http://er-web.co.jefferson.wa.us/recorder/web/. Includes grantor/grantee index and records on the County Property (Tax Parcel) Database Tool, also plats and survey images.
Property, Taxation Records Search assessor data free at www.co.jefferson.wa.us/assessors/parcel/ParcelSearch.asp, but no names searching.

King County ***Recorded Documents*** www.kingcounty.gov/business/Recorders.aspx Access to the recorder's databases is free at http://146.129.54.93:8193/legalacceptance.asp?.
Property, Taxation Records Access property records free at www.kingcounty.gov/operations/GIS/Maps/VMC.aspx.

Kitsap County ***Recorded Documents*** www.kitsapgov.com/aud/default.htm Search property data free on the land information system site at http://kcwaimg.co.kitsap.wa.us/recorder/web/. Click on Public Login. Site may be down. Fee to print official documents. Also, subscription access to grantor/grantee index back to 8/26/1990, parcels back to 1/1972, recordings to 4/6/1988 and Superior court docs and tax rolls are available at www.landlight.com/. **$$$**
Property, Taxation Records Search property and tax data free on the land information system site at http://kcwppub3.co.kitsap.wa.us/ParcelSearch/. No name searching. Fee to print official documents.**$$$**

Kittitas County ***Property, Taxation Records*** Access property data free at www.co.kittitas.wa.us/taxsifterpublic/disclaimer.asp, no name searching.

Klickitat County ***Archived Documents Records*** https://wei.sos.wa.gov/county/klickitat/Pages/default.aspx Access to the archived documents free at www.digitalarchives.wa.gov/.
Property, Taxation Records Access GIS-mapping site free at http://69.30.47.122/kcmap/ but no name searching.

Lewis County ***Recorded Documents*** http://lewiscountywa.gov/auditor Search the index online at https://quickdocs.lewiscountywa.gov/recorder/web/. Both a basic and advanced search are offered.
Property, Taxation Records Access property data free at http://parcels.lewiscountywa.gov/. Search by parcel number at https://quickdocs.lewiscountywa.gov/recorder/web/ The GIS/Mapping data found for free at http://maps.lewiscountywa.gov/maps/maplib_index.html.

Lincoln County ***Property, Taxation Records*** Access to property search for free at www.co.lincoln.wa.us/Assessor/disclaimer.htm.

Mason County ***Property, Taxation Records*** Access to Assessor data is free at www.co.mason.wa.us/disclaimer.php and at http://property.co.mason.wa.us/Taxsifter/Disclaimer.aspx. Access parcel data free on the GIS-mapping site at www.co.mason.wa.us/gis/index.php, but not name searching.

Okanogan County ***Recorded Documents*** www.okanogancounty.org Access to images free at www.digitalarchives.wa.gov/home. Images from 1993 to present.
Property, Taxation Records Access to county property search is free at www.okanogancounty.org/Assessor/map.htm.

Pacific County ***Recorded Documents*** https://wei.sos.wa.gov/county/pacific/en/pages/auditorhome.aspx Access to recorded documents free at http://pacificwa.countygovernmentrecords.com/pacificwa/web/.
Property, Taxation Records Access County Auditor property data free on the TaxSifter system at http://pacificwa.taxsifter.com/taxsifter/disclaimer.asp.

Pend Oreille County ***Property, Taxation Records*** Access property records free at www.pendoreilleco.org/county/disclaimer_2.asp.

Pierce County ***Recorded Documents*** www.co.pierce.wa.us/index.aspx?nid=93 Search index back to 1984 and images back to 3/1998 on the auditor's recording database for free at https://armsweb.co.pierce.wa.us/. Unofficial copies of marriage records for free at this site also.
Property, Taxation Records Property records on County Assessor-Treasurer database are free at http://epip.co.pierce.wa.us/CFApps/atr/ePIP/search.cfm.

San Juan County ***Recorded Documents*** www.sanjuanco.com/auditor/default.aspx Free access to the auditor database of real estate recording records found at www.sanjuanco.com/auditor/recordsearch.aspx.
Property, Taxation Records Access to assessor property records is free at http://69.30.47.122/kcmap/. No name searching. Access to parcel search info free at www.sanjuanco.com/assessor/parcelSearch.aspx.

Skagit County ***Recorded Documents*** www.skagitcounty.net/Common/asp/default.asp?d=Auditor&c=General&p=main.htm Access auditor's recorded documents as well as permits and marriages free at www.skagitcounty.net/Common/asp/Default.asp?D=AuditorRecording&C=Search&p=Search.asp&a=Recording.

Property, Taxation Records Search assessor data free at www.skagitcounty.net/Common/asp/default.asp?d=Home&c=General&P=main.htm Click on Record Searches, but no name searching.

Skamania County ***Property, Taxation Records*** Access to parcel information for free at http://skamaniawa.taxsifter.com/taxsifter/disclaimer.asp. Also, access to GIS/mapping free at http://skamaniawa.mapsifter.com/Disclaimer.aspx?ReturnUrl=%2fdefault.aspx.

Snohomish County ***Recorded Documents, Marriage Records*** www1.co.snohomish.wa.us/Departments/Auditor/ Access to the Auditor's office database back to 1997 is free at http://198.238.192.100/localization/menu.asp. Search on the recorded documents or marriage icons.
Property, Taxation Records Search the assessor property data for free at https://www.snoco.org/proptax/(o3rd3bylvwlsczrya511t555)/search.aspx, but no name searching.

Spokane County ***Recorded Documents (Index Only)*** www.spokanecounty.org/auditor/content.aspx?c=1527 Indexes of certain records available at https://recording.spokanecounty.org/recorder/web/. Must register for login.
Property, Taxation Records Search the County Parcel Locator database for free at www.spokanecounty.org/pubpadal/. No name searching. You may search sales by parcel number free at www.spokanecounty.org/pubpadal/SalesSearch.aspx.

Stevens County ***Property, Taxation Records*** Access to parcel information for free at http://stevenswa.taxsifter.com/Disclaimer.aspx.

Thurston County ***Recorded Documents*** www.co.thurston.wa.us/auditor/ Access the Auditor Recording data at www.co.thurston.wa.us/auditor/. Click on Public Record Index Available Online. Guests may log in using the \"Public Log In\" button. **$$$**
Property, Taxation Records Assessor and property data on Thurston GeoData database is free at www.geodata.org/parcelsrch.asp. No name searching.

Wahkiakum County ***Property, Taxation Records*** Access the yearly property sales list for free at www.co.wahkiakum.wa.us/agreement.html. Print out of current sales available free at www.co.wahkiakum.wa.us/depts/assessor/pdf/SalesThruApr2009.pdf.

Walla Walla County Auditor ***Recorded Documents*** www.co.walla-walla.wa.us Access to records found at http://recorder.co.walla-walla.wa.us/recorder/web/. Unofficial copies printed from images for free. Official copies must be requested at the office or by mail and fee is $3.00 for 1st page, $1.00 for each add'l page. **$$$**
Property, Taxation Records Access to the TaxSifter parcel search and sales is free at http://wallawallawa.taxsifter.com/taxsifter/disclaimer.asp.

Whatcom County ***Recorded Documents*** www.whatcomcounty.us/auditor/ Access to recorded records free at www.whatcomcounty.us/paris/. Records are from 1988 forward.
Property, Taxation Records Access to property records for free at http://property.whatcomcounty.us/.

Yakima County ***Recorded Documents*** www.yakimacounty.us/auditor/ The agency sends requesters to the Laredo system. Fees are based on a flat rate by usage ranging from $50 to $250 per month. The same vendor offers the Tapestry program with a $5.95 search fee and copies for $.50 per page. You can pay as you go with a credit card or be billed monthly with a $25.00 monthly minimum. Visit at www.fidlar.com or call 800-747-4600 at ext 271 or 324. **$$$**
Property, Taxation Records Assessor and property data on County Assessor database are free at http://yes.co.yakima.wa.us/assessor/Default.aspx. Access to the treasurer parcel database is free at https://yes.co.yakima.wa.us/ascend/(zjwf1z22ajfm3d550apmyhb2)/search.aspx. No name searching.

West Virginia

Capital: Charleston
Kanawha County
Time Zone: EST
Population: 1,855,413
# of Counties: 55

Useful State Links

Website: www.wv.gov
Governor: www.wvgov.org
Attorney General: www.doj.state.wi.us/ag/
State Archives: www.wvculture.org/history/wvsamenu.html
State Statutes and Codes: www.legis.state.wv.us/WVCODE/Code.cfm
Legislative Bill Search: www.legis.state.wv.us/Bill_Status/bill_status.cfm
Bill Monitoring: www.legis.state.wv.us/billstatus_personalized/persbills_login.cfm
Unclaimed Funds: https://apps.wvsto.com/eclaims_new/property_search.aspx

State Public Record Agencies

Sexual Offender Registry

State Police Headquarters, Sexual Offender Registry, www.statepolice.wv.gov/Pages/default.aspx Online searching is available from website, search by county or name, or by most wanted. Email questions to registry@wvsp.state.wv.us. Search the offender database to determine if a specific email address or username used on the internet belongs to a registered sex offender and has been reported.

Incarceration Records

West Virginia Division of Corrections, Records Room, www.wvdoc.com/wvdoc/ This agency offers a free search for active inmates and parolees at www.wvdoc.com/wvdoc/OffenderSearch/tabid/117/Default.aspx.

Corporation, LLC, LP, LLP, Trademarks/Servicemarks

Sec. of State - Business Organizations Division, 1900 Kanawha Blvd E, www.sos.wv.gov/business-licensing/Pages/default.aspx Corporation and business types records on the Secretary of State Business Organization Information System are available free online at http://apps.sos.wv.gov/business/corporations/. Search by organization name. Certified copies may be ordered online at http://apps.sos.wv.gov/ecomm/. An account is necessary. *Other Options:* Bulk sale of records is available in CD or DVD format, retrievable in CSV, Access or XML. Monthly or weekly updates are offered. Call 304-414-0265 for further details or visit https://apps.wv.gov/sos/bulkdata/Help/Default.aspx.

Uniform Commercial Code

Sec. of State - UCC Division, Bldg 1, Suite 157-K, www.sos.wv.gov/business-licensing/uniformcommercialcode/Pages/default.aspx There is a free service to search, and the website also gives the ability to order copies. Search the database free at http://apps.sos.wv.gov/business/uccsearch/index.aspx to determine if a specific individual/organization has active, expired or terminated liens filed. Results give UCC number, secured party, debtor and status. Online record requesters can be ordered by email - E-mail to ucc@wvsos.com. **$$$** *Other Options:* Bulk sale of records is available in CD or DVD format, retrievable in CSV, Access or XML. Monthly or weekly updates are offered. Call 304-414-0265 for further details or visit https://apps.wv.gov/sos/bulkdata/RegistrationInformation.aspx.

Driver License Information, Driver Records

Division of Motor Vehicles, Driving Records, www.transportation.wv.gov/dmv/Pages/default.aspx Online record access is available 24 hours a day. Batch requesters receive return transmission about 3 AM. Users must access through AAMVA. A contract is required and accounts must pre-pay. Fee is $5.00 per record. For more information, call 304-926-0708 Also, there is a free Status Check of a DL# at www.transportation.wv.gov/dmv/Pages/dlverify.aspx. $$$ *Other Options:* This agency will sell its DL file to commercial vendors, but records cannot be re-sold.

Voter Registration, Campaign Finance Reports, PACs

Sec of State - Election Division, Bldg 1 #157-K, www.sos.wv.gov/elections/Pages/default.aspx Search to see if someone is registered to vote at https://apps.sos.wv.gov/elections/voter/index.aspx. This shows the voter's polling place. Access campaign finance reports, including those for PACs, at www.sos.wv.gov/elections/campaignfinance/Pages/default.aspx. *Other Options:* Voter lists are available for political purposes for approx $.015 per name. A complete statewide list is approx. $6,800 ($.005 per name plus $1,000). Turnaround time is generally 48 hours. Call for further information.

Occupational Licensing Boards

Accountant-CPA .... www.boa.wv.gov/disciplinary/Pages/RevocationsandSuspensions.aspx
Aesthetician www.wvbbc.com/Home/LicenseeLookup/tabid/1856/Default.aspx
Amusement Ride Inspections .... www.wvlabor.com/newwebsite/Pages/Amusement_ride_inspectionsNEW.cfm
Amusement Ride Inspector .... www.wvlabor.com/newwebsite/Pages/Amusement_ride_inspectorNEW.cfm
Animal Technician .... www.wvbvm.org/Register_of_Licensees.html
Architect .... http://wvbrdarch.org/roster/lic/searchdb.asp
Asbestos Air Monitor-Clearance .... www.wvdhhr.org/rtia/allair.cfm
Asbestos Contractor .... www.wvdhhr.org/rtia/allcon.cfm
Asbestos Inspector .... www.wvdhhr.org/rtia/allinsp.cfm
Asbestos Laboratory .... www.wvdhhr.org/rtia/licensing.asp
Asbestos Project Designer/Planner .... www.wvdhhr.org/rtia/alldesign.cfm
Asbestos Supervisor .... www.wvdhhr.org/rtia/allsup.cfm
Asbestos Worker .... www.wvdhhr.org/rtia/allwork.cfm
Athlete Agent .... http://apps.sos.wv.gov/business/licensing/
Athletic Trainer https://wveis.k12.wv.us/certcheck/
Athletic Trainers-BOC www.wvbopt.com/documents/BOC%20listing%20-%20WV%20residents%20only4.pdf
Barber www.wvbbc.com/Home/LicenseeLookup/tabid/1856/Default.aspx
Barber/Beauty Culture School
.... www.wvbbc.org/MenuStructure/SchoolStudentInformation/SchoolStudentInformation/ListofSchools/tabid/1546/Default.aspx
Charitable Organization .... http://apps.sos.wv.gov/business/charities/help.html
Chiropractor .... www.boc.wv.gov/Pages/License-Search.aspx
Contractor, General .... www.wvlabor.com/newwebsite/Pages/contractor_searchNEW.cfm
Cosmetologist www.wvbbc.com/Home/LicenseeLookup/tabid/1856/Default.aspx
Counselor LPC, Professional .... www.wvbec.org/verificationoflicensure/namesofwvlpc.html
Counselor, Professional .... www.wvbec.org/verificationoflicensure/namesofwvlpc.html
Crane Operator .... www.wvlabor.com/newwebsite/Pages/crane_searchNEW.cfm
Cremation Education Providers .... www.wvfuneralboard.com/LinkClick.aspx?fileticket=cWNPacHMLk4%3d&tabid=652
Dental Hygienist www.wvdentalboard.org/verification%20instructions.htm
Dentist www.wvdentalboard.org/verification%20instructions.htm
Educational Audiologist https://wveis.k12.wv.us/certcheck/
Elevator Inspectors .... www.wvlabor.com/newwebsite/Pages/Safety_elevators_private_inspectorsRESULTS1.cfm
Engineer www.wvpebd.org/Home/LicensureVerification/ProfessionalEngineer/tabid/812/Default.aspx
Engineer, Retired www.wvpebd.org/Home/LicensureVerification/RetiredEngineer/tabid/814/Default.aspx
Engineering Authorized Co. www.wvpebd.org/Home/LicensureVerification/AuthorizedCompanyCOA/tabid/813/Default.aspx
Forester/Forestry Technician www.wvlicensingboards.com/foresters/roster-020612.pdf
Hearing Aid Dealer .... www.wvdhhr.org/wvbhadf/contactus.html
Insurance Adjuster www.wvinsurance.gov/LicensePrint/tabid/317/Default.aspx
Insurance Agent/Agency www.wvinsurance.gov/LicensePrint/tabid/317/Default.aspx
Landscape Architect .... http://wvlaboard.org/Portals/WVLABoard/docs/FY_2012_Roster.pdf
Lead Abatement Contractor .... www.wvdhhr.org/rtia/lead_contractors.cfm
Lobbyist/Lobbying Employer .... www.ethics.wv.gov/lobbyist/Pages/ListsandForms.aspx
Manicurist www.wvbbc.com/Home/LicenseeLookup/tabid/1856/Default.aspx
Manufactured Housing .... www.wvlabor.com/newwebsite/Pages/MH_contractor_license_search_NEW.cfm
Medical Corporation .... www.wvbom.wv.gov/licensesearch.asp

Medical License, Special Volunteer	www.wvbom.wv.gov/licensesearch.asp
Medical Professional LLC/Company	www.wvbom.wv.gov/licensesearch.asp
Milk Shipper	www.wvdhhr.org/phs/milk/records.asp
Mine Electrician	www.wvminesafety.org/PDFs/CERTS%20ELECTRICAL.pdf
Mine Surveyor/Foreman	www.wvminesafety.org/PDFs/SUPERCERTS.pdf
Miner, Underground/Surface	www.wvminesafety.org/certificationlists.htm
Minister License	http://apps.sos.wv.gov/business/licensing/
Notary Public	http://apps.sos.wv.gov/business/notary/
Nurse-LPN	https://apps.wv.gov/nursing/rnsearch/default.aspx
Nursing Schools	www.wvrnboard.com/default2.asp?active_page_id=86
Occupation'l Therapist/Asst/Practit'n'r	http://wvbot.org/dharris/members.pdf
Optometrist	www.wvbo.org/verify-license.php
Osteopathic Corporation	https://www.wvbdosteo.org/verify/
Osteopathic Physician/Phys'c'n Assist	https://www.wvbdosteo.org/verify/
Pesticide Applicat'n Business (RPAB)	www.kellysolutions.com/WV/RPAB/index.htm
Pesticide Applicator	www.kellysolutions.com/WV/Applicators/index.htm
Pesticide Applicator-Business	www.kellysolutions.com/WV/Business/index.htm
Pesticide Dealer, Restricted Use	www.kellysolutions.com/wv/Dealers/index.htm
Pesticide Registration	www.kellysolutions.com/WV/pesticideindex.htm
Pharmacies/Businesses	www.wvbop.com/index.php?option=com_wrapper&view=wrapper&Itemid=97
Pharmacist	www.wvbop.com/index.php?option=com_wrapper&view=wrapper&Itemid=97
Physical Therapis/Assistant	www.wvbopt.com/licensesearch.cfm
Physician/Medical Doctor/Assistant	www.wvbom.wv.gov/licensesearch.asp
Plumbers	www.wvlabor.com/newwebsite/Pages/plumber_searchNEW.cfm
Podiatrist	www.wvbom.wv.gov/licensesearch.asp
Private Investigator/Agency	http://apps.sos.wv.gov/business/licensing/
Psychologist	www.wvpsychbd.org/license_verification.htm
Radiologic Technologist	www.wvrtboard.org/LICENSESEARCH/tabid/358/Default.aspx
Radiologic Technology Accredited Schools	www.wvrtboard.org/LinkClick.aspx?fileticket=uyn4ZEu%2bXtA%3d&tabid=326
Radon Contractor/Trainer	www.wvdhhr.org/rtia/radon_contractor.cfm
Real Estate Appraiser (WV list)	www.appraiserboard.wv.gov/Roster/Pages/default.aspx
Respiratory Care Practitioner	www.wvborc.org/Home/LicenseVerifications/tabid/1117/Default.aspx
School Principal/CounselorSuperintendent	https://wveis.k12.wv.us/certcheck/
School Psychologist	www.wvpsychbd.org/license_verification.htm
School Psychologist/Nurse	https://wveis.k12.wv.us/certcheck/
School Social Svcs/attendance Invest'r	https://wveis.k12.wv.us/certcheck/
Security Guard	http://apps.sos.wv.gov/business/licensing/
Service of Process	http://apps.sos.wv.gov/business/service-of-process/
Shot Firer	www.wvminesafety.org/PDFs/CERTS%20TASK.pdf
Social Worker	www.wvsocialworkboard.org/licenseverification/licenseverification.asp
Speech/Language Pathologist	https://wveis.k12.wv.us/certcheck/
Supervisor of Instruction	https://wveis.k12.wv.us/certcheck/
Surveyor, Land/Business	www.wvbps.wv.gov/Pages/default.aspx
Teacher	https://wveis.k12.wv.us/certcheck/
Veterinarian	www.wvbvm.org/Register_of_Licensees.html
Water Bottler	www.wvdhhr.org/phs/bottledwater/records2.asp
Water Brands, Bottled	www.wvdhhr.org/phs/bottledwater/records3.asp

State and Local Courts

State Court Structure: The trial courts of general jurisdiction are the Circuit Courts which handle civil cases at law over $300 or more or in equity, felonies and misdemeanor and appeals from the Family Courts. The Magistrate Courts, which are akin to small claims courts, issue arrest and search warrants, hear misdemeanor cases, conduct preliminary examinations in felony cases, and hear civil cases with $5,000 or less in dispute. Magistrates also issue emergency protective orders in cases involving domestic violence.

The Circuit Courts hear appeals of Magistrate Court cases. Probate is handled by the Circuit Court. The highest court is the Supreme Court of Appeals of West Virginia.

Family Courts were created by constitutional amendment of January 1, 2002. Family Courts hear cases involving divorce, annulment, separate maintenance, family support, paternity, child custody, and visitation. Family Court judges also conduct final hearings in domestic violence cases. For further court details, see www.wvlrc.org/westvirginiacourtsystem2.htm.

Appellate Courts: Opinions and Calendar with Docket are available at courtswv.gov.

Statewide Court Online Access: There is no statewide access, but two designated vendors have relationships in many courts as described below.

1. Thirty-nine Circuit Courts provide details from the court record dockets at https://www.wvcircuitexpress.com/Default.aspx. There is a $125 sign-up fee and a monthly flat fee of $ 38.00 plus connect charge of $ 1.00 a minute. Records are available from 02/1997. Search by name or case number. A number of details are provided, however no identifiers are provided beyond the name, limited images are available. The WV Supreme Court prohibits court-related websites from displaying personal identifiers.

The Counties on Circuit Court Express are:

Barbour	Grant	Marshall	Ohio	Summers
Boone	Hampshire	Mason	Pendleton	Taylor
Brooke	Hancock	McDowell	Pocahontas	Webster
Calhoun	Hardy	Mercer	Preston	Wetzel
Clay	Jackson	Mineral	Putnam	Wirt
Doddridge	Jefferson	Mingo	Raleigh	Wood
Fayette	Kanawha	Monroe	Ritchie	Wyoming
Gilmer	Logan	Nicholas	Roane	

2. At present three Circuit Courts now are connected with a service offered by www.Clerkepass.com to view or obtain certified documents and non-certified documents. There is no name searching. A "User" can request and view Certified as well as Non-Certified documents. A "View" can only view Certified documents ordered by other users but cannot request any documents. A "Guest User" is a User who can request documents without registering with ClerkePass.com. The web page states it will charge a CAF (customized access fee) plus the existing court fees. The fees are detailed at the individual court URLs for this site.

   Each county on the Clerkepass platform has a separate URL; they are shown in the profiles are listed below.

Jefferson County

Circuit Court www.jeffcowvcircuitclerk.com/index.html

Certified or non-certified documents may be ordered online at https://www.clerkepass.com/FormsePass/Jefferson/. This is not a name search - the document number must be provided. **$$$**

Kanawha County

Circuit Court www.courtswv.gov/lower-courts/circuit-courts.html

Certified or non-certified documents may be ordered online at https://www.clerkepass.com/FormsePass/Kanawha/. There are added fees which depend on the type of document ordered. Per state law no identifiers shown. The site may not indicate when a case is bound over to a second court. **$$$**

Wood County

Circuit Court www.woodcountywv.com/

Civil: Certified or non-certified documents may be ordered online at https://www.clerkepass.com/FormsePass/wood/. This is not a name search - the document number must be provided. The site also provides access to vital records. **$$$**

Recorders, Assessors, and Other Sites of Note

Recording Office Organization: 55 counties, 55 recording offices. The recording officer is the County Clerk. All federal and state tax liens are filed with the County Clerk.

Statewide or Multi-Jurisdiction Access: There is no statewide sertvice fo access to recorded documents or assessor data. However a growing number of counties offer online access.

- Private company Digital Software offers subscription access to land book **assessment information for all counties** at http://digitalcourthouse.com. A user agreement is required.
- Private company Software Systems offers free access to property tax information for at least 25 counties at www.softwaresystems.com/ssi/taxinquiry/. Participating counties: Berkeley, Boone, Cabell, Fayette, Greenbrier, Hancock, Harrison, Jackson, Jefferson, Kanawha, Lewis, Logan, Marion, Marshall, Mineral, Mingo, Monongalia, Morgan, Nicholas, Ohio, Ritchie, Roane, Putnam, Taylor, and Upshur.

County Sites:

Berkeley County ***Property, Taxation Records*** Access property tax data free at www.softwaresystems.com/ssi/taxinquiry/. Also, access property data free at www.onlinegis.net/WvBerkeley/asp/controlVersion.asp. Click on Display Map then Search, no name searching. Also, access to GIS/mapping free at http://maps.berkeleywv.org/berkeleyonline/. Access sheriff tax sale data free at http://planning.berkeleycountycomm.org:8003/.

Boone County ***Property, Taxation Records*** Access property tax data free at http://boone.softwaresystems.com:8003/index.html.

Brooke County ***Property, Taxation Records*** Access to tax records for free at www.brookecountysheriff.com/tax/Search.aspx.

Cabell County ***Property, Taxation Records*** Access property tax data free at www.softwaresystems.com/ssi/taxinquiry/.

Fayette County ***Property, Taxation Records*** Access to property record data for free at www.fayetteassessor.com/search. Also, access property tax data free at www.softwaresystems.com/ssi/taxinquiry/.

Greenbrier County ***Property, Taxation Records*** Access property tax data free at www.softwaresystems.com/ssi/taxinquiry/.

Hampshire County ***Property, Taxation Records*** Access to GIS/mapping for free at http://ags.hampshirewv.com/map/.

Hancock County ***Property, Taxation Records*** Access to records for free at http://hancock.wvassessor.com/assrweb/Default.aspx. Also, access property tax data free at www.softwaresystems.com/ssi/taxinquiry/.

Hardy County ***Recorded Documents*** www.hardycounty.com/hardy-county-clerk Access recorded index free at http://216.27.81.171/hardywvnw/disclaimer.asp. Index goes back to 1/1993. **$$$**

Harrison County ***Recorded Documents*** www.harrisoncountywv.com/countyclerk.aspx Access to records free at www.harrisoncountywv.com/warning.aspx.
Property, Taxation Records Access to Assessor's parcel ownership/GIS/mapping for free at www.harrisoncountyassessor.com/searchdisclaimer.aspx. Also, access property tax data free at www.softwaresystems.com/ssi/taxinquiry/.

Jackson County ***Property, Taxation Records*** Access to Assessor's database free at http://portal.jacksonwvassessor.com/portal/. Also, access property tax data free at www.softwaresystems.com/ssi/taxinquiry/.

Jefferson County ***Recorded Documents*** www.jeffersoncountyclerkwv.com/ Access to county records free at www.jeffersoncountyclerkwv.com/. Click on Jefferson County document inquiry.
Property, Taxation Records Access property tax data free at www.softwaresystems.com/ssi/taxinquiry/.

Kanawha County ***Property, Taxation Records*** Access property tax data free at www.softwaresystems.com/ssi/taxinquiry/.

Lewis County ***Property, Taxation Records*** Access property tax data free at www.softwaresystems.com/ssi/taxinquiry/.

Logan County ***Property, Taxation Records*** Access property tax data free at www.softwaresystems.com/ssi/taxinquiry/.

Marion County ***Property, Taxation Records*** Access property tax data free at www.softwaresystems.com/ssi/taxinquiry/.

Marshall County ***Recorded Documents*** www.marshallcountywv.org/county.asp Access to records free at http://129.71.117.225/.
Property, Taxation Records Access to property data for free at http://portal.marcoassessor.org/portal/. Also, access property tax data free at www.softwaresystems.com/ssi/taxinquiry/.

Mercer County ***Property, Taxation Records*** Access to assessor web portal for free at http://portal.mercerassessor.com/portal/.

Mineral County ***Property, Taxation Records*** Access property tax data free at www.softwaresystems.com/ssi/taxinquiry/.

Mingo County ***Property, Taxation Records*** Access property tax data free at www.softwaresystems.com/ssi/taxinquiry/.

Monongalia County ***Recorded Documents*** www.monongaliacountyclerk.com/ Access to county records free at 1.http://searchrecords.monongaliacountyclerk.com/

Property, Taxation Records Access the County Parcel Search database free at www.assessor.org/parcelweb/. Search by a wide variety of criteria including owner name and address. Also, access property tax data free at www.softwaresystems.com/ssi/taxinquiry/.

Monroe County ***Property, Taxation Records*** Access to tax inquiry info for free at www.monroecountywv.net/Tax/Inquiry/. Must have name and year to search.

Morgan County ***Recorded Documents*** www.morgancountywv.gov/CountyClerk/default.aspx Access to Morgan County database free at http://129.71.205.187/

Property, Taxation Records Access property tax data free at www.softwaresystems.com/ssi/taxinquiry/.

Nicholas County ***Recorded Documents*** www.nicholascountywv.org/county-offices/countyclerk.aspx Access to records free at https://cotthosting.com/wvnicholas/User/Login.aspx?ReturnUrl=%2fwvnicholas%2fIndex.aspx. Can sign in as a guest or get an account.

Property, Taxation Records Access property tax data free at www.softwaresystems.com/ssi/taxinquiry/.

Ohio County ***Property, Taxation Records*** Access property tax data free at www.softwaresystems.com/ssi/taxinquiry/.

Pocahontas County ***Property, Taxation Records*** Access to property database for free at www.pocahontascountyassessor.com/disclaimer.htm.

Preston County ***Recorded Documents*** www.prestoncountywv.org/countyclerk.php Access to records free at www.prestoncountywv.org/disclaimer.php. Records from 1/1/1900 to present.

Putnam County ***Property, Taxation Records*** Access property tax data free at www.softwaresystems.com/ssi/taxinquiry/.

Raleigh County ***Property, Taxation Records*** Access to records free at http://mapping.raleighcountyassessor.com/portal/search_all.php.

Randolph County ***Recorded Documents*** www.randolphcountycommissionwv.org/index.php/county-government/county-offices/county-clerk Access records free at http://129.71.117.90/.

Property, Taxation Records Search County Assessor information at www.randolphcountyassessor.com/portal/ (requires username and password to login).**$$$**

Ritchie County ***Recorded Documents*** www.ritchiecounty.wv.gov/countygovernmentagencies/Pages/countyclerk.aspx Access to record indexing free at https://www.uslandrecords.com/uslr/UslrApp/index.jsp. Subscription required for more detailed information and viewing. With the exception of UCC's and vital records, all records are available beginning 7/1/85. **$$$**

Property, Taxation Records Access property tax data free at www.softwaresystems.com/ssi/taxinquiry/.

Roane County ***Property, Taxation Records*** Access property tax data free at www.softwaresystems.com/ssi/taxinquiry/.

Summers County ***Property, Taxation Records*** Access the tax inquiry database free at http://summerscountywv.org/index.php?page=online-tax-inquiry.

Taylor County ***Property, Taxation Records*** Access property tax data free at www.softwaresystems.com/ssi/taxinquiry/.

Tucker County ***Recorded Documents*** Access to records free at www.tuckerwv.net/. Use \"user\" for username and \"welcome\" for password.

Upshur County ***Property, Taxation Records*** Access property tax data free at www.softwaresystems.com/ssi/taxinquiry/.

Wayne County ***Recorded Documents*** www.waynecountywv.us Access recorded document index back to 4/1/1989 free at www.waynecountywv.us/WEBInquiry/.

Property, Taxation Records Access property tax data free at www.waynecountywv.us/WEBTax/Default.aspx.

Wood County ***Recorded Documents, Will, Death, Birth, Marriage Records*** www.woodcountywv.com/page/page14.php Access at http://129.71.205.120/webinquiry/. Some records go back to the 1800's.

Property, Taxation Records Access to the tax inquiry for free at http://129.71.205.120/webtax/. Also, access property data on the GIS-mapping site free at www.onlinegis.net/WvWood/asp/controlVersion.asp. Click on Display Map then Search; no name searching.

Wisconsin

Capital: Madison
Dane County
Time Zone: CST
Population: 5,726,398
# of Counties: 72

Useful State Links

Website: www.wisconsin.gov
Governor: www.wisgov.state.wi.us
Attorney General: www.doj.state.wi.us/ag/
State Archives: www.wisconsinhistory.org/libraryarchives/
State Statutes and Codes: 'http://legis.wisconsin.gov/rsb/stats.html
Legislative Bill Search: 'http://legis.wisconsin.gov/Pages/default.aspx
Bill Monitoring: 'https://notify.legis.wisconsin.gov/login?ReturnUrl=%2f
Unclaimed Funds: http://165.189.60.41/UCPWeb/ucpsearch.aspx

State Public Record Agencies

Criminal Records

Wisconsin Department of Justice, Crime Information Bureau, Record Check Unit, www.doj.state.wi.us/dles/cib/crime-information-bureau The agency offers Internet access at http://wi-recordcheck.org. Access 1) with an account with PIN is required, or 2) pay as you go with Visa/MC credit card. Records must be "picked up" at the website within 10 days. They are not returned by mail. Fee is $7.00 per request. agency. **$$$**

Sexual Offender Registry

Department of Corrections, Sex Offender Registry Program, http://offender.doc.state.wi.us/public/ There are three separate searches available form the home page - by either name, ZIP Code or by mapping location. Exact address of residence is available.

Corporation, LP, LLC, LLP

Division of Corporate & Consumer Services, Corporation Record Requests, www.wdfi.org Selected elements of the database ("CRIS" Corporate Registration Information System) are available online on the department's website at https://www.wdfi.org/apps/CorpSearch/Search.aspx?. A Certificate of Status can be ordered online for $10.00 at https://www.wdfi.org/apps/ccs/directions.asp. To place orders for status, copy work, or ID Reports go to https://www.wdfi.org/apps/oos/. Also, search securities companies and investment advisors free at www.wdfi.org/fi/securities/licensing/licensee_lists/default.asp. **$$$** *Other Options:* Some data is released in database format and is available electronically via email or on CD.

Trademarks/Servicemarks, Trade Names

Dept of Financial Institutions, Tradenames/Trademarks, www.wdfi.org/Notary_Public_and_Trademarks/default.htm Search by trademark description or trade name at https://www.wdfi.org/apps/TrademarkSearch/Search.aspx. *Other Options:* Bulk access is offered - requests are handled on an individual basis.

Uniform Commercial Code, Federal & State Tax Liens

Department of Financial Institutions, CCS/UCC, www.wdfi.org/ucc/ The URL at www.wdfi.org/ucc/search/ provides free search for most records. You may search by filing number or debtor name. Filing submitted online are available immediately, otherwise there is a 3-5 day delay. The search includes federal tax liens. FYI there is a statewide real estate search at https://propertyinfo.revenue.wi.gov/iasWorld/Main/Home.aspx. *Other Options:* Bulk Index data is available on CD. The initial subscription is $3,000, monthly updates of images are $250.00 per month.

Vital Records

WI Deprtment of Health Services, Vital Records, www.dhs.wisconsin.gov/vitalrecords/ Records may be ordered online via www.vitalchek.com, a state approved vendor. **$$$**

Driver Records

Division of Motor Vehicles, Driver Records, www.dot.wisconsin.gov/drivers/ Interactive service is available for approved requesters. Records are provided in PDF format for $5.00 each. The program is called PARS. Call 608-266-0928 or email pars@dot.wi.govfor more information. PARS participants can also participate in an employer notification program. Employers can enroll CDL drivers and will be notified when activity occurs on the employees record. The fee is also $5.00 per record when accessed. WI drivers may order their own record online at www.dot.wisconsin.gov/drivers/drivers/request-record.htm. The fee is $5.50 per record, use of a credit card is required. Also, a free status check of a DL is at www.dot.wisconsin.gov/drivers/online.htm. Must submit either DL, SSN, and DOB, or submit full name and DOB **$$$** *Other Options:* The entire DL of the license file (without convictions, accidents, withdrawals, etc.) is available for $250. The file does not include those who have opted out or who hold merely an ID Card. Purchase of data cannot be used for marketing or solicitations.

Vehicle Ownership & Registration

Department of Transportation, Vehicle Records Section, www.dot.wisconsin.gov/drivers/vehicles/index.htm Wisconsin offers a free license plate check and free lien look-up at online www.dot.wisconsin.gov/drivers/online.htm. Another free service exists at See www.dot.wisconsin.gov/drivers/vehicles/incidents.htm. At this site one may check if a driver has any restrictions (incidents) that would restrict the driver from obtaining a vehicle product (such as a title, registration, etc.). There is an Interactive online inquiry for ongoing, approved requestors. See the PARS program at www.dot.wisconsin.gov/drivers/drivers/pars/introduction.htm#vehicle. Available records include name and address of titled owners or lessees, plate info, vehicle information, and lien data. Fees involved. Also WI drivers may order their own vehicle record abstract online at www.dot.wisconsin.gov/drivers/vehicles/request-record.htm. The fee is $5.50 per record, use of a credit card is required. **$$$** *Other Options:* This agency offers a variety of methods of obtaining bulk registration lists on CD. FTP output by a specific request list is available only on certain files. Call 608-266-1466 for more information. All DPPA restrictions apply.

Voter Registration, Campaign Finance, Lobbyists

Government Accountability Board, Elections and Ethics, http://gab.wi.gov/ The home page for the campaign finance system is at http://cfis.wi.gov/. Filed reports may be viewed.

Occupational Licensing Boards

Accountant Firm .... http://online.drl.wi.gov/LicenseLookup/LicenseLookup.aspx
Accountant-CPA .... http://online.drl.wi.gov/LicenseLookup/IndividualCredentialSearch.aspx
Acupuncturist .... http://online.drl.wi.gov/LicenseLookup/MultipleCredentialSearch.aspx
Adjustment Service Company .... www.wdfi.org/fi/lfs/licensee_lists/
Aesthetics Establishm't/School .... http://online.drl.wi.gov/LicenseLookup/LicenseLookup.aspx
Aestjetician/Aesthetics Instructor .... http://online.drl.wi.gov/LicenseLookup/IndividualCredentialSearch.aspx
Appraiser, Real Estate/Gen/Residential .... http://online.drl.wi.gov/LicenseLookup/IndividualCredentialSearch.aspx
Architect .... http://online.drl.wi.gov/LicenseLookup/IndividualCredentialSearch.aspx
Architectural Corporation .... http://online.drl.wi.gov/LicenseLookup/LicenseLookup.aspx
Art Therapist .... http://online.drl.wi.gov/LicenseLookup/MultipleCredentialSearch.aspx
Asbestos Worker/Investigators/Contractors. www.dhs.wisconsin.gov/asbestos/AsbCompanies/Companyindex.htm
Athlete Agent/Trainer .... http://online.drl.wi.gov/LicenseLookup/IndividualCredentialSearch.aspx
Attorney .... www.wisbar.org/forpublic/ineedalawyer/pages/lris.aspx
Auction Company .... http://online.drl.wi.gov/LicenseLookup/LicenseLookup.aspx
Auctioneer .... http://online.drl.wi.gov/LicenseLookup/IndividualCredentialSearch.aspx
Audiologist .... http://online.drl.wi.gov/LicenseLookup/MultipleCredentialSearch.aspx
Bank .... www.wdfi.org/fi/banks/licensee_lists/default.asp?Browse=Banks
Barber School .... http://online.drl.wi.gov/LicenseLookup/LicenseLookup.aspx
Barber/Appren./Instruct./Mgr. .... http://online.drl.wi.gov/LicenseLookup/IndividualCredentialSearch.aspx
Behavior Analyst .... http://online.drl.wi.gov/LicenseLookup/IndividualCredentialSearch.aspx
Boiler Repairer .... http://apps.commerce.state.wi.us/SB_ServiceAgent/SB_RegObjMain.jsp
Boxer/Judge/Timekeeper .... http://online.drl.wi.gov/LicenseLookup/IndividualCredentialSearch.aspx
Boxing Club, Amateur/Prof. .... http://online.drl.wi.gov/LicenseLookup/LicenseLookup.aspx
Boxing Show .... http://online.drl.wi.gov/LicenseLookup/LicenseLookup.aspx
Building Inspector .... http://apps.commerce.state.wi.us/SB_ServiceAgent/SB_RegObjMain.jsp
Cemetery Authority/Warehouse .... http://online.drl.wi.gov/LicenseLookup/LicenseLookup.aspx

Cemetery Pre-Need Seller	http://online.drl.wi.gov/LicenseLookup/IndividualCredentialSearch.aspx
Cemetery Salesperson	http://online.drl.wi.gov/LicenseLookup/IndividualCredentialSearch.aspx
Charitable Organization	http://online.drl.wi.gov/LicenseLookup/LicenseLookup.aspx
Check Seller	www.wdfi.org/fi/lfs/licensee_lists/
Chiropractor	http://online.drl.wi.gov/LicenseLookup/MultipleCredentialSearch.aspx
Collection Agency	www.wdfi.org/fi/lfs/licensee_lists/
Cosmetologist	http://online.drl.wi.gov/LicenseLookup/IndividualCredentialSearch.aspx
Cosmetology Instr/Mgr/Apprentice	http://online.drl.wi.gov/LicenseLookup/IndividualCredentialSearch.aspx
Cosmetology School	http://online.drl.wi.gov/LicenseLookup/LicenseLookup.aspx
Counselor, Professional	http://online.drl.wi.gov/LicenseLookup/MultipleCredentialSearch.aspx
Credit Service Organization	https://www.wdfi.org/apps/CorpSearch/Search.aspx?
Credit Union	http://researchcu.ncua.gov/Views/FindCreditUnions.aspx
Currency Exchange	www.wdfi.org/fi/lfs/licensee_lists/
Dance Therapist	http://online.drl.wi.gov/LicenseLookup/MultipleCredentialSearch.aspx
Debt Collector	www.wdfi.org/fi/lfs/licensee_lists/
Dental Hygienist	http://online.drl.wi.gov/LicenseLookup/MultipleCredentialSearch.aspx
Dentist	http://online.drl.wi.gov/LicenseLookup/MultipleCredentialSearch.aspx
Designer, Engineering Systems	http://online.drl.wi.gov/LicenseLookup/IndividualCredentialSearch.aspx
Dietitian	http://online.drl.wi.gov/LicenseLookup/MultipleCredentialSearch.aspx
Drug Distributor/Mfg	http://online.drl.wi.gov/LicenseLookup/LicenseLookup.aspx
Electrical Inspector	http://apps.commerce.state.wi.us/SB_ServiceAgent/SB_RegObjMain.jsp
Electrician	http://apps.commerce.state.wi.us/SB_ServiceAgent/SB_RegObjMain.jsp
Electrologist/Electrology Instructor	http://online.drl.wi.gov/LicenseLookup/IndividualCredentialSearch.aspx
Electrology Establishment/School	http://online.drl.wi.gov/LicenseLookup/LicenseLookup.aspx
Employee Benefits Plan Administrator	https://ociaccess.oci.wi.gov/ProducerInfo/PrdIndividual.oci
EMT/Paramedic	https://www.wi-emss.org/public/wisconsin/default.cfm?page=public_lookup
Engineer/Engineer in Training	http://online.drl.wi.gov/LicenseLookup/IndividualCredentialSearch.aspx
Engineering Corporation	http://online.drl.wi.gov/LicenseLookup/LicenseLookup.aspx
Fertilizer	http://datcp.wi.gov/uploads/Environment/xls/FertLicense_Aug08.xls
Firearms Certifier	http://online.drl.wi.gov/LicenseLookup/IndividualCredentialSearch.aspx
Firearms Permit	http://online.drl.wi.gov/LicenseLookup/LicenseLookup.aspx
Fireworks Manufacturer	http://apps.commerce.state.wi.us/SB_ServiceAgent/SB_RegObjMain.jsp
Fund Raiser, Professional	http://online.drl.wi.gov/LicenseLookup/IndividualCredentialSearch.aspx
Fund Raising Counsel	http://online.drl.wi.gov/LicenseLookup/LicenseLookup.aspx
Funeral Director/Director Apprentice	http://online.drl.wi.gov/LicenseLookup/IndividualCredentialSearch.aspx
Funeral Establishment	http://online.drl.wi.gov/LicenseLookup/LicenseLookup.aspx
Funeral Pre-Need Seller	http://online.drl.wi.gov/LicenseLookup/IndividualCredentialSearch.aspx
Geologist	http://online.drl.wi.gov/LicenseLookup/IndividualCredentialSearch.aspx
Geology Firm	http://online.drl.wi.gov/LicenseLookup/LicenseLookup.aspx
Hearing Instrument Specialist	http://online.drl.wi.gov/LicenseLookup/MultipleCredentialSearch.aspx
HMO	https://ociaccess.oci.wi.gov/CmpInfo/CmpInfo.oci
Home Inspector	http://online.drl.wi.gov/LicenseLookup/IndividualCredentialSearch.aspx
HVAC Contractor	http://apps.commerce.state.wi.us/SB_ServiceAgent/SB_RegObjMain.jsp
Hydrologist	http://online.drl.wi.gov/LicenseLookup/IndividualCredentialSearch.aspx
Hydrology Firm	http://online.drl.wi.gov/LicenseLookup/LicenseLookup.aspx
Indian Gaming Vendor	www.doa.state.wi.us/category.asp?linkcatid=843&linkid=117&locid=7
Insurance Company	https://ociaccess.oci.wi.gov/ProducerInfo/PrdIndividual.oci
Insurance Intermediary	https://ociaccess.oci.wi.gov/ProducerInfo/PrdIndividual.oci
Insurance Premium Financier	www.wdfi.org/fi/lfs/licensee_lists/
Insurance Producer	https://ociaccess.oci.wi.gov/ProducerInfo/PrdFirm.oci
Interior Designer	http://online.drl.wi.gov/LicenseLookup/IndividualCredentialSearch.aspx
Investment Advisor/Advisor Rep	www.wdfi.org/fi/securities/licensing/licensee_lists/default.asp
Land Surveyor	http://online.drl.wi.gov/LicenseLookup/IndividualCredentialSearch.aspx
Landscape Architect	http://online.drl.wi.gov/LicenseLookup/IndividualCredentialSearch.aspx
Loan Company	www.wdfi.org/fi/lfs/licensee_lists/

Loan Solicitor/Originator	www.wdfi.org/fi/lfs/licensee_lists/default.asp
Lobbying Organization, Principal	https://lobbying.wi.gov/Directories/DirectoryOfLicensedLobbyists/2013REG
Lobbyist	https://lobbying.wi.gov/Directories/DirectoryOfLicensedLobbyists/2013REG
Manicurist Establ./Specialty School	http://online.drl.wi.gov/LicenseLookup/LicenseLookup.aspx
Manicurist/Manicurist Instructor	http://online.drl.wi.gov/LicenseLookup/IndividualCredentialSearch.aspx
Marriage & Family Therapist	http://online.drl.wi.gov/LicenseLookup/MultipleCredentialSearch.aspx
Massage Therapist/Bodyworker	http://online.drl.wi.gov/LicenseLookup/MultipleCredentialSearch.aspx
Matchmaker	http://online.drl.wi.gov/LicenseLookup/IndividualCredentialSearch.aspx
Midwife	http://online.drl.wi.gov/LicenseLookup/MultipleCredentialSearch.aspx
Mixed Artial Arts Contest	http://online.drl.wi.gov/LicenseLookup/LicenseLookup.aspx
Mobile Home & RV Dealer	www.wdfi.org/fi/lfs/licensee_lists/
Mortgage Banker/Broker	www.wdfi.org/fi/lfs/licensee_lists/default.asp
Motor Club	https://ociaccess.oci.wi.gov/CmpInfo/CmpInfo.oci
Motorcycle Dealer	www.wdfi.org/fi/lfs/licensee_lists/
Music Therapist	http://online.drl.wi.gov/LicenseLookup/MultipleCredentialSearch.aspx
Notary Public	https://www.wdfi.org/apps/NotarySearch/SearchCriteria.aspx
Nurse-RN/LPN	http://online.drl.wi.gov/LicenseLookup/MultipleCredentialSearch.aspx
Nursing Home Administrator	http://online.drl.wi.gov/LicenseLookup/IndividualCredentialSearch.aspx
Occupational Therapist/Assistant	http://online.drl.wi.gov/LicenseLookup/MultipleCredentialSearch.aspx
Optometrist	http://online.drl.wi.gov/LicenseLookup/MultipleCredentialSearch.aspx
Osteopathic Physician	http://online.drl.wi.gov/LicenseLookup/MultipleCredentialSearch.aspx
Payday Lender	www.wdfi.org/fi/lfs/licensee_lists/
Pesticide Applicator Business	http://datcp.wi.gov/Plants/Pesticides/Pesticide_Databases/index.aspx
Pesticide Applicator/Dealer	http://datcp.wi.gov/Plants/Pesticides/Pesticide_Databases/index.aspx
Pesticide Manufacturer/Labeler	http://datcp.wi.gov/Plants/Pesticides/Pesticide_Databases/index.aspx
Pesticide Vet Clinic	http://datcp.wi.gov/Plants/Pesticides/Pesticide_Databases/index.aspx
Pharmacy (instate/out of state)	http://online.drl.wi.gov/LicenseLookup/LicenseLookup.aspx
Pharmacy/Pharmacist	http://online.drl.wi.gov/LicenseLookup/MultipleCredentialSearch.aspx
Physical Therapist	http://online.drl.wi.gov/LicenseLookup/MultipleCredentialSearch.aspx
Physician/Medical Doctor/Surgeon/Asst	http://online.drl.wi.gov/LicenseLookup/MultipleCredentialSearch.aspx
Plumber	http://apps.commerce.state.wi.us/SB_ServiceAgent/SB_RegObjMain.jsp
Podiatrist	http://online.drl.wi.gov/LicenseLookup/MultipleCredentialSearch.aspx
Private Detective Agency	http://online.drl.wi.gov/LicenseLookup/LicenseLookup.aspx
Private Investigator	http://online.drl.wi.gov/LicenseLookup/IndividualCredentialSearch.aspx
Psychologist	http://online.drl.wi.gov/LicenseLookup/MultipleCredentialSearch.aspx
Radiographer/X-Ray Machine Operator	http://online.drl.wi.gov/LicenseLookup/IndividualCredentialSearch.aspx
Rate Service Org	https://ociaccess.oci.wi.gov/CmpInfo/CmpInfo.oci
Real Estate Agent/Broker/Sales	http://online.drl.wi.gov/LicenseLookup/IndividualCredentialSearch.aspx
Real Estate Appraiser	http://online.drl.wi.gov/LicenseLookup/IndividualCredentialSearch.aspx
Real Estate Business Entity	http://online.drl.wi.gov/LicenseLookup/LicenseLookup.aspx
Respiratory Care Practitioner	http://online.drl.wi.gov/LicenseLookup/MultipleCredentialSearch.aspx
Risk Purchasing Group	https://ociaccess.oci.wi.gov/CmpInfo/CmpInfo.oci
Sales Finance/Loan Company	www.wdfi.org/fi/lfs/licensee_lists/
Savings & Loan Financer	www.wdfi.org/fi/lfs/licensee_lists/
Savings Institution	www.wdfi.org/fi/savings_institutions/licensee_lists/
School Librarian/Media Specialist	https://www2.dpi.wi.gov/lic-tll/home.do
School Psychology Private Practice	http://online.drl.wi.gov/LicenseLookup/MultipleCredentialSearch.aspx
Securities Broker/Dealer/Agent	www.wdfi.org/fi/securities/licensing/licensee_lists/default.asp
Security Guard	http://online.drl.wi.gov/LicenseLookup/IndividualCredentialSearch.aspx
Sign Language Interpreter	http://online.drl.wi.gov/LicenseLookup/IndividualCredentialSearch.aspx
Social Worker	http://online.drl.wi.gov/LicenseLookup/MultipleCredentialSearch.aspx
Soil Science Firm	http://online.drl.wi.gov/LicenseLookup/LicenseLookup.aspx
Soil Scientist	http://online.drl.wi.gov/LicenseLookup/IndividualCredentialSearch.aspx
Soil Tester	http://apps.commerce.state.wi.us/SB_ServiceAgent/SB_RegObjMain.jsp
Speech Pathologist/Audiologist	http://online.drl.wi.gov/LicenseLookup/MultipleCredentialSearch.aspx

Teacher https://www2.dpi.wi.gov/lic-tll/home.do
Timeshare Salesperson .... http://online.drl.wi.gov/LicenseLookup/IndividualCredentialSearch.aspx
Veterinarian/Veterinary Technician .... http://online.drl.wi.gov/LicenseLookup/MultipleCredentialSearch.aspx
Viatical Settlement Broker .... https://ociaccess.oci.wi.gov/ProducerInfo/PrdIndividual.oci
Welder .... http://apps.commerce.state.wi.us/SB_ServiceAgent/SB_RegObjMain.jsp

State and Local Courts

State Court Structure: **Circuit Courts** have original jurisdiction in all civil and criminal matters within the state, including juvenile, and some traffic matters, as well as civil and criminal jury trials. The Small Claims limit is $5,000. The Clerk of Court is the record custodian.

The majority of **Municipal Court** cases involve traffic and ordinance matters. **Probate filing** is a function of the Circuit Court; however, each county has a **Register in Probate** who maintains and manages the probate records, guardianship, and mental health records.

Appellate Courts: Appellate Courts and Supreme Court opinions are available from http://wicourts.gov.

Statewide Court Online Access: All courts participate in the system described below.

The Wisconsin Circuit Court Access (WCCA) is a public access website that provides open record information per state law §§ 19.21-.39. Users may view **Circuit Court** case information at http://wcca.wicourts.gov. Access is free. With the recent addition of Portage county, data is now available from all counties.

Searches can be conducted either statewide or by a specific county. WCCA provides detailed information about circuit cases including criminal, civil and traffic. A docketed civil judgment search is also offered. Data throughput dates vary by county, but in general most counties have participated since the early 1990s.

The search allows a search by name, but for example if searching civil records you cannot designate in the search that the subject is a plaintiff or a defendant. Also, the search result page may not reveal multiple defendant parties, the entire case must be reviewed. As a result, this can be quite cumbersome.

Search results generally include the middle initial. The DOB is shown some of the time, and sometimes the DOB is only the month and year. The probate records are included for all counties. Confidential court records not included are restricted cases, adoptions, juvenile delinquency, child protection, termination of parental rights, guardianship, and civil commitments.

WCCA data is also available through a Simple Object Access Protocol (SOAP) interface and RSS Feeds on a subscription basis. For subscription, contact and technical information see http://wcca.wicourts.gov/index.xsl.

A Cautionary Note - While the information contained on the WCCA Web site has been entered by the official record-keepers in each county, it does consist of information voluntarily provided by county court staff. There is no mandate that all information must be reported. Note that WI has legislated that the WI Department of Justice to be the official record holder of criminal record information. It is advised to check with an attorney if using the WCCA for pre-employment screening purposes.

Other County Sites, Not Including the Statewide Site Mentioned Above:

Dane County

The Dane County Sheriff's Office provides an online request only site for accident reports, incident reports, and other records. See www.danesheriff.com/records.aspx.

Milwaukee County

Municipal Court
Criminal: Criminal case records on Milwaukee Municipal Court Case Information System database are free at http://query.municourt.milwaukee.gov/. Search ordinace and traffic violations by case or citation number, or by name..

Portage County

Circuit Court (Branches 1, 2 & 3) www.co.portage.wi.us/
Civil: Internet access is upon approval. Request in writing to Data Processing Dept, 1462 Strong Ave, Stevens Point 54481. Explain purpose of record requests. Online results show DOB most of time; however, sometimes DOB is month and year only on the index. **$$$** *Criminal:* same **$$$**

Recorders, Assessors, and Other Sites of Note

Recording Office Organization: 72 counties, 72 recording offices. The recording officers are the Register of Deeds for real estate and Clerk of Court for state tax liens. County Clerks hold marriage records and state tax liens.

Federal tax liens on personal property of businesses are filed with the Secretary of State. Only federal tax liens on real estate are filed with the county Register of Deeds. State tax liens are filed with the Clerk of Court, and at the State Treasurer at the State Department of Revenue.

Statewide or Multi-Jurisdiction Access: There is no statewide access to recorder and assessor records, but several cities and a growing number of counties offer online. One vendor has a wide range of coverage, see below.

- The Wisconsin Register of Deeds Association website at www.wrdaonline.org/RealEstateRecords offers helpful guidance to which counties are online. But their map has not been updated since 2007.
- Access recorder land data is available online in 23 counties by subscription from the Tapestry system. Fees are based on a flat rate by usage ranging from $50 to $250 per month plus a slight per minute if usage is surpassed. There is a $5.95 fee per search and copies can be generated for $.50 per page. You can pay as you go with a credit card or be billed monthly with a $25.00 monthly minimum. Visit at https://tapestry.fidlar.com. Participating counties are shown in the profiles below.

County Sites:

Adams County ***Real Estate, Deed, Lien Records*** www.co.adams.wi.gov/Departments/RegisterofDeeds/tabid/82/Default.aspx Access Register of Deeds data free at www.adamscountylandrecords.com/.

Property, Taxation Records Access assessor parcel data free at www.adamscountylandrecords.com but no name searching.

Ashland County ***Real Estate, Grantor/Grantee, Deed Records*** www.co.ashland.wi.us/departments/register-of-deeds Access to a general index to land related information free at http://ashlandwi.roddirect.com. Document images may be purchased using a credit card, establishing an escrow account or by paying a monthly fee for a subscription. **$$$**

Barron County ***Recorded Documents*** www.barroncountywi.gov/index.asp?Type=B_BASIC&SEC={4E43BDA8-057A-4774-A3AA-FB80457689E9} Access to records for a fee at https://tapestry.fidlar.com/Tapestry2/Default.aspx. Contact 309-794-3283 or kylec@fidlar.com for subscription information. Search fee is $5.95 each, printed images $.50 each unless otherwise noted. Find land records free at www.co.barron.wi.us/GCSWebPortal/Search.aspx. **$$$**

Property, Taxation Records Access to GIS/mapping for free at http://barroncowi.wgxtreme.com/.

Bayfield County ***Recorded Documents*** www.bayfieldcounty.org/register-of-deeds.asp Access to records for a fee at https://tapestry.fidlar.com/Tapestry2/Default.aspx. Contact 309-794-3283 or kylec@fidlar.com for subscription information. Search fee is $5.95 each, printed images $.50 each unless otherwise noted. **$$$**

Property, Taxation Records Access to property tax and land record information free at http://novus.bayfieldcounty.org:8081/. Also, access to mapping free at www.bayfieldcounty.org/map/.

Brown County Register of Deeds ***Recorded Documents*** www.co.brown.wi.us/departments/?department=e7fb85d94ba9 Access to records for a fee at https://tapestry.fidlar.com/Tapestry2/Default.aspx. Contact 309-794-3283 or kylec@fidlar.com for subscription information. Search fee is $5.95 each, printed images $.50 each unless otherwise noted. **$$$**

Property, Taxation Records Access to land records at www.co.brown.wi.us/departments/?department=133c6a3594a2. Also, land records can be downloaded from an ftp site; contact the Land Information office at 920-448-6295 to register and user information. Also, GIS/mapping site at http://maps.gis.co.brown.wi.us/geoprime/#ymax=618078.2783470246;ymin=477670.29223591334;xmax=197109.93930060434;xmin=30009.2448561598. Also, search for property data free at www.co.brown.wi.us/planning_and_land_services/land_information_office/.

Buffalo County ***Recorded Records Records*** www.buffalocounty.com/Buffalo%20County%20Register%20of%20Deeds.htm Access to recorded records free at www.buffalocounty.com/GCSWebPortal/Search.aspx.

Burnett County ***Real Estate Records*** www.burnettcounty.com/index.aspx?nid=100 Access to records free at http://burnettwi.roddirect.com/. Copies of document images may be purchased with credit card.

Property, Taxation Records Access to limited county property and assessment records is free at www.burnettcounty.org/. No name searching. For full data, an online subscription service is $100 per year. Also, access to GIS/mapping free at http://burnettwi.mapping-online.com/BurnettCoWi/.**$$$**

Calumet County ***Property, Taxation Records*** Access to assessor property tax data is free at http://calum400.co.calumet.wi.us/nsccalo/nsclndrec.

Chippewa County ***Recorded Documents*** www.co.chippewa.wi.us/index.php?option=com_content&view=article&id=121&Itemid=43 Access to records for a fee at https://tapestry.fidlar.com/Tapestry2/Default.aspx. Contact 309-794-3283 or kylec@fidlar.com for subscription information. Search fee is $5.95 each, printed images $.50 each unless otherwise noted. **$$$**

Property, Taxation Records Search property assessment and property tax database free at http://cctax.co.chippewa.wi.us/CCTax/Taxrtr?. Also, access to real property data free at www.assessordata.org/.

Clark County ***Recorded Documents, Delinquent Property Records*** www.co.clark.wi.us/index.aspx?nid=397 Real estate recording, property data, and delinquent tax info is available by subscription, see https://secure.propertymanagementportal.com/pmp/wi/clark/default.aspx. Fee is $25 per month and $1.20 per transaction, or $1.80 per transaction for casual users. **$$$**

Columbia County ***Recorded Documents*** www.co.columbia.wi.us/ColumbiaCounty/registerofdeeds/RegisterofDeedsHomePage/tabid/52/Default.aspx Access to records for a fee at https://tapestry.fidlar.com/Tapestry2/Default.aspx. Contact 309-794-3283 or kylec@fidlar.com for subscription information. Search fee is $5.95 each, printed images $.50 each unless otherwise noted. **$$$**

Property, Taxation Records Access the county tax parcel system free at http://lrs.co.columbia.wi.us/lrsweb/search.aspx. Also, search property info free on the GIS-mapping site at http://lrs.co.columbia.wi.us/website/ColumbiaCo/ColumbiaCo.asp.

Crawford County ***Recorded Documents*** www.crawfordcountywi.org/registerofdeeds/index.htm Access to land records index at https://landshark.crawfordcountywi.org/LandShark/login.jsp?url=https%3A%2F%2Flandshark.crawfordcountywi.org%2FLandShark%2Fsearchname.jsp. Fees invloved. **$$$**

Property, Taxation Records Access to GIS/mapping and tax and assessment data for free at http://crawfordwi.mapping-online.com/CrawfordCoWi/.

Dane County ***Recorded Documents*** http://countyofdane.com/regdeeds/default.aspx Access to records for a fee at https://tapestry.fidlar.com/Tapestry2/Default.aspx. Contact 309-794-3283 or kylec@fidlar.com for subscription information. Search fee is $5.95 each, printed images $.50 each unless otherwise noted. **$$$**

Property, Taxation Records Access to GIS/mapping for free at http://dcimap.countyofdane.com/OnPointWebsite/WebPages/Map/FundyViewer.aspx. Also, City of Madison tax assessor data is at www.cityofmadison.com/assessor/property/index.cfm. Search Sun Prairie property at http://db.sun-prairie.com/property/ and death list at http://db.sun-prairie.com/deathlist/. Also, search property info for Cross Plains, Mazomanie, Black Earth villages at www.wendorffassessing.com/municipalities.htm.

Dodge County ***Recorded Documents*** www.co.dodge.wi.us/index.aspx?page=65 Search Register of Deeds data at http://landshark.co.dodge.wi.us/LandShark/login.jsp?url=http%3A%2F%2Flandshark.co.dodge.wi.us%2FLandShark%2Fsearchname.jsp, index search is free, but fees apply for images and copies, $2.00 1st page, $1.00 2nd page. **$$$**

Property, Taxation Records Access to land records for free at http://dr1.co.dodge.wi.us/lrst/default.asp.

Door County ***Real Estate, Deed, Lien Records*** Access to land records images is by internet subscription or on CD-ROM. Subscription or CD is $300 monthly; call Register of Deeds 920-746-2270 for info and signup or escrow account. **$$$**

Douglas County ***Recorded Documents*** www.douglascountywi.org/ Access to the county Landshark system is at http://rdlandshark.douglascountywi.org/LandShark/login.jsp. Free registration is required.

Property, Taxation Records Access county land and property tax records free at www.gcssoftware.com/douglas/Search.aspx.

Dunn County ***Recorded Documents*** www.dunncountywi.govoffice2.com/ Access to records for a fee at https://tapestry.fidlar.com/Tapestry2/Default.aspx. Contact 309-794-3283 or kylec@fidlar.com for subscription information. Search fee is $5.95 each, printed images $.50 each unless otherwise noted. **$$$**

Property, Taxation Records Access to GIS/mapping data for free at www.dunncountywi.govoffice2.com/index.asp?Type=B_BASIC&SEC={D8E5BD75-3819-4CF2-960D-909DA05BFF43}.

Eau Claire County ***Recorded Documents*** www.co.eau-claire.wi.us Access to records for a fee at https://tapestry.fidlar.com/Tapestry2/Default.aspx. Contact 309-794-3283 or kylec@fidlar.com for subscription information. Search fee is $5.95 each, printed images $.50 each unless otherwise noted. **$$$**

Property, Taxation Records Access to GIS/mapping for free at http://eauclairecowi.wgxtreme.com/.

Florence County ***Property, Taxation Records*** Access to GIS/mapping free at www.florencewisconsin.com/GCSWebPortal/Search.aspx.

Fond du Lac County ***Property, Taxation Records*** Access to parcel data is free through the GIS-mapping site at www.fdlco.wi.gov/Index.aspx?page=1083. Also, access to tax parcel data search from free go to http://landinfo.fdlco.wi.gov/ascent/Parcel/SelectParcel.aspx.

Forest County ***Recorded Documents*** www.co.forest.wi.gov/localgov_departments_details.asp?deptid=392&locid=145 Access to the county Landshark system is at http://69.179.87.74/LandShark/login.jsp?url=http%3A%2F%2F69.179.87.74%2FLandShark%2Fsearchlegal.jsp. Free registration is required. No fee to search, fee for images. Also, access to real estate and grantor/grantee information free at https://propertyinfo.revenue.wi.gov/iasWorld/Search/Disclaimer2.aspx?FromUrl=../Search/GenericSearch.aspx?mode=owner. **$$$**

Property, Taxation Records Access to county property and assessor data free is at www.gcssoftware.com/forest/Search.aspx.

Grant County ***RE Tax, Grantor/Grantee Records*** http://grantcounty.org Subscription to all tax information and grantor/grantee index call John Anderson at 608-723-2666. **$$$**

Property, Taxation Records Access to county property and assessor data is at www.gcssoftware.com/Products/WebSearch.aspx and click on Grant County. Registration, $200.00 annual fee, username, and password required; call John at the Tax Lister office, 608-723-2666. Access to TriCounty GIS/mapping free at http://rmgis2.ruekert-mielke.com/tricounty/. This covers Grant, Iowa and Lafayette counties; free registration required.**$$$**

Green County ***Property, Taxation Records*** Access to parcel data is free on the GIS-mapping site at http://gis.msa-ps.com/greencounty/publicviewer/startup.htm.

Green Lake County ***Recorded Documents*** www.co.green-lake.wi.us/departments.html?Department=18 Access to records for a fee at https://tapestry.fidlar.com/Tapestry2/Default.aspx. Contact 309-794-3283 or kylec@fidlar.com for subscription information. Search fee is $5.95 each, printed images $.50 each unless otherwise noted. **$$$**

Property, Taxation Records Search GIS-mapping site for property data free at http://gis.co.green-lake.wi.us/website/GIS_Viewer_limit/viewer.htm but no name searching.

Iowa County ***Property, Taxation Records*** Access to TriCounty GIS/mapping for free at http://iowagrant.ims.ruekert-mielke.com/. This covers Grant and Iowa counties. Free registration required.

Iron County ***Real Estate, Grantor/Grantee, Deed Records*** www.co.iron.wi.gov/ Access to land records is available at http://records.ironcountywi.org/LandShark/login.jsp registration is required. No fee to search, but fee for images. Records go back to 1994. **$$$**

Jackson County ***Real Estate, Grantor/Grantee Records*** www.co.jackson.wi.us/index.asp?Type=B_BASIC&SEC={EBDF6BC5-8296-4082-86C7-1F77C1F49B1D} Access to document search (images only) free at http://jacksonwi.roddirect.com/. Copies may be purchased. **$$$**

Property, Taxation Records Access to property records are available online for free at http://jacksoncowi.wgxtreme.com/.

Jefferson County ***Real Estate, Grantor/Grantee, Deed, Lien Records*** www.jeffersoncountywi.gov/jc/public/jchome.php?page_id=158 Access parcel data free at www.jeffersoncountywi.gov/jclrs/LIO/LIO_Search.php, but no name searching. To order full records online using your credit card, see http://lrs.co.jefferson.wi.us/. Call 920-674-7254 for info, fees, and signup. Land records data is available by subscription on JCLRP; fee is $45 per month paid quarterly; document images $30 monthly plus $1 per page viewed. **$$$**

Property, Taxation Records Search assessment records free at www.jeffersoncountywi.gov/jc/public/jchome.php?page_id=1077, but no name searching. Also, search property data free on the GIS-mapping site at http://lrs.co.jefferson.wi.us/jcgis/main.do but no name searching.

Juneau County ***Real Estate, Deed, Mortgage Records*** www.co.juneau.wi.gov/localgov_departments_details.asp?deptid=444&locid=151 The ROD offers subscription, escrow and credit card services for Real Estate access; online docs go back to 01/01/1999 at https://landshark.co.juneau.wi.us/LandShark/. **$$$**

Property, Taxation Records Search the GIS-mapping site for property and assessment data free at http://gis.co.juneau.wi.us/pvweb22/index.htm. Click on free account login, then click \"Search Data\" but no name searching. Also a subscription service for complete property data. To search land sales by town, click on Land Sales at www.co.juneau.wi.gov/.**$$$**

Kenosha County ***Recorded Documents*** www.co.kenosha.wi.us/index.aspx?nid=522 Access to land records is available at https://landshark.co.kenosha.wi.us/LandShark/login.jsp registration is required. Fees to search. Records go back to 1994. Also, for non-name search of real estate see www.co.kenosha.wi.us/apps/propinq/index.phtml. No fee. **$$$**

Property, Taxation Records Search the Kenosha City Assessor's property database for free at www.kenosha.org/departments/assessor/search.html. No name searching. Access real estate records free at www.co.kenosha.wi.us/index.html and select under Property, Mapping & Environment. Also access parcel data free on the GIS-mapping site free at http://kcmapping.co.kenosha.wi.us/mapping_public/.

Kewaunee County ***Recorded Documents*** www.kewauneeco.org/ Access to the Register of Deeds CherryLAN Indexing and Imaging System is available for a monthly subscription fee of $300. Escrow subscription with an initial $100 deposit are also available. Index back to 10/12/89. **$$$**

Property, Taxation Records Search land/tax records free at www.kewauneeco.org/GCSWebPortal/search.aspx. Also, search parcel maps and property tax data free on the GIS mapping site at www.kewauneeco.org/. Subscription required for full data. Click on Land Records.**$$$**

La Crosse County ***Recorded Documents*** www.co.la-crosse.wi.us/Departments/departments.htm Access to records for a fee at https://tapestry.fidlar.com/Tapestry2/Default.aspx. Contact 309-794-3283 or kylec@fidlar.com for subscription information. Search fee is $5.95 each, printed images $.50 each unless otherwise noted. **$$$**

Property, Taxation Records Search for property owner and land data for free at www.co.la-crosse.wi.us/landrecordsportal/default.aspx.

Lafayette County ***Recorded Documents*** www.co.lafayette.wi.gov/localgov_departments_details.asp?deptid=315&locid=152 Access to records for a fee at https://tapestry.fidlar.com/Tapestry2/Default.aspx. Contact 309-794-3283 or kylec@fidlar.com for subscription information. Search fee is $5.95 each, printed images $.50 each unless otherwise noted. **$$$**

Property, Taxation Records Access to TriCounty GIS/mapping for free at http://rmgis2.ruekert-mielke.com/tricounty/. This covers Grant, Iowa and Lafayette counties. Free registration required.

Langlade County ***Recorded Documents, Birth Records*** www.co.langlade.wi.us/registerofdeeds.htm Access county birth index free at www.co.langlade.wi.us/Births/, from 1882 to 1909 Also, access to parcel search free at www.langladecogiws.com/LangladeCoWi/.

Property, Taxation Records Access property data free at www.langladecogiws.com/LangladeCoWi/ but no name searching.

Lincoln County Service Center ***Recorded Documents*** www.co.lincoln.wi.us/departments/?department=aa384fe82c0c Access to records for a fee at https://tapestry.fidlar.com/Tapestry2/Default.aspx. Contact 309-794-3283 or kylec@fidlar.com for subscription information. Search fee is $5.95 each, printed images $.50 each unless otherwise noted. **$$$**

Manitowoc County ***Real Estate, Deed Records*** www.manitowoc-county.com/department/dept_home.asp?ID=23 Access to Register of Deeds recorded land records system requires username and password at http://rod.manitowoc-county.com/landweb.dll; contact Register of Deeds office for sign-up. Indexes available from 3/1/1991 to present. **$$$**

Property, Taxation Records Access tax records free at http://manitowoc-county.com/taxquery/main.htm but no name searching. Search on GIS-map site at http://webmap.manitowoc-county.com/website/pasystem/. Foreclosures- www.manitowoc-county.com/ftp/treasurer/Reference/Foreclosed.htm. Manitowoc City Assessor database free at http://assessor.manitowoc.org/CityAssessor/search.aspx?sn=-. No name searching.

Marathon County ***Property, Taxation Records*** Access to county property records is free at www.co.marathon.wi.us/online/apps/lrs/index.asp. No name searching. Access by subscription is also available for full data. Also, access parcel/property data on the GIS-mapping site fee at http://gismaps.co.marathon.wi.us/gisweb/ccdcc_pub/ccdcc.asp. No name searching.**$$$**

Marinette County ***Real Estate, Deed Records*** www.marinettecounty.com/departments/?department=2ce81d5e7364 Access to real estate index at http://landshark.marinettecounty.com/LandShark/registration.jsp. Requires account. Search index free but $2.00 fee (plus $1.00 each add'l.) to view document. Registration and escrow account required. **$$$**

Property, Taxation Records Access to GIS/mapping for free at http://webgis.marinettecounty.com/.

Marquette County ***Property, Taxation Records*** Access to land records for free at http://marquettewi.mapping-online.com/MarquetteCoWi/.

Milwaukee County ***Recorded Documents*** http://county.milwaukee.gov/RegisterofDeeds7722.htm Access to records for a fee at https://tapestry.fidlar.com/Tapestry2/Default.aspx. Contact 309-794-3283 or kylec@fidlar.com for subscription information. Search fee is $5.95 each, printed images $.50 each unless otherwise noted. **$$$**

Property, Taxation Records Assessment data & sales data on Milwaukee City (not county) database at http://city.milwaukee.gov/DataampDataSearches673.htm. Search Franklin- at http://taxassessment.franklinwi.gov/assessmentsearch.cfm. Glendale- http://ts.glendale-wi.org; West Allis- http://apps.westalliswi.gov/property_search/search.aspx. Greendale at http://98.103.253.166/search.aspx.

Monroe County ***Property, Taxation Records*** Access assessment data on the GIS/mapping site free at http://monroecowi.wgxtreme.com/.

Oconto County ***Grantor/Grantee, Real Estate, Tax Lien Records*** www.co.oconto.wi.us/departments/?department=13771fafd73f Access to Registrar of Deeds available by subscription or escrow account at https://landshark.co.oconto.wi.us/LandShark/. You may also purchase a document with a credit card. **$$$**

Property, Taxation Records Access to the county SOLO tax parcel search is free or by subscription at http://solo.co.oconto.wi.us/ocontoco/. The free service does not include name searching. Subscription fee for full data is $300 per calendar year. Phone 920-834-6800 for more info.**$$$**

Oneida County ***Property, Taxation Records*** Access to property tax data is available free at http://octax.co.oneida.wi.us/ONCTax/Taxrtr. Also, search land records by name on the GIS mapping site at http://ocgis.co.oneida.wi.us/oneida/index.htm.

Outagamie County ***Real Estate, Deed, Mortgage, Judgment, Property Records*** www.outagamie.org/index.aspx?page=72 Access recorded documents data at https://landshark.co.outagamie.wi.us/LandShark/login.jsp. Registration and fees required for full data. Also, access to real estate taxes and maps free at www.outagamie.org/. Click on GIS/Maps & Taxes/Deeds. **$$$**

Property, Taxation Records Search property data free at http://outagamiecowi.wgxtreme.com/property, no name searching. Also, access a variety of property records at www.outagamie.org/index.aspx?page=76.**$$$**

Ozaukee County ***Recorded Documents*** www.co.ozaukee.wi.us Access to records for a fee at https://tapestry.fidlar.com/Tapestry2/Default.aspx. Contact 309-794-3283 or kylec@fidlar.com for subscription information. Search fee is $5.95 each, printed images $.50 each unless otherwise noted. **$$$**

Pepin County Register of Deeds ***Real Estate, Grantor/Grantee, Tax Lien Records*** www.wrdaonline.org/Biography/pepin.htm Access to records free at http://pepinwi.roddirect.com/Search/Search.aspx?showdisclaimer=1.

Property, Taxation Records Access maps, land records and tax data free at www.co.pepin.wi.us/.

Pierce County ***Recorded Documents*** www.co.pierce.wi.us/Register%20of%20Deeds/Register_Deeds_Main.html Access to records for a fee at https://tapestry.fidlar.com/Tapestry2/Default.aspx. Contact 309-794-3283 or kylec@fidlar.com for subscription information. Search fee is $5.95 each, printed images $.50 each unless otherwise noted. **$$$**

Property, Taxation Records Access to county property data is free at www.co.pierce.wi.us/Land%20Information%20Disclaimer.html. Click on Property Data Search.

Polk County ***Real Estate Records*** www.co.polk.wi.us Access to records free at http://polkwi.roddirect.com/.
Property, Taxation Records Access to GIS-mapping records free at http://polkcowi.wgxtreme.com/.

Portage County ***Recorded Documents*** www.co.portage.wi.us/rod/ Access to county records is free at https://landshark.co.portage.wi.us/LandShark/login.jsp. Registration required; searching is free; fee for copies of images. Property tax data does not include Stevens Point City. Access to records for a fee at https://tapestry.fidlar.com/Tapestry2/Default.aspx. Contact 309-794-3283 or kylec@fidlar.com forsubscription information. Search fee is $5.95 each, pringed images $.50 each unless otherwise noted. **$$$**
Property, Taxation Records Search the county tax application database free at http://pctax.co.portage.wi.us/PCTax/Taxrtr?action=taxdefault but no name searching. Property data on the GIS mapping site free at http://gisinfo.co.portage.wi.us/realestate/.

Price County ***Tax Rolls/Assessment, GIS Maps Records*** www.co.price.wi.us Access to public access records free at www.co.price.wi.us/government/CountyTreasurersOffice/DefaultPagePublicAccess.htm. Click on Real Estate or Personal Property.
Property, Taxation Records Access to land record/GIS for free at http://pricecowi.wgxtreme.com/.

Racine County ***Real Estate, Deed Records*** www.racineco.com/registerofdeeds/index.aspx Real estate record access is via a dial-up system; email or call the Racine County Register of Deeds Office, 262-636-3208, or see www.racineco.com/registerofdeeds/. **$$$**
Property, Taxation Records Tax inquiry is available free at http://services.racineco.com/propertytax/

Richland County ***Real Estate, Grantor/Grantee, Deed Records*** www.rclrs.net/rod/default.asp Search recorded land index for free at http://richlandwi.roddirect.com/ but fees apply to print images. Records go back to 9/1/1988. **$$$**
Property, Taxation Records Access parcel data free from the Land Information office at http://richlandwi.mapping-online.com/RichlandCoWi/. Also, access property data free at http://gis.msa-ps.com/MAPS/WI/Counties/Richland/Publicviewer/viewer.htm but no name searching.

Rock County ***Recorded Documents*** www.co.rock.wi.us/index.php/departments/departments-m-z/register-of-deeds Access to records for a fee at https://tapestry.fidlar.com/Tapestry2/Default.aspx. Contact 309-794-3283 or kylec@fidlar.com for subscription information. Search fee is $5.95 each, printed images $.50 each unless otherwise noted. Also, access for free to GIS/mapping information go to http://199.233.45.152/Rock/. **$$$**
Property, Taxation Records Access to GIS/mapping for free at www.co.rock.wi.us/index.php/property-division-maps.

Rusk County ***Real Estate Records*** www.ruskcounty.org/departments/register-of-deeds/ To access the document database free at http://ruskwi.roddirect.com/.
Property, Taxation Records Access assessor land data free at http://ruskcowi.wgxtreme.com/.

St. Croix County ***Recorded Documents*** www.co.saint-croix.wi.us/index.asp?Type=B_BASIC&SEC={4618BCA5-3876-4F9A-9667-9BC2E046557C} Access to records for a fee at https://tapestry.fidlar.com/Tapestry2/Default.aspx. Contact 309-794-3283 or kylec@fidlar.com for subscription information. Search fee is $5.95 each, printed images $.50 each unless otherwise noted. **$$$**
Property, Taxation Records Access to tax and assessment data and GIS/mapping for free at http://stcroixcowi.wgxtreme.com/.

Sauk County ***Recorded Documents*** https://www.co.sauk.wi.us/registerofdeeds Access to recorder's land records is available by subscription at http://landshark.co.sauk.wi.us/LandShark/login.jsp?url=http%3A%2F%2Flandshark.co.sauk.wi.us%2FLandShark%2Fsearchname.jsp. Registration required; setup account thru Recorder office. Occasional users search free, but view documents for $2 first page, $1 each add'l. **$$$**
Property, Taxation Records Search Village of Spring Green property data free at www.wendorffassessing.com/Spring_Green_options.htm. No name searching. Also, search Village of Plain property data at www.wendorffassessing.com/Plain_options.htm.

Sawyer County ***Recorded Documents*** www.sawyercountygov.org/CountyDepartments/RegisterofDeeds/tabid/110/Default.aspx Access to records for a fee at https://tapestry.fidlar.com/Tapestry2/Default.aspx. Contact 309-794-3283 or kylec@fidlar.com for subscription information. Search fee is $5.95 each, printed images $.50 each unless otherwise noted. **$$$**
Property, Taxation Records Access to the land records portal for free at www.sawyercountygov.org/CountyDepartments/LandRecords/LandRecordsPortal/tabid/117/Default.aspx.

Shawano County ***Real Estate Records*** www.co.shawano.wi.us Access to recorder's land records is available free or by escrow for full-time access at http://landshark.co.shawano.wi.us/LandShark/about.jsp?aboutKey=LandShark. Registration required; setup account thru Recorder office. Occasional users search free, but view documents for $2 first page, $1 each add'l. **$$$**
Property, Taxation Records Access parcel data free at http://gis.co.shawano.wi.us/portal/ but no name searching.

Sheboygan County ***Recorded Documents*** www.sheboygancounty.com/government/departments-r-z/register-of-deeds Access to records for a fee at https://tapestry.fidlar.com/Tapestry2/Default.aspx. Contact 309-794-3283 or kylec@fidlar.com for subscription information. Search fee is $5.95 each, printed images $.50 each unless otherwise noted. **$$$**
Property, Taxation Records Lookup parcel and property tax data free at www.co.sheboygan.wi.us/landinformation/(pyeg3k45vzjhdqrorb2oop55)/portal_public.aspx, but no name searching. Also, lookup parcel, property tax, and GIS mapping and surveys free at www.co.sheboygan.wi.us/landinformation/(vev2o545zwbmqkan1o1zjb55)/portal_public.aspx, but no name searching.

Taylor County ***Recorded Documents*** www.co.taylor.wi.us/deparments/register-of-deeds/ Access county land records back to 1/1998 with subscription to Landshark at https://landshark.co.taylor.wi.us/LandShark/login.jsp?url=https%3A%2F%2Flandshark.co.taylor.wi.us%2FLandShark%2Fsearchname.jsp. Index search is free; images are $2.00 1st page, $1.00 each add'l. **$$$**

Property, Taxation Records Search property and tax data free at http://taylorcowi.wgxtreme.com/.

Trempealeau County ***Recorded Documents*** www.tremplocounty.com/RegisterofDeeds/default.asp Access to real estate, tax/assessment and online mapping for a fee at www.tremplocounty.com/default/disclaimer.asp. Also, access to records for a fee at https://tapestry.fidlar.com/Tapestry2/Default.aspx. Contact 309-794-3283 or kylec@fidlar.com forsubscription information. Search fee is $5.95 each, pringed images $.50 each unless otherwise noted. **$$$**

Property, Taxation Records Access to the county assessor's database is free at www.tremplocounty.com/Search/Search.asp. GIS and mapping found at www.tremplocounty.com/landrecords/PickaMap.html.

Vernon County ***Recorded Documents*** www.vernoncounty.org/ROD/index.htm Access to document search free at www.vernoncounty.org/GCSWebPortal/Search.aspx.

Vilas County ***Recorded Documents*** www.co.vilas.wi.us/dept/rod.html Access to recorded documents free at http://vilaswi.roddirect.com/Default.aspx. Copies of records are charged a fee. **$$$**

Property, Taxation Records Access property data free by municipality name at http://webtax.co.vilas.wi.us/index.cfm but no name searching.

Walworth County ***Recorded Documents*** www.co.walworth.wi.us Search the Register of Deeds index for free on the county e-government public search page at www.co.walworth.wi.us/. Online records go back to 1973. Also, access to parcel index free at https://rodapps.co.walworth.wi.us/LandShark/login.jsp?url=http%3A%2F%2Frodapps.co.walworth.wi.us%2FLandShark%2Fsearchname.jsp. A fee is required if you want images. Click on the \"About\" to learn how to set up an subscription. Also, access to a private company free records available at http://publicrecords.searchsystems.net/.

Property, Taxation Records Search the treasurer's tax roll list under \"Tax Roll Documents\" at www.co.walworth.wi.us/.

Washington County ***Real Estate, Deed Records*** www.co.washington.wi.us/ Access to Landshark for real estate records available for a fee at https://landshark.co.washington.wi.us/LandShark/login.jsp. **$$$**

Waukesha County ***Real Estate, Deed, Lien, Marriage, UCC Records*** www.waukeshacounty.gov/defaultwc.aspx?id=37826 Access the recording database free at http://dwprd.waukeshacounty.gov/applications/production/ROD_TRACT_DOCUMENTS/.

Property, Taxation Records Search assessor property data at www.ci.waukesha.wi.us/Parcel/DataInquiry1.jsp and search county tax listings at http://tax.waukeshacounty.gov/. Waukesha City sales lists are free at www.ci.waukesha.wi.us/web/guest/PropertySalesInfo.

Waupaca County ***Real Estate, Deed Records*** www.co.waupaca.wi.us/Departments/RegisterofDeeds.aspx Access county land records back to 1/1998 with subscription to Landshark at https://landshark.co.waupaca.wi.us/LandShark/login.jsp/. Index search is free; images are $2.00 1st page, $1.00 each add'l. **$$$**

Property, Taxation Records Access land information office data free at http://public1.co.waupaca.wi.us/GISviewer/index.html?config=config_parcel.xml. Also, access to GIS/mapping free at http://public1.co.waupaca.wi.us/LandInformation/mapsAndApps/mapps.html.**$$$**

Waushara County ***Real Estate, Parcel, GIS-Mapping Records*** www.co.waushara.wi.us/register_of_deeds.htm Search property data free on the county land information system at www.co.waushara.wi.us/Website/WausharaPA/viewer.htm.

Property, Taxation Records Search property data free on the county land information system at www.co.waushara.wi.us/Website/WausharaPA/viewer.htm.

Winnebago County ***Recorded Documents*** www.co.winnebago.wi.us Access to records for a fee at https://tapestry.fidlar.com/Tapestry2/Default.aspx. Contact 309-794-3283 or kylec@fidlar.com for subscription information. Search fee is $5.95 each, printed images $.50 each unless otherwise noted. **$$$**

Property, Taxation Records Property records on the City of Oshkosh assessor database are free at www.ci.oshkosh.wi.us/oshkosh_ias/Search/Disclaimer2.aspx?FromUrl=../Search/GenericSearch.aspx?mode=owner. Also, access the City of Menasha Tax Roll Information database free at www.cityofmenasha-wi.gov/content/departments/finance/(3)tax_roll_information.php.

Wood County ***Recorded Documents*** www.co.wood.wi.us/Departments/ROD/ Access to records for a fee at https://tapestry.fidlar.com/Tapestry2/Default.aspx. Contact 309-794-3283 or kylec@fidlar.com for subscription information. Search fee is $5.95 each, printed images $.50 each unless otherwise noted. **$$$**

Property, Taxation Records Access to land maps/records for free at www.co.wood.wi.us/Departments/PZ/LandRecords.aspx/website/Public/viewer.htm.

Wyoming

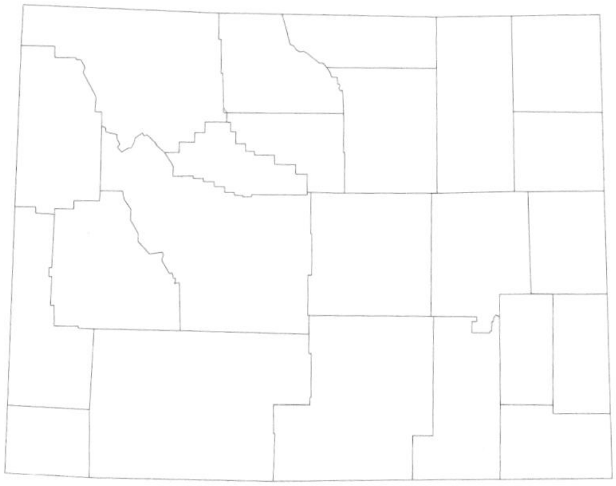

Capital: Cheyenne
Laramie County
Time Zone: MST
Population: 576,412
# of Counties: 23

Useful State Links

Website: http://wyoming.gov/
Governor: http://governor.wy.gov/
Attorney General: http://attorneygeneral.state.wy.us
State Archives: http://wyoarchives.state.wy.us/
State Statutes and Codes: http://legisweb.state.wy.us/LSOWEB/wyStatutes.aspx
Legislative Bill Search: http://legisweb.state.wy.us/LSOWEB/GeneralInfo.aspx
Unclaimed Funds: http://treasurer.state.wy.us/uphome.asp

State Public Record Agencies

Sexual Offender Registry

Division of Criminal Investigation, ATTN: WSOR, http://wysors.dci.wyo.gov/sor/home.htm The Internet is the search method offered by this agency to the public. Search is by last name, street name, city, county or ZIP. Data includes name including AKA, physical address, date and place of birth, date and place of conviction, crime for which convicted, photograph and physical description.

Corporation, LLC, LP, Fictitious Name, Trademarks/Servicemarks, Trade Names

Business Division, Attn: Records, http://soswy.state.wy.us/Business/BusEntOverview.aspx Information is available at https://wyobiz.wy.gov/Business/FilingSearch.aspx. You can search by corporate name or registered filing ID.

Uniform Commercial Code, Federal Tax Liens

Secretary of State, UCC Division - Records, http://soswy.state.wy.us/Business/Business.aspx One may email requests to SOSRequest@wyo.gov. The online filing system permits unlimited record searching, see https://ucc.state.wy.us/ExLogin.asp. Subscribers are entitled to do filings at a 50% discount. There is a $150 annual fee, with no additional fees charged for searches. Visit the webpage for more information. **$$$** *Other Options:* Lists of filings on CD or diskette are available for purchase. Download the database for $2,000 per year.

Driver License Information, Driver Records

Wyoming Department of Transportation, Driver Services, www.dot.state.wy.us/home/driver_license_records.html Electronic access is available using Web service, fee is $5.00 per record. Only approved vendors and permissible users are supported. Call Marianne Zivkovich at 307-777-4830 or write to the above address for details. **$$$** *Other Options:* The entire driver license file may be purchased for $2,500. This is only available with a signed contract and compliance with the DPPA.

Voter Registration, Campaign Finance

Secretary of State - Election Division, 200 W 24th Street, http://soswy.state.wy.us/Elections/Elections.aspx The agency provides a number of reports and searches for campaign finances, PACs, and donations at https://www.wycampaignfinance.gov/WYCFWebApplication/Reports/ResearchToolsAndLists.aspx. *Other Options:* An order form for bulk purchase is found at http://soswy.state.wy.us/Forms/Elections/General/VoterProductOrderForm.pdf.

Occupational Licensing Boards

Accountant Firm	http://cpaboard.state.wy.us/firm.aspx
Accountant-CPA	http://cpaboard.state.wy.us/holder.aspx
Architect	http://plboards.state.wy.us/architecture/Directory.asp
Attorney	www.wyomingbar.org/index.html
Bank	http://audit.state.wy.us/banking/banking/bankingregulatedentities.htm
Barber School/Shop	https://wyboc.glsuite.us/glsuiteweb/clients/wyboc/public/verificationsearch.aspx
Check Casher	http://audit.state.wy.us/banking/uccc/uccclicensees.htm
Child Care Licensee	https://sites.google.com/a/wyo.gov/early-childcare-and-licensing/contacts-childcare-facilities
Child Care Subsidy	https://sites.google.com/a/wyo.gov/early-childcare-and-licensing/contacts-childcare-facilities
Collection Agency	http://audit.state.wy.us/banking/cab/cablicensees.pdf
Controlled Substance Registrants	http://pharmacyboard.state.wy.us/OLV.aspx
Cosmetologist	https://wyboc.glsuite.us/glsuiteweb/clients/wyboc/public/verificationsearch.aspx
Cosmetology Instructor/School	https://wyboc.glsuite.us/glsuiteweb/clients/wyboc/public/verificationsearch.aspx
Dental Assistant/Hygienist	http://plboards.state.wy.us/dental/Directory.asp
Dentist	http://plboards.state.wy.us/dental/Directory.asp
Electrical Inspectors	http://wyofire.state.wy.us/electricalsafety/inspectors.html
Engineer, Professional	http://engineersandsurveyors.state.wy.us/roster/rosterSearch.aspx
Esthetician	https://wyboc.glsuite.us/glsuiteweb/clients/wyboc/public/verificationsearch.aspx
Funeral Pre-Need Agent	https://www.sircon.com/ComplianceExpress/Inquiry/consumerInquiry.do?nonSscrb=Y
Geologist/Geologist-in-training	http://wbpg.wy.gov/RosterSearch.aspx
Insurance Claims Adjuster	https://www.sircon.com/ComplianceExpress/Inquiry/consumerInquiry.do?nonSscrb=Y
Insurance Consultant/Producer/Service Rep	https://www.sircon.com/ComplianceExpress/Inquiry/consumerInquiry.do?nonSscrb=Y
Landscape Architect	http://plboards.state.wy.us/architecture/Directory.asp
Lender, Supervised	http://audit.state.wy.us/banking/uccc/uccclicensees.htm
Lobbyist	http://soswy.state.wy.us/Elections/docs/2012-2013_WY_Lobbyist_List.pdf
Manicurist/Nail Technician	https://wyboc.glsuite.us/glsuiteweb/clients/wyboc/public/verificationsearch.aspx
Motor Club Agent	https://www.sircon.com/ComplianceExpress/Inquiry/consumerInquiry.do?nonSscrb=Y
Nurse-LPN/RN/Aide/CAN-Discipline	https://nursing-online.state.wy.us/Default.aspx?page=37
Nurse-LPN/RN/Aide/CAN-List	https://nursing-online.state.wy.us/Verifications.aspx
Occupational Therapist/Assistant	http://ot.state.wy.us/search.aspx
Optometrist	www.arbo.org/index.php?action=findanoptometrist
Outfitter	http://outfitters.state.wy.us/PDF/directory/OutfitterDirectory.pdf
Pawnbroker	http://audit.state.wy.us/banking/uccc/uccclicensees.htm
Pharmacist/Pharmacy Technician	http://pharmacyboard.state.wy.us/OLV.aspx
Pharmacy, Institutional	http://pharmacyboard.state.wy.us/OLV.aspx
Physical Therapist/Assistant	http://plboards.state.wy.us/PTherapy/Directory.asp
Physician Assistant	https://wybom.glsuite.us/GLSuiteWeb/Clients/WYBOM/Public/LicenseeSearch.aspx?SearchType=PA
Physician/Medical Doctor/Psychiatrist	https://wybom.glsuite.us/GLSuiteWeb/Clients/WYBOM/Public/LicenseeSearch.aspx
Physicians - Disciplinary Actions	http://wyomedboard.state.wy.us/PDF/Menu/AlphabeticalDisciplinaryActionList.pdf
Podiatrist	http://plboards.state.wy.us/podiatry/PDF/ApplicationPackets/LicenseDirectory.pdf
Prescription Drugs/Substances Mfg/Seller	http://pharmacyboard.state.wy.us/OLV.aspx
Property Appraiser	https://www.arello.com/?SHOWNAV=1
Psychologist/Psychological Practitioner	http://plboards.state.wy.us/psychology/Directory.asp
Radiologic Technologist/Technician	http://plboards.state.wy.us/radiology/LicenseDirectory.asp
Real Estate Agent	https://www.arello.com/?SHOWNAV=1
Real Estate Appraiser	https://www.arello.com/?SHOWNAV=1
Reinsurance Intermediary	https://www.sircon.com/ComplianceExpress/Inquiry/consumerInquiry.do?nonSscrb=Y
Rent-to-own Company	http://audit.state.wy.us/banking/uccc/uccclicensees.htm
Rental Car Agents	https://www.sircon.com/ComplianceExpress/Inquiry/consumerInquiry.do?nonSscrb=Y
Retail Pharmacy	http://pharmacyboard.state.wy.us/OLV.aspx
Risk Retention	https://www.sircon.com/ComplianceExpress/Inquiry/consumerInquiry.do?nonSscrb=Y
Sales Finance Company	http://audit.state.wy.us/banking/uccc/uccclicensees.htm

Savings & Loan Association .... http://audit.state.wy.us/banking/banking/bankingregulatedentities.htm
School Psychologist/Specialist .... http://plboards.state.wy.us/psychology/Directory.asp
Surplus Line Broker, Resident .... https://www.sircon.com/ComplianceExpress/Inquiry/consumerInquiry.do?nonSscrb=Y
Surveyor, Land .... http://engineersandsurveyors.state.wy.us/roster/rosterSearch.aspx
Third Party Administrator .... https://www.sircon.com/ComplianceExpress/Inquiry/consumerInquiry.do?nonSscrb=Y
Travel & Baggage Agent .... https://www.sircon.com/ComplianceExpress/Inquiry/consumerInquiry.do?nonSscrb=Y
Trust Company .... http://audit.state.wy.us/banking/banking/bankingregulatedentities.htm
Water Dist/Collection Operator .... http://deq.state.wy.us/wqd/npdes/
Water/Waste Treatm't Plant Operator .... http://deq.state.wy.us/wqd/npdes/

State and Local Courts

State Court Structure: Each county has a **District Court** which oversees felony criminal cases, large civil cases, and juvenile and probate matters. The District Courts are run by the individual counties, therefore employees are county employees and are not state employees.

The **Circuit Court** is of limited jurisdiction and oversee civil cases when the amount sought does not exceed $50,000 (raised from $7,000 effective 07/2011) and small claims to $5,000. Circuit Courts also hear family violence cases and all misdemeanors. Three counties have two Circuit Courts each: Fremont, Park, and Sweetwater. Cases may be filed in either of the two court offices in those counties, and records requests are referred between the two courts. Effective January 1, 2003, all Justice Courts became Circuit Courts and follow Circuit Court rules. The Circuit Court is run by the state and employees are state employees.

Municipal Courts operate in all incorporated cities and towns; their jurisdiction covers all ordinance violations and has no civil jurisdiction. The Municipal Court judge may assess penalties of up to $750 and/or six months in jail.

Appellate Courts: Supreme Court opinions are listed by date at www.courts.state.wy.us/Opinions.aspx.

Statewide Court Online Access: Wyoming's statewide case management system is for internal use only. Planning is underway for a new case management system that will ultimately allow public access. **But at this time there is no online access to civil, criminal, or other court case files or dockets.**

County Court Online Sites: None

Recorders, Assessors, and Other Sites of Note

Recording Office Organization: 23 counties, 23 recording offices. The recording officer is the County Clerk. Federal tax liens on personal property of businesses are filed with the Secretary of State. Other federal and all state tax liens are filed with the County Clerk.

Statewide or Multi-Jurisdiction Access: There is no statewide database of county recorder or assessor data. However a growing number of counties offer online access to various property records and databases of recorded documents.

County Sites:

Albany County ***Recorded Documents*** www.co.albany.wy.us/Clerk.aspx For subscription services contact IT Department at 307-721-5500. **$$$**

Property, Taxation Records Search the county assessor database free at http://assessor.co.albany.wy.us.

Big Horn County ***Recorded Documents*** www.bighorncountywy.gov/dep-clerk.htm Access to subscription contact Ms Dori Noyes at 307-568-2357. **$$$**

Campbell County ***Property, Taxation Records*** Search property records free at www.ccgov.net/assessor/online/index.html.

Carbon County ***Grantor/Grantee, Real Estate, Deeds, Mortgages, Marriage License, Tract Indices Records*** www.carbonwy.com The county site is at http://news2.arcasearch.com/uswycb/. Also access to records free at https://idoc.csa-inc.net/carbonwy/Default.aspx. Must register to access site.

Property, Taxation Records Access to GIS/mapping for free at http://gis.carbonwy.com/. Also, access to property data free at http://assessor.carbonwy.com/.

Converse County ***Property, Taxation Records*** Access to Assessor's maps for free at http://conversecounty.org/gov-admin/county-assessor/maps.

Crook County ***Recorded Documents*** www.crookcounty.wy.gov/elected_officials/clerk/index.php Access to records for a fee at www.crookcounty.wy.gov/elected_officials/clerk/online_land_records.php. Fee is $250.00 annually or $25.00 per month. Must have a valid username and password to access the site. **$$$**

Property Records Access property ownership maps free at www.crookcounty.wy.gov/elected_officials/assessor/property_ownership_maps/index.php.

Fremont County ***Real Estate, UCC Records*** http://fremontcountywy.org/county-clerk/ Access to records database for a fee at http://fremontcountywy.org/county-clerk/land-recording-information/ for EagleWeb application. Some older documents are available by accessing ArcaSearch at http://news2.arcasearch.com/uswyfr/.

Goshen County ***Property, Taxation Records*** Access to property searches for free at http://goshencounty.org/index.php/property-search.

Hot Springs County ***Property, Taxation Records*** Access GIS/mapping data for free at http://cama.state.wy.us/DISTRICTS/MAPS_ONLINEDOCUMENTS/ShowMAPS_ONLINEDOCUMENTSTable.aspx

Johnson County ***Recorded Documents*** www.johnsoncountywyoming.org/government/clerk/ Access to records for a fee at https://www.idocmarket.com/. Must subscribe to access. **$$$**

Laramie County ***Recorded Documents, Marriage Records*** www.laramiecountyclerk.com Indices from 1985 back to patent are available at https://news2.arcasearch.com/uswylar/.

Property, Taxation Records Search property data free at http://arcims.laramiecounty.com/ but no name searching.

Natrona County ***Property, Taxation Records*** Access to property search information for free at www.natronacounty-wy.gov/index.aspx?NID=311.

Park County ***Property, Taxation Records*** Search the county tax database by property owner or by address or by property Tax ID at http://itax.parkcounty.us/.

Sheridan County ***Property, Taxation Records*** Access county property tax records free at http://webtax.csa-inc.net/sheridanwy/. Also, a GIS-mapping site provides parcel data free at www.sheridancounty.com/info/gis/overview.php.

Sublette County ***Property, Taxation Records*** Access property data and GIS-mapping free at www.sublettewyo.com/index.aspx?NID=35.

Sweetwater County ***Recorded Documents*** www.sweet.wy.us/index.aspx?nid=65 There is both a free and subscription service at http://idoc.sweet.wy.us/. User may need to load software. **$$$**

Property, Taxation Records Search property tax and assessements at www.sweet.wy.us/index.aspx?NID=210

Teton County ***Recorded Documents*** www.tetonwyo.org/cc Access to the Clerk's database of scanned images is free at http://maps.greenwoodmap.com/tetonwy/clerk/query/. Search for complete documents back to 7/1996; partial documents back to 4/1991.

Property, Taxation Records Access to Assessor's Tax Roll and GIS system for free at http://tetonwy.greenwoodmap.com/gis/download/. Must register first time.

Chapter 7

Searching Federal Court Records

Searching records at the federal court system can be one of the easiest or one of the most frustrating experiences that public record searchers may encounter. Although the federal court system offers advanced electronic search capabilities, at times it is practically impossible to properly identify a subject when searching civil or criminal records. Before reviewing searching procedures, a brief overview is in order.

Federal Court Structure

At the federal level, all cases involve federal or U.S. constitutional law or interstate commerce. The federal court system includes three levels of courts, plus several specialty courts. The home page for the U.S. Courts is www.uscourts.gov.

U. S. District Courts

The United States District Courts are the **trial courts** of the federal court system. District Courts have jurisdiction over civil and criminal matters.

Overall, there are 94 federal judicial districts, with at least one district in each state, the District of Columbia and Puerto Rico. The three territories of the United States (the Virgin Islands, Guam, and the Northern Mariana Islands) also have District Courts that hear federal cases.

Technically Bankruptcy Courts are actually units of the U.S. District Courts.

U. S. Bankruptcy Courts

Each of the 94 federal judicial districts handles bankruptcy matters through the U.S. Bankruptcy Courts. The Bankruptcy Courts generally use the same hearing locations (building) as the District Courts. If court locations differ, the usual variance is to have fewer Bankruptcy Court locations.

In some states, such as Colorado, the U.S. District Court or the Bankruptcy Court is comprised of a single judicial district. Others states, such as California, are composed of multiple judicial districts – Central, Eastern, Northern, and Southern. Also, within each judicial district there can be multiple divisions. Counting all the divisions and districts, there are actually over 280 U.S. District Court locations and nearly 195 U.S. Bankruptcy Court locations.

United States Court of Appeals

The 94 judicial districts are organized into 12 regional circuits, each of which has a United States Court of Appeals. A Court of Appeals hears appeals from the district courts located within its circuit, as well as appeals from decisions of federal administrative agencies.

In addition, the Court of Appeals for the Federal Circuit has nationwide jurisdiction to hear appeals in specialized cases, such as those involving patent laws and cases decided by the Court of International Trade and the Court of Federal Claims.

Supreme Court of the United States

The Supreme Court of the United States is the court of last resort in the United States. The Supreme Court is located in Washington, DC and it hears appeals from the United States Courts of Appeals and from the highest courts of each state.

Other Federal Courts

Three significant additional courts were created to hear cases or appeals for certain areas of litigation that demand special expertise. These courts are the U.S. Tax Court, the Court of International Trade, and the U.S. Court of Federal Claims.

U.S. Court of Federal Claims

The Court of Federal Claims is authorized to primarily hear money claims in regard to federal statutes, executive regulations, the Constitution, or contracts, expressed- or implied-in-fact, with the United States. Approximately a quarter of the cases involve complex factual and statutory construction issues in tax law. About a third of the cases involve government contracts. Cases involving environmental and natural resource issues make up about ten percent of the caseload. Another significant category of cases involve civilian and military pay questions. In addition, the Court hears intellectual property, Indian Tribe, and various statutory claims against the United States by individuals, domestic and foreign corporations, states and localities, Indian Tribes and Nations, and foreign nationals and governments.

Direct questions to the U.S. Court of Federal Claims, Attention: Clerks Office, 717 Madison Place, NW, Washington, DC 20005, or call 202-357-6400. See www.uscfc.uscourts.gov

U.S. Tax Court

The jurisdiction of the U.S. Tax Court includes the authority to hear tax disputes concerning notices of deficiency, notices of transferee liability, certain types of declaratory judgment, readjustment and adjustment of partnership items, review of the failure to abate interest, administrative costs, worker classification, relief from joint and several liability on a joint return, and review of certain collection actions.

Docket information is available for cases filed on or after May 1, 1986. Call Docket Information at 202-521-4650. For case records, call Records and Reproduction at 202-521-4688. Direct questions to the U.S. Tax Court at 400 Second Street, NW, Washington, DC 20217. The main number is 202-521-0700. Dockets and opinions also may be searched on the web at www.ustaxcourt.gov.

U.S. Court of International Trade

The U.S. Court of International Trade oversees disputes within the international trade community for individuals, foreign and domestic manufacturers, consumer groups, trade associations, labor unions, concerned citizens, and other nations.

The geographical jurisdiction of the United States Court of International Trade extends throughout the U.S. The court is also authorized to hold hearings in foreign countries. Appeals from final decisions of the court may be taken to the United States Court of Appeals for the Federal Circuit and, ultimately, to the Supreme Court of the United States.

The court provides online access to opinions and judgments. From 1999-2006, the Court published only the slip opinions online. Since January 1, 2007, the online postings contain both the slip opinion and judgment in each case. Registered users of the CM/ECF system have the ability to open a case as of October 11, 2006.

The Court's Administrative Office is located at One Federal Plaza, New York, New York 10278-0001, or call 212-264-2800. See www.cit.uscourts.gov

How Federal Trial Court Case Records are Organized

Indexing and Case Numbering

When a case is filed with a federal court, a case number is assigned. District courts index cases by the defendant and plaintiff names as well as by case number. Bankruptcy courts usually index cases by the debtor name and case number.

Therefore, when you search by name you will first receive a listing of all cases where the name appears, both as plaintiff and defendant.

To view case records you must know or find the applicable case number. Thus, searching the index by name should lead to the case file number.

Case numbering procedures are not consistent throughout the federal court system. One judicial district may assign numbers by district while another may assign numbers by location (division) within that judicial district or by judge within the division. Remember that case numbers appearing in legal text citations may not be adequate for searching unless they appear in the proper form for the particular court.

Docket Sheet

Same as in the state court systems, information from cover sheets and from documents filed as a case goes forward is recorded on the docket sheet. While docket sheets differ somewhat in format, the docket sheet is consistent from court to court because it shows the case history from initial filing to its current status. All docket sheets contain—

- Name of court, including location (division) and the judge assigned;
- Case number and case name;
- Names of all plaintiffs and defendants/debtors;
- Names and addresses of attorneys for the plaintiff or debtor;
- Nature and cause (e.g., U.S. civil statute) of action;
- Listing of documents filed in the case, including the date, docket entry number, and a short description (e.g., 12-2-92, #1, Complaint).

Assignment of Cases and Computerization

At one time, all cases were assigned to a specific district or division based on the county of origination. Although this is still true in most states, computerized tracking of dockets has led to a more flexible approach to case assignment. For example in Minnesota and Connecticut, rather than blindly assigning all cases from a county to one judge, their districts use random numbers and other methods to logically balance caseloads among their judges.

This trend may appear to confuse the case search process. But actually, finding cases has become significantly easier with the wide availability of Case Management/ Electronic Case Files (CM/ECF) and the PACER Case Locator (see descriptions to follow).

Case information and images of documents are stored at the courthouse for a timeframe determined by the individual court and then are forwarded to one of the Federal Records Centers (FRCs). Most case files created prior to 1999 were maintained in paper format only. Now all cases are files electronically through CM/ECF.

Court Locations, Contact Information, and Web Pages

One may use the Court Locator page at www.uscourts.gov/Court_Locator.aspx to find the exact address, phone number and web page for all the court locations. a wealth of information about each court.

An important fact to keep in mind is that most case files created prior to 1999 are maintained in paper format only. Closed case files and paper case files are stored at the courthouse for a timeframe determined by the individual court and then are forwarded to one of the Federal Records Centers (FRCs). A case file may be obtained through the court or directly from the FRC. A list of all the FRCs appears later in this chapter.

Record Searching - Electronic Access to Federal Court Records

There are important acronyms in regards to federal court case information – CM/ECF and PACER.

Case Management/Electronic Case Files (CM/ECF)

CM/ECF is the case management system for the Federal Judiciary for all bankruptcy, district, and appellate courts. The CM/ECF system allows courts to accept case filings over the Internet. Attorneys use CM/ECF to file documents and manage official documents related to a case.

CM/ECF permits concurrent access to case files by multiple parties, and offers expanded search and reporting capabilities. The system also offers the ability to: immediately update dockets and make them available to users, file pleadings electronically with the court, and download documents and print them directly from the court system.

A significant fact affecting record researchers is the CM/ECF Rules of Procedure that require filers redact certain personal identifying information. This means filings cannot include Social Security or taxpayer-identification numbers, full dates of birth, names of minor children, financial account numbers, and in criminal cases, home addresses, from their filings.

For further information on CM/ECF, visit www.pacer.gov/cmecf/index.html.

PACER and the PACER Case Locator

PACER. an acronym for **P**ublic **A**ccess to **E**lectronic **C**ourt **R**ecords, is the electronic service that allows the public to obtain case and docket information from the U.S. District, Bankruptcy, and Appellate courts.

You must know and search the individual court where the case was filed or held. Therefore, a researcher will likely need to use the **PACER Case Locator,** a national index for U.S. District, Bankruptcy, and Appellate courts. Using the Case Locator, a researcher can determine whether or not a party is involved in federal litigation and if so the the court location.

One may find more information or register online for PACER at www.pacer.gov.

The information gathered from the PACER system is a matter of public record and may be reproduced without permission. Essentially each court maintains its own database of case information and decides what to make available on PACER. PACER normally provides the following information

- A listing of all parties and participants including judges, attorneys, trustees
- A compilation of case related information such as cause of action, nature of suit, dollar demand
- A chronology of dates of case events entered in the case record
- A claims registry
- A listing of new cases each day in the bankruptcy courts
- Appellate court opinions
- Judgments or case status
- Types of case documents filed for certain districts.

PACER Fees

There are fees to use PACER. Electronic access to any case document, docket sheet, or case specific report is $0.10 per page, not to exceed the fee for thirty pages. The fee to access an audio file of a court hearing via PACER: $2.40 per audio file. If an account holder does not accrue charges of more than $15.00 in a quarterly billing cycle there is no fee charged.

Voice Case Information System (VCIS) or McVCIS

VCIS – Voice Case Information System – .is a means of accessing information regarding OPEN bankruptcy cases information 24/7 by using a touch-tone telephone. An automated voice response system will read a limited amount of bankruptcy case information directly from the court's database in response to Touch-Tone telephone inquiries. The advantage? There is no charge. Individual names are entered last name first with as much of the first name as you wish to include. For example, Joe B. Cool could be entered as COOLJ or COOLJOE. Do not enter the middle initial. Business names are entered as they are written, without blanks.

At one time each Bankruptcy Court had its own VCIS telephone number. But now nearly all Bankruptcy Courts provided access through a centralized VCIS phone number at 866-222-8019. Some court refer to this as McVCIS, which stands for Multi-Court Voice Case Information System.

Federal Court Record Searching Hints

Check the assigned counties of jurisdiction for each court within a state. Usually accessible from the web, this is a good starting point for determining where case records may be found.

The biggest problem with search federal court records is the lack of identifiers. Approximately 5 percent of the criminal records in the U.S. are records of federal offenses. As mentioned, very few identifiers are entered in the CM/ECF system. Thus federal courts no longer provide means to accurately identify a subject of a search. A handful will provide the last four digits of the SSN, or they may provide the birth month and year of birth, but not the day.

A well-known concern of the employment screening industry is the fact it is next to impossible for employers to verify that a new hire does not have a federal criminal record. Sometime the only starting point is to call the court. Some courts may be more willing than others to give out information by telephone. This is because most courts have fully computerized indexes that clerks can access while on the phone.

When Record Search Results Do Not Include Identifiers

This is a struggle and a tough problem to solve, especially if a searcher is dealing with a common name. Here are several ideas to use when for trying to ferret out a false-positive.

View Case Files

If possible, review the documents found in the case files for any hints of identification. At some district courts, clerks will look at paper case file records, if any, to determine if other identification exists that can match the requester's identifiers.

Call an Attorney Involved in the Case

The docket will list the attorney (or prosecuting attorney) involved in a case. Sometime these are great resources to determine the identity of a subject.

Check Incarceration Records

Searching prison records is sometimes an excellent alternative means for identity verification. Search the Bureau of Prisons at www.bop.gov/.

Check the News Media

Some record searchers have been successful in confirming an identity by using news media sources such as newspapers and web news media. Even blogs may help.

Obtaining Closed Case Files and the Federal Records Centers

After a federal case is closed, the documents are held by the federal courts location for a predetermined time. This can be as little as immediately or perhaps six months or more. The closed cases are then sent to and stored at a designated Federal Records Center (FRC). These offices are administered by the National Archives and Records Administration (NARA). See www.archives.gov/research. This procedure applies to all closed bankruptcy, civil, criminal, and court of appeals case files

The National Archives and Records Administration (NARA) provides access to archived court records exclusively by online ordering or by mail or fax. NARA no longer provides on-site court case review services to the public at its Federal Records Centers. Access to court cases is now available only via online ordering at www.archives.gov/research/court-records or by mail or fax at these facilities:

Anchorage Records Facility

Regional Records Services Facility
654 W 3rd Ave
Anchorage, AK 99501-2145
Phone: 907-261-7820
URL: www.archives.gov/anchorage
Holds records for courts from theses states: Alaska (most civil and criminal records)

Atlanta Records Facility (Ellenwood)

Regional Records Services Facility
4712 Southpark Blvd
Ellenwood, GA 30294
Phone: 404-736-2820 main
URL: www.archives.gov/atlanta
Holds records for courts from theses states: Alabama, Georgia, Florida, Kentucky, Mississippi, North Carolina, South Carolina and Tennessee

Boston Records Facility (Waltham)

Regional Records Services Facility
380 Trapelo Rd.
Waltham, MA 02452-6399
Phone: 781-663-0144
URL: www.archives.gov/boston
Holds records for courts from theses states: Connecticut, Maine, Massachusetts, New Hampshire, Rhode Island and Vermont

Chicago Records Facility

Regional Records Services Facility
7358 South Pulaski Road
Chicago, IL 60629-5898
Phone: 773-948-9030
URL: www.archives.gov/chicago
Holds records for courts from theses states: Illinois, Indiana, Michigan, Minnesota, Ohio and Wisconsin. See Dayton for recent Ohio bankruptcy records.

Dayton Records Facility

Regional Records Services Facility
3150 Springboro Rd
Dayton, OH 45439-1883
Phone: 937-425-0609
URL: www.archives.gov/frc/dayton
Holds records for courts from theses states: Ohio (Bankruptcy records: Northern District-1993 forward: Southern District-1995 forward)

Denver Records Facility

Regional Records Services Facility
17101 Huron St
Broomfield, CO 80023
Phone: 303-604-4740
URL: www.archives.gov/denver
Holds records for courts from theses states: Colorado, Montana, New Mexico, North Dakota, South Dakota, Utah and Wyoming

Fort Worth Records Facility

Regional Records Services Facility
PO Box 6216
Fort Worth, TX 76115-0216
Phone: 817-831-5900
URL: www.archives.gov/fort-worth
Holds records for courts from theses states: Arkansas, Louisiana, Oklahoma and Texas

Lee's Summit (Missouri) Records Facility

Regional Records Services Facility
200 Space Center Dr
Lee's Summit, MO 64064-1182
Phone: 816-268-8100
URL: www.archives.gov/frc/lees-summit
Holds records for courts from theses states: Now houses records from Bayonne, NJ for New Jersey, New York, Puerto Rico and Virgin Islands. See Kansas City location for Midwestern states

Lenexa (Kansas) Records Facility

Regional Records Services Facility
17501 W. 98th, Suite 47-48
Lenexa, KS 66219
Phone: 913-563-7600
URL: www.archives.gov/frc/lenexa
Holds records for courts from theses states: Iowa, Kansas, Missouri and Nebraska. See Lee's Summit location for records transferred from Bayonne for New Jersey, New York, Puerto Rico and Virgin Islands

Northeast Philadelphia Records Facility

Regional Records Services Facility
14700 Townsend Rd.
Philadelphia, PA 19154-1096
Phone: 215-305-2000, 305-2020
URL: www.archives.gov/philadelphia
Holds records for courts from theses states: Delaware, Maryland, Pennsylvania, Virginia and West Virginia (some older Maryland, Virginia, and West Virginia cases may be found at the Washington, DC facility)

Riverside (Perris) Facility

Regional Records Services Facility
23123 Cajalco Road
Perris, CA 92570-7298
Phone: 951- 956-2011
URL: www.archives.gov/riverside
Holds records for courts from theses states: Arizona, Southern California counties (Imperial, Inyo, Kern, Los Angeles, Orange, Riverside, San Bernardino, San Luis Obispo, Santa Barbara and Ventura), and Clark County Nevada

San Francisco Records Facility (San Bruno)

Regional Records Services Facility
1000 Commodore Drive
San Bruno, CA 94066-2350
Phone: 650-238-3500, 238-3488
www.archives.gov/facilities/ca/san_francisco.html
Holds records for courts from theses states: All Northern California counties, Hawaii, Nevada (except counties covered by the Las Vegas Division), and American Samoa

Seattle Records Facility

Regional Records Services Facility
6125 Sand Point Way NE
Seattle, WA 98115-7999
Phone: 206-336-5115
URL: www.archives.gov/facilities/wa/seattle.html
Holds records for courts from these states: Idaho, Oregon, Washington and Alaska (bankruptcy and some civil and criminal records)

Washington National Records Center (Suitland, MD)

Regional Records Services Facility
Use courier address for all mail
Suitland, MD, 20746
Phone: 301-778-1600
URL: www.archives.gov/facilities/md/suitland.html
Holds records for courts from these states: District of Columbia; all military bases; some older case records from Maryland, Virginia and West Virginia

Meet the Authors

Cynthia Hetherington, CFE has more than 18 years of experience in research, investigations, and corporate intelligence. She is the founder of Hetherington Group (hetheringtongroup.com), a consulting, publishing, and training firm focusing on intelligence, security, and investigations. Cynthia was named the 2012 James Baker Speaker of the Year for the Association of Certified Fraud Examiners.

A widely-published author, Cynthia authored *Business Background Investigations* (2007) as well as the third edition of this book. She is the publisher of Data2know.com: Internet & Online Intelligence Newsletter and has co-authored articles on steganography, computer forensics, Internet investigations, and other security-focused monographs.

She is also recognized for providing corporate security officials, military intelligence units, and federal, state, and local agencies with training on online intelligence practices.

To contact Ms. Hetherington, please email her at ch@hetheringtongroup.com.

Michael Sankey is founder and CEO of BRB Publications, Inc. and is Director of the Public Record Retriever Network, one of the nation's largest membership organization of professionals in the public record industry. Michael has more than 30 years of experience in research and public record access. He has authored or edited over 75 publications and editions including *The Sourcebook to Public Record Information*, *The Public Record Research TIPS Book*, and *The MVR Access and Decoder Digest*.

In the 1980s, he was president and CEO of Rapid Info Services, a national vendor of electronic-processed driving records. Rapid Info was the first vendor to offer online access of driving records to their clientele.

Michael was a member of the Steering Committee that founded the National Association of Professional Background Screeners (NAPBS), a professional trade association for the screening industry. He was also elected to the first Board of Directors in 2004 and served two years.

He is regarded as a leading industry expert in public records, criminal record access, state DMV policies and procedures, as well as knowing who's who in the commercial arena of public information vendors.

To contact Michael, please email him at mike@brbpublications.com.